THE FISHING HANDBOOK

Second Edition.
Editor: Richard Thomas.

The Fishing Handbook is designed to give comprehensive information on all bodies, organisations and companies involved with the sport of angling. Every conceivable product, service or contact connected with coarse angling is included in this book. For the serious angler the book should prove as important an item as his rod and reel.

Beacon Publishing
Jubilee House, Billing Brook Road,
Weston Favell, Northampton
Telephone: (0604) 407288
Telex: 312242 MIDTLXG

© Beacon Publications Limited 1982.

THE FISHING HANDBOOK

The Ultimate Source of Information for the Angler

Second Edition

£8.50

ISBN 0 906358 22 1

Whilst every care has been made to obtain accurate and reliable information, the Publisher cannot accept liability for any errors or omissions in this publication.

The Game Fishing Handbook

Introduction

Angling is one of the most popular participation sports and consequently involves a great number of people and organisations to both administer and supply equipment and services. The range and complexity involved is fertile ground for the publication of a reference work and we hope that The Fishing Handbook fulfills, and will continue to fulfill, a need for information on behalf of the individual angler and the angling trade.

It is our intention to produce the book annually and in order for the publication to properly serve the needs of the angler, it is essential that we continually strive to improve and enlarge upon our editorial. We would therefore very much welcome the contribution of our readers in drawing to our attention any inaccuracies or omissions. We would also welcome any suggestions on how we can make the book more useful to the reader.

Acknowledgements

A book containing the volume of information such as The Fishing Handbook could not be produced without the support and assistance of people directly connected with the sport of angling. Such people are too numerous to name individually ranging from members of the angling trade, fishing tackle retailers, angling club secretaries, fisheries staff of water authorities and the members of angling governing bodies. We would like to thank all who have talked to us, corresponded with us, helped us and encouraged us for their contribution to this book.

Contents
Section 1

uble, which fold independently, giving remarkable seat/load versatility.

No other estate car gives you such exibility.

PEUGEOT DESIGN EXCELLENCE

The name Peugeot is synonymous ith design excellence. The 505 Family state fully reflects this and boasts a vel of refinement that is hard to rival.

Power steering is standard and an strument panel with no less than four- en separate functions adds up to total riving control. There's an internal head- mp adjuster which varies the angle of e headlamp beam, to compensate for rrying loads, and even an econoscope that the driver can ensure fuel is sed efficiently.

With sumptuous tweed upholstery

and a special air ducting system which heats and ventilates all parts of the car evenly, passenger comfort is unsurpassed. The massive glass area and panoramic heated rear window, complete with wash/wipe, provides the ultimate in all round visibility.

Peugeot have designed the car with the utmost precision, even the spare wheel is located beneath the rear load area for easy access.

No other large estate gives you such a high level of refinement.

PEUGEOT ESTATE CAR HERITAGE

Only Peugeot have a true estate car heritage. We spend three years designing and testing our estates with particular attention to wheelbase and suspension engineering – not simply

an adaptation of the existing saloon configuration. Whether fully loaded or not we have ensured that the handling, comfort and ride remain excellent.

Each car and its components is thoroughly tested by a quality control team representing over 12% of the workforce.

So we feel confident in offering the Peugeot six-year anti-corrosion warranty on all our models.

No other manufacturer can claim the same level of estate car expertise.

PEUGEOT VALUE FOR MONEY

We believe that a 505 Estate is the finest you can own. **Prices start from just £7,199.**

Look up your local dealer in Yellow Pages. He'll be happy to demonstrate the unique Peugeot 505 Estate range.

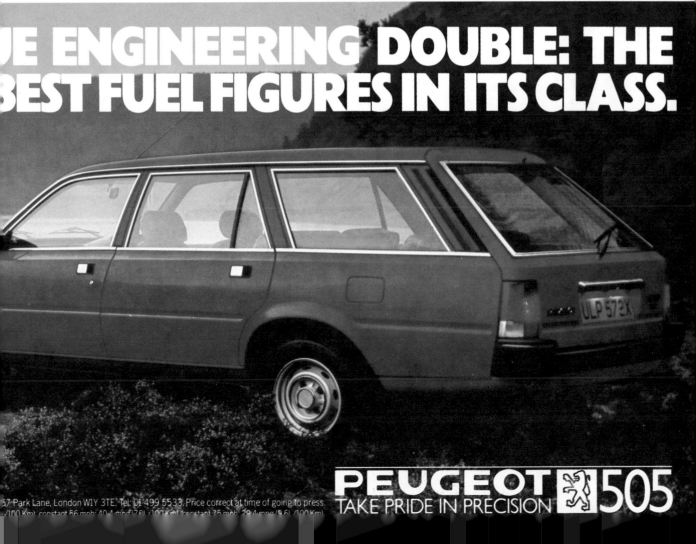

UE ENGINEERING DOUBLE: THE BEST FUEL FIGURES IN ITS CLASS.

ULP 572X

57 Park Lane, London W1Y 3TE. Tel: 01-499 5533. Price correct at time of going to press.
/100 Km), constant 56 mph: 40.4 mpg (7.0L /100 Km) constant 75 mph: 29.4 mpg (9.6L /100 Km)

PEUGEOT 505

TAKE PRIDE IN PRECISION

Scottish Angling News
tells you all about Fishing in Scottish waters

For the How, Why & Where of Fishing in Scotland, get Scottish Angling News - *The* magazine, for Sea, Coarse, Salmon and Trout Fishing news and information.

The Game Fishing Handbook

Specimen Hunting – or big fish for all ≡

Rod Hutchinson

Specimen Hunting — or big fish for all

G. Bontoff with a magnificent perch.

Probably the most used phrase in the popular press when reading the weekly angling columns, is, 'The fish of a life time' continuing in the vein that Joe Bloggs has been fishing thirty years before he finally caught a two pound reach, twenty pound carp, or seven pound tench etc. The impression given that the capture of big fish is down to luck, and the average angler must hope that one day Lady Luck will smile on him.

Yet at the same time, some anglers keep popping up week after week, with beaming smiles holding huge fish of all species. Obviously luck does play its part, but when some anglers consistently catch big fish, that part is very small indeed. What those anglers have done is to pick out a given species, select water where that species is known or thought to grow large, and then set about a method which will hopefully select those large fish, and put them on the bank.

There are no earth shattering new methods, indeed nothing that is beyond the realms of the average angler. The simple fact is that if an angler wishes to be successful with big fish, then that angler has to be selective in species, casting out and hoping a big fish will pick up, is not the way to success.

Selection of Species This is really down to the individual. Some dream of holding two pound roach, while to others the dream will be big carp or double figure bream. However, to be realistic, unless one is prepared to travel the length of the country, it is far better to pick a species for which your area is known. Without travelling for instance, there is little point in dreaming of big catfish unless you live in the Leighton Buzzard area, around which are the waters in which that species is concentrated. Although there are exceptions in individual lakes or rivers, as a general guide these are the species most likely to grow large in a given area.

Specimen Hunting – or big fish for all

Norfolk/Suffolk — Pike, Reach, Chub, Tench.
Fenland system of drains — Pike, Zander.
Lancs. Cheshire, Potteries — Bream, Carp, Tench.
Yorkshire Rivers — Barbel, Chub, Grayling.
Essex, Kent, Home Counties — Carp, Tench, Pike, Perch, Bream.
Southern Counties — Roach, Barbel, Chub, Grayling.
West Country — Carp, Chub, Tench, Roach.
Midlands — Bream, Roach, Catfish, Pike.

Selection of Venue

Having decided on the species an angler would most like to catch, he then comes to picking out the venue most likely to hold that fish. Fish of any species grow large in a water because the environment is suited to them, i.e. there is plenty of the type of food they prefer, available. Again with few exceptions dirty cloudy lakes are unlikely to hold big fish. Photosynthesis the key to aquatic life depends on light penetrating the water, which in turn promotes plant life, which harbours insects and crustacea, which provide the proteins essential for fish to grow. So as a general rule of thumb, **the clearer the water, the more likely fish are to grow large**. The exceptions to this rule are:

1. When preditors i.e. pike, zander, eels, catfish are the species sought after. Many lakes and drains are cloudy because they are too heavily populated by small fish species which are forced in their need for food to continually churn up the bottom. Here that abundance of small fish provides a regular food supply for the preditors to grow large on.

2. When the species of that water were introduced at a time when food supplies were high. They grew well until such a time as food became sparse, generally through additional stockings of that water. In the time of good feeding species such as carp could well grow to even thirty pounds. When food supplies become limited the carp would lose a certain amount of weight, but may still be able to sustain a weight over twenty pounds.

3. When the water concerned is used for land drainage and the colour is really artificial, being created by muddy water drawn off the fields.

Winter Wonderland and a specimen roach in the snow.

7

Specimen Hunting – or big fish for all

Tim Richardson, took notice of where the small fry had shoaled, suspecting that also super pike like the one he is holding would be present.

There is a general misconception amongst occasional angler that the bottom feeding species i.e. carp, tench and bream, need a thick muddy bottom in which to survive well. The muddy bottomed farm ponds which are often full of these fish may at first light look to support this view. In fact these water are usually full of stunted fish, because the waters cannot support them. The clear watered gravel pits with their lush, green weed growth are far better habitats, for those fish to grow large. The food sources being of a larger size i.e. mussel snails, shrimps, etc., on which fish quickly pack on weight.

Those same reasons apply to the clear rivers, that often run over chalk or gravel. Note the Hampshire rivers, i.e. Test, Avo Stour, which provide the food for barbel, chub and roach t grow to exceptional sizes. In many parts of the country thes ideal river locations are used as game fisheries, but it can als be said with near certainty that big coarse fish will be presen Many owners of the game fishing, will allow coarse fishing o of the game season, providing those fish caught are remove from their fishery. When this is the case, you have first class fi to stock up waters of your own. If it is not possible to gain permission to these waters, the adjoining water downstream the fisheries is the best place to look.

Although my preference is gravel pits when in pursuit of bottom feeding species, clay bottomed lakes can also produ fish of a large size. The meres of Cheshire, Salop and South Lancashire are such waters. The key here would seem to be their generally large acreage, combined with a low head of fis The food source may not be of as high a quality as that found the clear gravel pits, but the sheer abundance of bloodwor and all forms of the aquatic fly larvae compensates for this. Many of the meres also have massive explosions of daphnia each summer which, although I personally doubt are of mu benefit to large fish, certainly provide extra food for the younger fish of the species.

The key to it all is that a fish has to have abundant food to grow large. You are unlikely to find a water teeming with fish of large size. The specimen hunter doesn't expect to fill his ne every time he goes fishing. He is more likely to catch one or tw good sized fish, if he has selected his water properly.

Specimen Hunting – or big fish for all

Short Cuts Many anglers not unreasonably refuse to give away the venue from which they catch specimen fish. However, by reading the angling press carefully enough clues appear to piece together an area or water that produces good sized fish regularly. For instance, when half a dozen anglers all living within a few miles of each other report large tench. It is odds on that they are not all travelling far for their fishing. A glance through the ordinance survey map of that area should soon reveal those waters worth investigating. Take a look at them all and choose the one that appears to have those characteristics necessary for big fish.

Also the Match reports and the childrens pages of the Angling journals are well worth reading. Both sets of anglers are less likely to be secretive, and will more likely than not even name the water from where they've caught certain fish. A few years ago, a close friend of mine was well rewarded for following the Match reports. Two certain swims on a Yorkshire river, were creating problems for the Match anglers. They would get continually broken up by large fish, or if they managed to stay attached, the fish would take them into unseen snags, from which they had to pull for a break.

My friend moved into one of the swims immediately a match had finished. Instead of fine match tackle, he upped the strength of his line to eight pound breaking strain, combined with a large forged hook and a powerful carp red. Within an hour he had succeeded in putting two specimen barbel on the bank! A species few anglers even realised existed in that length of the river.

In a similar vein, a youngster reported a large carp from an Essex water. Not having a large enough set of scales he estimated the fish at over twenty pounds. Now some youngsters often quite innocently do over estimate the size of a fish, and few people took much notice of the report, as the water had no reputation for producing big fish. However one of the local carp anglers decided to take a look and his results were exceptional to say the least. In the space of a week he caught two carp of over thirty pounds and another of twenty eight pounds. What is more the fish fell to simple baits and tactics because they were simply naive, having never been fished specifically for, by any of the regular anglers on the water.

Gravelpit Whopper. Brian Hawkins with a super tench over 8lbs.

Specimen Hunting – or big fish for all

Methods and Tactics

Brian Hankins with a specimen eel.

Portrait of a specimen perch.

The story of the match anglers losing the large barbel regularly, well illustrates my first point, in that, tackle must be of a sufficient strength as to be able to cope with the size of fish the angler is after. It is far better to get one bite and land your fish, then get half a dozen bites and not land any, due to insufficient tackle strength. The two most important items being the line and the hook. Don't buy the cheapest, buy the best. Those few pence you save by buying the cheaper varieties could cost you the fish of a lifetime. Look for a line that is consistent all the way through, in strength and diameter. When it shows signs of wear, replace it. When it comes to hooks, simply buy the strongest available in the size you wish to use, and sharpen them up on an oilstone. Don't be afraid of using a larger hook than you usually would. The larger the hook, the greater the area of mouth or lip that is attached, and so the chances of the hook hold giving way are reduced.

It is difficult to generalise on rods when covering the whole spectrum of coarse fishing, but certain rules apply. Whatever the species, the rod should have sufficient power to set the hook, yet still have the ability to cushion the final lunges of fish beneath the rod top. The greater the distance being fished, so the power of the rod should be increased, as striking the hook home becomes more difficult. It also pays to use a rod increased length when fishing at any distance. The extra length enabling line to be picked up that much quicker. For close in fishing a rod often feet in length will sufficice, while once I'm fishing at distances greater than fifty yards, I prefer a twelve foot rod.

Feeding Times

Large fish of all species generally feed best in times of low light intensity. The first few hours after dawn and the last two hours in the evening are prime examples. Also days of heavy low cloud can be expected to be fruitful, so try to plan your visits to coincide with these times. While it is often thought that night fishing produces most big fish, this is not the case. The main benefits of night fishing are that the angler is settled in his swim during the productive periods, and is unlikely to scare away fish by unknowingly casting on their heads, or baiting up over feeding fish. The night anglers groundbait and hookbaits will already be in position when fish come on to feed.

roundbait and Hookbaits

he author with a carp anyone ould be proud to catch, weighing ver 30lbs.

Preditory fish i.e. pike, perch, eels, zander, will be in the areas containing their natural food, the small bait fish. This being so groundbaiting is not needed. The specimen hunter will find those areas containing plenty of food fish and know that the preditors will not be far away.

Most other species though will quickly take advantage of any regular food source, and as such, regular prebaiting has many advantages for the specimen hunter. The area chosen to prebait is best in the face of the wind to a great degree, and this will ensure that numbers of fish quickly realise there is an easy food supply in a given area.

Roach, bream and tench respond well to prebaiting with cereal groundbaits, which also contain a mixture of the following: Worms, maggots, hemp, sweetcorn, or wheat. When the time comes to fish, it is best to tackle up two rods, each baited with a different one from that list. The baits are switched about until it is found which one the fish have a preference for, and then both hooks will be baited with that food.

These species and also barbel and chub in rivers also respond well to swim feeder tactics. A large open ended swim feeder packed with the same foods as used in the prebaiting, ensures a continuous supply of food close to the hookbait. Although very successful, swimfeeders are not essential, and simple link legering, or fishing on a fixed paternoster, should provide good results with these species.

radled like a baby. Another 30 ounder to the author.

Carp being the largest growing of the bottom feeding species require a more selective approach. Larger and often harder baits are used both for prebaiting and for hookbaits, the idea being to introduce a food the smaller species are incapable of eating. While small foods like sweetcorn, beans, nuts, maggots and hamp can and do catch plenty of carp, they are not recommended for prebaiting in a mixed fishery, simply because they are not selective. All the afore mentioned species can eat these foods with ease.

Specimen Hunting – or big fish for all

Why chuck and chance when a little effort could see three beauties like these roach in your net.

Prebaiting is usually carried out with baits of a similar size to those used for the hookbait. The size can be anything from the size of a cherry to golf ball size. Boiling the baits in a sauce pan for between thirty seconds to three minutes will ensure a thin skin on the baits, other species find hard to breakdown. The longer the bait is boiled, the harder the skin becomes. Just how much bait is used in prebaiting depends on how many carp can be expected to find the bait. If only little is present, the fish are unlikely to associate the prebaited area as an easy food source. Generally between one and two pounds of bait, rolled into hook sized portions are used for prebaiting.

Carp will eat an enormous range of foods and although many of the carp anglers recipes are kept secret, lots of good baits can be made from ingredients found on the supermarket shelf. Dog and cat foods, beefburgers, sausages, luncheon meat, corned beef, cheeses, meat spreads, will all make excellent carp bait. Luncheon meat and cheeses, merely need to be cut to size, while the other food are made into a paste and stiffened up adding either sausagemeat, flour, crushed weetabix, groundrice, milk powder or semolina. Little extra additives are also well worth trying like, a spoonful of treacle or condensed milk, or a few drops of flavour essence. Adding three eggs to a pound of bait mixture, will ensure a skin if the angler wishes to boil his baits.

Terminal tackle is up to the individual, but to the fact two rods are often used, and at times of low light intensity, float fishing not generally used. As the baits are quite heavy, the angler may choose to freeline, with nothing on the line but a hook. However I much prefer to link leger, as I find it more responsive to bite indication.

Care of Fish

Finally let me say that I hope some readers will have gained the enthusiasm from this article to go out and catch their dream fish by design. It should always be remembered though that the fish of your dreams, also is the focus of many other anglers dreams. So should you be fortunate to catch it, please treat it with the respect it deserves. Weigh it in a soft mesh or wet sack. Keep it wet at all times and do not let it dry out. Keep it out of the water for the minimum amount of time possible. Photograph it and put it back to fight another day. The joy you've had in capturing that fish can be the joy of others in years to come.

Fishing Rod Manufacturers and Distributors

The following listings show the leading rod brand names and their manufacturer or distributor in the United Kingdom. Only major brands have been included and these are the brands under which a range of products are promoted and marketed. Each entry has been broken down into the main use of rods marketed under that particular brand name i.e. into Fly, Coarse or Sea.

FISHING ROD MANUFACTURERS AND DISTRIBUTORS

ABU *FLY, COARSE, SEA*
Manufacturer: ABU (Great Britain) Ltd.
Clydebank Industrial Estate,
Dunbartonshire
Tel: 041 952 6381

ACROD *FLY, COARSE, SEA*
Manufacturer: Appleton & Cragg,
1, Egloshayle Road, Wadebridge,
Cornwall
Tel: 020881 3321

AIKENS SUPERFLEX *FLY, COARSE, SEA*
Manufacturer: Aiken, Henry W. Ltd.
139/147, Kirkdale, Sydenham, London
SE26
Tel: 01 699 1141

ALBATROSS *SEA*
Distributor: H. Steade & Sons Ltd.
49, Catley Road, Sheffield, Yorks.
Tel: 0742 449454

ALPHA *FLY, COARSE, SEA, POLES*
Manufacturer: **Shakespeare Co.**
P.O. Box 1, Redditch, Worcs.
Tel: 0527 21570
See Advertisement on Inside Back Cover

ATR *FLY, COARSE, SEA*
Manufacturer: **Avon Tournament Rods**
55 Hatton Garden, London EC1N 8HP
See Advertisement this Section

AUGER *FLY, COARSE, SEA, POLES*
Manufacturer: Auger Accessories Ltd.
Auger Works, Crowland Road, London
N15
Tel: 01 802 0077

BERKLEY *FLY, SEA*
Distributor: Vince Lister Agency,
1, Send Road, Caversham, Reading
Tel: 0734 479641/481117

BOB CHURCH *FLY, COARSE*
Manufacturer: Bob Church & Co. Ltd.
16, Lorne Road, Northampton
Tel: 0604 713674

BRENT *COARSE, SEA*
Manufacturer: Brent (Hailsham) Limited
156, Station Road, Hailsham, East Sussex
Tel: 0323 840094

BRUCE & WALKER *FLY, COARSE, SEA*
Manufacturer: Bruce & Walker Limited,
Huntingdon Road, Upwood,
Huntingdon, Cambs.
Tel: 0487 813764

CAUDLE & RIVAZ *FLY*
Manufacturer: Caudle & Rivaz Ltd.
1, Chester Close, Heolgerrig, Merthyr
Tydfil
Tel: 0685 71404

CENTURY XXI *FLY, COARSE, SEA*
Manufacturer: **Shakespeare Company,**
P.O. Box 1, Redditch, Worcs.
Tel: 0527 21570
See Advertisement on Inside Back Cover

CHALLENGE *FLY*
Manufacturer: Foster Sporting Services,
32, St Johns Street, Ashbourne,
Derbyshire
Tel: 0335 43135

CHURCH HILL GOLD *FLY*
Manufacturer: Church Hill Farm,
Mursley, Bucks
Tel: 0296 72 524

CLARKE *COARSE*
Manufacturer: W.B. Clarke,
Crescent Works, Mount Pleasant,
Redditch
Tel: 0527 43310

COPPERHEAD *FLY*
Manufacturer: Sue Burgess Fishing
Tackle,
Glyn Celyn, Becon, Powys
Tel: 0874 4448

CRADDOCK *FLY, COARSE, SEA*
Manufacturer: E.R. Craddock Ltd.
Heming Road, Redditch, Worcs.
Tel: 0527 28301
Distributor: Richard Forshaw & Co. Ltd.
Colonsay House, Tarron Way, Moreton,
Merseyside
Tel: 051 678 7878

CUMBRIA *FLY*
Manufacturer: McHardys of Carlisle,
South Henry Street, Carlisle, Cumbria
Tel: 0228 23988

DAIWA *FLY, COARSE, SEA, POLES*
Manufacturer: Daiwa Sports Limited,
Netherton Industrial Estate, Wishaw
Tel: 069 83 61313
Telex: 777479 DAIWA G

D.A.M. *FLY, COARSE, SEA, POLES*
Distributor: D.A.M. Tackle Ltd.
P.O. Box 40, Leamington Spa, Warks.
Tel: 0926 313237

DAVID NORWICH *FLY*
Manufacturer: David Norwich,
467 Eglinton Street, Glasgow
Tel: 041 429 8302

DIAMONDBACK *FLY*
Manufacturer: Sue Burgess Fishing
Tackle,
Glyn Celyn, Powys, Wales
Tel: 0874 4448

DICMAR *FLY*
Manufacturer: John Dickson & Son,
21, Frederick Street, Edinburgh
Tel: 031 225 4218

ENGLISH LAKES
Manufacturer: The Gun Shop,
Jubilee Bridge, Lorton Road,
Cockermouth, Cumbria
Tel: 0900 822058

FOTHERGILL & HARVEY *FLY, COARSE, SEA*
Manufacturer: Fothergill & Harvey,
Composites Division, Summit,
Littleborough, Lancashire
Tel: 0706 78831

GARBOLINO *POLES*
Distributor: Sundridge,
Vicarage Lane, Hoo, Nr Rochester, Ke■
Tel: 0634 252104

GEOFFREY BUCKNALL *FLY*
Manufacturer: Sundridge,
Vicarage Lane, Hoo, Nr Rochester, Ke■
Tel: 0634 252104

GOLDCREST *FLY, COARSE, SEA*
Manufacturer: The Rodrill Co. Ltd.
Collingwood Road, London N15
Tel: 01 800 0018

GOLDEN LION *FLY, COARSE, SE*
Manufacturer: BFTC/Oakly Fishing
Tackle,
Heming Road, Washford Industrial
Estate, Redditch, Worcs.
Tel: 0527 24509

GREYS *FLY*
Manufacturer: **Greys of Alnwick,**
Wagon Way Road, Alnwick
Tel: 0665 602696

HARDY *FLY, COARSE, SEA*
Manufacturer: Hardy Bros (Alnwick)
Ltd.
Willowburn, Alnwick, Northumberland
Tel: 0665 602771

Rods

HI-LINE *FLY, COARSE, SEA*

Distributor: East Anglian Rod Co. Ltd.
Rookery House, Newmarket, Suffolk
Tel: 0638 5831

HORIZON *FLY, COARSE, SEA*

Manufacturer: **Horizon Fishing Company,**
47 Prospect Hill, Redditch, Worcs
Tel: 0527 62421
See Advertisement this Section

IAN HEAPS *POLES*

Distributor: **C.J. Field (Polynet) Ltd.**
Union Estate, Union Road,
Macclesfield, Cheshire
Tel: 0625 611077

JOHN GODDARD *FLY*

Manufacturer: F. Goddard (Efgeeco) Ltd.
26 Balham Hill, London SW12
Tel: 01 673 1177

KEVIN ASHURST *COARSE*

Manufacturer: Sundridge,
Vicarage Lane, Hoo, Nr Rochester, Kent
Tel: 0634 252104

KOPESCA *SEA*

Distributor: **Anglemark,**
P.O. Box 35, Sandbach, Cheshire
Tel: 09367 61484

KUNNAN *FLY, COARSE, SEA*

Distributor: **Normark Sports Ltd.**
Bossel Road, Buckfastleigh, Devon
Tel: 03644 2597

LERC *POLES*

Distributor: East Anglian Rod Co. Ltd.
Rookery House, Newmarket, Suffolk
Tel: 0638 5831

Distributor: Aiken, Henry W. Ltd.
139/147, Kirkdale, Sydenham, London
SE26
Tel: 01 699 1141

LITE-RODS *SEA*

Manufacturer: Lite-Rods,
David Street, Bridgend Industrial Estate,
Bridgend, Mid Glamorgan
Tel: 0656 50884

MARCO *FLY, COARSE, SEA*

Manufacturer: Modern Arms Co. Ltd.
Pembroke Road, Bromley, Kent
Tel: 01 460 3483

MARCUS WARWICK *FLY*

Manufacturer: Marcus Warwick
58 High St. West, Uppingham, Leics
Tel: 057282 2487

MILBRO *FLY, COARSE, SEA, POLES*

Manufacturer: **Millard Brothers Limited,**
Tantallon Road, North Berwick, Scotland
Tel: 0620 4661
See Advertisement this Section

MONCRIEFF ADJUSTABUTT *SEA*

Distributor: F. Goddard (Efgeeco) Ltd.
26, Balham Hill, London SW12
Tel: 01 673 1177

OAKLY *FLY, COARSE, SEA*

Manufacturer: B.F.T.C. Oakly Fishing
Tackle Ltd.
Heming Road, Washford Industrial
Estate, Redditch, Worcs.
Tel: 0527 24509

OLYMPIC *FLY, COARSE, SEA, POLES*

Distributor: Wisden-Edwards Ltd.
Pershore Trading Estate, Pershore,
Worcs.
Tel: 03865 2411/2/3

ORVIS *FLY*

Manufacturer: Orvis UK,
Nether Wallop Mill, Stockbridge,
Hampshire
Tel: 026 478 212

PARTRIDGE *FLY*

Manufacturer: **A.E. Partridge & Sons**
Ltd. Crescent Works, Mount Pleasant,
Redditch, Worcs.
Tel: 0527 41380

PATEKE MORTON *FLY, COARSE, SEA*

Manufacturer: Pateke Morton Ltd.
59, Hutton Close, Crowther, Indus. Est.
Washington, Tyne & Wear
Tel: 0632 466404

PELICAN *COARSE*

Manufacturer: Pelican Fishing Tackle,
118, Ashley Road, Parkstone, Poole,
Dorset
Tel: 0202 743291

PEZON ET MICHEL *FLY, POLES*

Distributor: Anglers Masterline Ltd.
Cotteswold Road, Tewkesbury, Glos.
Tel: 0684 294210
See Advertisement under Lines

PIONEER *SEA*

Manufacturer: Bruce & Walker Ltd
Huntingdon Road, Upwood,
Huntingdon, Cambs.
Tel: 0487 813764

RAPIER

Manufacturer: Taylor & Johnson Ltd.
Palmers Road, East Moons Moat,
Redditch, Worcs.
Tel: 0527 29030/21030

RODCRAFT *FLY, COARSE, SEA*

Manufacturer: Rodcraft of Redditch,
Tudor Works, Marsden Road, Redditch
Tel: 0527 62525

ROYAL *FLY*

Manufacturer: William Powell & Son
Ltd. 35, Carrs Lane, Birmingham
Tel: 021 643 0689

SHAKESPEARE *FLY, COARSE, SEA, POLES*

Manufacturer: **Shakespeare Company,**
P.O. Box 1, Redditch, Worcs.
Tel: 0527 21570
See Advertisement on Inside Back Cover

HARPES *FLY*

Manufacturer: **C. Farlow & Co.**
Limited, 151, Fairview Road,
Cheltenham, Glos.
Tel: 0242 518690

SIGMA *FLY, COARSE, SEA, POLES*

Manufacturer: **Shakespeare Company,**
P.O. Box 1, Redditch. Worcs.
Tel: 0527 21570
See Advertisment on Inside Back Cover

SIGMA SUPRA *FLY, COARSE*

Manufacturer: **Shakespeare Company,**
P.O. Box 1, Redditch. Worcs.
Tel: 0527 21570
See Advertisement on Inside Back Cover

SPECIALIST *FLY*

Manufacturer: Berkley,
Distributor: Vince Lister Agency,
, Send Road, Caversham, Reading
Tel: 0734 479641/481117

STARGLASS *POLES*

Distributor: Hampton Sports Asso. Ltd.
Unit J, Southampton Airport,
Southampton, Hampshire
Tel: 0703 611870

St CROIX *COARSE POLES*

Distributor: Anglemark,
P.O. Box 35, Sandbach, Cheshire
Tel: 09367 61484

STEADFAST *POLES*

Distributor: H. Steade & Sons Limited,
9, Catley Road, Sheffield, Yorks
Tel: 0742 449454

STREAMLINE *COARSE*

Manufacturer: Streamline Tackle,
9/51, Tickhill Road, Maltby, S. Yorks.
Tel: 0709 812559

SUNDRIDGE *FLY, COARSE, SEA*

Manufacturer: Sundridge,
Vicarage Lane, Hoo, Nr. Rochester,
Kent.
Tel: 0634 252104

SYDNEY JARVIS *FLY, COARSE, SEA*

Manufacturer: Sydney Jarvis,
5, Chestnut Road, Astwood Bank,
Worcs
Tel: 052789 2765

TARN RODS *FLY, COARSE*

Manufacturer: **D.P. Hulme,**
'Caen-y-Mynydd', Dolanog,
Welshpool, Powys.
Tel: 0938 810830
See Advertisement this Section

TAYLORS

Manufacturer: Taylors Fishing Tackle,
3, Western Avenue, Buckingham
Tel: 02802 3881

TERRY EUSTACE *FLY, COARSE, SEA*

Manufacturer: **Terry Eustace Rods & Blanks,**
2a, Booths Lane, Great Barr,
Birmingham
Tel: 021 360 9669
See Advertisement this Section

TONY FORDHAM *FLY, COARSE, SEA*

Manufacturer: Fordham & Wakefield,
Kinvale, Third Street, Langton,
Tunbridge Wells, Kent
Tel: 089286 3153

TROSSACHS *FLY*

Manufacturer: Trossachs Rod Building
Co. Ltd. Nethybridge, Invernesshire
Tel: 0479 82676

TYCOON FIN-NOR *SEA*

Distributor: Butler's Marine,
Woods Way, Mulbery Industrial Estate,
Goring-By-Sea, Sussex
Tel: 0903 502221

UGLY STIK *FLY, SEA*

Manufacturer: **Shakespeare Company,**
P.O. Box 1, Redditch. Worcs.
Tel: 0527 21570
See Advertisement on Back Inside Cover

VIKING *FLY, COARSE, SEA*

Distributor: Rollins & Sons (London) Ltd.
Rollins House, Mimram Road, Hertford
Tel: 0992 57555

VORTEX *FLY, COARSE, SEA*

Manufacturer: **E.T. Barlow & Sons
(Vortex) Ltd.**
Pond House, Weston Green, Thames
Ditton, Surrey
Tel: 01 398 3826
Distributor: Rodco,
Pond House, Weston Green, Thames
Ditton, Surrey
Tel: 01 398 2405
See Advertisement this Section

WESSEX RODS *FLY, COARSE, SEA*

Manufacturer: **Wessex Rods,**
Dorchester, Dorset
Tel: 0305 62277
See Advertisement this Section

YORKSHIRE *FLY*

Distributor: Mackenzie-Philps Limited,
Deer Springs, Stockeld, Wetherby,
Yorks.
Tel: 0937 63646

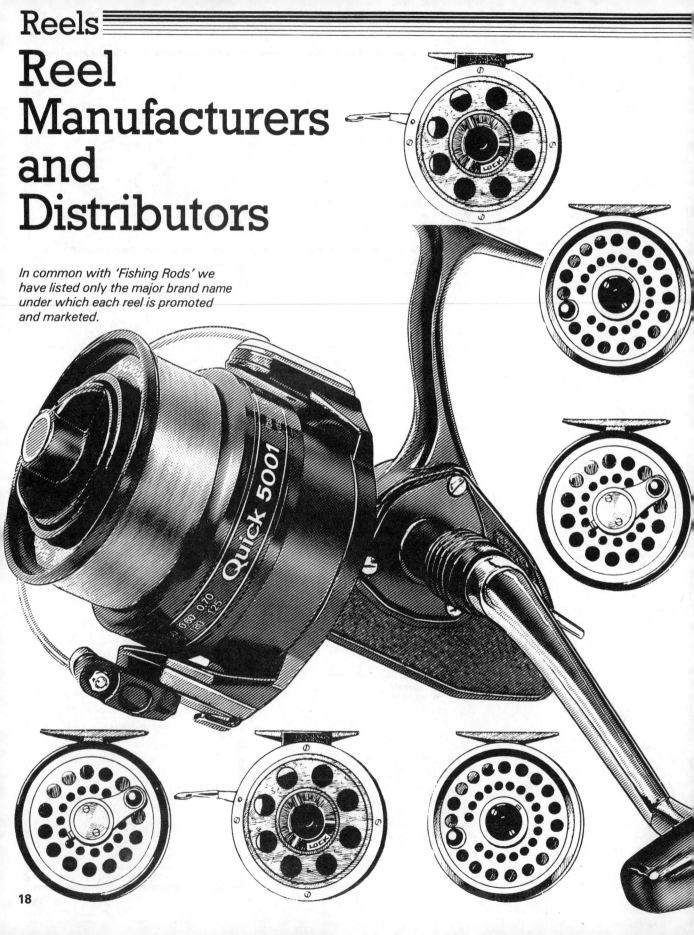

Reels

Reel Manufacturers and Distributors

In common with 'Fishing Rods' we have listed only the major brand name under which each reel is promoted and marketed.

REEL MANUFACTURERS AND DISTRIBUTORS

BU 500 SERIES
Manufacturer: ABU (Great Britain) Ltd.
Clydebank Industrial Estate,
Dunbartonshire
Tel: 041 952 6381

ABUMATIC
Manufacturer: ABU (Great Britain) Ltd.
Clydebank Industrial Estate,
Dunbartonshire
Tel: 041 952 6381

ALPHA
Manufacturer: **Shakespeare Company,
P.O. Box 1, Redditch, Worcs.
Tel: 0527 21570
See Advertisement on Inside Back
Cover**

ALVEY
Distributor: Auger Accessories Ltd.
Auger Works, Crowland Road, London
N15 6UP
Tel: 01 802 0077

AMBASSADEUR
Manufacturer: ABU (Great Britain) Ltd.
Clydebank Industrial Estate,
Dunbartonshire
Tel: 041 952 6381

BERKLEY
Distributor: Vince Lister Agency,
, Send Road, Caversham, Reading
Tel: 0734 479641

BEAULITE
Manufacturer: **Shakespeare Company,
P.O. Box 1, Redditch, Worcs.
Tel: 0527 21570
See Advertisement on Inside Back
Cover**

BLACK SEAL
Distributor: Wisden-Edwards Ltd.
Pershore Trading Estate, Pershore,
Worcs.
Tel: 03865 2411/2/3

CARDINAL
Manufacturer: ABU (Great Britain) Ltd.
Clydebank Industrial Estate,
Dunbartonshire
Tel: 041 952 6381

CHARGER
Distributor: Pegley-Davies Ltd.
Hersham Trading Estate, Walton-on-
Thames, Surrey
Tel: 093 22 40481

CONDEX
Manufacturer: **Shakespeare Company,
P.O. Box 1, Redditch, Worcs.
Tel: 0527 21570
See Advertisement on Inside Back
Cover**

CONTACT
Distributor: Sundridge,
Vicarage Lane, Hoo, Nr. Rochester,
Kent
Tel: 0634 252104

DAIWA
Distributor: Daiwa Sports Ltd.
Netherton Industrial Estate, Wishaw,
Strathclyde
Tel: 069 83 61313
Telex: 777479 DAIWA G

D.A.M.
Distributor: D.A.M. Tackle Ltd.
P.O. Box 40, Leamington Spa CV32
Tel: 0926 313237
Telex: 311932 MARFIN

DIPLOMAT
Manufacturer: ABU (Great Britain) Ltd.
Clydebank Industrial Estate,
Dunbartonshire
Tel: 041 952 6381

DRAGONFLY
Manufacturer: Netnia Ltd.
Intrepid Works, Falmouth, Cornwall
Tel: 0326 72441
Distributor: Leeda Tackle,
14, Cannon Street, Southampton, Hants
Tel: 0703 772131

GEARFLY
Manufacturer: Netnia Ltd.
Intrepid Works, Falmouth, Cornwall
Tel: 0326 72441
Distributor: Leeda Tackle,
14, Cannon Street, Southampton, Hants
Tel: 0703 772131

GLADIATOR
Distributor: Modern Arms Co. Ltd.
Pembroke Road, Bromley, Kent
Tel: 01 460 3483

GEOFFREY BUCKNALL
Manufacturer: Sundridge Tackle Ltd,
Vicarage Lane, Hoo, Rochester, Kent
Tel: 0634 252104

GRICE & YOUNG
Manufacturer: Grice & Young Ltd.
Somerford, Christchurch, Dorset
Tel: 0202 483636/7
Telex: HPA-G 418293

HARDY
Manufacturer: Hardy Bros. (Alnwick)
Ltd. Willowburn, Alnwick,
Northumberland
Tel: 0665 602771

KASSNAR
Distributor: Richard Forshaw & Co. Ltd.
Colonsay House, Tarran Way, Moreton,
Merseyside
Tel: 051 678 7878

LINESHOOTER
Manufacturer: Bob Church & Co. Ltd.
16, Lorne Road, Northampton
Tel: 0604 713674

MARCO

Distributor: Modern Arms Co. Ltd.
Pembroke Road, Bromley, Kent
Tel: 01 460 3483

MARRYAT

Distributor: Sue Burgess Fishing Tackle,
Glyn Celyn, Brecon, Powys
Tel: 0874 4448

MATSUO

Distributor: Pelican Fishing Tackle
118, Ashley Road, Parkstone, Poole,
Dorset
Tel: 0202 743291

MITCHELL

Distributor: Leeda Tackle,
14, Cannon Street, Southampton
Tel: 0703 772131

NEWELL

Distributor: Bruce & Walker Ltd,
Huntingdon Road, Upwood,
Huntingdon, Cambs.
Tel: 0487 813764

OFMER

Distributor: Modern Arms Co. Ltd.
Pembroke Road, Bromley, Kent
Tel: 01 460 3483

OLYMPIC

Distributor: Wisden-Edwards Ltd.
Pershore Trading Estate, Pershore,
Worcs.
Tel: 03865 2411/2/3

OMNI

Manufacturer: **Shakespeare Company,
P.O. Box 1, Redditch, Worcs.
Tel: 0527 21570**
See Advertisement Inside Back Cover

ORLANDO

Manufacturer: Grice & Young Ltd.
Somerford, Christchurch, Dorset
Tel: 0202 483636/7
Telex: HPA-G 418293

ORVIS

Distributor: Orvis Co. Inc,
Nether Wallop Mill, Stockbridge,
Hampshire
Tel: 026 478 212

PENN

Distributor: M. Ward Duckworth,
Littleton House, Crawley Ridge,
Camberley, Surrey
Tel: 0276 63910

POLICANSKY MONITOR

Distributor: F. Goddard (Efgeeco) Ltd.
26, Balham Hill, London SW12
Tel: 01 673 1177

RIMFLY

Manufacturer: Netnia Ltd.
Intrepid Works, Falmouth, Cornwall
Tel: 0326 72441
Distributor: Leeda Tackle,
14, Cannon Street, Southampton, Hants.
Tel: 0703 772131

RYOBI

Distributor: **Anglers Masterline Ltd.
Cotteswold Road, Tewkesbury, Glos
Tel: 0684 294210**
See Advertisement under Lines

SAGARRA

Distributor: Bruce & Walker Ltd,
Huntingdon Road, Upwood,
Huntingdon, Cambs.
Tel: 0487 813764

SHAKESPEARE

Manufacturer: **Shakespeare Company,
P.O. Box 1, Redditch, Worcs.
Tel: 0527 21570**
*See Advertisement on Inside Back
Cover*

SIGMA

Manufacturer **Shakespeare Company,
P.O. Box 1, Redditch, Worcs.
Tel: 0527 21570**
*See Advertisement on Inside Back
Cover*

SIGMA SUPRA

Manufacturer: **Shakespeare Company,
P.O. Box 1, Redditch, Worcs.
Tel: 0527 21570**
See Advertisement Inside Back Cover

SPECIALIST

Distributor: Vince Lister Agency,
1, Send Road, Caversham, Reading
Tel: 0734 479641/481117

SPEEDEX

Manufacturer: **Shakespeare Company,
P.O. Box 1, Redditch, Worcs.
Tel: 0527 21570**
See Advertisement Inside Back Cover

SUNDRIDGE

Manufacturer: I & C Carbonyte Ltd.
Vicarage Lane, Hoo, Nr Rochester, Ken
Tel: 0634 250901
Distributor: Sundridge,
Vicarage Lane, Hoo, Nr. Rochester,
Kent
Tel: 0634 252104

TARN

Manufacturer: **D.P. Hulme,
Coen-y-Mynydd, Dolanog, Welshpool
Powys
Tel: 0938 810830**
See Advertisement this Section

TATLER

Manufacturer: Grice & Young Ltd.
Somerford, Christchurch, Dorset
Tel: 0202 483636/7

VIKING

Manufacturer: Rollins & Son (London)
Ltd. Rollins House, Mimram Road,
Hertford
Tel: 0992 57555

ZEBCO

Distributor: **Vince-Lister Agency,
1, Send Road, Caversham, Reading
Tel: 0734 479641/481117**
See Advertisement this Section

Fishing Line Manufacturers and Distributors

In common with 'Fishing Rods' we have listed only the major brand names under which each line is promoted and distributed.
To aid the reader we have divided the entries into:
Fly, which would be used exclusively for fly fishing.
Monofilaament, which could be used under different circumstances in all types of fishing.
Braided, which would be used primarily by the sea angler but could also be used in other types of fishing.
Wire, which would also be used primarily by the sea angler.

FISHING LINE MANUFACTURERS AND DISTRIBUTORS

ABU Matchline – Spinline – Sealine
MONOFILAMENT
Manufacturer: ABU (Great Britain) Ltd.
Clydebank Industrial Estate,
Dunbartonshire
Tel: 041 952 6381

ABULON *FLY*
Manufacturer: ABU (Great Britain) Ltd.
Clydebank Industrial Estate,
Dunbartonshire
Tel: 041 952 6381

AIR CEL *FLY,*
Distributor: Leeda Tackle,
14, Cannon Street, Southampton, Hants
Tel: 0703 772131

ASPON-C *MONOFILAMENT*
Distributor: **Anglemark,**
P.O. Box 35, Sandbach, Cheshire
Tel: 09367 61484

ATLAS *MONOFILAMENT*
UK Agent: Frank Wallace, Yeomanry
House, Castle Hill, Reading
Tel: 0734 589703
   ATLAS ELITE
   Distributor: H.E. Watson & Son Ltd.
   9, Vernon Street, Sutton, Surrey
   Tel: 01 643 7993
   ATLAS KROIC

Distributor: C. Farlow & Co. Ltd.
151, Fairview Road, Cheltenham
Tel: 0242 518690

**BAYER PERLON
BAYER SUPER SOFT**
MONOFILAMENT
Distributor: Aiken Henry W. Ltd.
139/147, Kirkdale, Sydenham,
London SE26
Tel: 01 699 1141

BERKLEY *FLY, MONOFILAMENT,*
  BRAIDED
Distributor: **Vince Lister Agency,**
1, Send Road, Caversham, Reading,
Berks
Tel: 0734 479641/481117
See Advertisement this Section

BLACK SEAL *MONOFILAMENT*
Distributor: Wisden-Edwards Ltd.
Pershore Trading Estate, Pershore,
Worcs
Tel: 03865 2411

BRENT *MONOFILAMENT*
Distributor: Brent (Hailsham) Limited,
156, Station Road, Hailsham, East Sussex
Tel: 0323 840094

CANADIAN NORTHERN *FLY*
Distributor: Bob Church & Co. Ltd.
16, Lorne Road, Northampton
Tel: 0604 713674

CAPSTAN *MONOFILAMENT*
Distributor: Aiken, Henry W. Ltd.
137/147 Kirkdale, Sydenham,
London SE26
Tel: 01 699 1141

COMPETITOR *MONOFILAMENT*
Distributor: Sussex Tackle Ltd.
12, North Parade, Horsham, Sussex
Tel: 0403 67168

CORTLAND *FLY*
Distributor: **Normark Sports Limited,**
Bossell Road, Buckfastleigh, Devon
Tel: 03644 2597/2368
Telex: 42657 NORSPO G
See Advertisement under Rod Fitting
and Rod Rings

COURIER *FLY*
Manufacturer: C.E.D. Harris & Co. Lt
2a, Church Green West, Redditch,
Worcs.
Tel: 0527 64409
Distributor: Alfred Brooker & Co. Ltd.
Arthur Street, Redditch, Worcs.
Tel: 0527 26974
See Advertisement under Tackle
Retailers

**DAIWA MONFIL AND
PROLINE** *MONOFILAMENT*
Manufacturer: Daiwa Sports Limited,
Netherton Industrial Estate, Wishaw,
Tel: 069 83 61313

DAMYL *MONOFILAMENT*
Distributor: D.A.M. Tackle Ltd.
P.O. Box 40, Leamington Spa
Tel: 0926 313237
Telex: 311932 MARFIN

EFGEECO *MONOFILAMENT*
Distributor: F. Goddard (Efgeeco) Ltd
26 Balham Hill, London SW12
Tel: 01 673 1177

**FARLOWS
KROIC** *MONOFILAMENT*
Manufacturer: **C. Farlow & Co. Ltd.**
151, Fairview Road, Cheltenham
Tel: 0242 5158690

FISH HAWK *MONOFILAMENT*
Manufacturer: **Shakespeare Compan**
P.O. Box 1, Redditch, Worcs.
Tel: 0527 21570
See Advertisement on Inside Back
Cover

FORLINE   *MONOFILAMENT*
Distributor: Richard Forshaw & Co. Ltd.
Colonsay House, Tarran Way, Moreton, Merseyside
Tel: 051 678 7878

GALION   *FLY*
Distributor: Leeda Tackle,
14, Cannon Street, Southampton, Hants
Tel: 0703 772131

GANTEL   *MONOFILAMENT*
Distributor: Pelican Fishing Tackle
118, Ashley Road, Parkstone, Poole, Dorset
Tel: 0202 743291

GARCIA   *FLY*
Distributor: ABU (Great Britain) Limited,
Clydebank Industrial Estate, Dunbartonshire
Tel: 041 952 6381

GLADDING   *FLY, MONOFILAMENT, BRAIDED*
Distributor: D.A.M. Tackle Ltd.
P.O. Box 40, Leamington Spa, Warks.
Tel: 0926 313237

GOLDEN MARLIN   *MONOFILAMENT*
Distributor: Telltrade Limited,
104 Christchurch Road, Ringwood, Hants
Tel: 04254 3932

GUDEBROD   *FLY, BRAIDED*
Distributor: **Anglers Masterline Ltd.
Cotteswold Road, Tewkesbury, Glos.
Tel: 0684 294210
*See Advertisement this Section***

HARDY   *FLY, MONOFILAMENT, BRAIDED*
Manufacturer: Hardy Bros. (Alnwick) Ltd. Willowburn, Alnwick, Northumberland
Tel: 0665 60 2771

HERON   *FLY*
Distributor: Anglo American (Field Sports) Ltd. 6 Wardour Lodge, Sunningdale, Berkshire
Tel: 0990 20549
Telex: 849323 AEGIS G

JET   *MONOFILAMENT*
Manufacturer: **Shakespeare Company.
P.O. Box 1, Redditch, Worcs.
Tel: 0527 21570
*See Advertisement on Inside Back Cover***

LEEDS SEA DACRON   *BRAIDED*
Distributor: Leeda Tackle,
14, Cannon Street, Southampton, Hants
Tel: 0703 772131

LUXORKROIC   *MONOFILAMENT*
Distributor: **Anglers Masterline Ltd.
Cotteswold Road, Tewkesbury, Glos.
Tel: 0684 294210
*See Advertisement this Section***

MAGIC MONO   *MONOFILAMENT*
Distributor: Auger Accessories Ltd.
Auger Works, Crowland Road, London N15
Tel: 01 802 0077

MARLIN   *MONOFILAMENT, WIRE*
Distributor: Telltrade Limited,
104 Christchurch Road, Ringwood, Hants
Tel: 04254 3932

MASTERLINE   *FLY*
Manufacturer: **Anglers Masterline Ltd.
Cottesworld Road, Tewkesbury, Glos.
Tel: 0684 294210
*See Advertisement this Section***

Lines

MAXIMA *MONOFILAMENT*
Distributor: Millard Bros Ltd.
Tantallon Road, North Berwick, Scotland
Tel: 0620 4661

MILBRO *MONOFILAMENT*
Distributor: Millard Bros Ltd.
Tantallon Road, North Berwick, Scotland
Tel: 0620 4661

MILWARD SEARANGER *BRAIDED*
Manufacturer: **C. Farlow & Co. Ltd.**
151, Fairview Road, Cheltenham
Tel: 0242 518690

NEW CENTURY *FLY*
Manufacturer: **Shakespeare Company,**
P.O. Box 1, Redditch, Worcs.
Tel: 0527 21570
See Advertisement Inside Back Cover

OLYMPIC *MONOFILAMENT*
Distributor: Wisden-Edwards Ltd.
Pershore Trading Estate, Pershore,
Worcs.
Tel: 03865 2411/2/3

OPTIMA *MONOFILAMENT*
Distributor: C.J. Field (Polynet) Limited,
Union Road Estate, Union Road,
Macclesfield, Cheshire
Tel: 0625 611077

P.D.Q. *MONOFILAMENT,*
Distributor: Pegley-Davis Ltd.
Hersham Trading Estate, Walton-on-
Thames, Surrey KT12 3QE
Tel: 093 22 40481

PERLYL *MONOFILAMENT*
Manufacturer: Sportex Fishing Limited,
London Road, Stanstead, Essex.
Tel: 0279 812202

PLATIL *MONOFILAMENT*
Distributor: Leeda Tackle,
14, Cannon Street, Southampton
Tel: 0703 772131

PROFESSIONAL *FLY*
Manufacturer: **Shakespeare Company,**
P.O. Box 1, Redditch, Worcs.
Tel: 0527 21570
See Advertisement Inside Back Cover

ROYAL MARLIN *MONOFILAMENT*
Distributor: Telltrade Ltd.
104 Christchurch Road, Ringwood,
Hants
Tel: 04254 3932

SEA ACE *BRAIDED*
Manufacturer: Auger Accessories Ltd.
Auger Works, Crowland Road,
London N15
Tel: 01 802 0077

SHAKESPEARE *FLY,*
MONOFILAMENT, BRAIDED, WIRE
Manufacturer: **Shakespeare Company,**
P.O. Box 1, Redditch, Worcs.
Tel: 0527 21570
See Advertisement on Inside Back Cover

SIGMA *FLY, MONOFILAMENT,*
BRAIDED
Manufacturer: **Shakespeare Company,**
P.O. Box 1, Redditch, Worcs.
Tel: 0527 21570
See Advertisement on Inside Back Cover

SPECIALIST *FLY*
Distributor: Vince Lister Agency,
1, Send Road, Caversham, Reading,
Berks.
Tel: 0734 479641/481117
See Advertisement this Section

STREN *MONOFILAMENT*
Distributor: **Normark Sports Limited,**
Bossell Road, Buckfastleigh, Devon
Tel: 03644 2597
Telex: 42657 NORSPO G

SUPERFLEX
Distributor: Aiken, Henry W. Ltd.
139/147, Kirkdale, Sydenham,
London SE26
Tel: 01 699 1141

SUPERLINE *MONOFILAMENT*
Distributor: Leeda Tackle,
14, Cannon Street, Southampton, Hants.
Tel: 0703 772131

SYLCAST *FLY, MONOFILAMENT,*
BRAIDED
Distributor: Modern Arms Co. Ltd.
Marco Works, Pembroke Road, Bromley,
Kent.
Tel: 01 460 3483

TORTUE *MONOFILAMENT*
Distributor: Afad Limited,
38, Elizabeth Street, London, SW1 9NZ
Tel: 01 730 9831

TRILENE *MONOFILAMENT,*
Distributor: Vince Lister Agency,
1, Send Road, Caversham, Reading,
Berks.
Tel: 0734 479641
See Advertisement this Section

Clothing Manufacturers and Distributors

We have included in this section a wide range of both manufacturers and major clothing suppliers. All of these companies supply outdoor clothing suitable for the angler.

Clothing

Abu (Great Britain) Ltd.

Clydebank Industrial Estate,
Dunbartonshire
Tel: 041 952 6381

Manufacturers of Abu Thermo clothing

**AFONWEN WOOLLEN CO.
LTD.**

**Llangernyw, Abergele, North Wales
Tel: 0745 76350**
See Advertisement this Section

J. Barbour & Sons Ltd.

Simonside, South Shields, Tyne & Wear
Tel: 08943 2251

Manufacturers of outdoor clothing

Beaver of Bolton Ltd.

Nortex Mill, 105 Chorley Old Road,

Bolton, Lancashire
Tel: 0204 386899

**Manufacturers of 'Beaver' thermal
insulated garments, waterproofs and
quilted jackets**

Belstaff International Ltd.

Caroline Street, Longton, Stoke-On-
Trent
Tel: 0782 317261

**Manufacturers of waistcoats and
waxproofed outdoor clothing**

Blacks of Greenock

Port Glasgow, Renfrewshire, Scotland
Tel: 0475 42333

Manufacturers of outdoor clothing

Bob Church & Co. Ltd.

16 Lorne Road, Northampton
Tel: 0604 713674

**Manufacturers of waterproof and quilted
clothing**

Burton McCall Ltd.

Samuel Street, Leicester
Tel: 0533 538781
Telex: 341484

**Distributors of the Bridgedale range of
woollen sweaters, socks and thermal
underwear**

Calverton Sports Waterproofs

109 Front Street, Arnold, Nottingham
Tel: 0602 269174

Suppliers of Dartex fishing garments

Cambrian Fly Fishers

The Old Vicarage, Trevor, Llangollen,
North Wales
Tel: 0978 821789

**Suppliers of a complete range of outdoor
wear**

Casual Country Clothing

7 West Street, Farnham, Surrey
Tel: 0252 721163

**Suppliers of Slumberdown quilted
clothing**

Catworth Manufacturing Co. Ltd.

34 Market Road, Thrapston, Northants.
NN14 4JU
Tel: 08012 3280

Courtaulds Ltd.

Viscose Division, 13/14, Margaret Street,
London W1
Tel: 01 580 8501

**Manufacturers of Viloft thermal
underwear**

Clares Carlton Ltd.

Clares Country Clothing, Wells,
Somerset
Tel: 0749 73900
*Distributors of Waterproof Clothing
Manufacturers of protective clothing for
the angler*

Custom Rods (Oxford)

5 Pond Way, Cowley Centre, Oxford
Tel: 0865 775218

Manufacturers of waterproof clothing

Daiwa Sports Ltd.

Netherton Industrial Estate, Wishaw,
Strathclyde

el: 06983 61313
uppliers of Daiwa Specialist fishing
lothing

.A.M. Tackle Ltd.
.O. Box 40, Leamington Spa,
Warwickshire
el: 0926 313237
uppliers of a range of clothing for
nglers

amart Ltd.
owling Green Mills, Bradley Street,
ingley, West Yorkshire
el: 0274 568211
anufacturers of thermal underwear,
loves etc.

ane Valley Weatherwear
ane Mill, Broadhurst Lane, Congleton,
heshire
el: 02602 77969
uppliers of clothing for anglers

eArcy Fashions
Fareham Park Road, Fareham, Hants
el: 0329 42289
uppliers of outdoor waterproof clothing

"DERRIBOOTS"
ower Lane, Warmley, Bristol
el: 0272 679121
ee Advertisement this Section

Dorimac Products Ltd.
2 Canning Street, Hebburn, Tyne &
Wear
el: 0632 833223
uppliers of elasticated balaclava
elmets

DOUGLAS FRASER & SONS
SALES) LTD.
ackle & Guns Division,
riockheim, Angus, Scotland, DD11 4TU
el: 02412 341
ee Advertisement this Section

C. Farlow & Co. Ltd.
51 Fairview Road, Cheltenham, Glos.
el: 0242 518690

C.J. Field (Polynet) Ltd.
nion Road Estate, Macclesfield,
heshire
el: 0625 611077
anufacturer of Polytherm thermal
nderwear

FJALLRAVEN Sports Equipment
.O. Box 5, Harrogate
el: 0765 5363
uppliers of the Greenland fishermans
acket

owler Bros.
owsham, Lincoln
el: 06527 231
uppliers of a complete range of
lothing for the angler

Hadrian Country Clothing
51 High Street East, Wallsend, Tyne &
Wear
uppliers of a wide range of outdoor
lothing

Hardy Bros. (Alnwick) Ltd.
Willowburn, Alnwick, Northumberland
Tel: 0665 602771
Suppliers of 'Hardy' brand clothing for
the angler

Heron Anglers
The Heron, Unit 12, Dryden Court
Precinct, Renfrew Road, London
SE11 4NH
Tel: 01 582 9775
Suppliers of the Heron buoyancy
waistcoat

Husky of Tostock Ltd.
Box 8, Bury Street, Stowmarket, Suffolk
Tel: 044 92 4471
Manufacturers of thermo-insulated
outdoor clothing

**INDUSTRIAL SAFETY
(BIRMINGHAM)**
**Langley Drive, Chester Road
Industrial Estate, Castle Bromwich,
Birmingham, B35 7AD
Tel: 021 749 4433**
Clothing Waterproof, Thermal
Undergarments, Waders, Wellingtons,
etc.

John Brocklehurst
Matlock Street, Bakewell, Derbyshire
Tel: 062 981 2089
Suppliers of a wide range of country
clothing

John Partridge
New Power Station Road,

Trent Meadow, Rugeley, Staffs
Tel: 08894 4438
Manufacturers of clothing for Fishermen.

Kingswood Weatherwear
Dane Mill, Congleton, Cheshire
Tel: 02602 77969
Manufacturers of thermal and
weatherproof suits and accessories

**LAMIFLEX LTD.
Bury Ground, Carlyle Street, Bury,
Lancashire
Tel: 061 764 4926
See Advertisement this Section**

Kingfisher Ltd.
Litchfield Street, Rugeley, Staffs
Tel: 08894 5032
Manufacturers of waterproof jackets and
leggings

The Lavenham Rug Co. Ltd.
Long Melford, Suffolk
Tel: 078 725 535
Manufacturers of the Lavenham Fishing
Coat

Le Tricoteur & Co. Ltd.
Pitronnerie Road, St Peter Port,
Guernsey, Channel Islands
Tel: 0481 26214
Manufacturers of traditional Guernsey
sweaters

Macaseta Ltd.
Goodall Street, Macclesfield
Tel: 0625 22411
Manufacturers of personalised ties,
T-Shirts and sweatshirts for angling
clubs

Clothing

Multifabs Ltd.
Osmaston Works, Osmaston Road, Derby
Tel: 0232 3721

Nicko Sports Ltd.
43-45 Newtown Shopping Centre, Birmingham
Tel: 021 359 6568
Manufacturers of the Nicko Fishing Jacket

Penny Crowe
1 Sutton Close, Sutton Poyntz, Weymouth
Tel: 0305 833001
The Penny Crowe fishing jersey

PETER BARROW & CO.
Main Street, Hoveringham, Notts. NE14 7JR
Tel: 060 745 4286
See Advertisement this Section

Peter Storm
14 High Pavement, Nottingham, Notts.
Tel: 0602 50702
Manufacturers of foul weather gear and sweaters

P.R.M. Services Ltd.
3 Woodrise, Eastcote, Pinner, London
Tel: 089 56 73141
Manufacturers of "Supa' waders and wellingtons

Puffa Duvet Clothing Ltd.
Park Street, Hungerford, Berkshire
Tel: 04886 3237
Manufacturers of outdoor jackets and waistcoats

Q.T. Fashions (Kettering) Ltd.
53 Havelock Street, Kettering, Northants
Tel: 0536 520472
Le Grant fishing suits

Rob Jackson
65 High Street, Blairgowrie, Perthshire
Tel: 0250 3859
Retailer of branded fishing apparel

SHAKESPEARE CO.
P.O. Box 1, Redditch. Worcs
Tel: 0527 21570
Suppliers of a complete range of angling clothing.
See Advertisement on Inside Back Cover

Skye Crotal Knitwear
Camus Ohros, Isle of Skye
Islander wool sweaters

Sporting Developments International
210 Hermitage Road, Coalville, Leicester LE6 3EH
Tel: 0530 37236
Manufacturers of "Keeper" brand outdoor jackets

28

Sportsman's clothing by Mail Orde

STYLE 6520 YEOMAN QUILTED WAISTCOAT
A stylish and practical garment giving extra protection from the Mandarin collar. Made from shower resistant Polyester/Cotton and 6 oz Polyester quilting, the waistcoat features full button up front, two deep front pockets and a large inside zipper pocket.
Colours: White, Grey, Olive, Black, Navy, Red, Brown.
£14.95 + 75p p&p.

SIZES AVAILABLE: XS (32-34"), S (36"), M (38-40"), L (42-44"), XL (44-48").
All products carry our replacement or full money back guarantee.
Allow up to 28 days for delivery.

STYLE 4510 HEAVY DUTY OILED COTTON JACKET
A tough outdoor jacket featuring thick brushed cotton lining, corduroy collar, hand warmer pockets, large patch pockets, washable inner game pocket, wind cuffs and a heavy duty zip with storm flap. Tremendous value at **£33.95** + £1.50 p&p.

STYLE 4951 CAMOUFLAGE WATERPROOF JACKET
A fully weatherproof garment used by British Soldiers all over the world. Features of the jacket are 4 large pockets, hood, wind cuffs, heavy duty zip with full storm flap.
£21.15 + 75p p&p.

RANGE OF OUTDOOR CLOTHING

Send Cheque or P.O. to Peter Barrow
Hoveringham, Notts. NG14 7JR. Telephone: Lowdham 4286.

Stephens (Birmingham) Ltd.
Beach Road, Sparkhill, Birmingham
Tel: 021 772 4011
Manufacturers of waterproof jackets and leggings

Sue Burgess Fishing Tackle
Glyn Celyn, Brecon, Powys
Tel: 0874 4448
Manufacturers of specialist clothing for fly fishers

Sussex Countryman
Annington Cottage, Annington, Steyning, Sussex
Tel: 0903 812261
Suppliers of a full range of country clothing

Taylors Fishing Tackle
13 Western Avenue, Buckingham
Tel: 02802 3881

Thwaites Country Clothing
Bank End South Industrial Estate, Jedburgh, Roxburghshire
Tel: 08356 2470

Thornproof Manufacturing Co. Ltd.
Unit 32, Power Station Road, Trent Meadows, Rugeley, Staffs
Tel: 08894 6631/2

Thoroughbred Ground Bait Co. Ltd.
Weaths Yard, The Avenue, Acocks Green, Birmingham
Tel: 021 706 4509

Uniroyal Ltd.
Footwear Division, 62 Horseferry Londo SW1P 2AH
Tel: 01 222 5611

Walrus Waterproofs Ltd.
Mersey Street, Bullwell, Nottingham
Tel: 0602 277736

G. R. Woodford Ltd.
St. Marys Works, St. Marys Plain, Norwich
Tel: 0603 26604
Telex: 97320
Manufacturers of Pak Evac Survival Sui

Yorkshire Angler
Waterside House, Grove Farm Crescen Leeds
Tel: 0532 675615
Suppliers of outdoor clothing

Zacharias & Co.
26/27 Cornmarket Street, Oxford
Tel: 0865 43776
Manufacturers of waterproof clothing

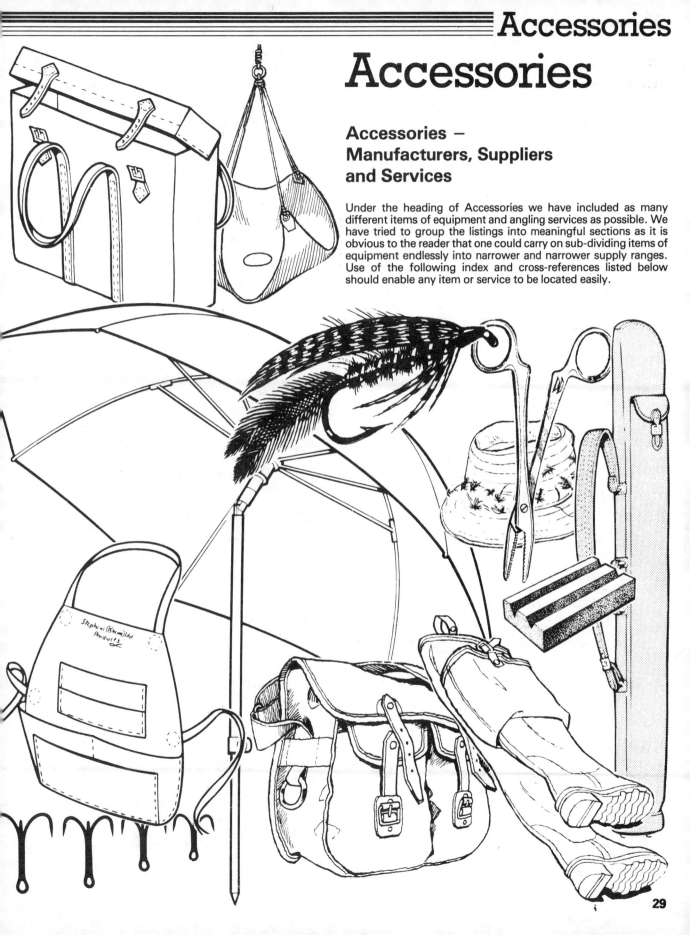

Accessories

Accessories –
Manufacturers, Suppliers
and Services

Under the heading of Accessories we have included as many different items of equipment and angling services as possible. We have tried to group the listings into meaningful sections as it is obvious to the reader that one could carry on sub-dividing items of equipment endlessly into narrower and narrower supply ranges. Use of the following index and cross-references listed below should enable any item or service to be located easily.

Accessories

Index
Accessories

FISHING EQUIPMENT ACCESSORIES

ERATION PUMPS

.A.M. Tackle Ltd.
O. Box 40, Leamington Spa,
arwicks
l: 0926 313237

HAKESPEARE CO.
O. Box 1, Redditch, Worcs
l: 0527 21570
*e Advertisement on Inside Back
over*

AIT BOXES, APRONS & ARRIERS

ou (Great Britain) Ltd.
ydebank Industrial Estate,
nbartonshire
l: 041 9526381

F.T.C./Oakly Fishing Tackle
d.
ming Road, Washford Industrial
tate, Redditch
l: 0527 24509
*nufacturers and distributors of bait
xes*

roxhead Joinery
dford, Bordon, Hants
l: 04203 4159

J. Field (Polynet) Ltd.
ion Road Estate, Union Road,
cclesfield
l: 0625 611077

ank Wallace
omanry Hse, Castle Hill, Reading
l: 0734 589703
K. Representative of H.H.R.

Goddard (Efgeeco) Ltd.
geeco Works, Balham Hill, London
V12
l: 01 673 1173

Karobes Ltd.
Queensway, Leamington Spa, Warks.
Tel: 0926 27911

Perry, Dean & Woods
P.O. Box 4, Ashbourne, Derbyshire
Tel: 053 86 491

Peter Drennan
Leopold St. Oxford
Tel: 0865 49580

Smiths Tackle Co.
55 Boverton Avenue, Brockworth, Glos.
Tel: 0452 823865
Manufacturers of bait aprons

Stephens (Birmingham) Ltd.
Beach Road, Sparkhill, Birmingham
Tel: 021 772 4011

BAIT CLEANING MACHINES, SIEVES & RIDDLES

Asco Products
St. John Street, Horwich, Bolton, Lancs
Tel: 0204 691737

Coventry Angling Supplies Ltd.
6 Arne Road, Walsgrave-on-Sowe, Nr.
Coventry
Tel: 0203 612299
Suppliers of Maggot Riddles

Mel Spence Fishing Tackle
Abbey National Yard, Market Place,
Pontefract, West Yorks.
Tel: 0977 797461
Suppliers of Maggot Riddles

BAIT DELIVERY SYSTEMS

Asco Products
St John Street, Horwich, Bolton, Lancs.
Tel: 0204 691737

BFTC/Oakley Fishing Tackle Co.
Heming Road, Washford Industrial
Estate, Redditch
Tel: 0527 24509

W.B. Clarke (Fishing) Ltd.
Crescent Works, Mount Pleasant,
Redditch, Worcs
Tel: 0527 43310

Dinsmores Ltd.
Westgate, Aldridge, Staffs
Tel: 0922 56421/2

C.J. Field (Polynet) Ltd.
Union Road Estate, Union Road,
Macclesfield, Cheshire
Tel: 0625 611077

G. C. Harris & Co. Ltd.
Double Century Works, High Street,
Astwood Bank, Redditch, Worcs
Tel: 052 789 3600

INTAKL ANGLING LTD.
P.O. Box 8, Beccles, Suffolk
See Advertisement this Section

Middy Floats
Ladysmith Road, Borrowash, Derby
Tel: 0332 677075

Perry, Dean & Woods
PO Box 4, Ashbourne, Derbyshire
Tel: 053 86 491

Peter Drennan
Leopold Street, Oxford
Tel: 0865 49580

Ray Benton Angling Aids
136 Oxford Road, Cowley, Oxford
Tel: 0865 711410
*Manufacturers of the Ray Benton
Catapult range*

Smiths Tackle Co.
55 Boverton Avenue, Brockworth, Glos.
GL3 4ER
Tel: 0452 823865

Thamesley Fishing Tackle Co.
278 Kingsland Road, London E8
Tel: 01 249 1954

BAIT SUPPLIERS – GROUNDBAIT

H & L ALDERSON
Higher Barn Farm, Turton Road,
Tottington, Nr. Bury, Lancs
Tel: 020488 3268

Bob Church & Co.
16 Lorne Road, Northampton, Northants
Tel: 0604 713674

BRITISH GROUNDBAITS
Four Elms Mills, Bardfield, Saling, Nr.
Braintree, Essex
Tel: 0371 850247
See Advertisement this Section

Bromley Bait Co.
13 Hampden Avenue, Beckenham, Kent
Tel: 01 650 6059

Carp Bait Suppliers
114a Eastwick Road, Taunton, Somerset
Tel: 0823 85919

Cherwell Bait Farm
3 Somerville Drive, Bicester, Oxon.
Tel: 08692 41677
Wholesalers of Groundbait
C. & J. Coles
Laithes Farm, Weedshaw Lane,
Cudworth, Barnsley
Tel: 0226 710184

E. W. Coombs Ltd.
25 Frindsbury Road, Stroud, Kent
Tel: 0634 79886/7
Suppliers of breadcrumbs
DONALD COOKE
**Corn Merchants, Bridge Mill,
Greasborough Road, Rotherham,
S60 1RD**
Tel: 0709 65968
Manufacturers of Pure Breadcrumbs
Duncan Kays Angling Services
15 Manor Way, Higham Ferrers,
Northampton
Tel: 09334 4395

Frank Wallace
Yeomanry House, Castle Hill, Reading,
Berks
Tel: 0734 589703

Genic
Manchester Street, Derby
Tel: 0332 42514

House & Co.
68 Lower Buckland Road, Lymington,
Hampshire
Tel: 0590 76806

John E. Haith
Park Street, Cleethorpes, Humberside
Tel: 0472 57515
Specialist suppliers of seed baits

KALIUM PRODUCTS LTD.
Albert Street, Redditch, Worcs.
Tel: 0527 64433
See Advertisement this Section

Penge Angling Supplies
7 Croydon Road, London SE20
Tel: 01 778 4652
Wholesalers of Hemp seed bait.

Phillips Yeast Products Ltd.
Park Royal Road, London NW10
Tel: 01 965 7533
High-Pro high protein bait

Polarset Ltd.
15 Cook Street, St Mary's, Southampton
Hants.
Tel: 0703 20645 436089

Stayon Fishing Bait Ltd.
Croft Farm, Chadwick End, Lapworth,
Solihull, West Midlands
Tel: 05643 2161
Suppliers of preserved baits, seed and groundbaits

Super Bait '78 Ltd.
103 Chingford Mount Road, Chingford
London E4
Tel: 01 531 4519
Suppliers of Carp bait and Sensas Continental groundbait

Tamplins Stayon Fishing Bait Ltd.
Croft Farm, Chadwick Eve, Lapworth,
W. Midlands
Tel: 05643 2161
Suppliers of Preserved groundbait and additives

Thoroughbred Groundbait Co. Ltd.
Weates Yard, The Avenue, Acocks
Green, Birmingham
Tel: 021 706 4509

Trafford Angling Supplies
34 Moss Road, Stretford, Manchester
Tel: 061 864 1211

BAIT SUPPLIERS — MAGGOTS, WORMS & SEABAITS

Alan Clarke
52 Methven Street, Southampton
Tel: 0703 30387
Suppliers of Live ragworm and lugworm

Ammodytes Co. Ltd.
Penbeagle Industrial Estate, St. Ives,
Cornwall
Tel: 073679 5424
Suppliers of blast frozen sea bait

dford Baits
ldington Airfield, Bedford
: 0234 781378

ent (Hailsham) Ltd.
Station Road, Hailsham, East Sussex
: 0323 840094
opliers of Fresh, Frozen and
served sea baits

omley Bait Co.
Hampden Avenue, Beckenham, Kent
: 01 650 6059
ggots, lobworms, brandlings, crabs,
odworms etc

erwell Bait Farm
omerville Drive, Bicester, Oxford
: 08692 41677
opliers of Maggots and Worms

Cowell
Norwood Drive, South Benfleet, Essex
: 03745 52549
opliers of Fresh and Frozen seabaits

I. Curtis
Macgillycuddy's Reek, Whalebone Yard,
High Street, Wells-next-the-sea, Norfolk

Davis, M.
Priory Piece Farm, Inkberrow, Worcs
Tel: 0386 792789
Suppliers of Brandling worms

Don Bait Co. Ltd.
Adwick Road, Mexborough, South Yorks
Tel: 0709 582220
Suppliers of Maggots

Don Singleton
2 Farr Close, Worsley, Mesnes, Wigan
Tel: 0942 39550
Suppliers of Bloodworms and Maggots

R. Ely
515 Christchurch Road, Boscombe
Tel: 0202 37070
Suppliers of Ragworm

Emrow Earth Products
Forest Green House, Forest Green,
Dorking, Surrey
Tel: 01 730 0982

Lime Tree Worm Farm
198 Ilkeston Road, Nottingham
Tel: 0773 806976

Maggot Farms Yorkshire Ltd.
Denbrook, Clifton Lane, Conisbrough,
Doncaster
Tel: 0709 862884
Suppliers of Maggots, Worms and
Groundbaits

Matchbait
North Barn Farm, Lancing, Sussex
Tel: 09063 63737
Suppliers of Maggots, Worms and
Lugworm

F. & B. W. PENDLEBURY
Gilligants Farm, Smithills, Bolton
Tel: 0204 41212
See Advertisement this Section

Penrhos Barn Products
Bankside House, Penrhos, Llanymynech,
Powys
Tel: 093875 435
Suppliers of all kinds of worms

Phil Cobb
112 Green Road, Poole, Dorset
Tel: 02013 3576
Suppliers of Ragworm

Polarset Ltd.
15 Cook Street, St Mary's, Southampton,
Hants.
Tel: 0703 20645 436089

Standardised Ltd.
2 Brook Road, Bitterne, Southampton
Tel: 04218 7917
Suppliers of Sea baits

Tamplins Stayon Fishing Bait Ltd.
Craft Farm, Chadwick Eve, Lapworth,
W. Midlands
Tel: 05643 2161
Suppliers of Preserved Sea Bait

Trafford Angling Supplies
34 Moss Road, Stretford, Manchester
Tel: 061 864 1211
Suppliers of Sea Baits

G. Voules
24 Dower Road, Four Oaks, Sutton
Coldfield, Warwickshire
Tel: 021 308 4955
Suppliers of Lobworms

Walker G. R.
6 Newland Gardens, Newbold,
Chesterfield
Tel: 0246 79085
Suppliers of Red Worms

C. Wenner
9 Gayton Road, Kings Lynn, Norfolk
Tel: 0553 671479
Suppliers of Lugworm

BASKETS, SEAT BASKETS & CREELS

Asco Products
St John Street, Horwich, Bolton, Lancs.
Tel: 0204 691737

C. J. Field (Polynet) Ltd.
Union Estate, Union Road, Macclesfield
Tel: 0625 611077

Mordex Ltd.
St Christopher House, Eyre Street,
Sheffield, S1 3GH
Tel: 0742 28005
Telex: Chamcom 547676 (forvere)
Suppliers of Willow fishing Baskets

Richard Forshaw & Co. Ltd.
Colonsay House, Tarran Way, Moreton,
Merseyside
Tel: 051 678 7878
Telex: 627083 Tackle G

Turners Baskets
Sydney Street, Cleethorpes, South
Humberside
Tel: 0472 43313

BITE ALARMS

Auger Accessories Ltd.
85b Crowland Road, Tottenham,
London N15
Tel: 01 802 0077
Manufacturers of the Heron bite alarm

Beacon Bite Indicators
Distributor: East Anglian Rod Co.
Rookery House, Newmarket, Suffolk
Tel: 0638 5831

Bitek Ltd.
The School House, Chartham Hatch,
Canterbury, Kent
Tel: 022789 352

B. J. Tackle & Co.
13 Brown Street North, Leigh, Lancs
Tel: 0942 605449

Cruz, Doyle & Tratt Products
Kinwood, Faygate, Horsham, Sussex
Tel: 029 383584
Manufacturers of "Magno" bite alarms

Dellareed Ltd.
20 Eagle Hill, Ramsgate, Kent.
Tel: 0843/582157
Manufacturers of the Optonic Bite Alarm

Electro Automation Ltd.
19 Lavender Way, Hitchin, Herts.
Tel: 0462 51096

F. Goddard (Efgeeco) Ltd.
26 Balham Hill, London SW12
Tel: 01 673 1177
Distributors of Optonic Bite Alarms

Sundridge
Vicarage Lane, Hoo, Nr. Rochester,
Kent
Tel: 0634 252104
Distributors of Buz Bite Alarms

Superbait '78 Ltd.
103 Chingford Mount Road, London E4
Tel: 01 531 4519
Distributors of AJS Alarms

BITE DETECTORS

Arrow Angling
16/18 Granby Row, Manchester
Tel: 061 236 6805

Asco Products Ltd.
St. John Street, Horwich, Bolton, Lancs
Tel: 0204 691737

B.F.T.C./Oakley Fishing Tackle Ltd.
Heming Road, Washford Industrial
Estate, Redditch
Tel: 0527 24509
Manufacturers of bite detectors

Dellareed Ltd.
20 Eagle Hill, Ramsgate Kent
Tel: 0843 582157
Manufacturers of See-Tip Bite Detectors

Evdon Manufacturing Co.
Neptune Works, Beoley Road West,
Redditch, Worcs
Tel: 0527 62027

C. J. Field (Polynet) Ltd.
Union Road Estate, Union Road,
Macclesfield, Cheshire
Tel: 0625 611077
Suppliers of the 'Ian Heaps' range of products

Frank Harlow Engineering Ltd.
Catley Road, Sheffield
Tel: 0742 441495

HOPKINS AND HOLLOWAY LTD.
**Brickyard Lane, Dudley, Warwickshire
Tel: 052785 3822**

*Manufacturers of accessories
and fittings for swing and
quiver tips, suppliers to
Manufacturers & Wholesalers
only*

John Roberts
21 Margate Road, Ramsgate, Kent
CT11 7SR
Tel: 0843 581678
Manufacturers of Specimen Hunters Run Clips

Matchman Fishing Equipment Ltd.
Green Lane New Factory, Heywood,
Lancashire
Tel: 0706 621311

Middy Floats
Ladysmith Road, Borrowash, Derby
Tel: 0332 677075

Modern Arms Co. Ltd.
Pembroke Road, Bromley, Kent
Tel: 01 460 3483
Manufacturers of Peg Bells

Peter Drennan
Leopold Street, Oxford
Tel: 0865 49580

PIRANHA PRODUCTS LTD.
**Box 33, Bishops Stortford, Herts
Tel: 0279 870867**
See Advertisement this Section

BOAT BUILDERS & SUPPLIERS

AC Mouldings
Cory Way, Barry Docks, Glamorgan
Tel: 0446 739671

ANGLESEY BOAT CO. LTD.
**Gallows Point, Beamaris, Anglesey
LL58 8Y1
Tel: 0248 810359**
*Tackle the Bait Problem
with us.
It's as easy as a b c.
Open 7 days a week for your
Sea Fishing requirements*

Avon Inflatables Ltd.
Dafen, Llanelli, Dyfed, South Wales
Tel: 05542 59171
Manufacturers of inflatable boats

Barry Marine Centre Ltd.
633, Caubridge Road, East Cardiff
Tel: 0222 562000

Boat Showrooms of London
286-290 Kensington High Street,
London W14
Tel: 01 602 0123

o Spalding Ltd.
ional Fishing Boat Centre, St.
justine's Roundabout, Felixstowe
d, Ipswich
0473 79891

NWITCO BOAT BUILDERS
brington Street, Kingsbridge,
on TQ1 DE
0548 2453
Advertisement this Section

tler's Marine
ods Way, Mulberry Industrial Estate,
ing-by-Sea, Sussex
0903 502221
nts for Striker Aluminium Yachts

leman Marine (London) Ltd.
Norwood High Street, West Norwood,
don SE27
01 670 5161

& P. (Marine Fabrications)
.
n Street, Brandesburton, Nr.
field, North Humberside, Yorkshire
0401 42866

bler Dinghies Ltd.
. Box 8, Rugeley, Staffs
05436 5999

G.W. Dolling & Son
207 Dalton Road, Barrow in Furness,
Cumbria
Tel: 0229 23708

Dorado Boats Ltd.
250 Main Road, Southbourne, Emsworth,
Hants.
Tel: 0243 71641

Dunean Craft Ltd.
Unit 3, Brittania Mill, Barley Holme
Road, Crawshawbooth, Rossendale,
Lancs.
Tel: 07062 223446

Freeward Marine Services Ltd.
Freeward House, Gosport Street,
Lymington, Hants
Tel: 0590 77155

Granta Boats
Ramsey, Huntingdon
Tel: 0487 813777

J.M. Henshaw (Marine) Ltd.
Verrington Lodge, Wincanton, Somerset
Tel: 0963 33237

Hibbing Ltd. (Boat Division)
147 Connaught Avenue, Frinton-on-Sea,
Essex
Tel: 02556 71565

Horne Brothers (Boatbuilders)
Ltd.
Ranalagh Works, Fishbourne, Isle of
Wight
Tel: 0983 883245

Island Plastics
Edward Street, Ryde, Isle of Wight
Tel: 0983 64911

Leakey Boats
Sutcliffe House, Settle, Yorks
Tel: 07292 3506
Manufacturers of folding boats

Les Brown & Son (Boatbuilders)
94 Castle Street, Fareham, Hants
Tel: 0705 374038

Lewis Marines
Mill Lane, Near Maidenhead, Berks
Tel: 0628 32788

Messrs J. W. Mackay
Newton Boatyard, Falkland Park Road,
Ayr
Tel: 0292 81586

Marina B. H. Ltd.
318 Alcester Road, Wythall, Nr.
Birmingham
Tel: 0564 822494

C. J. R. Marine Co.
Woodroffe Road, Tollesbury, Essex
Tel: 062186 497

Marine Mechanical
Temple Hill, Troon, Ayrshire, Scotland
Tel: 0292 313400

McNulty Marine Services
Victoria Road, South Shields, Tyne &
Wear
Tel: 0632 563196
The Northumbrian range of fishing boats

Meaghans Boatyard
402 Locksway Road, Portsmouth, Hants
Tel: 0705 733 649

Milton Smallcraft Ltd.
16 Stem Lane Industrial Estate, New Milton, Hants
Tel: 0425 610328
Telex: 477284 MATCOM

Orkney Boats Ltd.
Ford Lane Industrial Estate, Yapton, Arundel, Sussex
Tel: 0243 551456

**'PETERS MARINE'
BISHOPTON 050-586-2782
FOR ALL YOUR YAMAHA
NEEDS**

Pevensey Bay Marine
57-63 Eastbourne Road, Pevensey Bay, East Sussex
Tel: 0323 761714

Pilot International
30 Linsey Street, Epping, Essex
Tel: 01 228 1559

Reading Marine Services Ltd.
Scours Lane, Oxford Road, Reading
Tel: 0734 27155/27350

Rotork Marine Ltd.
Lake Avenue, Hamworthy, Poole, Dorset
Tel: 02013 81458

Solar Glassfibre Products Ltd.
35 Cross Street, Farnborough, Hants
Tel: 0252 40628

Sowerby Bridge Boat Centre Ltd
The Wharf, Sowerby Bridge, West Yorkshire
Tel: 0422 32922

Sportsfishing Boats
Oakham Grange, 26 Manor Close, Ferndown, Dorset
Tel: 0202 645539

Winsor Brothers
Unit 9, Common Fields, Upper Northam Drive, Hedge End, Southampton
Tel: 0703 464 757

Treeve Marine Ltd.
Treeve Lane, Hayle, Cornwall
Tel: 0736 752214

Virgo Marine Co.
Plump Road, Wallasey Dock, Four Bridges, Birkenhead
Tel: 051 647 4277

Yorkshire Marine
Clayfields Industrial Estate, Tickhill Road, Balby, Doncaster
Tel: 0302 853064
Manufacturers of "Pebble" boats

36

BOUYANCY AIDS & FLOTATION SUITS

Avon Inflatables Ltd.
Dafen, Llanelli, Dyfed, South Wales
Tel: 05542 59171

**SHAKESPEARE CO.
P.O. Box 1, Redditch, Worcs
Tel: 0527 21570**
See Advertisement on Inside Back Cover

G. R. Woodford Ltd.
St. Mary's Works, St. Mary's Plain, Norwich, Norfolk
Tel: 0603 26604
Manufacturers of Flotation Suits

CAR ROD CLAMPS

F. Goddard (Efgeeco) Ltd.
26 Balham Hill, London, SW12
Tel: 01 673 1177

Richard Wheatley & Son Ltd.
Century Works, Midland Road, Willehall, W. Midlands
Tel: 0922 23729

DISGORGERS

Asco Products
St John Street, Horwich, Bolton, Lancs.
Tel: 0204 691737

Auger Accessories Ltd.
Auger Works, Crowland Road, London N15
Tel: 01 802 0077

B.F.T.C./Oakley Fishing Tackle Co.
Hemming Road, Washford Industrial Estate, Redditch
Tel: 0527 24509

G. C. Harris & Co. Ltd.
Double Century Works, High Street, Astwood Bank, Redditch, Worcs
Tel: 052 789 3600

PKF Engineering
Unit 4, Newtown Trading Estate, Chase Street, Luton, Beds.
Tel: 0582 412110
*Manufacturers of Valley Disgorgers
Distributed by Vince Lister Agency*

Redditch Tackle Co.
Unit 15, Alders Drive, Moons Moat Estate, Redditch, Worcs
Tel: 0527 29030

Shakespeare Co.
P.O. Box 1, Redditch, Worcs
Tel: 0527 21570

Sussex Tackle Co.
12 North Parade, Horsham, Sussex
Tel: 0403 67168

DROGUES

Bob Church & Co. Ltd.
16 Lorne Road, Northampton
Tel: 0604 713674

G. C. Commodities
46a Church Street, Flint, North Wale

Datum Products Ltd.
Princess Works, Station Road, Beesto Notts
Tel: 0602 259347

C. J. Field (Polynet) Ltd.
Union Road Estate, Union Road, Macclesfield
Tel: 0625 611077
Manufacturer of Polydrogue

Shakespeare Co.
P.O. Box 1, Redditch, Worcs
Tel: 0527 21570

Sue Burgess
'Glyn Celyn', Felin Fach, Brecon, Po
Tel: 0874 4488

ELECTRONIC FISH FINDING EQUIPMENT

East Anglian Rod Co. Ltd.
Rookery House, Newmarket, Suffolk
Tel: 0638 5831

Goads (Chandlers) Ltd.
14 Goldsworth Park Trading Estate, Woking, Surrey
Tel: 04862 20404

Hartronics (Marine) Ltd.
Watsons Walk, St. Albans, Herts
Tel: 0727 60820

Karnclarke Ltd
1-4 Swan Mead, Tower Bridge Road, London SE1

Marelco Trading & Distributio Co. Ltd.
21 Ridley Road, Dalston, London E8
Tel: 01 952 4656
The fish Hawk ph meter

Pumpkin Marine
27 Holborn Viaduct, London EC1
Tel: 01 353 5571
Depth Finders

ssex Marine

Marina, St. Leonards on Sea,
tings
0424 425882

tton Marine Ltd.

on Jetty, Sutton Harbour, Plymouth,
von
0752 24777
*tributors of Kelvin Hughes Echo
unders*

iftech Ltd.

. Box 7, Basingstoke, Hampshire
0256 54248
*tributors of Echo Sounders and
th Indicators*

chtex Ltd.

Prince Avenue, Westcliff-on-Sea,
ex
0702 331188

SHING BAGS

co Products

ohn Street, Horwich, Bolton, Lancs.
: 0204 691737

ger Accessories Ltd.

ger Works, Crowland Road,
don N15
: 01 802 0077

BILLINGHAM & CO.

t 2, Lye Valley Industrial Estate,
mley Street, Lye, Stourbridge
Advertisement this Section

b Church & Co. Ltd.

Lorne Road, Northampton
: 0604 713674

ennan & Hickman Angling
oducts

kery Street, Wednesfield, West
lands
: 0902 738783

David Nickerson (Tathwell) Ltd.

The Old Vicarage, Tathwell, Louth,
Lincs.
Tel: 047287 536

C. Farlow & Co. Ltd.

151 Fairview Road, Cheltenham, Glos.
GL52 2EY
Tel: 0242 518690

F. Goddard (Efgeeco) Ltd.

26 Balham Hill, London SW12
Tel: 01 673 1177

Hardy Bros. (Alnwick) Ltd.

Willowburn, Alnwick, Northumberland
Tel: 0665 602771

Karobes Ltd.

Queensway Trading Estate, Leamington
Spa, Warwicks
Tel: 0926 27911

Lanner Field Sports

Granville Chambers, Midland Road,
Wellingborough, Northants
Tel: 0933 224482

Liddlesdale Fishing Bag Co. Ltd.

Douglas Square, Newcastleton,
Roxburghshire
Tel: 054121 616

Richard Forshaw & Co. Ltd.

Colonsay House, Tarran Way, Moreton,
Merseyside
Tel: 051 678 7878
Telex: 627083 Tackle G

SHAKESPEARE CO.

P.O. Box 1, Redditch, Worcs
Tel: 0527 21570
*See Advertisement on Inside Back
Cover*

Stephens (Birmingham) Ltd.

Beach Road, Sparkhill, Birmingham
Tel: 021 772 4011

Sue Burgess

Glyn Celyn, Felin Fach, Brecon, Powys
Tel: 0874 4488

FISH SMOKING EQUIPMENT

Abu (Great Britain) Ltd.

Clydebank Industrial Estate,
Dunbartonshire
Tel: 041 952 6381

Brooks Home Smokers

1a Compton Road, Southport,
Merseyside
Tel: 0704 67068

Hardy Bros. (Alnwick) Ltd.

Willowburn, Alnwick, Northumberland
Tel: 0665 602771

Lodel Products Ltd.

Sussex House, High Street, Billinghurst,
Sussex
Tel: 040381 4343
Stainless Steel Fish Smokers

SHAKESPEARE CO.

P.O. Box 1, Redditch, Worcs
Tel: 0527 21570
*See Advertisement on Inside Back
Cover*

FISH TRAPS

Eelfare

Church Farm, Burton-on-Stather,
Scunthorpe, S. Humberside
Tel: 0724 720898

R & B Leakey

Sutcliffe House, Settle, Yorks
Tel: 07292 3506

FISH STOCK SUPPLIERS

Alleron Fish Farm

Loddiswell, Nr. Kingsbridge,
South Devon
Tel: 054 855 306

Annandale Trout Farm
Carse of Ae, Lochmaben, Dumfries
Tel: 038 786 246

Avington Trout Fisheries Ltd.
Avington, Winchester, Hants
Tel: 096278 312

Avon Coarse Fish Farm Ltd.
The Gables, Old Alresford
Tel: 096273 2849

Bakewell Trout Farm
Riverside Works, Bakewell, Derbyshire

Beaver Fish Supplies
Waylands Farm, Approach Road,
Tatsfield, Kent
Tel: 09598 707

Berkshire Trout Farm
Hungerford, Berks
Tel: 04886 2520

Bibury Trout Farm
Bibury, Cirencester, Gloucestershire
Tel: 028574 215

Bondyke Fisheries
Sandholme Grange, Newport, North
Humberside
Tel: 0430 40624

Castle Fisheries
Inverary, Argyll
Tel: 0499 2233

Chirk Fishery Co. Ltd.
Chirk, Wrexham
Tel: 069 186 2420

Four Ways Fisheries
Edlesborough, Nr. Dunstable
Tel: 0525 220581

Franklyns Fish Farm Ltd.
Itchen Abbas, Winchester, Hants
Tel: 096 273

Heron Coarse Fish Supplies
31 Henbury Road, Acocks Green,
Birmingham
Tel: 021 706 7054

Hooke Springs Trout Farm
Beaminster, Dorset
Tel: 0308 862553

Howietoun Fish Farm
Bannockburn, Stirling
Tel: 0786 812473

Humberside Fisheries
Cleaves Farm, Skerne, Driffield, North
Humberside
Tel: 0377 43613

Munton & Fison
Stowmarket, Suffolk
Tel: 04492 2401

Northern Fisheries
78 Ashton Road, Newton-Le-Willows,
Lancs
Tel: 09252 5996

Orchard Mill Trout Farm Ltd.
11 Himley Green, Linslade, Leighton
Buzzard, Beds
Tel: 0525 371304

Oughton Fishery
Bedford Road, Hitchin, Herts
Tel: 0462 52855/4201

Packington Fisheries
Fishery Lodge, Broadwater, Maxstoke
Lane, Meriden, Warks.
Tel: 0676 22754

Selcoth Fisheries Ltd.
Moffat, Dumfreis
Tel: 0683 20509

Sinnington Trout Farm
Sinnington, York
Tel: 0751 31948

Stambridge Trout Fisheries
Nr. Rochford, Essex
Tel: 037 06 274

Trent Fish Culture Co. Ltd.
Mercaston, Brailsford, Nr. Derby
Tel: 033 528 318

Water Lane Fish Farm
Burton, Bradstock, Dorset
Tel: 030889 685

Watermill Trout Farms Ltd.
Westgate Mill, Louth
Tel: 0507 602524

FLIES

Alex Harper
Drill Hall, Thurso, Caithness
Tel: 0847 3179

ALFRED BOOKER & CO.
Arthur Street, Redditch, Worcs
Tel: 0527 27056
Distributors of "Courier" brand flies

Bessie Brown
Heatherdale, Lochton Road, Banchory,
Kincardineshire

Bob Church & Co. Ltd.
16 Lorne Road, Northampton
Tel: 0604 713674

A. D. Bradbury
16 The Square, Hale Barns, Altrincha
Tel: 061 980 2836

Campbell Black of Chelmsford
142-144 High Street, Ongar, Essex
Tel: 0277 364749
Telex: 995481

Chris Ingram
52 Station Road, Great Bowden, Mark
Harborough, Leicestershire
Tel: 0858 67562

Church Hill Farm
Mursley, Bucks
Tel: 029672 524
*See Advertisement in Day Permits
Section*

T. G. Clegg
Henley House, 99 Hook Road, Goole,
North Humberside
Tel: 0405 2207

Datam Products Ltd.
Princess Works, Station Road, Beeston
Nottinghamshire
Tel: 0602 259347

Davy Wotton
424 Margate Road, Ramsgate
Tel: 0843 69662

Deeside Tackle
Delene Cottage, Drumoak, Banchory,
Kincardineshire
Tel: 033 08 404

**Esmond Drury (Salmon Flies)
Ltd.**
Langton, Spilsby, Lincs
Tel: 0790 52353

C. J. Field (Polynet) Ltd.
Union Road Estate, Union Road,
Macclesfield, Cheshire
Tel: 0625 611077
*Distributors of Fordham & Wakefield
Flies*

D. & G. Flydressers
3 Wood Street Lane, Aberdeen
Tel: 0224 872170

Flymail
6 Nantesilo, Penrhyncoch, Nr.
Aberystwyth
Tel: 0970 828765

Fordham & Wakefield
Kinvale, Third Street, Langton Green,
Tunbridge Wells, Kent
Tel: 089286 3153

Foster Sporting Services
32 St. John's Street, Ashbourne,
Derbyshire
Tel: 0335 43135

...ling Mill Flies
...Arlington Drive, Carshalton, Surrey
...01 647 8258

...aham Trout Flies
...rton, Brampton Abbotts, Ross-on-
...e, Herefordshire
...0989 2430

...rdy Bros. (Alnwick) Ltd.
...lowburn, Alnwick, Northumberland
...0665 602771

...E. D. Harris & Co. Ltd.
...Church Green West, Redditch,
...rcs
...0527 64409

...WKES AND BLACK
View, Winkleigh, North Devon
083 783 430
Advertisement this Section

...n Veniard Ltd.
...High Street, Westerham, Kent
...0959 64119

...ckenzie-Philps Ltd.
...r Springs, Stockeld, Wetherby,
...ks
...0937 63646
range of flies including salmon
seat trout flies

...rtinez and Bird Ltd.
...lge Works, Redditch, Worcs
...0527 62131

...Hardys of Carlisle
...th Henry Street, Carlisle, Cumbria
...0228 23988

...rrisons
...Mount Street, Wrexham, Clwyd
...0978 364460

MUSTAD & SONS LTD.
**7 Farraday Road, North East Industrial
Estate, Peterlee, Co. Durham
Tel: 0783 869 553**
*Flies — Assorted Pack, Twin
Pack or Bulk*
*See Advertisement in Hooks
Section*

Peter Deane
Hide Hollow, Langley, Nr. Eastbourne
Tel: 0323 761069

Richard Forshaw & Co. Ltd.
Colonsay House, Tarran Way, Moreton,
Merseyside
Tel: 051 678 7878

Richard's
47 Merlin Way, Swindon, Wilts
Tel: 0793 38872
*Wholesaler of Trout, Sea Trout and
Salmon flies*

Riding Bros
135a Church Street, Preston, Lancs
Tel: 0772 23954

Robert McHaffie
33 Glengivlin Avenue, Limavady, Co.
Londonderry, Northern Ireland

SHAKESPEARE CO.
**P.O. Box 1, Redditch, Worcs
Tel: 0527 21570**
*See Advertisement on Inside Back
Cover*

Sheila Hassam & Son
48 Station Road, Chiseldon, Swindon
Tel: 0793 740765

Sid Knight
6 Uplands Drive, Bridgenorth,
Shropshire
Tel: 07462 2600

Speyside Salmon Flies
Stonefield Cottage, Grantown on Spey,
Merseyside
Tel: 0479 2735

Sue Burgess Fishing Tackle
Glyn Celyn, Brecon, Powys
Tel: 0874 4448

Tim Daniels (Church Hill Gold)
Church Hill Farm, Church Lane,
Mursley, Bucks
Tel: 029 672524

H. Turrall & Co. Ltd.
Dolton, Winkleigh, Devon
Tel: 08054 352
Manufacturer of artificial flies

FLY BOXES AND WALLETS

ANGLERS MASTERLINE LTD.
**Cotteswold Road, Tewkesbury, Glos.
Tel: 0684 294 210
See Advertisement under Lines**

Auger Accessories Ltd.
Auger Works, Crowland Road,
London N15
Tel: 01 802 0077

Bradbury A. D.
16 The Square, Hale Barns, Altrincham,
Cheshire
Tel: 061 980 2836

Brennan & Hickman Angling
Products
Rookery Street, Wednesfield, West
Midlands
Tel: 0902 738783

Daiwa Sports Ltd.
Netherton Industrial Estate, Wishaw,
Strathclyde
Tel: 06983 61313

F. Goddard (Efgeeco) Ltd.
26 Balham Hill, London SW12
Tel: 01 673 1177

Hardy Bros. (Alnwick) Ltd.
Willowburn, Alnwick, Northumberland
Tel: 0665 602771

Henry W. Aiken Ltd.
139/147 Kirkdale, Sydenham,
London SE26
Tel: 01 699 1141
Aikens Superflex fly boxes

Leascot
2 Charles Street, Kilmarnock, Ayr
Mail order supplies of Fly Wallets

Morrisons
40 Mount Street, Wrexham, Clwyd
Tel: 0978 4460

Normark Sport Ltd.
Bossell Road, Buckfastleigh, Devon
TQ11 0DD
Tel: 03644 2597
*See also Advertisements under Rod
Rings and Rod Fittings*

Richard Forshaw & Co. Ltd.
Colonsay House, Tarran Way, Moreton,
Merseyside
Tel: 051 678 7878
A wide range of quality fly boxes

Richard Wheatley & Sons Ltd.
Century Works, Midland Road, Walsall,
West Midlands
Tel: 0922 23729

SHAKESPEARE CO.
P.O. Box 1, Redditch, Worcs
Tel: 0527 21570
*See Advertisement on Back Inside
Page*

Sue Burgess Fishing Tackle
Glyn Celyn, Brecon, Powys
Tel: 0874 4448

Tara Designs
Victoria House, Norwich Road, Reepham
Tel: 060526 678

Tarn Rods
Caen-y-Mynydd, Dolanog, Welshpool,
Powys
Tel: 0938 810830
*See Advertisements under Rods and
Reels*

Sue Burgess Fishing Tackle
Glyn Celyn, Brecon, Powys
Tel: 0874 4448

Tarn Rods
Caen-y-Mynydd, Dolanog, Welshpool,
Powys
Tel: 0938 810830
*See Advertisements under Rods and
also Reels*

Tom C. Saville
Unit 7, Salisbury Square, off Ilkstone
Road, Nottingham
Tel: 062 784 248

H. Turrall & Co.
Dolton, Winkleigh, Devon
Tel: 08054 352

E. Veniard Ltd.
138 Northwood Road, Thornton Heath,
Surrey
Tel: 01 653 3565
*Suppliers of the Fish Hawk brand of
flytying materials and tools*

John Wilkins
62 Nelson Street, Buckingham, Bucks.
Tel: 02802 4495

FLYTYING MATERIALS TOOLS & EQUIPMENT

ALFRED BOOKER & CO.
Arthur Street, Redditch, Worcs. B98 8JY
Tel: 0527 26974
*See Advertisement Under Tackle
Shops*

ANGLERS MASTERLINE LTD.
Cotteswold Road, Tewkesbury, Glos
Tel: 0684 294210
See Advertisement under Lines

Ashby Lock & Line
Mill Lane Mews, Ashby De La Zouch,
Leics
Tel: 053 04 4157

BFTC/Oakley Fishing Tackle Ltd.
Heming Road, Washford Industrial
Estate, Redditch
*Manufacturers and Suppliers of fly
tying materials*

Brian Ogden
254 Church Street, Blackpool
Tel: 0253 21087

BRYSTAN
**122 Brynhyfryd, Croesyceiliog,
Cwmbran, Gwent NP44 2LX**
Tel: 06333 4785
See Advertisement under Lures

Campbell Black of Chelmsford
142/144 High Street, Ongar, Essex
Tel: 0277 364749 Telex 995481

Chris Ingram
52 Station Road, Great Bowden, Market
Harborough, Leics
Tel: 0858 67562

Ellis Slater
47 Bridgecross Road, Chase Terrace,
Walsall
Tel: 05436 71377

Fordham & Wakefield
Kinvale, Third Street, Langton Green,
Tunbridge Wells, Kent
Tel: 089286 3153

Gordon Griffiths Plastics
Lifford Way, Binley Industrial Estate,
Coventry
Tel: 0203 440859
Cobweb fly-tying thread

HAWKES and BLACK
Tor View, Winkleigh, North Devon
Tel: 083 783 430
See Advertisement Under Flies

P. J. Hood
Bicton Hill, Fordingbridge, Hampshire
Tel: 0425 52412

JOHN VENIARD LTD.
4/6 High Street, Westerham, Kent
Tel: 0959 64119
See Advertisement this Section

MACKENZIE-PHILPS LTD.
**Deer Springs, Stockeld, Wetherby,
Yorks**
Tel: 0937 63646
*A complete range of flytying
materials of high quality.
Comprehensive yearly
catalogue. Hand made hooks
and many exclusive items.
Day ticket fishing instruction
by prior appointment.*

McHardys of Carlisle
South Henry Street, Carlisle, Cumbria
Tel: 0228 23988

MEDWAY FEATHER CO.
3 Ingram Road, Gillingham, Kent
Tel: 0634 52841
See Advertisement this Section

Mayo Flycraft
Rathbawn Drive, Castlebar, Co. Mayo
Eire
Tel: 094 22757

rman Phillips
Griston Road, Watton, Norfolk
0953 882966
**ufacturer of and sole distributor of
lips Winging Machines**

Stuart Morgan
Brynhyfryd, Croescyceiliog,
nbran, Gwent
06333 4785

OATS

co Products Ltd.
John Street, Horwich, Bolton, Lancs
0204 691737

ger Accessories Ltd.
er Works, Crowland Road,
don N15
01 802 0077

T. Barlow & Son (Vortex) Ltd.
d House, Thames Ditton, Surrey
01 398 3826

tack Products Ltd.
ingdon Grove, Sudbury, Suffolk
0787 72028

ck & White (Sports) Ltd.
r Close Industrial Estate, Evesham,
rcs.
0386 45032
Advertisements under Lures

b Church & Co. Ltd.
orne Road, Northampton
0604 713674

mafloat
Waterside, Chesham, Bucks
02405 2596

& C. Carbonyte Ltd.
arage Lane, Hoo, Nr. Rochester,
t
0634 250901

Castafloat
7 Twyford Close, West Hallam,
Derbyshire
Tel: 0602 302517

W. B. Clarke (Fishing) Ltd.
Crescent Works, Mount Pleasant,
Redditch, Worcs
Tel: 0527 43310

CONTINENTAL POLE TACKLE CO.
**10-12 Prospect Way, Chatteris, Cambs.
Tel: 03543 5127**

Cruz, Doyle and Tratt Products
Kinwood, Faygate, Horsham, Sussex
Tel: 029383 584
Manufacturers of "Electrolight" Floats

Daiwa Sports Ltd.
Netherton Industrial Estate, Wishaw,
Strathclyde
Tel: 06983 61313
Ivan Marks/Daiwa Floats

D.A.M. Tackle Ltd.
P.O. Box 40, Leamington Spa, Warks
Tel: 0926 313237

David Kiddy
28 Barton Road, Torquay, Devon
Tel: 0803 23999
Manufacturers of polystyrene floats

East Anglian Rod Company Ltd.
Rookery House, Newmarket, Suffolk
Tel: 0638 5831

C. J. FIELD (POLYNET) LTD.
**Union Road Estate, Union Road,
Macclesfield, Cheshire
Tel: 0625 611077**

> **"Ian Heaps" Floats
> used by anglers all over
> Europe. Made from selected
> materials to Ian's design.
> Available in a range of
> patterns. Ask to see them at
> your local stockist.**

Frank Wallace
Yeomanry House, Castle Hill, Reading
Tel: 0734 589703

John Burton & Co. (Angling) Ltd.
Rough Hey Road, Ribbleton, Preston
Tel: 0772 797070

John Wilkins
62 Nelson Street, Buckingham, Bucks.
Tel: 02802 4495

Kalium Products Ltd.
Albert Steet, Redditch, Worcs.
Tel: 0527 64433
**Manufacturers of fluorescent and
waterproof float paint**

Kimberley Fishing Tackle Services
5a Regent Street, Kimberley,
Nottingham
Tel: 0602 383931
Manufacturer of fishing floats

S. Lacey & Co. Ltd.
Signal Works, 1-3 Station Works, Long
Eaton, Notts
Tel: 060 76 2972
Manufacturers of Signal Floats

Middy Floats
Ladysmith Road, Borrowash, Derby
Tel: 0332 677075

Modern Arms Co. Ltd.
Pembroke Road, Bromley, Kent
Tel: 01 460 3483

Newark Needle Floats
Manor Works, North Muskham, Newark,
Notts
Tel: 0636 702457

Peter Drennan
Leopold Street, Oxford
Tel: 0865 49580

SHAKESPEARE CO.
**P.O. Box 1, Redditch, Worcs
Tel: 0527 21570
See Advertisement on Inside Back
Cover**

Sima-Adams (G.B.) Ltd.
132 West Regent Street, Glasgow
Tel: 041 221 9106

Sundridge
Vicarage Lane, Hoo, Nr. Rochester,
Kent
Tel: 0634 252104

Ultra Fishing Tackle Ltd
34 Longfield Road, Sydenham Ind. Est.
Leamington Spa, Warks.
Tel: 0926 24722

Accessories: Float Wallets

FLOAT WALLETS & HOLDERS

Asco Products
St John Street, Horwich, Bolton, Lancs.
Tel: 0204 691737

Auger Accessories Ltd.
Auger Works, Crowland Road,
London N15
Tel: 01 802 0077

B.F.T.C./Oakly Fishing Tackle Ltd.
Heming Road, Washford Industrial
Estate, Redditch
Tel: 0527 24509
Manufacturers and distributors of float wallets and holders

C. Farlow & Co. Ltd.
151 Fairview Road, Cheltenham, Glos.
Tel: 0242 518690

F. Goddard, (Efgeeco) Ltd.
26 Balham Hill, London SW12
Tel: 01 673 1177

Henry W. Aiken Ltd.
139/147 Kirkdale, Sydenham,
London SE26
Tel: 01 699 1141

Shakespeare Co.
P.O. Box 1, Redditch, Worcs.
Tel: 0527 21570

GAFFS, TAILERS & PRIESTS

Abu (Great Britain) Ltd.
Clydebank Industrial Estate,
Dunbartonshire
Tel: 041 952 6381

Auger Accessories
Auger Works, Crowland Road,
London N15
Tel: 01 802 0077

BFTC/Oakley
Hemming Road, Washford Industrial
Estate, Redditch
Tel: 0527 24509

Bob Church & Co. Ltd.
16 Lorne Road, Northampton
Tel: 0604 713674
Manufacturers of Priests

C. Farlow & Co. Ltd.
151 Fairview Road, Cheltenham, Glos.
GL52 2EY

C. J. Field (Polynet) Ltd.
Union Road Estate, Union Road,
Macclesfield
Tel: 0625 611077

F. Goddard (Efgeeco) Ltd.
Efgeeco Works, Balham Hill, London
SW12
Tel: 01 673 1177

Hardy Bros (Alnwick) Ltd.
Willowburn, Alnwick, Northumberland
Tel: 0665 602771

G. C. Harris & Co. Ltd.
Double Century Works, High Street,
Astwood Bank, Redditch, Worcs
Tel: 052 789 3600

Keenets Ltd.
Furlong House, East Street, Warminster
Tel: 0985 215273

Redditch Tackle Co.
Unit 15, Alders Drive, Moons Moat
Estate, Redditch
Tel: 0527 29030

SHAKESPEARE CO.
P.O. Box 1, Redditch. Worcs
Tel: 0527 21570
See Advertisement on Inside Back Cover

Sue Burgess
'Glyn Celyn', Felin Fach, Brecon,
Powys.

Tarn Rods
Caen-y-Mynydd, Dolanog, Welshpool,
Powys
Tel: 0938 810830
See Advertisements under Rods and Reels

Wilco Sports
Tantallan Road, Nth Berwick, East
Lothian
Tel: 0620 3686

HANDLINES

BFTC/Oakley Fishing Tackle Ltd.
Heming Road, Washford Industrial
Estate, Redditch
Tel: 0527 24509
Manufacturers and suppliers of Handlines

Dutton & Co. (Fishing Tackle) Ltd.
20a Seaside, Eastbourne
Tel: 0323 23491

Kent & Co. (Twines) Ltd.
Hartley Trading Estate, Long Lane,
Liverpool
Tel: 051 525 1601

Modern Arms Co. Ltd.
Pembroke Road, Bromley, Kent
Tel: 01 460 3483

Richard Forshaw & Co. Ltd.
Colonsay House, Tarran Way, Moreto
Merseyside
Tel: 051 678 7878
Telex: 627083 Tackle G

Shakespeare Co.
P.O. Box 1, Redditch. Worcs
Tel: 0527 21570

HATS

Hardy Bros. (Alnwick) Ltd.
Willowburn, Alnwick, Northumberlan
Tel: 0665 602771

James Lock & Co. Ltd.
6 St James's Street, London SW1
Tel: 01 930 5849

HOOKS & HOOKS TO NYLON

Asco Products
St John Street, Horwich, Bolton, Lanc
Tel: 0204 691737

ANGLERS MASTERLINE LTD.
Cotteswold Road, Tewkesbury, Glos
Tel: 0684 294210
See Advertisement under Lines

Auger Accessories Ltd.
Auger Works, Crowland Road,
London N15
Tel: 01 802 0077

BFTC/Oakley Fishing Tackle C
Heming Road, Washford Industrial
Estate, Redditch
Tel: 0527 24509

Breakaway Tackle Developmen Co. Ltd.
376 Bramford Road, Ipswich
Tel: 0473 41393

Campbell Dixon Ltd.
Duck Lane, Maids Moreton, Buckingh
Tel: 028 02 2912
Distributor of Mustad and Partridge hooks

W. B. Clarke & Co. Ltd.
Crescent Works, Mount Pleasant,
Redditch, Worcs
Tel: 0527 43310

Esmond Drury Ltd.
Langton, Spilsby, Lincs
Tel: 0790 52352

C. Farlow & Co. Ltd.
151 Fairview Road, Cheltenham, Glos
Tel: 0242 518690

C. J. Field (Polynet) Ltd.
Union Road Estate, Union Road,
Macclesfield, Cheshire
Tel: 0625 611077
Suppliers of 'Tan Heaps' Hooks

Frank Wallace
Yeomanry House, Castle Hill, Reading,
Berks
Tel: 0734 589703
Distributors of Au Lion D'or Hooks

C.E.D. Harris & Co. Ltd.
2a Church Green West, Redditch,
Worcs.
Tel: 0527 64409

Henry W. Aiken Ltd.
139/147 Kirkdale, Sydenham,
London SE26
Tel: 01 699 1141
*Superflex and Strike One hooks to
nylon*

Mackenzie-Philps Ltd.
Deer Springs, Stockeld, Wetherby,
Yorks
Tel: 0937 63646

Martinez and Bird Ltd.
Bridge Works, Redditch, Worcs
Tel: 0527 62131

O. MUSTAD & SONS LTD.
**7 Farraday Road, North East Industrial
Estate, Peterlee, Co. Durham**
Tel: 0783 869553
See Advertisement this Section

A. E. Partridge & Sons Ltd.
Crescent Works, Mount Pleasant,
Redditch, Worcs
Tel: 0527 41380

Peter Drennan
Leopold Street, Oxford
Tel: 0865 49580

Sprite Fishing Tackle
75 Besley Road, Redditch, Worcs
Tel: 0527 65164

Sue Burgess Fishing Tackle
Glyn Celyn, Brecon, Powys
Tel: 0874 4448

Sundridge
Vicarage Lane, Hoo, Nr. Rochester,
Kent
Tel: 0634 252104
Distributors of VMC Hooks

H. Turrall & Co.
Dolton, Winkleigh, Devon
Tel: 080 54 352

Taylor & Johnson Ltd.
Palmers Road, East Moons Moat,
Redditch, Worcs
Tel: 0527 29030/21030
Suppliers of Stiletto Hooks

VINCE LISTER AGENCY
**1 Send Road, Caversham, Reading,
Berks**
Tel: 0734 479641
*Distributors of 'Lignham' Hooks to
Nylon*

M. WARD DUCKWORTH
**Littleton House, Crawley Ridge,
Camberley, Surrey**
Tel: 0276 63910

H. E. Watson & Son Ltd.
9 Vernon Road, Sutton, Surrey
Tel: 01 643 7993

INSECT SPRAYS

East Anglian Rod Co. Ltd.
Rookery House, Newmarket, Suffolk
Tel: 0638 5831

KNIVES

Asco Products
St John Street, Horwich, Bolton, Lancs.
Tel: 0204 691737

Burton McCall Ltd.
Samuel Street, Leicester
Tel: 0533 538781
*Full range of Knives including the
Normack Range*

Campbell Dixon Ltd.
Duck Lane, Maids Moreton, Buckingham
Tel: 02802 2912
Distributors of Wenger Swiss Knives

Daiwa Sports Ltd.
Netherton Industrial Estate, Wishaw,
Strathclyde
Tel: 06983 61313

C. Farlow & Co. Ltd.
151 Fairview Road, Glos.
Tel: 0242 518690

East Anglian Rod Co. Ltd.
Rookery House, Newmarket, Suffolk
Tel: 0638 5831

Accessories: Knives – Lures

Frank Harlow Engineering Ltd.
Catley Road, Sheffield, S. Yorks.
Tel: 0742 441495
Manufacturers of weedcutters

Hardy Bros. (Alnwick) Ltd.
Willowburn, Alnwick, Northumberland
Tel: 0665 602771

John Clarke & Son Ltd.
65 Garden Street, Sheffield

Malcberry Ltd.
366 Croydon Road, Beckenham, Kent
Tel: 01 650 2255

NORMARK SPORT LTD.
Bossell Road, Buckfastleigh, Devon
Tel: 036 44 2597/2368
See Advertisement under Rod Fittings
and Rod Rings

Pelican Fishing Tackle
118 Ashley Road, Parkstone, Poole,
Dorset
Tel: 0202 743291

Scalemead Arms Company
Dept. TG, Diplocks Way, Hailsham,
Surrey
Tel: 0323 845272

SHAKESPEARE CO.
P.O. Box 1, Redditch. Worcs
Tel: 0527 21570
See Advertisement on Inside Back
Cover

Telltrade Ltd.
104 Christchurch Road, Ringwood,
Hants.
Tel: 04254 3932

Whitby & Co.
The Old Fire Station, Aynam Road,
Kendal, Cumbria
Tel: 0539 21032

LINE & FLY GREASERS, SPRAYS & FLOATANTS

ANGLERS MASTERLINE LTD.
Cotteswold Road, Tewkesbury, Glos
Tel: 0684 294210
See Advertisement under Lines

Chubbs of Edgware Ltd.
33 South Parade, Mollison Way,
Edgware, Middlesex
Tel: 01 952 1579
Distributors of Perma aids

E. R. CRADDOCK LTD.
Heming Road, Redditch, Worcs
Tel: 0527 28301

C. Farlow & Co. Ltd.
151 Fairview Road, Cheltenham, Glos.
Tel: 0242 518690

Hardy Bros. (Alnwick) Ltd.
Willowburn, Alnwick, Northumberland
Tel: 0665 602771

John Roberts
21 Margate Road, Ramsgate, Kent
Tel: 0843 581678
Manufacturers of the Flymate
applicator

Leeda Tackle
14 Cannon Street, Southampton, Hants
Tel: 0703 772131

SHAKESPEARE CO.
P.O. Box 1, Redditch. Worcs
Tel: 0527 21570
See Advertisement on Inside Back
Cover

Sue Burgess Fishing Tackle
Glyn Celyn, Brecon, Powys
Tel: 0874 4448

LINE TRAYS

Auger Accessories Ltd.
Auger Works, Crowland Road,
London N15
Tel: 01 802 0077

Bob Church & Co. Ltd.
16 Lorne Road, Northampton
Tel: 0604 713674

Brennan and Hickman Angling
Products
Rookery Street, Wednesfield, West
Midlands
Tel: 0902 738783

C. J. Field (Polynet) Ltd.
Union Road Estate, Union Road,
Macclesfield, Cheshire
Tel: 0625 611077

F. Goddard (Efgeeco) Ltd.
26 Balham Hill, London SW12
Tel: 01 673 1177

Rayex
62 Crantock Road, Perry Barr,
Birmingham
Tel: 021 356 5695

Redport Net Co. Ltd.
Asker Works, 94 East Street, Bridport,
Dorset
Tel: 0308 22592

SHAKESPEARE CO.
P.O. Box 1, Redditch. Worcs
Tel: 0527 21570
See Advertisement on Inside Back
Cover

Smiths Tackle Co.
55 Boverton Avenue, Brockworth, Gl
Tel: 0452 823865

Sue Burgess
'Glyn Celyn,' Felin Fach, Brecon, Po
Tel: 0874 4488

LURES & ARTIFICIAL BAITS

Abu (Great Britain) Ltd.
Clydebank Industrial Estate,
Dunbartonshire
Tel: 041 952 6381

Alfred Booker & Co.
Arthur Street, Redditch, Worcs
Tel: 0527 27056
Distributors of 'Courier' Brand Lures

Asco Products Ltd.
St. John Street, Horwich, Bolton, Lar
Tel: 0204 691737

Auger Accessories Ltd.
Auger Works, Crowland Road,
London N15
Tel: 01 802 0077

BFTC/Oakley Fishing Tackle
Heming Road, Washford Industrial
Estate, Redditch
Tel: 0527 24509
Manufacturers and Suppliers of Lu
and artificial bait

BLACK & WHITE (SPORTS)
LTD.
Briar Close Industrial Estate, Evesh
Worcs
Tel: 0386 45032
See Advertisement this Section
See Also Advertisement under Rod
Rests, Holders and Bank Sticks

Brent (Hailsham) Ltd.
156 Station Road, Hailsham, East Sus
Tel: 0323 840094

BRYSTAN
122 Brynhyfryd, Croesyceiliog,
Cwmbran, Gwent NP44 2LX
Tel: 06333 4785
See Advertisement this Section

Butler's Marine
Woods Way, Mulberry Industrial Est
Goring-By-Sea, Sussex
Tel: 0903 502221
Distributors of Ferro Jet Lures and
Zuri trolling lures.

O. Crowther
Main Street, Frodsham, Cheshire
: 0928 31901

iwa Sports Ltd.
herton Industrial Estate, Wishaw,
athclyde
: 06983 61313

A.M. TACKLE LTD.
Box 40, Leamington Spa, Warks
: 0926 313237

xter Products Ltd.
nerch Road, Llanfairfechan,
ynedd
: 0248 680003

BRO LTD.
llington Road, Liverpool
: 051 928 4211
Advertisement this Section

st Anglian Rod Co. Ltd.
okery House, Newmarket, Suffolk
: 0638 5831

dystone International Angling
oducts
Efford Road, Higher Compton,
mouth
: 0752 771954
nufacturers and distributors of the
dystone Eel

Farlow & Co. Ltd.
Fairview Road, Cheltenham,
ucestershire
: 0242 518690

ank Wallace
omanry House, Castle Hill, Reading
: 0734 589703
tributors of Au Lion D'or Lures

Goddard (Efgeeco) Ltd.
Balham Hill, London SW12
: 01 673 1177

E.D. Harris & Co. Ltd.
Church Green West, Redditch,
rcs
: 0527 64409

C. Harris & Co. Ltd.
ble Century Works, High Street,
wood Bank, Redditch, Worcs
: 052 789 3600

enets Ltd.
long House, East Street, Warminster,
ts
: 0985 215273

nt & Company (Twines) Ltd.
rtley Trading Estate, Long Lane,
erpool
: 051 525 1601

Leeda Tackle
14 Cannon Street, Southampton, Hants
Tel: 0703 772131
Agents for Rublex Lures

Mackenzie-Philps Ltd.
Deer Springs, Stockeld, Wetherby,
Yorks
Tel: 0937 63646

MILLARD BROS. LTD.
Tantallon Road, North Berwick,
Scotland
Tel: 0620 4661
See Advertisement under Rods

O. MUSTAD & SONS LTD.

7 Farraday Road, North East Industrial
Estate, Peterlee, Co. Durham
Tel: 0783 869 553
For Lures, Flies, Hooks & Split
Rings, Assorted Pack or Bulk.
See Also Advertisement in
Hooks Section

NORMARK SPORT LTD.

Bossell Road, Buckfastleigh, Devon
Tel: 03644 2597/2368
See Also Advertisements under Rod
Rings and Rod Fittings

NORMARK SPORT LTD.
Bossell Road, Buckfastleigh, Devon
Tel: 03644 2597/2368
See Also Advertisement under Rod
Rings and Rod Fittings

F. Perkins Ltd.
48c Commercial Road, Hereford
Tel: 0432 4152
Manufacturers of Devon Spinners

Richard Forshaw & Co. Ltd.
Colonsay House, Tarran Way, Moreton,
Merseyside
Tel: 051 678 7878
Telex: 627083 Tackle G

Seaway Suppliers
6 Oban Road, Bournemouth
Tel: 0202 528221

SHAKESPEARE CO.
P.O. Box 1, Redditch. Worcs
Tel: 0527 21570
See Advertisement on Inside Back
Cover

Sima-Adams
27 Wellington Street, Glasgow
Tel: 041 221 9106

H. Steade & Sons Ltd.
49 Catley Road, Sheffield, Yorks
Tel: 0742 449454
Agents for Mister Twister Sea Fishing
Lures

Sundridge
Vicarage Lane, Hoo, Nr. Rochester,
Kent
Tel: 0634 252104
Distributors of Jensen Spinners

Telltrade Ltd.
104 Christchurch Road, Ringwood,
Hants
Tel: 04254 3932
Distributors of deep sea fishing lures

H. Turrall & Co.
Dolton, Winkleigh, Devon
Tel: 08054 352
Manufacturers of lures and streamers
for trout fishing

Universal Fishing Tackle Co.
Highfield Works, 107 Oakley Road,
Redditch, Worcs
Tel: 0527 62869
Manufacturers of a wide range of lures

Victoria Forge
William Street, Nelson, Lancs
Tel: 0282 691644
Manufacturers of Devon Minnows

Vince Lister Agency
1, Send Road, Caversham, Reading,
Berks.
Tel: 0527 41380
Distributors of Mepps Lures

Warwick Paravan
Common Cottage, Bishops Sutton,
Alresford, Hants
Tel: 096279 549

Western Seabaits
Blowinghouse Hill, St. Austell, Cornwall
Tel: 0726 5681
Main Distributors of Redgill Lures

MAGAZINE PUBLISHERS

Anglers Mail
I.P.C. Magazines Ltd.
Kings Reach Tower, Stamford Street,
London SE1
Tel: 01 261 6025

Angling Times
E.M.A.P. National Publications Ltd.
Bretton Court, Bretton, Peterborough
Tel: 0733 266222

Coarse Angler
281 Ecclesall Road, Sheffield
Tel: 0742 686132

Coarse Angling Monthly
Burlington Publishing Co. Ltd.
10 Sheer Street, Windsor, Berks.
Tel: 07535 56061

COARSE FISHERMAN
32 Daventry Road, Norton, Nr.
Daventry, Northants
Tel: 03272 4751

Tackle & Guns
E.M.A.P. National Publications Ltd.
Bretton Court, Bretton, Peterborough
Tel: 0733 26466

Rod & Line
James Paton Ltd.
18-20 Gordon Street, Paisley, Scotland
Tel: 041 889 8873

SCOTTISH ANGLING NEWS
S.A.N. Promotions Ltd. Block 5, Unit 1,
Burnside Industrial Estate, Garrell
Road, Kilsyth, Scotland
See Advertisement in Colour Section

Sea Angler
E.M.A.P. National Publications Ltd.
Bretton Court, Bretton Centre,
Peterborough
Tel: 0733 264666

Sea Angling Monthly
Burlington Publishing Co. Ltd.
10 Sheet Street, Windsor, Berks
Tel: 07535 56061

Trout and Salmon
E.M.A.P. National Publications Ltd.
21 Church Walk, Peterborough
Tel: 0733 264666

Trout Fisherman
E.M.A.P. National Publications Ltd.
Bretton Court, Bretton Centre,
Peterborough
Tel: 0733 264666

NETS-DRAG

BRIDPORT GUNDRY LTD.
(MARINE DIVISION)
Court Works, Bridport, Dorset
Tel: 0308 56666
> *Offers a complete range of*
> *fully rigged drag seine nets*
> *and accessories for clearing*
> *ponds, lakes and reservoirs.*
> *Free catalogue available on*
> *request.*

C. J. FIELD (POLYNET) LTD.
Union Road Estate, Union Road,
Macclesfield, Cheshire
Tel: 0625 611077

R. & B. Leakey
Sutcliffe House, Settle, Yorkshire
Tel: 07292 3506

Redport Net Co. Ltd.
Asker Works, 94 East Street, Bridport,
Dorset
Tel: 0308 22592
Manufacturers of Drag Nets

NETS-KEEP

Asco Products
St John Street, Horwich, Bolton, Lanc
Tel: 0204 691737

Auger Accessories Ltd.
Auger Works, Crowland Road,
London N15
Tel: 01 802 0077

B.F.T.C./Oakly Fishing Tackle
Ltd.
Heming Road, Washford Industrial
Estate, Redditch, Worcs
Tel: 0527 24509
Manufacturers and distributors of ke
nets

**ACK & WHITE (SPORTS)
D.**
ar Close Industrial Estate, Evesham,
rcs
: 0386 45032
*Advertisement under Rod Rests,
ders & Bank Sticks*

B. Clarke (Fishing) Ltd.
scent Works, Mount Pleasant,
.ch, Worcs
: 0527 43310

lfare
urch Farm, Burton-on-Stather,
nthorpe, South Humberside
: 0724 720898

J. FIELD (POLYNET) LIMITED
ion Road Estate, Union Road,
cclesfield, Cheshire
: 0625 611077
*ery World Champion since
1977 has used an 8ft
licromesh' Keepnet to hold
is world winning weight.*

Goddard (Efgeeco) Ltd.
eeco Works, Balham Hill,
don SW12
: 01 673 1177

C. Harris & Co. Ltd.
ble Century Works, High Street,
wood Bank, Redditch, Worcs
: 052789 3600

use & Co.
Lower Buckland Road, Lymington,
its
: 0590 76806

enets Ltd.
long House, East Street, Warminster
: 0985 215273

ORDEX LTD.
Christopher House, Eyre Street,
ffield S1 3GH
: 0742 28005
ex: Chamcom 547676 (forvere)

DPORT NET COMPANY LTD.
er Works, 94 East Street, Bridport,
set
: 0308 22592
Advertisement this Section

Steade & Sons Ltd.
Catley Road, Sheffield, Yorks
0742 449454

nity Sand Nets Ltd.
s Mill, James Street, York
0904 411199

NETS — LANDING NETS, FRAMES AND HANDLES

Abu (Great Britain) Ltd.
Clydebank Industrial Estate,
Dunbartonshire
Tel: 041 952 6381

Asco Products Ltd.
St. John's Street, Horwich, Bolton, Lancs
Tel: 0204 691737

Auger Accessories Ltd.
Auger Works, Crowland Road,
London N15
Tel: 01 802 0077

B.F.T.C./Oakly Fishing Tackle
Ltd.
Heming Road, Washford Industrial
Estate, Redditch, Worcs
Tel: 0527 24509
*Manufacturers and distributors of
landing nets*

Black & White (Sports) Ltd.
Briar Close Industrial Estate, Evesham,
Worcs
Tel: 0386 45032
*See Advertisement Under Rod Rests,
Holders and Bank Sticks*

CARROL McMANUS LTD.
**9, Sybron Way, Jarvis Brook,
Crowborough, Sussex
Tel: 08926 64388**
See Advertisement under Rod Blanks

W. B. Clarke (Fishing) Ltd.
Crescent Works, Mount Pleasant,
Redditch, Worcs
Tel: 0527 43310

Daiwa Sports Ltd.
Netherton Industrial Estate, Wishaw,
Strathclyde
Tel: 06983 61313

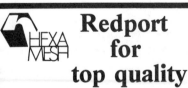

DINSMORE LTD.
**Westgate, Aldridge, Staffs
Tel: 0922 56421**
*Manufacturers of Landing Net Frames
and Handles*

C. Farlow & Co. Ltd.
151 Fairview Road, Cheltenham, Glos.
Tel: 0242 518690

C. J. FIELD (POLYNET) LTD.
**Union Estate, Union Road,
Macclesfield, Cheshire
Tel: 0625 611077**

Foster Sporting Services
32 St John's Street, Ashbourne,
Derbyshire
Tel: 0335 43135

Frank Harlow Engineering Ltd.
Catley Road, Sheffield
Tel: 0742 441495
*Manufacturers of extending Landing
Net Handles*

F. Goddard (Efgeeco) Ltd.
Efgeeco Works, Balham Hill, London
SW12
Tel: 01 673 1177

Hardy Bros (Alnwick) Ltd.
Willowburn, Alnwick, Northumberland
Tel: 0665 602771

G.C. Harris & Co. Ltd.
Double Century Works, High Street,
Astwood Bank, Redditch, Worcs
Tel: 052789 3600

House & Co.
68 Lower Buckland Road, Lymington,
Hants
Tel: 0590 76806

Keenets Ltd.
Furlong House, East Street, Warminster
Tel: 0985 215273

Modern Arms Co. Ltd.
Pembroke Road, Bromley, Kent
Tel: 01 460 3483

MORDEX LTD.
**St. Christopher House, Eyre Street,
Sheffield S1 3GH
Tel: 0742 28005
Telex: Chamcom 547676 (FORVERE)**

Pelican Fishing Tackle Ltd.
118 Ashley Road, Parkstone, Poole,
Dorset

REDPORT NET COMPANY LTD.
**Asker Works, 94 East Street, Bridport,
Dorset
Tel: 0308 22592**
See Advertisement under Nets-keep

Richard Forshaw & Co. Ltd.
Colonsay House, Tarran Way, Moreton,
Merseyside
Tel: 051 678 7878

Richard Wheatley & Sons Ltd.
Century Works, Midland Road, Walsall,
West Midlands
Tel: 0992 57555

Rollins & Sons (London) Ltd.
Rollins House, Mimram Road, Hertford,
Herts
Tel: 0992 57555
Distributors of Viking Landing Nets

SHAKESPEARE CO.
P.O. Box 1, Redditch, Worcs
Tel: 0527 21570
See Advertisement on Inside Back
Cover

Stephens (Birmingham) Ltd.
Beach Road, Sparkhill, Birmingham
Tel: 021 772 4011
Manufacturers of Landing Net Handles

Sue Burgess Fishing Tackle
Glyn Celyn, Brecon, Powys
Tel: 0874 4448

Tarn Rods
Coen-y-Mynydd, Dolanog, Welshpool,
Powys
Tel: 0938 810830
See Also Advertisement under Rods
and Reels

Wilco Sports
Tantallon Road, Nth Berwick, East
Lothian
Tel: 0620 3686

REEL CASES

Anglemark
P.O. Box 35, Sandbach, Cheshire
Tel: 09367 61484

Asco Products
St John Street, Horwich, Bolton, Lancs.
Tel: 0204 691737

Auger Accessories Ltd.
Auger Works, Crowland Road,
London N15
Tel: 01 802 0077

B.F.T.C./Oakly Fishing Tackle
Ltd.
Heming Road, Washford Industrial
Estate, Redditch, Worcs
Tel: 0527 24509
Manufacturers and distributors of reel
cases

Bob Church & Co. Ltd.
16 Lorne Road, Northampton
Tel: 0604 713674

Brennan & Hickman Angling
Products
Rookery Street, Wednesfield, West
Midlands
Tel: 0902 738783

Daiwa Sports Ltd.
Netherton Industrial Estate, Wishaw,
Strathclyde
Tel: 06983 61313

F. Goddard (Efgeeco) Ltd.
26 Balham Hill, London SW12
Tel: 01 673 1177

Hardy Bros (Alnwick) Ltd.
Willowburn, Alnwick, Northumberland
Tel: 0665 602771

Karobes Ltd.
Queensway Trading Estate, Leamington
Spa, Warks
Tel: 0926 27911

Roach Fishing Tackle
89 Baillie Street, Rochdale
Tel: 0706 33267

Smiths Tackle Co.
55 Boverton Avenue, Brockworth, Glos.
GL3 4ER
Tel: 0452 82 3865

Stephens (Birmingham) Ltd.
Beach Road, Sparkhill, Birmingham
Tel: 021 772 4011

Sue Burgess
'Glyn Celyn' Felin Fach, Brecon, Powys
Tel: 0874 4488

ROD BAGS AND HOLDALLS

Asco Products
St John Street, Horwich, Bolton, Lancs.
Tel: 0204 691737

Auger Accessories Ltd.
Auger Works, Crowland Road,
London N15
Tel: 01 802 0077

Brennan & Hickman Angling
Products
Rookery Street, Wednesfield, West
Midlands
Tel: 0902 738783

S.D. Crowther
67a Main Street, Frodsham, Cheshire
Tel: 0923 31901

Custom Rods (Oxford)
5 Pound Way, Cowley Centre, Oxford
Tel: 0865 775218

F. Goddard (Efgeeco) Ltd.
26 Balham Hill, London SW12
Tel: 01 673 1177

Henry W. Aiken Ltd.
139/147 Kirkdale, Sydenham, London
SE26
Tel: 01 699 1141

Karobes Ltd.
Queensway, Leamington Spa, Warks.
Tel: 0926 27911

Lanner Field Sports
Granville Chambers, Midland Road,
Wellingborough
Tel: 0933 224482

Liddlesdale Fishing Bag Co. Lt
Douglas Square, Newcastleton,
Roxburghshire, Scotland
Tel: 054121 616

RICHARD FORSHAW & CO.
LTD.
Colonsay House, Tarran Way,
Moreton, Merseyside
Tel: 051 678 7878
Telex: 627083 Tackle G
> *A wide selection of high*
> *quality rod bags and rod*
> *holdalls.*

Roach Fishing Tackle
89 Baillie Street, Rochdale
Tel: 0706 33267

Smiths Tackle Co.
55 Boverton Avenue, Brockworth, Glo
Tel: 0452 823865
Manufacturers of Rod holdalls and
bags

Stephens (Birmingham) Ltd.
Beach Road, Sparkhill, Birmingham
Tel: 021 772 4011

TACKLE TRADING CO.
286, High Street, Rochester, Kent
Tel: 0634 47654
See Advertisement this Section

ROD BLANKS

Aiken, Henry W. Ltd.
139/147 Kirkdale, Sydenham, London
SE26 4QW
Tel: 01 699 1141

Avon Tournament Rod Co.
55 Hatton Garden, London EC1N 8HF
See Also Advertisements under Rod

...uce & Walker Ltd.
...ntingdon Road, Upwood,
...ntingdon, Cambs.
...: 0487 813764

...RROLL McMANUS LTD.
...ybron Way, Jarvis Brook,
...owborough, Sussex
...: 08926 64388
...e Advertisement this Section

... Chapman Sports Equipment
...wling Road, Ware

...aiwa Sports Ltd.
...therton Industrial Estate, Wishaw,
...athclyde
...: 06983 61313

...avid Norwich
...7 Eglinton Street, Glasgow
...: 041 429 8302
...nufacturers of Bamboo Rod Blanks

...batube Ltd.
...llowburn, Alnwick, Northumberland
...: 0665 602771
...e Advertisement this Section

...rdham & Wakefield
...nvale, Third Street, Langton Green,
...nbridge Wells, Kent
...: 089286 3153
*...ents for Dale Clemens graphite fly
...d blanks*

Fothergill & Harvey Ltd.
Composites Division,
Summit, Littleborough, Lancs
Tel: 0706 78831

Frank Wallace
Yeomanry House, Castle Hill, Reading
Tel: 0734 589703
Distributors of C.A.P. Blanks

Going Bros
8 High Street, Southend, Essex
Tel: 0702 62351
Suppliers of Conolon Surf Blanks

Hardy Bros (Alnwick) Ltd.
Willowburn, Alnwick, Northumberland
Tel: 0665 602771

NORMARK SPORT LTD.
Bossell Road, Buckfastleigh, Devon
Tel: 03644 2597/2368

North Western Blanks
100 Lord Street, Leigh, Lancs
Tel: 0942 605449
See Advertisement this Section

Pateke Morton Ltd.
59 Hutton Close, Crowther, Washington
Ind. Est., Tyne & Wear
Tel: 0632 466404

SPORTEX FISHING LTD.
London Road, Stanstead, Essex
Tel: 0279 812202
See Advertisement this Section

Sue Burgess
'Glyn Celyn' Felin Fach, Brecon, Powys
Tel: 0874 4488

Taylors Fishing Tackle
13 Western Avenue, Buckingham
Tel: 02802 3881

Terry Eustace Rods & Blanks
2a Booth Lane, Great Bar, Birmingham
Tel: 021 360 9669

ROD FITTINGS

(CORKS, ROD HANDLES, REEL SEATS, REEL FITTINGS, BUTT CAPS, WHIPPING CORD, VARNISH)

ANGLERS MASTERLINE LTD.
Cotteswold Road, Tewkesbury, Glos
Tel: 0684 294210
See Advertisement under Lines

AVON TOURNAMENT RODS
55 Hatton Garden, London EC1N 8HP
*For all your Rod Fittings
requirements.*
*See Advertisement under Rods
Section.*

E. T. Barlow & Sons (Vortex) Ltd.
Pond House, Weston Green, Thames
Ditton, Surrey
Tel: 01 398 3826

C. H. Beatson & Sons
12 Sidney Street, Sheffield
Tel: 0742 25338
*Manufacturers of alloy sliding winch
fittings*

Caudle & Rivaz Ltd.
1 Chester Close, Heolgerrig, Merthyr
Tydfil
Tel: 0685 71404

David Norwich
467 Eglinton Street, Glasgow
Tel: 041 429 8302
Manufacturers of Reel Fittings

E.R. Craddock Ltd.
Heming Road, Redditch, Worcs
Tel: 0527 28301

George M. Forbes & Co. Ltd.
51 St. Vincent Crescent, Glasgow
Tel: 041 248 3882
Manufacturers of Varnish

GREY OF ALNWICK
Station Yard, Wagon Way Road, Alnwick, Northumberland NE66 2NP

Gordon Griffiths Plastics
Lifford Way, Binley Industrial Estate, Coventry
Tel: 0203 410859

Aiken, Henry W. Ltd.
139/147 Kirkdale, Sydenham, London SE26 4QW
Tel: 01 699 1141

John Roberts
21 Margate Road, Ramsgate, Kent
Tel: 0843 581678
Manufacturers of Realfit winch fittings

Kalium Products Ltd.
Albert Street, Redditch, Worcs
Tel: 0527 64433
Manufacturers of Kalium Varnish

Modern Arms Co. Ltd.
Marco Works, Pembroke Road, Bromley, Kent
Tel: 01 460 3483
Suppliers of "Modalock" rod & reel fittings

NORMARK SPORT LTD.
Bossel Road, Buckfastleigh, Devon
Tel: 03644 2597
See Advertisement this Section

North Western Blanks
100 Lord Street, Leigh, Lancs
Tel: 0942 605449
See Advertisement under Rod Blanks

VINCE LISTER AGENCY
1 Send Road, Caversham, Reading, Berks
Tel: 0734 479641
Distributors of Varmac Fittings

Wayland Automatic Products Ltd.
Brickyard Lane, Studley, Warks.
Tel: 052785 3822
Manufacturers of reel seats
Suppliers to Manufacturers and Wholesalers only

A. J. Worthington & Co. (Leek) Ltd.
Portland Mills, Leek, Staffs
Tel: 0538 383122
Manufacturers of Elephant and Talbot Brand rod binders
Available through all major wholesalers

Richard Forshaw & Co. Ltd.
Colonsay House, Tarran Way, Moreton, Merseyside
Tel: 051 678 7878
Telex: 627083 Tackle G

Sue Burgess
'Glyn Celyn' Felin Fach, Brecon, Powys
Tel: 0684 4488

ROD REPAIRS AND RENOVATORS

Abbas Sport
'The Workshop', Grove Lane, Stalbridge, Nr. Sturminster, Dorset
Tel: 0963 63005
U.K. Repairer for Kunnan Rods from Tiawan

Avon Tournament Rod Co.
55 Hatton Garden, London EC1N 8HP
See Advertisements under Rods and Rod Fittings

Anthony William Croft
Grove Lane, Stalbridge, Dorset
Tel: 0963 63005

David Norwich
467 Eglinton Street, Glasgow
Tel: 041 4298302

The Covert
East Street, Petworth, West Sussex
Tel: 0798 43118

Downham Tackle
24 Downham Way, Downham, Bromley Kent
Tel: 01 698 2723

Marcus Warwick
58 High Street West, Uppingham, Lei
Tel: 057282 2487

Otter Fly Fishing
3 South Exchange Court, 77 Queen Street, Glasgow
Tel: 041 226 5379

D. P. Hulme
Caen-y-Mynydd, Dolanog, Welshpool Powys.
Tel: 0938 810830

A. E. Partridge & Sons Ltd.
Crescent Works, Mount Pleasant, Redditch, Worcs
Tel: 0527 41380
Repairs for all types of rod

A. G. Topple
Unit 3, Bridgefount House, Buntingfor Herts
Tel: 0963 63005

Rodcraft
Reef House, 46 Artillery Road, Guildford, Surrey
Tel: 0483 77360

WESSEX RODS
Dorchester, Dorset
Tel: 0305 62277
See Also Advertisement under Rods

William Powell & Son Ltd.
35 Carrs Lane, Birmingham
Tel: 021 643 0689

ROD REST HOLDERS & BANK STICKS

Asco Products Ltd.
St. John Street, Horwich, Bolton, Lancs
Tel: 0204 691737

Auger Accessories Ltd.
Auger Works, Crowland Road, London N15
Tel: 01 802 0077

B.F.T.C./Oakly Fishing Tackle Ltd.
Heming Road, Washford Industrial Estate, Redditch, Worcs
Tel: 0527 24509
Manufacturers and distributors of rod rest holders and bank sticks

BLACK & WHITE (SPORTS) LTD.
Briar Close Industrial Estate, Evesham, Worcs
Tel: 0386 45032
See Advertisement this Section
See Also Advertisement under Lures

Breakaway Tackle Development Co. Ltd.
376 Brompton Road, Ipswich
Tel: 0473 41393

Brent (Hailsham) Ltd.
156 Station Road, Hailsham, East Sussex
Tel: 0323 840094

Bridgerest
151 Charles Henry Street, Birmingham B12
Tel: 021 622 3878

E. R. Craddock Ltd.
Heming Road, Redditch, Worcs
Tel: 0527 28301

D.A.M. Tackle Ltd.
P.O. Box 40, Leamington Spa, Warks
Tel: 0926 313237

David Peacock (Manufacturing Joiner)
Olivers Lane, Bridlington, East Yorkshire
Tel: 0262 602949

Dellareed Ltd.
20 Eagle Hill, Ramsgate, Kent
Tel: 0843 582157
Manufacturers of Elite rod rests

Dinsmores Ltd.
Westgate, Aldridge, Staffs
Tel: 0922 56421/2

East Anglian Rod Co. Ltd.
Rookery House, Newmarket, Suffolk
Tel: 0638 5831

Gardner Tackle
Hullbrook Farm, Shamley Green, Guildford, Surrey
Tel: 0483 893973

F. Goddard (Efgeeco) Ltd.
Efgeeco Works, Balham Hill, London SW12
Tel: 01 673 1177

G. C. Harris & Co. Ltd.
Double Century Works, High Street, Astwood Bank, Redditch, Worcs
Tel: 052 789 3600

House and Co.
68 Lower Buckland Road, Lymington, Hants
Tel: 0590 76806

Keenets Ltd.
Furlong House, East Street, Warminster, Wilts
Tel: 0985 215273

Modern Arms Co. Ltd.
Marco Works, Pembroke Road, Bromley Kent
Tel: 01 460 3483

MORDEX LTD.
St Christopher House, 121 Eyre Street Sheffield S1 3GH
Tel: 0742 28005
Telex: Chamcom 547676 (for Vere)

Pittmatic Anchors (UK) Ltd.
Oak Farm, Green Street Green, Orpington, Kent
Tel: 0689 51339
Manufacturers of the Pittmatic Rod Holder

Redditch Tackle Co.
Unit 15, Alders Drive, Moons Moat Estate, Redditch
Tel: 0527 29030

Richard Forshaw & Co. Ltd.
Colonsay House, Tarran Way, Moreton Merseyside
Tel: 051 678 7878
Telex: 627083 Tackle G

Shakespeare Co.
P.O. Box 1, Redditch, Worcs.
Tel: 0527 21570

H. Steade & Sons Ltd.
49 Catley Road, Sheffield, Yorks
Tel: 0742 449454

Stephens (Birmingham) Ltd.
Beach Road, Sparkhill, Birmingham
Tel: 021 772 4011

Super Bait '78
103 Chingford Mount Road, Chingford London E4
Tel: 01 531 4519
Distributors of BK Multiple rod rests

Taycol Components
587 Rawreth Industrial Estate, Rayleigh Essex
Tel: 0268 773281

V. C. M. Rod Holders
54 Central Parade, Herne Bay, Kent
Tel: 02273 4977/62195
VCB Boat rod holders

M. Ward Duckworth
Littleton House, Crawley Ridge, Camberley, Surrey
Tel: 0276 63910
Agent for 'College' rod holders

Wilco Sports
Tantallon Road, Nth. Berwick, East Lothian
Tel: 0620 3686

OD RINGS

NGLERS MASTERLINE LTD.
tteswold Road, Tewkesbury, Glos
: 0684 294210
e Advertisement under Lines

iwa Sports Ltd.
therton Industrial Estate, Wishaw,
athclyde
: 06983 61313

don Manufacturing Co.
ptune Works, Beeley Road West,
dditch, Worcs
: 0527 62027

OPKINS & HOLLOWAY LTD.
ickyard Lane, Studley, Warks
: 052 785 3822
nufacturers of Seymo Rod Rings
e Advertisement this Section

ayers Green
Bolitho Road, Penzance
: 0736 61197

ORMARK SPORTS LTD.
ssell Road, Buckfastleigh, Devon
: 03644 2597
e Advertisement this Section

rry, Dean & Woods
O. Box 4, Ashbourne, Derbyshire
l: 053 86 491

apphrite Laurels Ltd.
rk Farm Industrial Estate, Pipers
ad, Redditch, Worcs
: 0527 26041

ue Burgess
lyn Celyn', Felin Fach, Brechin,
wys.
l: 0874 4488

elltrade Ltd.
4 Christchurch Road, Ringwood,
nts.
l: 04254 3932

INCE LISTER AGENCY
Send Road, Caversham, Reading,
rks
l: 0734 479641
stributors of Varmac Rod rings

ODS – CUSTOM BUILT

bbas Sport
he Workshop', Grove Lane,
albridge, Nr. Sturminster, Dorset
l: 0963 63005

Allan Brown
118 Nightingale Road, Hitchin, Herts
Tel: 0462 59918

Anthony William Croft
Grove Lane, Stalbridge, Dorset
Tel: 0963 63005

Avon Tournament Rod. Co.
55 Hatton Garden, London, EC1N 8HP
**See Also Advertisements under Rods
and Rod Fittings**

Browns Fishing Tackle Ltd.
682 Romford Road, Manor Park,
London E12
Tel: 01 478 0389

Croydon Angling Centre
65 London Road, Croydon, Surrey
Tel: 01 688 7564

Custom Rods (Oxford)
5 Pound Way, Cowley Centre, Oxford
Tel: 0865 775218

D. A. P. Customised Rods Ltd.
Whitesheet Cottage, Donhead St
Andrew, Nr. Shaftesbury, Dorset
Tel: 074788 680

David Norwich
467 Eglinton Street, Glasgow
Tel: 041 429 8302

Essex Angling Centre
109 Leigh Road, Leigh-on-Sea, Essex
Tel: 0702 711231

Fulling Mill Flies
118 Arlington Drive, Carshalton, Surrey
Tel: 01647 8258

Gentrys Tackle
42 Park View Road, Welling, Kent
Tel: 01 303 3155

Going Brothers
8 High Street, Southend-on-Sea, Essex
Tel: 0702 62351

Greenway H. & Sons
10 Chester Road, Pype Hayes,
Birmingham
Tel: 021 373 0057

House of Howard (Grimsby) Ltd.
42 Augusta Street, Grimsby
Tel: 0472 55066

D.P. Hulme
Caen-y-Mynydd, Dolanog, Welshpool,
Powys.
Tel: 0938 810830

Marcus Warwick
58 High Street West, Uppingham, Leics
Tel: 057282 2487
Custom Built fly and coarse rods

Molesley Angling Centre
96 Walton Road, Molesley, Surrey
Tel: 01 979 9083

Otter Fly Fishing
3 South Exchange Court, 77 Queen
Street, Glasgow
Tel: 041 226 5379

F. Perkins Ltd.
48c Commercial Road, Hereford
Tel: 0432 4152

Richard Balm
71 High Street, Burnham, Bucks
Tel: 06286 5023

Ron Lees Fishing Tackle
27 High Street, Droitwich
Tel: 09057 3557

Roy Huins Fishing Tackle
138 Worcester Road, Bromsgrove

Simpsons of Turnford
Nunsbury Drive, Turnford, Broxbourne,
Herts
Tel: 09924 68799

South London Angling
91 Ladywell Road, Ladywell, Lewisham,
London SE13
Tel: 01 690 3609

Taylors Fishing Tackle
Unit 3, Iver Works, Lenborough Road,
Buckingham
Tel: 02802 3881

**TERRY EUSTACE RODS AND
BLANKS**
2a Booths Lane, Great Barr,
Birmingham
Tel: 021 360 9669
See Advertisement under Rods

Tony Allen Fishing Tackle
168a Silver Road, Norwich
Tel: 0603 412124

WESSEX RODS
Dorchester, Dorset
Tel: 0305 62277
See Also Advertisement under Rods

SEAT BOXES

Auger Accessories Ltd.
Auger Works, Crowland Road, London
N15
Tel: 01 802 0077

**Brennan & Hickman Angling
Products**
Rookery Street, Wednesfield, West
Midlands
Tel: 0902 738783

Broxhead Joinery
Lindford, Bordon, Hants
Tel: 04203 4159

C. J. FIELD (POLYNET) LTD.
Union Road Estate, Union Road,
Macclesfield, Cheshire
Tel: 0625 611077

F. Goddard (Efgeeco) Ltd.
26 Balham Hill, London SW12
Tel: 01 673 1177

Protector Tackle
463 Borough Road, Birkenhead,
Merseyside
Tel: 051 653 6845

Roach Fishing Tackle
89 Baillie Street, Rochdale
Tel: 0706 33267

Stephens (Birmingham) Ltd.
Beach Road, Sparkhill, Birmingham
Tel: 021 772 4011

K. L. Tackle
Mornington Street, Keighley, West
Yorkshire
Tel: 0535 67574
*Manufacturers of 'Black Match' seat
boxes*

SHOT AND LEADS

Alfred Booker & Co.
Arthur Street, Redditch, Worcs
Tel: 0527 26974/27056

**B.F.T.C./Oakly Fishing Tackle
Ltd.**
Heming Road, Washford Industrial
Estate, Redditch, Worcs
Tel: 0527 24509
*Manufacturers and distributors of shot
and leads*

**BLACK & WHITE (SPORTS)
LTD.**
Briars Close Industrial Estate,
Evesham, Worcs
Tel: 0386 45032
*See Advertisement under Rod Rests,
Holders and Bank Sticks*

**Breakaway Tackle Development
Co. Ltd.**
376 Bramford Road, Ipswich
Tel: 0473 41393

W. B. Clarke (Fishing) Ltd.
Crescent Works, Mount Pleasant,
Redditch, Worcs
Tel: 0527 43310

David Kiddy
28 Barton Road, Torquay, Devon
Tel: 0803 23999

Dinsmores Ltd.
Westgate, Aldridge, Staffs
Tel: 0922 56421

**Dutton & Co. (Fishing Tackle)
Ltd.**
20a Seaside, Eastbourne
Tel: 0323 23491

Mr. R. Dyer
2 The Fradgan, Newlyn, Penzance,
Cornwall
Tel: 0736 61781

Frank Wallace
Yeomanry House, Castle Hill, Reading
Tel: 0734 589703
*Distributors of Lemer and Sonde
Practique Weights*

Menwal Design Ltd.
The Kiln, Noble Street, Wem
Tel: 0939 32148

Modern Arms Co. Ltd.
Marco Works, Pembroke Road, Bromle
Kent
Tel: 01 460 3483

Norman May & Co.
Robsons Yard, 91/93 High Street,
Bridlington, Nth Humberside
Tel: 0262 78040
Distributors of Bimoco Leads

Thamesley Fishing Tackle Co.
278 Kingsland Road, London E8
Tel: 01 249 1954

SHOT AND LEAD
MOULD SUPPLIERS

Asco Products
St John Street, Horwich, Bolton, Lancs.
Tel: 0204 691737

Brian Rowe
96 Nolton Street, Bridgend, Mid
Glamorgan
Tel: 0656 58254

Brent (Hailsham) Ltd.
156 Station Road, Hailsham, East Susse
Tel: 0320 840094

Buckleys Angling Supplies
6 Leading Post Street, Scarborough
Tel: 0723 63202

C. A. Moulds
Lon Isa, Rhiwbina, Cardiff

arquiss Products
Blenheim Way, Flimwell, Wadhurst, E.
ssex
: 058087 442
**anufacturers of Kingcast D.I.Y. Lead
ulds**

WIVELS

sco Products
John Street, Horwich, Bolton, Lancs.
l: 0204 691737

bu (Great Britain) Ltd.
ydebank Industrial Estate,
nbartonshire
: 041 952 6381

ager Accessories Ltd.
ger Works, Crowland Road,
ndon N15
l: 01 802 0077

**LACK & WHITE (SPORTS)
D.**
ar Close, Industrial Estate,
esham, Worcs.
l: 0386 45032
e Advertisement Under Lures

D. Crowther
a Main Street, Frodsham, Cheshire
l: 0928 31901

exter Products Co.
anerch Road, Llanfairfechan,
wynedd
: 0248 680003

Farlow & Co. Ltd.
l Fairview Road, Cheltenham Glos.
l: 0242 518690

ARDY BROS. (ALNWICK) LTD.
illowburn, Alnwick, Northumberland
l: 0665 602771

C. Harris & Co. Ltd.
uble Century Works, High Street,
twood Bank, Redditch, Worcs
l: 052 789 3600

ollins & Sons (London) Ltd.
ollins House, Mimram Road, Hertford,
rts
l: 0992 57555
stributors of Viking swivels

elltrade Ltd.
4 Christchurch Road, Ringwood,
ants.
l: 0202 04254

Sundridge Tackle Ltd.
Vicarage Lane, Hoo, Rochester, Kent
Tel: 0634 252104

TACKLE BOXES

Abu (Great Britain) Ltd.
Clydebank Industrial Estate,
Dunbartonshire
Tel: 041 952 6381

Aiken, Henry W. Ltd.
139/147 Kirkdale, Sydenham, London
SE26 4QW
Tel: 01 699 1141

ANGLERS MASTERLINE LTD.
Cotteswold Road, Tewkesbury, Glos
Tel: 0684 294210
See Advertisement under Lines

Arrow Angling
16/18 Granby Row, Manchester
Tel: 061 2366805

Belstaff International Ltd.
Caroline Street, Longton, Stoke on Trent
Tel: 0782 317261

B.F.T.C./Oakly Fishing Tackle
Heming Road, Washford Industrial
Estate, Redditch
Tel: 0527 24509

**BLACK & WHITE (SPORTS)
LTD.**
**Briar Close Industrial Estate, Evesham,
Worcs.**
Tel: 0386 45032
See Advertisement under Lures

Brennan & Hickman Angling
Products
Rookery Street, Wednesfield, West
Midlands
Tel: 0902 738783

Brozal Ltd.
5 College Drive, Sandrock Road,
Tunbridge Wells, Kent
Tel: 0892 41744

Coventry Angling Supplies Ltd.
6 Arne Road, Walsgrave on Sow, Nr
Coventry
Tel: 0203 612299

Daiwa Sports Ltd.
Netherton Industrial Estate, Wishaw,
Strathclyde
Tel: 06983 61313

C. J. FIELD (POLYNET) LTD.
**Union Road Estate, Union Road,
Macclesfield**
Tel: 0625 611077

Frank Wallace
Yeomanry House, Castle Hill, Reading
Tel: 0734 589703
U.K. Representative of B.H.R.

F. Goddard (Efgeeco) Ltd.
26 Balham Hill, London SW12
Tel: 01 673 1177

Grice & Young Ltd.
Somerford, Christchurch, Dorset
Tel: 0202 483636

Hardy Bros (Alnwick) Ltd.
Willowburn, Alnwick, Northumberland
Tel: 0665 602771

I. & C. Carbonyte Ltd.
Vicarage Lane, Hoo, Nr. Rochester,
Kent
Tel: 0634 250901

Malcolm Scott
84 Station Road, Northwich, Cheshire
Tel: 0606 6543

Millard Bros Ltd.
Tantallon Road, North Berwick, Scotland
Tel: 0620 4661
See Advertisement under Rods

NORMARK SPORT LTD.
Bossell Road, Buckfastleigh, Devon
Tel: 03644 2597/2368
*See Also Advertisement under Rod
Rings and Rod Fittings*

Pelican Fishing Tackle Ltd.
118 Ashley Road, Parkstone, Poole,
Dorset
Tel: 0202 743291

**RICHARD FORSHAW & CO.
LTD.**
**Colonsay House, Tarran Way,
Moreton, Merseyside**
Tel: 051 678 7878
Telex: 627083 Tackle G

SHAKESPEARE CO.
P.O. Box 1, Redditch. Worcs
Tel: 0527 21570
*See Advertisement on Inside Back
Cover*

Smiths Tackle Co.
55 Boverton Avenue, Brockworth, Glos.
Tel: 0452 823865

Stephens (Birmingham) Ltd.
Beach Road, Sparkhill, Birmingham
Tel: 021 772 4011

Tara Designs
Victoria House, Norwich Road, Reepham
Tel: 060526 678

Taylors Fishing Tackle
Unit 3, Iver Works, Lenborough Road,
Buckingham
Tel: 02802 3881

West Riding Anglers Supply Ltd.
938 Leeds Road, Bradford, West Yorks
Tel: 0274 663767

TACKLE TROLLEYS

Auger Accessories Ltd.
Auger Works, Crowland Road,
London N15
Tel: 01 802 0077

Brennan & Hickman Angling
Products
Rookery Street, Wednesfield, West
Midlands
Tel: 0902 738783

Camberley Automation
Printing House Lane, Hayes, Middlesex
Tel: 01 573 7033

Stuart D. Crowther
67a Main Street, Frodsham, Cheshire
Tel: 0928 31901

F. Goddard (Efgeeco) Ltd.
26 Balham Hill, London SW12
Tel: 01 673 1177

House & Co.
68 Lower Buckland Road, Lymington,
Hampshire
Tel: 0590 76806

R. Phillips M/C Engineering
Works
Woodlands Street, Smethwick, Warley
Tel: 021 558 5942

Shakespeare Co.
P.O. Box 1, Redditch. Worcs
Tel: 0527 21570

TANGLE REMOVERS

Anglemark
P.O. Box 35, Sandbach, Cheshire

TAXIDERMISTS

A. Allison
The Lodge, East Brackley, Kinross,
Scotland
Tel: 0577 63115

Bradleys Taxidermy Service
Glen View, 72 Prospect Avenue,
Darwen, Lancs
Tel: 0254 74859

V. Davis
Chelfam House, Chelfam, Barnstaple,
Devon
Tel: 0271 82 373

C. Elliot
3 Holts Meadow, Redbourne, Herts
Tel: 058285 3487

A. E. Hall
1 The Bourne, Cockshot Lane,
Dormston, Inkberrow, Worcester
Tel: 0386 792101

K.J. Hampton
Farnham, Surrey
Tel: 0252 710525

John C. Metcalf
The Garden House, Noseley, Nr.
Billesdon, Leics
Tel: 0537 55604

John Hajiloizi
28 New Road, Wood Green, London N22
Tel: 01 888 3483

Hew Dale
The Fly Box, Station Road, Birnam,
Dunkeld, Perthshire
Tel: 035 02316

John W. Greaves
Castle Ashby, Northants
Tel: 0601 29302

R. Land
36 Link Road, Chesterfield
Tel: 0246 2267

Snowdonia Taxidermy Studio
Llanrwst, Gwynedd
Tel: 0492 640664

PETER STONE
38 Elmthorpe Road, Wolvercote,
Oxford OX2 8PA
Tel: 0865 59542
*If you have a fish for
mounting, then why not give
me a ring — or if you wish
inspect my work first.*

Tackle Box, The
272 Earlsfield Road, Wandsworth,
London SW18
Tel: 01 870 3831

M. Windham-Wright
Minard Farmhouse, Lerags, Oban,
Argyll
Tel: 0631 64936

N. R. Wood
Covertside, The Soss, Misterton,
Doncaster
Tel: 0427 890243

TERMINAL TACKLE (WIREWORK)

Asco Products
St John Street, Horwich, Bolton, Lancs.
Tel: 0204 691737

Auger Accessories Ltd.
Auger Works, Crowland Road,
London N15
Tel: 01 802 0077

B.F.T.C./Oakly Fishing Tackle
Ltd.
Heming Road, Washford Industrial
Estate, Redditch, Worcs
Tel: 0527 24509
*Manufacturers and suppliers of
terminal tackle*

BLACK & WHITE (SPORTS) LTD.
Briar Close Industrial Estate, Eveshan
Worcs
Tel: 0386 45032
*See Advertisement under Rod Rests,
Holders and Bank Sticks*

ent (Hailsham) Ltd.
6 Station Road, Hailsham, East Sussex
el: 0320 840094

. E. D. Harris & Co. Ltd.
Church Green West, Redditch,
orcs
el: 0527 64409

.D. Crowther
7A Main Street, Frodsham, Cheshire
el: 0928 31901

exter Products Co.
lanerch Road, Llanfairfechan,
wynedd
el: 0248 680003

M. R. Dyer
The Fradgan, Newlyn, Penzance,
Cornwall
el: 0736 61781

eenets Ltd.
urlong House, East Street, Warminster,
Jilts
el: 0985 215273

ent & Co (Twines) Ltd.
artley Trading Estate, Long Lane,
iverpool
el: 051 525 1601

Marquiss Product
Blenheim Way, Flimwell, Wadhurst,
ast Sussex
el: 058087 442
*Manufacturers of Kingcast D.I.Y.
Terminal Tackle*

Modern Arms Co. Ltd.
Pembroke Road, Bromley, Kent
Tel: 01 460 3483

Richard Forshaw & Co Ltd.
Colonsay House, Tarran Way, Moreton,
Merseyside
Tel: 051 678 7878
Telex: 627083 Tackle G

SHAKESPEARE CO.
**P.O. Box 1, Redditch. Worcs
Tel: 0527 21570
*See Advertisement on Inside Back
Page***

Telltrade Ltd.
104 Christchurch Road, Ringwood,
Hants.
Tel: 04254 3932

VINCE LISTER AGENCY
**1 Send Road, Caversham, Reading,
Berks
Tel: 0734 479641
*See Advertisement this Section***

TROPHIES

Brunwin Engraving
1 The Avenue, Brentwood, Essex
Tel: 0277 214073
*Manufacturers and engravers of
trophies and badges*

E. A. Clare & Son Ltd.
46/48 St Annes Street, Liverpool L3
Tel: 051 207 1336

Dover Street Trophies Ltd.
13 Dover Street, London W1
Tel: 01 493 8308

Engravia Trophy Centre
306 High Street, Kirkcaldy, Scotland
Tel: 0592 67635

H.B.S. Trophies Ltd.
102/104 Lionel Street, Birmingham B3
Tel: 021 233 1121

Kent Trophies Ltd.
362 High Road, Tottenham, London N17
Tel: 01 801 3544

Marks of Distinction Ltd.
124, Euston Road, London NW1
Tel: 01 382 3772

Swinnertons Ltd.
Union Street, Walsall
Tel: 0922 26081

Thanet Sports Trophies
89/90 Trinity Square, Margate, Kent
Tel: 0843 23178

Thos. Padmore & Sons Ltd.
180 Lozells Road, Birmingham
Tel: 021 523 6308

Thurston & Co. Ltd.
220 Camden High Street, London NW1
Tel: 01 267 5367

Vernon & Wilson Ltd.
56 Spencer Street, Birmingham 18
Tel: 021 236 1437

Victorcity Ltd.
12 Abbotsbury Road, Morden, Surrey
Tel: 01 640 3991

UMBRELLAS AND UMBRELLA TENTS

Asco Products
St John Street, Horwich, Bolton, Lancs.
Tel: 0204 691737

D. E. Barnes
21 Northdown Park Road, Margate, Kent
Tel: 0843 26740
Manufacturer and retailer of The Dave Barnes Specialist Umbrella Tent

Brennan & Hickman Angling Products
Rookery Street, Wednesfield, West Midlands
Tel: 0902 738783

Custom Rods (Oxford)
5 Pound Way, Cowley Centre, Oxford
Tel: 0865 775218
Manufacturers of Umbrella Tents

East Anglian Rod Co.
Rookery House, Newmarket, Suffolk
Tel: 0308 24342

F. Goddard (Efgeeco) Ltd.
Efgeeco Works, Balham Hill, London SW12
Tel: 01 673 1177

Intoleisure Ltd.
Claremont House, St Peters Footpath, Margate, Kent

MORDEX LTD.
St. Christopher House, Eyre Street, Sheffield S1 3GH
Tel: 0742 28005
Telex: Chamcom 547676 (for Vere)

Shakespeare Co.
P.O. Box 1, Redditch. Worcs
Tel: 0527 21570

H. Steade & Sons Ltd.
49 Catley Road, Sheffield, Yorks
Tel: 0742 449454

Stephens (Birmingham) Ltd.
Beach Road, Sparkhill, Birmingham
Tel: 021 772 4011

Sundridge Tackle Ltd.
Vicarage Lane, Hoo, Rochester, Kent
Tel: 0634 252104

H.E. Watson & Son Ltd
52 Firtree Road, Banstead, Surrey
Tel: 07373 54417

VIDEOS

DRAGON VIDEO PRODUCTIONS LTD.
2 Stratton House, Stratton Terrace, Westerham, Kent
Tel: 0959 64119
Video tapes on fly tying, casting and other aspects of fly fishing. Learn from experts 'The Gentle Art' in all its absorbing facets.

Intervision Ltd.
Unit 1, McKay Trading Estate, London W1
Tel: 01 960 8211

IPC Video Ltd.
Surrey House, Throwley Way, Sutton, Surrey
Tel: 01 643 8040

TFI Leisure Ltd.
159 Great Portland Street, London W1N 5FD
Head Office: St Mary's Street, Whitchurch, Shropshire
Tel: 0948 3341

Video Image Publications
Tower House, Fishergate, York.
Produce Fly Casting and Game Fishing Videos.

Wessex Flyfishing School
Lawrences Farm, Tolpuddle, Dorchester, Dorset
Tel: 0305 84460
Produce "Fly Casting Explained" video

WADERS, BOOTS & WELLINGTONS

Allan Brown
118 Nightingale Road, Hitchin, Herts.
Tel: 0462 59918

Bob Church & Co. Ltd.
16 Lorne Road, Northampton
Tel: 0604 713674

Belstaff International Ltd.
Caroline Street, Longton, Stoke-on-Trent, Staffs.
Tel: 0782 317261

C & V Products
GPO Box 63, 38 Merchiston Avenue, Edinburgh

Campbell Dixon Ltd.
Duck Lane, Maids Moreton, Buckingha
Tel: 028 02 2912
Chest & Thigh Waders by 'Ocean'

Clearwater Products
Ludbridge Mill, East Hendred, Wantag
Oxon.

Copnor Services Ltd.
Gurnard House, Westlands, Birdham, Chichester, Surrey
Tel: 0243 512797
Distributors of Le Chameau boots and waders

David Nickerson (Tathwell) Ltd.
The Old Vicarage, Tathwell, Louth, Lincs
Tel: 047287 536

DERRIBOOTS
10 Tower Lane, Warmley, Bristol
Tel: 0272 679121
See Advertisement under Clothing Manufacturers.

Dunlop Footwear Ltd.
176 Rice Lane, Liverpool L9
Tel: 051 525 1691

C. Farlow & Co. Ltd.
151 Fairview Road, Cheltenham, Glos
Tel: 0242 518690
The exclusive importers of American 'Seal-Dri' Latex waders.
Available from all good tackle dealers.

wler Brothers
wsham, Lincoln
: 06527 231
ppliers of a wide range of waders
d wellingtons

ala Angling Suppliers Ltd.
nghaugh Industrial Estate, Galashiels
: 0896 3069

M. GOODCHILD
st Common Lane, Scunthorpe, South
mberside, DN16 1DE
l: 0724 848200
e Advertisement this Section

rainger Street Supplies Ltd.
lsbury House, 27 Heaton Road,
wcastle Upon Tyne
: 0632 656607

dustrial Safety (Birmingham)
ngley Drive, Chester Road Industrial
ate, Castle Bromwich, Birmingham
l: 021 749 4433
e Advertisement under Clothing
ction

miflex Ltd.
ry Ground, Carlyle Street, Bury,
ncs
l: 061 764 4926

. R. Marrum (Sports) Ltd.
rth Portway Close, Round Spinney
dustrial Estate, Northampton
l: 0604 499131
mika Field Boots
ner Industrial & Sportswear (Ltd)

R.M. Services Ltd.
Woodrise, Eastcote, Pinner, Middlesex
l: 08956 73141
anufacturers of 'Supa' Waders.
e Advertisement under Clothing
anufacturers.

chmond Field Boots
Brancaster Lane, Purley, Surrey

Richard Forshaw & Co. Ltd.
Colonsay House, Tarran Way, Moreton,
Merseyside
Tel: 051 678 7878
Telex: 627083 Tackle G

SKEE-TEX LTD.
Battlesbridge, Essex
Tel: 03744 68282
See Advertisement this Section

Sundridge
Vicarage Lane, Hoo, Nr. Rochester,
Kent
Tel: 0634 252104
**Distributors of "La Bougnatte" Waders
and Boots**

Uniroyal Ltd.
62 Horseferry Road, London SW1
Tel: 01 222 5611
*Manufacturers of the hand-crafted
'Streamfisher' series of waders.*

M. Ward Duckworth
Littleton House, Crawley Ridge,
Camberley, Surrey
Tel: 0276 63910
Agents for 'Boudon' waders

Westgate Industrial Rubbers Ltd.
345 Shields Road, Newcastle Upon Tyne
Tel: 0632 654858

Zero Point Nine
17 Lodge Farm Estate, Barn Way,
Northampton
Tel: 0604 583341
Distributors of Eskimo Boots

WEIGHING SCALES

Avon Scale Co.
77 Fore Street, Edmonton, London N18
Tel: 01 807 6347

CONTESTA
*The Match Scale with the
5 Year Guarantee.
Capacities
14lb x 4 Dram Divisions
30lb x 8 Dram Divisions
Sturdy, Compact and
Extremely Accurate
Details from:
Contesta Scales
32 High Street,
Haliberton,
Tiverton,
Devon EX16 7AG
Tel: 0884 820712*

D.A.M. TACKLE LTD.
P.O. Box 40, Leamington Spa, Warks
Tel: 0926 313237

Hardy Bros. (Alnwick) Ltd.
Willowburn, Alnwick, Northumberland
Tel: 0665 602771

Reuben Heaton (Scales) Ltd.
2 Alfred Street, West Bromwich, West
Midlands
Tel: 021 553 0392

Salter Abbey Weighing Machine
Ltd.
St. Botolphs Lane, Bury St. Edmunds,
Suffolk
Tel: 0284 61321

Mail Order

The companies listed under this heading specialise in supplying the public direct with a range of angling equipment. In all cases a catalogue of the equipment on offer will be available on request.

Angling Holiday Operators and Organisers

The companies listed under this heading specialise in arranging holidays for the angler.

Fishing Tackle Wholesalers

The companies listed under this heading are the major trade angling wholesalers of general fishing tackle. It should be clearly understood that these companies would in their capacity as wholesalers, supply the fishing tackle trade only.

FISHING TACKLE WHOLESALERS

iken, Henry W. Ltd.
9/147 Kirkdale, Sydenham, London
E26 4QW
el: 01 699 1141

LFRED BOOKER & CO.
rthur Street, Redditch,
orcestershire
el: 0527 27056
e Advertisement under Lines

sco Products Ltd.
. Johns Street, Horwich, Bolton,
ancashire
el: 0204 691737

shdown Fieldsports
a High Street, East Grinstead, Sussex
el: 0342 312794

ob Church & Co. Ltd.
Lorne Road, Northampton
el: 0604 713674

reakaway Tackle Development
o. Ltd.
6 Bramford Road, Ipswich
el: 0473 41393

rent (Hailsham) Ltd.
6 Station Road, Hailsham, East Sussex
el: 0323 840094

ampbell Dixon Ltd.
ck Lane, Maids Moreton,
ckinghamshire
l: 028 02 2912

.B. Clarke (Fishing) Ltd.
escent Works, Mount Pleasant,
dditch, Worcs.
l: 0527 43310

D. Crowther
a Main Street, Frodsham, Cheshire
l: 0928 31901

utton & Co.
ishing Tackle) Ltd.
a Seaside, Eastbourne, East Sussex
l: 0323 23491

East Anglian Rod Co.
Rookery House, Newmarket, Suffolk
Tel: 0638 5831

C. FARLOW & CO. LTD.
151 Fairview Road, Cheltenham,
Gloucestershire
Tel: 0242 518690

C.J. FIELD (POLYNET) LTD.
Union Road Estate, Union Road,
Macclesfield, Cheshire
Tel: 0625 611077

Field Sports Scotland
5 Bruce Street, Dunfermline
Tel: 0383 22435

Fog Fishing Tackle
Ross on Wye, Herefordshire
Tel: 0989 4686

George Wilkins & Sons
Crown Works, 98 Alcester, Studley,
Warwickshire
Tel: 052 785 3862

George M. Forbes & Co. Ltd.
51 St. Vincent Crescent, Glasgow,
Strathclyde
Tel: 041 248 3882

F. Goddard (Efgeeco) Ltd.
26 Balham Hill, London SW12
Tel: 01 673 1177

HAWKES & BLACK
Tor View, Winkleigh, North Devon
Tel: 083 783 430
See Advertisement Under Flies

International Fish Hook Co. Ltd.
New Victoria Mills, Wellington Street,
Elton, Bury, Lancashire
Tel: 061 761 1300

JOHN ADAMS FISHING TACKLE
98 Lincoln Road, Boston, Lincs.
PE21 7EW
See Advertisement this Section
Tel: 0205 61950

John Burton (Angling) Ltd.
Pyramid Works, Rough Hey Road
Trading Estate, Preston, Lancashire
Tel: 0772 797070

John Rothery (Wholesale)
Co. Ltd.
22 Stamshaw Road, Portsmouth,
Hampshire
Tel: 0705 67323

W.H. Lane & Son
Cash and Carry Wholsale
31 & 33 London Road, Coventry
Tel: 0203 23316

Malmac Fishing Tackle
89 Reidvale Street, Glasgow, Strathclyde
Tel: 041 556 2667

Matchplan Fishing Tackle
1010 Chester Road, Pype-Hayes,
Birmingham
Tel: 021 382 3600

Midland Tackle
Headland Farm, West End,
Longclawson, Leics
Tel: 0664 822 054

Millard Bros. Ltd.
Tantallon Road, North Berwick, Scotland
Tel: 0620 4661
See Advertisement under Rods

Modern Arms Co. Ltd.
Marco Works, Pembroke Road, Bromley,
Kent
Tel: 01 460 3483

Napier & Craig
27 Wellington Street, Glasgow
Tel: 041 221 1731

Oakly Fishing Tackle Ltd.
Heming Road, Washford Industrial
Estate, Redditch
Tel: 0527 24509

Wholesalers

Pegley-Davies Ltd.
Hersham Trading Estate, Walton on
Thames, Surrey
Tel: 093 22 40481

Percy Wadhams Ltd.
Furlong House, East Street, Warminster,
Wiltshire
Tel: 0985 214551

Warr Associates
22 Bridge Street, Usk
Tel: 02913 3311

Peter Lyons Wholesale Suppliers
The Mallards, Underbank Avenue,
Charlestown, Hebden Bridge, West
Yorkshire
Tel: 042 284 3114

Richard Forshaw & Co.
Colonsay House, Tarron Way, Moreton,
Wirral, Merseyside
Tel: 051 678 7878

Rodrill Co. Ltd.
Collingwood Road, Tottenham, London
N15 4LD, Greater London
Tel: 01 800 0018

K. Stamford
105 Arnold Avenue, Gleadless, Sheffield
Tel: 0742 396959

Sue Burgess Fishing Tackle
Glyn Celyn, Brecon, Powys
Tel: 0874 4448

H. Steade & Sons Ltd.
49 Catley Road, Sheffield, South
Yorkshire
Tel: 0742 449454

Sussex Tackle Ltd.
12 North Parade, Horsham, Sussex
Tel: 0403 67168/65632

Sydney Jarvis
15 Chestnut Road, Astwood Bank, Worcs
Tel: 052 789 2765

Taylor & Johnson Ltd.
Palmers Road, East Moons Moat,
Redditch, Worcs.
Tel: 0527 29030/21030

Telltrade Ltd.
104 Christchurch Road, Ringwood,
Hants
Tel: 04254 3932

Thoroughbred Groundbait Ltd.
Weates Yard, The Avenue, Acocks
Green, Birmingham, West Midlands
Tel: 021 706 4509

John Veniard Ltd.
4/6 High Street, Westerham, Kent
Tel: 0959 64419

VORTEX
P.O. Box 135A, Thames Ditton, Surrey
Tel: 01 398 3826
See Advertisement under Mail Order
and Rods — Custom Built

H.E. Watson & Son Ltd.
9 Vernon Road, Sutton, Surrey
Tel: 01 643 7993

Western Seabaits
Blowinghouse Hill, St. Austell, Cornwall
Tel: 0726 5681

William Lindop Ltd.
Manchester, London, Bristol
Tel: 061 236 1151, 01 837 4475, 0272
40296

MAIL ORDER

nnetts of Sheffield Ltd.
nley Street, Sheffield
: 0742 760221

l Knott
unt Haven, Marazion, Cornwall
: 0736 711191

D. Bradbury
The Square, Hale Barns, Altrincham,
eshire
: 061 980 2836

**BURR & SON LTD. (THE
ELD SPORTS CENTRE)**
**West Street, Bridlington,
mberside**
: 0262 71770
*e Advertisement under Fishing
kle Retailers*

tlers Marine
ods Way, Mulberry Industrial Estate,
ring-By-Sea, Sussex
: 0903 502221
pliers of Big Game Fishing
uipment

mpbell Black of Chelmsford
/144 High Street, Ongar, Essex
: 0277 364749
ex: 995481

as W. Shelton Ltd.
th Street, Stanground, Peterborough
: 0733 65287

ventry Angling Supplies Ltd.
rne Road, Walsgrave on Sowe, Nr.
ventry
: 0203 612299

n Gray
Grange Way, Whitehall Road,
chester, Essex
: 0206 65333

ntry's Tackle
Park View Road, Welling, Kent
: 01303 3155

Garry Evans
105 Whitchurch Road, Cardiff
Tel: 0222 42361

Jim Johnson
1577/87 London Road, Norbury,
London SW16
Tel: 01 764 9711

John Norris
21 Victoria Road, Penrith, Cumbria
Tel: 0768 64211

Mackenzie-Philips Ltd.
Deer Springs, Stockeld, Weatherby,
Yorks, LS22 4AZ
Tel: 0937 63646

Marks & Marlow Ltd.
39 Tudor Road, Leicester
Tel: 0533 537714

McHardys of Carlisle
South Henry Street, Carlisle, Cumbria
Tel: 0228 23988

Mortimers
61 High Street, Grantown on Spey
Tel: 0479 2684

IAN LITTLE MAIL ORDER
**8 Dulverton Court, Bideford Green,
Leighton Buzzard, Beds.
Tel: 0525 378023**
See Advertisement this Section

RODCO
**Pond House, Weston Green, Thames
Ditton, Surrey**
Tel: 01 398 2405
See Advertisement this Section

Simpsons of Turnford
Nunsbury Drive, Turnford, Broxbourne
Tel: 09924 68799

MULLARKEY & SONS
**184/5 Waterloo Street, Burton-on-Trent,
Staffs**
Tel: 0283 66777
See Advertisement this Section

Mail Order

Normark Sport Ltd.
Bossell Road, Buckfastleigh, Devon
Tel: 03644 2597
See Also Advertisements under Rod Fittings and Rod Rings

SHELTONS GUNS & TACKLE

67 South Street, Stanground, Peterborough
Tel: 0733 65287
See Advertisement under Tackle Retailers Section

Sportsmail Ltd.
3 Allensbank Road, Cardiff
Tel: 0222 43166/396881

Sue Burgess Fishing Tackle
Glyn Celyn, Brecon, Powys
Tel: 0874 4448

Taylors Fishing Tackle
Unit 3, Iver Works, Lenborough Road, Buckingham
Tel: 02802 3881

TERRY EUSTACE RODS & BLANKS

2A Booth Lane, Great Barr, Birmingham
Tel: 021 360 9669
A fast postal service on a wide range of Coarse, Sea and Game tackle. Send three 1st Class Stamps for 80 page Catalogue.

The Tackle Shop
42 Tooley Street, Gainsborough, Lincs
Tel: 0427 3002

TOM C. SAVILLE LTD.

Princess Works, Station Road, Beeston, Notts
Tel: 0602 255655
Top Quality Fly-Tying and Game-fishing Equipment Suppliers Our 128 page annual Catalogue costs only 70p. We give the Service that YOU demand! Armchair Shopping at its Best DISCOUNT BARGAINS GALORE

Veals Fishing Tackle
61 Old Market Street, Bristol 2
Tel: 0272 20790

John Veniard Ltd.
416 High Street, Westerham, Kent
Tel: 0959 64419

Walkers of Trowell
Nottingham Road, Trowell, Nottingham
Tel: 0602 301816

ANGLING HOLIDAY OPERATORS AND ORGANISERS

…bey Gate Travel
31 The Parade, Oadby, Leics
: 0533 714915
…gling Holidays to Denmark and Spain

…tion Tours
Blackheath Village, London SE3 9LD
: 01 852 0025

…gling Holidays Travel Agency
Queensway, Burton Latimer,
…thants
: 053672 4226/5453

…& I Line
…ance House, Water Street, Liverpool
051 236 8325
…gling Holidays to Ireland

…ubsport Travel
…ames Street, London
01 629 5204

…ton Angling Holidays
High Street, Dover, Kent
: 0304 203607
…gling Holidays to Norway

…nstan Brearley Travel
High Street, Wombwell, Barnsley
: 0226 754197

…h America
Rowans, Nether Tabley, Knutsford,
…eshire
: 056581 2094

…orge Aitken
Offley Road, Kennington, London
…9
: 01 582 7087
…ut Fishing Holidays in New Zealand

…eshwater Fishing Parties
Brechin Place, London SW7 4QA
: 01 373 0493/5835
…me Fishing holidays to Northern
…in

Guides — Chasse Ltd.
Townend of Caprington, Kilmarnock,
Ayrshire
Tel: 0563 23757
**Salmon and Sea trout angling holidays
in Scotland**

Intourist Moscow Ltd.
292 Regent Street, London W1R 6QL
Tel: 01 580 4974
Fishing Holidays to Russia

Martin's World Travel
25 Market Place, Bolsover, Derbyshire
Tel: 0246 823763
**Angling Holidays to Ireland, Denmark
and Canada**

Mike McCormick's Field Sports Services Ltd.
Carlton Cottage, Maidwell, Northants
Tel: 0858 31880/31905
**Fishing Holidays to Norway, Kenya,
Mexico, New Zealand and Alaska**

M. T. S. Safaris
6 Bank Street, Malvern, Worcs
Tel: 06845 64545
**Fishing Holidays in East and South
Africa**

Normanton Express Travel
P.O. Box 94, Derby
Tel: 0332 380152
**Specialists in Angling Holidays to
Ireland**

P & O Ferries
P.O. Box 5, Jamieson's Quay, Aberdeen
Tel: 0224 572615

P. O. Ferries
94 High Street, Barnsley
Tel: 0232 23636

Stallard International Holidays
29 Stoke Newington Road, London N16
Tel: 01 254 6444
Big game Fishing Holidays to Mauritius

World of Sport Holidays
26 Castle Street, Hereford
Tel: 0432 59555
Wide range of angling holidays overseas

Yorkshire Tours
49 Thornton Lodge Road, Huddersfield
Tel: 0484 24269

Fishing Tackle Retailers

The following is a county by county list of Retailers in the United Kingdom. As well as selling fishing tackle a large number will also be able to supply you with fishing permits.

Index

Fishing Tackle Retailers

FISHING TACKLE RETAILERS

ENGLAND

AVON

AVON SHOOTING
2 Market Place, Radstock, Bath
Tel: 0761 33167
See Advertisement this section.

I.M. Crudgington Ltd.
37 Broad Street, Bath
Tel: 0225 66325 or 64928

Fishcraft
27 Brougham, Hayes, Bath
Tel: 0225 28157

Guncraftsman Ltd.
35 Orchard Street, Weston-Super-Mare
Tel: 0934 33111

Molly's
410 Wells Road, Bristol 4
Tel: 0272 772633

Omnia Sports Centre Ltd.
3 Chapel Hill, Clevedon
Tel: 0272 873196

Pet & Aquatic Food Stores
212 Cheltenham Road, Bristol
Tel: 0272 45642

Scott Tackle
42 Soundwell Road, Staple Hill, Bristol
Tel: 0272 567371

Scott Tackle
117 Bell Hill Road, St. George, Bristol
Tel: 0272 673941

Shepherds
46 Bond Street, Bristol BS1 3LZ
Tel: 0272 23351

S. Ship & Co.
7 Victoria Street, Staple Hill, Bristol
Tel: 0272 566985

J.B. Sport
31a Sandy Park Road, Brislington, Bristol 4
Tel: 0272 772633

Sportscene
24-50 South Parade, Yate Shopping Centre, Yate, Bristol
Tel: 0454 316629

Sportscene
Yate Branch, 29 South Walk, Yate, Bristol
Tel: 0454 316629

Sportscene
Knowle Branch, Broadwalk Shopping Centre, Knowle, Bristol
Tel: 05645 712008

Sportscene
Nailsea Branch, 18 Colliers Walk, Nailsea, Bristol
Tel: 027 55 4058

Sportscene
Bath Branch, The Mall, Southgate Centre, Bath
Tel: 0225 62421

Talbots Tackles
1 North Street, Bedminster, Bristol
Tel: 0272 663701

Veals Fishing Tackle
61 Old Market Street, Bristol 2
Tel: 0272 20790

Watersport Fishing Tackle
17a High Street, Keynsham
Tel: 02756 67135

Weston Model Aero & Angling Supplies
1 Oxford Street, Weston-Super-Mare
Tel: 0934 21031

BEDFORDSHIRE

Ampthill Angling & Sports Centre
14a Woburn Street, Ampthill
Tel: 0525 403469

Bleak Hall & Bird Farm
1 High Street, Kempston
Tel: 913 852530

lly's Tackle & Bait
Cheddington Road, Pitstone,
ghton Buzzard
: 0296 668803

XON BROS.
Tavistock Street, Bedford
: 0234 67145
e Advertisement this Section.

ighton Tackle Centre
Bridge Street, Leighton Buzzard
: 0525 373089

slies
Park Street, Luton
: 0582 35740

DDERS ANGLING STORES
Victoria Street, Dunstable
: 0582 68643
e Advertisement this Section.

ERKSHIRE

okes Tackle Shop
Northumberland Avenue, Reading
: 0734 82216

dy's Anglers' Kiosk
lers Lane, Bracknell
: 0344 21019

ld and Stream
Bartholomew Street, Newbury
0635 43186

illoud Ltd.
2 Old Crown Buildings, Windsor
d, Slough
0753 20437

C. Sports
Barkham Road, Wokingham
0734 781712

gs Fishing Tackle
Ray Street, Maidenhead
0628 29283

Phil Smart Fishing Tackle
20 Queens Road, Newbury
Tel: 0635 48660

Reading Aquarist
64 Kings Road, Reading
Tel: 0734 53632

Roxton Sporting Ltd.
10 Bridge Street, Hungerford
Tel: 04886 3222

SLOUGH SPORTS & ANGLING CENTRE
**245 Farnham Road, Slough
Tel: 0753 21055**
See Advertisement this Section.

Slough Sports and Angling Centre
Bracknell Market, Bracknell
Tel: 0344 21055

Trents Leisure Ltd.
25-26 Cheap Street, Newbury
Tel: 0635 46004

Tull Supplies
258 Kentwood Hill, Tilehurst, Reading

Turners of Reading
21 Whitley Street, Reading
Tel: 0734 84361

Windsor Angling Centre
157 St. Leonards Road, Windsor
Tel: 07535 67120

Windsor Fieldsports
5 St. Leonards Road, Windsor
Tel: 07535 56553

Wokingham Timber and Angling Supplies
105 London Road, Wokingham
Tel: 0734 787122

Wyers Fishing Tackle
479 Oxford Road, Reading
Tel: 0734 55614

BUCKINGHAMSHIRE

Agora Sports
A.W. Eagles
Church Street, Wolverton, Milton Keynes
Tel: 0908 317024

Church Hill Farm
Mursley, Bucks.
Tel: 029672 524

Coarse Angler
Angling House, Britannia Street, Aylesbury
Tel: 0296 82029

Dots Tackle Den
19-21 Victoria Road, Bletchley, Milton Keynes
Tel: 0908 74400

High Wycombe Angling Centre
69 West Wycombe Road, High Wycombe
Tel: 0494 445915

Lake Bros.
28 Stratford Road, Wolverton, Milton Keynes
Tel: 0908 313142

Peerless Angling & Sports Ltd.
264 Desborough Road, High Wycombe
Tel: 0494 27975

Rods'n'Guns
Rickmansworth Lane, Chalfont St Peter
Tel: 02407 5326

The Sports Centre
58 High Street, Stony Stratford, Milton Keynes
Tel: 0908 563389

The Tackle Box
3 Oliver Road, Bletchley, Milton Keynes
Tel: 0908 72393

CAMBRIDGESHIRE

Beecroft's
207 Cherryhinton Road, Cambridge
Tel: 0223 49010

Bloom & Wake Ltd.
Wisbech Road, Outwell, Wisbech
Tel: 0945 712578

Cochrane & Son
24-25 Old Market, Wisbech
Tel: 0945 3863

Cooper Bros.
12 Milton Road, Cambridge
Tel: 0223 65987

A Crowson (March) Ltd.
Bridge House, High Street, March
Tel: 03542 3327

Deryk's Fishing Tackle
1 Scargells Lane, March
Tel: 03542 55292

Mr. F.J. Farrington
2-4 Serry Lane, Chesterton
Tel: 0223 62378

Frank Wade & Son
247 High Street, Fletton, Peterborough
Tel: 0733 65159

Gallyon & Sons (Peterboro) Ltd.
5 Cowgate, Peterborough PE1 1LR
Tel: 0223 43152

Hunts Angling & Sports
35 Chequers Court, Huntingdon
Tel: 0480 55379

Leisuretime
35 Chequers Court, Huntingdon
Tel: 0480 55379

Nene Sports
Town Bridge, Peterborough
Tel: 0733 67353

Nene Sports
312 Lincoln Road, Peterborough
Tel: 0733 69993

Robin's Peg
721 Lincoln Road, New England, Peterborough
Tel: 0733 44899

SHELTONS GUNS & TACKLE
67 South Street, Stanground, Peterborough
Tel: 0733 65287
See Advertisement this Section.

Soham Sports & Tackle
27 High Street, Soham
Tel: 0353 720454

Thornton & Son
46 Burleigh Street, Cambridge
Tel: 0223 358709

Tight Lines Tackle
28a Hardwick Road, Eynesbury, St. Neots
Tel: 0480 212108

Mr. W.R. Webb
196 Newark Avenue, Peterborough
Tel: 0733 66466

CHESHIRE

Aband Camping & Angling Centre
10-12 Halton Road, Runcorn
Tel: 09285 76757

Anglers Corner
1a/1b Kingsway South, Latchford, Warrington
Tel: 0925 30716

Mr. Barry Hett
Market Street, Hyde
Tel: 061 368 9200

A.D. Bradbury
16 The Square, Hale Barns, Altricham
Tel: 061 980 2836

The Complete Angler
104 Gainsborough Road, Warrington
Tel: 0925 56441

Cooks Fishing Tackle
London Road, Hazel Grove, Stockport
Tel: 061 483 2589

Don of Disley
24 Market Street, Disley, Nr. Stockport
Tel: 06632 5370

Eric's Tackle & Pet Supplies
20A High Street, Weaverham, Northwich
Tel: 0606 85 3126

G A & M Fear
12 Welles Street, Sandbach
Tel: 09367 7493

Fishermans Mecca
Fennel Street, Warrington
Tel: 0925 33050

Frank Fellows
22 Shaw Heath, Stockport
Tel: 061 480 6046

David Gibson
Grosvenor Precinct, 13 Pepper Row, Chester
Tel: 0244 316132

Mr. V. Hedley
46 Lower Bridge Street, Chester
Tel: 0244 24421

The Hobby Shop
28 Church Street, Runcorn
Tel: 092 85 73614

H.G. Hopkins & Sons
55 High Street, Sandbach
Tel: 093 67 2404

Hylands Ltd.
121 Witton Street, Northwich
Tel: 0606 2768

Jim Challinor Sports
Padgate Lane, Padgate, Warrington
Tel: 0925 30765

Mr. F.J. Jones
87 Victoria Street, Crewe
Tel: 0270 212458

Steven A. Jones
29 Church Street, Wilmslow
Tel: 0625 528831

Kab's Cabin
228 Broad Street, Crewe
Tel: 0270 212708

Lymm Sports Centre
8 The Cross, Lymm, Warrington
Tel: 092 575 3021

. D. Malam
6A West Street, Crewe
: 0270 214751

atch Tac
Waters Green, Macclesfield
: 0625 23007

ddlewich Angling Supplies
Whetlock Street, Middlewich,
eshire CW10 9AB
: 0606 84 3853

nry Monk (Gunmakers) Ltd.
Foregate Street, Chester
: 0244 20988

oulton & Marsh
eam Street, Nantwich
: 0270 65775

rthwich & District Angling
ntre
London Road, Northwich
: 0606 2916

d'n'Reel
29 Enfield Road, Ellesmere Port
: 051 356 0687

d'n'Reel
tsford Road, Warrington
: 0925 344856

y Newton
ark Lane, Macclesfield
0625 24978

y Vernon & Son
Stockport Road, Timperley
061 980 3069

otts
34 Station Road, Northwich
0606 6543

ckle Shop
Market Street, Disley, Nr. Stockport
06632 5370

ry's of Congleton
Road Hill, Congleton CW12 1LG
026 02 3770

liam H. Worrall
3 Green Street, Sankey Green,
rington
0925 30960

ngs & Fins Ltd
ueens Parade, Winsford
060 65 54363

CLEVELAND

Anglers Corner
121/123 Abingdon Road, Middlesbrough
Tel: 0642 313103

Anglers Services Ltd.
27 Park Road, Hartlepool
Tel: 0429 74844

Bill Beattie
72 Queensway, Billingham
Tel: 0642 552615

F & K Flynn Ltd.
12 Viro Terrace, Stockton on Tees
Tel: 0642 66473

Mr. J.F. Gent
161 York Road, Hartlepool
Tel: 0429 72585

Harry Brough Ltd.
20 West Terrace, Redcar
Tel: 0642 482142

Priory Sports
23 Church Street, Guisborough
Tel: 0287 33480

D. Smith Ltd.
23 Station Road, Redcar
Tel: 0642 486827

Ward Thompson Bros.
87 Brough Road, Middlesbrough
Tel: 0642 247206

CORNWALL

A.B. Harvey & Sons Ltd.
1 & 2 Market Strand, Falmouth
Tel: 0326 312796

The Angling Centre
10A Victoria Place, St Austell
Tel: 0726 63377

Mr. B. Baird
40 Fore Street, Copperhouse, Hayle
Tel: 0736 752238

Bill Knott
The Shop, Newtown, Near Penzance

Bill's Tackle Box
34 Arwenack Street, Falmouth
Tel: 0326 315849

Mr. J. Bray
The Quay, Looe
Tel: 05036 2504

Central Sports
2 Crantock Street, Newquay
Tel: 06373 4101

The Fishermans Co-Op
The Wharf, St Ives
Tel: 0736 796276

The Gift and Sports Shop
10 Esplanade, Fowey
Tel: 072683 2207

A.P. Gilbert and Sons (Helston)
Ltd.
34 Meneage Street, Helston
Tel: 03265 2527

Hector Finch (Firearms) Ltd.
Bugle Shooting & Fishing Centre,
50 Fore Street, Bugle, St Austell
Tel: 0726 850955

Helston Sports
6 Wendran Street, Helston
Tel: 03265 2097

Mr. J. Langdons
20 St Mary Street, Truro
Tel: 0872 2207

R A & M A North
Church Square, Bodmin
Tel: 0208 2557

The Quay Shop
18 Quay Street, Penzance
Tel: 0736 3397

The Rod & Line
Little Green, Polperro, Nr. Looe
Tel: 0503 72361
*Caters for Sea Angling with
some Game and Coarse.*

Sports & Leisure & Cornwall
Fishing Tackle Supplies
4 Fernlea Terrace, St. Ives.
Tel: 0736 795626
*Caters for Sea Angling with a
little Game Angling.*

Tackle Box
4 Market Square, Mevagissey
Tel: 072684 3513

Tackle Box
11 Trinity Street, St Austell
Tel: 0726 5114
*Specialist in wreck and shark
fishing trips.*

Tony Kennedy
6 & 8 Church Street, Launceston
Tel: 0566 4465

Torpoint Sports & Tackle
13 Fore Street, Torpoint
Tel: 0752 813697

West Cornwall Angling Centre
25 Penpol Terrace, Hayle
Tel: 0736 754292

CUMBRIA

Allsports
Victoria Buildings, Royal Square,
Bowness on Windermere
Tel: 0966 23945

Angling & Hiking Centre
1 Astra Cinema Buildings, Abbey Road,
Barrow in Furness
Tel: 0229 29661

Carlisle Angling Centre
2 Globe Lane, Carlisle
Tel: 0228 24035

Carlson's Fishing Tackle
64 Kirkland, Kendal
Tel: 0539 24867

The Compleat Angler
4 King Street, Whitehaven
Tel: 0946 5322

Cumbria Countryman
Market Place, Ambleside

Geoff Wilson Practical
Gunsmiths
36 Portland Place, Carlisle
Tel: 0228 31542

The Gun Shop
Jubilee Bridge, Lorton Road,
Cockermouth
Tel: 0900 822058

Hannays of Barrow
50-52 Crelin Street, Barrow in Furness
Tel: 0229 22571

Harvey Jackson
Market Place, Ulverston
Tel: 0229 52247

W.N. Holmes & Son
45 Main Street, Egremont
Tel: 0946 820368

D.W. Lothian
35 Main Street, Cockermouth

McHardys of Carlisle
South Henry Street, Carlisle
Tel: 0228 23988

Mr. J. Norris
21 Victoria Road, Penrith
Tel: 0768 64211

A. Parker
23 Market Street, Ulverston
Tel: 0229 52061

R. Raine & Co.
21 Warwick Road, Carlisle
Tel: 0228 23009

Reg Thompson
127 Crosby Street, Maryport
Tel: 0990 81 2310

The Tackle Box
67 Main Street, Kirby Lonsdale
Tel: 0468 71663

Mark Taylor
2-4 Murray Road, Workington
Tel: 0900 3280

Mark Taylor
20-21 King Street, Whitehaven
Tel: 0946 2252

Temple Sports
9 Station Street, Keswick
Tel: 0596 72569

DERBYSHIRE

Anglers Corner
344 Osmaston Road, Derby
Tel: 0332 43870

ARTISAN ANGLING
141 London Road, Derby
Tel: 0332 40981

Arundel Aquatics and Angling
Supplies
56 Arundel Street, Glossop
Tel: 04574 3409

Mr. J.A. Barradell
976 London Road, Alvaston, Derby
Tel: 0332 71472

Bit'N'Bait Country Sports
97C Sitwell Street, Spondon
Tel: 0332 678824

Bradley Brothers Ltd.
9 Stephenson, Chesterfield
Tel: 0246 34908

Bridge Tackle Shop
30 Derby Road, Long Eaton
Tel: 06076 68338

D. & M. Calvert
64 Church Street, Eckington
Tel: 024 683 2755

Coarsea Angling Services Ltd.
1 Ward Street, Derby
Tel: 0332 31050

Fosters Sporting Services Ltd.
32 St John Street, Ashbourne DE6 1GH
Tel: 0335 43135

Horshoe Fishing Tackle
1 & 3 Station Road, Long Eaton
Tel: 06076 2972

Pickering & Goforth
34 Chester Street, Chesterfield
Tel: 0246 71366

Roach Pole
246 St Thomas Road, Derby
Tel: 0332 760682

Tackle Cabin
Rotherham Road, Harlesthorpe Dam,
Clowne, Chesterfield
Tel: 0246 810231

Wilf Mosley
88 Derby Road, Heanor
Tel: 07737 62640

D.A. Wright
136 Cotmanhay Road, Ilkeston
Tel: 0602 301610

DEVON

Anglers Den
13 Bolton Street, Brixham
Tel: 08045 3181

Babbacombe Sea Chest
84 Babbacombe Road, Torquay
Tel: 0803 35005

Mr. D.G. Baglow
85 Cadewell Lane, Shiphay, Torquay
Tel: 0803 63398

B & K Angling Supplies
14 The Quay, Appledore, Bideford
Tel: 02372 4613

Blacks Camping & Leisure Ltd
181 Sidwell Street, Exeter
Tel: 0392 76423

Bovey Sports & Tackle Shop
15 Town Hall Place, Bovey Tracey
Tel: 0626 832437

W S & G L Brokenshire
194 Saltash Road, Keyham, Plymouth
Tel: 0752 51291

Clem's Tackle Shop
5 The Quay, Ilfracombe
Tel: 0271 63460

Country Sports
9 William Street, Tiverton
Tel: 08842 4770

Dawlish Sports
15 Brunswick Place, Dawlish
Tel: 0626 862722

Sports
Exeter Street, Plymouth
0752 663483

Sports
h Devon House, 88 Vauxhall Street,
ican, Plymouth
0752 662361

l Sports.
3 Bank Street, Teignmouth
06267 2634

m Sports
ourtenay Street, Newton Abbot
0626 5333

ter Angling Centre
ty Arcade, Fore Street, Exeter
0392 36404

Exmouth Tackle Shop
he Strand, Exmouth
03952 74918

cher Sports
et Street, Torquay
0803 27035

d Statham's Tackle Box
Head, Exmouth
03952 72129

E. Gale & Son Ltd.
lill Street, Bideford
02372 2508

Gale & Son Ltd.
igh Street, Barnstable
0271 2244

s Sports
Torquay Road, Preston, Paignton
0803 523023

& H V Jeffrey Ltd.
Old Town Street, Plymouth
0752 665559

Keep
rook Street, Tavistock
0822 2509

bett's
2 High Street, Ilfracombe EX34 9QE
0271 62974

orne & Cragg
retonside, Plymouth
0752 23141

cy Hodge (Sports) Ltd.
106 Queen Street, Newton Abbot
0626 4923

Pethericks
22 High Street, Bideford
Tel: 078 988 3217

The Sea Chest
8 Northumberland Place, Teignmouth
Tel: 06267 3543

Sea Haven, Angling Access
4 Newcomen Road, Dartmouth
Tel: 08043 2093

Sports Centre
139 High Street, Ilfracombe
Tel: 0271 64546

Sportsman's Rendezvous
16 Fairfax Place, Dartmouth
Tel: 08043 3509

The Tackle Box
83 Exeter Street, Plymouth
Tel: 0752 23421

Tuckerman's Angling Centre
141 St Marychurch Road, Torquay
Tel: 0803 36216

The Variety Sports Shop
23 Broad Street, Ilfracombe EX34 9EE
Tel: 0271 62039

John Webber (Sports) Ltd.
79 Queen Street, Exeter
Tel: 0392 74975

West of England School of Game
Angling
Caynton House, Mill Street, Torrington
Tel: 080 52 3256
Caters for Game Angling

DORSET

The Anglers Tackle Store
56 Park Street, Weymouth
Tel: 0305 782624

Brac 'n' Tac
33 Catherine Hill, Frome
Tel: 0373 830478

Custom Tackle
904 Wimbourne Road, Moordown,
Bournemouth
Tel: 0202 514345

Davis Fishing Tackle
75 Bargates, Christchurch
Tel: 0202 485169

Dereck Case Angling Agency
5 High Street, Poole
Tel: 02013 6597

Dick's Fishing Tackle
66A High Street, Poole
Tel: 02013 79622

Hales Tackle
258 Barrack Road, Christchurch
Tel: 0202 484518

S.C. Hayman
13 Trinity Road, Weymouth
Tel: 0305 784786

J. & M. Hockaday
114 Portland Road, Wyke Regis
Tel: 0305 783145

C.J. Jeffrey & Son Ltd.
25 High East Street, Dorchester
Tel: 0305 2332

Les James Fishing Tackle
19 High Street, Poole
Tel: 02013 4409

Lyme Bay Marine
The Green, West Bay, Bridport
Tel: 0308 23478

Minster Sports
8 West Street, Wimborne
Tel: 0202 2240

Nimrod
Castle Parade, Iford Bridge,
Bournemouth
Tel: 0202 478224

The Sports Shop
37 West Street, Bridport
Tel: 0308 24403

The Tackle Shop
1 West Bay Road, West Bay, Bridport
Tel: 0308 23475

The Tackle Shop
17A Chiswell, Portland
Tel: 0305 820931

Tuck & Discount Tackle
52 Fortunes Well, Portland
Tel: 0305 820527

DURHAM

Adams Fishing Tackle & Guns
42 Duke Street, Darlington
Tel: 0325 68069

Anglers Services Ltd.
45 Claypath, Durham City
Tel: 0385 47584

Angling Supplies (Seaham) Ltd.
5 North Terrace, Seaham
Tel: 0783 813962

F. Armstrong Fishing Tackle
21 North Burns, Chester le Street
Tel: 0385 882154

Mr. J. Bond
80 High Street, Willington, Crook
Tel: 038882 6273

Dalesport
35 Market Place, Barnard Castle
Tel: 0833 38607

ELVET GAME CENTRE
8 New Elvet, Durham City
Tel: 0385 46713

Herdmans Pet Stores
121 Newgate Street, Bishop Auckland
Tel: 0388 2109

Kenneth Richardson
31 St Johns Road, Shildon
Tel: 038 884 3490

Peterlee Sports
45 Foden Way, Peterlee
Tel: 0783 862396

J. Raine & Sons
25 Market Place, Middleton in Teesdale
Tel: 08334 406

Windrow Sports
5-7 Fore Bondgate, Bishop Auckland
Tel: 0388 603759

J.W. Wright & Son
107 Parkgate, Darlington
Tel: 0325 63159

EAST SUSSEX

Mr. S.A. Anderson
9 Cliffe High Street, Lewes
Tel: 07916 3207

Anglers Kiosk
Hastings Pier, Hastings
Tel: 0424 433404

The Book and Bacca Shop
8 Bridge Street, Newhaven
Tel: 07912 3054

Brighton Fishing Tackle Shop
72 Beaconsfield Road, Brighton
Tel: 0273 502426

Compleat Angler
22 Pevensey Road, Eastbourne
Tel: 0323 24740

H.W. Daynes Tackle Shop
Pierhead, Eastbourne
Tel: 0323 33618

Eastbourne Tackle Shop
183 Langney Road, Eastbourne
Tel: 0323 20146

Harbour Tackle Shop
107 Fort Road, Newhaven
Tel: 07912 4441

Hastings Angling Centre
33-35 The Bourne, Hastings
Tel: 0424 432178

Lagoon Bait & Tackle Shop
327-329 Kingsway, Hove
Tel: 0273 415879

The Leather Man
2 Claremont Road, Seaford
Tel: 0323 893925

Redfearns Tackle Shop
8 Castle Street, Hastings
Tel: 0424 422094

Rice Brothers
1 High Street, Lewes BN7 2AD
Tel: 079 16 2176

Sussex Armoury
Sturton Place, Station Road, Hailsham
Tel: 0323 844544

The Tackle Box
Brighton Marina, Brighton
Tel: 0273 696477

Tony's Tackle Shop
211 Seaside, Eastbourne
Tel: 0323 31388

ESSEX
See also Greater London

Anglers Corner
114-116 Wantz Road, Maldon
Tel: 0621 52885

Abbey Angling & Pet Stores
15 Sun Street, Waltham Abbey
Tel: 0992 713968

Avenue Fishing Tackle
22a Woodford Avenue, Gants Hill, Ilford
Tel: 01 550 7815

The Bait Box
5 Grover Walk, Corringham
Tel: 03756 78821

L. Bowler
Photograph and Fishing Tackle
3 Cinema Parade, Dagenham
Tel: 01 592 3273

Mr. W.C. Brainwood
57-59 Clarence Road, Grays
Tel: 0375 4080

BROMAGES '75' (FISHING TACKLE) LTD.
666 Green Lane, Goodmayes, Ilford Essex
Tel: 01 590 3521
Ilford & Dagenham's leading tackle specialist. Fresh Sea & Coarse baits always in stock. Open 6 days a week and to 7.00 pm Friday. ACCESS/VISA cards welcome.

Brown's Fishing Tackle
71 Corbets Tey Road, Upminster
Tel: 04022 22177

Campbell Black of Chelmsford
142 High Street, Ongar
Tel: 0277 364749

Clarks Fishing Tackle
10 Bush House, Bush Fair, Harlow
Tel: 0279 22453

E.G. Coates & Son
16 Church Street, Witham
Tel: 0376 512255

Discount Guns & Tackle
44/45 Duke Street, Chelmsford
Tel: 0245 353715

Dubery's
19 Billet Lane, Hornchurch
Tel: 04024 49241

Edko Sports Services
136 North Street, Romford
Tel: 0708 61181

Edwards Fishing Tackle
7 Broomfield Road, Chelmsford
Tel: 0245 357689

Essex Angling Centre
109 Leigh Road, Leigh-on-Sea
Tel: 0702 711231

Fine Art Tackle
6 Chequers Parade, Dagenham
Tel: 01 592 8816

Gardener Bros.
19 Centre Way, Wickford
Tel: 03744 4530

G & B TACKLE
355/357 Victoria Avenue, Southend-Sea
Tel: 0702 32598
A good selection of all Sea and Freshwater Tackle and all Baits — Rods handbuilt to specification — Boat Angling Trips organised — Open 9am – 5.30pm Mon & Tues

9am – 1pm Weds
9am – 6pm Thurs, Fri, Sat.

odfreys
Moulsham Street, Chelmsford
0245 84562

ing Brothers
gh Street, Southend-on-Sea
0702 66439 and 0702 62351 (Rod
ding)

& B. HALL FISHING TACKLE
Highbridge Street, Waltham Abbey
0992 711932
Advertisement this Section.

ok & Line
r Pond Road, Rochford
0702 544696

y Anglers
astern Esplanade, Southend-on-Sea
0702 611826

n Metcalfe
cton Pier, Marine Parade,
cton-on-Sea
0255 25295

John Metcalfe
ewgate Street, Walton on Naze
02556 5680

.TEX
Station Road, Burnham on Crouch
0621 784189
Fishing Tackle and Bait.
Shakespeare — Daiwa —
tchell Milbro, East Anglian
d Co. Guns, Airguns and
tguns B.S.A. — Webley —
ikal Pellets and Cartridges
d Ammunition Regd. Fire
Arms Dealer

wall (Woodford) Ltd.
Chigwell Road, Woodford Bridge
01 504 1929

Last's Sports
79 High Street, Maldon
Tel: 0621 53982

Mr. McDowells
2 Rayne Road, Braintree
Tel: 0376 20207

Micks Tackle Shop
1 High Street, Old Harlow
Tel: 0279 415168

KEN'S TACKLE & GUNS
13 Radford Way, Billericay CM12 0AA
Tel: 02774 4846
★ *Super Clean Bait*
★ *Finest Selection of Tackle in*
the Area
★ *Agent for Anglian, Southern*
and Thames Licences
★ *Access & Barclaycard*
Welcome

The Old Cottage Shop
47 London Road, Stanway, Colchester
Tel: 0206 76647

Pope & Smith Ltd.
20 High Street, Chelmsford
Tel: 0245 774342

Pope & Smith Ltd.
20 High Street, Rayleigh
Tel: 0268 774342

E.J. Porter
43 Pallister Road, Clacton on Sea
Tel: 0255 25992

Mr. F.W. Price
9 Royston Avenue, Southend on Sea
Tel: 0702 614095

ROMFORD ANGLING CENTRE
209-211 North Street, Romford
Tel: 0708 63370
Major stockists of all leading
makes of Tackle, Rods,
Clothing etc.

Bait available 6 days a week.
Sea Fishing Specialists.
Extensive Trout & Game
Fishing area.
Access & Barclaycard
Welcome.
John, Geoff and Ernie look
forward to your visit.

Ronnie Crowe
63 Maldon Road, Gt. Baddow,
Chelmsford
Tel: 0245 71246

Sea Tackle
5 Pier Approach, Southend on Sea
Tel: 0702 611066

Sherwood Tackle
6 The Kingsway, Dovercourt, Harwich
Tel: 02555 4602

Southend Sports Centre Ltd.
639 Southchurch Road, Southend-on-Sea
Tel: 0702 67688

The Tackle Shop
52 High Street, Shoeburyness
Tel: 03708 3683

Woodhall Pet Stores
65 Wingletye Lane, Hornchurch
Tel: 04024 43419

GLOUCESTERSHIRE

Allsports
84-86 Barton Street, Gloucester
Tel: 0452 22756/27324

Allsports
2 Bath Road, Cheltenham
Tel: 0242 24289

D & J Sports
75 Cricklade Street, Cirencester
Tel: 0285 2227

Ed's Tackle
"Eboracum", High Street, South Cerney

Fred Harvey & Co. Ltd.
18 Barton Street, Gloucester
Tel: 0452 21609

Gloucester Angling Centre
45 Bristol Road, Gloucester
Tel: 0452 20074

Gloucester Rod & Gun Room
67 Alvin Street, Gloucester
Tel: 0452 410444

Mr. Ian Coley
444 High Street, Cheltenham
Tel: 0242 22443/582270

Tackle Retailers: Hampshire – Hereford

Jeff Aston Fishing Tackle
78 High Street, Gloucester
Tel: 0452 23009

Riverside (Lechlade) Ltd.
Park End Wharf, Lechlade
Tel: 0367 52229

Sports & Leisure
4 Market Place, Coleford
Tel: 0594 33559

Sportscene
48b Long Street, Wotton under Edge,
Tel: 045385 2742

The Tackle Shop
56 Church Street, Tewkesbury,
Gloucester
Tel: 0684 293234

Tredworth Fishing Tackle
78 High Street, Tredworth
Tel: 0452 23009

HAMPSHIRE

Avon Guns & Tackle
5 Whitefield Road, New Milton
Tel: 0425 617091

Alresford Flyfishers
528 West Street, Alresford
Tel: 096 273 4864

Basingstoke Angling Centre
5/6 Queens Parade, New Street,
Basingstoke
Tel: 0256 51264

Bim Osborne
80 Gregson Avenue, Bridgemary,
Gosport
Tel: 0329 280181

Central Sports
96/100 Kingston Road, Portsmouth
Tel: 0705 62523

Cordings (Gun & Sports Dealers)
18 New Market Square, Basingstoke
Tel: 0256 22255

Cordings (Gun & Sports Dealers)
67 High Street, Andover
Tel: 0264 2833

The Countryman
46 The Hundred, Romsey
Tel: 0794 512103

The Creel
36 Station Road, Aldershot
Tel: 0252 20871

Cupits
24 Bridge Road, Gore, Farnborough
Tel: 0252 42939

Ed's Tackle Shop
5-6 Selbourne Terrace, Fratton Bridge,
Portsmouth
Tel: 0705 25210

Handleys
11 Romsey Road, Southampton
Tel: 0703 772046

Hansfords
55 Portland Street, Fareham
Tel: 0329 280213

Hillary's
2 Park Way, Havant
Tel: 0705 484801

Home Stores
68 High Road, Swaythling, Southampton
Tel: 0703 551974

Hunters Hardwear & Tackle
33/39 High Street, Fordingbridge
Tel: 0425 53170

Jack Shephard Ltd.
1 Eastern Lane, Winnall, Winchester
Tel: 0962 65313

John Eadie Ltd
5B Union Street, Andover
Tel: 0264 51469

John Eadie Ltd.
22 The Square, Winchester
Tel: 0962 64188

Noels Fishing Tackle
314 Fernhill Road, Camberley
Tel: 0276 32488

Nobes & Co. Ltd.
55-57 Stoke Road, Gosport
Tel: 07017 81578

Patstone & Cox Sports Ltd.
25 High Street, Southampton
Tel: 0703 26672

Raison Bros
2 Park Road, North Camp, Farnborough
Tel: 0252 43470

Ringwood Tackle
5 The Bridges, West Street, Ringwood
Tel: 9924 5155

The Rod Box
52 St. Georges Street, Winchester
Tel: 0962 61561

Rovers
135a High Street, Lee on Solent,
Gosport
Tel: 0705 551757

Sea Anglers Supplies
427 Millbrook Road West, Southampt
Tel: 0703 772958

Southsea Sports
14 Highland Road, Southsea
Tel: 0705 735526

St. Denys Sea Bait & Tackle
53 St. Deny's Road, St. Denys,
Southampton
Tel: 0703 555750

Tackle Toys
7 Marine Parade West, Lee-on-Solent
Gosport
Tel: 0703 550209

Tackle Up
151-153 Ash Hill Road, Ash Vale,
Aldershot
Tel: 0252 27828

Toomer's Sports House
19 London Road, Southampton
Tel: 0703 23694

Tracey's
4 Chalet Hill, Bordon
Tel: 042 03 2544

Twoguys (D.I.Y.) Ltd.
27 Burnaby Close, Basingstoke
Tel: 0256 64981

Waterhouse & Conning
6 & 8 Portsmouth Road, Woolston
Tel: 0703 447595

Waterlooville Sports & Leisure
Centre
240 London Road, Waterlooville
Tel: 07014 3367

Western Fuels
151 Fleet Road, Fleet
Tel: 02514 4066

Wheelhouse International Ltd
67 Highland Road, Southsea
Tel: 0705 735144

HEREFORD & WORCESTER

Al's Tackle
26 Malvern Road, St Johns
Tel: 062 471 422107

H.W. Beacham
toke Road, Aston Fields,
sgrove
0527 73632

Durrant & Son
alcheapen Street, Worcester
0905 25247

ing Tackle Shop
oat Lane, Evesham
0386 3278
aters for coarse fishing.

d Perkins Ltd.
Commercial Road, Hereford
0432 4152

Sports
oad Street, Ross-on-Wye
0989 3723

M.A. Grinnall
rk Street, Stourport on Severn
02993 2212

ingways
orcester Road, Linktop, Malvern
068 45 3031

ert Hatton Fishing Tackle
Owen Street, Hereford
0432 2317

's Tackle
ven Street, Stourport-on-Severn

ury Tackle Centre
Southend, Ledbury
531 2768

Storey
utton Road, Kidderminster
562 745221

hore Leisure Centre
gh Street, Pershore
3865 3094

ells Ltd.
unt Pleasant, Redditch
0527 62669

C C Reynolds Sports &
bies
h Street, Bromyard
8852 2489

rside Service Station
aterside, Evesham
386 6593

Lees Fishing Tackle
y House, High Street, Droitwich
90 57 3557

Mr. R. Russell
93 Coventry Street, Kidderminster
Tel: 0562 64040

Severn Aquatics
103 Sidbury, Worcester
Tel: 0905 354512

Mr. G. Shinn
21-23 Old Street, Upton-on-Severn
Tel: 06846 2102

Stan Lewis
2 Severnside South, Bewdley
Tel: 0299 403358

J. White (Fishing Tackle)
11 Raven Street, Stourport
Tel: 029 93 71735

P. L. & M. R. Williams
The Chalet, Abbots Salford Caravan
Park, Abbots Salford, Nr. Evesham
Tel: 0386 870324

HERTFORDSHIRE
See also Greater London

Alan Brown
118 Nightingale Road, Hitchin
Tel: 0462 59918

Angling Centre
405 Whippendell Road, Watford
Tel: 0923 34952

**ARNOLDS RODS & TACKLE
LTD**
**2 New Road, Stanborough, Welwyn
Garden City**
Tel: 070 73 27332
See Advertisement this Section.

Arnolds Rods & Tackle
127 Hatfield Road, St. Albans

BARNET ANGLING CENTRE
228 High Street, Barnet
Tel: 01 440 8964
*For your complete satisfaction
in tackle requirements, why not
give us a call?
Stockists of all leading brands.
Barclaycard welcome.
Free parking.*

B K Leisure & Sports
51 High Street, Stevenage
Tel: 0438 50941

J. Collins Fishing Tackle
62 High Street, Stansted Abbott, Ware
Tel: 0920 871489

Fin'n'Fur
40 Hockerill Street, Bishop's Stortford
Tel: 0279 57061

House of Ross
3 Amwell Street, Hoddesdon
Tel: 099 24 62044

Howes & Drage
The Wynd, Letchworth
Tel: 04626 74861

Lee Sports & Marine Ltd.
34 Amwell End, Ware
Tel: 0920 5394

Leslies
14-16 Catherine Street, St. Albans
Tel: 0727 60721

LINKS SCHOOL OF FLY CASTING

C. Harrison-Baker (Principal)
Midhurst, 142 Links Way, Croxley
Green, Rickmansworth
Tel: 0923 44195

*Fly fishing, fly casting and fly
dressing tuition.*
Courses Available:—
Trout Preliminary 'A'
Trout Final 'B'
Fly Dressing
(Salmon & Trout) 'C'
Salmon & Sea Trout 'D'
(Including spinning)
Special Weekend (Trout) 'E'

*Your Salmon & Trout casting
problems and tuition
individually dealt with under
ideal conditions.
Weekend and personalised
courses designed to suit
individual requirements. All
tackle provided, flies tied to
order. Demonstration fly
casting projects undertaken.
River fishing, wading and
rivercraft gillieing for fishermen
can be arranged with
instruction for any period of
time.
National Anglers' Council and
Salmon & Trout Association
Approved Game Fishing
Instructor Grade 1.*

Mecca Angling
1 Parliament Square, Hertford
Tel: 0992 52049

Old Town Angling Centre
58 High Street, Hemel Hempstead

Olivers of Knebworth
123 London Road, Knebworth
Tel: 0438 812330

Oxhey D.I.Y. & Angling Centre
28 Pinner Road, Nr. Watford

Padaway
200 Watford Road, Croxley Green,
Rickmansworth
Tel: 0923 20603

Peartree Tackle
Peartree Lane, Welwyn Garden City

Popletts Tackle
12 The Hyde, Stevenage
Tel: 0438 52415

Queensway Pet Stores & Angling
Supplies
52 Queensway, Hemel Hempstead
Tel: 0442 54723

Sargent & Son
165a Uxbridge Road, Rickmansworth
Tel: 092 37 73314

The Ship Stores
Canalside, Marsworth, Nr Tring
Tel: 044282 668209

SIMPSONS OF TURNFORD
Nunsbury Drive, Turnford, Broxbourne
Tel: 09924 68799
See Advertisement this Section.

THE TACKLE CARRIER
157 St. Albans Road, Watford
Tel: 0923 32393
See Advertisement this Section.

Verdict Rods
103 The Green, Stotfold, Hitchin
Tel: 0462 730836

HUMBERSIDE

L & F Andrews
150 Ashby High Street, Scunthorpe
Tel: 0724 62585

Arcade Angling Centre
19 The Arcade, Goole
Tel: 0405 60676

Barry's
23 Westfield Avenue, Goole
Tel: 0405 2869

Bennetts
70 Frodingham Road, Scunthorpe
Tel: 0724 2042

Mr. D. Boyall
5 High Street, Barton on Humber
Tel: 0652 32706

D. BURR & SON LTD.
22 West Street, Bridlington
Tel: 0262 71770
See Advertisement this Section.

Castaline
58 High Street, Cleethorpes
Tel: 0472 690256

Chris Barugh'
Newbegin, Hornsea
: 04012 4947

Duncans
Paragon Square, Hull
: 0482 28150

& C FISHING TACKLE
Holderness Road, Hull
: 0482 701384

. Y.E. Everett
Flemingate, Beverley
: 0482 882653

e Fishing Basket
Beverley Road, Hull
: 0482 445284

inton Aviaries
Humberville Road, Immingham
: 0469 72446

Humberside Armoury & Angling
.
Lady Smith Road, Grimsby
: 0472 52029

W. Hutchinson & Co.
29 Anlaby Road, Hull
0482 223869

D Ledger Fishing Tackle
544 Anlaby Road, Hull
Tel: 0482 51994

F.W. Lightwoods
172 Cleethorpes Road, Grimsby
Tel: 0472 43536

Linfords
12 Hilderthorpe Road, Bridlington
Tel: 0262 78045

Mr. R. Little
567 Holderness Road, Hull
Tel: 0482 783621

Mallard Angling Supplies
5 Harbour Road, Bridlington
Tel: 0262 73103

Mereton Ltd.
59-60 Southgate, Hornsea
Tel: 04012 2650

Y & E Murray Ltd.
19 Chemical Lane, Barton on Humber
Tel: 0652 32237

Padgetts
413 Weelsby Street, Grimsby
Tel: 0472 52922

Pets Pantry
245 Grimsby Road, Cleethorpes
Tel: 0472 61766

Mr. B. Sipling
10 Market Place, Brigg
Tel: 0652 52343

Spark Bros
Haycroft Avenue, Grimsby
Tel: 0472 42613

Vic Peers
722 Holderness Road, Hull
Tel: 0482 51994

W & G Woolsey
4 Market Hill, Scunthorpe
Tel: 0724 2153

W & G Woolsey
278a Ashby High Street, Scunthorpe
Tel: 0724 66829

ISLE OF WIGHT

W. Bates & Son
5 Spring Hill, Ventnor
Tel: 0983 852175

Don Sports
21 Cross Street, Ryde
Tel: 0983 2912

Isle of Wight Sea Tac
6-8 Wilkes Road, Sandown
Tel: 0983 403654

A.P. Scott & Sons Ltd.
10 Lugley Street, Newport
Tel: 0983 2115

The Sports Shop
74 Regent Street, Shanklin
Tel: 0983 862454

KENT
See also Greater London

Anglers Cabin
20 East Milton Road, Gravesend
Tel: 0474 22793

Anglers Den
10 Franklin Road, Gillingham
Tel: 0634 52180

Bills Bait & Tackle
130 Snargate Street, Dover
Tel: 0304 204542

Boultings
33 Harbour Street, Whitstable
Tel: 0227 273680

Brazil's of Dover
162 Snargate Street, Dover
Tel: 0304 201457

Cartiers
75-81 High Street, Strood
Tel: 0634 724134

Cassidy's
106 Milton Road, Swanscombe
Tel: 0322 843563

Channel Angling
Beach Street, Deal
Tel: 03045 3104

DARTFORD ANGLING CENTRE
84 Lowfield Street, Dartford
Tel: 0322 28532
See Advertisement this Section.

Deans
20 East Street, Sittingbourne
Tel: 0795 72870

Don Gray Sports
7 Railway Street, Chatham
Tel: 0634 43032

Doughty's
358 High Street, Rochester
Tel: 0634 42574

The Dover Tackle Shop
146 Shargate Street, Dover
Tel: 0304 203742

The Downs Tackle Centre
29 The Strand, Walmer CT14 7DS
Tel: 03045 2811

Downham Sports Centre
435 Bromley Road, Downham
Tel: 01 697 2175

Downham Tackle
24 Downham Way, Downham

3 F's Fishing Tackle
7 Malling Road, Snodland
Tel: 0634 240596

Fishermans Corner
6 Kent Place, Ramsgate
Tel: 0843 582174

Fishermans Workshop
66 Oxford Street, Whitstable
Tel: 0227 274605

Foc'sle Fishing Tackle Stores
33 Beach Street, Deal
Tel: 03045 4013

The Friendly Fisherman
25 Camden Road, Tunbridge Wells
Tel: 0892 28677

Garry's (Milton & Smith)
12 Tontine Street, Folkestone
Tel: 0303 53881

Gentrys Tackle
42 Park View Road, Welling
Tel: 01 303 3155

Geoffs
36 Fort Hill, Margate
Tel: 0843 26386

S & E Gerrard
29 William Street, Herne Bay
Tel: 02273 2503

G K M Fishing Tackle
3 Parkside Parade, Northend Road,
Dartford
Tel: 0322 529146

Gravesham Angling Centre
16 Dover Road, Northfleet
Tel: 0474 26059

Greenfields Tackle
4-5 Upper Bridge Street, Canterbury
Tel: 0227 62638

Hobby House
10 Upper Street North, New Ash Green
Dartford
Tel: 0474 872136

Invicta Fishing Tackle
30 Wallers Road, Ospringe
Tel: 079582 5292

James Outram
63/65 High Street, Sevenoaks, Kent
Tel: 0732 53568

John Veniard Ltd.
4-6 High Street, Westerham
Tel: 0959 64119

Jones Tackle Shop
32 Cooling Road, Frindsbury, Strood
Tel: 0634 723666

Just Fishing
3 Bourne End, Bexley, Kent
Tel: 0322 51409

N BROWN
lomesdale Road, Bromley
: 01 460 5809
e Advertisement this Section.

ngfisheries
King Street, Margate
: 0843 23866

gsdon Angling Centre
² High Street, Edenbridge
: 0732 862704

anklows Kit & Tackle
Seal Road, Sevenoaks
: 0732 54952

arnies Ltd.
88 High Street, New Romney
: 06793 2172

dway Fishing Tackle
³ Shipbourne Road, Tonbridge
: 0732 355127

lton Bait & Tackle Shop
³ High Street, Milton Regis
: 0795 21212

pington Angling Supplies
³ High Street, St. Marys Cray, Kent
: 0689 34905

A Pikes Angling Supplies
79 High Street, Orpington, Kent
: 0689 37779

msgate Bait & Tackle
Vestcliff Arcade, Ramsgate
: 0843 53195
Caters for Sea Angling

n Edwards
52 High Street, Herne Bay
02273 2517

afare
ork Street, Broadstairs
0843 64953

Scotts Sports Equipment
Regency House, 7 Overy Street,
Dartford, Kent
Tel: 0322 21576

F.W. Simes & Son Ltd.
71 New Road, Gravesend
Tel: 0474 52350

F.W. Simes & Son Ltd.
78-80 High Street, Rainham
Tel: 0634 31255

F.W. Simes & Son Ltd.
157 High Street, Rochester
Tel: 0634 44975

The Tackle Box
1 Brunswick Street, Maidstone
Tel: 0622 671762

Town Tackle & Bait
95 King Street, Ramsgate
Tel: 0843 52924

Toyes Tackle
84 Broadway, Bexleyheath
Tel: 01 303 4349

J.B. Walker (Fishing Tackle) Ltd.
7-9 Marine Walk Street, Hythe CT21 5HP
Tel: 0303 66228

Neil Warwick
27 High Street, Tenterden
Tel: 05806 2407

LANCASHIRE

Anglers Den
19 Blackburn Road, Darwen
Tel: 0524 76713

Boyces
44 Manchester Road, Nelson
Tel: 0282 64412

Brian Ogden
254 Church Street, Blackpool
Tel: 0253 21087

Charlton & Bagnall
15 Yorkshire Street, Morecambe
Tel: 0524 410282

Chorley Anglers
12 Gillibrand Street, Chorley
Tel: 025 72 63513

Cleveleys Outdoor Centre
St Georges Lane, Cleveleys
Tel: 0253 821521

Cockers Sports
58 Kierby Walk, Church Street, Burnley
Tel: 0282 25830

Colne Angling Centre
66 Windsor Street, Colne
Tel: 0282 864076

Darwen & Gough
6 Moor Lane, Lancaster
Tel: 0524 64913

Edmondsons Fishing Tackle
15 Chapel Brow, Leyland
Tel: 077 44 21318

S.J. Fawcett
7 Great John Street, Lancaster
Tel: 0524 62033

The Fishermans Haunt
161 Blackburn Road, Accrington
Tel: 0254 34148

Fishing Tackle
36 Chorley Road, Adlington
Tel: 0257 482215

Fred's Angling Centre
35 Beach Road, Cleveleys, Blackpool
Tel: 0253 860 616

Halstead & Hartley
1 Cow Lane, Burnley
Tel: 0282 26943

C.E. Howarth
128 Watson Road, Blackpool
Tel: 0253 44016

Jacksons Fishing Tackle
27 Albion Street, Earby, Colne BB8 6QA
Tel: 028284 3333

K Tackle
39 Long Ing Lane, Barnoldswick, Colne
Tel: 0282 81 3553

Ken Varey
4 New Market Street, Clitheroe
Tel: 0200 23267

Langhorne's
80 Poulton Road, Fleetwood
Tel: 03917 2653

Le Moine Harry
22 Accrington Road, Blackburn
Tel: 0254 58719

Leyland Angling
13 Golden Hill Lane, Leyland
Tel: 077 44 21953

R. Marsden & Son Ltd.
115 Church Street, Preston
Tel: 0772 53314

McBrides
33a Parliament Street, Burnley
Tel: 0282 27386

Mike Roberts
Park Hill, Garstang, Preston
Tel: 09952 3925

R & E Millington
32 Steeley Lane, Chorley
Tel: 02572 72392

D.J. Nicholson
41 Warley Road, Blackpool
Tel: 0253 22557

NORTHERN GAMEFISHERS
(The Petman) 142 Stamford Street,
Ashton-under-Lyme
Tel: 061 330 4701
We are retailers of tackle, bait
and clothing for COARSE, SEA
and GAME ANGLERS
(including fly-tying materials)
and stockists of the leading
manufacturers, including
HARDY, ABU, BRUCE &
WALKER, BOB CHURCH,
MITCHELL, STEPHENS,
EFGEECO, VENIARDS.
8 miles from Manchester.
4 miles from the M62.
Licences available.

Porter
35 Beach Road, Cleveleys
Tel: 0253 860616

Ray Fox
48 Bolton Street, Chorley
Tel: 025 72 2938

Riding Bros Ltd.
135a Church Street, Preston
Tel: 0772 23954

Roe Lee Tackle Box
336 Whalley New Road, Blackburn
Tel: 0254 676977

Taylors
5 Penny Street, Blackburn
Tel: 0254 52007

P. Taylor Fishing Tackle
66 Windsor Street, Colne
Tel: 0282 864076

Ted Carter
87 Church Street, Preston
Tel: 0772 53476

Wade & Son
102 Burnley Road, Padiham
Tel: 0282 72461

S. Waterhouse & Son
38 Cookson Street, Blackpool
Tel: 0253 26159

J. Wiggans
15 Preston Road, Leyland
Tel: 077 44 21870

G.F. Wilkins
79 Banktop, Blackburn
Tel: 0772 21484

LEICESTERSHIRE

Angling Man
228-230 Melton Road, Leicester
Tel: 0533 65579

Arbon & Watts Ltd.
39 Sherrard Street, Melton Mowbray,
Leicester
Tel: 0664 62876

Bennetts
9 Market Place, Mountsorrell, Leicester
Tel: 0533 302818

Birstall Pet Shop
62 Front Street, Birstall
Tel: 0533 674039

Mr. R. Bolstridge
32 High Street, Coalville
Tel: 0530 32515

Charnwood Gun & Tackle
48 Chapel Street, Ibstock
Tel: 0530 60901

G. Grant
724 Melton Road, Thurmaston
Tel: 0533 693908

Mr. John F. Green
36 Nottingham Street, Melton Mowbray
Tel: 0664 4757

F.A. Holloway
Malt Mill Bank, Barwell
Tel: 0455 42078

Tony Horton
98 Wolvey Road, Burbage, Hinckley
Tel: 0455 32269

Jons Fishing Tackle
54 London Road, Oadby
Tel: 0533 719513

Kens Fishing Tackle
225 Saffron Lane, Leicester
Tel: 0533 831757

Loughborough Gun & Angling Centre
34 Nottingham Road, Loughborough
Tel: 0509 30627

Marks & Marlow Ltd.
39 Tudor Road, Leicester
Tel: 0533 537714

K R & P R Marston
62 Front Street, Birstall
Tel: 0533 674039

Roberts & Brooks Ltd.
1309 Melton Road, Syston
Tel: 0533 609941

Rutland Sports
20-22 Catmose Street, Oakham, Rutland
Tel: 0572 2675

Sports & Leather
Market Place, Oakham
Tel: 0572 2042

Sports & Toys
7 St Mary's Road, Market Harborough
Tel: 916 64046

Stamford Angling Centre
(Rutland Water) Whitwell Lodge,
Whitwell, Rutland
Tel: 0780 5454

Thurmaston Fishing Tackle
724 Melton Road, Thurmanston
Tel: 0533 693908

J.C. Townsend Ltd.
394 Humberstone Road, Leicester
Tel: 0533 766393

Wadsworth Fishing Tackle
90a Narborough Road, Leicester
Tel: 0533 549657

Wigston Tackle Shop
51 Leicester Road, Wigston
Tel: 0533 883571

E J & J M Wilkinson
26 Goward Street, Market Harborough
Tel: 916 2978

Norman Woodward
24 Braunstone Gate, Leicester
Tel: 0533 548850

LINCOLNSHIRE

Abbey Tackle
263 Monks Road, Lincoln
Tel: 0522 27024

L & F Andrews
150 Ashby High Street, Scunthorpe
Tel: 0724 62585

Belas Sports Shop
54-56 High Street, Hablethorpe
Tel: 05213 3328

Boundary Pet Stores
6 Bunters Hill, Lincoln
Tel: 0522 20772

rne Angling Centre
eadowgate, Bourne
07782 2114

den's
hend, Swineshead, Boston
020582 474

taline
) Upgate, Louth
0507 2149

J. Clayton
Main Ridge, Boston
0205 63118

Derek T. Ball
wthorn Bank, Spalding
0775 4001

& G M Hargrave
arket Place, Horncastle
06582 3366

risons & Sons
Croft Street, Lincoln
0522 23834

ok Line 'n' Sinker
Roman Bank, Skegness
0754 3623

eside Leisure Ltd.
ch Lane, Chapel St Leonards
0754 72631

e Newport Tackle Shop
Newport, Lincoln
0522 25861

obs
man Street, Lincoln
0522 24365

obs
High Street, Lincoln
0522 30501

mers
High Street, Skegness
0754 4404

yse's of Grantham
Welby Street, Grantham
0476 66079

aford Sports
he Shopping Precinct, Seaford
: 0529 303579

ngbys (Guns) Ltd.
Westgate, Sleaford
: 0529 302836

orts & Hobbies
ll Saints Street, Stamford
: 0780 4524

STAMFORD ANGLING CENTRE
13a Foundry Road, Stamford
Tel: 0780 54541

Stamford Gunshop Ltd.
8 St Mary's Hill, Stamford
Tel: 0780 2796

Storrs
Market Place, Wainfleet, Skegness
Tel: 0754 880378

THE TACKLE SHOP (Trevor S. Moss) GAINSBOROUGH
42 Tooley Street, Gainsborough
Tel: 0247 3002
*Stockist of all makes of fishing
tackle. Specialists in fishing
tackle for the specimen hunter.
Custom Rod Manufacturer —
full range of rod building
materials. Reservoir fly fishing
tackle — fresh bait always
available.*

Welland Tackle Shop
Bond Street Court, Spalding
Tel: 0775 61732

GREATER LONDON
See also Home Counties

Alans Sports
14 High Street, Yiewsley, West Drayton
Tel: 0895 443034

Anglers Complete Tackle Ltd.
170 Sydenham Road, Sydenham, London
SE26
Tel: 01 778 4860

Anglers Complete Tackle
5/6 Tudor Parade, Wellhall Road,
Eltham, London SE9
Tel: 01 859 2901

Anglers Corner
16 Swingate Lane, Plumstead, London
SE18
Tel: 01 854 3221

Anglers Shop
167 Ferndale Road, Clapham SW4
Tel: 01 274 5618

Ashpoles
15 Green Lanes, Islington, London N16
Tel: 01 226 6575

BAIT 78
103 Chingford Mount, London E4
Tel: 01 531 4519
See Advertisement this Section.

THE BAIT BOX
125 Dulwich Road, London SE24
Tel: 01 274 3297
See Advertisement this Section.

Benwoods Fishing Tackle
60 Church Street, Edgware Road,
London NW8
Tel: 01 723 9970

Birch Sport and Fishing Tackle
207 Royal College Street, London NW1
0SG
Tel: 01 485 9087

W. BIRCHALL
201 Old Oak Road, East Acton, London W3
Tel: 01-743 3381
NEWLY OPENED
General Fishing Tackle,
Coarse, Match, Fly, Sea, Suits,
Waders, Bait Etc.
Also at our shop (50 yds away)
Shotguns, Airguns, Sports and
Camping Equipment.

Birch's Fishing Tackle Shop
207 Royal College Street, London NW1
Tel: 01 485 9087

Browns Fishing Tackle
682 Romford Road, Manor Park, London E12
Tel: 01 478 0389

Cartiers
Chase Lane, Barkingside, Ilford
Tel: 01 551 4421

Chubbs of Edgware Ltd.
33 South Parade, Mollison Way, Edgware
Tel: 01 952 1579

H.F. Clarke & Son
57 Northcross Road, East Dulwich, London SE22
Tel: 01-693 4302

Cliff Glenton
186 Northfield Avenue, London W13
Tel: 01 567 3101

Croydon Angling Centre
65 London Road, Croydon, London
Tel: 01 688 7564

Croydon Fish & Tackle
94 Church Street, Croydon, London
Tel: 01 686 6792

Dawsons
1 Chatterton Road, Bromley
Tel: 01 460 7609

D & D Pets
14 Sutton Court Road, Hillingdon
Tel: 0895 34542

DELLS TACKLE
213 St John's Hill, Battersea, London SW11
Tel: 01 228 1320
See Advertisement this Section.

Dons of Edmonton
246 Fore Street, Edmonton
Tel: 01 807 5219

Downham Tackle
24 Downham Way, Downham, Bromley
Tel: 01 698 2723

Edgar Thurston
360 Richmond Road, East Twickenham
Tel: 01 892 4175

FARLOWS OF PALL MALL
5 Pall Mall, London. SW1Y 5NP
Tel: 01 839 2423

Farrer's of Tottenham
709 Seven Sisters Road, Tottenham
Tel: 01 800 3618

Fine Art Tackle
6 Chequers Parade, Dagenham
Tel: 01 592 8816

Line

Mitcham Road, Tooting, London

01 636 6029

ing Tackle Specialists

Old Kent Road, London SE1
01 703 3670

n' Tackle

ilcox Road, Lambeth, London SW8
01 622 0138

MES FISHING TACKLE

he Broadway, Edgware Road, W.
on, London NW9
01 202 0264

*of Britain's Largest Tackle
Displays. Coarse, Trout,
non and Sea. Large stocks
ds and reels. Materials for
-tying and rod building.
t high waders, knee boots,
Moon Boots, guaranteed
       against cold feet.
bber ankle boots, Wader
rogues, one piece suits,
hermal and polar wear.
Freshwater & Sea Baits.
ARD ACCESS ACCEPTED*

nk Johnson Jnr.

Ferndale Road, Brixton SW9
01 733 1722

rn Barnet Angling Supplies

Woodhouse Road, Friern Barnet,
on N12
01 368 8799

stys Darts and Fishing Tackle

igh Street, Hornsey, London N8
01 340 9310

orges Tackle

Mare Street, Hackney
01 986 6811

E Gerry

Whitehorse Road, Croydon
01 684 0380

rrys of Wimbledon

172 The Broadway, Wimbledon,
on SW19
01 542 7792

Glenton

Northfield Avenue, Ealing
01 567 3101

ne Fishing Tackle

High Road, Leytonstone E11
01 539 8522

rdon Lowes

-174 Sloane Street, London SW1
01 235 8484

Guns & Tackle

81 High Street, Whitton, Twickenham
Tel: 01 898 3129

Harefield Tackle

9 Park Lane, Harefield
Tel: 089 582 2900

HOUNSLOW ANGLING CENTRE

265/267 Bath Road, Hounslow
Tel: 01 570 6156
See Advertisement this Section.

The House of Hardy

61 Pall Mall, London SW1 5JA
Tel: 01 839 5515/6/7

J.T. Hunt (Aquapets) Ltd.

12 Spring Bridge Road, Ealing
Broadway
Tel: 01 567 3259

Jack Frost

43 Western Road, Southall
Tel: 01 574 8449

Johns Tackle Box

244 Woodhouse Road, Friern Barnet,
London N12

J. Johnson

1577 London Road, Norbury, London
SW16
Tel: 01 764 9711

Judd's of Hillingdon Ltd.

3 Westbourne Parade, Uxbridge Road,
Hillingdon
Tel: 01 573 0196

Keanes

65 Bloomfield Road, Plumstead SE18
Tel: 01 854 1731

Kennington Fishing Tackle
Supplies

191 Kennington Lane, London SE11
Tel: 01 403 2409

Ken's of Lewisham

126 Loampit Vale, Lewisham, London
SE13
Tel: 01 692 2565

THE KENSINGTON ANGLER

50 Golborne Road, North Kensington,
London W10
Tel: 01-960 4878
See Advertisement this Section.

Keswall (Woodford) Ltd.

618 Chigwell Road, Woodford Bridge
Tel: 01 504 1929

J.H. Lee

Jons Fishing Tackle Shop
116 Columbia Road, London E2 7RG

Lees Tackle Shop

397 Roman Road, London E3
Tel: 01 980 1130

MACDONALDS FISHING TACKLE

40 Eastcote Lane, South Harrow
Tel: 01 422 4375
See Advertisement this Section.

G. Matthews

31 Silver Street, Enfield
Tel: 01 363 0876

Micky Bonner

484 Barking Road, East Ham E6
Tel: 01 552 8902

Middlesex Angling Centre
1288 Greenford Road, Greenford,
Tel: 01 422 8311

Mikes Fishing Tackle & Pet Shop
6 West Lane, Bermondsey, London
SE16 PW4

Milwards at Lillywhites
4th Floor, Piccadilly Circus, London
SW1
Tel: 01 930 7146

J. Mitchell
410 Kingsland Road, London E8
Tel: 01 254 9333

Morgans of Kingston Bridge
17 High Street, Hampton Wick, Kingston
Upon Thames, Surrey
Tel: 01 977 6013

Molesey Angling Centre
96-98 Walton Road, East Molesey,
Surrey
Tel: 01 979 9083

Patone Sports Angling Centre
2 Spring Corner, High Street, Feltham,
Middx.
Tel: 01 751 3741

Paul's Fishing Tackle
47 Denmark Hill, Camberwell, London
SE5
Tel: 01 701 8502

Penge Angling Supplies
7 Croydon Road, Penge, London
SE20 7TJ
Tel: 01 778 4652

PLATTS
**988/990 Uxbridge Road, Hayes,
Middlesex**
Tel: 01 573 6857
See Advertisement this Section.

Riley's
94 Church Street, Croydon, Surrey
Tel: 01 686 6792

Robs Rods Angling Centre
287 Portland Road, South Norwood,
London SE25
Tel: 01 656 9123

Roberts Bros.
114 Carshalton Road, Sutton, Surrey
Tel: 01 642 6222

ROBERTSONS
**37 Prince Regents Lane, Plaistow,
London E13**
Tel: 01 476 3726
See Advertisement this Section.

Rob's Rods Angling Centre
287 Portland Road, South Norwood,
London SE25
Tel: 01 656 9123

Rod & Line
70-72 Loampit Vale, Lewisham, London
SE13 7AY
Tel: 01 852 1421

Ron's Fishing Tackle
465 Upper Richmond Road West, East
Sheen SW14
Tel: 01 876 4897

Sharp's Fishing Tackle
162 Malden Road, Kentish Town,
London NW5
Tel: 01 485 1759

SOUTH LONDON ANGLING
**91 Ladywell Road, Ladywell, London
SE13**
Tel: 01 690 3609
See Advertisement this Section.

Stablers
350/2 Garratt Lane, Earlsfield, London
SW18
Tel: 01 874 4683

Staines Leisure Sport
47/49 Church Street, Staines, Middx.
Tel: 0784 61831

STANOBS
**982 Harrow Road, Kensal Green,
London NW10 5JS**
Tel: 01 969 1142
See Advertisement this Section.

Sussex Armoury
1 Adelaide Street, London WC2
Tel: 01 379 6151

The Tackle Box
272 Earlsfield Road, Wandsworth,
London SW18
Tel: 01 870 3831

TERRY'S OF ENFIELD
**740 Hertford Road, Freezywater,
Enfield**
Tel: 0992 768322
See Advertisement this Section.

Thames Angling
11 Feltham Road, Ashford, Middx.
Tel: 078 42 43185

Todd's Tackle Shop
123 Lee Road, Blackheath SE3 9DS
Tel: 01 852 1897

Tony's Tackle
227 Chingford Mount Road, Chingfo
London E4
Tel: 01 529 2156

's Walthamstow Angling
ntre

Fulbourne Road, Walthamstow,
don E17
01 527 1135

ody's of Wembley
High Road, Wembley
01 902 7217

ngs of Harrow
& C Station Road, Harrow
01 427 0119

REATER MANCHESTER

& A Accessories
Tyldsley Road, Atherton
0942 883207

disons
High Street, Lees, Oldham OL4 5AQ
061 624 1308

dy Tackle
-250 Manor Road, Droylsden,
nchester 35
061 370 2038

gling Centre
Rochdale Road, Bury, Lancs
061 764 4571

e Aquarium
St Marys Gate, Rochdale, Lancs
0706 47211

quarium & Pet Supplies
Ashton Road, Oldham
061 652 9605

rowsmith
Gorton Lane, West Gorton,
nchester M12
061 223 2393

rrie Hett
Market Street, Hyde
061 368 9200

E.J. Battersby
57 Worsley Road, Swinton
Tel: 061 794 2784

A.D. BRADBURY
16 The Square, Hales Barn, Altrincham
Tel: 061 980 2836
See Advertisement this Section.

Burnden Tackle
137 Newport Street, Bolton
Tel: 0204 24408

Cooks Fishing Tackle
395 London Road, Hazel Grove,
Stockport
Tel: 061 483 2589

J.A. Downs
13 Preston Road, Standish
Tel: 0257 422561

Dysons
72 Manchester Road, Altrincham
Tel: 061 928 1068

E & S Aquariums
253 Heywood Road, Prestwich
Tel: 061 773 7212

Edgeley Sports & Fishing Depot
45 Greek Street, Edgeley, Stockport
Tel: 061 480 2511

F. Fallows Fishing Tackle Dealers
222 Shaw Heath, Stockport
Tel: 061 480 6046

Georges Fishing Tackle
15 Frog Lane, Wigan
Tel: 0942 41932

IA & BM Gilder
532 Oldham Road, Failsworth
Tel: 061 681 2538

Hardie Bott Ltd.
9 Hanging Ditch, Manchester 4
Tel: 061 834 0420

Heywood Sports & Tackle Shop
83 Manchester Street, Heywood
Tel: 0706 69300

J.H. Kelly Fishing Tackle &
Sports
238 Market Street, Hyde
Tel: 061 368 5938

Ken Booth
566 Middleton Road, Chadderton,
Oldham

R. Kitchen
303 Chester Road, Hulme, Manchester
15
Tel: 061 872 5586

Leatherbarrow Angling Supplies
198 Church Road, Urmston
Tel: 061 748 0959

Leighs
94 Gorton Road, Reddish, Nr Stockport
Tel: 061 432 6559

Len Tobutt Sports
505 Blackburn Road, Hillview Centre,
Astley Bridge, Bolton
Tel: 0204 58506

Mossley Angling Centre
137 Manchester Road, Mossley
Tel: 04575 3523

Northern Angler
29 Market Place, Middleton
Tel: 061 643 3524

The Petman (Northern
Gamefishers)
142 Stamford Street, Ashton under Lyme
Tel: 061 330 4701

Pets Corner
239 Lower Broughton Road, Salford
Tel: 061 792 3362

Platt Bridge Tackle
663 Liverpool Road, Platt Bridge, Wigan
Tel: 0942 863791

A.J.J. Roberts
22 Heath Street, Golborne
Tel: 0942 73894

Ronnies Tackle Shop
219 Manchester Road, Kearsley
Tel: 0204 71691

Roxy Aquatics
171 Queens Road, Ashton under Lyme
Tel: 061 330 7714

Sam Aldred
57 Market Street, Westhoughton, Bolton
Tel: 0942 812341

Tackle Retailers: Merseyside – Norfolk

F.H. Smith
167 Regent Road, Salford
Tel: 061 872 1367

The Sportsman
438 Palatine Road, Northenden,
Manchester M22 4JT
Tel: 061 998 7881

Steves of Bolton
237 Bridgeman Street, Bolton
Tel: 0204 20428

Sussex Armoury
8 Shambles Square, Manchester
Tel: 061 834 7533

The Tackle Shop
359 Ainsworth Road, Radcliffe
Tel: 061 723 3088

A. Taylor
48 Parrin Lane, Honton, Eccles
Tel: 061 789 4608

A. Taylor
333 Wellington Road North, Stockport
Tel: 061 432 0913

Tom Blackledge
8 The Weind, Wigan
Tel: 0942 44648

Trafford Angling Supplies
34 Moss Road, Stretford, Manchester
Tel: 061 864 1211

West Pennine Angling Supplies Ltd.
204 Yorkshire Street, Rochdale
Tel: 0706 524 911

T. & F. Wilcox Ltd.
2 Stockport Road, Crown Point, Denton
Tel: 061 336 6048

Windetts
84 Bradshawgate, Bolton
Tel: 0204 22899

MERSEYSIDE

Calverts Sports
29 South Parade, Speke, Liverpool
Tel: 051 486 9040

Harrison Bait & Tackle
74 Smithdown Road, Liverpool 7
Tel: 051 733 9664

W.J. & J. Harrison
18 St Helens Road, Prescott
Tel: 051 426 5011

Heslop & Dunkinfield Ltd.
48 Stanley Street, Liverpool
Tel: 051 236 4851

W. Hitchell & Son Ltd.
47 Oxton Road, Birkenhead
Tel: 051 652 2785

Hoppy's
10/14 Sefton Street, Liverpool 21
Tel: 051 928 5435

Howard Sports Ltd.
8-10 Hoghton Street, Southport,
Tel: 0704 34111

Ken Hopkins
19 Upton Road, Moreton, Wirrall,
Tel: 051 677 8092

Ken Watson Sports
Victoria Road, New Brighton, Wirrall,
Tel: 051 638 4505

Liverpool Angling Centre
429 Smithdown Road, Liverpool L15 3JL
Tel: 051 733 2591

Maghull Rod & Tackle
332 Moorhey Road, Maghull
Tel: 051 531 0045

Matchwinner Sports
186a Rufford Road, Crossens, Southport
Tel: 0704 29455

The Outrigger
90 Banks Road, West Kirby, Wirral
Tel: 051 625 9001

Mr. John A. Parkes
173-175 New Chester Road, New Ferry, Wirrall
Tel: 051 645 3202

W. Richards
India Buildings, 42 Brunswick Street, Liverpool
Tel: 051 236 2925

J.E. Robinson & Son
71 Sussex Road, Southport PR9 0SP
Tel: 0704 34136

Mr. S. Skinner
469 Rice Lane, Liverpool
Tel: 051 525 5574

Sports Forum
Unit B, Belle Vale Shopping Centre, Liverpool
Tel: 051 498 461

Sports Life Ltd.
250 Telegraph Road, Heswall, Wirral
Tel: 051 342 2340

Star Angling Centre
101 Duke Street, St Helens

The Tackle Box
72 Seaview Road, Liscard, Wallasey
Tel: 051 638 3281

Taskers Tackle Ltd.
165-171 County Road, Walton, Liverpool 4
Tel: 051 523 7522

J.K. Valentines
196 Islands Brow, Haresfinch, St. Hel
Tel: 0744 32527

Wirrall Angling Centre
463 Borough Road, Birkenhead
Tel: 051 653 6845

NORFOLK

Baker & O'Keefe Ltd.
7 Pier Walk, Gorleston, Great Yarmo
Tel: 0493 62448

Barric Sports & Travel
11 High Street, Holt
Tel: 026 371 2390

A.C. Browne & Son
6 Timber Hill, Norwich NOR 13LB
Tel: 0603 27668

Len Bryer Fishing Tackle and F Supplies
1 Norwich Street, Fakenham NR21 9A
Tel: 0328 2543

Bungay Angling Centre
54 St Mary's Street, Bungay
Tel: 0986 3842

Catch 22
23 Victoria Road, Diss
Tel: 0379 3272

Chambers Angling Centre
Market Place, East Dereham
Tel: 0362 2006

C. Clarke
30 Market Place, Aylsham
Tel: 026 373 3110

Coastal Supplies Ltd.
15 Beeston Road, Sheringham
Tel: 0263 822587

Cochrane & Son
86 Lynn Road, Downham Market
Tel: 036 63 3177

Colin Stevens
55 London Road, Kings Lynn
Tel: 0553 5852

Dennys & Sons Ltd.
et Place, Harlestone
0379 852248

. I.R. Flaxman
n Lane, Caister-on-Sea
0493 728563

lyon & Sons Ltd.
dford Street, Norwich NR2 1AN
0603 21241/22845

pers Gun & Tackle Shop
ailway Road, Downham Market
03663 3408

cham Tackle Carrier
enwood Road, Heacham
0485 70477

ning Bait & Tackle Supplies
er Street, Horning
0692 6307

n's Tackle Den
ridewell Alley, Norwich
0603 614114

Markham
South Market Road, Great Yarmouth
0493 2346

hols & Hosier
St Peter's Road, Great Yarmouth
0493 3409

rfolk Tackle
Norfolk Street, Kings Lynn
0553 65534

ter Roach Fishing Tackle
St Augustine Street, Norwich
: 0603 27896

kards Fishing Tackle
Hill, Long Stratton
: 0508 30262

wnall & Sons
Regent Road, Great Yarmouth
: 0493 2873

lham Pet & Leisure Shop
nehouse, High Street, Stalham
: 0692 81800

etford Sports & Toy Centre
White Hart Street, Thetford
: 0842 3338

m Boulton
3 Drayton Road, Norwich
: 0606 46834

ny Allen Fishing Tackle
3A Silver Road, Norwich
: 0603 412124

Wroxham Angling & Gift Centre
Station Road, Wroxham
Tel: 06053 2453

NORTHAMPTONSHIRE

Albert Watts
4 Herriotts Lane, Wellingborough
Tel: 97 223919

The Angling Centre & Gunroom
85 St Leonards Road, Northampton
Tel: 0604 64847

Anglers World
86 Rockingham Road, Corby
Tel: 9126 2900

Beck Sports
28 High Street, Daventry
Tel: 92 2773

Bielby Sports
Queens Square, Corby
Tel: 9126 4830

Billing Aquadrome Ltd.
Little Billing, Northampton
Tel: 0604 408181

BOB CHURCH & CO. LTD.
16 Lorne Road, Northampton
Tel: 0604 713674

Brackley Gunsmith Ltd.
83 High Street, Brackley
Tel: 0280 702519

Burford & Prigmore
40 Wimbledon Street, Northampton
Tel: 0604 53771

Frank's Fishing Tackle
38 Wellington Street, Kettering
Tel: 0536 514509

Gilders
250/252 Wellingborough Road,
Northampton
Tel: 0604 36723

C.H. Green & Sons Ltd.
3 The Market Place, Oundle
Tel: 08322 3518

J. & M. Leach
26 Church Street, Rushden
Tel: 918 53007

R. & J. Smith
76 Kingsley Park Terrace, Northampton
Tel: 0604 713521

Sports & Tackle
47/51 High Street, Daventry
Tel: 92 3284

Sportsmans Lodge
44 Kingsthorpe Road, Kingsthorpe
Hollow, Northampton
Tel: 0604 713399

Tebro Sports
4 Market Square, Corby
Tel: 9126 3005

T.H. Thursby & Son
16 Sheep Street, Northampton
Tel: 0604 38225

Webster & Sons
37 High Street, Irthling Borough
Tel: 97 650110

Webster & Sons
9 Brook Street, Raunds
Tel: 97 622029

NORTHUMBERLAND

G.L. Coulson & Sons Ltd.
4 Road Ends, Prudhoe
Tel: 0661 32402

M. Cropp & Son
8 Have Lock Street, Blyth
Tel: 067 06 2574

GREYS OF ALNWICK
Station Yard, Wagon Way Road,
Alnwick
Tel: 0665 602696

Game Fair
12 Marygate, Berwick on Tweed
Tel: 0289 5119

Greggs Sports
6 Battle Hill, Hexham
Tel: 0434 605456

R.L. Jobson & Son
Tower Showrooms, Alnwick
Tel: 0665 602135

John Gregg & Sons (Sports) Ltd.
Market Place, Haltwhistle
Tel: 0498 20255

McDermotts
112 Station Road, Ashington
Tel: 0670 812214

Murraysport
2 Narrowgate Street, Alnwick
Tel: 0665 60 2462

H.A.B. Pyle
15 Hencotes, Hexham
Tel: 0434 60 5333

Tackle Retailers: Yorkshire North – Notts

YORKSHIRE NORTH

J. Anderson & Son
4 Saville Street, Halton
Tel: 0653 2367

Anglers Corner
41 Huby Court, Walmgate Bar
Tel: 0904 29773

Buckleys Angling Supplies
6 Leading Post Street, Scarborough
Tel: 0723 63202

Bulmers Selling Service
Fishing Tackle, Monk Bar
Tel: 0904 54070

Eric Walker Tackle Shop
Finkle Street, Thirsk
Tel: 0845 23248

Filey Fishing Tackle
12 Hope Street, Filey
Tel: 0723 513732

The Fisherman
29 George Hudson Street, York,
Tel: 0904 31061

G.E. Hill
40 Clarence Street, York
Tel: 0904 24561

Hookes of York Ltd.
28 Coppergate, York
Tel: 0904 55073

M. H. & C. Johnson
2 Briggate, Knaresborough
Tel: 0423 863065

Linfords
12 Hilderthorpe Road, Bridlington
Tel: 0262 78045

MacKenzie Philps Ltd.
Deer Springs, Stockeld, Wetherby,
LS22 4AN
Tel: 0937 63646

Mallard's
5 Harbour Road, Bridlington
Tel: 0262 73103

A.C. Pritchard
56 Eastborough, Scarborough YO11 1NJ
Tel: 0723 74017

Richmond Sports
14 Finkle Street, Richmond
Tel: 0748 2225

Selby Angling Centre
69 Brook Street, Selby
Tel: 0757 703471

J.R. & P.H. Smith
28 High Street, Knaresborough
Tel: 0423 863322

C. Swift
25 Castlegate, Malton
Tel: 0653 4580

Whitby Angling Supplies
65 Haggersgate, Whitby
Tel: 0947 3855

NOTTINGHAMSHIRE

Aqualand
217 Bobbersmill Road, Nottingham
Tel: 0602 703460

Aquarist and Angler
8 Westdale Lane, Gedling NG4 3FY
Tel: 0602 612657

Archie Tizley
100 Bunbury Street, Meadows,
Nottingham
Tel: 0602 868960

Horace Burrows
91 Outram Street, Sutton in Ashfield
Tel: 0623 557816

Clifton Angling & Pet Supplies
5 Sandham Walk, Clifton
Tel: 0602 841662

Colin Walton Fishing Tackle Specialists
2 Brisbane Court, Balderton, Newark
Tel: 0636 705742

R.M.C. Dibble
40 Belvedere Street, Mansfield
Tel: 0623 23214

Eastwood Pets Garden & Fishing Centre
64 Nottingham Road, Eastwood
Tel: 07737 2624

Forest Town Fishing Tackle & Pet Shop
113 Clipstone Road, Forest Town West,
Nottingham
Tel: 0623 27422

J.T. Guy
59 Annesley Road, Hucknall
Tel: 0602 632868

J. & M. Hartley
14/16 Station Street, Mansfield
Woodhouse
Tel: 0623 23443

J & S Tackle
59 West Street, Arnold
Tel: 0602 262 644

K D R Angling
2 Garnet Street, Netherfield
Tel: 0602 248449

Ken Ward Ltd.
6 Carlton Road, Worksop
Tel: 0909 472904

Kindon Angling
1 Broxtowe Avenue, off Broxtowe La
Nottingham

W. Lloyd Fishing Tackle
45 Castlegate, Newark
Tel: 0636 702758

Matchmen
5 Bannerman Road, Bulwell
Tel: 0602 278859

Ollerton Aquarium
Sherwood Drive, New Ollerton, Newa
Tel: 0623 860478

Radcliffe Sports
3 Cropwell Road, Radcliffe on Trent
Tel: 06073 5269

Ray Leach
19 Boar Lane, Newark
Tel: 0636 74232

Redmayne & Todd Ltd.
46 Canal Street, Nottingham
Tel: 0602 51904

Richmonds Tackle
26 Midworth Street, Mansfield
Tel: 0623 33790

Sabre Sport and Dart Centre
42/44 Outram Street, Sutton in Ashfie
Tel: 0623 512849

C. Smith & Sons (Newark) Ltd.
Clinton House, Lombard Street, Newa
Tel: 0636 703839

The Tackle Box
Trent Bridge, West Bridgford
Tel: 0602 866121

Terry Dorman
272 Denman Street, Nottingham
Tel: 0602 781695

Tom C. Saville Ltd.
Unit 7 Salisbury Square, Middleton
Street, Radford NG7 2AB
Tel: 0602 784248
Caters for Game Angling

Tomlinson's Tackle
84 Gateford Road, Worksop
Tel: 0909 475773

n Watson & Son Ltd.
Ilkeston Road, Nottingham
0602 786990

n Watson & Son Ltd.
ak Street, Carrington, Nottingham
0602 609561

opliss
hay Bridge, Annesley Road,
knall
0602 633430

lkers of Trowell
Nottingham Road, Trowell
0602 301816

XFORDSHIRE

G. Alderton DIY & Fishing
kle
Brasenose Road, Didcot

. Allmond
e Causeway, Bicester
08692 2767

weathers Tackle
Wantage Road, Didcot
0235 814877

. Bridgeman
High Street, Witney
0993 2587

st-a-Way Fishing Tackle
Warwick Road, Banbury
0295 54274

LLS TACKLE LTD.
Oxford Road, Cowley, Oxford
0865 711410
Advertisement this Section.

es Sports Toys and Cycles
lvescot Road, Carterton OX8 3JL
0993 842396

Henley Sports
1/3 Greys Road, Henley on Thames
Tel: 049 12 3687

Ian Hayden Fishing Tackle
33 The Vine Yard, Abingdon
Tel: 0235 26579

Ian Hayden Fishing Tackle
13 Mill Street, Wantage
Tel: 0235 74989

**JOHN WILKINS FISHING
TACKLE**

39A James Street, Oxford
Tel: 0865 43469
Oxfordshire's largest stockists
of Fishing Tackle
Game/Coarse/Sea
Custom Built Rods
Clothing
Quality Bait
Rod and Reel Repairs
Licences, Club Cards
Access/Barclaycard Welcome

Mill Street Pets & Fishing Tackle
127 Mill Street, Kidlington
Tel: 086 75 2030

Musketoon
3 Market Place, Woodstock
Tel: 0993 811005

North Oxford Tackle
95 Islip Road, Summertown, Oxford
OX2 7SP
Tel: 0865 56955
Caters for Coarse Angling only

A.K. Parrot
Riverside, Henley on Thames
Tel: 049 12 2380

Seal Seam Sports
Chestnuts Yard, Upper High Street,
Thame
Tel: 084 421 2129

Standlake Fishing Tackle
29 High Street, Standlake

The Sportsman
193-195 Barns Road, Cowley Centre,
Oxford
Tel: 0865 779604

The Sportsman
15 High Street, Witney
Tel: 0993 3161

Suit Case
3A Church Lane, Banbury
Tel: 0295 3614

Ted Turner Ltd.
87 High Street, Wheatley
Tel: 086 77 2404

Turners Tackle & Bait
4a Station Road, Farringdon
Tel: 0367 21044

J. Venables & Sons
St Aldate's, Oxford
Tel: 0865 44257

Wallingford Sports
71 High Street, Wallingford
Tel: 0491 37043
Caters for Coarse Angling

J. Wilkins
39a James Street, Oxford
Tel: 0865 43469

G.H. Williams
115 London Road, Headington
Tel: 0865 62664

SHROPSHIRE

W. Clay & Sons
5a Scotland Street, Ellesmere
Tel: 069171 2542
Caters for Coarse Angling

Country Sports
Imperial Chambers, Bull Ring, Ludlow
Tel: 0584 4557

Ebralls
Smithfield Road, Shrewsbury
Tel: 0743 3048

G. Forrest
2 Wyle Cop, Shrewsbury
Tel: 0743 56878

Forster & Ellison
11 Watergate Street, Whitchurch
Tel: 0948 2809

Guns & Ammo
95 Beatrice Street, Oswestry
Tel: 0691 3761

H.W. Philips & Son
9 Abbey Foregate, Shrewsbury
Tel: 0743 56449

The Rod & Gun
3 High Street, Dawley, Telford
Tel: 0952 503550

S & S Bait & Tackle Supplies
26 Allen Gardens, Market Drayton
Tel: 0630 4835

A.B. Smith
11 Market Street, Craven Arms
Tel: 05882 2368

Speeds
6/8 Watergate Street, Whitchurch
Tel: 0948 2289

Tackle Retailers: Somerset – Yorkshire South

Sport & Leather
16 Kings Street, Ludlow
Tel: 0584 2351
Caters for Coarse Angling

C. Stokes
15 Queen Street, Market Drayton
Tel: 0630 4679

Herbert Tucker
The Square, Newport TF10 7AU
Tel: 0952 810002

Stuart Williams
5 Underhill Street, Bridgnorth
Tel: 074 62 2832

SOMERSET

Brac n' Tack
33 Catherine Hill, Frome
Tel: 0373 830478

Bridge Sports (Taunton) Ltd.
21 Bridge Street, Taunton
Tel: 0823 81537

Bridge Sports Ltd.
22-24 Eastover, Bridgwater
Tel: 0278 423843

Bridgwater Guns Ltd.
22 St Marys Street, Bridgwater
Tel: 0278 423441

Exmoor Guns & Fishing
3 The Parade, Minehead
Tel: 0643 2736

George Hinton & Sons Ltd.
62 Bridge Street, Taunton
Tel: 0823 72548

Hagas Fishing Tackle & Guns
29 Princess Street, Yeovil
Tel: 0935 4600

E. Hobley & Sons
27 High Street, Shepton Mallet
Tel: 0749 2072

Lance Nicholson Fishing and Guns
High Street, Dulverton
Tel: 0398 23409

Marney's Fishing Tackle Ltd.
3 Bond Street, Yeovil
Tel: 0935 23257

Minehead Sports
55 The Avenue, Minehead
Tel: 0643 3423

H. Nicholls & Son
50 High Street, Street
Tel: 0458 42785

A.W. Rule
8 Parret Close, Langport
Tel: 0458 250649

Sports of Bond Street
Bond Street, Yeovil
Tel: 0935 23368

The Sports Shop
2 Bath Street, Frome
Tel: 0373 2712

Topp Tackle
61 Station Road, Taunton
Tel: 0823 82518

H.U. Tout
High Street, Dulverton
Tel: 0398 23382

A. Twigger
8 The Square, Wiveliscombe
Tel: 0984 23445

A.A. Woodbury & Son Ltd.
36-38 High Street, Wellington
Tel: 082 347 2105

YORKSHIRE SOUTH

Andy's Fishing Tackle
274 Langsett Road, Sheffield
Tel: 0742 343352

Arthur Turner Ltd.
33/35 West Bar, Sheffield
Tel: 0742 22560

C.H. Beatson & Sons (Discount Fishing Tackle)
12 Sidney Street, Sheffield S1 4RN
Tel: 0742 25338

Bennetts of Sheffield Ltd.
1-5 Stanley Street, Sheffield
Tel: 0742 760221

Billy Clarke
6 Woodhead Road, Sheffield S2 4TA
Tel: 0742 51145

S.U. Calcott (Anglers Paradise)
2 Ladys Bridge, Sheffield
Tel: 0742 22817

Clegg Bros
62 Doncaster Road, Barnsley
Tel: 0226 83750

Concord Tackle Shop
283 Hatfield House Lane, Sheffield
Tel: 0742 386060

Conisbrough Sports
52 Church Street, Conisbrough, Nr Doncaster
Tel: 0709 864367

David Parkes Fishing Tackle
28 Westgate, Rotherham
Tel: 0709 63085

W.G. Dawsons
70 Holme Lane, Sheffield
Tel: 0742 343682

J. Edwards
757 City Road, Sheffield 12
Tel: 0742 399994

N. & J. Exley & Son
7 Stubbin Lane, Sheffield 5
Tel: 0742 387740

Franco's Angling Supplies
148 High Street, Bentley, Doncaster
Tel: 0302 874888

F.G. Gale & Son
26 Copley Road, Doncaster
Tel: 0302 68950

T. Grice & Son
14 The Guardian Centre, Rotherham
Tel: 0709 65454

Hardy's Gunshop
White Lane, Gleadless, Sheffield
Tel: 0742 656705

Howards Fishing Tackle
20 Main Street, Hackenthorpe, Sheffield S12 4LB
Tel: 0742 484895

Jack Purchase
71 Lonsdale Avenue, Intake, Doncaster
Tel: 0302 26007

Lakins
626 Chesterfield Road, Sheffield 8
Tel: 0742 53234

Lakins
640 Stamforth Road, Sheffield 9
Tel: 0742 442939

Myatt Fishing Tackle
207 Carrhouse Road, Bellevue, Doncaster
Tel: 0302 63629

News
Wales Road, Kiveton Park, Sheffield
0909 771978

...l's Fishing Tackle
Barnsley Road, Sheffield
0742 385837

...ls Tackle Shop
...caster Road, Denaby Main, Nr
...caster
0709 862558

...rtfishers
...Street, Hatfield, Doncaster
0302 840287

...rts and Angling
...Newbegin, Hornsea
04012 4947

...Stamford
Attercliffe Common, Sheffield
0742 442398

...amline Tackle
...1 Tickhill Road, Maltby, Rotherham
0709 812599

...ry & Johns Fishing Tackle
Buchanan Road, Sheffield S5 8AU
0742 343337

...Thackeray
Nursery Street, Sheffield
0742 29986

...rne Pet & Angling Centre
...e Green, Thorne, Nr Doncaster
0405 814056

...Wait
Cheserfield Road, Woodseats,
...field
0742 585133

...Welbon & Sons
Attercliffe Common, Sheffield
0742 441106

...& O. Woodhouse
Worksop Road, Swallow Nest,
Sheffield
0742 873070

STAFFORDSHIRE

...dy Kelsall
...ert Street, Stone
0785 3708

...thony Smith (Sports) Ltd.
...rton Lane, Great Wyrley, Walsall
0922 415950

Bacchus & Rhone
129 High Street, Woodville
Tel: 0283 216870

Barkers of Bloxwich Ltd.
184 High Street, Bloxwich, Walsall
Tel: 0922 75026

G. Bate
7 Market Square, Stafford
Tel: 0785 44191

D. Berrisford
57 Stockwell Street, Leek
Tel: 05382 4186

Burton Fishing Tackle Centre
87 High Street, Burton on Trent
Tel: 0283 32967

C & F Charsley
130 Northwood Park Road, Hanley,
Stoke on Trent
Tel: 0782 29436

Chase Matchman
130 Belt Road, Hednesford
Tel: 05438 71292

T. Cooper
30 Pall Mall, Hanley, Stoke on Trent
Tel: 0782 21589

H.C. Durbar
8 William Clowes Street, Burslem, Stoke
on Trent
Tel: 0282 814941

Gerald Heath Fishing Tackle
97 Rugeley Road, Chase Terrace,
Walsall
Tel: 054 36 2420

Greenways Fishing Tackle
23 Lichfield Street, Tamworth
Tel: 0827 66701

Gresley Tackle
23 Castle Road, Castle Gresley, Nr.
Burton on Trent
Tel: 0283 221513

E.J. Hambry
6 Tamworth Road, Polesworth, Nr.
Tamworth
Tel: 0827 895011

F. Holt Fishing Tackle
104 Wolverhampton Road, Stafford
Tel: 0785 59262

F. Holt Fishing Tackle
122 Marston Road, Stafford
Tel: 0785 51073

John Birks (Sports)
293 Uttoxeter Road, Normacot, Stoke on
Trent ST3 5LQ
Tel: 0782 319939

John Edwards
5 Church Street, Lichfield
Tel: 05432 28179

C. Linford Ltd.
High Green, Cannock
Tel: 054 35 3118

B. Mellor
30 Brunswick Street, Hanley, Stoke on
Trent
Tel: 0782 266742

Mullarkey & Sons
184/185 Waterloo Street, Burton on
Trent
Tel: 0283 66777

Princes Fishing Tackle
142 Elder Road, Cobridge, Stoke on
Trent
Tel: 0782 21700

Rod & Tackle Shop
52 Bridge Street, Uttoxeter
Tel: 08893 4740

I. Smith Fishing Tackle
82 Weston Road, Meir, Stoke on Trent
Tel: 0782 317399

Specialists Military Sales
103 Hednesford Road, Heath Hayes,
Cannock
Tel: 0543 78347

The Sports Shop
7 Brunswick Street, Newcastle
Tel: 0782 628334

The Tackle Box
97 High Street, Wolstanton, Newcastle
under Lyne
Tel: 0782 625577

Tackle Box
34 Hartshill Road, Stoke on Trent
ST4 7QT
Tel: 0782 412253

Tony Scott Fishing Tackle
22 Uxbridge Street, Burton on Trent
Tel: 0283 48540

SUFFOLK

Angling Depot
17 Commodore Road, Oulton Broad
Tel: 0502 4811

Bowmans of Ipswich
37/39 Upper Orwell Street, Ipswich
Tel: 0473 51195

Tackle Retailers: Surrey

Breakaway Tackle Development Co. Ltd.
376 Bramford Road, Ipswich
Tel: 0473 41393

Mr. M.R. Brien
2a Bent Hill, Felixstowe
Tel: 03942 5318

Bungay Angling Centre
54 St Marys Street, Bungay
Tel: 0986 3842

Crack Sports
7 Blyburgate, Beccles NR34 9TA
Tel: 0502 712045

S. & G. Gowen
57 Lorne Park Road, Lowestoft
Tel: 0502 81943

Ipswich Angling Centre
199 Felixstowe Road, Ipswich
Tel: 0473 78004

Jeckells Yacht & Caravan Supply Co. Ltd.
128 Bridge Road, Oulton Broad, Lowestoft
Tel: 0502 65007

Jim's Tackle & Sports
46 High Street, Haverhill
Tel: 0440 3127

Johns Fishing Tackle
127 All Saints Road, Newmarket
Tel: 0638 2724

Lowestoft Angling Centre
189-191 London Road South, Lowestoft
Tel: 0502 3392

R.A. Markham
717 Wood Bridge Road, Ipswich
Tel: 0473 77841

Rod & Gun Shop
62 The Thorough Fare, Woodbridge
Tel: 039 432377

SAM HOOK (LOWESTOFT) LTD.
132 Bevan Street, Lowestoft
Tel: 0502 65821

W. Simpson & Sons
37/39 Bury Street, Stowmarket
Tel: 04492 2914

Southwold Angling Centre
64 High Street, Southwold
Tel: 0502 722985

Sports Lodge
High Street, Leiston
Tel: 0728 830167

Stebbing Sports
6 Mill Street, Mildenhall
Tel: 0638 713196

The Swim & Pitch
23 Gainsborough Street, Sudbury
Tel: 0787 74066

Swine & Pitch
17 Gaol Lane, Sudbury
Tel: 0787 74066

E. Taylor
Suffolk House, 11 High Street, Saxmundham
Tel: 0728 2102

Tackle — Up
49a St Johns Street, Bury St Edmonds
Tel: 0284 5022

Ted Bean Fishing Tackle
175 London Road North, Lowestoft
Tel: 0502 65832

Viscount Fishing Tackle
207 Clapgate Lane, Ipswich
Tel: 0473 78179

SURREY
See also Greater London

A. & G. Allchorne
42 Bridge Street, Godalming
Tel: 048 686602

Angling Plus
62 Central Road, Worcester Park
Tel: 01 330 4892

APOLLO SALES & SERVICE
2B Woodham Lane, New Haw, Addlestone
Tel: 0932 48354
For the best in fishing tackle and baits. Full selection of coarse, game and sea equipment. Rods made to your own specifications. Expert advice on tackle, bait and fishing venues in Surrey. Day tickets available for local private lakes.

S. Baker
151 Goldsworth Road, Woking
Tel: 04862 73957

Cheam Tackle
705 London Road, North Cheam
Tel: 01 330 4787

Chertsey Angling Centre
40 Guildford Street, Chertsey
Tel: 09328 62701

Coopers
1 Wythe Green Road, Carshalton
Tel: 01 647 7642

Conns Guns 'n' Tackle
67 High Street, Camberley

Croydon Angling Centre
65 London Road, Croydon
Tel: 01 688 7564

Croydon Fish & Tackle
94 Church Street, Croydon

Den's
129 Princess Road, Maybury, Woking
Tel: 04862 60551

H.W. Finch (Fishing Tackle)
327 Lower Addiscombe Road, Croyd
Surrey CR0 9RF
Tel: 01 654 6144

Freewheels
92 Brighton Road, Horley
Tel: 02934 71421

Fulford Fishing Tackle
32 Abbey Street, Farnham
Tel: 0252 713735

S.C. Fuller
28 South Street, Dorking
Tel: 0306 882407

J. & E. Gerry
298 Whitehorse Road, Croydon
Tel: 01 684 0380

S.J. Jeffrey & Son
134 High Street, Guildford
Tel: 0483 72297

Ken Collings (Angling) Ltd.
114a Carshalton Road, Sutton
Tel: 01 642 6222

Kenleys
66/68 Church Street, Weybridge
Tel: 0932 52265

Leisure Sport Angling Centre Tackle Shop
47/49 Church Street, Staines
Tel: 0784 61831

Lightwater Angling Centre
81 Guildford Road, Lightwater
Tel: 0276 72734

R. Maynard
58 The Market, Rose Hill, Sutton
Tel: 01 641 1654

Molesey Angling Centre
96-98 Walton Road, East Molesey
Tel: 01 979 9083

gan's of Kingston Bridge
gh Street, Hampton Wick
1 977 76013

Is Fishing Tackle
ndon Road, Blackwater

Tackle
e Broadway, Plough Lane,
ington
1 681 2060

de Pets and Angling Centre
gh Street, Sandhurst, Camberley

y of Croydon
hurch Street, Croydon
0168 66792

Williams
Park Road, Kingston on Thames
1 546 9082

'n' Tackle
igh Street, Caterham Hill

lors Tackle
St Michael's Road, Caterham
0883 43807

mes Tackle
Burlington Road, New Malden
1 942 1215

pkins Bros
Parade, London Road, Dorking
0306 87716

ton Cycles & Tackle
ridge Street, Walton on Thames
09322 21424

ton Tackle Shop
Station Road, Addlestone
0932 42528

ybridge Guns & Tackle
Oatlands Drive, Weybridge
0932 42675

slow Tackle
Gilders Road, Chessington
1 391 1777

NE & WEAR

. Aggas
outh Frederick Street, South Shields
0632 565195

nall & Kirkwood Ltd.
rey Street, Newcastle on Tyne
0632 25873

ry Carr Sports
lc, The Galleries, Washington
0632 473361

Dave Miller
314/5 High Street West, Sunderland
Tel: 0783 59666

The Fishbowl
3 Burdon Road, Sunderland
Tel: 0783 71026

W.B. & P.A. Gibbard
Lane Head, Ryton
Tel: 089 422 2626

J. McDougall
206-208 Ocean Road, South Shields
Tel: 0632 563953

Mr. J. Robertson
101 Percy Street, Newcastle upon Tyne
Tel: 0632 22018

J. Robson
22 Vine Place, Sunderland
Tel: 0783 4103

R.S. TACKLE
36 Collingwood Street, Newcastle
Tel: 0632 25731

W. Temple Ltd.
43 Ocean View, Whitley Bay
Tel: 0632 526017

WARWICKSHIRE

Anglers Corner
1246 Pershore Road, Stirchley,
Birmingham 29
Tel: 021 459 4899

D. Ashby & Son Ltd.
The Tackle Shop, 182 Leythalls Lane,
Coventry
Tel: 0203 87900

Astwood Guns
4 High Street, Studley
Tel: 052 785 4963

Baileys Fishing Tackle
55 The Saltisford, Birmingham Road,
Warwick
Tel: 0926 41984

Banks & Burr
27 Claremont Road, Rugby
Tel: 0788 76782

Cook & Ryder
125 Long Street, Atherstone
Tel: 082 77 3153

A.F. Cooper
17 Willes Road, Leamington Spa
Tel: 0926 22539

A.F. Cooper
115 Abbey Street, Nuneaton
Tel: 0682 66326

A.F. Cooper
37 Greenhill Street, Stratford upon Avon
Tel: 0789 292778

H. Greenway & Son
55 Mill Street, Bedworth
Tel: 0203 312392

The Gun Shop
62a Lawford Road, Rugby
Tel: 0788 75198

Mr. W.H. Norris
24 Russell Terrace, Leamington Spa
Tel: 0926 26067

Rookes Leather & Fishing Tackle
Centre
25B Clemens Street, Leamington Spa
Tel: 0926 26848

WEST MIDLANDS

Acocks Green Sports Centre
1208 Warwick Road, Acocks Green,
Birmingham 28
Tel: 021 706 0763

Aldridge Tackle
48a Paddock Lane, Aldridge
Tel: 0922 58653

A & J Allen
5/6 New Road, Great Bridge, Tipton
Tel: 021 557 1074

G.A. Allport
2a West Street, Leamore, Walsall
Tel: 0922 75762

Anglers Corner
1246 Piershore Road, Stirchley,
Birmingham
Tel: 021 459 4899

D. Ashby
182 Lythalls Lane, Coventry
Tel: 0203 87900

K. Austin
2 Alfred Street, West Bromwich
Tel: 021 553 0392

Barkers of Bloxwich Ltd.
184 High Street, Bloxwich, Walsall
Tel: 0922 75026

G. Bate
16 Colmore Circus, Birmingham 4
Tel: 021 236 7451

Beasley Sports & Fishing Tackle
125 Walsall Road, Willenhall
Tel: 0902 67639

G. Beddow
425 Bilston Street, Wolverhampton
Tel: 0902 41045

T.N. Birch
5 Silver Court, High Street, Brownhills
Tel: 054 33 2395

F.R. Blacow
467 Holyhead Road, Coventry
Tel: 0203 591774

A.G. Britton
171 Walsgrave Road, Coventry
Tel: 0203 458708

A.E. Brookes
958 Bristol Road South, Northfield,
Birmingham
Tel: 021 475 2859

J. Chaplain
884 Alum Rock Road, Birmingham 8
Tel: 021 327 4193

A.G. Clarkes
1 Blakenhall Lane, Leamore
Tel: 0922 407398

Clarkes
Unit 6, Woodlands Centre, Short Heath,
Birmingham
Tel: 0922 78903

A. Clissett
666 Alum Rock Road, Birmingham
Tel: 021 326 6932

Mr. A. Clissett
1801 Pershore Road, Cotteridge,
Birmingham
Tel: 021 458 2797

Clive Smith
212 New Road, Rubery, Birmingham
Tel: 021 453 5434

G. Cooke
49/50 High Street, Rowley Regis, Warley
Tel: 021 559 1046

Coventry Angling Supplies Ltd.
6 Arne Road, Walsgrave on Sowe, Nr.
Coventry
Tel: 0203 612299

Cyril Cooper
153 Station Street East, Coventry
Tel: 0203 87555

Eric Willmont Sports Centre
1049 Stratford Road, Hall Green,
Birmingham
Tel: 021 777 1758

Fanci That
156 Weoley Castle Road, Birmingham 19
Tel: 021 427 1336

Fenwicks of Wolverhampton
Pitt Street, Wolverhampton
Tel: 0902 24607

The Fishing Lodge
1770 Coventry Road, Birmingham
Tel: 021 743 0448

The General Stores
Stratford Road, Wootton Wawen,
Solihull
Tel: 05642 2119

Goodes Fishing Tackle
44 Union Street, Wednesbury
Tel: 021 556 0602

Greenways Fishing Tackle
1010 Chester Road, Pype Hayes,
Birmingham
Tel: 021 373 0057

Greenways Fishing Tackle
5-7 Warren Farm Road, Kingstanding,
Birmingham
Tel: 021 373 2558

Greenways Fishing Tackle
815 Warwick Road, Tyseley,
Birmingham
Tel: 021 706 2049

Greenways Fishing Tackle
66 Church Road, Yardley, Birmingham
Tel: 021 706 5133

Greenways Fishing Tackle
225 Heathway, Shard End, Birmingham
Tel: 021 747 6838

Greenways Fishing Tackle
55 Mill Street, Bedworth
Tel: 0203 312392

Greenways Fishing Tackle
Shop 2, 51 High Street, Brockmoor,
Nr. Brierley Hill
Tel: 0384 71519

R. Hawkins
73 Thornbridge Avenue, Birmingham
Tel: 021 357 4676

A.G. Heath
97 Rugeley Road, Chase Terrace,
Walsall
Tel: 054 36 2420

J. Hickman
211 Station Road, Stechford,
Birmingham
Tel: 021 783 2104

S.W. Homer
197 Wolverhampton Road West, Wa
Tel: 0922 29454

Jacksons Tackle
113 Toll End Road, Tipton
Tel: 021 556 0875

**Roy Jarvis Fishing Tackle &
Sports**
364 Shirley Road, Acocks Green
Tel: 021 706 0550

John's Fishing Tackle
806 Alcester Road South, Kings Hea
Birmingham
Tel: 021 430 5177

Keepers Lodge
10a Mill Street, Sutton Coldfield
Tel: 021 354 7612

W.H. Lane & Sons
31 London Road, Coventry
Tel: 0203 29346/23316

Leisure Sports
100 Jardine Crescent, Tile Hill North
Coventry
Tel: 0203 466314

Mal Storey
236 Hagley Road, Hasbury, Halesow
Tel: 021 5501 830

G.H. & D. Matthews
255 Longmore Road, Shirley, Solihu
Tel: 021 744 8828

**Olympic Cycles Guns & Fishi
Tackle**
3 Moor Street, Brierley Hill,
Tel: 0384 77325

Olympic Sports
90a Worcester Road, West Hagley
Tel: 0562 885475

Parkington Fisheries
Fishery Lodge, Maxstoke Lane, Meri
Nr Coventry
Tel: 0676 22754

Pennant Fishing Tackle
44 Union Street, Wednesbury
Tel: 021 556 2070

Peter Gordon
84 High Street, Dudley
Tel: 0384 52413

S.R. Redding
269 Bearwood Road, Warley
Tel: 021 429 8564

Baker
we Street, Whitmore Reans,
erhampton
902 711227

Haynes
afford Street, Wolverhampton
902 23777

Jarvis Fishermans
dise
hirley Road, Acocks Green,
ngham
21 706 0550

um's
afford Street, Walsall
922 26684

haw
all Road, Willenhall
0902 67639

don Sports
Coventry Road, Sheldon,
ngham
021 742 3384

Simmonds & G.L. Priddey
atford Road, Shirley, Solihull
021 744 1376

Smith
Witton Road, Aston, Birmingham
021 356 8736

nape
Aldermans Green Road, Coventry
0203 365635

rt & Tackle
anks Lane, Wombourne
0902 896432

rt n' Tackle
igh Street, Bilston
0902 46200

Jones Fishing Tackle
addlebarn Road, Selly Oak,
ingham
021 472 2035

tevens
Ann's Road, Cradley Heath, Warley
0384 67778

B. Stretton
Brettle Lane, Amblecote,
rbridge
03843 2741

merfield Sports Centre
Dudley Road, Birmingham
021 454 7585

TERRY EUSTACE RODS & BLANKS

2A Booths Lane, Great Barr, Birmingham
Tel: 021 360 9669
See Advertisement under Custom Built Rods.

William Powell & Son Ltd.
35/37 Carrs Lane, Birmingham
Tel: 021 643 8362

Woodward Bros.
92 Lower Litchfield Street, Willenhall
Tel: 0902 61191

W & W Tropical Fish
552-554 Walsall Road, Birmingham
B42 1LR
Tel: 021 358 6238

WEST SUSSEX

F.A. Anderson
4 Middle Row, East Grinstead
Tel: 0342 25604

The Anglers Den
35 East Street, Shoreham by Sea
Tel: 07917 2014

Angling Specialists
27 Queen Street, Horsham
Tel: 0403 64644

Burgess Hill Angling Centre
143 Church Road, Burgess Hill
Tel: 04446 2287

Clarke's Sports
11 East Street, Horsham
Tel: 0403 65379

Clarksports
39/49 Queensway, Bognor Regis
Tel: 02433 21376

The Covert
East Street, Petworth
Tel: 0798 43118

Fishermans Quay Angling Centre
146 Pier Road, Littlehampton
Tel: 09064 5766

Grosvenor Marine & Sports
13 Coronation Buildings, Brougham Road, Worthing
Tel: 0903 37177
Caters mainly for Sea Angling with some Coarse.

Henfield Angling Specialists
3 Commercial Buildings, High Street, Henfield
Tel: 079155 3996

Ken Dunman
2 Marine Place, Worthing
Tel: 0903 39802

Kirkmans (Crawley) Ltd.
40 The Broadway
Tel: 0293 26670

Russel Hillsdon Ltd.
46 South Street, Chichester
Tel: 02437 83811

Shoreham Sports Centre
24 Brunswick Road, Shoreham by Sea
Tel: 07917 2580

Town Angler
54 Ewhurst Road, West Green, Crawley
Tel: 0923 21186

Tropicana of Littlehampton
5 & 6 Pier Road, Littlehampton
Tel: 09064 5190

Sporting Guns Ltd.
76 Crossgates Road, Leeds
Tel: 0532 648824

West Park Angling
574 Thornton Road, Girlington, Bradford
Tel: 0274 495142

West Riding Anglers Supply
938 Leeds Road, Bradford
Tel: 0274 663767

Wetherby Angling Centre
7 Crossley Street, Wetherby
Tel: 0937 63769

Whingate Pets & Tropicals
94 Town Street, Armley, Leeds LS12 3HJ
Tel: 0532 633215

Willis Walker Ltd.
105/109 Cavendish Street, Keighley
Tel: 0535 60 2928

WILTSHIRE

Angling Centre
Manchester Road, Swindon
Tel: 0793 22701

Calne Sports
3 Phelps Parade, Calne
Tel: 0249 812572

Cannon & Son Sports
34 High Street, Wootton Basset, Swindon
Tel: 079 370 2261/2

Cole & Son Sports Ltd.
6 Market Place, Chippenham
Tel: 0249 3624

Cole & Son Sports Ltd.
33 The Market Place, Devizes
Tel: 0380 2059

Tackle Retailers: Yorkshire West

G. & K. Sports Ltd.
6 Station Hill, Chippenham
Tel: 0249 56200

J.W. & P.M. Henderson Tackle Shop
32 Roundstone Street, Trowbridge
Tel: 022 14 5472

House of Angling
59/60 Commercial Road, Swindon
Tel: 0793 693460

John Eadie
20 Catherine Street, Salisbury
Tel: 0722 28535

Reg Smith & Ford Sports Shop
2a The Shambles, Bradford-on-Avon
Tel: 022 16 2339

Reg Smith & Ford Sports
10 Warminster Road, Westbury
Tel: 0373 822318

Reg Smith & Ford Sports
24 Three Horseshoes Mall, Warminster
Tel: 0985 213287

Robinsons
13 Bath Road, Melksham
Tel: 0225 702219

Rod & Reel
11 Sidmouth Street, Devizes SN10 1LD
Tel: 0380 5431

Sportscene
17 Brunel Plaza, Swindon
Tel: 0793 27881

Swindon Angling Centre Ltd.
175 Manchester Road, Swindon
Tel: 0793 22701

Wests
32 Roundstone Street, Trowbridge
Tel: 022 14 5472

WILTSHIRE ROD & GUN
23-25 High Street, Swindon SN1 3ES
Tel: 0793 47455
Rods, Reels, Tackle, Bait and clothing, from Shakespeare, Daiwa and many others.
Special section for the Game fisherman including flying tying materials.
Full range of Bob Church tackle
3m from M4. Free Parking.
BARCLAYCARD & ACCESS WELCOME

YORKSHIRE WEST

Fred Alexander
3 The Springs, Wakefield
Tel: 0924 373820

A.S.A. Angling
31 Horton Street, Halifax
Tel: 0422 51684

Angling Stores Ltd.
938/940 Leeds Road, Bradford
Tel: 0274 663767

Brian Worsnop Fishing Tackle
98 Northgate, Huddersfield
Tel: 0484 45032

Burtons Sports Centre
30/32 Front Street, Pontefract
Tel: 0977 702191

Calder Angling Supplies
38 Gooder Lane, Rostrick, Brighouse
Tel: 0484 711063

Carters of Bradford Ltd.
15 Bridge Street, Bradford BD1 1RY
Tel: 0274 26215

G.A. Cullimore
29a Park Road, West Yorks
Tel: 0274 565913

Davids of Harehills
267 Harehills Lane, Leeds 8

Fred Alexander
The Springs, Wakefield
Tel: 0924 73820

Gledhills
60 The Headrow, Leeds 1
Tel: 0532 455336

THE GUN SHOP & ANGLING SUPPLIES
36 Cross Green, Pool Road, Otley, West Yorkshire
Tel: (0943) 462770
Stockists of all leading tackle and bait. Day Permits available. Try us for your requirements.

Headingley Angling Centre
58 North Lane, Leeds 6
Tel: 0532 784445

Holme Valley Sports
76 Huddersfield Road, Holmfirth, Huddersfield HD7 1AZ
Tel: 048 489 4128

Huddersfield Angling Centre
22 Chapel Hill, Huddersfield
Tel: 0484 29854

Mr. A.J. Jewson
1 Westgate, Halifax
Tel: 0422 54146

Ken Jackson
47a Queen Street, Morley, Leeds
Tel: 0532 537688

Kendall & Watson
5 Grand Arcade, Leeds
Tel: 0532 457768

Kirkgate Anglers
95 Kirkgate, Leeds LS1 7DJ
Tel: 0532 34880

K.L. Tackle
Mornington Street, Keighley
Tel: 0535 67574

Linsley Bros Ltd.
28 Kirkgate, Leeds LS2 7DR
Tel: 0532 452790

Match Anglers
99 Westgate, Wakefield
Tel: 0924 78878

Mathers & Craven
Market Street, Dewsbury
Tel: 0924 463660

Mel Spence Fishing Tackle
Abbey National Yard, Market Place, Pontefract
Tel: 0977 77461

Pheasant Valley (Helmsley) L
430 Oxford Road, Gomersal, Cleckheaton
Tel: 0274 870618

D. Richmond
10 Morley Street, Bradford
Tel: 0274 21042

J.T. Rogers
12 Barwick Road, Seacroft, Leeds
Tel: 0532 641195

Sporting Guns Ltd.
76 Crossgates Road, Leeds
Tel: 0532 648824

West Park Angling
574 Thornton Road, Girlington, Brad
Tel: 0274 495142

West Riding Anglers Supply
938 Leeds Road, Bradford
Tel: 0274 663767

Wetherby Angling Centre
7 Crossley Street, Wetherby
Tel: 0937 63769

Whingate Pets & Tropicals
94 Town Street, Armley, Leeds LS12
Tel: 0532 633215

Willis Walker Ltd.
105/109 Cavendish Street, Keighley
Tel: 0535 60 2928

FISHING TACKLE RETAILERS

...ompiling this list we are aware that ...e of those included may not be able ...eet all of your tackle needs. On the ...r hand there may be shops which ...ide a first-class service. The list is to ...iewed as an aid to visiting anglers.

...LAND SOUTHERN

...ARLOW

...O'Donoghue
...astle Street, Carlow

...ssrs Tully's Sports Centre
...Tullow Street, Carlow

...A. McCullagh
...et Square, Muine Bheag

...ne & Dawson Ltd.
...Street, Tullow

...VAN

...cMahon
...ly Stores, Belturbet

...Brian Mulligan
...Street, Cootehill

...O'Reilly
...Street, Cavan

...net Sports Stores
...Hall Street, Cavan

...Donoghue
...idge Street, Cavan

...CLARE

...eogh's
...a, Killaloe

...T. McNamara
...tshannon

Dressco Ltd.
Unit 12/13, Shannon Town Centre, Shannon

CO CORK

Mr. J. O'Sullivan
4 Patrick St., Fermoy

Vickery & Co.
Main Street, Bantry

Mr. J. O'Sullivan
The Pier, Courtmacsherry

T. W. Murray & Co. Ltd.
87 Patrick Street, Cork

Roche's Leisure Shop
17 Patrick Street, Cork

The Tackle Shop
6 Lavitts Quay, Cork

Atkins & Co. Ltd.
The Square, Dunmanway

Messrs. P. Twohig
Strand Street, Kanturk

Mylie Murphy Ltd.
The Garage, Kinsale

Mallow Sports Centre
21 Bridge Street, Mallow

CO DONEGAL

Messrs. D. McLaughlin
7 West End, Buncrana

Pat Barrett
Bundoran

C. J. Doherty
Main Street, Donegal

Mr. J. J. McCrossan
Lower Main Street, Letterkenny

B. O'Neill
Bridgend, Lifford P.O.

Eamonn Martin
The Border Shop, Lifford

CO DUBLIN

Garnetts & Keegan Ltd.
31 Parliament Street, Dublin 2

J. W. Elvery & Co. Ltd.
Suffolk Street, Dublin 2

A.B.C. Stores
15 Mary's Abbey, Dublin 1

Moorkens Ltd.
11 Upper Abbey Street, Dublin 7

Watts Bros. Ltd.
18 Upper Ormond Quay, Dublin 7

Rory's
17a Temple Bar, Dublin 2

Angling & Sports Centre
13 Main Street, Blackrock

Fishermans Wharf
(Mick Macs), 8 Railway Road, Dalkey

Clinton's Ltd.
Tackle & Gunsmiths, Ballydowd, Lucan

CO GALWAY

Messrs T. Cheevers
North Gate Street, Athenry

Galway City Sports
(The Great Outdoors)
Eglinton Street, Galway

T. Naughton & Sons Ltd.
35 Shop Street, Galway

Freeney's
High Street, Galway

Mr. Hugh Duffy
5 Mainguard Street, Galway

K. Duffy & Son
Main Street, Headford

Keller Bros.
Ballinasloe

Keogh's Ltd.
Main Street, Oughterard

Garry Kenny
Palmerstown Stores, Portumna

Thomas Tuck
Main St., Oughterard

CO KERRY

Moriarty
Seaview, Fenit

Handy Stores
Kenmare Place, Killarney

Mrs. M. O'Neill
6 Plunkett Street, Killarney

Messrs. D. N. Foley
2 Main Street, Killarney

Benner & Co.
28 Bridge Street, Tralee

Henberry Sports
50 Ashe Street, Tralee

Mrs. A. J. Huggard
Angler's Rest, Waterville

CO KILDARE

P. Mulhall
20 Emily Square, Athy

Paul Cullen
Moore Street, Monasterevan

John Cahill
Sallins Road, Naas

Patrick A. Fleming
New Row, Naas

Newbridge Rod & Gun
Henry Road, Newbridge

McWey
Round Tower House, Kildare

CO KILKENNY

J. O'Leary & Son
Lr. Main Street, Graiguenamanagh

Michael McGrath
3 Lr. Patrick Street, Kilkenny

Kilkenny Sports Scene
1 Irishtown, Kilkenny

CO LAOIS

Messrs. Lawlor
The Square, Durrow

CO LEITRIM

Conroy
Ruskey, Carrick-on-Shannon

Phil's Fishing Tackle
Main Street, Ballinamore

The Creel
Main St., Carrick-on-Shannon

CO LIMERICK

McMahon's
Sports Shop, Roches Street, Limerick

Limerick Sports Stores
10 William Street, Limerick

Nestor Bros. Ltd.
28 O'Connell Street, Limerick

CO LONGFORD

Denniston
Central Stores, Longford

CO LOUTH

Olraine Agencies
Unit 13, Abey Shopping Centre, West
Street, Drogheda

R. Q. O'Neill Ltd.
Earl Street, Dundalk

Emerald Sports
Earl Street, Dundalk

Magee Sports
Shopping Centre, Dundalk

CO MAYO

Messrs. O'Connor
Main Street, Ballycastle

John Walkin
Tone Street, Ballina

V. Doherty
Bridge Street, Ballina

Wm. Coyle
American Street, Belmullet

Angler's Lounge
Lower Main Street, Swinford

J. J. O'Connor
15 Spencer Street, Castlebar

Messrs Staunton Sports Shop
Main Street, Castlebar

Pat Quinn Tackle
Main Street, Castlebar

CO MEATH

"Tomas" (Murray)
Farrell Street, Kells

The Rod & Gun Sports Shop
Abbeylands, Navan

Londis Ltd
39 Trimgate Street, Navan

CO MONAGHAN

T. J. Hanberry
3/4 Fermanagh Street, Clones

CO ROSCOMMON

W. T. Wynne
Main Street, Boyle

C. J. Finn
Main Street, Roscommon

CO OFFALY

M. Madden
29 Main Street, Birr

T. Holt
Main Street, Edenderry

J. Hiney
Main Street, Ferbane

CO SLIGO

M. J. Creegan
2/4 Main Street, Ballymote

Barton Smith Ltd.
Hyde Bridge, Sligo

F. Nelson & Sons Ltd.
42 Castle Street, Sligo

CO TIPPERARY

O'Keeffe
O.K. Garage, New Street, Carrick-on-
Suir

John Kavanagh
Westgate, Clonmel

Sheahan's Stores
66 Pearse Street, Nenagh

Mr. Ken Henderson
Main Street, Roscrea

G. W. Kilroy
The Mall, Thurles

CO WATERFORD

Messrs Morgan Carroll & Co.
The Square, Ballybricken, Waterford

O. Bowman & Sons
6 Mary Street, Dungarvan

Mark's Fishing Tackle Store
35 Parnell Street, Waterford

Barnett
Street, Tramore

WESTMEATH

Halley Fishing Tackle
ominick St., Mullingar

J. Murray
ingar Sports Centre, Castle Street,
ingar

's Fishing Tackle
hurch Street, Athlone

Denis Connell Tackle
Dublin Gate Street, Athlone

Sean Egan Tackle
59 Connaught St., Athlone

S.G.S. Marine
Ballykernan, Athlone

CO WEXFORD

Paddy Lennon
26 Main Street, Enniscorthy

John Webb
100 Main Street, Gorey

Peter Goggin
56 South Street, New Ross

Jim Mooney & Co. Ltd.
North St., New Ross

George Bridges
14 Selskar Street, Wexford

Michael Goggin
34 North Main Street, Wexford

CO WICKLOW

George O'Toole Ltd.
Lr. Main Street/Bridge Street, Arklow

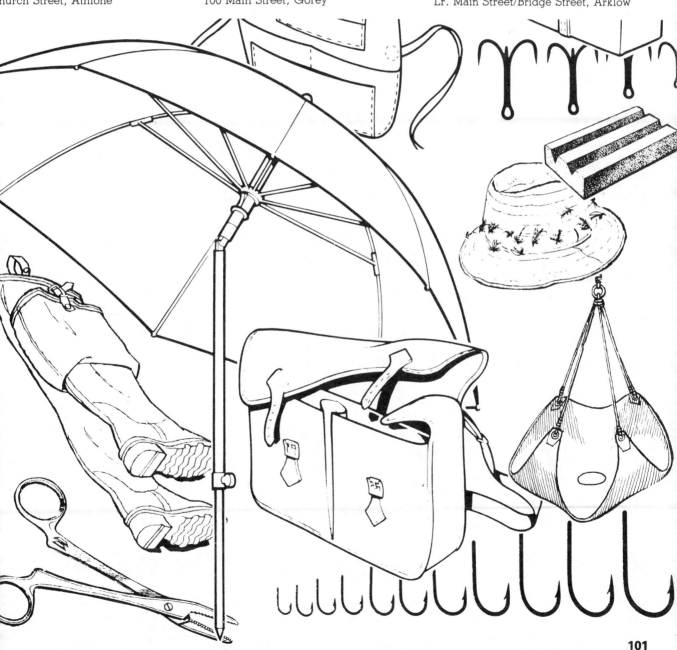

FISHING TACKLE RETAILERS

SCOTLAND

BORDERS

Anglers Choice
High Street, Melrose, Roxburghshire
Tel: 089 682 3070

R.B. Crawley
29 High Street, Innerleithen
Tel: 0896 830411

R. Grieve & Sons
26 High Street, Eyemouth
Tel: 0390 50270

Ian Frazer (Sports)
Northgate, Peebles
Tel: 0721 20979

John Dickson & Son
35 The Square, Kelso
Tel: 05732 2687

D. & H. McDonald
9-11 High Street, Selkirk
Tel: 0450 21398

Pet Store & Fishing Tackle Shop
1 Union Street, Hawick
Tel: 0450 3543

Stothart
6 High Street, Hawick
Tel: 0450 2231

J. & A. Turnbull
30 Bank Street, Galashiels
Tel: 0896 3191

CENTRAL

Alex Smith & Sons
140 Carronshore Road, Carronshore,
Falkirk
Tel: 03245 2903

D. Crockart & Son
15 King Street, Stirling
Tel: 0786 3443

James Bayne
76 Main Street, Callander
Tel: 0877 30218

J.K. Angling & Guns
101 Mary Square, Laurieston, by Falkirk
Tel: 0324 23156

McClarens
4 Allenvale Road, Bridge of Allan
Tel: 0786 833530

McClarens
13 Callendar Riggs, Falkirk
Tel: 0324 34805

M. Rae
10 Cow Wynd, Falkirk
Tel: 0324 29919

Sports Emporium
Unit 5, Newmarket Street, Falkirk
Tel: 0324 31119

FIFE

Alex Constables
39a High Street, Kirkcaldy
Tel: 0592 60770

The Anster Gift Box
44 Shore Street, Anstruther
Tel: 0333 310389

W. & M. Byers
62 High Street, Cowdenbeath
Tel: 0383 513777

Davesports
14a Bridge Street, Leven
Tel: 0333 25115

Eldor Sports
26/28 East Port, Dunfermline
Tel: 0383 24516

The Fishing Lodge
Loch Fitty, Kingseat
Dunfermline
Tel: 0383 23162

Hobby & Model
10-12 New Row, Dunfermline
Tel: 0383 22582

James Grubb
367 High Street, Kirkcaldy
Tel: 0592 60441

Lock Fitty Lodge
The Lodge, Lock Fitty, by Dunferml
Tel: 0383 23162

J. Mitchell & Son
120 Main Street, Lochgelly
Tel: 0592 780 587

D.L. & D.S. Ross
2 Mill Lane, Tayport
Tel: 08 265 2518

F.D. Simpson
28 West Preston Street, Edinburgh
Tel: 031 667 3058

Sportshop (Fife) Ltd.
31 Esplanade, Kirkcaldy
Tel: 0592 69416

Sportshop (Fife) Ltd.
13 Glenwood, Glenrothes
Tel: 0592 752767

Sportshop (Fife) Ltd.
280 High Street, Cowdenbeath
Tel: 0383 512643

Sportshop (Fife) Ltd.
1 Sandwell Street, Buckhaven
Tel: 0592 712480

We're Game (Shooting & Fishing)
3 Park Road, Kirkcaldy
Tel: 0592 54301

DUMFRIES & GALLOWAY

Castle Douglas Guns & Tackle
9 St Andrews Street, Castle Douglas
Tel: 0556 2977

A. Coltart & Son
Drumlanrig Street, Thornhill
Tel: 0848 30464

Gordon M.N. Pattie & Son
109 Queensbury Street, Dumfries
Tel: 0387 2891

Gordons Sports
65 High Street, Lockerbie
Tel: 057 62 2400

M. McCowan & Son
43 High Street, Dalbeattie
Tel: 0556 610270

M. McCowan & Son
52 King Street, Castle Douglas
Tel: 0556 2009

McMillan
iars Venell, Dumfries
0387 2075

e Sports Shop
George Street, Stranraer
0776 2705

Steel (Sporting Supplies) Ltd.
urray Street, Annan
046 12 2365

. White
ket Place, Langholm, Dumfries
0541 80274

RAMPIAN

gling Centre
ss Street, Elgin
0343 7615

Brown & Co.
Belmont Street, Aberdeen
0224 21692

ıce's
West Church Street, Buckie
0542 32161

S. Clark
Cross Street, Fraserburgh
03462 4427

S. Clark
k Street, Peterhead
034 62 4427

k's Sports
Broad Street, Fraserburgh
03462 4120

Dickson & Son Ltd.
Belmont Street, Aberdeen
0224 20480

orge D. Manson
47 Gordon Street, Huntly
0466 2482

orge Smith & Co.
Bridge Street, Ballater
033 82 432

Masson (Sports) Ltd.
Main Street, Turriff AB5 7BJ
088 82 2428

tee Sports
ow Street, Bannff
026 12 5821

Millington — Jefferies
New Street, Rothes, Moray
03403 407

J.A.J. Munro
95 High Street, Aberlour on Spey
Tel: 03405 220

Ritchie's of Ellon
61 Bridge Street, Ellon
Tel: 0358 20440

Robertson Sports
1 Kirk Street, Peterhead
Tel: 0779 2584

Slater Sports
5 High Street, Buckie, Banffshire
Tel: 0542 31769

J. Somers & Son
40 Thistle Street, Aberdeen
Tel: 0224 50910

The Tackle Shop
188 High Street, Elgin
Tel: 0343 3129

The Tackle Shop
77 High Street, Aberlour on Spey
Tel: 03405 570

The Tackle Shop
97b High Street, Forres
Tel: 0309 72936

LOTHIAN

Anglers Corner
3 Churchill Place, Edinburgh
Tel: 031 447 3676

J. Dickson & Son Ltd.
21 Frederick Street, Edinburgh
Tel: 031 225 4218

Field & Stream
61 Montrose Terrace, Abbeyhill,
Edinburgh
Tel: 031 661 4282

The Golf Centre
58 Dalry Road, Edinburgh
Tel: 031 337 5888

Gun & Fishing Tackle Shop
28a Haddington Place, Edinburgh
Tel: 031 556 9384

Shooting Lines Ltd.
23 Roseburn Terrace, Edinburgh
Tel: 031 337 8616

F.D. Simpson Ltd.
28 West Preston Street, Edinburgh
Tel: 031 667 3058

The Sports Angle
11 West Main Street, Whitburn
Tel: 0501 40666

Sportsman's Emporium
4-6 Jarvey Street, Bathgate
Tel: 031 556 3244

Thomas Wilson & Son
11 South Street, Dalkeith
Tel: 031 663 2182

HIGHLANDS & ISLANDS

Angus Stuart
60 High Street, Grantown on Spey
Tel: 0479 2612

Archibald Brown & Son
21 Main Street, Tobermory, Isle of Mull
Tel: 0688 2020

Cairdsport
The Aviemore Centre, Aviemore,
Inverness
Tel: 0479 810296

A. Cameron & Sons
Kinburn Stores, Ardgay, Ross-Shire
Tel: 086 32 359

Charles McLaren (Fishing
Tackle)
Invermudale, Altnaharra, Sutherland
Tel: 054 981 225

Eric G. Kemp
31-33 Bridge Street, Kirkwall, Orkney
Tel: 0856 2137

J. Graham & Co.
71 Castle Street, Inverness
Tel: 0463 33178

Gray & Co.
30 Union Street, Inverness
Tel: 0463 33225

Harper Fly Fishing Service
Drill Hall, Sinclair, St. Thurso
Tel: 0847 3179

Hay & Co.
47 Commercial Road, Lerwick, Shetland
Tel: 0595 3057

James A. Manson
88 Commercial Street, Lerwick,
Shetland
Tel: 0595 3448

Leisuropa Ltd.
6-8 Inglis Street, Inverness
Tel: 0463 39427

Robins Brae Supplies
Robins Brae, Dunrossness
Tel: 0950 60556

Tackle Retailers: Tayside

Lindsay & Co.
Main Street, Golspie, Sutherland
Tel: 040 83 212

The Longship
Broad Street, Kirkwall, Orkney
Tel: 0856 3251

A.A. MacDonald
23 Sinclair Street, Thurso
Tel: 0847 2819

W.A. MacDonald
Castle Street, Dornoch, Sutherland
Tel: 086 281 301

R. Macleod & Son
14 Lamington Street, Tain
Tel: 0862 2171

A.M. Morgan
Albert Street, Kirkwall, Orkney
Tel: 0856 2471

Nicol Spence & Son
26 Bridge Street, Kirkwall, Orkney
Tel: 0856 2162

Osprey Fishing Tackle
The Craft Village, Aviemore Centre,
Aviemore
Tel: 0479 810767

The Outdoor Shop
Canal Bank, Fort Agustus
Tel: 0320 6477

Pentland Sport Emporium
14 Olrig Street, Thurso
Tel: 0847 2473

Robin's Brae Supplies
Dunrossness, Shetland
Tel: 0950 60556

Rob Wilson
Fountain Square, Brora, KW9 6NX
Tel: 04082 373

A. Sandison
Altona, Mid Yell, Shetland
Tel: 0957 2037

Sporting Stores
Tulloch Street, Dingwall, Ross-Shire
Tel: 0349 62346
Caters for Trout and Sea Trout

W.S. Sinclair
27 John Street, Stromness, Orkney
Tel: 0856 850469

Mortimers
61 High Street, Grantown-on-Spey
Tel: 0479 2684

Outdoor Shop
Canal Side, Fort Augustus
Tel: 0320 6477

W.S. Sinclair
23-27 John Street, Stromness, Orkney
Tel: 0856 850469

Skye Marine & Leisure Centre
Willow Bank, Broadford, Isle of Skye
Tel: 047 12 271

Sport in Scotland Ltd.
Ormiston & MacDonald, 22 Market Brae,
Inverness
Tel: 0463 222757

The Sports Shop
6 North Beach Street, Stornaway, Isle of
Lewis
Tel: 0851 5464

Stove & Smith
98 Commercial Street, Lerwick,
Shetland
Tel: 0595 3383

Wilson & Nolf
1 Francis Street, Wick
Tel: 0955 4284

TAYSIDE

Angus Gun & Tackle Room
98 Beoughty Ferry Road, Dundee
Tel: 0382 453668

Wm. Cook & Sons
19 High Street, Crieff
Tel: 0764 2081

J. Crockart & Son
26 Allen Street, Blairgowrie
Tel: 0250 2056

David Brown & Son
157 High Street, Kinross
Tel: 0577 62451

David Simpson (Sports)
Post Office, Coupar Angus, Perthshire
Tel: 082 82 329

Duncan of Brechin Ltd.
19 Clerk Street, Brechin
Tel: 035 62 2700

J.R. Gow & Sons Ltd.
12 Union Street, Dundee
Tel: 0382 25427

Highland Guns & Tackle
Blair Atholl, Perthshire
Tel: 079681 303

L.M. Jamieson
41 Dunkeld Street, Aberfeldy
Tel: 08872 385

P.D. Malloch (Field Sports)
24 Scott Street, Perth
Tel: 0738 21631

McKerchar & McNaughton Ltd
Bridgend, Kinloch Ramock, Pitlochry
Perthshire
Tel: 08822 306

R. & M. Murdie
37-39 South Street, Milnathort, Kinros
Tel: 0577 63179

Peter D. Malloch
Atholl Road, Pitlochry
Tel: 0796 2228

W. Phillips
180 High Street, Montrose
Tel: 0674 2692

Rob Jackson Fishing Tackle &
Sports
65 High Street, Blairgowrie
Tel: 0250 3859

Ruthven P. Smith
287-291 Brook Street, Broughty Ferry,
Dundee
Tel: 0382 77351

Shotcast Ltd.
8 Whitehall Crescent, Dundee
Tel: 0382 25621

Sporting Guns & Ammo
55 North Methven Street, Perth
Tel: 0738 23679

The Sports Shop
22-24 High Street, Brechin
Tel: 03562 2491

Tayside Guns & Tackle
259 Old High Street, Perth
Tel: 0738 32316

mas Clark & Sons
High Street, Arbroath
0241 73467

Shop
ll Street, Dunkeld
03502 556

RATHCLYDE

drie Sports
High Street, Airdrie
02364 65921

en Ltd.
est Nile Street, Glasgow
041 221 0484

sports
itchfield Street, Kilmarnock
0563 23922

glers Rendezvous
altmarket, Glasgow
041 552 4662

gling & Sport Shop
High Street, Johnstone
0505 29733

gling Supplies
Glaisnock Street, Cumnock
0290 20002

an Sea Angling Centre
re Station, The Beach, Brodick, Isle
rran
0770 2192

Brown & Son
Main Street, Tobermory, Isle of Mull
0688 2020

Cafaro Bros
140 Renfield Street, Glasgow
Tel: 041 332 6224

The Carousel
3/4 West Clyde Street, Helensburgh
Tel: 0436 2790

Caurnie Pets & Tackle
105 Cowgate, Kirkintilloch, by Glasgow
Tel: 041 776 4458

Country Sports
135 Neilston Road, Paisley
Tel: 041 884 6833

Currie Sports
32 High Street, Irvine
Tel: 0294 78603

Wm R. Findlater
Main Street, Arrochar
Tel: 030 12 304

Gamesports
60 Sandgate, Ayr
Tel: 0292 63822

R. & J. Gibbons
Blair Crescent, Galston, Ayrshire
Tel: 0563 820207

D. Graham
9-13 Combie Street, Oban
Tel: 0631 2069

J.M. Grant
120 Stirling Street, Airdrie
Tel: 02364 55532

Hugh MacArthur (Sports)
37 Lochnell Street, Lochgilphead, Argyll
Tel: 0546 2212

Inverawe Fisheries
Taynuilt, Argyll
Tel: 086 62 262

James Kent
2380 Dumbarton Road, Glasgow 14
Tel: 041 952 1629

James Kirk
25 Kyle Street, Ayr
Tel: 0292 63390

John Dickson & Son
20 Royal Exchange Square, Glasgow
G1 3AG
Tel: 041 221 6794

Kerr Bros
143-145 Quarry Street, Hamilton
Tel: 0698 282956

Lanark Sports
66 High Street, Lanark
Tel: 0555 61231

Lawrie Renfrew
514 Great Western Road, Glasgow
Tel: 041 334 3635

J. MacKenzie & Son
175 Dalrymple Street, Greenock
Tel: 0475 21408

Martin Sports
13 Minard Road, Glasgow
Tel: 041 632 4864

McCririck & Sons
38 John Finnie Street, Kilmarnock
Tel: 0563 25577

T. McGall & Co.
7-9 Main Street, Alexandria,
Dunbartonshire
Tel: 0389 56063

T. McGall & Co.
9 Villafield, Main Road, Cardross
Tel: 038 984 521

Pitchers Sports
23-25 Moss Street, Paisley, Renfrewshire
Tel: 041 889 6969

I.C. Purdie
25 Argyll Street, Dundon
Tel: 0369 3232

Sports 90
90 Main Street, Barrhead, Renfrewshire
Tel: 041 881 5873

Tackle & Books
Main Street, Tobermory, Isle of Mull
Tel: 0688 2336

The Tackle Shop
6 Aird Place, Oban
Tel: 0631 3933

Tackle & Textiles
62 Shore Street, Gourock
Tel: 0475 34102

Tansney's Sports
34 Alexander Street, Clydebank
Tel: 041 952 1283

Viking Sports
32 Burnbank Road, Hamilton
Tel: 0698 281951

William Robertson & Co. Ltd.
27 Wellington, Glasgow G2
Tel: 041 221 6687

FISHING TACKLE RETAILERS

WALES

CLWYD

Anglers Den
29 Queen Street, Rhyl
Tel: 0745 54765

Arthur H. Fogarby
29 Queen Street, Rhyl
Tel: 0745 54765

Blue Shark
Quay Street, West Parade, Rhyl
Tel: 0745 50267

Sports Shop
4A Meliden Road, Prestatyn
Tel: 07456 2390

T.L.L. Morrisons & Co. (Retail) Ltd.
38 Mount Street, Wrexham
Tel: 0978 364460

The Tackle Box
50-52 Sea View Road, Colwyn Bay
Tel: 0492 31104

Trigger & Tackle
South Prior House, Clwyd Street, Ruthin
Tel: 082 42 3739

William Roberts Ltd. (Tackle & Tack)
123-131 High Street, Rhyl
Tel: 0745 53031

Wings & Fins
9 Lord Street, Wrexham
Tel: 0978 59657

DYFED

Barry Llwellyn Sports
Cowell Precinct, Llanelli
Tel: 05542 3720

Biers Pool Autofill Sports
London Road, Pembroke Dock
Tel: 064 63 4548

Chapmans
Nun Street, St Davids
Tel: 043788 301

County Sports
3 Old Bridge, Haverfordwest
Tel: 0437 3740

Dudley Marine
Charles Street, Milford Haven
Tel: 064 62 2787

R.O. Evans
10 High Street, St Davids
Tel: 043 78 339

Fishermans Friend
Willing House, Main Street, Pembroke
Tel: 06463 2893

Fishguard Yacht & Boat Co.
Main Street, Goodwick, Fishguard
Tel: 0348 873377

Frank Donovan & Co.
61 Bush Street, Pembroke Dock
Tel: 064 68 2756

W.T.V. Humber
46-48 Dimond Street, Pembroke Dock
Tel: 064 63 2132

John Evans
1 Alban Square, Aberaeron
Tel: 054553 356

John James Anglers Corner
65 Robinson Street, Llanelli
Tel: 055 42 3981

C. Jones & Son
Emlyn Boot Stores, Newcastle Emlyn
Tel: 0239 710405

Lyric Sports Centre
Lyric Buildings, King Street, Carmarthen
Tel: 0267 7166

Malcolm Sports
Sycamore Street, Newcastle Emlyn
Tel: 0239 710756

Megicks
Corner Shop, Lampeter
Tel: 0570 422226

Morgan Davies
14 Bridge Street, Kidwelly
Tel: 055 43

Morris Bros
Troy House, St Julian Street, Tenby
Tel: 0834 2105

Morris Bros
Bank House, High Street, Tenby
Tel: 0834 2306

Morris Bros
37 Main Street, Pembroke
Tel: 064 63 5767

T. Newing & Sons Ltd.
13 Hamilton Terrace, Milford Haven
Tel: 064 62 3180

Sports Gear
24 Main Street, Pembroke
Tel: 064 63 3445

J.E. Rosser
3 Queen Street, Aberystwyth
Tel: 0970 7451

Sportsmans Corner
13 College Street, Ammanford
Tel: 0269 2834

Teifi Sports
4/5 Black Lion Mews, Cardigan
Tel: 0239 3679

Toms Sports Ltd.
10 Market Street, Haverfordwest
Tel: 0437 3653

Towy Sports
9 King Street, Llandeilo
Tel: 055 82 2637

M. & A. Williams
10A Pendre, Cardigan
Tel: 0239 2038

GWENT

Angling Centre
47 Church Street, Ebbw Vale
Tel: 0495 302518

rc Tackle
Caerleon Road, Newport
l: 0633 215785

ave Richards (Angling
pplies)
Church Road, Newport
: 0633 54910

raham Willis Tackle & Sports
Tredegar Street, Risca
: 0633 612513

n Rowe Fishing Tackle
t 1 Ruskin Avenue, Rogerstone,
wport
: 063343 5950

J. Larcombe
ortland Buildings, Commercial
et, Pontypool
: 049 553935

H. Powell & Sons
Chapel Street, Pontnewydd,
mbran
06333 2465

M. Fishing Tackle
Monk Street, Abergavenny
0873 3175

eets Fishing Tackle
hycarne Street, Usk
02913 2552

WYNEDD

sports & Hobbies
ch Road, Barmouth
0341 280240

glers Den
Madoc Street, Llandudno
0492 79931

gling & Gun Centre
3 High Street, Porthmadog
0766 2464

nbrian Supplies
le Street, Conway
049263 2275

wy Angling Centre
se Hill Street, Conwy

nty Sports
nty Buildings, Stanley Street,
head
0407 2059

Castle Gift Shops Ltd.
High Street, Llanberis
Tel: 028 682 379

B.W. Davies
Lord Street, Blaenau Ffestiniog
Tel: 076 681 414

I. & O. Davies
Siop-y-Llan, Dolwyddelan
Tel: 069 06237

YR Eryr Sports & Tackle
31/33 High Street, Bala
Tel: 0678 520370

W.D. Evans & Son
London House, 4/5 Seaview Terrace,
Aberdovey
Tel: 065 472 353

M.T. Houghton
1/3 Mona Street, Amlwch
Tel: 0407 830267

Howards Fishing Tackle
72 Pool Street, Caernarfon
Tel: 0286 2671

D. Huxley Jones
1/3 South Penrallt, Caernarfon
Tel: 0286 3186

J's Fishing Parlour
16 Newry Street, Holyhead
Tel: 0407 4171

Ken Johnson
Devon House, Water Street, Menai
Bridge
Tel: 0248 714508

Millsports
21 Church Street, Llangefni
Tel: 0248 723938

R.P. Owen
Stanley House, Old Market Square,
Holyhead
Tel: 0407 2458

G. Payne
Derwen, Peny Bryn, Blaenau Ffestiniog
Tel: 076 676 2787

W.E. Pugh
74 High Street, Bala
Tel: 0678 520 248

Ron Edwards
6 Dean Street, Bangor
Tel: 0248 2811

Tackle & Guns
Devon House, Water Street, Menai
Bridge
Tel: 0248 714508

Trade Winds Sports Shop
The Harbour, Abersoch
Tel: 075881 2530

Westmorlands
19 Lloyd Street, Llandudno
Tel: 0492 77126

R.T.M. Wilkes
Marine & Caravan Supplies, Calder
Stores, Llwyngwril
Tel: 0341 250394

MID GLAMORGAN

W.G. Bale
Coed Y Brain, 4 Bartlett Street,
Caerphilly
Tel: 0222 882802

Brian Rowe
96 Nolton Street, Bridgend
Tel: 0656 58254

Coey-y-Brain
4 Bartlett Street, Caerphilly
Tel: 0222 882802

Lloyds Sports
40 Cannon Street, Aberdare
Tel: 0685 873717

Meadbro Sports
52 Hannah Street, Porth
Tel: 044 361 3905

The Merthyr Angling Shop
Unit 4, Station Arcade, High Street,
Merthyr Tydfil
Tel: 0685 812740

Pontypridd Angling Supplies
Masonic Buildings, High Street, Groug,
Pontypridd
Tel: 0443 407747

Pyle Marine Ltd.
Garden & Leisure Centre, Pyle Nr
Bridgend
Tel: 0656 742431

Ralph Evans (Sports)
31 Commercial Street, Kenfighill,
Bridgend
Tel: 0656 741178

Tony's Tackle Shop
18 Castle Street, Caerphilly
Tel: 0222 885409

POWYS

W. Cook
The Medical Hall, Llanwrtyd Wells
Tel: 059 13207

Home Handicrafts
15 Short Bridge Street, Newtown
Tel: 0686 26917

G.H. Lindup
North Road, Llanymynech
Tel: 0691 830 027

Sue Burgess Fishing Tackle
The Industrial Estate, Brecon
Tel: 0874 4621

Tom Aylward Sports
21 Maengwyn Street, Machynlleth
Tel: 0654 2438

SOUTH GLAMORGAN

Angling Supplies
172 Penarth Road, Cardiff
Tel: 0222 20723

Astoria Sports
15 Holton Road, Barry
Tel: 0446 735165

A. Bale & Sons
3 Frederick Street, Cardiff
Tel: 0222 29929

Barry Chandlers & Marine Services
20 Plymouth Road, Barry
Tel: 0446 742204

Berkeley Stores
Rhoose, Barry
Tel: 0446 71024

Clanfields
23 Winston Square, Colcot
Tel: 0446 741707

The Fishing & Angling Centre
109 High Street, Barry
Tel: 0446 746 598

Garry Evans
105 Whitchurch Road, Cardiff
Tel: 0222 42361

Home & Gardening Supplies
64/68 Countisbury Avenue, Llanrumney, Cardiff
Tel: 0222 78036

L.M. Sports Place Ltd.
2 The Precinct, Llantwit Major
Tel: 04465 2332

Sportsmail Ltd.
3 Allensbank Road, Heath, Cardiff
Tel: 0222 4316

Vale Fisheries
Llandow Industrial Estate, Cowbridge
Tel: 04463 4848

WEST GLAMORGAN

Capstan House
Beach Street, Swansea
Tel: 0792 54756

G.L. Davies
Cross Road, Loughor, Swansea
Tel: 0792 892142

Derek Jones
South Dock Bridge, Swansea
Tel: 0792 466096

T.G. Hughes
87 High Street, Gorseinon, Swansea
Tel: 0792 894218

Linnard Sports Ltd.
25 High Street, Swansea
Tel: 0792 55631

P.E. Mainwaring
9 Dillwyn Road, Sketty, Swansea
Tel: 0792 22245

Selwyn Jenkins Sports Co. Ltd.
45 Station Road, Port Talbot
Tel: 0639 882787

Sports Outfitters
36 Windsor Road, Neath
Tel: 0639 2152

ISLE OF MAN

J. Mead
9 Parliament Street, Ramsey
Tel: 0624 813092

Nods for Rods
11 Castle Street, Douglas
Tel: 0624 21562

R.C. Turner
Victoria Street, 12 Villiers Buildings, Douglas
Tel: 0624 5950

Sporting Sams
Church Road, Port Erin
Tel: 0624 832181

CHANNEL ISLANDS

Bakers
43 The Pollet, St. Peter Port, Guernse
Tel: 0481 21139

G.L.F. Domaille
The Bridge, St. Sampson, Guernsey
Tel: 0481 44542

R.E. Duplain
23 Victoria Street, Alderney
Tel: 048 182 2414

The Fishing Centre
20 Sand Street, St. Helier, Jersey
Tel: 0534 25095

Marquand Bros. Ltd.
North Quay & Pier Steps, St. Peter Pc
Guernsey
Tel: 0481 20962

D. Peacock
Les Rocquettes, St. Annes, Alderney
Tel: 048 182 2702

PJN Fishing Tackle
7 Beresford Market, St. Helier, Jersey
Tel: 0534 74875

Stewart Hunt
71 King Street, 28 Broad Street, Jerse
Tel: 0534 23458

Tackle & Accessories Centre
Street Market, St. Helier, Jersey
Tel: 0534 71855

Tackle & Accessories Centre
30 Bordage, St. Peter Port, Guernsey
Tel: 0481 45335

F.R. Wheway
16 Broad Street, St. Helier, Jersey
Tel: 0534 20194

Your Guide to
Day Permit Fishing

Day Permit Fishing

Day Permit Fishing

This section is intended to provide, wherever possible, two essential pieces of information. Firstly, to provide the name and telephone number of an individual or organisation directly concerned with the water in question. In practice this normally means the riparian owner. The visiting angler therefore has an information source available so that questions can be asked in advance of a planned fishing excursion about the nature of the fishing, the tackle requirements, type of bait to be used etc. At the same time the exact location and the access points to the water can be discovered. Secondly, to provide information on exactly where to purchase the permit to fish the particular water. Exceptionally, we have included details of some weekly and season permit waters. The reason for including season permit information is that where the cost of a season permit is low a visitor might like to have the option of fishing those waters and still consider it a worthwhile expense.

Visiting new fisheries where different skills and techniques may well have to be employed and enjoying the excitement of a new challenge and environment is one of the great pleasures open to the angler. It is sad therefore that the increasing trend is for waters to be closed for day permits and to cater only for season permits or restricted syndicates. Much of the blame for this trend must fall on a small minority of unthinking anglers who spare no though for others. Unruly behaviour, discourteous handling of your enquiry to a day permit water or leaving litter strewn around the fishing banks are certain ways to ensure that more and more waters will become closed. If you use this book to visit new fisheries then we hope that as a serious angler you will act responsibily and leave behind you a feeling of goodwill.

British Water Authority Boundaries & Divisions

1. SCOTLAND
2. NORTHUMBRIAN
3. NORTH-WEST
4. YORKSHIRE
5. WELSH
6. SEVERN-TRENT
7. ANGLIAN
8. THAMES
9. SOUTH-WEST
10. WESSEX
11. SOUTHERN

Anglian

GRIMSBY

BRIGG

Ancholme
Waithe Beck
Louth
LOUTH
SKEGNESS
Steeping
Eau
Barlings
Fossdyke Canal
LINCOLN
Witham
Bain
Witham
Slea
Sibsey Trader
BOSTON
South Forty Foot
GRANTHAM
Ui Glen
SPALDING
Welland
Nene
Glen
STAMFORD
Gwash
Sibson Fisheries
Rutland Water
PETERBOROUGH
Chater
Eyebrook Res.
Welland
MARCH
Alconbury Bk.
Old Bedford
New Bedford
ELY
KETTERING
Nene
Grafham Water
HUNTINGDON
Kym
Pitsford Res.
Brampton Branch
Bedford Ouse
CAMBRIDGE
Cam
Ravensthorpe Res.
NORTHAMPTON
Ouse
Ivel
Rhee
BEDFORD
Granta
Grand Union Canal
Ouse
BUCKINGHAM
MILTON KEYNES

KING'S LYNN
Nar
WISBECH
Ely Ouse
Wissey
Little Ouse
Lark
Cut Off Channel
BURY ST. EDMUNDS

Glaven
Bure
Ant
Wensum
DEREHAM
Tud
Yare
NORWICH
Yare
GT. YARMOUTH
Bure
Tas
Thet
Waveney
Blyth
Dove
Deben
Aide
Gipping
IPSWICH
Orwell
Stour
Brett
Colne
Ardleigh Res.
COLCHESTER
Pant
Abberton Res.
Chelmer
Blackwater
Cam
CHELMSFORD
Hanningfield Res.
Wid
Crouch
Roach
SOUTHEND-ON-SEA
Mar Dyke
Thames

Locator map
LINCOLNSHIRE
WELLAND AND NENE
GREAT OUSE
NORFOLK AND SUFFOLK
ESSEX

N

WHERE TO FISH—COARSE

Anglian Water Authority

Ambury Road,
Huntingdon
Tel: 0480 56181

Assistant Director (Fisheries):
A. J. Miller

Regional Biologist & Fisheries Scientist:
Dr. R. S. J. Linfield

Rod Licences
A regional rod licence allowing the holder to fish in all five river division areas is available. Alternatively each river division has a rod licence for fishing in that division area only. Rod licences are available from division offices or from tackle shops throughout the area.

Essex River Division

Rivers House
Springfield Road
Chelmsford
Tel: 0245 64721

Fisheries Officer: E. Pearson

RIVERS

River Can
CENTRAL & ADMIRALS PARKS, CHELMSFORD
Chelmsford District Council
Free fishing

River Chelmer
NR. VICTORIA ROAD, CHELMSFORD
Free fishing
See Chelmer & Blackwater Navigation Canal

River Colne
Colnes' A.S.
Sec: K. W. Murrells
Tel: 07875 3371

River Stour
BURES AND LITTLE HORKESLEY
Colnes' A.S.
Sec: K. W. Murrells
Tel: 07875 3371

CATTAWADE BRIDGE NR. MANNINGTREE
Lawford A.C.
Sec: R. W. Nunn
Mistley Hall Cottage, Clacton Road, Mistley

DEDHAM
Clovers Ltd., Flour Mills, Dedham
Tel: 0206 322226
Permits available in normal office hours

FLATFORD MILL
Elm Park Hornchurch & District A.A.
Sec: P. W. Darling
Tel: 04023 43246
Permits also available from bailiff on bank

GLEMSFORD TO RODBRIDGE
Long Melford & District A.A.
Sec: N. Mealham
6 Springfield Terrace, East Street, Sudbury
Tel: 0787 77139
Permits only available by advance booking in writing

GREAT HENNY, NR. SUDBURY
Great Cornard A.C.
Sec: P. Franklin
48 Queensway, Grt. Cornard, Sudbury
Tel: 0787 73766
Day permits in advance from secretary. Two weeks notice

GREAT HENNY, NR. SUDBURY
The Swan Public House
Mr May
Tel: 078729 238
Permits available on river bank or from above

RODBRIDGE, SUDBURY, HENNY & GREAT CORNARD
Sudbury & District A.A.
Sec: W. J. Gabbey
Tel: 0787 71597
Permits from bailiffs on bank or local tackle shops

River Wid
WRITTLE BRIDGE, NR. CHELMSFORD
Marconi A.S.
Sec: T. S. Palmer
Tel: 0245 71806
Permits by advance application to:
3 The Westerings, Great Baddow, Chelmsford

STILLWATERS

ABBERTON RESERVOIR
Layer-de-la-Haye, Nr. Colchester
Essex Water Co.
Tel: 020 634 356 or 234
Permits best booked in advance for popular dates either by writing or telephone

ALTON WATER RESERVOIR
Holbrook
Gipping A.P.S.
General Manager: G. Alderson
19 Clover Close, Ipswich
Tel: 0473 211402
Day permits also available from local tackle shops or general store near reservoir

AQUATELS LAKE
Basildon
Rentaplay Aquatels Ltd., Cranes Farm Road, Basildon
Tel: 0628 25118
Permits available on site

CENTRAL PARK LAKE
Chelmsford
Chelmsford District Council
Free fishing

CORRINGHAM FISHING POND
Corringham
Owner: C. Wood
Culham House, Church Road, Corringham
Tel: 03756 3799
Season permits only

DANBURY LAKES
Danbury Country Park
Essex County Council
Estates & Valuation Dept.
Tel: 0245 67222
Permits from warden at lakeside

GLOUCESTER PARK LAKE
Basildon
Basildon District Council
Tel: 0268 22881
Permits available on bank

GOSFIELD LAKE
Gosfield, Nr. Halstead
Halstead & Hedingham A.C.
Permits available from bailiff on bank

LAKE MEADOWS
Billericay
Basildon District Council
Tel: 0268 22881
Permits available on bank

LAKE WALK
Clacton on Sea
Lake View A.C.
Weekly tickets only, Monday to Friday from: E. J. Porter Tackle Shop, Clacton
Tel: 0255 25992

MILL LAKES
Holbrook
G. Nunn
Tel: 0473 328249
Coarse fishing permits available on site. Advance booking for trout fishing advisable

NORTHLAND LAKE
Pitsea
Basildon District Council
Tel: 0268 22881
Permits available on bank

OLD HALL POND
Thorndon Country Park
Essex County Council
Estates & Valuation Dept.
Tel: 0245 67222
Permits from warden at lakeside

PRIORY PARK LAKE
Southend
Southend Borough Council
Sports & Recreation Dept.
Tel: 0702 49451
Permits available on bank

ROCHFORD RESERVOIR
Rochford A.C.
Membership Sec: M. Freund
Tel: 0702 555143
Permits available from the Horse & Groom Public House adjacent to reservoir

DEBURY PARK LAKE
hend
hend Borough Council
rts & Recreation Dept.
0702 49451
mits available on bank

UTH OCKENDON CARP FISHERY
th Ockendon
oster
0702 42148
mits available on site

UTH OCKENDON PIT
th Ockendon
rrock A.C.
D. Nutt
04025 4832

ARFIELD PITS
on, Nr. Long Melford
g Melford & District A.A.
N. Mealham
ringfield Terrace, East Street, Sudbury
0787 77139
mits only available by advance booking
writing

ORNDON COUNTRY PARK
Old Hall Pond

ORPE PITS
Thorpe
wedon & District A.C.

E WARREN
nford-le-Hope
sure Sport A.C.
0784 61831
mits from bailiff on bank

E WARREN
nford-le-Hope
ll Club Angling Section
J. W. Deaves
03756 2107

EALD LAKE
ald Country Park
th Weald, Brentwood
ex County Council
ates & Valuation Dept.
0245 67222
mits available at lakeside

CANALS

helmer & Blackwater
avigation Canal
ELMSFORD TO MALDON
elmsford A.A.
D. C. Wilson
0245 87014
mits available from bailiff on towpath

NDON LOCK TO STONEHAMS
CKS
rconi A.S.
T. S. Palmer
0245 71806
mits available from lady at Sandon Lock
see notice board

GREAT OUSE RIVER DIVISION

Great Ouse River Division
Great Ouse House
Clarendon Road
Cambridge
Tel: 0223 61561

Fisheries Scientist:
C. A. Klee

RIVERS

River Cam
DIMMOCKS COTE
Histon & District A.S.
Sec: R. Cooper
Tel: 0954 502764
Permits available from local tackle shops
or: Cooper Bros. Tackle, Cambridge
Tel: 0223 65987

PIKE & EEL PUBLIC HOUSE TO GRANTCHESTER MEADOWS
Cambridge
Free Fishing

DIMMOCKS COTE
Cambridge Albion A.S.
Sec: D. Turpin
Tel: 0223 312032
Permits available from bailiff

CAMBRIDGE
Cambridge Fish Preservation & A.S.
Sec: A. C. Moden
Tel: 03543 3896
Permits from local tackle shops or bailiff on bank

CLAYHYTHE BRIDGE TO LEWINS WASH
Gt. Ouse Fishery Consultative Association
Day permits available from treasurer
L. C. Collins

River Delph
See Old Bedford River

River Great Ouse
Source to Bedford

BEDFORD & ENVIRONS
Bedford A.C.
Sec: Mrs Appleton
Tel: 0234 54708
Permits must be obtained in advance of fishing from:
Dixon Bros., Tavistock Street, Bedford
Tel: 0234 67145

BEDFORD
Bedford Town Centre
Free fishing on extensive stretches of the river

STONY STRATFORD/BETWEEN WOLVERTON & HAVERSHAM
Milton Keynes A.A.
Sec: M. D. Sands
6 Kipling Drive, Newport Pagnell
Tel: 090862 6534
Day permits available from local tackle shops

BUCKINGHAM
Buckingham District A.A.
Sec: T. Young
Tel: 029 671 3742
Permits available from:
John Wilkins, Tackle Shop, Buckingham

BLETSOE, NR. BEDFORD
Falcon Inn
Bletsoe
Tel: 0234 781464
Permits available from Inn

WHITINGS
Iron Trunk, G.V.C. to Haversham Viaduct
Milton Keynes A.A.
Sec: M. D. Sands
6 Kipling Drive, Newport Pagnell
Tel: 0908 62 6534
Day permits

River Great Ouse
(Including Old West River)

BEDFORD TO KING'S LYNN
Earith
Earith & District A.C.
Sec: T. A. Mitchell
Tel: 0487 842090
Permits available from Earith Post Office or The Crown Hotel, Earith

EARITH TO COTTENHAM
Histon & District A.S.
Sec: R. Cooper
Tel: 0954 502764
Permits available from local tackle shops or Cooper Bros Tackle, Cambridge
Tel: 0223 65987

HOUGHTON & HEMINGFORD
Houghton & Wyton & Hemingfords A.S.
Sec: A. J. Wilkinson
5 Thicket Road, Houghton
Annual, weekly and day permits from secretary or bailiff on bank

HUNTINGDON
Huntingdon A. & F.P.S.
Sec: W. Wallis
Tel: 0480 58935
Permits available from:
Hunts Angling, Huntingdon
Tel: 0480 55379

ST. NEOTS
St. Neots & District A. & F.P.S.
Sec: S. E. Smith
Tel: 0480 75995
Permits from above or bailiff on bank

ST. IVES
St. Ives A. & F.P.S.
Sec: P. Keepin
Tel: 0480 61165
Permits available from:
Handycrafts, Bridge Street, St. Ives
Kings Tackle, St. Ives

STRETHAM
Cambridge Albion A.S.
Sec: D. Turpin
Tel: 0223 312032
Permits available from bailiff

WHERE TO FISH—COARSE

NR. ELY
Cambridge Fish Preservation & A.S.
Sec: A. C. Moden
Tel: 03543 3896
Access via Randalls Farm at Barway
Permits from Cambridge tackle shops or from bailiff on bank

OFFORD
Offord & Buckden A.S.
Sec: A. Plumb
Tel: 0480 810595
Permits available from the car park, Offord

TEN MILE BANK TO DENVER
King's Lynn A.A.
Sec: G. T. Bear
1 Cock Drove, Downham Market
Tel: 03663 87114
Day and week permits from bailiff on bank

GODMANCHESTER
Godmanchester A. & F.P.S.
Sec: B. P. Doherty
5 Kisby Avenue, Godmanchester
Tel: 0480 54365
**Day permits from bailiff on bank and Stanjay Sports, Godmanchester
Carp to around 20lb**

ELY
Ely Town Centre
Free fishing

HOLYWELL TO EARITH
Over & Swavesey District A.S.
Sec: D. Cook
Tel: 0954 31141
Season permits only from above

LITTLEPORT TO ELY
Littleport A.C.
Sec: J. W. Shelsher
Tel: 0353 860787
Permits from above or local tackle shops

WATERBEACH
Waterbeach A.C.
Sec: C. Rickards
Tel: 0223 861162
Permits, weekdays only, available from The Lockhouse, Waterbeach

River Ivel
LANGFORD TO BROOM
Shefford & District A.A.
Sec: I. Anderson
44 Ampthill Road, Shefford, Beds
Tel: 0462 811577
Permits by written application to secretary

River Lark
BARTON MILLS TO WEST ROW
Lark A.P.S.
Sec: G. J. Amiss
22 Cricks Road, West Row, Bury St. Edmunds
Tel: 0638 715976
Day permits available from above or local tackle shops

NR. LITTLEPORT
Littleport A.C.
Sec: J. W. Shelsher
Tel: 0353 860787
Permits from above or local tackle shops

114

ISLEHAM
Isleham A.C.
Sec: E. G. Woodbridge
Tel: 06378 659
Permits from the Post Office, Isleham

River Little Ouse
WILTON BRIDGE, NR. LAKENHEATH
Brandon & District A.C.
Sec: P. Cooper
16 High Street, Feltwell, Thetford IP26 4AF
Tel: 0842 828448
Day permits from above and Edward's Shop, Brawdon

THETFORD AND SANTON DOWNHAM
Thetford & Breckland A.C.
Treasurer: J. H. Corston
Tel: 0842 61706
**Permits available from:
Thetford Sports & Toys
White Hart Street, Thetford
Tel: 0842 3338**

River Nar
NARBOROUGH
Owner: R. Munford
Belgrave House, The Maltings, Narborough
Tel: 0760 337266
Permits from above

SETCHEY TO KING'S LYNN
King's Lynn A.A.
Sec: G. T. Bear
1 Cock Drove, Downham Market
Tel: 03663 87114
Day and weekly permits available

Old River Nene
March
March Town Centre
Free fishing

NEAR MARCH
March Working Mens A.C.
Sec: H. Davies
Tel: 03542 3956
**Permits available from:
Derek Hawkes Tackle, March or bailiff on bank**

RAMSEY ST. MARYS AND BENWICK
Ramsey & District A.S.
Sec: P. E. Aldred
9 Blackmill Road, Chatteries
Tel: 03543 2232
Day, week or season permits from Wades Tackle, Ramsey or bailiff on bank

LOW CORNER FARM
Wisbech & District A.A.
Sec: Bryan Lakey
Tel: 0945 5465
Permits from above or from local tackle shops

STANGROUND TO HORSEY TOLL
Peterborough & District A.A.
Sec: W. W. Yates
Tel: 0733 67952
Permits from local tackle shops

New Bedford River
EARITH TO SUTTON GAULT BRIDGE
Cambridge Fish Preservation & A.S.

Sec: A. C. Moden
Tel: 03543 3896
Permits from: Chequers Public House, Sutton or Lockeeper at Earith

Old Bedford River/ River Delph
MEPAL, MANEA AND SUTTON
Cambridge Albion A.S.
Sec: D. Turpin
Tel: 0223 312032
**Permits available from the Three Pickle Public House, Mepal
Permits at Manea and Sutton available f bailiff**

MEPAL
Wisbech & District A.A.
Sec: Bryan Lakey
Tel: 0945 5465
Permits from above or local tackle shop

MANEA
Manea A.C.
Sec: R. M. Field
Tel: 03542 55286
Permits from above

Sheffield & District A.A.
Bailiff: T. Canham
Church Drove, Outwell
Tel: 094571 3492
**Permits from above or:
Three Holes Post Office
Welney Post Office**

River Ouzel
BLETCHLEY TO WILLEN
Milton Keynes A.A.
Sec: M. D. Sands
6 Kipling Drive, Newport Pagnell
Tel: 0908 6534
Day permits from local tackle shops

OLD LINSLADE
Gladiators A.A.
Sec: C. Green
Tel: 052527 446
**Permits from above or
Leighton Buzzard Tackle Centre**

SPARKS MEADOW
Milton Keynes A.A.
Sec: M. D. Sands
6 Kipling Drive, Newport Pagnell
Tel: 0908 62 6534

River Thet
KILVERSTONE AND BARNHAM
Thetford & Breckland A.C.
Treasurer: J. H. Corston
Tel: 0842 61706
**Permits available from: Thetford Sports & Toys, White Hart Street, Thetford
Tel: 0842 3338**

River Wissey
HILGAY AND STOKE FERRY
King's Lynn A.A.
Sec: G. T. Bear
1 Cock Drove, Downham Market
Tel: 03663 87114
Day and week permits from shop at Hilgay Bridge

KE FEN FERRY, NR. SOUTHERY
don Anglers Assoc.
01-520 7477
mits from bailiff at farm

CANALS

and Union Canal
KE HAMMOND TO
EDDINGTON
n A.C.
D. Rayner
0582 24583
mits from bailiff on bank

LVERTON
eon A.A.
G. E. Young
0908 76651
mits from Galleon Public House, Old
lverton or from bailiff on bank

KE HAMMOND
on Keynes A.A.
M. D. Sands
ling Drive, Newport Pagnell
090962 6534
permits from local tackle shops

TCHLEY TO WOOLSTON
chley Working Mens Club
mits available from local tackle shops

FENLAND DRAINS

t Drain
AR MARCH
ch Working Mens A.C.
H. Davies
03542 3956
mits available from:
ek Hawkes Tackle, March or bailiff on
k

ITTLESEY
ittlesey A.A.
L. Mumby
0733 203245
mits from tackle shops in Whittlesey or
erborough

t Drain
ffield & District A.A.
iff: T. Canham
rch Drove, Outwell
094571 3492
mits from above or
ee Holes Post Office
lney Post Office

atteris Working Mens A.C.
B. F. Kightly
Vest Street, Chatteris
03543 2015
and week permits from Jim's Corner
p, West Park Street, Chatteris
. Payne, Market Hill, Chatteris
yck's Tackle Shop, 1 Scargills Lane,
ch, Cambs.
wsons Tackle Shop, High Street, March
tteris Working Mens Club, Station
et, Chatteris

Hundred Foot Drain
See New Bedford River

Middle Level Main Drain
Sheffield & District A.A.
Bailiff: T. Canham
Church Drove, Outwell
Tel: 094571 3492
Permits from above or:
Three Holes Post Office
Welney Post Office

Whittlesey Dyke
Whittlesey A.A.
Sec: L. Mumby
Tel: 0733 203245
Permits from tackle shops in Whittlesey or
Peterborough

Counter Drain
Whittlesey A.A.
Sec: L. Mumby
Tel: 0733 203245
Permits from tackle shops in Whittlesey or
Peterborough

Fishers Dyke
Godmanchester A. & F.P.S.
Sec: B. P. Doherty
5 Kisby Avenue, Godmanchester
Tel: 0480 54365
Day permits from bailiff on bank or Stanjay
Sports, Godmanchester

Forty Foot Drain
**WELLSBRIDGE TO PUDDOCKS
BRIDGE**
Ramsey & District A.S.
Sec: P. E. Aldred
9 Black Mill Road, Chatteris
Tel: 03543 2232
Day, week and season permits from Wades
Tackle, Ramsey or bailiff on bank

**PUDDOCKS BRIDGE TO HORSEWAY
SLUICE**
Chatteris Working Mens A.C.
Sec: B. F. Kightly
18 West Street, Chatteris
Tel: 03543 2015
Day and week permits from Jim's Corner
Shop, West Park St., Chatteris
G. A. Payne, Market Hill, Chatteris
Deryck's Tackle Shop, 1 Scargill's Lane,
March, Cambs.
Crowsons Tackle Shop, High Street, March
Chatteris Working Men's Club, Station St.,
Chatteris

Yaxley Lode, Northwest Cut, Black Ham, Kings Dyke
Yaxley A.C.
Sec: K. G. Burt
55 Windsor Road, Yaxley, Peterborough
PE7 3JA
Tel: 0733 241119
Season permits from Peterborough tackle
shops, bailiff or secretary

Bevills Leam
Bevills Leam F.C.
Sec: Mrs Chapman
The Elms, Benwick
Tel: 035477 209

Pophams Eau
Sheffield & District A.A.
Bailiff: T. Canham
Church Drove, Outwell
Tel: 094571 3492
Permits from above or
Three Holes Post Office

Relief Channel
**DENVER, NR. DOWNHAM MARKET
TO KING'S LYNN**
Anglian Water Authority
Great Ouse River Division
Tel: 0223 61561
Bailiff: C. Cawkwell
Tel: 055385 336
Permits from AWA office or local tackle
shops

Cut off Channel
**WEREHAM ROAD BRIDGE TO
WISSINGTON**
Anglian Water Authority
Great Ouse River Division
Tel: 0223 61561
Bailiff: C. Cawkwell
Tel: 055385 336
Permits from AWA office or local tackle
shops

OTHER WATERS

Lees Brook
Godmanchester A. & F.P.S.
Sec: B. P. Doherty
5 Kisby Avenue, Godmanchester
Tel: 0480 54365
Day permits from bailiff on bank or Stanjay
Sports, Godmanchester

Reach Lode
NR. BURWELL
Cambridge Fish Preservation & A.S.
Sec: A. C. Moden
Tel: 03543 3896
Permits from bailiff or
Johns Tackle, Newmarket

Burwell Lode
BURWELL
Cambridge Fish Preservation & A.S.
Sec: A. C. Moden
Tel: 03543 3896
Permits from bailiff or
Johns Tackle, Newmarket

STILLWATERS

AIRMAN PIT
Shefford
Shefford & District A.A.
Sec: I. Anderson
Tel: 0462 811577
Permits available from:
Camp Stores, Hemlow Camp

BARKERS LANE PITS
Bedford
Bedford A.C.
Sec: Mrs Appleton
Tel: 0234 851429
Permits available from
Dixon Bros, Tavistock Street, Bedford
Tel: 0234 67145

WHERE TO FISH—COARSE

BLUE LAGOON
Bletchley
Milton Keynes A.A.
Sec: M. D. Sands
6 Kipling Drive, Newport Pagnell
Tel: 0908 62 6534
Day permits from local tackle shops

BUCKENHAM PITS
Mundford
Mundford A.C.
Sec: R. Whiting
9 Council House, Ickburgh, Thetford
Permits from above

COSGROVE LODGE PARK LAKES
Stony Stratford
Tel: 0908 563360
Permits available on site

ELEVENACRE LAKE
Stowe A.C.
Sec: C. Hawkins
Homelea, Dadford, Buckingham MK18 5JX
Tel: 02802 3973
Day permits from secretary only

EMBERTON PARK LAKES
Olney
Leighton Buzzard A.C.
F. McLellan
Tel: 0525 374702
Permits available on site

GRACE FISHERY
Purls Bridge, Nr. Manea
J. Possemis
Tel: 035478 316
Permits available on site

LITTLE PAXTON FISHERY
Little Paxton, Nr. St. Neots
Manager: Ian May
8 Davis Close, Little Paxton
Tel: 0480 212059
Permits must be obtained in advance

LOUGHTON LAKE
Milton Keynes A.A.
Sec: M. D. Sands
6 Kipling Drive, Newport Pagnell
Tel: 0908 62 6534
Day permits

LYNFORD LAKE
Mundford
Mundford A.C.
Sec: B. Whiting
9 Council Houses, Ickburgh, Thetford
Permits from above

Manea Pit
Manea
Manea A.C.
Sec: R. M. Field
Tel: 03542 55286
Permits from bailiff at pit

MILTON LAKE
Milton, Nr. Cambridge
Histon & District A.S.
Sec: R. Cooper
Tel: 0954 50274
Four permits per day by advance booking from: Cooper Bros. Tackle, Cambridge
Tel: 0223 65987

OCTOGAN LAKE
Stowe A.C.
Sec: C. Hawkins
Homelea, Dadford, Buckingham MK18 5JX
Tel: 02802 3973
Day permit available from secretary only

PRINGLES PIT
Mepal
Wisbech & District A.A.
Sec: Bryan Lakey
Tel: 0945 5465
Permits from above or local tackle shops

SCOULTON MERE
Between Watton and Hingham
Permits from keepers cottage on roadside

SNETTERTON PITS
Snetterton Gravel Co
Permits available on site

STOCKGROVE PARK
Leighton Buzzard
South Bedfordshire District Council
Tel: 0582 65061
Permits available on bank

STOWE LAKES
Stowe School, North Buckingham
Stowe A.C.
Sec: A. Summers
Tel: 0280 703725
Permits only from above

SWAN LAKE
Woolpit, Nr. Bury St. Edmunds
Mr Baker
Tel: 0359 40293

THOMPSON WATER
Nr. Watton
Permits available on bank

TRINDERS PIT
Soham
Mr. J. Trinder
Permits obtainable from the Post Office, Soham

WEST STOW COUNTRY PARK
Nr. Bury St. Edmunds
Bury St. Edmunds A.A.
Sec: N. J. Bruton
Tel: 0284 66074
Permits available on site

WILLEN LAKE
Milton Keynes
Milton Keynes A.A.
Sec: M. D. Sands
6 Kipling Drive, Newport Pagnell
Tel: 0908 62 6534
Day permits from local tackle shops

WILLOW VALE FARM
Steeple Claydon, Nr. Buckingham
Permits available on site

WOODLAKES CARAVAN & CAMPING PARK
Stowbridge, Nr. King's Lynn
Mr. Gorbould
Tel: 0553 810414
Permits from office on site

WYBOSTON PITS
Permits available from:
A. P. James, The Golf House
Wyboston Lakes, Nr. St. Neots

LINCOLNSHIRE RIVER DIVISION

Lincolnshire River Division
50 Wide Bargate, Boston
Tel: 0205 65661

Fisheries Officer: P. Kalinowski

RIVERS

River Ancholme
Scunthorpe & District A.A.
Sec: I. Robertson
Tel: 0724 845466
Permits available from local tackle shop
bailiff on bank

River Bain
Mostly private fishing

CONINGSBY
Kirkstead A.C.
Sec: M. Barnsdale
Tel: 0526 53359
Season permits only from above

River Slea (Kyme Eau)
CHAPEL HILL
Witham & District Joint Anglers Fed.
Sec: R. H. Hobley
Tel: 0522 683688
Permits from Crown Inn, Chapel Hill or bailiff on bank

River Steeping
Witham & District Joint Anglers Fed
Sec: R. H. Hobley
Tel: 0522 683688
Permits from local tackle shops or bailiff bank

River Till
THORPE BRIDGE – BRANSBY – OLD
Lincoln & District A.A.
Sec: T. McCarthy
Tel: 0522 29006
Permits available from Lincoln tackle sh

River Witham
BASSINGHAM TO BECKINGHAM
Lincoln and environs
Lincoln & District A.A.
Sec: T. McCarthy
Tel: 0522 29006
Permits available from Lincoln tackle sh
or bailiff on bank

LINCOLN TO BOSTON
Witham & District Joint Anglers Fed.
Sec: R. H. Hobley
Tel: 0522 683688
Permits from local tackle shops or bailiff bank

CANALS

Fossdyke Canal
HARDWICK

shalls A.C.
nits available from 'The Tackle Shop',
sborough
0427 3002

LINCOLN

am & District Joint Anglers Fed.
R. H. Hobley
0522 683688
nits available from the Pyewipe Inn,
tackle shops or bailiff on bank

antham Canal

ANTHAM TO WOOLSTHORPE

ntham A.A.
W. Hutchins
0476 75628
permits from tackle shops in Grantham

cester & District A.A.
J. C. Padmore
Churchill Road, Thurmaston
permits from tackle shops in Grantham

E RUTLAND ARMS INN

lsthorpe-by-Belvoir to Redmile Bridge,
s.
esford & District A.A.
C. George
infold Lane, Bottesford
0949 43357
and season permits from Rutland Arms
and Bull Inn, Bottesford

ts A.A.
L. E. Simpson
Main Street, Bulwell, Nottingham
permits available

uth Canal

WINGHAM FEN TO TETNEY LOCK

am & District Joint Anglers Fed.
R. H. Hobley
0522 683688
nits from bailiff or ticket dispenser at
ey Lock

OTHER WATERS

rgate & Sibsey Trader Drain

ston & District A.A.
: J. D. McGuire
hurchill Drive, Boston PE21 0NH
0205 64949
and annual permits available from
cle shops in Boston

linghay Skirth

TATTERSHALL

ham & District Joint Anglers Fed.
: R. H. Hobley
0522 683688
mits from Pub at Tattershall Bridge or
iff on bank

st and West Fen Catchwater

STON TO HAGNABY

ton & District A.A.
: J. D. McGuire
hurchill Drive, Boston PE21 0NH
and annual permits available from
cle shops in Boston

bhole

ton & District A.A.

Sec: J. D. McGuire
6 Churchill Drive, Boston PE21 0NH
Day and annual permits available from
local tackle shops

South Forty Foot Drain

Boston & District A.A.
Sec: J. D. McGuire
6 Churchill Drive, Boston PE21 0NH
Day and annual permits available from
tackle shops in Boston

Timberland Delph

Witham & District Joint Anglers Fed.
Sec: R. H. Hobley
Tel: 0522 683688
Permits from Pub and tackle shop at
Kirkstead Bridge

Wainfleet Relief Channel

Witham & District Joint Anglers Fed.
Sec: R. H. Hobley
Tel: 0522 683688
Permits from local tackle shops or bailiff on
bank

STILLWATERS

BARTON BROADS
Barton on Humber
Owner: Mr. Murray
Tel: 0652 32237
Advance booking advisable for carp lake
only. Otherwise permits available on site

BOULTHAM PARK LAKE
Lincoln
Lincoln & District A.A.
Sec: T. McCarthy
Tel: 0522 29006
Permits available from local tackle shops

CASTLE LEISURE PARK
Tattershall
Tel: 0526 43193
Permits available on site

CHAPEL BOATING LAKE
Nr. Skegness
Tel: 0754 72631
Permits available on site

DENTON RESERVOIR
Denton, Nr. Grantham
Grantham A.A.
Sec: W. Hutchins
Tel: 0476 75628
Permits available from Grantham tackle
shops

ELMERS ROAD PIT
Horncastle
Permits available on bank

GILBERTS
Oasby, Nr. Sleaford
Permits available on site

HARTSHOLME LAKE
Lincoln & District A.A.
Sec: T. McCarthy
Tel: 0522 29006
Permits available from local tackle shops

HATTON TROUT FISHERY
Nr. Wragby
Permits available on site

HILL VIEW FISHERY
Hogsthorpe, Nr. Skegness
Owner: Mr. Raynor
Tel: 0754 72979

HOLLANDS PIT
Nr. Skegness
Permits available on site

MOAT FARM LAKE
Nr. Skegness
Permits available on site

NORTH SOMERCOATES LAKE
Nr. Grimsby
Permits available on site

PARTNEY LAKE
Partney, between Skegness & Horncastle
Permits from nearby Shell Garage

REVESBY RESERVOIR
Revesby
The Revesby Estate
Permits available on bank

RICHMOND LAKES
North Hykeham, Lincoln
Tel: 0522 688026
Permits available on bank

STARMERS PIT
Lincoln
Lincoln & District A.A.
Sec: T. McCarthy
Tel: 0522 29006
Permits from local tackle shops

STICKNEY BRICK PITS
Nr. Boston
Permits available on site

SUTTON LAKE
Sutton-on-Sea
Permits available on site

SWANHOLME LAKES
Lincoln
Witham & District Joint Anglers Fed.
Sec: R. H. Hobley
Tel: 0522 683688
Permits available on site

SYCAMORE LAKE
Burgh Le Marsh, Nr. Skegness
Tel: 0754 810749
Permits available on site

WEST ASHBY GRAVEL PIT
Horncastle
Permits available on site

NORFOLK & SUFFOLK RIVER DIVISION

Yare House
62-64 Thorpe Road
Norwich
Tel: 0603 61561

Fisheries Officer: C. K. Jones

WHERE TO FISH—COARSE

RIVERS

River Ant
LUDHAM TO HOW HILL
Anglian Water Authority
Norfolk & Suffolk River Division
Tel: 0603 615161
Free fishing

River Bure
ACLE & BURGH MARSHES
Anglian Water Authority
Norfolk & Suffolk River Division
Tel: 0603 615161
Free fishing

BUREBANK TROUT FISHERIES
Itteringham, Nr. Aylsham
D. Green
Tel: 026387 666
Limited permits by advance booking
Closed 1982/83 Season
Open again 1983/4 Season

BURGH
T. Crix
Mill House, Burgh
Tel: 026373 2117
Permits by arrangement in advance

BUXTON
L. Ford
Old Mill Hotel, Buxton
Tel: 060546 846761
Permits from above

ST. BENETS
Norwich & District A.A.
Sec: Mr Wigg
Tel: 0603 43625
**Permits available from cottage near water
but access difficult to find for newcomers**

**SOUTH WALSHAM & UPTON/
WOODBASTWICK**
Anglian Water Authority
Norfolk & Suffolk Rivers Division
Tel: 0603 615161
Free fishing

River Deben
Framlingham & District A.C.
Sec: B. Finbow
Tel: 0728 860123
Permits from above

WICKHAM MARKET
Woodbridge & District A.C.
Permits available from:
Rod & Gun Shop, Woodbridge
Tel: 03943 2377

River Gipping
SPROUGHTON BRIDGE NR. IPSWICH
Gipping A.P.S.
General Manager: G. Alderson
Tel: 0473 211402
Permits also available from:
Local tackle shops in Ipswich

River Thurne
COLDHARBOUR
Norwich & District A.A.
Sec: Mr Wigg
Tel: 0603 43625

Permits available from cottage near water
but access difficult to find for newcomers

**POTTER HEIGHAM—LUDHAM AREA
MARTHAM AND REPPS AREA
THURNE SOUTH AND NORTH
MARSHES**
Anglian Water Authority
Norfolk & Suffolk River Division
Tel: 0603 615161
Free fishing

River Waveney
BUNGAY COMMON
Suffolk County Amalgamated A.A.
Sec: G. Howard
Tel: 0502 4024
**Permits available from Bungay Angling
Centre, Bungay**
Tel: 0986 3842

Diss & District A.C.
Sec: M. R. Howard
7 Masefield Road, Diss
Tel: 0379 51494
Annual membership required

EARSHAM TO GELDSTON
Bungay Cherry Tree A.C.
Sec: I. R. Gosling
Tel: 0986 2982
**Weekly permits available from Bungay
Angling Centre, Bungay**
Tel: 0986 3842
**Good Bream water with fish to 8 & 9lbs.
Also good Roach and Chub**

Harleston, Wortwell & District A.C.
Sec: J. Adamson
Tel: 0379 3952
**Season permits only (£4 in 80-81 season)
from: G. Denny & Sons Ltd., Market Place,
Harleston**
Tel: 0379 852248

**NEEDHAM AND WEYBREAD
EARSHAM/BARSHAM/
WORLINGHAM**
Anglian Water Authority
Norfolk and Suffolk River Division
Tel: 0603 615161

WAINFORD MILL
Anglian Water Authority
Norfolk and Suffolk River Division
Tel: 0603 615161
Permits available from above

River Wensum
LENWADE
London Anglers Association
Tel: 01 520 7477
Bailiff: G. Fisher
Tel: 0603 404288
Permits available from bailiff on bank

LYNG, LYNG EASTAUGH
Dereham & District A.C.
Sec: H. E. Mortram
Yaxham Road, Mattishall
Tel: 0362 850151
**Day permits from Chambers Tackle Shop,
Dereham**

NORWICH CITY CENTRE
Norwich City Council Amenities Dept.
Tel: 0603 22233

SWANTON MORLEY
Permits available from Waterfall Cottage
Swanton Morley
Tel: 036283 424

UPPER WENSUM
Fakenham A.C.
Sec: G. Twite
16 Back Street, Hempton, nr. Fakenham
Tel: 0328 4637
Day permits available from:
Len Bryers Tackle Shop
Bridge Street, Fakenham
Tel: 0328 2543

River Yare
**BUCKENHAM FERRY/CANTLEY/
ROCKLAND CLAXTON/LANGLEY**
Anglian Water Authority
Norfolk and Suffolk River Division
Tel: 0603 615161
Free fishing

**EASTON/BAWBURGH/COLNEY/
EARLHAM**
Anglian Water Authority
Norfolk and Suffolk River Division
Tel: 0603 615161
Permits available from above

STILLWATERS

ALDERFEN BROAD
Neatishead
Mr G. Haylett
George Haylett Tackle Shop, Wroxham
Tel: 06053 2453
**Limited number of permits daily. Fishing
from rowing boat. Advance booking
advisable**

BARTON BROAD
Free fishing
Boats for hire from Cox Bros.
Tel: 069260 206

BEESTON LAKE
Neatishead
**Permits available by advance booking:
Keepers Cottage, Beeston Park
Neatishead, Nr. Norwich**
Tel: 0692 630688

BILLINGFORD PIT
Billingford, Nr. Dereham
Dereham & District A.C.
Sec: H. E. Mortram
Yaxham Road, Mattishall, Dereham
Tel: 0362 850141
**Day permits from Chambers Tackle Shop
Dereham**

BLICKLING LAKE
Blickling Hall, Blickling
Nr. Aylsham
Anglian Water Authority
Norfolk and Suffolk River Division
Tel: 0603 615161
Authority Water Bailiff: Tel: 026373 3106
Permits from A.W.A. or local tackle shop

BOOTON CLAY PITS
Cawston, Nr. Aylsham
Aylsham & District A.S.
Sec: Mr Sutton
Tel: 026373 2433

its from bailiff of
ston Post Office
es Tackle Shop, Aylsham

GE LAKES
vade
on Anglers Association
01 520 7477
its available from bailiff

OME PITS
ne, Nr. Bungay
ire at Bungay Angling Club, Bungay
0986 3842

STON HALL PONDS
ingham
lingham & District A.C.
0728 860123
its from above

CHINGHAM PIT
ungay
ay Cherry Tree A.C.
I. R. Gosling
0986 2982
kly permits obtained from
ay Angling Centre, Bungay
0986 3842

BRIGG LAKE
rigg Estate, Roughton
ooth
026375 444
six permits per day. Must be booked
vance

Y BROAD
fishing, boat only
s available from: Mr Thompson
049377 250

TON DECOY LAKE
on, Nr. Lowestoft
Green
0502 703568
fishing only – advance booking
sable

TON LAKE
Great Yarmouth
den: W. Mussett
049379 208
nits available on site

EAT LODGE PONDS
hlingham
hlingham & District A.C.
0728 860123
nits available from above

EAT ORMESBY BROAD
fishing, boat only
s available from Eels Foot Hotel
0493 730217

EAT WITCHINGHAM LAKES
vade
on Anglers Association
01 520 7477
nits available from bailiff on bank

TON PARK LAKE
h of Norwich
nits available on site

RDLEY MARSHES
on

Permits available from:
P. Nicholls
14 Market Place, Loddon

HAVERINGLAND LAKE
Nr. Cawston
Anglian Water Authority
Norfolk and Suffolk River Division
Tel: 0603 615161
Permits available from above or
The Post Office, Cawston
Tel: 060542 322

HEVENINGHAM LAKE
Heveningham Hall Estate
Nr. Halesworth
Permits available from bank

HEVINGHAM LAKES
Hevingham, Nr. Aylsham
Mr C. Matthewson
Tel: 060548 368
Permits available at entrance to Lakes

HICKLING BROAD AND HEIGHAM SOUND
Norfolk Naturalists Trust
Warden Tel: 069261 276
Permits available on site

HOLKHAM LAKE
Holkham Park
Nr. Wells-next-the-Sea
Permits available from the main gate

HOMERSFIELD LAKE
Homersfield
Mr M. Symonds
Tel: 098686 676 or 530
Permits available from shop on site of
Waveney Valley Lakes, Wortwell

HOLTON GRAVEL PITS
Nr. Halesworth
Permits available from:
Rod & Gun Shop, Woodbridge
Tel: 03943 2377

HORSEY MERE
Nr. Great Yarmouth
Mr J. Buxton
Tel: 049376 235
Permits available from above at Horsey Hall
or from the bailiff Mr Tubby in village

LETHERINGSETT LAKE
Letheringsett, Nr. Holt
Permits available from bank

LITTLE ORMESBY BROAD
Free fishing, boat only
Boats through G. French
Tel: 0493 732173

LONELY FARM LEISURE PARK
Nr. Saxmundham
Tel: 0728 3344
Permits for coarse and trout fishing
available on site

LYNG EASTAUGH PIT
Dereham & District A.C.
Sec: H. E. Mortram
Yaxham Road, Mattishall
Tel: 0362 850141
Day permits available from Chambers
Tackle Shop, Dereham

REDGRAVE LAKE
Botesdale, Nr. Diss
Private owner at Redgrave Hall
Tel: 0473 2318449
Permits available from bailiff on bank

REDHOUSE FARM MOAT
Dennington
Framlingham & District A.C.
Tel: 0728 860123
Permits available from above

ROLLESBY BROAD
Free fishing, boat only
Boats available through Mr Milstead
Tel: 0493 748232

SELBRIGG LAKE
Hempstead, Nr. Holt
Permits available from:
Mr Wright, Wrights Farm

STATION PIT
Bungay
Suffolk County Amalgamated A.A.
Sec: G. Howard
Tel: 0502 4024
Free fishing

SWAN LAKE
Woolpit, Nr. Bury St. Edmunds
Mr Baker
Tel: 0359 40293
Permits available on bank

SWANTON MORLEY LAKES
Nr. East Dereham
Tel: 036283 424
Permits obtainable on site before
commencing fishing

TAVERHAM PITS
See Costessey Pits

THORPENESS MERE
Nr. Leiston
Free fishing

WAVENEY VALLEY LAKES
Wortwell
M. Symonds
Tel: 098386 530 or 676
Permits available from shop on site

WEYBREAD PITS
Nr. Harleston
Harleston, Wortwell & District A.C.
Sec: J. Adamson
Tel: 0379 3952
Day and week permits also available from:
G. Denny & Sons Ltd., Market Place,
Harleston
Tel: 0379 852248
Brockdish Service Station, Brockdish
Bungay Angling Centre, Bungay
C. G. Saye, 20 The Common, Harleston

WICKHAM MARKET RESERVOIR
Woodbridge & District A.C.
Permits available from:
Rod & Gun Shop, Woodbridge
Tel: 03943 2377

WOMACK WATER
Free fishing from bank

WORTHING PIT
North Elmham, Nr. Dereham
Dereham & District A.C.
Sec: H. E. Mortram
Yaxham Road, Mattishall, Dereham
Tel: 0362 850141
Permits available from Chambers Tackle Shop, Dereham

WELLAND & NENE RIVER DIVISION

Welland & Nene River Division
North Street, Oundle
Tel: 0832 73701

Fisheries Office: D. Moore

RIVERS

River Folly
PEAKIRK
Anglian Water Authority
Welland & Nene River Division
Tel: 0832 73701
Permits from local tackle shops

River Glen
SURFLEET – SPALDING
Spalding F.C.
Sec: D. Taylor
Tel: 0775 5117
Permits from:
Derek T. Ball Tackle, Spalding
Tel: 0775 4001
or bailiff on bank

SURFLEET TO RIVER MOUTH
Free fishing

River Nene
NASSINGTON – ELTON – FOTHERINGAY
Leicester & District Amalgamated Soc. of Anglers
Sec: L. H. Barnsley
Tel: 0533 704142
Permits from bailiff on bank

WELLINGBOROUGH
Road bridge to Down Stream Fence only
Wellingborough & District Nene A.C.
Sec: G. W. Barker
139 Knox Road, Wellingborough
Tel: 0933 223823
Day permits available from:
Albert Watts Tackle, Wellingborough
Tel: 0933 223919 or bailiff

DENFORD TO BARNWELL TO OUSE HARROLD AREA
Season permits only from local dealers or secretary, Wellingborough & District Nene A.C.

NORTHAMPTON – BECKETTS PARK MIDSUMMER MEADOWS AND BARNS MEADOWS
Northampton Borough Council
Tel: 0604 34734
Free fishing

WANSFORD – PETERBOROUGH – DOG IN A DOUBLET
Peterborough & District A.A.

Sec: W. W. Yates
75 Lawn Avenue, Peterborough PE1 3RA
Tel: 0733 67952
Day permits from local tackle shops or bailiffs

PETERBOROUGH
Anglian Water Authority
Welland & Nene River Division
Tel: 0832 73701
Permits from local tackle shops or the Dog in a Doublet Lock-keeper

NORTHAMPTON
Northampton Nene A.C.
Sec: S. H. Battison
Tel: 0604 409361
Permits available from Northampton tackle shops

COTTERSTOCK
Cotterstock A.A.
Sec: Mrs J. Popplewell
Tel: 0832 73671
Permits available from:
Church Farm, Cotterstock

OUNDLE
Oundle A.A.
Sec: D. Laxton
Tel: 0832 72289
Permits available from:
Riverside Hotel, Oundle
Greens Newsagents, Market Place, Oundle

WHISTON LOCK, EARLS BARTON TO HARDWATER LOCK, DODDINGTON
Earls Barton A.C.
Sec: B. F. Hager
113 Station Road, Earls Barton, Northampton
Tel: 0604 810888
Annual permits from M. Perkins (Shop), The Square, Earls Barton

River Welland
MARKET DEEPING SEVERAL FISHERY
MARKET DEEPING – CROWLAND
Deeping St. James A.C.
Sec: J. Cran
53 Castle Drive, Northborough
Tel: 0778 343691
Day permits available from Market Deeping Aquarium (personal callers only)

STAMFORD
Stamford Town Centre
Free fishing

CROWLAND – SPALDING
Anglian Water Authority
Welland & Nene River Division
Tel: 0832 73701
Permits from local tackle shops or The Golden Ball Inn, Spalding

TALLINGTON WEIR
Anglian Water Authority
Welland & Nene River Division
Tel: 0832 73701
Permits from local tackle shops

BARROWDEN – UFFINGTON
Stamford Welland A.A.
Sec: G. E. Bates
Tel: 0780 51060

Permits from local tackle shops or bailiff on bank

UFFINGTON – TALLINGTON
Stamford A.C.
Chairman: C. Howard
Tel: 0780 54542
Permits available from:
Stamford Angling Centre, Stamford
Tel: 0780 54541

CANALS

Coventry Canal
BISHOP STREET WHARF, COVENTRY TO BULL'S HEAD BRIDGE, POLESWORTH
Coventry & District A.A.
Sec: P. O'Connor
48 Loxley Close, Wood End, Coventry
Tel: 0203 612880
Day permits

Grand Union Canal
BUCKBY WHARF TO MUSCOTT M BRIDGE
Coventry & District A.A.
Sec: P. O'Connor
48 Loxley Close, Wood End, Coventry
Tel: 0203 612880
Day permits

FENNY STRATFORD AREA
Coventry & District A.A.
Sec: P. O'Connor
48 Loxley Close, Wood End, Coventry
Tel: 0203 612880
Day permits

WELFORD ARM
Coventry & District A.A.
Sec: P. O'Connor
48 Loxley Close, Wood End, Coventry
Tel: 0203 612880
Day permits

Leicester Canal
SECTION OF GRAND UNION CAN NORTON LOCK TO CRICK TUNNE
Coventry & District A.A.
Sec: P. O'Connor
48 Loxley Close, Wood End, Coventry
Tel: 0203 612880
Day permits

HARBOROUGH ARM
Market Harborough & District A.S.
Sec: J. W. Ashton
Tel: 0858 67301
Permits available from:
Sports & Toys, 7 St. Marys Road, Market Harborough
J. E. Wilkinson, Goward Street, Market Harborough

YELVERTOFT & HUSBANDS BOSWORTH
Leicester & District Amalgamated Societ of Anglers
Sec: L. H. Barnsley
Tel: 0533 704142
Permits from bailiff on bank

WEEDON – YARDLEY GOBION
Northampton Nene A.C.
Sec: S. H. Battison

0604 409361
mits available from Northampton tackle
ps

**LKINGTON AND NUNEATON
STRICT**
ventry & District A.A.
:: P. O'Connor
Loxley Close, Wood End, Coventry
: 0203 612880
y permits

ford Canal
NBURY BRIDGE TO NELL BRIDGE
ventry & District A.A.
:: P. O'Connor
Loxley Close, Wood End, Coventry
: 0203 612880
y permits

OTHER WATERS

**rnatt Drain
uth Drove Drain
rth Drove Drain
unter Drain
w River Drain
urth District Drain**
alding F.C.
:: D. Taylor
l: 0775 5117
mits from:
rek T. Ball Tackle, Spalding
l: 0775 4001
from bailiff on bank

oronation Channel
ALDING
glian Water Authority
elland & Nene River Division
l: 0832 73701
mits from local tackle shops or
e Golden Ball Inn, Spalding

reatford Cut
ARKET DEEPING
glian Water Authority
elland & Nene River Division
l: 0832 73701
mits from local tackle shops

axey Cut Drain
glian Water Authority
elland & Nene River Division
l: 0832 73701
mits from local tackle shops

oretons Leam Drain
TERBOROUGH – GUYHIRN
glian Water Authority
elland & Nene River Division
l: 0832 73701
mits from local tackle shops or
e Dog in a Doublet lock-keeper

STILLWATERS

INGTON PARK LAKE
rthampton
rthampton Borough Council
: 0604 34734
e fishing

ALVECOTE FISHERY
near Polesworth
Coventry & District A.A.
Sec: P. O'Connor
48 Loxley Close, Wood End, Coventry
Tel: 0203 612880
Day permits available

BARNWELL PICNIC PARK
Oundle
Permits available on bank

BECKETTS PARK LAKE
Northampton
Northampton Borough Council
Tel: 0604 34734
Free fishing

BILLING AQUADROME
Northampton
Tel: 0604 408181
Permits available on site

BILLING BROOK LAKES
Northampton
Northampton Borough Council
Tel: 0604 34734
Free fishing

CASTLE ASHBY LAKES
Castle Ashby
Bailiff: S. Greaves
Tel: 060129 302
Permits available on site

CRANSLEY RESERVOIR
Nr. Kettering
Anglian Water Authority
Northampton Water Division
Tel: 0604 21321
Permits from pump house at reservoir

DAVENTRY RESERVOIR
Daventry Country Park
Daventry County Council
Warden: 03272 77193
Permits available from vending machine on
site

DITCHFORD LAKE
Wellingborough & District Nene A.C.
Sec: G. W. Barker
139 Knox Road, Wellingborough
Tel: 0933 223823
Season permits from local dealers and
secretary

EAST FIELD PARK LAKE
Northampton
Northampton Borough Council
Tel: 0604 34734
Free fishing

FAWSLEY PARK
Nr. Daventry
Northampton Nene A.C.
Sec: S. H. Battison
Tel: 0604 409361
Permits from local tackle shops

GUNWADE LAKE
Peterborough
Peterborough Development Corporation
Tel: 0733 68931
Permits available on site

HOLLOWELL RESERVOIR
Ravensthorpe
Anglian Water Authority
Northampton Water Division
Tel: 0604 21321
Permits obtainable from automatic vending
machine

LAUNDE ABBEY LAKES
Nr. Uppingham
Permits available on bank

MAXEY PIT
Nr. Peterborough
Peterborough & District A.A.
Sec: W. W. Yates
75 Lawn Avenue, Peterborough, PE1 3RA
Tel: 0733 67952
Day permits from local tackle shops or
bailiffs

NAPTON RESERVOIRS
near Napton
Coventry & District A.A.
Sec: P. O'Connor
48 Loxley Close, Wood End, Coventry
Tel: 0203 612880
Day permits available

OVERSTONE PARK LAKES
Northampton
Overstone Solarium
Tel: 0604 45255
Permits available on site

RANSOME ROAD GRAVEL PITS
Northampton
Northampton Nene A.C.
Sec: S. H. Battison
Tel: 0604 409361
Permits from Northampton tackle shops

RANSOME ROAD LAKE
Northampton
Northampton Borough Council
Tel: 0604 34734
Free fishing

SIBSON FISHERIES
Stibbington, Nr. Peterborough
Tel: 0780 782621
Bailiff: Mr Bettinson
Tel: 0780 782733
Six coarse fishing permits per day
Four trout fishing permits per day
Advance booking advisable

SYWELL LAKE
Wellingborough & District Nene A.C.
Sec: G. W. Barker
139 Knox Road, Wellingborough
Tel: 0933 223823
Season permits from local dealers and
secretary

THRAPSTON GRAVEL PITS
Coventry & District A.A.
Sec: P. O'Connor
48 Loxley Close, Wood End, Coventry
Tel: 0203 612880
Day permits from bailiff on bank

WICKSTEED PARK LAKE
Kettering
Kettering Thrapston & District A.A.
Sec: L. Garrett
Tel: 0536 517665
Permits available on bank

Anglian Water Authority

Ambury Road, Huntingdon
Tel: 0480 56181

Assistant Director (Fisheries):
A. J. Miller
Regional Biologist & Fisheries Scientist:
Dr R. S. J. Linfield

ESSEX RIVER DIVISION

Rivers House
Springfield Road
Chelmsford
Tel: 0245 64721

Fisheries Officer: E. Pearson

Rod Licences
A regional rod licence allowing the holder
to fish in all five river division areas is
available. Alternatively each river division
has a rod licence for fishing in that division
area only. Rod licences are available from
division offices or from tackle shops
throughout the area.

STILLWATERS

ARDLEIGH RESERVOIR
Nr. Colchester on A137
Colchester – Manningtree Road
Anglian Water Authority/
Tendring Hundred Waterworks Co
Fishery Manager: R. Connell
Tel: 0206 230642
Day permits available on site

CHESTERFORD TROUT FISHERIES
Gt. Chesterford, Saffron Walden
Day tickets available from
Tel: 0799 30493. Advance booking
essential

EAST HANNINGFIELD LAKE
Nr. Chelmsford
Essex Water Co
Hanningfield Works, South Hanningfield,
Chelmsford
Tel: 0245 400381
Day permits available by advance booking
from D. Benson
Tel: 0245 400269

MILL LAKES
Holbrook
G. Nunn
Tel: 0473 328249
Coarse fishing permits available on site
Advance booking for Trout fishing
advisable

GREAT OUSE RIVER DIVISION

Great Ouse River Division
Great Ouse House
Clarendon Road
Cambridge
Tel: 0223 61561

Fisheries Scientist: C. A. Klee

RIVERS

River Lark
BARTON MILLS TO WEST ROW
Lark A. & P.S.
Sec: G. J. Amiss
Tel: 0638 715976
Permits available from above or local
tackle shops

———

NR. LITTLEPORT
Littleport A.C.
Sec: J. W. Shelsher
Tel: 0353 860787
Permits from above or local tackle shop

ISLEHAM
Isleham A.C.
Sec: E. G. Woodbridge
Tel: 063878 659
Permits from the Post Office, Isleham

River Nar
NARBOROUGH
Owner: R. Munford
Belgrave House, the Maltings, Narboroug
Tel: 0760 337266
Permits from above

SETCHEY TO KING'S LYNN
King's Lynn A.A.
Sec: G. T. Bear
Tel: 03663 4114

STILLWATERS

BLOCK FEN FISHERY
Nr. Chatteris
Permits from:
Chatteris Aqua Sports Ltd.
Block Fen, Nr. Chatteris

CHURCH HILL FARM
Mursley, Bucks
Tel: 029672 524
Day permits available from T. Daniels
Church Hill Farm, Mursley MK17 0RS
See Advertisement this Section

GRAFHAM WATER
Nr. Huntingdon
Anglian Water Authority
Bedford Water Division
Tel: 0480 810247
Fishing Lodge
Tel: 0480 810531
Permits available on site

HATCHERY HOUSE FISHERY
Barrow, Nr. Bury St. Edmunds
Suffolk
Day permits: Rutters,
18 Angel Hill, Bury St. Edmunds, Suffolk
Tel: 0284 62131
Permits bookable in advance

LINFORD LAKES
Nr. Newport Pagnell
Tel: 0865 882215

CHURCH HILL FARM TROUT FISHERY

FISHING IN PEACEFUL BUCKINGHAMSHIRE COUNTRYSIDE THE CIVILISED WAY

The fishing consists of 2 lakes with a total of 10 acres of water. Stock Density is high and maintained by daily restocking. The average catch is just over two fish per rod and the average size of the fish is a little more than 2lb. Price £11.75 per day (2 brace limit), evening £6 (1 brace limit). Fishing starts 9am, finishes 9pm.
Lunches are served daily and are freshly prepared every day except Sunday. The price is £3.50 or £1.50 for Ploughman's Lunch.
The shop on the premises provides the angler with the opportunity of buying his requirements including most popular flies for the water. One may also try one of the range of the New Church Hill Gold Carbon Fibre Rods.

Enquiries to:
TIM DANIELS, CHURCH HILL FARM, MURSLEY, BUCKS MK17 0RS
Tel: Mursley (029672) 524 or S.A.E. please

...TLE HEATH FARM
...e Heath Road, Gamlingay, Nr. Sandy
...0767 50301
...permits by advance booking from
...ve

...GHTON FISHERY
...ord Trout Farm
...Hitchin
...0462 4201

...ING LAKE TROUT FISHERIES
...linge, Nr. Bury St. Edmunds
...R. C. Nunn
...ckle Up'', St. John's Street,
...St. Edmunds
...0284 5022
...permits limited, advance booking
...ntial

...GRITH TROUT FARM
...rith, Nr. Milton Keynes
...permits on site
...0525 714012

...ARAGE SPINNEY LAKE
...e Linford, nr. Newport Pagnell
...permits in advance only from
...). Sando, 6 Kipling Drive,
...vport Pagnell, MK16 8EB
...0908 62 6534

...ODLAKES CARAVAN & ...MPING PARK
...bridge, Nr. King's Lynn
...Gorbould
...0553 810414
...nits from office on site

LINCOLNSHIRE RIVER DIVISION

Lincolnshire River Division
50 Wide Bargate, Boston
Tel: 0205 65661

Fisheries Officer: P. Kalinowski

STILLWATERS

BUCKMINSTER PARK LAKE
Buckminster
Tel: 0476 860472

CASTLE LEISURE PARK
Tattershall
Tel: 0526 43193
Permits available on site

HILL VIEW TROUT LAKE
Hogsthorpe, Nr. Skegness
Owner: K. Raynor
Hill View Trout Lake, Skegness Road, Hogsthorpe, Skegness, Lincs
Tel: 0754 72979
Day permits available in advance from above

SWANHOLME LAKES
Nr. Lincoln
Mr J. Pickard
Tel: 0522 690087

TOFT NEWTON RESERVOIR
Market Rasen
Anglian Water Authority
Lincolnshire River Division
Tel: 0205 65661
Bailiff Tel: 06737 453
Permits available at reservoir

NORFOLK & SUFFOLK RIVER DIVISION

Yare House
62-64 Thorpe Road
Norwich
Tel: 0603 61561

Fisheries Officer: C. K. Jones

STILLWATERS

BUREBANK TROUT FISHERIES
Itteringham, Nr. Aylsham
Mr D. Green
Tel: 026387 666
Limited permits – advance booking advisable
Closed 1982/83 season. Open again 1983/84 season

EAST TUDDENHAM FISHERY
Nr. Norwich
Norfolk and Suffolk Flyfishers Society
Chairman: S. Walker
Tel: 0603 49038
Day tickets only available to members of Society – subscription £5.00

EDGEFIELD HALL LAKE
Edgefield Hall, Nr. Holt
Tel: 026371 2437
Permits available on site

LONELY FARM LEISURE PARK
Nr. Saxmundham
Tel: 0728 3344
Permits for coarse and trout fishing available on site

SHERMANBURY PLACE FISHER
Nr. Henfield
Enquiries and season permits from Fishery Manager, G. Rowles, Lakeview, Old Bury Hill, Dorking
Day permits available for short while in order that anglers can try out fishery

SWANTON MORLEY LAKES
near East Dereham, Norfolk
Day permits available from Waterfall Cottage
Swanton Morley after 8am
Tel: 036283 424
Permits must be acquired before fishing commences.
Season permits available form Water Recreation, 47 Clockhouse Lane, Ashford, Middx (S.A.E. please)

WELLAND & NENE RIVER DIVISION

Welland & Nene River Division
North Street, Oundle
Tel: 08322 3701

Fisheries Officer: D. Moore

STILLWATERS

ELINOR TROUT FISHERY
Aldwincle, Nr. Thrapston
Owner: J. Popplewell
40 North Street, Oundle, Peterborough
PE8 4AL
Tel: 0832 73671
Permits bookable by telephone. Advance booking advisable

EYEBROOK RESERVOIR
Caldecott, Uppingham, Leics
Corby (Northants) & District Water Co.
Geddington Road, Corby
Tel: 9123 64298
Fisheries attendant
Tel: 0536 770264
Day and evening permits available on site

PITSFORD RESERVOIR
Pitsford, Nr. Northampton
Anglian Water Authority
Northampton Water Division
Tel: 0604 21321
For information contact Head Bailiff
G. Wood
Tel: 060126 350
Permits available on site

———

RAVENSTHORPE RESERVOIR
Ravensthorpe
Anglian Water Authority
Northampton Water Division
Tel: 0604 21321
For information contact G. Wood
Tel: 060126 350
Permits available from pumphouse at reservoir
Tel: 060125 210

RINGSTEAD GRANGE TROUT FISHERY
Ringstead, Nr. Kettering
Owner: H. Foster
Tel: 0933 622960
Day and evening permits on site
Advance booking advisable
See Advertisement this Section

RUTLAND WATER
Empingham, Nr. Oakham
Anglian Water Authority
Administration
Tel: 078086 321
Fishing enquiries and boat hire bookings
Tel: 078086 770
Day and evening permits available on site

SIBSON FISHERIES
Stibbington, Nr. Wansford
Tel: 0780 782621
Bailiff: V. Bettinson
Tel: 0780 782621
**Six coarse fishing permits per day
Four trout fishing permits per day
Advance booking advisable**

RIVERS

River Bure
ACLE & BURGH MARSHES
Anglian Water Authority
Norfolk & Suffolk River Division
Tel: 0603 615161
Free fishing

BUREBANK TROUT FISHERIES
Itteringham, Nr. Aylsham
D. Green
Tel: 026387 666
**Limited permits by advance booking.
Closed 1982/83 season. Opens again
1983/84 season**

BURGH
T. Crix
Mill House, Burgh
Tel: 026373 2117
Permits by arrangement in advance

BUXTON
L. Ford
Old Mill Hotel, Buxton
Tel: 060 846 761
Permits from above

ST. BENNETTS
Norwich & District A.A.
Sec: Mr Wigg
Tel: 0603 43625
**Permits available from cottage near wat
but access difficult to find for newcome**

**SOUTH WALSHAM &
UPTON/WOODBASTWICK**
Anglian Water Authority
Norfolk & Suffolk River Division
Tel: 0603 615161
Free fishing

River Glaven
CLEY, NORFOLK
Anglian Water Authority
Yare House, Thorpe Road, Norwich
Tel: 0603 615161
Day permits also available from:
P. Suckling
The Old Manor, Cley
Tel: 0263 740863
1982 season only

River Wensum
LENWADE
London Anglers Association
Tel: 01 520 7477
Bailiff: G. Fisher
Tel: 0603 404288
Permits available from bailiff on bank

LYNG, LYNG EASTAUGH
Dereham A.C.
Treasurer: B. Fanthorpe
11a Neatherd Road, Dereham
Tel: 0362 2094
Permits available from above

NORWICH CITY CENTRE
Norwich City Council
Amenities Dept.
Tel: 0603 22233

SWANTON MORLEY
near East Dereham, Norfolk
**Day permits available from
Waterfall Cottage, Swanton Morley, afte
8am**
Tel: 036283 424
**Permits must be acquired before fishing
commences. Season permits available f
Water Recreation, 47 Clockhouse Lane,
Ashford, Middx (S.A.E. please)**

Upper Wensum
Fakenham A.C.
Sec: G. Parsons
Tel: 0328 4637
**Permits available from:
Len Bryers Tackle Shop
Bridge Street, Fakenham**
Tel: 0328 2543

North-West

1. EDEN AND BORDER ESK
2. WEST AND SOUTH WEST CUMBRIA
3. SOUTH CUMBRIA
4. EAST CUMBRIA, NORTH AND CENTRAL LANCASHIRE
5. SOUTH LANCASHIRE, GREATER MANCHESTER AND MERSEYSIDE
6. CHESHIRE

North West Water Authority

North West Water Authority
Dawson House, Great Sankey
Warrington WA5 3LW
Tel: 092 572 4321
Regional Fisheries Officer:
J. D. Kelsall
New Town House, Buttermarket Street
Warrington
Tel: 0925 53999

For administrative purposes the Authority is divided into two areas:

Northern Area:
River Lune catchment and all catchments to the North

Area Fishery Officer:
Dr C. Harpley, North Cumbria Area Office
Chertsey Hill, London Road, Carlisle
Tel: 0228 25151

Southern Area:
River Wyre and all catchments to the South including Upper Ribble

Area Fishery Officer:
R. D. Parker, Bancroft House
Liverpool Road, Great Sankey
Warrington
Tel: 092 572 4161

Regional rod licences are issued by most local tackle shops and by some hotels throughout the Authority's area.

For ease of location the Authority's area is shown by river division (please see map for clarification).

DIVISIONAL OFFICES

Head Office:
Dawson House, Great Sankey
Warrington
Tel: 092 572 4321
Central Division:
New Town House, PO Box 30
Buttermarket Street, Warrington
Tel: 0925 53922
Eastern Division:
Oakland House, Talbot Road
Old Trafford, Manchester
Tel: 061 872 5919

Northern Division:
PO Box 36, Holme Head, Carlisle
Tel: 0228 36321
Pennine Division:
London House, Oldham Road
Middleton
Tel: 061 643 1188
Ribble Division:
Pennine House, Stanley Street, Preston
Tel: 0772 59455
Rivers Division:
New Town House, Buttermarket Street
Warrington
Tel: 0925 53999
Southern Division:
Allport/Bridle Road, Bromborough
Merseyside
Tel: 051 327 1275
Western Division:
Merton House, Bootle, Merseyside
Tel: 051 922 7260

CHESHIRE AREA
RIVERS

River Dane

Davenham A.C.
Sec: A. Cook
Tel: 0606 41838
Permits also available from:
Hylands Pet Stores Ltd
121 Witton Road, Northwich
Tel: 0606 2768
Northwich & District Angling Centre
25 London Road, Northwich
Tel: 0606 2916

Middlewich A.S.
Sec: G. Stainer
Tel: 060 684 695
Permits also available from:
Middlewich Angling Supplies
Wheelock Street, Middlewich
Tel: 060 684 3853 or from
Association bailiff on bank

Northwich A.A.
Sec: E. Moore
Struma, Gadbrook Road, Rudheath,
Northwich
Tel: 0606 2986
Day and week permits available from bailiff on bank

River Weaver

Middlewich A.S.
Sec: G. Stanier
Tel: 060 684 3695
Permits also available from:
Middlewich Angling Supplies
Wheelock Street, Middlewich
Tel: 060 684 3853

Northern A.A.
Sec: G. Wilson
Tel: 02572 65905
Permits also available from:
Local tackle shops

Northwich A.A.
Sec: E. Moore
Struma, Gadbrook Road, Rudheath,
Northwich
Tel: 0606 2986
Day and week permits available from bailiff on bank

STILLWATERS

ARROWE PARK LAKE
Metropolitan Borough of Wirral
Department of Leisure Services
8 Rivedale Road, West Kirby, Wirral
Tel: 051 625 9441
Permits also available from:
The Golf Pro Shop, Arrowe Park
Tel: 051 677 1527

BILLINGE GREEN POOLS
Northwich A.A.
Sec: E. Moore
Tel: 0606 2986
Permits also available from:
Erics Tackle & Pet Supplies
20a High Street, Weaverham
Tel: 0606 853126
Daves Angling Supplies, Middlewich
Tel: 0606 3853
Hylands Pet Stores Ltd,
121 Witton Street, Northwich
Tel: 0606 2768
Scott's, 84 Station Road, Northwich
Tel: 0606 6543

BIRKENHEAD PARK (LOWER LAKE
Metropolitan Borough of Wirral
Department of Leisure Services
8 Riverside Road, West Kirby, Wirral
Tel: 051 625 9441
Permits also available from:
Grange Road West Sports Centre
Birkenhead
Tel: 051 652 9336

BOSLEY RESERVOIR, NR. MACCLESFIELD
Moss Side Social A.S.
Sec: R. W. Harrop
1 Fulham Avenue, Newton Heath,
Manchester M10 6TI
Tel: 061 682 5370
Day permits also available from:
J. Arnold, 1 Lakeside Estate, Bosley
Tel: 02603 450

CAPESTHORNE HALL, NR. CHELFORD
Stoke on Trent A.S.
Sec: S. F. Broadgate
Tel: 0782 618833
Permits also available from:
A. Bradley, The Lodge, Capesthorne H
Nr. Chelford
Tel: 0625 861584

CAPTAINS PIT, WALLASEY
Metropolitan Borough of Wirral
Department of Leisure Services
8 Riverdale Road, West Kirby, Wirral
Tel: 051 625 9441
Permits also available from:
Guinea Gap Baths, Wallasey
Tel: 051 639 9792

GREAT BUDWORTH MERE
Northwich A.A.
Sec: E. Moore
Struma, Gadbrook Road, Rudheath,
Northwich
Tel: 0606 2986
Day and week permits available from b
on bank

HER WHITLEY SAND QUARRY
sham & District A.C.
D. Chow
0928 715099
mits by written application

TS POOL, BRADWELL
dlewich A.S.
G. Stainer
060 684 3695
mits also available from:
dlewich Angling Supplies
eelock Street, Middlewich
060 684 3853 or from
ociation bailiff on bank

G GEORGE V POOL
ncham
ford Borough Council
eation & Amenities Officer
n House, Talbot Road, Stretford,
chester
061 872 2101

DBEATERS RESERVOIR
ce Albert A.S.
C. Sparkes
0625 26311
mits also available from:
ewton Fishing Tackle
d Park Lane, Macclesfield
0625 24978

DON COMMON LAKE
clesfield Borough Council
rt House, Macclesfield
0625 21955
ermits necessary

NGBARN PARK PIT
rington Borough Council
eation Dept, 80 Sankey Street
rington
0925 35961
mits also available on banks

M DAM
m A.C.
J. S. Graham
oswell Avenue, Warrington, Cheshire
4 6DQ
0925 54942
permits also available from:
al tackle shops or bailiff on bank

WCOW PIT, BYLEY
dlewich A.S.
G. Stainer
060 684 3695
mits also available from:
dlewich Angling Supplies
eelock Street, Middlewich
060 684 3853 or from Association bailiff
bank

W POOL
sford & District A.A.
J. S. Bailey
06065 3902
nbers only by special permit

WBRIDGE POOL
sford & District A.A.
J. S. Bailey
06065 3902
mits also available from:
Blackburn

---

447 Station Road, Winsford
Tel: 06065 4818

THE OCEAN, WINSFORD
Winsford & District A.A.
Sec: J. S. Bailey
Tel: 06065 3902
Permits also available from:
J. L. Blackburn
447 Station Road, Winsford
Tel: 06065 4818

PETTY POOL, WHITEGATE
Middlewich A.S.
Sec: G. Stainer
Tel: 060 684 3695
Permits also available from:
Middlewich Angling Supplies
Wheelock Street, Middlewich
Tel: 060 684 3853 or from
Association bailiff on bank

Northwich A.A.
Sec: E. Moore
Struma, Gadbrook Road, Rudheath,
Northwich
Tel: 0606 2986
Day and week permits available from bailiff
on bank

Winsford & District A.S.
Sec: J. S. Bailey
Tel: 06065 3902
Permits also available from:
J. L. Blackburn
447 Station Road, Winsford
Tel: 06065 4818

PRITCHARDS PIT, DAVENHAM
Davenham A.C.
Sec: A. Cook
Tel: 0606 41838

REDESMERE
Prince Albert A.S.
Sec: C. Sparkes
Tel: 06235 26311
Permits also available from:
A. Bradley, The Lodge, Capesthorne Hall,
Nr. Chelford
Tel: 0625 861584

SHAKERLEY MERE, ALLOSKOCK
Cheshire County Council
40a Church Street, Davenham
Tel: 0606 3874
Permits also available from the bank

SHERWINS PIT
Middlewich A.S.
Sec: G. Stainer
Tel: 060 684 3695
Permits also available from:
Middlewich Angling Supplies
Wheelock Street, Middlewich
Tel: 060 684 3853

SOUTH PARK POOL
Macclesfield Borough Council
Stuart House, Macclesfield
Tel: 0625 21955
Permits also available from the pavilion

STATHAM POOL
Lymm A.C.
Sec: J. Graham
15 Boswell Avenue, Warrington WA4 6DQ
Tel: 0925 54942

Day permits from secretary, bailiff on bank
and local tackle shops

TATTON MERE, WEST BANK
Cheshire County Council
40a Church Street, Davenham
Tel: 0606 3874
Permits also available from:
Knutsford gate entrance

WIDE HOLE, HIGHER POYNTON
Northern A.A.
Sec: G. Wilson
Tel: 02572 65909
Permits also available from:
Local tackle shops

WIRRAL COUNTRY PARK THURSTASTON
Metropolitan Borough of Wirral
Dept. of Leisure Services
8 Riverdale Road, West Kirby
Tel: 051 625 9441
Permits also available from:
Visitors Centre, Wirral Country Park,
Station Road, Thurstaston

WOODS MEADOW
Davenham A.C.
Sec: G. Sparkes
Tel: 0625 26311

CANALS

Bridgewater Canal
RUNCORN TO PRESTON BROOK
Halton Joint Anglers
Sec: W. Durr
Footbridge Cottage, Canal Street, Runcorn
Tel: 09285 77508
Season permits also available from:
Local tackle shops

BROADHEATH BRIDGE TO LEIGH
Northern A.A.
Sec: G. Wilson
11 Guildford Avenue, Chorley
Control arm of canal as far as Corn Brook
Bridge
Day permits from bailiffs

LENGTH BETWEEN MANCHESTER AND LEIGH
Northern A.A.
Sec: G. Wilson
11 Guildford Avenue, Chorley
and
Leigh and District A.A.
Sec: J. Scotson
28 Glover Street, Leigh

Macclesfield Canal
Northern A.A.
Sec: G. Wilson
Tel: 02572 65905
Permits also available from local tackle
shops

Prince Albert A.S.
Sec: C. Sparkes
Tel: 0625 26311
Permits also available from:
R. Newton Fishing Tackle
3 Old Park Lane, Macclesfield
Tel: 0625 24978

WHERE TO FISH – COARSE

BRIDGES 72 TO 75
Kidsgrove & District A.S.
Sec: C. E. Woodcock
29 Mitchell Avenue, Talke
Day permits from secretary

BRIDGES 75 TO 77
Congleton A.S.
Sec: N. J. Bours
8 Norfolk Road, Congleton
Day permits available

BRIDGE 80 TO 80A
Robin Hood A.C.
Sec: K. Wilson
52 Beach Drive, Kidsgrove
Day permits from secretary

WATERY LANE AQUEDUCT TO HALL GREEN LOCK
Crewe L.M.R. Sports Club
Sec: A. Jones
290 Crewe Road, Cresty
Day permits on towpath

Peak Forest Canal
ASHTON JUNCTION TO WOODLEY TUNNEL
Hyde & District Fed. of Anglers
Sec: B. Smart
20 Kingston Gardens, Hyde
Day permits on towpath

WOODLEY TUNNEL TO WHALEY BRIDGE
Stockport & District A.F.
Sec: C. Holland
121 Northgate Road, Edgeley, Stockport
Day permits on towpath

Shropshire Union Canal
Shropshire Union Canal A.A.
Sec: R. Brown
Tel: 0942 76917
Permits also available from
The bailiff

Trent & Mersey Canal
DUTTON TO MIDDLEWICH
Northwich A.A.
Sec: E. Moore
Struma, Gadbrook Road, Rudheath, Northwich
Tel: 0606 2986
Day and week permits from bailiff on bank

Warrington A.A.
Sec: J. S. Jackson
Tel: 0925 37525
Permits also available from
Erics Tackle & Pet Supplies
20a High Street, Weaverham
Tel: 0606 853126
Daves Angling Supplies
Middlewich
Tel: 0606 3853
Hyland Pet Stores Ltd
121 Witton Street, Northwich
Tel: 0606 2768
Northwich & District Angling Centre
25 London Road, Northwich
Tel: 0606 2916
Scott's
84 Station Road, Northwich
Tel: 0606 6543

Trent & Mersey Canal
KIDSGROVE TO RODE HEATH
North Staffs Association of Anglers
Official: F. Bassett
Tel: 0782 46633

EAST CUMBRIA, NORTH & CENTRAL LANCASTER AREA

RIVERS

River Lune
Kirby Lonsdale A.C.
Sec: G. Clough
Permits also available from:
The Tackle Box, Kirby Lonsdale
Via Carnforth, Lancashire
HALTON & SKERTON FISHERIES
North West Water Authority
Tel: 0925 53999
Permits available from:
Mrs Curwen, Greenup Cottage,
Hornby Road, Caton, Nr. Lancaster
Tel: 0524 770078
Darwen and Gough, 6 Moor Lane,
Lancaster
Tel: 0524 64913
Lancaster & District A.A.
Sec: C. T. Preston
Tel: 0468 71574
Permits also available from:
Mrs A. Curwen, Greenup Cottage,
Hornby Road, Caton
Tel: 0524 770078
Darwen & Gough, 6 Moorlane, Lancaster
Tel: 0524 64913
Lansil A.C.
Denny Beck to Howgill Beck
Sec: J. Barnes

88 West End Road, Morecambe
Tel: 0524 416006
Annual permits from the secretary
Sedbergh A.A.
Sec: J. P. Lowis
Tel: 0587 20868
Permits also available from:
Lowis's (Sedbergh) Ltd., Main Street,
Sedbergh, Cumbria
Tel: 0587 20446

SKERTON PARK FISHERY
Lonsdale A.C.
Sec: G. Parkinson
166 Dorrington Road, Lancaster LA1 4T
Day permits from secretary or local tac
shops

Tebay & District A.C.
Sec: H. Riley
Tel: 05874 376
Permits also available from:
Cross Keys Hotel, Tebay
Tel: 05874 240
Junction Hotel, Tebay
Tel: 05874 232

River Rawthey
Sedbergh A.A.
Sec: J. P. Lowis
Tel: 0587 20868
Permits also available from:
Lowis's (Sedbergh) Ltd., 45 Main Street,
Sedbergh, Cumbria
Tel: 0587 20446

River Ribble
Co-operative Wholesale Society
Withgill Estate, Higher Hodder, Clither
Lancashire
Annual permits available from:
R. Hill, The Fishermans Haunt,
161 Blackburn Road, Accrington
Tel: 0254 34148
H. Le-Moine Fishing Tackle
22 Accrington Road, Blackburn
Tel: 0254 58716

Northern Anglers Association
Preston Centre
Enquiries: G. Jones
1 Carnarvon Road, Preston

Northern Anglers Association
Wigan Centre
Enquiries: W. Gratton
66 Balcarres Road, Aspull, Wigan
Tel: 0942 492376

Ribble Valley Borough Council
Church Brow, Clitheroe
Tel: 0200 25111
Permits also available from:
K. Varey, 4 New Market Street
Clitheroe
Tel: 0200 23267

Settle A.A.
Sec: M. G. Riley
Tel: 07292 3501
Permits also available from:
Royal Oak Hotel, Market Place, Settle
Tel: 07292 2561

Wigan A.A.
Committee Member: W. Gratton
Tel: 0942 492376
Permits from local tackle shops

...r Twiss
...ton A.C.
...mittee Member: Mr Creswell
...eborough Park Drive
...ton, Yorkshire
...its also available from
...M. Berry, Newsagents, Main Street,
...ton, via Carnforth
...0468 41683

...r Wyre
...stang & District A.A.
...D. E. Irvin
...09952 3312
...kly permits available from Sec

...ichael's Angling Assoc.
...A. Moss
...its also available from:
...G. Martin, Bridge Cottage
...ichael's-on-Wyre, Nr. Preston
...09958 228
...Roberts Fishing Tackle & Guns
...Hill, Garstang, Nr. Preston
...09952 3925

...an A.A.
...mittee Member: W. Gratton
...0942 492376
...its from local tackle shops

STILLWATERS

...ILRIDGE LOWER RESERVOIR
...ing Sec: Mrs J. C. Peate
...he Anchorage, Skipton Old Road,
...ridge, Colne, Lancs
...0282 863993
...its also available from:
...aylor, Fishing Tackle
...indsor Street, Colne, Lancs
...0282 864076

...NLEY DEEP PIT
...an A.A.
...mittee Member: W. Gratton
...0942 492376
...its available on site

...LLING NO. 1
...an A.A.
...mittee Member: W. Gratton
...0942 492376
...its available on site

...TTON FISHERY
...th West Water Authority
...rs Division, Newtown House,
...ermarket Street, Warrington
...0925 53999
...its also available from:
...M. M. Hayes, Mitton Hall Farm, Mitton,
...Whalley, Lancs
...025486 281

...D POND
...an A.A.
...mittee Member: W. Gratton
...0942 492376
...its available on site

...RN HALL RESERVOIR
...rington & District F.C.
...A. Balderstone
...0254 33517
...its also available from:
...arratt, 8 Stanley Street, Oswaldtwistle
...0254 31272

STANLEY PARK LAKE
Blackpool Park A.C.
M. Jap
Permits available from local tackle shops
and bailiff at lake

SWANTLEY LAKE
Lonsdale A.C.
Sec: G. Parkinson
166 Dorrington Road, Lancaster
Day permits available from local tackle
shops

WIDDOWS LAKE
Wigan A.A.
Committee Member: W. Gratton
Tel: 0942 492376
Permits available on site

CANALS

Lancaster Canal
Northern A.A.
Sec: G. Wilson
Tel: 02572 65905
Day permits also available from:
Local tackle shops

EDEN AND BORDER ESK AREA

RIVERS

River Petteril
Penrith Angling Association
Sec: R. F. Allison
Tel: 0768 62256
Permits available from:
Charles R. Sykes, 4 Great Dockery, Penrith,
Carlisle
Tel: 0768 62418

STILLWATERS

HIGH STANDS POND
Nr. Cotehill, Carlisle
Permits available from:
Wigan & District A.C.
Asst Sec: K. Hogg, 95 Holne Terrace,
Wigan
Tel: 0942 492376

SWINDALE
Permits by written application to:
North West Water Authority
Eastern Division

THIRLMERE
Permits by written application to North
West Authority Eastern Division

ULLSWATER
No permits required although local
permission should be obtained

SOUTH CUMBRIA AREA
RIVERS
River Gilpin
Northern Anglers Association

Sec: G. Wilson
Tel: 02572 65905
Permits also available from:
Local tackle shops

River Kent
Burneside Anglers Association
Chairman: E. Sykes
Tel: 0539 24020
Permits also available from:
The Jolly Anglers Hotel, Burneside
Nr. Kendal, Cumbria
Tel: 0539 24020

Kent Anglers Association
Sec: J. C. Parkin
Tel: 0539 22386
Permits also available from:
T. Atkinson & Son, Sports Depot
19 Stricklandgate, Kendal
Tel: 0539 20300

L. Parsons
Lower Leven Farm, Nr. Kendal, Cumbria
Tel: 0448 60435

Staveley Anglers Association
Sec: D. A. Taylor
Tel: 0539 821002
Permits also available from:
R. L. Smith, Newsagent, Staveley
Tel: 0539 821253

River Lickle
Furness Fishing Association
Committee Member: Mr Groundwell
1 Astra Buildings, Abbey Road,
Barrow-in-Furness
Tel: 0229 29661
Permits available from above
c/o Angling & Hiking Centre

STILLWATERS

BIGLAND HALL COARSE FISHERY
Bigland Hall Sporting Estate
Blackbarrow, Nr. Ulverston, Cumbria
Tel: 0448 31 728

BURN HOLE PIT
Furness F.A. (coarse section)
Sec: D. Jackson
117 Chapel Street, Dalton-in-Furness
Tel: 0229 62275
Day and week permits on application in
writing to the secretary

CONISTON WATER
No fishing
National Trust Land
National Trust, "Broadlands", Borrans
Road, Ambleside
Tel: 09663 3003

ESTHWAITE LAKE
Esthwaite Estates Ltd., Graythwaite Hall
Estate Office, Graythwaite, Nr. Ulverston,
Cumbria
Tel: 0448 31248
Permits also available from:
Mr T. A. Taylor
Esthwaite How Farm, Nr. Sawrey
Hawkshead, Cumbria
Tel: 09666 331
Mr B. Raistrick, The Post Office
Hawkshead, Cumbria
Tel: 09666 201

HIGH POND PIT
Furness F.A. (coarse section)
Sec: D. Jackson
117 Chapel Street, Dalton-in-Furness
Tel: 0229 62275
Day and week permits on application in writing to secretary

HOLEHIRD TARN
Cumbria County Council
Estates & Valuation Dept., Arroyd Block
The Castle, Carlisle, Cumbria
Permits – limited to 8 per day
Mr N. Bleese, Holehird Gardens Staff
Tel: 09662 4743

KILLINGTON LAKE
Kent (Westmorland) Anglers Association
Sec: J. C. Parkin
11a Blea Tarn Road, Kendal
Tel: 0539 22386
Day, week and season permits also available from Keepers Cottage on East Bank

LOUGHRIGG TARN
National Trust, 'Broadlands', Borrans Road, Ambleside
Tel: 09663 3003
Permits also available from:
Mrs Murphy, Tarn Foot Farm, Loughrigg
Nr. Ambleside, Cumbria
Tel: 09663 2596

LAW POND PIT
Furness F.A. (coarse section)
Sec: D. Jackson
117 Chapel Street, Dalton-in-Furness
Tel: 0229 62275
Day and week permits on application in writing to secretary

MARTIN OPENWORKS
Furness Fishing Association
Committee Member: Mr Groundwell
1 Astra Buildings, Abbey Road,
Barrow-in-Furness
Tel: 0229 29661
Permits available from above
c/o Angling & Hiking Centre
Barrow-in-Furness

ORMSHILL RESERVOIR
Furness Fishing Assocation (coarse section)
Sec: D. Jackson
117 Chapel Street, Dalton-in-Furness
Tel: 0229 62275
Day and week permits available on application in writing to secretary

RITA PIT
Furness Fishing Assocation (coarse section)
Sec: D. Jackson
117 Chapel Street, Dalton-in-Furness
Tel: 0229 62275
Day and week permits available on application in writing to secretary

RYDAL LAKE
Windermere, Ambleside & District A.A.
Sec: J. B. Cooper
Tel: 09662 3768
Permits also available from:
Mr Cowking, Ghyllside Cycles
The Slack, Ambleside
Tel: 09663 3592
Glen Rothay Hotel, Rydal, Nr. Ambleside
Tel: 09663 2524

Mr B. Raistrick, The Post Office,
Hawkshead, Cumbria
Tel: 09666 201
J. & C. H. Smythe, Ash Street,
Bowness-on-Windermere, Cumbria
Tel: 09662 3750
J. & P. M. Stobbart, Church Street,
Ambleside, Cumbria
Tel: 09663 2656

Windermere
South Lakeland District Council
Tourism & Recreation Dept., Ashleigh,
Windermere, Cumbria
Tel: 09662 2244
Permits also available from:
Kendal Sports Shop, 28 Stramongate,
Kendal, Cumbria
Tel: 0539 21554
J. & C. H. Smythe, Ash Street, Bowness-on-Windermere, Cumbria
Tel: 09662 3750

CANALS

Ulverston Canal
Ulverston Angling Association
Sec: H. B. Whittam
Tel: 0229 52232
Permits also available from:
Mr A. Parker Fishing Tackle
23 Market Street, Ulverston
Tel: 0229 52061
Angling & Hiking Centre
1 Astra Buildings, Abbey Road,
Barrow-in-Furness, Cumbria
Tel: 0229 29661

SOUTH LANCASHIRE, GREATER MANCHESTER & MERSEYSIDE AREA

RIVERS

River Crossens
Southport & District A.A.
Sec: C. Russell
41 Longacre, Southport PR9 9TB
Tel: 0704 213521
Day and week permits also available from:
J. Robinson & Son, 71 Sussex Road,
Southport
Tel: 0704 34136
Mrs Rothwell, 186 Rufford Road, Crossens
Southport
Tel: 0740 20874

River Irwell
Northern A.A.
Sec: G. Wilson
Tel: 02572 65905
Permits also available from:
Local tackle shops

STILLWATERS

ABBEY LAKES
Northern A.A. – Orell & District
Sec: R. Crank
Tel: 0942 213815
Permits also available from:
Georges Fishing Tackle, 15 Frog Lane,
Wigan
Tel: 0942 41932
Ron's, 6 St James Road, Orell

AINSDALE LAKE, NR. SOUTHPOR[...]
Liverpool & District A.A.
Sec: J. Johnson
Tel: 051 526 4083
Permits also available from:
Local tackle shops and on bank

ANGLEZARKE RESERVOIR
See Rivington Group Reservoirs

BLACKLEACH RESERVOIR
Farnworth & District A.A.
Sec: A. Johnson
Tel: 0204 75989
Permits also available from:
Salters Sports & Tackle, Market Street,
Farnworth
Tel: 0204 73287
Battersby's Tackle Shop, 57 Worsley R[...]
Swinton
Tel: 061 494 2784

BLACKLEY NEW ROAD UPPERLA[...]
City of Manchester Recreational Servic[...]
Town Hall, Manchester
Tel: 061 236 3377
Permits from: McMahons Newsagents,
Riverdale Road, Manchester

BOAT SHED, WALKDEN
Farnworth & District A.A.
Sec: A. Johnson
Tel: 0204 75989
Permits also available from:
Battersby's Tackle Shop, 57 Worsley R[...]
Swinton
Tel: 061 494 2784
Salters Sports & Tackle, Market Street,
Farnworth
Tel: 0204 73287

GART HOLE CLOUGH,
CKLEY
f Manchester Recreational Dept.
n Square, Manchester
61 236 3377
ts also available from:
dant on duty

DFORD LODGE
ss by gate on Melville Street only
n & District A.A.
. A. Shanahan
204 63770
n permits also available from:
tackle shops

GEWATER RESERVOIR
vorth & District A.A.
A. Johnson
204 75989
n permits also available from:
rsby's Tackle Shop, 57 Worsley Road,
on
61 494 2784
rs Sports & Tackle, Market Street,
vorth
204 73287

L HILL, BOLTON
ss via Hall Lane
n & District A.A.
J. A. Shanahan
204 63770
n permits also available from:
tackle shops

BUNK, FIRWOOD LANE,
TON
n & District A.A.
J. A. Shanahan
204 63770
its also available from:
tackle shops

GESS'S POND, WIDNES
n & District A.A.
K. Philcock
051 423 1627
its also available from:
man's Tackle Shop, 22 Albert Road,
nes
051 424 2580
ennington, 273 Warrington Road,
nes

SCOUGH BRICK LAKE
Ormskirk
pool & District A.A.
J. Johnson
051 526 4083
its also available from:
tackle shops and on the bank

CALDERBROOK DAMS
Todmorden A.S.
Sec: D. Howorth
Tel: 070 681 4443
Permits also available from:
Pet Shop, Hare Hill Road, Littleborough,
Lancs
Tel: 0706 78452
Steve's Tackle Shop, Rochdale, Lancs

CHORLTOM'S RESERVOIR, MOSS LANE, WALKDEN
Farnworth & District A.A.
Sec: A. Johnson
Tel: 0204 75989
Permits also available from
Battersby's Tackle Shop, 57 Worsley Road,
Swinton
Tel: 061 494 2784
Salters Sports & Tackle, Market Street,
Farnworth
Tel: 0204 73287

DEBDALE LOWER RESERVOIR, GORTON
City of Manchester Recreational Dept.
Crown Square, Manchester
Tel: 061 236 3377
Permits also available from bank

DEBDALE UPPER RESERVOIR
City of Manchester Recreational Dept.
Crown Square, Manchester
Tel: 061 236 3377
Permits available from bank

DIXON GREEN RESERVOIR, FARNWORTH
Farnworth & District A.A.
Sec: A. Johnson
Tel: 0204 75989
Permits also available from:
Battersby's Tackle Shop, 57 Worsley Road,
Swinton
Tel: 061 494 2784
Salters Sports & Tackle, Market Street,
Farnworth
Tel: 0204 72387

DOFFCOCKER RESERVOIR
Bolton & District A.A.
Sec: J. A. Shanahan
Tel: 0204 63770
Season permits also available from:
Local tackle shops
Species caught: Bream, Pike, Tench,
Perch, Carp and Roach

DRINKWATER PARK LAKE, PRESTWICH
Greenall Whitley A.A.
Sec: J. Robinson
Tel: 061 224 3174
Permits also available from:
Local tackle shops

DUNSCAR 1 & 2, GLEAVES, SHORE LODGE
Bolton & District A.A.
Sec: J. A. Shanahan
Tel: 0204 63770
Season permits also available from:
Local tackle shops

ELTON RESERVOIR, BURY
Bury A.A. & Elton Sailing Club
Mr Taylor
Tel: 061 764 2858
Permits also available from:
The banks

FAN LODGE, BICKERSHAW
Northern A.A., Ashton Centre
Sec: R. Brown
Tel: 0942 76917
Permits also available from:
Local tackle shops

FIRS PARK LAKE
Leigh & District A.A.
Sec: J. Scotson
Tel: 0942 674944
Permits available from:
Bank Ranger

FIR TREE FLASH
Fir Tree Angling Society
Sec: R. Newport
Tel: 0942 675403
Permits available from:
The banks

FIRWOOD, FIRWOOD LANE, BOLTON
Bolton & District A.A.
Sec: J. A. Shanahan
Tel: 0204 63770
Season permits also available from:
Local tackle shops

WHERE TO FISH—COARSE

GORSE PIT, WALKDEN
Farnworth & District A.A.
Sec: A. Johnson
Tel: 0204 75989
Permits also available from:
Battersby's Tackle Shop, 57 Worsley Road,
Swinton
Tel: 061 494 2784
Salters Sports & Tackle, Market Street,
Farnworth
Tel: 0204 73287

HEATON PARK BOATING LAKE
City of Manchester Recreational Dept.
Crown Square, Manchester
Tel: 061 236 3377
Permits also available from:
Ticket office
Note: Restricted fishing during public
boating season

HILL MILL RESERVOIR, CROMPTON WAY, HALLIWELL
Bolton & District A.A.
Sec: J. A. Shanahan
Tel: 0204 63770
Season permits also available from:
Local tackle shops

JUMBLES RESERVOIR
North West Water Authority
Pennine Division, London House, Oldham
Road, Middleton, Manchester
Tel: 061 643 1188
Fishing free
Possession of N.W.W. licence essential

LIVERPOOL PARK LAKES
Liverpool City Council
Recreation & Open Spaces Dept.
Mansion House, Calderstones Park,
Liverpool
Tel: 051 724 2371

LOWERBROOK LAKE
Rainow
Bollington & Royal Oak A.S.
Sec: T. Barber
10 George Street, West Macclesfield
SK11 6ES
Day permits from Millbrooke Pool Lodge or
bankside

LOWER AND UPPER RODDLESWORTH
See Rivington Group Reservoirs

MERTONS 1 & 2, SHARPLES ASTLEY BRIDGE
Bolton & District A.A.
Sec: J. Shanahan
Tel: 0204 63770
Season permits also available from:
Local tackle shops

MILLBROOKE POOL
Rainow
Bollington & Royal Oak A.S.
Sec: T. Barber
10 George Street, West Macclesfield
SK11 6ES
Day permits from lodge at side of pool or
bankside

MYRTLE ROAD LODGES
Middleton Angling Society
Sec: P. Iddle
Tel: 061 795 7691
Permits available on site

Ogden Reservoir
Oldham & District United A.A.
Sec: H. Garside
Tel: 04577 5993
Permits also available from:
Local tackle shops

PENNINGTON FLASH
Pennington Flash A.A.
Sec: J. Scotson
Tel: 0942 674944
Permits also available from:
Association bailiffs

PLATT FIELDS PARK, RUSHOLME
City of Manchester Recreational Dept.
Crown Square, Manchester
Tel: 061 236 3377
Permits also available from:
The banks
Banks suitable for the disabled

POYNTON POOL
Stockport Federation of Anglers
Sec: C. Holland
Tel: 061 480 9888
Limited permits from bank

QUEENSMERE
Swinton & Pendlebury
Sec: A. Richards
Tel: 061 794 9910

RIVINGTON GROUP RESERVOIRS
North West Water Authority
Western Division, Merton House
Stanley Road, Bootle
Tel: 051 922 7260
Permits also available from:
A. Leach, 78-80 Lee Lane, Horwich
Tel: 0204 67625
Harry Le-Moine, 22 Accrington Road,
Blackburn
Tel: 0254 58716
W. J. Salmon, Rivington Hall, Rivington,
Bolton
Tel: 0204 67738

SAYCES POND, WIDNES
Halton & District A.A.
Sec: K. Philcock
Tel: 051 423 1627
Permits also available from:
Herriman's Tackle Shop
22 Albert Road, Widnes
Tel: 051 424 2580
D. Pennington, 273 Warrington Road,
Widnes

Smiths Reservoir, Smiths Road, Bolton
Bolton & District
Sec: J. A. Shanahan
Tel: 0204 63770
Season permits also available from:
Local tackle shops
Noted for large carp

SOUTH LANE POND, WIDNES
Halton & District A.A.
Sec: K. Philcock
Tel: 051 423 1627
Season permits also available from:
Herriman's Tackle Shop
22 Albert Road, Widnes
Tel: 051 424 2580
D. Pennington
273 Warrington Road, Widnes

SPRINGWOOD LODGE, RAMSBOTTOM
T. Robinson (Springwood) A.C.
Sec: S. Petch
Tel: 070 682 4999
Permits also available from:
Ramsbottom Library
Carr Street, Ramsbottom
Tel: 070 682 2484

STRINESDALE UPPER RESERVOIR
Oldham & District Amalgamated A.A.
Sec: H. Garside
Tel: 04577 5993
Permits also available from:
Local tackle shops

SWINESHAW MILL DAM, MILLBROOK
Oldham & District Amalgamated A.A.
Sec: H. Garside
Tel: 04577 5993
Permits also available from:
Local tackle shops

TERRACE DELPH
Rainford Junction A.S.
Sec: E. J. Eastham
Tel: 074488 4593

TOMMY WALKERS, WALKDEN
Farnworth & District A.A.
Sec: A. Johnson
Tel: 0204 75989
Permits also available from:
Battersby's Tackle Shop
57 Worsley Road, Swinton
Tel: 061 494 2784
Salters Sports & Tackle
Market Street, Farnworth
Tel: 0204 73287

WAYOH RESERVOIR
North West Water Authority
Pennine Division, London House
Oldham Road, Middleton, Manchester
Tel: 061 642 1188

WHELMAR'S QUARRY
Leigh & District A.A.
Sec: J. Scotson
Tel: 0942 674944
Permits also available from:
Bank Ranger

ITTLEBOOK RESERVOIR, LKDEN

worth & District A.A.
A. Johnson
0204 75989
its also available from:
ersby's Tackle Shop
orsley Road, Swinton
061 494 2784
rs Sports & Tackle
ket Street, Farnworth
0204 73287

RTHINGTON LAKES

n West Water Authority
ral Division, Newtown House,
rington
0925 53922
its also available from:
den or ticket machine in car park

EST & SOUTH WEST UMBRIA AREA

STILLWATERS

SENTHWAITE LAKE

e District Planning Board
er Walk, Kendal, Cumbria
0539 24555
its available from:
& Sports, Main Street, Kendal,
bria
0539 74396
. Lothian, 35 Main Street,
kermouth, Cumbria
0900 822006
onal Park Information Centre, Moot

0539 72803
cholson, The Gun Shop, Lorton Road,
kermouth
0900 822058
ples Sports Shop, Station Street,
vick, Cumbria
0596 72569

YTON POND

its available from:
Ward, Home Farm, Brayton, Aspatria,
Carlisle
0965 20262

TERMERE

onal Trust, 'Broadlands', Borrans Road,
leside
096 63 3003
its also available from:
cholson, The Gun Shop, Lorton Road,
kermouth
0900 822058
T. Richardson, Gatesgarth Farm,
rmere, Cumbria
059 685 256

CRUMMOCK WATER

National Trust, 'Broadlands', Borrans Road,
Ambleside
Tel: 096 63 3003
Permits also available from:
Mrs L. Beard, Rannerdale Farm,
Buttermere, Cumbria
Tel: 059 685 232
I. Nicholson, The Gun Shop, Lorton Road,
Cockermouth
Tel: 0900 822058

DERWENTWATER

Keswick Angling Association
Sec: W. Ashcroft
Tel: 0596 72703
Permits also available from:
Temples Sports Shop, Station Street,
Keswick, Cumbria
Tel: 0596 72569

LOWESWATER

National Trust, 'Broadlands', Borrans Road,
Ambleside
Tel: 096 63 3003
Permits also available from:
Kirkstile Inn, Loweswater
Tel: 090 085 232
I. Nicholson, The Gun Shop, Lorton Road,
Cockermouth
Tel: 0900 822058
Mrs T. Richardton, Gatesgarth Farm,
Buttermere, Cumbria
Tel: 059 685 256

MOCKERKIN TARN

Permits available from:
The Gun Shop, Jubilee Bridge, Lorton
Road, Cockermouth, Cumbria
Tel: 0900 822058

WASTWATER

National Trust, 'Broadlands', Borrans Road,
Ambleside
Tel: 096 63 3003
Permits by written application:
The Warden, National Trust Camp Site,
Wasdale Head

CANALS

Bridgewater Canal

Northern A.A.
Sec: G. Wilson
Tel: 02572 65905
Permits also available from:
Local tackle shops

Huddersfield Narrow Canal

Oldham & District Amalagamated Anglers
Sec: H. Garside
Tel: 04577 5993
Permits also available from:
A. Haynes, 12 Hollins Crescent,
Greensfield, Oldham
Tel: 04577 6297

Leeds and Liverpool Canal

LIVERPOOL TO HALSALL
Liverpool & District A.A.
Sec: J. Johnson
97 Liverpool Road North, Maghull

HALSALL TO WIGAN
Wigan D.A.A.
Sec: T. A. Blackledge
16 Florence Street, Wigan
Day permits available

Northern A.A.
Sec: G. W. Wilson
11 Guildford Avenue, Chorley
Day permits on towpath

Marsden Star A.C.
Day permits available

Leeds and Liverpool Canal A.A.
Sec: S. Watmough
8 Moor View Court, Sandbeds, Keighley
Day permits available

WIGAN TO LEIGH
Leigh & District A.A.
Sec: J. Scotson
26 Glover Street, Leigh
Tel: 0942 677944
Day permits from bailiffs

RUFFORD ARM
Liverpool D.A.A.
Sec: J. Johnson
97 Liverpool Road North, Maghull
Day permits at the waterside

Manchester, Bolton and Bury Canal

HINDS BRIDGE, ELTON TO WITHINS BRIDGE, RADCLIFFE
Bury & District A.A.
Sec: F. Booth
142 Bury Road, Tottington, Nr. Bury
Day permits available

BAILEYS BRIDGE TO WITHINS BRIDGE AND HALL LANE AND NOB HILL, LITTLE LEVER
Bolton & District A.A.
Sec: A. Riding
34 Higher Swan Lane, Bolton
Day permits are available

Rochdale Canal

Greenall Whitley A.A.
Sec: J. Robinson
Tel: 061 224 3174
Permits also available from:
Local tackle shops

Rufford Canal

Liverpool & District A.A.
Sec: J. Johnson
Tel: 051 526 4083
Permits also available from:
Local tackle shops

St. Helens Canal

Newton-le-Willows A.A.
Sec: E. Marcroft
Tel: 09252 5680
Season and day permits also available
from: C. Pardoe
13 Pine Avenue, Newton-le-Willows
Tel: 09252 7919
or canal bank

WHERE TO FISH—GAME

North West Water Authority

North West Water Authority
Dawson House, Great Sankey
Warrington WA5 3LW
Tel: 092 572 4321

Regional Fisheries Officer:
J. D. Kelsall
New Town House, Buttermarket Street,
Warrington
Tel: 0925 53999

For administrative purposes the Authority
is divided into two areas:

Northern Area:
River Lune catchment and all catchments
to the North

Area Fishery Officer:
Dr C. Harpley, North Cumbria Area Office
Chertsey Hill, London Road, Carlisle
Tel: 0228 25151

Southern Area:
River Wyre and all catchments to the
South including Upper Ribble

Area Fishery Officer:
R. D. Parker, Bancroft House
Liverpool Road, Great Sankey
Warrington
Tel: 092 572 4161

Regional rod licences are issued by most
local tackle shops and by some hotels
throughout the Authority's area.

For ease of location the Authority's area is
shown by river division (please see map for
clarification).

DIVISIONAL OFFICES

Head Office:
Dawson House, Great Sankey
Warrington
Tel: 092 572 4321

Central Division:
New Town House, PO Box 30
Buttermarket Street, Warrington
Tel: 0925 53922

Eastern Division:
Oakland House, Talbot Road
Old Trafford, Manchester
Tel: 061 872 5919

Northern Division:
PO Box 36, Holme Head, Carlisle
Tel: 0228 36321

Pennine Division:
London House, Oldham Road
Middleton
Tel: 061 643 1188

Ribble Division:
Pennine House, Stanley Street, Preston
Tel: 0772 59455

Rivers Division:
New Town House, Buttermarket Street
Warrington
Tel: 0925 53999

Southern Division:
Allport/Bridle Road, Bromborough
Merseyside
Tel: 051 327 1275

Western Division:
Merton House, Bootle, Merseyside
Tel: 051 922 7260

CHESHIRE AREA

RIVERS

River Dane
Davenham A.C.
Sec: A. Cook
Tel: 0606 41838
Permits also available from:
Hylands Pet Stores Ltd
121 Witton Road, Northwich
Tel: 0606 2768
Northwich & District Angling Centre
25 London Road, Northwich
Tel: 0606 2916

Middlewich A.S.
Sec: G. Stainer
Tel: 060 684 695
Permits also available from:
Middlewich Angling Supplies
Wheelock Street, Middlewich
Tel: 060 684 3853 or from
Association bailiff on bank

Northwich A.A.
Sec: E. Moore
Tel: 0606 2986
Permits also available from:
Erics Tackle & Pet Supplies
20a High Street, Weaverham
Tel: 0606 853126
Hylands Pet Stores Ltd
121 Witton Street, Northwich
Tel: 0606 2768
Scott's
84 Station Road, Northwich
Tel: 0606 6543

River Weaver
Middlewich A.S.
Sec: G. Stanier
Tel: 060 684 3695
Permits also available from:
Middlewich Angling Supplies
Wheelock Street, Middlewich
Tel: 060 684 3853

Northern A.A.
Sec: G. Wilson
Tel: 02572 65905
Permits also available from:
Local tackle shops

Northwich A.A.
Sec: E. Moore
Tel: 0606 2986
Permits also available from:
Erics Tackle & Pet Supplies
20a High Street, Weaverham
Tel: 0606 853126
Hylands Pet Stores Ltd
121 Witton Street, Northwich
Tel: 0606 2768
Scott's
84 Station Road, Northwich
Tel: 0606 6543

STILLWATERS

BILLINGE GREEN POOLS
Northwich A.A.
Sec: E. Moore
Tel: 0606 2986
Permits also available from:
Erics Tackle & Pet Supplies
20a High Street, Weaverham
Tel: 0606 853126
Daves Angling Supplies
Middlewich
Tel: 0606 3853
Hylands Pet Stores Ltd
121 Witton Street, Northwich
Tel: 0606 2768
Scott's
84 Station Road, Northwich
Tel: 0606 6543

TTOMS RESERVOIR, LANGLEY
Macclesfield
ce Albert A.S.
C. Sparkes
0625 26311
permits also available from:
ewton Fishing Tackle
rk Lane, Macclesfield
0625 24978

NEBRIDGE FISHERY
cle, Macclesfield
Wood
026 07 603 or 026 07 293
y and day permits available from
e. Advance bookings only

EAT BUDWORTH MERE
hwich A.A.
E. Moore
na, Gadbrook Road, Rudheath,
vich
0606 2986
and week permits available from bailiff
ank

HER WHITLEY SAND QUARRY
sham & District A.C.
D. Chow
0928 715099
its by written application

ALOAD RESERVOIR
Macclesfield
ce Albert A.S.
C. Sparkes
0625 26311
permits also available from:
ewton Fishing Tackle
k Lane, Macclesfield
0625 24978

DBEATERS RESERVOIR
ce Albert A.S.
C. Sparkes
0625 26311
its also available from:
ewton Fishing Tackle
k Lane, Macclesfield
0625 24978

TON HOLE
ford & District A.A.
. S. Bailey
06065 3902
bers only

TON LAKE FISHERY
n Farm, Tetton
lewich
27077 271
its from above

E HOLE, HIGHER POYNTON
ern A.A.
G. Wilson
2572 65909
its also available from local tackle
s

EAST CUMBRIA, NORTH & CENTRAL LANCASTER AREA

RIVERS

River Calders
Northern Angler Association
Sec: G. Wilson
Tel: 02572 65905
Permits also available from:
Local tackle shops

River Clough
Sedbergh A.A.
Sec: J. P. Lowis
Tel: 0587 20868
Permits also available from:
Lowis's (Sedbergh) Ltd., 45 Main Street, Sedbergh, Cumbria
Tel: 0587 20446

River Dee
Sedbergh A.A.
Sec: J. P. Lowis
Tel: 0587 20868
Permits also available from:
Lowis's (Sedbergh) Ltd., 45 Main Street, Sedbergh, Cumbria
Tel: 0587 20446

River Doe
Ingleton A.C.
Committee Member: Mr Cresswell
4 Ingleborough Park Drive, Ingleton, Yorkshire
Permits also available from:
P. & M. Berry, Newsagents, Main Street, Ingleton, via Carnforth, Yorkshire
Tel: 0468 41683

River Greta
Ingleton Angling Club
Committee Member: Mr Cresswell
4 Ingleborough Park Drive, Ingleton, Yorkshire
Permits also available from:
P. & M. Berry, Newsagents, Main Street, Ingleton, via Carnforth
Tel: 0468 41683

River Keer
Carnforth & District A.A.
Sec: A. McCartney
Permits also available from:
I. K. McCartney, 20 Coniston Road, Carnforth, Lancs
Tel: 0524 734160

River Lune
Kirby Lonsdale A.C.
Sec: G. Clough
Permits also available from:
The Tackle Box, Kirby Lonsdale, via Carnforth, Lancashire

HALTON & SKERTON FISHERIES
North West Water Authority
Tel: 0925 53999
Permits available from:
Mrs Curwen, Greenup Cottage, Hornby Road, Caton, Nr. Lancaster
Tel: 0524 770078
Darwen and Gough, 6 Moor Lane, Lancaster
Tel: 0524 64913

Lancaster & District A.A.
Sec: C. T. Preston
Tel: 0468 71574
Permit also available from:
Mrs A. Curwen, Greenup Cottage, Hornby Road, Caton, Nr. Lancaster
Tel: 0524 770078
Darwen & Gough, 6 Moor Lane, Lancaster
Tel: 0524 64913

Lansil A.C.
Sec: J. Barnes
Tel: 0524 416006
Permits also available from:
J. Clayton, Lansil Sports & Social Club, Caton Road, Lancaster
Tel: 0524 2016

Sedbergh A.A.
Sec: J. P. Lowis
Tel: 0587 20868
Permits also available from:
Lowis's (Sedbergh) Ltd., Main Street, Sedbergh, Cumbria
Tel: 0587 20446

Tebay & District A.C.
Sec: H. Riley
Tel: 05874 376
Permits also available from:
Cross Keys Hotel, Tebay
Tel: 05874 240
Junction Hotel, Tebay
Tel: 05874 232

River Ribble
Co-operative Wholesale Society
Withgill Estate, Higher Hodder, Cliteroe, Lancashire
Annual permits available from:
R. Hill, The Fishermans Haunt, 161 Blackburn Road, Accrington
Tel: 0254 34148
H. Le-Moine Fishing Tackle
22 Accrington Road, Blackburn
Tel: 0254 58716

Northern Anglers Association
Preston Centre
Enquiries: G. Jones
Carnarvon Road, Preston

Northern Anglers Association
Wigan Centre
Enquiries: W. Gratton
66 Balcarres Road, Aspull, Wigan
Tel: 0942 492376

Ribble Valley Borough Council
Church Brow, Clitheroe
Tel: 0200 25111
Permits also available from:
K. Varey, 4 New Market Street, Clitheroe
Tel: 0200 23267

MITTON BRIDGE TO HODDER FOOT
North West Water
Day permits available from:
Mrs M. M. Haynes, Mitton Hall Farm, Mitton, near Whalley, Lancs

Settle A.A.
Sec: M. G. Riley
Tel: 07292 3501
Permits also available from:
Royal Oak Hotel, Market Place, Settle
Tel: 07292 2561

Wigan A.A.
Committee Member: W. Gratton
Tel: 0942 492376
Permits from local tackle shops

River Ure

Hawes & High Abbotside A.A.
Sec: A. H. Barnes
Marridene, Gayle, Hawes
Tel: 870 384
Season, monthly and weekly permits also available from Masons, Newsagents, Board Hotel, Crown Hotel, all in Hawes

River Wenning

Bentham Anglers Association
Sec: A. R. Green
The Post Office, Main Street, Bentham,
Lancaster LA2 7HL
Tel: 0468 61650
Day and week permits also available from:
Mr Mottram, Station Road, Bentham
Nr. Lancaster
Tel: 0468 61886

River Wyre

Garstang & District A.A.
Sec: D. E. Irvin
33 High Street, Garstang, Preston
PR3 1EA
Weekly permits available from Sec

St. Michael's Angling Assoc
Sec: A. Moss
Permits also available from:
Miss G. Martin, Bridge Cottage,
St. Michael's-on-Wyre near Preston
Tel: 09958 228
Mike Roberts Fishing Tackle & Guns
Park Hill, Garstang, nr. Preston
Tel: 09952 3925

Wigan A.A.
Committee Member: W. Gratton
Tel: 0942 492376
Permits from local tackle shops

STILLWATERS

HIGHER & LOWER ANTLEY RESERVOIRS
Accrington & District F.C.
Sec: A. Balderstone
Tel: 0254 33517
Permits also available from:
T. Barratt, 8 Stanley Street, Oswaldtwistle
Tel: 0254 31272

AUDLEY RESERVOIR
Accrington & District F.C.
Sec: A. Balderstone
Tel: 0254 33517
Permits also available from:
T. Barratt, 9 Stanley Street, Oswaldtwistle
Tel: 0254 31273

BANK HOUSE FISHERY, LOW MILL
D. J. Dobson, Bank House, Lancaster Road,
Caton, Lancaster
Tel: 0524 770412
Day, ½ day and evening permits available from above. Advance booking advisable

BARNSFOLD
Nr. Gossnargh, Preston
Day permits by advance booking only from
F. Casson, 34 Blackburn Road, Ribchester,
near Preston
Tel: 025 484 202

CLAPHAM & AUTSWICK BECK
Ingleborough Estate Office, Clapham, via
Lancaster
Dr J. A. Farrer
Tel: 04685 302
Weekly permits from above

EARNSDALE RESERVOIR
Sunnyhurst, Darwen
Tel: 0254 75348

GRIZEDALE LEA RESERVOIR
Oakenclough
Kirkham & District Flyfishers
Sec: Mr Hinchcliffe
Permits available from:
Ye Olde Fishing Tackle Shoppe
8 Preston Street, Kirkham
Tel: 0772 685333

MITCHELL HOUSE RESERVOIR
Accrington & District F.C.
Sec: A. Balderstone
Tel: 0254 33517
Permits also available from:
T. Barratt, 8 Stanley Street, Oswaldtwistle
Tel: 0254 31272

MITTON FISHERY
North West Water Authority
Rivers Division, Newtown House,
Buttermarket Street, Warrington
Tel: 0925 53999
Day permits also available from
Mrs M. M. Haynes, Mitton Hall Farm,
Mitton, nr. Whalley, Lancs
Tel: 0254 86281

PARSONAGE RESERVOIR
Blackburn A.A.
Sec: B. Hogarth
1 Moorfield Road, Leyland, Lancashire
Tel: 07744 24018
Day permits from Roe Lee Tackle
Box 336, Whalley New Road, Blackburn
Tel: 0254 676977

SABDEN LODGE
Accrington & District F.C.
Sec: A. Balderstone
Tel: 0254 33157
Permits also available from:
T. Barratt, 8 Stanley Street, Oswaldtwistle
Tel: 0254 31272

WHALLEY ABBEY RESERVOIR
Black Dog Fisheries, Mill Lane, Cossall,
Notts
Permits also available from:
Ken Varey, 4 New Market Street, Clitheroe,
Lancs
Tel: 0200 23267

EDEN AND BORDER ESK AREA

RIVERS

River Border Esk
GLENZIER ESTATES
Baten Bush Farm, Longtown, Cumbria
Tel: 0228 791235

J. Mavir
Fauld Bungalow, Longtown, Cumbria
Tel: 0228 791496

River Caldew
Beck & Leslie Ltd.
Denton Street, Carlisle
Tel: 0228 24145

Dalston Parish Council
Dalston, Carlisle
Mr S. A. Cope
Tel: 0228 710485

River Eamont
Penrith Angling Association
Sec: R. F. Allinson
7 Scaws Drive, Penrith
Tel: 0768 62256
Day, week and season permits available
from: Charles R. Sykes
4 Great Dockery, Penrith, Cumbria
Tel: 0768 62418

River Eden
BRACKEN BANK LODGE
Lazonby, Nr. Penrith, Cumbria
Tel: 076 883 241
Permits by written application only to
Mr Burton

...sle Angling Association
...E. Cave
...228 20833
...its available from:
...sle Angling Centre, 2 Globe Lane,
...sle
...228 24035
...ardy's, South Henry Street, Carlisle
...228 23988
...ine & Co., 21 Warwick Road, Carlisle
...228 23009

...by Stephen A.A.
...B. Owen
...903 51591
...its available from:
...sons, 2 Market Street,
...y Stephens, Cumbria
...930 71519

...ith Angling Association
...R. F. Allinson
...ws Drive, Penrith
...768 62256
...nd week permits available from:
...les R. Sykes, 4 Great Dockery, Penrith,
...bria
...768 62418

...RWICK HALL WATERS
...its available from:
...Elwes, Warwick Hall, Carlisle
...228 60291

...er Irthing
...pton Angling Association
...T. Donockley
...069 76 518
...its available from:
...pton Sports, Front Street, Brampton

...er Lowther
...ith Angling Association
...R. F. Allinson
...ws Drive, Penrith
...768 62256
...nd week permits available from
...les R. Sykes, 4 Great Dockery, Penrith,
...bria
...768 62418

STILLWATERS

...VESWATER
...on permits only
...en application to:
...n West Water
...ern Division, Oakland House, Talbot
..., Old Trafford, Manchester M16 0QF
...061 872 5919

...TON DALE
...its by written application to:
...n West Water
...ern Division

...ERWATER FISH FARM LTD
...Plains, Armathwaite, Carlisle
...076 885 271

THIRLMERE
Permits by written application to:
North West Water
Rivers Division

THURSTONFIELD LOUGH
Nr. Carlisle
Mr H. Stordy
Lough House, Thurstonfield, Carlisle
Tel: 022 876 431
Day and season permits from above.
Advance booking advisable

ULLSWATER
No permits required although local
permission should be obtained

WESTMORLAND HOLME
Penrith Angling Association
Sec: R. F. Allinson
7 Scaws Drive, Penrith
Tel: 0768 62256
Day and week permits available from
Charles R. Sykes, 4 Great Dockery, Penrith,
Cumbria
Tel: 0768 62418

WET SLEDDALE
North West Water
Eastern Division, Oakland House,
Talbot Road, Old Trafford, Manchester
M16 0QF
Tel: 061 872 5919
Season permits only

SOUTH CUMBRIA AREA

RIVERS

River Bathay
Windermere, Ambleside & District A.A.
Sec: J. B. Cooper
Rylstone, Limethwaite Road, Heathwaite,
Windermere LA23 2BQ
Day, week and season permits also
available from local tackle shops and
Tourist Information Centres

River Kent
Kent (Westmorland) A.A.
Sec: J. C. Parkin
11a Blea Tarn Road, Kendal
Tel: 0539 22386
Day and week permits available from
T. Atkinsons Sports Depot, Kendal

Kirby Pool
Furness Fishing Association
Committee Member: Mr Groundwell
Tel: 0229 29661
Permits available from above
c/o Angling & Hiking Centre

River Rothay
Windermere, Ambleside & District A.A.
Sec: J. B. Cooper
Rylstone, Limethwaite Road, Heathwaite,
Windermere LA23 2BQ
Day, week and season permits also
available from local tackle shops and
Tourist Information Centres

River Sprint
Burneside Anglers Association
Chairman: E. Sykes
Tel: 0539 24020
Permits also available from:
The Jolly Anglers Hotel, Burneside
Nr. Kendal, Cumbria
Tel: 0539 24020

River Troutbeck
Windermere, Ambleside & District A.A.
Sec: J. B. Cooper
Rylstone, Limethwaite Road, Heathwaite,
Windermere LA23 2BQ
Day, week and season permits also
available from local tackle shops and
Tourist Information Centres

River South Tyne
Allendale A.A.
Visitors weekly permits available from the
Post Office, Allendale. Annual permits by
writing to J. W. Smith, Dalegarth, Allendale,
Hexham

Alston & District A.A.
Sec: L. S. Pattison
Belvedere, Park Lane, Alston
Tel: 049 881222
Day and week permits also available from:
D. & P. Jackson, Ironmongers,
High Market, Front Street, Alston, Cumbria

Haltwhistle & District A.C.
Sec: J. Mason, 27 Woodhead Park,
Haltwhistle
Weekly permits also available from:
John Greggs Sports Shop
Main Street, Haltwhistle, Northumberland
Tel: 0498 20255

GARRIGILL, ALSTON AREA
The Research and Development Co. Ltd.,
Alston, Cumbria
Yearly permits available from above

River Till
Chatton A.A.
Sec: A. Jarvis, New Road, Alnwick

Coldstream & District A.A.
Sec: M. Patterson
Tel: 0890 2719
Permits from: Head Gamekeeper
Nesbit Cottage, Fenton, Wooler
Tel: 066 86 243

Ford & Etal F.C.
Head Keepers Cottage
Ford & Etal Estates Office, Ford Village,
Nr. Berwick upon Tweed
Tel: 089 082 224
Permits also available from:
The Post Office, Ford Village,
Nr. Berwick upon Tweed
Tel: 089 082 230

STILLWATERS

BIGLAND HALL TROUT FISHERY
Newby Bridge, Cumbria
Contact: R. Bigland
Backbarrow, Ulverston LA12 8PB
Tel: 0448 31728
Day, evening and season permits available

BLEA TARN
National Trust, 'Broadlands'
Borrans Road, Ambleside
Tel: 09663 3003
Permits also available from:
Blea Tarn Farmhouse, Little Langdale
Nr. Ambleside, Cumbria
Tel: 09667 614

BLECHAM TARN
National Trust, 'Broadlands',
Borrans Road, Ambleside
Tel: 09663 3003
Permits by written application to:
The Warden, Low Wray Camp Site
Nr. Ambleside, Cumbria

BROTHERSWATER
Free fishing
National Trust Water
Borrans Road, Ambleside
Tel: 09667 614

————

CONISTON WATER
National Trust, 'Broadlands',
Borrans Road, Ambleside
Tel: 09663 3003
No fishing

DRUNKEN DUCK FARM
Hawkeshead, Nr Ambleside
Permits available form the Duck Inn,
Hawkeshead
Tel: 096 66 347

ESTHWAITE LAKE
Esthwaite Estates Ltd, Graythwaite Hall
Estate Office, Graythwaite, Nr. Ulverston,
Cumbria
Tel: 0448 31248
Permits also available from:
Mr T. A. Taylor
Esthwaite How Farm, Nr. Sawrey,
Hawkeshead, Cumbria
Tel: 09666 331
Mr B. Raistrick, The Post Office,
Hawkeshead, Cumbria
Tel: 09666 201

GLEASTON BECK
Furness Fishing Association
Committee Member: Mr Groundwell
1 Astra Buildings, Abbey Road,
Barrow-in-Furness
Tel: 0229 29661
Permits available from above
c/o Angling & Hiking Centre

GRASMERE LAKE
No permits required but access permission
should be obtained from local owners

GRIZEDALE BECK
Grizedale Angling Club
Sec: Alan Hilton
Tel: 09666 582
Permits also available from:
Mrs J. F. Taylforth, Camp Warden
Grizedale, Ambleside, Cumbria
Tel: 022 984 287

HIGH ARNSIDE TARN
Windermere, Ambleside & District A.A.
Sec: J. B. Cooper
Rylstone, Limethwaite Road, Heathwaite,
Windermere LA23 2BQ
**Day, week and season permits also
available from local tackle shops and
Tourist Information Centres**

KENTMERE TARN
Staveley & District A.A.
Sec: D. A. Taylor
Tel: 0539 821002
**Season permits only, direct from Staveley &
District A.A.**

KILLINGTON LAKE
Kent (Westmorland) Anglers Association
Sec: J. C. Parkin
11a Blea Tarn Road, Kendal
Tel: 0539 22386
**Day, week and season permits also
available from:**
Keepers Cottage on East Bank

MOSS ECCLES TARN
Windermere, Ambleside & District A.A.
Sec: J. B. Cooper
Rylstone, Limethwaite Road, Heathwaite,
Windermere LA23 2BQ
**Day, week and season permits also
available from local tackle shops and
Tourist Information Centres**

SCHOOL KNOT TARN
Windermere, Ambleside & District A.A.
Sec: J. B. Cooper
Rylstone, Limethwaite Road, Heathwaite,
Windermere LA23 2BQ
**Day, week and season permits also
available from local tackle shops and
Tourist Information Centres**

URSWICK TARN
Urswick Tarn Association
Sec: Mrs C. M. Clutton-Brock
1 Church View, Great Urswick, Ulverston,
Cumbria
Tel: 0229 56642
Permits also available from:
The Derby Arms, Great Urswick, Ulverston,
Cumbria
Tel: 0229 56348

WINDERMERE
South Lakeland District Council
Tourism & Recreation Dept., Ashleigh
Windermere, Cumbria
Tel: 09662 2244
Permits also available from:
Kendal Sports Shop, 28 Stramongate,
Kendal, Cumbria
Tel: 0539 21554
J. & C. H. Smythe, Ash Street,
Bowness-on-Windermere, Cumbria
Tel: 09662 3750

YEW TREE TARN
Coniston & Torver District A.A.
Sec: D. E. Lancaster
Wetherlam, Mount Pleasant, Greenod
Ulverston, Cumbria
Tel: 022 986 307
Day permits also available from:
Mr Raven, Gift & Tackle Shop, Yewda
Road, Coniston, Cumbria LA21 8DU

SOUTH LANCASHIRE GREATER MANCHESTER & MERSEYSIDE AREA

STILLWATERS

BLACKLEY NEW ROAD UPPERLA
City of Manchester Recreational Servi
Town Hall, Manchester
Tel: 061 236 3377
Permits from: McMahons Newsagents
Riverdale Road, Manchester

**BOTTOMS RESERVOIR,
TINTWHISTLE, GLOSSOP**
North West Water
Eastern Division, Bottoms Office
Tel: 045 74 2064
Season and day permits also available
site

BRADFORD LODGE
Bolton & District A.A.
Sec: J. A. Shanahan
Tel: 0204 63770
**Season permits also available from loc
tackle shops**

CALDERBROOK DAMS
Todmorden A.S.
Sec: D. Howorth
Tel: 070 681 4443
Permits also available from:
Pet Shop, Hare Hill Road, Littleborou
Lancs
Tel: 0706 78452
Steve's Tackle Shop, Rochdale, Lancs

TLESHAW RESERVOIR
am & District United A.A.
. K. Lees
61 624 5176
its also available from:
tackle shops

E LODGE RESERVOIR, GLOSSOP
West Water
rn Division, Bottoms Office
45 74 2064
n and day permits also available on

N RESERVOIR (EARNSDALE
RVOIR), DARWEN
. Priestley
owlesly Road, Darwen, Lancs
NE
254 75348
ermits also available from:
wistle, 'County Sports'
worth Street, Darwen
254 72187

DALE LOWER RESERVOIR,
TON
of Manchester Recreation Dept.
n Square, Manchester
61 236 3377
its also available from bank

LE RESERVOIR
West Water
ine Division, Parkfield House,
hester Old Road, Middleton,
hester
61 643 1188
al permits only

FCOCKER RESERVOIR
n & District A.A.
. A. Shanahan
204 63770
n permits also available from local
e shops

NKWATER PARK LAKE,
TWICH
nall Whitley A.A.
. Robinson
61 224 3174
its also available from local tackle
s

SCAR 1 & 2, GLEAVES, SHORE
GE
n & District A.A.
. A. Shanahan
204 63770
n permits also available from local
e shops

NSDALE RESERVOIR
ean Reservoir

ELTON RESERVOIR, BURY
Bury A.A. & Elton Sailing Club
Mr Taylor
Tel: 061 764 2858
Permits also available from the banks

ENTWISTLE RESERVOIR
North West Water
Pennine Division, Parkfield House,
Manchester Old Road, Middleton,
Manchester
Tel: 061 643 1188
Annual permits only

FIRS PARK LAKE
Leigh & District A.A.
Sec: J. Scotson
Tel: 0942 674944
Permits available from Bank Ranger

FIR TREE FLASH
Fir Tree Angling Society
Sec: R. Newport
Tel: 0942 675403
Permits available from the banks

**FIRWOOD, FIRWOOD LANE,
BOLTON**
Bolton & District A.A.
Sec: J. A. Shanahan
Tel: 0204 63770
Season permits also available from local
tackle shops

HEATON RESERVOIR
North West Water
Pennine Division, Parkfield House,
Manchester Old Road, Middleton,
Manchester
Tel: 061 643 1188
Annual permits only

**HILL MILL RESERVOIR, CROMPTON
WAY**
Halliwell
Bolton & District A.A.
Sec: J. A. Shanahan
Tel: 0204 63770
Season permits also available from local
tackle shops

JUMBLES RESERVOIR
North West Water
Pennine Division, Parkfield Lane,
Manchester Old Road, Middleton,
Manchester M24 4EA
Tel: 061 643 1188
Day and ½ day permits available from
warden

KITCLIFFE RESERVOIR
Oldham & District Amalgamated Anglers
Sec: H. Garside
Tel: 04577 5993
Permits also available from:
Local tackle shops

LIVERPOOL PARK LAKES
Liverpool City Council
Recreation & Open Spaces Dept
Mansion House, Calderstones Park,
Liverpool
Tel: 051 724 2371

**LOWER AND UPPER
RODDLESWORTH**
See Rivington Group Reservoirs

**MERTONS 1 & 2, SHARPLES ASTLEY
BRIDGE**
Bolton & District A.A.
Sec: J. Shanahan
Tel: 0204 63770
Season permits also available from local
tackle shops

OGDEN RESERVOIR
Oldham & District United A.A.
Sec: H. Garside
Tel: 04577 5993
Permits also available from local tackle
shops

PENNINE TROUT FISHERY
5 miles from Junction 21 on M62
Calderbrook Lake, Calderbrook Road,
Littleborough, Nr. Rochdale, Lancs
Tel: 070681 6829

PENNINGTON FLASH
Pennington Flash A.A.
Sec: J. Scotson
Tel: 0942 674944
Permits also available from Association
bailiffs

RIVINGTON GROUP RESERVOIRS
Nr. Bolton, Lancs
North West Water
Western Division, Merton House, Stanley
Road, Bootle
Tel: 051 922 7260
**Season and day permits also available from
local tackle shops**

SMITHS RESERVOIR, SMITHS ROAD, BOLTON
Bolton & District A.A.
Sec: J. A. Shanahan
Tel: 0204 63770
**Season permits also available from local
tackle shops**

———————

STRINESDALE UPPER RESERVOIR & STRINESDALE LOWER RESERVOIR
Oldham & District Amalgamated A.A.
Sec: H. Garside
Tel: 04577 5993
**Permits also available from local tackle
shops**

SWINESHAW MILL DAM, MILLBROOK
Oldham & District Amalgamated A.A.
Sec: H. Garside
Tel: 04577 5993
**Permits also available from local tackle
shops**

VALE HOUSE RESERVOIR
Tintwhistle
North West Water
Eastern Division, Bottoms Office
Tel: 045 74 2064
**Season and day permits also available on
site**

WALKERWOOD RESERVOIR
North West Water
Pennine Division, Parkfield House,
Manchester Old Road, Middleton,
Manchester
Tel: 061 643 1188
Annual permits only

WAYOH RESERVOIR
North West Water
Pennine Division, Parkfield House,
Manchester Old Road, Middleton,
Manchester
Tel: 061 642 1188
Annual permits only

WORTHINGTON LAKES
North West Water
Central Division, New Town, Buttermarket
Street, Warrington
Tel: 0925 53922
Permits also available from:
Warden or ticket machine in car park

WEST & SOUTH WEST CUMBRIA AREA
RIVERS

River Cocker
Cockermouth A.A.
Tel: 0900 823570
Day, week and season permits available

from
D. Lothian, 35 Main Street, Cockermouth
Tel: 0900 822006
I. Nicholson, The Gun Shop, Larton Road,
Cockermouth
Tel: 0900 822058

River Derwent
Cockermouth A.A.
Dr J. Abernethy
5 Sunscales Avenue
Tel: 0900 823 570
D. Lothian, 35 Main Street, Cockermouth
Tel: 0900 822006
I. Nicholson, The Gun Shop, Larton Road,
Cockermouth
Tel: 0900 822058

Keswick Anglers Association
Sec: W. Ashcroft
Springhaven, How Lane, Portinscale,
Keswick
Tel: 0596 72703
Day and week permits available from:
Local tackle shops or S.A.E. to Sec

River Ehen
Egremont Angling Association
Sec: C. Fisher
Tel: 0946 820855
Permits available from:
M. Bell, Magnus Maximus Design Ltd.
Frizington, Cumbria
Tel: 094 686 771

Wath Brow & Ennerdale A.A.
Sec: D. Edwards
Tel: 0946 811912
Permits available from:
Wath Post Office, Cleator Moor, Cumbria
Tel: Mr W. Bound, 0946 810377

River Ellen
Permits available from
R. & J. Holt, The Colour Shop
Outgang Road, Aspatria
Tel: 0956 20514

River Esk
Muncaster Castle Estates
Permits available from:
Pennington Arms Hotel
Ravenglass, Cumbria
Tel: 065 77 222

River Greta
Keswick Anglers Association
Sec: W. Ashcroft
Springhaven, How Lane, Portinscale,
Keswick
Tel: 0596 72703
Day and week permits available from:
Local tackle shops or S.A.E. to Sec

River Irt
Lutwidge Arms Hotel
Holmrook, Cumbria
Permits available from:
Tel: 094 04 230 C. Simpson

River Marron
BRANTHWAITE MILL
Branthwaite, Workington
Permits available from:
Tel: 0900 5089 D. Talbot

STILLWATERS

BASSENTHWAITE LAKE
Lake District Planning Board
Busher Walk, Kendal, Cumbria
Tel: 0539 24555

BURNMOOR TARN
National Trust Water
Borrans Road, Ambleside
Tel: 096 63 3003

BUTTERMERE
National Trust, 'Broadlands', Borrans ▮
Ambleside
Tel: 096 63 3003
Permits also available from:
I. Nicholson, The Gun Shop, Lorton R◀
Cockermouth
Tel: 0900 822058
Mrs T. Richardson, Gatesgarth Farm,
Buttermere, Cumbria
Tel: 059 685 256

COGRA MOSS, NR. LAMPLUGH
Cockermouth Angling Association
Tel: 0900 823570
Day, week and season permits also
available from:
D. Lothian, 35 Main Street, Cockermo◀
Cumbria
Tel: 0900 822006
I. Nicholson, The Gun Shop, Lorton R◀
Cockermouth
Tel: 0900 822058
W. E. Litt, Dockray Nook Farm, Lampl▮
Tel: 09186 432

DERWENTWATER
Keswick Angling Association
Sec: W. Ashcroft
Springhaven, How Lane, Portinscale,
Keswick
Tel: 0596 72703
Day and week permits also available ▮
Local tackle shops or S.A.E. to Sec

———————

LOWESWATER
National Trust, 'Broadlands', Borrans ▮
Ambleside
Tel: 096 63 3003
Permits also available from:
Kirkstile Inn, Loweswater
Tel: 090 085 232
I. Nicholson, The Gun Shop, Lorton R◀
Cockermouth
Tel: 0900 822058
Mrs T. Richardson, Gatesgarth Farm,
Buttermere, Cumbria
Tel: 059 685 256

OVERWATER FISHERY
Nr. Uldale
Permits from:
D. Lothian Tackle, Main Street,
Cockermouth

WASTWATER
National Trust, 'Broadlands', Borrans ▮
Ambleside
Tel: 096 63 3003
Permits by written application:
The Warden, National Trust Camp Sit◀
Wasdale Head

Northumbrian

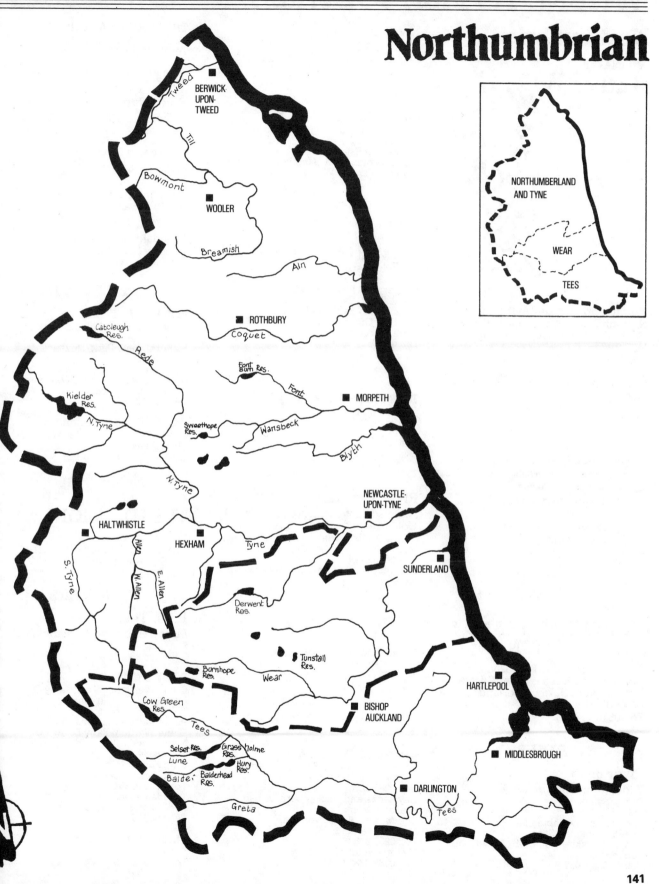

BERWICK-UPON-TWEED

Tweed

Till

Bowmont

WOOLER

Breamish

Aln

Catcleugh Res.

ROTHBURY

Coquet

Rede

Font Burn Res.

Font

Kielder Res.

N. Tyne

Sweethope Res.

MORPETH

Wansbeck

Blyth

N. Tyne

NEWCASTLE-UPON-TYNE

HALTWHISTLE

HEXHAM

Tyne

Allen

W. Allen

E. Allen

SUNDERLAND

S. Tyne

Derwent Res.

Tunstall Res.

Burnhope Res.

Wear

HARTLEPOOL

Cow Green Res.

Tees

BISHOP AUCKLAND

Selset Res.

Grassholme Res.

Lune

Hury Res.

MIDDLESBROUGH

Balder

Balderhead Res.

Greta

DARLINGTON

Tees

Inset map

NORTHUMBERLAND AND TYNE

WEAR

TEES

WHERE TO FISH—COARSE

Northumbrian Water Authority

Northumbrian Water Authority
Northumbria House, Regent Centre
Gosforth, Newcastle-upon-Tyne
NE3 3PX
Tel: 0632 843151

Chief Fisheries Officer: A. S. Champion
Fishery Officer: J. D. Cave

Regional Rod Licences
Rod Licences are obtainable from the Head
Offices and other selected outlets.
A full list is obtainable on request.

Rod Licences for Scaling Dam are available
from Yorkshire Water Authority, 21 Park
Square South, Leeds.

NORTHUMBERLAND & TYNE DIVISION

Northumberland & Tyne Division
Northumbria House, Town Centre,
Cramlington, Northumberland
NE23 6UP
Tel: 0670 713322

RIVERS

River Blyth

Bedlington & Blagdon A.A.
Sec: S. Symons
Tel: 0670 822011
Permits also available from:
The Professionals Shop
Bedlington-shire Golf Club, Acorn Bank,
Bedlington
Tel: 0670 822087

River Till

Chatton A.A.
Sec: A. Jarvis, New Road, Alnwick

Coldstream & District A.A.
Sec: Mr Patterson
Tel: 0890 2719
The Fenton Estate
Permits from: Head Gamekeeper, Nesbit
Cottage, Fenton, Wooler
Tel: 066 86 243

Ford & Etal F.C.
Head Keepers Cottage
Ford & Etal Estates Office, Ford Village,
Nr. Berwick upon Tweed
Tel: 089 082 224
Permits also available from:
The Post Office, Ford Village, Nr. Berwick
upon Tweed
Tel: 089 082 230

TILLMOUTH PARK HOTEL
Cornhill on Tweed
Tel: 0890 2255

River Tweed

See also Scotland (Borders Region)
Coldstream & District A.A.
Sec: E. M. Paterson
Market Square, Coldstream
Tel: 0890 2719
Day and week permits also available from
bank

Kelso Angling Association
Sec: C. Hutchinson
Tel: 05732 3440

Ladykirk & Norham A.A.
Sec: R. G. Wharton, 8 St. Cuthberts Square,
Norham, Berwick-on-Tweed
Tel: 0289 82467
Day, week and season permits also
available from:
The Masons Arms, Norham,
Northumberland
Tel: 0289 82326
Victoria Hotel, Norham
Tel: 0289 82237

TILLMOUTH PARK HOTEL
Cornhill on Tweed
Tel: 0890 2255

For additional information see also Rive
Till this section

River Tyne

Haltwhistle & District A.C.
Sec: J. Mason, Castle Hill Ho., Haltwhis
Permits also available from:
John Greggs Sports Shop,
Main Street, Haltwhistle
Tel: 0498 20255

Northumbrian A.F.
Sec: P. A. Hall
Tel: 0632 21987

Tynedale District Council
Prospect House, Hexham
Tel: 0434 60411

STILLWATERS

BOLAM LAKE, BELSAY
Northumberland National Parks &
Countryside Dept.
Estburn, South Park, Hexham
Tel: 0434 605555
Permits also available from:
Mr Andrew Miller, The Warden
Bolam Lake, Nr. Belsay
Tel: 066 181 234

Whittle Dene Reservoirs
Gateshead & Newcastle Water Co.
Mr F. Palmer
Whittle Dene Reservoirs
Tel: 06614 3210
Day permits available

TEES DIVISION

Tees Division
Trenchard Avenue, Thornaby
Stockton-on-Tees TS17 0EQ
Tel: 0642 62216

RIVERS

River Tees

Bishop Auckland & District A.C.
Sec: L. Mallam
Tel: 0388 896575

RABY ESTATES
Game Warden, Raby Estates Office
Staindrop, Co. Durham
Tel: 0833 60416
Permits also available from:
Game Warden, Raby Estates Office
Middleton-in-Teesdale
Tel: 08334 209
High Force Hotel
High Force, Teesdale
Tel: 0833 22264
Teesdale Hotel
Middleton-in-Teesdale
Tel: 08334 264

Thornaby A.A.
Sec: D. Speight
Tel: 0642 62099

NORTHUMBRIAN

m A.A.
: Mr Flynn
: 0642 66473
mits also available from:
K. Flynn, The Tackle Shop,
Varo Terrace, Stockton-on-Tees
: 0642 66473

STILLWATERS

ACKTON RESERVOIR
thumbrian Water Authority
es Division Office
nchard Avenue, Thornaby,
ckton-on-Tees
: 0642 62216
permits available on site

ALING DAM
thumbrian Water Authority
es Division Office
nchard Avenue, Thornaby,
ckton-on-Tees
: 0642 62216
mits also available from:
ing Lodge at reservoir

TILERY LAKE
Wingate, Co. Durham
Hartlepool & District A.C.
Sec: K. Hewitson
16 Heathfield Drive, Hartlepool
Tel: 042969882 or 69025
Restricted day permits from
Anglers Services Ltd, 27 Park Road,
Hartlepool
Anglers Services Ltd, Claypath, Durham

WEAR DIVISION

Wear Division
Wear House, Abbey Road, Pity Me
Durham DH1 5EZ
Tel: 0385 44222

RIVERS

River Wear
Bishop Auckland & District A.C.
Sec: L. Mallam
Tel: 038889 6595

Chester-le-Street & District A.C.
Sec: T. Wright
156 Sedgletch Road, Houghton-Le-Spring
DH4 5JY
Tel: 0783 848211
Day and annual permits also available from:
Photographic & Sports Centre
139 Front Street, Chester-le-Street
Tel: 0385 882557

FINCHALE ABBEY
Mr E. M. Welsh
The Farmhouse, Finchale Abbey, Durham
Tel: 0385 66528

Willington & District A.C.
Sec: R. Lumb
Permits also available from:
Bonds Tackle Shop
High Street, Willington
Tel: 038889 6273

Durham City Anglers
Sec: G. Hedley
Tel: 0385 64603

WHERE TO FISH—GAME

Northumbrian Water Authority

Northumbrian Water Authority
Northumbria House, Regent Centre
Gosforth, Newcastle-upon-Tyne
NE3 3PX
Tel: 0632 843151
Chief Fisheries Officer: A. S. Champion
Fishery Officer: J. D. Cave

NORTHUMBERLAND & TYNE DIVISION

Northumberland & Tyne Division
Northumbria House, Town Centre,
Cramlington, Northumberland
NE23 6UP
Tel: 0670 713322
Regional Rod Licences
Rod Licences are obtainable from the Head
Offices and other selected outlets.
A full list is obtainable on request.
Rod Licences for Scaling Dam are available
from Yorkshire Water Authority, 21 Park
Square South, Leeds.

RIVERS

River Aln

Aln Angling Association
Sec: F. J. R. Moir
Tel: 0665 602771
Day, week, month and season permits also
available from:
R. Murray (Sports) Ltd., 2 Narrow Gate,
Alnwick

River Blyth

Bedlington & Blagdon A.A.
Sec: S. Symons
8 Moorland Drive, Bedlington
Tel: 0670 822011
Day permits also available from:
The Professionals Shop
Bedlington-shire Golf Club, Acorn Bank,
Bedlington
Tel: 0670 822087

River Coquet

Northumbrian Anglers Federation
Sec: P. A. Hall
24 Ridley Place, Newcastle upon Tyne
NE1 8LF
Tel: 0632 321987
Week, fortnight and season permits
available by writing to Head Bailiff.
A. Bagnall, Thirston Mill, West Thirston,
Felton, Morpeth, Northumberland

Tillmouth Park Hotel
Cornhill on Tweed
Tel: 0890 2255

River Tweed

See also Scotland (Borders Region)
Coldstream & District A.A.
Sec: Mr Patterson
Tel: 0890 2719
Permits also available from:
Berwick Sports Centre
Bridge Street, Berwick upon Tweed
Tel: 0289 6116
The Crown Hotel
Coldstream, Borders
Tel: 0890 2558
Tourist Information Centre, Caravan
Coldstream, Borders
Tel: 0890 2607

Kelso Angling Association
Sec: C. Hutchinson
Tel: 05732 3440

Ladykirk & Norham A.A.
Sec: R. G. Wharton, 8 St. Cuthberts Square,
Norham
Permits also available from:
The Mason's Arms
Norham, Northumberland
Tel: 0289 82326
Victoria Hotel
Norham
Tel: 0289 82237

Tillmouth Park Hotel
Cornhill on Tweed
Tel: 0890 2255

River Tyne

Haltwhistle & District A.C.
Sec: J. Mason, Castle Hill Ho., Haltwhistle
Permits also available from:
John Greggs Sports Shop
Main Street, Haltwhistle
Tel: 0498 20255

Northumbrian Anglers Federation
Sec: P. A. Hall
24 Ridley Place, Newcastle upon Tyne
NE1 8LF
Tel: 0632 321987
Week, fortnight and season permits
available by writing to
Head Bailiff, A. Bagnall, Thirston Mill, West
Thirston, Felton Morpeth, Northumberland

Tynedale District Council
Prospect House, Hexham
Tel: 0434 60411
Day and season permits available from
above

River Wansbeck

Wansbeck District Council
Day and monthly permits from:
Warden, Riverside Park, Ashington
Tel: 0670 812323

for Tributary see River Font

Rothbury & Thropton A.C.
Sec: J. H. Whiteley
'Sandaig', Hillside, Rothbury
Permits also available from:
James Renvoise, Fishing Tackle Shop, High
Street, Rothbury

River Derwent

Axwell Park & Derwent Valley A.A.
Sec: Mr Ransome
5 Naylor Avenue, Winlaton Mill, Blaydon
Tyne & Wear
Day permits available from above

River East Allen

Allendale A.A.
Sec: Mr Smith
Dalegarth, Allendale, Hexham
Tel: 043 483 375
Weekly permits also available from:
The Post Office
Allendale, Nr. Hexham
Tel: 043 483 201

River Font

Northumbrian A.F.
Sec: P. A. Hall
Tel: 0632 21987

River North Tyne

Falstone F.C.
Sec: G. W. Robson
3 Mousey Haugh, Falstone, Nr. Hexham
Day, week and season permits also
available from:
Black Cock Inn
Falstone, Nr. Hexham
Tel: 0660 40200

The George Hotel
Chollerford, Northumberland
Tel: 043 481 205

River Rede

Otterburn Towers Hotel
Otterburn, Northumberland
Tel: 0830 20673
Day Trout permits available from above

Percy Arms Hotel
Otterburn, Northumberland
Tel: 0830 20261
Trout permits available to residents only

STILLWATERS

BAKETHIN RESERVOIR
Nr. Kielder, North Tyne Valley
Northumbrian Water Authority
Northumberland & Tyne Division
Northumbria House, Cramlington
Tel: 0670 713322
Day permits on site from fishing lodge
Tel: 0660 50260

FONTBURN RESERVOIR
Off Scots Gap Road
Northumbrian Water Authority
Northumberland & Tyne Division
Northumbria House, Cramlington
Tel: 0670 713322
Mr N. Roberts, Superintendent
The Fishing Lodge, Fontburn Reservoir
Tel: 0669 20465
Day permits on site

KIELDER RESERVOIR
Nr. Bellingham
Northumbrian Water Authority
Northumberland & Tyne Division
Northumbria House, Cramlington
Tel: 0670 713322
Permits available from

Fishing Centre', Matthews, Kielder,
umberland
660 50260
permits on site

ETHOPE LOUGH
y, day and evening permits available

S. P. Wood
h House, Sweethope Lough, Harle,
castle upon Tyne
830 40249

TTLE DENE RESERVOIRS
castle & Gateshead Water Co
permits available from
mer, Whittle Dean Reservoirs
66 14 3210

ES DIVISION
chard Avenue, Thornaby,
kton-on-Tees TS17 0EQ
0642 62216

RIVERS
er Tees
op Auckland & District A.C.
L. Mallam
388 896575

Y ESTATES
e Warden, Raby Estates Office,
drop, Co. Durham
833 60416
its also available from
e Warden, Raby Estates Office,
leton-in-Teesdale
8334 209
Force Hotel
Force, Teesdale
833 22264
dale Hotel
leton-in-Teesdale
8334 2674

naby A.A.
D. Speight
ainsby Gate, Stainsby Hill, Thornaby,
eland
642 620799
ission to fish may be obtained by
g to above enclosing S.A.E.

A.C.
Mr Flynn
642 66473
its also available from:
. Flynn, The Tackle Shop,
ro Terrace, Stockton-on-Tees
642 66473

STILLWATERS
DERHEAD RESERVOIR
arnard Castle, Co. Durham
umbrian Water Authority
Division Office
chard Avenue, Thornaby
ton-on-Tees
642 62216
permits available from:
t machine on site

CKTON RESERVOIR
otherstone
umbrian Water Authority
Division Office
chard Avenue, Thornaby,
ton-on-Tees

Tel: 0642 62216
Day permits available from fishing lodge at
reservoir

COW GREEN RESERVOIR
Nr. Middleton-in-Teesdale
Northumbrian Water Authority
Tees Division Office
Trenchard Avenue, Thornaby,
Stockton-on-Tees
Tel: 0642 62216
Day permits also available from:
Fishing Lodge at reservoir

GRASSHOLME RESERVOIR
Nr. Barnard Castle, Co. Durham
Northumbrian Water Authority
Tees Division Office
Trenchard Avenue, Thornaby,
Stockton-on-Tees
Tel: 0642 62216
Day permits available on site

HURY RESERVOIR
Nr. Balderstone, Co. Durham
Northumbrian Water Authority
Tees Division Office
Trenchard Avenue, Thornaby,
Stockton-on-Tees
Tel: 0642 62216
Permits available on site

LARTINGTON FISHERIES
Lartington Hall Estates
Permits available from:
M. Innis
'Riversdale', Lartington, Barnard Castle
Tel: 0833 50632

LOCKWOOD BECK RESERVOIR
Teesdale
Northumbrian Water Authority
Tees Division Office
Trenchard Avenue, Thornaby,
Stockton-on-Tees
Tel: 0642 62216
Permits also available on site

SCALING DAM
on Guisborough-Whitby Road
Northumbrian Water Authority
Tees Division Office
Trenchard Avenue, Thornaby,
Stockton-on-Tees
Tel: 0642 62216
Day permits available from Fishing Lodge
at reservoir

SELSET RESERVOIR
Nr. Middleton-in-Teesdale
Northumbrian Water Authority
Tees Division Office
Trenchard Avenue, Thornaby,
Stockton-on-Tees
Tel: 0642 62216
Day permits also available from:
Fishing Lodge at reservoir

TILERY LAKE
Hartlepool & District A.C.
Sec: K. Hewitson
Tel: 0429 69882
Permits also available from:
Anglers Service
45 Claypath, Durham
Tel: 0385 47584
Anglers Service
27 Park Road, Hartlepool
Tel: 0429 74844

WEAR DIVISION
Wear Division
Wear House, Abbey Road, Pity Me
Durham DH1 5EZ
Tel: 0385 44222
RIVERS
River Browney
Bishop Auckland & District A.C.
Sec: L. Mallam
Tel: 038889 6575

Durham City Anglers
Sec: G. Hedley
Tel: 0385 64603

River Wear
Bishop Auckland & District A.C.
Sec: L. Mallam
Tel: 038889 6595
For permit information contact D. Naisbitt,
Windrow Sports, Bishop Auckland

Chester-le-Street & District A.C.
Sec: T. Wright
Tel: 0783 848211
Day and season permits also available
from:
Photographic & Sports Centre
139 Front Street, Chester-le-Street
Tel: 0385 882557

FINCHALE ABBEY
E. B. Welsh
The Farmhouse, Finchale Abbey, Durham
Tel: 0385 66528
Day permits available from above

Willington & District A.C.
Sec: R. Lumb
18 Shipley Terrace, West View Estate,
Crook
Day and week permits also available from:
Bonds Tackle Shop
High Street, Willington
Tel: 038889 6273
Mrs Newton, The Brown Trout, Sunnybrow
H. Roberts (Newsagents), 2 East Bridge
Street, Crook
A. Coates, Sports and Tackle Shop, Hope
Street, Crook
Anglers Services, Claypath, Durham

Durham City Anglers
Sec: G. Hedley
Tel: 0385 64603

STILLWATERS
BURNHOPE RESERVOIR
Northumbrian Water Authority
Wear Division
Abbey Road, Pity Me, Durham
Tel: 0385 44222
Day permits available from the reservoir
lodge

DERWENT RESERVOIR
Edmundbyers, nr. Consett, Co. Durham
Sunderland & South Shields Water Co.
29 St. John Street, Sunderland
Tel: 0783 57123
Day permits available from above

TUNSTALL RESERVOIR
Nr. Wolsingham, Weardale
Northumbrian Water Authority
Wear Division
Abbey Road, Pity Me, Durham
Tel: 0385 44222
Day permits available from site

OSWESTRY

Llyn Vyrnwy

Afon Tanat

Afon Cain

Pen-y-Gwely

WELSHPOOL

Roden

Perry

MARKET
DRAYTON

Tern

Trent
STAFFORD

Banwy

Rhiw

Shropshire
Union Canal

Severn

Meverley

SHREWSBURY

Roden

Afon Trannc

Severn

Afon Dulas

LLANIDLOES

NEWTOWN

MONTGOMERY

Red
Brook

Camd
Brook

Aston

Severn

TELFORD

NEWTOWN

Staffs and
Worcs Canal

Cannock Chase
Reservoirs

Teme

Clun

Omy

WOLVERHAMPTON

Severn

BIRMINGHAM

Teme

Rea

Stour

Stour

KIDDERMINSTER

Cole

Cole

Blythe

Elmley
Brook

Worcs and
Birmingham
Canal

WORCESTER

Teme

MALVERN

EVESHAM

Alne

Grand Union Canal

Leadon

Laughern
Brook

Ripple

PERSHORE

Isbourne

Arrow

Avon

LEAMINGTON
SPA

Leadon

Stour

STRATFORD-UPON-AVON

Dene

SEVERN

Gloucester
and
Berkeley
Canal

GLOUCESTER

Little Avon

146

Severn-Trent

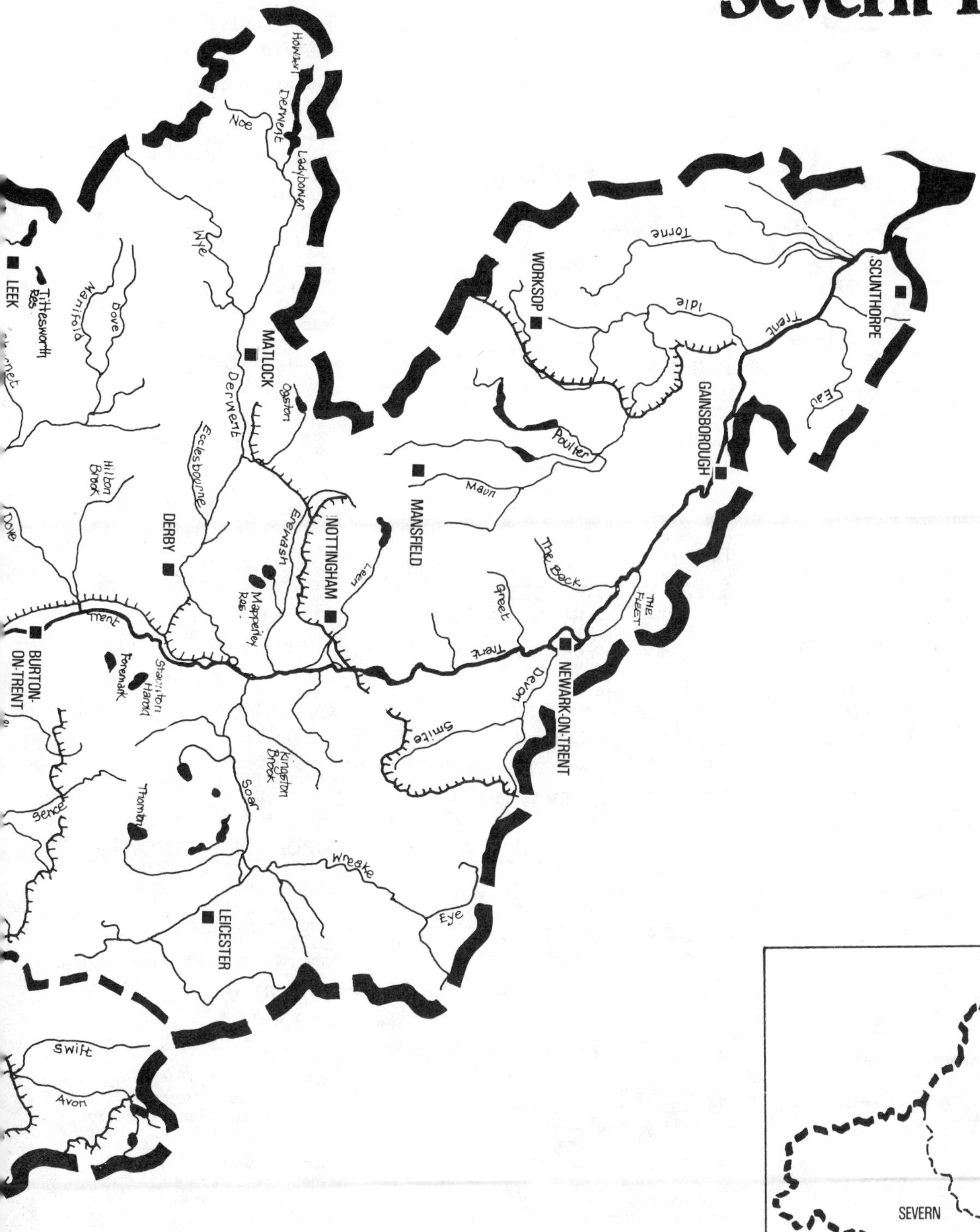

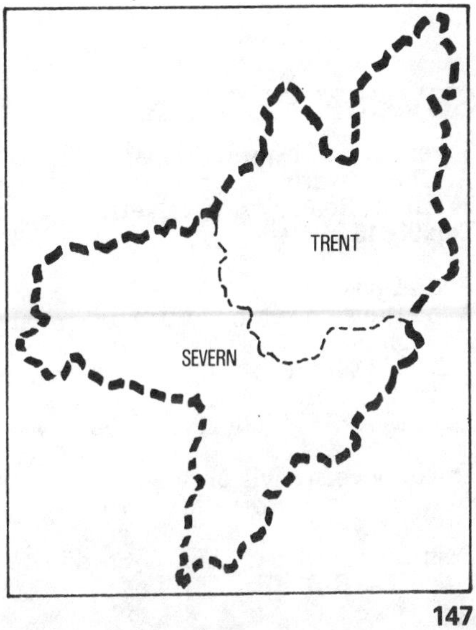

Howarf

Derwent

Noe

Wye

Ladybower

Titlesworth Res.

LEEK

Manifold

Dove

Derwent

MATLOCK

Ogston

Ecclesbourne

Hilton Brook

Dove

DERBY

Everash

Mapperley Res.

NOTTINGHAM

Leen

Trent

Trent

Sence

BURTON-ON-TRENT

Tame

Fonmark

Staunton Harold

Kingston Brook

Thornton

Soar

Smite

Devon

LEICESTER

Wreake

Eye

Swift

Avon

WORKSOP

Torne

Idle

Poulter

Maun

Trent

MANSFIELD

The Beck

Greet

The Fleet

SCUNTHORPE

Trent

Eau

GAINSBOROUGH

NEWARK-ON-TRENT

TRENT

SEVERN

WHERE TO FISH–COARSE

Severn Trent Water Authority

Abelson House, 2297 Coventry Road
Sheldon, Birmingham B26 3PU
Tel: 021 743 4222

Assistant Director of Scientific
Services: Mr M. L. Parry

Regional Rod Licences
Regional rod licences are available from
S.T.W.A. offices as given below and in
Severn Region listing, Monday to Friday
8.30am – 5.00pm or from Authority's many
licence distributors throughout the area.
Licence enables holder to fish entire
region.

Dial-a-Report
For information regarding water levels and
conditions:
Trent Area: 0602 866405
Upper Severn Area: 0743 8037
Lower Severn Area: 0684 296929

SEVERN REGION

Severn Area Fisheries Manager:
A. Churchward
64 Albert Road North, Malvern
Tel: 06845 61511

Avon Division
Avon House, De Montford Way
Cannon Park, Coventry
Tel: 0203 416510
District Fisheries Officer: A. Starkie
Tel: 06845 61511 Ext. 261

Lower Severn Division
64 Albert Road North, Malvern
Tel: 06845 61511
District Fisheries Officer: A. Starkie
Tel: 06845 61511 Ext. 261

Upper Severn division
Shelton, Shrewsbury
Tel: 0743 63141
District Fisheries Officer: J. Wollard
Tel: 0743 63141 Ext. 320

RIVERS

River Avon
CLEVE PRIOR
Seven Trent Water Authority
Free fishing
Details available from
Tel: 06845 61511

**ECKINGTON, STRENSHAM LOCK
BIRLINGHAM**
Cheltenham A.C.
Sec: F. J. Selley
Tel: 0242 28586
Permits available from:
The Bell Inn, Eckington

EVESHAM, HAMPTON FERRY
E. Huxley
Hampton Ferry House, Evesham
Tel: 0386 2458

**EVESHAM TOWN STRETCH,
COMMON ROAD STRETCH**
Evesham A.A.
Permits available from bailiff on bank

PERSHORE
Severn Trent Water Authority
Free Fishing
Details available from
Tel: 06845 61511

PERSHORE – RIVER WICK
Kinver Freeliners
Sec: D. H. Barnett
2 Glenwood Close, Brierley Hill,
W. Midlands
Permits available from above with S.A.E.

RUGBY AND ENVIRONS
Rugby Federation of Anglers
Sec: H. P. Wagstaff
4 Crick Road, Hillmorton, Rugby
Contact above for details

**STRATFORD-ON-AVON, TOWN
WATER**
Fisheries Bailiff, Council Offices
14 Rother Street, Stratford-on-Avon
Permits also available from:
A. C. Claridge Tackle
Greenhill Street, Stratford

WELFORD, UPTON AVON
Permits available from:
The Four Alls Inn
Welford-on-Avon

River Banwy
BANWY
Northern A.A.
Sec: G. Wilson
Tel: 02572 65905
Permits available from above

HENIARTH WATER
H. Ellis
Lyn-y-Wern, Llanfair Caereinion,
Welshpool
Permits available from above

Llanfair Caereinion
Montgomeryshire A.A.
Sec: P. Craig
6 Prince of Wales Drive, Welshpool
Permits available from:
The Lion Hotel and Newsagents,
Welshpool

Halton District A.A.
Sec: D. K. Philcock
68 Belvoir Road, Widnes,
Cheshire WA8 6HR
Tel: 051 423 1627
Season permits from secretary

LLANGADFAN
Montgomeryshire A.A.
Sec: P. Craig
6 Prince of Wales Drive, Welshpool
Permits available from:
The Lion Hotel and Newsagents,
Welshpool

LLANGADFAN WATER
Mr Leake
Cann Office Hotel, Llangadfan, Welshpo
Tel: 093 888 202
Permits available from above

NEUADD WATER
Mr Edwards
Neuadd Bridge Farm, Caravan Park
Llanfair Caereinion, Nr. Welshpool

River Camlad
FORDEN
Montgomeryshire A.A.
Sec: P. Craig
6 Prince of Wales Drive, Welshpool
Permits available from above

FORDEN BRIDGE WATER
Welshpool & District A.A.
Sec: R. Fairbrother
Tel: 068 687 345
Permits available from:
Mrs Thompson
Dolvorwyn Hall, Abermule, Powys

River Rhiw
BERRIEW
Montgomeryshire A.A.
Sec: P. Craig
6 Prince of Wales Drive, Welshpool
Permits available from:
Dolvorwyn Hall Hotel, Abermule

FELINDRE MILL FARM
Welshpool & District A.A.
Sec: R. Fairbrother
Tel: 068 687 345
Permits available from:
T. Lewis, Felindre Mill Farm, Berriew

River Roden
Whitemore Reans Constitutional A.A
Sec: R. H. Hughes
Star Chambers, Princes Square,
Wolverhampton
Permits available from above with S.A.E.

er Salwarpe

OITWICH
er Freeliners
D. H. Barnett
enwood Close, Brierley Hill,
Midlands
mits available from above with S.A.E.

er Severn

ERMULE
thern A.A.
G. Wilson
02572 65905
mits available from above

CHAM
ern Trent Water Authority
e fishing
ails from
0743 63141

DGNORTH
tmore Reans Constitutional A.A.
R. H. Hughes
Chambers, Princes Square,
verhampton
mits available from above with S.A.E.

CEWYDD
ern Trent Water Authority
e fishing
ails from
0743 63141

EEVE PRIOR, NR. EVESHAM
ern Trent Water Authority
e fishing
ails from
06845 61511

ALPORT, IRON BRIDGE
ern Trent Water Authority
e fishing
ails from
0743 63141

GLIS (RIGHT BANK ABOVE WEIR)
ern Trent Water Authority
e fishing
ails from
, 0743 63141

GLIS WEIR
ORCESTER
rcester & District United A.A.
: Mr E. Davis
ntre Course Buildings, Pitchcroft,
rcester
mits available from: Seven Aquatics, 103
bury, Worcester
o from: Al's Tackle Shop, 26 Malvern
d, Worcester

L LLYS FARM
Evans
Llys Farm, Llanidloes
mits available from above

DINGTON BROOK, QUATFORD,
DGNORTH AND ALVELEY
ver Freeliners
: R. Oliver
High Street, Kiner, West Midlands
038 483 3255
mits available from above with S.A.E.

LINCOMB WEIR
Severn Trent Water Authority
Free fishing
Details from
Tel: 0743 63141

LION HOTEL WATER
W. A. Bengry
The Lion Hotel, Caerhowell, Montgomery
Permits available from above

LLANDINAM, NR. CAERSWS
Severn Trent Water Authority
Upper Severn Division
Tel: 0743 63141
Permits available from:
The Lion Hotel, Llandinam
Tel: 068 684 233

LLANIDLOES
Severn Trent Water Authority
Free fishing
Details from:
S.T.W.A. Shrewsbury
Tel: 0743 63141

LLANIDLOES TOWN WATER
Llanidloes A.C.
Sec: J. D. Davies
Tel: 05512 2644
Permits available from:
Owen Chemists, Llanidloes

LOWER LEIGHTON, WELSHPOOL
Montgomeryshire A.A.
Sec: P. Craig
6 Prince of Wales Drive, Welshpool
Permits available from:
Bonds, Hall Street, Welshpool or
Millingtons, Church Street, Welshpool

HALFWAY, MONTGOMERY
G. Watkins
Red House Farm, Halfway, Montgomery
Permits available from above

HARBOUR INN, ARLEY
Permits from Inn or bankside

IRON BRIDGE
Iron Bridge A.S.
Sec: P. A. Wilcox
Tel: 095 245 3279
Permits available from bailiff on bank

Dawley A.S.
Sec: K. Brown
48 Fellows Close, Little Dawley, Telford
Tel: 0942 592611
Day permits available from bailiff on bank

KEMPSEY
Severn Trent Water Authority
Free fishing
Details from
Tel: 06845 61511

LOWER SEVERN BETWEEN
TEWKESBURY & GLOUCESTER
Gloucester United A.A.
Sec: P. Farnworth
Tel: 0531 820183
Permits available from local tackle shops or
Bailiff at Haw Bridge and Boat House,
Lower Lode. No night fishing

MAESMAWR HALL HOTEL
Permits available from:
The Manager, Maesmawr Hall Hotel,
Caersws
Tel: 068 684 255

NR. MALVERN, WORCS
Upton A.A.
Sec: W. K. R. Tainton
Tel: 06845 64581
Permits available from:
G. Shinn Tackle Shop, Upton-on-Severn

MELVERLEY
Severn Trent Water Authority
Free fishing
Details from S.T.W.A. Shrewsbury
Tel: 0743 63141

MONTFORD BRIDGE
Wingfield Arms, Montford Bridge
Permits available from above

NEWTOWN
Montgomeryshire A.A.
Sec: P. Craig
6 Prince of Wales Drive, Welshpool
Permits available from:
H.L. Bebb Tackle Shop, Newtown

NEWTOWN
Northern A.A.
Sec: G. Wilson
Tel: 02572 65905
Permits available from above

NEWTOWN
Severn Trent Water Authority
Free fishing
Details from
S.T.W.A. Shrewsbury
Tel: 0743 63141

PENARTH
Severn Trent Water Authority
Free fishing
Details from
S.T.W.A. Shrewsbury
Tel: 0743 63141

PENARTH, NR. NEWTOWN
Northern A.A.
Sec: G. Wilson
Tel: 02572 65905
Permits available from above

PERSHORE
Severn Trent Water Authority
Free fishing
Details from
Tel: 06845 61511

PITTS ISLAND
HAMPTON LOADE
Permits available from:
M. Storey Fishing Tackle
Sutton Road, Kidderminster or
A. Hooper
Post Office Stores, Stourton

PITTS WATER
HAMPTON LOADE
Permits available from:
Eye Hall, Hampton Loade
or on bank

WHERE TO FISH – COARSE

POOL QUAY
Northern A.A.
Sec: G. Wilson
Tel: 02572 65905
Permits available from above

RED HOUSE FARM WATER
G. Watkins
Red House Farm, Halfway, Montgomery
Permits available from above

RIPPLE
Severn Trent Water Authority
Free fishing
Details from
Tel: 06845 61511

RIVER BRIDGE, MONTGOMERY
W. A. Bengry
The Lion Hotel, Caerhowell, Montgomery
Permits available from above

ROSSALL ESTATES, SHREWSBURY
Shropshire A.F.
Sec: P. C. Moody
Tel: 0952 603779
Permits available from Rossall Cottage

**SEVERN GREEN WATER,
NEWTOWN – PENSTROWEDD FARM**
Newtown & District F.C.
Sec: J. A. Walker
Tel: 0686 27987
Permits available from:
L. Bebb Tackle, Newtown

**SHELDON HEATH WATERS,
TRIMPLEY**
Sheldon Heath Social Club
26 Brays Road, Sheldon, Birmingham
Permits available from above

SHIP INN, HIGHLEY
Permits at Ship Inn or bankside

SHREWSBURY, MONTFORD BRIDGE
Whitmore Reans Constitutional A.A.
Sec: R. H. Hughes
Star Chambers, Princes Square,
Wolverhampton
Permits available from above with S.A.E.

SHREWSBURY
Ditherington A.S.
Sec: G. E. Williams
Tel: 0743 860835
Match bookings: J. Almond
Tel: 0743 242271
Permits available from local tackle shops in
Shrewsbury

SHREWSBURY TOWN
Shrewsbury & Atcham Borough Council
Fisheries Officer
Tel: 0743 61411
Permits available from local tackle shops or
Council Offices

STOURPORT C.
Lyttleton A.A.
Sec: E. Wilkes
Tel: 02993 6269
Permits available on bank

STOURPORT MOORINGS
¼ mile of Left Bank
Free fishing

**STOURPORT POWER STATION
WATERS**
Permits available from:
M. Storey, Fishing Tackle
Sutton Road, Kidderminster

UNICORN INN, HAMPTON LOADE
Permits available from Inn

UNITY HOUSE WATER, ARLEY
Unity House Farm, Arley
Permits available from above

UPTON
Severn Trent Water Authority
Free fishing
Details from
Tel: 06845 61511

River Swift
RUGBY AND ENVIRONS
Rugby Federation of Anglers
Sec: M. P. Wagstaff
4 Crick Road, Hillmorton, Rugby
Details available from above

Tanat River
HENSTENT FARM WATER
M. Roberts
Henstent Farm, Llangynog, Oswestry
Permits available from above

LLANGEDWYN WATER
Mr Atherton
Green Inn, Llangedwyn, Oswestry
Tel: 069181 234
Permits available from above

LLANYBLODWELL
P. Hindley
Horse Shoe Inn, Llanyblodwell
Nr. Oswestry
Permits available from above

PARC FARM WATER
R. E. Hughes
Parc Farm, Penybontfawr, Nr. Oswestry
Tel: 069174 293
Permits available from above

River Teme
BACHE POOL
S. C. Evans
Bache Pool, Craven Arms, Shropshire
Permits available from above

KNIGHTWICK
Permits available from:
Talbot Hotel, Knightwick

LUDLOW
Ludlow A.C.
Sec: R. J. Deakin
9 Downton View, Ludlow
Permits available from:
J. Smith Tackle Shop, Ludlow

PEACOCK INN
Boraston, Tenbury Wells
Permits also available from:
Mrs. Goddard
Farm Cottage, Eardiston, Tenbury Wells
Bailiff: F. Mills
Stemeside Close, Tenbury Wells

River Tern
Whitmore Reans Constitutional A.A.
Sec: R. H. Hughes
Star Chambers, Princes Square,
Wolverhampton
Permits available from above with S.A.

MARKET DRAYTON
Severn Trent Water Authority
Free fishing
Details from
Tel: 06845 61511

River Twrch
FOEL
Montgomeryshire A.A.
Sec: P. Craig
6 Prince of Wales Drive, Welshpool
Permits available from above

Tawe & Tributaries A.A.
Sec: K. Jones
Tel: 0639 843916
Permits available from above

River Vyrnwy
BRONYMAIN, MEIFOD
R. N. Jones
Bronymain, Meifod
Permits available from above

BRYN VYRNWY
D. Williams
Bryn Vyrnwy, Llansantffraid
Permits available from above

CIL BACH, MEIFOD
Mr Goolden
Cil Bach, Meifod, Powys
Permits available from above

DYFFRYN, MEIFOD
J. R. Wilkinson
Dyffryn, Meifod, Powys
Permits available from above

GODA BRIDGE, MEIFOD
Liverpool & District A.A.
Sec: J. Johnson
Tel: 051 526 4083
Permits available from above

MEIFOD AREA
Halton & District A.A.
Sec: D. K. Philcock
68 Belvoir Road, Widnes WA8 6HR
Tel: 051 423 1627
Season permits from secretary

GODR FACH WATER
A. Murgatroyd
Godr, Llansantffraid
Tel: 069 181 397
Permits available from above

LLANSANTFFRAID
G. Millis
Cross Keys Inn, Llansantffraid, Gwern-y
Cilan
Permits available from above

LLANYMYNECH
Montgomeryshire A.A.
Sec: P. Craig
6 Prince of Wales Drive, Welshpool
Permits available from:
Lindup Tackle, Llanymynech

ANYMYNECH
oenix A.C.
: J. A. Mobley
Greenhill Road, Halesowen
021 422 1161
y permits available from above

ANYMYNECH AND MEASBROOK
rthern A.A.
: G. Wilson
: 02572 65905
mits available from above and bailiff on
k

CANALS

oucester & Sharpness Canal
MILE STRETCH
ish Waterways Board
. Lovesy, Area Amenity Assistant,
ck Office, Gloucester
: 0452 25524
r and year permits and details from
ve, and also from local tackle shops
l canal bridgemen

and Union Canal
AUNSTON
ventry & District A.A.
:: P. O'Connor
oxley Close, Wood End, Coventry
: 0203 612880
y permits available from bailiff on bank

ICK TO ELKINGTON
gby Federation of Anglers
:: M. P. Wagstaff
rick Road, Hillmorton, Rugby
mits available from:
ks & Burr
Claremont Road, Rugby

ARWICK TO NAPTON
al Leamington Spa A.A.
:: E. G. Archer
outh Way, Leamington Spa
: 0926 34185
y and season permits available from
liff on bank and local tackle shops

dney Canal
dney & District A.C.
:: E. J. Mathews
: 0594 23649
rmits available from:
ter James Sports Shop, Lydney

ontgomery Canal
BERBECHAN
by A.C.
:: F. Evans
MacAlpine Close, Upton
: 051 678 7619
y and week permits from
Cubbins, 96 Waterpark Road,
kenhead or bailiff

ewport Canal
ifnal A.C.
:: Mrs E. Mountford
: 0952 883037
mits available from bailiff on bank

Oxford Canal
WILLERBY TO BRINKLOW
Rugby Federation of Anglers
Sec: M. Wagstaff
4 Crick Road, Hillmorton, Rugby
Permits available from:
Banks & Burr, 27 Claremont Road, Rugby

Shropshire Union Canal
ABERMULE
P. J. Davies
Byles Lock, Abermule
Permits available from above

STILLWATERS

ARROW VALLEY PARK LAKE
Redditch District Council
Permits available from wardens hut

BLAKEMERE
Nr. Ellesmere
Ellesmere A.C.
Sec: W. Benkoff
Tel: 093 922 317
**Permits available from local tackle shops
and on bank**

CAPTAIN'S POOL
Phoenix A.C.
Sec: J. A. Mobley
155 Greenhill Road, Halesowen
Tel: 021 422 1161
Season permits available from above

**COMPTON VERNEY LAKES, TOP
LAKE**
Warwick
Permits available from J. Shuman
171 St. Peters Road, Kineton
Tel: 0926 640570

COMPTON VERNEY BOTTOM LAKE
Warwick
Permits available from A. Yates
Park Farm, Compton Verney
Tel: 0926 640241

COOMBE POOLE
Binley
Permits available from bailiff at pool

EARLSWOOD LAKE
Between Shirley & Kings Heath
Mrs Palmer
Permits available at lake

HAMPTON FERRY
Evesham
E. W. Huxley & Son
Tel: 0386 2458
Permits available from cafe on bank

HAWK LAKE
Hawkstone Park, Hodnet
Shropshire A.F.
65 Broadway Avenue, Trench, Telford
Sec: P. C. Moody
Tel: 0952 603779
Day permits available from bailiff on bank
Wem A.C.
Sec: R. A. Salisbury
1 The Paddock, Whitchurch Road, Wem
Tel: 0939 33720
Day permits available from bailiff on bank

HORSHAY POOL
Telford
Dawley A.S.
Sec: K. Brown
48 Fellows Close, Little Dawley, Telford
Tel: 0942 592611
**Day permits available from above and also
on bank**

LYDNEY LAKE
Lydney & District A.S.
Sec: E. J. Mathews
Tel: 0594 23649
Permits available from:
Peter James Sports, Lydney

MORTON COPPICE POOL
Telford
Dawley A.C.
Permits available from bailiff on bank

NEWBOLD QUARRY
Empire Anglers
Sec: R. Cooknell
5 Easenhall Road, Harboro Magna, Rugby
Permits available from above

STIRCHLEY POOLS
Telford
Dawley A.C.
Sec: K. Brown
48 Fellows Close, Little Dawley, Telford
Tel: 0942 592611
**Day permits available from above and also
on bank**

SULBY LAKE
Welford Grange, Welford
Permits available on bank

SUNDERTON POOL (THE DELL)
Ditherington A.S.
Sec: G. E. Williams
Tel: 0743 860835
**Permits available from local tackle shops in
Shrewsbury**

TENBURY
Geltrend Ltd.
S. R. Lewis
2 Severnside, South Bewdley, Worcs.
Tel: 0299 403358
Permits available from above in advance

TRENCH POOL
Sommerfields A.C.
Sec: S. Harris
Tel: 0952 590605
Permits available on bank

WHITEMERE
Nr. Ellesmere
Ellesmere A.C.
Sec: W. Benkoff
Tel: 093 922 317
**Permits available from local tackle shops
and on bank**

WILDEN POOL
Stourport
Permits available from:
Ron Russell Fishing Tackle
Coventry Street, Kidderminster

WHERE TO FISH—COARSE

WITHY POOL
Dawley A.C.
Sec: K. Brown
48 Fellows Close, Little Dawley, Telford
Tel: 0942 592611
Day permits available from bailiff on bank

TRENT REGION

Trent Area Fisheries Manager:
R. Templeton
Meadow Lane, Nottingham
Tel: 0602 865007

Derwent Division
Raynesway, Derby
Tel: 0332 61481
Divisional Fishery Officer:
M. Cathcart
Tel: 0602 865007

Lower Trent Division
Mapperley Hall, Lucknow Avenue
Nottingham
Tel: 0602 608161
Divisional Fishery Officer:
M. Cathcart
Tel: 0602 865007

Soar Division
Leicester Water Centre, Gorse Hill
Anstey, Leicester
Tel: 0533 352011
Divisional Fishery Officer:
M. Cooper
Tel: 0602 865007

Tame Division
Tame House, 156-170 Newhall Street
Birmingham
Tel: 021 233 1616
Divisional Fishery Officer:
M. Cooper
Tel: 0602 865007

Upper Trent Division
Trinity Square, Horninglow Street
Burton-on-Trent
Tel: 0283 44511
Divisional Fishery Officer:
M. Cooper
Tel: 0602 865007

RIVERS

River Churnet
LEEK
Leek & Moorlands F.C.
Sec: D. White
Tel: 0538 371526
Limited permits available from above

River Derwent
DERBY TO BORROWASH
Earl of Harrington A.C.
Sec: J. Callaghan
Tel: 0332 751126
Permits available from local tackle shops

DUFFIELD
Derbyshire A.F.
Sec: P. W. Fox
Tel: 0332 840042
Permits available from local tackle shops or
at Bridge Inn and Cottage opposite Inn at
Duffield

MATLOCK BATH
Matlocks A.C.
Sec: R. N. E. Walsh
5 Derby Road, Homesford, Matlock
Tel: 062 982 2535
Day permits available from:
Midland Hotel, Matlock Bath
and bailiffs on bank

River Devon
ELSTON GRANGE
Bottesford & District A.A.
Sec: B. C. Cross
12 The Square, Bottesford
Permits available on bank

River Idle
HAXEY GATE
Scunthorpe & District A.A.
Sec: I. A. Robertson
35 Merton Road, Bottesford, Scunthorpe
Tel: 0724 845466
Day permits available from bailiff on bank
or local tackle shops

LANGHOLME BOUNDARY TO TRENT
Sheffield & District A.A.
Sec: J. W. Taylor
12 West Lane, Aughton, Sheffield
Details from above

MISSION
Doncaster & District A.A.
Sec: A. Slater
Tel: 0302 852675
Permits available from:
Doncaster and Bawtry tackle shops

**THRUMPTON STRETCH AND
HARDMOORS STRETCH**
Bridon Wire A.C.
Sec: P. Ware
67 Albert Road, Retford
Tel: 0777 705748
Day and season permits from bailiff or
secretary

River Manifold
HULME END
Leek & Moorlands F.C.
Sec: D. White
Tel: 0538 371526
Limited permits available from above

River Penk
PENKRIDGE DISTRICT
Whitmore Reans Constitutional A.A.
Sec: R. H. Hughes
Star Chambers, Princes Square,
Wolverhampton
Permits available from above with S.A.E.

River Soar
BARROW-ON-SOAR, KEGWORTH
Loughborough Soar A.S.
Sec: M. Downs
273 Alan Moss Road, Loughborough
Tel: 050 68472

Day permits available from
Mrs Gee, 9 Pasture Lane,
Sutton Bonington

THE CLIFFS AT SUTTON BONINGTON
Sutton Bonington A.S.
Sec: M. Moseley
Tel: 0509 843035
Permits also available from:
The Old Plough, Sutton Bonington

KEGWORTH, RADCLIFFE DEEPS
Long Eaton & District A.F.
Sec: W. A. Parker
Tel: 06076 67164
Permits available from local tackle shops

KEGWORTH, RADCLIFF-ON-SOAR
Long Eaton Victoria A.S.
Sec: D. L. Kent
Tel: 06076 64813
Permits available on the bank and
Bridge Tackle
Derby Road, Long Eaton

LEICESTER TO BARROW-ON-SOAR
Leicester & District A.S.A.
Sec: L. H. Barnsley
Tel: 0533 704142
Permits available from bailiff on bank,
Barrow
Proctors Pleasure Park Lakes and River,
Barrow-on-Soar
Permits available from slot machine at gate

RACLIFFE ON SOAR
Adjacent to Redhill Lock, access via farm
track at Radcliffe
Zingari A.C.
Sec: C. Shepherd
Tel: 03317 2170

River Stowe
GREAT BRIDGEFORD, STAFFORD
Whitmore Reans Constitutional A.A.
Sec: R. Hughes
Star Chambers, Princes Square,
Wolverhampton
Permits available from above with S.A.E.

River Torne
ROSSINGTON BRIDGE, TRENT
Doncaster & District A.A.
Sec: A. Slater
Tel: 0302 58873
Permits available on the bank and local
tackle shops

River Trent
**BURTON-ON-TRENT TO
NOTTINGHAM
CAYTHORPE TO HOVERINGHAM**
Midland A.S.
Sec: J. Bradbury
19 Ethel Avenue, Linby, Hucknall
Tel: 0602 634487
Day and season permits from bailiff on
bank

CLIFTON, SOUTH BANK
Royal Ordnance Factory A.S.
Sec: K. Ingers
Tel: 0602 279241

SEVERN TRENT Trent

HOLME PIERREPOINT
National Water Sports Centre
Tel: 0602 866301
Permits available from ranger on bank

LONG EATON, NR. THRUMPTON
Long Eaton Victoria A.S.
Sec: D. L. Kent
Tel: 06076 64813
Permits available on bank or
Bridge Tackle
Derby Road, Long Eaton

NOTTINGHAM
Nottingham A.A.
Sec: J. Collin
Tel: 0602 877558

NOTTINGHAM CITY CENTRE
Embankment
Free fishing

RADLEY
Warrington Arms Water
Warrington Arms
Permits available from bailiff on bank

STOKE BARDULPH, HAZELFORD, CLIFTON GROVE, RADCLIFFE-ON-TRENT AND FLINTHAM ESTATE
Nottingham & District Federation A.S.
Sec: W. Belshaw
Tel: 0602 216645
Permits available from bailiff on bank

WARKESTONE TO WILLINGTON
Derby A.A.
Sec: T. Hickton
Tel: 0332 362458
Permits available from local tackle shops or bailiff on bank

TRENT BRIDGE
Earl Manvers A.C.
Sec: G. R. Dennis
Deabill Street, Netherfield
Tel: 0602 240201
Day permits available from bailiff on bank

TRENT LOCK TO CRANFLEET CANAL
Long Eaton Victoria A.S.
Sec: D. L. Kent
Tel: 06076 64813
Permits available on bank or
Bridge Tackle, Derby Road, Long Eaton

TRENT LOCK, SOUTH BANK
Long Eaton & District A.F.
Sec: W. A. Parker
Tel: 06076 67164
Permits available from local tackle shops

NOTTINGHAM TO FLIXBOROUGH, BESTHORPE TO COLLINGHAM
Sheffield Amalgamated A.S.
Sec: A. Baynes
39 Sparken Hill, Worksop S80 1AL
Tel: 0909 474365
Day permits available from bailiff on bank

R. COLLINGHAM
Collingham A.A.
Sec: Mrs J. Wilson
Tel: 0636 892 700
Permits available from bailiff on bank

COLWICK PARK
Severn Trent Water Authority
Lower Trent Division
Tel: 0602 865007
Permits available from above and
The Lodge, Colwick Park
Tel: 0602 247152

DUNHAM
Sheffield & District A.A.
The Mission Hall, Clay Street, Attercliffe, Sheffield
Sec: J. W. Taylor

FISKERTON TO ROLLESTON
Nottingham & Piscatorial Soc.
Permits available from Gunsmiths, Newark

HIGH MARNHAM
Mansfield & District A.A.
Sec: A. Quick
158 Huthwaite Road, Sutton in Ashfield
NG17 2GX
Tel: 0623 511479
Day permits available from bailiff on bank

KELHAM
Newark County Council
Permits available from bailiff on bank

LOW MARNHAM
Chesterfield A.A.
Sec: B. E. Thorley
Tel: 0246 39541
Permits available from bailiff on bank

NEWARK DYKE
Newark Piscatorial Federation
Sec: J. Garland
Tel: 0636 2962
Permits available from bailiff on bank

NORTH CLIFTON AND LAUGHERTON
Lincoln & District A.A.
Sec: T. McCarthy
Tel: 0522 29006
Permits available from local tackle shops and bailiff on bank

NORTH CLIFTON AND SOUTH CLIFTON
Sheffield Amalgamated A.S.
Sec: A. Baynes
39 Sparken Hill, Worksop S80 1AL
Tel: 0909 474365
Day permits available from bailiff on bank

TORKSEY
Ye Old Ram Inn A.C.
Sec: D. Richmond
Tel: 0623 33790
Permits available from:
Richmond Tackle, 26 Midworth Street, Mansfield

TORKSEY LOCK, COTTAM SITE, SUTTON GIRTON, NORMANTON, CROMWELL
Sheffield & District A.A.
Bailiff: Mr Jordan
29 Crow Park Avenue, Sutton-on-Trent
Permits available from above

WINTHORPE
Newark Piscatorial Federation
Sec: J. Garland
Tel: 0636 2962
Permits available from bailiff on bank

WINTHORPE
Severn Trent Water Authority
Lower Trent Division
Tel: 0602 865007
Permits available from above and
Mrs Potter, The Level Crossing, Winthorpe

WINTHORPE, HOLME MARSH, FOOTITTS MARSH, NESS FARM, NEWARK
Worksop & District A.A.
Sec: G. Rollinson
Tel: 0909 473109
Permits from bailiff on bank

River Wreake
THREE MILE STRETCH FROM MELTON MOWBRAY
Asfordby Society of Anglers
Sec: H. Birch
Tel: 0664 812364
Permits available by advance booking from above

EAST GOSCOTE
Acresford Sand & Gravel Co
Permits available on bank

CANALS

Ashby or Moira Canal
BULKINGTON BRIDGES 1 TO 11 AND DADLINGTON BRIDGE 22 TO MARKET BOSWORTH BRIDGE 45
Coventry D.A.A.
Sec: M. Williams
134 Scots Lane, Coundon, Coventry
Day permits from towpath or from local tackle dealers

MARKET BOSWORTH AT BRIDGE 45
Shackerstone A.A.
Sec: Mrs B. Andrews
6 Church Road, Shackerstone, Nuneaton
Day permitrs on towpath or from secretary

SNARESTONE
Measham A.C.
Sec: J. Wainwright
6 The Square, Oakthorpe, Burton-on-Trent
Season permits available

Beeston Canal
Nottingham Fed. A.S.
Sec: W. Belshaw
17 Spring Green, Clifton Estate, Nottingham
Day permits in advance from local tackle dealers

Nottingham A.A.
Sec: L. E. Simpson
92 Main Street, Bulwell, Nottingham
Day permits in advance from local tackle dealers

Birmingham and Fazeley Canal
Fazeley Victory W.M.C. A.S.
Permits available on towpath

153

WHERE TO FISH – COARSE

Birmingham Canal Navigations
RUSHALL CANAL AND DAW END BRANCH
British Waterways Board Fishery
Season and day permits available from bailiff on bank and
P.W. Chapman
1 Whitehorse Road, Brownhills, Walsall

Wyrley & Essington Canal
Edward St. W.M.C. A.C.
Sec: I. H. Jones
101 Edward Street, Broomhill, Cannock
Day and season permits from secretary or
Mr Coyne, Pelsall Stop, Canal Side, Pelsall

BROWNHILLS
L.C.P. Steel Products A.C.
Sec: W. H. Day
56 Willenhall Street, Darlaston
Tickets from bailiff on bank

PELSALL
Albion Pressed Metal A.C.
Sec: P. Weaver
21 Harrison Road, Cannock
Day permits from secretary

Freemasons A.C.
Sec: J. D. Fletcher
22 Benton's Lane, Great Wyrley, Walsall
Day permits from secretary

NEW INVENTION
Swan A.C.
Sec: J. Wakelin
68 High Road, Lane Head, Willenhall
Day permits from secretary .

WEDNESFIELD
Whitmore Reans C.A.A.
Sec: R. H. Hughes
Star Chambers, Princes Square, Wolverhampton
Day permits from secretary

Jenks & Cattell A.C.
Sec: T. C. Gilson
25 Reedley Road, Sneyd Park, Essington, Wolverhampton
Day permits from above

Caldon Canal
MILTON TO HAZELHURST JUNCTION
Burslem Izaak Walton A.S.
Sec: R. W. H. Burdon
Tel: 0782 618807
Permits available on bank

Chesterfield Canal
DRAKEHOLES TO WEST STOCKWITH
Sheffield & District A.A.
Sec: J. W. Taylor
Tel: 0742 24910
Day permits available from lock keeper, Gringley, Notts

WEST RETFORD BRIDGE TO CHURCH LANE, CLAYWORTH
Worksop & District A.A.
Sec: G. Rollinson
Tel: 0909 473109
Day permits available from bailiff on bank

WORKSOP
Grafton A.A.
Sec: K. Hill
102 Cavendish Road, Worksop
Tel: 0909 476944
Day and season permits available from bailiff on bank
Lockhouse, Bracebridge
Grafton Hotel, Worksop

Erewash Canal
LONG EATON
Long Eaton & District Fed. of Anglers
Sec: W. Parker
75 College Street, Long Eaton
Permits from local tackleists

Long Eaton Victoria A.S.
Sec: G. Plummer
18 Sandford Avenue, Long Eaton
Permits from local tackleists

TROWELL
Horse and Groom A.C.
Sec: A. A. Bishop
13 Hazel Drive, Larkhill Estate, Nuthall
Permits available

SANDIACRE
Sandiacre Alexandra F.C.
Sec: E. Jones
Sudbury Avenue, Sandiacre
Day permits available

LANGLEY MILL
NCB No. 5 Area F.C.
Sec: D. A. Allsop
27 Hardy Barn, Shipley
Permits available

Cotmanhey A.C.
Sec: E. Stratham
169 Ladywood Road, Ilkeston
Tel: 0602 320784
Permits from bailiffs

Leicester Canal
KILBY BRIDGE
Wigston Angling Society
Sec: A. Keleher
20 Estad Avenue, Leicester
Permits from Wigston Tackle Shop
51 Leicester Road, Wigston

NORTH BRIDGE, LEICESTER TO GLEN PARVA ROAD BRIDGE
Leicester A.S.
Sec: P. A. Jayes
Tel: 0533 832045
Permits available from above and also bailiff on bank

BARROW ON SOAR TO KEGWORTH FOOTBRIDGE
Loughborough Soar A.S.
Sec: M. Downs
273 Alan Moss Road, Loughborough
Tel: 0509 68472
Day permits

Nottingham Canal
5 MILE STRETCH
Bottesford & District A.A.
Sec: B. C. Cross
12 The Square, Bottesford
Permits available on bank

Staffordshire & Worcestershire Canal
PENKRIDGE AND WEDNESFIELD
Whitmore Reans Constitutional A.A.
Sec: R. H. Hughes
Star Chambers, Princes Square, Wolverhampton
Permits available from above with S.A.E.

STAFFORD
Izaak Walton (Stafford) A.A.
Sec: R. Wilton
Tel: 0785 661429
Permits available from:
Mr Exton, 2 Marlborough Avenue, Staffo
Advance booking only

Stainforth & Keadby Canal
KEADBY CANAL
Keadby Canal Committee
Sec: D. Parkes
Tel: 0709 584308
Permits available from bailiff on bank

PRESERVED DRAINS AND DOUBLE RIVERS
Sheffield & District A.A.
Sec: J. W. Taylor
Tel: 0742 24910
Permits available from above

Trent and Mersey Canal
BLACKPOOL & BASIN
Ukrainian Youth Centre
The Old Cliffe House, Weston-on-Trent
Permits available from Club House

FRADLEY AND COLWICH
British Waterways Board
Details from J. G. Taylor
B.W.B. Basin End, Chester Road, Nantwic
Tel: 0270 65122

SHARDLOW TO EGGINGTON
Derby A.A.
Sec: T. Hickton
Tel: 0332 362458
Permits available from local tackle shops

WYCHNOR TO CLAYMILLS
Burton Mutual A.A.
Sec: D. J. Clerk
Permits available from local tackle shops

STILLWATERS

ALLESTREE LAKE
Allestree Park
Derby City Council, Parks Dept
Tel: 0332 31111
Day tickets available on bank

ALVASTON LAKE
Alvaston Park
Derby City Council, Parks Dept
Tel: 0332 31111
Day tickets available on bank

ASHBOURNE LAKE
Ashbourne
Wine Tavern A.C.
Permits available from:
Fosters Sporting Services
Tel: 0335 43135

ENBOROUGH LAKE
...ton
...re Sport A.C.
...pe Park, Staines Lane, Chertsey
...hits also available from above or bailiff
...ank

DLES LAKE
Goscote
...esford Sand & Gravel Co
...act: R. J. A. Hawkesley
...0533 609545
...hits available from fishing office on site

VOIR LAKE
...oir Castle
...hits available from Estate Office

OOKVALE PARK
...ngton
...ingham City Council
...021 235 3022
...hits available on site

RSLEM LAKE
...e-on-Trent
...e-on-Trent City Council
...hits available from patrolman on bank

TERLEY RESERVOIR
...ey & District A.C.
...R. Turner
...0773 45876
...hits available from bailiff on bank

NNON HILL PARK
...eley
...ingham City Council
...021 235 3022
...hits available on site

ARNWOOD WATER
...ghborough
...rnwood District Council
...hits available from Charnwood Leisure
...tre, Browns Lane, Loughborough

MBER LAKE
...ngham City Council
...hits available from bailiff on bank

NOR PARK RESERVOIR
...ey & District A.C.
...R. Turner
...0773 45876
...hits available from bailiff on bank

EMERE
...Ellesmere
...e-on-Trent A.S.
...S. F. Broadgate
...0782 618833
...hits available from:
...mere Post Office
...lay & Sons, Ellesmere

WICK PARK RESERVOIR
...ngham
...rn Trent Water Authority
...hits available from:
...Fishing Lodge
...0602 247152 or
...Tackle Box, Trent Bridge, Nottingham
...0602 866121

AKEMARSH POOL
...Rochester
...k & Moorlands F.C.

Sec: D. White
Tel: 0538 371526
Permits available from above

DIXONS LAKE
Melton Mowbray
Sec: G. Dixon
Tel: 0664 5101
Limited permits available, advance booking necessary

DUNHAM
Between Newark and Gainsborough
Sheffield & District A.A.

EDGBASTON RESERVOIR
Edgbaston
Birmingham City Council
Tel: 021 235 3022
Permits available on site

FIELD MILL DAM
Mansfield & District A.A.
Sec: A. Quick
158 Huthwaite Road, Sutton in Ashfield
Tel: 0623 511479
Day permits from bailiff on bank

FOREST PARK
Hanley
Stoke-on-Trent City Council
Permits available on bank

FOX HOLLIES PARK
Acocks Green
Birmingham City Council
Tel: 021 235 3022
Permits available on site

GUNTHORPE GRAVEL PIT
Nottingham & District Federation A.S.
Sec: W. Belshaw
Permits available on bank

HANLEY PARK LAKE
Stoke-on-Trent City Council
Permits available on bank

HARLESTHORPE DAM
Clowne
Permits available from:
Mr Sibbring, Tackle Cabin
Tel: 0246 810231

HIMLEY HALL POOL
Dudley Metropolitan Borough Council
Permits available on site

HOLME PIERPOINT GRAVEL PIT
Nottingham & District Federation A.S.
Sec: W. Belshaw
Tel: 0602 216645
Permits available from bailiff on bank

ILAM LAKE
Ilam
Permits available from:
W. Hudson
Isaac Walton Farm, Ilam
Tel: 033529 329

KEDLESTON LAKE
Kedleston Hall
Tel: 0332 840396
Permits available from Curator at Lodge

KNOSSINGTON CARP LAKE
Nr. Oakham
Permits available from:
D. H. Pryke
Tel: 066 477 305
Permits available by advance booking only

LANGOLD LAKES
Worksop
Bassetlaw District Council
Permits available on site

LAUNDE LAKE
Nr. Tilton
James Brough & Sons
Tel: 057 286 202
Permits available on site
LIDO
Fenton
Stoke-on-Trent County Council
Permits available on bank
LIFFORD RESERVOIR
Kings Norton
Birmingham City Council
Tel: 021 235 3022
Permits available on bank
LONG CLAWSON
Old Manor Pond
Permits available on bank
LONGTON PARK LAKE
Stoke-on-Trent City Council
Permits available from patrolmen on bank
MANOR FARM POND
Tibshelf
Ye Old Ram Inn A.C.
Sec: D. Richmond
Tel: 0623 33790
Permits available from:
Richmond Tackle
26 Midworth Street, Mansfield
MANOR FLOODS
Ilkeston
Cotmanhay A.C.
Sec: E. Statham
Tel: 0602 320784
Permits available from:
D. Wright Tackle Shop, Cotmanhay and on bank
MAPPERLEY RESERVOIR
Derbyshire County Council
Ranger Post: 07737 5480
Limited permits available on site
MARKEATON LAKE
Markeaton Park
Derby City Council, Parks Dept.
Tel: 0332 31111
Day tickets available on bank

MILL FARM FISHERY
Gilmorton
Contact: T. R. Baker
Tel: 04555 2392
Permits available from above

NEWLANDS POND
Coupes Farm, Clipston
Permits available on bank

WHERE TO FISH – COARSE

NORMAN CHAMBERLAIN PLAYING FIELDS POOL
Shard End
Birmingham City Council
Tel: 021 235 3022
Permits available on site

NORTON POOLS
Nr. Brownhills
Whitmore Reans Constitutional A.A.
Sec: R. H. Hughes
Star Chambers, Princes Square,
Wolverhampton
Permits available from above with S.A.E.

OLD HALL POOL
Bentley, Walsall
Walsall Borough Council
Free fishing

OSBORNES POND
Shipley Park
Derbyshire County Council
Ranger Post: 077 37 5480
Limited permits available on site

PARK HALL POOL
Walsall Borough Council
Tel: 0922 26418
Permits available on site

PERRY PARK
Perry Barr
Birmingham City Council
Tel: 021 235 3022
Permits available on site

POOL HALL FARM
Mr & Mrs Dickenson
Lower Pen, Wolverhampton
Tickets available from above

PROCTORS PLEASURE PARK LAKES & RIVER
Barrow-on-Soar
Tel: 0509 42434
Permits from slot machine at gate

PYPE HAYES PARK
Erdington
Birmingham City Council
Tel: 021 235 3022
Permits available on site

RADCLIFFE POND
Nottingham & District Federation A.S.
Sec: W. Belshaw
Tel: 0602 216645
Permits available on bank

RHODESIA POND NR. WORKSOP
Grafton A.A.
Sec: K. Hill
102 Cavendish Road, Worksop
Tel: 0909 476944
Day and season permits from bailiff on bank
Lockhouse, Bracebridge
Grafton Hotel, Worksop

RUDYARD LAKE
British Waterways Board
Bailiff: I. L. Nixon
Lake House, Rudyard, Leek
Permits also available on bank

SALFORD PARK
Aston
Birmingham City Council
Tel: 021 235 3022
Permits available on site

SANDHILLS LAKE
Worksop & District A.S.
Sec: G. Rollinson
Tel: 0909 473109
Permits available from bailiff on bank

SCARCLIFFE POND
Mansfield & District A.A.
Sec: A. Quick
158 Huthwaite Road, Sutton in Ashfield
Tel: 0623 511479
Day permits available from bailiff on bank

SHARDLOW MARINA
Bailiff: J. D. Burrows
Tel: 0332 792625
Limited permits available from above

SHARDLOW PONDS
Shardlow
Long Eaton & District A.F.
Sec: W. A. Parker
Tel: 06076 67164
Permits available from local tackle shops

SMALL HEATH PARK
Small Heath
Birmingham City Council
Tel: 021 235 3022
Permits available on site

STAUNTON HAROLD LAKE
Nr. Melbourne
Severn Trent Water Authority
Soar Division
Bailiff: K. Harris
18 Alma Street, Melbourne
Tel: 03316 3144
Permits also available from:
Melbourne Sports
15 Market Place, Melbourne

STOW POOL
Lichfield
Lichfield District Council
St. John Street, Lichfield
Permits also available from bailiff on bank

SUTTON PARK – FIVE POOLS
Sutton Coldfield
Birmingham City Council
Tel: 021 235 3022
Permits available on site

SWAMP, HOLDEN BRIDGE
Hanley
Stoke-on-Trent City Council
Permits available on bank

SWANS HURST PARK
Kings Heath
Birmingham City Council
Tel: 021 235 3022

SWARKESTONE GRAVEL PIT
Nr. Swarkestone
Derby A.A.
Sec: T. Hickton
Tel: 0332 362548
Permits available from bailiff on bank or local tackle shops

TRENTHAM GARDENS
Stoke-on-Trent
Permits available from gate

TRITTIFORD MILL
Yardsley Wood
Birmingham City Council
Tel: 021 235 3022
Permits available on site

TUNSTALL PARK
Stoke-on-Trent City Council
Permits available from patrolman on site

VICAR WATER
Clipstone
Clipstone Colliery A.C.
Sec: F. W. Welch
Tel: 0623 34924
Permits available on bank

WALSALL ARBORETUM
Walsall Borough Council
Tel: 0922 26418
Permits available on site

WARD END PARK
Saltley
Birmingham City Council
Tel: 021 235 3022
Permits available on site

WEST MIDLAND SAFARI PARK
Permits available from November to Ma
Tel: 0299 402114

WESTPORT LAKE
Stoke-on-Trent City Council
Permits available from patrolmen on ba

WILLESLEY LAKE
Measham, Ashby
Leicestershire & South Derbyshire
Welfare A.A.
Sec: T. Wood
77 Shortheath Road, Moira, Burton-on-T
Permits available from Matchmans Peg,
Woodville

WINFIELD LAGOON
National Water Sports Centre
Tel: 0602 866301
Permits available from rangers on bank

WINTHORPE LAKE
Nr. Newark
Severn Trent Water Authority
Permits available from:
S.T.W.A. Office
Tel: 0602 865007
Mrs Potter, The Level Crossing, Wintho

WOODHALL LAKE
Bulwell
Permits available from
Walkers of Trowell
Nottingham Road, Trowell
Tel: 0602 301816

WOODSETTS QUARRY POND
Worksop & District A.A.
Sec: G. Rollinson
Tel: 0909 473109
Permits available from bailiff on bank

evern Trent
ater
uthority

elson House, 2297 Coventry Road
ldon, Birmingham B26 3PU
: 021 743 4222
istant Director of Scientific
vices: Mr M. L. Parry

ional Rod Licences

ional rod licences are available from
.W.A. offices as given below and in
ern Region listing, Monday to Friday
am-5.00pm or from Authority's many
ce distributors throughout the area.
nce enables holder to fish entire
on.

-a-Report

information regarding water levels and
ditions:
nt Area: 0602 866405
per Severn Area: 0743 8037
er Severn Area: 0684 296929

EVERN REGION

ern Area Fisheries Manager:
Churchward
lbert Road North, Malvern
: 06845 61511
on Division
on House, De Montford Way
nnon Park, Coventry
: 0203 416510
rict Fisheries Officer: A. Starkie
: 06845 61511 Ext. 261
ver Severn Division
lbert Road North, Malvern
: 06845 61511
rict Fisheries Officer: A. Starkie
: 06845 61511 Ext. 261
per Severn division
lton, Shrewsbury
: 0743 63141
rict Fisheries Officer:
tarkie – Avon & Lower Severn
ision
090 566 678
ollard – Upper Severn Division
074 37 6312

RIVERS

er Banwy
NWY
thern A.A.

A Trout Menu for all Tastes....

May we recommend our reservoirs — made by man, but graced by nature, and well
stocked with excellent fighting trout?
Quiet, peaceful surroundings, away from the crowds, with well equipped boats
should the fancy take you.

Draycote Reservoir, Nr. Rugby 600 acres
Fishery opens April 9th until October 24th.
Day tickets and information from Kites Hardwick Filling
Station, 300 yards from Draycote entrance gate on the
Banbury side. Tel: 0788 812018.

Foremark Reservoir, Nr. Burton-on-Trent
230 acres
Fishery opens April 7th until 15th October.
Day tickets available from Bendalls Farm Shop, adjacent
to entrance of reservoir (0283 703294). Information and
season permits available from Leicester Water Centre,
Gorse Hill, Anstey, Leicester (0533 352011).

Ladybower Reservoir, North Derbyshire
504 acres
Fishery opens 8th April until 15th October.
Day tickets and information available from STWA Office,
Dimple Road, Matlock (0629 55051) or Fishery Office at
Ladybower Reservoir (0433 51254). Information and
advance booking only available from STWA Office, Bamford,
Nr. Sheffield (0433 4424).

Linacre Reservoir, Nr. Chesterfield 44 acres
(Requires Yorkshire Water Authority rod licence). Fishery
opens 1st April (season tickets), 8th April (day tickets) until
30th September.
Day tickets and information available from STWA Office,
Dimple Road, Matlock (0629 55051), Mr. Hall, 9 Beetwell
Street, Chesterfield, (0246 73133) or Fishery Warden,
Linacre Reservoir (weekends 10am to 4pm only).

Ogston Reservoir, Nr. Chesterfield 203 acres
Fishery opens 1st April until 15th October.
Day tickets and information available from STWA Office,
Dimple Road, Matlock (0629 55051) or New Napoleon Inn,
Wolley Moor, Near Ogston Reservoir (0246 590413).

Shustoke Reservoir, Nr. Coleshill 100 acres
Fishery operated by Cambrian Fisheries, opens 12th March
until 15th October.
Information and advance booking available from Cambrian
Fisheries, Afonwen, Nr. Mold, Clwyd, Telephone 035282
589. Permits available on site from 1st March.

Thornton, Nr. Leicester 75 acres
Operated by Cambrian Fisheries. Fishery opens 1st April
until 15th October.

Information and advance booking available from Cambrian
Fisheries, Afonwen Nr. Mold, Clwyd, Telephone 035282
589. Permits and information available on site from 1st
March (053021 7107).

Trimpley, Nr. Kidderminster 29 acres
Operated by Trimpley Anglers Association. Fishery opens
2nd April until 15th October. Permits only available to
members of the Trimpley Anglers Association.
Information and permits available from Mr. R F Pratt,
Trimpley Anglers Association, 24 Lea Wood Grove,
Kidderminster, Worcs. Telephone Kidderminster 60448.

Colwick Park 65 acres
Fishery opens March 18th until October 15th.
Day tickets and information available from the Fishing
Lodge, Colwick Park off Mile End Road, Nottingham
(0602 247152); The Tackle Box, Trent Bridge, Nottingham
(0602 866121); Mr. P Bramman, 187 Carlton Road,
Nottingham; Eastwood Pets, 64 Nottingham Road,
Eastwood, Nottingham; after 5th May KDR Angling, 2 Garnet
Street, Netherfield, Nottingham (0602 248449).

Tittesworth Reservoir, Nr. Leek, Staffs
109 acres
Fishery opens 9th April until 15th October.
Day tickets and information available from STWA Office,
Westport Road, Burslem, Stoke-on-Trent (0782 85601) or
the Fishing Lodge, Tittesworth Reservoir (053834 389).

Llandinam (River Fishery), Nr. Caersws
approx. 4 miles
Fishery opens 18th March until 30th September.
Information and permits available from The Lion Hotel,
Llandinam, Powys (068684 233). Information only available
from Dr. J Woolland, Fisheries Office, STWA, Upper Severn
Division, Shelton, Shrewsbury (0743 63141).

Diglis Weir, Worcester, Approx. 300 yards
Operated by Worcester and District United Anglers
Association. Fishery opens 2nd February until 30th
September.
Day tickets and information available from Al's Tackle Shop,
26 Malvern Road, Worcester (0905 422107) on odd days,
or Severn Aquatics, 103 Sidbury, Worcester (0905 354512)
on even days.

SEVERN TRENT WATER

Sec: G. Wilson
Tel: 02572 65905
Permits available from above

HENIARTH WATER
H. Ellis
Lyn-y-Wern, Llanfair Caereinion
Welshpool
Permits available from above

LANFAIR CAEREINION
Montgomeryshire A.A.
Sec: R. Thomas
128 Oldford Rise, Welshpool
Tel: 0938 3488
Day and weekly permits available from:
H. L. Bebb, Tackle Shop, Newtown
Bonds, Hall Street, Welshpool
The Vaults, White Lion Hotel, Welshpool;
Cottage Inn, Montgomery; Green Dragon,
Buttington; T. Lewis, Felindre Mill; Berriew,
Edderton Hall; Cock Hotel, Forden;
Dolforwyn Hall Hotel, Abermule; Mr.
Lindop, Tackle Shop; Mr. Burgess; Telford
A.A., Telford; Ebrall Bros, Severnside,
Shrewsbury

LLANGADFAN
Montgomeryshire A.A.
Sec: R. Thomas
128 Oldford Rise, Welshpool
Tel: 0938 3488
Day and weekly permits available from:
H. L. Bebb, Tackle Shop, Newtown
Bonds, Hall Street, Welshpool
The Vaults, White Lion Hotel, Welshpool;
Cottage Inn, Montgomery; Green Dragon,
Buttington; T. Lewis, Felindre Mill; Berriew,
Edderton Hall; Cock Hotel, Forden;
Dolforwyn Hall Hotel, Abermule; Mr.
Lindop, Tackle Shop; Mr. Burgess; Telford

A.A., Telford; Ebrall Bros, Severnside,
Shrewsbury

River Camlad
Welshpool & District A.A.
Day, week and season permits from
Mrs Thompson, Dolvorwyn Hall, Abermule
L. Bebb, Short Bridge Street, Newtown

LLANGADFAN WATER
Mr. Leake
Cann Office Hotel, Llangadfan, Welshpool
Tel: 093 888 202
Permits available from above

NEUADD WATER
Mr. Edwards
Neuadd Bridge Farm, Caravan Park,
Llanfair Caerionion, Nr. Welshpool

Mule River
ABERMULE
Montgomeryshire A.A.
Sec: R. Thomas
128 Oldford Rise, Welshpool
Tel: 0938 3488
Day and week permits available from:
Dolvorwyn Hall Hotel, Abermule

ABERMULE TO KERRY
Lower Pengelly Farm
Kerry, Newtown
Tel: 068 688 610
Permits available from above

CAPTAINS BRIDGE WATER, ABERMULE
Welshpool & District A.A.

Sec: R. Fairbrother
Tel: 068 687 345
Permits available from:
Mrs Thompson
Dolvorwyn Hall, Abermule or
L. Bebb, Short Bridge Street, Newtown

River Rhiew
BERRIEW
Montgomeryshire A.A.
Sec: R. Thomas
128 Oldford Rise, Welshpool
Tel: 0938 3488
Day and week permits available from:
Dolvorwyn Hall Hotel, Abermule

FELINDRE MILL FARM
Welshpool & District A.A.
Sec: R. Fairbrother
Tel: 068 687 345
Permits available from:
T. Lewis, Felindre Mill Farm, Berriew

River Severn
WORCESTER
Worcester & District United A.A.
Sec: Mr E. Davis
Centre Course Buildings, Pitchcroft,
Worcester
Day permits available from:
Seven Aquatics, 103 Sidbury, Worcester
Tel: 0905 354512
Al's Tackle Shop, 26 Malvern Road,
Worcester
Tel: 0905 422107

LION HOTEL WATER
W. A. Bengry
The Lion Hotel, Caerhowell, Montgomery
Day, weekend, week, month and season
permits available from above

LLANDINAM, NR. CAERSWS
Severn Trent Water Authority
Upper Severn Division
Tel: 0743 63141
Day and season permits available from:
The Lion Hotel, Llandinam
Tel: 068 684 233

LOWER LEIGHTON, WELSHPOOL
Montgomeryshire A.A.
Sec: R. Thomas
128 Oldford Rise, Welshpool
Tel: 0938 3488
Day and week permits available from
Bonds, Hall Street, Welshpool
The Vaults, White Lion Hotel

HALFWAY, MONTGOMERY
G. Watkins
Red House Farm, Halfway, Montgomery
Day, weekend and week permits available
from above

LEIGHTON
Liverpool & District A.A.
c/o J. Johnson
97 Liverpool Road, North Maghull
Tel: 051 506 4083
Season and day permits available from
above

NEWTOWN, WELSHPOOL
Montgomeryshire A.A.
Sec: R. Thomas
128 Oldford Rise, Welshpool
Tel: 0938 3488

Day and week permits available from
H. L. Bebb Tackle Shop, Newtown
RED HOUSE FARM WATER
G. Watkins
Red House Farm, Halfway, Montgomery
Day, weekend and week permits available
from above

UPPER PENRHYLLAN
S. Price
Upper Penrhyllan, Dolwen, Llanidloes
Permits available from above

Tanat River
HENSTENT FARM WATER
M. Roberts
Henstent Farm, Llangynog, Oswestry
Permits available from above

LLANGEDWYN WATER
Mr Atherton
Green Inn, Llangedwyn, Oswestry
Tel: 069181 234
Permits available from above

LLANYBLODWELL
P. Hindley
Horse Shoe Inn, Llanyblodwell
Nr. Oswestry
Permits available from above

PARC FARM WATER
R. E. Hughes
Parc Farm, Penybontfawr, Nr. Oswestry
Tel: 069174 293
Permits available from above

BRYN TANAT HOTEL
Llansantffraid, Nr. Oswestry
Tel: 069181 259
Permits from hotel

River Teme
PEACOCK INN
Boraston, Tenbury Wells
Permits also available from:
Mrs Goddard
Farm Cottage, Eardiston, Tenbury Wells
Bailiff: F. Mills
Stemeside Close, Tenbury Wells

River Twrch
FOEL
Montgomeryshire A.A.
Sec: R. Thomas
128 Oldford Rise, Welshpool
Tel: 0938 3488
Day and week permits available from
above

Tawe & Tributaries A.A.
Sec: K. Jones
21 St. Davids Road, Ystalyfera
Tel: 0639 843916
Season, week and day permits available
from above and D. Watkins, Tawe Sports,
Commercial Street, Ystradgynlais

River Vyrnwy
BRONYMAIN, MEIFOD
R. H. Jones
Bronymain, Meifod
Permits available from above

DYFFRYN, MEIFOD
J. R. Wilkinson

Dyffryn, Meifod, Powys
Permits available from above
GODR FACH WATER
A. Murgatroyd
Godr, Llansantffraid
Tel: 069 181 397
Permits available from above
VYRNWY LAKE
Lt. Col. Sir John Baynes
Lake Vyrnwy Hotel, via Oswestry
Tel: 069173 244
Permits available from above

STILLWATERS
DRAYCOTE RESERVOIR
Nr. Rugby
Severn Trent Water Authority
Avon Division
Day permits available from Fishing Lodge
on site
Tel: 0788 811107
FACHWEN POOL
Aberhafesp
Montgomeryshire A.A.
Sec: P. Craig
6 Prince of Wales Drive, Welshpool
Permits available from:
The Grapes Inn, Newtown
Bebb's Tackle Shop, Newtown

FAIROAKS POOLS
Nr. Rugeley
J. R. Fairclough
Tel: 0543 480984
Limited permits available by advance
booking from above

GUILSFIELD BROOK
Montgomeryshire A.S.
Sec: P. Craig
6 Prince of Wales Drive, Welshpool
Permits available from local tackle shops

HIMLEY HALL ROCK POOL AND HIMLEY HALL GREAT POOL
Nr. Dudley
Permits available from bailiff on bank

LLYN CLYWEDOG RESERVOIR
Llanidloes A.C.
Sec: J. D. Davies
Tel: 05512 2644
Permits available from above

LLYN TARW
Pontdolgoch
Montgomeryshire A.A.
Sec: R. Thomas
128 Oldford Rise, Welshpool
Tel: 0938 3488
Permits available from:
Bebb's Tackle, Newtown

PEATSWOOD LAKE
Market Drayton
Tern Fisheries, Broomhall Lodge
Tel: 0630 4505
Permits available from above

SHOWELL MILL POOL
Sambrook
Nicklin Bros.
Showell Mill Farm, Sambrook, Newport
Permits available from above

SULBY LAKE
Welford Grange, Welford
Permits available on bank

NWY LAKE
Llanwddyn
ol. Sir John Baynes
Vyrnwy Hotel, via Oswestry
69 173 244
ermits available from above

ENT REGION

t Area Fisheries Manager:
empleton
dow Lane, Nottingham
0602 865007

RIVERS

er Churnet

& District Fly Fishing Association
A. K. Bridgett, 34 Windsor Drive, Leek
0538 373163
ed season permits available from
e

er Derwent

BY TO BORROWASH
f Harrington A.C.
. Callaghan
332 751126
its available from local tackle shops

FIELD
yshire A.F.
. W. Fox
332 840042
its available from local tackle shops or
dge Inn and Cottage opposite Inn at
eld

LOCK
cks A.C.
R. N. E. Walsh
62 982 2535
its available from:
s Newsagents
Road, Matlock

LOCK BATH
cks A.C.
R. N. E. Walsh
062 982 2535
its available from:
and Hotel, Matlock Bath

er Dove

EDALE
& District Fly Fishing Association
A. K. Bridgett, 34 Windsor Drive, Leek
0538 373163
ed season permits available from
e

er Manifold

ME END
& Moorlands F.C.
D. White
538 371526
ed permits available from above

NDE LAKE
ilton
s Brough & Sons
57 286 202
its available on site

ACRE RESERVOIR
hesterfield
permits available from
V.A. Office, Dimple Road, Matlock
629 55051 or
all, 9 Beetwell Street, Chesterfield
246 73133
site

MILL FARM FISHERY

Gilmorton
Contact: T. R. Baker Tel: 04555 2392
Day and evening permits available from above. Advance booking advisable.

OGSTON RESERVOIR

Nr. Chesterfield
Severn Trent Water Authority
Derwent Division
Limited day permits available from:
New Napoleon Inn, Woolly Moor
Tel: 0246 590413
S.T.W.A. Office, Matlock
Tel: 0629 55051

PACKINGTON FISHERIES

Meriden, Nr. Coventry
Tel: 0676 22754
Permits available from site
See Advertisement this Section

PATSHULL PARK FISHERY

Patshull Road, Nr. Wolverhampton
Patshull Developments
Tel: 0902 700173
Permits available from above and also from
Temple Hotel
Tel: 0902 700100

SHELMORE TROUT FISHERY

Off A518 between Gnosall and Norbury
For permits telephone 078 574 205

SHUSTOKE

Nr. Coleshill
Tame House, Newhall Street, Birmingham 3
Tel: 021 233 1616

THORNTON RESERVOIR

Nr. Leicester
Cambrian Fisheries
22 West Sherbourne St. John
Nr. Basingstoke, Hampshire
Day permits on site

TITTESWORTH RESERVOIR

Nr. Leek
Severn Trent Water Authority
Upper Derwent Division
Day permits available from:
S.T.W.A. Office, Stoke-on-Trent
Tel: 0782 85601
Fishing Lodge on site
Tel: 0538 34389

STILLWATERS

COLWICK PARK RESERVOIR

Nottingham
Severn Trent Water Authority
Day and evening permits available from:
The Fishing Lodge
Colwick Park, off Mile End Road
Tel: 0602 247152 or
The Tackle Box, Trent Bridge, Nottingham
Tel: 0602 866121
K.D.R. Angling, 2 Garnet Street,
Netherfield
Tel: 0602 248449

COPES ROUGH LODGE

Boulters Lane, Baddesley Ensor,
Atherstone. Warks Tel: 0827 873365
Day, evening and season permits available

CROMWELL LAKE

Nr. Newark
Cromwell Fly Fishers
Sec: J. Holt
Tel: 0636 812235
Day permits in advance from Mr. Stock,
Carlton Service Station, Cromwell, Newark

FAIROAKES POOLS

Nr. Rugeley
J. R. Fairclough
Home Farm, Hints, Nr. Tamworth
Tel: 0543 480984
Limited permits available from above

FOREMARK RESERVOIR

Nr. Burton-on-Trent
Severn Trent Water Authority
Soar Division
Day permits available from:
Bendalls Farm Shop, adjacent to entrance
to reservoir
Tel: 0283 703294
Information from STWA Office, Leicester
Water Centre, Gorse Hill, Anstey,
Leicester
Tel: 0533 352011

GAILEY TROUT FISHERY

Gailey Lea Lane, Penkridge, Cannock
Permits available from
Mr Buxton
Tel: 078 571 4855
Day and evening permits

HAMPS VALLEY FISHERY

Winkhill, Nr. Leek
Tel: 053 86 255
Day permits from above advance booking necessary

HATFIELD MARINA

Hatfield, Nr. Thorne
Tickets from Marina

HIGHAM FARM TROUT FISHERY

Old Higham, Nr. Alfreton
Tel: 0773 833812
Day permits from above

LADYBOWER RESERVOIR

Nr. Bamford, Nth Derbyshire
At junction of A57 and A6013
Severn Trent Water Authority
Derwent Division
Day permits available from:
Fishery Officer on site
Tel: 0433 51254
S.T.W.A. Office, Dimple Road, Matlock
Tel: 0629 55051

EASTERN DIVISIO

WESTERN
DIVISION

AXMINSTER

SIDMOUTH

EXETER

TORQUAY

DARTMOUTH

ILFRACOMBE

BARNSTAPLE

OKEHAMPTON

TAVISTOCK

PLYMOUTH

BUDE

LAUNCESTON

BOSCASTLE

BODMIN

ST. AUSTELL

NEWQUAY

TRURO

FALMOUTH

ST. IVES

PENZANCE

LANDS END

N

outh West
Water
Authority

5 Barnfield Road
eter, Devon

ncipal Fisheries & Recreation
ficer: Dr E. R. Merry

heries Information Office
ormation Officer: P. R. Muggeridge
: 0392 31666

gional Rod Licences
d Licences are not supplied by
rdens, however they are obtainable
m distributors throughout the region. A
of these locations is available from the
eries Information Office. The Office
supplies Rod Licences by return post.

ere is no statutory Coarse fishing close
son in Cornwall and Devon but owners
impose their own.

W.W. WESTERN AREA

toria Square
min, Cornwall
0208 3131

eries Officer: E. S. Bray
0208 3131

d Warden: A. D. Mills
Penna, Tavistock
0822 3993

STILLWATERS

ADLER QUARRY POND
Launceston
Contact: R. Westlake
Alder Farm, Lewdown, Okehampton
Tel: 055683 241

COLLEGE RESERVOIR
Penryn
Warden: R. P. Evans
Tel: 0326 72544
Permits available from the self-service unit
on site

DUTSON LAKE
Launceston
Contact: E. J. Broad
Lower Dutson Farm, Launceston
Tel: 0566 2607

ROCHE ANGLING CLUB PONDS
St. Austell
Roche Angling Club
Sec: D. E. Minards
Tel: 06373 5669
Permits available from the following
locations:
Bugle: Hector Finch
Bodmin: Sports & Cycles, Bunts
Mevagissey: Shark Centre
Newquay: Central Sports, Vickers
Roche: Post Office
St. Austell: Angling Centre
Truro: John Langdon
Wadebridge: Appleton & Cragg

ST. BURYAN POND
Penzance
Contact: V. B. Care
Downs Barn, St. Buryan
Tel: 073 672 220

ST. EARTH POOL
Marazion A.C.
Sec: T. Tompkins
Tel: 073676 3329
Day permits also available from:
West Cornwall Angling Centre, Hayle
Tel: 0736 754292

SALTASH LAKE AT ST. GERMANS
Royal Albert Bridge A.C.
Permits from the Tackle Box, Plymouth

SHILLAMILL LAKES
Looe
Contact: J. Facey
Tel: 05032 271

STEVENSTONE LAKE
Torrington
Contact: R. W. Parnell, Owner
Deerpark, Stevenstone
Tel: 080 522102
Permits available on site

STONE LAKE
Launceston
Contact: W. P. Ponsford
Stone Farm, Bridestowe, Okehampton
Tel: 083786 253

STOWFORD POND
Launceston
Permits available from
D.K. Sports, Plymouth
Tel: 0752 663483

TAMAR LAKES
Bude
Warden: K. Spalding
Tel: 028 882 262
Permits available from self-service unit by
the dam

TINDEEN FISHERS
Penzance
Permits available from
G. J. Laity and Sons
Bostraze Goldsitnney, Penzance
Tel: 073 676 3486

TREDIDON BARTON LAKE
Launceston
Contact: G. Jones
Tel: 056 686 288

TRENCREEK LAKES
St. Austell
Contact: David and Jane Borradaile
Trencreek Farm Camping Park
Tel: 0726 882540

TRENESTRALL LAKE
St. Mawes
Contact: W. Palmer
Trenestall Farm
Philleigh Ruan High Lanes
Tel: 032 66 662

WHEAL GREY POOL
Helston Penzance
Marazion A.C.
Sec: T. Tompkins
Tel: 073676 3329
Day permits also available from:
Bill Knott
Tel: 0736 76 2542

CANALS

Bude Canal

Bude Canal Angling Association
Sec: B. Putt
2 Orchard Close, Pughill, Bude
Tel: 0288 3992
Day permits also available from:
B. Sampson, The Boathouse, Bude
North Cornwall Pet Supplies, Bude

EASTERN AREA

3-5 Barnfield Road, Exeter, Devon
Tel: 0392 50861

Fisheries Office: C. V. M. Davies,
B.Sc. M.I. Biol.
Assistant Fisheries Officer:
M. J. Chudley
Tel: 064 74 278

Head Wardens:
D. K. Clifton
Tel: 0626 68906
L. Thompson
Tel: 029 74 2850
T. Ford
Tel: 0271 73192

RIVERS

River Clyst
Exeter & District Angling Association
Sec: D. L. Beaven

Tel: 0392 75925
Permits available from Exeter Angling
Centre
Tel: 0392 36404

River Creedy

Exeter & District Angling Association
Sec: D. L. Beaven
Tel: 0392 75925
Permits available from Exeter Angling
Centre
Tel: 0392 36404

Newton Abbot Fishing Association
Sec: P. Goss
Tel: 0803 863953

River Culm

Exeter & District Anglers Association
Sec: D. L. Beaven
Tel: 0392 75925
Permits available from Exeter Angling
Centre
Tel: 0392 36404

HEMYOCK
Upper Culm Fishing Association
Sec: T. A. Blackmore
'Sunset', Claylidon
Tel: 082 368 485
Permits also available from H. M. Sanders
The Bakery, Hemyock, Devon
S.A.E. please

UFFCULME
Contact: Lt. Cdr. T. L. Metters, Owner
The Old Parsonage Farmhouse
Uffculme, Devon
Tel: 0884 40205

River Exe

Warden Lower Exe: A. Sheppard
Tel: 0392 74230

COWLEY BRIDGE
Newton Abbot Fishing Association
Sec: P. Goss
Tel: 0803 863953
Permits also available from local tackle
shops

DULVERTON
Contact: Mrs T. Howells
Tel: 0398 23302

Exeter & District Angling Association
Sec: D. L. Beaven
Tel: 0392 75925
Permits available from Exeter Angling
Centre
Tel: 0392 36404

EXETER (3 MILES)
South West Water Authority
3/5 Barnfield Road, Exeter
Tel: 0392 31666

TIVERTON
Tiverton & District A.A.
Sec: Bob Coles
Tel: 08842 4416
Permits from Country Sports
9 William Street, Tiverton
Tel: 088 42 4770

TIVERTON
Hartnoll Country House Hotel

Contact: Q. S. Buckland
Bolham, Tiverton
Tel: 088 42 2777

THORVERTON BRIDGE
Permits available from
T. Mortimer, High Banks
Latchmore, Thorverton
Tel: 0392 860241

STILLWATERS

ABBROOK POND
Kingsteignton
Exeter & District Angling Association
Sec: D. L. Beaven
Tel: 0392 75925
Permits available from Exeter Angling
Centre
Tel: 0392 36404

BUTTLEIGH PONDS NR. TIVERTON
Tiverton & District A.C.
Sec: M. Trump
Tel: 08842 57761

BUZZACOTT MANOR LAKE
Combe Martin
Permits from lakeside

CHARD POND
Perry St. Chard
Contact: G. Bartlett
20 Fore Street, Chard

CULLOMPTON FISHERY
See Stout Fishery

DARRACOTT RESERVOIR
Darracott
Warden: H. Reeves
Tel: 02372 2957
Permits available from self-service unit on
site

HARCOMBE HOUSE POND
Chudleigh
Tel: 0626 852227

HOME FARM POND
Exeter & District Angling Association
Sec: D. L. Beaven
Tel: 0392 75925
Permits available from Exeter Angling
Centre
Tel: 0392 36404

PRESTON PONDS
Newton Abbot Fishing Association
Sec: P. Goss
Tel: 0803 863953

RACKERHAYES PONDS
Newton Abbot
Newton Abbot Fishing Association
Sec: P. Goss
Tel: 0803 863953
Permits also available from local tackle
shops
The Anglers Den, Brixham
The Tuck Box and Smokerie, Kingsteignton
Percy Hodge (Sports) Ltd.
Drum Sports, Newton Abbot
H. Cove Clarke & Paignton Sports,
Paignton
Doel Sports, Teignmouth
Fletcher Sports & Tuckermans, Torquay
Blake Sports, Totnes

SAMPFORD PEVERELL POND
Exeter & District Angling Association
Sec: D. L. Beaven
Tel: 0392 75925
Permits available from
Exeter Angling Centre
Tel: 0392 36404

SLAPTON LEY
Dartmouth
Fishing from boats only
Permits available from
Slapton Ley Field Centre
Slapton, Kingsbridge
Tel: 0548 580466

SQUABMOOR RESERVOIR
Knowle
Warden: T. Davies
Tel: 040481 2208
Permits available from
Knowle Post Office
The Tackle Shop, 20 The Strand
Exmouth (open Sunday mornings)
Exeter Angling Centre, City Arcade
Fore Street, Exeter

STOUT FISHERY
Cullompton
Mr E. J. Berry
Billingsmoor Farm, Nr. Butterleigh
Cullompton
Tel: 08845 248
Bookings in advance for permits

STOVER LAKE
Newton Abbot
Devon County Council
Contact: The County Estates Surveyor
County Hall, Exeter
Tel: 0392 77977
Permits available on site

VENN POND
Barnstaple & District Angling Associatic
Sec: C. E. Arnold
135 High Street, Ilfracombe
Tel: 0271 65656
Day permits also available from
Rod 'n Reel, Bear Street, Barnstaple
E. Gale & Sons Ltd, 59 High Street,
Barnstaple

CANALS

Exeter Canal

Exeter & District Angling Associati
Sec: D. L. Beaven
46 Hatherleigh Road, Exeter
Tel: 0392 75925
Day and week permits available from l
tackl dealers or The Bridge Café, Cou
Wear, Exeter

Grand Western Canal

Devon County Council
Leased to Tiverton A.S.
Tel: 0392 77977
Day permits available from
Country Sports Tackle Shop, Tiverton
Tel: 08842 4770
Council Offices and Post Office, Samp
Peverell

…uth West
…ater
…uthority

…Barnfield Road
…er, Devon

…cipal Fisheries & Recreation
…er: Dr E. R. Merry

…eries Information Office
…mation Officer: P. R. Muggeridge
…0392 31666

…onal Road Licences
…Licences are not supplied by
…ens, however they are obtainable
…distributors throughout the region. A
…f these locations is available from the
…ries Information Office. The Office
…supplies Rod Licences by return post.

…e Seasons
…rt of the Authority's strategy on
…on cropping, the season on some
…has been changed. Therefore it is
…able to check with the S.W.W.A.
…nation Office or the Fishery owner
…selecting your River.

…is no statutory Coarse fishing close
…n in Cornwall and Devon but owners
…mpose their own.

…W. EASTERN AREA
…rnfield Road, Exeter, Devon
…392 50861

…ries Officer: C. V. M. Davies BSc,
…iol

…ant Fisheries Officer:
…Chudley
…64 74 278

Head Wardens:
D. K. Clifton
Tel: 0626 68906
L. Thompson
Tel: 029 74 2850
T. Ford
Tel: 0271 73192

RIVERS

River Avon
Warden: G. A. Stickland
Tel: 036 47 2230

SOUTH BRENT – AVETON GIFFORD
Avon Fishing Association
Weekly permits only
Chairman: Mr. Schofield
c/o Carlton House, The Terrace, Torquay
Permits also available from
Loddiswell Post Office
Diptford Post Office
D. M. Blake, Fore Street, Totnes
Molyneux Sports, Fore Street, Kingsbridge

River Axe
Warden: T. K. G. Davies
Tel: 040 481 2208

Axminster
George Hotel, Axminster
Tel: 0297 32209
Permits only available if not required by
hotel guests

LONGBRIDGE STOCKLAND
Contact: Mr. Summerhayes
Ulcombe Farm, Upottery
Near Honiton, Devon
Tel: 040 486 230

WINSHAM
Contact: G. Bartlett
20 Fore Street, Chard, Somerset
For daily ticket

River Barle
DULVERTON
Contact: Mrs T. Howells
Carnarvon Arms Hotel
Tel: 0398 23302

SIMONSBATH
Contact: T. G. Woodward (Proprietor)
Exmoor Forest Hotel
Tel: 064 383 341

WINSFORD
Contact: M. Warner
Tarr Steps Hotel
Tel: 064 385293

River Bovey
Lower Teign Fishing Association
Sec: J. Michelmore
c/o H. G. Michelmore & Co.
Market Street, Newton Abbot
Tel: 0626 2404

Permits available from
Percy Hodge (Sports)
104 Queen Street, Newton Abbot

River Bray
BRAYFORD
Owner: Mr. & Mrs. C. Hartnoll
Little Bray House
Brayford, Barnstaple
Tel: 05988 295
Permits available from above

SOUTH MOLTON
Poltimore Arms, North Molton
Contact: Mrs Hobson
Tel: 059 84 338
Permits available from above

South Molton Angling Club
Sec: I. T. S. Binding
Tel: 076 95 2161
Permits also available from
Gun and Sports Centre
130 East Street, Molton

River Creedy
Exeter & District Angling Association
Sec: D. L. Beaven
Tel: 0392 75925
Permits available from Exeter Angling
Centre
Tel: 0392 36404

River Culm
Exeter & District Angling Association
Sec: D. L. Beaven
Tel: 0392 75925
Permits available from Exeter Angling
Centre
Tel: 0392 36404

HEMYOCK
Upper Culm Fishing Association
Sec: T. A. Blackmore
'Sunset', Claylidon
Tel: 082 368 485
Permits also available from H. M. Sanders,
The Bakery, Hemyock, Devon. S.A.E.
please

UFFCULME
Contact: Lt. Cdr. T. L. Metters, Owner
The Old Parsonage Farmhouse
Uffculme, Devon
Tel: 0884 40205

River Dart
Warden Lower Dart: G. J. Yunnie
Tel: 080 421 413

Warden Upper Dart: D. J. French
Tel: 03643 301

BUCKFASTLEIGH TOTNES WEIR
POOL
Dart Angling Association
Sec: J. F. Butler
Tel: 0803 63742
Permits available from
Blakes Sport Shop, Totnes
Sports Shop, Buckfastleigh
Percy Hodge Sports, Newton Abbot
Tuckermans Fishing Tackle, Torquay

SOUTH WEST Eastern

BUCKFASTLEIGH
Buckfast Blue Fisheries
Permits available from
The Sports Shop, 35/36 Fore Street
Buckfastleigh
Tel: 036 44 3297

PRINCETOWN
EAST AND WEST DART
Upper Dart Fishing Association
Permits also available from
The Sports Shop at Newton Abbot
The Forest Inn, Hexworthy
James Bowden & Son, Chagford
Princetown Post Office
Postbridge Post Office
Percy Hodge Sports, Newton Abbot

River Little Dart
CHUMLEIGH
Fox and Hounds Hotel
Eggesford, North Devon
Tel: 07698 345
Permits available from above

River Erme
Warden: G. A. Stickland
Tel: 03647 2230

IVYBRIDGE
Contact: Mrs B. S. Sparrow (Owner)
Cleeve, Ivybridge, Devon
Tel: 075 54 2534
Limited permits to members of Anglers Co-
operative Association only. Subscription
available on site

River Exe
Warden Lower Exe: A. Sheppard
Tel: 0392 74230

COWLEY BRIDGE
Newton Abbot Fishing Association
Sec: A. H. Preston
Tel: 0803 69360
Permits also available from local tackle
shops

DULVERTON
Carnarvon Arms Hotel
Contact: Mrs T. Howells
Tel: 0398 23302

Exeter & District Angling Association
Sec: D. L. Beaven
Tel: 0392 75925
Permits available from Exeter Angling
Centre
Tel: 0392 36404

EXETER (3 MILES)
South West Water Authority
3/5 Barnfield Road, Exeter
Tel: 0392 31666

TIVERTON
Tiverton & District A.A.
Sec: Bob Coles
Tel: 08842 4416
Permits from Country Sports, 9 William
Street, Tiverton
Tel: 088 42 4770

TIVERTON
Hartnoll Country House Hotel
Contact: Q. S. Buckland

Bolham, Tiverton
Tel: 088 42 2777

THORVERTON BRIDGE
Permits available from
T. Mortimer, High Banks, Latchmore,
Thorverton
Tel: 0392 860241

River Lew
The West of England School of Game
Angling
Caynton House, Torrington
Contact: John Gawesworth
Tel: 08052 3256

River Lyn
Warden: D. J. Christelow
Tel: 059 85 3586

EAST LYN, NORTH DEVON
Permits available from
Mrs Stevens, Glebe House
Brendon, Lynton

EAST LYN
Rockford Inn
Contact: J. Hayhoe
Tel: 05987 214

EASTLYN
Doone Valley Riding Stables
Malmsmead, Brendon

**WATERSMEET AND GLENTHORNE
FISHERIES**
South West Water Authority
Permits available from the following
locations:
The Warden: Coombe Park Lodge, Lynton
Tel: 05985 3586
Hillsford Bridge, Lynton
Mr. Hill, The Esplanade, Lynmouth
Mr. Parfrey, Stag Hunters Inn, Brendon
Mr. Lynn, Ironmongers, High Street,
Porlock
Anglers Corner, Imperial Buildings, Castle
Hill, Lynton
Mrs. Pile, Oakleigh, Tors Road, Lynmouth
Permits also available from
Fisheries Office S.W.W.A.
3/5 Barnfield Road, Exeter
Tel: 0392 31666

River Mole
South Molton A.C.
Sec: I. T. S. Binding
Tel: 076 952161

SOUTH MOLTON
Permits available from
A. W. Youings, Garramarsh
Queen's Nympton
Tel: 076 97360

UMBERLEIGH
Fortescue Arms Hotel, Umberleigh
Tel: 07698 214

River Okement
OKEHAMPTON
Hill Barton Farm
Owner: Mr Pennington
Tel: 0837 2454

The West of England School of Game
Angling
Caynton House, Torrington
Contact: John Gawesworth
Tel: 08052 3256

River Otter
Warden: T. K. G. Davies
Tel: 040 481 2208

BUDLEIGH SALTERTON
Free fishing for Anglers holding S.W.W
Licence
1st April to 30th September

OTTERY ST. MARY
Venn Ottery Guest House
Venn Ottery, Ottery St. Mary, Devon

WESTON
Mr C. P. May, Bridge House
Weston, Near Honiton, Devon
Tel: 0404 2738

WESTON
Permits available from
L. L. Stevenson (Owner)
Otter Inn, Weston, Near Honiton, Dev
Tel: 0404 2594

WESTON
Permits available from
J. R. O. Boswell, Combe House Hotel
Gittisham, Near Honiton, Devon
Tel: 0404 2756

WESTON
Permits available from
Mr & Mrs Noar, Deer Park Hotel
Weston, Near Honiton, Devon
Tel: 0404 2064

River Taw
Warden: A. Morton
Tel: 02372 6236
Warden Lower Taw: J. Guard
Tel: 036 35 344

**Barnstaple & District Angling
Association**
Sec: M. J. Andrew
Tel: 0271 814474
Permits also available from
Barnstaple tackle shops

CHUMLEIGH
Fox and Hounds Hotel
Eggesford, Chumleigh
Tel: 07698 345

CREDITON
J. O. Yates, Gemini, Lanham Lane,
Winchester, Hants
Tel: 0962 61681
Permits also available from
R. Drayton, 46 Godfreys Gardens, Bov
Crediton
Tel: 03633 417

NORTH TAWTON
Owner: Mr K. Dunn
The Barton, North Tawton
Tel: 083782 230

'ICKLEPATH
ntact: Mr French, Owner
vencourt, Sticklepath, Okehampton,
von
l: 083784 325

MBERLEIGH
rtescue Arms Hotel
berleigh
: 07698 214

MBERLEIGH
rmits subject to hotel bookings available
m
e Rising Sun Hotel
nager: M. A. F. Tate
: 076 96 447

ver Teign
rden Lower Teign: R. Collett
: 0626 61676

rden Upper Teign: R. J. Peardon
: 06474 545

AGFORD UPPER TEIGN
er Teign Fishing Association
A. J. Price
ons Meadow, Chagford
064 73 3253
week and season permits availble

Anglers Rest
le Bridge, Drewsteignton

er Teign Fishing Association
J. Michelmore
H. G. Michelmore & Co.
ket Street, Newton Abbot
0626 2404
its available from
y Hodge (Sports), 104 Queen Street,
ton Abbot

er Torridge
FORD
act: Group Captain Norton Smith
Warham, Beaford, Winkleigh
08053 317

TON
act: R. Cusden
Inn, Dolton
8054 244

SWORTHY
ford Bridge Hotel
r: R. M. Vincent
Damerel, Near Holsworthy
40 926 252

er Torridge Fisheries
ct: C. R. Rowe
olt, Appledore, Bideford,
Devon
3 723 126
ts bookable in advance

PWASH
oon Inn
: Wing Cdr. Inniss
wash, Beaworthy, North Devon
0 923 376

The West of England School of Game Angling
Caynton House, Torrington
Contact: John Gawesworth
Tel: 08052 3256

WEARE GIFFORD
Contact: A. Hooper
Post Office, Riverdale, Weare Gifford, Bideford
Tel: 02372 2479

River Yarty
LONGBRIDGE STOCKLAND
Contact: Mr Summerhayes
Ulcombe Farm, Upottery, Near Honiton
Tel: 040 486 230

STILLWATERS

AVON DAM
South Brent
Warden: G. A. Stickland
Tel: 03647 2230
No permit required
Anglers must have current Rod Licence

BELLBROOK VALLEY TROUT FISHERY, OAKFORD
West of Tiverton on Rackenford Road
Contact: J. Braithwaite
Oakford, Tiverton, Devon
Tel: 039 85 292
Day permits

CULLOMPTON FISHERY
See Stout Fishery

DARRACOTT RESERVOIR
Darracott
Warden: H. Reeves
Tel: 02372 2957
Permits available from self-service unit on site

EAST BATSWORTHY FISHERIES
Rackenford, Nr. Tiverton
Contact: Mr. Gardner
Tel: 088 488 278
Advance booking advisable. Day permits

EXE VALLEY FISHERY
Dulverton
½ day permits limited. Advance booking advisable
Contact: The Fishery
Tel: 0398 23328

FERNWORTHY RESERVOIR
Chagford
Warden: P. Hatton
Tel: 06473 2440
Day and evening permits available from self-service unit on site

GAMMATON RESERVOIR, BIDEFORD
Torridge Flyfishing Club
Sec: F. J. Witt
Tel: 02372 4602

GENNETS RESERVOIR, BIDEFORD
Torridge Flyfishing Club
Sec: F. J. Witt
Tel: 023 72 4602

KENNICK RESERVOIR
Nr. Bovey Tracey, Devon
Warden: R. L. Davison
Tel: 0626 833199
Day and evening permits available from self-service unit on site

SLADE RESERVOIR
Ilfracombe
Warden: R. Bickley
Tel: 0271 62870
Day permits available from self-service unit on site

SPURTHAM FISHERY
Up Ottery, Nr. Honiton
Day and evening permits available.
Advance booking advisable
Tel: 040 486 209

SQUABMOOR RESERVOIR
Nr. East Budleigh
Warden: T. Davies
Tel: 040481 2208
Permits available from Knowle Post Office
The Tackle Shop, 20 The Strand, Exmouth
(open Sunday mornings)
Exeter Angling Centre, City Arcade, Fore Street, Exeter

STAFFORD MOOR FISHERY
Dolton, Winkleigh
Contact: A. Joynson
Brightly Barton, Dolton, Winkleigh
Tel: 080 54360
Day and evening permits available.
Advance booking advisable
Tel: 08054 371/363 or 360

STOUT FISHERY
Billingsmoor, near Cullompton, Devon
Mr E. J. Berry
Billingsmoor Farm, Nr. Butterleigh, Cullompton
Tel: 08845 248
Bookings in advance for day permits

TOTTIFORD RESERVOIR
Nr. Bovey Tracey, Devon
Warden: R. L. Davison
Tel: 0626 833199
Day and evening permits available from self-service unit on site

TRENCHFORD RESERVOIR
Moretonhamstead
Warden: R. L. Davison
Tel: 0626 833199
Permits available from site

VENFORD RESERVOIR
Ashburton
Warden: D. French
Tel: 03643 301
Permits not required
Anglers must have current Rod Licence

WEST BACKSTONE FARM
Rackenford, Nr. Tiverton
Contact: C. L. Thomas
Tel: 088488 251
Advance booking only. Day permits

WHITE SHEET FARM TROUT LAKES
Off A31 Ringwood-Wimborne Rd. Turn right for Holt then first right
Permits from White Sheet Farm, White Sheet, Wimborne, Dorset
Tel: 0202 884504

WIMBLEBALL RESERVOIR
Brompton Regis, Somerset
Warden: B. Poole
Tel: 03987 372
Day and evening permits available from self-service unit on site. Bookings only on first day
Tel: 03987 372 or 0392 31666

WISTLAND POUND RESERVOIR
Barnstaple, Devon
Warden: G. Rogers
Tel: 07695 2429
Day and evening permits available from self-service unit on site

S.W.W. WESTERN AREA

Victoria Square
Bodmin, Cornwall
Tel: 0208 3131

Fisheries Officer: E. S. Bray
Tel: 0208 3131

Assistant Fisheries Officer:
B. Letts
Tel: 0566 2857

Head Warden: A. D. Mills
Nr. Penna, Tavistock
Tel: 0822 3993

RIVERS

River Allen
Wadebridge & District Angling Association
Sec: E. J. Renals
Coppins, Whiterock Close
Wadebridge, Cornwall
Tel: 020881 3239
Day permits available from
Messrs. A. V. Cave and Sons
Polmorla Road, Wadebridge
Tel: 020 881 2591

River Camel
Warden: F. T. Bartlett
Tel: 084 02 3396

Bodmin Anglers Association
Sec: Lt. Col. H. M. Ervine Andrews V.C.
The Old Barn, St. Neot, Liskeard, Cornwall
Tel: 0579 20799
Day, week, season permits available from
A. Cowl, Camel Cottage, Dunmere, Bodmin
S.A.E. please

Liskeard & District Angling Club
Sec: B. G. Wilson
The Bruff, Rilla Mill, Callington
Day and week permits also available from the following locations:
Post Office, Rilla Mill, Callington
Tony Kennedy Sports, 6 Church Street, Launceston
Sams Camping and Fishing, Buller Street, East Looe
Godfreys Stores, Barn Street, Liskeard

Wadebridge & District Angling Association
Sec: E. J. Renals
Coppins. Whiterock Close, Wadebridge
Tel: 020881 3239
Day permits also available from
Messrs A. V. Cave & Sons
Polmorla Road, Wadebridge
Tel: 020 881 2591

River Carey
Arundel Arms Hotel
Lifton
Mrs Ann Voss-Bark
Tel: 056 684244
Permits available after first consideration to hotel guests

River Claw
Bude Angling Association
Sec: Lt. Cdr. S. F. W. Blackall R.N.
4 Ward Close, Stratton Bude, Cornwall EX23 9BB
Tel: 0288 4354
Day, week and month permits available from
C. & M. Tidball, D.I.Y. Centre, The Square, Holsworthy, Devon
Tatham Rod Sports, Belle Vue, Bude, Cornwall

Rivers East & West Looe
Warden: P. V. Brewer
Tel: 0208 872642

Liskeard & District Angling Club
Sec: B. G. Wilson
The Bruff, Rilla Mill, Callington
Day and week permits also available from the following locations:
Post Office, Rilla Mill, Callington
Tony Kennedy Sports Shop, 6 Church Street, Launceston
Sams Camping and Fishing, Buller Street, East Looe
Godfrey Stores, Barn Street, Liskeard

River Fowey
Warden: M. J. Manning
Tel: 0208 3178

Bodmin Angling Association
Sec: Col. H. M. Ervine Andrews V.C.
Tel: 0579 20799
Permits available from:
A. Cowl, 1 Camel Valley
Dunmere, Bodmin
S.A.E. please

Lanhydrock Angling Association
Permits available from the National Trust
The Estate Office, Lanhydrock Park, Bodmin, Cornwall
Tel: 0208 4281

Liskeard & District Angling Club
Sec: B. G. Wilson
The Bruff, Rilla Mill, Callington
Day and week permits also available from the following locations:
Post Office, Rilla Mill, Callington
Tony Kennedy Sports Shop,
6 Church Street, Launceston
Sams Camping and Fishing, Buller Street, East Looe
Godfreys Stores, Barn Street, Liskeard

Lostwithiel Fishing Assocation
Sec: S. E. Brewer
Tel: 0208 872542
Season permits also available from:
Angling Centre, 6 Victoria Place, St. Austell
Messrs. Penhaligon, 15 Queen Street, Lostwithiel
Tackle Box, 11 Trinity Street, St. Austell
Messrs. North, Church Square, Bodmin

River Inny
Liskeard & District A.C.
Sec: B. G. Wilson
The Bruff, Rilla Mill, Callington
Day and weekly permits available from
Tony Kennedy Sports, 6 Church Street, Launceston
Sams Camping & Fishing, Buller Street, East Looe
The Post Office, Rilla Mill, Callington
Godfreys Stores, Barn Street, Liskeard

River Lyd
Arundel Arms Hotel
Lifton
Mrs. Ann Voss-Bark
Tel: 056 684244
Permits available after first consideratic hotel guests

Forestry Commission
Okehampton
Contact: C. Friend, Southern House, Lydford, Okehampton
Tel: 0837 2585

River Lynher
Warden: L. Maddever
Tel: 0566 3181

Liskeard & District Angling Club
Sec: B. G. Wilson
The Bruff, Rilla Mill, Callington
Day and week permits available from t following locations:
Post Office, Rilla Mill, Callington
Tony Kennedy Sports, 6 Church Street Launceston
Sam's Camping and Fishing, Bullet Str East Looe
Godfreys Stores, Barn Street, Liskeard

er Meavy

y Walkham and Plym Fishing Club
Rear Admiral G. W. Gay
hiteford Road, Mannamead, Plymouth
0752 664486
its available from The Keep Tackle
, Tavistock and Jefferys & D.K. Sports,
outh

er Menalhyl

lawgan Angling Club
it available from
Trevenna, Lanvean House,
awgan, Newquay
06374 316
. please

er Ottery

aceston Angling Association
M. R. Jones
0566 2422
its also available from
rs. Raddals
Gate Street, Launceston

er Plym

den: R. S. Armstrong
082 285 2564

outh & District Freshwater A.A.
. Evans
g Cottage, Hemerdon, Plympton
its available from
Sports, 204 Exeter Street, Plymouth
0752 63483

, Walkham & Plym Fishing Club
Rear Admiral G. W. Gay
hiteford Road, Mannamead, Plymouth
752 664486
its also available from:
Keep Tackle Shop, Tavistock
ys and D.K. Sports, Plymouth

r Seaton
den: P. V. Brewer
0208 872642

ard & District Angling Club
. G. Wilson
ruff, Rilla Mill, Callington
nd week permis also available from
llowing locations:
Office, Rilla Mill, Callington
Kennedy Sports Shop, 6 Church
, Launceston
Camping and Fishing, Buller Street,
ooe
eys Stores, Barn Street, Liskeard

r Tamar

den: P. Hinde
752 45492

len for Mid Tamar: L. Maddever
566 3181

Angling Association
. Cdr. S. F. W. Blackall R.N.
d Close, Stratton Bude, Cornwall
9BB
88 4354
s available from the following
ns:
Centre, The Square, Holsworthy,

Devon
C. & M. Tidball, Tatham Rod Sports, Belle
Vue, Bude, Cornwall

Launceston Angling Association
Sec: M. R. Jones
Tel: 056 62422
Permits also available from
Messrs. Raddals, West Gate Street,
Launceston

MILTON ABBOT
Endsleigh House
Milton Abbot, Nr. Tavistock
Tel: 082287 248
Weekly permits for hotel residents

Arundel Arms Hotel
Lifton, Devon
Mrs. Ann Voss-Bark
Tel: 056 684244
**Permits available after first consideration to
hotel guests**

River Tavy
Warden: C. H. De Quick
Tel: 0822 3705

Tavy, Walkham & Plym Fishing Club
Sec: Rear Admiral G. W. Gay
29 Whiteford Road, Mannamead, Plymouth
Tel: 0752 664486
Permits also available from
The Keep Tackle Shop, Tavistock
and Jefferys and D.K. Sports, Plymouth

River Thrushel
Arundel Arms Hotel
Lifton
Mrs. Ann Voss-Bark
Tel: 056 684244
**Permits available after first consideration to
hotel guests**

River Walkham
Warden: R. S. Armstrong
Tel: 082 285 2564

Tavy, Walkham & Plym Fishing Club
Sec: Rear Admiral G. W. Gay
29 Whiteford Road, Mannamead, Plymouth
Tel: 0752 664486
Permits also available from
The Keep, Tavistock and
Jefferys and D.K. Sports, Plymouth

River Wolf
Arundel Arms Hotel
Lifton
Mrs Ann Voss-Bark
Tel: 056 684244
**Permits available after first consideration to
hotel guests**

STILLWATERS

ARGAL RESERVOIR
Penryn, off B3291
Warden: R. P. Evans
Tel: 0326 72544
**Day and evening permits available from
the self service unit on site**

BURRATOR RESERVOIR
Nr. Yelverton
Warden: R. S. Armstrong
Tel: 082 285 2564
**Permits available from self-service unit on
site**

COLLEGE FISHERY
Penryn
Warden: R. P. Evans
Tel: 0326 72544
Tickets available on site

CROWBY RESERVOIR
Camelford
Warden: F. T. Barlett
Tel: 08402 3396
Day permits available on site

DRIFT RESERVOIR
Penzance
Day and evening permits available from
Chyandour Estate Office, Cyandour
Tel: 0736 3021
T. Shorland (Bailiff)
Tel: 0736 3869

MELDON RESERVOIR
Nr. Okehampton, Devon
Warden: M. Hancock
Tel: 040 926 366
**No permit required for this Reservoir.
However anglers must have current
S.W.W.A. rod licence**

PORTH RESERVOIR
Newquay
Warden: D. Parkyn
Tel: 06373 2701
**Evening and day permits available from the
self-service unit on site**

SIBLYBACK RESERVOIR
Nr. Upton Cross Liskeard (off B3254)
**Day and evening permits available from
the self-service unit on site**

STITHIANS RESERVOIR
Nr. Redruth, Cornwall
Warden: N. K. Vogwill
Tel: 0872 3541
Day permits available from
E. Williams, Middle Boswin, 9 Maidens
Road, Porkellis, Cammanellis, Redruth or
self service by dam

TAMAR LAKES
Bude
Warden: K. Spalding
Tel: 028 882 262
**Permits available from self-service unit by
the dam**

TRENCREEK LAKES
St. Austell
Contact: David and John Borradaile
Trencreek Farm, Camping Park, Hewas
Water, St. Austell
Tel: 0726 882540
Day permits available

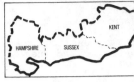

LYMINGTON
Lymington
Beaulieu
ROMSEY
SOUTHAMPTON
WINCHESTER
ANDOVER
NEWPORT
Test
Itchen
Hamble
Meon
PORTSMOUTH
PETERSFIELD
Chichester Canal
Lavant
CHICHESTER
Rother
PETWORTH
Arun
WORTHING
Adur
BRIGHTON
HORSHAM
HAYWARDS HEATH
Bewl Bridge Res.
Ardingly Res.
Bargate Res.
Ouse
E. GRINSTEAD
Weir Wood Res.
Eden
Arlington Res.
EASTBOURNE
Cuckmere
Bough Beech Res.
ROYAL TUNBRIDGE WELLS
HASTINGS
Darwell Res.
Powdermill Res.
Brede
Medway
Beult
Tillingham
Rother
Bewl Bridge Res.
MAIDSTONE
RYE
Royal Military Canal
SITTINGBOURNE
ASHFORD
Gt. Stour
E. Stour
CANTERBURY
FOLKESTONE
Nail Bourne
Little Stour
Stour
DOVER
MARGATE

KENT
HAMPSHIRE
SUSSEX

N

168

Southern Water Authority

Sandbourne House
Worthing, Sussex

Principal Fisheries Officer:
C. Chandler, B.Sc.

Assistant Fisheries Officer:
. Roberts
0903 205252

National Rod Licences
Licences are not issued by bailiffs but be obtained from most tackle dealers m the secretaries of many angling

e of difficulty, licences can be t from the Authority's headquarters.

HAMPSHIRE AND E OF WIGHT RIVER VISIONS

eigh House
et Street, Eastleigh

ries Inspector: D. Paterson
703 614622

RIVERS

r Meon
sfield & District A.C.
. A. McKee
30 66382

mouth & District A.C.
. Snook
05 62986

r Test
KBRIDGE
eyhound Inn, Stockbridge
6 481 833

WAR MEMORIAL PARK, ROMSEY
Test Valley Borough Council
Duttons Road, Romsey
Tel: 0794 515117
Two permits per day available from above office

The Rod Box, Winchester
Proprietor: Col. E. Hay
Permits issued on a careful discriminatory basis
Tel: 0962 713458

STILLWATERS

ABSHOT POND
Portsmouth & District A.C.
Sec: R. Snook
Tel: 0705 62986

ALRESFORD POND
Alresford A.C.
Sec: M. G. Handoll
Oakcroft, Jacklyns Lane, Alresford
Tel: 096273 2474
Day permits from Alresford Fly Fishers, Bakehouse Yard, West Street, Alresford

BAFFINS POND
Portsmouth & District A.C.
Sec: R. Snook
Tel: 0705 62986
Permits available from Southsea Sports Shop
Tel: 0705 735526

BROADLANDS LAKE COARSE FISHERY
Ower, Nr. Romsey
Ringwood & District A.A.
Sec: J. Steel
30 Monsal Avenue, Ferndown
Tel: 0202 893748
Day and week permits available on site

BROCKHURST MOAT, GOSPORT
Portsmouth & District A.C.
Sec: R. Snook
Tel: 0705 62986

BROWNWITCH POND
Gosport
Portsmouth & District A.C.
Sec: R. Snook
Tel: 0705 62986

BUTTOCKS HEATH RESERVOIR
Permits available from bailiff on site
Tel: 04892 433041

CADMANS POOL
New Forest South of Fritham
Forestry Commission, Lyndhurst
Tel: 042128 2801
Permits from any camping permit office or local tackle shops

CARRON ROW FARM PONDS
Titchfield
Tel: 0329 45102

CHANDLERS FORD LAKE
Eastleigh Borough Council
Permits from Council Offices
Leigh Road, Eastleigh
Tel: 0703 614646
Permits restricted to children under 16

COOMBE POND
Titchfield
Portsmouth & District A.C.
Sec: R. Snook
Tel: 0705 62986
Permits available from
Southsea Sports Shop
Tel: 0705 735526

FISHERS POND
Colden Common, Nr. Winchester
Permits available from pondside cottage

FOXCOTE LAKE
Charlton
Andover F.C.
Sec: C. M. Elms
Tel: 0264 64835
Permits available from John Eadies and Cordings tackle shops, Andover

HATTCHET POND
Nr. Beauleigh
Forestry Commission, Lyndhurst
Tel: 042128 2801
Permits from any camping permit office or local tackle shops

HAWLEY LAKE
Permits available from
Cupits
24 Bridge Road, Cove, Farnborough
Tel: 0252 42939

HAYLING LAKE
Denmead
Bognor Regis F.W.A.C.
Sec: R. Thomas
Tel: 024 353 465

HILSEA MOAT
Portsmouth
Portsmouth & District A.C.
Sec: R. Snook
Tel: 0705 62986
Permits also available from:
The Southsea Sports Shop
14 Highland Road, Southsea
Tel: 0705 735526

KINGFISHER LAKE
Testwood
Romsey & District A.S.
Sec: K. R. Pack
Tel: 0703 781556
Permits by advance application to above

KINGHAM LAKE
Winnalmoors, Winchester
Winchester A.C.
Sec: P. J. Allen
Tel: 0962 3929 (day)
Permits from above. No Sunday fishing or on Saturday match days
24 hours notice required

LEIGH PARK LAKE
Havant
Southern A.A.
Sec: T. A. Irons
Tel: 0705 597017

NUTSEY LAKE
Testwood
Romsey & District A.S.
Sec: K. R. Park
Tel: 0703 781556
Permits by advance application to above

SINAH LAKE
Hayling Island
Portsmouth & District A.C.
Sec: R. Snook
Tel: 0705 62986
**Permits available from
Southsea Sports Shop**

SOAKE POND
Denmead
Portsmouth & District A.C.
Sec: R. Snook
Tel: 0705 62986
**Permits available from
Southsea Sports Shop**

OTHER WATERS

STREAMS IN THE NEW FOREST
Forestry Commission, Lyndhurst
Tel: 042128 2801
Permits for trout fishing by fly on streams
running through certain sections of the
New Forest. Permits available from any
camping permit office or from local tackle
shops

ISLE OF WIGHT

River Yar
East Cowes A.S.
Sec: R. Gustar
Tel: 0983 524757

Isle of Wight Freshwater A.A.
Sec: W. Kingswell
Tel: 0983 403994
**Permits also available from tackle dealers
throughout the Island**

STILLWATERS

GUNVILLE POND
Carisbrooke
Isle of Wight Freshwater A.A.
Sec: W. Kingswell
Tel: 0983 403994
**Permits also available from tackle dealers
throughout the Island**

SOMERTON RESERVOIR
Cowes
Isle of Wight Freshwater A.A.
Sec: W. Kingswell
Tel: 0983 403994
**Permits also available from tackle dealers
throughout the Island**

KENT RIVER AND WATER DIVISION

54 College Road, Maidstone, Kent

Fisheries Inspector: B. Joslin
Tel: 0622 671711

170

RIVERS

River Beult
A.C.T. Fisheries Ltd.
Enquiries to:
170 Sydenham Road, London SE26

Paddock Wood A.C.
Sec: G. E. F. Haynes
23 Bramley Gardens, Paddock Wood
Tel: 089 283 2730
Day permits from secretary

River Brede
Rye & District A.A.
Sec: D. Bird
1 Freeland Road, Ealing, W5
Tel: 01 992 3943
**Day and week permits available from
Cottage at Iden Lock; The Globe, Military
Road, Rye; Ashdowns, Peasmarsh, nr. Rye;
Marnies Ltd, High Street, New Romney;
Post Office, Old Romney; The Stone Ferry,
Stone in Oxney**

River Eden
EDENBRIDGE
Fire Station Corner to First Bridge
Free fishing
Details from Logsdon Angling Centre
Tel: 0732 862704

SALMANS FARM
Penshurst
Bailiff: E. Dockerty
Tel: 0892 870328
Permits available at farm

River Medway
Crowborough & District A.A.
Sec: K. J. B. Wilson
Elysium, 35 Southridge Road, Crowborough
Tel: 08926 4722
**Day permits available from the
Bald Faced Stag, Ashurst
Tel: 089274 321**

Maidstone Victory A. & Medway
Preservation S.
Sec: R. Edmunds
31 Allington Gardens, Wateringbury,
Maidstone
Tel: 0622 812904
**Day membership also available from local
tackle shops**

TONBRIDGE AREA
Tonbridge & District A. & F.P.S.
Sec: A. S. Wolfe
Tel: 0732 351541
Permits available from bailiff on bank

Royal Tunbridge Wells A.A.
Sec: A. R. Woodhams
Tel: 0892 30766

Paddock Wood A.C.
Sec: G. E. F. Haynes
23 Bramley Gardens, Paddock Wood
Tel: 089 283 2730
Day permits from secretary

River Rother
Bodiam A.C.
Sec: A. T. Weddle

Tel: 058 083 646
Permits available from bailiff on bank

Clive Vale A.C.
Sec: D. Swain
Tel: 0424 713240

IDEN BRIDGE TO SCOTS FLOAT
Southern Water Authority
Fisheries Office
Tel: 0622 671771
Free fishing from the roadside bank

Rother Fishing Association
Booking Officer: W. S. Rudd
Tel: 058085 430
**No day tickets to individuals – but clu
bookings accepted**

Rye & District A.A.
Sec: D. Bird
1 Freeland Road, Ealing W5
Tel: 01 992 3943
**Day and week permits available from
cottage at Iden Lock; The Globe, Milit
Road, Rye; Ashdowns, Peasmarsh, nr.
Marnies Ltd., High Street, New Romne
Post Office, Old Romney; The Stone Fe
Stone-in-Oxney**

River Stour
Betteshanger Colliery W.A.S.
Sec: A. Herbert
22 James Hall Gardens, Walmer, nr. D
Tel: 03045 64179
**Stretch at Plucks Gutter from bailiff on
bank. Day and year permits from secre**

Canterbury & District A.A.
Sec: N. S. N. Stringer
Riversdale, 14 Mill Road, Sturry,
Canterbury CT2 0AF
Tel: 0227 710830
Day and week permits available on ba

Sandwich & District A.A.
Sec: D. W. R. Daniels
Tel: 0403 613658
Day permits available from bailiff on b

River Tillingham
Rye & District A.A.
Sec: D. Bird
1 Freeland Road, Ealing W5
Tel: 01 992 3943
**Day and week permits available from
cottage at Iden Lock; The Globe, Milit
Road, Rye; Ashdowns, Peasmarsh, nr.
Marnies Ltd., High Street, New Romne
Post Office, Old Romney; The Stone F
Stone-in-Oxney**

STILLWATERS

BROOKLANDS LAKE
Dartford & District A. & P.S.
Sec: D. E. Reeve
Tel: 0322 26728
Permits from bailiff on bank

CHILHAM LAKE
Nr. Canterbury
Mid Kent Water Co., Ashford
Tel: 0634 240313
**Five tickets per week – booked in
advance**

VE VALE RESERVOIR
e Vale A.C.
D. Swain
0424 713240
ickets from above or Harold Road
tshop

CLESBOURNE RESERVOIR
e Vale A.C.
D. Swain
0424 713240

GES LAKE
ock Wood A.C.
G. E. F. Haynes
amley Gardens, Paddock Wood
089 283 2730
ermits from secretary

FIN LAKES
tham, Nr. Canterbury
its available on bank

TON KIRBY LAKE
ord & District A.P.S.
D. E. Reeve
322 26728
its from bailiff on bank

NSONS LAKE
eld
its from bailiff on bank
. Fisheries: J. Joslin
58 084 219

FIELD LAKE
y
Mill A.C.
. Scriven
echwood Road, Caterham, Surrey
ts also available from bailiff on bank

E PARK LAKE
stone
ts available from Recreation Dept,
an House, King Street, Maidstone
622 671361
al tackle shops

E LAKE
sham
sham A.C.
. P. Baldock
79582 3240
ts available from bailiff on bank

ARSH BALLAST PIT
the
ts available from bailiff on bank

POOLS
elsea
rn Water Authority
22 55211
s available from Market Stores, Pett
or Area Fishing Officer, Miller
, Lower Stone Street, Maidstone

TYMANS PONDS
lms, Nr. Edenbridge
s available from
on Angling Centre, Edenbridge
32 862704

OR PARK
tone
s available on site

SCARLETS LAKE
Cowden, Nr. East Grinstead
Bailiff: J. Jackson
Scarlets Farm, Furnace Lane, Cowden
Tel: 034286 414

WEIR WOOD RESERVOIR
East Grinstead
Permits from Recreation Officer
Tel: 034282 2731 or 0444 892453

OTHER WATERS

NORTH AND SOUTH STREAMS
Deal Marshes
Sandwich & District A.A.
Sec: D. W. R. Daniels
Tel: 0304 613658

ROMNEY MARSH DRAINS
Rye & District A.A.
Sec: D. Bird
1 Freeland Road, Ealing W5
Tel: 01 992 3943
Day and week permits from the cottage at Iden Lock; The Globe, Military Road, Rye; Ashdowns, Peasmarsh, nr. Rye; Marnies Ltd., High Street, New Romney; Post Office, Old Romney; The Stone Ferry, Stone-in-Oxney

CANALS

Royal Military Canal
WEST HYTHE DAM TO IDEN LOCK
Ashford & District A.A.
Sec: C. J. Hyder
37 Northumberland Avenue, Kennington, Ashford
Day and week permits available from bailiff on bank, tackle shops in Hythe, Ashford and New Romney

SUSSEX RIVER DIVISION

Southern Water Authority
Falmer, Brighton

Fisheries Inspector: Dr. B. Buckley Ph.D BA
Tel: 0273 506766

RIVERS

River Adur
STEYNING
Pulborough & Steyning A.S.
Sec: M. Booth
Tel: 079 881 525
Permits from local tackle shops

SHERMANBURY PLACE FISHERY
Nr. Henfield
Fishery Manager: G. Rowles
Tel: 0306 883621

WINEHAM
Small stretch
Free fishing

Worthing & District Piscatorial Soc.
Sec: R. P. Tunnicliff
Tel: 0273 413368
Permits also available from Dunmans Tackle, Worthing

BRAMBER
Sussex County A.A.
Sec: Mrs J. Cranford
5 Myrtle Terrace, Weavers Lane, Henfield
Tel: 0273 492714
Day and week permits available from newsagents near bridge

River Arun
PULBOROUGH
Central Association of London & Provisional A.C.
Sec: J. Watts
Tel: 01 686 3199
Permits also available from Swan Corner Shop, Pulborough

ARUNDEL
Sussex County A.A.
Sec: Mrs J. Cranford
5 Myrtle Terrace, Weavers Lane, Henfield
Tel: 0273 492714
Day and week permits available from The Black Rabbit Public House, Arundel The George & Dragon Public House, Arundel

Petersfield & District A.C.
Sec: G. A. McKee
Tel: 0730 66382

Portsmouth & District A.A.
Sec: R. Snook
Tel: 0705 62986

LOWER REACHES
Southern Water Authority
Fisheries Office
Tel: 0273 506766
Free fishing for licence holders

HOUGHTON
Worthing & District Piscatorial Soc.
Sec: R. P. Tunnicliff
Tel: 0273 413368
Permits also available from Dunmans Tackle, Worthing

River Cuckmere
Complete Angling & F.C.
Sec: V. W. Honeyball
Tel: 0323 54598
Permits also available from Complete Angler Tackle Shop, Eastbourne

Hailsham A.A.
Sec: G. R. Verral
Tel: 0323 841716

River Ouse
Haywards Heath & District A.A.
Sec: S. F. Whetstone
Tel: 044 473059
Weekly holiday tickets only

LEWIS TOWN CENTRE
Free fishing

OLD MILL FARM AREA
Browns Boatyard, Barcombe
Permits available from bailiff at farm

SOUTHERN Sussex

River Pevensey Avon

Hailsham A.A.
Sec: G. R. Verral
Tel: 0323 841716
Day permits from above or
Tonys Tackle Shop, Eastbourne
Sussex Armoury, Hailsham

River Rother

Petersfield & District A.A.
Sec: G. A. McKee
Tel: 0730 66382

Petworth A.C.
Sec: D. A. Pugh
Tel: 0798 42866
Permits also available from
Howards Tackle and The Red Lion,
Petworth

Portsmouth & District A.C.
Sec: R. Snook
Tel: 0705 62986

NORTH MILL
Rother A.C.
Sec: C. C. Boxall
4 Half Moon Cottages, Petersfield Road,
Midhurst
GU29 9LL
Day permits available from
Rice Bros. Tackle Shop, West Street,
Midhurst
Burchnalls, North Street, Midhurst

Southern Anglers
Sec: T. A. Irons
Tel: 0705 597017

STILLWATERS

ABBOTS LAKE
Abbotswood, Arlington
Hailsham A.A.
Sec: G. R. Verrall
Tel: 0323 841716
Day permits from above

ARDINGLY COLLEGE
Rev. Waters
3 Stangrove Cottages, Ardingly

BALCOMBE LAKE
Haywards Heath & District A.S.
Sec: S. F. Whetstone
Tel: 0444 73059
Weekly holiday tickets only

BENNET PARK FARM
Heathfield
Permits from the farm

BUCKSHOLE RESERVOIR
Alexander Park, Hastings
Hastings Bexhill & District A.A.
Sec: J. Gutsell
Tel: 0424 421422
Permits also available from
Park Bailiff, T. Barton
51 St. Helens Park Road, Hastings
Tel: 0424 421317

BURTON MILL POND
Nr. Petworth
Bailiff, 390a High Hoes, Petworth
Tel: 0798 42647
Permits from above

CLIVE VALE RESERVOIR
Clive Vale A.C.
Sec: D. Swain
Tel: 0424 713240

COOMBE POND
Petersfield & District A.C.
Sec: G. A. McKee
Tel: 0730 66382

CROWHURST RESERVOIR
See Wishingtree Reservoir

FARTHINGS LAKE
Battle
Bailiff: B. Buss
23 Marley Rise, Battle, Sussex
Permits also available from:
Roy's Newsagent, Battle
Reenies Tackle Shop, Bexhill
Hastings Angling Center, Bexhill
Tony's Tackle Shop, Eastbourne
Tel: 0323 31388

HAYLING ISLAND GRAVEL PIT
Petersfield & District A.C.
Sec: G. A. McKee
Tel: 0730 66382

HEATH POND
Also known as Petersfield Pond
Petersfield & District A.C.
Sec: G. A. McKee
Tel: 0730 66382

LONG LAKE
see Quarry Lake

MICHLEHAM PRIORY
Hailsham
Permits available on site

PETERSFIELD POND
Also known as Heath Pond
Portsmouth & District A.C.
Sec: R. Snook
Tel: 0705 62986

PEVENSEY HAVEN
Compleat Angler
Sec: V. W. Honeyball
Tel: 0323 54598
Day permits also available from the
Complete Angler Tackle Shop, Eastbourne

PILTDOWN POND
Piltdown
Free fishing

PIDDINGHOE POND
Piddinghoe Pond
Seaford A.C.
Sec: Mr B. White
Tel: 0273 38513

QUARRY LAKE
Chichester
Chichester & District A.S.
Permits available from
Russel Hillson Ltd., Chichester
Tel: 02437 83811
Weekly permits only

SHERMANBURY PLACE
Nr. Henfield
Private Controller: Mr Rowles
Tel: 0306 883621

SOUTHERN LEISURE CENTRE
Chichester
Coarse fishery, six lakes
Tel: 0243 787715

VALE BRIDGE MILL POND
Burgess Hill
Haywards Heath & District A.A.
Sec: S. F. Whetstone
Tel: 0444 73059
Weekly holiday tickets only

WHYKE LAKE
see Quarry Lake

WISHINGTREE RESERVOIR
Hastings
Hastings Bexhill & District A.A.
Sec: J. Gutsell
Tel: 0424 421422
Permits also available from
Park Bailiff, T. Barton
51 St Helens Park Road, Hastings
Tel: 0424 421317

OTHER WATERS

Wallers Haven
Hailsham A.A.
Sec: G. R. Verrall
Tel: 0323 841716
Day permits from above or
Tony's Tackle Shop, Eastbourne
Sussex Armoury, Hailsham

Compleat Angler
Sec: V. W. Honeyball
Tel: 0323 54598
Day permits also available from
Compleat Angler Tackle Shop, Eastb

Seaford A.C.
Sec: Mr B. White
Tel: 0273 38513
Day permits available from Star Inn du
opening hours

CANALS

Chichester Canal
Bognor Regis A.A.
Sec: R. Thomas
Tel: 024 353 465
Permits available from tackle shops in
Bognor Regis

Chichester Canal A.A.
Sec: B. Misselbrook
c/o Autocare Garage, Bognor Regis
Permits available from tackle shops in
Chichester

Petworth A.C.
Sec: D. A. Pugh
Tel: 0798 42866

Petersfield & District A.C.
Sec: G. A. McKee
Tel: 0730 66382

Portsmouth & District A.C.
Sec: R. Snook
Tel: 0705 62986

Southern Water Authority

Regional Rod Licences

Rod licences are not issued by bailiffs but may be obtained from most tackle dealers or from the secretaries of many angling clubs.

In case of difficulty, licences can be bought from the Authority's headquarters.

HAMPSHIRE AND ISLE OF WIGHT RIVER DIVISIONS

Eastleigh House
Market Street, Eastleigh

Fisheries Inspector: D. Paterson
Tel: 0703 614622

...ldbourne House
...rthing, Sussex

...cipal Fisheries Officer:
... Chandler, B.Sc.

...stant Fisheries Officer:
... Roberts
...0903 205252

RIVERS

River Anton

Andover A.A.
Hon. Sec: C. M. Elms
60 Gallaghers Mead, Andover
Day permits from Cordings Tackle Shop and John Eadie Ltd.

Manager, Rooksbury Mill, Rooksbury Road, Andover
Day permits
The Rod Box, Winchester
Proprietor: Col. E. Hay
Tel: 0962 713458

River Beaulieu

The Rod Box, Winchester
Proprietor: Col. E. Hay
Permits issued on a careful discriminatory basis

River Itchen

EASTLEIGH BOROUGH COUNCIL
Bishopstoke
Permits from Council Offices
Leigh Road, Eastleigh
Tel: 0703 614646
Permits restricted to children under 16

SOUTHAMPTON
Woodmill to Mansbridge
Public fishing on left bank
Coarse fishing only

WINCHESTER
The Weirs, Winchester
Winchester City Council
Tel: 0962 68166
Free fishing

The Rod Box
Proprietor: Col. E. Hay
Permits issued on a careful discriminatory basis
Tel: 0962 713458

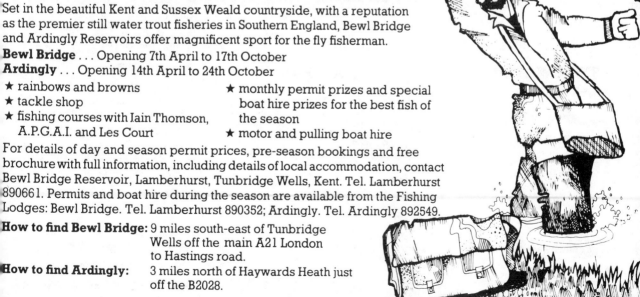

cast a line ...
at Southern Water Trout fisheries

Set in the beautiful Kent and Sussex Weald countryside, with a reputation as the premier still water trout fisheries in Southern England, Bewl Bridge and Ardingly Reservoirs offer magnificent sport for the fly fisherman.

Bewl Bridge ... Opening 7th April to 17th October
Ardingly ... Opening 14th April to 24th October

★ rainbows and browns
★ tackle shop
★ fishing courses with Iain Thomson, A.P.G.A.I. and Les Court
★ monthly permit prizes and special boat hire prizes for the best fish of the season
★ motor and pulling boat hire

For details of day and season permit prices, pre-season bookings and free brochure with full information, including details of local accommodation, contact Bewl Bridge Reservoir, Lamberhurst, Tunbridge Wells, Kent. Tel. Lamberhurst 890661. Permits and boat hire during the season are available from the Fishing Lodges: Bewl Bridge. Tel. Lamberhurst 890352; Ardingly. Tel. Ardingly 892549.

How to find Bewl Bridge: 9 miles south-east of Tunbridge Wells off the main A21 London to Hastings road.

How to find Ardingly: 3 miles north of Haywards Heath just off the B2028.

Southern Water Authority

SOUTHERN Kent

River Lymington
BROCKENHURST TO FOREST BOUNDARY
Forestry Commission, Lyndhurst
Tel: 042128 2801
Permits available from any camping permits officer or from local tackle dealers

The Rod Box
Winchester
Proprietor: Col. E. Hay
Permits issued on a careful discriminatory basis
Tel: 0962 713458

River Meon
Petersfield & District A.C.
Sec: G. A. McKee
Tel: 0730 66382

Portsmouth & District A.C.
Sec: R. Snook
Tel: 0705 62986

River Rother
HABIN BRIDGE, NEAR ROGATE
Southern Anglers
Hon. Sec: T. Irons
7 Nelson Crescent, Horndean, Portsmouth
PO8 9LZ

River Test
STOCKBRIDGE
The Greyhound Inn, Stockbridge
Tel: 026 481 833

WAR MEMORIAL PARK, ROMSEY
Test Valley Borough Council
Duttons Road, Romsey
Tel: 0794 515117
Two permits per day available from above office

The Rod Box, Winchester
Proprietor: Col. E. Hay
Permits issued on a careful discriminatory basis
Tel: 0962 713458

STILLWATERS

ALRE FISHERY
Alresford
Tel: 096 273 2837

AVINGTON TROUT FISHERIES
Avington, Winchester
Tel: 096278 312
**Advance booking required
Day permits**

BOTLEY GRANGE LAKE
Botley Grange Hotel
Nr. Southampton
Tel: 04892 5611
4 permits per day by advance booking

BULL MEADOW LAKE
Boldre, Lymington
P. Perry, Manager
Portmore Farm, Boldre, Lymington
Tel: 0590 73810
Day permits

JOHN O'GAUNT LAKE
Mr Simms
Jasmine Cottage, Kings Somborne
Stockbridge
Tel: 07947 353
Day permits available from Farm

LADYWELL LAKES TROUT FISHERY
Entrance to fishery off the Dean, Alresford
B. H. Dening,
Arle House, Ladywell Lane, Alresford
Tel: 096273 2317
Day permits on site

LEOMINSTEAD TROUT FISHERY
Emery Down, Lyndhurst
Controller: Mr. Jarmal
Emery Down, Lyndhurst SO4 7GA
Tel: 042 128 2610
**Advance booking advisable
Day permits**

LITTLE UPLANDS
Droxford
Contact: N. Gussman
Tel: 04897 8507
Day permits

ROOKSBURY MILL TROUT FISHERY
Rooksbury Mill, Rooksbury Road, Andover
Tel: 0265 52921
Day permits from manager at above address

KENT RIVER AND WATER DIVISION

54 College Road, Maidstone, Kent

Fisheries Inspector: B. Joslin
Tel: 0622 671771

RIVERS

Bartley Mill Stream
BAYHAM ESTATE, LITTLE BAYHAM
Permits available from the Garage
Little Bayham — Mr Bulman
Tel: 0892 890201

River Rother
Bodiam A.C.
Sec: A. T. Weddle
Tel: 058 083 646
Permits available from bailiff on bank

Clive Vale A.C.
Sec: D. Swain
Tel: 0424 713240

IDEN BRIDGE TO SCOTS FLOAT
Southern Water Authority
Fisheries Office
Tel: 0622 671771
Free fishing from the roadside bank

Rother Fishing Association
Booking Officer: W. S. Rudd
Tel: 058085 430
No day tickets to individuals — but club bookings accepted

Rye & District A.A.
Sec: J. Fiddimore
Tel: 07978 384
Permits available from cottage at Iden I or William the Conqueror Pub at Iden

River Stour
Betteshanger Colliery A.S.
Sec: A. Herbert
Tel: 03045 64179
Stretch at Pluck's Gutter from bailiff on bank. Day permits also available from Focsule Tackle Shop, Deal

Canterbury A.A.
Sec: N. S. N. Stringer
Tel: 0227 710830

Sandwich & District A.A.
Sec: D. W. R. Daniels
Tel: 0403 613658
Day permits available from bailiff on ba

STILLWATERS

BAYHAM LAKE
Lamberhurst, Tunbridge Wells
Day permits from J. Parkman
Bayham Abbey, Kent
Tel: 0892 890276

BEWL BRIDGE RESERVOIR
Lamberhurst
Southern Water Authority
**Day permits available from Manager, Bewl Bridge Reservoir, Lamberhurst, Tunbridge Wells
During season from Fishing Lodge**
Tel: 0892 890352

BORINGWHEEL FISHERY
Nutley, Nr. East Grinstead
Permits available on site

CHIDDINGSTONE CASTLE LAKE
Tel: 058 084 219
Permits available from Castle

COOMBE FARM FISHERY
See Tenterden Trout Waters

DARWELL LAKE
Battle
Hastings Flyfishers Club Ltd.
Mountfield, Robertsbridge
Tel: 0580 880407
Day permits from above

HAYES FARM TROUT FISHERY
Hayes Lane, Bromley
Tel: 01 656 2270
Permits available on site

ATHLY FISHERY
berhurst, Tunbridge Wells
permits from
thly Farm, Clay Hill Road, Hook Green,
berhurst
0892 890235

OH CORNER
enden, Cranbrook
permits from I. Thomson
Corner, Rolvenden, Cranbrook
058 084 219
permits available. Advance booking
sable

TERDEN TROUT WATERS
TERDEN
OMBE FARM: B. EVANS
: 058 06 3201
PERMITS AVAILABLE

SSEX RIVER DIVISION
hern Water Authority
ner, Brighton

eries Inspector:
. Buckley PhD, BA
0273 506766

RIVERS

r Arun
BOROUGH
ral Association of London &
sional A.C.
. Watts
1 686 3199
its also available from
Corner Shop, Pulborough

ndel River
ex County A.A.
Mrs B. Mitchell
antley Estate, Henfield
its available from
lack Rabbit Public House, Arundel
eorge Public House, Arundel

sfield & District A.C.
G. A. McKee
730 66382

mouth & District A.C.
R. Snook
705 62986

LOWER REACHES
Southern Water Authority
Fisheries Office
Tel: 0273 506766
Free fishing for licence holders

HOUGHTON
Worthing & District Piscatorial Society
Sec: R. P. Tunnicliff
Tel: 0273 413368
Permits also available from
Dunmans Tackle, Worthing

River Ouse
AVINS BRIDGE, LINDFIELD TO GOLD BRIDGE, NEWICK
Haywards Heath & District A.A.
Sec: S. F. Whetstone
2 West View Cottages, Lindfield, Haywards
Heath RH16 2LJ
Tel: 044 473059
Weekly holiday tickets only

LEWIS TOWN CENTRE
Free fishing

OLD MILL FARM AREA
Browns Boatyard, Barcombe
Permits available from bailiff at farm

River Rother
Petersfield & District A.C.
Sec: G. A. McKee
25 North Lane, Buriton, Petersfield
Tel: 0730 66382
Day permits available from Petersfield Tackle Shop

Petworth A.C.
Sec: D. A. Pugh
Tel: 0798 42866
Permit also available from
Howards Tackle and The Red Lion,
Petworth

Portsmouth & District A.C.
Sec: R. Snook
Tel: 0705 62986

Rother A.C.
Match Sec: R. Stevens
Tel: 073081 3897
Permits available
Rice Bros. Tackle Shop, Midhurst

STILLWATERS

ARDINGLY RESERVOIR
Off College Road, Ardingly, Nr. Haywards
Heath, West Sussex
Southern Water Authority
Fisheries Officer
Tel: 034 2822731
Day permits available from bailiff on Ardingly
Tel: 0444 892549

ARLINGTON RESERVOIR
Nr. Eastbourne
Eastbourne Water Co.
Tel: 0323 21371
Bailiff: 0323 870815
Advance booking advisable

BALCOMBE LAKE
Haywards Heath & District A.S.
Hon. Sec: S. F. Whetstone
2 West View Cottages, Lindfield, Haywards
Heath RH16 2LJ
Weekly holiday permits only

BORINGWHEEL FISHERY
Nutley
Permits available on site

DARWELL LAKE
Battle
Hastings Flyfishers Club Ltd.
Mountfield, Robertsbridge
Tel: 0580 880407
Day permits from above

FEN PLACE MILL ESTATE
Turners Hill
T. J. Nelson
Tel: 0444 52871 or 0342 715466
Permits by prior appointment only

NEWELLS LAKE
T. Cotton
Bodiams, Two Mile Ash, Christs Hospital,
Horsham
Day permits by advance booking

PECKHAMS COPSE
Southern Leisure Centre, Vinnetrow Road,
Chichester
Fishing Department
Tel: 02437 87715
Day permits available from bailiff

POWDERMILL LAKE
Nr. Sedlescombe
Hastings Flyfishers Club Ltd
Mountfield, Robertsbridge
Tel: 0580 880407
Day permits from above

WATTLEHURST LAKE
Nr. Horsham
Private Controller: G. Nye
Tel: 030 679341
Six rods only — advance booking advised

YEW TREE TROUT FISHERY
Between Rotherfield and Mark Cross
(off B2100)
**Permits from J. Schumacher, Yew Tree
Farm, Yew Tree Lane, Rotherfield
Crowborough, Sussex**
Tel: 089 285 2529

Thames

BANBURY

CHIPPING
NORTON

BICESTER

Cherwell

Oxford Canal

Ray
(Ottmoor)

Evenlode

Windrush

WITNEY

Thame

Thames

CIRCENCESTER

Churn

Coln

Leach

Ghill Brook

OXFORD

Ampney
Brook

Cole

Ock

DIDCOT

SWINDON

Lambourn

READING

Kennet

Lodde

MARLBOROUGH

Kennet & Avon Canal

NEWBURY

Kennet & Avon Canal

Kennet

BASINGSTOKE

PETERSFIELD

1. WESTERN
2. EASTERN
3. NORTHERN
4. SOUTHERN
5. METROPOLITAN

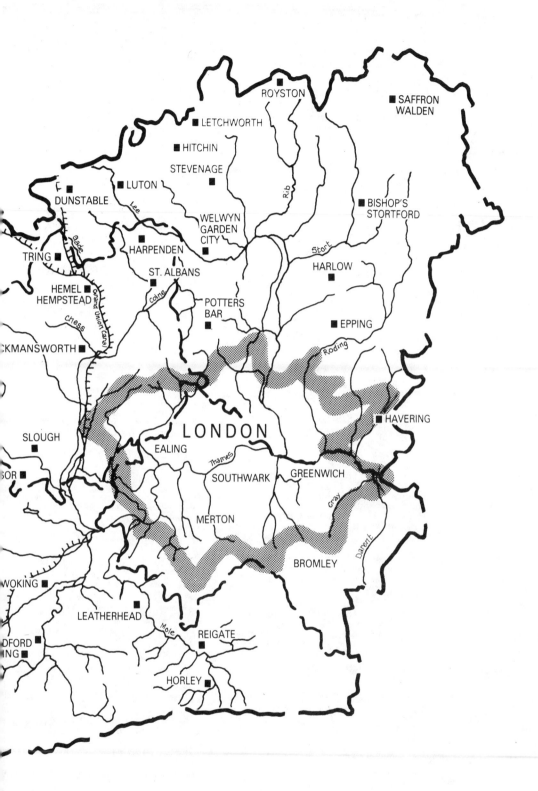

ROYSTON

SAFFRON
WALDEN

LETCHWORTH

HITCHIN

STEVENAGE

LUTON

DUNSTABLE

Lee

WELWYN
GARDEN
CITY

Rib

BISHOP'S
STORTFORD

TRING

Gade

HARPENDEN

Stort

HARLOW

Grand Union Canal

ST. ALBANS

HEMEL
HEMPSTEAD

Chess

Colne

POTTERS
BAR

EPPING

CKMANSWORTH

Roding

LONDON

HAVERING

SLOUGH

EALING

Thames

SOR

SOUTHWARK

GREENWICH

MERTON

Cray

Darent

BROMLEY

WOKING

LEATHERHEAD

Mole

REIGATE

DFORD
NG

HORLEY

N

177

Thames Water Authority

New River Head, Rosebery Avenue
London EC1R 4TP
Tel: 01 837 3300

Fisheries Manager: D. Paton
T.W.A. Reading Bridge House
Reading
Tel: 0734 583583

Regional Rod Licences
A Thames Water Authority rod licence is
required by all anglers aged 12 and over.
One licence covers all the divisions shown
below.

EASTERN AREA

The Grange
Crossbrook Street
Waltham Cross
Herts EN8 8LX

Senior Fisheries Officer:
Mr Reeves Tel: 0992 23611

RIVERS

River Beane
HARTHAM COMMON FISHERY
Hertford Town Centre
Access off Port Hill (B158) onto swimming
pool access road
Boundary from point of access of Port Hill
for 1 mile downstream to River Lee
confluence. Both banks
Chub, Dace, Roach, Perch and Pike
Operated by Herts County Council, County
Hall, Hertford
Tel: 0992 54977
Permits not required. Public fishery

River Lee
OFF A6129 AT BROCKET PARK
Access off A612 at Lemsford and Brocket
Park
Boundary from Warren Farm downstream
to Lemsford Mill. Both banks of river and
broadwater

Mixed coarse fishery
Operated by Brocket Park Estate, Estate
Office
Tel: 070 73 23999
Season Permits from Estate office

WARE MILLSTREAM
The Priory, Priory Street, Ware, Herts
Pedestrian access through Ware Priory off
Priory St
Boundary from Glaxo Ltd boundary fence
downstream to confluence with river Lee
Navigation
Mixed fishing including Roach, Chub,
Dace, Perch and Pike
Operated by Ware Town Council, Priory
Office, Priory St., Ware, Herts
Tel: 0920 61261
**Day Permits available on Bank, Season
Permits from council offices**

SMALL RIVER LEE
Wormley, Herts; Waltham Abbey, Essex;
Enfield, Middx
Access via various road bridges and
footpaths from Lee Navigation Tow Path
Boundary from Aqueduct Lock, Wormley,
Herts downstream for approx 4 miles to
confluence with River Lee Navigation at
Brimsdown
Chub, Roach, Dace and Perch
Operated by Local District Councils
Public fishing. Permits not required

KINGSWEIR FISHERY
Off A1170 at Wormley, Herts
Access along Slipe Lane off A1170 at
Wormley
Pedestrian access over railway and over
river Lee Navigation
Boundary from Kingsweir Cottage
downstream for ¾ mile on left banks and to
sluice on right bank
Coarse fishing primarily Barbel and Chub
Operated by Kingsweir Fishery
Sec: W. Newton, Kingsweir Cottage, Slipe
Lane, Wormley, Herts
Tel: 09924 68394
Day permits available on bank

RIVER LEE
Off A1010 at Enfield, Middx
Access off Swan and Pike Road, via
Ordnance Road, off A1010
Boundary from Swan and Pike Road
downstream for ½ mile to confluence with
River Lee Flood Channel, right bank
Barbel, Chub, Pike, Roach, Tench, Eels
Operated by Lee Valley Regional Park
Authority
Tel: 0992 717711
Public fishing. Permits not required

NEW CUT
Off Marsh Lane, near Northumberland
Park Station
Access 1 mile right bank fishing footpath
from Stonebridge Locks
Boundary from Chalk Bridge Sluices
downstream to Stonebridge Locks. Right
bank only
Chub, Dace, Roach, Bream, Pike and
occasional Trout
Free fishing. Permits not required

RIVER LEE
Hackney Marshes, London E9
Access from Lea Bridge Road/Temple Mill

Road/Carpenters Road
Boundary from Lea Bridge Road
downstream for 2 miles to Carpenters R
Chub, Dace, Roach, Barbel and occasic
Grayling
Operated by London Borough of Hackn
Public fishing. Permit not required

RIVER LEE FLOOD CHANNEL
Netherhall Channel
Off Dobb's Weir Road, Hoddesdon, He
Access upstream of Dobb's Weir Road,
adjacent to Flood Control Gates
Boundary from Fieldes Weir downstrea
to Dobb's Weir Road. Both banks
Mixed coarse fishery including Chub,
Roach, Perch, Bream and Pike
Operated by Redland Aggregates Ltd,
Woolmer Green, Knebworth, Herts
Tel: 0438 811811

RIVER LEE FLOOD CHANNEL
Meadgate Lane Lagoons
Meadate Lane, near Broxbourne, Herts
Pedestrian access from car park in
Meadgate Lane to North Lagoon, Centr
Lagoon and South Lagoon
Boundary from Dobb's Weir Road
downstream 1¼ miles to Nazeing New
Road
Mixed fishing including Pike, Carp, Te
Chub, Bream, Roach and Eels
Operated by Leisure Sport Angling Clu
47-49 Church Street, Staines, Middx
Tel: 0784 61831
**Season Permits available on application
the Angling Manager**

RIVER LEE FLOOD CHANNEL
Kia-ora Channel
Off Nazeing New Road, Nazeing, Essex
Pedestrian access off Nazeing New Roa
Green Lane adjacent to Gravel Workin
Boundary from Nazeing New Road
downstream for ¾ mile to Kia-ora Flood
Control Gates
Mixed fishing including Chub, Roach,
Perch, Bream and Pike
Operated by Redland Aggregates Ltd,
Woolmer Green, Knebworth, Herts
Tel: 0438 811811

RIVER LEE FLOOD CHANNEL
Holy Field Lake
Off Green Lane, Nazeing, Essex
Access via footpath from end of Green
Lane to Kia-ora Flood Control Gates
Boundary from Kia-ora Flood Control
Gates, down stream for ½ mile to Long
Crest Weir. Right bank
Mixed fishing including Pike, Carp, Te
Bream and Roach
Operated by Kingsweir Fishery
Sec: W. Newton, Kingsweir Cottage, Sl
Lane, Wormley, Herts
Tel: 099 24 68394
Permits available on bank
Season permits available upon applica

RIVER LEE FLOOD CHANNEL
Holy Field Lake
Off Green Lane, Nazeing, Essex
Access via footpath from end of Green
Lane to Kia-ora Flood Control Gates
Boundary from Kia-Ora Flood Control
Gates, downstream for ½ mile to Long
Crest Weir. Left bank
Mixed fishing including Pike, Carp, Te

m and Roach
rated by Redland Aggregates Ltd,
lmer Green, Knebworth, Herts
0438 811811

ER LEE FLOOD CHANNEL
field Channel
Crooked Mile (B194) near Waltham
ey, Essex
ess via Stubbings Hall Lane off
oked Mile near Waltham Abbey
dary from Longcrest Weir
nstream for ¾ mile to confluence with
River Lee
d fishing including Chub, Roach,
h, Bream and Pike
rated by Redland Aggregates Ltd,
lmer Green, Knebworth, Herts
0438 811811

ER LEE FLOOD CHANNEL
RELIEF CHANNEL FISHERY
A121, near Waltham Abbey
ess via footpath from Fishers Green
ge downstream to Waltham Abbey 1¼
s
ndary from Fishers Green Lane
nstream 1¼ mile to Waltham Abbey,
ex. Right bank only
rse fishing with occasional Brown Trout
erated by Thames Water Authority,
tham Cross
0992 23611
mits available from Thames Water
hority or P. & B. Hall Fishing Tackle, 44
hbridge Street, Waltham Abbey, Essex
0992 711932
mits not available on bank

ER LEE
A121 at Waltham Abbey, Essex
ess via footpath from Abbeyview Road
21) Waltham Abbey
ndary from Abbeyview Road upstream
¾ mile to confluence with Cornmill
am. Left bank
ub, Roach, Bream
erated by Waltham Abbey Angling
sortium
: P. King, 32 Ashdown Crescent,
eshunt, Herts EN8 0BY
mits available from P. & B. Hall Fishing
kle, 44 Highbridge Street, Waltham
bey, Essex
: 0992 711932

RNMILL STREAM
A121 at Waltham Abbey, Essex
acent via footpath off Highbridge Street,
acent to Abbey
ndary from Highbridge Street,
tream for ¾ mile to confluence with
er Lee. Both banks
ub, Roach, Bream, Rudd
erated by Waltham Abbey Angling
sortium
: P. King, 32 Ashdown Crescent,
eshunt, Herts EN8 0BY
mits available from P. & B. Hall Fishing
kle, 44 Highbridge Street, Waltham
bey, Essex
: 0992 711932

VER LEE FLOOD CHANNEL
A121 at Waltham Abbey
cess via service road adjance to River.
y holders only
ndary from Waltham Abbey
vnstream to King George's Reservoir.
h banks
arse fishing including specimen Barbel,

Chub and Dace
Operated by Thames Water Authority
Tel: 0992 23611
**Private fishing leased to Angling Clubs
from Thames Water Authority
Permits not available**

RIVER LEE NAVIGATION
Ordnance Road, off A1010 Enfield Wash
Access via towing path for 1 mile
Boundary from Rammey Marsh Lock
downstream to Enfield Lock
Roach, Tench, Bream and Chub
Operated by British Waterways Board
Tel: 0992 764626
Public fishing. Permits not required

RIVER LEE NAVIGATION
Ordnance Road, Enfield or off Lea Valley
Road (A110) Ponders End
Access via towing path for 2 miles
Boundary Enfield Lock downstream to
Ponders End Lock
Roach, Tench, Pike and Perch
Operated by British Waterways Board
Tel: 0992 764626
Public fishing. Permits not required

RIVER LEE NAVIGATION
Off Lea Valley Road or off Picketts Lock
Lane, N9
Access via left bank towing path for 1¼
miles
Boundary from Ponders End Lock
downstream to Picketts Lock
Perch, Roach, Bream and Chub
Operated by British Waterways Board
Tel: 0992 764626
Public fishing. Permits not required

RIVER LEE NAVIGATION
Off Waltham Cross
Access via towing path for 1 mile
Boundary from Waltham Common Lock
downstream to Waltham Town Lock
Roach, Chub, Tench and Pike
Operated by British Waterways Board
Tel: 0992 764626
Public fishing. Permits not required

RIVER LEE NAVIGATION
Off A121 Waltham Cross
Access via towing path for 1 mile
Boundary from Waltham Town Lock
downstream to Rammey Marsh Lock
Tench, Roach and Chub
Operated by British Waterways Board
Tel: 0992 764626
Public fishing. Permits not required

River Lee Navigation
Off Cadmore Lane, Cheshunt
Access via towing path for ½ mile
Boundary from Cheshunt Lock downstream
to Waltham Common Lock
Roach, Pike, Chub and Tench
Operated by British Waterways Board
Tel: 0992 764626
Public fishing. Permits not required

RIVER LEE NAVIGATION
Off Picketts Lock Lane, N9
Access from Picketts Lock Lane
Boundary from inside Picketts Lock Leisure
Centre boundary fence, right hand bank
Perch, Roach, Bream, Chub
Operated by Lea Valley Regional Park

Authority
Tel: 0992 717711
Permits from Warden on bank

RIVER LEE NAVIGATION
Off A406 North Circular Road, N18
Access via towing path for 2¾ miles
Boundary from Pickett's Lock downstream
to Stonebridge Lock
Roach, Chub, Tench, Bream and Pike
Operated by British Waterways Board
Tel: 0992 764626
Public fishing. Permits not required

RIVER LEE NAVIGATION
Off Ferry Lane, Tottenham
Access via towing path for ½ mile
Boundary from Stonebridge Lock
downstream to Tottenham Lock
Dace, Roach, Chub and Bream
Operated by British Waterways Board
Tel: 0992 764626
Public fishing. Permits not required

RIVER LEE NAVIGATION
Many entrances to towpath off road bridges
Access via towing path for 4 miles
Boundary from Tottenham Lock
downstream to Old Ford Lock
Roach, Bream and Carp
Operated by British Waterways Board
Tel: 0992 764626
Public fishing. Permits not required

RIVER LEE NAVIGATION
Off road bridges onto towpath
Access via towing path for 1¾ miles
Boundary from Old Ford Lock downstream
to Bow Creek
Roach and Bream
Operated by British Waterways Board
Tel: 0992 764626
Public fishing. Permits not required

RIVER LEE NAVIGATION
Off road bridges to towpath
Access via towing path for 2 miles
Boundary from Bow Lock downstream to
confluence with River Thames
Coarse fish and some tidal species
Operated by British Waterways Board
Tel: 0992 764626
Public fishing. Permits not required

RIVER LEE NAVIGATION
Hertford Castle downstream to Hertford
Lock
Access via towing path
Boundary from Hertford Castle A414
downstream to Hertford Lock off Mead
Lane
Bream, Roach, Rudd, Tench, Perch and
Pike
Operated by British Waterways Board
Tel: 0992 764626
Public fishing. Permits not required

RIVER LEE NAVIGATION
Priory Street, Ware, Herts
Pedestrian access on towing path, off Mead
Lane, Hertford and Priory Street, Ware
Boundary from Hertford New Gauge
downstream to Ware Lock, towing path
only
Chub, Dace, Roach, Bream, Perch and Pike
Operated by British Waterways Board
Tel: 0992 764626 and Thames Water
Authority, Ware Lock House
Public fishing. Permits not required

RIVER LEE NAVIGATION
Off Ware Road at Ware, Herts
Pedestrian access along towing path off
Ware High Street and Ware Road
Boundary from Ware Lock along towing
path downstream to Hardmead Lock, right
bank only
Dace and Bream
Operated by British Waterways Board
Tel: 0992 764626
Public fishing. Permits not required

RIVER LEE NAVIGATION
Off Ware Road, near Stanstead Abbots
Pedestrian access along towing path
Boundary from Hardmead Lock
downstream to Stanstead Lock, right bank
only
Roach, Tench, Bream, Perch and Pike
Operated by British Waterways Board
Tel: 0992 764626
Public fishing. Permits not required

RIVER LEE NAVIGATION
Off A414 at Stanstead Abbots (St.
Margarets)
Access ¾ mile downstream from Stanstead
Lock along right bank towing path
Boundary from Stanstead Lock downstream
to London Anglers Association sign at
Woods Paint Factory, right bank only
Mixed coarse fish
Operated by British Waterways Board
Tel: 0992 764626
Public fishing. Permits not required

RIVER LEE NAVIGATION
Off Rye Road or Rattys Lane, Hoddesdon
Access via towing path from Rye House
Road Bridge (downstream section)
Boundary from Rye House downstream to
Railway Bridge. Right bank only
Usual coarse fish
Operated by British Waterways Board
Tel: 0992 764626
For details contact J. Arnold, 5 Downfield
Close, Downfield Road, Hertford Heath,
Herts
Public fishing. Permits not required

RIVER LEE NAVIGATION
Off Rattys Lane, Hoddesdon
Access via towing path from Railway
Bridge downstream to London Anglers
Association notice board at Dobb's Weir
Boundary as above, right bank only
Tench
Operated by West Ham A.S.
Sec: M. J. Groman, 46 Cobden Road,
Leytonstone, E11
Tel: 01 556 4819
**Permits from bailiff on bank or lock keeper
Tel: 09924 62474**

DOBBS WEIR
Off Dobbs Weir Road, Hoddesdon
Boundary Weirpool from road bridge
round to weir then towpath upstream to the
West Ham A.S. notice board and
downstream to Dobbs Weir Lock
Mixed coarse fishing including Barbel and
Bream
Operated by London Anglers Association
183 Hoe Street, Walthamstow E17
Tel: 01 520 7477
**Permits available from bailiff on bank. No
fishing on island which is strictly private.
The left bank of Dobb's weirpool is**

controlled as a Day Permit fishery by the
onsite fishery owner. Permits available on
bank

RIVER LEE NAVIGATION
Off the Nazeing New Road, near
Broxbourne
access via towing path for approx 4½ miles
Boundary from Dobbs Weir Lock
downstream via Crown Bridge to Pony
Gate above Kingsweir Fishery
Mixed coarse fish including Chub
Operated by Crown Fishery
Sec: Mr P. Brill, Carthagena Lock,
Broxbourne
Tel: 099 24 61048
Permits available from Bailiff on bank

AQUEDUCT FISHERY, WORMLEY
Off A1170 at Wormley
Access over level crossing gates to river
Boundary from notice board before Crown
Meadow downstream to notice board
above Aqueduct Lock
Chub, Roach and Tench
Operated by London Anglers Association
Sec: 183 Hoe Street, Walthamstow E17
Tel: 01 520 7477
Permits available from Bailiff on bank

RIVER LEE NAVIGATION
Off A1010 at Turnford or from Windmill
Lane, Cheshunt
Access via towing path for 1 mile below
Cheshunt Lock
Boundary from Notice Board at Aqueduct
Lock downstream to Cheshunt Lock
Roach, Perch, Tench, Chub etc
Operated by British Waterways Board
Tel: 0992 764626
Public fishing. Permits not required

River Mimram
Welwyn Garden city off A1000
Access via A1000 Hertford Road Bridge
Boundary from A1000 Hertford Road
Bridge to Digswell Park Road Bridge ⅔
mile. Both banks
Brown Trout, Dace and Chub
Operated by Welwyn and Hatfield New
Towns Commission Angling Club
Sec: W. Stone, 3 New Fields, Welwyn
Garden City, Herts
Permits not available. Apply to above

New River
WARE TO STOKE NEWINGTON
No access allowed
Boundary the whole river from Ware to
Stoke Newington
Trout and coarse fish
Operated by Thames Water Authority
**Private fishing to selected angling clubs
No public fishing or access. Permits not
available**

River Roding
Stapleford Tawney on A113
Access via footpath from Passingford
Bridge
Boundary from Passingford Bridge
upstream for 1 mile to Green Farm
Cottages, left bank
Chub, Roach, Dace, Bream with occasional
Brown Trout
Operated by Elm Park & Hornchurch
District A.C.

Sec: P. Darling, 40 Rosslyn Avenue, Ha
Wood, Essex
Permits available on bank

RIVER RODING
Buckhurst Hill off A121
Access via footpath via Recreation Gro
Boundary from Loughton Bridge (Chigv
Lane) downstream for 1½ miles to Rodi
Lane Bridge
Chub, Roach, Dace, Perch and Pike
Operated by Epping Forest District
Council, Parks Officer
Tel: 0378 77344
Public fishing. Permit not required

RIVER RODING
Woodford, Essex off A104/A121
Access via various footpaths, and
Luxborough Lane off A113
Boundary for 2¾ miles to Southend Roa
Bridge (A12)
Chub, Roach and Perch
Operated by Epping Forest District
Council, Parks Officer
Tel: 0378 77344
Public fishing. Permit not required

RIVER RODING
Wanstead, London E11
Access via footpaths from Wanstead Pa
and Ilford Golf Course
Boundary from A12 Southend Bridge R
downstream for 1¾ miles to Romford R
Bridge A118
Chub and Roach
Operated by Epping Forest District
Council, Parks Officer
Tel: 0378 77344
Public fishing. Permit not required

RIVER RODING
Ilford/Barking
Access via Barking Creek and various
footpaths
Boundary from A118 Roadbridge, via
Barking Creek to River Thames approx
miles
Mixed coarse fish and some estuarine
species
Operated by various local Councils
Public fishing. Permit not required

River Stort
Spellbrook, off A1184
Access via towpath for ½ mile from Stat
Road upsream
Boundary from the outlet to the Thorley
Marsh Ditch to the Lock by-pass on the
right bank, and from opposite Thorley
Marsh Ditch to footpath by Wallbury Ca
on the left bank
Carp, Tench, Roach, Rudd, Perch and F
Operated by London Anglers Associatic
183 Hoe Street, Walthamstow E17
**Day and season permits available to
residents of Harlow**

RIVER STORT
Spellbrook off A1184
Access from A1184 right into Spellbrook
Lane East, then by foot on towing path
Boundary from opposite confluence off
Spellbrook downstream to confluence o
Little Hallingbury Brook left hand bank
Roach, Carp, Bream and Tench
Operated by London Anglers Associatic
183 Hoe Street, Walthamstow E17
**Day and season permits available to
residents of Harlow**

R STORT

.1184, Harlow Mill
strian access along towing path left

dary from Feakes Lock by-pass to
4 road bridge
h, Rudd, Bream, Carp, Pike and Perch
ated by Harlow and District A.S.
L. A. Hatwell, 262 Fullers Mead,
w, Essex
it details not known

R STORT

w Town Park area Fishery
ss via Edinburgh Way, Harlow turn
River Way
dary from Eastwick Mead upstream to
w Mill left hand bank and to Bishop
ford Fishery on the right hand bank
h, Bream, Carp, Pike and Perch
rated by London Anglers Association,
loe Street, Walthamstow E17
bers plus day and season permits
able to residents of Harlow

r Stort Navigation

don, Essex
ss off B181 at Roydon Station
dary from B181 road bridge
nstream for ¼ mile to Roydon Mill
h, Dace, Rudd, Perch and Pike
ed by British Waterways Board
0992 764626
rated by British Waterways Board
lic fishing. Permits not required

R STORT NAVIGATION

don, Essex
ss off Roydon High Street B181
dary from Roydon Mill downstream
½ miles to confluence with river Lee
igation towing path
h, Rudd, Dace, Perch, Pike and Tench
rated by Lychnobite A.S.
T. G. Fisher, 15 Underwood Road,
gford E4
permits available from Brick Lock

OTHER RIVERS

ppermill Stream

in Walthamstow Reservoir complex,
ry Lane, Tottenham
access tel: 01 808 1527
dary approx 1 mile of fishing within
ervoir complex downstream from Ferry

ed coarse fishing including Grayling,
b and Roach
erated by Thames Water, New River
d, Rosebery Avenue, London EC1
01 837 3300 Ext 2420
and season permits available

STILLWATERS

EXANDRA LAKE

A116 Aldersbrook Road
estrian access only from road side
cies: Carp, Tench, Roach, Pike and
ch
erated by Epping Forest Conservators
01 508 2266
lic fishing. Permits not required

BALDWINS HILL POND

Off A121 Debden, into Baldwins Hill
Access from Roadside Walk North West,
visible from Road
Species: Carp, Tench, Roach, Rudd, Perch
and Pike
Operated by Epping Forest Conservators
Tel: 01 508 2266
Public fishing. Permits not required

BEDFORDS PARK LAKE

Off B175 at Chase Cross, near Brentwood
Access from A12 take B175 to Chase Cross
then Lower Bedfords Road
Species: Mixed coarse fish mainly Carp
and Roach
Operated by North Romford A.S.
Sec: Mrs Partridge
Tel: 0708 24461
Permits from bailiff on bank

BERWICK PONDS

Off A13 near Rainham, Essex
Access from A13 turn into Launders Lane
then turn into Berwick Pond Road. Entrance
on left
Species: Mixed coarse fish
Operated by Elm Park, Hornchurch and
District A.S.
Sec: P. W. Darling
Tel: 04023 43246
Permits from bailiff on bank

BOWYERS LAKE

Waltham Cross
Access via Trinity Lane off A1010 at
Waltham Cross
Species: Carp, Tench, Bream, Roach, Eels
Operated by Duke of Wellington A.S.
Chairman: A. Curson
Tel: 01 527 1639 or 01 985 5255
Permits from bailiff on bank or gatekeeper

BRACKEN POOL

Broxbourne, Herts
Access off Meadgate Lane, Broxbourne,
Herts. Pedestrian access from Meadgate
Lane Car Park
Species: Pike, Carp, Bream and Roach
Operated by Leisure Sport A.C., Angling
Manager, 47-49 Church Street, Staines,
Middx
Tel: 0784 61831
**Season permit only on application to
Angling Manager**

BRETONS LAKE, DAGENHAM

Off A125 Rainham Road
Access via Bretons Social Centre off A125
to Lakeside
Species: Carp, Tench and Roach
Operated by Bretons A.C.
Sec: B. R. Breeze, 112 Canonsleigh Road,
Dagenham, Essex
Permits available from above address

CHASE GRAVEL PITS

Off A124 into Dagenham Road, Barking
Access via car park in the Chase off
Dagenham Road, Barking
Species: Carp, Tench, Roach, Rudd,
Bream, Perch and Pike
Operated by White Hart A.S.
Sec: A. Tickle, 157 Dagenham Road, Rush
Green, Romford RM7 0TL
Permits from bailiff on bank or gatekeeper

CHESHUNT NORTH RESERVOIR

Off Brookfield Lane, Cheshunt
Access via A10 to Brookfield Lane then into
Cheshunt Park
Species: Carp, Tench, Roach, Rudd,
Bream, Perch etc.
Operated by Kings Arms and Cheshunt
A.C.
Sec: J. Connor
Tel: 0992 762414
10 permits per day only. Available from
Simpsons of Turnford, Tackle Dealer,
Nunsbury Drive, Turnford, Broxbourne
Tel: 09924 68799

CHIGBORO' FISHERIES

Chigborough Road, Maldon
Enquiries to Bailiff
Tel: 0621 57368
See Advertisement this Section

CLAVERHAMBURY CARP LAKE

Galley Hill Road, Waltham Abbey
Access: Lake is situated at end of Galley
Hill Road (Claverhambury Road), Waltham
Abbey, Essex
Species: Carp
Operated by A.D. Huxter & Sons,
Claverhambury Farm, Upshire, Waltham
Abbey, Essex
Tel: 099 289 2114
Permits limited to 10 per day. Available
from P. & B. Hall Fishing Tackle, 44
Highbridge Street, Waltham Abbey, Essex
Tel: 0992 711932

CLISSOLDS PARK LAKES

Stoke Newington, London N16
Access: Park is situated at Junction of
Green Lanes (A105) and Brownswood Road
Species: Carp, Tench, Roach and Perch
Operated by London Borough of Hackney
Public fishing. Permits not required

CONNAUGHT WATER

Off A1069 Rangers Road, Chingford to A11 road
Access via car park on roadside 50 yards from lake
Species: Roach, Tench, Carp and Pike
Operated by Epping Forest Conservators
Tel: 01 508 2266
Public fishing. Permits not required

COPTHALL PARK LAKE

Off B1393 near Epping
Access via Private road off B1393 next to Bell Motel, Epping
Species: Carp
Operated by Mr. Watford, Gamekeeprs Cottage, Copped Hall Estate, Epping
Season permits only from Mr Watford

CROWN FISHERY

Broxbourne, off Nazeing New Road
Access via gravel workings or Carthagena Lock
Species: Mixed coare fish
Operated by Crown Fishery
Resident Manager: P. Brill
Tel: 09924 63656
Permits available from bailiff on site

EAGLE POND

A1007 Snaresbrook Road
Access: fishing from road side of pond only
Species: Carp, Tench, Roach, Rudd, Pike and Perch
Operated by Epping Forest Conservators
Tel: 01 508 2266
Public fishing. Permits not required

EPPING FOREST PONDS

There are many additional small ponds throughout the forest available for public fishing
Species: Carp, Tench and other pond species
Operated by Epping Forest Conservators
Tel: 01 508 2266
Public fishing. Permits not required

FAIRLANDS VALLEY LAKE

Off A1(M) Stevenage
Access in Six Hills Way, Stevenage
Species: Carp, Roach, Perch, Bream and Pike
Operated by Stevenage Borough Council
Park Warden
Tel: 0438 5324
Permits from bank

FAIRLOP PLAIN LAKE

Romford, Essex
Access off Forest road from A123
Proposed coarse fish
Operated by London Borough of Redbridge Parks Dept
Tel: 01 551 0911
Permit undecided yet

FINSBURY PARK LAKE

Off A105 at Manor House
Pedestrian access
Species: Mixed coarse fish
Operated by London Borough of Haringey
Free public fishing. Permits not required

FRIDAY LAKE

Off A121, Cheshunt, Herts
Pedestrian access only, along towing path

to Waltham Common Lock, cross Lee Navigation, follow footpath to Lake
Species: Carp, Roach, Tench, Pike
Operated by Kings Arms and Cheshunt Angling Society
Sec: J. Connor
Tel: 0992 762414
Permits available from bailiff on bank

GERPINS LANE POND

Off Park Farm Road, Upminster, Essex
Access via Gerpins Lane
Species: Carp, Tench, Roach, Rudd
Operated by Ms J. Balment, Leprechaun Farm, Gerpins Lane, Upminster, Essex
Day permits available from farm

GOBIANS LAKE

The Grove, off Moffats Lane, near Brookmans Park, North Mymms
Pedestrian access from car park
Species: Carp, Roach, Rudd, Perch and Tench
Operated by North Mymms Parish Council
Enquiries Park Warden, H. Wade
Tel: 070 72 66972
Permits not generally issued. Parish residents preferred

GOLDINGS HILL PONDS

Off A121 Debden Green
Access: Two ponds adjacent to A121 Debden Green
Species: Carp, Tench, Roach, Rudd, Perch and Pike
Operated by Epping Forest Conservators
Tel: 01 508 2266
Public fishing. Permits not required

GOODMAYES PARK LAKE

Off A124 Junction with Goodmayes Lane
Pedestrian access from car park
Species: usual coarse fish
Operated by London Borough of Barking
Public fishing. Permits not required

GROVELANDS PARK LAKE

Off A111 near Southgate
Pedestrian access from car park
Species: Mixed coarse fish
Operated by Enfield Borough Council, Park Keeper
Tel: 01 886 8405
Permits available on bank

HAINAULT FOREST LAKE

Off A112 at Hainault Forest and Recreation area
Pedestrian access from car park
Species: Carp, Tench, Roach, Rudd, Bream, Perch and Pike
Operated by Greater London Council
Tel: 01 633 1705
Free public fishing. Permits not required

HARLOW COMMON POND

Adjacent to Harlow Common Road, off

London Road, Potter Street, Harlow, Es
Pedestrian access only
Species: Rudd
Operated by Harlow District Council
Tel: 0279 446611
Free public fishing. Permits not requir

HARROW LODGE LAKE

Harrow Lodge Park, Hornchurch
Acces off A125 Upper Rainham into Pa
Species: Roach, rudd, Carp, Perch and Pike
Operated by Southern Essex Group Angling Bodies Consultative
Sec: R. Smith
Tel: 01 592 0348
Permits from bailiff on bank

HATFIELD FOREST LAKES

Hatfield Forest, Takeley, near Bishops Stortford
Pedestrian access along footpaths from Forest Car Parks
Species: Carp, Roach, Pike, Bream and Tench
Operated by National Trust
Head Ranger: Mr Jolly
Tel: 0279 870447
Permits available from bailiff on bank

HIGHAMS PARK LAKE

Off Chingford Lane, Woodford Green
Pedestrian access from park entrances
Species: Carp, Tench, Roach, Rudd, Pik and Perch water
Operated by Epping Forest Conservato
Tel: 01 508 2266
Public fishing. Permits not required

HOLLOW POND

Off A114 Whipps Cross Road
Access park by roadside then by foot
Species: Carp, Tench, Roach, Rudd, Pik and Perch
Operated by Epping Forest Conservato
Tel: 01 508 2266
Public fishing. Permits not required

HOLYWELL HYDE LAKE

Cole Green, Herts
Access off B195 near Welwyn Garden c
via Holywell Hyde Lane
Species: Carp, Tench, Roach and Rudd
Operated by Redland Aggregates Ltd, Woolmer Green, Knebworth, Herts
Tel: 0438 811811
Permits available on site

HOOKS MARSH PIT

Fishers Green Lane, Waltham Abbey
Access off B194 at Waltham Abbey into park at bottom of Fishers Green Lane
Species: Carp, Tench, Roach, Rudd, Per Bream and Pike
Operated by Leisure Sports A.C.
Tel: 0784 61831
Permits available from bailiff on bank or from P. & B. Hall Fishing Tackle, 44 Highbridge Street, Waltham Abbey, Ess Tel: 0992 711932

JACKS LAKE, HADLEY COMMON

Hadley Common, New Barnet
Access off A110 at New Barnet, access to lake is from North Field Road
Species: Carp, Tench, Roach, Perch and Pike
Operated by Local Authority and, Londo

gh of Enfield
1 366 6565
c fishing. Permits not required
Two adjacent lakes on Golf Course
rivate, No Fishing

GSDON LANE POND
don Lane, Potter Street, Harlow,
k
ss: Parking in Kingsdon Lane
les: Pike, Perch, Roach, Rudd, Carp
ench
ated by Harlow District Council
279 446611
public fishing. Permits not required

GSWEIR-PAYNES LANE CARP
E
194 at Nazeing
ess from Nazeing New Road (B194) turn
Paynes Lane and Fishery is on right
ies: Carp
rated by Kingsweir Fishery
ager: W. Newton, Kingsweir Cottage,
Lane, Wormley
09924 68394
nits available from bailiff on bank

PITS LAKE
desdon, Herts
ss at Lampits Housing Estate
ies: Rudd and Tench
rated by Residents Association
dents only

YESBROOK PARK LAKES
odge Avenue (A1153) at Barking,
esbrook Park
estrian access from car park
ies: Roach, Rudd, Carp, Tench, Perch
Pike
rated by Southern Essex Group
ling Bodies Consultative
R. Smith
01 592 0348
nits from local tackle shops only

TESWELL POND, HARLOW
nd Avenue, Harlow New Town
estrian access only
ies: Carp, Roach, Tench, Perch, Pike

rated by Harlow District Council
0279 446611
e public fishing. Permits not required

RTH MET. PIT
B176 into Cadmore Lane, Cheshunt
estrian access from Cadmore Lane or
n towing path on Lee Navigation,
eshunt Lock
ies: Mixed coarse fish, notably Tench
erator not known
mits available from bailiff on bank

KMERE PARK POND
A1000 at Potters Bar
cess from car park in Oakmere Park
ecies: Usual coarse fish
erated by local council
mits available from bailiff on bank (see
ns at Oakmere Park)

KWOOD POND, HARLOW
Fourth Avenue, Harlow into Hodings
ad
destrian access only
ecies: Carp and Tench

Operated by Harlow District Council
Tel: 0279 446611
Free public fishing. Permits not required

OLD LOOP, NEW RIVER
Enfield Town Park
Fishing in river Enfield Town Park only
(Old Loop)
Species: Mixed coarse fish
Operated by Enfield Town Hall, Silver
Street, Enfield
Tel: 01 366 6565 ext 2343
Permits available from bailiff on bank

ORNAMENTAL WATER, WANSTEAD
Off A12 Redbridge Station Roundabout
Access by foot from Park gates in
Wanstead Park Road
Species: Carp, Tench, Pike, Roach, Rudd
and Perch
Operated by Epping Forest Conservators
Tel: 01 508 2266
Day permits available from Park Keepers
on bank

PARKLANDS LAKE
Corbets Tey
Access off B1421, Corbets Tey Road,
Upminster, Essex
Species: Carp, Tench, Roach, Rudd, Perch
and Pike
Operated by Southern Essex Group
Angling Bodies Consultative
Sec: R. Smith, 46 Shortcrofts Road,
Dagenham, Essex
Tel: 01 592 0348
Permits available from bailiff on bank

PERCH POND
Off A116 Aldersbrook Road, Wanstead
Access by foot from Northumberland
Avenue
Species: Carp, Tench, Perch, Pike, Roach
and Rudd
Operated by Epping Forest Conservators
Tel: 01 508 2266
Day permits available from park keeper on
bank

RAPHAEL PARK LAKE
Off A12 at Gidea Park
Access from A12 turn into Pettits Lane, then
into Parland Avenue
Species: Carp, Tench, Roach, Rudd, Perch
and Pike
Operated by Southern Essex Group
Angling Bodies Consultative
Sec: R. Smith, 46 Shortcrofts Road,
Dagenham, Essex
Tel: 01 592 0348
Permits available from bailiff on bank

RODING VALLEY LAKE
Off A121 onto B170 near Buckhurst Hill
Access from B170 turn into Rows Road then
into Green Walk, Buckhurst Hill
Species: Usual coarse fish
Operated by Roding Valley A.C.A.
Sec: L. Lee Esq., 12 Charteris Road,
Woodford Green
Tel: 01 504 9934
Permit details from council offices

SOUTH PARK LAKE
Off A1083 near Seven Kings, Ilford
Access from A1083 into South Park Road
Species: Usual coarse fish
Operated by London Borough of

Redbridge
Tel: 01 551 0911
Free public fishing. Permits not required

SOUTH WEALD LAKE
Weald Park (Country Park) near
Brentwood
Access to park in Weald Road near A12
Brook Street Junction
Species: Carp, Tench, Roach, Bream,
Perch and Pike
Operated by Essex County Council
Tel: 0277 216297
Permits available from bailiff on bank

STANBOROUGH SAILING LAKE
Off A6129 near Welwyn Garden City
Pedestrian access from Stanborough Lane
Species: Carp, Tench, Roach and Bream
Operated by Welwyn Garden City A.C.
Sec: V. Sutton, 30 Timber Croft, Welwyn
Garden City
Tel: 070 73 23500
Permits available from bailiff on bank

ST. MARGARET'S PONDS
Off A1161 near St. Margaret's Hospital
Access: Parking on right off A1161, north St.
Margaret's Hospital, ponds on both sides of
road
Species: Carp, Tench, Rudd, Roach, Pike
and Perch
Operated by Epping Forest Conservators
Tel: 01 508 2266
Public fishing. Permits not required

THEYDON GREEN POND
Theydon Green off B172 Theydon Bois
Access across Green from adjacent roads
Species: Roach, Carp, Tench, Rudd, Pike
and Perch
Operated by Epping Forest Conservators
Tel: 01 508 2266
Public fishing. Permits not required

TRENT PARK LAKES
Off A111 near Cockfosters
Access via Private Park Road off A111
Species: Usual coarse fish
Operated by Greater London Council, Park
Manager, The Rookery, Trent Park,
Cockfosters
Tel: 01 633 1705
Permits available from bailiff on bank or
Park Manager. Permits limited to 10 per
day

TURNFORD CONSORTIUM WATERS
Off A1170 into Slipe Lane, Wormley
Pedestrian access from car park in Slipe
Lane
Species: Carp, Tench, Roach, Rudd, Perch,
Pike and Bream
Operated by Turnford Consortium, Lea
Valley Regional Park Authority
Tel: 0992 717711
Limited number of permits available from
Simpsons of Turnford, Tackle Dealer,
Nunsbury Drive, Turnford
Tel: 09924 68799

VALENTINES PARK LAKE
Gants Hill, Ilford, Essex
Access off A123 at Gants Hill
Species: Usual coarse fish
Operated by London Borough of
Redbridge
Permit details not known

THAMES Metropolitan

WAKE VALLEY PONDS
Adjacent to A11 between Robin Hood and Wake Arms Roundabouts
Access from London Road on left hand side, car parks adjacent to pond. Second pond on East side A11
Species: Tench, Carp, Roach, Rudd, Pike and Perch
Operated by Epping Forest Conservators
Tel: 01 508 2266
Public fishing. Permits not required

WALTHAMSTOW, NO. 1 RESERVOIR
Ferry Lane, Tottenham, London
Species: Carp and Tench
Operated by Thames Water Authority, New River Head, Rosebery Avenue, London EC1
Tel: 01 837 3300 Ext 2418
Day permits and season permits available on site at site entrance
Tel: 01 808 1527

WALTHAMSTOW, NOS. 2 & 3 RESERVOIRS
Ferry Lane, Tottenham, London
Species: Bream, Roach, Carp, Tench and Pike
Operated by Thames Water Authority, New River Head, Rosebery Avenue, London EC1
Tel: 01 837 3300 Ext 2418
Day permits and season permits available on site at site entrance
Tel: 01 808 1527

WALTHAMSTOW GROUP, HIGH MAYNARD RESERVOIR
Ferry Lane, Tottenham, London
Species: Perch, Roach, Carp, Bream and Rudd
Operated by Thames Water Authority, New River Head, Rosebery Avenue, London EC1
Tel: 01 837 3300 Ext 2418
Day permits and season permits available on site at site entrance
Tel: 01 808 1527

WALTHAMSTOW GROUP, LOW MAYNARD RESERVOIR
Ferry Lane, Tottenham, London
Species: Bream, Pike, Carp, Roach and Tench
Operated by Thames Water Authority, New River Head, Rosebery Avenue, London EC1
Tel: 01 837 3300 Ext 2418
Day permits and season permits available on site at site entrance
Tel: 01 808 1527

WALTHAMSTOW GROUP, WEST WARWICK RESERVOIR
Ferry Lane, Tottenham, London
Species: Pike, Bream and Carp
Operated by Thames Water Authority, New River Head, Rosebery Avenue, London EC1
Tel: 01 837 3300 Ext 2418
Day permits and season permits available on site at site entrance
Tel: 01 808 1527

WANTZ BOATING LAKE
Off A124 near Fords Sport Ground
Access: Car park in Wood Lane (A124),

Romford, Essex
Species: Roach, Perch, Carp and Tench
Operated by Southern Essex Group Angling Bodies Consultative
Sec: R. Smith, 46 Shortcrofts Road, Dagenham, Essex
Tel: 01 592 0348
Permits available from local tackle shops

WARREN POND
Off A1069 into Warren Pond Road, Chingford
Access by foot from roadside
Species: Carp, Tench, Roach, Rudd, Perch and Pike
Operated by Epping Forest Conservators
Tel: 01 508 2266
Public fishing. Permits not required

WORMLEYBURY LAKE
Off A1170 into Church Lane at Wormley, Herts
Access from Church Lane, cross over A10 by-pass, turn immediately left in to Wormleybury
Species: Carp, Tench, Roach and Perch
Operated by Mr G. Barnes, Wormleybury Estate
Season permits only from Mr Barnes
Tel: 099 24 65375

METROPOLITAN AREA

Senior Fisheries Officer: J. Percival
Rivers House, Cross Ness Works, Abbey Wood, London SE2
Tel: 01 310 5500

RIVERS

River Cray
FIVE ARCHES MEADOW, NEAR BEXLEY, KENT

Access via footpath from St James' Church off North Cray Bypass
Boundary approx ½ mile up and downstream, both banks from Five Arches Bridge
Roach, Tench, Carp and Brown Trout
Operated by London Borough of Bexley, Gravel Hill, Bexleyheath, Kent
Free public fishing. Permits not required

River Lee
THREE MILLS WALL RIVER/PRESCOTT CHANNEL

Off High Street, Stratford, London E15
Access via Bisson Road, off High Street, Stratford (A11)
Boundary from High Street, Stratford downstream for ¾ mile to Bow Creek Flood Gates
Mixed coarse fish mainly Roach and Tench
Operated by London Borough of Newham
Public fishing. Permits not required

River Thames

The tidal Thames is fishable from Teddington Weir down to the sea. Fish is free and access from the banks unrestricted with certain exceptions around lock structures or where private dwellings adjoin the water.
Coarse fish may be caught as far downstream as Wapping. Eels, through the length, Brown and Rainbow Trout upper reaches. A continuous public footpath exists along almost the entire bank from Teddington to Putney
Further information can be obtained from The Thames Angling Preservation Soc
Hon. Sec: A. E. Hodges, 'The Pines', The Kiln Lane, Bexley, Kent DA5 2BB
Tel: 0322 525575

WATERWORKS RIVER/CITY MILL RIVER/BOW BACK RIVER
at Stratford Marsh, London E15
Access via footpaths from Carpenters and High Street, Stratford
Boundary Carpenters Road, downstream for 1 mile to Bow flyover (A11)
Mixed coarse/estuarine fish including Chub, Roach and Dace
Operated by London Borough of Newham

Public fishing. Permits not required

TEDDINGTON TO RICHMOND BRIDGE

Access at Teddington from Ferry Road from the North and by footpath from Riverside Drive, Richmond from the South
Access at Ham Car Park, near Ham House
River Lane, Petersham and Richmond Town Centre all on the South Bank
Dace, Roach, Bream and Barbel. Brown Trout stocked into the weirpool by Thames Water Authority

Free public fishing. Permits not required

RICHMOND BRIDGE TO KEW BRIDGE

Access via Water Lane and Cholmondeley Walk, Richmond and Ferry Lane, off Kew Green, Kew
Usual tidal species

Free public fishing. Permits not required

KEW BRIDGE TO CHISWICK BRIDGE

Access by Cambridge Cottages, Kew and Chiswick Bridge both on South bank. The Strand on the Green is accessible on the North bank
Dace, Roach, Eels and occasional trout

Free public fishing. Permits not required

CHISWICK BRIDGE TO PUTNEY BRIDGE

Access via Ship Lane and Dukes field, Mortlake; Chiswick Mall; Hammersmith Bridge and the Embankment near Putney Bridge

Free public fishing. Permits not required

NEY BRIDGE TO WAPPING
ss via access steps, fishing restricted
foreshore in centre of London. Such
are at Battersea Park adjacent to
hall Bridge in front of Festival Hall and
apping. These stairs are often locked
, Roach, Eels, Flounders, Trout and
sional Carp
public fishing. Permits not required

STILLWATERS

XANDRA PALACE LAKE
well Hill, Haringey, London
estrian access from car park in
andra Park
l coarse species
rated by the London Borough of
ngey
fishing. Thames Water Authority
nit required

TTERSEA PARK BOATING LAKE
ersea Park SW11
ss via park entrances in Queenstown
, Prince of Wales Drive and Albert
ge Road SW11
ling restricted to short section of bank
Northern side
, Roach, Perch, Tench and Eels
rated by Greater London Council,
s Department, The County Hall, SE1
public fishing. Permits not required

SHY PARK PONDS
na Fountain, Heron Pond, Leg o' Mutton
d, Long Water and Rick Pond
tact: G. W. Cook, Superintendent of
s, Hampton Court Palace, East
esey, Surrey
01 977 1328
0 season permits only. Apply in writing
or after April 1st

OOKLANDS LAKE
tford, Kent
cess from Princess Road or Powder Mill
e, Dartford
rp, Tench, Pike, Roach, Bream and Eels
erated by Dartford and District Angling
Preservation Society, 'Lake House', 2
lnut Tree Avenue, Wilmington, Kent
11 1LJ
y permits available from bailiff at water

ANON HILL COMMON POND
non Hill Lane, Bushey Mead, Merton
cess via Canon Hill Lane
ach, Bream, Carp, Tench and occasional
e and Perch
erated by Council of the London
rough of Merton, Recreation and Arts
pt., Morden Park House, London Road,
rden, Surrey SM4 5QU
rmits available from park keeper on
non Hill Common

**LAPHAM COMMON – MOUNT
ND AND EAGLE POND**
apham Common SW4
unt Pond is adjacent to The Avenue
205, South Circular)
gle Pond is on Clapham Common south
e
rp, Roach, Bream, Tench and Pike
erated by London Borough of Lambeth,
rk Superintendent Mr Franklin, 164

Clapham Park Road, London SW4 7DD
Tel: 01 622 6655
Free public fishing. Permits not required

CRYSTAL PALACE BOATING LAKE
Crystal Palace Park, Penge
Entrance in Thicket Road, SE20
Angling allowed around one half of the lake
Roach, Bream, Perch, Tench, Carp and
Pike
Operated by Greater London Council,
Parks Dept., The County Hall SE1
**Day permits available from park keeper on
bank. Season permits also available**

DANSON PARK LAKE
Danson Road, Bexleyheath, Kent
Access via park gates in Danson Road or
Lakeside Close
Angling restricted to South Bank
Mixed coarse fish notably Roach
Operated by London Borough of Bexley,
Gravel Hill, Bexleyheath
Day, week and season permits available

**HAMPSTEAD PONDS (2) AND VALE
OF HEALTH POND**
Hampstead Heath NW3
Access from South Hill Park and South End
Road, near Hampstead Heath Station. Vale
of Health Pond is reached from East Heath
Road
Roach, Bream, Tench, Perch, Carp and
Pike
Operated by Greater London Council,
Parks Dept., County Hall, SE1. Park
Manager: D. King, GLC Storeyard,
Parliament Hill Fields, Highgate Road NW5
Free public fishing. Permits not required

HIGHGATE PONDS (2)
Parliament Hill Fields NW5
Access via Millfield Lane
Roach, Perch, Bream, Carp and Eels
Operated by Greater London Council,
Parks Dept., County Hall, SE1. Park
Manager: D. King, GLC Storeyard,
Parliament Hill Fields, Highgate Road NW5
Free public fishing. Permits not required

**HORTON KIRBY LAKES (3 GRAVEL
PITS)**
Horton Road, Horton Kirby, Kent
Access via track from Horton Road
Carp, Tench, Pike, Bream, Roach and
Perch
Operated by Dartford and District Angling
and Preservation Society, Lake House, 2
Walnut Tree Avenue, Wilmington, Kent
DA11 1LJ
**Day permits available from bailiff in hut by
entrance or on bank**

KESTON PONDS
Off Westerham Road, Keston Mark,
Bromley, Kent
Access via Fishponds Road
Carp, Roach, Tench, Perch, Pike and
occasional Bream and Eels
Operated by London Borough of Bromley,
Park Manager: Mr Long, 83 Tweedy Road,
Bromley BR1 1DA
Tel: 01 464 3833
Free public fishing. Permits not required

THE MODEL BOAT POND
Darenth, near Dartford
Access via public footpath from Roman

Villa Lane, Darenth
Roach, Bream, Tench, Perch, Carp, Pike
and Chub
Operated by Leisure Sports Ltd., Angling
Manager: J. E. Newby, 47-49 Church Street,
Staines
Tel: 0784 61831
Day permits available on bank

**ONE ISLAND POND AND SEVEN
ISLAND POND**
Mitcham Common, Mitcham
One Island Pond is South and Seven Island
is North of Croydon Road which crosses
Mitcham Common
Mirror, Common and Crucian Carp, Tench,
Roach, Rudd, Pike, Perch and Gudgeon
Operated by the Council of the London
Borough of Merton, Recreation and Arts
Dept., Morden Park House, London Road,
Morden, Surrey SM4 5QU
Free public fishing. Permits not required

POTOMAC POND
Gunnersbury Park, Brentford W3
Access through park via entrance in Popes
Lane
Roach, Tench, Carp and Bream
Operated by London Borough of Hounslow,
Parks and Open Spaces
Tel: 01 992 2247
Day permits available from bailiff on bank

REGENTS CANAL DOCK
Limehouse, E14
Access via gate to south of Commercial
Road, near Stepney East Station or via
Island Row
Eels, Roach, Perch and Bream
Operated by British Waterways Board
Also operated by the Thames Angling
Preservation Society
Hon. Sec: A. E. Hodges, 'The Pines', Tile
Kiln Lane, Bexley, Kent DA5 2BB
Day tickets available on bank

RUXLEY LAKES
Ruxley Corner, Footscray, Kent
Access off A20 Sidcup Bypass
Three lakes, largest available to non-club
members
Roach, Pike, Carp, Bream, Perch, Rudd
and Tench
Operated by Orpington and District
Angling Association
Hon. Sec.: R. Bright, 133 The Drive, Bexley,
Kent
Tel: 01 303 5945
**Limited number of permits for weekdays
only
Obtainable in advance from Orpington
Angling Supplies, 304 High Street, St Mary
Cray, Kent**

**SOUTH EAST LONDON AQUATIC
CENTRE**
Woolwich Dockyard, London SE18
Supt. David Shukar
Access from Europe Road, west of
Woolwich Ferry
Carp, Rudd, Roach, Tench and Perch
Operated by London Borough of
Greenwich, Baths and Sports Dept
Tel: 01 855 0131
Day permits available on site

185

THAMES Northern – Southern

SOUTHMERE LAKE
Thamesmead SE2
Access via Belvedere Road
Fishing restricted to east bank
Roach, Carp, Perch and Eels
Rudd and Tench in Summer
Operated by Greater London Council,
Parks Dept., The County Hall, SE1
Day permits available on bank

SOUTH NORWOOD LAKE
South Norwood, Croydon
Access via Woodvale Avenue, off South
Norwood Hill
Roach, Bream, Carp, Pike, Perch and
Tench
Operated by London Borough of Croydon,
Auckland Road
Tel: 01 771 1896
**Day permits available from park keepers
on bank. Season permits available**

SURREY DOCK
Rotherhithe SE16
Access via main gate in Lower Road,
Rotherhithe, opposite Rotherhithe Public
Baths
Roach, Perch, Tench, Bream, Pike and Eels
Operated by Southwark Angling and
Preservation Society
Hon. Sec.: P. King, 15 Coxson Way, Fair
Street, Bermondsey SE16
Tel: 01 403 0274
Permits available on bank

TOOTING BEC LAKE
Tooting Bec Common, Tooting SW17
Lake is north of A214, Tooting Bec Road
Carp, Roach, Bream, Pike, Perch and
Tench
Operated by London Borough of
Wandsworth, Tooting Bec Common
Tel: 01 672 6354
Free public fishing. Permits not required

VICTORIA PARK LAKE
London Borough of Tower Hamlets, near
Old Ford Road
Pedestrian access from car park
Usual coarse species
Operated by Greater London Council,
Parks Superintendent
Tel: 01 985 1957
Free public fishing. Permit not required

WANDSWORTH COMMON POND
Wandsworth Common, SW11
Access via Baskerville Road, off A214
Trinity Road (from west) or off Bellevue
Road, near Wandsworth Common Station
(from south)
Roach, Bream, Perch, Pike with Carp and
Tench in summer
Operated by London Borough of
Wandsworth, SW18
Tel: 01 874 1841
Free public fishing. Permits not required

CANALS

Grand Union Canal
HAYES TO OSTERLEY
Access via Station Road, Harlington; Bulls
Bridge; Glade Lane, Southall; Trumpers
Ways; Hanwell
Boundaries at Lock 98 (Osterley) and
Bridge 200 (Hayes)

Roach, Bream, Carp, Perch, Pike and Eels
Operated by London Anglers Association
Sec: Mr P. Ellis, 183 Hoe Street,
Walthamstow E17 3AP
Tel: 01 520 7477
Permits available from bailiffs on towpath

Grand Union Canal (Paddington Canal)
LITTLE VENICE, PADDINGTON TO BULLS BRIDGE, SOUTHALL
Access at Little Venice; Scrubs Lane,
Hammersmith; Disraeli Road, off Acton
Lane, NW10; Abbey Road, Park Royal;
Horsenden Lane South, Greenford; Bulls
Bridge
Roach, Bream, Carp, Tench, Perch,
Gudgeon and Eels
Operated by London Anglers Association
Sec: Mr P. Ellis, 183 Hoe Street,
Walthamstow E17 3AP
Tel: 01 520 7477
Permits available from bailiffs on towpath

Herts Union Canal
HACKNEY, LONDON E9
Access off Old Ford Road, or footpath from
Victoria Park and Carpenters Road
Boundary from Grand Union Canal (Old
Ford Road) downstream for 1¼ miles to
confluence with River Lee at Carpenters
Road
Roach, Bream, Tench and Dace
Operated by London Borough of Twoer
Hamlets
Public fishing. Permits not required

Limehouse Cut
BROMLEY BY BOW, LONDON E3
Access off A102, Northern Approach at
Gillender Street
Boundary from Bow Creek for 1¼ miles to
Commercial Road (A13)
Roach, Tench and Bream
Operated by London Borough of Tower
Hamlets
Public fishing. Permits not required

Regents Canal
REGENTS CANAL FROM SALMONS LOCK TO LITTLE VENICE, PADDINGTON
Access via Salmon Lane, Limehouse E14;
Old Ford Road, E2; Colebrook Row,
Islington, N1; Lisson Grove, Marylebone,
NW1
Boundary at Little Venice, 10 miles of
towpath
No fishing from private bank adjoining
private property, or in Little Venice basin
Roach, Bream, Gudgeon, Eels, Carp,
Tench and Pike
Operated by Raven AC
Hon. Sec: E. Mears, Esq., 16 Broomhouse
Road, London SW6
Tel: 01 736 5581
Permits available from bailiff on bank

NORTHERN DIVISION

**The Grange, Crossbrook Street,
Waltham Cross, Herts EN8 8LX**

Senior Fisheries Officer: Mr Reeves
Tel: 0992 23611

RIVERS

River Thames
FROM HENLEY TO WINDSOR
Weir permits for the following weirs:
Hambledon, Marlow and Bray covered
one single permit available from
Thames Water Authority
Finance Dept., Nugent House
Vastern Road, Reading
Tel: 0734 593333

STILLWATERS

ALDENHAM RESERVOIR
Access A411 Bushey-Elstree Road,
Aldenham Road entrance to Aldenham
Country Park. Boats available
Operated by Herts County Council
Warden: J. Deacon
Tel: 01 953 9602
Day permits available from warden on s

BLACK PARK LAKE
Access in Black Park Road off A412 Slo
road
No night fishing
Free public fishing

COWLEY LAKE
Access off Packet Boat Lane, West Dray
Operator not known
Permits available on site

FARLOWS LAKE
Access in Ford Lane off B470 Iver-West
Drayton Road
Tench, Bream, Pike; Trout fishing by an
method in coarse season
Operated by Wm. Boyers Ltd
Tel: 08954 45141
**Permits available on site from cafe or
bailiffs on bank. Night fishing permitted**

LITTLE BRITAIN LAKE
Access along Packet Boat Lane, West
Drayton
Owner not known
Permits available on bank

PIX FARM LAKE
Fishing available on application to Mr G.
Gaywood
Tel: 092 77 69863

RICKMANSWORTH AQUADROME
Access via car park off Frogmoor Lane,
Rickmansworth
Operated by Three Rivers District Counc
Free public fishing

RUISLIP LIDO
Reservoir Road, Ruislip
Manager on site Mr Prescott
Tel: 08956 34081
Day permits available on site

SAVAY FARM
Moor Hall Lane, Denham, Bucks
Roach, Perch, Tench, Pike and Carp
Operated by Redland Angling Scheme
Manager: G. Love, 41 Lincoln Road, North
Harrow, Middx

n permits and night syndicate by
n application only. Day permits
ble at Balfours Newsagents, Denham;
to fishing and Judds of Hillingdon Ltd,
gdon

RTWOOD COMMON PONDS
es, Middx
ss via Shortwood Avenue, off A30 near
ked Billet Roundabout
public fishing

DE OAK PIT
ss via Little Marlow Sewage Works on
5 Marlow-Bourne road
rated by Marlow A.C.
G. W. Hoing
062 85 22405
permits available from local tackle
s

NMORE COMMON PONDS
nore Hill, Middx
e small ponds
ch, Roach and Carp
public fishing

CKWOOD PARK LAKE
n
rated by Hon. Secretary: C. J. Withey,
igh Wood Close, Luton
0582 36818
nits available from above

STHORPE FARM
ess via Westhorpe Farm A4155
low-Bourne End Road
rated by M. J. Randall
0279 4275
icularly noted for large catches of
cian Carp

CANALS

and Union Canal
NG STATION TO HUNTON
DGE LOCK, KINGS LANGLEY
erated by London Anglers Association
permits available at Dacorum Council
ces, Hemel Hempstead

NTON BRIDGE LOCK TO GROVE
Ll
cess via Grove Mill Lane on A411 Hemel
npstead to Watford Road
erated by Kings Langley A.S.
n. Sec: A. Anderson
0442 59341
mits available from bailiff on bank

**CROXLEY GREEN LOCKS 78-80 TO
DICKINSONS & MOOR POUNDS**
Access by various points mainly via track to
Croxley Mills and Moor off A412 near
Croxley Green Metropolitan Line Tube
Station
Operated by Watford Piscators
Hon. Sec: N. F. Brandon, 25 Leaford
Avenue, Watford
Tel: 0923 27019
Permits available on bank

**CROXLEY GREEN TO
RICKMANSWORTH**
Moor Pound Lock to Rickmansworth Lock
Operated by Sceptre A.S.
Hon. Sec: D. Hobbs
Tel: 09273 71391
Day permits available on bank

M40 TO BULL'S BRIDGE, SOUTHALL
Operated by London Anglers Association
Day permits available on bank

Grand Union Canal, Slough Arm

**SLOUGH BASIN TO JUNCTION WITH
MAIN CANAL**
Access at various points along canal
Operated by London Anglers Association
Day permits available on bank

RICKMANSWORTH LOCK TO M40
Approx 7 miles canal towpath
Access via Frogmoor Lane, Batchworth;
Springwell Lane, Mill End; Coppermill
Lane, Harefield; and Moorhall Lane,
Denham
Operated by Blenheim A.S.
Hon. Sec: F. W. Lancaster
Tel: 01 749 0033
Permits available on bank

SOUTHERN DIVISION

Thames Water Authority
Ladymead, By Pass Roads,
Guildford, Surrey
Tel: 0483 77655

Senior Fisheries Officer:
Dr. A. Butterworth

RIVERS

River Kennet
BARTON COURT FARM
Kintbury
E. D. Hill
Tel: 04885 226

Permits for weekdays only by prior
arrangement

CRAVEN FISHERY
Off the A4 about 3 miles west of Newbury
Fishery Bailiff: B. Edwards
Fisher Cottage, Craven Estate, Hampstead
Marshall, Newbury
Tel: 0635 40505
**Permits must be booked at least one week
in advance by telephone or writing**

OLD MILL PRIVATE HOTEL
Aldermaston
Tel: 073 521 2365

READING
Boundary right bank downstream Blakes
Lock to mouth
Access via Orts Road
Free public fishing. Permits not required

Twickenham Piscatorial Society
Next to A4 about 1 mile east of Newbury
Access by footbridge behind Inn
Boundary 500 yards from footbridge
upstream to Greenham Lock
Mixed coarse fish
Permits available from the White House
Inn, Newbury
Tel: 0635 42614

River Loddon
HURST
Access through Dinton Pastures Country
Park off B3030 Winnersh to Twyford Road
Boundary right bank downstream from
Reading Road Bridge for approx 1 mile
Chub, Roach and occasional Barbel
**Permits available from Country Park
Wardens**
Tel: 0734 342016
See Advertisement this Section

SINDLESHAM
Access from Mill Cottage off Sindlesham
Lane
Boundary from overspill weir to
roadbridge, backstream right bank
Chub and Barbel
Permits available from Mill Cottage

SINDLESHAM
Access from Sindlesham Lane
Boundary upstream of Sindlesham Mill to
above motorway bridge. Main river, right
bank
Mixed coarse fish
**Permits in advance from Farnham A.S.,
Sec: R. T. Frost, Danefort, Cambridge
Road, Farnborough
Tel: 0252 42809**

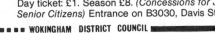

River Mole

DEEPDENE FISHERY

Off A25 Dorking
Access via tarmac drive from A25 west of
Deepdene Bridge
Boundary 500 yards downstream from
Deepdene Bridge, left bank only
Chub, Dace and Roach
Operated by S. C. Fuller, 28 South Street,
Dorking, Surrey
Tel: 0306 882407
**Permits available from above or bailiff on
bank**

River Thames

Weir permits for the following weirs:
Boveney Lock, Bell Weir Lock,
Shepperton, Sunbury and Molesley main,
covered by one single permit are available
from:
**Thames Water Authority
Finance Dept., Nugent House
Vastern Road, Reading
Tel: 0734 593333**

FROM BENSON TO HENLEY

Weir permits for the following weirs:
Goring, Shiplake and Marsh Lock covered
by one single permit are available from:
**Thames Water Authority
Finance Dept., Nugent House
Vastern Road, Reading
Tel: 0734 593333**

COOKHAM

Boundary right bank upstream of Cookham
Bridge to Railway Bridge
Access via towpath
Operated by Cookham and District A.C.
Sec: T. Butter
Tel: 0494 49402
**Permits available from Kings Fishing
Tackle, 18 Ray Street, Maidenhead.
Tel: 0628 29283 and other local tackle
shops**

DORNEY

Boundary left bank upsream from Boveney
Lock to beginning of gardens at Dorney
Reach
Access via towpath from car park at
Boveney Common
Operated by Maidenhead and District
A.A., Chairman: G. W. Rance, Ivydene,
Forlease Road, Maidenhead
Tel: 0628 27448
Permits available from above

HURLEY

Boundary right bank upstream to Hurley
Lock
Access through Hurley Village
Operated by London Anglers Association
Tel: 01 520 7477
**Permits available on bank
Thames Water Authority licence required**

MAIDENHEAD

Boundary right bank downstream from My
Lady Ferry to beginning of gardens
Access via towpath from car park
Operated by Maidenhead and District
A.A., Chairman: G. W. Rance, Ivydene,
Forlease Road, Maidenhead
Tel: 0628 27448
Permits available on bank

Boundary right bank Boulton Lock to
Maidenhead Bridge
Access from Ray Head Road. And left bank
Maidenhead Bridge to end of Public
Gardens, access via Ellington Road
Mixed coarse fish
Free public fishing. Permits not required

MARLOW

Boundary left bank upstream from Marlow
Bridge to opposite Temple Island
Access via towpath
Operated by Marlow and District A.
Sec: G. W. Hoing, 15 Greenlands,
Flackwell Heath, High Wycombe
Tel: 06285 22405
**Permits available from Kings Fishing
Tackle, 1 Ray Street, Maidenhead
Tel: 0628 29283 and other local tackle
shops**

Boundary downstream from Marlow Lock
to end of Riverwoods Drive, left bank
Mixed coarse fish
Free public fishing. Permits not required

Boundary left bank from Riverwoods Drive
to opposite first islands
Access via towpath
Mixed coarse fish
Operated by Marlow and District A.
Sec: G. W. Hoing, 15 Greenlands,
Flackwell Heath, High Wycombe
Tel: 0625 22405
**Permits available from Kings Fishing
Tackle, 1 Ray Street, Maidenhead
Tel: 0628 29283 and other local tackle
shops**

READING

Boundary right bank from Caversham
Bridge approx 1½ miles upstream
Access at free car park off Richfield
Avenue just upstream of bridge
Mixed coarse fish
Operated by Reading Borough Council
Tel: 0734 55911 Ext 2167
Permits available on bank

Boundary right bank from upstream limit of
Reading Borough Council section for
approx 1100 yds
Access via Scours Lane off A329 at
Tilehurst
Mixed coarse fish
Operated by Thames Water Authority
Free public fishing. Permits not required

REMENHAM

Boundary right bank downstream from
Leander clubhouse to within 100 yds of

Hambledon Lock except for short
signposted London A.A. stretch in mid
Access via Remenham Church
Operated by Remenham A.S.
Sec: Mrs A. E. Fenn
Tel: 04912 6490
Day permits available on bank

RUNNYMEDE

·Boundary right bank from Runnymede
House to Bellweir Lock
Access from National Trust car park at
Runnymede
Free public fishing. Permits not require

STAINES

Boundary downstream of Staines, all
accessible banks
Free public fishing. Permits not require

The Thames Angling Preservation Soci
has acquired a considerable amount of
knowledge about the River Thames fro
Staines down to the sea. Free advice to
on receipt of S.A.E.

WINDSOR AND ETON

Boundary left bank upstream from A332
Roadbridge to Long Bridge
Access from car park off Meadow Lane
Operated by Salt Hill A.S.
Sec: H. W. Mayo, 16 Old Way Lane,
Cippenham, Slough
Tel: 062 86 63574
**Permits available from Windsor Angling
Centre, 157 St Leonards Road, Windsor
Tel: 075 35 67210**

Boundary left bank downstream, Railwa
Bridge to Windsor Town Bridge
Access via Meadow Lane and right ban
downstream from A332 Roadbridge to
Windsor Town Bridge
Access from Bath Island car park
Mixed coarse fish
Free public fishing. Permits not require

Boundary Romney Island and right bank
downstream from Romney Lock to Railw
Bridge
Access from car park near Railway Stati
Mixed coarse fish
Operated by Old Windsor A.A.
Sec: D. Meakes, 51 Bulkly Avenue,
Windsor
Tel: 07535 52741
**Day permits available from Windsor
Angling Centre, 157 St Leonards Road,
Windsor
Tel: 075 35 67210**

Boundary right bank from Victoria Bridg
upstream to Railway Bridge
Access from Victoria Bridge via towpath
Mixed coarse fish
Free public fishing. Permits not require

Boundary right bank Albert Bridge to Ha
Lane
Access via towpath from Albert Bridge
Mixed coarse fish
Operated by Old Windsor A.A.
Sec: D. Meakes, 51 Bulkly Avenue,
Windsor
Tel: 07535 52741

**Permits available from Windsor Angling
Centre, 157 St Leonards Road, Windsor
Tel: 075 35 67210**

...dary Eton Wick left bank from
...ey Lock for approx 1 mile
...ss via towpath
...d coarse fish
...ated by London Anglers Association
...1 520 7477
...its available on bank
...es Water Authority Licence required

...r Wey

...DALMING, SURREY

...dary from Godalming Town Bridge
... to Broadford Bridge, Shalford, left
...h, Dace, Chub, Perch, Pike with
...sional carp, bream and trout
...ated by Godalming A.S.
...permits available from A. & G.
...orne, Tackle dealer, 42 Bridge Street,
...lming

...LDFORD, SURREY

...dary from Shalford to Send approx 9
...s, also some short free stretches in the
... centre
...ed coarse fish
...rated by Guildford A.S.
...permits available from bailiff on bank

...KING, PYRFORD

...dary right bank downstream
...rcourt Lock to Swing Gate
...ss from Newark Lane via towpath
...rated by Woking and District A.A.
... B. Candler, 58 Nursery Road, Knaphill,
...king
...nits in advance from J. Cobbett,
...dlands, Coldharbour Road, Pyrford

STILLWATERS

...DERMERE LAKE

...ham Common, near Wisley, Surrey
...ess via Old Lane, off A3 southbound
...iageway
...am, Roach and Pike
...erated by Valuation and Estates Office,
...ey County Council, Surrey House,
...den Street, Kingston-upon-Thames
...01 549 6111
...e public fishing. Permits not required

...ACKNELL MILL POND

...cknell, Berks
...ess from Wildridings Road
...erated by Bracknell District Council
...e public fishing. Permits not required

...TTENS POND

...obswell near Guildford, Surrey
...cess off Worplesdon Road from A320
...king Road, north of Guildford
...mmon and Crucian Carp, Tench and
...ch
...eated by Guildford A.S.
...: G. Pank, 72 St Philips Avenue,
...rcester Park
...: 01 337 5692
...y permits available from bailiff on bank

...CHAN PARK LAKE

...chan Park, Horsham Road, Crawley,
...Sussex
...cess off A264 west of Crawley
...am, Carp, Roach and Pike
...y permits available from Town Angler,
...ewhurst Road, West Green, Crawley

Tel: 0293 21186 and
Kirkmans, 40 The Broadway, Crawley
Tel: 0293 26670

DEANS FARM READING

Access via Star Road, Reading
Parking at Farm
Includes length of River Thames adjacent
to lake
Operated by Redland Angling Scheme
Day permits available on site at Farm

EARLSWOOD LAKES

Woodhatch, near Reigate, Surrey
Access via Woodhatch Road
Mixed coarse fish, notably carp
Operated by Reigate and Banstead
Borough Council, Town Hall, Reigate,
Surrey
Free public fishing. Permits not required

FOUR WENTS POND

Holmwood, Dorking, Surrey
Access via Mill Road
Mixed coarse fish including carp and
perch
Operated by National Trust, Polesden
Lacy, Surrey
Tel: 0372 53401
Free public fishing. Permits not required

FRENSHAM GREAT POND

Frensham, Surrey
Access from A287 1 mile south of Frensham
Tench, Pike, Roach and Perch
Operated by Farnham A.S.
Sec: R. T. Frost, Danefort, Cambridge
Road, Farnborough
Tel: 0252 42809
Permits available from above

FRENSHAM SMALL POND

near Frensham, Surrey
Access via narrow road running east off the
A287 in Frensham Village
Tench, Rudd, Roach, Pike, Perch and Carp
Operated by Farnham A.S.
Sec: R. T. Frost, Danefort, Cambridge
Road, Farnborough
Tel: 0252 42809
Permits available from above

GOSSOPS GREEN MILL POND

Access via Lea Close
Mixed coarse fish
Operated by Crawley Borough Council,
Town Hall, Boulevard, Crawley, W. Sussex
Tel: 0293 2744
Permits available from warden on bank

HENFOLD LAKES FISHERY

Henfold Lane, Newdigate, Surrey
Access via Henfold Lane
Pike, Carp in bottom lake; Tench, Roach in
top lake
Operated by Ernest Green, Henfold Lanes
Fishery, Henfold Lane, Beare Green,
Surrey
Tel: 0306 6549
**Permits available on site or advance
bookings form above**

HOLLYBUSH LANE FISHERIES

Farnborough, Hants
Access in Hollybush Lane off Lynchford
Road, Farnborough
3 lakes with Bream, Roach, Tench, Carp
and Pike

Operated by Redland Fisheries
Manager: G. Rowles, Lakeview, Old Bury
Hill, Westcott, Dorking
Tel: 0306 883621
Day permits for car park lake only, from
Raison Bros, Park Road, Farnborough
Tel: 0252 43470 and other local tackle
shops
See Advertisement this Section

LANGHAM POND

Runnymede, near Windsor, Surrey
Access via footpath through field opposite
National Trust car park at Runnymede
Roach, Tench and Pike
Operated by Old Windsor A.S.
Sec: D. Meakes, 51 Bulkley Avenue,
Windsor
Tel: 075 35 52741
**Day permits available from Windsor
Angling Centre, 157 St Leonards Road,
Windsor**
Tel: 075 35 67210

LITTLETON LAKES

Littleton Lane, Shepperton
Entrance via Junction of Littleton Lane and
Chertsey Road
**Permits must be obtained prior to fishing
from Mrs Clark, at Westray Bungalow after
8a.m.**
**Day and annual permits available from
Thames Angling, 11 Feltham Road,
Ashford, Middx**
Operated by Redland Angling Scheme

LODGE POND

Farnham, Hants
Access through Alice Holt Forest off the
A325, signs for lake past the Forestry
Commission Office
Roach, Tench, Pike, Carp
Operated by Farnham A.S.
Sec: R. T. Frost, Danefort, Cambridge
Road, Farnborough
Tel: 0252 52809
**Permits available from above or Forestry
Commission Office**

LONG LAKE, THATCHAM

Off Lower Way, Thatcham
Operated by Thatcham A.A.
Sec: K. Roberts
Tel: 0635 63346
**Permits available from Dorcis Hardware
Shop**

LONGMOOR LAKE

Barkham near Wokingham, Berks
Access through California Country Park off
Nine Mile Ride
Operated by Wokingham District Council
**Permits available from wardens office on
site**

MILL POND

Addlestone, Surrey
Access via Allied Mills, Bourneside Road,
Addlestone
Mixed coarse fish
Permits available from the Mill Office
Tel: 0932 52944

189

MYTCHETT FARM LAKE
Mytchett, Surrey
Access from Mytchett Road, opposite Hazel Road
Bream, Tench, Roach, Pike and Crucian Carp
Permits available from Raison Bros Tackle Shop, Farnborough
Tel: 0252 43470

OLD BURY HILL LAKE
Westcott, Dorking, Surrey
Access via tarmac drive off A25 just west of Dorking
Pike, Carp, Zander, Tench
Operated by Mr G. Rowles, Lakeview, Old Bury Hill, Westcott, Dorking, Surrey
Permits available by post or from site

SILVERMERE LAKE
Cobham, Surrey
Access via Redhill Road
Bream with occasional Carp and Pike
Operated by Silvermere Golf and Country Club, Redhill Road, Cobham, Surrey
Tel: 093 26 7275
Permits available from office or by post from above

SUMMERLEAZE GRAVEL PIT
Bray, near Maidenhead, Berks
Access from Monkey Island Lane
Roach, Bream and Tench
Operated by Summerleaze Gravel Co Ltd
Day permits available from Gravel Co Office or Kings Fishing Tackle, 18 Ray Street, Maidenhead
Tel: 0628 29283

TILGATE PARK LAKES
Tilgate Estate, Crawley
Access via Titmus Road
Mixed coarse fish
Operated by Crawley Borough Council
Town Hall, Boulevard, Crawley, W. Sussex
Tel: 0293 28744
Permits available from warden on bank

TRILAKES
Sandhurst, near Camberley, Surrey
Access form Yateley Road
Mixed coarse fish and trout
Operated by Trilakes Ltd., C. Homewood, Yateley Road, Sandhurst, Surrey
Tel: 0252 873191

WAGGONERS WELLS LAKES
Grayshott, Surrey
Access via signposted road off B3002 1 mile west of Grayshott
Trout lake stocked with brown trout
Coarse lake contains Roach, Perch and Carp
Operated by National Trust
Permits available from Warden on bank

WELLINGTON COUNTRY PARK
Riseley, near Reading, Hants
Access from roundabout off A32 South Riseley
Gravel pit with coarse fish
Permits available from Country Park Office

WEY FARM LAKE
Oltershaw, Surrey
Access signposted from A320 Chertsey-Woking Road
Roach, Perch, Tench and Carp

Permits available from house at entrance to fishery, local tackle dealers or by post from G. Rowles, Lakeview, Old Bury Hill, Westcott, near Dorking, Surrey

WHITE SWAN LAKE
Hurst, near Wokingham, Berks
Access through Dinton Pasture Country Park off the B3030 Winnersh to Twyford Road
Roach, Perch, Carp and Pike
Operated by Wokingham District Council
Permits available from wardens on site
See Advertisement this Section

WILLOWAY LAKES
Ash Vale, Hants
Access off Showfield Road, Ash Vale
Larger Lake with Tench, Carp and Roach
Smaller lake stocked with Trout
Operated by Stillwater Fisheries
Permits available on site or from Raison Bros, Park Road, Farnborough

YATELEY COMMON PONDS
Yateley, Hants
Access from A30
Carp, Tench, Bream and Pike
Operated by Hampshire County Council
Permits available by advance booking only from the warden
Tel: 0252 874346

CANALS

Basingstoke Canal
ALDERSHOT TO BYFLEET, SURREY
Canal still to be renovated, some fishing in Mytchett area
Access via towpath
Operated by Basingstoke Canal Surrey Angling Amalgamation
Sec: R. M. Hatcher, 80 Hillview Court, Guildford Road, Woking
Day permits available from bailiff on bank

NORTH WANBOROUGH TO ASH, HAMPSHIRE
Angling centres at Odiham, Dogmersfield, Crookham, Fleet and Aldershot
Access via towpath only
Roach, Bream and Carp
Operated by Hamshire Basingstoke Canal Angling Amalgamation
Sec: L. A. Harris, 24 Hampton Court, Woolford Way, Basingstoke
Tel: 0256 57596
Day permits in advance from local tackle shops

Kennet and Avon Canal
HUNGERFORD
Hungerford Canal A.A.
Chairman: W. Radbourne
Tel: 04886 2131
Permits from Paul Good Ironmongers High Street, Hungerford

KINTBURY
Kintbury A.C.
Sec: A. J. Broughton
Tel: 04885 793
Permits available from Mrs Robinson, 7 Kennet Road, Kintbury
Tel: 04885 8955

THATCHAM
Thatcham A.A.
Sec: K. Roberts
Tel: 0635 63346
Permits available on bank

Wey Navigation Canal
9 miles of canal from Newark Bridge, Ripley to Thames Lock, Weybridge
Chub, Roach, Bleak, Gudgeon and Ca
Operated by Wey Navigation Amalgamation
Day permits available on tow path

WESTERN DIVISION

Senior Fisheries Officer:
Dr P. Spiller
Tel: 0865 721125
Seacourt Tower, West Way, Botley, Oxford

RIVERS

River Cherwell
CROPEDRY TO BANBURY AND NELLBRIDGE TO BLETCHINGDON
Access at Cropedry, Grimsbury, Some and Heyford
Banbury & District A.A.
Sec: P. M. Handley
Tel: 029578 491
Permits available from tackle shops in Banbury

OXFORD/KIDLINGTON
Boundaries signposted right hand bank
Water Eaten to A40 and left hand bank
Sparsey Meadow
Access off A40 and via Islip
Abingdon & Oxford Anglers Alliance
Sec: M. J. Ponting
Tel: 0865 67008
7 day permits from above or tackle shop in Abingdon/Oxford Area

KIRTLINGTON
Cherwell at Northbrook 1½ miles upstre to Northbrook Bridge left hand bank
Access off A4095
Bicester & District A.A.
Sec: W. Barker
Tel: 086 92 43675
Permits T.A. Allmond Tackle Shop, Bicester
Tel: 08692 2767

BIBURY
Between two footbridges 200yds on righ hand bank
Fly only
Operated by Swan Hotel, Bibury
Tel: 028 574 204
Permits available to residents only

...ver Evenlode
...NSHAM
...Cassington and upstream of A40
...e meadow upstream of A40 both banks
...e meadow downstream of A40 right
...nk only
...ingdon & Oxford Anglers Alliance
...c: M. J. Ponting
...: 0865 67008
...out, fly only, from April 1st
...ay permits from above or tackle shops
...Abingdon/Oxford area

...ver Ock
...Abingdon
...rporate Fishery, downstream of
...kbridge Childrens fishery, Town Clerk,
...atton Lodge, Bath Street, Abingdon

...ver Ray
...IP VILLAGE
...m notice 200m below Oddington to Islip
...nt bank only. Both banks of confluence
...h Cherwell
...cess via Islip
...ingdon & Oxford A.A.
...: M. J. Ponting
...: 0865 67008
...ay permits from above or tackle shops
...Oxford/Abingdon Area

...NCOT
...undary 1 mile each side of Fencot bridge
...cess and parking via bridge
...ester & District A.A.
...: W. Barker
...: 08692 43675
...mits from T. A. Allmond Tackle Shop,
...ester
...: 08692 2767

...ver Thame
...ABBINGTON ISLAND
...ghton Buzzard A.C.
...: F. McLellan
...: 0525 374702
...mits available from: Old Fisherman Inn,
...g Crendon
...: 0844 201247

...ver Thames
...OM LECHLADE TO BENSON
...ir Permits for the following weirs:
...afton, Radcot, Rushey, Shifford,
...sham, Sandford, Culham and Day's
...k covered by one single permit
...ilable from
...mes Water Authority, Finance Dept.,
...gent House, Vastern Road, Reading
...: 0734 593333

...NGDON CORPORATE FISHERY
...e to residents
...mits to visitors available from Town
...rk, Stratton Lodge, Bath Street

...SCOT, OXON
...CHLADE TO BUSCOT
...ess off A417
...erated by London Anglers Assoc.
...: V. R. Cooke
...: 01 520 7447
... permits available from bailiff on bank.
...mes Water Authority Licence required

BUSCOT TO GRAFTON LOCK
Car park at Kelmscot
Match fishery 100+ pegs
**Permits available from Turners Tackle & Bait, Faringdon
Tel: 0367 21044**

EYNSHAM, SANDFORD AND CLIFTON-HAMPDEN
Access via Eynsham Bridge, Clifton-Hampden Bridge
Operated by Abingdon & Oxford Anglers Alliance
Sec: M. J. Ponting
Tel: 0865 67008
7 day permits from local tackle shops in Abingdon/Oxford area

GODSTOW TO SEACOURT OVERSPILL AND SEACOURT STREAM FROM OVERSPILL TO A420
Access via Godstow car park
Operated by North Oxford A.S.
Sec: J. Humm
Tel: 0865 45051
Permits from above. Club bookings welcomed

RADCOT, GRAFTON LOCK TO OLD MAN'S BRIDGE
Towpath side access and car park at Radcot
Match fishers 100+ pegs. Disabled facilities
Operated by Fadcot A.C.
Sec: C. R. Neville
Tel: 036781 362
**Day, 7 day or season permits available from the Swan Hotel, Radcot or Turners Tackle, Faringdon
Tel: 0367 21044**

NEWBRIDGE, NEWBRIDGE 2 FIELDS UPSTREAM, RIGHT HAND BANK
Operated by Stroud and District A.A.
Sec: J. Starkey
Tel: 0453 45535
Permits available from Naybush Pub at Newbridge. Permits also at Newbridge Farm by prior arrangement

CLANFIELD, OLD MAN'S BRIDGE TO RUSHEY LOCK
Left hand bank
Access via Radcot Bridge or by arrangement with Clanfield A.C.
Operated by Clanfield A.C.
Sec: F. Baston, Mill Lane, Clanfield, Oxon
Permits by writing in advance from above

OXFORD RESIDENTS FISHERY
Pout Meadow left hand bank Godstow to Medley, car park at Godstow

MEDLEY TO A420 TOWPATH AND AT SANDFORD
Access via Osney Bridge, car parking at Medley
Operated by O.D.A.A.
Sec: P. Weston
Tel: 08692 44533

LECHLADE, ST. JOHNS LOCK TO HAPENNY BRIDGE
Right hand bank
Operated by Trout Inn, Lechlade
Tel: 0367 52313
Permits available on site

SANDFORD TO NUNEHAM BRIDGE TOWPATH ALSO DUXFORD
Access difficult
Operated by Abingdon & District Angling & Restocking Association
Sec: R. Pitson
Tel: 0235 25140
7 day permits available from local tackle shops. Included in permit of Abingdon & Oxford Alliance Fisheries

SANDFORD KENNINGTON SOCIAL CLUB
Off Island above weir
Operated by R. Leach, 33 Henley Road, Kennington
Permits and match bookings by arrangement

SHILLINGFORD – WALLINGFORD
Shillingford Bridge Hotel
Tel: 086 732 8567
Permits available from the hotel

TADPOLE BRIDGE TO TENFOOT BRIDGE
Right hand bank
Access and car park at Tadpole
Coarse match fishery 100+ pegs
Operated by Trout Inn, Buckland, near Faringdon
Tel: 036 787 234
Permits available from above

River Thames and River Windrush, Newbridge
2 fields downstream on left hand bank at Newbridge and from road bridge to confluence left hand bank River Windrush
Access via Newbridge car park on site
Coarse fish and Trout
Operated by Rose Revived Hotel, Newbridge, nr. Standlake
Tel: 086 731 221
Permits available from Hotel

River Windrush
BURFORD
Access via Burford Bridge and Town Car Park
Burford A.S.
Sec: L. R. Lavigne
Tel: 0895 52208
Permits from Public Houses in Burford

THAMES Western

STILLWATERS

ABBEY LAKE
Abbey Grounds, Cirencester
Access via Market Square or footpath from
Spital Gate. Car parking at both sites
Permits available from Cirencester Town
Council, also through local tackle dealers

ADLESTROP LAKE
Adlestrop
Car parking adjacent to water
Carp
Moreton in the Marsh A.C.
Sec: F. D. Wilsdon
Tel: 0451 21018
Permits from Hoopers Newsagent, Moreton
in the Marsh

BLENHEIM PALACE LAKE
Woodstock
Access off A34
Boat fishing only for non-residents
Blenheim Palace Estate Office
Tel: 0993 811432 (Office Hours)
Permits must be booked in advance

COATE WATER COUNTRY PARK
Marlborough Road
Off Junction 15 M4
Car park on site
Match fishery
Bream, Tench, Roach, rudd, Pike
Thamesdown Borough Council
Information Tel: 0793 22837
Day permits available on site

COMMODORE LAKE
Fairford, Nr. Lechlade
Access off A417 east of Fairford
Car park on site, lake used on some
weekends for water skiing
Newlands A.C.
Permits from Clubhouse

DORCHESTER LAKE
Dorchester
Access opposite Plough Public House on
A423
Abingdon & Oxford Anglers Alliance
Sec: M. J. Ponting
Tel: 0865 67008
7 day permits from local tackle shops

DUKES LAKE
Wolvercote, nr. Oxford
Access via wooden steps off A40 near
canal crossing, North Oxford
Operated by Mr Hamm
Tel: 0865 45051
Permits available from local tackle shops

HINKSEY LAKE
Hinksey Park, Oxford
Access via Lake Street off Abingdon Road
Bream, Carp and Tench
Oxford City Council
Information tel: 0865 58490
Permits available at lake

HORCOTT LAKES
Fairford
Off A417 Fairford follow sign marked RAF
Fairford off main road and turn right
opposite Carriers Arms. Car park on site
Horcott A.C.
Sec: D. Reeve
82 Okus Road, Swindown
Tel: 0793 34378
By arrangement permits can be made
available on site

HORSESHOE LAKE
Lechlade
Access off A361 north of Lechlade on
Bunford Road
Car parking on site
Linch Hill fisheries
Tel: 0865 882215
Warden: Mr Martin
Tel: 0367 52448
Day permits available on site

KEYNES PARK
Nr. Ashton Keynes
Signposted off Spine Road east of
Somerford Keynes
Car parking on site
Tench, Roach and Bream
Ashton Keynes A.C.
Sec: J. Parker
Tel: 079370 2028
Day permits available on site at wardens
office

MARLBOROUGH POOL
Cassington Village
Access off A40. Car Park
Abingdon & Oxford Anglers Alliance
Sec: M. J. Ponting
Tel: 0865 67008
7 day permits from local tackle shops from
1st November

MILTON POOLS FARMS
Junction 7, M40 London to Oxford
J. Rust
Tel: 08446 8150
Permits available on site

NORTHMOOR LAKE
Ashton Keynes
South Cerney A.C.
Sec: H. J. Franklin
Tel: 0285 830362
Permits from ticket machine at bank

SOUTH CERNEY PITS
HAM LANE POOL, HILL'S LAKE
AND BRADLEY'S MAIN PIT
Access via South Cerney Village. Car park
Tench
South Cerney A.C.
Sec: H. J. Franklin
Tel: 0285 830362
Day permits available on site from club
house or ticket machine

TELFORDS POND
Cheyney Manor, Swindon
Near Steam Train Public House
Day permits weekdays only from House

TRING RESERVOIRS
Tench, Catfish, Bream, Roach, Pike and
occasional carp
Bailiff: B. Double Esq. Tel: 044282 2379
Day permits on bank for Wilstone, Starto
and Marsworth

TUCKWELLS PIT
Radley, Nr. Abingdon
Access difficult via road to Thrupp Lakes
Abingdon & Oxford Anglers Alliance
Sec: M. J. Ponting
Tel: 0865 67008
7 day permits from local tackle shops

CANALS

Grand Union Canal, Aylesbur Arm
AYLESBURY BASIN TO RED HOUSE LOCK
Access at various points, mainly Brought
Operated by A.C. Delco
Hon. Sec: G. Munday
Tel: 029 661 2671

COOKS WHARF TO TRING STATIO
Carp
Operated by Tring Anglers
Hon. Sec: J. A. Smith
Tel: 0296 688777
Permits available on bank

RED HOUSE LOCK TO MARSWORT BASIN (MAIN CANAL)
Access limited at Red House end
Good carp at Marsworth end
Operated by Tring Anglers
Hon. Sec: J. A. Smith
Tel: 0296 688777
Permits available on bank

Oxford Canal
BANBURY TO CROPEDRY AND NELLBRIDGE TO BLETCHINGDON
Banbury & District A.A.
Sec: P. M. Handley
Tel: 029578 491
Permits from tackle shops in Banbury

CLAYDON
Boundaries signposted
London A.A.
Sec: V. R. Cooke
Tel: 01 520 7477
Permits from bailiff on bank

KIDLINGTON TO NAPTON
Coventry A.A.
Sec: P. O'Connor
Tel: 0203 612880

OXFORD TO KIDLINGTON
N. Oxford A.S.
Sec: J. Humm
Tel: 0865 45051
Day permit available from Dells Tackle I
136 Oxford Road, Cowley, Oxford

hames Water uthority

w River Head, Rosebery Avenue,
don EC1R 4TP
: 01 837 3300

heries Manager: D. Parton
V.A., Reading Bridge House,
ading
: 0734 583583

gional Rod Licences

hames Water Authority rod licence is
uired by all anglers aged 12 and over.
e licence covers all the divisions shown
ow.

EASTERN DIVISION

The Grange, Crossbrook Street,
Waltham Cross, Herts EN8 8LX
Senior Fisheries Officer:
Mr Reeves
Tel: 0992 23611

RIVERS

River Beane

WOODHALL PARK BROADWATER FISHERY
Watton-at-Stone on A602
Access via Woodhall Park entrance off
A602 1½ miles South of Watton-at-Stone
Boundary B1001 to first weir 1 mile
downstream
Stocked Trout Fishery (proposed for 1983)
Operated by Estate Manager, Woodhall
Park Estate, Nr Watton-at-Stone, Herts
Tel: 0920 830246
Permits on application

River Lee

NEW CUT
Off Marsh Lane, Near Northumberland
Park Station
Access 1 mile right bank fishing footpath
from Stonebridge Locks
Boundary from Chalk Bridge Sluices
downstream to Stonebridge Locks. Right
bank only
Chub, Dace, Roach, Bream, Pike and
occasional Trout
Free fishing. Permits not required

River Lee Flood Channel

LEE RELIEF CHANNEL FISHERY
Off A121, near Waltham Abbey

Access via footpath from Fishers Green
Bridge downstream to Waltham Abbey 1¼
miles
Boundary from Fishers Green Lane
downstream 1¼ miles to Waltham Abbey,
Essex. Right bank only
Coarse fishing with occasional Brown Trout
Operated by Thames Water Authority,
Waltham Cross
Tel: 0992 23611
**Permits available from Thames Water
Authority or P. & B. Hall Fishing Tackle,
44 Highbridge Street, Waltham Abbey,
Essex**
Tel: 0992 711932
Permits not available on bank

River Mimram

WELWYN GARDEN CITY
Off A1000
Access via A1000 Hertford Road Bridge
Boundary from A1000 Hertford Road
Bridge to Digswell Park Road Bridge ⅔
mile. Both banks
Brown Trout, Dace and Chub
Operated by Welwyn and Hatfield New
Town Commission Angling Club
Sec: W. Stone, 3 New Fields, Welwyn
Garden City, Herts
Permits not available. Apply to above

RIVER MIMRAM

B1000 at Welwyn Garden City
Access via public footpath, 1 mile south of
railway viaduct, off B1000 on left
Boundary from B1000 Road Bridge to Tewin
Road Bridge 1¼ miles. Both banks
Brown and Rainbow Trout to 5lb
Operated by Tewin Fly Fishers
Sec: M. Neal, 47 Herns Lane, Welwyn
Garden city, Herts

Tel: 070 73 31549
Permits not available. Apply to above
RIVER MIMRAM
B1000 at Welwyn Garden City
Access via Public footpaths at Tewinbury
and Tewin Mill, off B1000
Boundary from Tewin Road Bridge to King
Bridge 1 mile both banks
Brown and Rainbow Trout to 5lb
Operated by Palmers Green Angling
Society
Trout Secretary: P. G. King, 32 Ashdown
Crescent, Cheshunt, Herts EN8 0BY
Permits not available. Apply to above
RIVER MIMRAM
B1000 between Welwyn Garden City and
Hertford
Access via footpath ½ mile downstream of
Tewin Mill
Boundary from Kingsbridge to B1000 Road
Bridge, near Hertford, ¾ mile both banks
Brown and Rainbow Trout to 5lb
Operated by Tewin Fly Fishers
Sec: M. Neal, 47 Herns Lane,
Welwyn Garden City, Herts
Tel: 070 73 31549
Permits not available. Apply to above
New River
WARE TO STOKE NEWINGTON
No access allowed
Boundary the whole river from Ware to
Stoke Newington
Trout and coarse fish
Operated by Thames Water Authority
**Private Fishing to selected Angling Clubs
No Public Fishing or access. Permits not
available**
River Roding
STAPLEFORD TAWNEY
On A113
Access via footpath from Passingford
Bridge
Boundary from Passingford Bridge
upstream for 1 mile to Green Farm
Cottages, left bank
Chub, Roach, Dace, Bream with occasional
Brown Trout
Operated by Elm Park & Hornchurch
District A.C.
Sec: P. Darling, 40 Rosslyn Avenue,
Harold Wood, Essex
Permits available on bank

STILLWATERS

ADMIRALS WALK LAKE
Off A1170 near Hoddesdon
Access from A1170 at Hoddesdon into
Yewlands then Admirals Walk
To be developed as Trout fishing
Opeated by Lee Valley Regional Park
Authority, Middleton House, Bullcross,
Enfield EN9 9HG
Tel: 0992 717711
Permit details not yet available

CHIGBORO' FISHERIES
Chigborough Road, Maldon
Enquiries to Bailiff
Tel: 0621 57368
See Advertisement this Section

NETHERHALL TROUT FISHERY
Off A1170 near Hoddesdon
Access from A1170, turn into Essex Road,
then into Dobb's Weir Road, fishery on left
Species: Brown and Rainbow Trout. Put and
Take Fishery

Operated by Mr A. H. Harris, The
Bungalow, Carthagena Lock, Broxbourne,
Herts
Tel: 09924 43013
**Permits available on site. Advance
bookings advised**

SOUTHEND FARM RESERVOIR
Off A121 near Skillet Hull, Waltham Abbey
Access from A121 turn into Woodgreen
Road, then into Southend Lane
Species: Rainbow Trout
Operated by J. F. Orman Esq, Southend
Farm, Southend Lane, Waltham Abbey,
Essex
Tel: 0992 716480
Permits available on site

WALTHAMSTOW, NO. 4 RESERVOIR
Ferry Lane, Tottenham, London
Species: Rainbow and Brown Trout. Fly
only, bank and boat
Operated by Thames Water Authority,
New River Head, Rosebery Avenue,
London EC1
Tel: 01 837 3300 Ext. 2418
**Day permits available on site at site
entrance**
Tel: 01 808 1527
**Advance bookings can be made from
Thames Water Authority**

WALTHAMSTOW, NO. 5 RESERVOIR
Ferry Lane, Tottenham, London
Species: Rainbow and Brown Trout. Fly
only, bank only
Operated by Thames Water Authority,
New River Head, Rosebery Avenue,
London EC1
Tel: 01 837 3300 Ext. 2418
**Day permits available on site at site
entrance**
Tel: 01 808 1527
**Advance bookings can be made from
Thames Water Authority**

WALTHAMSTOW GROUP, EAST WARWICK RESERVOIR
Ferry Lane, Tottenham, London
Species: Rainbow Trout, any method fishing
Operated by Thames Water Authority,
New River Head, Rosebery Avenue,
London EC1
Tel: 01 837 3300 Ext. 2418
**Day Permits available on site at site
entrance**
Tel: 01 808 1527
**Advance bookings can be made from
Thames Water Authority**

METROPOLITAN AREA
Senior Fisheries Officer:
J. Percival

Rivers House, Cross Ness Works,
Abbey Wood, London SE2
Tel: 01 310 5500

RIVERS

River Cray
FIVE ARCHES MEADOW, NEAR BEXLEY, KENT
Access via footpath from St James' Churc
off North Cray Bypass
Boundary approx ½ mile up and
downstream, both banks from Five Arche
Bridge
Roach, Tench, Carp and Brown Trout
Operated by London Borough of Bexley,
Gravel Hill, Bexleyheath, Kent
Free public fishing. Permits not required

River Thames
The tidal Thames is fishable from
Teddington Weir down to the sea. Fishin
is free and access from banks unrestrict
with certain exceptions e.g. around lock
structures or where private dwellings
adjoin the water.
Coarse fish may be caught as far
downstream as Wapping. Eels througho
the length, Brown and Rainbow Trout in
upper reaches. A continuous public
footpath exists along almost the entire So
bank from Teddington to Putney.
Further information can be obtained from
The Thames Angling Preservation Socie
Hon Sec: A. E. Hodges, 'The Pines', Tile
Kiln Lane, Bexley, Kent DA5 2BB
Tel: 0322 525575
TEDDINGTON TO RICHMOND BRIDGE
Access at Teddington from Ferry Road
from the North and by footpath from
Riverside Drive, Richmond from the Sou
Access at Ham Car Park, near Ham Hou
River Lane, Petersham and Richmond
Town Centre all on the South Bank
Dace, Roach, Bream and Barbel. Brown
Trout stocked into the weirpool by Tham
Water Authority
Free public fishing. Permits not required
RICHMOND BRIDGE TO KEW BRIDGE
Access via Water Lane and Cholmonde
Walk, Richmond and Ferry Lane, off Kew
Green, Kew
Usual tidal species
Free public fishing. Permits not required
KEW BRIDGE TO CHISWICK BRIDG
Access by Cambridge Cottages, Kew ar
Chiswick Bridge both on South bank. Th
Strand on the Green is accessible on the
North bank
Dace, Roach, Eels and occasional Trout
Free public fishing. Permits not required
CHISWICK BRIDGE TO PUTNEY BRIDGE
Access via Ship Lane and Dukes Field,
Mortlake, Chiswick Mall, Hammersmith
Bridge and the Embankment near Putne
Bridge
Free public fishing. Permits not required

STILLWATERS

BARN ELMS RESERVOIR
Barnes, SW13
Access via Methyr Terrace, Castelneau
SW13
Operated by the Thames Water Authori

y and part day permits available at
tehouse
: 01 748 3423
vance bookings Tel: 01 837 3300
. 2418
g limit: whole day permits – 6 fish
half day permits – 4 fish

MPTON PARK WEST RESERVOIR
nworth
ames Water Authority
: 01 837 3300 (Ask for Kempton Park)
mits can be booked in advance or from
ekeeper on site

ORTHERN DIVISION

e Grange, Crossbrook Street,
ltham Cross, Herts EN8 8LX

ior Fisheries Officer:
Reeves
: 0992 23611

STILLWATERS

OXLEY HALL WATERS
ess via All Saints Lane off A412
kmansworth
ee lakes of trout fishing
erated by P. Sansom-Timms
092 37 72068 or 092 37 78290
permits 4 fish limit
ht permits 2 fish limit

NFORD FISHERIES
el Wilson
s Head, Pig Lane, Kintbury, Berks
04885 539

RLOWS LAKE
ess in Ford Lane off B470 Iver-West
yton Road
ch, Bream, Pike; Trout fishing by any
nod in coarse season
rated by Wm. Boyers Ltd
08954 45141
nits available on site from café or
ffs on bank. Night fishing permitted

GS LANGLEY TROUT FISHERY
ess via Sunderlands Meadow, Church
e, Kings Langley
season 23rd March to 14th November
permits 4 fish limit
ning permit 2 fish limit
and Half Rods available for 1982
fish 1981 7½lb Rainbow
bag 1981 15lb 4 fish
rated by Mr G. J. Gaywood
092 77 69863
Advertisement this Section

IMER PARK LAKES
ess via B485 Chesham-Rickmansworth
er: C. W. Cansdale
024 04 2396
permits 4 fish limited, bookable 1
k in advance
ning permits 2 fish limit, bookable 1
th in advance
and half rods available
Rainbow 1981 7lb 8ozs
Brown 1981 5lb 11ozs
age weight 2lb 2ozs

EN MOTHER RESERVOIR
n Road, Colne Brook, Slough
ries Manager: Mr R. Haines
7843 6656
g is fly only from boats
nd season tickets available from
pril 1982 at Reservoir

SOUTHERN DIVISION
Thames Water Authority
Ladymead, By-Pass Roads, Guildford,
Surrey
Tel: 0483 77655
Senior Fisheries Officer:
Dr A. Butterworth

RIVERS

River Kennet
BARTON COURT FARM
Kintbury
E. D. Hill
Tel: 04885 226
**Permits for weekdays only by prior
arrangement**

River Tillingbourne
ALBURY, NEAR GUILDFORD
Access through Bottings Mill off Chilworth
to Albury Road
Rainbow Trout, any method fishing
Limited permits available from
Tillingbourne Trout Farm, Albury Mill,
Albury
Tel: 048 641 2567

River Wey
GODALMING, SURREY
Boundary from Godalming Town Bridge
down to Broadford Bridge, Shalford, left
bank
Roach, Dace, Chub, Perch, Pike with
occasional carp, bream and trout
Operated by Godalming A.S.
Day permits available from
A. & G. Allchorne, Tackle Dealer,
42 Bridge Street, Godalming

River Whitewater
The Rod Box
Winchester
Proprietor: Col. Eric Hay
**Permits issued on a careful discriminatory
basis**
Tel: 0962 713458

STILLWATERS

BAGWELL GREEN FISHERY
Winchfield near Hartley, Wintney, Hants
Access approx 1½ miles along small road
off B3016
Two lakes stocked with Rainbow and
Brown Trout
**Permits in advance from Mrs J. Marshall,
Greenways Farm, Winchfield**
Tel: 025 671 2292

RUSHMOOR TROUT LAKE
Rushmoor, near Hindhead, Surrey
Access off the Churt to Tilford Road, just
north of the 'Pride of the Valley' Hotel
Rainbow and Brown Trout
**Limited number of permits from Benwoods,
Edgeware Road, London**
Tel: 01 923 9970 or
Sporting Guns, Haslemere
Tel: 0428 51913

SPRINGWATER LAKE
Greywell, near Basingstoke, Hants
Access from Greywell to Up Nately Road
Rainbow, Brown and Brook Trout, stocked
**Limited permits by advance booking from
Mr R. Barder, Andwell Mill Trout Farm,
Hook**
Tel: 025 672 2756

STRATFIELD SAYE TROUT LAKES
Stratfield Turgis near Basingstoke, Hants
Access off A33 by Wellington Arms Hotel
Rainbow, Brown and Brook Trout, stocked
Operated by Wellington Estates
**Day permits by advance booking from
A. Elliss, Fishery Bungalow, Stratfield
Turgis**
Tel: 0256 882543
See Advertisement this Section

TRILAKES
Sandhurst, near Camberley, Surrey
Access from Yateley Road
Mixed coarse fish and trout
Operated by Trilakes Ltd., C. Homewood,
Yateley road, Sandhurst, Surrey
Tel: 0252 873191

WAGGONERS WELLS LAKES
Grayshott, Surrey
Access via signposted road off B3002 1 mile
west of Grayshott
Trout lake stocked with brown trout
Coarse lake contains roach, perch and
carp
Operated by National Trust
Permits available from Warden on bank

WILLINGHURST FISHERY
Shamley Green, Surrey
Access off Alderbrook Lane from B2128
south of Shamley Green
4 lakes stocked with Rainbow and Brown
Trout
**Limited day permits available by advance
booking from Mr M. Syms**
Tel: 048 66 71238
See Advertisement this Section

THAMES Western

WILLOWAY LAKES
Ash Vale, Hants
Access off Showfield Road, Ash Vale
Larger lake with Tench, Carp and Roach
Smaller lake stocked with Trout
Operated by Stillwater Fisheries
Permits available on site or from Raison Bros., Park Road, Farnborough

WONERSH TROUT FISHERY
Chilworth, Surrey
Access from Blacksmith Lane off A248 at Chilworth
Lake and part of R. Tillingbourne stocked with Rainbow, Brown and Brook Trout
Limited humber of day permits from
Tel: 0483 33407 (office hours) or 0483 77360

WESTERN DIVISION
Senior Fisheries Officer:
Dr P. Spillet
Tel: 0865 721125
Seacourt Tower, West Way, Botley, Oxford

RIVERS

River Churn
CIRENCESTER
Fishing in public parks within town boundaries
Trout
Permits available from D & J Sports, Cricklade Street, Cirencester

River Coln
FAIRFORD
Downstream of townbridge 1 mile left hand bank
Access via public footpath. Parking in Fairford Square
Trout and Grayling. Fly only
Operated by Bull Hotel, Fairford
Tel: 0285 712535
Permits available on site to non-residents as well

River Evenlode
EYNSHAM
At Cassington and upstream of A40
One meadow upstream of A40 both banks
One meadow downstream of A40 right bank only
Abingdon & Oxford Anglers Alliance
Sec: M. J. Ponting
Tel: 0865 67008
Trout, fly only, from April 1st
7 day permits from above or tackle shops in Abingdon/Oxford area

River Thames and River WINDRUSH, NEWBRIDGE
2 fields downstream on left hand bank at Newbridge and from road bridge to confluence left hand bank River Windrush
Access via Newbridge car park on site
Coarse fish and Trout
Operated by Rose Revived Hotel, Newbridge, nr. Standlake
Tel: 086 731 221
Permits available from Hotel

River Windrush
BURFORD
Access via Burford Bridge and Town Car Park
Burford A.S.
Sec: L. R. Lavigne
Tel: 0895 52208
Permits from Public Houses in Burford

STILLWATERS

ABBEY FISHERY
Hayfields, Waltham Abbey
Tel: 09972 65772

BUSHY LEAZE FISHERY
Near Lechlade
Tel: 0865 882215

FARMOOR RESERVOIR
Cumnor Road, Farmoor, Nr. Oxford
Thames Water Authority
Denton House, Iffly Turn, Oxford
Tel: 0865 778921
Permits available on site

HORSESHORE LAKE TROUT FISHERY
South Cerney, Cirencester
Access via old railway bridge at South Cerney
Two lakes. Fly fishing. Operated by Gerrards Cross Fisheries Ltd.
Tel: 049481 2555 or 0285 861034
Permits and car park on site. Prior booking advisable. Permits also available from House of Angling, 59/60 Commercial Road, Swindon

LECHLADE TROUT FARM FISHERY
Lechlade
Tel: 0367 52754

LINCH HILL FISHERY
Stanton Harcourt, Nr. Oxford
Access signposted off Stanton Harcourt-Standlake Road (B449)
2 lakes, fly fishing only
Car parking and disabled facilities
Tel: 0865 882215
Operated by A.R.C.
Day, season and evening

LOCKINGE ESTATE
East Hendred 200
Flyfishing only
Operated by Mr King, The Post Office, Ardington, off Reading-Wantage Road
Day permits available from Post Office

LOWER MOOR FISHERY
Oaksey, Nr. Malmesbury
Signposted off Oaksey, Somerford Keynes road
Car parking on site
2 fly fishing lakes
Operated by G. Raines
Tel: 066640 232
Advance booking advisable early in season and bank holidays etc.

SNIPE LAKE
Cerney Wick
Tel: 0793 750016
22 acres of water
Day permits

SPINNAKER LAKE
Cerney wick
Tel: 0793 750016
55 acre fly only fishery
Day and season permits

TRING RESERVOIRS
Tench, Catfish, Bream, Roach, Pike and occasional carp
Bailiff: B. Double Esq
Tel: 044 282 2379
Day permits on bank for Wilstone, Start and Marsworth
Apply to bailiffs

WICK WATER TROUT FISHERY
South Cerney
Access off Spine Road car park
Fly fishing only
South Cerney A.C.
Sec: H. J. Franklin
Tel: 0285 860362
Permits available from May 1st on site

WROUGHTON RESERVOIR
Access via Overtown Hill, Wroughton
Car park on site. Boats available maxim 8 rods
Thames Water Authority
Cotswold Division
Tel: 0793 24331 Ext 242
Permits in advance from E. Jones at Cotswold Division, 17 Bath Road, Swin

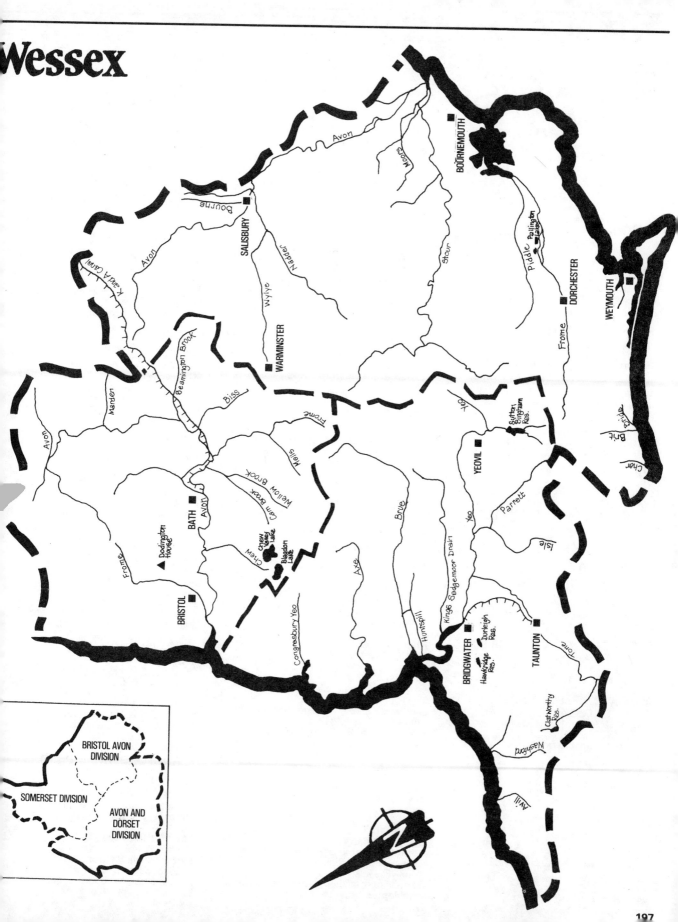

Wessex

BRISTOL AVON DIVISION

SOMERSET DIVISION

AVON AND DORSET DIVISION

WESSEX Avon

Wessex Water Authority

Regional Operations Centre
Wessex House, Passage Street
Bristol BS18 8XH

Chief Fisheries Officer:
Tel: 0272 290611

Regional Rod Licences
Rod licences are not issued by bailiffs.
However these can be obtained from most
tackle dealers or from the secretaries of
many angling clubs. Licences are available
from the Operations Centre.

AVON AND DORSET DIVISION

2 Nuffield Road, Poole
Dorset BH17 7RL
Fisheries Officer: Dr D. R. Wilkinson
Tel: 02013 71144

RIVERS

River Avon
AVON, NR. CHRISTCHURCH
New Queen Hotel
Tel: 0425 72432
Permits available after first option to hotel
guests from 1st August to 31st January

BREAMORE, NR. FORDINGBRIDGE
Bat & Ball Inn
Tel: 07257 252
Permits from above

BURGATE, NR. FORDINGBRIDGE
Salisbury & District A.C.
Sec: A. C. Amos
Tel: 0425 52660
Permits obtainable from:
V. J. Stallard
Burgate Manor Farm, Burgate,
Fordingbridge
Tel: 0425 53908

CHALFORD
Downton A.A.
Sec: R. E. Wyatt
Tel: 0725 20604
Permits from
Anthony Hadleys Hairdressers, Downton

CHALFORD
Salisbury & District A.C.

Sec: R. W. Hillier
Tel: 0425 21164
Permits available from the
Downton Newsagency, The Headlands,
Downton

CHRISTCHURCH
Royalty Fishery
West Hants. Water Co
Mill Road, Christchurch
Tel: 0202 483361
Fishery Manager: Capt. P. Green
Fishery Bailiff: K. Keynes
Tel: 0202 485262
Permits available from:
Davis Fishing Tackle, Christchurch
Tel: 0202 485169

NR. CHRISTCHURCH
Winkton Fishery
Permits available from:
Davis Fishing Tackle, 75 Bargates,
Christchurch
Tel: 0202 485169
Permits available from 1st July to 31st
January

DOWNTON
Bull Hotel, Downton
Tel: 0725 20374
Permits available from above

FORDINGBRIDGE
Hunters Island
Mr Dixon
Tel: 0425 52194
Permits by advance application only

FORDINGBRIDGE
Recreation Grounds
Free fishing

NR. FORDINGBRIDGE
Sandy Balls Holiday Centre
Godshill, Fordingbridge
Tel: 0425 53042
Permits available from above

RINGWOOD
Christchurch A.C.
Sec: E. G. Chislett
Tel: 0202 478224 (day)
Permits from Nimrod Tackle, Christchurch
or Ringwood Tackle Shop, Ringwood

RINGWOOD
SEVERALS FISHERY
Ringwood & District A.A.
Sec: J. Steel
30 Monsal Avenue, Ferndown
Tel: 0202 893748
Day, week and 2 week permits must be
obtained in advance from:
Ringwood Tackle Shop, West Street,
Ringwood
Tel: 04254 5155

RINGWOOD
Upper Severals Fishery
Owner: Mr Ferguson
Permits available from bailiff on bank

NR. RINGWOOD
Bisterne Fishery
Permits available from the bailiff
28 Bisterne, Nr. Ringwood
Tel: 04254 4828
Permits only available from 1st August to
30th September

SALISBURY
Salisbury & District A.C.
Sec: R. W. Hillier
Tel: 0425 21164
Permits available from:
M. & E. Braban Newsagents
187 Wilton Road, Salisbury

Bickerley Mill Stream
RINGWOOD
Ringwood & District A.A.
Sec: J. Steel
30 Monsal Avenue, Ferndown
Day permits available from:
Ringwood Tackle Shop
Tel: 04254 5155

River Frome
Dorchester F.C.
Sec: J. J. Fisher
Tel: 03030 306
Two permits only on Tuesday, Thursday
and Saturday, after 15th June
Advance booking required

FRAMPTON
Permits available from:
C. J. Jeffrey & Son
High Street, Dorchester
Tel: 0305 2332
One permit per day

WAREHAM TO POOLE HARBOUR
Wessex Water Authority
Avon & Dorset Division
Tel: 02013 71144
Free fishing

WOOL, NR. WAREHAM
Woolbridge Manor Hotel
Tel: 0929 462313
Two permits available on Saturday only
Advance booking required

River Lydden
NR. STALBRIDGE
Stalbridge A.S.
Sec: A. M. Cairns
Tel: 0963 62562
Permits available from
Chas Meaders Ltd., General Store,
Stalbridge

River Nadder
SALISBURY
Salisbury & District A.C.
Sec: R. W. Hillier
Tel: 0425 21164
Permits available from:
M. & E. Braban Newsagents
187 Wilton Road, Salisbury

River Stour
BLANDFORD AND ENVIRONS
Blandford & District A.C.
Sec: M. D. Stone
Tel: 0258 54054
Permits available from Conyers Tackle
Shop, West Street, Blandford

BOURNEMOUTH
Throop Fishery
Permits available from:
E. Leah, South Lodge
Holdenhurst, Nr. Bournemouth
Tel: 0202 35532

ISTCHURCH
e Farm Meadow Caravan Site
way, Christchurch
ylor
202 483597
its available on site

FE MULLEN
cke
ill Petrol Station, Corfe Mullen
25885 261
its available from above

WESTON
reston A.S.
. H. Tatchell
258 54803
its limited to ten per day
C. Light, 4 Water Lane, Durweston

ngham & District A.A. Ltd.
P. J. Rolfe
tts Mead, Shaftesbury
747 2744
nd week permits from secretary

RD BRIDGE, NR.
ISTCHURCH
tchurch A.C.
D. Chislett
d Milton Road, New Milton
425 610304
nd week permits from Davis Tackle
ales Tackle

THBOURNE
er: Mrs Haig
dge Place, Northbourne
2016 2851
its available from above from June to
f October

LBRIDGE
ridge A.C.
A. M. Cairns
963 6562
its available from:
Meaders Ltd., General Store
idge

RMINSTER NEWTON
inster & Hinton A.A.
T. J. Caines
be Gate, The Bridge, Sturminster
on
258 72355
nd week permits available from:
Sports Shop, Sturminster Newton

STURMINSTER NEWTON
hester A.S.
A. J. Trickey
rrow Close, Castle Park, Dorchester
its available from:
Jeffrey & Son, Dorchester
305 2332

STILLWATERS

SHFORD LAKES
wood
tchurch A.C.
E. G. Chislett
202 478224 (day)
ted number of permits available from
od Tackle, Christchurch

RISTCHURCH HARBOUR
tchurch A.C.

Sec: D. Chislett
Tel: 0202 478224 (day)
Permits from local tackle shops

CROSSWAYS LAKE
Dorchester & District A.S.
Sec: A. J. Trickey
10 Barrow Close, Castle Park, Dorchester

EDINGTON LAKE
Salisbury & District A.C.
Sec: R. W. Hillier
Tel: 0425 21164
Permits available from:
G. Drewett
Priory Farm, Eddington, Westbury

GASPER LAKES
Stourhead
Tel: 074 784 624
Permits available on site

HIGHTOWN LAKE
Ringwood
Ringwood & District A.A.
Sec: J. Steel
30 Monsal Avenue, Ferndown
Tel: 0202 893748
Day and week permits available from:
Ringwood Tackle, West Street
Ringwood
Tel: 04254 5155

KINGFISHER LAKE
Ringwood
Permits available from:
M. Clark
Kingfisher House, 33 North Poulner Road
Ringwood
Tel: 04254 4222

KINGSBRIDGE LAKES
Off Organford Road, Organford, Poole
J. Hadfield
Tel: 0202 622220
Limited number of permits available
See Advertisement this Section

LONGLEAT LAKES
Longleat House, Longleat, Warminster
Tel: 09853 551 or 324
Permits available from the House

MOREYS LAKE
Nr. Ringwood
Ringwood & District A.A.
Sec: J. Steel
30 Monsal Avenue, Ferndown
Tel: 0202 893748
Day permits available from Ringwood
Tackle, West Street, Ringwood

PALLINGTON LAKES
Dorchester
Wessex & Water Authority
Avon & Dorset Division
Tel: 02013 71144
Permits available on site but advance
booking advisable

RADIPOLE LAKE
Weymouth
Weymouth Borough Council
Permits available from:
The Tackle Shop, Park Street, Weymouth
Tel: 0305 782624

WARMWELL LAKES
Warmwell

Warmwell Holiday Village
Nr. Dodington
Permits available on site

CANALS
Kennet and Avon Canal

Devizes A.A.
Sec: B. K. Nisbeck
20 Blackberry Lane, Potterne, Devizes
Tel: 0380 5718
Day permits from local shops, secretary,
Barge Inn, Honeystreet, Barge Inn, Seend

Pewsey & District A.A.
Sec: Mrs H. E. Bewley
11 Chisenbury Court, East Chisenbury

BRISTOL AVON DIVISION

P.O. Box 95
Broad Quay
Bath, Avon BA1 2YP

Fisheries Officer: M. J. Amey
Tel: 0225 313500

RIVERS

River Avon
KELSTON & SALTFORD AREAS
Bathampton A.A.
Sec: D. Crookes
25 Otago Terrace, Larkhall, Bath
Tel: 0225 27164
Day permits from Crudgingtons, Broad
Street, Bath
Fishcraft, Brougham Hayes, Bath
or secretary

WESSEX Avon

BATH CITY CENTRE
Free fishing on towpath only
Information from local tackle shops

NEAR BATH
Bath A.A.
Sec: B. Storey
Tel: 0225 25072
Monthly tickets only available by writing to Secretary

BARTON AND STAVERTON
Bradford on Avon & District A.A.
Sec: B. Webster
Garland Farm, The Midlands, Holt, nr. Trowbridge
Tel: 0225 782170
Day and week permits from Smith & Ford Sports, Bradford on Avon
Wests Tackle, Roundstone Street, Trowbridge or Secretary

BRISTOL
Beeses Tea Garden
Free fishing to holders of Wessex Water Authority licence on towpath only

CHARFORD LIONS FISHERY
Downton A.A.
Sec: Maj. D. S. M. Mackenzie
Rose Cottage, Charlton All Saints, Salisbury
Tel: 0725 21764
Day permits from
Tony's Hairdressers, The Borough
Stag Inn, Ringwood, Downton

CHIPPENHAM
Chippenham A.C.
Sec: Mrs M. Steele
21 Braemar Road, Colne
Tel: 0249 815903
Day and week permits available from local tackle shops

KEYNSHAM, BATH, LIMPLEY STOKE MELKSHAM, CHIPPENHAM CHRISTIAN MALFORD, MELMERSBURY
Bristol & District Amalgamated Anglers
Sec: J. S. Parker
Tel: 0272 672977
Season permits only

TROWBRIDGE
Ushers A.C.
Sec: R. Rudd
Tel: 02214 63775
Permits from Hendersons Tackle, Trowbridge
Tel: 02214 5472

River Chew
Bristol and District Amalgamated Anglers
Sec: J. S. Parker
Tel: 0272 672 977
Season permits only

River Frome (Bristol)
BRISTOL
EASTVILLE PARK
Bristol City Council
Tel: 0272 26031
Free fishing

BRISTOL
OLDBURY COURT ESTATE
Bristol City Council
Tel: 0272 26031
Free fishing

River Frome (Somerset)
RODE
Bristol & District Amalgamated Anglers
Sec: J. S. Parker
Tel: 0272 672977
Season permits only

FROME AND ENVIRONS
Frome
Sec: R. J. Lee
103 The Butts, Frome
Tel: 0373 61433
Day permits available from
Secretary or local tackle shops

River Marden
Calne Angling Association
Sec: R. J. Reeves
16 Wessex Close, Calne, SN11 8NY
Tel: 0249 814516
Day and weekly permits from Secretary or Dumb Post Inn, Bremhill, nr. Calne
L. Wilkins, Tackle Dealer,
3 Wood Street, Calne

OTHER WATERS

Semington Brook
Bradford on Avon & District A.A.
Sec: J. B. Webster
Garland Farm, The Midlands, Holt, nr. Trowbridge
Tel: 0225 782170
Day and week permits from Smith & Ford Sports, Bradford on Avon; Wests Tackle, Roundstone Street, Trowbridge or Secretary

STILLWATERS

ABBOTS POND
South West of Abbots Leigh
Permits available from
Woodspring District Council
Leisure Services Dept.
Tel: 0934 413040
Free fishing

BERKLEY LAKE
Frome
Frome & District A.A.
Sec: R. J. Lee
Tel: 0373 61433
Permits from Brian Neal
Fosters Menswear, West Way Precinct, Frome

BITTERWELL LAKE
South of Frampton Cotterell, Nr. Bristol
Westerleigh Parish Council
Permits available on site

BRISTOL CITY DOCKS
Baltic Wharf Water Leisure Centre
off Cumberland Road, Bristol
Tel: 0272 297608
Permits from above

BROKERS WOOD
Woodland Park
Tel: 0373 822238
Nr. Westbury
Permits must be booked in advance as only 5 permits per day

DODINGTON HOUSE
Permit information available from
The Agent, Dodington House,
Chipping Sodbury, Glos.
Tel: 0454 318899

DUNKIRK POND
Devizes
Permits available from the site

EASTVILLE PARK LAKE
Eastville, Bristol
Bristol City Council
Parks Dept.
Tel: 0272 26031
Free fishing

EDEN VALE LAKE
Westbury
Permits from the bank

ERLESTOKE LAKE
Lavington Angling Club
Sec: M. D. Gilbert
Tel: 0380 830245
Permits also available from the
Bailiff — Badger Lane Cottage
Erlestoke, and
Rod and Reel Tackle Shop, Devizes
Permits restricted to 10 per day

HENLEAZE LAKE
Bristol
Permits available June 16th to October from Lake

LAKESIDE
Nr. Devizes
Tel: 0380 2767
Permits available on site

LONGLEAT LAKES
Warminster
Permit information from the Agent
Longleat House, Warminster
Tel: 09853 551 or 324

ST. GEORGE'S PARK LAKE
St. George, Bristol
Bristol City Council
Parks Dept.
Tel: 0272 26031
Free fishing

STATION POND
Westbury
Eden Vale A.A.
Sec: R. E. Sims
Tel: 0985 215451
Permits available Tuesday and Thursday only

WITHAM FRIARY POND
Nr. Frome
Mr E. D. H. Miles
Witham Hall Farm
Tel: 037384 239
Permits available from the farm

WOODLAND PARK LAKE
See Brokers Wood, Westbury

WOOTTON BASSETT LAKE
Wootton Bassett Angling Club
Sec: T. Strange
Tel: 0793 851178
Permits from Cannon & Sons Sports Shop, High Street, Wootton Bassett

Tel: 0272 26031
Free fishing

CANALS

ennet and Avon Canal

VONCLIFFE TO SEMINGTON
adford-on-Avon District Angling
sociation
c: J. B. Webster
rland Farm, The Midlands, Holt, nr.
owbridge
: 0225 782170
y and week permits from
th & Ford Sports, Bradford on Avon
sts Tackle, Roundstone Street,
wbridge or Secretary

TH
hampton Angling Association
: D. Crookes
Otago Terrace, Larkhall, Bath
: 0225 27164
permits from Crudgingtons, Broad
et, Bath
craft, Brougham Hayes, Bath or
retary

vizes Angling Association
: B. K. Nisbeck
Blackberry Lane, Potterne, Devizes
0380 5718

eder Canal

STOL
tol & West of England Federation of
lers
V. Tyrrell
0272 500165
nits available from
s Tackle Shop, Bristol

OMERSET DIVISION

. Box 9
g Square
dgwater
merset TA6 2EA
eries Officer: C. Arden
0278 57333

RIVERS

er Axe

ARE
h Somerset Association of Anglers
R. Newton
levedon Road, Tickenham, Clevedon,
n BS21 6RD
and week permits available from
ia Sports, Chapel Hill, Clevedon
vans, Orchard Street, Weston-super-

tol & District Amalgamated
lers
J. S. Parker
0272 672977
on permits only

OM BRIDGE, NEAR CHARD
d & District A.C.
D. Lemon
anvill Avenue, Chard, Somerset
1EU
0460 61281
nd season permits available from
d Cycle Co., Holyrood Street, Chard

er Brue

GLASTONBURY
on Manor A.A.

Sec: P. Daye
Tel: 0458 42025
**Permits from Nichols Sports
Street, or other local tackle shops**

HIGHBRIDGE
North Somerset Association of Anglers
Sec: R. Newton
64 Clevedon Road, Tickenham, Clevedon,
Avon BS21 6RD
**Day and week permits available from G.
Jotcham, High Street, Burnham-on-Sea**

Bristol & District Amalagamated Anglers
Sec: J. S. Parker
Tel: 0272 672977
Season permits only

River Congresbury, Yeo
**Bristol & District Amalgamated
Anglers**
Sec: J. S. Parker
Tel: 0272 672977
Season permits only

River Huntspill

**(Continues as South Drain above Gold
Corner – see other waters)
Bridgwater A.A.**
Sec: P. D. Summerhayes
4 Raleigh Close, Bridgwater, Somerset
TA6 4NL
Tel: 0278 424718
**Permits from local tackle shops or
L. A. Williams, 7 Webber Way, Puritan,
Bridgwater
Tel: 0278 684027**

River Isle
DONYATT AND ILMINSTER
Chard & District A.C.
Sec: D. Lemon
38 Glenvill Avenue, Chard, Somerset
TA20 1EU
**Season and day permits from Chard Cycle
Co.
Holyrood Street, Chard**

ILMINSTER
Ilminster & District A.A.
Sec: A. Green
Tel: 04605 3363
**Permits available from:
Clapps Newsagents, Ilminster
Rules Tackle Shop, Langport
Newton Abbot F.A.**
Sec: P. Goss
Tel: 0803 863953
Permits available from bailiff on bank

LANGPORT
Wessex Federation of Angling Clubs
Sec: J. J. Mathrick
Tel: 0458 32304
**Permits are obtainable from any of the
Federations member clubs which issue
day permits. Effectively these are all the
major clubs in the region and most tackle
shops will be able to supply a relevant
permit**

River Kenn
North Somerset Association of Anglers
Sec: R. Newton
64 Clevedon Road, Tickenham, Clevedon,

Avon BS21 6RD
**Day and week permits from
Omnia Sport, Chapel Hill, Clevedon
W. Evans, Orchard Street, Weston-super-
Mare**

King Sedgmoor Drain
Bridewater A.A.
Sec: P. D. Summerhayes
4 Raleigh Close, Bridgwater, Somerset
TA6 4NL
**Day and week permits available from local
tackle shops or
L. A. Williams, 7 Webber Way, Puriton,
Bridgwater
Tel: 0278 684027**

River New Blind Yeo
NR. CLEVEDON
North Somerset Association of Anglers
Sec: R. Newton
64 Clevedon Road, Tickenham, Clevedon,
Avon BS21 6RD
Permits from local tackle shops

River Parrett
LANGPORT
Langport & District A.A.
Sec: Mrs I. Barlow
Florissant, Northfield, Somerton TA11 6JJ
Tel: 0458 72119
**Day, week and season permits from A. W.
Rule Fishing Tackle Specialist, 8 Parrett
Close, Langport or Secretary
LANGPORT**
Wessex Federation of Angling Clubs
Sec: J. J. Mathrick
Tel: 0458 32304
**Permits are obtainable from any of the
Federations member clubs which issue
day permits. Effectively these are all the
major clubs in the region and most tackle
shops will be able to supply a relevant
permit**
**MARTOCK AND STOKE SUB
HAMDON**
Stoke Sub Hamdon & District A.A.
Sec: M. Prescott
Homemead, Rimpton Road, Marston
Magna, Yeovil, Somerset BA22 8DS
Tel: 0935 850426
**Weekly permits available from
Hagas Tackle, Princes Street, Yeovil
or secretary**

River Tone
**Creech St Michael and Ham
Taunton A.A.**
Sec: G. P. Horrell
Tel: 0823 81537 (Business)
**Permits available from
Bridge Sports or Topp Tackle, Taunton**
NR. TAUNTON AND WELLINGTON
Taunton Fly Fishing Club
Sec: J. S. Hill
Tel: 0823 71530
**Day, week and month permits available
from tackle shops in Taunton and
Wellington
Topp Tackle, Station Road, Taunton
Bridge Sports, Bridge Street, Taunton
A. Woodbury, High Street, Wellington**

West Sedgmoor Drain
Taunton A.A.
Sec: G. P. Horrell
Tel: 0823 81537 (Business)
**Permits available from
Bridge Sports or Topp Tackle, Taunton**

River Yeo (Yeovil)

ILCHESTER
Ilchester and District A.A.
Sec: R. Hughes
23 St. Cleers Orchard, Somerton, Somerset
Tel: 0458 72128
Day permits available from
Tony Coles Florist, The Square, Ilchester
and local tackle shops in Yeovil

YEOVIL AND YETMINSTER
Yeovil and Sherborne A.A.
Sec: N. Garrett
Tel: 0935 71889
**Permits from Hagas Tackle, Yeovil or
Marneys Sports, Yeovil**

STILLWATERS

APEX LAKE
Burnham
North Somerset Association of Anglers
Sec: R. Newton
64 Clevedon Road, Tickenham, Clevedon,
Avon BS21 6RD
**Day and week permits from G. Jotcham,
High Street, Burnham on Sea**

ASHFORD RESERVOIR
Nr. Bridgwater
Bridgwater A.A.
Sec: P. D. Summerhayes
4 Raleigh Close, Bridgwater, Somerset
TA6 4NL
Tel: 0278 424718
**Day and week permits from local tackle
shops**

ASH POND
Chard & District A.C.
Sec: D. Lemon
38 Glanvill Avenue, Chard, Somerset
TA20 1EU
Tel: 0460 61281
**Day and season permits available from
Chard Cycle Co., Holyrood Street, Chard**

BRICKYARD PONDS
Pawlett, Bridgwater
Bristol & District Amalgamated Anglers
Sec: J. S. Parker
Tel: 0272 672977
Season permits only

BRIDGWATER DOCKS
Bridgwater A.A.
Sec: P. D. Summerhayes
4 Raleigh Close, Bridgwater, Somerset
TA6 4NL
Tel: 0278 424718
**Day and week permits from local tackle
shops or L. A. Williams, 7 Webber Way,
Puriton, Bridgwater
Tel: 0278 684027**

COMBWICH PONDS
Nr. Cannington
Bridgwater A.A.
Sec: P. D. Summerhayes
4 Raleigh Close, Bridgwater, Somerset
TA6 4NL
Tel: 0278 424718
**Day and week permits from local tackle
shops or L. A. Williams, 7 Webbers Way,
Puriton, Bridgwater
Tel: 0278 684027**

DUNWEAR PONDS
Bridgwater

Bridgwater A.A.
Sec: P. D. Summerhayes
4 Raleigh Close, Bridgwater, Somerset
TA6 4NL
Tel: 0278 424718
**Day and week permits from local tackle
shops or L. A. Williams, 7 Webbers Way,
Puriton, Bridgwater
Tel: 0278 684027**

NEWTOWN POND
Highbridge
North Somerset Association of Anglers
64 Clevedon Road, Tickenham, Clevedon,
Avon BS21 6RD
**Day and week permits from G. Jotcham,
High Street, Burnham-on-Sea**

NORTON PONDS
Taunton A.A.
Sec: G. P. Horrell
Tel: 0823 81537 (Business)

PERRY STREET POND
Nr. Chard
Chard & District A.C.
Sec: D. Lemon
38 Glanvill Avenue, Chard, Somerset
TA20 1EU
Tel: 0460 61281
**Season and day permits from
Chard Cycle Co., Holyrood, St. Chard**

RED LYNCH LAKE
Between Wincanton and Bruton
Permits available on site

SCREECH OWL PONDS
Nr. Bridgwater
Bridgwater A.A.
Sec: P. D. Summerhayes
4 Raleigh Close, Bridgwater, Somerset
TA6 4NL
Tel: 0278 424718
**Day and week permits from local tackle
shops and L. A. Williams, 7 Webber Way,
Puriton, Bridgwater
Tel: 0278 684027**

TAUNTON ROAD POND
Bridgwater A.A.
Sec: P. D. Summerhayes
4 Raleigh Close, Bridgwater, Somerset
TA6 4NL
Tel: 0278 424718
**Day and week permits from local tackle
shops or L. A. Williams, 7 Webber Way,
Puriton, Bridgwater
Tel: 0278 684027**

OTHER WATERS

18rh Rhyne
Bridgwater A.A.
Sec: P. D. Summerhayes
4 Raleigh Close, Bridgwater, Somerset
TA6 4NL
Tel: 0278 424718
**Day and week permits from local tackle
shops and L. A. Williams, 7 Webber Way,
Puriton, Bridgwater
Tel: 0278 684027**

Langacre Rhyne
Bridgwater A.A.
Sec: P. D. Summerhayes
4 Raleigh Close, Bridgwater, Somerset
TA6 4NL
Tel: 0278 424718

**Day and week permits from local tackle
shops and L. A. Williams, 7 Webber Way
Puriton, Bridgwater
Tel: 0278 684027**

North Drain
Bridgwater A.A.
Sec: P. D. Summerhayes
4 Raleigh Close, Bridgwater, Somerset
TA6 4NL
Tel: 0278 424718
**Day and week permits from local tackle
shops and L. A. Williams, 7 Webber Way
Puriton, Bridgwater
Tel: 0278 684027**

South Drain
Bridgwater A.A.
Sec: P. D. Summerhayes
4 Raleigh Close, Bridgwater, Somerset
TA6 4NL
Tel: 0278 424718
**Day and week permits from local tackle
shops and L. A. Williams, 7 Webber Wa
Puriton, Bridgwater
Tel: 0278 684027**

North Somerset Association of Angl
Sec: R. Newton
64 Clevedon Road, Tickenham, Clevedo
Avon BS21 6RD
**Day and week permits from G. Jotcham,
High Street, Burnham-on-Sea**

NR. GLASTONBURY
Glaston Manor A.A.
Sec: P. Daye
Tel: 0458 42025
**Permits from Nichols Sports Street, or ot
local tackle shops**

Westmoor/Southmoor/Thorneymoor and Long Load Drains

LANGPORT AREA
Ilchester & District A.A.
Sec: R. M. Hughes
Tel: 0458 72128

Bridgwater A.A.
Sec: P. D. Summerhayes
4 Raleigh Close, Bridgwater, Somerset
TA6 4NL
Tel: 0278 424718
**Day and week permits from local tackl
shops and L. A. Williams, 7 Webber W.
Puriton, Bridgwater
Tel: 0278 684027**

CANALS

Bridgwater and Taunton Can
Bridgwater A.A.
Sec: P. D. Summerhayes
4 Raleigh Close, Bridgwater, Somerset
TA6 4NL
Tel: 0278 424718
**Day and week permits from local tackl
shops and L. A. Williams, 7 Webber W
Puriton, Bridgwater
Tel: 0278 684027**

NR. TAUNTON
Taunton A.A.
Sec: G. P. Horrell
Tel: 0823 81537 (Business)
**Day permits available from Bridge Spo
or Topp Tackle, Taunton**

essex Water uthority

onal Operations Centre
ssex House, Passage Street
ol BS18 8XH

f Fisheries Officer:
0272 290611

onal Rod Licences
licences are not issued by bailiffs.
ever these can be obtained from most
e dealers or from the secretaries of
y angling clubs. Licences are available
the Operations Centre.

ON AND DORSET VISION

ffield Road, Poole
et BH17 7RL

eries Officer: Dr D. R. Wilkinson
0202 61144

RIVERS

er Avon

N, NR. CHRISTCHURCH
Queen Hotel
0425 72432
its available after 1st optional to hotel
ts from 1st August to 31st January

AMORE, NR. FORDINGBRIDGE
Ball Inn
07257 252
its from above

GATE, NR. FORDINGBRIDGE
oury & District A.C.
R. W. Hillier
ew Zealand Avenue, Salisbury
0722 21164
and annual permits obtainable from:
Stallard
ate Manor Farm, Burgate,
ingbridge
0425 53908

CHALFORD
Downton A.A.
Sec: Major D. S. M. Mackenzie
Rose Cottage, Charlton All Saints, Salisbury
Tel: 0725 21764
**Day and annual permits from
Anthony Hadleys Hairdressers, Downton**

CHALFORD
Salisbury & District A.C.
Sec: R. W. Hillier
29 New Zealand Avenue, Salisbury
Tel: 0722 21164
**Day and annual permits available from the
Downton Newsagency, The Headlands,
Downton**

CHRISTCHURCH
Royalty Fishery
West Hants Water Co.
Mill Road, Christchurch
Tel: 0202 483361
Fishery Manager: Capt. P. Green
Fishery Bailiff: K. Keynes
Tel: 0202 485262
**Permits available from:
Davis Fishing Tackle, Christchurch
Tel: 0202 485169**

NR. CHRISTCHURCH
Winkton Fishery
**Permits available from:
Davis Fishing Tackle, Christchurch
Tel: 0202 485169
Permits available from 1st July to 31st
January**

DOWNTON
Bull Hotel, Downton
Tel: 0725 20374
Permits available from above

FORDINGBRIDGE
Hunters Island
Mr Dixon
Tel: 0425 52194
Permits by advance application only

FORDINGBRIDGE
Recreation Grounds
Free fishing

NR. FORDINBRIDGE
Sandy Balls Holiday Centre
Godshill, Fordingbridge
Tel: 0425 53042
Permits available from above

RINGWOOD
Christchurch A.C.
Tel: 0202 478224 (day)
**Day and week permits from Ringwood
Tackle Shop, Ringwood**

RINGWOOD
Severals Fishery
Ringwood & District A.A.
Sec: M. D. Winslade
Tel: 0202 824805
**Permits must be obtained in advance from:
Ringwood Tackle Shop, West Street,
Ringwood
Tel: 04254 5155**

RINGWOOD
Upper Severals Fishery
Owner: Mr Ferguson
Permits available from bailiff on bank

NR. RINGWOOD
Bisterne Fishery
**Permits available from the bailiff
28 Bisterne, Nr. Ringwood
Tel: 04254 4828
Permits only available from 1st August to
30th September**

SALISBURY
Salisbury & District A.C.
Sec: R. W. Hillier
29 New Zealand Avenue, Salisbury
Tel: 0722 21164
**Permits available from:
M. & E. Braban Newsagents
187 Wilton Road, Salisbury**

River Frome
Dorchester F.C.
Sec: J. J. Fisher
'Red' Hollow, Godmanstone, Dorchester
Tel: 03030 306
**Two permits only on Tuesday, Thursday
and Saturday after 15th June. Advance
booking required. Annual and day permits**

FRAMPTON
**Permits available from
C. J. Jeffrey & Son
High Street, Dorchester
Tel: 0305 2332
One permit per day**

WAREHAM TO POOLE HARBOUR
Wessex Water Authority
Avon & Dorset Division
Tel: 02013 71144
Free fishing

WOOL, NR. WAREHAM
Woolbridge Manor Hotel
Tel: 0929 462313
**Two permits available on Saturday only.
Advance booking required**

River Stour
BLANDFORD AND ENVIRONS
Blandford & District A.C.
Sec: M. D. Stone
4 Cadley Close, Blandford Forum, Dorset
Tel: 0258 54054
**Day and week permits available from
Conyers Tackle Shop, West Street,
Blandford**

BOURNEMOUTH
Throop Fishery
**Permits available from:
E. Leah, South Lodge, Holdenhurst,
Nr. Bournemouth
Tel: 0202 35532**

CHRISTCHURCH
Grove Farm Meadow Caravan . Site
Stourway, Christchurch
G. Taylor
Tel: 0202 483597
Permits available on site

CORFE MULLEN
P. Locke
Old Mill Petrol Station, Corfe Mullen
Tel: 025885 261
Permits available from above

DURWESTON
Durweston A.S.
Sec: J. H. Thatchell
Methody, Durweston
Tel: 0258 54803
Annual and day permits limited to ten per day from C. Light, 4 Water Lane, Durweston

Gillingham & District A.A.
Sec: P. J. Rolfe
Tel: 0747 2744

ILFORD BRIDGE, NR. CHRISTCHURCH
Christchurch A.C.
Tel: 0202 478224 (day)
Permits from local tackle shops

NORTHBOURNE
Owner: Mrs Haig
8 Bridge Place, Northbourne
Tel: 02016 2851
Permits available from above from June to end of October

STALBRIDGE
Stalbridge A.C.
Sec: A. M. Cairns
Tel: 0963 62562
Permits available from:
Chas Meadars Ltd., General Store, Stalbridge

STURMINSTER NEWTON
Sturminster & Hinton A.A.
Sec: T. J. Caines
Coombe Gate, The Bridge, Sturminster Newton
Tel: 0258 72355
Day, week and annual permits available from:
The Sports Shop, Sturminster Newton

NR. STURMINSTER NEWTON
Dorchester & District A.S.
Sec: D. A. J. Pride
47 Mellstock Avenue, Dorchester
Day permits available from:
C. J. Jeffrey & Son, Dorchester
Tel: 0305 2332

DAMERHAM FISHERIES
M. Davies
South End, Fordingbridge
Day permit
Tel: 07253 446
Advance booking advisable

FLOWERS FARM LAKES
Nr. Batcombe Down, Cerne Abbas, Dorchester
Tel: 03003 351
Advance booking advisable

GARDEN POOL, BICKTON
See Bickton Mill Trout Lake

KINGSBRIDGE LAKES
Off Organford Road, Organford
J. Hadfield
Tel: 0202 622220
Limited number of permits available
See Advertisement this Section

MARTIN'S TROUT LAKE
Wimborne, Dorset
Day permits: W. Ball, Martin's Farm, Woodlands, Wimborne, Dorset
Tel: 020123 2335

PALLINGTON LAKES
Dorchester
Wessex Water Authority
Avon & District Division
Tel: 02013 71144
Day permits available on site but advance booking advisable

TOLPUDDLE TROUT FISHERY
Wessex Flyfishing School, Tolpuddle
Contact: R. Slocock NAC, Lawrences Farm, Tolpuddle
Tel: 0305 84460
Day, ½ day, evening and season permits available. Advance booking advisable

WHITESHEET FARM LAKE
Holt, Nr. Wimborne
P. T. Cook
Tel: 0202 884504 or 883687
Advance booking advisable

STILLWATERS

ALLENS FARM TROUT LAKES
Rockbourne Road, Sandleheath, Nr. Fordinbridge
Tel: 07253 313
Day, ½ day & evening permits available on site but advance booking advisable

BICKTON MILL TROUT LAKE
Bickton, Nr. Fordingbridge
Bailiff: P. White
Tel: 0425 52236
Permits available on site

BRISTOL AVON DIVISION

P.O. Box 95
Broad Quay
Bath, Avon BA1 2YP

Fisheries Officer: M. J. Amey
Tel: 0225 313500

The Bristol and District Amalgamated Anglers control very extensive fishing rights in the Bristol Avon Division. Although no day tickets are available, club membership is open to all and is very reasonably priced
Membership is available through any tackle shop in the area.

RIVERS

River Chew
Bristol & District Amalgamated Anglers
Sec: J. S. Parker
16 Lansdown View, Kingswood, Bristol BS15 4AW
Tel: 0272 672 977
Season permits only

Wellow Brook
NEAR BATH
Bath A.A.
Sec: A. J. Smith
14 Hampton House, Grosvenor Road, London Road, Bath
Monthly permits only obtainable by writing to Secretary

STILLWATERS

BARROW RESERVOIRS 1, 2 AND 3
Nr. Bristol
Bristol Waterworks Company
Woodford Lodge, Chew Stoke
For information
Tel: 027589 2339
Day and season permits available from Reservoir

AGDON LAKE
. Bristol
stol Waterworks Company
oodford Lodge, Chew Stoke
r information
l: 027589 2339
y and season permits available from
ke
l: 0761 62527

AMELEY LAKES
vately owned by
J. Harris
crest Farm, Cameley
details on fishing
: 0761 52423/52790

EW VALLEY LAKE
ew Stoke, Nr. Bristol
stol Waterworks Company
oodford Lodge, Chew Stoke
information
027589 2339
son and day permits available from lake

DINGTON HOUSE
nit information available from
Agent, Dodington House
pping Sodbury, Glos
0454 318899

NGWATER LAKE
stoke
er: D. Hampton
0380 830294
nits available on site

ALGAR'S FARM LAKE
t Woodlands, Nr. Frome
09853 233
ance booking required

MERSET DIVISION
Box 9, King Square,
gwater, Somerset TA6 2EA

eries Officer: C. Arden
0278 57333

RIVERS
er Cheddar, Yeo

Somerset Association of Angling
s
R. Newton
artins, 64 Clevedon Road, Tickenham,
edon
02755 6107
permits from local tackle shops

River Isle
DONYATT
Chard A.A.
Chairman: D. Lemon
38 Glanville Avenue, Chard
Day permits from Chard Cycle Co.
Holyrood Street, Chard

Ilminster & District A.A.
Sec: A. Green
10 Hillview Terrace, Ilminster
Tel: 04605 3363
Day permits available from:
Clapps Newsagents, Ilminster
Rules Tackle Shop, Langport

Newton Abbot F.A.
Sec: P. Goss
Tel: 0803 863953
Permits available from bailiff on bank

STILLWATERS

CLATWORTHY RESERVOIR
Nr. Wivelscombe, Taunton
Wessex Water Authority
Somerset Division
Tel: 0278 57333
Reservoir Ranger: R. Deer
Tel: 0984 23549
**Permits available from the
Fishing Lodge on site**

DURLEIGH RESERVOIR
Bridgwater
Wessex Water Authority
Somerset Division
Tel: 0278 57333
Reservoir Ranger: B. Jones
Tel: 0278 424786
**Day permits available from the self-service
unit at the Fishing Lodge**

HAWKRIDGE RESERVOIR
Spaxton, Nr. Bridgwater
Wessex Water Authority
Somerset Division
Tel: 0278 57333
Reservoir Ranger: B. Jones
Tel: 0278 424786
**Day permits available from the self-service
unit at the shelter near the car park**

NUTSCALE RESERVOIR
T.C.B. Guy
The Great House, Timberscombe
Tel: 064 384 345
Limited permits only by advance booking

OTTERHEAD LAKES
Nr. Churchingford, Taunton
Wessex Water Authority
Somerset Division
Tel: 0278 57333
**Permits available from
Otterhead Lodge**

SUTTON BINGHAM RESERVOIR
Yeovil
Wessex Water Authority
Somerset Division
Tel: 0278 57333
Reservoir Ranger: P. Hill
Tel: 0935 872389
**Day permits available from Fishing Lodge
on site**

LANGPORT
Wessex Federation of Angling Clubs
Sec: J. J. Mathrick
25 Ashwell Lane, Glastonbury BA6 8BG
Tel: 0458 32304
**Permits are obtainable from any of the
Federations member clubs which issue
day permits. Effectively these are all the
major clubs in the region and most tackle
shops will be able to supply a relevant
permit**

River Parrett
LANGPORT
Langport & District A.A.
Sec: Mrs I. Barlow
Florissant, Northfield, Somerton TA11 6SJ
**Day permits from Rules Tackle Shop,
Langport**

LANGPORT
Wessex Federation of Angling Clubs
Sec: J. J. Mathrick
25 Ashwell Lane, Glastonbury BA6 8BG
Tel: 0458 32304
**Permits are obtainable from any of the
Federations member clubs wich issue day
permits. Effectively these are all the major
clubs in the region and most tackle shops
will be able to supply a relevant permit**

**MARTOCK AND STOKE SUB
HAMDON**
Stoke Sub Hamdon & District A.A.
Sec: M. Prescott
Homemead, Rimpton Road, Marston
Magna, Yeovil
Tel: 0935 850426
**Day permits available from
Hagas Tackle, Yeovil**

River Tone
**Creech St. Michael and Ham Taunton
A.A.**
Sec: G. P. Horrell
Tel: 0823 81537 (Business)
**Permits avaialble from Bridge Sports or
Topp Tackle, Taunton**

NR. TAUNTON AND WELLINGTON
Taunton Flyfishing Club
Sec: J. S. Hill
21 Manor Road, Taunton
Tel: 0823 71530
**Permits available from tackle shops in
Taunton and Wellington**

River Yeo (Yeovil)
ILCHESTER
Ilchester and District A.A.
Sec: R. Hughes
32 St. Cleers Orchard, Somerton
Tel: 0458 72128
**Permits available from
Tony Coles Florist, The Square, Ilchester**

YEOVIL AND YETMINSTER
Yeovil and Sherborne A.A.
Sec: N. Garrett
18 Springfield Road, Yeovil
Tel: 0935 71889
**Permits from Hagas Tackle, Yeovil or
Marneys Sports, Yeovil**

Yorkshire

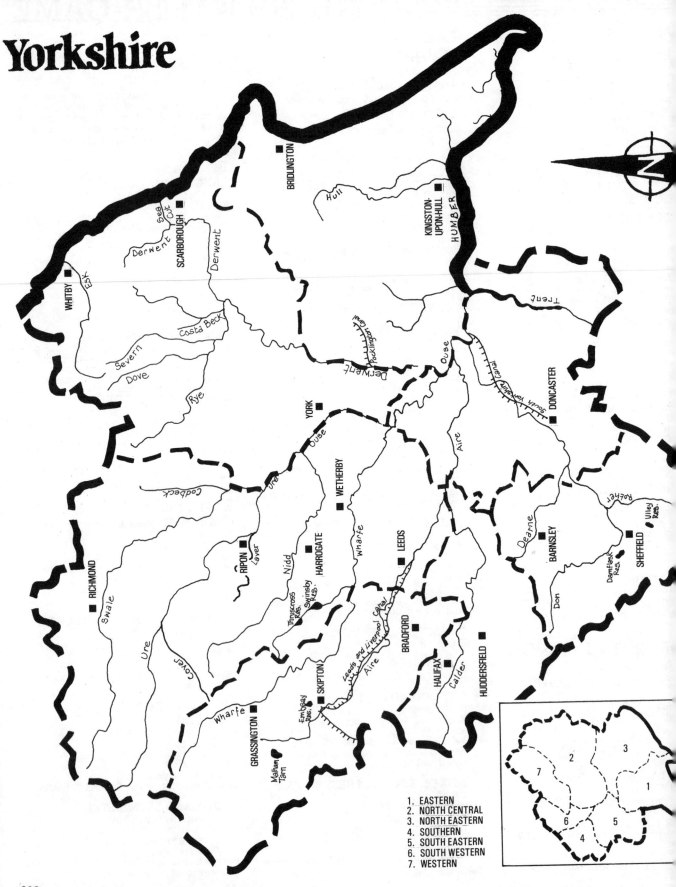

1. EASTERN
2. NORTH CENTRAL
3. NORTH EASTERN
4. SOUTHERN
5. SOUTH EASTERN
6. SOUTH WESTERN
7. WESTERN

orkshire
ater
uthority

st Riding Houe
lbion Street
ds LS1 5AA

enity, Fisheries & Recreation
cer: Dr D. J. Shillcock
eries Officer: S. Bailey

ional Rod Licences
kshire Water Authority Licences are
ded in all cases and are readily available
n almost all fishing tackle shops in
kshire or direct from Amenity, Fisheries
Recreation Officer at Head Office,
ds.

ASTERN DIVISION

North Bar Within
erley
17 8OB

ior Fisheries Inspector: C. J. Firth
0482 881218 Ext 36

RIVERS

er Derwent
k A.A.
irman: T. Ridsdale
but Bridge Farm, Thornton
bourne, York
07593 219
mits are also available from the above
also
orsley
urnholme Grove, Burnholme, York
e Bell Inn, East Cottingwith, York
07593 240
llington Oak, Canal Head, Nr.
klington, Yorks
07592 361

er Hull
VERLEY TO HEMPHOLM ONLY
e fishing to all Yorkshire Water
hority licence holders, although
etimes access may be in private
ership

BUTARY
dingham Beck
e fishing to all Yorkshire Water
hority licence holders

STILLWATERS

BAKERS POND
Newport Gilberdyke, Nr. Goole
Permits available on site

BEVERLEY & BARMSTON DRAIN
Free fishing to all Yorkshire Water
Authority licence holders
For further information:
Yorkshire Water Authority, C. J. Firth,
Senior Fisheries Inspector,
37 North Bar Within, Beverley HU17 8DB
Tel: 0482 881218 Ext 36

BROOMFLEET PONDS
Broomfleet
Free fishing to all Yorkshire Water
Authority licence holders
For further information:
Yorkshire Water Authority
37 North Bar Within, Beverley HU17 8DB
Tel: 0482 881218 Ext 36

FISH TRADES POND
Newport Gilberdyke, Nr. Goole
Permits available on site

HOLDERNESS DRAIN
Free fishing to all Yorkshire Water
Authority licence holders
For further information
Yorkshire Water authority
C. J. Firth, Senior Fisheries Inspector
37 North Bar Within, Beverley HU17 8DB
Tel: 0482 881218 Ext 36

KILPIN POND
Howden, Nr. Goole
Permits available on site

NORTH HOWDEN
Nr. Howden, Goole
Permits available on site

STONE CREEK & PATRINGTON HAVEN
Free fishing to all Yorkshire Water
Authority licence holders (Flounders and
Eels only)
For further information:
Yorkshire Water Authority
C. J. Firth, Senior Fisheries Inspector
37 North Bar Within, Beverley HU17 8DB
Tel: 0482 881218 Ext 36

CANALS

Leven Canal
LEVEN TROUT FISHERY
Nr. Hull
Permits: Trailer & Marina (Leven) Ltd.
Sandholme Lane, Sandholme Park, Leven,
Hull

Hull & District A.A.
Sec: K. Bone
44 Barrington Avenue, Cottingham Road,
Hull HU5 4BD
Tel: 0482 493296
Season and day permits from caravan site,
11 The Meadows, Leven and from tackle
shops in Hull and Beverley

Market Weighton Canal
Free fishing to all Yorkshire Water

Authority licence holders
Match bookings available

Pocklington Canal
York A.A.
Chairman: T. Ridsdale
Walbut Mill Farm, Thornton, Melbourne,
York Bridge
Tel: 07593 219
Permits available from the above and
J. Horsley
20 Burnholme Grove, Burnholme, York
Blue Bell Inn, East Cottingwith, York
Tel: 075 93 240
The Wellington Oak, Canal Head,
Nr. Pocklington
Tel: 07592 3854
College Arms, Bielby, Nr. Melbourne
Tel: 07593 361

NORTH CENTRAL DIVISION

Spenfield
182 Otley Road
West Park
Leeds 16
Tel: 0532 781313

Senior Fisheries Inspector:
Mr A. Ingles
Tel: 0532 892744

RIVERS

River Bain
Richmond & District A.S.
Sec: J. Legge
9 St. Johns Road, Hipswell, Catterick
Garrison, DL9 4BQ
Tel: 0748 833478
Day, week and season permits available
from secretary. Day and week permits from
local tackle shops in Richmond

River Cod Beck
Thirsk A.C.
Sec: K. Kilvington
Tel: 0845 22515
Permits available from:
Richmond Farm, Topcliff, Nr. Thirsk, also
J. Mayes, Dalton Bridge House, Topcliffe,
Nr. Thirsk, also
B. Taylor, Dalton Cottage Farm, Dalton

River Dove
SPARROW HALL
South Fields, Nr. Kirkby Moorside
Permits at the Hall

River Nidd
KNARESBOROUGH AREA
Lido Caravan Site
Knaresborough
Contact Mr Harper
Tel: 0423 865169

Scotton A.C.
Sec: M. B. Vallance
Tel: 09014 282
Permits available from
Rothwells/Scotton Post Office
Main Street, Scotton
Tel: 0423 863218

PATELEY BRIDGE AREA

Nidderdale A.C.
Sec: Mrs J. Dalton
Tel: 0765 4004
Permits available from:
Richmond Shoe Shop, High Street, Pateley
Bridge
T. Pool
Tel: 0423 711638 or
The Post Office, Glasshouses
Tel: 0423 711395 or
The Post Office, Summerbridge
Tel: 0423 780428

RAMSGILL AREA

Bradford No. 1 A.C.
Sec: C. W. Smith
Tel: 0274 815630
Permits available from local tackle shops

Leeds & District Amalgamated Society of Anglers

Sec: G. Copley
Tel: 0532 705059
Permits from local tackle shops or from the
Society's address by application in
advance
75 Stoney Rock Lane, Leeds 9

SKIP BRIDGE AEA

York & District Amalgamation of Anglers
Sec: E. Woodward
204 Salisbury Terrace, York YO2 4XP
Tel: 0904 58298
Day permits available from:
Skip Bridge Garage, Skip Bridge
Tel: 0901 30365

TOCKWITH AREA

York & District Amalgamation of Anglers
Sec: E. Woodward
204 Salisbury Terrace, York YO2 4XP
Tel: 0904 58298
Day permits available from:
G. E. Hill, 40 Clarence Street, York
Bulmers Selling Service, Lord Mayor's
Walk, York

WILSTROP AREA

York & District Amalgamation of Anglers
Sec: E. Woodward
204 Salisbury Terrace, York YO2 4XP
Tel: 0904 58298
Day permits available from/and anyone
who intends to arrive or depart after dark
must notify:
W. Blacker, Wilstrop Hall Farm, Wilstrop
Tel: 0901 215

River Swale
MAUNBY AREA

Bradford No. 1 A.A.
Sec: C. W. Smith
44 Fleet Lane, Queensbury, Bradford
BD13 2JQ
Tel: 0274 815630
Day permits available from Buck Inn,
Maunby

MORTON ON SWALE AREA

Northallerton & District A.C.
Sec: G. Easby
Tel: 0609 5464 Ext 242 (Daytime only)
Permits available from
J. Grainger
Morton on Swale (signposted in village) or
W. Metcalf & Son
Central Arcade, Northallerton
Tel: 0609 3398

RICHMOND AREA

Below Richmond Falls
Richmond & District A.S.
Sec: J. Legge
9 St. Johns Road, Hipswell, Catterick
Garrison DL9 4BQ
Tel: 0748 833478
Week permits available from
Secretary or Metcalfes Sports Shop and
Sports & Tackle Shop, Richmond

ELLERTON ABBEY

Leeds and & District Amalgamated Society
of Anglers
Sec: G. Copley
Tel: 0532 70509
Permits from Society headquarters
75 Stoney Rock Lane
Beckett Street, Leeds

THIRSK AREA

Skipton Bridge to Baldersby
Thirsk A.C.
Sec: Mr K. Kilvington
Tel: 0845 22515
Permits available from
Eric Walkers Tackle Shop, Finkle Street,
Thirsk
Tel: 0845 23248 or
Scotts the Saddlers, Market Place, Thirsk
Tel: 0845 22048 or
The Kings Arms, Sand Hutton, Thirsk
Tel: 0845 587263

TOPCLIFFE AREA

(South to R. Ouse)
Helperby A.C.
Sec: J. Wiles
Tel: 09016 660
Permits available from
H. Ploughman Render, Main Street,
Helperby
Tel: 09016 685 or
Messrs. Driffield Brothers, c/o Golden
Lion, Main Street, Helperby
Tel: 09016 269 or
Myton Grange, Myton on Swale
Permits on site

CUNDALL

Lodge Farm
Cundall
T. Barker
Tel: 09016 203

CUNDALL HALL FARM

Cundall
F. R. Bewlay
Tel: 09016 252

SHEEP HILLS FARM

Asenby
Mrs Kitson
Nr. Topcliffe

WHITE SWAN HOTEL

Topcliffe
B. Pritchard
Tel: 08457 207

Leeds & District Amalgamated Socie of Anglers

Sec: G. Copley
Tel: 0532 70509
Permits available from
White Swan Hotel, Topcliffe
B. Pritchard
Tel: 08457 207

River Ure
BAINBRIDGE AREA

Wensleydale A.A.
Sec: Mr Leyland
Tel: 0969 50210
Permits available at Mill Garth, Bainbridg
Leyburn, West Yorkshire
The Rose & Crown
Bainbridge, Nr. Leyburn
Tel: 0969 50225
The King Arms, Askrigg
Tel: 0969 50258
Victoria Hotel, Worton

LANGTHORPE-BOROUGHBRIDGE AREA

Boroughbridge A.C.
Sec: G. Whitaker
Permits available from
I. Topham
The Post Office, Boroughbridge
Tel: 09012 2560

MIDDLEHAM & SPENNITHORNE AREA

Leeds & District Amalgamated Society o
Anglers
Sec: G. Copley
Tel: 0532 70509
Tel: 0532 482373 for fishing information
Permits available from
the Old Horn Inn
Spennithorne, Mr. Leyburn
Tel: 0969 22370

RIPON AREA

Ripon A.C.
Sec: A. R. Trees
Tel: 0765 3143
Permits available from
R. C. Hodgson (Gunsmith)
The Old Market Place, Ripon
Tel: 0765 3029

WESTWICK-NEWBY HALL AREA

Permits from
Mr Greenwood
Newby Hall Estate
Tel: 09012 2583

River Wharfe
BOSTON SPA AREA

Boston Spa A.C.
Sec: A. Waddington
Tel: 0937 842664
Permits available from:
Spa Baths Tackle Shop
Boston Spa
F. Murray
Tel: 0937 842337

OTLEY AREA
POOL-IN-WHARFEDALE
Pool fishery
Leeds & District Amalgamated Society of Anglers
Sec: G. Copley
Tel: 0532 70509
Tel: 0532 482373 for fishing enquiries
Permits available from
The Stores, Hanson Coyle, Pool
Also from tackle shops in Leeds

RYTHER AREA
Cawood Caravan Park
Ryther Road, Cawood
Mr Douthwaite
Tel: 075 786 450

Leeds & District Amalgamated Society of Anglers
Sec: G. Copley
Tel: 0532 70509
Tel: 0532 482373 for fishing enquiries
Permits available from
Ulleskelf Arms, Ulleskelf
Softly
Tel: 0937 2136

TADCASTER AND EASDIKE AREA
Leeds & District Amalgamated Society of Anglers
Sec: G. Copley
Tel: 0532 70509
Tel: 0532 482373 for fishing enquiries
Permits from:
The Britannia Inn, Commercial Street, Tadcaster
Wood
Tel: 0937 832168 during opening hours

Tadcaster A.C.
Sec: D. Wilkinson
Sandfield Terrace, Tadcaster
24 8AN
Tel: 0937 834610
Day permits available from
The Britannia Inn, Commercial Street, Tadcaster
Wood
Tel: 0937 832168 during opening hours or
Westmorlands Newsagents
Commercial Street, Tadcaster
Tel: 0937 832397 open from 6 a.m.

WETHERBY AREA
Wetherby & District A.C
Sec: P. F. Burnett
Tel: 0937 62171
Permits available from
Knight, Wetherby Angling Centre, Crossley Street, Wetherby
Tel: 0937 63769 or
George & Dragon, North Street, Wetherby

STILLWATERS

D BECK RESERVOIR
Yorkshire Water Authority
Fisheries Office
Tel: 0532 781313
Permits also available from
Osmotherley Sub Post Office
West end, Osmotherley
Tel: 060 983 201

HAROLD PARK LAKE FISHERY
Bradford No. 1 A.A.
Sec: C. W. Smith
44 Fleet Lane, Queensbury, Bradford
BD13 2JQ
Tel: 0274 815630
Day permits available from
T. K. Patel, 446 Halifax Road, Bradford 6
Richmonds, Morley Street, Bradford

LONGBOTTOM DAM
Birstall, Nr. Leeds
Spenborough & District A.A.
Sec: J. P. Farrar
Tel: 0924 475068
Permits available from local tackle shops

MANN DAM
Cleckheaton, Nr. Leeds
Spenborough & District A.A.
Sec: J. P. Farrar
Tel: 0924 475068
Permits available from local tackle shops

ROUNDHAY PARK FISHERY
Leeds
Leeds & District Amalgamated Society of Anglers
Sec: G. Copley
Tel: 0532 482373
Permits available from local tackle shops and
Roundhay Park Cafe
Roundhay Park, Leeds

SEMERWATER LAKE
Wensleydale
Permits from
Wensleydale A.C.
Sec: H. G. Leyland
Tel: 0969 50210

Private section also available:
Mr Metcalfe
Tel: 0969 50436

Richmond & District A.S.
Sec: J. Legge
9 St. Johns Road, Hipswell, Catterick Garrison
DL9 4BQ
Tel: 0748 833478
Day, week and season permits from secretary. Day and week permits from local tackle shops in Richmond

SHERBURN LAKE
Wheatsheaf A.C.
Sec: J. Jeffery
Tel: 0977 682866

SHIPTON LAKE
Bradford City A.A.
Sec: A. Scaife
Tel: 0274 47799
Permits available from local tackle shops

STAVELEY LAKE
F. Pickles
Tel: 0274 24281

UPPER LAKE
See Roundhay Fishery

WATERLOO LAKE
See Roundhay Fishery

YEADON TARN
Permits available for stretches owned by
a) Aireborough & District A.A.
b) Yeadon & District A.A.
Permits from:
R. Holgate
64 Leeds Road, Otley, W. Yorks
Tel: 0943 461757

NORTH EASTERN DIVISION

Tosti
20 Avenue Road
Scarborough
Tel: 0723 66655

Divisional Fisheries Office:
L. Smith
Tel: 0751 73770

RIVERS

River Derwent
BUBWITH & ELLERTON
Howden & District A.C.
Sec: M. Redman
46 Marshfield Avenue, Goole, N. Humberside
Tel: 0405 61836
Day and yearly permits from
White Swan, Bubwith
Boot and Shoe, Ellerton
or Secretary

ELVINGTON & SUTTON ON DERWENT
Leeds & District Amalgamated Society of Anglers
Sec: G. Copley
Tel: 0532 70509
Permits available from Headquarters
75 Stoney Rock Lane, Beckett Street, Leeds 9
Tel: 0532 482373

MALTON AREA
Old Fitswilliam Malton Estate
The Estate Office, Malton
Tel: 0653 2849
Permits available from the above and also
The Royal Oak, Old Malton
Tel: 0653 2503

York A.A.
Chairman: T. Ridsdale
Walbut Mill Farm, Thornton, Melbourne
Tel: 07593 219
Permits for stretches of the Derwent available from the above and also
J. Horsley, 20 Burnholme Grove, Burnholme

STAMFORD BRIDGE AREA
York & District Amalgamation of Anglers
Sec: E. Woodward
204 Salisbury Terrace, york YO2 4XP
Tel: 0904 58298
Day permits available from
The Post Office, Stamford Bridge
Tel: 0759 71251

WHYKHAM AREA
Scarborough Mere A.C.
Sec: W. Scott
Cemetery Lodge, 30 Dean Road,
Scarborough YO12 7JH
Tel: 0723 76253
Day permits available from
St. Helens in the Park Caravan Site
Whykham

YEDINGHAM AREA
Leeds & District Amalgamated Society of
Anglers
Sec: G. Copley
Tel: 0532 70509
Permits available from:
The Providence Inn, Yedingham
Tel: 09445 231

Tributaries:
COSTA
Pickering Fishery Association
Sec: C. Hardy
Tel: 0751 72212
Permits and information available from
above at
3 Westbourne Grove, Pickering

PICKERING BECK
Pickering Fishery Association
Sec: C. Hardy
Tel: 071 72212
Permits and information available from
above at
3 Westbourne Grove, Pickering

THORNTON BECK
Pickering Fishery Association
Sec: C. Hardy
Tel: 0751 72212
Permits and information available from
above at
3 Westbourne Grove, Pickering

River Esk
DANBY AREA
Danby A.C.
Sec: F. Farrow
Tel: 02876 385
Permits available from the above at
The Butchers Shop
Danby, Nr. Whitby

EGTON AREA
Egton Estates
Egton Bridge, Whitby
Tel: 0947 85346
Permits available for the above from
The Estates Office
Bookings available in advance

RUSWARP AREA
Stretch owned by Yorkshire Water
Authority
Permits available from
Mr Perry at
The Boat landing area, Ruswarp
Also from Fisheries Office, Highcaster Mill,
Pickering
L. Smith
Tel: 0751 73161

River Ouse
Huttons Ambo A.C.
Sec: S. King
Tel: 065 381 596
Permits available from the above and also
The Post Office
Whitewell on the Hill
Tel: 065 381 328

York & District Amalgamated Society of Anglers
Sec: E. Woodward
204 Salisbury Terrace, York YO2 4XP
Tel: 0904 58298
Day permits available from
The Post Office, Nether Poppleton
D.M. Club Supplies, Church Lane, Nether
Poppleton

ACASTER
Leeds & District Amalgamated Society of
Anglers
Sec: G. Copley
Tel: 0532 70509
Permits available from
Manor Country Guest House, Acaster
Tel: 0904 706723

FULFORD
York & District Amalgamated Society of
Anglers
Sec: E. Woodward
204 Salisbury Terrace, York YO2 4XP
Tel: 0904 58298
Day permits available from
Hoe's Bakery, Main Street, Fulford
Tel: 0904 28298

NETHER POPPLETON AREA
Leeds & District Amalgamated Society of
Anglers
Sec: G. Copley
Tel: 0532 70509
Tel: 0532 482373 for fishing information

NEWTON ON OUSE & BENINGBOROUGH
York & District Amalgamated Society of
Anglers
Sec: E. Woodward
204 Salisbury Terrace, York YO2 4XP
Tel: 0904 58298
Day permits available from
G. E. Hill, 40 Clarence Street, York
Bulmers Selling Service, Lord Mayor's
Walk, York

NUN MONKTON
Permits available from
R. Arrowsmith
Tel: 0901 30303

POPPLETON
York & District Amalgamated Society of
Anglers
Sec: E. Woodward
204 Salisbury Terrace, York YO2 4XP
Tel: 0904 58298
Day permits available from
Mr Rainbow
Nether Poppleton Post Office
Nether Poppleton
Tel: 0904 794351

WIDDINGTON AREA
York & District Amalgamated Society of
Anglers

Sec: E. Woodward
204 Salisbury Terrace, York YO2 4XP
Tel: 0904 58298
Day permits available from
G. E. Hill, 40 Clarence Street, York
Bulmers Selling Service, Lord Mayor's
Walk, York

River Rye
HAWNBY AREA
Lord Mexborough Estate
Arden Hall, Hawnby
Tel: Gamekeeper 043 96 213
Permits available from
Hawnby Hotel, Hawnby
Tel: 043 96 202

NUNNINGTON TO HOLBECK
Nunnington Hall Estates Office, Nunningto
Tel: 043 95 202
Permits available from the Estate Office c
The Keeper, Nunnington Hall
Tel: 043 95 247

OLD FITSWILLIAM MALTON ESTAT
The Estate Office, Malton
Tel: 0653 2849
Permits available from the above and als
The Royal Oak, Old Malton
Tel: 0643 2503

BRAWBY AND RYTON
York & District Amalgamated Society of
Anglers
Sec: E. Woodward
204 Salisbury Terrace, York YO2 4XP
Tel: 0904 58298
Day permits from
Manor Farm, Brawby

River Seven
Yorkshire Water Authority
Permits available from
The Sun Inn, Normansby
Tel: 0751 31051

BARUGH BRIDGE AREA
York & District Amalgamated Society of
Anglers
Sec: E. Woodward
204 Salisbury Terrace, York YO2 4XP
Tel: 0904 58298
Day permits from Manor Farm, Brawby

STILLWATERS

ELVINGTON LAKE
York
S. Britton
Lake Cottage, Elvington, York
Tel: 090 485 255

THE SCARBOROUGH MERE
Scarborough Mere A.C.
Sec: W. Scott
Cemetery Lodge, 30 Dean Road,
Scarborough
YO12 7JH
Tel: 0723 76253
Day permits from bailiff on the bank and
local tackle shops
Buckleys Tackle Shop
Leeding Post Street, Eastborough,
Scarborough
Tel: 0723 63202
Phillips Tackle
Victoria Road, Scarborough

OUTH EASTERN
DIVISION

pley House
aterdale
oncaster

sheries Inspector: G. Moss
el: 0302 22199

STILLWATERS

KERN LAKE
by Road, Doncaster
ncaster Metropolitan Council
rmits available from attendant on bank
: 0302 700581

RTON BROADS
rton
oprietor: J. Murray
l: 0524 32237

JSWORTH LAKES
sworth, Nr. Doncaster
ncaster Metropolitan Council
rmits available from attendant on bank
: 0302 785732

E DELVES LAKE
by Road, Thorne
rne & Moorends A.A.
: J. Armstrong
Houps Road, Thorne
: 0405 814151
mits available on the bank

LLOWGARTH PONDS
ksey
caster
mits available on site

CANALS

w Junction
stleford & D.A.A.
: E. Ward
ynwood Crescent, Pontefract
permits from lock keeper at
ehouse or local tackle dealers

uth Yorkshire Navigation
nal
AINFORTH PARISH COUNCIL
nforth
caster
0302 700386
rly permits available (£1) from council
es, or
ellers Rest Farm, Norton, Doncaster

ncaster & District A.A.
A. Slater
0302 58873
information re permits please contact
ve

SOUTHERN DIVISION

P.O. Box 15
Castle Market Building
Exchange Street
Sheffield S1 1GB
Tel: 0742 26421

RIVERS

River Dearn
L.N.E.R. A.C.
Sec: H. F. Smallman
35 Sycamore Road, Mexborough,
South Yorks
Permits from local tackle shops

STILLWATERS

ARBOURTHORNE PARK
Eastern Avenue
Sheffield City Council
Tel: 0742 56244
Permits from bailiff on bank

COLD HIENDLEY RESERVOIRS
Coal Industry Social Welfare Organisation
Sec: J. Wood
Tel: 0226 5241
Permits available on the bank

CRABTREE POND
Sheffield
Sheffield City Council
Tel: 0742 56244

CROOKES VALLEY DAM
Western Park Complex
Sheffield City Council
Tel: 0742 56244
Permits available from bailiff on the bank

DAMFLASK RESERVOIR
Low Bradfield, Nr. Sheffield
Yorkshire Water Authority
Fisheries Office
Tel: 0742 26421
Permits available from vending machine on
site

FRESHFIELD POND
Sheffield
Sheffield City Council
Tel: 0742 56244
Permits from bailiff on site

GRAVES PARK
Sheffield
Sheffield City Council
Tel: 0742 56244
Permits available from the park-keeper

HILLSBOROUGH PARK
(Juniors only)
Sheffield
Sheffield City Council
Tel: 0742 56244
Permits available from the park-keeper

LINACRE RESERVOIR
Nr. Chesterfield
Severn Trent Water Authority
Tel: 0629 55051
(Requires Y.W.A. rod licence)
Permits available from:
F. Hall
9 Beetwell Street, Chesterfield
Tel: 0246 73133

NEWBIGGIN RESERVOIR
High Green
Chapeltown & District A.A.
Sec: J. W. Rowlinson
8 Brook Road, High Green, Sheffield
S30 4GG
Tel: 0742 848242
Day permits available from secretary,
water bailiffs or Roes Pet Shop, High Green

RIVELIN VALLEY
Eastern Avenue
Sheffield City Council
Tel: 0742 56244
Permits from bailiff on bank

ULLEY RESERVOIR
Nr. Rotherham
Yorkshire Water Authority
Fisheries Office
Tel: 0742 26421
Permits available from vending machine on
site

UNDERBANK RESERVOIR
Nr. Stocksbridge, Sheffield
Yorkshire Water Authority
Fisheries Office
Tel: 0742 26421
Permits available from vending machines
on site

WENTWORTH RESERVOIR
Sheffield & District A.A.
Sec: J. W. Taylor
Tel: 0742 24910

WESTWOOD RESERVOIR
High Green
Chapeltown & District A.A.
Sec: J. W. Rowlinson
8 Brook Road, High Green, Sheffield
S30 4GG
Tel: 0742 848242
Day permits available from secretary,
water bailiff and Roes Pet Shop, High
Green

WINTERSETT RESERVOIR
Coal Industry Social Welfare Organisation
Sec: J. Wood
Tel: 0226 5241
Permits available on the bank

WORSBOROUGH RESERVOIR
Nr. Barnsley
Barnsley & District Amalgamated Anglers
Society
Sec: A. Noble
9 Coronation Drive, Birdwell, Barnsley
**Permits available from Reservoir House
and bailiffs**

CANALS

Chesterfield Canal

Grafton Angling Club
Sec: R. A. Mee
157 Anston Avenue, Workshop
Permits available from
Grafton Hotel, Gateford Road, Worksop
Tel: 0909 3505

**Worksop & District Amalgamated
Association of Anglers**
Sec: G. Rollinson
Tel: 0909 3109

SOUTH WESTERN DIVISION

**Thrum Hall Lane
Halifax
HX1 4QX
Tel: 0422 62421**

Fisheries Inspector: M. Hall
Tel: 0924 37201

RIVERS

River Calder

Bradford No. 1 A.A.
Sec: C. W. Smith
Tel: 0274 815630
Permits available from local tackle shops

SOWERBY BRIDGE AREA
Ryburn A.S.
Sec: L. Kitching
Tel: 0274 671944
Permits available from above and
F. Fairburn
123 St. Peters Avenue, Sowerby or
Dewsons Tackle Shop, Halifax

River Dearne

Flanshaw A.S.
Sec: L. D. White
Tel: 0924 66432
Permits available from
Fred Alexnader
The Springs, Wakefield
Tel: 0924 73820 and
R. Jennings
99 West Gate, Wakefield

STILLWATERS

BLACK MOSS RESERVOIR
Slaithwaite & District A.C.
Sec: A. Bamforth
43 Binn Road, Marsden, Huddersfield
HD7 6HF
Tel: 0484 844119
**Day permits available from Angling
Centre, Huddersfield;
Worsnors, Huddersfield**

BROOKFOOT LAKE
Brookfoot, Brighouse
Brighouse A.A.
Sec: P. M. Hoyle
155 Foxcroft Drive, Brighouse HD6 3UP
Tel: 0484 714691
**Day permits available from
Calder Angling Supplies
38 Gooder Lane, Brighouse
Tel: 0484 711063**

DOL ROYD MILLS DAM
Scholes
Paris Piscatorial Society
Sec: R. Sykes
Tel: 0924 66432
**Permits available from
The Post Office, Scholes
Tel: 0274 873184**

HILL TOP RESERVOIR
Slaithwaite & District A.C.
Sec: A. Bamforth
43 Binn Road, Marsden, Huddersfield
HD7 6HF
Tel: 0484 844119
**Day permits available from:
Huddersfield Angling Centre
22 Chapel Hill, Huddersfield
Tel: 0484 29854
Worsnors, Huddersfield**

LEE MILLS DAM
Scholes
Paris Piscatorial Society
Sec: R. Sykes
Tel: 0924 66432
**Permits available from
The Post Office, Scholes
Tel: 0274 873184**

MARCH HAIGH RESERVOIR
Standedge, Marsden
Slaithwaite & District A.C.
Sec: A. Bamforth
43 Binn Road, Marsden, Huddersfield
HD7 6HF
Tel: 0484 844119
**Day permits available:
Huddersfield Angling Centre
22 Chapel Hill, Huddersfield
Tel: 0484 29854
Worsnors, Huddersfield**

NOSTELL PRIORY FISHERIES
Nostell Priory, Nr. Wakefield
Tel: 0924 863562
**Permits available from Head Bailiff
on site or
Foulby Lodge
Foulby, Nr. Wakefield**

RED BROOK RESERVOIR
Standedge, Marsden
Slaithwaite & District A.C.
Sec: A. Bamforth
43 Binn Road, Marsden, Huddersfield
HD7 6HF
Tel: 0484 844119
**Day permits available
Huddersfield Angling Centre
22 Chapel Hill, Huddersfield
Tel: 0484 29854
Worsnors, Huddersfield**

SPARTH RESERVOIR
Slaithwaite & District A.C.
Sec: A. Bamforth
43 Binn Road, Marsden, Huddersfield
HD7 6HF
Tel: 0484 844119
**Permits available from:
Worsnop & Smith
98 North Gate, Huddersfield
Tel: 0484 45032
and Huddersfield Angling Centre
22 Chapel Hill, Huddersfield
Tel: 0484 29854**

SWELLANDS RESERVOIR
Standedge, Marsden
Slaithwaite & District A.C.
Sec: A. Bamforth
43 Binn Road, Marsden, Huddersfield
HD7 6HF
Tel: 0484 844119
**Day permits available from Huddersfield
Angling Centre,
22 Chapel Hill, Huddersfield
Tel: 0484 29854;
Worsnors, Huddersfield**

TUNNEL END RESERVOIR
Standedge, Marsden
Slaithwaite & District A.C.
Sec: A. Bamforth
43 Binn Road, Marsden, Huddersfield
HD7 6HF
Tel: 0484 844119
**Day permits available from
Huddersfield Angling Centre
22 Chapel Hill, Huddersfield
Tel: 0484 29854
Worsnors, Huddersfield**

CANALS

Huddersfield Narrow Canal
LONGROYD BRIDGE TO TUNNEL
END
Slaithwaite & District A.C.
Sec: A. Bamforth
43 Binn Road, Marsden, Huddersfield
HD7 6HF
Tel: 0484 844119
**Day permits available from
Huddersfield Angling Centre
22 Chapel Hill, Huddersfield
Tel: 0484 29854
Worsnors, Huddersfield
or Albion Inn, Longroyd Bridge**

K 30 TO LOCK 24, LANCASHIRE
eworth & District A.S.
C. T. Johnson, 3 Birch Road,
rmill, Oldham
ermits available

**K 24 (SADDLEWORTH) TO
GE 85 AT GREENFIELDS**
am & District A.A.A.
H. Garside, 60 Queensway,
nfield, Saddleworth, Oldham
ermits from local tackle shops or on
ath

GE 85 TO LOCK 9 (MOSSLEY)
eworth & District A.S.
C. T. Johnson, 3 Birch Road,
rmill, Oldham
ermits available

**TON-UNDER-LYNE TO
TSHEAD POWER STATION**
nfield Astley A.C.
P. Hill, 174 Chapel Street, Dukinfield,
hire
nd season permits available

ESTERN DIVISION
dacre House
Box 201
r Lane
ford BD1 5PZ
0274 306063

RIVERS

er Aire
ley A.C.
P. Exley
hfield Road, Frizinghall, Bradford
4HY
0274 493409
permits available from tackle shops in
ford and Bingley

ford City A.A.
A. Scaife
hetley Hill, Bradford BD8 8NQ
0274 47799
ermits available at Village Store in
shills and Cononley

Listerhills Old Boys A.A.
Sec: Mrs S. C. Harrison
8 Lime Street, Bradford
Permits available from local tackle shops

Saltaire A.A.
Sec: W. M. Troman
Tel: 0274 583088
Permits available from local tackle shops in
Bradford area

KEIGHLEY AREA
Keighley A.C.
Sec: Mr Brocklesby
Tel: 0535 67699
Permits available from the above at
11 Ellholme Yew Street, Beechcliff,
Keighley
W. Walker
109 Cavendish Street, Keighley
Tel: 0535 602928
K.L. Tackle
131 North Street, Keighley
Tel: 0535 67574
Rileys Tackle, Cross Hills

SKIPTON AREA
Skipton A.A.
Sec: J. W. Preston
Tel: 0756 5435
Permits from club officials only
Contact Mr Preston for details

River Wharfe
GRASSINGTON AREA
Bradford City A.A.
Sec: A. Scaife
Tel: 0274 47799
Permits available from local tackle shops or
for Buckden Area
The Buck Inn, Buckden
Tel: 075 656 227

Linton Threshold & Grassington A.C.
Treas: I. Patrick
Tel: 0756 752014
Permits available from
Grassington Post Office
Main Street, Grassington
Tel: 0756 752226

KILNSEY AREA
Bradford No. 1 A.A.
C. W. Smith
Tel: 0274 815630
Permits available from tackle shops in
Bradford and Bingley

Kilnsey A.C.
Sec: J. A. Croft
Tel: 075676 267
Permits *only* available from
The Tenants Arms, Kilnsey
Tel: 0756 752301

SALTAIRE A.A.
Sec: W. M. Troman
Tel: 0274 583088
Permits available from local tackle shops in
Bradford area

TILKLEY AREA
Ilkley & District A.A.
Sec: J. A. Cockerill
Tel: 0943 608310
Permits available from
Crees Pet Stores
Leeds Road, Ilkley
Tel: 0943 609594
and Runnymede News Agents
Leeds Road, Ben Rhydding
Tel: 0943 607406

STILLWATERS

Malham Tarn
Malham Tarn Field Centre, Settle
Tel: 072 93 331
Permits available from above
Fishing from boats only

PILLEYS LAKE
Eccleshill, Nr. Bradford
Permits from
Listerhill Old Boys A.A.
Mrs S. C. Harrison
8 Lime Street, Bradford

CANALS
Leeds and Liverpool Canal
Various stretches controlled by the
following:

Leeds & Liverpool Canal A.A.
Sec: W. M. Troman
Tel: 0274 583088

Bingley A.C.
Sec: P. Exley
Tel: 0274 93409

Bradford No. 1 A.A.
Sec: C. W. Smith
Tel: 0274 815630

Keighley A.C.
Sec: L. W. Brocklesby
Tel: 0535 67699

Permits for the sections controlled by the
above clubs and associations are readily
available from tackle shops throughout the
area

EARBY AREA
Marsden Star A.S.
Sec: S. P. Cunliffe
122 Halifax Road, Nelson
Tel: 0282 699743
Day and week permits available from local
tackle shops

Yorkshire Water Authority

West Riding House
67 Albion Street
Leeds LS1 5AA
Tel: 0532 448201
Amenity, Fisheries & Recreation
Officer:
Dr D. J. Shillcock
Fisheries Officer: S. Bailey

Regional Rod Licences
Yorkshire Water Authority Licences are
needed in all cases and are readily available
from almost all fishing tackle shops in
Yorkshire or direct from Amenity, Fisheries
and Recreation Officer at Head Office,
Leeds.

EASTERN DIVISION

37 North Bar Within
Beverley
HU17 8OB
Senior Fisheries Inspector: C. J. Firth
Tel: 0482 881218 Ext 36

STILLWATERS

FISH TRADES POND
Newport Gilberdyke
Nr. Goole
Permits available on site

CANALS

Driffield Canal
SNAKEHOLME LOCK TO DRIFFIELD
LOCK
Permits available on production of Y.W.A.
licence from
Wansford Post Office
Wansford, Nr. Great Driffield
Tel: 0377 84359

NORTH CENTRAL DIVISION

Spenfield
182 Otley Road
West Park, Leeds 16
Tel: 0532 781313

Senior Fisheries Inspector: Mr A.
Ingles
Tel: 0532 892744

RIVERS

River Cod Beck
Thirsk A.C.
Sec: K. Kilvington
Tel: 0845 22515
Permits available from:
Richmond Farm, Topcliff, Nr. Thirsk
also J. Mayes, Dalton Bridge House,
Topcliffe, Nr. Thirsk also
B. Taylor, Dalton Cottage Farm, Dalton

River Cover
SPENNITHORNE AREA
The Cover Bridge Inn
East Witton
North Yorks

Crakehall Beck
**CRAKEHALL
BEDALE**
Crakehall A.C.
Sec: J. Pontefract
Tel: 0677 22877

River Laver
Ripon A.C.
Sec: A. R. Trees
55 Borrage Lane, Ripon
Tel: 0765 3143
Day permits available from
R. C. Hodgson Tackle Shop
The Old Market Place, ripon
Tel: 0765 3029

River Nidd
KNARESBOROUGH AREA
Lido Caravan Site
Knaresborough
Contact: Mr Harper
Tel: 0423 865169

Scotton A.C.
Sec: M. B. Vallance
Tel: 09014 282
Permits available from
Rothwells/Scotton Post Office
Main Street, Scotton
Tel: 0423 863218

PATELEY BRIDGE AREA
Nidderdale A.C.
Sec: Mrs J. Dalton
Tel: 0765 4004
Permits available from:
Richmond Shoe Shop
High Street, Pateley Bridge
T. Pool
Tel: 0423 711638 or
The Post Office, Glasshouses
Tel: 0423 711395 or
The Post Office, Summerbridge
Tel: 0423 780428

RAMSGILL AREA
Bradford No. 1 A.C.
Sec: C. W. Smith
Tel: 0274 815630
Permits available from local tackle shops

**Leeds & District Amalgamated Society
of Anglers**
Sec: G. Copley

Tel: 0532 705059
Permits from local tackle shops or from th
Society's address by application in
advance
75 Stoney Rock Lane, Leeds 9

SKIP BRIDGE AREA
York & District Amalgamation of Anglers
Sec: E. Woodward
Tel: 0904 58298
Permits available from
Skip Bridge Garage, Skip Bridge
Tel: 0901 30365

TOCKWITH AREA
York & District Amalgamation of Anglers
Sec: E. Woodward
Tel: 0904 58298
Permits available from:
Crown Inn, Kirk Hammerton
Tel: 0901 30341

WILSTROP AREA
York & District Amalgamation of Anglers
Sec: E. Woodward
Tel: 0904 58298
Permits available from/and anyone who
intends to arrive or depart after dark mus
notify:
W. Blacker, Wilstrop Hall Farm, Wilstrop
Tel: 0901 215

River Skell
Ripon A.C.
Sec: A. R. Trees
55 Garage Lane, Ripon
Tel: 0765 3143
Day permits available from
R. C. Hodgson Tackle Shop, The Old
Market Place, Ripon
Tel: 0765 3029

River Swale
GATENBY AREA
Preston Park A.C.
Sec: N. G. Wickman
7 Skelwith Road, Berwick Hills,
Middlesbrough, Cleveland TS3 7PT
Tel: 0642 211139
Holiday permits up to 2 months available
from above

MAUNBY AREA
Bradford No. 1 A.C.
Sec: C. W. Smith
Tel: 0274 815630
Permits available from local tackle shops

RICHMOND AREA
Reeth to Catterick Bridge
Richmond & District A.S.
Sec: J. Legge
9 St. Johns Road, Hipswell,
Catterick Garrison
Permits available from the above and als
Mr. Hutchinson, Crosslane, Richmond
Tel: 0748 3767
W. Metcalf & Son
Central Arcade, Northallerton
Tel: 0609 3398
Sports & Leisure, Northallerton
Tel: 0609 70548
F. & K. Flynn (Tackle Shop)
12 Viro Terrace, Stockton on Tees
Tel: 0642 66473 also
Adams Fishing Tackle & Guns
Duke Street, Darlington
Tel: 0325 68069

ver Ure
AINBRIDGE AREA
ensleydale A.A.
c: Mr Leyland
l: 0969 50210
rmits available at Mill Garth, Bainbridge,
yburn, West Yorkshire
e Rose & Crown
inbridge, Nr. Leyburn
l: 0969 50225
e Kings Arms, Askrigg
l: 099 50258
ctoria Hotel, Worton

ANGTHORPE-BOROUGHBRIDGE
REA
roughbridge A.C.
c: G. Whitaker
rmits available from
opham
e Post Office, Boroughbridge
l: 09012 2560

IDDLEHAM & SPENNITHORNE
REA
eds & District Amalgamated Society of
glers
c: G. Copley
l: 0532 70509
l: 0532 482373 for fishing information
rmits available from
e Old Horn Inn, Spennithorne, Nr.
yburn
l: 0969 22370

PON AREA
on A.C.
c: A. R. Trees
Borrage Lane, Ripon
: 0765 3143
y permits available from
C. Hodgson Tackle Shop
e Old Market Place, Ripon
: 0765 3029

ESTWICK-NEWBY HALL AREA
rmits from
Greenwood
wby Hall Estate
l: 09012 2583

ver Wharfe
STON SPA AREA
ton Spa A.C.
: A. Waddington
: 0937 842664
mits available from:
Baths Tackle Shop
ton Spa
Turray
: 0937 842337

LEY AREA
l-in-Wharfedale
l Fishery
ds & District Amalgamated Society of
glers
: G. Copley
0532 70509
0532 482373 for fishing enquiries
mits available from
Stores
son Coyle, Pool
from tackle shops in Leeds

THER AREA
vood Caravan Park

Ryther Road, Cawood
Mr. Douthwaite
Tel: 075 786 450

Leeds & District Amalgamated Society of Anglers
Sec: G. Copley
Tel: 0532 70509
Tel: 0532 482373 for fishing enquiries
Permits available from Ulleskelf Arms,
Ulleskelf
B. Softly
Tel: 0937 2136

TADCASTER AND EASDIKE AREA
Leeds & District Amalgamated Society of
Anglers
Sec: G. Copley
Tel: 0532 70509
Tel: 0532 482373 for fishing enquiries
Permits from
The Britannia Inn,
Commercial Street, Tadcaster
P. Wood
Tel: 0937 832168 during opening hours

Tadcaster A.C.
Sec: D. Wilkinson
Tel: 0937 834610
Permits available from
The Britannia Inn
Commercial Street, Tadcaster
P. Wood
Tel: 0937 32168 during opening hours or
Westmorlands Newsagents
Commercial Street, Tadcaster
Tel: 0937 832397 open from 6 a.m.

WETHERBY AREA
Wetherby & District A.C.
Sec: P. F. Burnett
Tel: 0937 62171
Permits available from
D. Knight
Wetherby Angling Centre
10 Crossley Street, Wetherby
Tel: 0937 63769 or
George & Dragon
North Street, Wetherby

STILLWATERS
COD BECK RESERVOIR
Nr. Northallerton
Yorkshire Water Authority
Fisheries Office
Tel: 0532 781313
Day permits available from Osmotherly
Post Office, 4 West End, Osmotherly
Tel: 060 983 201

FARMIRE FISHERY
Knaresborough
Day permits available in advance only.
By post from
B. Morland, Farmire House, Farmire
Fishery, Stang Lane, Farnham,
Knaresborough or
M. H. & C. Johnson, 4 Briggate,
Knaresborough
Tel: 0423 683065

FEWSTON RESERVOIR
Nr. Blubbershouses, Otley
Y.W.A. Fisheries Office
Tel: 0532 781313
Day permits available on site

LEIGHTON RESERVOIR
Healey, Nr. Masham
Estate Office, Swinton, Masham, Ripon
Tel: 076 582 224
Day permits from vending machine on site

LONGBOTTOM DAM
Birstall, Nr. Leeds

Spenborough & District A.A.
Sec: J. P. Farrar
Tel: 0924 475068
Permits available from local tackle shops

ROUNDHAY PARK FISHERY
Leeds
Leeds & District Amalgamated Society of
Anglers
Sec: G. Copley
Tel: 0532 482373
Permits available from local tackle shops
and Rounday Park Cafe, Roundhay Park,
Leeds

SHIPTON LAKE
Bradford City A.A.
Sec: A. Scaife
Tel: 0274 47799
Permits available from local tackle shops

STAVELEY LAKE
F. Pickles
Tel: 0274 24281

SWINSTRY RESERVOIR
Nr. Blubbershouses, Otley
Y.W.A. Fisheries Office
Tel: 0532 781313
Day permits available on site

THORNTON STEWARD RESERVOIR
Y.W.A. Fisheries Office
Tel: 0532 781313
Permits available from
Finghall Sub Post Office

THRUSCROSS RESERVOIR
Nr. Otley
Y.W.A. Fisheries Office
Tel: 0532 781313
Day permits from machine on site

UPPER LAKE
See Roundhay Fishery

WASHBURN VALLEY RESERVOIRS
(Fewston, Swinsty, Thruscross)
Y.W.A. Fisheries Office
Tel: 0532 781313
Permits available from vending machines
located on all sites

WATERLOO LAKE
See Roundhay Fishery

NORTH EASTERN DIVISION
Tosti
20 Avenue Road
Scarborough
Tel: 0723 66655
Divisional Fisheries Office:
L. Smith
Tel: 0751 73770

RIVERS
River Derwent
Elvington & Sutton on Derwent
Leeds & District Amalgamated Society of
Anglers
Sec: G. Copley
Tel: 0532 70509
Permits available from Headquarters
75 Stoney Rock Lane, Beckett Street, Leeds
9
Tel: 0532 482373

MALTON AREA
Old Fitswilliam Malton Estate
The Estate Office, Malton
Tel: 0653 2849
Permits available from the above and
also The Royal Oak, Old Malton
Tel: 0653 2503

York A.A.
Chairman: T. Ridsdale
Walbut Mill Farm, Thornton, Melbourne
Tel: 07593 219
Permits for stretches of the Derwent available from the above and also
J. Horsley, 20 Burnholme Grove, Burnholme

STAMFORD BRIDGE AREA
York & District Amalgamation of Anglers
Sec: E. Woodward
Tel: 0904 58298
Permits available from
The Post Office, Stamford Bridge
Tel: 0759 71251

YEDINGHAM AREA
Leeds & District Amalgamated Society of Anglers
Sec: G. Copley
Tel: 0532 70509
Permits available from
The Providence Inn, Yedingham
Tel: 09445 231

River Esk

DANBY AREA
Danby A.C.
Sec: F. Farrow
Tel: 02876 385
Permits available from the above
at The Butchers Shop
Danby, Nr. Whitby

Preston Park A.C.
Sec: N. G. Wickman
7 Skelwith Road, Berwick Hills,
Middlesbrough, Cleveland TS3 7PT
Tel: 0642 211139
Holiday permit up to 2 months available from above

River Ouse

Huttons Ambo A.C.
Sec: S. King
Tel: 065 381 596
Permits available from the above
and also the Post Office
Whitewell on the Hill
Tel: 065 381 328

York & District Amalgamated Society of Anglers
Sec: E. Woodward
Tel: 0904 58298

ACASTER
Leeds & District Amalgamated Society of Anglers
Sec: G. Copley
Tel: 0532 70509
Permits available from
Manor Country Guest House, Acaster
Tel: 0904 706723

FULFORD
York & District Amalgamation of Anglers
Sec: E. Woodward
Tel: 0904 58298
Permits available from
Hoe's Bakery
Main Street, Fulford
Tel: 0904 28298

NETHER POPPLETON AREA
Leeds & District Amalgamated Society of Anglers
Sec: G. Copley
Tel: 0532 70509
Tel: 0532 482373 for fishing information

NEWTON ON OUSE & BENINGBOROUGH
York & District Amalgamation of Anglers
Sec: E. Woodward
Tel: 0904 58298

Permits available from
Dawnay Arms
Newton on Ouse
Tel: 03474 345

NUN MONKTON
Permits available from
R. Arrowsmith
Tel: 0901 30303

POPPLETON
York & District Amalgamation of Anglers
Sec: E. Woodward
Tel: 0904 58298
Permits available from
Mr Rainbow
Nether Poppleton Post Office
Nether Poppleton
Tel: 0904 794351

WIDDINGTON AREA
York & District Amalgamation of Anglers
Sec: E. Woodward
Tel: 0904 58298
Permits available from
Dawnay Arms
Newton on Ouse
Tel: 03474 345

River Rye

HAWNBY AREA
Lord Mexborough Estate
Arden Hall, Hawnby
Tel: Gamekeeper 04396 213
Permits available from Hawnby Hotel, Hawnby
Tel: 043 96 202

NUNNINGTON TO HOLBECK
Nunnington Hall
Estates Office
Nunnington
Tel: 043 95 202
Permits available from the
Estate Office or The Keeper
Nunnington Hall
Tel: 043 95 247

OLD FITSWILLIAM MALTON ESTATE
The Estate Office
Malton
Tel: 0653 2849
Permits available from the above and also
The Royal Oak, Old Malton
Tel: 0643 2503

STILLWATERS

ARDEN LAKE
Near Mott
Permits available from
Arden Hall, Nr. Mott
Tel: 043 96 343

CASTLE HOWARD LAKE
Permits available from
Leisure Ways
26 Victoria Road, Scarborough
Tel: 0723 68777 also
Castle Howard Estate
Estate Office
Castle Howard
Tel: 065 384 333

ELMHAG LAKE
Oldstead
P. Bradley
Tel: 034 76 223

ELVINGTON LAKE
York
S. Britton
Lake Cottage, Elvington, York
Tel: 090 485 255

LORD MEXBOROUGH ESTATES
Arden Hall, Nr. Hawnby
Permits available from the

Gamekeepers at the Hall

RIEVAULX LAKES
Rievaulx Abbey
Mr Birkett
Tel: 043 96 230

SOUTH EASTERN DIVISION
Copley House
Waterdale
Doncaster
Fisheries Inspector: G. Moss
Tel: 0302 22199

STILLWATERS

BARTON BROADS
Barton
Proprietor: J. Murray
Tel: 0524 32237

CROMWELL LAKE
Cromwell Fly Fishers
Manager: J. Holt
Tel: 0636 812235

THRYBERGH RESERVOIR (Fly only)
Rotherham Borough Council
Tel: 0709 2121 Ext 3228
Permits available from
Amenities & Recreation Dept.
Welgate, Rotherham

SOUTHERN DIVISION
P.O. Box 15
Castle Market Building
Exchange Street
Sheffield S1 1GB
Tel: 0742 26421

STILLWATERS

DAMFLASK RESERVOIR
Low Bradfield, Nr. Sheffield
Yorkshire Water Authority
Fisheries Office
Tel: 0742 26421
Day and ½ day permits available from vending machine on site

LINACRE RESERVOIR
Nr. Chesterfield
Severn Trent Water Authority
Tel: 0629 55051
Permits available from
F. Hall
9 Beetwell Street, Chesterfield
Tel: 0246 73133

MOREHALL RESERVOIR
Bolsterstone, Nr. Sheffield
Yorkshire Water Authority
Fisheries Office
Tel: 0742 26421
Day permits available from vending machine on site

SCOUT DIKE RESERVOIR
Nr. Penistone, Sheffield
Yorkshire Water Authority
Fisheries Office
Tel: 0742 26421
Day permits available from vending machine on site

ULLEY RESERVOIR
Nr. Rotherham
Yorkshire Water Authority
Fisheries Office
Tel: 0742 26421
Day and ½ day permits available from vending machine on site

DERBANK RESERVOIR
tockbridge, Sheffield
shire Water Authority
eries Office
0742 26421
and ½ day permits available from
ing machines on site

NTWORTH RESERVOIR
field & District A.A.
J. W. Taylor
0742 24910

UTH WESTERN
VISION

m Hall Lane
fax HX1 4QX
0422 62421

eries Inspector: M. Hall
0924 37201

STILLWATERS

URN RESERVOIR
onden
onden Flyfishers
H. Hamer
0422 72596 (Business)
72427 (Home)
mits from
Shaw
ewbarton, Sowerby, Nr. Halifax
0422 31205

LTON HALL TROUT FISHERY
kefield
0924 257911
mits from above

ESTERN DIVISION

adacre House
. Box 201
ar Lane
dford BD1 5PZ
: 0274 306063

RIVERS

r Aire
gle A.C.
P. Exley
0274 493409
nits available from tackle shops in
ley and Bradford

dford No. 1 A.A.
C. W. Smith
0274 815630
nits available from tackle shops in
ford and Bingley

dford City A.A.
A. Scaife
0274 47799
nits available from tackle shops in
ford and Bingley

erhills Old Boys A.A.
Mrs S. C. Harrison
ne Street, Bradford
nits available form local tackle shops

Saltaire A.A.
Sec: W. M. Troman
Tel: 0274 583088
Permits available from local tackle shops in
Bradford area

KEIGHLEY AREA
Keighley A.C.
Sec: Mr Brocklesby
Tel: 0535 67699
Permits available from the above at
11 Ellholme Yew Street, Beechcliff,
Keighley
W. Walker
109 Cavendish Street, Keighley
Tel: 0535 602928
K.L. Tackle
131 North Street, Keighley
Tel: 0535 67574
Rileys Tackle, Cross Hills

SKIPTON AREA
Skipton A.A.
Sec: J. W. Preston
18 Beech Hill Road, Carleton, Skipton BD23
3EN
Tel: 0756 5435
Day and week permits from club officials
only
Contact Mr. Preston for details

River Wharfe
GRASSINGTON AREA
Bradford City A.A.
Sec: A. Scaife
Tel: 0274 47799
Permits available from local tackle shops or
for Buckden Area
The Buck Inn, Buckden
Tel: 075 656 227

Linton Threshfield & Grassington A.C.
Sec: H. T. Astley
Shiel, Raines Meadows, Grassington
BD23 5NB
Tel: 0756 752720
Day and week permits available from
Grassington Post Office
Main Street, Grassington
Tel: 0756 752226

KILNSEY AREA
Bradford No. 1 A.A.
C. W. Smith
Tel: 0274 815630
Permits available from tackle shops in
Bradford and Bingley
Kilnsey A.C.
Sec: J. A. Croft
Tel: 075676 267
Permits only available from Tenants Arms,
Kilnsey
Tel: 0756 752301

Saltaire A.A.
Sec: W. M. Troman
Tel: 0274 583088
Permits available from local tackle shops in
Bradford area

ILKLEY AREA
Ilkley & District A.A.
Sec: J. A. Cockerill
31 Grange Estate, Valley Drive, Ilkley
LS29 8NL
Tel: 0943 608310
Day and week permits available from
Crees Pets, Leeds Road, Ilkley
Ben Rhydding News Agency, Leeds Road,
Ilkley

STILLWATERS

DOE PARK RESERVOIR
Bradford City A.A.
Sec: A. Scaife
Tel: 0274 47799
Permits available from above and local
tackle shps

EMBSAY RESERVOIR
Skipton A.A.
Sec: J. W. Preston
18 Beech Hill Road, Carleton, Skipton
BD23 3EN
Tel: 0756 5435
Day permits available from club officials
and also
K. Tackle, Water Street, Skipton

FEWSTON RESERVOIR
Blubberhouse, Otley
Tickets avaialble on site

GREENFIELD LAKE & BECK
Northwest of Buckden, Upper Wharfedale
Contact: A. Sedgley, Low Greenfield,
Buckden, Skipton
Tel: 0756 76858
Day permits available from above
Advance booking advisable

JENNYGILL RESERVOIR
Skipton A.A.
Sec: J. W. Preston
18 Beech Hill Road, Carleton, Skipton
BD23 3EN
Day permits available from club officials
and K. Tackle, Water Street, Skipton

LEEMING RESERVOIR
Bradford City A.A.
Sec: A. Scaife
Tel: 0274 47799
Permits available from above and local
tackle shops

MALHAM TARN
Malham Tarn Field Centre, Settle
Tel: 072 93 331
Permits available from above
Fishing from boats only

SUNNYDALE RESERVOIR
East Morton
Bingley A.C.
Sec: P. Exley
Tel: 0274 493409
Permits from above and also
The Pantry, Morton
Also local tackle shops

SWINSTRY RESERVOIR
Blubberhouse, Otley
Tickets available on site

WHINNYGILL RESERVOIR
Skipton A.A.
Sec: J. Preston
18 Beech Hill Road, Carleton, Skipton
BD23 3EN
Tel: 0756 5435
Day permits available from club officials
and also K. Tackle, Water Street, Skipton

Scotland

ORKNEY

Kirkwall

SHETLAND

Lerwick

Thurso
Dunnet
Keiss
Wick

Lewis

Lochinver

Naver

Black
Water

Shin

Loch Shin

Thurso

Summer Isles
Ullapool
Embo
Dornoch
Portmahomack
Tain

Harris

WESTERN ISLES

Aultbea
Poolewe

Moray Firth
Lossiemouth Portknockie
Gardenstown
Fraserburgh
Buckie
Portsoy
Lossie
Spey
Deveron
Ugie
Petershead
Ythan
Urie
Don

Uig

SKYE

Shieldaig

HIGHLAND

Kyle of Lochalsh

Loch Ness

GRAMPIAN

Dee

ABERDEEN

Spey

Eigg

Stonehaven

Coll

Tobermory

Mull

Oban

TAYSIDE

DUNDEE
Arbroath
Tayport

St. Andrews

FIFE

Anstruther
Pittenweem
Buckhaven Methil

Arrochar

CENTRAL

Garelochead
Clynder
Helensburgh

North Berwick
Dunbar

Ardentinny

Loch Fyne

Dunoon
Gourock

Queensferry South
EDINBURGH
Cockenzie
Tyne

Clyde

Eyemouth

Tarbert

Rothesay
Largs
Millport

GLASGOW

LOTHIAN

Kilchattan Bay

STRATHCLYDE

Blackadder

Islay

Loch Ranza
Arran
Ardrossan
Firth of Clyde
Troon
Whiting Bay

Saltcoats
Irvine

Douglas

Yarrow

BORDERS

Prestwick
AYR

Campbeltown

Girvan

Nith

DUMFRIES AND GALLOWAY

L. Ken

Stranraer

Kippford

Port Patrick

Port William
Garlieston
Kirkcudbright

Port Logan
Drummore
Isle of Whithorn

SCOTLAND

ough, historically, Scotland was the
area to develop a system of Water
orities and 'Divisions', a lead which
and and Wales followed, power for
r has now devolved to Local District
ncils.

only area bodies in Scotland are the
nal Purification Boards. These,
ever, do not fulfil a direct role related
hing. Scotland also differs in respect
ving no National Rod Licence. The
us laws and requirements are imposed
ly. Subsequently, the editorial format
he Scotland section has been altered
cordance with these differences.

BORDERS REGION

RIVERS

en River
o A.A.
Mr Hutchinson
057 32 3440
its also available from
Mrs Morris
m East Mill, Kelso

Water
& Liddle Fisheries Assoc.
R. J. B. Hill
of Scotland Buildings, Langholm
0541 80428
on and week permits available from J.
g Wylie, Head River Watcher,
burnfoot, Canonbie

e River
raham, Gamekeeper
ers House, Eckford
083 55 255

Kale Water
A. Graham, Gamekeeper
Keepers House, Eckford
Tel: 083 55 255

R. B. Anderson W.S.
Royal Bank Buildings, Jedburgh
Tel: 083 56 3202

Leet
Coldstream & District A.S.
Sec: E. M. Patterson
Tel: 0890 2719
Permits also available from:
Crown Hotel, Coldstream

Liddle Water
Esk & Liddle Fisheries Assoc.
Sec: R. J. B. Hill
Bank of Scotland Buildings, Langholm
Tel: 0541 80428
Weekly Tickets only from
J. D. Ewart, Drapers
Newcastleton
Tel: 054 121 257

WHITHAUGH PARK
Newcastleton
Tel: 054 121 220

Lyne Water
Peebleshire Trout Fishing Assoc.
c/o David G. Fyfe
Tel: 0721 20131
Permits also available from:
I. Fraser
1 Brigegate, Peebles
Tel: 0721 20979

Slitrig Water
STOTHARTS
6 High Street, Hawick
Tel: 0450 2231

PET STORES
1 Union Street, Hawick
Tel: 0450 3543

River Teviot
KELSO – JEDBURG AREA
Kelso A.A.
Sec: C. Hutchison
Tel: 057 32 3440
Permits also available from:
Redpatch & Co
55 Horsemarket, Kelso
Tel: 057 32 2578
Gamekeeper
Keeper's Cottage, Eckford
Tel: 083 55 255

Jedforest A.A.
Sec: A. Whitecross
Tel: 083 56 3615
Trout permits only available from:
Jedburgh Gun & Sports Shop
Kenmore Toll, Jedburgh
Tel: 083 56 2377

JEDBURG AREA TO SOURCE
Hawick Angling Club
Sec: R. Johnson
Tel: 0450 2266
Stotharts
6 High Street, Hawick

Tel: 0450 2231
Pet Stores
1 Union Street, Hawick
Tel: 0450 3543

River Till
Chatton A.A.
Sec: A. Jarvis
New Road, Chatton, Alnwick
Permits also available from:
Head Gamekeeper, Nesbit Cottage, Fenton,
Wooler
Tel: 066 86 243
Ford Post Office
Head Keepers House, Ford

River Tweed
See also Lothian Region
STANHOPE – THORNIE LEE
Peebleshire Trout Fishing Assoc.
c/o David G. Fyfe, 39 High Street, Peebles
Tel: 0721 20131
Permits available from:
Ian Fraser, 1 Bridgegate, Peebles
Tel: 0721 20979
Stobo Post Office, Stobo
The Crook Inn, Tweedsmuir
The Lucken Booth
55 High Street, Innerleithen
The George Inn, Walkerburn
Tel: 089 687 220
John Dickson & Son, 21 Frederick Street,
Edinburgh
F. & D. Simpson, 28 West Preston Street,
Edinburgh

RAE BURN – MANOR BRIDGE
I. Fraser
1 Bridgegate, Peebles
Tel: 0721 20979

WIRE BRIDGE POOL – SCROGBANK
Peebleshire Salmon Fishing Assoc.
c/o Blackwood & Smith W.S.
Tel: 0721 20131
I. Fraser
1 Bridgegate, Peebles
Tel: 0721 209 79

WALKERBURN AND FAIRNILEE
Tweed Valley Hotel
Walkerburn
Tel: 089 687 220
Permits available to non residents

GALASHIELS
Day permits available on Saturdays
Gala A.A.
Sec: R. Watson
Tel: 0896 56330
Permits also available from:
Kingsknownes Hotel, Galashiels
Tel: 0896 3478
Permits available to non residents

Tweed Valley Hotel
Walkerburn
Tel: 089 687 220
Permits available to non-residents

GALASHIELS, SUNDERLAND HALL
R. Smyly
Sunderland Hall, Galashiels
Tel: 0750 21298

GALASHIELS – BOLESIDE BEAT
Galashiels A.A.

SCOTLAND Borders – Central

Sec: R. Watson
41 Balmoral Avenue, Galashiels
Permits also available from:
L. Bald
Fisherman's Cottage, Boleside
Tel: 0750 2792

LOWOOD BRIDGE
L. B. Smith
Darnlee, Darnick, Melrose

MELROSE
Trout permits available from
Melrose & District A.A.
Sec: J. Broomfield
Tel: 089 682 2219
Permits also available from:
Angler's Choice
High Street, Melrose
Tel: 089 682 3070

All other permits
Tweedswood Ghillie
Fisherman's Cottage, Nowstead
Tel: 089 682 2076

MELROSE (ST. AIDANS)
The Brother Superior
St. Aidans, Gattonside

ST. BOSWELLS
St. Boswells & Newtown A.A.
Sec: R. Black
Tel: 083 52 3271
Permits also available from
Newsagents in the village such as:
C. D. Grant, Newsagent, St. Boswells
Also available by contacting:
Mr. Law
Main Street, St. Boswells
W. Brown
49 Springfield Road, St. Boswells
River Watchers on the bank

Earlston A.A.
Sec: W. W. Lothian
Tel: 089 684 559

ST. BOSWELLS
Dryburgh Abbey Hotel
St. Boswells
Tel: 083 52 2261
Permits available to non-residents

KELSO
Kelso A.A.
Sec: C. Hutchison
Tel: 057 32 3440
Permits also available from:
Forrest & Son
The Square, Kelso
Tel: 057 32 2578
Sportswize
Roxburgh Street, Kelso
River Watchers on the bank

BIRGHAM DUB AND LOWER BIRGHAM
The Hon. Caroline Douglas-Home
The Hirsel, Coldstream

LENNEL BOAT AND COLDSTREAM (TOWN WATER)
Coldstream & District A.A.
Sec: E. M. Paterson
Market Square, Coldstream
Tel: 0890 2719
Day and week permits available from bank

LADYKIRK
Ladykirk & Norham A.A.
Sec: R. G. Wharton
8 St. Cuthberts Square, Norham, Berwick-on-Tweed
Tel: 0289 82467
Day, week and season permits also available from:
Masons Arms, Norham
Tel: 0289 82326
Victoria Hotel, Norham
Tel: 0289 82237
Permits should be available to non residents from both hotels

NORHAM
Farm House
West Newbiggin, Norham

STILLWATERS

ALEMOOR LOCH
Hawick Angling Club
Sec: R. Johnston
Tel: 0450 3771
Permits also available from:
D. Stotharts, Tackle Shop
High Street, Hawick
Tel: 0450 2231
S. Spiers
Alemoor, Roberton, Hawick

CROOKED LOCH
Stotharts
6 High Street, Hawick
Tel: 0450 2231
Pet Shop
1 Union Street, Hawick
Tel: 0450 3543

HELLMORE LOCH
Hawick Angling Club
Sec: R. Johnson
Tel: 0450 3771
Stotharts
6 High Street, Hawick
Tel: 0450 2231
Pet Shop
1 Union Street, Hawick
Tel: 0450 3543

LOCH OF THE LOWES
St. Mary's Angling Club
Sec: J. Miller
Tel: 031 447 2192
Permits also available from:
The Glen Cafe, Cappercleuch
Gordon Arms Hotel, Yarrow
Permits available to non residents
Fishing Tackle Shop
Innerleithern
Tel: 0896 411
Shooting Lines
23 Roseburn Terrace, Edinburgh
Tibbie Shiels Hotel, Cappercleuch
Rodono Hotel, St. Mary's Loch
Tel: 075 04 232
Weekly Tickets only available from:
Resident Keeper
Henderland East Cottage, Cappercleuch
Tel: 075 04 243

ST. MARY'S LOCH
St. Mary's Angling Club
Sec: J. Miller
Tel: 031 447 2192

Permits also available from:
The Glen Cafe, Capporcleuch
Gordon Arms Hotel, Yarrow
Tibbieshiels Hotel
Rodono Hotel, St. Mary's Loch
Tel: 075 04 232
Tackle Shop, Innerleithen
Tel: 0896 411
Anglers Choice
High Street, Melrose
Tel: 089 682 3070
Keeper
Henderland East Cottage, Cappercleuch
Tel: 075 04 243
Permits available to non residents from hotels

WILLESTRUTHER LOCH
Hawick Angling Club
Sec: R. Johnson
Tel: 0450 3771
Stotharts
6 High Street, Hawick
Tel: 0450 2231
Pet Shop
1 Union Street, Hawick
Tel: 0450 3543

WINDYLAWS LOCH
Hawick Angling Club
For coarse fishing permits only:
Sec: R. Johnson
Tel: 0450 3771
Coarse and Game fishing permits:
Stotharts
6 High Street, Hawick
Tel: 0450 2231
Pet Shop
1 Union Street, Hawick
Tel: 0450 3543

CENTRAL REGION

RIVERS

Dochart River
See also Tayside Region
Killin Breadalbane A.C.
Sec: D. Allan
Tel: 056 72 362
Permits also available from Sec. at his shop
D. & S. Allan Fishing Tackle, Main Street, Killin

Forth River
GALTMORE BRIDGE TO BUCHLYVIE
A. E. Billet
Glenhead Cartmore
Tackle shops in Glasgow, Kirkintilloch

GARTMORE BRIDGE UPSTREAM
Mrs Ferguson
Station Buildings, Aberfoyle

Messrs D. Crockart & Son
15 King Street, Stirling
Tel: 0786 3443

Glasgow Telephones & Civil Service A.A.
Sec: D. Taylor
Tel: 041 221 4251 (work)
        0236 772939 (home)

STILLWATERS

CHRAY LOCH
ch Achray Hotel
e Trossachs by Callander
el: 087 72 229
rmits available to non-residents

OCHAN-NA-LARIGE
lin Breadalbane A.C.
ec: D. Allan
l: 056 72 362
rmits also available from Sec. at his shop
& S. Allan Fishing Tackle, Main Street,
lin

AY LOCH
lin Breadalbane A.C.
c: D. Allan
l: 056 72 362
rmits also available from Sec. at his shop
& S. Allan Fishing Tackle, Main Street,
lin

UMFRIES & ALLOWAY REGION

RIVERS

ver Annan
nandale and Egremont A.C.
c: P. A. W. Hope Johnstone
l: 057 64 317

mmissioners for Royal Four Towns
hing
c: W. Graham
.: 038 781 220

per Annandale A.A.
:: J. Black
: 0683 20104

D HOUSE HOTEL
mphray, Moffat
.: 057 64 214

NE COUNTRY GUEST HOUSE, MPHRAY
: 057 67 367

dnoch River
wton Stewart A.A.
V. McDowall
: 0671 3252
rthur Street, Newton Stewart
eat Hotel, Newton Stewart
ngowan Hotel, Creetown
House o' Hill, Bargrennan

& G. Nelson
Sports Shop
7 Victoria Street, Newton Stewart
0671 2858

yfewater
olegirth Estate
Upper Annandale A.A.
: J. Black
0683 20104

k River
also Lothian Region

All waters ticket. Weekly ticket only
Esk & Liddle Fisheries Assoc.
Sec: R. J. B. Hill
Bank of Scotland Buildings, Langholm
Tel: 0541 80428
Weekly permits also available from:
J. Irving Wylie, River Watcher
Byreburn Foot, Canonbie
Tel: 05415 279

Canonbie Ticket. Weekly tickets only
Esk & Liddle Fishers Assoc.
Sec: R. J. B. Hill
Bank of Scotland Buildings, Langholm
Tel: 0541 80428
Weekly permits also available from:
J. Irving Wylie, River Watcher
Byreburn Foot, Canonbie
Tel: 05415 279
P. Lillie
19 Rowanburn, Canonbie
Tel: 05415 224
Langholm Guest House, Langholm
Tel: 0541 80378
Cross Keys Hotel, Canonbie
Riverside Inn, Canonbie

Ken River
New Galloway A.A.
c/o Clydesdale Bank, New Galloway
Sec: N. Birch
Tel: 064 42 404
Permits also available from:
Ken Bridge Hotel, New Galloway
Contact: Mrs Forrest
Tel: 064 42 211
Cross Keys Hotel, New Galloway

Kirtle Water
Gretna A.A.
Sec: J. G. Graham
126 Currock Park Avenue, Carlisle
Cumbria CA2 4DH
Permits also available from:
Hunters Lodge Hotel, Gretna
Tel: 046 13 214

Malzie Water
Crosemalzie Water
Port William
Tel: 098 886 254

Minoch River
Newton Stewart A.A.
Sec: R. W. D. McDowall
Tel: 0671 3252

Nith River
Buccleuch Estates
Thornhill
Tel: 0848 30482

TIDAL STRETCH
Nithdale District Council
Finance Department
Duccleuch Street, Dumfries
Tel: 0387 3166

UPPER STRETCH
Upper Nithdale Angling Club
Sec: W. Forsyth
Tel: 065 92 241
Permits also available from
D. McMillan
6 Friars Vennel, Dumfries
Tel: 0387 2075

Mennockfoot Lodge Hotel, Sanquhar
Tel: 065 92 382

Palnure Burn
Newton Stewart A.A.
Sec: R. W. McDowall
Tel: 0671 3252

Penkiln Burn
Newton Stewart A.A.
Sec: R. W. McDowall
Tel: 0671 3252

Royal Four Towns Water
Castle Milk Estates Office
Lockerbie, Dumfries
Tel: 057 65 203/4
Commissioners for Royal Four Towns
Fishings
Sec: W. Graham
Tel: 038 781 220

Tarf Water
CROSEMALZIE HOUSE
Portwilliam
Tel: 098 886 254

THREE LOCH'S CARAVAN SITE
Kirkcowan
Tel: 067 183 304

TARF HOTEL
Kirkcowan
Tel: 067 183 325

Urr River
Castle Douglas & District A.A.
Sec: A. Muir
Tel: 0556 2351 (work)
     0556 2849 (home)
Permits also available from:
Tommy's Sports Shop
20 King Street, Castle Douglas
Tel: 0556 2851

Dalbeattie A.A.
Sec: D. Bomphray
Tel: 0556 610241
Advisable to contact Ticket Secretary to
book:
Mr N. Parker
30 High Street, Dalbeatty
Tel: 0556 610448

Water of Milk
ECCLEFECHAN HOTEL
Ecclefechan
Tel: 057 63 213
Permits available to non-residents

Wauchope Water
Esk & Liddle Fisheries Assoc.
Sec: R. J. B. Hill
Bank of Scotland Buildings, Langholm
Tel: 0541 80428
Season and week permits also available
from:
Adam Grieve
82/84 High Street, Langholm

White Esk River
Weekly Tickets Only
Esk & Liddle Fisheries Assoc.
Sec: R. J. B. Hill

Bank of Scotland Buildings, Langholm
Tel: 0541 80428
Permits also available from:
Eskdale Hotel, Langholm
Tel: 0541 80357

STILLWATERS

BRACK LOCH
Milton Park Hotel, Dalry
Tel: 064 43 286
Permits available to non-residents

BUSH LOCH
Cally Estates Office
Gatehouse of Fleet
Tel: 055 74 361

CLATTERINGSHAWS LOCH
Newton Stewart Angling Club
Sec: R. W. McDowall
Tel: 0671 3252

DEE LOCH
Forestry Commission
South Scotland Conservancy
55 Moffat Road, Dumfries
Tel: 0387 2425
Recreation Planning Officer
D. F. C. Forbes
Galloway Deer Museum
Clatteringshaws, New Galloway
Talnotry Caravan Park, Newton Stewart
Dundeugh Forest Officer

FLEET LOCH
Cally Estates Office
Gatehouse of Fleet
Tel: 055 74 361

GARWACKIE LOCH
Forestry Commission
South Scotland Conservancy
55 Moffat Road, Dumfries
Tel: 0387 2425
Recreation Planning Officer:
D. F. C. Forbes

GRANNOCH LOCH
Cally Estates Office
Gatehouse of Fleet
Tel: 055 74 361

HERON LOCH
A. & G. Nelson, The Sports Shop
15/17 Victoria Street, Newton Stewart
Tel: 067 183 2858
B. Stevens
Three Lochs Caravan Park
Kirkcowan, Newton Stewart

HIGHLANDS AND ISLANDS
RIVERS

Halladale River
Forsinard Hotel
Forsinard, Halladale
Tel: 064 17 221

Nairn River
Nairn A.A.
Sec: Mrs W. R. Mackay
Tel: 0667 53768

Nevis River
Fort William A.A.
Sec: A. E. Reece

Tel: 0379 2068
Permits also available from tackle shops in
Fort William

Oich River
Outdoor Shop
Canal Bank, Fort Augustus
Tel: 0320 6477

South Ford
South Uist A.C.
Sec: E. E. Dunn
Tel: 0870 2336 Daytime
     0870 2427 Evening

Tarff River
Fort Augustus A.A.
Sec: Mr Wooley
Tel: 0320 6477

Wester River
Wilson & Nolf
1 Frances Street, Wick
Tel: 0955 4284

For Rivers on the Island of Skye
– Rivers Lealt, Brogaig, Staffin, Conon, Rha
Portree A.A.
Sec: O. M. Burd
Tel: 0478 2437

STILLWATERS

A'Chroisg Loch
Ledgowan Lodge Hotel, Achnasheen
Tel: 044 588 252

ASCOG LOCH
Isle of Bute A.A.
Sec: S. W. Squires
Tel: 0700 2730

BLAIRS LOCH
The Tackle Shop
97b High Street, Forres
Tel: 0309 72936

FAD LOCH
Isle of Bute A.A.
Sec: S. W. Squires
Tel: 0700 2730

GARRY LOCH
Tomdoun Hotel
Glengarry
Tel: 080 92 218
Permits available to non-residents

HEMPRIGGS LOCH
Wilson & Nolf
1 Frances Street, Wick
Tel: 0955 4284

LOCHINDORB
Angus Stuart
60 High Street, Grantown-on-Spey
Tel: 0479 2612

LOCH LUICHART
Dingwall A.C.
Permits available from
A. Shanks
Sporting Stores, Dingwall
Tel: 0349 2346

HOWIE LOCH
Milton Park Hotel, Dalry
Tel: 064 43 286
Permits available to non-residents

KEN LOCH
Tommy's Sports Shop
20 King Street, Castle Douglas
Tel: 0556 2851

KERRIOCH LOCH
Newton Stewart A.A.
Sec: R. W. McDowall
Tel: 0671 3252

MACKIE LOCH
Nithdale District Council
Finance Department
Duccleugh Street, Dumfries
Tel: 0387 3166

MANOCH LOCH
Lidderdale & Gillespie
National Bank Building, Castle Douglas
Tel: 0556 2314

OCHILTREE LOCH
Newton Stewart A.A.
Sec: R. W. McDowall
Tel: 0671 3252
Permits also available from
Tarf Hotel, Kirkcowan
Tel: 067 183 325

ORNOCKENOCH LOCH
Cally Estates Office
Gatehouse of Fleet
Tel: 055 74 361

RONALD LOCH
B. Stevens
Three Lochs Caravan Park
Kirkcowan, Newton Stewart
Tel: 067 183 304
A. & G. Nelson, The Sports Shop
15/17 Victoria Street, Newton Stewart
Tel: 067 183 2858

SKERROW LOCH
Cally Estates Office
Gatehouse of Fleet
Tel: 055 74 361

SPECTACLE LOCH
Forestry Commission
South Scotland Conservancy
55 Moffat Road, Dumfries
Tel: 0387 2425
Recreation Planning Officer:
D. F. C. Forbes

STROAN LOCH
New Galloway A.A.
Sec: Mr Laurie
Tel: 064 42 239

WEE LOCH
Newton Stewart A.A.
Sec: R. W. McDowall
Tel: 0671 3252

WHINYEON LOCH
Murray Arms Hotel
Gatehouse of Fleet
Tel: 055 74 491

WOODHALL LOCH
Culgruff House Hotel
Crossmichael by
Castle Douglas
Tel: 055 627 230
Mossdale Post Office
Castle Douglas

FE REGION
RIVERS
en River
also Tayside Region
hil Haven A.C.
B. Stewart
cIntosh Crescent, Leven
its also available from:
esports
Bridge Street, Leven
0333 25115
mation only available from:
Artisans A.C.
A. Japp
0383 830635
STILLWATERS
hurlie Reservoir
n A.C.
R. McMillan
0592 3291
its also available from:
esports, 14A Bridge Street, Leven
0333 25115

W LOCH
by Model Shop
New Row, Dunfermline
0383 22582

AMPIAN REGION
RIVERS
rn River
rge Smith & Co.
ridge Street, Ballater
033 82432

e River
sthill & Elrick A.C.
ident: R. Findlay
0224 741704

r Ugie A.A.
Captain J. Q. P. Curzon
046 46 638
its also available from:
n Milne, Newsagent, 3 Ugie Road,
rhead
ard Duthie, c/o Dicks Sports, 54 Broad
et, Fraserborough
orrison, c/o Charles Bruce,
monger, 10 Chapel Street, Peterhead

an River
e A.A.
G. A. Joss
065 16 233
its available from all the following
ces:
esdale Bank Limited, Fyvie
065 16 233
n Bar, Fyvie
Hotel, Fyvie
Supermarket, Fyvie
ling Tor Cafe, Fyvie
an Hotel, Ellon
0358 20208

WBURGH
y & Oudwick Estates
E. Forbes
r Manager
03586 297
H NAN LANN
ckie Lodge Hotel

White Bridge
Tel: 045 63 276
Permits available to non-residents

MAO VALLEY
Ben Loyal Hotel, Tongue
Tel: 080 05 216

MNOR LOCH
G. G. Mortimer, Tackle and Guns
61 High Street, Grantown-on-Spey
Tel: 0479 2684

QUEIN LOCH
Isle of Bute A.A.
Sec: S. W. Squires
Tel: 0700 2730

RUARD LOCH
Wilson & Nolf
1 Frances Street, Wick
Tel: 0955 4284

SIONASCAIG LOCH
Royal Hotel, Ullapool
Tel: 0854 2181

STEMPSTER LOCH
Wilson & Nolf
1 Francis Street, Wick
Tel: 0955 4284

LOTHIAN REGION
RIVERS
Clyde River
United Clyde Angling Improvement
Assoc. Ltd.
Treasurer: J. Owgley

Lyne River
St. Mary's A.C.
Sec: Mr J. Miller
Tel: 031 447 2192

Tweed River
See also Borders Region
Peebleshire Trout Fishing Assoc.
Sec: D. G. Fyfe
Tel: 0721 20131

St. Mary's A.C.
Sec: Mr J. Miller
Tel: 031 447 2192
STILLWATERS
DANSKINE LOCH
The Lodge, Danskine
Near Gifford, East Lothian
CANALS
Union Canal
British Waterways Board
Applecross Street, Glasgow G4 2SP

STRATCHLYDE REGION
RIVERS
Add River
Poltalloch Estate Office

Annick River
Kilmaurs A.C.
Sec: J. Watson
Tel: 056 381 267
Currie Sports Shop, Town Head

Clyde River
LOWER STRETCHES (TO MOUTH)
United Clyde Angling Protective Assoc.
Ltd.
Sec: R. C. Sharp
Tel: 0698 62960
Permits also available from:
Most tackle dealers in Glasgow,
Edinburgh and main West of Scotland
towns

CLYDE RIVER
Upper stretches
Lanark & District Angling Club
Sec: A. C. McLean
Tel: 0555 4879
(Please enclose S.A.E. to 137 St. Leonards
Street, Lanark)

CLYDE RIVER
Roberton – Thankerton Stretch
United Clyde Angling Protective Assoc.
Ltd.
Sec: R. C. Sharp
Tel: 0698 62960

Lamington Angling Protective Assoc.
Sec: J. Hyslop
Tel: 0899 20616
Bailiff on banks

Coyle River
Drongan Youth Angling Club
Treasurer: M. Harvey
Tel: 029 258 840

Leven River
Loch Lomond Angling Improvement
Assoc.
c/o Messrs R. A. Clement & Co.
Sec: C. A. Ingram
224 Ingram Street, Glasgow
Permits also available from:
Various tackle makers

Inverbeg Hotel
Near Luss
Tel: 043 686 279
STILLWATERS
ASCOG LOCH
Kyles of Bute Angling Club (Game fishing)
Sec: A. Morrison
Tel: 070 081 458
Permits also available from:
Shops in Kames & Tighnabruaich
Bute Estate Office (Coarse fishing)
Rothesay, Isle of Bute
Tel: 0700 2627

FAD LOCH
Bute Estate Office
Rothesay, Isle of Bute
Tel: 0700 2627

HARELAW LOCH
Port Glasgow A.C.
Sec: I. Tucker
Tel: 0475 705012
LOMOND LOCH
Loch Lomond Angling Improvement Assoc.
c/o Messrs R. A. Clement & Co.
C. A. Ingram
Tel: 041 221 0068
Permits also available from:
Various tackle makers
Inverbeg Hotel, Near Luss

223

Tel: 043 686 279
Ardlui Hotel, Ardlui
Loch Lomond, by Arrochar
Tel: 030 14 243

TROMLEE LOCH
Chief Forester
Forestry Commission
21 Dalavich, Taynuilt
Tel: 086 62 258
Kilchrenan Trading Post
Tel: 086 63 232

CANALS
Forth and Clyde Canal
British Waterways Board
Applecross Street, Glasgow G4 9SP
R. Southgate
31 Morris Street, Hamilton
Tel: 0698 429245
Season permits

BANKNOCK AND TWECHAR
Glasgow & West of Scotland C.A.A.
Day permits available

CASTLE CARY TO BONNYBRIDGE
Edinburgh & East of Scotland C.A.A.
Day permits available

OLD KILPATRICK TO BOWLING
Kirkintilloch A.C.
Day permits available

Union Canal
British Waterways Board
Applecross Street, Glasgow G4 9SP

TAYSIDE REGION
RIVERS
Ardle River
Corriefodly Hotel
Bridge of Cally, Blairgowrie
Tel: 025 086 236

The Log Cabin Hotel
Glen Derby, Kirkmichael
Tel: 025 081 288

Bridge of Cally Hotel
Bridge of Cally
Tel: 025 086 231

Dean Water
Rescobie Loch Development Assoc.
Sec: R. Herdman
Bailiff: J. Yule
Tel: 030 781 384

Canmore Angling Club
Sec: E. Mann
44 Sheriff Park Gardens, Forfar, Angus

Strathmore Angling Improvement Assoc.
Sec: J. Christie
51 Broadford Terrace, Broughty Ferry, Dundee
Tel: 0382 736462
Permits also available from:
J. R. Gow & Sons
12 Union Street, Dundee
Shotcast
Whitehall Crescent, Dundee
Mr Carnegie
Crathie Bridge, Meigle

C. Kerr
1 West High Street, Forfar

Kerbert Water
Canmore Angling Club
Sec: E. Mann
44 Sheriff Park Gardens, Forfar

Lee Loch
Rescobie Loch Development Assoc.
Sec: R. Herdman
Permits available from:
Bailiff: J. Yule
Tel: 030 781 384
and Mr Ostler
Tel: 035 67208

Leven River
See also Fife Region
River Leven Trust
Sluice House, Loch Leven
Tel: 059 284 225

Lunan Water
Rescobie Loch Development Association
Sec: R. Herdman
Permits available from:
Bailiff: J. Yule
Tel: 030 781 384
and T. Clark & Sons

River North Esk
GALLERY AND HATTON BEATS
Links Hotel
Montrose
Tel: 0674 2288
CRAIGO BEAT
Montrose & District A.C.
Sec: G. S. Taylor
Tel: 0674 3904
KINABER ROAD BRIDGE TO MORPHIE DAM
Rescobie Loch Development Assoc.
Sec: R. Herdman
Permits available from:
Bailiff: J. Yule
Tel: 030 781 384
and Dalhousie Estates
Swan Street, Brechin
Johnstone Ltd, Salmon Fisheries, Montrose

Tay River
Aberfeldy A.C.
Sec: D. Campbell
Tel: 088 74 354
Loch Tay Guest House
Kenmore
Tel: 088 73 236
Dunkeld House Hotel
Dunkeld
Tel: 035 02 243
Ballathie Estate Office
Ballathie Farms near Stanley
Tel: 025 083 250
Royal George Hotel
Tay Street, Perth
Logierait Hotel
Ballinluig
Tel: 079 682 253
Post Offices
Dunkeld & Birnam
R. Scott Miller
Top Shop, Atholl Street, Dunkeld
Tel: 035 02 556
Weem Hotel
Weem, by Aberfeldy
Tel: 088 72 381

Grandtully Hotel
Strathtay
Tel: 088 74 207
Tummel River
Pitlochry Angling Club
c/o Pitlochry Tourist Office
28 Atholl Road, Pitlochry
Sec: Mr Gardner
Tel: 0796 2157 (after 17.30 hrs)
The Pine Trees Hotel
Pitlochry
Tel: 0796 2121
J. Wildblood
Y.M.C.A. Bonskeid House, Pitlochry
Tel: 079 684 208

STILLWATERS

CLUNNIE LOCH
Dunkeld & Birnam A.A.
Sec: J. Duncan
Permits available from:
R. Scott-Miller
Top Shop, Atholl St., Dunkeld
Tel: 035 02556

FASKALLY LOCH
P. Williamson
Boathouse, Loch Faskally
Pitlochry
Tel: 0796 2919

FITTY LOCH
D. Crombie
Regional Water Engineer
Fife Regional Council
Water Division, Glenrothes, Fife
Tel: 0592 756541

FORFAR LOCH
Canmore Angling Club
Sec: E. Mann
44 Sheriff Park Gardens, Forfar
Permits also available from
C. Kerr
1 West High Street, Forfar

FRENCHIE LOCH
Dunkeld & Birnam A.A.
Sec: J. Duncan
Permits available from:
R. Scott-Miller, Top Shop
Atholl Street, Dunkeld
Tel: 035 02 556
GLOW LOCH
D. Crombie, Regional Water Engineer
Fife Regional Council, Water Division
Glenrothes, Fife
Tel: 0592 756541
LUNAN WATER
Arbroath A.C.
Sec: J. Gibb
Tel: 0241 76901
MONKSMYRE LOCH
Keithwick A.C.
Sec: J. Watt
Tel: 082 82 205
RESCOBIE LOCH
Rescobie Loch Development Assoc.
Bailiff: J. Yule
Tel: 030 781 384
Canmore A.C.
Sec: E. S. Mann
44 Sheriff Park Gardens, Forfar
TUMMEL LOCH
Queens View Hotel
Strathtummel, by Pitlochry

SCOTLAND

...ough, historically, Scotland was the ...t area to develop a system of Water ...horities and 'Divisions', a lead which ...land and Wales followed, power for ...er has now devolved to Local District ...ncils.

... only area bodies in Scotland are the ...ional Purification Boards. These, ...vever, do not fulfil a direct role related ...shing. Scotland also differs in respect ...aving no National Road Licence. The ...ous laws and requirements are imposed ...lly. Subsequently, the editorial format ...he Scotland section has been altered ...ccordance with these differences.

...RDERS REGION

RIVERS

...er Ale
...arts
...h Street, Hawick
...450 2231

...ick Angling Club
...R. Johnston
...n', 6 Raeson Park, Hawick
...450 2266
...week and season permits available from
...tores
...on Street, Hawick
...450 3543
... Premises, 5 Sandbed, Hawick
...man (Saddlers), Denholm
...Guest House, Bridge Street, Hawick
...l. Rennie, Bourtree Place

...n Water
...tores
...on Street, Hawick
...450 3543

Blackadder
ALLANTON
Greenlaw A.C.
Sec: A. Lamb
Waterford, Wester Row, Greenlaw
Tel: 03616 246
Day and season permits available

BLACKADDER MAINS TO ALLENBANK
W. P. Harrowe
Tofthill, Allanbank
Tel: 089 081 302

WHITELAW STRETCH
Mr Scott
Whitelaw Farmhouse, Duns

KIMMERGHAME MILL TO MOUTH BRIDGE
C. McCosh
Kimmerghame Mill
Tel: 03612 2263

A. Bigger
Kimmerghame Heugh

Blackadder Tributaries
Greenlaw A.C.
Sec: A. Lamb
Tel: 03616 246
Permits also available from
Post Office, Greenlaw
All hotels in area

River Borthwick
Hawick Angling Club
Sec: R. Johnston
'Kelvin', 6 Raeson Park, Hawick
Tel: 0450 2266
Day, week and season permits available from
Stotharts
6 High Street, Hawick
Tel: 0450 2231
Pet Stores
1 Union Street, Hawick
Tel: 0450 3543
Club Premises, 5 Sandbed, Hawick
Dickman (Saddlers), Denholm
Elm Guest House, Bridge Street, Hawick
J.H.M. Rennie, Bourtree Place

Bowmont Water
Yetholm A.A.
Sec: A. J. Turnbull
Tel: 04674 2311

Cadden Water
J. & A. Turnbull
30 Bank Street, Galashiels
Tel: 0896 3191

Dye Water
Whiteadder A.A.
Sec: R. Welsh
Abbey Street, Bathans, Duns
Tel: 03614 210
Day and season permits also available from:
James Boyd
St. Leonards, Polwarth, Greenlaw
A. Murray
15 Home Place, Duns
D. Graham
The Square, Duns
Mr Speedie
Whitchester, Elmford

Red Lion Hotel, Allenton
White Swan Hotel, Duns

Earn River
Gordon F.C.
Sec: W. A. Virtue
Kircaig, Manse Street, Galashiels

Eddleston Water
I. Fraser
1 Bridgegate, Peebles
Tel: 0721 20979

Eden River
Kelso A.A.
Sec: Mr Hutchinson
Tel: 057 32 3440
Permits also available from:
Mr & Mrs Morris
Ednam East Mill, Kelso

Eden Water
UPPER STRETCH
Gordon Fishing Club
Sec: W. A. Virtue
Kircaig, Manse Street, Galashiels
Permits also available from:
Mr J. Hay
Station Road, Gordon
Mr D. Virtue
Swallow Eaves, Westruther

LOWER STRETCH
Forrest & Sons
The Square, Kelso

Redpath & Co
55/57 Horsemarket, Kelso
Tel: 05732 2578

Sportswise
Roxburgh Street, Kelso
Permits also available on site from:
River Watchers

Ettrick Water
Selkirk & District A.A.
Sec: Mr A. Murray
Tel: 0750 21534
Permits also available from
Post Offices at Ettrick, Yarrowford
Yarrow and Ettrickbridge

Ettrickshaws Lodge Hotel
Ettrickbridge
Tel: 075 05 229
Permits available to non residents

Eye Water
Eyewater Angling Club
Sec: J. Gillie (Water Bailiff)
24 Haymons Cove, Eyemouth
Tel: 0390 50038
Day, week, fortnight and season permits also available from:
R. Grieve
26 High Street, Eyemouth
Tel: 0390 50270
A. S. Davidson & Sons
Berrybank, Reston
Mr Darling
Springwood Hill, Reston
D. McIntosh
Howburn, Reston

Gala Water

Gala A.A.
Sec: R. Watson
Tel: 0896 56330
Post Office, Stow
J. & A. Turnbull
30 Bank Street, Galashiels
Tel: 0896 3191

Royal Hotel
Stow
Permits available to non residents

Jed Water

Jedforest A.A.
Sec: A. Whitecross
Tel: 08356 3615

Jedforest Country House Hotel
Camptown
Tel: 083 54 274
Permits available to non residents

Kale River

A. Graham, Gamekeeper
Keepers House, Eckford
Tel: 083 55 255
Day permits available

Kale Water

A. Graham, Gamekeeper
Keepers House, Eckford
Tel: 083 55 255
Day permits available

R. B. Anderson W.S.
Royal Bank Buildings, Jedburgh
Tel: 083 56 3202

River Leader

UPPER, MIDDLE AND LOWER STRETCHES
Earlston A.A.
Sec: Mr Lothian
10 Westfield, Earlston
Tel: 089 684 559
Day and season permits also available
from: J. McQuillen,
Market Place, Earlston
L. Rutherford, Market Place, Earlston

LEADER WATER AND TRIBUTARIES FROM WHITSLAID BRIDGE TO CARFRAEMILL
Lauderdale A.A.
Sec: D. M. Milligan
2 Sidegate Mews, Haddington
Tel: 062 082 5161
Day and season permits also available
from:
Lauder Post Office, Market Place, Lauder
Mrs E. P. McDonald, Market Place, Lauder
Anglers Choice, High Street, Melrose

Liddle Water

Esk & Fisheries Association
Sec: R. J. B. Hill
Solicitor, Langholm, Dumfriesshire
Tel: 0541 80428
Season and weekly tickets only from
J. D. Ewart, Drapers, Newcastleton
Tel: 054 121 257

WHITHAUGH PARK
Newcastleton

Tel: 054 121 220
Day permits available

River Lyne

Peebleshire Trout Fishery Association
Sec: David G. Fyfe
39 High Street, Peebles
Tel: 0721 20131
Day, week and season permits also
available from:
I. Fraser
1 Brigegate, Peebles
Tel: 0721 20979
and various local tackle shops and hotels

Megget Water

Rodono Hotel
St Mary's Loch
Tel: 075 04 232
Permits available to non residents

Oxnam Waters

Jedforest A.A.
Sec: A. Whitecross
Tel: 083 56 3615
Permits also available from:
Jedburgh Gun & Sports Shop
Kenmore Toll, Jedburgh
Tel: 083 56 2377
W. Shaw
Cannongate, Jedburgh

River Rule

Hawick Angling Club
Sec: R. Johnston
'Kelvin', 6 Raeson Park, Hawick
Tel: 0450 2266
Day, week and season permits available
from
Stotharts
6 High Street, Hawick
Tel: 0450 2231
Pet Stores
1 Union Street, Hawick
Tel: 0450 3543
Club Premises, 5 Sandbed, Hawick
Dickman (Saddlers), Denholm
Elm Guest House, Bridge Street, Hawick
J.H.M. Rennie, Bourtree Place

River Slitrig

Hawick Angling Club
Sec: R. Johnston
'Kelvin', 6 Raeson Park, Hawick
Tel: 0450 2266
Day, week and season permits available
from
Stotharts, 6 High Street, Hawick
Pet Stores, 1 Union Street, Hawick
Club Premises, 5 Sandbed, Hawick
Dickman (Saddlers), Denholm
Elm Guest House, Bridge Street, Hawick
J.H.M. Rennie, Bourtree Place

River Teviot

KELSO-JEDBURG AREA
Kelso A.A.
Sec: C. Hutcheson
Tel: 057 32 3440
Day permits also available from:
Redpath & Co
55 Horsemark, Kelso
Tel: 057 32 2578
Gamekeeper
Keeper's Cottage, Eckford
Tel: 083 55 255

ECKFORD
Gamekeeper, Keeper's House, Eckford
Tel: 083 55 255
Day permits available

Jedforest A.A.
Sec: A. Whitecross
Tel: 083 56 3615
Trout permits only available from
Jedburgh Gun & Sports Shop
Kenmore Toll, Jedburgh
Tel: 083 56 2377

JEDBURGH AREA TO SOURCE
Hawick Angling Club
Sec: R. Johnston
'Kelvin', 6 Raeson Park, Hawick
Tel: 0450 2266
Day, week and season permits available
from
Stotharts
6 High Street, Hawick
Tel: 0450 2231
Pet Stores
1 Union Street, Hawick
Tel: 0450 3543
Club Premises, 5 Sandbed, Hawick
Dickman (Saddlers), Denholm
Elm Guest House, Bridge Street, Hawick
J.H.M. Rennie, Bourtree Place

River Till

Chatton A.A.
Sec: A. Jarvis
New Road, Chatton, Alnwick
Permits also available from:
Head Gamekeeper
Nesbit Cottage, Fenton, Wooler
Tel: 066 86 243
Ford Post Office
Head Keepers House, Ford

River Tweed

See also Lothian Region
STANHOPE-THORNIE LEE
Peebleshire Trout Fishing Assoc.
Sec: David G. Fyfe, 39 High Street, Peeb[
Tel: 0721 20131
Day, week, fortnight and season permit[
available from:
Ian Fraser, 1 Bridgegate, Peebles
Tel: 0721 20979
Stobo Post Office, Stobo
The Crook Inn, Tweedsmuir
The Lucken Booth
55 High Street, Innerleithen
The George Hotel, Walkerburn
Tweed Valley Hotel, Walkerburn
Tel: 089 687 220
John Dickson & Son, 21 Frederick Stree[
Edinburgh
F. & D. Simpson, 28 West Preston Street[
Edinburgh
Blackwood & Smith, 39 High Street,
Peebles
Edmund H. S. Fraser, High Street,
Innerleithen

RAE BURN-MANOR BRIDGE
I. Fraser
1 Bridgegate, Peebles
Tel: 0721 20979

WIRE BRIDGE POOL-SCROGBAN[
Peebleshire Salmon Fishing Assoc.
c/o Blackwood & Smith W.S.
Tel: 0721 20131

Fraser
Bridgegate, Peebles
l: 0721 209 79
y permits available from above. Season
rmits only from Blackwood & Smith W.S.

ALKERBURN AND FAIRNILEE
eed Valley Hotel
alkerburn
l: 089 687 220
rmits available to non residents

GALASHIELS
y permits available on Saturdays
la A.A.
c: R. Watson
: 0896 56330
mits also available from
gsknowes Hotel, Galashiels
: 0896 3478
mits available to non residents

eed Valley Hotel
lkerburn
089 687 220
mits available to non residents

LASHIELS, SUNDERLAND HALL
myly
derland Hall, Galashiels
0750 23298

LASHIELS-BOLESIDE BEAT
ashiels A.A.
R. Watson
almoral Avenue, Galashiels
mits also available from:
ald
erman's Cottage, Boleside
0750 2792

WOOD BRIDGE
Smith
lee, Darnick, Melrose

LROSE
t permits available from
ose & District A.A.
J. Broomfrield
ensbourne, Douglas Road, Melrose
089 682 2219
week and season permits also
able from:
er's Choice
Street, Melrose
089 682 3070

ther permits
edswood Ghillie
ermans Cottage, Nowstead
089 682 2076

ROSE (ST. AIDANS)
Brother Superior
dans, Gattonside

OSWELLS
swells & Newtown A.A.
R. Black
83 52 3271
its also available from
agents in the village such as:
Grant, Newsagent, St. Boswells
available by contacting:
aw
Street, St. Boswells
oan
ringfield, St. Boswells
Watchers on the bank

Earlston A.A.
Sec: W. W. Lothian
Tel: 089 684 559

ST. BOSWELLS
Dryburgh Abbey Hotel
St. Boswells
Tel: 083 52 2261
Day, week and month permits available to
non residents

KELSO
Kelso A.A.
Sec: C. Hutchison
Tel: 057 32 3440
Permits also available from:
Forrest & Son, The Square, Kelso
Redpath & Co
55/57 Horsemarket, Kelso
Tel: 057 32 2578
Sportswize
Roxburgh Street, Kelso
River Watchers on the bank

**BIRGHAM DUB AND LOWER
BIRGHAM**
The Hon. Caroline Douglas-Home
The Hirsel, Coldstream

**LENNEL BOAT AND COLDSTREAM
(TOWN WATER)**
Coldstream & District A.A.
Sec: E. M. Patterson
Tel: 0890 2719
Permits also available from:
Crown Hotel, Coldstream
Tourist Information Centre
(Town Water only)

LENNEL-LADYKIRK
Coldstream & District A.A.
Sec: E. Patterson
Tel: 0890 2719
Trout only:
The Manager
Milne Garden, Coldstream

LADYKIRK
Ladykirk & Norham A.A.
Sec: R. G. Wharton
8 St. Cuthberts Square, Norham
Permits also available from:
Masons Arms, Norham
Tel: 0289 82326
Victoria Hotel, Norham
Tel: 0289 82237
Permits should be available to non
residents from both hotels

NORHAM
Farm House, West Newbiggin, Norham

Whiteadder

See also Lothian Region
Whiteadder A.A.
Sec: R. Welsh
Abbey street, Bathans, Duns
Tel: 03 614 210
Season permits also available from:
Red Lion Hotel, Allanton
White Swan Hotel, Duns

Berwick & District A.A.
Sec: A. R. Manderson
11 Westfield Avenue, Berwick
River Watcher on bank
Permits also available from:

Berwick Sports Centre
Bridge Street, Berwick

Earlston A.A.
Sec: W. W. Lothian
10 Westfield Street, Earlston
Tel: 089 684 559
Day permits only from secretary or
H. McAlpine, Readerfoot Cottage, Melrose

Yarrow Water

Selkirk & District A.A.
Sec: A. Murray
Tel: 0750 21534
Pet Stores
1 Union Street, Hawick
Tel: 0450 3543

STILLWATERS

ACREKNOWE RESERVOIR
Hawick Angling Club
Sec: R. Johnston
'Kelvin', 6 Raeson Park, Hawick
Tel: 0450 2266
Day, week and season permits available
from
Stotharts
6 High Street, Hawick
Tel: 0450 2231
Pet Stores
1 Union Street, Hawick
Tel: 0450 3543
Club Premises, 5 Sandbed, Hawick
Dickman (Saddlers), Denholm
Elm Guest House, Bridge Street, Hawick
J.H.M. Rennie, Bourtree Place

ACREMOOR LOCH
Hawick Angling Club
Sec: R. Johnston
'Kelvin', 6 Raeson Park, Hawick
Tel: 0450 2266
Day, week and season permits available
from
Stotharts
6 High Street, Hawick
Tel: 0450 2231
Pet Stores
1 Union Street, Hawick
Tel: 0450 3543
Club Premises, 5 Sandbed, Hawick
Dickman (Saddlers), Denholm
Elm Guest House, Bridge Street, Hawick
J.H.M. Rennie, Bourtree Place

ALEMOOR LOCH
Hawick Angling Club
Sec: R. Johnston
'Kelvin', 6 Raeson Park, Hawick
Tel: 0450 2266
Day, week and season permits available
from
D. Stotharts, Tackle Shop
6 High Street, Hawick
Tel: 0450 2231
A. Spiers
Alemoor, Roberton, Hawick

COLDINGHAM LOCH
Dr E. J. Wise
West Loch House, Coldingham
Tel: 039 03 270
Day and evening permits

FRUID RESERVOIR
Lothian Regional Council
Dept. of Water Supply Services
Comiston Springs
55 Buckstone Terrace, Edinburgh
Tel: 031 445 4141

GLADHOUSE RESERVOIR
Lothian Regional Council
Dept. of Water Supply Services
55 Buckstone Terrace
Fairmile Head, Edinburgh

GOOSE LOCH
Stotharts
6 High Street, Hawick
Tel: 0450 2231
Pet Shop
1 Union Street, Hawick
Tel: 0450 3543

HELLMOOR LOCH
Hawick Angling Club
Sec: R. Johnston
'Kelvin', 6 Raeson Park, Hawick
Tel: 0450 2266
Day, week and season permits available from
Stotharts
6 High Street, Hawick
Tel: 0450 2231
Pet Stores
1 Union Street, Hawick
Tel: 0450 3543
Club Premises, 5 Sandbed, Hawick
Dickman (Saddlers), Denholm
Elm Guest House, Bridge Street, Hawick
J.H.M. Rennie, Bourtree Place

LINDEAN RESERVOIR
Selkirk & District A.A.
Sec: Mr A. Murray
Tel: 0750 21534
D. & H. McDonald
9-11 High Street, Selkirk
Tel: 0750 2139

LOCH OF THE LOWES
St. Mary's Angling Club
Sec: J. Miller
6 Greenbank Loan, Edinburgh EH10 5SH
Tel: 031 447 2192
Day and week permits also available from:
The Glen Cafe, Cappercleuch
Gordon Arms Hotel, Yarrow
Permits available to non residents
Crook Inn, Tweedsmuir
Anglers Choice, Tackle Shop,
High Street, Melrose
Tibbie Shiels Hotel, St. Mary's Loch
Tel: 075 04 232
Weekly tickets only available from:
Resident Keeper, Henderland East
Cottage, Cappercleuch
Tel: 075 04 243
Galloway Deer Museum, Clatteringshaw,
New Galloway & Talnotry Caravan Park,
Newton Stewart
Day and week permits available

NORTH USK RESERVOIR
M. Jones
Fairliehope Farm, Carlops By Penicuik
Tel: 0896 86 425

OXNAM RIVER
Jedforest A.A.
Sec: A. Whitecross

Tel: 083 46 3615

POTMORE LOCH
Bank tickets available at Loch side
Boat bookings
Tel: 0968 73904 in advance

ROSEBERRY RESERVOIR
Lothian Regional Council
Water Supply Services
55 Buckstone Terrace
Fairmile Head, Edinburgh
Tel: 031 445 4141

ST. MARY'S LOCH
St. Mary's Angling Club
Sec: J. Miller
6 Greenbank Loan, Edinburgh EH10 5SH
Tel: 031 447 2192
Day and week permits also available from:
The Glen Cafe, Cappercleuch
Gordon Arms Hotel, Yarrow
Tibbieshiels Hotel
Rodono Hotel, St. Mary's Loch
Tel: 075 04 232
Crook Inn, Tweedsmuir
Anglers Choice
High Street, Melrose
Tel: 089 682 3070
Keeper
Henderland East Cottage, Cappercleuch
Tel: 075 04 243
Permits available to non-residents from hotels

ST. MARY'S LOCH
Loch Leven Trout
Gordon Arms Hotel, Yarrow, Selkirkshire
Day permits available

STANTLING CRAIGS COMPENSATION POND
Galashiels A.A.
Sec: R. Watson
4 Balmoral Avenue, Galashiels
Gala A.A.
Sec: R. Watson
Tel: 0896 56330
Permits also available from:
J. & A. Turnbull
30 Bank Street, Galashiels
Tel: 0896 3191

TALLA RESERVOIR
Lothian Regional Council
Dept. of Water Supply Services
Comiston Springs
55 Buckstone Terrace, Edinburgh
Tel: 031 445 4141

WATCH RESERVOIR
Whiteadder A.A.
Sec: J. Boyd
Tel: 03612 2377

WILLIESTRUTHER LOCH
Hawick Angling Club
Sec: R. Johnston
'Kelvin', 6 Raeson Park, Hawick
Tel: 0450 2266
Day, week and season permits available from
Stotharts, 6 High Street, Hawick
Pet Shop, 1 Union Street, Hawick
Club Premises, 5 Sandbed, Hawick
Dickman (Saddlers), Denholm
Elm Guest House, Bridge Street, Hawick
J.H.M. Rennie, Bourtree Place

WOODEN LOCH
Gamekeeper
Keepers House, Eckford
Tel: 083 55 255
Day permits available

CENTRAL REGION

RIVERS

Allan Water
Allan Water Angling Improvement Assoc.
Sec: P. Nicholls
5 Lister Court, Bridge of Allan
D. Crockart & Son
15 King Street, Stirling
Tel: 0786 3443
Allanbank Motel
Greenloaning, Dunblane
Tel: 078 688 205
Day permits available to non residents

Devon River
See also Fife Region
Devon Angling Association
Sec: R. Breingan
33 Redwell Place, Alloa
Tel: 0259 215185
Season and day permits available from
Arthur West Emporium
Primrose Street, Alloa
Messrs D. Crockart & Son
15 King Street, Stirling
Tel: 0786 3443

Dochart River
See also Tayside Region
Killin Breadalbane A.C.
Sec: D. Allan
Tel: 056 72 362
Permits also available from Sec at his sho
D. & S. Allan Fishing Tackle
Main Street, Killin

Endrick River
Loch Lomond Angling Improvemen Assoc.
Sec: c/o R. A. Clement
Tel: 041 221 0068
Permits also available from:
Bailiff: 0360 40692

Forth River
GALTMORE BRIDGE TO BUCHLYV
A. E. Billet
Glenhead, Cartmore
Day and season permits available from
Tackle shops in Glasgow, Kirkintilloch

GARTMORE BRIDGE UPSTREAM
Mrs Ferguson
Station Buildings, Aberfoyle

Messrs D. Crockart & Son
15 King Street, Stirling
Tel: 0786 3443
Day and season permits available

Glasgow Telephones & Civil Service A.A.
Sec: D. Taylor

enfield Avenue, Glasgow
041 221 4251 (work)
0236 722939 (home)
permits available

rell Burn
rth Fish Protection Assoc.
S. Gillies
ngston Flats, Kilsyth
0236 822511
um Sales & Service Station
ng Road, Kilsyth
0236 822003

zert River
ertbank Hotel
oxtown, Stirlingshire
0360 310303

hay River
Breadalbane A.C.
D. Allan
56 72 362
nd week permits also available from
at his shop:
S. Allan, Fishing Tackle Shop
Street, Killin
Hotel, Killin
56 72 296

h River
rockart & Son
ng Street, Stirling
786 3443
ermits available

STILLWATERS

RAY LOCH
Achray Hotel
rossachs by Callander
87 76 229
ermits available to non residents

TON LOCH
h Fish Protection Association
S. Gillies
ngstone Flats, Kilsyth
236 822511
nd season permits also available

um Sales & Service Station
g Road, Kilsyth
236 822003

RON VALLEY RESERVOIR
irector of Finance
al Regional Council
orth, Stirling
786 3111 Extn. 333
ermits available

LTER LOCH
rt & Stenhousemuir Angling Club
A. McArthur
wood, 11 Bellsdyke Road, Larbert
32 45 2581
ermits available

END LOCH
ridge A.C.
Neil
dostoun Cres., Harthill

OF MENTEITH
Hotel

Port of Monteith, by Stirling
Tel: 087 75 258
Day fishing permits available

LILLIE LOCH
Blackridge A.C.
Sec: A. Neil
9 Murdostoun Cres., Harthill

LOCHAN-NA-LARIGE
Killin Breadalbane A.C.
Sec: D. Allan
Tel: 056 72 362
Permits also available from Sec. at his shop
D. & S. Allan Fishing Tackle
Main Street, Killin

LOMOND LOCH
Loch Lomond A.A.
Sec: c/o R. A. Clement & Co
Tel: 041 221 0068
Inversnaid Hotel, Inversnair
Tel: 087 786 223
The Winnock Hotel, Drymen
Tel: 0360 60 245
or 0360 60 204
also available from:
Bailiff
Tel: 0360 40692
Permits available on non residents from hotels

TAY LOCH
Killin Breadalbane A.C.
Sec: D. Allan
Tel: 056 72 362
Permits also available from Sec. at his shop:
D. & S. Allan Fishing Tackle
Main Street, Killin

DUMFRIES & GALLOWAY REGION

RIVERS

Ae Water
Upper Annandale A.A.
Sec: J. Black
Tel: 0683 20104
Day, week and month permits available
from J. P. M. Johnstone, Glenae, Amisfield, Dumfries

River Annan
Annandale and Egremont A.C.
Sec: P. A. W. Hope Johnstone
Tel: 057 64 317

Commissioners for Royal Four Towns Fishing
Sec: W. Graham
Tel: 038 781 220

Upper Annandale A.A.
Sec: J. Black
1 Rosehill, Grange Road, Moffat DG10 9HT
Season permits from Secretary only
Day and week permits available from
Red House Hotel
Wamphray, Moffat
Tel: 057 64 214
Gordon Sports, High Street, Lockerbie
F. Cowin, Victoria Wines, High Street,

Lockerbie
J. Graham, Agricultural Engineer,
Millhousebridge

Bladnoch River
Newton Stewart A.A.
J. Stuart Coy
Park Cottage, Creetown, Newton Stewart
Tel: 067182 332
Day and week permits available from
The Gun Shop, 40 Queen Street, Newton
Stewart

A. & G. Nelson
The Sports Shop
15/17 Victoria Street, Newton Stewart
Tel: 0671 2858

Border Esk
Esk & Liddle Fisheries Assoc.
Sec: R. J. B. Hill
Tel: 0541 80428
Weekly tickets only

Cairn Water
Nithdale District Council
Finance Department
Duccleugh Street, Dumfries
Tel: 0387 3166
Permits also available from:
H. I. Renwick
Dellcairn House, Moniave
Tel: 084 82 353 or
H. I. Renwick
Castlehill Farm, Moniave
Tel: 084 82 321
Day and week permits available from
D. McMillan, 6 Friars Vennel, Dumfries

Castle Milk Water
Castle Milk Estates Office
Lockerbie, Dumfries
Tel: 057 65 203/4
Day and season permits available

Crawick Water
Upper Nithdale Angling Club
Sec: W. Forsyth
Tel: 065 92 214
Permits also available from:
Menockfoot Lodge Hotel, Sanquhar
Tel: 065 92 382
Hotel can arrange for permit available by prior arrangement from the Bailiff

Cree River
Newton Stewart A.A.
Sec: J. Stuart Coy
Park Cottage, Creetown, Newton Stewart
Tel: 067182 332
Day and week permits also available from:
The Gun Shop, 40 Queen Street, Newton
Stewart

Cross Water of Luce
Stranraer & District A.A.
c/o 90 George Street, Stranraer
Sec: D. McDiarmid
Tel: 0776 2705
Day and week permits also available from:
North West Castle Hotel, Stranraer
Tel: 0776 2644
And other Hotels, Sports Shops,
Ironmongers, Caravan & Camping Sites in
Stranraer & District

Doon River

Drumgrange & Keirs Angling Club
Sec: M. MacDonald
Palace Bar, Waterside Stores, Dunaskin
Tel: 029 253 204/245
Day and season permits available

Esk River

See also Lothian Region
All Waters Ticket. Weekly Ticket Only
Esk & Liddle Fisheries Assoc.
Sec: R. J. B. Hill
Solicitor, Langholm, Dumfriesshire
Tel: 0541 80428
Week and season permits also available from:
J. Irving Wylie, River Watcher
Byreburn Foot, Canonbie
Tel: 05415 279

CANONBIE TICKET
Weekly Tickets Only
Esk & Liddle Fisheries Assoc.
Sec: R. J. B. Hill
Tel: 0541 80428
J. Irving Wylie, River Watcher
Byreburn Foot, Canonbie
Tel: 05415 279
P. Lillie
19 Rowanburn, Canonbie
Tel: 05415 224
Langholm Guest House, Langholm
Tel: 0541 80378
Cross Keys Hotel, Canonbie
Riverside Inn, Canonbie

Euchar Water

Upper Nithdale Angling Club
Sec: W. Forsyth
Tel: 065 92 241

Evan Water

The Red House Hotel
Newton Wamphray, Moffat
Tel: 057 64 214

Ewes Water

Esk & Liddle Fisheries Assoc.
Sec: R. J. B. Hill
Tel: 0541 8428
Permits also available from:
Eskdale Hotel, Market Place, Langholm
Tel: 0541 80357
Langholm Restaurant
81 High Street, Langholm

Fleet River

Murray Arms Hotel
Gatehouse of Fleet
Tel: 055 74 491
Permits available to non residents

Hoddom Water

P. Helm
22 Fernlea Crescent, Annan
Tel: 046 12 2922
Day permits available

Kello Water

Upper Nithdale Angling Club
Sec: W. Forsyth
Tel: 065 92 241

Ken River

New Galloway A.A.
c/o Clydesdale Bank, New Galloway
Sec: N. Birch
Tel: 064 42 404
Permits also available from:
Ken Bridge Hotel, New Galloway
Contact: Mrs Forrest
Tel: 064 42 211
Cross Keys Hotel, New Galloway

River Kinnel

Upper Annandale A.A.
Sec: J. Black
1 Rosehill, Grange Road, Moffat DG10 9HT
Tel: 0683 20104
Season permits from secretary only
Day and week permits available from
Red House Hotel, Wamphray, Moffat
Gordons Sports, High Street, Lockerbie
F. Cowin, Victoria Wines, High Street,
Lockerbie
J. Graham, Agricultural Engineer,
Millhousebridge

Liddle Water

Esk & Liddle Fisheries Assoc.
Sec: R. J. B. Hill
Tel: 0541 80428
Permits also available from:
Mrs Elliot, River Watcher
Thistlesyke, Newcastleton
Tel: 054 121 200
Langholm Guest House, Langholm
Tel: 0541 80378

Mennock Water

Upper Nithdale Angling Club
Sec: W. Forsyth
Tel: 065 92 241

Milk River

Castle Milk Estates Office
Lockerbie, Dumfries
Tel: 057 65 203/4
Day, week and season permits available

Minoch River

Newton Stewart A.A.
Sec: J. Stuart Coy
Park Cottage, Creetown, Newton Stewart
Tel: 067182 332
Day and week permits available from
The Gun Shop, 40 Queen Street, Newton
Stewart

Moffat Water

Upper Annandale A.A.
Sec: J. Black
Tel: 0683 20104

New Ashby Pow

New Abbey A.A
c/o Abbey Arms Hotel, New Abbey
Tel: 038 785 366

Nith River

Buccleuch Estates
Thornhill
Tel: 0848 30482

TIDAL STRETCH
Nithdale District Council
Finance Department
Duccleuch Street, Dumfries
Tel: 0387 3166

MIDDLE STRETCH
Mid Nithdale A.A.
Sec: R. W. Coltart
c/o A. Coltart & Son, Shoe Shop
Thornhill
Tel: 0848 30464
Day and week permits also available f
George Hotel, Thornhill
Tel: 0848 30326

UPPER STRETCH
Upper Nithdale Angling Club
Sec: W. Forsyth
Solicitor, Sanquhar, Dumfriesshire
Tel: 065 92 241
Day, week and season permits also available from:
D. McMillan
6 Friars Vennel, Dumfries
Tel: 0387 2075
Mennockfoot Lodge Hotel, Sanquhar
Tel: 065 92 382

Palnure Burn

Newton Stewart A.A.
Sec: J. Stuart Coy
Park Cottage, Creetown, Newton Stew
Tel: 067182 332
Day and week permits available from
The Gun Shop, 40 Queen Street,
Newton Stewart

Penkiln Burn

Newton Stewart A.A.
Sec: J. Stuart Coy
Park Cottage, Creetown, Newton Stew
Tel: 0671 82 332
Day and week permits available from
Gun Shop, 40 Queen Street, Newton
Stewart

Royal Four Towns Water

Castle Milk Estates Office
Lockerbie, Dumfries
Tel: 057 65 203/4
Commissioners for Royal Four Towns
Fishings
Sec: W. Graham
Tel: 038 782 220
Day, week and season permits availab

Sark River

Gretna A.A.
Sec: J. G. Graham
126 Currock Park Avenue,
Carlisle, Cumbria CA2 4DH
Permits also available from:
Hunters Lodge Hotel, Gretna
Tel: 046 13 214

Tarras Water

Esk & Liddle Fisheries Assoc.
Sec: R. J. B. Hill
Tel: 0541 80428
Permits also available from:
Eskdale Hotel
Market Place, Langholm
Tel: 0541 80357
J. M. White
Market Place, Langholm

rr River
astle Douglas & District A.A.
ec: I. T. Bendall
 King Street, Castle Douglas
el: 0556 2851
ay and week permits available from
mmy's Sports, 20 King Street,
astle Douglas

ater of Milk
clefechan Hotel
clefechan
l: 057 63 213
rmits available to non residents

hite Esk River
eekly tickets only
k & Liddle Fisheries Assoc.
c: R. J. B. Hill
icitor, Langholm, Dumfriesshire
l: 0541 80428
eek and season permits also
ailable from
kdale Hotel, Langholm
l: 0541 80357

STILLWATERS

TON RESERVOIR
wn Hotel, New Cumnock
029 04 251
mits available to non-residents

RFAD LOCH
f Hotel, Kirkcowan
067 183 325

RSCOBE LOCH
Hugh Wontner
scobe, Balmaclellan
064 42 245
4 42 294
permits available

CK ESK RESERVOIR
& Liddle Fisheries Assoc.
R. J. B. Hill
itor, Langholm, Dumfriesshire
0541 80428
permits also available from:
holm Guest House, Langholm
0541 80378

CK LOCH
stry Commission, South Scotland
ervancy
offat Road, Dumfries
0387 2425
eation Planning Officer, D.F.C. Forbes
evens
e Lochs Caravan Park
owan, Newton Stewart
067 183 304
way Deer Museum
ering Shaws, New Galloway
try Caravan Park, Newton Stewart
G. Nelson, The Sports Shop
Victoria Street, Newton Stewart
67 183 2858
euch Forest Office, Dundeuch

NTIS LOCH
on Stewart A.A.
Stuart Coy

Park Cottage, Creetown, Newton Stewart
Tel: 067182 332
**Day and week permits available from the
Gun Shop, 40 Queen Street,
Newton Stewart**

CALLY LOCH
Cally Hotel
Gatehouse of Fleet
Tel: 055 74 341
**Day, week and month permits available to
non-residents**

CARSFAD LOCH
Dalry A.A.
c/o Glenkens Cafe, Dairy
Sec: J. Kentley
Tel: 064 42 211

CLATTERINGSHAWS LOCH
Newton Stewart A.A.
Sec: J. Stuart Coy
Park Cottage, Creetown, Newton Stewart
Tel: 067182 332
**Day and week permits available from the
Gun Shop, 40 Queen Street,
Newton Stewart**

DALBEATTY RESERVOIR
Dalbeatty A.C.
Sec: G. D. Bomphray
Tel: 0556 610421
**Advisable to contact Ticket Secretary to
book:**
N. Parker
30 High Street
Dalbeatty DG5 4AA
Tel: 0556 610448
Day, week and season permits available

DEE LOCH
Forestry Commission
South Scotland Conservancy
55 Moffat Road, Dumfries
Tel: 0387 2425
Recreation Planning Officer:
D. F. C. Forbes
Galloway Deer Museum
Clatteringshaws, New Galloway
Talnotry Caravan Park, Newton Stewart
Dundeugh Forest Officer
Day and week permits available

DINDINNIE RESERVOIR
Stranraer & District A.A.
c/o 40 George Street, Stranraer
Tel: 0776 2705
And Hotels, Sports Shops, Ironmongers
Caravan & Camping Sites in Stranraer &
District
Day and week permits available

EARLSTOUN LOCH
Milton Park Hotel, Dalry
Tel: 064 43 286
Permits available to non-residents

GLENAMEUR LOCH
Newton Stewart A.A.
Sec: J. Stuart Coy
Park Cottage, Creetown, Newton Stewart
Tel: 067182 332
**Day and week permits available from the
Gun Shop, 40 Queen Street,
Newton Stewart**

GLENKILN RESERVOIR
Forestry Commission

South Scotland Conservancy
55 Moffat Road, Dumfries
Tel: 0387 2425
Recreation Planning Officer:
D. F. C. Forbes

HERON LOCH
A. & G. Nelson, The Sports Shop
15/17 Victoria Street, Newton Stewart
Tel: 067 183 2858
B. Stevens
Three Lochs Caravan Park
Kirkcowan, Newton Stewart

KNOCKQUASSEN RESERVOIR
Stranraer & District A.A.
c/o 40 George Street, Stranraer
Tel: 0776 2705
And Hotels, Sports Shops, Ironmongers
Caravan & Camping Sites in Stranraer &
District
Day and week permits available

LAURIESTON LOCH
Gatehouse & Kirkcudbright A.A.
Sec: D. A. Lamont
Tel: 0577 30492

LILIES LOCH
Forestry Commission
South Scotland Conservancy
55 Moffat Road, Dumfries
Tel: 0387 2425
Recreation Planning Officer:
D. F. C. Forbes
Galloway Deer Museum
Clatteringshaws, New Galloway
Talnotry Caravan Park
Newton Stewart
Day permits available

LOCHENBRECK LOCH
Gatehouse & Kirkcudbright A.A.
Sec: D. A. Lamont
Tel: 0577 30492

LOCHNAW LOCH
Lochnaw Castle Hotel, Nr. Stranraer
Tel: 077 687 227
Permits available to non-residents

OCHILTREE LOCH
Newton Stewart A.A.
Sec: J. Stuart Coy
Park Cottage, Creetown, Newton Stewart
Tel: 067182 332
**Day and week permits available from the
Gun Shop, 40 Queen Street,
Newton Stewart**

PENWHRIN RESERVOIR
Stranraer & District A.A.
c/o 40 George Street, Stranraer
Tel: 0776 2705
And Hotels, Sports Shops, Ironmongers
Caravan & Camping Sites in Stranraer &
District
Day and week permits available

REE LOCH
Stranraer & District A.A.
c/o 40 George Street, Stranraer
Tel: 0776 2705
Day and week permits also available from:
And Hotels, Sports Shops, Ironmongers
Caravan & Camping Sites in Stranraer &
District

ROAN LOCH
Castle Douglas & District A.A.
Sec: I. T. Bendall
20 King Street, Castle Douglas
Tel: 0556 2851
Day permits available from
Tommy's Sports Shop
20 King Street, Castle Douglas
Tel: 0556 2851

RONAL LOCH
B. Stevens
Three Lochs Caravan Park
Kirkcown, Newton Stewart
Tel: 067 183 304
A. & G. Nelson, The Sports Shop
15/17 Victoria Street
Newton Stewart
Tel: 067 183 2858

SKATE LOCH
Milton Park Hotel, Dalry
Tel: 064 43 286
Permits available to non-residents

SOULSEAT LOCH
Stranraer & District A.A.
c/o 90 George Street, Stranraer
Tel: 0776 2705
Day and week permits also available from:
And Hotels, Sports Shops, Ironmongers
Caravan & Camping Sites in Stranraer &
District

WHINYEON LOCH
Murray Arms Hotel
Gatehouse of Fleet, Kirkcudbrightshire
Tel: 055 74 491

FIFE REGION

RIVERS

River Ceres Burn
Eden A.A.
Sec: J. Fyffe
Tel: 082 82 53588
Permits also available from:
John R. Gow & Sons (Fishing Tackle)
Union Street, Dundee
Tel: 0382 25427

Strathmore Angling Improvement
Assoc.
Sec: J. Christie
Tel: 0382 25427

Devon River
See also Central Region
Devon A.A.
c/o Hobby Model
10-12 New Row, Dunfermline
Tel: 0383 22582

Earn River
See also Tayside Region
Dunfermline Artisan A.A.
c/o Hobby Model
10-12 New Row, Dunfermline
Tel: 0383 22582

Eden River
Eden A.A.
Sec: J. Fyffe
67 Braehead, Cupar
Tel: 082 82 53588
Day and season permits also available
from:
John R. Gow & Sons, (Fishing Tackle)
Union Street, Dundee
Tel: 0382 25427

Strathmore Angling Improvement
Assoc.
Sec: J. Christie
Tel: 0382 736462
Permits from J. R. Gow & Sons
Union Street, Dundee
Tel: 0382 25427

Hobby Model
10-12 New Row, Dunfermline
Tel: 0383 22582

STILLWATERS

CAMERON RESERVOIR
St. Andrews Angling Club
Sec: P. F. Malcolm
Tel: 0334 76347
**Permits also available from bailiff on the
bank**

CLATTO LOCH
Crawford Priory Estate
c/o Mr Colombo
West Lodge, Crawford Priory Estate,
Cupar

FITTY LOCH
Game Fisheries
"Loch Fitty Lodge" Shop, Kingseat
Dunfermline
Tel: 0383 23162
Information only, especially regarding fly
fishing on loch available from:
The Canmore A.C.
Sec: L. W. Mitchell
Tel: 0383 31561
Day permits available

LEVEN LOCH
Information, especially regarding fly
fishing on loch available from:
The Canmore A.C.
Sec: L. W. Mitchell
Tel: 0383 31561

Ore Loch
Fishing Lodge Lochore
Meadows Country Park
Crosshill, Lochgelly
Kelty Co-operative
Chemist Branch, Kelty
Sports Shop
High Street, Cowdenbeath

RAITH LAKE
Kirkcaldy
Tel: 0383 23162

ROSCOBIE RESERVOIR
Townhill A.C.
Sec: J. Macdonald
5 Witch Brae, Dunfermline

GRAMPIAN REGION

RIVERS

Avon River
Delnashaugh Hotel
Ballindalloch, Banffshire
Tel: 080 72 210
Also see entry under Strathclyde region

Bervie Water
Laurencekirk & District A.A.
Sec: R. Stewart
Tel: 056 17 680

Bogie River
Clerk of Fishings
Duke Street, Huntley
Tel: 0466 2291
Day, week, month and season permits
available

Dee River
Ardoe House Hotel
Banchory
Tel: 0224 867355

Banchory Lodge Hotel
Banchory
Tel: 033 02 2625

Mar Lodge
Braemar, Aberdeenshire
Tel: 033 82 216

Invercauld Arms Hotel
Braemar
Tel: 033 83 605
Day and week permits available

Deveron River
Turriff A.A.
Sec: I. Masson
Tel: 088 82 2428
Week permits only

Clerk of Fishings
Duke Street, Huntly
Tel: 0466 2291
Day, week, month and season permits

Forbes Arms Hotel
Rothiemay, Huntly
Tel: 046 681 248
Day and week permits

Deveron House Hotel
Union Road, Macduff
Tel: 0261 32309
Day and week permits available to no
residents from hotels

County Hotel
32 High Street, Banff
Tel: 026 12 2846
Day permits available

Don River
KEMNAY FISHING
F. J. & Mrs S. L. Milton
Kemnay House, Kemnay
Tel: 046 74 2220

NCLUNE BEAT/KILORUMMY BEAT
erdeen & District A.A.
o Messrs Clark & Wallace
l: 0224 53481

verurie A.A.
c: T. H. Dunderdale
l: 0467 53481
mits also available from:
Duncan
West High Street, Inverurie
: 0467 20310
Hillary
ne Circle, Glenkinoie
: 097 53 335

lquhonnie Hotel
athdon
: 097 52 210

drummy Castle Hotel
drummy, by Alford
033 65 288
permits available

nt Arms Hotel
ymusk
046 77 226
mits available to non-residents from
els

dhorn River
also Highlands Region
es A.A.
P. Garrow
bertson Place, Forres IV36 0EU
kly permits available from
. Lilley, Tackle Shop, 97B High Street,
es

River
k of Fishing
e Street, Huntly
0466 2291
week, month and season permits
able

sie River
A.A.
. Mackay
llies Drive, Elgin
0343 45168
nd week permits available from local
e shops

emouth A.A.
. B. Clark
34 381 2380
ts also available from:
e dealers in Elgin

er Water
ncekirk & District A.A.
. Stewart
56 17680

kle Burn River
y Estates Development Co.
s Office, Forres, Moray
309 72213
and day permits available

River
lso Highlands Region
formation contact:

Mortimers (Tackle Shop)
High Street
Grantown on Spey, Moray
Tel: 0479 2684
Weekly permits available from above

BLAIRFINDY LODGE HOTEL
Glenlivet, Ballindalloch
Banff, Grampian
Tel: 080 73 376
See Advertisement under Hotels

Craigellachie Hotel
Craigellachie
Tel: 034 04 204
Advance booking only. Weekly permits

Aberlour Hotel
Aberlour
Tel: 034 05 287
Day permits

Palace Hotel
High Street, Grantown on Spey
Tel: 0479 2706
Weekly permits

Uglie River
Westhill & Elrick A.C.
President: R. Findlay
Tel: 0224 741704

River Ugie A.A.
Sec: Captain J. Q. P. Curzon
Dalvaine, Rhynie, Huntly, Aberdeenshire
AB5 4HL
Tel: 046 46 638
**Day, week and season permits also
available from:**
Gavin Milne, Newsagent
3 Ugie Road, Peterhead
Dicks Sports, 54 Broad Street,
Fraserborough

Ythan River
Fyvie A.A.
Sec: G. A. Joss
Bank House, Fyvie, Turriff, Aberdeenshire
Tel: 065 16 233
**Day and season permits available from all
of the following sources:**
Clydesdale Bank Ltd., Fyvie
Tel: 065 16 233
Ythan Bar, Fyvie
Vale Hotel, Fyvie
Spar Supermarket, Fyvie
Sheiling Tor Cafe, Fyvie
PLC, Fyvie

NEWBURGH
Udny & Oudwick Estates
Tel: E. Forbes
Fishery Manager
Tel: 03586 297

HADDO HOUSE STRETCH, RIGHT BANK
Day permits available from
S. French & Son, Methlick, and
Estate Office, Haddo House, Aberdeen
Tel: 065 15 664

STILLWATERS

ARTLOCH FISHERY
Huntly
Tel: 0466 2448

BLAIRS LOCH
G. Lilley, Tackle Shop
97b High Street, Forres
Tel: 0309 72936

LOCH CUT
A. P. Brown & McRae (Solicitors)
35 Frithside Street
Fraserborough
Tel: 034 62 4761

LOCHINDORB
Moray Estates Development Co
Estates Office
Forres, Moray
Tel: 0309 72213

LOCH OF STRATHBEG
A. P. Brown & McRae, Solicitors
35 Frithside Street, Fraserburgh
Tel: 034 62 4761
Tufted Duck Hotel, St. Combs
Tel: 034 65 2481
Day permits available

MILLBUIES LOCH
Department of Recreation
Moray District Council
30/32 High Street
Elgin, Moray

SAUCH LOCH
Drumtochty Arms Hotel
Auchen Blae
Tel: 056 12 210
Day permits available to non-residents

HIGHLANDS AND ISLANDS

RIVERS

Alness River
Loch Achenachie Angling Club
Sec: M. Burr
Tel: 099 72 561

Coul House Hotel
Contin, by Strathpeffer
Tel: 099 72 487
Day permits available

Dunraven Lodge Hotel
Strathpeffer
Tel: 099 72 210

Badachro River
Principal: Gairloch Estates
Permits available from:
Shieldaig Lodge Hotel, Gairloch
Tel: 044 583 250
Contact: Mrs S. Thornton

Balgy River
Mr Doe, Keeper
Balgy Lodge, Shieldaig
Tel: 044 587 231

Loch Torridon Hotel
Torridon by Achinasheen
Tel: 044 587 242
Permits available to non-residents

Beauly River
Beauly Angling Club & Lovat Estate Office
Beauly
Tel: 046 371 2205

Berriedale River
Portland Arms Hotel
Lybster, Caithness
Tel: 059 32208
Permits available to non-residents

Blackwater River
Loch Achonachie Angling Club
Sec: M. Burr
Tel: 099 72 561

Craigdarroch Lodge Hotel
Craigdarroch Drive, Contin
by Strathpeffer
Tel: 099 72 265

Broadford River
Broadford Hotel
Broadford, Isle of Skye
Tel: 047 12 204/5
Day permits available to non-residents

Calder River
Mains Hotel
Main Street, Newtonmore
Tel: 054 03 206
Permits available to non-residents

Carron River
Renton Finlayson
Estates Office, Bonar Bridges, Sutherland

Clachnaharry River
Moray Firsth Salmon Fisheries Co. Ltd.
2 Ness Walk, Inverness
Tel: 0463 33714
Permits also available from:
Gray & Co. (Tackle Shop)
30 Union Street, Inverness
Tel: 0463 33225
The Post Office
North Kessock
Tel: 046 373 201

Cluanie River
Cluani Inn
Glenmoriston
Tel: 0320 51238
Permits available to non-residents

Conon River
Loch Achonachie Angling Club
Sec: M. Burr
Tel: 099 72 561

Dingwall A.C.
Sec: A. Shanks
The Sporting Stores
Tulloch Street, Dingwall
Tel: 0349 62346
Day, week and season permits available
from above

Creed River
The Factor
Stornoway Trust Estate Office
Stornoway, Isle of Lewis
Tel: 0851 2002

Dulnain River
Strathspey Angling Improvement Assoc.
Sec: G. Mortimer
Tel: 0479 2684
No day permits fishing, contact above for
further information

Dundonnell River
Dundonnell Hotel
Dundonnell, by Garve
Tel: 085 483 204
Day permits available

Enrick River
Kilmartin Hall
Glenurquhart
Tel: 045 64 269

Feshie River
Osprey Fishing School
Tel: 0479 810767

Invereshie House Hotel
Kincraig, by Kingussie
Tel: 050 04 332

Fhorsa River
And 60 Lochs
Uig Lodge Hotels
by Stornoway, Isle of Lewis
Tel: 085 05286
Permits available to non-residents

Findhorn River
See also Grampian Region
Freeburn Inn
Tomatin
Tel: 080 82 205
Logie Farm
Glenferness, Nairn
Tel: 030 95 226

Finnan River
Glenfinnan House Hotel
Glenfinnan
Tel: 039 783 235

Garry (Upper) River
Garry Gualach Ltd.
Invergarry
Tel: 080 92 230
Day, week and month permits available

Tomdoun Hotel
Glen Garry
Tel: 080 92 218
Permits available to non-residents

Garvie River
Royal Hotel
Ullapool
Tel: 0854 2181

Halladale River
Helmsdale River Board
Fishery Office
Strathnaver, Kinbrace
Tel: 064 16 201
Weekly permits available from
A. Jappy & Sons Ltd, Shore Road,
Helmsdale

Kerry River
Principal: Gairloch Estates
Gairloch A.C.
Hon. Sec: T. A. Bell
Tel: 044 583247

Creag Mor Hotel
Gairloch, Wester Ross
Tel: 0445 2068
Day permits

Kirkaig River
Culag Hotel
Lochinver
Tel: 057 14 209
      057 14 255

Meig River
East Lodge Hotel
Strathconon
Tel: 099 77 222

Moriston River
Glenmoriston Estates Office
Glenmoriston
Tel: 0320 51202

Mudale River
And Various Lochs in Area
Angling Centre
Altnaharra Fishing
Altnaharra, by Lairg
Tel: 054 981 225

Nairn River
Nairn A.A.
Sec: Mrs W. R. Mackay
36 Mill Road, Queenspark, Nairn IV12 5
Tel: 0667 53768
Day, week and fortnight permits availab
from secretary, evenings only or
Pat Fraser's Sports Shop, High Street,
Nairn, daytime only

Ness River
Inverness A.C.
Sec: J. Fraser
33 Hawthorn Drive, Inverness
Tel: 0463 36193
Day and week permits

North Dessock River
Moray Firth Salmon Fisheries Co. L
2 Ness Walk, Inverness
Tel: 0463 33714
Permits also available from:
Gray & Co
30 Union Street, Inverness
Tel: 0463 33225
The Post Office
North Kessock
Tel: 046 373 201

North Ford
South Uist A.C.
Sec: Dr I. Logan Jack
Griminish, Benbecula
Tel: 08702215/2068
Day and week permits available from

Oykel River
Renton Finlayson
Estates Office

r Bridge
oykel Lodge Hotel
oykel by Ardgay
54 984 200

y River
l Hotel
ool
854 2181

River
60 Other Lochs
odge Hotel
rnoway, Isles of Lewis
85 05 286

River
Bridge Hotel
ean Bridge
39 781 236

ddle River
our Hotel
rt William
85 55 225
ermits

achan River
chan Hotel
han, Isle of Skye
47 852 204
ermits available (free to residents)

rt River
ost House Hotel
ost, Isle of Skye

Tel: 047 032 202

Spean River
Spean Bridge Hotel
Spean Bridge
Tel: 039 781 250

The Rod & Gun Shop
18 High Street, Fort William

Spey River
See also Grampian Region
(Contact Clubs and Associations for
Designated Areas Information)
**Abernethy Angling Improvement
Assoc.**
Sec: Mayor McClaren
Tel: 047 982 204
**Day and weekly permits available from
Kellmans Stores, Boat of Garton
Tel: 047 983 205**

Badenoch A.A.
Sec: Mrs J. Waller
39 Burnside Avenue, Aviemore
Tel: 0479 810798
**Day, week and season permits from
Mains Hotel, Newtonmore
Tel: 054 03 206**

Invereshie House Hotel
Kincraig by Kingussie
Tel: 054 04 332
Permits from above

Osprey Fishing School
Aviemore Centre, Aviemore

Tel: 0479 810767
Sec: J. Cornfoot
Day and week permits available

**Strathspey Angling Improvement
Assoc.**
Sec: G. Mortimer, c/o Mortimers Tackle
Shop, High Street, Grantown on Spey
Tel: 0479 2684 for information and weekly
permits
The Boat Hotel
Boat of Garten
Tel: 047 983 258
Day and week permits

Silverfjord Hotel
Kingussie
Tel: 054 02 292

Thurso River
Thurso A.A.
Sec: J. Robertson
Tel: 0847 2819
**Association was granted stretch of water
by Lord Thurso**

THURSO FISHERIES LTD
Thurso East, Thurso, Caithness KW14 8HW
Tel: 0847 3134
Sec: P. J. W. Blackwood
Day or week permits available
See Advertisement this Section

Torridon River
Loch Torridon Hotel
Torridon, by Achnasheen
Tel: 044 587 242

Truim River
Badenoch Angling Assoc.
Sec: Mrs J. WAller
Tel: 0479 810798
Permits also available from:
Mains Hotel
Main Street, Newtonmore
Tel: 054 03 206

Ullapool River
Highland Coastal Estates
(Rhidorroch) Office
Shore Street, Ullapool

Upper Moriston
Cluanie Inn
Glenmoriston
Tel: 0320 51238

STILLWATERS

ABAINN AN UIRD
And Various Lochs and Small Rivers in
South Skye
An Oilfig Eilean Iarmain
Isle of Skye
Tel: 047 13 266
Day, week and month permits

ABHAINN ELSEORT
An Oilfig Eilean Iarmain
Isle of Skye
Tel: 047 13 266
Day, week and month permits

ACHALL LOCH
Highland Coastal Estates
(Rhidorroch) Office
Shore Street, Ullapool

ACHILTIBUIE
Badentarbat Lodge
Achiltibuie, Ullapool
Tel: 085 482 225
Day, week and season permits

ACHONACHIE LOCH
Loch Achonachie Angling Club
Sec: M. Burr
Tel: 099 72 561
Day and week permits

AFFRIC HILL LOCHS
Forest Office
Cannich, Beauly

AILSH LOCH
Oykel Bridge Hotel, by Lairg

ALVIE LOCH
Lynwilg Hotel
Loch Alvie, Aviemore
Tel: 0479 810602

AN DUIN LOCH
Fisheries for Scotland
Balivanich, Isle of Benbecula
Tel: 0870 2346
Season permits

AN OIS LOCH
The Factor, Stornoway
Trust Estate Office
Stornoway, Isle of Lewis
Tel: 0851 2002

ARDTORNISH ESTATE
Ardtornish Estate Office
Morvern, by Oban
Tel: 096 784 288

ARKAIG LOCH
The West Highland Estates Office
33 High Street, Fort William
Tel: 0397 2433
039 782 217

ASSYNT LOCH
Inchnadamph Hotel
Inchnadamph, Sutherland
Tel: 057 12 202
Culay Hotel, Lochinver
Tel: 057 14 209/255

ASSYNT (34 LOCHS)
Assynt Angling Club
Sec: A. M. McKenzie
Tel: 057 14 253
Tourist Information Office
Lochinver
Tel: 057 14 330
Day, week, fortnight, month or season
permit available

AVIELOCHAN
Mrs M. McCook
Avielochan, Aviemore
Tel: 0479 810450
G. G. Mortimer & Son (Fishing Tackle)
61 High Street
Grantown-on-Spey, Moray
Tel: 0479 2684

AWE LOCH
Inchnadamph Hotel, Inchnadamph
Tel: 057 12 202

BADACHRO LOCH
Plus 7 Other Hill Lochs
Principal: Gairloch Estate
Day permits available to non-residents
from:
Shieldaig Lodge Hotel, Gairloch
Tel: 044 583 250
Mrs S. Thornton

BADAGYLE LOCH
Royal Hotel, Ullapool
Tel: 0854 2181

BADANLOCH
Navidale House Hotel, Helmsdale
Tel: 043 12258

BALMACARA ESTATE LOCHS
Balmacara Hotel
By Kyle of Lochalsh
Tel: 0599 283
Day permits

BA LOCH AND
LOCHAN NA LACHLAIN
Kingshouse Hotel, Glencoe
Tel: 085 56 259
Day permits available from above

BEANNACH LOCH
Sutherland Arms Hotel, Lairg
Tel: 0549 2291

BEANNACHARAN LOCH
East Lodge Hotel, Strathconon
Tel: 099 77 222

BEANNACH LOCH
Culag Hotel, Lochinver
Tel: 057 14 209
057 14 255

BENBECULA LOCHS
Over 300 Lochs on Benbecula and South
Uist
South Uist A.C.
Sec: Dr I. Logan Jack
Griminish, Benbecula
Tel: 0870 2215/2068
Day and week permits available from Se

BENEVEAN LOCH
J. Graham & Co. Ltd.
27 Union Street, Inverness
Tel: 0463 33178

BHARABHAIG LOCH
An Oilfig Eilean Iarmain
Isle of Skye
Tel: 047 13 266

BLACK LADY LOCH
H. Davis
Creag Mor Hotel
Gairloch, Wester Ross
Tel: 0445 2068

BORVE LOCH
Borve Lodge, Isle of Harris
Tel: 085 985 202

BRAN LOCH
Whitebridge Hotel, Stratherrick
Tel: 045 63 272

BRORA LOCH
Loch Brora A.C.
Sec: J. Mackay
Tel: 040 82512
Sutherland Estates
Golspie
Tel: 040 83268
Estate Office
Gordonbrush, Brora
Tel: 040 82 323
Day, week and month permits availabl

BUIDHE LOCH
Dornoch & District A.A.
Sec: W. A. MacDonald
Castle Street, Dornoch
Tel: 082 281 301
Day and week permits available from

CALDER LOCH
A. A. MacDonald
23 Sinclair Street
Thurso, Caithness
Tel: 0847 2819

CAM LOCH
Ford Post Office
21 Dalavich, Taynuilt, Argyll

CAOL LOCH
Bettyhill Hotel, Bettyhill
Tel: 064 12 202

CARRON LOCH
Borve Lodge, Isle of Harris
Tel: 085 985 202

CATRINE LOCH
Inveroykel Lodge Hotel

rathoykel by Ardgay
el: 054 984 200

LACHAN LOCH
e Factor, Stornoway Trust
tate Office, Stornoway
e of Lewis
el: 0851 2002
y permits available

LAISSE LOCH
ılag Hotel, Lochinver
1: 057 14 209
057 14 255

AR LOCH
vidale House Hotel, Helmsdale
1: 043 12 258

JUANIE LOCH
chfour Estate Office
chgarroch by Inverness
: 046 386 218/9
y permits available

OLLAM LOCH
e Manager, Neil MacDonald
iraclete, Tarbert
e of Harris
: 0859 2464

OR NA MANG LOCH
vidale House Hotel, Helmsdale
: 043 12 258

AGGIE LOCH
Loyal Hotel, Tongue
080 05 216
el Bridge Hotel, by Lairg
ek and day permits available

AITE LOCH
yhill Hotel, Bettyhill
064 12 202

AICH LOCH
enoch A.A.
Mrs J. Waller
0479 810 798
Local tackle shops in Kingussie
, week and season permits also
able from:
pers House, Cuaich, Dalwhinnie

IL NA CAILLICH LOCH
cipal: Forestry Commission
ıs Post Office, Beauly
046 371 419
permits available

LCE NA LOCHEN
Loyal Hotel, Tongue
080 05 216
and week permits

AG LOCH
y Hotel, Lochinver
057 14 209
057 14 255

FRAOICH LOCH
g Hotel, Lochinver
057 14 209
057 14 255

LAS LOCH
Mortimer & Son, High Street
town-on-Spey, Moray

Tel: 0479 2648
Mrs M. McCook
Avielochan, Aviemore
Tel: 0479 810450

DEADMAN'S LOCH
Lands Officer
Dept. of Agric. & Fisheries for Scotland
Balivanich, Isle of Benbecula
Tel: 0870 2346
Season permit

DOCHFOUR LOCH
Dochfour Estate Office
Dochgarroch by Inverness
Tel: 046 386 218
046 386 230
Day, week and season permits available

DRINISHADER LOCH
The Manager, Neil MacDonald
7 Diraclet, Tarbert
Isle of Harris
Tel: 0859 2464

DRUMBEG LOCHS
20 Lochs near Hotel
Drumbeg Hotel
Assynt, by Lairg
Day: 057 12 236
**Day and week permits (free to hotel
residents)**

DUBH LOCH
Assynt Angling Club
Sec: S. McClelland
Tel: 057 14 253
J. P. T. Mellor
Barndromin Farm
Knipoch, by Oban
Tel: 085 26 273

DUINTE LOCH
Bettyhill Hotel, Bettyhill
Tel: 064 12 202

EILLANEICH LOCH
Altnaharra Hotel
Altnaharra, by Lairg

EILT LOCH
Lochailort Inn, Lochailort
Tel: 068 77 208

ERICHT LOCH
Badenoch A.A.
Sec: Mrs J. Waller
Tel: 0479 810 798
Day, week and season permits

FADA LOCH
Lands Officer
Dept. of Agric. & Fisheries for Scotland
Balivanich, Isle of Benbecula
Tel: 0870 2346
Day, week and season permits available
South Uist A.C.
Sec: E. E. Dunn
Tel: 0870 2336 Daytime
0870 2427 Evening
But the North End of Loch is not fishable
with South Uist A.C. permit (see
"Benbecula Lochs entry)

FADA LOCH
Skye
Portree A.A.

Sec: D. M. Burd
Tel: 04782437

FEARNAN LOCH
Navidale House Hotel, Helmsdale
Tel: 043 12 258

FESHIE LOCH
Osprey Fishing School
The Fishing Centre, Aviemore
Tel: 0479 810767

FINCASTLE LOCH
Borve Lodge, Isle of Harris
Tel: 085 985 202

FIONN LOCH
Gairloch A.C.
Hon Sec: T. A. Bell
Tel: 044 583 247
Culag Hotel, Lochinver
Tel: 057 14 209
or 057 14 255
Creag Mor Hotel, Gairloch
Tel: 0445 2068
Day permits available

FUARLOCH
Sutherland Arms Hotel
Lairg, Scotland
Tel: 0549 2291

GARBAIG LOCH
H. DAvis
Creag Mor Hotel
Gairloch, Wester ross
Tel: 0445 2068

GARRY LOCH
Garry Gualach Ltd., Invergarry
Tel: 080 92 230
Day and week permits available

GHRIAMA LOCH
Overscaig Hotel
Overscaig by Lairg
Tel: 054 983 203

GILLAROO LOCH
Inchnadamph Hotel, Inchnadamph
Tel: 057 12 202

GIRDH GREAGAN LOCHAN
Bettyhill Hotel, Bettyhill
Tel: 064 12 202

GLASCARNOCH LOCH
Aultguish Inn, by Garve
Tel: 099 75 254
Day, week and month permits

GLENMORISTON
22 Hill Lochs
Glenmoriston Estate Office
Glenmoriston
Tel: 0320 51202
Day permits

GRASSY LOCH
The Manager, Neil MacDonald
7 Diraclete, Tarbert
Isle of Harris
Tel: 0859 2464

GROSEBAY LOCH
The Manager, Neil MacDonald
7 Diraclete, Tarbert
Isle of Harris
Tel: 0859 2464

GRUAGACH LOCH
Inchnadamph Hotel, Inchnadamph
Tel: 057 12 202

HAKEL LOCH
Ben Loyal Hotel, Tongue
Tel: 080 05 216
Day and week permits

HOPE LOCH
Altnaharra Hotel
Altnaharra, by Lairg

HORSACLEIT LOCH
N. MacDonald
The Manager,
7 Diraclete, Tarbert
Isle of Harris
Tel: 0859 2464

HOSPITAL LOCHAN
Weekly permits only
The Warden, Glencoe Camp site
Forestry Commission, Glencoe

HOUSE LOCH
The Manager, Neil MacDonald
7 Diraclete, Tarbert
Isle of Harris
Tel: 0859 2464

INCHLAGGAN LOCH
Garry Gualach Ltd., Invergarry
Tel: 080 92 230

KEOSE LOCH
Loch Keose A.A.
Sec: Dr I. K. McIntosh
Tel: 085 186 222

KIRKTOMY LOCH
Bettyhill Hotel, Bettyhill
Tel: 064 12 202

KNOCKIE LOCH
Knockie Lodge Hotel
White Bridge
Tel: 045 63 276
Permits available to non-residents
Whitebridge Hotel, Stratherrick
Tel: 045 63 272

KYLE OF SUTHERLAND
Kyle of Sutherland A.A.
Permits available from:
R. Macleod & Sons
14 Lamington Street, Tain
Tel: 0862 2171
Invershin Hotel, Invershin, Lairg
Tel: 054 982 202
Inveroykel Lodge Hotel
Strathoykel, by Ardgay
Tel: 054 984 200

LAGGAN LOCH
Badenoch A.A.
Sec: Mrs J. Waller
Tel: 0479 810 798
Day, week and season permits also
available from:
Loch Laggan Filling Station

LANNSAIDH LOCH
Dornoch & District A.A.
Sec: W. A. MacDonald
Castle Street, Dornoch
Tel: 082 281 301
Day and week permits available from Sec.

LAOIGH LOCH
Dornoch & District A.A.
Sec: W. A. MacDonald
Castle Street, Dornoch
Tel: 082 281 301
Day and week permits available from Sec.

LAXDALE LOCH
Borve Lodge, Isle of Harris
Tel: 085 985 202

LEATHAN LOCH
Skye
Portree A.A.
Sec: D. M. Burd
Tel: 0478 2437

LETTERESSIE LOCH
Inchnadamph Hotel, Inchnadamph
Tel: 057 12 202

LOCH AN EILEIN
An Oilfig Eilean Iarmain
Isle of Skye
Tel: 04713 266

LOCH AN IASGAICH
An Oilfig Eilean Iarmain
Isle of Skye
Tel: 047 13 266

LOCHDHU HILL LOCHS
The Ulbster Arms Hotel
Halkirk, Caithness
Tel: 084 783 641 and 206
Manageress: Miss Keith
Daily permits available (free to residents of hotel)

LOCHMADDY
See "North Uist Estate Lochs"

LOCH NESS
Inverness A.C.
Sec: J. Fraser
Fort Augustus A.A.
Sec: Mr Wooley
Tel: 0320 6477
Glenmoriston Estate Office
Glenmoriston
Tel: 0320 51202
Foyers Hotel, Foyers
Tel: 045 63216
Permits available to non-residents
Permits also available from local tackle shops in area

LOYAL LOCH
Ben Loyal Hotel, Tongue
Tel: 080 05 216
Altnaharra Hotel
Altnaharra, by Lairg
Day and week permits

LUICHART LOCH
Dingwall & District A.C.
Sec: A. Shanks
The Sporting Stores
Tulloch Street, Dingwall
Tel: 0349 62346

Day, week and season permits available from above

LURGAN LOCH
Royal Hotel, Ullapool
Tel: 085 2181

MAOVALLY
Ben Loyal Hotel
Tongue
Tel: 080 05 216
Week and day permits

MAREE LOCH
Gairloch A.C.
Hon Sec: T. A. Bell
Tel: 044 583 247
Shieldaig Lodge Hotel, Gairloch
Tel: 044 583 250
Mrs S. Thornton
Permits available to non-residents
Loch Maree Hotel
Tel: 044 589 200
Kinlochewe Hotel
Kinlochewe, by Achnasheen
Tel: 044 582 253

MEADIE LOCH
Altnaharra Loch
Altnaharra, by Lairg
Bettyhill Hotel, Bettyhill
Tel: 064 12 202

MEIG LOCH
Loch Achonachie Angling Club
Sec: M. Burr
Tel: 099 72 561
East Lodge Hotel, Strathconon
Tel: 099 77 222

MELVICH HILL LOCHS
Melvich Hotel
Melvich, by Thurso
Tel: 064 13 206

MERKLAND LOCH
Overscaig Hotel
Overscaig, by Lairg
Tel: 054 983 203

MIGDALE LOCH
Dornoch & District A.A.
Sec: W. A. MacDonald
Castle Street, Dornoch
Tel: 082 281 301
Day and week permits available from Se

MODSAIRE LOCH
Ben Loyal Hotel, Tongue
Tel: 080 05 216
Day and week permits

MOR LOCH
G. G. Mortimer
61 High Street, Grantown-on-Spey
Tel: 0479 2684
Bettyhill Hotel, Bettyhill
Tel: 064 12 202

MORLICH LOCH
Glenmoriston Estates Office
Glenmoriston
Tel: 0320 51202

NA CEARDAICH LOCH
Lands Officer
Dept. of Agric. & Fisheries for Scotland

linvanich, Isle of Benbecula
ason permit

AM BREAC LOCH
ch Keose A.A.
c: Dr I. K. McIntosh
l: 085 186 222

AM GEADH
nds Officer
pt. of Agric. & Fisheries for Scotland
linvanich, Isle of Benbecula
l: 0870 2346
ason permit

A MUILNE LOCH
ch Keose A.A.
c: Dr I. K. McIntosh
l: 085 186 222

AN LOAGH LOCH
ttyhill Hotel, Bettyhill
: 064 12 202

AVER LOCH
naharra Hotel
anaharra, by Lairg
: 054 981 222

RTH UIST ESTATE LOCHS
acipal: Factor
th Uist Estates
hmaddy, North Uist
mits for all fishing can be obtained at
Estate Office, Lochmaddy and at:
th Uist A.C.
: D. L. Cockburn
084 63205

HTOW LOCHAN
eroykel Lodge Hotel
thoykel, by Ardgay
054 984 200

YOULISH LOCH
. Mortimer
igh Street, Grantown-on-Spey
0479 2684

LY LOCHS
Middle and Lower
acDonald
rpolly, Ullapool
057 14 252
permits

LARDEN LOCH
ey Fishing School
more Centre
0479 810767

DICH LOCH
in
Arms Hotel, Fort Augustus
320 6206
week and month permits

NASGAIL LOCH
60 Other Lochs
odge Hotel
ornoway, Isle of Lewis
85 05 286

DALE LOCH
dale House Hotel, Helmsdale
43 12 258

RUTHVEN NESS
Whitebridge Hotel, Stratherrick
Tel: 045 63 272
J. Trotter
Brin Holiday Estates, Farr
Tel: 080 83211
Leisuropa Ltd.
6-8 Inglis Street, Inverness
Tel: 0463 39427

SHEEP LOCH
The Manager, Neil MacDonald
7 Diraclete, Tarbert
Isle of Harris
Tel: 0859 2464

SHETLAND'S WATERS
1000 Lochs and Voes
Shetland A.A.
Sec: A. Miller
3 Gladstone Terrace, Lerwick
Tel: 0595 3729
Shetland and practically all Lochs are
under control of Shetland A.A.
Weekly tickets only available from
Hon. Treasurer, c/o Bank of Scotland,
Lerwick

SHIEL LOCH
Strontian A.C.
D. Macaulay, Dalilea Farm
Acharacle, Argyll
Tel: 096 785 253
Creel Fishing Facilities Co.
Creel Cottage, Acharacle
Tel: 096 785 281
Ben View Hotel
Strontian, Argyll
Tel: 0967 2333
Glenfinnan House Hotel
Glenfinnan
Tel: 039 783 235
Stage House Inn
Glenfinnan
Tel: 039 783 246

SHIN LOCH
Lairg Angling Club
Sec: J. M. Ross
Post Office House, Lairg, Sutherland
IV27 4DD
Tel: 0549 2010
Day 0549 2025
Permits are not issued at Post Office (above
address) but are available at:
Local Hardware Fishing Tackle Shop
Club Warden, Club Hut at Lochside

SKYE LOCHS
Skye
Portree A.A.
Sec: D. M. Burd
Tel: 0478 2437
12 Hill lochs in North Skye

SLACSAVAT LOCH
And 60 Other Lochs
Uig Lodge Hotel
by Stornoway, Isle of Lewis
Tel: 085 05 286

SLUICE LOCH
Borve Lodge, Isle of Harris
Tel: 085 985 202

SOUTH UIST LOCHS
Over 300 Lochs on Benbecula and South
Uist

Day and week permits to cover most
fisheries available from:
South Uist A.C.
Sec: Dr I. Logan Jack
Griminish, Benbecula
Tel: 0870 2215/2068

SOVAL ESTATE LOCHS
Soval A.A.
Sec: E. Young
Tel: 0851 2204

SPEY DAM
Badenoch A.A.
Sec: Mrs J. Waller
39 Burnside Avenue, Aviemore
Tel: 0479 810798
Day, week and season permits

SPEY LOCH
Osprey Fishing School
The Fishing Centre, Aviemore
J. Cornfoot
Tel: 0479 810767

STAINCH LOCH
Altnaharra Hotel
Altnaharra, by Lairg

STOOR LOCHS
Skye
Portree A.A.
Sec: D. M. Burd
Tel: 0478 2437

STRATH KANAIRD LOCH
Highland Coastal Estates (Rhidorroch)
Offices, Shore Street, Ullapool

TARFF NESS
Whitebridge Hotel, Stratherrick
Tel: 045 63 272

TERGAVET LOCH
Lands Officer
Department of Agric. & Fisheries for
Scotland, Balavanich
Isle of Benbecula
Tel: 0870 2346
Season permit available

TIGH NA CREIGE LOCH
Inveroykel Lodge Hotel
Strathoykel, by Ardgay
Tel: 054 984 200

ULBSTER ARMS HOTEL
12 Hill Lochs
Ulbster Arms Hotel
Halkirk, Caithness
Tel: 084 783 206
or 084 783 641
Day permits

UNAPOOL LOCH
Kylesku Hotel, Kylesku
Tel: 097 183 231/200

URIGILL LOCH
Inveroykel Lodge Hotel
Strathoykel, by Ardgay
Tel: 054 984 200

VAA LOCH
Mrs M. Cook
Aviemore
Tel: 0479 810 450
G. G. Mortimer & Son, Tackle and Guns
61 High Street, Grantown-on-Spey
Tel: 0479 2684

VERAGAVAT LOCH
Lands Officer
Dept. of Agric. & Fisheries for Scotland
Balivanich, Isle of Benbecula
Tel: 0870 2346
Season permit available

WATTEN LOCH
Loch Watten Hotel
Watten, Caithness
Tel: 095 582 232
Wilson & Nolf
1 Francis Street, Wick
Tel: 0955 4284

WESTER LOCH
Wilson & Nolf
1 Francis Street, Wick
Tel: 0955 4284

OTHER WATERS

Caledonian Canal
Dochfour Estate Office
Dochgarroch, by Inverness
Tel: 046 386 218
or 046 386 230

LOTHIAN REGION

RIVERS

Almond River
River Almond A.A.
Tel: 0506 33813

Birns Water
East Lothian A.A.
c/o Messrs J. S. Main
87 High Street, Haddington
River Watchers on Bank

BOTHWELL BURN
Bailiff: R. Graham
Cranshaws
White Swan Hotel, Duns
Barnikon Hotel, Duns

Esk River
See also Dumfries Region
Esk Valley Angling Improvement Assoc.
c/o 26 Eldendean Terrace, Bennyrigg
T. Mealyon
Sports Shops
11 Newbiggin, Musselburgh

River Waters of Musselburgh & District A.A.
G. R. Scott
9 Sherwood View, Bonnyrigg
Tel: 031 663 4919

Faseny Burn
Bailiff: R. Graham
Cranshaws
White Swan Hotel, Duns
Barnikon Hotel, Duns

Keith Water
East Lothian A.A.
c/o J. S. Main
87 High Street, Haddington
River Watchers on Bank

Tyne River
East Lothian A.A.
Sec: J. Crombie
10 St. Lawrence, Haddington, East Lothian
EH41 3RL
Day and season tickets available from shops in Dunbar, East Linton and Haddington and Edinburgh tackle shops

Water of Leith
Director of Administration
Lothian Regional Council
Regional Headquarters
George IV Bridge, Edinburgh
Tel: 031 229 9292 Extn. 2553

Whiteadder Water
See also Borders Region
Whiteadder A.A.
Sec: R. Welsh
Tel: 036 14 210
Permits also availble from:
T. Speedy
Ellemford, Duns
Bailiff: R. Graham, Cranshaws
White Swan Hotel, Duns
Barnikon Hotel, Duns

STILLWATERS

BEECRAIGS LOCH
Department of Recreation & Leisure
West Lothian District Council
Council Buildings
High Street, Linlithgow
Tel: 050 684 3121

CLUBBIEDEAN RESERVOIR
Lothian Regional Council
Department of Water Supply Services
Comiston Springs
55 Buckstone Terrace, Edinburgh
Tel: 031 445 4141

CROSSWOOD RESERVOIR
Lothian Regional Council
Department of Water Supply Services
Comiston Springs
55 Buckstone Terrace, Edinburgh
Tel: 031 445 4141

DONOLLY RESERVOIR
Lothian Regional Council
Department of Water Supply Services
Alderston House
Haddington, East Lothian
Tel: 062 082 2109

FRUID RESERVOIR
Lothian Regional Council
Department of Water Supply Services
Comiston Springs
55 Buckstone Terrace, Edinburgh
Tel: 031 445 4141

GLADHOUSE RESERVOIR
Lothian Regional Council
Department of Water Supply Services
Comiston Springs
55 Buckstone Terrace, Edinburgh
Tel: 031 445 4141

GLENCORSE RESERVOIR
Lothian Regional Council
Department of Water Supply Services
Comiston Springs
55 Buckstone Terrace, Edinburgh
Tel: 031 445 4141

HARLAW RESERVOIR
Lothian Regional Council
Department of Water Supply Services
Comiston Springs
55 Buckstone Terrace, Edinburgh
Tel: 031 445 4141

HARPERRIG RESERVOIR
Lothian Regional Council
Department of Water Supply Services
Comiston Springs
55 Buckstone Terrace, Edinburgh
Tel: 031 445 4141

HOPES RESERVOIR
Lothian Regional Council
Department of Water Supply Services
Alderston House
Haddington, East Lothian
Tel: 062 082 2109

LINLITHGOW LOCH
Rod & Gun, 13 High Street
Boatman at The Loch

NORTH ESK RESERVOIR
Fairliehope Farm, Carlops

ROSEBERRY RESERVOIR
Lothian Regional Council
Department of Water Supply Services
Comiston Springs
55 Buckstone Terrace, Edinburgh
Tel: 031 445 4141

TALLA RESERVOIR
Lothian Regional Council
Department of Water Supply Services
Comiston Springs
55 Buckstone Terrace, Edinburgh
Tel: 031 445 4141

THREIPMUIR RESERVOIR
Flemings
42 Main Street, Balerno

WHITEADDER RESERVOIR
Lothian Regional Council
Department of Water Supply Services
Alderston House
Haddington, East Lothian
Tel: 062 082 2109

STRATHCLYDE REGIO

RIVERS

Add River
Poltalloch Estate Office

nick Water
eghorn Angling Club
: D. Muir
0294 213137
and week permits

ich River
permits available from
estry Office, Dalavich, by Taynuilt, Loch
ch 258

on River
n A.C.
: T. M. Hamilton
0698 793517
o see entry under Grampian Region

e River
ERAWE AND LORN BEAT
erawe Fisheries
erawe Barn, Taynuilt
086 62 262
anaiseig Hotel
arenan by Taynuilt
086 63 333
and week permits available

CKAIRN BEAT
and week permits from
. Nelson, Muckairn, Taynuilt 241

RRAGE BEAT (SOUTH BANK
LY)
ekly permits from Bell, Ingram,
burgh
031 225 3271

r River
A.C.
P. Mack
0292 60275

ngan Youth Group A.C.
M. Harvey
029 258 840

hinleck A.A.
J. McColm
Milne Avenue, Auchinleck
0290 21953
permits also available from:
ctor of Finance
n Buildings, Ayr
llan
yle Street, Ayr
esport, 60 Sandgate, Ayr
glish
nconner Avenue, Auchinleck
wood & Johnstone, Newsagent
Cross, Mauchline
amson, Post Office
n Street, Ochiltree

art River
winbanks
kle & Books, Main Street
ermory, Isle of Mull
0688 2336
permits available

ck Cart River
tle A.C.
E. W. Griffiths
Villiam Street, Johnstone

Burnock Water
Linwood & Johnstone
Newsagent, The Cross, Mauchline

A. Samson
Post Office
Main Street, Ochiltree

Carse Burn
Head Forester
Torinturk, West Loch Tarbert
Tel: 08802 566
Day permits

Cessnock Water
Hurlford A.C.
Sec: J. Miller
Tel: 0563 35122

Linwood & Johnstone
Newsagents, The Cross, Mauchline
Day and week permits available

A. Samson
Post Office
Main Street, Ochiltree

Clyde River
LOWER STRETCHES (TO MOUTH)
United Clyde Angling Protective Assoc.
Ltd.
Sec: R. C. Sharp
20 Cunningham Street, Motherwell
Tel: 0698 62960
Permits also available from:
Most Tackle Dealers in Glasgow,
Edinburgh and main West of Scotland
towns
Day and annual permits available

Clyde River
UPPER STRETCHES
Lanark & District Angling Club
Sec: A. C. McLean
Tel: 0555 4879
(Please enclose S.A.E. to 137 St. Leonards
Street, Lanark)

Clyde River
ROBERTON-THANKERTON STRETCH
United Clyde Angling Protective Assoc.
Ltd.
Sec: R. Sharp
20 Cunningham Street, Motherwell
Tel: 0698 62960
Day and annual permits available

Lamington & District Angling
Improvement Association
Sec: J. Hyslop
Donnachie Cottage, Biggar ML12 6EP
Tel: 0899 20616
Day, week and season permits available
from Bailiff on bank, Secretary and Bryden
Newsagent, Biggar

Coniglen Water
Kintyre Fish Protection and A.C.
Sec: Rev. J. McFie
Tel: 0586 2605

Coyle River
Drongan Youth Group Angling Club
Sec: J. Hunter
52 Bonnyton Avenue, Drongan, Ayrshire

KA6 7OG
Tel: 029 258 814
Season permits available from Secretary
and
James Kirk (Tackle Dealers), 5 Union
Arcade, Burns Statue Square, Ayr

Doon River
Dalrymple A.C.
Sec: J. Black
Portland Road, Dalrymple
No day permits available from above club

Drumgrange & Keirs A.C.
Sec: S. J. Taylor
9 Carsphairn Road, Dalmellington

Hollybush House Hotel
Hollybush
Tel: 029 256 214
Day permits available

Euchar River
J. T. P. Mellor
Barndromin Farm, Knipoch by Oban
Tel: 085 26 273
Day permits available

Mrs M. McCorkindale
Lochview, Kilninver by Oban
Tel: 085 26 200
Day permits available

Finnart River
Chief Forester
Forest Office, Benmore Forest
Kilmun, by Dunoon
Day permits available

Forsa River
Glenforsa Hotel
by Salen, Isle of Mull, Argyll
Day and week permits available

Tackle & Books
Main Street
Tobermory, Isle of Mull
Day permits available

Mr Duncan Swinbanks
Tel: 0688 2336

Fyne River
Arkinglas Estate Office
Cairndow, Argyll
Tel: 049 96 217
Cairndow Estate
Tel: 049 96 284
Day permits available

Garnock River
KILWINNING
Eglinton A.C.
Sec: M. S. Tudhope
Tel: 0294 53652

Glazert River
Kilmaurs A.C.
Sec: J. Watson
Tel: 056 381267

Goil River
Chief Forester
Forest Office, Ardgartan Forest, Arrochar

Gryffe River

Strathgryfe A.A.
Sec: F. Sinclair
'Dunedin', Port Glasgow Road, Kilmacolm
PA13 4QG
Tel: 549 2435
Day permits available from Cross Cafe,
Kilmacolm

Irvine River

Dreghorn Angling Club
Sec: D. Muir
Tel: 0294 213137
Day and week permits

Irvine & District Angling Club
Sec: R. Gilmour
58 Muir Drive, Irvine
Day and week permits also available from:
Currie's Sports Shop, Townhead
Season permits from secretary only

Hurlford A.C.
Sec: J. Miller
Tel: 0563 35122

Kilmarnock A.C.
Sec: H. Grubb
33 Lochnager Road, Bellfield, Kilmarnock
Tel: 0563 27574
Day and week permits available from
McCririck & Sons, 38 John Finnie Street,
Kilmarnock
Tel: 0563 25577

Leven River

Loch Lomond Angling Improvement Assoc.
c/o Messrs R. A. Clement & Co.
Sec: C. A. Ingram
224 Ingram Street, Glasgow
Day, week and season permits also
available from:
Various Tackle Makers

Inverbeg Hotel
Near Luss
Tel: 043 686 279

Liever River

Mrs Cameron
Ford Post Office, Ford 271
Tel: 054 681 271
Day permits available from above

Lugar River

Auchinleck A.A.
Sec: J. McColm
21 Milne Avenue, Auchinleck
Tel: 0290 21953
Day permits also available from:
J. English
1 Darnconner Avenue, Auchinleck
Linwood & Johnstone, Newsagent
The Cross, Mauchline
A. Sampson, Post Office
Main Street, Ochiltree

Machrie Water

J. T. Boscawan
The Estate Office
Killiechassie, Aberfeldy
Day and week permits available

North Esk

Melville Castle
Lesswade, Midlothian
Tel: 031 663 6633

Orchy River

DALMALLY BEAT AND AUCH WATER BEAT
Day permits from:
Croggan Crafts, Dalmally 201
Tel: 083 82 201

STRONMILCHAN BEAT
Permits from J.A. Tattersfield, Windy
Ridge, Brigg Road, Wressle
Tel: 0652 53235

CRAIG LODGE BEAT
Day permits from C. MacFarlane-Barrow,
Craig Lodge, Dalmally 216

CRAIG BEAT
Weekly permits from J. K. Miller,
Turnworth House, Blandford, Dorset
Tel: 0258 53166

UPPER CRAIG BEAT
Day permits from L. Campbell,
Arichastlich, Glen Orchy, Dalmally 282

INVERORAN HOTEL BEAT
Day permits from Hotel, Black Mount,
Bridge of Orchy, Tyndrum 220

STILLWATERS

AROS LOCH
Tobermory A.A.
Sec: A. D. Brown
Stronsaule, Tobermory
Tel: 0688 2331
Day and week permits available from
A. Brown & Son, 21 Main Street,
Tobermory, Isle of Mull

ARDTORNISH ESTATES HILLS LOCHS
Ardtornish Estate Office
Morvern, by Oban
Tel: 096 784 288
Day permits available

ARGYLL ESTATES HILL LOCHS
Argyll Estates Office
Cherry Park, Inveraray
Tel: 0499 2203
Permits available on application to above

ASGOG LOCH
Kyles of Bute Angling Club (Game Fishing)
Sec: A. Morrison
Tel: 070 081 458
Permits also available from:
Shops in Kames & Tighnabruaich
Bute Estate Office (Coarse Fishing)
Rothesay, Isle of Bute
Tel: 0700 2627

ASSOPOL LOCH
Argyll Arms Hotel
Bunessan, Isle of Mull
Tel: 068 17 240
Day, week and month permits available

AUCHALOCHY LOCH
Kintyre Fish Protection A.C.
Sec: Re. J. McFie
Tel: 0586 2605

AVICH LOCH
Chief Forester, Forest Office
Dalavich, by Taynuilt
Tel: 086 64 258
Day and week permits available from
above

AWE LOCH
Chief Forester, Forest Office
Dalavish, by Taynuilt
Tel: 086 64 258
Portsonachan Hotel
by Dalmally
Tel: 086 63 224

BRANDER BEAT
Day permits available from Hydro Board
Visitor Reception, Cruachan, Taynuilt 67

BA LOCH
Day permits available from
King's House Hotel, Glencoe, Argyll
Tel: 085 56 259

BALLOCK – MOSS LOCHANS
Gluddoch House Hotel, Langbank

BARCRAIGS RESERVOIR
Rowbank A.C.
Sec: A. C. Wilson
Tel: 041 889 3459

BARNLUASGAN LOCH
Chief Forester, Forest Office
Knapdale Forest, Cairnbaan, Lochgilphe
Tel: 0546 2304
Mrs Robertson
Barnluavsgan, Lochgilphead
Day permits available

BRADAN LOCH
R. Heaney
Talaminnoch, Straiton
Tel: 065 57 617
Day and week permits available

BROCKBOWIE LOCH
R. Heaney
Talaminnoch, Straiton
Tel: 065 57 617
Day permits available

BURNFOOT RESERVOIR
Kilmarnock A.C.
Sec: H. Grubb
33 Lochnagar Road, Bellfield, Kilmarnoc
Tel: 0563 27574
Day and week permits available from
McCririck & Sons, 38 John Finnie Street
Kilmarnock
Tel: 0563 25577

BUSBIE RESERVOIR
Bobby's Mini Market
Chapelhill Mount
The Tackle Shop

Harbour Road, Ardrossan
ay and week permits

AM LOCH
rs Cameron
rd Post Office, Ford 271
el: 054 681 271
ay permits available from above

ASTLE FISHERIES
ay permits available from
rm Kiosk, Inveraray 2233

OILLE BHAR LOCH
hief Forester, Forest Office
apdale Forest, Cairnbaan
chgilphead
el: 0546 2304
rs Robertson
rnluasgan, Lochgilphead

OLL ESTATE LOCHS
ay and week permits available from
ctor, Coll Estate House, Arinagour,
le of Coll, Argyll

RAIGENDUNTON RESERVOIR
lmarnock A.C.
c: H. Grubb
Lochnagar Road, Bellfield, Kilmarnock
el: 0563 27574
ay and week permits available from
cCririck & Sons, 38 John Finnie Street,
lmarnock
el: 0563 25577

ROSSHILL LOCH
ntyre Fish Protection & A.C.
c: Rev. J. McFie
l: 0586 2605

HU LOCH
Heaney
laminnoch, Straiton
l: 065 57 617
y permit available

JBH LOCH
y permits available from
. P. Mellor, Barndromin Farm, Knipoch,
Oban, Argyll
l: 085 26 273

JBH MOR LOCH
ief Forester, Forest Office
rcaldine, Connel
l: 063 172 203
y permit available

K LOCH
istleford Inn
ch Eck, by Dunoon
l: 036 986 250
y permit available

ERLINE HILL LOCHS
y permits from Ford Hotel, Ford 273

D LOCH
y and week permits available from
e Estate Office, Rothesay, Isle of Bute
l: 0700 2627

NLAS LOCH
las F.C.
: W. A. McMillan
: 0292 64002
day permits

GLASHAN LOCH
Lochgair Hotel
by Lochgilphead
Tel: 054 682 233
Day permit available

GLEANN A'BHEARRADCH LOCH
Cologin Homes Ltd
Lerags, by Oban
Tel: 0631 4501
The Barn Bar, Cologin
Lerags, by Oban
Day permits available

GLEN DUBH RESERVOIR
Chief Forester, Forest Office
Barcaldine, Connel
Tel: 063 172 203
Day permit available

GORM LOCH
Machrie Hotel
Port Ellen, Isle of Islay
Tel: 0496 2310
Port Charlotte Hotel
Isle of Islay
Tel: 049 685 321
Day permits available

GRYFFE LOCH (LOWER)
Port Glasgow A.C.
Sec: I. Tucker
Tel: 0475 705012

HELENSBURGH RESERVOIRS 1 & 2
Helensburgh A.C.
Sec: J. F. McCreath
37 Bain Crescent, Helensburgh G84 9DP
Tel: 0436 4850
**Day permits available by writing to
Club treasurer, 75 West Clyde Street,
Helensburgh**

INVERAWE FISHERIES
½ day and day permits available at
Fishing Hut, Taynuilt 262

KNOCKNAIRSHILL LOCH
Port Glasgow A.C.
Sec: I. Tucker
Tel: 0475 705012

KYPE RESERVOIR
The Keeper at The Reservoir
Tel: 0357 20114
Day permits available

LINFERN LOCH
R. Heaney
Talaminnoch, Straiton
Tel: 065 57 617

LINNHE LOCH
Chief Forester, Forest Office
Knapdale Forest, Cairnbaan
Lochgilphead
Tel: 0546 2304
Day permits available

LOCHAIN GHLEANN LOCHA
Kilchoan Hotel, Ardnamurchan
Tel: 097 23200
Day permits available

LOMOND LOCH
Loch Lomond Angling Improvement Assoc.
c/o Messrs R. A. Clement & Co.
C. A. Ingrams
Tel: 041 221 0068
Day and week permits also available from:
Various Tackle Makers
Inverbeg Hotel, near Luss
Tel: 043 686 279
Ardlui Hotel, Ardlui
Loch Lomond, by Arrochar
Tel: 030 14 243
Rowardennan Hotel, by Drymen
Tel: 036 087 273

LOSGUNN LOCH
The Chief Forester
Forest Office, Knapdale Forest,
Cairnbaan, Lochgilphead
Tel: 0546 2304

LUSSA LOCH
Kintyre Fish Protection & Angling Club
Sec: Rev. J. McFie
Lochend Manse, Campbeltown
Tel: 0586 2605
**Day, week and season permits also
available from:**
R. Armour & Sons
Longrow, Campbeltown

MILL RESERVOIR
Port Glasgow A.C.
Sec: I. Tucker
Tel: 0475 705012
Bobby's Mini Market
Chapelhill Mount
The Tackle Shop
4 Harbour Road, Ardrossan

MISHNISH LOCHS
Tobermory A.A.
Sec: A. D. Brown
Stronsaule, Tobermory
Tel: 0688 2381
Day and week permits available from
A. Brown & Son, 21 Main Street,
Tobermory, Isle of Mull

MUDLE LOCH
Kilchoan Hotel
Ardnamurchan
Tel: 097 23 200

NANT LOCH
Kilchronan Trading Post
Kilchronan
Tel: 086 63 232
Day permits available from above

NORTH CRAIG RESERVOIR
Kilmaurs A.C.
Sec: J. Watson
Tel: 056 381 267

PENWHAPPLE RESERVOIR
Penwhapple F.C.
Sec: J. H. Murray
3 & 120A Dalrymple Street, Girvan
Tel: 0465 2039
**Day and weekly permits available from
Bungalow at Loch**

243

POWDERWORKS RESERVOIR
(Upper and Lower Powder Dams)
Kyles of Bute Angling Club
Sec: A. Morrison
Tel: 070 081 458
Permits also available from:
Several Shops in Kames & Tighnabruaich

PRESTWICK RESERVOIR
Prestwick Angling Club
c/o The Wheatsheaf Inn
Main Street, Monkton
Sec: J. B. Gibson
67 Seaforth Road, Ayr
Day permits available

QUIEN LOCH
Bute Estate Office
Rothesay, Isle of Bute
Tel: 0700 2627
Day permits available

ROWBANK RESERVOIR
Rowbank A.C.
Sec: A. C. Wilson
Tel: 041 889 3459

RUAN LOCH
Kintyre Fish Protection & A.C.
Sec: Rev. J. McFie
Tel: 0586 2605

SCAMADALE LOCH
Mrs M. McCorkindale
Lochview, Kilninver, by Oban
Day permits available

SEAFIELD LOCH
The Chief Forester
Forest Office, Knapdale Forest,
Cairbaan, Lochgilphead
Tel: 0546 2304

SEIL LOCH
J. T. P. Mellor
Barndromin Farm, Knipoch, by Oban
Tel: 085 26 273
Day permits available

SKELLOCH LOCH
R. Heaney
Talaminnoch, Straiton
Tel: 065 57 617
Forestry Commission, Carrick
Forest Office, Barr
Weekly and day permits available

TARSAN LOCH
Dunoon & District Angling Club
Hon Sec: J. G. Lindsay Pate
Tel: 0369 2631
Day, week and season permits also available from:
G. Scott, Ironmonger
108 Argyle Street, Dunoon
Tel: 0369 2121

TIGHNABRUAICH RESERVOIR
Kyles of Bute Angling Club
Sec: A. Morrison
Tel: 070 081 458
Permits also available from:
Several shops in Kames & Tighnabruaich

TORR LOCH
D. Swinbanks
Tackle & Books, Main Street,
Tobermory, Isleof Mull
Tel: 0688 2336
Day permits available

TULLA LOCH
Permits available from
Inveroran Hotel, Black Mount,
Bridge of Orchy, Tyndrum 220

TAYSIDE REGION

RIVERS

Airneyfoul River
Sec: E. S. Mann
44 Sheriff Park Gardens, Forfar

Ardle River
Permits available from
Corriefodly Hotel, Bridge of Cally,
Blairgowrie
Tel: 025 086 236
Bridge of Cally Hotel, Bridge of Cally
Tel: 025 086 231
The Log Cabin Hotel, Glen Derby,
Kirkmichael
Tel: 025 081 288

Balvag River
Messrs D. Crockart & Son
15 King Street, Stirling
Tel: 0786 3443
Day and season permits available

Braan River
Dunkeld and Birnam A.A.
Sec: J. Duncan
c/o R. Scott-Miller
Top Shop, Atholl Street, Dunkeld
Tel: 035 02556

Amulree Hotel
Amulree, by Dunkeld
Tel: 035 05 218
Day permits available (free to hotel residents)

Dean Water
Rescobie Loch Development Assoc.
Sec: R. Herdman
112 Millfield Road, Arbroath, Angus
DO11 4HN
Strathmore Assoc. Water
Day and season permits available from T.
Clark & Sons, High Street, Arbroath

Canmore Angling Club
Sec: E. Mann
44 Sheriff Park Gardens

Forfar, Angus
Day and week permits available

Strathmore Angling Improvement Assoc.
Sec: J. Christie
51 Broadford Terrace
Broughty Ferry, Dundee
Tel: 0382 736462
Day and season permits also available from:
J. R. Gow & Sons
12 Union Street, Dundee
Shotcast
Whitehall Crescent, Dundee
Mr Carnegie
Crathie Bridge, Meigle
C. Kerr
1 West High Street, Forfar

Devon River
Rumbling Bridge Hotel

Dochart River
See also Central Region
D. & S. Allan, Fishing Tackle Shop
Main Street, Killin
Tel: 056 72 362
Day and week permits available

Earn River
See also Fife Region
St. Fillans & Lochearn A.A.
Sec Tel: 076 485 219
Permits available from Post Office,
St. Fillans
Tel: 076 485 220
Lochearnhead Post Office, Lochearnhead
Tel: 056 73 201
Royal Hotel, Melville Square, Comrie
Tel: 076 47 200
Day permits available (free to residents)

Eright River
Bridge of Cally Hotel
Bridge of Cally
Tel: 025 086 231

Gaur River
Moor of Rannoch Hotel
Rannoch Station
Tel: 088 23 238

River Girron Burn
Amulree Hotel
Amulree, by Dunkeld
Tel: 035 05 218
Day permits available (free to residents)

Glen Esk
Rescobie Loch Development Assoc
Sec: R. Herdman
112 Millfield Road, Arbroath, Angus
DD11 4HN
Day and season permits available from:
Dalhousie Estates, Swan Street, Brechin

Kerbert Water
Canmore Angling Club
Sec: E. Mann
44 Sheriff Park Gardens, Forfar
Day and week permits available

Loch

cobie Loch Development Assoc.
R. Herdman
Millfield Road, Arbroath, Angus
4HN
nd season permits available from
stler
35 67208

no River

nore A.C.
E. S. Mann
eriff Park Gardens, Forfar

hsie River

nunzie Hotel
shee
)25 085 224/5

ver Isla

hmore Angling Improvement
oc.
J. Christie
roadford Terrace
ghton Ferry, Dundee
)382 736462
its also available from:
Gow & Sons
nion Street, Dundee
cast, Whitehall Crescent, Dundee
Carnegie
hie Bridge, Meigle

an Water

cobie Loch Development Assoc.
R. Herdman
Millfield Road, Arbroath, Angus
1 4HN
roath A.C. waters
and season permits available from
lark & Sons, High Street, Arbroath

n River

ingall Hotel
ingall by Aberfelby
088 73 367
permits available

hieville Hotel
Aberfeldy
088 73 319
permits available

ran Water

more Angling Club
E. Mann
heriff Park Gardens, Forfar
and week permits available

er North Esk

LLERY AND HATTON BEATS
s Hotel
trose
0674 2288
permits available

CRAIGO BEAT
Montrose & District A.C.
Sec: G. S. Taylor
Tel: 0674 3904

KINABER ROAD BRIDGE TO MORPHIE DAM
Rescobie Loch Development Assoc.
Sec: R. Herdman
112 Millfield Road, Arbroath, Angus
DD11 4HN
Day and season permits available from:
Johnstone Ltd., Salmon Fisher, Montrose

South Esk River

Kirriemuir Angling Club
Sec: H. F. Burness
Tel: 057 52 3456
Permits in advance from secretary

Montrose & District A.C.
Sec: G. S. Taylor
Tel: 0674 3904

JUSTINHAUGE HOTEL SRETCH
Rescobie Loch Development Assoc.
Sec: R. Herdman
112 Millfield Road, Arbroath, Angus
DD11 4HN
Day and season permits available from:
Justinhaugh Hotel

GLEN CLOVA STRETCH
Rescobie Loch Development Assoc.
Sec: R. Herdman
112 Millfield Road, Arbroath, Angus
DD11 4HN
Day and season permits available from:
Ogilvie Hotel & Kirriemuir A.C.

Tay River

Aberfeldy A.C.
Sec: D. Campbell
Tel: 088 74 354

Loch Tay Guest House
Kenmore
Tel: 088 73 236

Director of Finances Offices
Perth
Day and week permits available

Kinloch House Hotel
Dunkeld Road, Blairgowrie
Tel: 025 084 237
Day permits avaiable

Muirton House Hotel
Essendy Road, Blairgowrie
Tel: 0250 2113
Day permits available

Dunkeld House Hotel
Dunkeld
Tel: 035 02 243
Day permits available

Ballathie Estate Office
Ballathie Farms near Stanley
Tel: 025 083 250
Week permits available

Royal Geoge Hotel
Tay Street, Perth

Logierait Hotel
Ballinluig
Tel: 079 682 253
Day and week permits available

Post Offices
Dunkeld & Birnam
Day and week permits available

R. Scott-Miller
Top Shop, Atholl Street, Dunkeld
Tel: 035 02 556
Day and week permits avail able

Weem Hotel
Weem, by Aberfeldy
Tel: 088 72 381
Day permits available

Grandtully Hotel
Strathtay
Tel: 088 74 207
Day permits available

WITHIN BOUNDARIES OF CITY OF PERTH
Director of Finance
Perth & Kinross District Council
1 High Street, Perth
Tel: 0738 21161
Day permits available

Tummel River

Pitlochry Angling Club
Sec: R. Harriman
Sunnyknowe, 7 Nursing Home Brae,
Pitlochry
Tel: 0796 2484
Day, week and season permits available
from Information Centre,
P. D. Malloch and Ballinluig Post Office

West Water

Brechin A.C.
Sec: D. E. Smith
3 Friendly Park, Brechin, Angus DD9 6RF
Day permits available from
The Sports Shop, Brechin

Rescobie Loch Development Assoc.
Sec: R. Herdman
112 Millfield Road, Arbroath, Angus
DD11 4HN
Day and season permits available from
Brian's, Lordburn Street, Arbroath
Leased by Arbroath A.C.

STILLWATERS

ACHRAY LOCH
Chief Forester
Achray Forest Office, Aberfoyle
Day permits available

BHAC LOCH
Pitlochry Angling Club
Sec: R. Harriman
Sunnyknowe, 7 Nursing Home Brae,
Pitlochry
Tel: 0796 2484
**Day permits available from Airdaniar Hotel,
Atholl Road, Pitlochry**
Tel: 0796 2266

BORDER HOLES LOCH
Brechin A.C.
Sec: W. Brooks
Tel: 035 62 3257

BUTTERSTONE LOCH
Bailiff:
Lochend Cottage, Butterstone
Tel: 035 04 238
Day and evening permits available

CARDNEY LOCH
Gamekeeper: C. Hitchings
Day permits available
Tel: 035 04 248

CHON LOCH
C. MacNair
Frenich Farm, Aberfoyle
Day permits available

CURRAN LOCH
The Log Cabin Hotel
Glen Derby, Kirkmichael
Tel: 025 081 288

DRUNKIE LOCH
Chief Forester
Achray Forest Office, Aberfoyle
Day permit available

DUNALASTAIR RESERVOIR
Dunalastair Hotel
Kinloch Rannoch
Tel: 088 22 323

EARN LOCH
St. Fillans & Loch Earn A.A.
Sec's Tel: 076 485 219
**Permits also available from:
Post Office, S. Fillans**
Tel: 076 485 220
**Lochearnhead Post Office
Lochearnhead**
Tel: 056 73 201

EIGHEACH LOCH
Rannoch & District Angling Club
Sec: J. Brown
The Square, Kinloch Rannock, by Pitlochry
PH16 5PN
Tel: 088 22 331
½ day, day, week, month and season
permits available from secretary above

FASKALLY LOCH
P. Williamson
Boathouse, Loch Faskally
Pitlochry
Tel: 0796 2919
Day permits available

FORFAR LOCH
Canmore Angling Club
Sec: E. Mann
44 Sheriff Park Gardens, Forfar
**Day and season permits also available
from:**
C. Kerr
1 West High Street, Forfar

GARRY LOCH
Pitlochry Angling Club
Sec: R. Harriman
Sunnyknowe, 7 Nursing Home Brae,
Pitlochry
Tel: 0796 2484
**Day permits from Airdaniar Hotel, Atholl
Road, Pitlochry and
Mr. Kennedy, Dalnaspidal Lodge**

GLENDEVON
Upper and Lower Reservoirs
D. Crombie, Regional Water Engineer
Fife Regional Council, Water Division
Glenrothes, Fife
Tel: 0592 756541

GLENFARG RESERVOIR
D. Crombie, Regional Water Engineer
Fife Regional Council
Water Division, Glenrothes, Fife
Tel: 0592 756541

GLENOGIL RESERVOIR
Canmore Angling Club
Sec: E. Mann
44 Sheriff Park Gardens, Forfar
Day permits available

KINARDOCHY LOCH
Pitlochry Angling Club
Sec: R. Harriman
Sunnyknowe, 7 Nursing Home Brae,
Pitlochry
Tel: 0796 2484
**Day permits available from
Airdaniar Hotel, Atholl Road, Pitlochry**
Tel: 0796 2266

LAIDON LOCH
Moor of Rannoch Hotel
Rannoch Station
Tel: 088 23 238

LEVEN LOCH
Loch Leven Fisheries
The Pier, Kinross
Tel: 0577 63407

LEVEN CUT
Loch Leven sluices to Auchmuir Bridge
River Leven Trust, Sluice House, Loch
Leven
Tel: 059 284 225
Day and season permits available

LOCHAN-NA-LARIGE
D. & S. Allan
Fishing Tackle Shop
Main Street, Killin
Tel: 056 72 362
Day and week permits available

RANNOCH LOCH
Loch Rannoch Conservation Assoc.
Sec: Dr S. Fordham
Cluain Na Coille, Dall, Rannoch Station
Tel: 088 22379
**Day and week permits also available from
Kinloch Rannoch hotels or shop or with
surcharge from bailiff on bank**

REOIDHTE LOCH
Chief Forester
Achray Forest Office, Aberfoyle
Day permits available

RESCOBIE LOCH
Rescobie Loch Development Assoc.
Sec: R. Herdman
112 Millfield Road, Arbroath, Angus
DD11 4HN
**Day and season permits available from
T. Clark & Sons, High Street, Arbroath**

SAUGH LOCH
Brechin Angling Club
Sec: D. E. Smith
3 Friendly Park, Brechin, Angus DD9 6RF
**Day permits also available from:
Sports Shop
High Street, Brechin**
Tel: 035 62 2491
**Ramsay Arms Hotel, Fettercairn
Drumtochty Arms Hotel, Auchenblae**

TAY LOCH
D. & S. Allan, Fishing Tackle Shop
Main Street, Killin
Tel: 056 72 362
Day and week permits available
Loch Tay Guest House, Kenmore
Tel: 088 73 236
Killin Hotel, Killin
Tel: 056 72 296
Day permits available (free to residents)
Adreonaig Hotel
South Loch Tayside, by Killin
Tel: 056 72 400
Day permits available
Ben Lawers Hotel, by Aberfeldy
Tel: 056 72 436

TULLOCHCURRAN LOCH
The Log Cabin Hotel
Glen Derby, Kirkmichael
Tel: 025 081 288

TUMMEL LOCH
Queens View Hotel
Strathtummel, by Pitlochry
(Free to residents)

VOIL LOCH
Ledcreich Hotel
Balquhidder by Lochearnhead
Tel: 087 74 230
Day permits available (free to resdents)

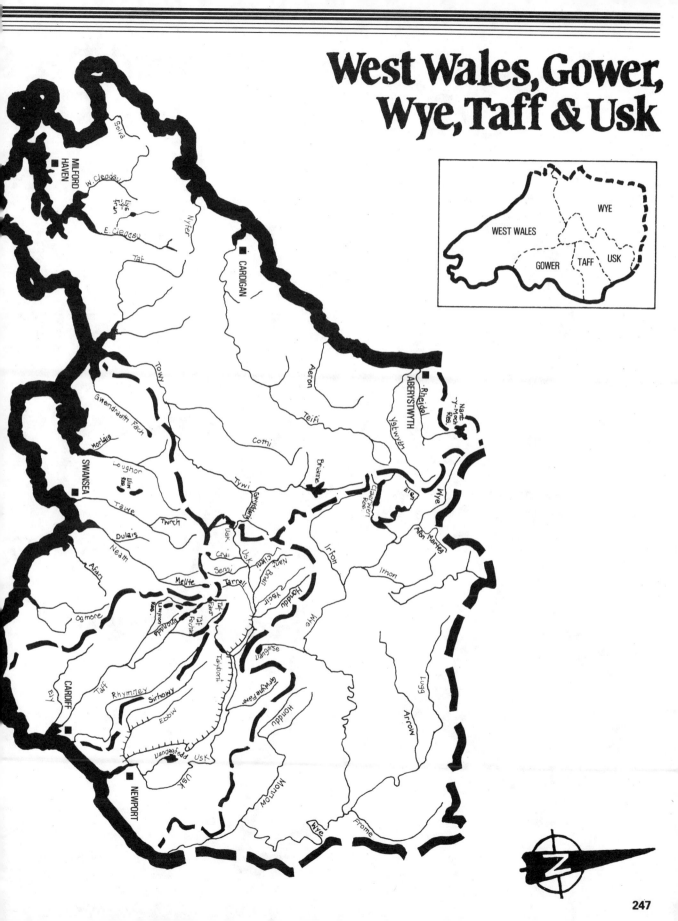

West Wales, Gower, Wye, Taff & Usk

WEST WALES

WYE

GOWER TAFF USK

MILFORD HAVEN

Solva

W. Cleddau

E. Cleddau

Nyfer

Taf

CARDIGAN

Aeron

Teifi

Towy

Gwendraeth Fach

Cothi

ABERYSTWYTH

Rheidol

Nant-y-Moch Res.

Ystwyth

SWANSEA

Morlais

Loughor

Lliw Res.

Tawe

Twrch

Tywi

Gwydderig

Brianne

Claerwen Res.

Elan

Wye

Afon Marteg

Dulais

Neath

Usk

Crai

Usk

Senni

Nant-Bran

Cledan

Irfon

Ithon

Afan

Mellte

Tarrell

Yscir

Honddu

Cynrig

 Clydach

Ogmore

Taf Fechan

Taf Fawr

Llangorse

Grwyne Fawr

Honddu

Wye

Lugg

Ely

CARDIFF

Taff

Rhymney

Sirhowy

Ebbw

Talybont

Llangynidr

Usk

Arrow

NEWPORT

Usk

Monnow

Wye

Frome

247

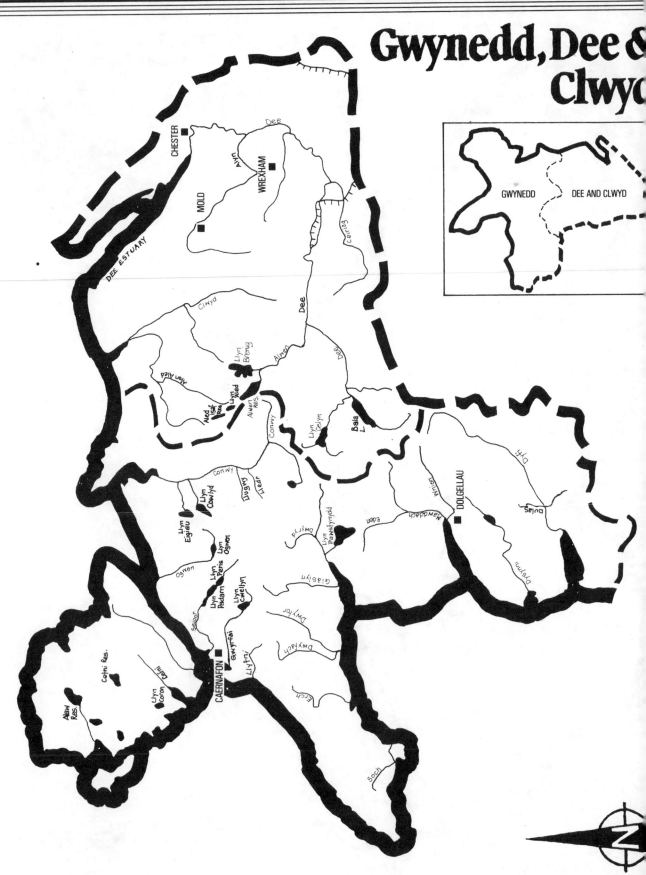

Gwynedd, Dee & Clwyd

CHESTER

WREXHAM

MOLD

DEE ESTUARY

Dee

Alyn

Ceiriog

Clwyd

Dee

Llyn Brenig

Alwen

Afon Aled

Llyn Aled

Aled Isaf Res.

Alwen Res.

Conwy

Llyn Celyn

Bala L.

Dee

Conwy

Llugwy

Lledr

Llyn Cowlyd

Llyn Eigiau

Ogwen

Llyn Ogwen

Dwyryd

Llyn Trawsfynydd

Eden

Mawddach

Wnion

DOLGELLAU

Dyfi

Dulas

Dysynni

Ogwen

Llyn Padarn

Llyn Peris

Llyn Cwellyn

Glaslyn

Seiont

Llyfni

Gwyrfai

CAERNAFON

Llyn Cwellyn

Dwyfor

Dwyfach

Erch

Soch

Cefni

Llyn Coron

Alaw Res.

Cefni Res.

GWYNEDD   DEE AND CLWYD

N

elsh
ater
uthority

Head Bailiff – South:
G. Thomas
Dolafon, Maerdy, Corwen, Clwyd
Tel: 049 081 413

Head Bailiff – North:
W. Forkings
Seven Springs, Caerwys, Nr. Mold
Tel: 035 282 511

RIVERS

Maelor A.A.
Sec: K. Bathers
Sunnyside Hill Street, Cefn Mawr, near Wrexham
Tel: 0978 820608
Day and week permits also available from:
Secretary and local tackle shops

CORWEN TO BALA
Chirk A.A.
Sec: J. L. Davies
Tel: 069 186 7378

Corwen & District A.C.
Sec: M. J. Green
Tel: 0490 2369

Bala A.A.
Sec: D. M. Rees
21 Tremyffridd, Bala

nbrian Way
con
vys
0874 3181
ntact: Public Information
partment

Dee River
CHESTER TO HOLT
Lavister A.C.
Sec: W. A. Smith
Tel: 097 883 2044
Permits also available from:
Tackle dealers in Chester

HOLT TO RUABON
Bangor A.A.
c/o The Stores, Bangor-on-Dee
Tel: 0978 780430
Chairman
Tel: 0978 780260

Glyndwr Preservers
Midland Fly Fishers
I. A. Morris, The Lodge
Biudd, Llangollen
Permits from Royal Hotel
Llangollen
Tel: 0978 860202

Holt & Farndon A.C.
Sec: R. Williams
Tel: 0829 270891

Liverpool & District A.A.
Sec: J. Johnson
Tel: 051 526 4083

OVERTON-ON-DEE
Boat Inn Water
Permits from J. Chamberlain
Tel: 097 873 243
Advance booking advisable

RUABON TO CORWEN
Bryn-y-Pys A.A.
Sec: H. V. Guest
Bryn-Hovah, Bangor-on-Dee, Wrexham
Day permits available from Mrs Jones, Tackle Shop, Wrexham

Liverpool & District A.A.
Sec: J. Johnson
Tel: 051 526 4083

Llangollen A.A.
Sec: W. N. Elbourne
12 Chapel Sreet, Llangollen LL20 8NN
Permits by written or personal application only

STILLWATERS

ALED ISAF RESERVOIR
Interpretation Centre, Brenig Reservoir
Cerrig-y-Drudion, Nr. Corwen, Clwyd
Tel: 049 082 463

ALWEN RESERVOIR
Reservoir Keeper, Alwen Reservoir
Cerrig-y-Drudion, Nr. Corwen, Clwyd
Tel: 049 082 208

BALA LAKE
(Llyn Tegid)
D. Bowen, Lake Warden
Permits also available from:
R. E. Evans, BradfordHouse
High Street, Bala

BOLESWORTH CASTLE LAKE
Stoke on Trent A.C.
Sec: S. F. Broadgate
Tel: 0782 618833

THE FLASH LAKE, GRESFORD
Permits available from local angling shops

LLYN ALED RESERVOIR
Interpretation Centre, Brenig Reservoir
Cerrig-y-Drudion, Nr. Corwen, Clwyd
Tel: 049 082 463

LLYN TEGID
See Bala Lake entry

WEPRE POOL
Connah's Quay A.C.
Sec: P. Roberts
Tel: 0244 815643

WIRRAL COUNTRY PARK PONDS
Head Ranger, Wirral Country Park Centre
Station Road, Thurstaston, Merseyside
Tel: 051 648 4371

e W.W.A. introduced a new fishing
nce structure in 1980. Each river has
en categorised from A to G on the basis
the potential and general quality of the
ing. The best waters are those of
ss A.

icence for a particular class of water
titles anglers (if permission has been
nted) to fish in all waters of the same or
er class but not water of a higher class.

EE AND CLWYD
IVISION

re Hall
old
1: 0352 58551

sheries, Recreation and Amenity
fier:
P. Hodgson BSc MSc
l: 0352 58551

ssistant Fisheries, Recreation and
nenity Officer:
M. Scutter BSc
l: 0352 58551

CANALS

Shropshire Union Canal
MAIN LINE, MIDDLEWICH AND LLANGOLLEN BRANCH
Shropshire Union Canal A.A.
Hon. Sec: R. Brown
Tel: 0942 76917

GOWER DIVISION

86 Kingsway, Swansea
Tel: 0792 468000

Divisional Fisheries & Recreation
Officer: A. G. Harvey

Supervisory Bailiff:
S. J. Williams
30 Bryn Morgru, Alltwen
Pontardawe, Swansea
Tel: 0792 863490

RIVERS

Neath River
Neath & Dulais A.A.
Hon. Sec: A. Beasley
Tel: 0639 50878

STILLWATERS

PWLL-Y-WAUN POND
Porthcawl Sea A.A. (Freshwater section)
Hon. Sec: J. Lock
Tel: 065 671 2876

SQUARE POND
Briton Ferry
Metal Box Coarse F.C.
Hon. Sec: J. Hall
Tel: 0639 50375

WILDERNESS POND
Porthcawl Sea A.A. (Freshwater section)
Hon. Sec: J. Lock
Tel: 065 671 2876

GWYNEDD DIVISION

Penrhosgarnedd, Bangor, Gwynedd
Tel: 0248 51144

Fishery, Recreation & Amenities
Officer:
P. J. Parkinson

Assistant Fishery, Recreation &
Amenities Officer:
B. R. Nelson

Area Head Bailiffs:
Dolwyddelan: E. Lloyd Price
Tel: 069 06 250
Criccieth: E. Owen
Tel: 076 671 2582
Dolgellau: D. T. Lloyd
Tel: 0341 422 338

RIVERS

Glyn River
Weekly Tickets Only
Talsarnau & District A.A.
Sec: M. Nelson
Tel: 0766 780254
Permits also available from:
The Post Office, Talsarnau
Tel: 0766 770201

STILLWATERS

CEFNI RESERVOIR
Cefni A.A.
Sec: W. J. Williams
Tel: 024 877 765

EIDDEW BACH
Weekly tickets only
Talsarnau & District A.A.
Sec: M. Nelson
Tel: 0766 780 254
Permits also available from:
The Post Office, Talsarnau
Tel: 0766 770201

EIDDEW MAWR
Weekly tickets only
Talsarnau & District A.A.
Sec: Mr Nelson
Tel: 0766 780 254
Permits also available from:
The Post Office, Talsarnau
Tel: 0766 770201

HAFOD-Y-LLYN
W. Jones
Penarth, Llanbedr, Gwynedd
Tel: 034 123 350

LLYN CORON
Meyrick Estate, Bodorgan Estate Office
Bodorgan, Anglesey
Tel: 040 787 253
Permits also available from Beat Keeper on site

LLYN FEDW
Weekly tickets only
Talsarnau & District A.A.
Sec: Mr Nelson
Tel: 0766 780254
Permits also available from:
The Post Office, Talsarnau
Tel: 0766 770201

LLYN PADARN
Gwynedd Division
Penrhosgarnedd, Bangor, Gwynedd
Fisheries Officer: P. J. Parkinson
Tel: 0248 51144
Permits also available from:
D. Jones, Shop, Goed, Llanberis

LLYN TECWYN UCHAF
Talsarnau & District A.A.
Sec: Mr Nelson
Tel: 0766 780254
Permits also available from:
The Post Office, Talsarnau
Tel: 0766 770201

LLYN TWR
Anglesey Freshwater F.C.
c/o D. John
Bacon Specialist Shop, Market Street,
Holyhead

TAFF DIVISION

Crwys House
Crwys Road
Cardiff
Tel: 0222 399961

Fisheries Officer: John Davies
Head Bailiff: Ivan Bevan

STILLWATERS

BRYN CAE OWEN POND
Merthyr Tydfil A.A.
Hon. Sec: T. Norman
Tel: 0685 76801

CYFARTHFA LAKE
Merthyr Tydfil A.A.
Sec: T. Norman
Tel: 0685 76801

DARREN LAKE
Glyncornell A.A.
Hon. Sec: J. M. Evans
Tel: 0443 439961
Permits also available from:
Sports shops in Rhondda Valley

NANTHIR RESERVOIR
Abadare & District A.A.
Hon. Sec: R. Hancock
Tel: 0685 875209

PENYWERN PONDS
Merthyr Tydfil A.A.
Hon. Sec: T. Norman
Tel: 0685 76801

PONTSTICILL RESERVOIR
The Stores
Pontsticill Reservoir, Nr. Merthyr Tydfil
Tel: 0685 2404
(self issue ticket machine)

ROATH PARK LAKE, CARDIFF
Keepers hut at lakeside

SK DIVISION

ation Buildings, Queensway
ewport, Gwent
el: 0633 840404

shery, Recreation & Amenity Officer:
W. Lambert

ssistant Fishery, Recreation &
nenity Officer: B. Benbow

strict Head Bailiff:
J. Stevens
Woolpitch, Greenmeadow,
wmbran, Gwent
l: 0633 64363

RIVERS

k River
K TO ABERGAVENNY
ergavenny
retches
mits from P.M. Fishing Tackle
Monk Street, Abergavenny
0873 3175

rthyr Tydfil A.A.
: T. R. Norman
0685 76801

ea Chief Clerk
n Hall, Abergavenny
0873 2721
mits also available from:
. Fishing Tackle
Monk Street, Abergavenny

Town Water Fishery Assoc.
C. E. Brain
0633 55587
mits from Sweets Fishing Tackle,
thycarne Street, Usk

ERGAVENNY TO BRECON
Whiting
rdy Cottage, Llanwenarth, Citra
0873 810642

Powell
n Garage, Ebbw Vale

Jay
ge End Inn, Circkhowell

CON TO SOURCE
. Davies
Drug Stores, Sennybridge, Brecon
087 482 221

G. Morgan
syrwyddfa, Sennybridge, Brecon
087 482 252

STILLWATERS

CWMBRAN BOATING LAKE
Torfaen Borough Council
Tel: 0633 67791
Permits available from boathouse keeper at lake

MACHINE POND
Brynmawr
Permits from Brutens
Ebbw Vale
Tel: 0495 303132

TREDEGAR HOUSE LAKE
Tredegar House park attendants

WOODSTOCK POND
Newport A.A.
Sec: P. Climo
Tel: 0633 841029
Permits also available from:
A.R.C. Tackle
60 Caerleon Road, Newport
Tel: 0633 215785
Richards Tackle
Church Road, Newport
Keepers on site

CANALS

Monmouthshire & Brecon Canal
Cwmbran A.C.
Sec: P. M. Guillford
Tel: 06333 5036

LLANGATOCK TO CRICKHOWELL
British Steel Corporation
Season permits from secretary

MAMHILAD
Pontllanfraith A.C.
Sec: L. Watkins
Tel: 0495 223271
Day permits from secretary

Pontypool A.A.
Hon Sec: A. Wakeman
Tel: 04955 4743
Day permits also available from:
Inspector of Waterways
Railway Buildings, Govilon, Gwent
Typoerh Stores, near Jockey Bridge
Sports Shop, Pontypool

CRUMLIN ARM
Permits on towpath or from tackleist in Risca

WEST WALES DIVISION

Meyler House, St. Thomas Green
Haverford West, Dyfed
Tel: 0437 5551

Fisheries, Recreation & Amenities
Officer: R. I. Millichamp

Assistant Fisheries, Recreation &
Amenities Officer: M. Harcup

District and Head Bailiffs:
Towy: D. Brown
Tel: 0550 20060
Pembroke: D. Worthington
Tel: 0994 230722
Upper Teifi: L. W. Laws
Tel: 09744 416
Lower Teifi: W. C. Jones
Tel: 057044 697

RIVERS

Rheidol River
Aberystwyth A.A.
Sec: Dr J. D. Fish
Tel: 0970 828433

Teifi River
Llandyssul A.C.
Sec: A. Jones
Tel: 055932 2317
Weekly permits only

Pontrhydfendigaid A.A.
Sec: D. Lloyd Jones
Rhydteif, Pontrhydfendigaid
Permits from R. Rees & Sons
Florida Shop, Pontrhydfendigaid

Tregaron A.A.
Sec: G. R. Phillips
Tel: 09744 207

COEDMORE
Coedmore Enterprises
Permits from Craft Shop
Cardigan Wildlife Park

Mr Ablett
Highmead Arms Hotel
Llanybydder, Dyfed
Tel: 0570 480258

STILLWATERS

BOSHERTON PONDS
Pembrokeshire & District A.C.
Sec: T. J. Caveney
Tel: 064 684 208

FALCONDALE LAKE
D. E. Davies
Teify Sports, high Street, Lampeter
Tel: 0570 422268

WYE DIVISION

4 St. John Street, Hereford
Tel: 0432 6313

Fisheries, Recreation & Amenities
Officer: E. M. Staite

Assistant Fisheries, Recreation &
Amenities Officer: P. G. Hilder
Head Bailiff:
C. Lloyd
Tel: 04974 227

RIVERS

Cammarch River
Cammarch Hotel
Llangammarch Wells
Tel: 05912 205
Permits available to non-residents

Ithon River
Llandrindod Wells A.A.
Sec: A. H. Selwyn
Tel: 0597 2397
Permits also available from:
C. Bradley
Bradleys Hardware, Builth Wells
Tel: 059 787 2310
C. Selwyn & Sons
4 Park Crescent, Llandrindod Wells
Tel: 0597 2397

Severn Arms Hotel
Penybont, Powys
Tel: 059 787 224
Permits available to non-residents

Walsh Arms Hotel
Llandwei, Llandrindod Wells
Tel: 059 787 227
Non-residential hotel

Irfon River
C. Bradley
Bradleys Hardware, Builth Wells
Tel: 059 787 2310

Cammarch Hotel
Llangammarch Wells
Tel: 05912 205

Llynfi River
Head Water Bailiff
W. N. Lloyd
Bridgend Cottage, Glasbury-on-Wye, via
Hereford
Tel: 049 74 227

Lugg River
HEREFORD, 7 MILE STRETCH
Hereford & District A.A.
Sec: I. Astley
Tel: 098122 283
Permits from local tackle shop

LUGG MILL
Mrs Garlick
Lugg Bridge House, Lugwqardine,
Hereford
Permits from above

Phoenix A.C.
Sec: J. A. Mobley
155 Greenhill Road, Halesowen
Tel: 021 422 1161
Day permits available from above

Wye River
Cwmbran A.A.
Sec: P. M. Gulliford
Tel: 06333 5036

FORD FAWR
W. N. Lloyd
Head Water Bailiff
Bridgend Cottage, Glasbury-on-Wye,
Hereford
Tel: 049 74 227
Permits on application from above

GABALUA WATER
Mrs Williams
Gabalua Farm, Whitney-on-Wye
Permits from above

GARNONS WATER
Garnons Estate Office
Bridge Sollars
Tel: 098 122 235
Permits from above

GLANWYE WATER
Mrs Potter
Hay-on-Wye
Tel: 0497 820368
Permits in advance from above

GLASBURY – BUILTH WELLS
Woosnam & Tyler Estate Agents
Dolgarreg, North Road, Builth Wells
Tel: 09822 3248
Permits from above

HAY CASTLE & CLYRO COURT WATER
W. N. Lloyd
Head Water Bailiff
Bridgend Cottage, Glasbury-on-Wye
Tel: 049 74 227
Permits from above in advance

HEREFORD 8 MILE STRETCH
Hereford & District A.A.
Sec: I. Astley
The Lindens, Bishopstone, Hereford HR4 7JG
Tel: 098122 283
Day and week permits from local tackle shops

HOLME LACY BEAT NO. 5
Permits from H. Hatton Fishing Tackle
64 St. Owen Street, Hereford

LONGWORTH HALL HOTEL STRETCH
Longworth Hall Hotel
Lugwardine
Mr. Smith
Permits from above

MOCCAS WATER
Red Lion Hotel
Bredwarine
Tel: 098 17 303
Permits in advance from above

Rhayader A.A.
Sec: Mrs Jones
Tel: 0597 810866
Mrs Powell
Garth House, Rhayader
Tel: 0597 810451
Vulcan Motel Doldowlod, Nr. Llandrindoc Wells
Tel: 0597 810438

ROSS ON WYE
Town Stretch
Sec: H. Webb
Permits from G. & B. Sports, 10 Broad Street, Ross on Wye

SUFTON WATER
Mordiford Bridge
Permits from Mrs E. Boulcott
Yew Tree Cottage, Mordiford

STILLWATERS

DDERW POOLS
D. Eckley
Dderw Farm, Nr. Llyswen, Brecon

LLANDRINDOD WELLS LAKE
Permits available from Lakeside shop

WEST END FARM WATER
M. Bozward
West End Farm, Docklow, Nr. Leominster

Welsh Water Authority

ambrian Way
econ
wys
l: 0874 3181
ontact: Public Information
epartment

e W.W.A. introduced a new fishing
ence structure in 1980. Each river has
en categorised from A to G on the basis
the potential and general quality of the
hing. The best waters are those of
ass A.

icence for a particular class of water
titles anglers (if permission has been
anted) to fish in all waters of the same or
ver class but not water of a higher class.

EE AND CLWYD IVISION

ire Hall
ld
l: 0352 58551

heries, Recreation and Amenity
icer:
P. Hodgson BSc MSc
l: 0352 58551

sistant Fisheries, Recreation and
nenity Officer:
M. Scutter BSc
l: 0352 58551

ad Bailiff – South:
Thomas
lafon, Maerdy, Corwen, Clwyd
l: 049 081 413

ad Bailiff – North:
Forkings
ven Springs, Caerwys, Nr. Mold
l: 035 282 511

RIVERS

Aled River

St. Asaph A.A.
Sec: I. D. Jones
18 Heol Afon, St. Asaph
Tel: 0745 582993
Day and week permits also available from:
G. Owen, Glasfryn Stores, Llansannen
Tel: 074 577 615
Bevins Newsagents, St. Asaph

Llansannen Sporting Club Water
Day, week and season permits from
G. Owen, Glasfryn Stores, Llansannen
Tel: 074 577 615

Alwen River

Owain Glyndwr Hotel
Corwen
Tel: 0490 2115
Day permits from hotel

Crown Hotel
G. K. Huxley, Crown Hotel, Llanfihangel
Day permits available from hotel

Alyn River

Season Tickets Only
Caergwrle A.C.
Sec: R. Mathers
29 Hawarden Road, Hope, Wrexham
Season permits from above

Llay Hall A.A.
N. Griffiths
Tan-y-Allt, Cefn-y-Bedd, Wrexham
Permits from above

Cegidog River

Llay Hall A.A.
c/o N. Griffiths
Tan-yr-Allt, Cefn-y-Bedd, Wrexham
Permits from above

Ceiriog River

**CHIRK CASTLE WATER AND
BRYNHYNALLT ESTATE WATER**
Chirk A.A.
Sec: J. L. Davies
76 Longfield, Chirk, nr. Wrexham
**Day and week permits available from
Secretary**

West Arms Hotel Water
2-day permits available from
Mr. Lowe, West Arms Hotel, Llanarmon

Clwyd River

SOURCE TO DENBIGH
Liverpool & District A.C.
Sec: J. Johnson
97 Liverpool Road, North Maghull
Nr. Liverpool
Tel: 051 526 4083
Day and season permits

Rhyl A.A.
Sec: H. I. Jones
Belmont, 51 Pendyffryn Road, Rhyl
Tel: 0745 50342
**Permits from A. H. Fogerty, 29 Queen
Street, Rhyl
Tel: 0745 54765**

DENIGH TO MOUTH
St. Asaph A.A.
Sec: I. D. Jones
16 Heol Afon, St Asaph
Tel: 0745 582993
Day and week permits also available from:
Bevins Newsagents
High Street, St. Asaph
Foxons Post Office
Lower Denbeigh Road, Penrhewl, St.
Asaph
Tel: 0745 583583

Dee River

DUNGARY HALL WATERS
Lower Wern Salmon Anglers
Bangor-on-Dee, Clwyd
Season permits available from
E. Vickars, Speeds Newsagents,
Whitchurch, Shropshire

Newbridge A.A.
Hon. Sec: P. Davies, 10 Lawton House,
Ruabon
**Day permits available from above
Tel: 097 881 2497**

CHESTER TO HOLT
Lavister A.C.
Sec: W. A. Smith
Tel: 097 883 2044
**Permits also available from tackle dealers
in Chester**

HOLT TO RUABON
Bangor A.A.
c/o The Stores, Bangor-on-Dee
Tel: 0978 780430
Chairman
Tel: 0978 780260
**Day and weekend permits available from
above for salmon
Day and season permits for trout**

GLYNDWR PRESERVES
Midland Fly Fishers
I. A. Morris, The Lodge, Biudd, Llangollen
**Day permits from Royal Hotel, Llangollen
Tel: 0978 860202**
Berwyn Arms Hotel, Glyndyfrdwy
Groes Lwyd Farm, Rhewl
**Day permits from hotel, contact
N. J. or G. M. Croft**

Holt & Farndon A.C.
Sec: R. Williams
Tel: 0829 270891

Ty-Isaf Farm
Mr. Evans
Permits from above

Ty-Tan-Derwen Farm
Mr Davies
Permits from above

Tan-y-Garth Farm
Mr. Thomas
Permits from above

OVERTON-ON-DEE
Boat Inn Water
Permits from J. Chamberlain
Tel: 097 873 243
**Advance booking advisable
3-day permits**

RUABON TO CORWEN

Bryn-y-Pys A.A.
Sec: V. Guest
Bryn-Howah, Bangor-on-Dee, Wrexham

Liverpool & District A.A.
Sec: J. Johnson
97 Liverpool Road, North Maghull, nr.
Liverpool
Tel: 051 526 4083
Day and season permits

Llangollen A.A.
S. I. Evans, The Dingle, Abbey Road,
Llangollen
Day and week permits available from W. N.
& H. N. Elbourn
12 Chapel Street, Llangollen LL20 8NN

Maelor A.A.
c/o N. I. Wright, 34 Heol Cefnydd, Cefn
Mawr
Tel: 097881 2592
Day and week permits available from
above and C. Roberts, 20 Daywell
Crescent, Gobowen, Salop

CORWEN TO BALA

Chirk A.A.
Sec: J. L. Davies
76 Longield, Chirk, nr. Wrexham
Day and week permits available from
secretary

Corwen & District A.C.
Sec: M. J. Green
Tel: 0490 23690

BALA TO LLANUWCHLLYN

Llanuwchllyn A.C.
Sec: Mr Gittins
Llanuchlyn, Gwynedd

Bala & District A.A.
Sec: D. M. Rees
21 Tremyffridd, Bala
Tel: 0678 520812
Day, week, month, winter and block
permits available from local tackle shops

Elwy River

St. Asaph A.A.
Sec: I. D. Jones
18 Heol Afon, St. Asaph
Tel: 0745 582993
Permits from Mr. Cosnett, Newsagent,
High Street, St. Asaph
Foxons Newsagents, Penrhewl, St. Asaph
Plas Elwy Hotel, The Roe, St. Asaph

Rhyl & District A.A.
Sec: H. I. Jones
Tel: 0745 50342

Bodelwyddan A.C.
Sec: R. G. Richardson
Tel: 0745 582693

Llafor River

Bala & District A.A.
Sec: D. M. Rees
21 Tremyffridd, Bala
Tel: 0678 520812
Day, week, month, winter and block
permits available from local tackle shops

Lliw River

Llanuwchllyn A.C.
Sec: Mr Gittins, Llanuchlyn, Gwynedd
Permits also available from:
Yr Eryr, High Street, Bala
Tel: 0678 520370

Bala & District A.A.
Sec: D. M. Rees
21 Tremyffridd, Bala
Tel: 0678 520812
Day, week, month, winter and block
permits available from local tackle shops

Twrch River

Llanuwchllyn A.C.
Sec: Mr Gittins
Llanuchlyn Gwynedd

STILLWATERS

ALED ISAF RESERVOIR
Interpretation Centre, Brenig Reservoir
Cerrig-y-Drudion, Nr. Corwen, Clwyd
Tel: 049 082 463

ALWEN RESERVOIR
Nr. Cerrigydrduion
Reservoir Keeper, Alwen Reservoir,
Cerrig-y-Drudion, Nr. Corwen, Clwyd
Tel: 049 082 208
Day permits available

BALA LAKE
(Llyn Tegid)
Sec: D. M. Rees
21 Tremyffridd, Bala
Tel: 0678 520812
Day, week, month, winter and block
permits also available from local tackle
shops

BRENIG RESERVOIR
Nr. Denbigh
Interpretation Centre, Brenig Reservoir
Cerrig-y-Drudion, Nr. Corwen, Clwyd
Tel: 049 082 463
Season, week and day permits on site

CAMBRIAN FISHERIES
See Ysceifiog Lake

CILCAIN RESERVOIRS
(five reservoirs in area)
Cilcain Fly F.A.
Sec: E. Williams
9 Maes Cilan, Cilcain, Mold
Tel: 035 282 554
Day and week permits bookable in
advance

CWM PRYSOR LAKE
Bala & District A.A.
Sec: D. M. Rees
21 Tremyffrid, Bala
Permits from R. E. Evans, Bradford House,
High Street; E. Evans, Yr Eyr, High Street;
W. E. Pugh, Sports Shop, High Street, all in
Bala

DOLWEN RESERVOIR
Reservoir Keeper
Plas Uchaf Reservoir, Llanefydd
Nr. Denbigh, Clwyd
Tel: 0745 590574
Day permits on site

THE FLASH LAKE, GRESFORD
Permits available from local angling shop

LLYN ALED RESERVOIR
Interpretation Centre, Brenig Reservoir
Cerrig-i-Drudion, Nr. Corwen, Clwyd
Tel: 049 082 463

LLYN CELYN
Nr. Bala
Fron-Goch Post Office, Fron-Goch, Bala
W. E. Pugh, 74 High Street, Bala
R. E. Evans, Bradford House, Bala
Information only from
Reservoir Keeper Tel: 0678 520368
Season and day permits locally available

LLYN TEGID
See Bala Lake entry

**PENYCAE RESERVOIRS,
UPPER & LOWER**
J. A. Jackson, Reservoir Keeper
Reservoir House, Penycae
Wrexham & East Denbighshire Water
Company
21 Egerton Wrexham
Tel: 0978 2259
Season permits from above

PLAS UCHAF RESERVOIR
Reservoir Keeper
Plas Uchaf Reservoir, Llanefydd
Nr. Denbigh, Clwyd
Tel: 0745 590574
Day permits on site

SEVEN SPRINGS LAKE
Caerwys, Mold
4-day permits from A.D. Maine, Caerwys
Gun and Tackle, Prestatyn; Anglers Den
Rhyl

WEPRE POOL
Connah's Quay A.C.
Sec: P. Roberts
Tel: 0244 815643

WIRRAL COUNTRY PARK PONDS
Head Ranger, Wirral Country Park Cent
Station Road, Thurstaston, Merseyside
Tel: 051 648 4371

**YSCEIFIOG LAKE (CAMBRIAN
FISHERIES)**
M. J. Bulleid
Cambrian Fishers, Afonwen, Nr Mold
Tel: 035282 589
Booking in advance advisable
Day and season permits from above

GOWER DIVISION

86 Kingsway, Swansea
Tel: 0792 468000

Divisional Fisheries & Recreation
Officer:
A. G. Harvey

Supervisory Bailiff:
S. J. Williams
30 Bryn Morgru, Alltwen
Pontardawe, Swansea
Tel: 0792 863490

RIVERS

fan River
an Valley A.A.
n. Sec: R. Hope
l: 0639 888328

wenny River
ncoed & District A.C.
c: Dr G. M. Gwilliam
l: 0656 860993
mits also available from
Withers
Felindre Road, Pencoed
l: 0656 861 324

arw River
gwr A.A.
c: F. J. Hughes
l: 0656 722077
mits also available from:
Rowe, Fishing Tackle
l: 0656 58254

an River
ngyfelach & District A.A.
: M. L. Griffiths
ldwyn Road, Cockett, Swansea SA5 5BU
: 0792 581711
ason and week permits available from
l Davies (Shop), 130 Woodfield Street,
rriston
l. Day, 27 Vicarage Road, Morriston
arrison, 110 Clase Road, Morriston
Haeney, 75 Tan-y-lan Road, Morriston

ynfi River
nfi Valley A.A.
n Sec: D. C. Edmonds
Bridgend Road, Maesteg

ughor River
manford A.A.
: A. S. Usherwood
: 0269 2173

elte River
nneath & District A.A.
: R. W. Cole
Woodlands Park Drive, Cadoxton, Neath
0639 55576
r and week permits available from
retary and Dinas Hotel, Pontneath;
ite Horse Inn, Pontneath; Craig Cafe,
mgwrach

ath River
ath & Dulais A.A.
Sec: A. Beasley
0639 50878

nneath & District A.A.
: R. W. Cole
Woodlands Park Drive, Cadoxton, Neath
0639 55576
and week permits available from the
retary, and Dinas Hotel, Pontneath;
ite Horse Inn, Pontneath; Craig Cafe,
mgwrach

dd Fach River
nneath & District A.A.
R. W. Cole
Woodlands Park Drive, Cadoxton, Neath

Tel: 0639 55576
Day and week permits available from the
secretary, and Dinas Hotel, Pontneath;
White Horse Inn, Pontneath; Craig Cafe,
Cwmgwrach

Ogmore River
Ogwr A.A.
Hon. Sec: F. J. Hughes
Tel: 0656 722077

Pyrddin River
Glynneath & District A.A.
Sec: R. W. Cole
24 Woodlands Park Drive, Cadoxton, Neath
Tel: 0639 55576
Day and week permits available from the
secretary, and Dinas Hotel, Pontneath;
White Horse Inn, Pontneath; Craig Cafe,
Cwmgwrach

Tawe River
Pontardawe & District A.A.
Weekly permits only from Clive Rowland's
Sports Shop, Woodfield Street, Morriston
Tel: 0792 75993

Tawe & Tributaries A.A.
Hon. Sec: K. Jones
21 St. Davids Road, Ystalyfera
Tel: 0639 843916
Season, week and day permits also
available from:
D. Watkins, Tawe Sport, Commercial
Street, Ystradgynlais
J. G. Davies, The Pharmacy, Brecon Road,
Abercraf
Mr. Hoare, General Stores, Penycae
Linnards Sports Shop, High Street, Swansea
D. C. Rowlands, Sports Shop, Gurnos Road,
Ystalyfera
C. Jones Sports Shop, Pontardawe

Dan-yr-Ogof Caves Ltd
Penycae, Swansea Valley
Tel: 063977 284
Day permits available from caves office

STILLWATERS

EGLWYS NUNYDD RESERVOIR
British Steel Corporation
Sports & Social Club, Groes, Margram,
Port Talbot
Sec: C. Jones
Tel: 0639 883161 Ext. 3368
Day and week permits available from
above

LLIEDI RESERVOIR
UPPER & LOWER
Welsh Water Authority
South West Wales River division
19 Pen-y-Fai Lane, Llanelli
Tel: 57031
Self issue booth at reservoir
Day permits also available from:
John James, Fishing Tackle
65 Robinson Street, Llanelli
Tel: 05542 3031/3012

LLYNFAWR RESERVOIR
Upper Rhonda A.A.
Sec: D. B. Davies
Tel: 0443 771296

LOWER LLIW RESERVOIR
Fisheries Officer
Tel: 0792 46800

PWLL-Y-WAUN POND
Porthcawl Sea A.A. (Freshwater section)
Hon Sec: J. Lock
Tel: 065 671 2876

UPPER LLIW RESERVOIR
Nr. Swansea
Fisheries Office
Tel: 0792 468000
Day permits from Gower Division Office,
86 The Kingsway, Swansea

WILDERNESS POND
Porthcawl Sea A.A. Freshwater Section
Hon Sec: J. Lock
Tel: 065 671 2876

YSTRADFELLTE RESERVOIR
Welsh Water Authority
Glamorgan River Division
Tremains House, Coychurch Road,
Bridgend
Tel: 0656 2217
Day and season permits available from
Llwyn Onn reservoir filter house

GWYNEDD DIVISION

Penrhosgarnedd, Bangor, Gwynedd
Tel: 0248 51144

Fishery, Recreation & Amenities
Officer:
P. J. Parkinson

Assistant Fishery, Recreation &
Amenities Officer:
B. R. Nelson

Area Head Bailiffs:

Dolwyddelan: E. Lloyd Price
Tel: 069 06 250
Criccieth: E. Owen
Tel: 076 671 2582
Dolgellau: D. T. Lloyd
Tel: 0341 422 338

RIVERS

Afon Teigl Water
Cambrian A.A.
Sec: E. Evans
Garth, Tyddyn Gwyn, Manod
Blaenau Ffestiniog
Day, week and season permits available
from J. E. Jones, Tackle Dealers,
Church Street, Blaenau Ffestiniog
Derwen Stores, Llan Ffestiniog

Artro River
Artro A.A.
Sec: G. Pierce
Tel: 034 123 288

Conwy River
National Trust Office
Dinas, Betws-y-Coed, Gwynedd

Dolgarrog A.A.
Sec: F. A. Currie
Tel: 049 269 651
Week and day permits

Llanrwst A.C.
Sec: D. Thomas
Tel: 0492 640596
**Weekly permits from The Library Tackle
Shop, Llanrwst
Tel: 0492 640 525
The Radio Shop, Watling Street, Llanrwst**

Gwydyr Hotel
Betws-y-Coed
Tel: 06902 217
**Private fishing, day permits can be
arranged by prior application for non-
residents**

Cyfnal Waters
Cambrian A.A.
Sec: E. Evans
Garth, Tyddyn Gwyn, Manod
Blaenau Ffestiniog
Day, week and season permits available
from J. E. Jones, Tackle Dealer, Church
Street, Blaenau Ffestiniog
Derwen Stores, Llan Ffestiniog

Dolgarrog River
Dolgarrog A.A.
Sec: F. A. Corrie
Tel: 049 269 651

Dwyfach River
Criccieth & Llanystumdwy A.A.
Sec: G. Hamilton
Tel: 076 671 2251

N. Jones
Ael-y-Bryn, Bontddu, Nr. Dolgellau
Tel: 034 149 241
Permits available from
The Post Office, Glanllwyd
Tel: 034 140209

Dwyfor River
Criccieth & Llanystumdwy A.A.
Sec: G. Hamilton
Tel: 076 671 2251

Dwyryd River
P. D. Tointon
Sylfaen, Barmouth
Tel: 0341 280461

Dysynni River
Mrs Ellis
Pen-o-Wern, Bryncrug, Tywyn
Co. J. F. Williams Wynne
Peniarth, Llanegryn, Nr. Tywyn
Tel: 0654 710328

Eden River
Prysor A.A.
Sec: D. G. Williams
Tel: 076 687 310

N. Jones
Ael-y-Bryn, Bontddu, Nr. Dolgellau
Tel: 034 149 241
Permits from
The Post Office, Ganllwyd
Tel: 034 140 209

Einion River
Talybont A.C.
Sec: J. W. Hughes
Tel: 034 17 449

Erch River
Pwllheli & District A.C.
Sec: G. W. Pritchard
Edwyfeld, 30 Lon Ceredigion, Pwllheli
Tel: 0758 3531
Week and day permits from
D. & E. Hughes, 24 Penlan Street, Pwllheli

Glaslyn River
Glaslyn A.A.
Porthmadog
Permit Sec: R. J. Gauler
Tel: 076 686 229
3-day, week and season permits from
Pugh's, 94 High Street, Porthmadog

Goedol Water
Cambrian A.A.
Sec: E. Evans
Garth, Tyddyn Gwyn, Manod
Blaenau Ffestiniog
Day, week and season permits available
from J. E. Jones, Tackle Dealer, Church
Street, Blaenau Ffestiniog
Derwen Stores, Llan Ffestiniog

Gwyrfai River
Seiont, Gwyrfai & Llyfni A.S.
Sec: H. P. Hughes
11 Eryri Estate, Bethel, Caernarfon
Tel: 0248 670 666
Season, day and week permits available
from A. Huxley Jones Tackle, Caernarfon;
A. D. Griffiths, Newsagent, Pen-y-roes;
secretary and treasurer

Leri River
Talybont A.C.
Sec: J. Hughes
Tel: 034 17449

Lledr River
Plas Hall Hotel and Restaurant
Pont-y-Pant, nr. Betws-y-Coed
Gwynedd LL25 0PH
Tel: 069 06 206

Dolwyddelan F.A.
Dolwyddelan
Permits from Siop-y-llan
Dolwyddelan
Tel: 069 06 137
E. Jones (secretary), 8 Llwyn Estyn,
Deganwy
Tel: 0492 84669

Llugwy River
Gwydyr Hotel, Betws-y-Coed
Tel: 06902 217
Day permits from hotel

Ty'n y Coed Hotel
Capel Curig, Gwynedd
Tel: 069 04 231
Permits from hotel

Llyfni River
Seiont, Gwyrfai & Llyfni A.S.
Sec: H. P. Hughes

11 Eryri Estates, Bethel, Caernarfon
Tel: 0248 670666
Season, day and week permits available
from A. Huxley Jones Tackle, Caernarfon
A. D. Griffiths, Newsagent, Pen-y-roes;
secretary and treasurer

Mawddach River
Dolgellau A.A.
Sec: W. E. Roberts
2 Muriau, Cader Road, Dolgellau LL40 1§
Tel: 0341 422360
Day, week and season permits also
available from
Local tackle shop – Tel: 0341 422388
D. McCaffrey, Celfi Diddan, Eldon Squa
Dolgellau; J. Morris, Ty Newydd Farm,
Ganllwyd (Bailiff) at home or on bank

Dolmelynllyn Hall Hotel
Ganllwyd, Dolgellau
Tel: 034 140 273
Permits from hotel

Merddwr River
Voelas Arms Hotel
Pentrefoelas, nr. Betws-y-Coed
Tel: 069 05 654
Day permits from above

Ogwen River
Ogwen Valley A.A.
Day permits from Buckley Wyn, Outfitte
40 High Street, Bethesda
Tel: 0248 600020

Rhydhir River
Pwllheli A.A.
Sec: G. W. Pritchard
Edwyfed, 30 Lon Ceredigion, Pwllheli
Tel: 0758 3531
Day and week permits also available fro
D. & E. Hughes, Penlan Street, Pwllheli

Seiont River
Seiont, Gwyrfai & Llyfni A.S.
Sec: H. P. Hughes
11 Eryri Estates, BEthel, Caernarfon
Tel: 0248 670 666
Season, day and week permits avialable
from A. Huxley Jones Tackle, Caernarfo
A. D. Griffiths, Newsagent, Pen-y-roes;
secretary and treasurer

Wnion River
Dolgellau A.A.
Sec: W. E. Roberts
2 Muriau, Cader Road, Dolgellau LL40
Tel: 0341 422360
Day, week and season permits also
available from:
Local tackle shop
Tel: 0341 422388
D. McCaffrey, Celfi Diddan, Eldon Squa
Dolgellau; J. Morris, Ty Newydd Farm,
Ganllwyd (Bailiff) at home or on bank

Wygyr River
Wygyr F.A.
Sec: F. Gough
Glanrafon Mountain Road, Llanfechel,
Amlwch, Anglesey

Ysbyty Ifan
National Trust
Dinas, Betws-y-Coed

WHERE TO FISH—GAME

STILLWATERS

...JI RESERVOIR
...A.A.
...V. J. Williams
...4 877 765

...YSTRADLLYN RESERVOIR
...ddgelen
...ystradllyn Reservoir Treatment
...s, Cwmystradllyn, Nr. Garn
...rnmaen
...76 675 255
...n and day permits on site

...TINIOG FISHERIES (TAN-Y-...AU LAKE)
...au Ffestiniog
...ies Administration Officer
...B., Bron Henlog
...udno Junction
...492 81248

...NMERIN LAKE
...i & District A.A.
...A. D. Woodvine
...s, Machynllerh, Powys
...65 473 273
...Tomlinson, Pentre, Corris
...65 473 252
...n permits available from
...es, Maelor Stores, Corris
...65 473 625 or
...ghes, Newsagent, Machynlleth

...ADAR
...rian A.A.
...Evans
..., Tyddyn Gwyn, Manod
...au Ffestiniog
...week and season permits available
...E. Jones, Tackle Dealer, Church
...t, Blaenau Ffestiniog
...en Stores, Llan Ffestiniog

...ALAW
...esey
...g Office, Llyn Alaw, Llanerchymedd,
...esey
...voir Warden
...40 788 762
...ermits on site

...CONACH
...ont A.C.
...Hughes
...34 17 449

...CORON
...ick Estate, Bodorgan Estate Office
...rgan, Anglesey
...40 787 253
...its also available from:
...keeper on site

...CRAIG-Y-PISTYLL
...ystwyth A.A.
...Dr J. D. Fish
...0970 828433

...CWMORTHIN
...brian A.A.
...E. Evans
...n, Tyddyn Gwyn, Manod
...nau Ffestiniog
...week and season permits available
...J. E. Jones, Tackle Dealer, Church

Street, Blaenau Ffestiniog
Derwen Stores, Llan Ffestiniog

LLYN CYNWCH
Dolgellau A.A.
Sec: W. E. Roberts
2 Murai, Cader Road, Dolgellau LL40 1SG
Day, week and season permits available from local tackle shop – Tel: 0341 422388
D. McCaffrey, Celfi Diddan, Eldon Square, Dolgellau; J. Morris, Ty Newydd Farm, Ganllwyd (Bailiff) at home or on bank

LLYN DUBACH
Cambrian A.A.
Sec: E. Evans
Garth, Tyddyn Gwyn, Manod
Blaenau Ffestiniog
Day, week and season permits available from J. E. Jones, Tackle Dealer, Church Street, Blaenau Ffestiniog
Derwen Stores, Llan Ffestiniog

LLYN DWFN
Talybont A.C.
Sec: J. Hughes
Tel: 034 17 449

LLYN EDNO
Glaslyn A.A.
Permit Sec: R. T. Gauler
Tel: 076 686 229

LLYN FFRIDD
Cambrian A.A.
Sec: E. Evans
Garth, Tyddyn Gwyn, Manod
Blaenau Ffestiniog
Day, week and season permits available from J. E. Jones, Tackle Dealer, Church Street, Blaenau Ffestiniog
Derwen Stores, Llan Ffestiniog

LLYN IDWAL
T. Jones
Windsor House, Bethesda

LLYN LLAGI
Cambrian A.A.
Sec: E. Evans
Garth, Tyddyn Gwyn, Manod
Blaenau Ffestiniog
Day, week and season permits available from J. E. Jones, Tackle Dealer, Church Street, Blaenau Ffestiniog
Derwen Stores, Llan Ffestiniog

LLYN MANOD
Cambrian A.A.
Sec: E. Evans
Garth, Tyddyn Gwyn, Manod
Blaenau Ffestiniog
Day, week and season permits available from J. E. Jones, Tackle Dealer, Church Street, Blaenau Ffestiniog
Derwen Stores, Llan Ffestiniog

LLYN MORWYNION
Cambrian A.A.
Sec: E. Evans
Garth, Tyddyn Gwyn, Manod
Blaenau Ffestiniog
Day, week and season permits available from J. E. Jones, Tackle Dealer, Church Street, Blaenau Ffestiniog
Derwen Stores, Llan Ffestiniog

LLYN NANT-Y-CAGL
Talybont A.C.
Sec: J. Hughes
Tel: 034 17 449

LLYNNAU GAMALLT
Cambrian A.A.
Sec: E. Evans
Garth, Tyddyn Gwyn, Manod
Blaenau Ffestiniog
Day, week and season permits available from J. E. Jones, Tackle Dealer, Church Street, Blaenau Ffestiniog
Derwen Stores, Llan Ffestiniog

LLYNNOED BARLWYD
Cambrian A.A.
Sec: E. Evans
Garth, Tyddyn Gwyn, Manod
Blaenau Ffestiniog
Day, week and season permits available from J. E. Jones, Tackle Dealer, Church Street, Blaenau Ffestiniog
Derwen Stores, Llan Ffestiniog

LLYN TECWYN ISAF
Weekly tickets only
Talsarnau & District A.A.
Sec: Mr Nelson
Tel: 0766 780254
Permits also available from:
The Post Office, Talsarnau
Tel: 0766 770201

TANYGRISIAU RESERVOIR
C.E.G.B. Ffestiniog Power Station, Blaenau Ffestiniog
Tel: 076 681 465
Permits available from power station

TAFF DIVISION

Crwys House
Crwys Road
Cardiff
Tel: 0222 399961

Fisheries Officer: John Davies
Head Bailiff: Ivan Bevan

RIVERS

Cynon River
Abadare & District A.A.
Hon Sec: R. Hancock
Tel: 0685 875209

Ely River
Bute A.A.
Sec: L. V. Powell
176 Clare Road, Grangetown, Cardiff

Rhondda River
Glyncornel A.A.
Sec: J. M. Evans
126 Ystrad Road, Ystrad, Rhondda
Tel: 0443 439961
Week and season permits also available from Sports Shop in Valley

Taff River
Bute A.A.
Sec: L. V. Powell
176 Clare Road, Grangetown, Cardiff

257

Merthyr Tydfil A.A.
Hon Sec: T. Norman
2 Wesley Close, Dowlais, Merthyr Tydfil
Tel: 0685 76801
**Day permits available from A. Rees,
13 Alexandra Avenue, Merthyr Tydfil
or E. Thompson, 1 Rowan Way, Gurnos
Estate, Merthyr Tydfil**

Whitland A.A.
Sec: R. M. Jones
Tel: 09944 523

Thaw River

Cowbridge & District A.A.
Sec: H. W. Roberts
Tel: 044 63 3241

STILLWATERS

BEACONS RESERVOIR
Nr. Brecon
Fishing Office, Llwyn-on Filter House,
Llwyn-on Reservoir, Nr. Merthyr Tydfil
Tel: 0222 399961
**Season and day permits from Llwyn-on
Reservoir**

CANTREF RESERVOIR
Nr. Merthyr Tydfil
Fishing Office, Llwyn-on Filter House
Llwyn-on Reservoir, Nr. Merthyr Tydfil
Tel: 0222 399961
**Season and day permits available from
Llwyn-on Reservoir**

CWMDARE PONDS
Abadare & District A.A.
Sec: R. Hancock
Tel: 0685 875209

CYFARTHFA LAKE
Merthyr Tydfil A.A.
Sec: T. Norman
Tel: 0685 76801

DOL-Y-GAER RESERVOIR
Nr. Talybont
The Stores, Pontsticill Depot
Pontsticill Reservoir, Nr. Merthyr Tydfil
Tel: 0222 399961
Season and day permits on site

LISVANE RESERVOIR
Nr. Cardiff
Reservoir Superintendant
Llanishen/Lisvane Reservoir, Cardiff
Tel: 0222 752236
Season and day permits on site

LLANISHEN RESERVOIR
Nr. Cardiff
Reservoir Superintendant
Llanishen/Lisvane Reservoir, Cardiff
Tel: 0222 752236
Season and day permits on site

LLWYN-ON RESERVOIR
Nr. Merthyr Tydfil
Fishing Office, Llwyn-on Filter House
Llwyn-on Reservoir, Nr. Merthyr Tydfil
Tel: 0222 399961
**Season and day permits on site at the Filter
House**

LOWER NEUADD RESERVOIR
Nr. Talybont
The Stores, Pontsticill Depot
Pontsticill Reservoir, Nr. Merthyr Tydfil
Tel: 0222 399961
**Season and day permits available from
Pontsticill Reservoir**

NANT MOEL CYNON
Abadare & District A.A.
Hon. Sec: R. Hancock
Tel: 0685 875209

PENYWERN PONDS
Merthyr Tydfil A.A.
Hon Sec: T. Norman
Tel: 0685 76801

PONTSTICILL RESERVOIR
Nr. Talybont
The Stores, Pontsticill Depot
Pontsticill Reservoir, Nr. Merthyr Tydfil
Tel: 0222 399961
Season and day permits on site

RHYMNEY BRIDGE RESERVOIR
Glyncornel A.A.
Hon Sec: J. M. Evans
126 Ystrad Road, Ystrad, Rhondda
Tel: 0443 439961
**Weekly and season permits available from
Sports Shops in Valley**

**TAFF FAWR RESERVOIR AND TAFF
FECHAN RESERVOIR**
Taff Angling Association
Sec: H. T. Gwynne
87 Shirley Drive, Heol Gerrig,
Merthyr Tydfil
Tel: 0685 4506
**Day and season permits available from
vending machine on site**

UPPER NEUADD RESERVOIR
Nr. Talybont
The Stores, Pontsticill Depot
Pontsticill Reservoir, Nr. Merthyr Tydfil
Tel: 0222 399961
Day permits from Pontsticill Reservoir

USK DIVISION

**Station Buildings, Queensway
Newport, Gwent
Tel: 0633 840404**

Fishery, Recreation & Amenity Officer:
J. W. Lambert

Assistant Fishery, Recreation &
Amenity Officer:
B. Benbow

District Head Bailiff:
J. L. Stevens
54 Woolpitch, Greenmeadow
Cwmbran, Gwent
Tel: 0633 64263

RIVERS

Afon Llwyd
PONTYPOOL
Pontypool A.A.
Hon. Sec: A. Wakeham
7 St. Hilas Road, Griffithstown, Pontypo
WP4 5HN
Tel: 04955 4743
Day permits also available from:
Larcombe Sports Shop
Commercial Street, Pontypool
Tel: 04955 3935

Caerfanell Brook
G. J. Owen
Maesmawr Farm, Talybont, Nr. Brecon

Usk Hotel
Talybont-on-Usk
Tel: 087 487 251
Day permits available

Cileni Brook
Aberdare & District A.A.
Sec: R. Hancock
Tel: 0685 875209

Ebbw
Islwyn & District Anglers
Sec: Mrs J. Meller
Tel: 049 526 357

Maesmawr Water
G. J. Owen
Maesmawr Farm, Talybont, Nr. Brecon

Nant Bran
J. Roderick
Llwyncoed Farm, Llanfihangel
Nant Bran, Nr. Brecon
Tel: 087 482 273

River Sirhowy
Islwyn & District Anglers
Sec: Mrs J. Meller
Tel: 049 526 357

Pontllanfraith A.C.
Sec: L. Watkins
Tel: 0495 223 271

South Wales Switchgear A.C.
Sec: G. Dingley
73 Meadow Close, Pengam, Blackwood
Gwent
Tel: 0443 833 642
Day permits available from club secreta

Tarrell River
Merthyr Tydfil A.A.
Sec: T. R. Norman
Tel: 0685 76801

Usk River
**LLANSPYDDID TO LLANFAES
BRIDGE**
Brecon A.S.
Brecon, Powys
Sec: L. Peters
53 Ffynnon Dewi, Llanfaes, Brecon
**Day permits from R. & C. Denman, 11
Watergate, Brecon
Tel: 0874 2071**

NFAES BRIDGE TO LITTLE
OD
on F.A.
he Town Clerk, The Guildhall,
on, Powys
ermits from R. & C. Denman
atergate, Brecon
874 2071

FAES
es Hotel, Crickhowell, Powys
874 730371 and 730372
ermits from hotel and P.M. Fishing
le, 12 Monk Street, Abergavenny
873 810563

CKHOWELL BRIDGE AREA
howell & District A.A.
Sec: J. Stenner Evans
fan, Ffawyddog, Llangattock,
howell
873 810563
its from the Vine Tree Inn,
attock
873 810514

NFOIST BRIDGE TO BELOW
ER BRIDGE
nouth District Council
cil Office, Whitecross Street,
nouth, Gwent
600 2122
its from P.M. Fishing Tackle,
nk Street, Abergavenny
ll's Sports Ltd, 53 Cross Street,
gavenny
e Inn, Llanfoist

TO ABERGAVENNY
gavenny
tches
its from P.M. Fishing Tackle
nk Street, Abergavenny
873 3175

hyr Tydfill A.A.
. R. Norman
685 76801

Chief Clerk
Hall, Abergavenny
873 2721
its also available from
Fishing Tackle
nk Street, Abergavenny

Town Water Fishery Assoc.
C. E. Brain
Julians Road, Newport, Cardiff
633 55587
permits from Sweets Fishing Tackle,
ycarne Street, Usk

RGAVENNY TO BRECON
hiting
y Cottage, Llanwenarth, Citra
873 810642

well
Garage, Ebbw Vale

ge Inn
Bridge, near Usk
873 880243
ermits available from hotel

CON TO SOURCE
Davis

The Drug Stores, Sennybridge, Brecon
Tel: 087 482 221

H. G. Morgan
Ynysyrwyddfa, Sennybridge, Brecon
Tel: 087 482 252

Yscir River
Aberdare & District A.A.
Sec: R. Hancock
Tel: 0685 875209

STILLWATERS

AFON LWYD
Cwmbran
Cwmbran A.C.
Hon. Sec: P. M. Gulliford
Tel: 06333 5036
Permits also available from:
D. H. Powell & Sons
Chapel Street, Pontnewydd

CRAI RESERVOIR
Cnewr Estate Ltd.
Tel: 087 482 207
Permits also available from:
Reservoir Keep on site

LLANDEGFEDD RESERVOIR
Nr. Cardiff
Sluvae Treatment Works
Llandegfedd Reservoir, Panteg, Pontypool
Tel: 04955 55333
Season and day permits available from above

OLWAY BROOK
Pontypool A.A.
Hon. Sec: A. Wakeham
7 St. Hilda's Road, Griffithstown, Pontypool
WP4 5HN
Tel: 04955 4743
Day permits also available from:
Greyhound Inn, Usk

PANTYREOS RESERVOIR
Nr. Bettws, Gwent
Reservoir Superintendant
Pantyreos Reservoir, Henllys, Cwmbran
Tel: 0633 612249
Season and day permits on site

PENYFAN POND
Islwyn & District Anglers
Sec: Mrs J. Meller
Tel: 049 526 357

PEN-YR-HEOL RESERVOIR
Pontypool A.A.
Sec: A. Wakeham
7 St. Hilda's Road, Griffithstown, Pontypool
WP4 5HN
Tel: 049 55 4743
Day permits also available from:
Larcombe Sports Shop
Commercial Street, Pontypool
Tel: 049 55 3935

TALYBONT RESERVOIR
Brecon
Gwent Water Division
Station Buildings, Station Approach,
Newport, Gwent
Tel: 0633 840404
Season and day permits also available

---

from:
Reservoir Superintendant
Talybont Reservoir, Talybont-on-Usk
Nr. Brecon
Tel: 087 487 237

USK RESERVOIR
Nr. Trecastle
Reservoir Keep
Usk Reservoir, Trecastle, Nr. Brecon
Tel: 0550 20422
Season and day permits on site

WENTWOOD RESERVOIR
Nr. Newport
Reservoir Superintendant
Wentwood Reservoir, Llanvaches, Penhow,
Newport
Tel: 0633 400213
Season and day permits on site

YNYSYFRO RESERVOIRS UPPER AND LOWER
Nr. Newport
Usk Water Division
Station Buildings, Queensway
Newport, Gwent
Tel: 0633 840404
Season and day permits also available from:
Reservoir Superintendant on site
Tel: 063 64374

WEST WALES DIVISION

Meyler House, St. Thomas Green
Haverfordwest, Dyfed
Tel: 0437 5551

Fisheries Recreation & Amenities
Officer:
R. I. Millichamp

Assistant Fisheries Recreation &
Amenities Officer:
M. Harcup

District and Head Bailiffs:

Towy: D. Brown
Tel: 0550 20060
Pembroke: D. Worthington
Tel: 0994 230722
Upper Teifi: L. W. Laws
Tel: 09744 416
Lower Teifi: W. C. Jones
Tel: 057044 697

RIVERS

Bran River
Llandovery A.A.
Season, day, fortnight and 8 day permits
available only from W. Aldred Thomas, 6
Kings Road, Llandovery
Tel: 0550 20267

Cennen River
Llandeilo A.A.
Sec: D. Richards
Tel: 05582 2672

Cleddau River

See Eastern or Western Cleddau

Cothi River

Carmarthern Amateur A.A.
Sec: G. James
50 St. Davids Street
Tel: 0267 7997
Permits from Messrs. Davies & Jones, King Stret, Carmarthen
Tel: 0267 7166

Carmarthen & District A.C.
Sec: D. T. Lewis
25 Park Hall, Carmarthen
Weekly permits only from J. M. Dark, Tackle Shop, 16 Chapel Street, Carmarthen; and Nantgaredig Post Office
Tel: 0267 201

Clwb Godre Mynydd Ddu
Sec: D. A. Bailey
Tel: 0269 822083

Cross Hands & District A.S.
Sec: L. R. Thomas
71 Caeglas, Crosshands, Llanelli

Nant Gwilw
Sec: G. Jones
Tel: 0269 822545
Permits also available from:
The Forest Arms Hotel, Brechfa, Dyfed

Cyrin River

Carmarthen Amateur A.A.
Sec: G. James
50 St. David's Street, Carmarthen
Tel: 0267 7997
Permits from Messrs. Davies & Jones, King Street, Carmarthen
Tel: 0267 7166

Dewi Fawr

Carmarthen & District A.C.
Sec: D. T. Lewis
25 Park Hall, Carmarthen

Dulas River

Corris & District A.A.
Sec: A. D. Woodvine
Ceinws, Machynlleth, Powys
Tel: 065 473 273
and B. Tomlinson, Pentre, Corris
Tel: 065 473 252
Season, week and day permits available from D. Rees, Maelor Street, Corris
Tel: 065 473 625

Llandeilo A.A.
Sec: D. Richards
Tel: 05582 2672

Llanidloes & District A.A.
Sec: J. D. Davies
Tel: 05512 2644

Neuadd Arms Hotel
Llanwrtyd Wells
Tel: 05913 236
Permits from above

Eastern Cleddau River

W. I. Griffiths
Hunters Lodge, Robeston Wathen,

Narberth
Tel: 0834 860270
Day, week and season permits from above or the Bush Inn, Robeston Wathen

Pembrokeshire Fly Fishers
H. W. Oliver, Red House
Llawhaden, Nr. Narbeth
Tel: 099 14 252
Permits from above

Robeston House Hotel
Mr G. Barratt
Tel: 0834 860932
Limited permits from above

Gwendraeth River

Carmarthen & District A.C.
Sec: H. Evans
25 Maple Crescent, Carmarthen
Tel: 0267 31945 Evenings
Day permits available from local tackle shops or secretary

Carmarthen Amateur A.A.
Sec: G. James
50 St. Davids Street, Carmarthen
Tel: 0267 7997
Permits from Messrs. Davies & Jones, King Street, Carmarthen
Tel: 0267 7166

Gwili River

Carmarthen & District A.C.
Sec: D. T. Lewis
25 Park Hall, Carmarthen
Weekly permits only covers all club waters available form J. M. Dark, Tackle Shop, 16 Chapel Street, Carmarthen F. M. & H. E. Davies, Newsagents, Bridge Street, Kidwelly

Carmarthen Amateur A.A.
Sec: G. James
50 St. Davids Street, Carmarthen
Tel: 0267 7997
Permits from Messrs. Davies & Jones, King Street, Carmarthen
Tel: 0267 7166

Gwydderig River

Llandovery A.A.
Season, day, fortnight and 8 day permits only from W. Aldred Thomas
6 King's Road, Llandovery
Tel: 0550 20267

Nevern River

Newport & District A.A.
Sec: Dr W. J. B. Owen
Gwynfa, Moylgrove, Cardigan SA43 3BU
Tel: 023986 619
Week and fortnight permits available from Lloyds Bank, Newport; Essex Havard, Newport; Beynon Williams Tackle Shop, Newprt; Salutation Inn, Felindre, Newport

Nevern Angling Syndicate
Sec: H. Betty
56 High Street, Fishguard, Dyfed
Tel: 0348 873215
Day permits available from secretary

Newport (Pembs) and District A.A.
Sec: W. Tucker, Parrog Road, Newport, Dyfed

Day, week and fortnight permits availa from Beynon's Fishing Tackle, Temple House, Newport
Tel: 0239 820265

Rheidol River

Aberystwyth A.A.
Sec: Dr J. D. Fish
P.O. Box 15, Aberystwyth, Dyfed
Tel: 0970 828433
Day, week and season permits availab from J. Rosser, The Tackle Shop, 3 Que Street, Aberystwyth; Aber Gun Supplie Terrace Road, Aberystwyth; E. H. Evan Erwyd Garage, Ponterwyd, Dyfed

Taf River

Carmarthen & District A.C.
Sec: D. T. Lewis
25 Park Hill, Carmarthen
Week permits available from secretary

Whitland A.A.
Sec: R. M. Jones
Tel: 09944 523
Day permits from Rees Garage Ltd., Sta Garage, Whitland
Tel: 09944 304

Teifi River

Sunny Hill Hotel
Tregaron, Dyfed
Tel: 09744 303
Day, week and season permits availab from hotel

Teifi Trout Association
Sec: C. Jones
Emlyn House, Newcastle, Emlyn
Tel: 0239 710405
Season and weekly permits available fr local tackle shops

Mrs. Davies
Stradmore Gardens
Cenarth, Nr. Cardigan, Dyfed
Season tickets only from above

Emlyn Arms Hotel
Newcastle, Emlyn, Dyfed
Tel: 0239 710317
Special rates for hotel guests

Llandysul A.C.
Sec: A. Jones
Siop-y-Jones, Llandysul
Tel: 055932 2317
Season, week and day permits aviabl from Megicks, Corner Shop, Harford Square, Lampeter
Tel: 0570 422 226

Pontrhydfendigaid A.A.
Sec: D. Lloyd Jones
Rhydteifi, Pontrhydfendigaid
Permits from R. Rees & Sons Florida Shop, Pontrhydfendigaid

Tregaron A.A.
Sec: G. R. Phillips
c/o Barclays Bank Ltd, Tregaron, Dyfe SY25 6JL
Day, week, month and season permits available from Barclays Bank, Tregaro Medical Hall, Tregaron; Sunny Hill Sho Tregaron; London House, Llanddewi B Post Office, Llanddewi Brefi; Post Offic Llanfair Clydogau; Megicks, Ironmong Lampeter

OEDMORE
edmore Enterprises
ermits from Craft Shop, Cardigan Wildlife
rk

r Ablett
ghmead Arms Hotel
anybydder, Dyfed
el: 0570 480258

wy River

armarthen Amateur A.A.
c: Mr G. James
St. Davids Street, Carmarthen
l: 0267 7997
rmits from Messrs. Davies & Jones; Lyric
orts Centre, King Street, Carmarthen
l: 0267 7166

rmarthen & District A.C.
c: D. T. Lewis
Park Hall, Carmarthen
eekly permits only, covers all club
ters from J. M. Dark, Tackle Dealer,
apel Street, Carmarthen

oss Hands & District A.A.
: L. R. Thomas
Caeglas, Cross Hands, Llanelli

ndeilo A.A.
: D. Richards
05582 2672

egaron A.A.
: G. R. Phillips
09744 207

wdor Estates
ates Office, Llangathen, Carmarthen

. Williams
y-y-Bere Farm, Rhandirmwyn
ndovery
05506 218

E. Thomas
n Farm, Rhandirmwyn Road,
dovery, Dyfed
20276
permits from Tonn Farmhouse

dovery A.A.
, season, fortnight and 8 day permits
able from W. Aldred Thomas, 6 King's
, Llandovery
0550 20267
distributors of permits

LBANK DYFED ESTATE
. Cooke & Arkwright, Estate Office,
garthen, Carmarthen SA32 8QF
055 84 494
on permits only from estate office or
ekeeper, J. S. Bellany, Ty Castell,
hvyn, Llandeilo, Dyfed
055 84 433

stern Cleddau River
brokeshire A.A.
Sec: Mr Summers
ty Road, Haverfordwest
its also available from:
ty Sports
Bridge Haverfordwest
437 3740

Ystwyth River

Aberystwyth A.A.
Sec: Dr J. D. Fish
P.O. Box 15, Aberystwyth, Dyfed
Tel: 0970 828433
Day, week and season permits available
from J. Rosser, The Tackle Shop, 3 Queen
Street, Aberystwyth; Aber Gun Supplies,
Terrace Road, Aberystwyth; E. H. Evans,
Erwyd Garage, Ponterwyd, Dyfed

Llanilar A.A.
Sec: Dr P. Callaghan
Tel: 09747 213
Day permits from J. E. Rosser, 3 Queen
Street, Aberystwyth

STILLWATERS

BRYMANLWG FARM LAKE
L. Gale
Brynamlwg Farm, Penuwch, Tregaron,
Dyfed

DINAS LAKE
CEGB Rheidol Fishery, Rheidol Power
Station, Capel Bangor, Aberystwyth
Day permits available from local agents
Evans Garage, Ponterwyd
See Advertisement this Section

LLANLLAWDDOG LAKE
Mr Olive
Home Farm, Llanllawddog, Carmarthen
Tel: 026 784 436
See Advertisement this Section

LLYN BERWYN
Tregaron A.A.
Sec: G. R. Phillips
c/o Barclays Bank Ltd, Tregaron
Tel: 09744 207
Day, week and season permits available
from bank; Medical Hall, Tregaron; Sunny
Hill Shop, Tregaron; London House,
Llanddewi Brefi; Post Office, Llanddewi
Brefi; Post Office, Llanfair Clydogau;
Megicks, Ironmongers, Lampeter

LLYS-Y-FRAN RESERVOIR
Nr. Maenchlochog
Day permits available from Reservoir
Superintendent
Tel: 09913 273
Also County Sports
3 Old Bridge, Haverfordwest
Tel: 0437 3740

NANT-Y-MOCH LAKE
Nr. Aberystwyth
CEGB Rheidol Fishery, Rheidol Power
Station, Capel Bangor, Aberystwyth
Day permits from local agents
See Advertisement this Section

PENBRYN LAKES
D. J. Owen
Penbryn, Bronant, Aberystwyth

PENRHYNCOCH LAKES
LLYN BLAENMELINDWR
LLYN CRAIG-Y-PISTYLL
LLYN PENDAM
LLYN RHOSGOCH
LLYN SYFYDRIN
Aberystwyth A.A.
Sec: Dr J. D. Fish
P.O. Box 15, Aberystwyth, Dyfed
Tel: 0970 828433
Day, week and season permits available
from J. Rosser, The Tackle Shop, 3 Queen
Street, Aberystwyth; Aber Gun Supplies,
Terrace Road, Aberystwyth; E. H. Evans,
Erwyd Garage, Ponterwyd, Dyfed

PONTERWYD LAKES
BRAY'S POOL
LLYN-YR-OERFA
Aberystwyth A.A.
Sec: Dr J. D. Fish
P.O. Box 15, Aberystwyth, Dyfed
Tel: 0970 828433
Day, week and season permits available
from J. Rosser, The Tackle Shop, 3 Queen
Street, Aberystwyth; Aber Gun Supplies,
Terrace Road, Aberystwyth; E. H. Evans,
Erwyd Garage, Ponterwyd, Dyfed

PRESCELLY RESERVOIR
Day and season permits available from
water bailiff, Blaenpant, Nr. New Inn,
Rosebush, Maenclochog

TEIFI POOLS
Near Tregaron
Fishery & Recreation Officer
Tel: 0437 5551
Permits also available from, Megicks
Corner Shop, Lampeter, Dyfed
Tel: 0570 422 226

TRISANT LAKES
LLYN FRONGOCH
LLYN GLANDWGAN
LLYN RHOSRHYDD
Aberystwyth A.A.
Sec: Dr J. D. Fish

P.O. Box 15, Aberystwyth, Dyfed
Tel: 0970 828433
Day, week and season permits available from J. Rosser, The Tackle Shop, 3 Queen Street, Aberystwyth; Aber Gun Supplies, Terrace Road, Aberystwyth; E. H. Evans, Erwyd Garage, Ponterwyd, Dyfed

WYE DIVISION

4 St. John Street, Hereford
Tel: 0432 6313
Fisheries, Recreation & Amenities Officer:
E. M. Staite
Assistant Fisheries, Recreation & Amenities Officer:
P. G. Hilder
Head Bailiff:
C. Lloyd
Tel: 04974 227

RIVERS

Cammarch River

Cammarch Hotel
Llangammarch Wells
Tel: 059 12 205
Permits available to non-residents

Humber Brook

G. Warren
Humber Grange, Humber, Nr. Leominster

Ithon River

Llandrindod Wells A.A.
Sec: A. H. Selwyn
Sports Shop, Park Crescent, Llandrindod Wells
Tel: 0597 2397
Permits also available from:
C. Bradley
Bradleys Hardware, Builth Wells
Tel: 059 787 2310
C. Selwyn & Sons
4 Park Crescent, Llandrindod Wells
Tel: 0597 2397
Severn Arms Hotels
Mr. Davies
Penybont, Powys
Tel: 059 787 224
Day and week permits available to non-residents
Walsh Arms Hotel
Llandwei, Llandrindod Wells
Tel: 059 787 227
Non residential hotel

Irfon River

C. Bradley
Bradleys Hardware, Builth Wells
Tel: 059 787 2310
Cammarch Hotel
Llangammarch Wells
Tel: 05912 205

Llynfi River

Head Water Bailiff
W. N. Lloyd
Bridgend Cottage, Glasbury-on-Wye, via Hereford
Tel: 049 74 227

Llyn Gwyn

Mrs Davies
Chemist Shop, West Street, Rhayader
Mrs Price
Nantmynach Farm, Nantmel, Rhayader

Lugg River

HEREFORD, 7 MILE STRETCH

Hereford & District A.A.
Sec: I. Astley
Tel: 098 122 283
Permits from local tackle shops

LUGG MILL
Mrs Garlick
Lugg Bridge House, Lugwardine, Hereford
Permits from above

Marteg River

Rhayader A.A.
Sec: Mrs Jones
Tel: 0597 810866
Permits also available from:
Mrs Powell
Garth House, Rhayader
Tel: 0597 810451
Vulcan Motel
Doldowlod, Nr. Llandrindod Wells
Tel: 0579 810438

MONNOW RIVER
Skenfrith
W. E. Price
The Malthouse Farm
Permits from G & B Sports, 10 Broad Street, Ross on Wye

PRIORY WATER
Priory Motel
Skenfrith
Tel: 060 084 210
Permits from above

Wye River

Cwmbran A.A.
Sec: P.M. Gulliford
Tel: 06333 5036
Black Lion Hotel
Llangurig, nr. Llanidloes
Tel: 0555 223
Day and week permits from above
Glansevern Arms Hotel
Pontmawr, Llangurig
Tel: 05515 240
Permits available from above
FORD FAWR
W. N. Lloyd
Head Water Bailiff
Bridgend Cottage
Glasbury-on-Wye, Hereford
Tel: 049 74 227
Permits on application from above
GABALVA WATER
Mrs Williams
Gabalva Farm, Whitney on Wye
Permits from above
GARNONS WATER
Garnons Estate Office
Bridge Sollars
Tel: 098 122 235
Permits from above
GLANWYE WATER
Mrs Potter
Hay-on-Wye
Tel: 0497 820368
Permits in advance from above
GLASBURY-BUILTH WELLS
Woosnam & Tyler Estate Agents
Dolgarreg, North Road, Builth Wells
Tel: 09822 3248
Permits from above
HAY CASTLE & CLYRO COURT WATER
W. N. Lloyd
Head Water Bailiff
Bridgend Cottage, Glasbury on Wye
Tel: 049 74 227
Permits from above in advance

HEREFORD 8 MILE STRETCH
Hereford & District A.A.
Sec: I. Astley
Tel: 098122 283
Permits from local tackle shops

HOLME LACY BEAT NO. 5
Permits from H. Hatton Fishing Tackle
64 St. Owen Street, Hereford
LONGWORTH HALL HOTEL STRETCH
Longworth Hall Hotel
Lugwardine
Mr Smith
Permits from above
MOCCAS WATER
Red Lion Hotel
Bredwardine
Tel: 098 17 303
Permits in advance
Rhayader A.A.
Sec: Mrs Jones
'Ty Gwyrth', South Street, Rhayader, Pow
Tel: 0597 810866
Day, week and season permits also available from:
Powells Newsagents
Garth House, Rhayader
Tel: 0597 810451
Davisports, Rhayader
J. Price, Nantymynach, Nantmel
Vulcan Motel, Doldowlod, Llandrindod Wells
ROSS ON WYE TOWN STRETCH
Sec: H. Webb
Permits from G & B Sports
10 Broad Street, Ross on Wye
SUFTON WATER
Mordiford Bridge
Permits from Mrs E. Boulcott
Yew Tree Cottage, Mordiford
WYE BRIDGE AREA
Montmouth District Council
Council Offices, Whitecross Street
Tel: 0600 2122
Day, week and season permits from abo

STILLWATERS

Elan Valley Lakes

Nr. Rhayader
Elan Estate Office
Elan Village, Rhayader, Powys
Tel: 0597 810449
Season, week and day permits available
Elan Valley Hotel
Elan Village
Tel: 059782 448
Day and week permits from hotel

LLYNGWYN LAKE
Rhayader A.A.
Sec: Mrs Jones
'Ty Gwyrth', South Street, Rhayader, Po
Tel: 0597 810866
Permits also available from:
Powells Newsagent
Garth House, Rhayader
Tel: 0591 810451
Davisports, Rhayader
J. Price, Nantymynach, Nantmel
Vulcan Motel, Doldowlod, Llandrindod Wells
Elan Valley Hotel, Elan Village
Tel: 059782 448
Day and week permits from hotel

TROEDYRHIW LAKES
D. W. Whelan
Troedyrhiw Isaf, Llangammarch Wells

Where you can fish

WHERE TO FISH

Englan

North-West

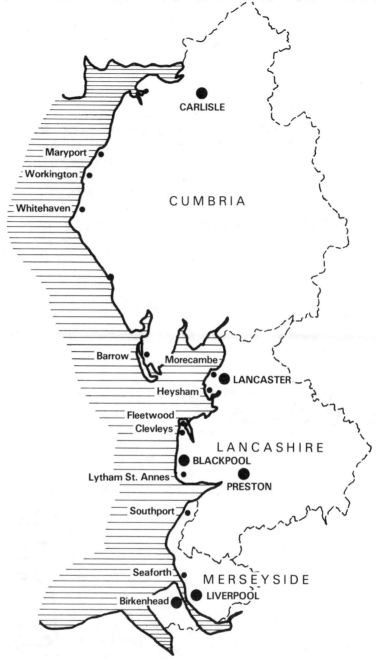

CARLISLE

Maryport

Workington

Whitehaven

CUMBRIA

Barrow

Morecambe

LANCASTER

Heysham

Fleetwood

Clevleys

LANCASHIRE

BLACKPOOL

Lytham St. Annes

PRESTON

Southport

Seaforth

MERSEYSIDE

Birkenhead

LIVERPOOL

Cumbria

MARYPORT   Good pier and shore fishing. The Promenade Beach and Grasslot Beach are both good beach fishing marks and among the species you can expect are Pollack, Pouting, Flounder and Plaice. Boat caught species include Bass, Dogfish, Coalfish, Skate, Mackerel, Conger and Cod in Winter.

WORKINGTON   Harrington Beach, 2 miles South of Workington is a much favoured beach fishing mark. Flatties, Mackerel, Cod and Silver Eels are what you can expect there. Another good beach mark is Siddick beach to the North of Workington. Some of the best boat fishing in the area can be had just one mile off Harrington. Skate, Pouting, Mackerel, Dogfish, Cod and Silver Eels are the main catches in deep water.

WHITEHAVEN Rock fishing is popular at Parton and St Bees Head. Wellington Beach and Whitehaven Harbour are quite productive. Species caught from shore include Pouting, Silver Eels, Whiting, Mackerel and Plaice. The best deep water species caught in the area are Cod, Mackerel and Skate.

BARROW IN FURNESS Good boat fishing marks around this area. Scaith Hole, Piel Island and Foulney Island are just three to look out for. The main species caught here include Bass, Plaice, Skate, Whiting and Cod.

Charters arranged by
Hamays Tackle Shop
Tel: 0229 22571

Lancashire

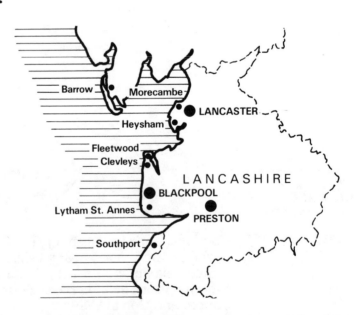

HEYSHAM All year round fishing from Heysham Harbour. Fish to be expected are Conger, Pouting, Mullet, Flounders and Dabs.

MORECAMBE All year round fishing. Beach fishing yields Plaice, Dabs, Bass and Flounders during the Summer and Autumn. Whiting can be expected during the Winter. Boat fishing off Morecambe fair and the most caught species are Conger, Mackerel, Dogfish and Cod.

FLEETWOOD Good boat and shore fishing. Beach fishing marks at Marine Beach and estuary of River Wyre quite productive. Species caught from shore include Cod, Bass, Plaice, Skate and Mullet. Boat fishing good with a variety of species including flatties, Dogfish, Pouting, Haddock, Whiting, Ling and Pollack.

Bay Fisher
Skipper: Bob Rayner
Tel: 0253 810241

Onceagain
Skipper: Guy Timmerman
Tel: 03917 71273

Viking II
Skipper: Gordon Wilson
Tel: 039 18 5339 or
Duncan Catterall
Tel: 0772 863184 after 6.15

Wandering Star & Viking II
Skipper: Gordon Wilson
Tel: 03917 5339

Karen Margaret
Skipper: Chris Donnelly
Tel: 0253 866462

CLEVELEYS The towns breakwater and the beach at Anchorsholme are good marks for Plaice, Dab, Flounder and Whiting. Boat fishing produces good catches of Conger, Mackerel, Sole and Tope.

BLACKPOOL Fishing from the North Pier is best from September through to the end of February. You can then expect good catches of Codling, Dabs and Whiting. Best boat fishing catches include Mackerel, Cod, Tope and Bass. All local beaches are poor in Summer but Winter time brings good sport with Pouting, Cod, Flounder and Dabs.

LYTHAM & LYTHAM ST. ANNES Fishing from the promenade is fair with the main catches being Cod, Flounder, Plaice and Dabs. Boat fishing also fair with more or less the same species as at Blackpool being caught.

Merseyside

SOUTHPORT   The flat sandy shore and weak tides make pier fishing the most productive at this location. The main species caught here in Win are Whiting, Codling and flatties. At varying times of the year species caught include Conger, Gurnard, Mullet, Bass and Dogfish. Boat fishing in the area produces good catches of Cod Whiting, Bass, Mackerel and the occasional Black Bream.

SEAFORTH   Fishing around Seaforth rocks is very good. During the Summe the main catches are Flounder, Dabs, Plaice and Dogfish. Durin the Winter Cod up to 25lbs, Whiting and the occasional Thornb are caught.

LIVERPOOL DOCKS   Mainly flatties but the occasional Whiting, Dogfish and Cod are also caught. Some big Congers under all the breakwaters. Be su to obtain permit from Mersey Docks and Harbour Company bef fishing here though.

Sultan
Skipper: Ron Martland
Tel: 051 6393061
30 foot, 10 rods

Hoyle Star
Tel: 051 632 3884
32 foot, 12 rods

The Bristol Channel

Avon

WESTON SUPER MARE — Shore and Boat fishing fair. During Winter the best catches are Pout, Cod and Whiting. During Spring and Summer, Flounder, Bass, Dabs, Skate, Conger and Sole are the main catches to be made.

Weston Star
Skipper: Ivan Nash
Tel: 0934 22788

Somerset

WATCHET — Good boat fishing location with lots of excellent marks. Steart Flats, near Watchet are productive with good catches of Flounders, Dabs and Rays. Shore fishing from Bassington and Dunster Beaches are reasonable for Dogfish and Conger. These beaches have produced three types of Ray.

MINEHEAD — Beach fishing reasonable for Flounder, Dabs and Bass. Boat fishing mainly for Conger, Cod, Bass and Dogfish. Some good catches of Mackerel in Summer. Harbour fishing for Mullet, Codling and Bass.

Joseph-Marrie II
Skipper: Dave Roberts
Tel: 0643 3892
33 ft, 10 rods

Pelican II
Tel: 0643 5272

Searcher
Tel: 0643 3687

Gay Spartan
Tel: 0643 2701

Sundown
Tel: 0643 5361

Minehead Angler
Skipper: T. Arnold
Tel: 0643 5730 or 4158

Michael I
Skipper: Roger Baker
Tel: 0643 3974

Miss Tilley
Tel: 0643 2674

South-West

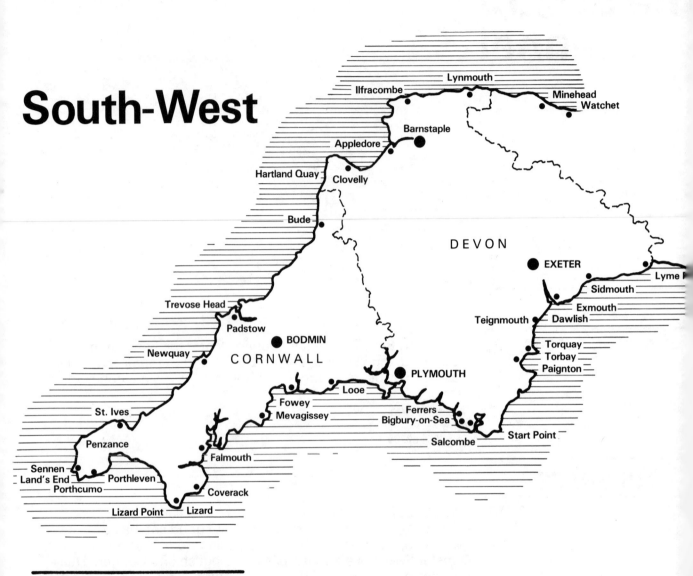

Map labels: Lynmouth, Ilfracombe, Minehead, Watchet, Barnstaple, Appledore, Hartland Quay, Clovelly, Bude, DEVON, EXETER, Lyme, Sidmouth, Exmouth, Teignmouth, Dawlish, Trevose Head, Padstow, BODMIN, Torquay, Torbay, Paignton, Newquay, CORNWALL, PLYMOUTH, St. Ives, Looe, Fowey, Mevagissey, Ferrers, Bigbury-on-Sea, Penzance, Salcombe, Start Point, Sennen, Land's End, Falmouth, Porthleven, Porthcumo, Coverack, Lizard Point, Lizard

Devon – North

LYNMOUTH Reasonable shore fishing and boat fishing. The usual species ca be expected if shore fishing. A variety of species including som good Mullet can be had when boat fishing in some of the rough waters. Good Shark fishing available.

ILFRACOMBE The pier provides good catches of Mackerel, Garfish, Bass and Flatties. Beach fishing produces good catches of Bass, Macker and Mullet. The best boat fishing takes place not far from the q where you can expect good hauls of Tope, Skate and Cod.

Exel
Skipper: Dave Clemence
Tel: 0271 63460

Princess
Skipper: J. Barbeary
Tel: 0271 64957

APPLEDORE Shore fishing is quite successful with the main catches being Bass and Flatties. Fishing from the quay may bring you, among other species, Bass, Flounders and Dabs. Boat fishing, especially Shark fishing is popular here.

CLOVELLY All year round fishing with a good variety of species available. Bull Huss, Conger, Cod, Whiting and Dogfish are among the species you can expect. Bass and Mackerel are prevalent in the Summer as are Ray in the Winter.

Janelle
Tel: 023 73 596

HARTLAND Excellent sea fishing with many species available including Whiting, Mullet and Pouting. Bass up to 13lbs have been caught. Congers are also a reasonably good size.

Devon – South

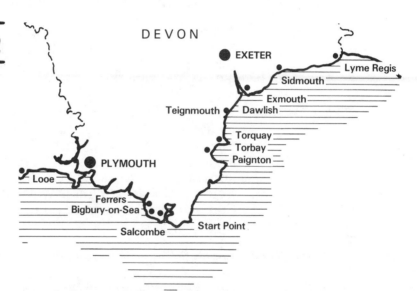

DEVON

EXETER
Lyme Regis
Sidmouth
Exmouth
Teignmouth — Dawlish
Torquay
Torbay
Paignton
PLYMOUTH
Looe
Ferrers
Bigbury-on-Sea
Start Point
Salcombe

PLYMOUTH Boat fishing offers deep water wrecks and reef fishing within a 40 mile radius of Plymouth. Conger, Ling, Pollack, Coalfish, Turbot and Electric Ray are some of the common catches. Plymouth harbour is good for Congers of up to 60lb. Also good for Ray. Trinity Pier is excellent for Flounders, Bass and Grey Mullet.

Buster
Skipper: J. Folland
Tel: 0752 668322
34 foot, 10 rods, accommodation can be arranged

The Gay Girls
Skipper: Bob Williamson
Tel: 0752 45975

June Lipet
Skipper: Jim Campbell
Tel: 0822 832652

Marco
Skipper: Colin Johns
Tel: 0752 339220
Day, weekly or evening charters

Satrat
Skippers: Harry Steptoe
Tel: 0752 708476
Terry Launce
Tel: 0752 261739
Wreck, shark, reef charters
Channel Isle charters can be arranged

Solan Goose
Furzeland Fishing & Charters
Tel: 0752 59673
Day or weekly charters
30 foot, 12 rods

Sunlight
Skipper: Ray Parsons
Tel: 0752 21722
Wreck, reef and shark fishing

NEWTON FERRERS Shore and boat fishing, both very good. Species caught from shore include Pollack, Bass and Flounders. Boat fishing produces good catches of Mackerel, Flatties, Mullet and Conger. The Shark season is from June to October.

BIGBURY-ON-SEA The long sandy beach here shelves very gradually and the bigger fish are in the deep water. The best catch here are excellent Bass – caught from shore and boat. Apart from Bass the most common species caught are Flatties.

SALCOMBE A good boat fishing location with plenty of excellent boat marks. The main catches here are Plaice, Turbot, Dabs and Flounder. The Gilt-head Bream is a common visitor to the area and they are often taken up to 6lbs.

START POINT The best time to fish here is early morning. The Skerries Bank not far away produces excellent catches of Turbot, Plaice, Dabs and Rays for boat anglers. Those fishing from the shore or rocks can also have good catches of Dabs, Rays and Plaice if they can cast into the sandy areas between the rocks. However, the best catch from beach here is Wrasse which are a good size here. In late Summer there are a good number of Black Bream to be had especially close to the shore line.

PAIGNTON Beach fishing good especially during Summer and Autumn. Species to expect here include Bass, Mullet, Mackerel and Bass. Boat fishing good for Mackerel in its season.

BRIXHAM Brixham's breakwater is ideal if you're after Conger, especially on Winter nights when there's a frost.

Tremlet Fisherman
Skipper: Albert King
Tel: 08045 6380
12 rods, fishing in the English Channel

DARTMOUTH Daytime fishing is best for Bass and Pouting. Dusk and after dark are best for Flounders, Dabs and the occasional Plaice. During the Summer large numbers of Mackerel gather here and the best time to catch them is early morning or late evening. Winter is best for Flounders and the best bait to use for them is peeler or soft-back.

Penny Louise
Skipper: Lawrie Dawson
Tel: 08043 28381
32 foot, 12 rods

Pisces
Skipper: B. Dash
Tel: 08043 3069
32 foot, 10 rods, wreck fishing

TORBAY
Best shore fishing mark is Hopes Nose, via the Marine Drive. One of many good catches in these waters is Wrasse — up to 7lbs are common. In the rocks to the right of the main area there are excellent Conger to be had. Best catches (40lbs +) are taken at night. Black Bream and Mullet are two more good sized catches often caught here.

Graham
Tel: 0803 55 9025

TORQUAY
Plenty of wreck fishing available along the Skerries Bank where there are excellent catches of Conger, Pollack, Bass, Flatties and Turbot to be made. Many good beach marks including Hopes Nose for Bass and Plaice, Abbey Sands and Anstey's Cove. Babbacombe Pier is excellent for Mackerel in its season.

TEIGNMOUTH
A good centre for Plaice, Flounders and Bass, the biggest catches coming between October and March. The rocks between Teignmouth and Dawlish are excellent for big catches of Bass.

DAWLISH
Excellent fishing all around the area but one of the best shore fishing marks is between Smuggler's Gap and Spray Point. There are some good catches of Mackerel in the Summer months. Dawlish breakwater sometimes produces memorable catches of a variety of species. About 1 mile out from Parson and Clerk Rocks boat anglers can have good sport with Conger and Dogfish.

EXMOUTH
The pier situated just opposite Dawlish Warren provides excellent sport. It is a great platform for those after Pollack, Wrasse, Bass, Pouting and Flatties. During Autumn the best time to fish for Bass, Garfish and Mackerel is at dusk and early morning. Flounder are common in Winter and Plaice are caught from time to time. Conger of up to 50lbs have been landed here.

SIDMOUTH
Excellent beach and boat fishing in Sidmouth Bay area. Mackerel are best during Spring and Summer as are Pollack. Bass to 13lbs, Skate to over 100lbs, good sized Tope and Bull Huss are common catches. Other common species here are Plaice, Turbot, Whiting, Dabs and Flounders.

Cornwall – North

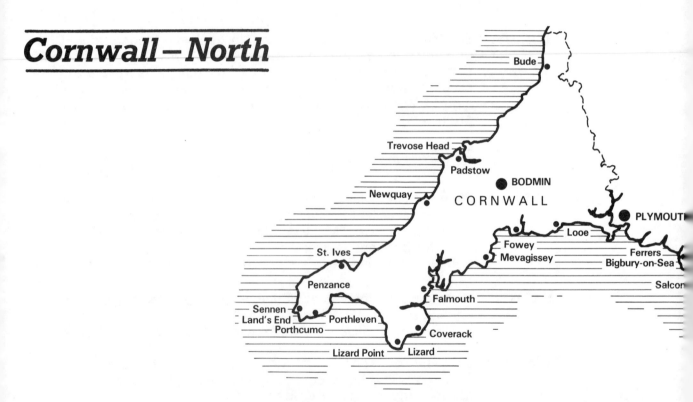

BUDE   Mainly shore fishing at any of the number of excellent shore-marks. Two of the best marks are Tretherick Point, and Stepper Point. Good catches of Bass, Dabs, Flounder and Ray to be had both marks especially during early morning and after dusk. Good sized Rays are common from the beach during Summer and Autumn.

PADSTOW   Boatfishing is excellent especially if you're after Porbeagle Shark. The best catches can be had less than a mile from the cliff as the sharks hunt over the rocky grounds close by. Tope give good sp from time to time. Other catches here from shore and boat are Plaice, Mackerel, Bass, Turbot, Mullet, Pollack and Whiting.

Baroness
Skipper: Clive Martin
Tel: 020 888 480

Lady Jane
Skipper: Ray Provis
Tel: 020 886 2239

TREVOSE HEAD One of the best shore fishing marks in the country but caution must be taken whilst fishing here. Because of the cliff erosion and huge swells it is very dangerous to fish from the lower edges. However the fishing here is excellent and there is a wide range of species to be had. One of the best catches is Tope which go up to 40lbs. Mackerel are caught, just off the headland, often to a very good weight. Wrasse, Garfish and Pollack are just three of other species caught often at this great beach mark.

NEWQUAY Best shore-fishing marks are on the rocks at either side of the bay. One in particular is Town Head where Mackerel, Garfish and Flatties are the main catch. Early morning and late evening are best times to fish at. The piers are also good fishing marks. Most common species caught in the area during the Summer are Pollack, Mackerel and Garfish. During Autumn there are good catches of Plaice and Dabs to be had especially at night time. Wintertime provides the shore angler with excellent catches of Codling and Spurdog, best catches being made at night. Bass and Dabs are also common catches during Winter.

ST IVES Beach fishing is good with lots of great beach and rock marks to choose from. Main shorefishing quarry is Bass. There are many species present here and some of the most common are Pollack, Mullet, Flatties and Garfish. One of the best catches taken by boats during Summer is Mackerel.

SENNEN Less than ½ mile from Lands End, Sennen Beach is subject to heavy surf making it ideal for Bass. Specimens of up to 13lbs have been caught here but it is thought that it is only a matter of time before that record is broken. Another good catch is Grey Mullet which arrive in massive shoals every couple of years. Sennen Harbour fishes well for a variety of species including Pollack, Mackerel, Wrasse, Garfish, Mullet and Bass. At Lands End itself Pollack of up to 10lbs are often taken.

PORTH CURNO Many excellent beach marks to fish from. Among the good catches to be had here are Bass, Garfish, Pollack, Wrasse, Mackerel and Small Eyed Ray. Turbot can be caught from the shore occasionally especially during early Winter.

Cornwall-South

MOUSEHOLE The Pier offers good fishing with a variety of species present. Some of the species you can expect at varying times of year are Mackerel, Pollack, Garfish, Wrasse, Bream and Whiting. Boat fishing is also productive especially for Sharks. One of the best boat marks is Runnel Stone.

PENZANCE Excellent boat, shore and pier fishing. Best time to fish here is between June and November. Among the species you can expec are Pollack, Bass, Mackerel and Mullet. Sharks provide some goc sport for those fishing from boats.

PORTHLEVEN Well known for its good hauls of Bass, they are best fished durin rising tide after dark. During early morning and late evening there is a variety of excellent catches to be made. Some of the species you can expect here are Grey Mullet, Wrasse, Mackerel, Garfish, Bass and Pollack.

THE LIZARD Britain's most southerly point provides good sport for anglers wit a wide range of species present. Large Wrasse are common no more than 100 yards away from the rocks. Mackerel and Bass are most common in early morning and late evening. Plenty of good Conger fishing points and the best time to try for them is well aft dark.

COVERACK Situated on the Eastern side of the Lizard this small town provide the shore angler with some excellent sport. Among the species you can expect here are Pollack, Wrasse, Garfish, Mackerel and Bass during Summer. Night time fishing from the harbour breakwater produces good catches of Conger and Bull Huss. To the east of Coverack is excellent for Wrasse.

MEVAGISSEY The southern breakwater produces some good catches all year round. Some of the species you can expect from this breakwater are Mackerel, Garfish, Bass and Pollack. After dark the breakwater is good for Bass and Conger. Mullet are another excellent catch round the whole harbour area. Boat fishing around Mevagissey is good, especially in the Summer with Shark being increasingly popular here.

Excalibur
Skipper: Ray Andrews
Tel: 0726 882214

FALMOUTH Many excellent shore and boat fishing marks in the Falmouth area. The Prince of Wales Pier and Quay are best fished at night and then the principle catches are Pollack, Mackerel, Flounder and Bass. Trefusis Point, a 1 mile long rocky beach fishes well for Mackerel, Wrasse, Pollack, Bass and the occasional Ray. At the entrance to Falmouth harbour, Pedennis Point has many a good of Wrasse and Pollack to be had. On the eastern side of the harbour is St Anthony's Head, a favourite mark for Wrasse. Fish under the head during Autumn and you should have good catches of Black Bream.

One of the best boat fishing marks in the area is just off Pendennis Point. Here there are good catches of Wrasse to be made and excellent Conger fishing at night. Black Rock, near Pendennis Point is good for Bass and Pollack.

Monkswood
Skipper: Frank Vinnicombe
Tel: 0326 72775

Philanderer
Skipper: Colin McGillivary
Tel: 0326 250711

FOWEY The harbour area provides some excellent fishing. Bass, Mullet and Flounder are the main quarry. Just past Bodinnick, there have been some fine catches of Conger at night. Some specimens have been 50lbs and more. Out past the jetties is a great location for Plaice and Flounder. The British record Flounder was landed here and it weighed in at 5lb 11oz.

LOOE Many excellent beach fishing marks around the area. Shark fishing is one of the most popular pastimes here, in fact Looe is fast becoming a household name in big-game angling. Some of the best beach marks to the West of Banjo Point are Wallace Beach, Leak Rock and Hannafore Point. These three marks are all good for Garfish, Conger, Mackerel, Wrasse and Pollack. Plaidy Beach, Seaton and Downderry, all to the east of Stinker Cover are all good for Bass and Pollack.

There are also some fine boat marks in the Looe area. Phillips Rock and Bretons are both excellent for Ling, Cod, Bream, Conger and Pollack. The area beyond the Eddystone is good for Shark, Blues up to 100lbs and Porbeagle up to 500lbs.

Sundancer
Skipper: John Hicks
Tel: 601 05035

Southern

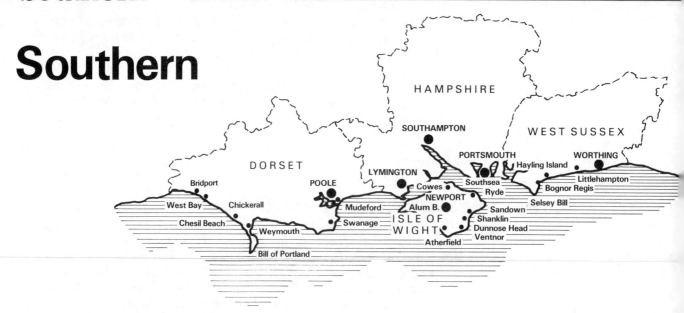

Dorset

LYME REGIS The small, sometimes extremely stormy harbour gives good spor[t] for Bass, as does the shore. The best times to go after Bass is at dusk and early morning. Mackerel are an excellent catch during Summer and Autumn. Conger of 20lbs and more are common around the harbour. The best boat caught species are Skate and Conger which are plentiful about 2-3 miles from shore. Other species are Pollack, Thornback Ray, Pouting, Bull Huss and Spurdog.

BRIDPORT Beach fishing produces some good catches of Pouting, Flatties, Bass, Whiting, Cod and Conger. Boat fishing in the West Bay area.

Avocet
Skipper: Bert Powell
Tel: 0308 23475

Mako
Skipper: Dave Dichter
Tel: 0308 23941

Tia Maria
Skipper: Jack Ellis
Tel: 0308 85338

WEST BAY West Bay harbour at the Western end of Cheshil Beach is best fished after dark. The main species caught here are Spurdog, Pollack, Bass, Pouting and Flatties. There are some good catch[es] of Mackerel and Garfish to be had after dusk especially during t[he] Summer.

CHESIL BEACH The 18 mile long Cheshil Beach fishes best after dark, offering a[t] least 20 species. December and January are best for Cod (up to 14lbs). Dabs, Whiting, Tope and Spurdog in Winter, are joined [by] Plaice during the Summer. Excellent sized Tope and Congers ar[e] often caught here.

CHICKERELL Near Chickerell is the fleet, a large, calm lagoon with excellent fishing to be had. Among the species you can expect here are Flounder, Silver Eels, Bass and Dabs.

BILL OF PORTLAND Very rocky and steep, caution must be taken when fishing here. One of the many excellent species taken from here are Congers of up to 60lbs. Mullet of up to 10lb are common. Other good catches include Bass and Pollack.

WEYMOUTH The Stone Pier Breakwater has some good catches of Flatties and Whitings to be had at the inshore end. Between the Stone Pier and Portland Breakwater excellent catches of Wrasse, Bass, Pout and Pollack can be made. Weymouth Bay is best after dark especially for Bass. Round the bay is Osmington Mills where the rocky ledges make for good catches of Bull Huss, Bass and Pout.

Geoff Hobson Boat Charter
Tel: 0305 785032
Challenger
Skipper: Alan Boram
Tel: 0305 784275

Flamer
Skipper: Sam Fowler
Tel: 03056 7068

LULWORTH COVE One of the country's leading areas for Conger. Specimens of 25-35lbs are not uncommon in this rocky terrain.

POOLE Excellent boat fishing venue with many good catches of Tope, Bass, Conger and Bream being made quite near the shore. Harbour fishing also good with the principle catches being Plaice, Flounders and Bass.

Neptune
Skipper: Bill Cooper
Tel: 020 13 79830
Kingfisher
Skipper: Bert Fray
Tel: 020 13 6597

Ivory Gull
Skipper: Norman Blow
Tel: 0202 33311

BOURNEMOUTH Beach fishing only fair with the only worthwhile catches being Sole, Dabs and Pout. The pier fishes well all year round with a good variety of species being taken. In Winter the favourite catches are Whiting, Codling, Pout and the occasional Plaice. In Summer the variety of species caught from the pier include Plaice, Dabs, Flounders, Sole, Bass, Pollack and Black Bream. Some good size Congers are often caught from under the Pier. About ½ mile from the pier the rocks yield good catches of Pollack. Further out there are excellent catches of Mackerel and Tope to be made during the Summer. East of Bournemouth, the Southbourne Rough is a good mixed fishing ground.

MUDEFORD Situated at entrance to Christchurch Harbour. Mudeford provides good all round sport for the sea angler. Beaches in the area are good for Flounders, Skate, Bass and Whiting. Boat fishing produces some good catches of Tope, Skate, Dogfish, Conger and some Thresher Shark.

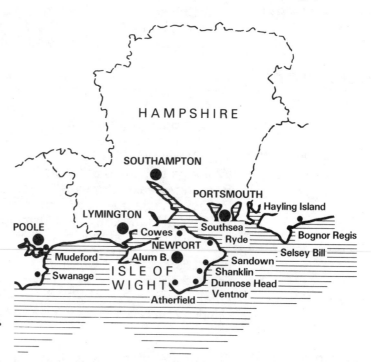

Hampshire

LYMINGTON Boat fishing is good with Skate, Conger, Dogfish and Pout not fa
out from the town. Further out excellent Tope is to be had with
some good cathes of Bass. Beach fishing in the area is restricted
as many of the beaches are privately owned. One of the most
popular is the one-mile long Park Shore. Here you can catch
Dogfish, Bass, Tope, Conger and Skate at varying times of the
year.

KEYHAVEN
Blue Ribbon
Skipper: Ron Bunday
Tel: 0703 776075

GOSPORT The towns Stoke Bay provides excellent catches of Flatties, Pou
Bass and Bream in the Summer for the shore fisherman. Around
the demolished pier good catches of Bass can be had. Boat fishi
around Stokes Bay is also good, some of the best catches being
Tope, Conger and Cod.

SOUTHSEA The Blocks, just off Southsea is an excellent boat fishing mark. I
gives excellent results with Bass and some good catches of Polla
and Plaice. Fishing from South beach produced Pout, Whiting,
Wrasse and Pollack. Cod and Turbot are occasionally caught in
Winter. Bass around the entrance of the harbour is the main cate
the boat fisher can expect.

PORTSMOUTH Fishing from the harbour is difficult because of all the traffic
coming in and out of the harbour. The Haslar Sea Wall near the
entrance to the harbour produces good results with Pout, Whitir
and Wrasse.

HAYLING ISLAND Beach fishing produces good results especially from the South Beach where you can expect catches of Plaice, Whiting, Dabs and Flounders at varying times throughout the year. Boat fishing in the Hayling Bay for Tope, Skate, Bass and Mackerel is good with one of the best areas being Church Rocks.

Porbeagle & Sea Jay
Skippers: Peter & Colin Johnson
Tel: 0734 787269/791672
Fishing around Selsey, Nab & Isle of Wight

SOUTHAMPTON The eastern side of Southampton Water is productive for anglers especially for those after Flatties. Flounders are caught easily at Weston Beach, near Netley. This beach is also very good for Bass. Equally good for Flounder and Bass is Hamble just along from Netley. Boat fishing in the area produces Flounder and Bass also but there are also some good mixed fishing grounds at Calshott and Greenland Buoy.

The Isle of Wight

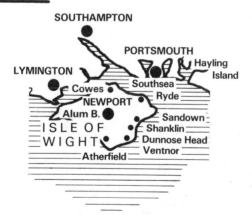

Tailing a big tope from the Solent. Careful handling allows us to return the fish alive – the commonsense approach these days.

SANDOWN BAY All beaches for Bass and Plaice. Red Cliff, to the left of the bay for good Conger. The Pier for Dabs, Plaice, Bass and Mullet.

ALUM BAY Very rocky terrain which attracts big specimens. Good sized Bass and occasionally a Thornback Ray. Alum Bay is one of the few spots on the island where Turbot are caught.

NEEDLES AREA

Blue Ribbon
Skipper: Ron Bunday
Tel: 0706 776075

Avocet
Skipper: Alan Warner
Tel: 0983 753467

SHANKLIN Best boat fishing marks are Horseshore Lodge and Luccombe. Here you can get results with Bass, Pollack and Conger. Fishing from Shanklin Pier is erratic but if you are patient Congers, Mackerel and Pollack are the species you can expect.

DUNNOSE HEAD A very rocky area with fierce tides, Dunnose Head has some goo marks for boat fishing. Most frequent catches here are Conger, Huss, Black Bream and Dogfish.

ATHERFIELD Best fishing is from boats, particularly after dark. Species you ca expect are Pouting, Tope, Bass and Conger.

VENTNOR Pier, Beach and Boat fishing. Pier fishing from April to Septemb with good variety of catches including Mackerel, Bream, Bass, Plaice, Flounder, Wrasse, Skate and Grey Mullet.

RYDE Good fishing from pier with principle catches being Plaice, Brear Grey Mullet, Pollack and Bass. Boat fishing fair with good catch of Dabs, Skate, Conger and Mackerel being taken. Beach caugh species include Sole, Bass and Plaice.

COWES Some excellent beach marks. Species you can expect here are Flounders, Bass, Whiting. Harbour fishing produces good variet of species including Pollack, Whiting and Pout.

Sussex-West

SELSEY BILL Most of the rock off Selsey produce good catches of many species. In the Summer Black Bream, Conger, Rays and Tope a caught frequently. Although the strong tides around the area create excellent fishing, care should be taken when both boat o beach fishing in this area. Beach fishing brings good results her with Bass and Bream in the Summer and Whiting and Cod in th Winter.

BOGNOR REGIS Boat fishing is excellent for Dogfish, Skate, Conger and Bull Huss with Bream in the Summer. You can add to these Cod and Whiting in the Winter. Beach fishing here can produce good results with Bass, Whiting and Flatties in Winter. There are good catches of Bass during the Summer months.

LITTLEHAMPTON Best known for its excellent Black Bream Littlehampton is probably one of the best boat fishing locations in West Sussex. Some of the best Black Bream marks are Kingsmere Rocks, about 5½ miles South of the town, the Ditches which are near the Kingsmere Rocks and a number of marks around the Winter Knoll which is just 1½ miles out. The Black Bream season lasts from April to June. Apart from Black Bream excellent catches of Bull Huss, Mackerel, Tope and Congers are common.

Best of All
Skipper: R. E. Hughes
Tel: 0903 44375
Wreck & Mark fishing day or night

Charlotte Newman
Skipper: Brian Barret
Tel: 0243 551666

Patricia A
Skipper: Alan Walker
Tel: 090 6433437

Starbreaker
Tel: 0256 61758
32 foot, 10 rods

Lisamarie of Arun
Skipper: Michael Driscol
Tel: 0243 821655

Tarka
Skipper: Ross Fisher
Tel: 024 369 4863

Jung Frau
Skipper: Ian Warren
Tel: 090 63 3976

Ariel
Skipper: Mike Pratt
Tel: 0798 42370

Our Gaye
Skipper: Brian Ferris
Tel: 090 64 4927

Tobermory
Skipper: Peter Hill
Tel: 090 64 5763

Margaret Elaine
Skipper: Tony Steel
Tel: 090 64 3870

WORTHING Boat fishing, up to a mile out of Worthing, produces good results with flatfish, especially Plaice. Beach fishing brings good results with not only the flatfish but Black Bream, Bass and Mullet in the Summer. Sole is a common catch during Autumn and Winter. Worthing Pier has some good fishing to offer with Flounders, Whiting and Sole in the Winter and Black Bream and Mullet during the Spring and Summer.

SHOREHAM (SHOREHAM HARBOUR)

John LL
Skipper: John Landale
Tel: 0273 594930

Cecilia Rose
Skipper: Ken Voice
Tel: 0273 592461

Buci
Skipper: Peter Lamont
Tel: 0273 418219

Blue Marlin
Skipper: Ron Saunders
Tel: 0273 417485

South-East

Sussex – East

HOVE Boat fishing produces good results with Plaice, Skate, Dabs and Mackerel in the Summer and Whiting in Winter. Beach fishing in Hove yields some quite good Flatties and Bass.

BRIGHTON Best beach fishing here is off the Blue Lagoon beaches. Night fishing produces best results with Flounders and Bass being the best catches. The Black Rock and its surrounding area situated the eastern area of the town is one of the best boat fishing mark It yields Conger, Skate and Whiting in Winter and good Bream Summer. Rock Taw produces excellent catches of Tope (40lbs during the Summer and Autumn as well as many other species.

Brighton Sea Angling Services
Tel: 0273 685713/689528
Wreck fishing & general fishing

Compass Rose
Skipper: Peter Hayles
Tel: 0273 689528

Royal Eagle
Skipper: Peter Blacklock
Tel: 044 46 3876

Nimrod
Skipper: Jim Hollingsworth
Tel: 07917 4793

Skintus II
Skipper: Fred Cox
Tel: 01647 8414

Sea Jay
Skipper: Robert Whitehead
Tel: 07917 3374

May Archer
Skipper: R. A. May
Tel: 0273 592251

Riptide
Skipper: Derek Dalmon
Tel: 0903 36759

Cee Heather
Skipper: Eric Collins
Tel: 0323 896793

Sea Break
Skipper: Brian
Tel: 0273 556601

NEWHAVEN Two of the best marks off Newhaven for boat fishing are the Dredger Dumping Grounds and the Red Shrave. The Red Shrave, just a mile out from the breakwater gives excellent catches of Whiting, Codling, Plaice, Dabs and Pout. A further mile out from here is the Dredger Dumping Grounds which is excellent if its Plaice, Dabs, Sole or Whiting you're after. Wrecks are many and some of the best lie about four miles out between Newhaven and Peacehaven. Here you can expect good catches of Conger, Pollack, Black Bream and Pout.

Beach fishing provides excellent catches of Bass from May to October. Pier fishing from either of the two piers is good with the main catch being Cod. Other species caught from the piers include Bass, Flounders, Congers, Dabs and Pout.

SEAFORD Some great beach fishing here. The promenade, with its sea wall provides some excellent marks for beach fishing. One of these is Tide Mills on the west end of the promenade. Here you can, during February, March and April, land excellent Plaice and Flounder. On the Eastern side of the Promenade lies the Buckle, a very rough area but during the Summer produces excellent catches of Conger. During the Summer the whole length of the Promenade offers a good Bass and Flatties mark. During Winter Codling, Whiting, Pout and Dabs are the main catches along the Promenade, although there are still excellent catches of Conger at night.

Boat fishing around Seaford is as good as the beach fishing here. At Tide Mills, on the West of the Promenade about 300 yards out, excellent hauls of Sole and Flounder are caught. At the opposite end of the town between Martello Towers and Splash Point, about 500 yards out lies Town Rock. This mark yields good catches of Bass in Summer and Cod and Whiting in the Winter. Another good mark is Martello Tower itself, where about 1 mile out there is Dogfish, Huss, Conger, Skate and Pout to be caught. Between Seaford and Cuckmere Haven, the Birling Gap has excellent catches of Bass.

BEACHY HEAD Strong tides off the head make this location dangerous to fish but the rewards are excellent. The best mark for Bass here is the Beachy Head Ledge, less than ½ mile away from the lighthouse. The best time for Bass is May to July. When the weather is calm around the head excellent catches of the fish can be caught.

Beachy Head is also well known for its Tope and the best catches of the fish are taken to the west of Beachy Head Ledge, in Summer. Another fish to look out for here during the Summer is Black Bream. A good mark for Plaice and Sole is called the Goldmine. It is just West of Sugar Loaf Rock at Hollywell. A small area of mud and sand, after high tide you can expect good results. As well as the marks already mentioned, Beachy Head and it's surrounding area provides excellent all year round fishing. Fishing off the rocks could land you with a number of species including Huss, Pout, Skate and even Whiting and Cod in the Winter.

EASTBOURNE Shore, boat and pier fishing available. Species to expect here at varying times in the year are Pouting, Plaice, Bream, Conger an Dabs.

BEXHILL-ON-SEA No pier. Beach fishing quite good. In Summer you can expect Bass, Rockling, Pout, Whiting and Dabs, Cod joins these for the Winter period. The best months for Bass are May, June and Ju

ST. LEONARDS Good all year round fishing from both boat and beach. Many species to be caught here including Bass, Mackerel, Whiting, C Bull Huss, Turbot and Flatties.

HASTINGS Boat fishing, especially wreck fishing can produce good results, with Conger, Cod, Pollack and Ling being what you can expect Inshore fishing mainly for Flatties but excellent Cod in Winter. E bait inshore are lugworms and in Winter squid or herring.

Hastings pier is excellent in Summer for Mackerel, Garfish, Dabs, Sole, Bass and Mullet. Winter brings Silver Whiting, Cod Flounders, and the occasional Plaice inshore. The best beach fishing is around the extensive areas of rocks, and the most popular baits to use are lugworm, white rag and peeler crab.

Helping Hand
Tel: 0424 433923
36 foot, 10 rods

RYE At Pett Level Beach the main catches are Bass and Flatties, especially Flounders and Dabs. In Rye Bay the main catches are Cod and Whiting inshore but the variety of species widens the further out you go. Deep water wrecking means fishing in the English Channel so do beware of the shipping traffic. Once you have found a suitable place the fish are excellent. Massive Cong are common as are big Tope. Spurdogs, Black Bream, Mackere Bull Huss, Pout and Dogfish are some of the others you will fin here at varying times throughout the year.

Closer inshore there are large numbers of Plaice and Dabs to taken with the occasional great Cod, often over 30lbs.

Kent

DUNGENESS Boat fishing to the South-East of Dungeness Point is a real haven for those after really big Congers. The great number of wrecks around here have been known to produce specimens of 60lbs and over. Other good catches from boats include Pollack, Bass and Conger. The best months for boat fishing are May to October. Shore fishing is also good here. Species to expect are Codling, Whiting, Pouting and Mackerel and the most productive months are October to February.

HYTHE Best fishing is from pier. Very good Bass here especially after dark. Boat fishing just out from the pier is also productive with Flounders being one of the best catches.

SANDGATE Some good fishing to be had here especially around the ridge of rock which extends for over 1 mile. This ridge is situated less than 50 yards out from the low water mark. During Spring and Summer the main species to expect are Plaice, Pouting, Whiting, Codling and Conger. Bass are excellent especially between July and October.

FOLKESTONE Good all round sea fishing location, with fishing productive from shore, pier and boat. Beach fishing is best after dusk when you can expect good catches of Conger and Bass. There are some excellent boat fishing marks around this location and among the species you can expect are Bream, Flatties, Pouting and Pollack. Cod are best from October to February and Mackerel are best from June to August. Conger of up to 50lbs have been caught here and probably the best place for them is near the pier.

Jenny
Tel: 032 24 46798
30 foot

Lady Anne
Skipper: Mick Fuller
Tel: 0303 56838
32 foot

Royal Charlotte: 38 foot
Portia: 36 foot
Tel: 030 382 2329
Cod fishing on the Varne Bank

Varne Angler
Skipper: Tom Wilks
Tel: 0303 56216

The easiest way to find a charter boat – and to enjoy sea fishing for the first time. Just go down to the harbour and wait for a mackerel trip.

DOVER Plans for a hoverport have disrupted the fishing here somewhat but the Southern breakwater and a few beaches are still availab[l] Cod, Whiting, Mackerel, Flatties and Skate are the main catche here.

Betty B
Skipper: Bill Solly
Tel: 0304 204542

DEAL All year round fishing activity. During Autumn and Winter there are good catches of Cod and Whiting to be made. In Spring an[d] Autumn the main catches are Bass, Mackerel, Skate, Dogfish, Black Bream, Flatties and Codling.

SANDWICH Species to expect here are Flounders, Codling, Grey Mullet, Pla and Pouting.

RAMSGATE Beach fishing good, but night fishing is best as during Summer beaches tend to be crowded. Boat fishing excellent with plenty good marks including Dumpton Gap for Flatties and the Rough Congers. In Spring and Summer the species you can expect ar[e] Soles, Dabs and Flounders with some excellent Bass from time time. In Winter the main species are Soles, Whiting, Cod, Flounders and Dogfish.

Bayside
Skipper: John Myers
Tel: 0843 583834

Enterprise
Skipper: Nigel Stephens
Tel: 0843 28437

Lady Sybil
Tel: 0843 582 702
32 foot, 12 rods, daily trips

Wendy Anne
Skipper: Wilkie Wilkinson
Tel: 0843 33617

BROADSTAIRS Shore and boat fishing quite good. Tope, Plaice, Bass, Pouting and Whiting are the main species you can expect here.

MARGATE A good all round fishing location with some fine catches to be made. Excellent catches of Cod during Spring and Autumn, up to 20lbs. Shore fishing for Bass very productive. Stone pier Cod in Winter and the wooden pier for some excellent Mullet. Good catches of Tope from boats.

HERNE BAY All year round fishing with good variety of fish available. Species to expect are Flounders, Dabs, Silver Eels, Mullet, Dogfish, Plaice and Skate. Excellent location for Tope fishing from May to September. Bass are also prevalent from June to September. Cod can be caught in good quantity during the Autumn and Winter.

Jacky
Skipper: Peter Neame
Tel: 022 73 62321

WHITSTABLE Excellent location for sea-fishing. During Winter there are some good catches of Cod to be made especially from Tankerton Beach. Other species you can expect here are Plaice, Bass, Dabs, Eels, Flounder and Skate.

QUEENBOROUGH
Kerry Louise
Skipper: Tony Kemsley
Tel: 0795 873246

Pamelakay
Skipper: Dave Ferigan
Tel: 0634 54203

Landward
Skipper: Mike Deller
Tel: 0634 573134

Ryland
Skipper: James Wright
Tel: 0634 573134

GILLINGHAM
Dyme Star
Skipper: Dave Allen
Tel: 0634 43137

Galatea
Skipper: Paul Gotts
Tel: 0634 57211

East Anglia

King's Lynn, New Hunstanton, Salthouse, Cley, Sheringham, Cromer, NORWICH, NORFOLK, GREAT YARMOUTH, Gorleston, Corton, LOWESTOFT, Southwold, SUFFOLK, Aldeburgh, IPSWICH, Felixstowe, HARWICH, COLCHESTER, Walton on the Naze, ESSEX, Clacton-on-Sea, CHELMSFORD, SOUTHEND-ON-SEA

Essex

SOUTHEND-ON-SEA   Fishing from Southend Pier is good with many species to be caught. Dabs, Plaice, Eels, Bass and Mullet are just a few of the

Sue Ann
Skipper: K. Glynn
Tel: 0702 547060
      0702 544696

The Fineart
Skipper: Ken George
Tel: 0702 540123
31 foot, fishing off shore Essex coast marks

WEST MERSEA
Miss Grace II
Skipper: Stuart Belbin
Tel: 0206 38 2681

Skeena
Skipper: Bryan Parkinson
Tel: 0202 38 2948

BRADWELL

Argonaut
Skipper: Owen Wooley
Tel: 0245 74584
12 rods, tuition available

Harrier
Skipper: Bob Cox
Tel: 0621 461

Woolin
Skipper: Tony Hornett
Tel: 0621 87492

BRIGHTLINGSEA

Sula J
Tel: 0255 3323
30 foot

BURNHAM ON CROUCH

Gemini Girl
Tel: 0268 778688
Essex off shore Cod fishing

Vanessa
Skipper: P. Bamonte
Tel: 0268 44112

CLACTON-ON-SEA Main fishing takes place during Autumn and Winter because of the tourist season. Boat fishing reasonable with Bass, Rays, Tope, Flatties and Dogfish the main species caught during the Summer with the addition of Cod and Whiting in the Winter.

WALTON ON THE NAZE Boat, Shore and Pier fishing all reasonably good. Species to expect here are Whiting, Flatties, Tope, Skate, Bass and Pouting. Good Cod can be caught from September through to March.

Mother of Pearl
Skipper: D. E. Murphy
Tel: 02556 4274
25 foot

HARWICH Best fishing is from boats. A variety of species caught including Whiting, Pouting and Codling during Autumn and Winter and Skate, Sole, Mullet, Bass and Flatties during Spring and Summer.

Suffolk

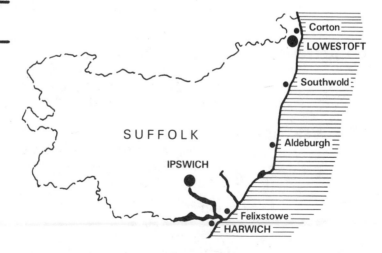

FELIXSTOWE Cod fishing excellent during Autumn and Winter. Bass and Skate fishing good in Summer, with the Skate being especially plentiful in the harbour area.

Our Times
Skipper: R. Brinkley
Tel: 03942 70853

291

Charter fishing with an experienced skipper is your shortcut to better sport. Don't crowd the boat – half a dozen on board is more comfortable than the full crew.

ALDEBURGH The three mile long Aldeburgh Beach is best for fishing at night. Between October and January however daytime fishing is fair. main species caught here are Cod, Tope, Garfish, Sole, Whiting and Flounder.

SOUTHWOLD Good beach fishing with a variety of species available. Winter is best for Sole, Whiting and Codling and Summer for Sole, Silver Eels and Bass. Main boat caught species are Sole, Mackerel, Skate, Turbot, Dogfish and the occasional shark.

LOWESTOFT Good beach fishing to be had from both South and North Beaches. Among the species present are Whiting, Flatties, Bass Tope and Ray. Excellent location for Cod fishing especially from October to May.

Jason M
Skipper: John Mann
Tel: 0603 743877

Happy Days
Tel: 0502 83220

CORTON Corton Beach gives good sport for Mullet, Whiting, Tope and Bass. Also good for Cod during Winter. Boat fishing gives an excellent variety of fish including Tope, Bass, Turbot, Monkfish Ling and Pollack.

Norfolk

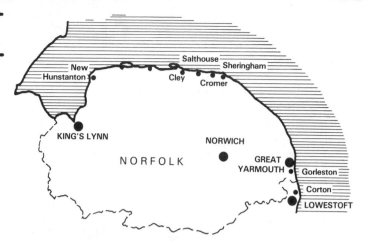

GREAT YARMOUTH Beach, boat and pier fishing all very successful here. Spring and Summer best for Tope, Eels, Skate and Flounders. Winter best for Cod, Whiting, Dogfish, Flounders and Dabs.

White Swan
Skipper: Claude Laws
Tel: 0606 867377

Norfolk Queen
Skipper: Jack Wells
Tel: 0493 720465

Marulu
Skipper: Brian
Tel: 0493 730354 after 6p.m.

Try
Skipper: F. Goodchild
Tel: 0493 720754

Pinicle Caroline
Skipper: Frank Pickering
Tel: 026 379 714

GORLESTON Beach fishing good for Whiting, Dabs and Flounders. Skate especially good from October to March. You can expect the usual boat caught species if fishing from boats.

CROMER Good all year round fishing. Cod excellent from September to end of March and Whiting and Dabs good in Summer. Fishing from shore and pier in Summer for Skate and Bass.

SHERINGHAM A haven for fishermen who are after Flatties as they are caught plentifully here all year round. Mackerel are caught from June to September. Autumn and Winter are best for Cod.

SALTHOUSE Very deep water close inshore. Shore and Boat fishing good here almost all year round. Flatties are excellent during Winter. Good catches of Mackerel and Bass are sometimes made during the Summer.

CLEY NEXT THE SEA Steep shingle beaches and excellent location for fishing. All year round beach and boat angling. Species caught from shore are Mullet, Conger, Flatties, Bass, Tope, Pollack and Pouting. Boat fishing good for Black Bream, Red Bream, Tope, Cod, Bass, Turbot, Gurnard, Dogfish and Angler Fish.

NEW HUNSTANTON Hunstanton Beach gives good sport for Tope, Bass, Flounders, Dab and Garfish. Boat fishing out in the Wash good for Skate, Conger, Mackerel, Tope, Bass and Gurnard.

North-East

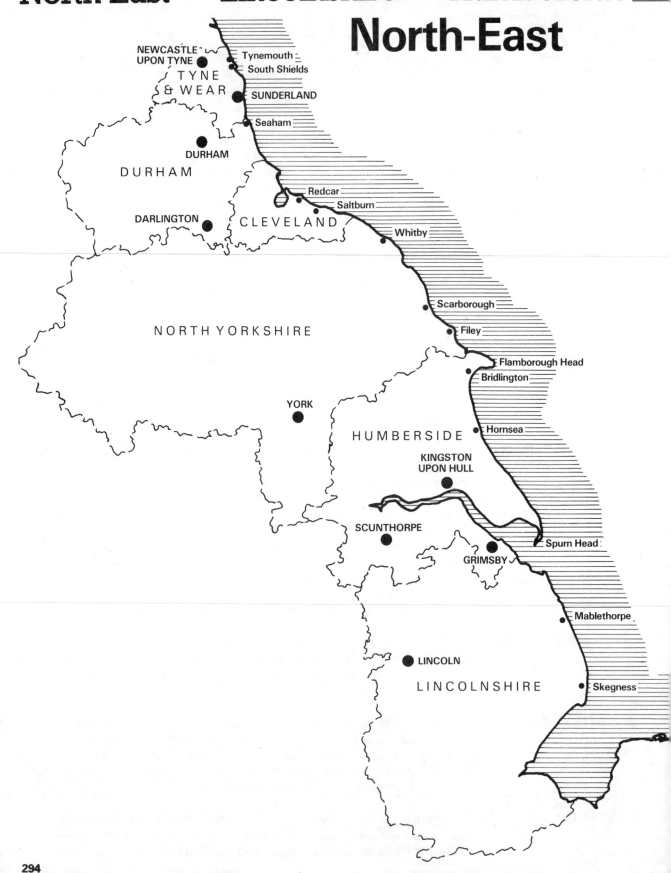

NEWCASTLE UPON TYNE

Tynemouth
South Shields

TYNE & WEAR

SUNDERLAND

Seaham

DURHAM

DURHAM

DARLINGTON

CLEVELAND

Redcar
Saltburn

Whitby

NORTH YORKSHIRE

Scarborough

Filey

Flamborough Head
Bridlington

YORK

HUMBERSIDE

Hornsea

KINGSTON UPON HULL

SCUNTHORPE

Spurn Head

GRIMSBY

Mablethorpe

LINCOLN

LINCOLNSHIRE

Skegness

Lincolnshire

SKEGNESS Good boat fishing available all year round. The species you can expect include Tope, Dogfish, Flounders, Dabs and Skate at varying times throughout the year. Beach fishing is good. Species to expect include Flounders, Dabs, Whiting, Cod and Silver Eels.

MABLETHORPE Beach fishing is reasonable with mainly Flatties being caught. Boat fishing is better with many species available. Amongst those you can expect good catches of, are Tope, Mackerel, Bass and Skate. Cod are best during September to December.

Humberside

GRIMSBY Good fishing can be had from boats along the Humber Bank. Shore fishing on the foreshore is also good at times. Main species caught at this location are Codling, Plaice, Flounders and Eels.

Undaunted
Skipper: Bill Dodgson
Tel: 0472 55349

SPURNHEAD Excellent fishing at Spurn Peninsula for Conger, Cod, Plaice, Dab and Mackerel. Other good beach marks are Kilnsea Corner and John's Point. Boat fishing fair with species caught as from beach with the addition of Mackerel and Skate.

HORNSEA Boat fishing is most productive at this location. Among the species you can expect here are Flatties, Tope, Cod and Haddock. In Spring and Summer the best catches are Whiting, Dabs and Skate. Good Bass can occasionally be had by fishing from the shore.

BRIDLINGTON Boat fishing best in Winter. The main species caught then are Ray, Codling and Flatties. Both the North and the South Pier produce good catches of Codling during Autumn and Winter. Other species you can expect from pier fishing at this location include Billet, Flatties and Whiting.

Kathleen
Skipper: Ian Taylor
Tel: 0262 79434
40 foot, 12 rods

Mary Ellen
Skipper: Dennis Brown
Tel: 0262 76930

North Wind
Skipper: Mr Cockerill
Tel: 0262 74605
40 foot, 12 rods

Our Freda
Skipper: Chris Wright
Tel: 0262 77530
40 foot, 12 rods

Young Tom
Skipper: Norman Orum
Tel: 0262 76018

FLAMBOROUGH HEAD Boats around the head take a variety of fish including Cod, Haddock, Mackerel and Plaice. In some of the more rocky areas you can occasionally take the odd Pollack and Coalfish.

Yorkshire – North

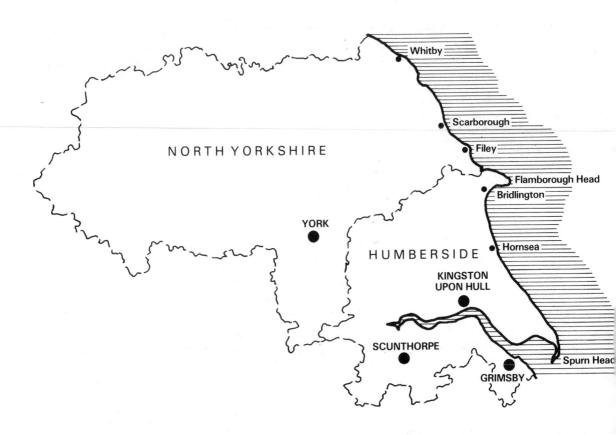

FILEY BRIGG Boat fishing quite good. Cod is caught all year round and some excellent Mackerel from July to September. Shore fishing quite good with mainly flatties being caught but Mackerel are good from June to September.

Jeremy Gordon II
Skipper: J. Smith
Tel: 0723 512114

SCARBOROUGH Best shore fishing takes place during Winter. The main species caught from shore are Cod, Bass, Flounder, Plaice, Dab, Whiting and Mackerel. Good boat fishing not far out of Scarborough. Whiting excellent in bay during Winter. Good catches of Codling from August onwards. Other boat caught species are Conger, Bass, Mackerel, Pollack and Cod.

Sea Quest
Skipper: Peter Messruther
Tel: 0723 71775

WHITBY East and West Piers, both very good fishing. Flounders, Dabs, Plaice, Coalfish and Mackerel all caught regularly off these piers. Boat fishing excellent with good catches of a variety of species including Wolf Fish, Ling, Haddock. Whiting, Cod and Flatties. Two of the best beach marks are Upgang and Newholme Beck. Flounder, Codling and Billet are all good catches at both locations.

MR. M. MARSDEN
43 HALL ROAD, MOORGATE, ROTHERHAM, S. YORKS
SEA FISHING – WHITBY
MFV TOILER, WRECK & REEF FISHING
VHF SOUNDER, RADAR
TEL: 0709 71071

Sea Trek
Skipper: Stuart Johnson
Tel: 0947 810606

Gina St Belle
Skipper: Paul Foster
Tel: 0947 604754

Jennifer Margret
Tel: 0947 603070

Skipper: Paul Foster
Tel: 0947 604754
Accommodation can be arranged

North Star
Skipper: John Grayson
Tel: 0947 810606

Sea Roma
Skipper: George Tabor
Tel: 0947 604825

Emily G
Skipper: Reginald Firth
Tel: 0947 602016

Cleveland

SALTBURN BY THE SEA Fishing from shore and boat quite good. Species to be expected are Mackerel, Gurnard, Flatties, Coalfish and Whiting. Some Bass in Summer and Haddock in early Winter. Pier fishing with main species caught being Codling.

REDCAR Shore and boat fishing good. Main catches are Flatties and Codling in late Winter and Spring, Whiting, Mackerel and Coalfish during the Summer. Best fishing from shore is just before and after high tide, expect the usual beach-caught fish.

HARTLEPOOL
Wayside Flower II
Skipper: D. W. Horsley
Tel: 0429 34007

WHERE TO FISH—SEA

Durham

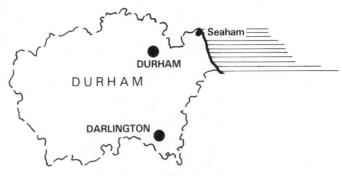

SEAHAM   Good beach fishing and pier fishing. Cod, Codling and Whiting the principle catches in Winter from the beach. Skate, Pouting Mackerel in the Summer. Boat fishing is good with main quarrie being Coalfish, Plaice and Flounders.

Tyne & Wear

SUNDERLAND   All year round fishing. Whiting, Cod and Codling are the best catches during the Winter. During the Summer the variety wide to include Flounders, Dabs, Plaice, Pouting, Skate and Gurnard Roker Pier is excellent for those after Cod and Flatfish especiall during the Winter.

SOUTH SHIELDS   All year round fishing. Boat, Beach and Pier fishing all good. M popular beach marks include Frenchmans Point, Herd Beach, South Beach and Black Rock. The pier also gives good sport. M beach caught species are Cod, Flounder, Plaice and Dabs. Boa fishing for species including Cod, Flounder, Plaice and Dabs.

Freia
Skipper: Martin Meling
Tel: 0632 550709
30 foot

TYNEMOUTH   Some of the best beach fishing marks are the Long Sands, Sou of Cullercoats, Tynemouth Haven and Long Sands. Rocks fishi marks worth a visit are at Sharpness Point and Cullercoats Harbour. Species caught from shore include Plaice, Flounder, (and Dabs. Same species caught from boats with the addition o Coalfish and Dogfish.

Scotland's for fishing!

©

Scotland is ideal for getting away from it all. You'll find plenty of areas for first class coarse, game and sea angling. Take your time, relax and enjoy the scenery. You'll find there's plenty of room for everyone.

Whether you're planning a holiday on your own, with your family or with a group of friends we can offer you a selection of accommodation to suit your needs. Remember many hotels and self catering sites have their own stretches of water and offer inclusive fishing holidays.

If you need further advice or would like any of our range of holiday publications contact any Tourist Information Centre in Scotland or:

Scottish Tourist Board, 23 Ravelston Terrace, Edinburgh EH4 3EU. Telephone: 031-332 2433.

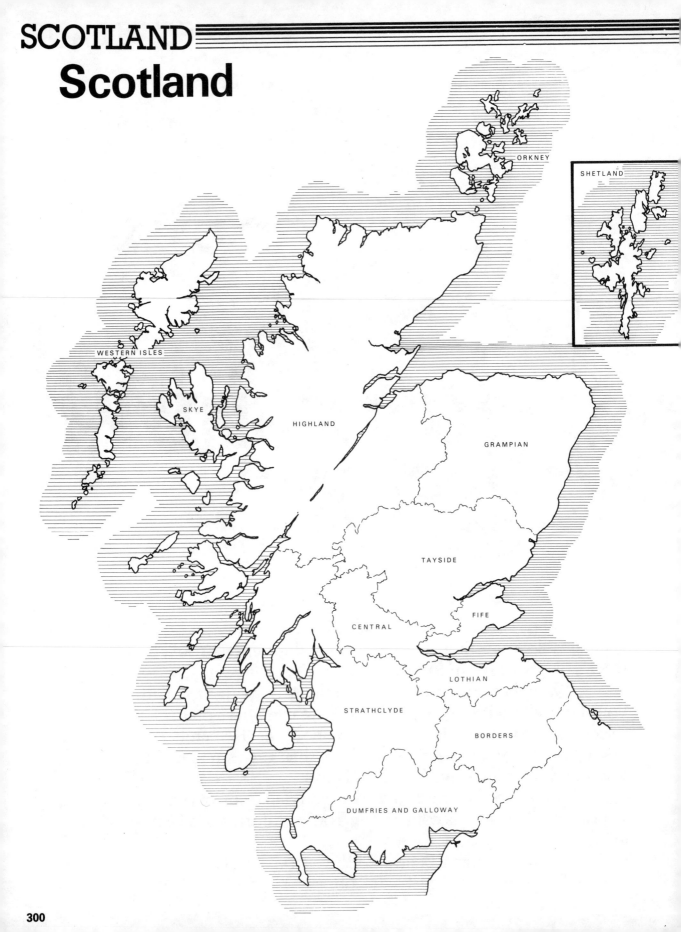

SCOTLAND
Scotland

ORKNEY

SHETLAND

WESTERN ISLES

SKYE

HIGHLAND

GRAMPIAN

TAYSIDE

FIFE

CENTRAL

LOTHIAN

STRATHCLYDE

BORDERS

DUMFRIES AND GALLOWAY

Dumfries and Galloway

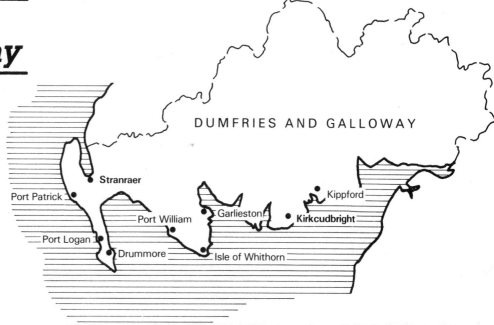

DUMFRIES AND GALLOWAY

Stranraer

Port Patrick

Port William

Garlieston

Kippford

Kirkcudbright

Port Logan

Drummore

Isle of Whithorn

KIPPFORD   On the Solway Firth which offers good flat fishing. Types to be found are Cod, Flounder and Plaice from the shore. Flatfish, including Turbot, Cod, Tope, Mackerel and Pollack from boats.

Skipper: J. Paterson
Tel: 055 662 232
Skipper: E. Grierson
Tel: 0387 4985

KIRKCUDBRIGHT   Approximately 3 miles from fishing grounds which offer excellent tope and good general fishing. Types to be found are Cod, Coalfish, Conger, Bass, Plaice, Flounders, Pollack and Dogfish from the shore. Cod, Coalfish, Conger, Dogfish, Mackerel, Haddock, Tope, Pollack, all types of Flatfish and Whiting from boats.

GARLIESTON   Several square miles of water sheltered by the land. Types of fish to be found are Mackerel, Cod, Pollack and Coalfish from the shore. Mackerel, Cod, Pollack, Ray, Plaice, Dab, Flounder and Coalfish from boats.

Mrs J. McGinn
Tel: 054 854 664

ISLE OF WHITHORN   The Isle Bay itself offers nearly a mile of sheltered water with many good rock fishing marks. Types of fish to be found are Cod, Coalfish, Dogfish, Conger, Pollack, Mackerel and Wrasse from the shore. Cod, Rays, Flatfish, Spurdog, Dogfish, Mackerel, Conger and Tope from boats.

Morning Light
Skipper: E. McGuire
Tel: 098 85 468

Starlight
Skipper: Mr. Nash
Tel: 098 85 521

PORT WILLIAM Is on the east side of Luce Bay. With Monreith Bay, still a good bass beach, to the south of it. Types of fish found are Tope, Spurdog, Rays, Cod, Pollack and Flatfish from boats. Bass, Wrasse, Codling and Pollack from shore.

Mr J. Hannah
Tel: 098 87 434

DRUMMORE Main port for fishing western side of Luce Bay. Many good shore marks on sandy beaches north of Drummore, while Mull of Galloway provides excellent shore fishing over rocky ground. Types of fish found are Pollack, Wrasse from rocky shores, Flatfish, Bass, Mullet, Porbeagle Shark and Rays from sandy beaches. Pollack, Coalfish, Cod, Wrasse, Whiting, Lesser Spotted Dogfish, Bullhuss, Spurdog, Tope, Rays and Conger from boats.

Harvester
Skipper: S. Woods
Tel: 077 684 372

PORT LOGAN Many good shore marks to north and south of village. Types of fish found are Pollack and Wrasse from rocky shores. Pollack, Coalfish, Cod, Wrasse, Whiting, Lesser Spotted Dogfish, Bullhuss, Spurdog, Tope, Rays and Conger from boats with an occasional Haddock.

PORTPATRICK Good shore fishing from many rocky points north and south, the best known being the Yellow Isle, ½ mile north of the harbour. Sandeel Bay, a little further north, and Killintringan Lighthouse. Types of fish found are Pollack, Coalfish, Plaice, Flounder, Codling, Mackerel, Dogfish, Conger, Wrasse and Tope occasionally.

STRANRAER & LOCH RYAN Stranraer, at the head of Loch Ryan, is a good point for starting off on many sea angling marks. The lower part of the Loch around Cairnryan and Lady Bay have produced many Scottish records from shore and boat. Types of fish found are Cod, Haddock, Whiting, Flatfish, (including some Turbot), Rays, Conger, Spurdog, Dogfish and occasional Tope.

Strathclyde

GIRVAN From the end of the pier good fishing for fair-sized Plaice and Flounders. Night fishing is good for Rock Cod. One mile south is the noted 'Horse Rock' a good shore mark. Types of fish found are Haddock, Plaice, Codling, Rays, Flounders, Whiting and Gurnard (mostly from boat). Mostly Coalfish, Cod, Pollack and Mackerel which are quite heavy towards Ailsa Craig.

Lenora V
Skipper: T. Harrison
Tel: 0465 2631

Morning Trade
Skipper: A. Ingram
Tel: 0465 2320

AYR Good shore fishing from Newton Shore, north of the harbour, from the harbour jetty and from the rocky coastline at the Heads of Ayr. Boat fishing in the bay for good catches of Cod, Haddock, Thornbacks, Spurdogs and Flatfish. Tope have also been taken from around the Lady Isle. Types of fish found are Flounder, Coalfish, Whiting, Skate, Eels, Dab, Cod Dogfish and Conger from the shore and pier. Spurdog, Cod, Pollack, Whiting, Dogfish, Coalfish, Skate, Eels, Flounders, Thornback Ray and Conger from Boats. Good Mackerel trolling in July and August.

M. Johnson
Tel: 0292 81638

T. Medina
Tel: 0292 85297

PRESTWICK Shore fishing is best after dark. Types of fish found are Cod, Flounder, Plaice, Dab, Coalfish, Dogfish and Mullet from shore. Cod, Flounder, Plaice, Dab, Coalfish, Dogfish, Tope, Rays, Thornbacks and Mackerel from boats.

TROON Good pier fishing from the harbour. Cod and Flatfish can be taken at low tide from Barassie Shore. Many good marks out on the bay with a small wreck off the Lady Isle. Types of fish found are Cod, Plaice, Flounder, Coalfish, Rays, Dogfish, Conger, Whiting and Pollack from shore. Cod, Plaice, Flounder, Coalfish, Rays, Dogfish, Conger, Whiting, Pollack, Thornback, Gurnard and very occasional Tope from boats.

Dusky Maid
Skipper: J. Wilson
Tel: 0292 313161

Scotland – Strathclyde

Coll

Tobermory

Mull

Oban

Arrochar

Garelochead

Ardentinny

Clynder

Helensburgh

Dunoon

Loch Fyne

Gourock

Tarbert

Rothesay

Largs

Millport

GLASGOW

Kilchattan Bay

Islay

Loch Ranza

STRATHCLYDE

Ardrossan

Saltcoats

Arran

Irvine

Firth of Clyde

Troon

Whiting Bay

Prestwick

AYR

Campbeltown

Girvan

IRVINE Good boat fishing area. One mile north or south out of the harbour provides good Cod fishing. Large Conger can be contacted mainly at dusk on the rough ground around Cappock Rock, south of Irvine Harbour. Spurdog are prolific at times all over Irvine Bay. Types of fish found are Flounder and Cod from shore. Cod, Flounder, Dogfish, Rays, Conger, Haddock, Whiting, Coalfish and very occasional Tope from boats.

Talisman
Skipper: H. Patterson
Tel: 0294 57209

SALTCOATS & ARDROSSAN Shore fishing from the South Bay and around the harbours. Approximately 3 miles north is Ardneil Bay which is prolific Cod ground. Good beach fishing in Irvine Bay, and small bay between Saltcoats and Ardrossan. Types of fish found are Cod, Haddock, Rays, Flounder, Coalfish, Dogfish, Conger, Whiting and Pollack from shore. Cod, Rays, Flounder, Coalfish, Dogfish, Conger, Whiting, Pollack, Haddock, Dabs, Gurnard and Thornbacks from boats.

ISLE OF ARRAN Good shore fishing around whole Island.

LAMLASH Main sea angling centre on Island. Boats to Whiting Bay & Pladda to the south. Types of fish found Cod, Haddock, Whiting, Coalfish, Pollack, Conger, Rays, Flatfish, Mackerel and Dogfish.

Mr. McClean
Tel: 077 087240

WHITING BAY Excellent fishing banks from Largiebeg Point to King's Cross Point. Types of fish mainly Whiting.

LOCHRANZA At northern end of Island. Types of fish found Cod, Conger and Haddock from shore. Cod, Conger and Haddock from boats.

CAMPBELTOWN Good for Cod, Haddock, Flatfish in Kildalliog Bay and from the Winkie, causeway between Davaar Island and mainland.

LOCH FYNE Longest sea loch in Scotland. Many shore marks.

INVERARAY On west side of loch. Types of fish found are Cod, Mackerel, Pollack, Coalfish, Ling, Dogfish, Conger Eel, Hake and Plaice.

TARBERT Sheltered harbour and adjacent coast of the loch near the lower end on the west shore are good fishing grounds. Types of fish found are Cod, Mackerel, Coalfish and Sea Trout from the shore. Mackerel, Cod, Coalfish, Rays, Haddock and Whiting from boats.

FIRTH OF CLYDE
TIGHNABRUAICH Good fishing banks on west side of the Bute and around Inchmarnock. Types of fish found are Mackerel and Coalfish from shore. Mackerel, Coalfish, Cod, Haddock, Flatfish, Whiting and Dogfish from boats.

ROTHESAY Many excellent shore marks. The deep water marks at Garroch Head are good for both boat and shore anglers. Types of fish found are Cod, Pollack, Plaice, Mackerel and Wrasse from shore. Cod, Pollack, Plaice, Mackerel, Conger, Spurdog, Thornback, Coalfish, Wrasse and Whiting from boat.

KEITH TODD
CARLEOL, 3 ALMA TERRACE,
ROTHESAY, ISLE OF BUTE
TEL: 0700 3716

KILCHATTAN BAY Good all year round fishing. At south end of Isle of Bute. Types of fish found are Cod, Pollack, Plaice, Mackerel, Conger, Dogfish, Wrasse and Whiting.

MILLPORT On Island of Greater Cumbrae. Good fishing at a bank between the SE point of Millport Bay and Keppel pier. Fintry Bay and the Piat Shoal, good sporting areas. Good shore marks in the Farland Point and Keppel area. Types of fish found are Mackerel, Pollack, Cod, Conger, Coalfish from shore. Cod, Haddock, Coalfish, Pollack, Dogfish and Mackerel from boats.

LARGS Several good fishing banks including the Piat Shoal and Skelmorlie Patch. Boating centre which caters for sea anglers. Types of fish found are Cod, Pollack, Haddock, Mackerel, Coalfish and Dogfish

Mitchell Hotel Services
Tel: 0549 672044

GOUROCK   Coastline from Largs to Greenock most popular area for shore fishing. At Wemyss Bay, angling is not permitted from the pier but good catches can be had to the south, and the Red Rocks about a mile north, noted for Codling. At Inverkip, a sandy beach, where large Flounders and other Flatfish can be taken. Cloch Point, Cloch along Gourock promenade to the swimming pool car park, and Greenock Esplanade all good marks for shore anglers. Dinghy anglers easy access to many Clyde marks including the Gantocks, where outsize Cod and Coalfish have been taken. Types of fish found are Codling, Whiting, Pouting, Conger, Flatfish, Mackerel and Rays from both shore and boat.

W. Irvine
Tel: 0475 33686

R. Wilson
Tel: 0475 36864

DUNOON   Best fishing marks near the Gantocks, on Warden's Bank in the East and West Bays. Dunoon, around Kirn and Hunters Quay in the Holy Loch and the southern part of Loch Long. Fishing available from pier. Types of fish found are Codling, Whiting, Pouting, Conger, Flatfish, Mackerel and Rays from both shore and boat.

ARDENTINNY   Types of fish found are Cod and Mackerel from the shore. Cod, Conger, Haddock, Ray, Plaice, Flounder, Whiting, Coalfish and Mackerel from boats.

Boat Centre
Tel: 036 981288

ARROCHAR   Fishing at northern end of Loch Long. Types of fish found are Cod, Conger, Pollack, Coalfish and Rays from shore. Cod, Haddock, Whiting, Conger, Pollack, Coalfish, Mackerel, Rays and Dogfish from boat.

CLYNDER   Fishing on west side of the Gareloch and one mile north of the popular Rhu Narrows. Types of fish found are Cod and Mackerel from shore. Cod, Conger, Rays, Plaice, Flounders, Dogfish, Whiting, Pouting and Mackerel from boats.

GARELOCHHEAD   Fishing centre of the area offering whole shoreline of Gareloch. Loch Goil and Upper and Lower Loch Long in easy reach. Types of fish found Cod, Coalfish, Pollack, Dab, Flounder, Plaice, Whiting, Haddock, Pouting, Rays, Mackerel, Spurdog and Lesser Spotted Dogfish.

HELENSBURGH Fishing on the Firth of Clyde at the southern end of Gareloch. Types of fish found are Cod, Flounder, Coalfish, Conger, Rays, Dogfish, Whiting, Dab, Haddock, Pollack and Mackerel from both shore and bank.

D. Nichol
Tel: 0436 2707

OBAN Fishing best off the south and west coasts of Kerrera Island, particularly near Bach Island and Shepherds Hat. Maiden Island and Oban Bay give good Mackerel in July and August. Types of fish found are Mackerel, Huss, Conger, Coalfish, Dogfish, Rays, Pollack and occasional Cod and Haddock from boats.

Highlands & Islands

MALLAIG Flatfish, Pollack, Conger, Mackerel, Coalfish in bay and from roc and new piers.

KYLE OF LOCHALSH Types of fish found are Conger, Coalfish, Pollack and Whiting from the harbour. Pollack, Cod, Coalfish, Mackerel and Whiting from boat.

SHIELDAIG Fishing in sea lochs of Shieldaig, Torridon and Upper Torridon. Types of fish found large Whiting, Haddock, Cod, Conger, Ling, Huss, Coalfish, Dabs, Sole and Mackerel.

GAIRLOCH Popular sea angling bay, especially good around Longa Island at entrance to loch. Types of fish found are Cod, Haddock, Whiting Pollack, Coalfish and Flatfish.

POOLEWE AND AULTBEA Offer sheltered waters of Loch Ewe. Types of fish found are Pollack, Coalfish, Dab and Codling from shore. Haddock, Cod, Codling, Gurnard, Skate, Whiting, Mackerel and Flatfish from boats.

SHETLAND

Lerwick

Kirkwall ORKNEY

Thurso
Dunnet
Keiss
Wick

Lewis

Lochinver

Summer Isles

Ullapool

Aultbea

Poolewe

Embo
Dornoch
Portmahomack
Tain

Lossiemouth Portknockie
Moray Firth
Buckie Portsoy

Harris

WESTERN ISLES

Uig

Shieldaig

SKYE

HIGHLAND

Kyle of Lochalsh

Eigg

Coll
Tobermory

ULLAPOOL & THE SUMMER ISLES

Good shore fishing at Morefield, Rhu and Achiltibuie. Loch Broo and the waters encircled by the Summer Isles offer excellent sea angling. Noted for large Skate. Types of fish found are Codling, Coalfish, Conger, Pollack, Mackerel, Dabs, Thornback, Dogfish, Flounders and Plaice from shore. Codling, Coalfish, Conger, Pollack, Mackerel, Ray, Dabs, Thornback, Dogfish, Flounders, Plaice, Haddock, Whiting, Wrasse, Ling, Megrim, Gurnard, Turb and Spurdog.

ULLAPOOL CHARTER CO.
MAREFIELD MOTEL, ULLAPOOL,
ROSS & CROMARTY, ROSS-SHIRE
TEL: 0854 2161/2425
See Advertisement this Section

LOCHINVER

Types of fish found Cod, Haddock, Whiting, Saithe, Gurnard, Ling, Halibut, Pollack, Mackerel, Wrasse, Conger and Skate from boats. Coalfish, Pollack, Cod and Mackerel from shore.

Dolphin
Skipper: J. Crooks
Tel: 057 14 832

INNER HEBRIDES
ISLE OF ISLAY

Port Ellen and Port Askaig good harbours. Types of fish found ar Cod, Haddock, Whiting, Coalfish, Pollack, Mackerel, Gurnard, Dogfish, Spurdog, Plaice, Flounder, Tope, Ling, Conger, Skate and Rays from boat.

ISLE OF MULL
SALEN

The Sound of Mull is becoming one of main Skate marks in Argy area, also yields a number of Tope, the largest being a specimen 50lbs. Types of fish found are Coalfish, Pollack, Cod, Wrasse, Flounder, Mullet, Sea Trout and Mackerel from shore. Ray, Skate Ling, Pollack, Coalfish, Cod, Spurdog, Tope, Conger and Gurnar from boats.

Forss
Skipper: Brian Burgess
Tel: 0688 2165

TOBERMORY In 1979 many Tope of between 35 and 40lbs were caught, ton-up Skate were tagged and returned alive, the largest a specimen 175lbs, double figure Cod and jumbo Haddock are numerous. Types of fish found are Tope, Skate, Rays, Pollack, Coalfish, Ling, Conger, Gurnard, Spurdog, Cod, Haddock, Flatfish (Plaice, Dabs and Turbot) and Whiting from boats. Coalfish, Pollack, Cod, Wrasse, Flounders, Grey Mullet, Sea Trout, Conger, Thornback and Mackerel from shore.

ISLE OF COLL Fishing from several rocks round island. Good sport on the Mull side and at the mouth of Arinagour Bay. Types of fish found are Mackerel, Coalfish, Pollack, Cod, Conger, Haddock, Skate and Flounder.

ISLE OF EIGG Types of fish found are Pollack, Conger, Spurdog, Skate, Cod and Mackerel.

ISLE OF SKYE
PORTREE Good fishing marks in and round the harbour. Types of fish found are Cod, Haddock, Whiting, Coalfish, Pollack and Mackerel.

UIG Loch Snizort and small islands at its entrance, with Ascrib Islands opposite, good fishing areas. Types of fish found are Coalfish, Mackerel, Pollack, Conger, Whiting, Haddock, Dogfish, Flatfish, Skate, Cod and Gurnard from boats. Coalfish, Mackerel, Pollack, Conger and Dogfish from shore.

LENDALE BY DUNVEGAN Shore fishing at Poolteil Pier, Glendale and Neist Point lighthouses. All types of fish from boats.

OUTER HEBRIDES
ISLE OF HARRIS
TARBERT Type of fish found are Mackerel, Ling, Coalfish, Cod, Rays, Pollack and Conger from shore. Plaice, Haddock and Flounder from boats.

ISLE OF LEWIS
STORNOWAY Type of fish found are Conger, Coalfish, Skate, Cod, Rays, Ling, Pollack, Whiting, Dabs, Bluemouth, Flounder, Wrasse, Dogfish and Haddock.

SHETLAND ISLES Offers the best Skate fishing in Europe. Type of fish found Coalfish, Pollack, Dogfish, Mackerel, Dabs, Conger and Cod fro shore. Skate, Halibut, Ling, Cod, Torsk, Haddock, Whiting, Coalfish, Pollack, Dogfish, Porbeagle Shark, Norway Haddock, Gurnard, Mackerel, Cuckoo and Ballan Wrasse.

LERWICK Superb Skate fishing, also excellent mixed fishing for Ling, Cod Tusk, Haddock, Pollack and Halibut.

Sula
Skipper: E. Manson
Tel: 0595 3488

ORKNEY ISLANDS The Old Man of Hoy, Scapa Flow and Marwick Head are well known angling marks. The Brough of Birsay, Costa Head and t Eday and Stronsay Firths are known marks for big Halibut and Skate. Fishing from Kirkwall or Stromness provides easy access Scapa Flow where wrecks provide homes for large Ling and Conger. Excellent shore fishing. Types of fish found are Sea Tr Plaice, Pollack, Coalfish, Mackerel and Wrasse from shore. Ska Halibut, Ling, Cod, Pollack, Haddock, Coalfish, Plaice and Dog from boats.

Sheltered waters in Scapa Flow hold variety of fish, including Skate, Halibut, Ling, large Cod and Pollack.

THURSO AND SCRABSTER Access to the Pentland Firth, where there are first class fishing grounds. Thurso Bay and Dunnet Head are sheltered and it is e to reach marks afloat. Excellent rock fishing at Scrabster and Conger can be caught from the harbour walls. Types of fish fou are Cod, Ling, Haddock, Conger, Pollack, Coalfish, Dogfish, Spurdog, Plaice, Wrasse, Mackerel, Dab, Whiting, Rays, Halib and Porbeagle Shark.

J. McKay
Tel: 0847 2868

Mr Maynard
Tel: 0847 4872

DUNNET Dunnet Sands beach worth shore angling from. Types of fish found are Cod, Ling, Haddock, Conger, Pollack, Coalfish, Dogfish, Spurdog, Plaice, Wrasse, Mackerel, Dab, Rays, Whiting, Halibut and Porbeagle Shark.

KEISS Good shore fishing from the rocks around Keiss and from the beach at Sinclair's Bay. Good Plaice, Sea Trout and Mackerel.

WICK Mainly rock fishing for Conger, Pollack, Coalfish, Cod, Haddock, Mackerel and Flatfish. Good points are Longberry, Boathaven, Sandigoe and Helman Head. Excellent Cod off Noss Head.

BRORA Types of fish Cod, Coalfish, Haddock, Rays and Conger from boats.

EMBO Grannies Heilan' Hame is a caravan holiday centre. Types of fish found are Coalfish, Mackerel and Flatfish from the pier. The rocks provide good Cod. Spinning for Sea Trout from the beach up to the mouth of Loch Fleet. Coalfish, Mackerel, Plaice, Cod, Haddock and Whiting at times from boats.

DORNOCH Access to the north coast banks of Dornoch Firth. Types of fish found are Sea Trout from shore. Flatfish, Haddock and Cod from boats.

TAIN Access to the south coast banks of Dornoch Firth for excellent Sea Trout. Types of fish found Wrasse, Flatfish, Pollack and Mackerel from shore. Haddock, Cod, Skate and Mackerel from boats.

PORTMAHOMACK Well protected harbour and sandy beach, on the Dornoch Firth. Types of fish found are Cod from shore. Haddock and Cod from boats.

MORAY FIRTH Famous for its fishing grounds. Types of fish found Cod, Haddock, Flatfish of many kinds, Pollack, Coalfish and Mackerel.

NAIRN Southern shore of Moray Firth. Most fishing from two small piers at entrances to the tidal harbour. Types of fish found are Mackerel, small Coalfish, Pollack, Dab and Cod.

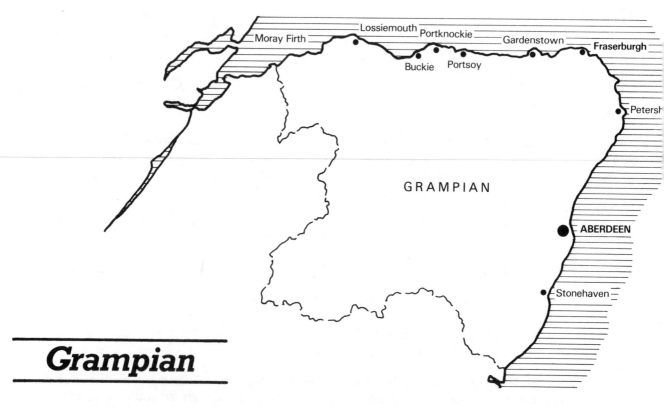

Grampian

LOSSIEMOUTH AND GARMOUTH

Off the east and west beaches Sea Trout and Finnock abound. Types of fish found are Sea Trout, Mackerel and Conger from the pier, Coalfish, Mackerel and Flatfish from the 6½ miles of shore fishing. Sea Trout between harbour and Boar's Head Rock and the old cement works Garmouth. Haddock, Cod, Plaice and Coalfish from boats.

BUCKIE

Offers fishing on the eastern side of Spey Bay from sandy beach and rugged cliff formations. Types of fish found are Cod, Coalfish, Conger, Pollack, Mackerel, Haddock, Whiting and Flatfish.

Buckie Boat Charters
Tel: 0343 820830

PORTNOCKIE

West of Cullen Bay. Small harbour is used by two small Mackerel boats. Type of fish found are Cod and Coalfish from the rocks, Mackerel from the piers. Haddock, Ling and Gurnard from boats.

PORTSOY

Types of fish found are Coalfish and Mackerel from the small pier, Cod from the east and west rocks. Mackerel, Cod, Haddock, Plaice, Coalfish and Dab from boats.

GARDENSTOWN AND CROVIE Mackerel plentiful here between June and September. Types of fish found are Coalfish, Pollack, Flatfish and Conger from shore. Mackerel, Cod, Haddock, Flounder, Plaice, Conger, Dab, Catfish, Gurnard and Ling from boats.

Mr C. F. Davidson
Tel: 026 15212

FRASERBURGH Offers fishing in the Moray Firth to the west and north, and the North Sea to the east. Types of fish found are Cod, Coalfish and Mackerel from both shore and boat.

PETERHEAD Excellent breakwaters, 1900ft and 2800ft long are the main shore marks. Types of fish found are Mackerel, Coalfish, Cod and Dab from the pier. Cod, Haddock, Dabs, Ling, Coalfish and Mackerel from boats.

ABERDEEN Excellent rock fishing for Codling, Coalfish, Mackerel, Whiting, Haddock and Flatfish.

STONEHAVEN Good rock fishing marks on both sides of Stonehaven. Great catches of Cod and Haddock are taken regularly from boats. Types of fish found are Cod, Haddock, Pollack, Coalfish, Flounder, Catfish and Mackerel from shore. Cod, Haddock, Coalfish, Pollack, Ling, Catfish, Plaice and other Flatfish, Ballan Wrasse, Cuckoo Wrasse, Whiting and Norway Haddock from boats.

Tayside

ARBROATH Types of fish found are Cod, Coalfish, Mackerel, Flounder, Conger, Plaice, Haddock and Pollack.

C. Ferrier
Tel: 0241 73360

DUNDEE On the estuary of the River Tay offers sea fishing in the city centre. Broughty Ferry, Easthaven and Carnoustie have sea fishing from piers, rocks and from boats. Good marks around the Bell Rock about 12 miles off shore. Types of fish found are Cod and Flatfish from shore. Cod, Haddock, Mackerel, Coalfish, Ling, Pollack, Pouting and Plaice from boats.

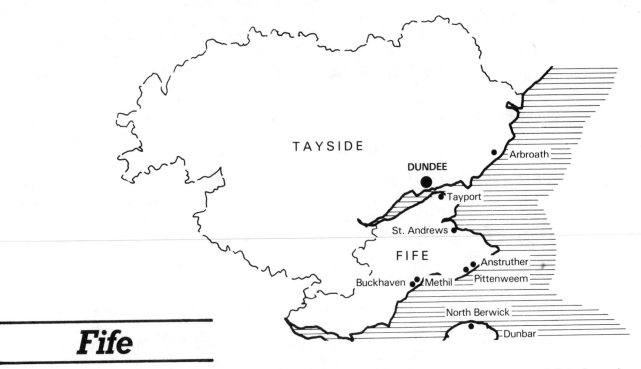

Fife

TAYPORT   Good shore fishing in sheltered waters. Types of fish found are Cod, Flounder and Plaice from shore, with occasional Sea Trout (permit required).

ST. ANDREWS   Shore fishing on the rocks between the bathing pool and the harbour.

ANSTRUTHER   Good catches of Rock Codling from the breakwater. Flounders from the pierhead. 200yds off the pier is a good bank for Cod and Mackerel. Also fishing marks off the Isle of May. Types of fish found are Cod, Coalfish, Haddock, Flounder and Wrasse from shore. Ling and Conger from boats.

Aquarius
Skipper: M. Peters
Tel: 0592 52242

PITTENWEEM   Good catches from the lighthouse pier including Rock Cod, Coalfish and Flatfish. At low tide is a big rock called 'Sandy Craig' a good mark. Types of fish found are Cod, Haddock, Coalfish, Wrasse, Flounder, Ling and Conger from boats. Cod, Haddock, Coalfish, Wrasse and Flounder from shore.

A. G. Marsh
Tel: 033 34 611

METHIL AND BUCKHAVEN   In Methil fishing from the sea wall and besides the dock is Methil Power Station which attracts Whiting, Haddock and good Mackerel in Summer. Types of fish found are Codling, Plaice and Mackerel from shore. Cod, Haddock, Whiting, Plaice and a few Catfish from boats.

Lothian

SOUTH QUEENSFERRY Types of fish found are Cod, Whiting, Coalfish, Mackerel and Flounder from both boat and shore in season.

EDINBURGH Several miles of sandy shoreline on the Forth Estuary. Best marks are at Cramond, round the mouth of the river Almond and the Seafield to Portobello area. Types of fish found are Flatfish, Codling, Ray's Bream, Whiting, Eels and Mackerel in season from shore.

COCKENZIE Mullet can be caught around the warm waters outfall to the east of Cockenzie Power Station and around the harbour. Other species include Flatfish, Codling and Mackerel.

NORTH BERWICK Good boat fishing out of North Berwick. The coastline between the town and Dunbar is good shore fishing. Types of fish found are Cod, Haddock, Plaice, Mackerel and Coalfish.

DUNBAR Rock, pier and beach fishing from Dunbar to Eyemouth. Types of fish found are Cod, Haddock, Flounder, Coalfish, Mackerel, Wrasse, Whiting, Pollack, Codling, Dabs, Plaice and Eels. Occasional Gurnard.

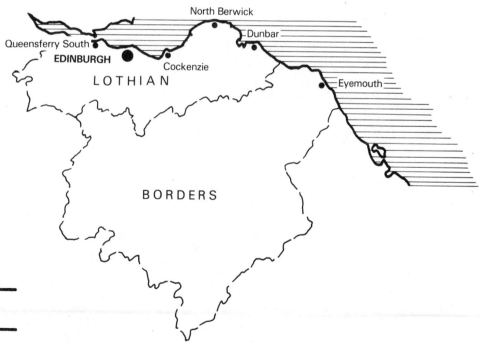

Borders

EYEMOUTH Rock and beach fishing. Boat fishing from Eyemouth, Burnmouth and St. Abbs. Types of fish found are Cod, Mackerel, Coalfish, Flounder, Plaice, Sole, Haddock, Catfish, Ballan Wrasse and Whiting from both boat and shore.

Mr. Johnson
Tel: 039 02 370

Mr. Aitchinson
Tel: 039 02 220

Wales

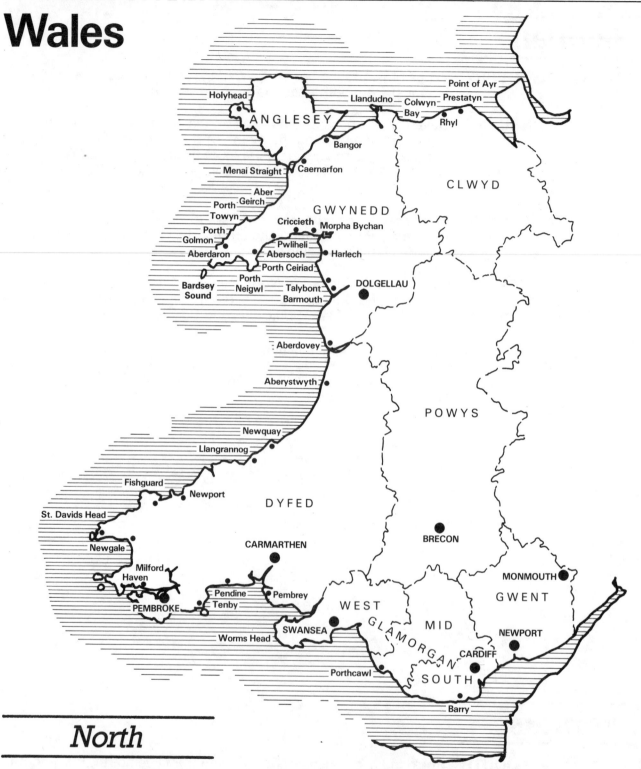

ANGLESEY

Holyhead

Llandudno
Colwyn
Bay
Prestatyn
Point of Ayr
Rhyl

Bangor

Menai Straight
Caernarfon

CLWYD

Aber
Geirch
Porth
Towyn
Porth
Golmon
Aberdaron

GWYNEDD

Criccieth
Morpha Bychan
Pwlheli
Abersoch
Harlech
Porth Ceiriad

Bardsey
Sound
Porth
Neigwl
Talybont
Barmouth

DOLGELLAU

Aberdovey

Aberystwyth

POWYS

Newquay

Llangrannog

Fishguard
Newport

DYFED

St. Davids Head

BRECON

Newgale

Milford
Haven

CARMARTHEN

MONMOUTH

GWENT

PEMBROKE
Pendine
Tenby
Pembrey

WEST

MID

Worms Head
SWANSEA
GLAMORGAN

NEWPORT

CARDIFF

Porthcawl
SOUTH

Barry

North

POINT OF AYR Between the Point and the West Hoyle Bank is the ½ mile wide Welsh Channel. There are some excellent catches to be made here. Species include Tope, Silver Eels, Flounders and good size Bass. Caution must be taken when fishing here as the tide floods very quickly.

PRESTATYN Daytime fishing is almost impossible on the beach due to the popularity of the location with tourists. Night time fishing is by far the more easier and productive. At night the main species you can expect here are Flounders, Bass, Dabs and Plaice.

RHYL Boat fishing is good at this location. Among the species to expect here are Dogfish, Dabs, Plaice, Conger and Tope. Further out, around Middle Patch Spit Buoy is a productive mark for Flatties, Monkfish, Gurnard, Ray and good Tope. Bass and Flounder are common near the harbour mouth.

Baaragutt
Skipper: Jack Quinn
Tel: 0745 55439

COLWYN BAY Beach and shore fishing reasonable. Old Colwyn Beach gives good results for Bass and Flounders and the occasional Tope. The Victoria Pier is available to the public in Summer only and then the main catches are Whiting, Bass and Dabs. A good beach mark is Rhos Point where good catches of Mackerel can be had. A short while out from Rhos Point you can catch Tope, Ray and Gurnard in Summer from boats. The main catches in the Winter around this mark are Whiting and Codling.

LLANDUDNO The holiday season makes Llandudno beach difficult for anglers to fish except in early morning and night time. The beach at Little Orme Head, at the eastern end of the promenade gives good sport in the shape of Bass, Codling, Whiting and Dabs. Another good beach fishing mark are the Black Rocks, just 1 mile from the West Shore. Dabs, Dogfish and good sized Bass are the species most caught there. The jetty near Llandudno produces good results all year round. The main species caught in Winter are Plaice, Dabs, Bass and Flounders and in the Summer, Codling and Whiting.

CONWY Conwy Bay provides excellent sport for boat fishermen. In the shallows the main catch is Bass and where the water is deeper you will find good catches of Codling, Whiting, Dabs, Plaice and Flounders. To the west of Conwy is Conwy Morfa an excellent shore fishing mark. Here you can catch, among other species, Bass, Plaice and Flounders.

MENAI STRAITS This 12 mile long and ½ mile wide channel between Anglesey and Gwynedd provides excellent sport for the sea angler. See the following two entries for details of the boat and shore fishing along the Menai Straits.

Wales – North

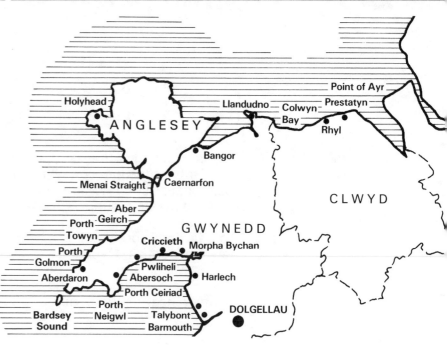

Map showing locations: Point of Ayr, Holyhead, ANGLESEY, Llandudno, Colwyn Bay, Prestatyn, Rhyl, Bangor, Menai Straight, Caernarfon, CLWYD, Aber, Porth Geirch, GWYNEDD, Towyn, Criccieth, Morpha Bychan, Porth Golmon, Pwllheli, Aberdaron, Abersoch, Harlech, Porth Ceiriad, Porth Neigwl, Talybont, DOLGELLAU, Bardsey Sound, Barmouth

BANGOR   Many good beach fishing marks around this area. Bangor foreshore itself produces good catches of Plaice, Bass, Whiting and Cod at varying times throughout the year. The shores aroun the Menai Bridge are more productive with a good selection of fi being taken. Among those you can expect here are Bass, Flounders, Mullet, Whiting, Cod, Pollack and Wrasse. Boat fishi from Bangor gives good results with Bass, especially around Traeth Lafan. The fast currents around the Menai Bridge make t a dangerous area in which to fish from boat unless you are a wel experienced sailor. No wonder this area is called the Swellies. Fi to expect here are Cod, Bass, Conger, Pollack and Plaice.

Faithfull II
Skipper: E. Haigh
Tel: 0248 4252

CAERNARFON   There are several good beach fishing marks along Caernarfon shore. Between Ysqubor Isaf and Tŷ Calch is excellent for really big Tope as well as Bass, Mullet and Flounders near the golf course there is same great sport to be had during the Winter wit Tope, Codling and Whiting being the best catches. If you are aft Mullet there is no better place than the Quay Wall at Caernarfon land really big catches. As well as Mullet the area around the qua is good for Flatties and Bass. Two of the best boat fishing marks around Caernarfon are the Belan Narrows and Traeth Melynog. the Belan Narrows the main species you can expect are Tope, Bass, Thornback Rays, Flounders, Dabs and Dogfish. Further along at Traeth Melynog there are some excellent catches of Flounders to be had as well as Bass in good numbers.

Badger
Skipper: John Evans
Tel: 0286 2492

Sweet Success
Tel: 0286 872482

ABER GEIRCH   A small creek surrounded by rocks, it fishes best from September to November when you can expect some good catches of Bass and Pollack.

PORTH TOWYN   Some good shore fishing to be had here. The area is very rocky and you can land some excellent specimens of Bass especially at evening time. Wrasse and Pollack are also frequent catches in the area.

PORTH GOLMON   This sandy beach bordered by rocks is good hunting ground for Bass and Tope. In Summer there are shoals of Mackerel passing by which make for a good catch. The Tripods just out from Porth Golmon is an underwater reef. Tricky to fish but well worth the effort. Here you will find Red Bream, Brill, Turbot and Plaice amongst others.

BARDSEY SOUND   Cliff bound area facing the sound. Most of the area is impossibly cliff-bound but there are a few good spots for the fisherman here. Best catch here is Bass but there are also some excellent catches of Pollack and Wrasse to be made. Best boatfishing in this area takes place nearest Bardsey Island. Quite close in here you will find Pollack, Bass and Coalfish.

ABERDARON   Beach fishing difficult in Summer beacause of the tourists so best time for fishing here is between September and April. Best species caught from shore is Bass. Two of the best boat fishing marks in the area are Ynys Gwylan Fawr and Ynys Gwylan Fach. These two small islands less than 1 mile South East of Aberdaron are excellent for Bass, Mackerel and Pollack. A further 2 miles beyond Ynys Gwylan Fach is Devil Ridge, another good boat mark. The ridge rises to within 30 foot of the surface in places and it's an excellent hunting ground for Tope, Bull Huss, Rays, Pollack and Cod, and Whiting in Winter.

Anglesey

AMLWCH Boat fishing best with many good catches. Skate, Herring, Mackerel, Conger and Tope up to 40lbs are taken here.

ANGLESEY
Rebecca Jane
Skipper: Roy Smith
Tel: 0407 831284

Starida
Skipper: D. Jones
Tel: 0248 810746

Exact
Skipper: Tony Ripper
Tel: 0248 810396

BEAUMARIS Good boat and shore fishing available. Flatties and Codling can caught from beach marks opposite Beaumaris and along the Straits.

HOLYHEAD Excellent beach and boat fishing. Many good shore marks, just some are at Trearddur Bay, Porthclafarch and on Stanley Embankment at Cymran. Species caught from beach marks include Flounder, Conger, Whiting, Bull Huss. Good boat fishir with Tope, Ling and Shark and many other species.

Jeanne D'Ark
Skipper: A. Williams
Tel: 0407 3184

Victoria
Skipper: Geordie McClay
Tel: 0407 4910

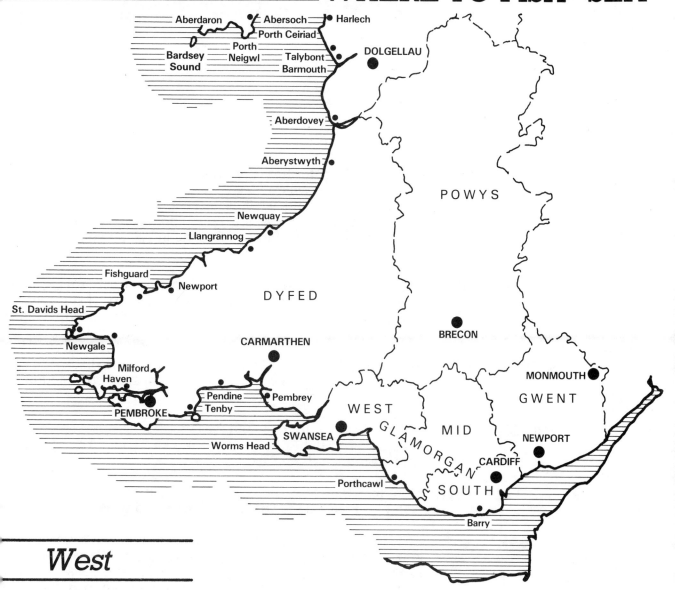

West

PORTH NEIGWL   A 4 mile long storm beach with a good surf even in fine weather. During Summer beach fishermen can land some good catches of Bass but the bigger specimens stay well off-shore. Other principle catches here are Dabs and Plaice.

PORTH CEIRIAD   A good beach mark and not as busy as most of the other beaches along the Lleyn coast. Principle catches here are Skate, Thornback Ray, Dabs, Whiting, Dogfish and Flounder.

ABERSOCH   Beach is best fished during early morning and late evening. Species caught from beach include Whiting, Bass and Flatties. The beach near Bennar Headland is good for Dabs in the Winter and Bass in the Autumn. About 1½ miles North West of Abersoch is St Tudwals Island, East and West. There are some good boat marks around the islands and the main catches are Pollack, Dogfish, Bull Huss and Thornback Rays.

PWLLHELI   Harbourt is best for Bass and Mullet. Shorefishing quite good a
Abererch Strand where Plaice, Flounder and Bass are the main
catches. Boat fishing is fair all year round. Seaward from Carreg
Ymbil, the Gimblet Shoal are a good boat fishing mark. Main
catches here are Whiting and Codling in Winter and Flatties,
Pollack and Ray in the Summer.

CRICCIETH   Beaches are best fished during early morning and late evening
when the main catches are Plaice and Bass. Boat fishing just of
Criccieth produces some good catches of Plaice, Skate, Dogfish
Tope and Flatties.

MORFA BYCHAN   Best fishing here is for Bass, especially from the Black Rock
Sands. Other species you can expect here are Dabs, Flounder a
Plaice.

HARLECH SANDS   Difficult location to reach but well worth the effort. There are
always good catches of Flatties, Bass and Tope to be had for th
who make the effort.

TALYBONT   More than 8 miles of sandy beach, best fished in Spring and
Autumn. Best catches here are Flatties and Bass.

BARMOUTH   Busy in Summer but there are still one or two worthwhle marks
look out for. Good Bass are common at Ynys y Brawd and the
Fairbourne railway bridge is good for Mullet and Bass. Boat fish
is best about 5-6 miles West of Barmouth where the principle
catches are Ray, Pollack and Skate.

BARMOUTH
Sea Bar
Skipper: Barrie Thomas
Tel: 0341 250537

BURRY POINT
Maxine
Skipper: W. Frost
Tel: 0834 813666

ABERDOVEY   Harbour is best for Bass and Flatties but the only time you can
really fish here, mainly because of the Summer holiday traffic, i
during Spring and Autumn. Ynystas Dunes is good beach fishin
mark and the principle catches are Flounder and Bass. Aberdov
Bar is a good boat fishing mark for those after Skate, Ray and
Pollack.

Ceffyl Mor
Skipper: W. Bartlett
Tel: 0654 710869

ABERYSTWYTH One of the best shore spots is Constitution Hill Rocks where the main catches are Whiting, Dogfish and Dabs. The harbour is often good for Mullet, Flounder and Pollack. The Stone Jetty on the south side of the harbour produces good catches of a variety of fish. In Winter the main catches are Dabs, Pouting, Whiting and Dogfish and in Summer, Pollack, Gurnard, Dabs, Pouting and Conger. Tanybwlch Beach on the South side of the stone jetty is an excellent Bass mark in Summer. Other species you will find at this mark are Flounder, Dabs, Pollack and Dogfish.

Boat fishing in the Cardigan Bay area, off Aberystwyth is very productive. From 10 miles and more out Thornback Rays of 12-22lbs are common. Porbeagle Sharks of up to 120lbs and Blue Sharks of up to 90lbs have been caught in the area. Other species you can expect are Conger, Cod, Turbot, Ling, Pollack and Monkfish. Nearer Aberystwyth there is still quite a variety of fish to be had. Among the species you can expect quite close to shore are Pollack, Whiting, Thornback and Homelyn Rays, Dogfish, Gurnard and Coalfish.

Boy Shamus
Tel: 0970 611980

Nissan
Skipper: Dave Taylor
Tel: 09970 828815

NEW QUAY The headland is a good mark for beach fishing. Among the species you can expect here are Mackerel, Pollack, Wrasse, Dogfish and the occasional Bass.

Iolanthe
Skipper: C. Davies
Tel: 0239 2832

LLANGRANNOG One of the best fishing spots in the area Ynys Lochtyn, a rocky headland, just North from Llangrannog beach. From the most northern point of the headland the main species you can expect good catches of are Bass, Dabs, Rockling, Rays, Conger, Pollack, Whiting, Mackerel and Huss. From the eastern side of the headland there are good catches Rockling, Pollack, Bass, Mackerel and Wrasse to be made. From the ledges on the Western side you can expect Mackerel, Bass, Dabs, Whiting and Dogfish.

NEWPORT Newport Sands are excellent if you're after Bass. Spring and Autumn are best for the species and dusk is usually the best time of day. Best off Dinas Head and Trwyn y Bwa. From both points the species you can expect are Skate, Ray, Mackerel, Huss, Monkfish, Turbot and Dogfish. Blue and Porbeagle Sharks are common enough quite near the shore.

FISHGUARD The harbour fishes quite well with Plaice, Dabs, Pouting, Pollac and Wrasse being the principle species found there. The main species caught from the beach here are Ray, Pouting, Conger a Bass. Fishguard Bay is a good venue for the boat fisherman. Winter species include Cod, Bass and Whiting. In Summer ther more variety of species in the area and the main ones are Gurna Conger, Pollack, Tope, Ray and Skate.

ST. DAVIDS HEAD Mackerel and Pollack are the main catch for the fisherman fishir from the headland. Other species caught are Wrasse, Tope and Bass. One of the best boat fishing marks in the area is Bishops Rocks which are about 3 miles West of St. Davids Head. This 1 mile long reef holds some good catches of Pollack, Tope and Bl Shark.

NEWGALE This 2 mile long beach is excellent for Bass nearly all year round Other good catches here are Plaice, Whiting, Flounder and Codling. Boat fishing in St Brides Bay is good for Tope, Pollack Brill, Plaice, Dabs and Spur.

MILFORD HAVEN There are many good beach and boat marks around the Milford Haven area. Bass fishing from Broad Haven at Basherton is bes during late Summer and Autumn. Another good mark is Kilpais where the main catches are Bass, Codling, Coalfish and Flatties Fishing from the piers and jetties inside the Haven is fine for Codling, Whiting, Pollack, Skate, Coalfish and Rays.

Dyfed Marine Services
Tel: 06464 600717

PEMBROKE Several good stretches of beach in the Pembroke area, producir some excellent fishing. The main beach caught species in the ar are Bass, Herring, Thornback Rays, Conger and Tope. A good boat fishing mark is between the Pembroke Ferry and H.M.S. Warrior in Pembroke Docks. Congers of up to 75lbs have been caught in this location which is known as the Conger Holes. Another good boat mark is just off St Gavans Head where there are fine catches of Tope, Ray, Bass and Pollack to be made.

TENBY Giltar Point at the extreme south west end of Tenby's Sands produces some good catches for the shore angler. The main catches from the point are Bass and Mullet. Monkstone Beach is also excellent for Bass during Spring and Autumn. Dabs and Skate are frequent visitors to the beach. The main catches for the boat fisherman in the Tenby area are Tope, Ray, Dogfish, Conger, Mackerel in Summer and Whiting in Winter.

TENBY
Deso
Skipper: B. Ryan
Tel: 0604 633672

James Rolfe
Skipper: Don Bowler
Tel: 0834 2663

SAUNDERSFOOT
Shimo-San
Skipper: W. Frost
Tel: 0834 813666

PENDINE Excellent location for the shore angler. The beach is long, uncrowded and although shallow it has a good run of surf. Almost any spot on the beach will bring you good catches of Bass, Flounders and Plaice.

PEMBREY Some excellent fishing to be had on the whole length of beach. Bass are best from May to November, good sized Tope caught during May and June. February and March are excellent for Flounder.

WORMS HEAD An excellent mark for Whiting in Autumn and early Winter. Good catches of Bass from the Southern side of the head. From North side Tope is the best catch especially from July to September. Boat fishing is quite good just off Worms Head and the best catch is Bass.

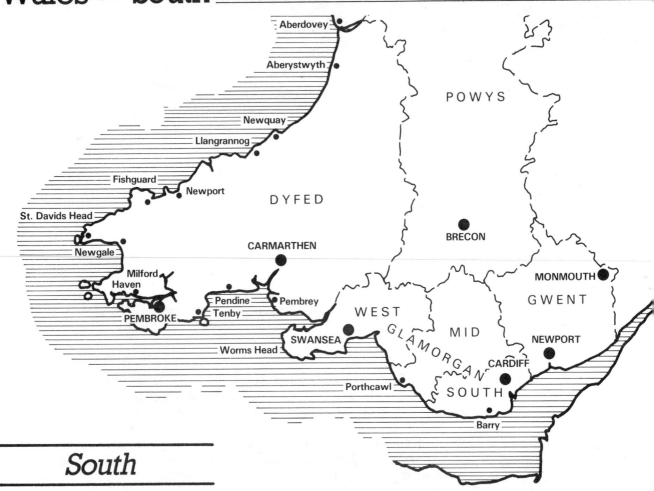

Map of South Wales showing: Aberdovey, Aberystwyth, Newquay, Llangrannog, Fishguard, Newport, St. Davids Head, Newgale, Milford Haven, PEMBROKE, Pendine, Tenby, Pembrey, CARMARTHEN, Worms Head, SWANSEA, Porthcawl, Barry, CARDIFF, SOUTH, MID, WEST GLAMORGAN, NEWPORT, GWENT, MONMOUTH, BRECON, POWYS, DYFED

South

SALTHOUSE POINT Shore fishing quite good with excellent Flounder from November to February and the occasional Bass from time to time. Boat fishing of the point is fair with the main catches being Whiting, Tope, Thornback Rays and the odd Porbeagle Shark.

SWANSEA Good shorefishing from Lighthouse Island near Mumbles Head. Species you can expect here are Bass, Cod, Whiting and tope. The pier is an excellent platform for Conger, Mackerel and Bass Summer and Whiting and Flatties in Winter. One of the best boat fishing marks in the area is the Outer Green Grounds, out from Mumbles Head. In Winter the main catches on these grounds are Whiting and Cod. Species to expect in during the Summer months are Tope, Dabs, Ray, Plaice and the occasional Conger.

Lady Helen
Skipper: Paul Radford
Tel: 0792 23388

June Veronica
Tel: 0792 583165

Gower Trader and Gower Ranger
Skipper: Ernie Bishopston
Tel: 044 128 2164

Mermaid
Skipper: Tony Whitehead
Tel: 0792 59924

Susan Jane
Tel: 0656 58254

PORTHCAWL Best shorefishing marks at at Sker Point and Ogmore by Sea. At Sker Rocks the main catches are Thornback Ray, Flatties, Bass and Dogfish. At Ogmore the main catches are Cod and Whiting in Winter and Bass in Summer. Boat fishing off Porthcawl is good with principle catches being Bass, Plaice and Thornback Rays in Summer and Flounder, Whiting and Cod in Winter.

Dolphin
Skipper: D. Tucker
Tel: 0656 714909

Our Sonia
Skipper: K. Parsons
Tel: 0656 56481

BARRY One of the best shorefishing marks in the area is at St Mary's Well Bay. The sand spit here produces some good Cod of up to 15lbs, Pouting and Whiting and Bass in Summer. At Lavernock Point fishing is best from November to April, best catch is Cod up to 8lbs. Cold Knapp, back at Barry is a steep pebble beach, fishes well for Cod, Whiting and Flounder in Winter. Boat fishing off Barry is good for Pout, Flounder, Whiting and Cod.

CARDIFF Foreshore at Cardiff Docks fishes well from 2 hours before and 2 hours after high water. Species you can expect here include Whiting, Flounder, Pout, Codling and Silver Eel. Boat fishing from Cardiff is fair with the main catches being Flatties, Rays, Dogfish, Conger Eels and Silver Eels, Whiting and Cod.

Alaine-Dominique
Tel: 0633 275907
Slomoshun
Tel: 01 845 3456 or
Cardiff 614200

Michele
Tel: 055 46 3315

NEWPORT St Brides Beach near Newport is a good beach fishing mark. Main species you can expect in Summer are Sole, Silver Eel, Plaice, Flounder and Bass. In Winter the main species from this beach are Pout, Whiting and a few Codling. Another good beach mark around Newport is Goldcliff where thare are some excellent catches of Pouting, Whiting, Cod and Flounder to be had. Redwick, two miles East of Goldcliff where there are some good catches of Whiting to be made.

ANGLING IN IRELAND

Ireland is truly an angler's paradise, whether your interests lie in coarse, game or sea angling. Bream, roach, tench and rudd abound in the clear, unpolluted waters of Ireland's rivers and

lakes. Where else would a 100lb catch be classed as normal! And coarse angling is free in Ireland, with no close season. The game angler will be equally delighted, whether pitting his skills against the true wild trout of the great western loughs or the sea trout

which enter the rivers from April to September. And Ireland offers the sea angler 3,500 miles of unspoilt coastline, with rock and beach fishing for wrasse, pollack, conger and bass, just waiting to be explored.

Or you can take a trip in one of the many fully equipped boats–with so many species present, you never know what will take your bait next. There are many easy, low cost ways to get to all this great sport, a wide choice of accommodation, and many inclusive angling packages too.

Come on over–you'll be very welcome. And you'll enjoy some of the finest angling in Europe.

For information on all aspects of angling in Ireland and reservations, contact your nearest Irish Tourist Board office.

✿ Ireland

LONDON 150 New Bond Street, W1Y 0AQ. 01-493 3201
BIRMINGHAM 6-8 Temple Row B2 5HG. 021-236 9724
MANCHESTER 28 Cross Street M2 3NH. 061-832 5981
GLASGOW 19 Dixon Street G1 4AJ. 041-221 2311

YOU COULD ONLY BE IN IRELAND.

Ireland
Southern

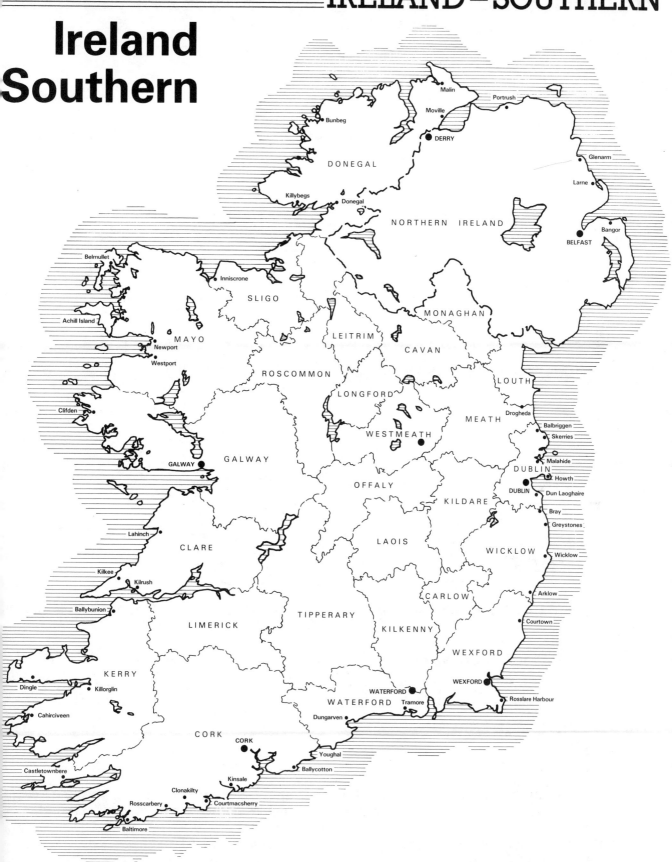

Malin

Moville

Portrush

Bunbeg

DERRY

Glenarm

DONEGAL

Larne

Killybegs

Donegal

NORTHERN IRELAND

Bangor

BELFAST

Belmullet

Inniscrone

SLIGO

MONAGHAN

Achill Island

LEITRIM

CAVAN

MAYO

Newport

Westport

ROSCOMMON

LONGFORD

LOUTH

Clifden

WESTMEATH

MEATH

Drogheda

Balbriggen

Skerries

GALWAY

GALWAY

Malahide

DUBLIN

OFFALY

Howth

DUBLIN

Dun Laoghaire

KILDARE

Bray

Lahinch

Greystones

CLARE

LAOIS

WICKLOW

Wicklow

Kilkee

Kilrush

CARLOW

Arklow

Ballybunion

Courtown

LIMERICK

TIPPERARY

KILKENNY

WEXFORD

KERRY

WEXFORD

Dingle

Killorglin

WATERFORD

Rosslare Harbour

WATERFORD

Tramore

Cahirciveen

Dungarven

CORK

Castletownbere

CORK

Youghal

Kinsale

Ballycotton

Clonakilty

Rosscarbery

Courtmacsherry

Baltimore

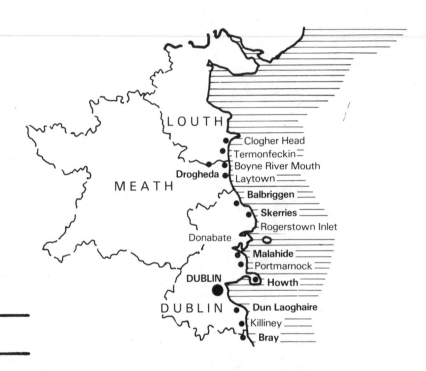

The map shows the following locations labelled along the coast: LOUTH, Clogher Head, Termonfeckin, Boyne River Mouth, Drogheda, Laytown, MEATH, Balbriggen, Skerries, Rogerstown Inlet, Donabate, Malahide, Portmarnock, DUBLIN, Howth, Dun Laoghaire, Killiney, Bray.

Louth

CLOGHER HEAD   Mackerel, small Pollack, Dabs and occasional Codling from pier. Pollack, Codling and Coalfish from rocks.

TERMONFECKIN   Flounders and occasional Bass from beach.

Meath

BOYNE RIVER MOUTH   Bass and Flatfish from beach. Bass from driftline fishing in estu... and at outflow from fish meal factory Mullet can be found.

LAYTOWN AND DELVIN RIVER MOUTH   Bass, Flounder and occasional Sea Trout from beaches.

Dublin

BALBRIGGAN   Harbour holds Mullet. Codling, Dogfish, Dabs, Whiting, small Pollack and small Coalfish can be had from boats.

SKERRIES   Mackerel, small Coalfish and small Pollack from pier. Mackerel and Wrasse from rocks at swimming place. Pollack, Codling, Coalfish, Plaice, Wrasse, Whiting, Dogfish, occasional Thornback Ray and Tope from boats.

ROGERSTOWN INLET   Bass can be found at low water on the sand bar at the mouth and during the flood tide inside the sand dunes.

DONABATE STRAND   Codling and occasional Bass from beach.

MALAHIDE   Mullet near railway line at Broadmeadows. Flounder and occasional Bass in pool below railway bridge and estuary.

PORTMARNOCK   The rocks around Martello Towers produce Bass and Flounders. Mackerel and some Flatfish in the Summer.

HOWTH   Mackerel, Flounder and small Pollack from pier.

RED ROCK   Channel fishing for Flatfish and Bass around low water. Occasional Tope near Martello Towers.

BULL WALL   From the lighthouse Flounder and occasional Bass. From the bridge Codling, Whiting, small Pollack and occasional Bass and Flounder.

POOLBEG   Mackerel, Conger and small Pollack from rocks below lighthouse. Flounder, Bass, small Conger and occasional Sea Trout at Half Moon swimming club. At outlet of power station Mullet can be found.

SANDYMOUNT STRAND   Cockle Lake, Blackrock Baths and back of dump provide beach fishing for Flounder and Bass.

DUN LAOGHAIRE   Plaice, Whiting, small Pouting, Conger and Codling from West pier and Mullet in Summer.

BULLOCK HARBOUR   Codling, Whiting, Plaice, Wrasse, Pollack etc from boats. Wrasse from rocks at back of harbour.

COLIEMORE HARBOUR   Small Pollack, Codling, Conger from the pier. Pollack, Whiting, Wrasse, Codling, Plaice etc from boats.

KILLINEY BEACH   Occasional Plaice, Bass and small Pollack from beach.

CORBAWN LANE   Crab Island for Codling. Bass, Flounder, Plaice, Codling, Dabs and Lesser Spotted Dogfish from the beach.

Wicklow

BRAY   Codling, Dogfish, Pollack and occasional Conger from pier. Bass, Flounder, Codling and Plaice from below promenade. Ray, Conger, Codling, Wrasse, Pollack and Dogfish from boats with Mullet during Summer.

NORTH BEACH   Dogfish and occasional Dab, Plaice, Turbot, Bass, Black Sole, Tope and Conger from beach especially at night.

GREYSTONES   Small Pollack, occasional Bass, Plaice and Codling from pier. Codling, Pollack and occasional Bass from rocks at Carrigeden and the Flat Rock.

SOUTH BEACH   Codling, Bass, Flounder, Pollack, Plaice, Dogfish, Gurnard and occasional Ray and Tope from all along the beach, best marks are Kilcoole, Newcastle, "The Point" and the Breeches especially at night. Occasional Lemon Sole can be found at the Breeches.

WICKLOW   Pollack, Flounder, Plaice, Codling and small Ray from the pier. Mullet from the harbour and Flounder from Broad Lough.

Sheelagh
Michael Greenwood
Tel: 0404 2297

SILVER STRAND   Bass, Flounder, Dogfish and occasional Plaice from the beach with Spurdogfish at night.

BRITTAS BAY   Bass, Dogfish, Whiting and Codling from the beach.

PENNYCOMEQUICK BRIDGE   Flounder, Bass, Codling, Whiting, Dogfish and occasional Plaice from near rocks and river mouth to the south. Best at night, for three hours either side of high water, in Winter.

ARKLOW   Flounder and Codling on Ferrybank. Codling, Dabs, Dogfish and Bass from rocks and beach.

CLOGGA (NUN'S) BEACH   Bass by float fishing on rocks at southern end.

Wexford

KILMICHAEL POINT Bass, Mackerel and Plaice from rocks.

CLONES STRAND Bass, Codling, Whiting and occasional Tope from beaches in Summer. Codling, Whiting and Flounder in Winter.

COURTOWN Flounder and Bass from beaches. Mullet from harbour.

POLLSHONE Flounder, Dabs, Bass, Dogfish, Plaice, Gurnard and occasional Tope from rocks.

CAHORE POINT Bass and Flatfish from beach, pier and rocks.

AURICE CASTLE STRAND Bass, Flounder, Tope, occasional Stingray and Thornback from beaches in season.

TINNABEARNA Tope, Dogfish, Bass and Flounder from beach.

BLACKWATER Ballyconnigar and Blue Pool for Bass, Tope, Flatfish and Flounder.

CURRACLOE Bass, Tope and Flounder from beach at night.

RAVEN POINT Flatfish, Bass and occasional small Ray from beach.

WEXFORD HARBOUR Occasional Ray from north side of breakwater. Flounder and Bass from Ferrybank, Cats Strand, Ardcavon Srand and the breakwater. Bass, Ray, Skate, Dogfish, Garfish, Gurnard and occasional Tope from boats.

FERRYCARRIG Bass and Flounder. Many Bass have to be, by law, returned alive to water because they are undersized. Shore and boat fishing.

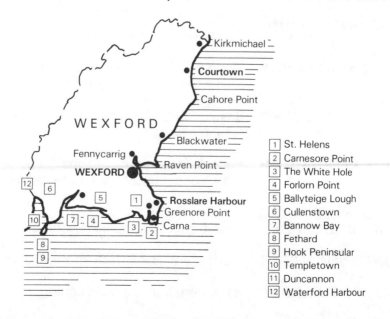

1	St. Helens
2	Carnesore Point
3	The White Hole
4	Forlorn Point
5	Ballyteige Lough
6	Cullenstown
7	Bannow Bay
8	Fethard
9	Hook Peninsular
10	Templetown
11	Duncannon
12	Waterford Harbour

ROSSLARE Shore and pier fishing for Conger. Channel below bridge for Flounder, Dogfish and Bass. Flounder and Dabs in harbour. Boat fishing to Tuskar Rock for Bass, also Tope and Flatfish, Cod, Pollack, Red Sea Bream, Pouting and Dogfish. Excellent Bass by spinning and trolling from Splaugh Rocks.

GREENORE POINT Bass, Flounder, occasional Dogfish on beach.

ST. HELENS Bass from rocks and south of pier.

CARNA Flounder from pier. Bass and Flatfish from shore.

CARNSORE POINT Bass, Wrasse, Flounder, Dogfish and small Pollack from rocks.

THE 'COOMBE' Bass, Sea Trout, Flounder and Tope by surf fishing. Lady's Island Lake good for Bass.

THE 'WHITE HOLE' Sea Trout, Bass and Tope by surf fishing and spinning.

KILMORE QUAY Bass, Flounder and Codling from beach, rocks and pier. Mullet from harbour. St. Patricks Bridge, which is a reef of rocks east of the harbour is a good boat mark for Bass and Flatfish. The Saltee Islands produce excellent Pollack, Tope and Bass.

FORLORN POINT Bass, Sea Trout, small Pollack from the shore by spinning.

BURROW SHORE Bass, occasional Tope and Flatfish by surf fishing.

BALLYTEIGE LOUGH Bass from spinning in channel. Bass and Tope from surf fishing.

CULLENSTOWN AND BLACKHALL Flounder and Bass by surf fishing.

BANNOW BAY Flounder, Bass and occasional Tope by spinning at mouth of bay. Surf fishing on both beaches.

FETHARD Bass and Flatfish on beaches and in sandy coves. Deep sea fishing.

HOOK PENINSULAR Pollack, Wrasse, occasional Tope and Bass from rocks. Best marks between Slade and Hook Head.

TEMPLETOWN, DOLLAR BAY AND BOOLEY BAY Bass from shore by float fishing and bottom fishing.

DUNCANNON FORT Flatfish and Bass from shore, Conger from harbour.

WATERFORD HARBOUR Bass from inshore boat fishing.

Waterford

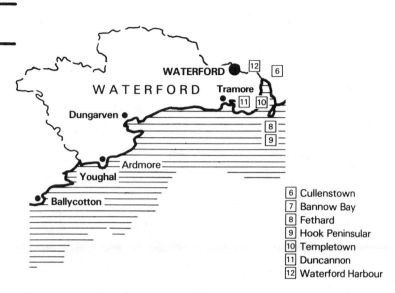

Map legend:

6	Cullenstown
7	Bannow Bay
8	Fethard
9	Hook Peninsular
10	Templetown
11	Duncannon
12	Waterford Harbour

TRAMORE STRAND Bass and Flatfish by surf fishing.

DUNGARVAN Shore fishing for Bass and Flatfish from Clonea Strand and Castle and Cunnigar Spit. Bass, Flatfish and Dogfish from Ballinacourty Pier. Bass and Flounder from Barnawee Railway Bridge and Road Bridge. Bass, Flounder and Mullet from Dungarvan town marks such as Pool above Railway Bridge, Railway Bridge, Pool between bridges and Quays. Conger from both Helvic Pier walls also Mullet, Flatfish and occasional Bass. Rock fishing at Helvic Head for Pollack, Wrasse and Mackerel. Boat fishing for Ray, Dogfish, Bass, Pollack, Tope, Spurdogfish. Deep sea angling for Blue Shark. Bass over sandbank at Cunnigar Point.

Kingfisher
Cormac Walsh
Tel: 058 41274

First Cork
T. E. Casey
Ballymacart 42

Tudor Lady
John Landers
Tel: 058 41873

Violet
Sean Whelan
Tel: 058 41642

ARDMORE Bass and Pollack at Fuges. Bass and Flatfish at Ballyquin Strand, and Whiting Bay sluice. Mackerel and Pollack at Blackrock, Lieanaun, Faill na g Cat, Gleann Piarais, Goileen, Falla Bawn and Faill an Iarainn. Bass, Flatfish and Sea Trout at Kiln and Ardmore Strand. Mackerel, Pollack, Sea Trout, Mullet and Wrasse from Ardmore Pier. Pollack, Wrasse, Mackerel and Gurnard from Mackerel Point. Pollack, Mackerel and Wrasse from Fr. O'Donnell's Well, Faillawaderr and Flat Rock. Bass, Flatfish, Coalfish, Dogfish and Sea Trout from Clash and Goat Island. Bass, Flatfish and Dogfish from Whiting Bay Bridge. Bass, Pollack, Wrasse, Sea Trout and Mackerel from Whiting Bay.

Ireland – Southern
Cork

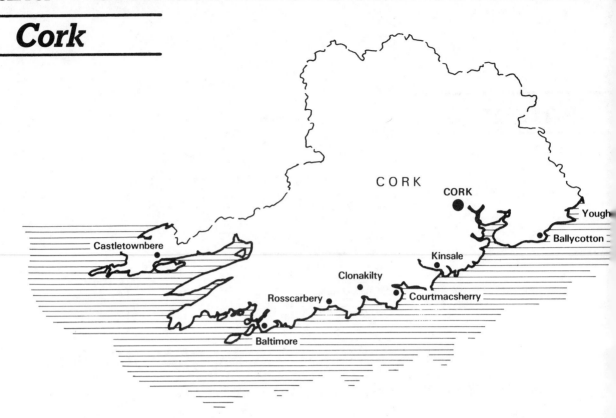

C O R K

CORK

Yough[

Ballycotton

Kinsale

Clonakilty

Courtmacsherry

Castletownbere

Rosscarbery

Baltimore

YOUGHAL Shore fishing for Bass and Flounder from Pillmore, Packs Mall Strand, Quays, Tourig, Blackwater and Ardsallagh. Bass and Mullet from Pill. Bass and Flatfish from Youghal Strand by surf fishing. Bass from Mollgoggins, Ferry Point, Monatrea, Easter Point, Blackball Head and Cabin Point. Flounder, Dogfish, Bass and Mackerel in season from Green Park Corner. Conger and occasional Bass at night from Pier Head. Bass and small Pollack from Old Bridge. Bass, Flounder and Dogfish from Mangan's Co and Caliso Bay

   Boat fishing for Flounder, Codling in Autumn. Good bass mar are 'The Narrows' between Ferry Point and Pier Head, and Youghal Harbour. Deep sea fishing for Blue Shark in the bay.

Visce Beatha
Capt. M. Vastenhout
Tel: 024 2313

BALLYCOTTON Blue Shark, Skate, Tope, Porbeagle, Cod, Ling, Pollack, Bass, Conger, Coalfish mostly from boats.
   Shore fishing from Knockadoon Head for Pollack and Wrasse Garryvoe Strand for Bass, Flounder, Plaice and Dab. Ballymona Strand for Bass, Flatfish and Sea Trout. Ballyandreen for Bass, Pollack, Dogfish and Mackerel. Ballycroneen for Bass, Dogfish, Flatfish and occasional Tope. Ballycotton harbour for Mullet, an Conger at the end of the pier.

CORK HARBOUR Bass fishing from many shore marks including Inch Strand, Gullies in Rock, The 'Foyle', Canavan's Point, Under Ruins, North of White Bay, Corkbeg Strand, Long Point, Under Castle, Saleen, Under Pilot Station, Paddy's Point, Lough More. Bass and Flatfish from Trabolgan Strand, Roche's Point Strand, Fisherman's Rock. Other shore marks are Powers Head, Gylen, The 'Dock' Carthy's Strand, The 'Gut', White Bay, Carlisle Pier, Gold Point, East Ferry Mouth, Barrack Hole, Railway Passover, a variety of fish including Pollack, Mackerel, Wrasse, Flatfish, Bass, Small Ray, Codling, Sea Trout, Flounder, Dogfish, Conger, Thornback Ray, at Railway Passover, can be found.

Boat fishing for Skate, Ray, Dabs, Plaice, Codling, Cod, Conger, Turbot, Ray, Pollack, Whiting, Dogfish, Tope at many marks.

Norma T and Barrcuda
Barry Twomey
Tel: 021 831448

Leaca Rua and Marwyn
Cork Harbour Boats Ltd.
Tel: 021 841348
021 841633

KINSALE HARBOUR Shore fishing for Bass and Flounder from Long Bridge, Gully Bridge, and Jagoe's Point. Conger from Conger Hole and Mullet from above Gully Bridge and Kinsale.

Inshore boat fishing for Bass, Dabs, Flatfish, Pollack, Conger, Codling, Whiting, Rays, Codfish, Wrasse, Dogfish, Mackerel, Gurnard, Coalfish and Sea Trout from marks such as Castle Hole, River Bandon, Conger Hole, Outside Farmers Rock, South and West of Charles Fort, Outside Sandy Cover Island, and South of Shronecan Point.

Deep sea fishing especially for Sharks, main marks are Ling, Rocks, Pango Reef, off the Old Heads and the wreck of the 'Lusitania'. Blue Shark, Skate, Ling, Conger, Dogfish, Rays, Coalfish, Pollack, Red Bream and Wrasse are all to be found.

Rapparee, Dromderrig, Moonlighter, Kern, Florence and Leacy
Trident Hotel
Tel: 021 72301

Skua, Shamrock Gannet and Luckyella
Kinsale Angling Centre Ltd.
Tel: 021 72611

COURTMACSHERRY BAY Bass and Flatfish from Garrettstown Strand. Bass, Flatfish and Mullet from Garranafeen Strand. Bass and Flatfish can be found at Argideen estuary, Timoleague, Sand Bank, Courtmacsherry Strand. Conger from Courtmacsherry Pier. Pollack, Mackerel and Dogfish from Land Point, Broadstand Bay, Quarry Point and Barry's Point.

St. Mologa, Mark Anthony, Naomh Anthony, Moby Dick, Larry O'Rourke, Blave Mari, Lowland and Onedin 2
John O'Sullivan
Tel: 023 46135

Ireland — Southern

CLONAKILTY BAY Bass and Flounder from Clonakilty Estuary, Virgin Mary's Point and Muckruss Estuary. Bass, Flounder and Codling from Bar Roc and Bass, Pollack, Wrasse and Mackerel from Ring Head.

ROSSCARBERY 3 beaches for Bass, also The Bar and Slip. Pollack and Wrasse from behind Pier. Bass, Mackerel, Dogfish from pier. Bass and Mullet in small harbour. Bass and Flounder from Boat Slip, Bridg Channel, Warren Strand, Ownahincy Strand, and Little Island Strand. Bass and Flatfish from The Long Strand.

WEST CORK (SKIBBEREEN COASTLINE) Flounder, Mullet, Bass, Sea Trout, Wrasse, Pollack, Conger, Dogfish, Mackerel, Flatfish, Ray from shores. Pollack, Wrasse, Mackerel and Flatfish from rocks. Deep sea fishing for Conger, Pollack, Mackerel, Wrasse and Gurnard.

BALTIMORE Boat fishing for Sharks, Skate, Conger, Ling, Tope, Cod, Pollack and Mackerel. Pollack, Bass and Mackerel from shore.

BALTIMORE
Baltimore Oriel
Ted Brown
Tel: Baltimore 27

CROOKHAVEN
Leda
Crookhaven Sea Angling Centre
Tel: 028 35153

SCHULL
Lilian Rose
Nick Dent

CASTLETOWNBERE Sheltered fishing in Berehaven, and offshore marks in Bantry Ba for Shark, Pollack, Conger, Skate, Ray, Ling, Huss, Pouting, Bream, Wrasse, Spurdog, Flounders, Gurnard, Grey Mullet, Plaice, Mackerel and Whiting.

Kerry

BALLKINSKELLIGS BAY Rock fishing for Pollack, Mackerel, Wrasse, Conger, Dogfish and occasional Bass. Surf fishing for Bass and Flatfish, especially at mouth of Inny and one mile either side.

CAHERCIVEEN Boat fishing to Valentia Island for Conger, Turbot, Halibut, Skate Red Bream, Bass, large Gurnard, Mackerel, Tope, Garfish and Blue Shark.
Rock fishing for Pollack, Mackerel, Wrasse, Dogfish at Culoo, Cooncrome Harbour west side, and Kells. Beach marks include Lough Kay, for Flatfish and occasional Ray. Pier fishing from Reenard Point for Flatfish, Mackerel and Bass. Bass and Flounde at Rossbehy Creek. Coonanna Harbour for Pollack, Wrasse and Mackerel on the western side. Portmagee harbour for Conger and Mullet, and small Dogfish and Pollack off bridge.

KILLORGLIN Bass and Flatfish with occasional Tope from Inch Strand. Bass and Flounder from Laune River and Ballycasane Pier. Cromane Point for Bass and Flatfish. Inshore fishing in channel between Rossbehy Point and Cromane Point for Ray, Flatfish, Tope and Dogfish. Glenbeigh for Bass, Flatfish. White Strand for Bass, Flatfish, Dogfish, occasional Ray and Tope. Bass and occasional Tope from Rossbehy Point.

DINGLE PENINSULAR Surf fishing for Bass at Smerwick, Cloghane and Castlegregory. Offshore fishing for Pollack, Coalfish, Conger, Ling, Sea Bream, Skate, Tope, Halibut and Turbot.

Bass and Flatfish from Black Rock, Banna Strand, Carrahane Sands, Barrow harbour, Fenit Island, Derrymore Island, Camp, Lough Gill Mouth, Magharees, Kilshannig Point, Scraggane Bay, Brandon Bay, Traghbawn, Dingle harbour, Trabey. Bass and Flounder from Blennerville. Flounder from Ferriter's Cove. Flatfish from Clogher and Coumeenoole, Dogfish from Ventry Pier. Bass, Flatfish, Dogfish and Ray from Ventry harbour. Bass from Minard, Annascaul. Fenit Pier for Bass, Skate, Ray, Tope, Dogfish, Monkfish, Pollack, Conger, Flatfish and Mullet. Inshore boat fishing at Fenit for Skate, Ray, Tope, Monkfish, Dogfish and Conger.

BALLYBUNION Cashen River for Bass, Flounder, Dogfish and Flatfish. Blackrock for Bass, Flatfish, Conger, Pollack and Wrasse. Bass and Flatfish from Ballybunion, Beal Strand and Littor Strand. Beach fishing at Beal Point for Turbot and Plaice.

Ireland – Southern
Clare

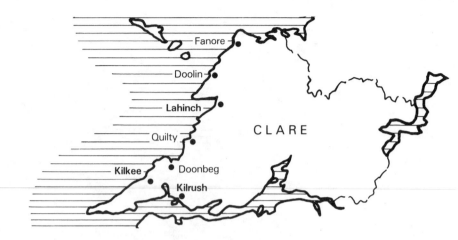

Fanore
Doolin
Lahinch
Quilty
Kilkee
Doonbeg
Kilrush
CLARE

KILRUSH Cappagh Pier for Conger, Dogfish and occasional Monkfish. Querrin for Flatfish, Tope, Monkfish and Ray. Flatfish from Qu Pier. Flounder from Kildysart Pier.

CARRIGAHOLT Dogfish from pier.

KILKEE Rock fishing at Ross Point for Mackerel, Pollack and Wrasse. South of town rocks for Pollack, Bass, Flatfish and Wrasse. Mackerel, Garfish, Wrasse, Spurdog, Pollack, Conger and To from Baltard.

DOONBEG Bass and Flatfish from Doughmore Strand, Lough Donnell an Seafield.

QUILTY Bass from back of pier and reef at west end of sea front road. and Flatfish from Spanish Point and White Strand. Rock fishir Freagh for Pollack, Mackerel and Wrasse. Green Island for Ga Pollack, Wrasse, Conger, Tope, Dogfish and occasional Porbe Shark.

LAHINCH Beach fishing for Flatfish and Bass. Boat fishing from Liscann for Porbeagle Shark. Inagh River mouth for Bass, Mullet, Flat and Sea Trout.

DOOLIN Rock fishing at Traghleachan for Wrasse, Mackerel, Pollack, Conger, Tope and Dogfish. Beach fishing at Doolin for Bass, Mackerel, Flatfish and Dogfish. Rock fishing at Poulcraveen a Ard na Glaise for Mackerel, Pollack, Wrasse, Garfish, Conger Dogfish. Ballyreen for Mackerel, Garfish, Wrasse, Pollack, Dogfish, Tope and occasional Porbeagle Shark.

Happy Hooker
Sea Arann Co. Ltd.
Tel: Lisdoonvarna 186 and 103

FANORE Beach fishing for Bass, Flatfish and Tope from rockier beach. Black Head for Dogfish, Mackerel, Conger, Pollack and Wrasse. Bass and Flatfish from Rynn Point. Bass, Mackerel and Tope from New Quay.

BALLYVAUGHAN	SEAFIELD PIER AND QUILTY
Missy Moo	**Barbara D**
Cormacruisers Limited	M. McMahon
Tel: 061 76251	Tel: 061 77244

Galway

CLIFDEN Boat fishing for Blue Shark, Tope, Coalfish, Pollack, Ray, Ling, Cod, Skate, Brill, Turbot and Plaice from Slyne Head, Barrister wreck off Inishark, Inishbofin, Inishturk and Fosteries Shoals. Bay marks are Ballinakill, Killary, Roundstone, Mannin Cleggan and Bunowen. Conger and Flounder and Cleggan Pier. Pollack, Wrasse, Mackerel from Aughrusbeg, Coolacloy, Beleek. Pollack, Wrasse and Conger from Omey Island. Conger from Streamstown. Pollack, Wrasse, Mackerel and Ray from Slopers Cliff, Hawks Nest (also Ray). Wrasse and Ray from White Lady, Boat Harbour, Ballinaga. Flounder, Plaice and small Turbot from Candoolin. Pollack, Wrasse and Conger from Salt Lake. Ray from Mannin Bay, Flounder and Turbot from False Bay and Doonloughan (also Plaice). All boat fishing marks.

GALWAY	CLIFDEN
Jean Elaine	**Maeve Marie**
Elmer Kavanagh	John Ryan
Tel: 091 64789 (O)	Tel: Clifden 108
091 23331 (H)	
	KILLARY HARBOUR
ROUNDSTONE	**Killary Bay**
Killaree	Balzer Deep Sea Fishing Centre
Joe Keane	Tel: Leenane 30
Tel: Roundstone 39	Ballinrobe 115

Belmullet

Gweesalia

Achill Island

MAYO

Newport

Westport

Mayo

WESTPORT Boat and shore fishing for Monkfish, Skate, Tope, Conger, Co
Codling, Pollack, Flounder, Plaice, Gurnard, Coalfish, Bass,
Wrasse, Turbot, Dogfish, White Skate, Porbeagle Shark, Blue
Shark and Tunny. Good marks are Clew Bay, Cloghormack bu
Pigeon Point, Tower in Inner Bay and off lighthouse.

WESTPORT
Finnaun
Francis Clark
Tel: Westport 459

MAID OF CLEW BAY
Padraic Conlon
Tel: Westport 371

LADY HELEN
Reg Roynon
Tel: Carrowholly 715

NEWPORT Clew bay for boat fishing for Mackerel, Tope, Skate, Conger,
Dogfish, Monkfish, Codfish, Whiting, Pollack, Sea Trout and
Gurnard.

ACHILL ISLAND Boat fishing for Conger, Tope, Ling, Pollack, Flatfish, Blue sha
Thresher, Porbeagle and Tunny. Tullaghan Bay for Flatfish.

DARBYS POINT, ACHILL
Dorren Patricia
Joe Kilbane
Tel: Achill Sound 70

GEESALA Sea Trout, Flounder and occasional Bass.

BELMULLET Blacksod Point for Pollack and Wrasse from rocks and Dogfish, occasional Ray and Conger from pier. Flatfish and Dogfish from Elly Bay. Mullet from Quay in Belmullet. Beach fishing for Flatfish, Dogfish, occasional Sea Trout and Bass, Pollack and Mackerel from rocks below tower, along stretch between Corraun Point and Glosh Tower. Flounder, Sea Trout, Dogfish and small Turbot from Cross. Pollack, Coalfish, Mackerel, Dogfish and occasional Conger from Annagh Head. Flounder, occasional Ray and Conger from Frenchport. Conger from Erris Head. Wrasse, Conger, Dogfish, Pollack and Coalfish from Glenlara. Sea Trout, Mackerel, Pollack and Flatfish from Blind Harbour. Beach fishing at Pollacoppal for Ray, Flounder and small Turbot, Mackerel and Pollack from rocks. Mackerel, Pollack, small Coalfish, Conger, Dogfish, Pouting and Wrasse from Ballyglass Lighthouse. Ray, Flounder, Turbot, Plaice, Dogfish, Codling, Coalfish, Pollack and Flatfish from Ballyglass Pier and beach. Sea Trout, Bass and Flatfish from Rossport, and Rinroe. Ray, Turbot, Flounder, Dogfish, Plaice, Dab, Gurnard, Wrasse, Mackerel, Coalfish and Pollack from Portacloy piers, and Flatfish with occasional Ray from beach. Flounder, Dab, Eel, Pollack, Coalfish and Mullet from Porturlin.

BLACKSOD

Girl Emer
Ed Sweeney
Tel: Blacksod 4

BALLINA & KILLALA

Cleona
John Walkin
Tel: 096 22442

Sligo

INNISCRONE Shore fishing for Pollack, Wrasse, Tope, Ray, Bullhuss, Dogfish from Downpatrick Head, Old Tower area, Lacken Head and Pier and Kilcummin Head. Sea Trout, Bass, Dabs and Flounder from Moy Estuary. Flounder, Dabs and Sea Trout from Inniscrone Beach. Conger, Mackerel, Coalfish, Pollack and Wrasse from Inniscrone Pier. Mackerel, Coalfish, Wrasse and Pollack from Rathlee Point and Pollahenny. Conger, Wrasse, Pollack and Coalfish from Temple Rocks and Aughris Head.

Boat fishing for Shark, Tope, Dogfish, Spurdog, Bullhuss, Smith Hound, Cod, Ling, Conger, Ray, Skate, Turbot, Brill, Pollack, Coalfish, Garfish, Whiting and Mackerel.

INNISCRONE

Dipper & Kingfisher
Jim Byrne
Tel: 096 36144

MULLAGHMORE

Salome
Mrs. S. Mulligan
Tel: 071 76126

Star of Ulster
Joe McGowan

Donegal

DONEGAL Conger, Wrasse and Pollack from St. Johns Point on rocks belo lighthouse. The Inishmurray Islands good boat marks for Tope, Skate, Blue Shark and Plaice.

KILLYBEGS Rock fishing for Pollack, Mackerel, Wrasse and Tope. Coalfish, Conger, Mackerel, Mullet and Pollack from harbour. Wrecks off Killybegs good boat marks for Conger, Ling, Pollack, Coalfish a Turbot.

LOUGHROS BEG Mackerel, Conger, Pollack, Wrasse and Coalfish from north sho Boat fishing off Gweebarra Bay for Pollack, Wrasse and Coalfish Between Gweebarra Bay and Aran Island Haddock, Cod, Ling a Whiting in Summer.

THE ROSSES From the beaches opposite Cruit Island, small Turbot, Tope, Flatfish and Dogfish are caught. On the rocks to the South Wrasse, Dogfish and Pollack are caught. Aran Island to Bloody Foreland boat mark for Cod, Haddock and Whiting. Tory Island boat mark for Cod, Coalfish, Turbot, Whiting, Rays, Plaice and Gurnard. Horn Head boat mark for Flatfish. Sheephaven Bay for Shark, Tope, Cod, Ling and Haddock.

FANAD HEAD Rock fishing for Pollack, Coalfish, Wrasse and occasional Sea Trout. Sandy bays for many Flatfish. Boat fishing in Lough Swill for Plaice, Dabs and inner loch for Tope in Summer.

MALIN HEAD Shore fishing for Coalfish and Pollack. Dunaff Head to Malin He boat fishing for Cod, Pollack, Dogfish and Rays. Malin Head to Lough Foyle boat fishing for Cod, Pollack and Coalfish.

MOVILLE Tope, Conger, Skate, Pollack, Cod, Gurnard, Plaice and Ling. Lough Foyle boat fishing for Dogfish, Skate, Gurnard and Mackerel.

ROSSAPENNA Good boat fishing for Tope.

DOWNINGS
Leontine Goreux
Carlton W. Buchanan
Tel: Downings 48

PORT NA BLAGH
Charlie Girl
John McClean
Tel: 074 22443

Northern Ireland

PORTSTEWART Offers fishing in Lough Foyle and River Bann. Pier, beach and rock fishing produce Mackerel, Pollack, Garfish, Coalfish, Flounder, Plaice, Sea Trout and Bass. Castlerock Strand produces good Bass fishing.

PORTRUSH Offers fishing in Lough Foyle and River Bann. Pier, beach and rock fishing produce Mackerel, Pollack, Garfish, Coalfish, Flounder, Plaice, Sea Trout and Bass.

GLENARM Boat, pier and rock fishing produce Pollack, Plaice, Mackerel, Codling and Flounders.

LARNE Larne Lough fishing for Mackerel, Pollack, Cod, Coalfish, Whiting etc. Herrings off 'The Maidens' some miles from shore.

WHITEHEAD AND CARRICKFERGUS Offers fishing in Belfast Lough for Pollack, Coalfish, Garfish, Cod, Mackerel, Sea Trout, Whiting from both shore and boats. Boats also offer Blue Shark, Skate, Tope, Bass and Flatfish.

BANGOR Offers fishing on Belfast Lough for Haddock, Whiting, Cod, Coalfish and Pollack. Mackerel after June. Boats offer Blue Shark, Skate, Tope, Cod, Bass and Flatfish.

DONAGHADEE Mackerel, Codling and Pollack from rocks or pier. Boats offering large Cod about 3m offshore.

STRANGFORD LOUGH Offers 24 species of sea fish such as Blue Shark, Skate, Tope, Cod, Bass and Flatfish.

ENGLAND

AVON

Avon Specimen Hunters

Secretary – S. Knee
42 Bowring Close, Hartcliffe, Bristol 3

Bathampton AA

Secretary – D. Crookes
25 Otago Terrace, Larkhall, Bath
Tel: 0225 27164

Membership – Unrestricted. Junior
membership available
Year Formed – 1930
No. of Members – 2300
Facilities – 10 Miles of fishing on Bristol Avon,
5 miles of trout fishing on tributaries of the
Bristol Avon 10 ponds and lakes offering
carp, tench etc. Hire out Newbridge —
Saltford — Kelston waters a total of 250 pegs.

Blandford & District AC

Secretary – D. Stone
4 Cadley Close, Blandford Forum
Tel: 0258 54054

Membership – Unrestricted
Year Formed – 1952
No. of Members – 275
Facilities – Dorset Stour. Slow moving river
fishing in and around Blandford.

Bristol Avon & District Anglers Consultative Assoc.

Secretary – C.F. Sutton
147 Sheridan Road, Twerton, Bath
Tel: 0225 28210

Bristol Golden Carp AA

Secretary – C. Golding
24 Queen Street, Two Mile Hill, Kingswood,
Bristol
Tel: 0272 677379

Bristol & District Amalgamated Anglers

Secretary – J.S. Parker
16 Landsdown View, Kingswood, Bristol
Tel: 0272 67977

Membership – Unrestricted
No. of Members – 600

Bristol & West of England Federation of Anglers

Secretary – V.D. Tyrrell
16 Falcon Close, Westbury-on-Trym
Tel: 0272 500165

Membership – Restricted
Year Formed – 1902
No. of Members – 7,500 anglers represented
Facilities – Bristol Avon, 3 miles right bank
downstream from confluence of Pipley Brook,
Swineford to confluence of Willsbridge
Brook, Willsbridge, Bristol including weir
and scours at Keynsham. Feeder canal from
Avon St. Bridge to Netham Lock (0.8 mile).

Ridgeway & District AA

Secretary – R.J. Walker
17 Birch Court, Keynsham, Bristol BS18 2RQ
Tel: 02756 5228

Membership – Unrestricted. Junior
membership available
No. of Members – 60
Facilities – Many stretches of River Avon,
Bristol stretches on River Brue, River Yeo,
River Chew, River Axe, Somerset, Frome,
Tockenham reservoir, Pawlett Ponds and
Nailsea Ponds. Hiring available on 40 peg
limit application in writing at least 6 months
in advance. For larger venue apply to Bristol
& District Amalgamated Anglers.
Tel: 0272 672977.

Sedgemoor Specimen Group

Secretary – M. Cattermole
1 Owen Drive, Failand, Bristol

Silver Dace

Secretary – J.C. Bedford
22 Kildare Road, Knowle, Bristol
Tel: 0272 633215

Stalbridge AS

Secretary – A.M. Cairns
33 Park Road, Stalbridge
Tel: 0963 62562

Membership – Unrestricted
Year Formed – 1950
No. of Members – 180
Facilities – 2 Miles of the River Stour
containing chub, roach, pike, perch, dace,
gudgeon. 1 Mile River Lydden also
containing chub, roach, eels, etc.

Sturminster & Hinton AA

Secretary – T.J. Caines
Coombe Gate, The Bridge, Sturminster,
Newton
Tel: 0258 72355

Membership – Restricted
Year Formed – 1905
No. of Members – 300
Facilities – River Stour — 7 miles both banks,
centred on Sturminster Newton.

Weston-Super-Mare & District AA

Secretary – J.A. Morgan
57 Earlham Grove, Weston-Super-Mare
Tel: 0934 31614

Membership – Unrestricted
Year Formed – 1902
No. of Members – 1000

BEDFORDSHIRE

Ampthill & District A & FPS

Secretary – I.R. Milford
5 Tudor Close, Barton-Le-Clay
Tel: 0582 882147

Membership – Unrestricted at moment
Year Formed – 1954
No. of Members – 1700
Facilities – Brogborough Pit — Tench, ca
roach, rudd, bream, perch, chub, pike,
Kempston Hardwick Pit, Ampthill Reservc
Marston Pit, Westminster Pool-Ampthill, I
Ouse, Carlton, Pavenham and Felmersha

Bedford AC

Secretary – M.E. Appleton
155 Marlborough Road, Bedford
Tel: 0234 851429 or 54708

Membership – Unrestricted
Year Formed – 1872
No. of Members – 800
Facilities – The club controls various type
water covering several miles River Great
Ouse. Narrow, wide, shallow and deep, a
and below Bedford. We also have a pit c
to Bedford town centre.

Dunstable & District Specimen Group

Secretary – C. Golder
90 Meadow Way, Leighton Buzzard

Gladiators Specimen Group

Secretary – N. Gilbert
63 Heath Road, Leighton Buzzard

Ivel Valley

Secretary – J. Dickinson
25 Osborn Road, Barton

Kempston AC

Secretary – D.J. King
64 Denns Road, Kempston, Bedford

Membership – Unrestricted
Year Formed – 1937
No. of Members – 180
Facilities – K.A.C. own the fishing rights
Kempston Mill to Queens Park on one b
Have a water sharing agreement with
Rushden AC which entitles K.A.C. men
to fish River Nene at Ditch Ford, the Riv
Ouse at Eaton Socon and Houghton Mil
Hartigdon.

Leighton Buzzard AC

Secretary – F. McLellan
49 Wing Road, Leighton Buzzard
Tel: 0525 374702

ghton Buzzard Specimen
up

etary – A. Beat
est Hill, Aspley Guise

on AC

etary – D.W. Rayner
ratton Gardens, Luton
0582 24583

bership – Unrestricted
of Members – 650 (inc. Juniors)
ities – 2 Areas of Middle Ouse at Eaton
and Lavendon Mill. Five acre lake at
oston. Approx. 14 miles of fishing on The
d Union Canal, (main line), between
ge 102 Stoke Hammond and bridge 126
ddington, Bucks.

on & District AA

etary – J.R. Bird
topsley Way, Luton LUZ 7UU
0582 20267

bership – Unrestricted
Formed – 1949
of Members – 25
ities – Gt. Linford Complex Newport
ell, Bucks by arrangement with
ingham AA. River Ouse and pit —
ersham, Bedfordshire.

efford & District AA

etary – J. Anderson
mpthill Road, Shefford
0462 811577

nbership – Unrestricted up to 1000
r Formed – 1898
of Members – 900
ities – River Ouse at Sharnbrook
enham and Great Barford. River Ivel and
Navigation Canal and Airman Pit,
ford.

rulam AC

etary – J.K. Trew
Benson Close, Bramingham Wood, Luton
3QR
0582 593798

nbership – Unrestricted. Junior
nbership available
r Formed – 1934
of Members – 600
ilities – River Lee. 1½ miles, 2 stretches.
ll fast river, 5 miles from St. Albans
vel Pit at Smallford, 2 miles from St.
ans. Deep lake, (big carp). Gravel Pit at
gmore, 5 miles from St. Albans, 3 Lakes,
eep. Converted watercress bed in St.
ans, 5' deep. Coarse and game fish. April
June 15. River Ouse, 8 miles north of
ford. 3½ miles in 3 stretches. Fast and
water.

RKSHIRE

Delco

Secretary – G. Munday
0926 612671

Bracknell & District Specimen Group

Secretary – R. Kemp
15 Bridge Road, Cove, Hants

Englefield Green

Secretary – R.A. Young
53 Ashbrook Road, Old Windsor
Tel: 07535 65151

Membership – Unrestricted
Year Formed – 1951
No. of Members – 150
Facilities – Section of River Bourne, Colne,
Wradisbury, Colnebrook.

Hungerford Canal AA

Chairman – W. Radbourne
17 Chiltern Way, Hungerford
Tel: 04886 2131

Kennet Valley Specimen Group

Secretary – M. Morris
14 High Street, Theale

Kingsmoor Anglers

Secretary – C. Gibbs
78 Monksfield Way, Slough SL2 1QT

Membership – Unrestricted (Applications in
writing). Junior membership available age 13
to 17
Year Formed – 1966
No. of Members – 530
Facilities – Several waters between
Maidenhead and Staines. Pleasure and
specimen fishing only. No match fishing.

Kintbury F.C.

Secretary – Mr. R.W. Wallace
24 Burtons Hill, Kintbury, Newbury
Tel: 04885 8857

Membership – Restricted
No. of Members – 200
Facilities – Fishing on the Kennet and Avon
Canal for bream, dace, roach, perch and
chub. Fishing also at Dundas Stream at the
River Kennet.

Maidenhead AS & District Assoc.

Chairman – G.W. Rance
'Ivydene' 35 Forlease Road, Maidenhead
Tel: 0628 27448

Membership – Unrestricted
No. of Members – 450
Facilities – Several good stretches of the
Thames. Club bookings welcomed.

Old Windsor AC

Secretary – D.A. Meakes
51 Bulkeley Avenue, Windsor Tel: 07535 52741

Membership – Restricted
Year Formed – 1945
No. of Members – 140
Facilities – 3 stretches of the Thames in and
around Windsor. Noted for Roach, Dace,
Chub, Bream, Barbel and Pike. Also 3
ponds/lakes within easy reach from Windsor.
Noted for Roach, Rudd, Perch, Tench and
Carp.

Reading & District AA

Secretary – D. Capon
8 Moats Crescent, Thame, Oxon
Tel: 084421 3760

An association of affiliated clubs. It controls
waters on the Thames, Kennet and the
Kennet/Avon Canal. Also controls six lakes
all within a 10 mile radius of Reading. Entry
is by membership of an affiliated club.

Salt Hill AS

Secretary – H.W. Mayo
16 Oldway Lane, Chippenham, Slough
Tel: 06286 63574

Thatcham AA

Secretary – K. Roberts
206 Benham Hill, Thatcham, Newbury
Tel: 0635 63346

Twickenham Piscatorial Society

Secretary – L. Pallett
37 Stuart Way, Windsor
Tel: 075 35 55977

Membership – Restricted
Year Formed – 1920
No. of Members – 250
Facilities – Newbury stretch of River Kennet
and Thame stretch of River Thame.

Twyford & District FC

Secretary – D. Metcalfe
Millwood, 10 Ambleside Close, Woodley
Tel: 0734 693955

Membership – Restricted to local residents
Year Formed – 1935
No. of Members – 700
Facilities – Rivers Lodden, Thames, St.
Patricks Stream at Charvil, Twyford. River
Lodden at Sandford, Woodley. All River
Fishing, no pits or lakes.
Day permits only if accompanied by a
member.

Wraysbury AC

Chairman – Bill Dick
5 Wharf Road, Wraysbury
Tel: 078481 2274

BUCKINGHAMSHIRE

Buckingham District AA

Secretary – T. Young
1 Demoram Close, Winslow
Tel: 029671 3742

Membership – Unrestricted
Year Formed – 1911
No. of Members – 750
Facilities – About 10 miles of the Gt. Ouse.

Cookham & District AC

Secretary – T. Butler
41 Bank Street, High Wycombe
Tel: 0494 449402

Membership – Restricted to 175
Year Formed – 1940
No. of Members – 150

Gerrards Cross & District AS

Secretary – H. Cordery
12 Fiddlers Walk, Wargrave
Tel: 073522 3402

Membership – Unrestricted
Year Formed – 1934
No. of Members – 300

Marlow AC

Secretary – G.W. Hoing
15 Greenlands, Flackwell Heath, High
Wycombe
Tel: 06285 22405/06284 72283

Membership – Unrestricted
Year Formed – 1937
No. of Members – 800
Facilities – Approximately 2 miles River
Thames above and below Marlow Bridge.
Members and day tickets. Approximately 1½
miles River Thame, Oxon. Members only. 3
Pits of approximately 100 acres in the Marlow
area.

Milton Keynes AA

Secretary – M.D. Sando
6 Kipling Drive, Newport Pagnell
Tel: 0908 62 6534

Waters available at Blue Lagoon at Water
Eaton, Bletchley, Sparks Meadow, Bletchley,
Willen Lake and Loughton Lake. Waters also
on the River Thames at Windsor, the River
Ouzel and the Grand Union Canal at Stoke
House

Newport Pagnell FA

Secretary – F.J. Read
19 Chicheley Street, Newport Pagnell
Tel: 911 610342

Membership – Unrestricted
Year Formed – 1887
No. of Members – 1200
Facilities – River Great Ouse from Kickles
Farm near M1 motorway to Ravenstone Mill,
distance approximately 7 miles, double bank
in most cases. Eight gravel pits. Total 65
acres. Day permits are not issued to visitors.
Each member allowed 2 guests permits on any
one day.

Prestwood & Dist. AC

Secretary – B. Putt
2 Five Acres, Chesham
Tel: 02405 72541

Membership – Unrestricted
No. of Members – 375
Facilities – Weston Turville Reservoir near
Aylesbury. 20 acre reservoir shared with
sailing club.

Steeple Claydon AC

Secretary – W. Edwards
16 Buckingham Road, Steeple Claydon
Tel: 029673 8993

Membership – Restricted
No. of Members – 110

Stowe AC

Secretary – C. Hawkins
Homelea Dadford, Buckingham MK18 5JX
Tel: 02802 3973

Membership – Restricted. Junior membership
restricted to 20
Year Formed – 1975
No. of Members – 100
Facilities – Stowe Lakes are situated in the
gardens of Stowe School, North Buckingham.
There are 2 lakes in idyllic surroundings, one
of 11 acres and one slightly smaller. Primarily
a Tench fishery, which has been restocked
with a large head of Tench. Also Roach and
Wild Carp, with Pike for the winter
fisherman.

CAMBRIDGESHIRE

Cambridge Albion AS

Secretary – R. Gentle
34 Ramsden Square, Cambridge
Tel: 0223 69820

Membership – Unrestricted
Year Formed – 1905
No. of Members – 1,000 +
Facilities – Dimmocks Cote, Cambridge, Old
Bedford at Mepal, Manea and Sutton, Old
West at Stretham. We have 41 miles of water
in total.

Cambridge FP & AS

Secretary – A.C. Moden
2 Birch Avenue, Chatteris
Tel: 03543 3896

Membership – Unrestricted
Year Formed – 1885
No. of Members – 1,500
Facilities – The Society has several fisheries in
the Cambridge area, the nature of which
varies from the very slow moving Reach and
Burwell Lodes and the slow rivers Cam and
Gt. Ouse to the tidal Hundred Foot River. All
types of coarse fish are present but Roach and
Bream predominate.

Chatteris Working Mens AC

Secretary – Mr. B. Knightly
18 West Street, Chatteris
Tel: 03543 2015

Membership – Unrestricted
No. of Members – 150
Facilities – 40ft drain and adjoining 16ft drain,
2 miles north of Chatteris. Bream, Tench,
Pike and Zander caught.

Deeping St. James AC

Secretary – J. Cran
53 Castle Drive, Northborough, Peterborough
Tel: 0778 343691

Membership – Restricted
Year Formed – 1890
No. of Members – 1,112
Facilities – River Welland (Market Deepin
and Deeping St. James). Gravel pits and
millstream at Maxey and Market Deeping.
Trout pits at West Deeping.

Earith & District AC

Secretary – T.A. Mitchell
33 High Street, Earith, Huntingdon
Tel: 0487 842090

Membership – Unrestricted
Year Formed – 1950
No. of Members – 50
Facilities – Middle Ouse: Approximately 1
yards on south bank at Earith (restricted t
full yearly members, at present £5.00 year
and visiting club matches). Two stretches
north bank, of 400 and 600 yards — day
tickets available, 1000 yards on Old West
River at Earith — day tickets available. M
fishing — Roach, Bream, Dace, Perch, Pi
and Zander.

Godmanchester A & FPS

Secretary – B.P. Doherty
5 Kisby Avenue, Godmanchester PE18 8B
Tel: 0480 54365

Membership – Restricted
Year Formed – 1943
No. of Members – 200
Facilities – River Great Ouse. Very varied
stretches includes wide deep slow moving
main river areas and weir pools, sluice po
gravel bed, faster areas holding chub, dac
etc. Bream, roach, pike, carp. Flattish
landscape but unspoilt backwaters i.e. not
easily accessible by boats.

Histon & District AS

Secretary – R. Cooper
236 Histon Road, Cottenham Tel: 0954 50

Membership – Unrestricted
No. of Members – 1,000
Facilities – 11 miles of Old West from Earit
Twenty Pence, Cottenham. Dimmicks Cote
(River Cam) Lake at Fen Road, Milton.

Houghton & Wyton AS

Secretary – A. Wilkinson
Thicket Road, Houghton, Huntingdon

Membership – Restricted
Year Formed – 1947
No. of Members – 40
Facilities – River Gt. Ouse and back waters
Houghton and Hemingford.

Huntingdon A & FPS

Secretary – Walters Wallis
8 Clayton's Way, Huntingdon Tel: 0480 58

Membership – Unrestricted
Year Formed – 1888
No. of Members – 200
Facilities – River Great Ouse at Huntingdo

Offord & Buckden AS

Secretary – A. Plumb
8 Latin Close, Offord Cluny, Huntingdon
Tel: 0480 810595

bership – Unrestricted
Formed – 1890
of Members – 400
ities – We own all our waters, a lot of the
rs are fishable without being bothered by
. There are about 4 miles of water, and
ent parts hold different species. Our
rs are bookable on a coach party basis,
y E. Blowfield, 4 Monks Cottages,
den, Huntingdon.

erborough & Dist. AA

etary – W.W. Yates
wn Avenue, Peterborough PE1 3RA
0733 67952

bership – Unrestricted. Junior
bership available
Formed – 1875
of Members – 1,800
ities – Greater part of River Nene from
p Bank Bridge, Wansford downstream to
in-a-Doublet, south bank. Part of
wade Lake situated in Ferry Meadows,
n. Gravel pits at Maxey, Nr.
rborough. Share part of Bourne Eau and
Glen with a federation of clubs.

orpres AC

etary – T.E. Turner
e Bower, Whittlesey, Peterborough
0733 204282

bership – Restricted
Formed – 1947
ities – We have the fishing rights of
lon Brick Pits, namely Central Pit
ittlesey) tench, perch, pike, bream — Eye
Eye Peterborough) Carp 30 lb plus,
m, roach, tench — Orton Pit well known
apture of present British Tench Record —
I. Pit large carp, bream, double figures,
h, tench — Norman Cross Pit good stock
nch and roach.

msey & District AS

etary – P.E. Aldred
ackmill Road, Chatteris Tel: 03543 2232

bership – Unrestricted. Junior
bership available
of Members – 500
ities – Old River Nene, Ramsey St.
vs, 40 pegs available for hire; Fortyfoot,
sey, 220 pegs available for hire; Old
r Nene, Halfpenny Toll, Benwick, 35 pegs
lable for hire. Bookings from J.J. Atkin,
he Ave, Ramsey.

Ives A & FPS

etary – P. Keepin
w Road, St. Ives, Huntingdon PE17 4BG
0480 61165

bership – Unrestricted
r Formed – 1880
of Members – 600 – 700
lities – Approximately 2 miles River Ouse
dle level and several pits offering all
cies of coarse fish.

Neotts & District Angling and h Preservation Society

etary – S.E. Smith
iver Terrace, St Neotts, Huntingdon
0480 75995

Membership – Unrestricted
Facilities – Control several stretches of the
Great Ouse and a large gravel pit near St
Neotts.

Waterbeach AC

Secretary – A. Ballaam
14 Rothleigh Road, Cambridge
Tel: 0223 358911 Ext. 2649

Membership – Unrestricted
Year Formed – 1936
No. of Members – 450
Facilities – Approximately 5 miles on the
River Cam, 1½ miles on Swoffham Lode plus
a 15 acre trout lake. (Membership restricted
to 50).

Yaxley Angling Club

Secretary – K.G. Burt
55 Windsor Road, Yaxley, Peterborough
PE7 3JA
Tel: 0733 241119

Membership – Unrestricted
No. of Members – 350

CHESHIRE

Bollington & Royal Oak AS

Secretary – T. Barber
10 George Street, West Macclesfield
SK11 6ES

Membership – Unrestricted. Junior
membership available
Year Formed – Pre 1940
No. of Members – 200
Facilities – Millbrook and Lowerbrook at
Rainow, Clarence, Lowerhouse and Ingersley
at Bollington, Hancock's Pool and Mayfield
Centre. We provide very good carp fishing.

Cheshire AA

Secretary – F.R. James
34 Sweet Briar Crescent, Crewe CW2 8PE
Tel: 0270 69855

Membership – Unrestricted
Year Formed – 1918
No. of Members – 7,000
Facilities – Montgomeryshire 6½ miles. R.
Severn and 1½ miles R. Camlad St. Staffs.
Knypersley Reservoir 33 acres, Serpentine
lake 14 acres Cheshire and Shropshire,
Shropshire Union Canal 50 miles, Llangollen
Branch 40 miles, Cheshire Trent and Mersey
Canal 7 miles. R. Dee 12 miles (in
conjunction with Dee AA) R. Dane 5 miles
(Somerford Booths Ches.).

Cheshire Specimen Group

Secretary – K. McNeil
21 Vale Road, Timperley, Altringham
WA15 7TQ
Tel: 061 980 3464

Membership – Restricted (Selection by
invitation only)
No. of Members – 5

Congleton AS

Secretary – N.J. Bours
8 Norfolk Road, Congleton CW12 1NY
Tel: 02602 77284

Membership – Unrestricted. Junior
membership available
Year Formed – 1954
No. of Members – 350
Facilities – Several stretches of River Dane,
Congleton area. 2 sections of Macclesfield
Canal. Several local pools. Day permits only
if accompanied by a member. Hiring out only
on Clubs Stretch of Macclesfield Canal at
Congleton.

Davenham AC

Secretary – A. Cook
41 Fairfield Road, Leftwich Estate, Northwich
CW9 8DG
Tel: 0606 41838

Membership – Unrestricted
Year Formed – 1954
No. of Members – 900
Facilities – 7 miles trout and coarse fishing on
River Dane. 4 pits — carp, roach, perch,
tench, chub. River Dane — roach, dace,
perch, gudgeon.

Halton District AA

Secretary – K. Philcock
68 Belvoir Road, Widnes WA8 6HR
Tel: 051423 1627

Membership – Unrestricted
Year Formed – 1898
No. of Members – 400
Facilities – 3 local ponds coarse fishing only.
½ mile River Banwy Llanfair Caerinion, ½
mile River Vyrnwy Meifod.

Halton Joint Anglers

Secretary – W. Durr
4 Ashley Road, Runcorn Tel: 09285 77508

Membership – Unrestricted
Year Formed – 1947
No. of Members – 237
Facilities – Approximately 4½ mile of the
Bridewater canal from Waterloo Bridge old
town Runcorn, to Cawleys bridge Preston
brook. About 500 pegs holding Roach, Rudd,
Bream, Perch, Carp.

I.C.I. AC

Secretary – J. Price
82 Pudding Lane, Mattersley, Hyde SK14 3HZ
Tel: 061 366 9423

Membership – Restricted
Year Formed – 1968
No. of Members – 240
Facilities – Works reservoir. 2 acres on I.C.I.
Hyde site. Holds large head of carp, bream,
some rudd, roach, perch, tench.

Irby AC

Secretary – Frank Evans
4 McAlpine Close, Upton, Wirral L49 6JR
Tel: 051 678 7619

Membership – Unrestricted
Year Formed – 1967
No. of Members – 600
Facilities – 25 small lakes and ponds (Wirral
area) SUC at Aberbechan. River Severn
Aberbechan (small stretches). Montgomery
Canal, Aberbechan, Bridge nos 150-153
available to hire for matches.

Lymm AC

Secretary – J.S. Graham
15 Boswell Avenue, Warrington WA4 6DQ
Tel: 0925 54942

Membership – Restricted (Members only accepted after induction meeting) Junior membership available
Year Formed – 1946
No. of Members – 1,700
Facilities – R. Bollin, Lymm — Several miles river — game and coarse fishery. Whitley Pool, Warrington — 3 acre coarse fishery. Village Pool, Whitley, Warrington — ¾ acre coarse fishery. Wincham Brook, Lostock Gralam, Northwich — 1 mile river — game and coarse species. Hatchmere, Norley, via Warrington — 12 acre coarse fishery. Lymmvale, Whitegate, Northwich — Unique mixed fishery — American Brook, Brown and Rainbow trout, tench, chub, grayling, orfe. R. Vrynwy, Llandrinio, Llanymynech, Powys — ¾ mile river — mixed fishery. R. Severn Llandrinio, Llanymynech, Powys — ¾ mile river — mixed fishery. River Rhiw, Manafon, Berriew, Powys — ½ mile river, mixed fishery, River Severn, Abermule, Newtown, Powys — ¾ mile river, mixed species. Hirings available are Lymm Dam (occasionally let out) 50 pegs maximum; Hatchmere — 15 pegs maximum; Statham Pool — 25 pegs maximum; R. Dane — 45 pegs maximum; R. Vrynwy — 30 pegs maximum; R. Severn — Llandrinio — 25 pegs maximum; R. Severn — Abermule — 30 pegs maximum.

Middlewich AS

Secretary – Geoffrey Stanier
43 Elm Road, Middlewich, Cheshire
Tel: 060 684 3695

Membership – Unrestricted
Year Formed – 1891
No. of Members – 600
Facilities – Coarse fishing on approximately 2 miles of the River Dane at Middlewich, trout fishing on 1 mile River Dane. Still water fishing on various local ponds. Shared fishing on River Weaver at Northwich.

Nantwich AS

Secretary – R.P. Dainty
Morningside, 85 Broad Lane, Stapeley, Nantwich, Cheshire   Tel: 0270 626536

Membership – Unrestricted
No. of Members – 300
Facilities – Derbyshire — Mid-Cheshire and Mid Wales. Mainly river fishing providing excellent trout, grayling, salmon and coarse fishing.

Northwich AA

Secretary – Eric Moore
'Struma' Gadbrook Road, Rudheath, Northwich
Tel: 0606 2986

Membership – Unrestricted. Junior membership available
No. of Members – 1000
Facilities – River Weaver at Hartford, Trent and Mersey Canal. Available to hire for matches applications to Match Secretary. W. Buckley, 13 Firthfields, Darenham, Northwich. Tel: 0606 41964.

Prince Albert AS

Secretary – C. Sparkes
High Lodge, Upton, Macclesfield
Tel: 0625 26311

Membership – Unrestricted
Year Formed – 1954
No. of Members – 5,000
Facilities – Rivers Severn, Ribble, Lune, Dovey, Dee, Banwy, Dove, Mawddach, Trent, Dane, Dean Vyrnwy. In addition to numerous lakes, reservoirs and pools plus Macclesfield Canal and Welsh arm of Shropshire Union Canal.

Shropshire Union Canal

Secretary – R. Brown
10 Dale Road, Golbourne, Warrington
Tel: 0942 76917

Tarporley & Dist. AA

Secretary – R.W. Cross
25 Burton Avenue, Tarporley Tel: 08293 2843

Membership – Restricted
Year Formed – 1919
No. of Members – 100
Facilities – 6 Cheshire Meres.

Warrington AA

Secretary – J.S. Jackson
23 Nora Street, Warrington WA1 2JG
Tel: 0925 37525

Membership – Unrestricted
Year Formed – 1891
No. of Members – 13,000
Facilities – 134 miles canal fishing, Bridgewater, Trent and Mersey, Shropshire Union, Grey Mist Mere, Ackers Pit, River Gowy, R. Alyn, R. Ribble, R. Dee, R. Severn, R. Banwy, R. Vyrnwy, R. Roden, Rea Brook, R. Cain, R. Dane, Cicely Mill Pool.

Winsford and District AA

Secretary – J.S. Bailey
22 Plover Avenue, Winsford Tel: 060 65 3902

Membership – Unrestricted
Year Formed – 1900
No. of Members – 1,500
Facilities – River Weaver, River Dane, (coarse and game river fishing). Pools — Top Flash Marton Hole, The Ocean, New Pool, Newbridge Pool, Sixes Hole (coarse fishing with exception of Marton Hole which is a game fishery).

Wyche AC

Secretary – F. McGarry
65 Queens Drive, Nantwich

Membership – Unrestricted
Year Formed – 1955
No. of Members – 1,350
Facilities – River Weaver, various, Nantwich, trout, dace, roach, bream, chub, River Dee, Holt, Nr. Wrexham, dace, roach, River Banwy, Meifor, North Wales, trout, dace, chub, roach, Osmere, Blakemere, Nr. Whitchurch, bream, roach, rudd, perch, pike, tench, Crewe, Aughtons Flash, Thomassons Flash, bream, rudd, carp. Also affiliated to Cheshire Anglers and ballot permits, various other waters.

CLEVELAND

Association of Teeside & Distr AC

Secretary – A. Allen
1 Scalby Grove, Stockton-on-Tees

Thornaby AA

Secretary – D. Speight
10 Stainsby Gate, Stainsby Hill, Thornab
Tel: 0642 62099

Membership – Unrestricted
No. of Members – 1,000 +
Facilities – 50-60 miles on R. Tees, Swiral Ure, Eden.

Yarm AC

Secretary – F.K. Flynn
12 Vard Terrace, Stockton
Tel: 0642 66473

Facilities – Coarse fishing at Neasham and

CORNWALL

Bude Canal AA

Secretary – B. Putt
2 Orchard Close, Poughill, Bude
Tel: 0288 3992

Membership – Unrestricted
No. of Members – Approx. 80

Essa AC

Secretary – J. Webber
2 Rashleigh Avenue, Saltash
Tel: 075 55 5594

Membership – Unrestricted
Year Formed – 1977
No. of Members – 50

Marazion AC

Secretary – T. Tompkins
1 Trewartha Road, Praa Sands, Nr. Penza
Tel: 073 676 3329

Membership – Unrestricted
Year Formed – 1976
No. of Members – 104
Facilities – 3½ Acres Wheal Grey Pool, Tresowes Nr. Ashton, Helston. Disused cla pit containing roach, rudd, carp, tench, perch, bream. 2½ Acres St. Earth Pool, S Earth Nr. St. Ives. Containing carp, tench roach, dace, bream. 2½ Acres Boscathno Reservoir, Penzance, same species as othe

Roche AC

Secretary – D.E. Minards
63 Porth Bean Road, Newquay
Tel: 063 73 5669

Membership – Restricted
Year Formed – 1960
No. of Members – 400
Facilities – Disused clay pits and stone quarries in Mid. Cornwall. 8 Pools in all ranging from 1½ acres to 7 acres. All our pools are fully stocked with a full range of fish. The pools are totally covered in trees and natural cover.

...unteer AC

Secretary – G. Eley
...ennis Road, Liskeard
...0579 45633

Membership – Unrestricted
...Formed – 1968
...of Members – 32

...UMBRIA

...mpton AA

Secretary – T. Donockley
...nton Crescent, Low Row Brampton
...069 76 518

Membership – Restricted
...Formed – 1870
...of Members – 300

...lisle Specimen Group

Secretary – C. Bowman
...Nicholas Street, Carlisle

...ness FA (Coarse Section)

Secretary – D. Jackson
...Chapel Street, Dalton-in-Furness

Membership – Restricted
...of Members – 300
...ities – Fishing in Ormsgill Reservoir for
...m, Roach, Rudd, Perch, Tench, Carp
...Pike.

...wick AA

Secretary – W. Ashcroft
...nghaven, How Lane, Portinscale, Keswick
...0596 72703

Membership – Restricted to residents only.
...or membership available
...Formed – Over 100 years
...of Members – 100
...ities – Part of River Greta (trout and
...on). Part of River Derwent (trout and
...on). Derwent water (coarse fish and
...).

...erston AA

Secretary – H.B. Whittam
...yndhurst Road, Ulverston
...0229 52322

...bership – Restricted on Game
...Unrestricted on Coarse
...Formed – 1890
...of Members – 400 +
...ities – Canal — excellent — used by
...s for matches. ¾ mile River Crake —
...bers only — salmon, sea-trout.
...tallow Tarn — trout (brown) members
...Sandhall Ponds — trout (rainbow)
...bers only.

...ndermere Ambleside &
...t. AA

Secretary – J.B. Cooper
...one, Limethwaite Road, Windermere
...096 62 3768

Membership – Restricted to local residents 10
miles radius of Ambleside. Junior membership
available
Year Formed – 1949
No. of Members – 219
Facilities – Headwaters of Lake Windermere
i.e., Brathay, Rothay and Troutbeck rivers,
together with 3 Tarns, School Knott —
Windermere, High Arnside — Skelwith
Bridge area and Moss Eccles — Far Sawrey,
stocked annually with brownies on put and
take basis. Rydal Lake, coarse fishing only.

DERBYSHIRE

British Gypsum AC

Secretary – Harry Mear
20 Church Avenue, Hatton Tel: 0283 813873

Membership – Restricted
No. of Members – 150
Facilities – 1 mile mill Fleam Tutbury
commencing from the waterfall to Tutbury
cricket field. ¼ mile River Dove at Hatton.

Chesterfield AA

Secretary – B.E. Thorley
98 St. Augustins Avenue, Birdholme
Tel: 0246 39541

Membership – Unrestricted
Year Formed – 1928
No. of Members – 824
Facilities – Stretches of Rivers Trent, Idle,
Derwent plus stillwaters.

Clay Cross AA

Secretary – G. Bull
9 Cromford Road, Holmgate, Clay Cross
Tel: 864299

Membership – Restricted
Year Formed – 1979
No. of Members – 370
Facilities – Coarse fishing on Meadow Farm
pond between Clay Cross and Holmgate.

Cotmanhay AC

Secretary – E. Statham
169 Ladywood Road, Ilkeston Tel: 0602 320784

Membership – Restricted
Year Formed – 1955
No. of Members – 100
Facilities – Manor Floods (Ilkeston) — 2 acre
lake with carp, tench, roach and pike (day
and season tickets) 1½ miles Ereloash Canal
at Cotmanhay with carp and tench. (Day and
season tickets). Shipley Gate pond ½ acre.
Members only.

Derby AA

Secretary – T. Hickton
7 Crecy Close, Derby DE3 3JU
Tel: 0332 362548

Membership – Unrestricted
Year Formed – 1899
No. of Members – 6,500
Facilities – River Trent from Swarkestone to
Willington. Trent Mersey Canal from
Shardlow to Eggington. Gravel pit at
Swarkestone. Anchor Church Pools at
Ingleby. Wanlip Country Club, sailing and
marina lakes (members only). Also a part of
River Soar at Wanlip.

Derbyshire County Council

Secretary – O.W. Handley
'Osprey' House, Ogston, Higham,
Derby DE5 6EL
Tel: 077 383 3595

Membership – Restricted
Year Formed – 1959
No. of Members – Full Members – 450
(Access to all waters)
Season Ticket Holders – 950
(Coarse fishing only on lower Derwent).

Earl of Harrington AC

Secretary – J. Callaghan
12 Spencer Street, Alvaston, Derby
Tel: 0332 751126

Membership – Unrestricted
Year Formed – 1900
No. of Members – 1000
Facilities – River Derwent between Derby and
the Road Bridge at Borrowash.

Glossop Amalgamated AS

Secretary – Mrs. Sylvia Hampson
24 Arundel Street, Glossop
Tel: Glossop 3409

Membership – Unrestricted
No. of Members – 250
Facilities – Waters at Hurst Lodge, Botany,
North Road, Heath Lodge, Padfield, Mottram
Ponds (The Mud) and 3 stretches at Dinting.

Kegworth AS

Secretary – D. Dakin
73 Nottingham Road, Kegworth, Nr. Derby
Tel: 050 97 3496

Membership – Restricted
Year Formed – Pre 1900
No. of Members – 80
Facilities – Hallstone Meadow in village of
Kegworth on River Soar. General coarse
fishing. Society also affiliated to the Long
Eaton Federation whose permits allow
members to fish downstream of Kegworth
Road Bridge to Ratcliffe on Soar locks and
other waters of the federation.

Long Eaton & Dist. AF

Secretary – W.A. Parker
75 College Street, Long Eaton
Tel: 060 76 67164

Membership – Open to clubs to federate
Year Formed – 1919
No. of Members – 2,600
Facilities – River Trent, Trent Lock, South
Bank. River Soar, Kegworth (Ratcliffe Deeps).
2 miles — Erewash Canal, Sandiacre lock to
Long Eaton lock 2 miles — 3 small ponds at
Shardlow.

Matlocks AC

Secretary – R.N.E. Walsh M.R.I.P.H.H.
5 Derby Road, Homesford, Matlock
Tel: 062 982 2535

Membership – Unrestricted. Junior
membership available
Year Formed – 1943
No. of Members – 250
Facilities – The club has a thriving game and
coarse fishery on the Derbyshire Derwent.
Matlock length, Matlock Bath length, 2 ponds
at Lumsdale. The Gas Works length at
Matlock, Darley Bridge length, Pic, Tor &
High Tor lengths. Oaker length, Darley Dale
Cricket Ground length, all members only.
Part of River Amber. Hire out Matlock Bath,
River Derwent, matches at discretion apply to
Secretary.

Moss Brook AC

Secretary – Derek Morton
17 Station Road, Eckington, Sheffield
Tel: 024683 435163

Membership – Restricted to 70 members
Year Formed – 1959
No. of Members – 70
Facilities – The Mois Valley from White
bridge downstream to Atco works. 2 miles
River Mois — stocked at least once a year.

NCB No. 5 Area FC

Secretary – Derek Allsop
27 Hardy Barn, Shipley
Tel: 077 37 67727

Membership – Restricted
No. of Members – 100
Facilities – Waters within Shipley Park.
Mapperley Reservoir, Osbornes Pond, Adams
Pond, Erewash Canal Langley Mill to 'Shipley
Boat Inn'.

Pride of Derby AA Limited

Secretary – A. Miller
16 Mercia Drive, Willington, Derby
Tel: 0283 702701

Membership – Restricted
Year Formed – 1895
No. of Members – 1,500
Facilities – River Derwent at Church Wilne
and Shardlow, Derby. River Trent at Sawley
near Long Eaton, Notts.

Ripley and District AC

Secretary – Raymond Turner
2a Argyll Road, Ripley
Tel: 0773 45876

Membership – Unrestricted
Year Formed – 1892
No. of Members – 1,010
Facilities – Butterley Reservoir (about 200
pegs). Codnor Park Reservoir (about 85
pegs). Both reservoirs have one boat each for
fishing from. Species are roach, bream,
perch, tench, carp, pike and rudd. Also
about 2 miles of River Amber from Sawmills
near Ambergate to South Wingfield (Trout
and coarse fish).

Swadlincote & District AA

Secretary – M. Salt
25 Pingle Farm Road, Newhall

Membership – Restricted

Zingari AC

Secretary – C. Shepherd
75 Belmont Avenue, Breaston,
Derby DE7 3AA
Tel: 03317 2170

Membership – Restricted
Year Formed – 1962
No. of Members – 40
Facilities – Adjacent Redhill lock on R. Soar.
Access via farm track at Radcliffe-on-Soar.

DEVON

Barnstaple & District AA

Secretary – M.J. Andrew
3 Wrafton Road, Braunton, North Devon
Tel: 0271 814474

Membership – Unrestricted C & G, Restricted
G
Year Formed – 1931
No. of Members – 300
Facilities – Coarse — ponds up to 2 acres in
size with small stretch of the river Jaw.

Bideford & District AC

Secretary – V.B. Eveleigh
21 Capern Road, Bideford, Devon EX39 3DY
Tel: 023 72 2470 Club: 023 72 77996

Membership – Unrestricted
Year Formed – 1964
No. of Members – 300 Male, 45 Female
60 Juniors, 100 Associates
Facilities – The only area the club controls
fishing is on a club lake situated at Langtree
Nr. Torrington, Devon. We have of course a
wonderful coastline for sea fishing. Game
fishing is available. The club has a
headquarters open to members of Angling
Clubs producing proof of AC membership.

Exe Valley Specimen Group

Secretary – P. Thompson
Crossmead Hall, Dunsford Hill, Exeter

Exter & District AA

Secretary – D.L. Beaven
46 Hatherleigh Road, Exter EX2 9LD
Tel: 0392 75925

Membership – Unrestricted
Year Formed – 1970
No. of Members – 3500
Facilities – Control is exercised over approx.
12 miles of river fishing on the Rivers Exe,
Culm, Clyst and Creedy. The Exeter ship
canal. Direct control over approx. 5 miles
both banks with ponds at Kingsteignton,
Tiverton and Mamhead.

South Devon Specimen Group

Secretary – P. Gregory
5 Diamond Road, Haven Banks, St Thomas,
Exeter

S.W.E.B. (Torbay District) AC

Secretary – T. Holtom
Electric House, Union Street, Torquay
TQ1 4BN
Tel: 0803 26200

Membership – Restricted
Year Formed – 1973
No. of Members – 70
Facilities – None, but have knowledge and
information about complete area.

Tiverton & District AC

Secretary – M. Trump
5 Lodge Road, Tiverton   Tel: 088 42 57761

Membership – Unrestricted
Year Formed – 1975
No. of Members – 200
Facilities – 3 Ponds at Butterleigh near
Tiverton with tench, carp, roach and rudd
(some crucian carp); 2 stretches of the River
Exe. 1. Exe walk in Tiverton. ½ mile appro×
down stream of road bridge in town. Dace,
grayling, roach and trout. 2. ¾ mile River
Exe in Exeter, stretching north of station ro×
dace, roach, grayling.

DORSET

Christchurch AC

Secretary – D. Chislett
Nimro 8 Sports, 9 Castle Parade, Ilford,
Bournemouth
Tel: 0202 478224

Membership – Unrestricted
Year Formed – 1938
No. of Members – 1800
Facilities – 40 Miles of Hampshire, Avon &
Dorset Stour plus 5 lakes.

Dorchester Angling & Boating Society

Secretary – A. Beattie
5 James Road, Dorchester Tel: 0305 66536

Membership – Restricted
Year Formed – 1977
No. of Members – 50
Facilities – Waters fished by club — sea fro×
Poole, Chesil Beach to Brixham. Coarse an
game fishing, most rivers and lakes open t×
public in Dorset, Hampshire, Somerset and
Devon.

Gillingham & District AA Ltd.

Secretary – P.J. Rolfe
12 Butts Mead, Shaftesbury Tel: 0747 274×

Membership – Unrestricted. Junior
membership available
No. of Members – 200
Facilities – Rivers Shreen and Stour. Seve×
small stillwater fisheries.

Ringwood & District AA

Secretary – J. Steel
30 Monsal Avenue, Ferndown Tel: 0202 89×

Membership – Unrestricted. Junior
membership available
Year Formed – 1949
No. of Members – 1000
Facilities – Hampshire Avon, 5 miles
Ringwood area including Severals and Ibs×
fisheries. Dorset Stour, 10 miles. Other riv×
3 miles. 6 lakes including Broadlands and
Moreys. Most waters available to hire for
matches.

rminster & Hinton AA

etary – T.J. Caines
nbe Gate, The Bridge, Sturminster
on
0258 72355

bership – Unrestricted. Junior
bership available
of Members – 250
ities – Approximately 7 miles of River
r (both banks) centred on town of
ninster Newton.

reham & District AS

etary – J. Thomas
ourne Drive, Wareham

bership – Restricted
Formed – 1930
of Members – 100
ities – River Frome, River Piddle. Various
s and lakes.

nborne & District

etary – J. Bass
ennyson Road, Walford, Wimborne
0202 883840

bership – Unrestricted
Formed – 1950
of Members – 800
ities – Dorset Stour — about 10 miles. 2
lakes and 4 coarse lakes.

RHAM

ester-le-St. and District AC

etary – T. Wright
Sedgeletch Road, Houghton-le-Spring,
& Wear
0783 848211

bership – Unrestricted
Formed – 1935
of Members – 500
ities – River Wear 4 miles game and
se fish. River Pont 5 miles brown trout

lington Brown Trout AA

etary – G.E. Coulson
ange Avenue, Hopworth Place, Nr.
ngton
0325 720246

bership – Restricted
Formed – Early 1900's
of Members – 550 +
ities – Middle to Upper reaches of Tees
Swale.

lington Fly FC

etary – F.C. Birkbeck
4 Nora Fenby House, 48 The Green,
erton, Darlington
0325 63896

bership – Restricted
ities – Egglestone and Abbey Bridge on
Coniscliffe and Croft. Six miles.

ham Co. Fed. of Anglers

tary – W. Craigs
eveland Place, Peterlee, Durham

Ferry Hill & District AC

Secretary – N. Davies
16 Conyers Terrace, Ferry Hill DL17 8AT
Tel: 0740 51522

Membership – Unrestricted. Junior
membership available
No. of Members – 700
Facilities – Control rights on Burnhope
Reservoir and Blackton Reservoir. Rivers
North Tyne, Tyne, Hear, Tees, Swale and
Ure. 2 ponds with coarse fish.

Hartlepool and District AC

Secretary – K. Hewitson
16 Heathfield Drive, Hartlepool, Cleveland
Tel: 69025/69882

Membership – Restricted to residents in
Hartlepool postal area. 'Outside' membership
(non-voting) is at present unrestricted.
No. of Members – 200
Facilities – Tilery Lake coarse fishery. Lake
Kenny, Hutton Henry; R. Wear, Durham;
Bolderhead Reservoir, Teesdale; 2
Corporation Park Lakes in Hartlepool,
Cleveland.

ESSEX

Basildon & District AS

Secretary – R.A. Drake
41 Edinburgh Avenue, Corringham, Stanford
Le Hope

Membership – Unrestricted
No. of Members – 300
Facilities – Control two waters — Moat House
Fishery and a water situated just outside
Billericay with easy access and parking. Both
waters hold good stocks of carp, tench,
roach, perch and rudd.

Beacontree and District AA

Secretary – A.C. Ward
173 Western Avenue, Dagenham
Tel: 01 593 0047

Becmain AS

Secretary – R. Smith
46 Short Crofts Road, Dagenham
Tel: 01 592 0348

Membership – Unrestricted

Bretons AS

Secretary – B.R. Breeze
112 Cannonsleigh Road, Dagenham
Tel: 01 592 7028

Billericay & District AC

Secretary – E.A. Dyer
159 Wood Street, Chelmsford
Tel: 0245 355575

Membership – Unrestricted
Year Formed – 1957
No. of Members – 2,500
Facilities – Rivers and lakes in Essex, 13
fisheries.

Castle AC (Ongar)

Secretary – K. Smith
130 Queens Way, Shelley, Ongar

Cedars PS

Secretary – R. Castley
116 Macon Way, Cranham, Upminster

Membership – Unrestricted
Year Formed – 1968
No. of Members – 15-20
Facilities – 2 lakes at East Hanningfield. All
banks controlled.

Chelmsford AA

Secretary – D.C. Willson
66 Marconi Road, Chelmsford CM1 1QD
Tel: 0245 87014

Membership – Unrestricted
Year Formed – 1922
No. of Members – 2,000
Facilities – 3½ miles River Chelmer, Gt.
Waltham — tench, pike, roach, rudd, carp.
Over 14 miles of Chelmer and Blackwater
Navigation Canal. Several weir pools and
backwaters including Kingmill, Paper Mills
and Hoe Mill. Broads Green Lake (near
Great Waltham), Danbury Trout Lake
(Rainbow and Brown) and Boreham Mere
Fisheries — bream, roach, tench, carp,
perch, pike.

Colnes AS

Secretary – K.W. Murrells
1 Hillie Bunnies, Earls Colne, Colchester
CO6 2RU
Tel: 078 75 3371

Membership – Unrestricted
Year Formed – 1910
No. of Members – Approx. 300
Facilities – Several miles of the River Colne
and either side of the village plus various
other lengths further down stream. Two
stretches of the Stour at Bures, Suffolk. Also a
small stretch at Little Horkesley (Essex-Suffolk
border).

Elm Park Hornchurch & District AS

Secretary – P.W. Darling
40 Rosslyn Avenue, Harold Wood, Romford
Tel: 04023 43246

Membership – Restricted
Year Formed – 1936
No. of Members – 300
Facilities – 4 lakes in locality, 3 stretches on
Suffolk Stour, 1 stretch River Roding.

Essex Angling Consultative Assoc.

Secretary – Mr. B.J.G. Wale
4 Longmore Avenue, Great Baddow,
Chelmsford, Essex
Tel: 0245 352145

Function – to act as a liaison between clubs
and public authorities such as the Water
Authorities. Also helps clubs with their
internal problems such as settling up fishing
leases. Has 49 member clubs.

Halstead and Hedingham AC

Secretary – P. Firman
9 Spansey Court, Halstead

Membership – Unrestricted
Facilities – Lakes, several pits and rivers.

Kelvedon & District AA

Secretary – T. Ladkin
68 Western Road, Silver End, Witham
Tel: 0376 83504

Membership – Unrestricted
Year Formed – 1948
No. of Members – 1200
Facilities – Roach, dace, chub, perch in 7½ miles of River Blackwater between Stisted and Wickham Bishops. Plus stretch of River Stour and 11 stillwaters in Silver End Birch, Tiptree areas. Sea fishing trips organised.

Maldon AS

Secretary – P. Revill
'Langford Limes' 94 Crescent Road,
Heybridge, Maldon CM9 SN
Tel: 0621 54765

Membership – Unrestricted. Junior membership available
No. of Members – 650 +
Facilities – Large gravel pit (6 acres), 2 acre reservoir, small carp water, approx 2½ miles of river Blackwater, 3 miles of Chelmer canal, roach, perch, pike, dace, carp, tench, chub, bream. All waters for members only. Occasionally hired for matches at committees discretion.

Marconi AS

Secretary – T.S. Palmer
3 The Westerings, Great Baddow, Chelmsford
Tel: 0245 71806

Membership – Unrestricted
Year Formed – 1925
No. of Members – 400
Facilities – 4 large lakes and approximately 3½ miles of river.

Mid Essex Specimen Group

Secretary – K.W. Lovell
20 Alefounder Close, Colchester

Moor Hall & Belhus AS

Secretary – N.A. Tilbrook
46 Mill Road, Aveley, South Ockendon
RM15 4SL
Tel: 040 26 3694

Membership – Restricted. Junior membership available
Year Formed – 1960
No. of Members – 160
Facilities – Hill Farm Fishery, South Road, South Ockendon, (7 acres). Ham River Pits, South Ockendon (leased).

Priory AC

Secretary – B.J.G. Wale
4 Longmore Avenue, Great Baddow,
Chelmsford
Tel: 0245 352145

Membership – Restricted
Year Formed – 1963
No. of Members – 85
Facilities – Private gravel pit — Upminster.

Roding Valley Anglers Consultative Assoc.

Secretary – L. Lee
12 Charteris Road, Woodford Green
Tel: 01 504 9934

Saffron Walden AC

Secretary – K.E. Richardson
2 Hilltop Lane, Saffron Walden

Membership – Restricted
Year Formed – 1960
No. of Members – 1000
Facilities – 3½ miles Great Ouse — 2 Sections, ½ mile of Old West River, 1 mile River Cam, 4 miles River Thet, 3 pits — 1 lake — average 2 acres each.

Selo AS

Secretary – R.H. Edmonds
55 Westwood Avenue, Brentwood
Tel: 027 219942

Shell Club AS

Secretary – J.W. Deaves
28 Rainbow Lane, Stanford Le Hope
SS17 0AS
Tel: 037 56 2107

Membership – Restricted
Year Formed – 1930
No. of Members – 300
Facilities – We have a 30 acre lake called 'The Warren', Wharf Road, Stanford-Le-Hope and the club is a works club. We have a varied coarse fishery (carp, tench, bream, roach, perch). Only a small amount of bank is measured for members, the remainder is open to public on day ticket basis.

Shore House Angling Group

Secretary – G. Govier
173 Church Road, Shoeburyness
Tel: 03708 3496

Membership – Restricted to local Residents
Year Formed – 1978
No. of Members – 23

South Essex Group Angling Consultative

Secretary – R. Smith
46 Short Crofts Road, Dagenham
Tel: 01 592 0348

Thurrock AC

Secretary – D. Nutt
94 Erriff Drive, South Ockendon RM15 5AY
Tel: 040 25 4832

Membership – Restricted
Year Formed – 1945
No. of Members – 640
Facilities – 10 acre clay pit South Ockendo — approximately 40 years old — all speci Excellent pike. Good carp — rented from Thurrock B.C. — 5 acre clay pit, Dunton years old — carp, roach, rudd, tench. 5 a sand and gravel pit. Rainham, Essex — owned freehold. All species coarse fish.

Tunnel AC

Secretary – J. Hunt
309 Somercotes, Basildon

Wangye AS

Secretary – R.S. Kendall
10 Dunmow Close, Chadwell Heath, Rom
Tel: 01 590 3751

Membership – Restricted
Year Formed – 1956
No. of Members – 175
Facilities – ¼ acre lake and 2000 yards of River Roding.

Westbarrow Hall AC

Secretary – R.M.F. Wright
40 Nicholson Road, Thundersley, Benfleet
Tel: 0702 558648

Membership – Restricted
Facilities – Small lake in Southend area.

Woodford AS

Secretary – L.G. Lee
12 Chartens Road, Woodford Green, Esse
Tel: 01 504 9934

Membership – Unrestricted
No. of Members – 125
Facilities – Stretch of River Roding from Passingford Bridge Shorts Mill. Also fishi Paynes Lane Lake.

White Hart AS

Secretary – A. Tickle
157 Dagenham Road, Rush Green, Romfo
Tel: 70 20963

Membership – Restricted to 60
No. of Members – 50
Facilities – 2 Lakes at Dagenham Road, Dagenham. Common Carp to 15lbs, Brea 8lbs.

GLOUCESTERSHIRE

Cheltenham AC

Secretary – F.J. Selley
2 Hollis Gardens, Hatherley, Cheltenham
GL51 6JQ
Tel: 0242 28586

Membership – Restricted
Year Formed – 1866
No. of Members – Limited 800
Facilities – About 7 miles of Lower Warwickshire, Avon at Bredon Eckington Strensham Lock and Birlingham. Deep slo water 12 ft. to 16 ft. Very good for bream catches of over 50 lbs made every year, g roach, some large chub and a lot of pike to 16-18 lbs (we return most).

...ucester United AA

...etary – P. Farnsworth
...he Butts, Newent, Gloucester
...0531 820183

...bership – Unrestricted
...of Members – 1300
...ities – Approximately 5 miles of lower
...n between Tewkesbury and Gloucester.
...ners Pool (7 acres) at Saul Nr.
...cester — Roach, perch, rudd, tench,
...n — better known for its large carp. ½
...stretch of Stroudwater canal at Framilode
...Gloucester — roach, perch, tench, rudd.

...cott AC

...etary – D. Reeve
...kus Road, Swindon, Wilts. SN1 4JP
...0793 34378

...bership – Restricted
...of Members – 200
...ities – Fishing in four gravel pits at
...ott Lane, Fairford, Glos.

...ney & District AC

...etary – E.J. Matthews
...ork Road, Cinderford, Gloucester
...0594 23649

...bership – Unrestricted
...Formed – 1962
...of Members – 700
...ities – Lydney Lake 4 acres and Lydney
...al 1 mile — carp, roach, tench, bream,
...e and rudd.

...reton in the Marsh AC

...etary – F.D. Wilson
...mberts Field, Bourton on the Water
...0451 21018

...cholt AC

...etary – J. Canwell
...ellsprings Road, Gloucester
...0452 27515

...bership – Restricted
...Formed – 1940
...of Members – 30

...th Cerney AC

...etary – H.J. Franklin
...rs Farm, South Cerney, Cirencester
...0285 860 362

...bership – Unrestricted
...Formed – 1936
...of Members – 980

...utshill AC

...etary – D.J. Carter
...hestnut Park, Kingswood, Wotton-Under-
...e
...045 385 3561

...bership – Restricted by a 10 mile radius.
...r membership restricted to 125
...Formed – 1960
...of Members – 150
...ities – A lake of 2.7 acres at the Stoutshill
...ol at Uley near Dursley, Glos. and 1 mile
...th banks on River Frome at Whitminster,
...cestershire. Hire for matches only to
...e in immediate area.

Stroud & District AA

Secretary – J. Storkey
3 Broadmere Close, Dursley
Tel: 0453 45535

GREATER LONDON

Bath Road PS

Secretary – C.L. Gardner
8 Lilac Gardens, Ealing, London W5 4LD
Tel: 01 579 6967

Membership – Unrestricted
Year Formed – Re-founded in 1952
No. of Members – 600 +
Facilities – River Thames (North Stoke), River
Colne (Poyle, 1 mile), Hithermore Lake and
ponds at Poyle.

Blenheim AS

Secretary – F.W. Lancaster
20 Hillary Road, Shepherds Bush, W12
Tel: 01 749 0033

Car-Pike Specimen Group

Secretary – C. Pocock
10 Onslow Gardens, Grange Park

Civil Service AS

Secretary – N.J. Day
74a Honor Oak Road, London SE23 3RR

Membership – Restricted
Year Formed – 1934
Facilities – Waters on Thames, Kennet and
Medway. Still waters in Middlesex and North
London.

Crystal Palace AA

Secretary – W.E.S. Beattie
175 Hermitage Road, Upper Norwood,
London SE19 3QJ
Tel: 01 653 0232

Membership – Restricted
Year Formed – 1924
No. of Members – 200 Seniors 25 Juniors
Facilities – Intermediate Lake — Crystal
Palace Park. (Still water fishery. All major
coarse fish).

Duke of Wellington AS

Chairman – A. Curzon
1 Alma Avenue, Highams Park, London E4
Tel: 01 985 5255

Firestone AC

Secretary – R. Cloves
42 Caryle Road, South Ealing, London W5
Tel: 01 568 1152

Membership – Unrestricted
Year Formed – 1979
No. of Members – 30

Harrow AS

Secretary – T. Skelton
"Hazeldean", Cheapside Lane, Denham, Bucks.
Tel: 0895 833867

Membership – Unrestricted
No. of Members – 350

Jubilee AS

Secretary – D. Seymour
Flat 5, 57 Grange Park Road, Leyton,
London E10
Tel: 01 556 4456

Membership – Unrestricted
Year Formed – 1935
No. of Members – 45

Leisure Sport AC

Angling Manager – J.E. Newby
47/49 Church Street, Staines
Tel: 0784 61831

Membership – Unrestricted
Year Formed – 1974
No. of Members – 16,000
Facilities – Ash Vale, Bedfont, Broxbourne,
Burghfield, Twyford, Frimley, Larkfield,
Rickmansworth, Ryemeads Shepperton,
Staines, Stanstead Abbotts, Theale,
Wraysbury Yateley and certain special
locations. Also St. Patricks stream Twyford,
stretches of R. Wey, R. Ouse, R. Ivel and
lakes at Fishers Green, Papercaut and Hooks
Marsh.

London AA

Secretary – V.R. Cooke
183 Hoe Street, Walthamstow,
London E17 3AP
Tel: 01 520 7477 (Day)

Membership – Unrestricted
Year Formed – 1884
No. of Members – Approx. 18,000
Facilities – Extensive fishing rights in London
and surrounding areas. Includes stretches of
Rivers Avon, Beult, Cam, Great Ouse, Stour,
Thames, Cole, Lee, Little Ouse, Stort, Ver,
Wensum, Wissey plus lakes, canals and
reservoirs.

Long Life AS

Secretary – R. Jordan
22 Barden Close, Harefield
Tel: 089 582 3060

Membership – Restricted
Year Formed – 1955
No. of Members – 200

Lychnobite Angling Soc.

Secretary – P. White
18 Margaret Avenue, St Albans
Tel: 0727 35510

Membership – Unrestricted. Junior
membership available
Year Formed – 1893
No. of Members – 261
Facilities – Rivers Lea, Stort, Avon, Roding.
All short stretches — Coarse. Pits at Nazing
— Coarse. River Pant — Game and Coarse.

New Studio Club AS

Secretary – D.M. Edwards
51 Poplar House, Wickham Road, Brockley,
London SE4 1NE
Tel: 01 691 4011

Membership – Restricted
Year Formed – 1939
No. of Members – 260
Facilities – 1 clay pit approximately 6 acres, 1 sand pit approximately 29 acres, both situated at Sevenoaks, Kent.

Palmers Green AS

Secretary – P.G. King
32 Ashdown Crescent, Cheshunt, Herts. EN8 0RS
Tel: 97 27238

Membership – Unrestricted
No. of Members – 44
Facilities – Are the managing club of the Waltham Abbey consortium of nine clubs.

Penge AC

Secretary – J.A. Nue
56 Bargrove Close, Averley, London SE20
Tel: 01 659 3311

Membership – Unrestricted
No. of Members – 100
Facilities – Fishing at Pevensey Haven from Chilley Bridge to Rickney Bridge. Most species of coarse fish may be caught.

S. Davall AS

Secretary – P.J. Pitt
4 Gordon Avenue, St Margarets on Thames, East Twickenham, Middlesex TW1 1NQ
Tel: 01 892 8113

Membership – Unrestricted
Year Formed – Approx. 1960
No. of Members – 100 +
Facilities – River Bourne, Nr. Woking, Potts and Hinksey Streay Oxford, Maple Durham Nr. Reading. Plus 21 exchange waters on Rivers, The Thane, Thames, Colne, Wey and Mole and 4 lakes.

Shadwell Basin & Angling & Preservation Society

Hon. Secretary – T.J. Nevill
Lansbury Institute, The Highway, E.1.
Tel: 01 981 5972

Facilities – Shadwell Basin (disused dock all major coarse fish).

Southfields Specimen Group

Secretary – A. Stone
7 Ambleside, Albert Drive SW19

Southwark Angling and Preservation Society

Secretary – P. King
15 Caxton Way, Fair Street, Bermondsey SE16
Tel: 01 403 0724

Thameside Specimen Group

Secretary – D. Smith
30 Mary's Road, Teddington

The Thames Angling Preservation Society

Hon. Secretary – A.E. Hodges
The Pines, 32 Tile Kiln Lane, Bexley, Kent DA5 2BB
Tel: Crayford 525575 (London) 2 525575
S.T.D. 0322 525575

Founded in 1838
To protect the fisheries of the River Thames.

GREATER MANCHESTER

Border Anglers & Naturalists (Mossley & Dist.)

Secretary – H. Garside
60 Queensway, Greenfield, Oldham OL3 7AH
Tel: 045 77 5993

Membership – Restricted – Junior Members
Year Formed – 1971/2
No. of Members – Approx. 250
Facilities – Hollingrove Dam, Coarse fishing — Greenfield Trout etc. River Tame, Alexandra Mill length only, Uppermill Claytons Pond Mossley area (Coarse fish), River Tame Greenfield Mossley area short lengths being developed for coarse fishing. (Milton Mill area Roaches area). We are a branch club for the Oldham and District AAA and help control their waters.

Bowker Vale AC

Secretary – T. Vinter
4 Cravenwood Road, Manchester
Tel: 061 740 9939

Membership – Unrestricted
Year Formed – 1972
No. of Members – 206
Facilities – 2 lodges about 2 acres each. Almost all species of coarse fish thrive along with a couple of hundred brown trout.

Bury District AS

Secretary – F. Booth
142 Bury Road, Tottington, Nr. Bury, Lancs BL8 3DX
Tel: 020488 2517

Membership – Unrestricted
Year Formed – 1903
No. of Members – Approx. 1300

Greater Manchester and Diggle AC

Secretary – D. Turner
32 Beech Avenue, Greenfield, Oldham
Tel: 04577 70194

Membership – Restricted
Year Formed – 1947/8
No. of Members – 272
Facilities – Tanners Dam at Saddleworth (coarse fishery). Hartshead Power Station at Stalybridge (coarse fishery) Reddish Vale. Waters at Reddish (coarse fishery with day tickets available at local tackle dealers).

Greenall Whitley, AA

Secretary – J. Robinson
6 Birch Polygon, Rusholme, Manchester M14 5HX
Tel: 061 224 3174

Membership – Unrestricted
Year Formed – 1908
No. of Members – 1,800
Facilities – Rochdale Canal — Slattocks Bridge to Manchester (6 miles), River We — Saltlength, River Dane — Sproston Gr Drinkwater Park Lake — Prestwich.

Heywood AS

Secretary – B.J. Hargreaves
11 Victor Street, Heywood, Lancs.
Tel: 0706 622445

Membership – Unrestricted
No. of Members – 200
Facilities – Two mill lodges near town cen adequate parking facilities.

Manley AS

Secretary – S.E. Myers
16 Balcarres Avenue, Whelley, Wigan, L
Tel: 0942 34430

Membership – Restricted
Year Formed – 1904
No. of Members – 25
Facilities – Haigh Brewery Lodge — 1200 Metres situated in farm land on what was Earl of Crawford and Balcarres Estate — gently sloping bottom between deeps and shallows which are conducive to good res in hot or cold weather. Meadow pit lodge 1000 sq. metres situated as above.

Milnthorpe Anglers

Secretary – T. Mort
41 Garstang Avenue, Breightmet, Bolton Lancs.
Tel: 0204 26386

Membership – Restricted
Year Formed – 1968
No. of Members – 45
Facilities – The club does not own any wa was formed solely for match fishing.

Moss Side Social AS

Secretary – R.W. Harrop
1 Fulham Avenue, Newton Heath, Manch M10 6TF   Tel: 061 682 5370

Membership – Unrestricted
No. of Members – 150
Facilities – Fishing for all species of coars fish at Todbrook Reservoir. All coarse species, particularly Bream and Pike may caught at Bosley Reservoir near Macclesfi

Norwest Specimen Group

Secretary – G.A. Waters
73 Newearth Road, Worsley, Manchester

Oldham & District Amalgamat AA

Secretary – H. Garside
60 Queensway, Greenfield, Oldham OL3 7AH   Tel: 045 77 5993

mbership – Unrestricted – full membership
clubs.
r Formed – 1950
of Members – Approximately 350 to 400
nting all categories.
ilities – Area Saddleworth, Oldham,
ybridge. Huddersfield Narrow Canal
arse and Trout) Lock 24 Saddleworth — to
dge 85 Greenfield. Swineshaw Mill Dam
ybridge area (trout and coarse). A water
takehill Nr. Oldham (Dam). Small pond at
tton Nr. Oldham (Coarse fish).

chdale & District AS

retary – F. Garvin
Queensway, Rochdale, Lancs.
0706 43035

mbership – Restricted
of Members – Approx. 150
ilities – A small club house — surrounded
lodges in a lightly wooded area. Lodges
tain most coarse fish with a good head of
.

chdale Walton AS

retary – D.R. Gent
Croft Head Drive, Milnrow, Rochdale,
ater Manchester
0706 342052

mbership – Restricted
r Formed – 1858
of Members – 200
ilities – Three still waters for coarse
ng. Approximately 5 acres.

inton & Pendlebury AC

retary – A, Richards
Moss Lane, Swinton, Lancs.
061 794 9910

mbership – Restricted
r Formed – 1973
of Members – Approx. 600
ilities – Our water is known as
ensmere and is at the Junction of the
6 Bolton to Manchester Road with Station
d and Queensway Pendlebury. Carp,
m, roach, tench, perch and rudd. Day
ets are obtainable by post at least 1 week
r to fishing enclosing a stamped
ressed envelope and cheque/Postal Order
correct amount.

lcome Anglers

retary – A.M. Rearden
arlborough Road, Royton, Oldham, Lancs
6AU
061 624 7777

mbership – Unrestricted
r Formed – 1870
of Members – 60
lities – Two local mills.

AMPSHIRE

esford AC

retary – M.G. Handoll
croft, Jacklyns Lane, Alresford
025273 2474

Membership – Unrestricted. Junior
membership available
Year Formed – 1979
No. of Members – 40
Facilities – The Alresford Pond

Basingstoke AC

Secretary – R. Branton
111 Wrekin Close, Basingstoke Tel: 0256 28819
Permit Secretary – A.M. Danes
97 Copland Close, Basingstoke Tel: 0256 50115

Membership – Unrestricted
Year Formed – 1962
No. of Members – 478
Facilities – Some small rivers in the
Basingstoke area, two lakes at the Vyne
National Trust and affiliated to:— Reading &
District Angling Association, Hampshire
Basingstoke Canal Anglers Association,
Kennet Valley Fishery Association, National
Federation of Anglers.

Bishops Waltham AC

Secretary – M. Creese
8 St. Andrews Green, Meonstoke
Tel: 048 97 664

Membership – Unrestricted
Year Formed – 1969
No. of Members – 83

Castle AC

Secretary – John Snowden
44 Westbury Court, Hedge End, Southampton
Tel: 048 92 81309

Membership – Unrestricted
No. of Members – 100
Facilities – Fishing at Butlocks Heath
Reservoir, Southampton

Christchurch AC

Secretary – B. Chislett
16 Old Milton Road, New Milton
Tel: 0425 610304

Membership – Unrestricted. Junior
membership available
No. of Members – 1800
Facilities – 40 miles of Stour and Avon 9
stillwater coarse fishing lakes 1 put and take
trout lake.

Cove AS

Chairman – D. Chambers
c/o Cupits, 24 Bridge Road, Farnborough
Tel: 0252 42939 (Day)

Membership – Restricted
No. of Members – 150
Facilities – Stretch of River Loddon and
gravel pit at Theale.

Eastleigh & District AC

Secretary – P.W. Bowman
325 Market Street, Eastleigh Tel: 0703 610987

Membership – Unrestricted
Year Formed – 1952
No. of Members – 940
Facilities – Majority of waters are man made
lakes, up to 6 acres in area. Fish mainly
stocked are carp, bream, tench, roach, rudd
and perch.

Farnborough & District

Secretary – J.G. Raison
2 Park Road, Farnborough
Tel: 0252 512134/43470

Membership – Restricted
Year Formed – 1933
No. of Members – 450
Facilities – 3½ miles river Whitewater
(Heckfield), 2¼ miles River Loddon
(Winnersh), 1¼ miles River Wey (Frensham),
roach, dace, chub, perch, trout, gudgeon,
pike, grayling (all rivers), 45 miles shared
fishing Basingstoke canal, 4 gravel pits at
Farnborough famous for carp, tench and
bream.

Farnham AS

Secretary – R.F. Frost
49 Cambridge Road, East Farnborough
GU14 6QB
Tel: 0252 42809

Membership – Unrestricted. Junior
membership available
Year Formed – 1910
No. of Members – 1000
Facilities – Stretches of River Loddon, River
Way and six lakes.

Hampshire Basingstoke Canal AA

Secretary – L.A. Harris
24 Hampton Court, Woolford Way,
Basingstoke
Tel: 0256 57596

Membership – Only through affiliated club.

Hartley Wintney AS

Secretary – E. Dunn
18 Vivian Close, Church Crookham
Tel: 02514 28391

Facilities – Stretch of the River Hart and
several stretches stillwaters.

Haslemere AS

Secretary – M.J. Traviss
21 Greenfield Close, Liphook
Tel: 0428 723389

Membership – Restricted
Year Formed – 1936
No. of Members – 450
Facilities – Shillinglee — Lake 32 acres,
Forkedpond — pond 8 acres, Wadesmarsh
pond 2 acres, Lythehill — pond 1 acre,
Imphams — pond 1 acre, River Rother —
River 4 miles (Shared).

Oakhanger AS

Secretary – M. Clarkson
9 South Hurst, Whitehill, Bordon
Tel: 04203 2157

Facilities – Several stillwaters

Pawn Brokers Specimen Group

Secretary – R. Gaynor
132 Pinewood Park, Love, Farnborough

Petersfield & District AC

Secretary – G.A. McKee
25 North Lane, Buritom, Petersfield
GU31 5RS

Membership – Restricted
Year Formed – Approx. 1932
No. of Members – 170
Facilities – Sussex Rother — Petworth,
Fittleworth, Trotton, Durford Bridge. Arun —
Pulborough, Watersfield River Meon —
Titchfield, Chichester Canal. Westhammet
gravel pit, Hayling Island gravel pit. Hilsea
moat Portsmouth, Heath Lake Petersfield.

Portsmouth & District AC

Secretary – R. Snook
86 Caernarvon Road, Portsmouth
Tel: 0705 62986

Membership – Unrestricted
Year Formed – 1947
No. of Members – 1200
Facilities – Extensive coarse fishery in
Hampshire and Sussex.

Ringwood & District AA

Secretary – J. Steel
30 Mansal Avenue, Ferndown
Tel: 0202 893748

Membership – Unrestricted. Junior
membership available
Year Formed – 1949
No. of Members – 1000
Facilities – Hampshire Avon, 5 miles
Ringwood area including Severals and Ibsley
fisheries. Dorset Stour, 10 miles. Other rivers
3 miles. 6 lakes including Broadlands and
Moreys. Most waters available to hire for
matches.

Salisbury & District AC

Secretary – A.C. Amos
28 Dudley Avenue, Fordingbridge
Tel: 0425 52660

Membership – Unrestricted
Year Formed – 1941
No. of Members – 1900
Facilities – Coarse fishing at Steeple
Langford, Petersfinger, Edington and Milford
Lakes. Also on Dorset Stour, Eye Mead.
Coarse/game on River Avon at Burgate,
Charford and Salisbury River Nadder at
Salisbury. Game only on River Avon at
Durnford, West Amesbury and Upper Avon,
River Wylye at Stapleford, Bapton and Wylye
Village.

Southampton Piscatorial Society

Hon. Secretary – B. Blakey
14 Furzedale Park, Hythe, Southampton
Tel: 0703 844042

Southern Anglers

Secretary – T.A. Irons
7 Nelson Crescent, Horndean, Portsmouth
Tel: 0705 597017

Facilities – 1½ miles on River Rother.

Winchester AC

Secretary – P.J. Allen
c/o 72a Parchment Street, Winchester
Tel: 0962 3929 (Day)

Membership – Restricted to local residents
No. of Members – 250

HEREFORD & WORCS

Evesham AA

Secretary – T.H. Pitcher
17 Charles Close, Evesham

Hereford and District AA

Secretary – I. Astley
The Lindens, Bishopstone, HR4 7JG
Tel: 098122 283

Membership – Unrestricted
Year Formed – 1921
No. of Members – Approx. 700 adults and 600
children.
Facilities – Approximately 8 miles of the River
Wye and 7 miles of the River Lugg near
Hereford. (Distances expressed as single
bank). Salmon, trout, and coarse fish
(particularly chub, dace, roach, perch and
pike).

Kidderminster & District AA

Secretary – M.R. Millinchip
246 Marlpool Lane, Kidderminster
Tel: 0562 63471

Membership – Restricted
Year Formed – 1892
No. of Members – 1800
Facilities – Bewdley. Above Bridge for about
one mile. Bewdley. Below bridge for about
three quarters of a mile. Winnalls. Below
Stourport for about one mile. Stewpony
Canal. For about one and a half miles.

Lyttelton AA

Secretary – E. Wilkes
31 Mostyn Road, Stourport-on-Severn
Tel: 029 93 6269

Membership – Restricted
Year Formed – 1911
No. of Members – 570
Facilities – Coarse fishing on River Severn at
Stourport. Mostly match fishing venue. Total
pegs 100.

Portobello AC

Secretary – J.R. Harries
17 Kingsbury Road, St Johns, Worcester
Tel: 0905 54598

Membership – Restricted
Year Formed – 1955
No. of Members – 85
Facilities – R. Tewe (¾ mile), Bow Brook (¾
mile) Mill pool — Reconstructed in 1971.

Upton AA

Secretary – W.K.R. Tainton
136 Poolbrook Road, Nr Halvern
Tel: 068 45 64581

Membership – Restricted
Year Formed – 1900
No. of Members – 150
Facilities – Good coarse fishing on the Rive
Severn adjacent to the town. Species barbe
chub, roach, bream, dace etc. The river is
slow and averages between 5ft. and 10ft.
deep. Best methods, swimfeeder with mago
or float fishing with caster and maggots.
Permit 1980, 40p per day. Available from C
Shinn fishing tackle shop, Upton-upon-
Severn.

Wye Valley Specimen Group

Secretary – C. Raymen
35 Dover Street, Mountain Ash, Mid
Glamorgan

HERTFORDSHIRE

Barnet & District AC

Chairman – E.G. Kent
6 Mansfield Avenue, East Barnet
Tel: 01 440 0965

Membership – Unrestricted
Year Formed – 1933
No. of Members – 650

Bishops Stortford & District AS

Secretary – C. Costema
31 Thornbera Road, Bishops Stortford
Tel: 0279 52151

Membership – Unrestricted
Year Formed – 1949
No. of Members – 950 +
Facilities – Several miles of the River Stort
and around Bishops Stortford and small la
Day tickets are available on the river only
at present a major restock is taking place c
some reaches after Thames Water flood
alleviation work.

Boxmoor & District AS Ltd.

Secretary – K. Charge
11 Cattsdell, Hemel Hempstead
Tel: 0442 52799

Membership – Restricted
Year Formed – 1927
No. of Members – 400

Colne Valley Anglers Consultative Assoc.

Secretary – T.H. Cockfield
39 Falcon Way, Garston, Watford
Tel: 092 73 76031

Fisheries AC

Secretary – D. Brown
P.O. Box 180, 88 Newhouse Crescent,
Garston, Watford
Tel: 09273 78884 or 79478

bership – Unrestricted (but waiting list)
of Members – 300
ities – 3 lakes of about 85 acres at
ters Farm, Cospermill Lane, West Hude,
mansworth, containing quality coarse fish
l species.

field & District AS

etary – E.F. Denchfield
ockbreach Road, Hatfield
07072 62791

bership – Restricted
Formed – 1952
of Members – 150
ities – Waters on Lord Salisbury's Estate,
eld, Herts. Large lake with River Lea
ing through it and a further 2 miles of the
r from Millgreen to Essendon. 52 seater
hes run every other Sunday to other
es.

tfordshire Federation of
glers

etary – Mr. P.A. Chapman
illcrest, Hatfield
07072 63140

bership – Restricted
Formed – 1950
of Members – 400
ities – The waters are controlled by
ber Clubs and open for individual
bership.

chin & District AA

etary – L. Day
hatchers End, Hitchin
0462 50612

bership – Unrestricted
Formed – 1932
of Members – 350
ities – Stretches on the Middle and Upper
e plus lakes.

gerford Canal AA

etary – W. Radbourne
04886 2131

gs Arms & Cheshunt AS

etary – J. Conner
alisbury Road, Enfield

bership – Unrestricted
of Members – 700

gs Langley AS

etary – A. Anderson
eadow Road, Hemel Hempstead
0442 59341

bership – Restricted (waiting list)
Formed – 1929
of Members – 200

chworth & District AA

etary – C.W.G. Matthews
nworth Corner Post Office, 2 Baldock
, Letchworth
04626 5019

Membership – Restricted
Year Formed – 1952
No. of Members – 700
Facilities – Own lakes (Disused gravel pits)
Henlow. Rented waters on River Ouse and
Old Bedford. Access to River Ivel.

North Harrow Waltonians

Secretary – H. Peplow
Bowsridge, Smokey Row, Great Kimble, Nr.
Aylesbury
Tel: 08444 3815

Membership – Restricted
Year Formed – 1931
No. of Members – 1100

Palmers Green AS

Secretary – P.G. King
32 Ashdown Crescent, Cheshunt, EN8 0RS
Tel: 0992 27238

Membership – Unrestricted
Year Formed – 1948
No. of Members – 41
Facilities – We are the managing club of the
Waltham Abbey Angling Consortium of nine
clubs. The W.A.A.C. has a private fishery of
about 1½ miles of water on the Old River Lea
and the Cornmill stream at Waltham Abbey,
Essex. Palmers Green A.S. has a 1½ mile
stretch on the New River between Ware and
Hertford, in Herts. Palmers Green has ¾ mile
trout fishery on River Mirmram at Tewin,
Herts.

Rickmansworth Conservative
Club & District AS

Secretary – A.R. Harris
158 Balmoral Road, Watford WD2 4EY
Tel: 0923 21360

Membership – Restricted (waiting list). Junior
membership available
No. of Members – 270
Facilities – Fishing at Pynesfield Lakes, West
Hyde, Rickmansworth in Herts.

Sceptre AS

Hon. Secretary – D. Hobbs
77 The Gossamers, Meriden Estate, Garston
Tel: 09273 71391

Facilities – Stretch of the Grand Union Canal
at Moor Pound Lock to Rickmansworth.

The Tring Anglers

Secretary – J.A. Smith
67 Lower Icknield Way, Marsworth, Nr. Tring
Tel: 0296 668 777

Membership – Unrestricted
Year Formed – 1947
No. of Members – Approx. 160
Facilities – B.W.B. Canal — Tring station —
Cooks Wharf Wendover Arm and Aylesbury
Arm (approx. 9 miles in all) River Thame at
Chearsley Nr. Aylesbury — River Ivel at
Shefford, Beds. Small pond at Marsworth.

Verulam AC (St. Albans)

Secretary – J. Trew
128 Benson Close, Luton, Beds. LU3 3QR
Tel: 0582 593798

Membership – Unrestricted. Junior
membership available
Year Formed – 1934
No. of Members – 600
Facilities – River Lee. 1½ miles, 2 stretches,
small fast river, 5 miles from St. Albans.
Gravel Pit at Smallford, 2 miles from St.
Albans. Deep lake (big carp). Gravel pit at
Frogmore, 5 miles from St. Albans, 3 lakes, 8'
deep. Converted watercress bed in St.
Albans, 5' deep. Coarse and game fish, April
1—June 15. River Ouse 8 miles north of
Bedford. 3½ miles in 3 stretches. Fast and
slow water.

Watford Piscators

Secretary – N.F. Brandon
25 Leaford Crescent, Watford
Tel: 0923 27019

Membership – Restricted
Year Formed – 1935
No. of Members – 700

Welwyn Garden City

Secretary – V. Sutton
30 Timbercroft, Welwyn Garden City
Tel: 07073 23500

Membership – Restricted (12 mile radius)
No. of Members – 500

HUMBERSIDE NORTH

Beverley & District AC

Secretary – P. Dodds
26 Wilbert Lane, Beverley
Tel: 0482 885270 or 0482 882197

Membership – Restricted
Year Formed – 1975
No. of Members – 35
Facilities – River Derwent Wressele,
approximately 1 mile. Fishing is £1.50 per
year. Permits available from the secretary.

Carlton FC

Secretary – J.T. Iball
10 The Pastures, Carlton, Goole
Tel: 0405 860 539

Membership – Unrestricted
Year Formed – 1970
No. of Members – 350 +
Facilities – 6 acre lake in village — tench
water. 3 miles of river (Drain type).

Driffield Hearts of Oak AC

Secretary – R.A. Porter
7 Driffield Road, Nafferton, Driffield
Tel: 0377 44477

Membership – Unrestricted. Junior
membership available
Year Formed – 1831
No. of Members – 42
Facilities – Our water consists of one lake. The
area is known as Emotland Nr. Frodingham.
There are other lakes in the area but these are
private but open to day tickets. All the lakes
have roach, bream, carp, rudd, perch and
pike.

Eggborough Power Station Sports and Social Club

Secretary – A. Kelly
35 Westfield Road, Eggborough, Goole
Tel: 0977 661061

Membership – Unrestricted
Year Formed – 1968
No. of Members – 60
Facilities – A man made Lagoon 110m x 60m, 4½ ft. deep stocked with roach, perch, rudd, tench, carp and chub.

Fisons AC

Secretary – G. Smith
Arcade Angling Centre, Goole
Tel: 0405 60676

Membership – Restricted
No. of Members – 70
Facilities – Decoy pond at Old Goole. Stretch Derwent at Buiswith, Humberside.

Goole & District AA

Secretary – D. Whitaker
39 Westbourne Grove, Goole, DN14 6NA
Tel: 0405 3513

Membership – Unrestricted
Year Formed – 1948
No. of Members – 350
Facilities – R. Derwent at Elvington — Breightom — Wressle 2½ miles. R. Trent at Laneham — Littleborough 1½ miles. Ponds at Foggathorpe — Rawcliffe — Cowick.

Howden & District AC

Secretary – M. Redman
46 Marshfield Avenue, Goole
Tel: 0405 61836

Membership – Unrestricted. Junior membership available
Year Formed – 1928
No. of Members – 40
Facilities – We have four miles of the Yorkshire Derwent on the east bank starting at Bubwith Bridge going upstream to Aughton and continuing upstream to Ellerton landing and beyond. Cost of joining the club is £8.00 (this is for those who wish to fish away matches on other clubs waters). Also yearly permits which run from January to December at a cost of £1.00 per year — very good value. Waters available to hire for matches. Permanent pegs.

Hull & District AA

Secretary – K. Bone
44 Barrington Avenue, Cottingham Road, Hull
Tel: 0482 493296

Membership – Unrestricted
Year Formed – 1893
No. of Members – 2,000
Facilities – N. Yorkshire Butterwick (R. Rye) trout, grayling and coarse. Brandesburton ponds (no close season) 11 ponds. Leven canal mixed fishery. River Derwent (Yorks) two stretches. Windmill pond, Lincs. Mixed fishery. River Trent (Notts) Carlton and Crankley point.

Hull Fish Trade AC

Secretary – D. Officer
406 Irton House, Cavill Place, Hull, Yorks
Tel: 0482 217976

Membership – Restricted
No. of Members – 40
Facilities – Pond at Newport (East Yorks). Approximately 30 pegs. Match bookings Mr. D. Dixon, 14 Canal Side East, Newport, East Yorkshire. River Rye at Swinton, N. Yorks about ¾ of mile. Members only.

Market Weighton AC

Secretary – T. Brown
19 Glenfield Avenue, Market Weighton
Tel: 06962 2779

Membership – Unrestricted
Year Formed – 1966
No. of Members – 45
Facilities – Waters within a radius of 15 miles of Market Weighton. 2 ponds within 4 miles of Market Weighton — well stocked all species. River Foulness approximately ½ mile — mainly bream, roach and dace. Low Catton — R. Derwent ¾ mile — mixed fishery including trout and grayling.

HUMBERSIDE SOUTH

Scunthorpe & District AA

Secretary – I. Robertson
35 Merton Road, Bottesford, Scunthorpe
Tel: 0724 845466

Membership – Unrestricted
No. of Members – Approx. 2,500 adults — 1,500 juniors
Facilities – The length of River Ancholme in the county of Lincolnshire and South Humberside, between Bishopbridge (in the south) and South Ferriby (north) where the river enters the River Humber. Also control a small stretch at West Stockwith, north west of Gainsborough. On the River Idle the rights are exercised between Misterton Soss and the Sluice Gates (at entry into the River Trent) At West Stockwith — county of Lincolnshire.

KENT

Ashford AS

Secretary – C.J. Hyder
37 Northumberland Avenue, Kennington, Ashford
Tel: 0233 26841

Membership – Unrestricted within 20 mile radius. Junior membership available
Year Formed – 1901
No. of Members – 850
Facilities – 14 miles — Royal Military Canal; Iden lock to west Hythe dam. 5 miles — river Stour, Ashford to Wye. (Members only). Individual clubs may book sections of Royal Military Canal with W. Hodgkin Esq. Tel: 0233 20997

Ashford Kingfishers AC

Secretary – Mr. W.L. Rolfe
82 Bredgar Close, Stanhope Estate, Ashford
Tel: 0233 39153

Membership – Unrestricted
No. of Members – 41
Facilities – Fishing on an irrigation pyke at the Royal Military Canal at Warehorne.

Betteshanger CWAS

Secretary – Mr. A. Herbert
22 James Hall Gardens, Walmer, Near De
Tel: 03045 64179

Membership – Restricted
No. of Members – 70
Facilities – Approx. 5 mile stretch of the Kentish Stour from Plucks Gutter Bridge t Richborough Castle.

Bodiam AC

Secretary – A.T. Weddle
4 The Green, Bodiam, Robertsbridge
Tel: 058 083 646

Membership – Restricted
Year Formed – 1950
No. of Members – 100
Facilities – The area is on the Kent and Su borders. The waters are on the Kentish Ro and enclosed ponds on local farms.

Bromley & District AS

Secretary – C.C. Wills
17 Dane Court, Coxheath, Maidstone

Membership – Restricted
Facilities – River and Stillwater fisheries in Kent including 2 large gravel pits and a stretch of River Darent at Bradbourne nr. Sevenoaks.

Canterbury & District AA

Secretary – N.S.N. Stringer
Riversdale, Mill Road, Sturry, Canterbury CT2 0AF
Tel: 0227 710830

Membership – Unrestricted. Junior membership available
Year Formed – 1928
No. of Members – 2,060
Facilities – Members — 200 acres Lakes, Fordwich & Westbere 8 miles River Stour Fordwich to Plucks Gutter. Day tickets — Grove Ferry — Plucks Gutter. Also availa to Hire for matches.

Dartford & District Angling & Preservation Society

Secretary – H.E. Gooding
298 Lowfield Street, Dartford
Tel: 0474 50236

Membership – Restricted
Year Formed – 1931
No. of Members – 2,400
Facilities – Brooklands Lake, Dartford. Lak at Sutton, Lakes at Horton Kirby, River Medway — Tonbridge, River Beult and Le Teise — Maidstone.

Edenbridge AS

Secretary – D.T. Gallard
1 Shoebridge Cottages, Furnace Farm, Cowden
Tel: 034286 711

mbership – Restricted
r Formed – 1950
of Members – 700
ilities – Both banks of River Eden from
cted to Penshurst. River Medway at Ashurst
, Withyham. Lakes at Hever Castle and
rsh Green.

lmesdale AS

airman – C. Cross
Filmer Lane, Sevenoaks
0732 55587

nbership – Unrestricted
r Formed – 1950 about
of Members – 700 approx.
ilities – Large Ballast pit, 2 smaller lakes,
nile of river and 1 mile stream.

thfield & District AC

retary – J. Martin
ndon Way, Lyminge, Folkestone
0303 862764

nbership – Unrestricted
r Formed – 1973
of Members – 100 approx.
ilities – Fresh water, ¾ mile dyke on
ney Marsh at Old Romney and limited
ess to various private lakes. Sea fishing,
e club competitions at Dungeness and
er breakwater. Boat competitions on
rtered boat off Dungeness.

nt Anglers Consultative Soc.

retary – J. Peters
dens House, Sherbourne Close, Dorset
d, Tunbridge Wells

gfisher Angling & servation Soc.

retary – A. Burrows
entley Close, New Barn, Longfield,
mouth

ilities – Coarse fishing water in Kent and a
t Lake near Shoreham.

idstone & District Motor vices Sport & Social Club

retary – L. Day
heppey Road, Maidstone
0622 45847

bership – Restricted
Formed – 1978
of Members – 90
ilities – Sea angling on Kent coast and
rs.

idstone Victory A & Medway servation Soc.

etary – R. Edmunds
llington Gardens, Wateringbury,
lstone
0622 812904

bership – Restricted to a set number
Formed – 1895
ities – River Medway for roach, chub,
m, dace, pike, perch, bleak and
eon. Teston and Yalding waters available
re for matches.

Orpington & District

Secretary – R. Bright
133 The Drive, Bexley
Tel: 01 303 5945

Facilities – 3 lakes at Ruxley Corner, near
Foots Cray, Kent.

Paddock Wood AC

Secretary – G. Haynes
23 Bramley Gardens, Paddock Wood
Tel: 089 283 2730

Membership – Unrestricted. Junior
membership available
No. of Members – 270
Facilities – River Medway — Stilstead Farm,
E. Peckham, Arnold and Nathan, E.
Peckham, River Medway — Tutsham Farm,
Teston, and Teston. R. Beult, Yalding and
Gedges Lake, Matfield all day ticket waters.
Beltring Pond, Beltring.

Penguin AC

Secretary – D. Palmer
3 White Wood Road, Eastry, Sandwich
Tel: 0304 611829

Membership – Unrestricted
No. of Members – 40

Penshurst AS

Secretary – M.A. Minns
3 Montgomery Road, Tunbridge Wells
Tel: 0892 38625

Membership – Restricted
Facilities – Private waters

Rye & District AS

Secretary – A.V. Curd
34 The Maltings, Peasmarsh, nr. Rye
Tel: 079 721 427

Membership – Unrestricted. Junior
membership available
Year Formed – 1920
No. of Members – 150
Facilities – Fishing on the Rivers Tillingham,
Brede and Rother. The latter being a well
known permanently pegged match water.
Most drains and dykes on the Romney Marsh.
All our waters are in or around Rye. Waters
available for closed events, club and league
matches only.

South Norwood AC

Secretary – R.A. Moore
29 Cordrey Gardens, Coulsdon
Tel: 01 668 4624

Membership – Unrestricted (waiting list)
Year Formed – 1936
No. of Members – 300
Facilities – Stretch of the River Eden at
Chiddingstone, Kent. Two ponds at
Edenbridge, Kent.

Tenterden & District Angling & Preservation Assoc.

Secretary – D.M. Burt
26 Aragon Close, Ashford TN23 2DH
Tel: 0233 36657

Membership – Restricted
Year Formed – 1920
Facilities – Fishing on River Rother, adjoining
dykes and streams, and local ponds.

Tonbridge & District A & F.P.S.

Secretary – A.S. Wolfe
59 Hunt Road, Tonbridge
Tel: 0732 351541

Membership – Unrestricted
Year Formed – 1875
No. of Members – 2000 + 500 juniors
Facilities – 4 miles of the River Medway
around Tonbridge. Single bank of River Eden
— roach and chub specimen water Hayesden
Lake — 7 acres recently stocked and Old
Ballast Pit near Tonbridge and 2 acre carp
and tench pool.

LANCASHIRE

Accrington & District FC

Secretary – A. Balderstone
42 Towneley Avenue, Huncoat
Tel: 0254 33517

Membership – Unrestricted
Year Formed – 1956
Facilities – Coarse and trout fishing on
reservoirs and rivers, salmon rivers.

B.I.C.C. AC

Secretary – J. Worthington
46 Landside, Leigh
Tel: 0942 605273

Membership – Restricted
Year Formed – 1934
No. of Members – 45

Bolton & District AA

Secretary – J.A. Shanahan
4 Sunninghill Street, Bolton BL3 6LX
Tel: 0204 63770

Membership – Unrestricted. Junior
membership available
No. of Members – 2,500 + 1,500 Juniors
Facilities – Bradford Lodge, Great Lever; Bull
Hill; Hall Lane; Bolton Canal, Little Lever;
Smith's Reservoir, Great Lever; Temple
Springs, Smithills; Mertons Loddes, Astley
Bridge; Firwood and the Bunk Reservoirs,
Tonge Moor; Dunscarnes land 2, Shore
Lodge and Gleaves; Dingle and Farm
Lodges, Little Lever. Hulton Park Lodge,
Over Hulton; Ingledene, Belmont Road,
Bolton. Some waters available to hire for
matches.

British Aircraft Corp/English Electric Angling Section

Secretary – W.J. Stammers
3 Cottam Lane, Ashton Preston
Tel: 734685

Membership – Restricted
No. of Members – 100 +
Facilities – Affiliated to the Northern Anglers
Ass.

Bury District Angling Society

Secretary – F. Booth
142 Bury Road, Tottington, nr. Bury
Tel: 020 488 2517

Membership – Unrestricted. Junior membership available
No. of Members – 1,034
Facilities – Parker's, Elton Vale, Kirklees, Tottington, Scholes Water, Tottington, Bury and Bolton Canal, Crompton's, Smethurst Waters, Woolford, Horse Shoe Lodge Ramsbottom, Bolholt Waters, Leaks Waters. Taylor and Nicholson's Wikes Water, Longcroft Waters trout, only.

Garstang & District AA

Secretary – D.E. Irvin
33 High Street, Garstang, Preston

Membership – Restricted
No. of Members – 60
Facilities – 3 mile stretch of the River Wyre at Garstang.

Hyndburn & Blackburn AA

Secretary – K.J. Lambert
79 Prospect Terrace, Whalley Road, Altham West, Accrington
Tel: 0254 395557

Membership – Unrestricted
Year Formed – 1977
No. of Members – 550
Facilities – Fishing on River Ribble, River Calder and nine still waters.

Lancaster Osprey Specimen Group

Secretary – W. Goff
6 Gardner Road, Lancaster

Lansil AC

Secretary – J.E.N. Barnes
88 West End Road, Morecambe
Tel: 0524 416006

Membership – Unrestricted
Year Formed – 1934
No. of Members – 200
Facilities – Fishing on both banks of River Lune from Howgill Beck upstream to Denny Beck — salmon, sea trout, brown trout, large bream, roach, dace, perch and pike. Access to River Ribble, Wyre, Rufford Canal and all Northern anglers waters. N.F.A. Affiliated.

Leyland & District AS

Secretary – G. Kelly
56 St Davids Road, Leyland PR5 2XX
Tel: 07744 24643

Membership – Unrestricted. Junior membership available
Year Formed – 1975
No. of Members – 50
Facilities – Lancaster Canal, Leeds/Liverpool Canal, Rivers Ribble and Trent.

Liverpool & District AA

Secretary – J. Johnson
97 Liverpool Road (North) Maghull, Merseyside
Tel: 051 526 4083

Membership – Unrestricted. Junior membership available
No. of Members – Approx. 2,500
Facilities – All waters available for matches.

Lonsdale A.C.

Secretary – G. Parkinson
166 Dorrington Road, Lancaster

Membership – Unrestricted
Year Formed – 1971
No. of Members – 260
Facilities – Fishing on Swantley Lake stocked with carp, tench, roach, perch and two smaller waters. Club issues Newsletter, monthly meetings, social evenings also regular matches and competitions.

Loveclough AC

Secretary – L.J. Thomas
5 Victoria Street, Haslingden, Rossendale
Tel: 07062 28424

Membership – Unrestricted
Year Formed – 1973
No. of Members – 100
Facilities – Fishing on two waters in the Rossendale Valley both fed by the River Limey.

Marsden Star AS

Secretary – S.P. Cunliffe
122 Halifax Road, Nelson BB9 0EL
Tel: 0282 699743

Membership – Unrestricted
Year Formed – Circa 1900
No. of Members – Approx. 650
Facilities – 9 Miles of Leeds and Liverpool Canal between Long Ing Bridge and Bank Newton also stretches of River Aire and Calder and several small waters in Lancashire and Yorkshire.

Northern AA

Secretary – G. Wilson
11 Guildford Avenue, Chorley
Tel: 02572 65905

Membership – Unrestricted
Year Formed – 1889
No. of Members – 12,000 Senior 2,000 Junior, 1,000 Pensioners
Facilities – Fishing on Lancaster Canal, Glasson Dock and Arm. Parts of Leeds and Liverpool Canal, Shropshire Union Canal, Bridgewater Canal. Wide Hole, Macclesfield Canal, Lower Peak Forest Canal. Also fishing on stretches of the following rivers: Ribble, Worthenbury Brook, Dee, Alyn, Calder, Vyrnwy, Gilpin, Banwy, Severn, Weaver and Old.

Orrell

Secretary – D. Bushell
62 Melwood Drive, Liverpool L12 8RW
Tel: 051 228 4522

Membership – Unrestricted. Junior membership available
No. of Members – 40
Facilities – River Dee, River Severn, River Vyrnwy, River Weaver, River Perry, Leeds, Liverpool Canal.

Preston Centre Federated Angl

Secretary – G. Jones
1 Carnarvon Road, Preston Tel: 0772 5686

Membership – Unrestricted
Year Formed – 1900
No. of Members – 4,000
Facilities – Fishing on Rivers Ribble, Wyre and Rufford Canal near Preston. Maps available from Secretary.

Southport & District AA

Secretary – C. Russel
41 Longacre, Southport

Membership – Restricted
No. of Members – 400
Facilities – Fishing on the River Crossons which runs through private estate and only club members have access.

Todmorden AS

Secretary – D. Howorth
42 Hallroyd Crescent, Todmorden
Tel: 070 681 4443

Membership – Unrestricted
Year Formed – 1935
No. of Members – 280 + 250 juniors
Facilities – Fishing on two trout lakes one coarse lake and 7 miles of Rochdale Canal

Withnell A.C.

Secretary – D. Hough
1 Lodge Bank, Brinscall, Nr. Chorley

Membership – Restricted
No. of Members – 250 +
Facilities – Croft Lodge, Brinscall — Stock with carp, roach, tench, perch. Cricket Fi Lodge, Withnell Fold — roach, bream. Perrite Lodge, Chorley — carp, roach, br perch and various small ponds in Withnell

LEICESTERSHIRE

Asfordby Society of Anglers

Secretary – H. Birch
Asfordby, Melton Mowbray
Tel: 0664 812364

Membership – Restricted to 12 mile radius Junior membership available
Year Formed – 1963
No. of Members – 350
Facilities – Fishing on 60 and 20 acre grav pits at Asfordby and Frisby, River Wreake North Gullet, Rivers Glen and Eau. River Wreake, only available to hire for matches maximum 100 pegs.

Bottesford and District AA

Secretary – Clive George
14 Pinfold Lane, Bottesford, Nottingham
Tel: 0949 43357

Membership – Unrestricted. Junior membership available
No. of Members – 300
Facilities – The Grantham canal between t Rutland Arms Inn Woolsthorpe-by-Belvoir and Redmile Bridge, Leicestershire. Up to pegs available on canal for matches.

Douglas Bader AC

Secretary – L.H. Barnsley
25 West Avenue, Leicester
Tel: 0533 704142

Membership – Restricted
Year Formed – 1970
No. of Members – 21
Facilities – Fishing on small private lake.

Hinckley AC

Secretary – John Evans
6 Azalea Drive, Burbage, Hinkley
Tel: 0455 614266

Membership – Unrestricted
Year Formed – 1922
No. of Members – 500
Facilities – 5 miles of Ashby-de-la-Zouch
Canal, ¾ mile River Sence and three small
local pools. Bream, Carp, Tench, Roach and
Perch may be caught in the canal.

Leicester AS

Secretary – P.A. Jayes
Alton Road, Leicester Tel: 0533 832045

Membership – Unrestricted
Year Formed – 1876
No. of Members – 500 + 500 Juniors
Facilities – Fishing on Leicester Canal and
stretches of Rivers Bime and Soar.

Leicester & District Amalgamated Society of Anglers

Secretary – L.H. Barnsley
5 West Avenue, Leicester
Tel: 0533 704142

Membership – Unrestricted
Year Formed – 1905
Facilities – Fishing on Rivers Soar, Wreake,
and Nene also Ashby Canal and Grand Union
Canal

Leicester & District Multiple Sclerosis AC

Secretary – L.H. Barnsley
West Avenue, Leicester Tel: 0533 704142

Membership – Restricted
Year Formed – 1970
No. of Members – 21

Loughborough Soar AS

Secretary – M. Downs
3 Alan Moss Road, Loughborough
Tel: 0509 68472

Membership – Unrestricted. Junior
membership available
Year Formed – 1865
No. of Members – 920
Facilities – Fishing on River Soar and Grand
Union Canal also Kegworth and Barrow
Locks. Matches can be booked on the Sutton
Bonington Normanton stretches.

Market Harborough & District Society of Anglers

Secretary – J.W. Ashton
Connaught Road, Market Harborough
Tel: 0858 67301

Membership – Unrestricted
Year Formed – Circa. 1900
No. of Members – 225 + 250 Juniors
Facilities – 6½ miles stretch of Grand Union
Canal at eight access points. Car parking
facilities. Disabled angling clubs allowed free
fishing if Secretary notified.

Measham & District AC

Secretary – J. Wainwright
6 The Square, Oakthorpe, Nr. Burton on
Trent DE12 7QS
Tel: 0530 71408

Membership – Unrestricted. Junior
membership available
Year Formed – 1950
No. of Members – 400
Facilities – Fishing on 1½ miles of Ashby
Canal and 2 miles of River Mease.

Quorn AS

Secretary – P. Hearn
272 Park Road, Loughborough
Tel: 0509 68483

Membership – Unrestricted
Year Formed – 1935
No. of Members – 400
Facilities – Fishing on middle reaches of River
Soar.

Shackerstone & District AA

Secretary – Mrs. B.M. Andrews
6 Church Road, Shackerstone, Nuneaton
Tel: 0827 880480

Membership – Unrestricted
Year Formed – 1927
No. of Members – 500 + 275 Juniors
Facilities – 7½ miles of Ashby Canal. Well
stocked with tench, roach, bream and carp.

Soar Valley Specimen Group

Secretary – L. Culley
16 Windsor Close, Quorn
Tel: 0509 43797

Membership – Restricted
No. of Members – 8
Facilities – Fishes locally and distant waters
for big fish of all species.

Stapleford Park AC

Secretary – R. Ecob
9 Mortimer Road, Melton Mowbray
Tel: 0664 5048

Membership – Restricted
No. of Members – Approx. 70

Sutton Bonington AS

Secretary – M. Moseley
39 Far Lane, Normanton on Soar,
Loughborough
Tel: 0509 843035

Membership – Unrestricted
Year Formed – 1936
No. of Members – 85 – 100
Facilities – The Cliffs

Wreake Valley Specimen Group

Secretary – Kevin Stephenson
3 Wayfarer Drive, East Goscote
Tel: 0533 607198

Membership – Restricted
No. of Members – 6 Maximum
Facilities – As many waters as possible locally
and all over the country in search of large
specimens.

Uppingham & District AS

Secretary – D.L. Johnson
3 High Street East, Uppingham, Rutland
Tel: 057 282 2334

Membership – Unrestricted
Year Formed – 1953
No. of Members – Approx. 300
Facilities – Approximately 10 miles of Upper
River Welland. The river is about 30ft. wide
with shallow glides and deep pools, stocked
with chub, roach and dace also bream, tench,
carp, pike and eels.

LINCOLNSHIRE

Boston & District AA

Secretary – J.D. McGuire
6 Churchill Drive, Boston PE21 0NH
Tel: 0205 64949

Membership – Unrestricted. Junior
membership available
Year Formed – 1890
No. of Members – 4,892
Facilities – Fishing on Bargate and Sibsey
Trader drain. Bellwater hobhole and West
Fen Drains. River Glen, Bourne Eau, River
Witham, River Steeping, Steeping relief
channel, Louth Canal, Fossdyke Canal and
south part of Forty Foot Drain. Match
applications for drains to Secretary. River
Glen confined to affiliated clubs only. Other
waters apply to R.H. Hobley, 30 Gunby Ave,
Lincoln.

Deeping St. James AC

Secretary – J. Cran Esq.
53 Castle Drive, Northborough, Peterborough
PE6 9DL Tel: 0778 343691

Membership – Restricted within 20 miles
No. of Members – 331 + 400 Juniors and OAP's
Facilities – River Welland (Market Deeping
Several Fishery) available for matches.

East Midland AF

Secretary – W.J.C. Hutchins
63 Huntingtower Road, Grantham

Membership – Restricted
No. of Members – Federation of 9 clubs
Facilities – Stretches of River Eay and River
Glen — both banks.

Gainsborough & Trentmans AC

Secretary – L. Smithson
42 Haldane Street, Gainsborough

Membership – Restricted
Year Formed – 1964
No. of Members – 20
Facilities – Stretches of River Trent at
Collingham.

Horncastle AC

President – S.A. North
23 Queen Street, Horncastle
Tel: 06582 2402

Membership – Restricted
Year Formed – 1880
No. of Members – 85
Facilities – Fishing on Horncastle Canal and two brick pits..

Lincolnshire Anglers Consultative Assoc.

Secretary – J.D. McGuire
6 Churchill Drive, Boston
Tel: 0205 64949

Membership – Unrestricted
Year Formed – 1951
No. of Members – 20,000
Facilities – No fishing rights. Body who liaises between the Licence Holders and Anglian Water Authority.

Lincoln & District AA

Secretary – A.D. Gilbert
Tel: 0522 685709

Membership – Unrestricted
Year Formed – 1868
No. of Members – 6,321
Facilities – Fishing on Rivers Trent and Witham, three lakes with area of 35 acres also Old River Witham, Wainfleet Relief channel, Steeping River, Rivers Till, Skerth, Barlings and Fossdyke and Swanholme Lakes Complex.

Louth L.A.W.A.C.

Secretary – G. Allison
15 Florence Wright Avenue, Louth
Tel: 0507 602587

Membership – Unrestricted
Year Formed – 1929
No. of Members – 60

Stamford Welland AA

Secretary – G.E. Bates
16a Austin Street, Stamford
Tel: 0780 51060

Membership – Unrestricted
Year Formed – 1878
No. of Members – 400
Facilities – Fishing on 22 miles of upper River Welland.

Witham & District Joint AF

Secretary – R.H. Hobley
30 Gunby Avenue, Hartsholme Estate, Lincoln
Tel: 0522 683688

Membership – Unrestricted
Year Formed – 1914
No. of Members – 40,000 +
Facilities – Fishing on 120 bank miles including River Witham, River Steeping, Wainfleet Relief Channel, Fossdyke Canal, Billinghay Skirth and Timberland Delph — all good mixed coarse fishing. Swanholme lakes at Lincoln — fly fishing for trout.

Witham Valley Specimen Group

Secretary – T. Richardson
3 The Smooting, Tealby

MERSEYSIDE

Brunswick AC

Secretary – Peter Hatton
42 Thornholme Crescent, Liverpool 11
Tel: 051 256 8975

Membership – Restricted
Year Formed – 1950
No. of Members – 12
Facilities – Montgomery canal Lannymynech between bridges 92-94.

Crosby & District AC

Secretary – M. Cain
40 Buttermere Gardens, Crosby, Liverpool, L23 0SF
Tel: 051-928 9364

Membership – Unrestricted. Junior membership available
Year Formed – 1971
No. of Members – 60
Facilities – No Club Waters, but members of Liverpool and Dist. AA, and N.F.A. Outings held on alternate Sundays, by coach to venues within approx. 100 mile radius. Meetings fortnightly which are well attended because of features such as talks, films, etc.

Hutton & District AA

Secretary – H.O. Palmer
143 Blue Bell Lane, Hutton
Tel: 051 489 4819

Membership – Restricted
Year Formed – 1886
No. of Members – 60
Facilities – River Dee, Bowling Bank, Nr Wrexham, North Wales

Irby AC

Secretary – Frank Evans
4 McAlpine Close, Upton, Wirral L49 6JR
Tel: 051 678 7619

Membership – Unrestricted
Year Formed – 1967
No. of Members – 600
Facilities – 25 Small lakes and ponds (Wirral area) (S.U.C. at Aberbechan). River Severn Aberbechan (small stretches). Montgomery Canal, Aberbechan, Bridge Nos. 150-153 available to hire for matches.

Liverpool City AA

Secretary – A.G. Chapman
50 Crosswood Crescent, Huyton, Liverpool L36 2QG
Tel: 051 480 9007

Membership – Unrestricted
Year Formed – 1900
No. of Members – 65
Facilities – 3½ miles River Vyrnwy, Llanymynech. N. Wales.

Liverpool & District AA

Secretary – Mr. John Johnson
97 Liverpool Road, Maghull
Tel: 051 526 4083

Membership – Unrestricted
No. of Members – 1500
Facilities – 30 mile stretch of the Leeds & Liverpool Canal between Liverpool and Halsall. 99 miles of the Shropshire Union Canal and a stretch of the Rufford Canal between Burscough and Tarleton. Various other waters. Contact club Secretary for more details.

Maghull & Lydiate AC

Secretary – J. Johnson
97 Liverpool Road, (North) Maghull
Tel: 051 526 4083

Membership – Unrestricted
Year Formed – 1911
No. of Members – 182
Facilities – Swan Pool, Liverpool Road Aughton, Burscough Brickworks, Abbey Lane Burscough, Barton Brook, Altcar Merser's Pool, Bells Lane, Lydiate Ainsdale Lake, Ainsdale, Lands, Moss Lodges, Skelmersdale (Joint ownership with Skem. Comrades).

Newton-le-Willows AA

Secretary – Edward Marcroft
4 Horridge Avenue, Newton-le-Willows
Tel: 09252 5680

Membership – Unrestricted
Year Formed – 1974
No. of Members – 821
Facilities – Our water is the Sankey St. Helens Canal. Approx. 1 mile at Newton-le-Willows in a low lying picturesque setting. It is split into two pounds, upper and lower. The lower pound offers good all round sport with over 70 pike caught this year. The upper pound offers excellent all round coarse fishing throughout the year including all species.

Orrell AC

Secretary – D. Bushell
62 Melwood Drive, Liverpool L12 8RW
Tel: 051 228 4522

Membership – Unrestricted
Year Formed – 1954
No. of Members – 44 Seniors, 7 Juniors
Facilities – 2 Miles off The River Perry. Near Montford Bridge.

Southport & District AA

Secretary – C. Russell
41 Longacre, Southport
Tel: 0704 213521

Membership – Restricted
Year Formed – 1906
No. of Members – 300
Facilities – River Crossens and Tributaries, Nr. Southport. Canalised Drainage Waterways. Permits issued for ½ mile of R. Crossens at banks near Southport.

St Helens Specimen Group

Secretary – R. Pendleton
32 Surrey Street, Parr, St Helens

ORFOLK

sham & District AS

etary – K. Sutton
own Lane, Aylsham
026 373 2433

bership – Unrestricted
Formed – 1953
of Members – 80
ities – 1 mile Upper Bure. 1 mile Upper
2 acre clay pit.

ndon & District AC

etary – Peter Cooper
igh Street, Feltwell, Thetford IP26 4AF
0842 828448

bership – Unrestricted. Junior
bership available
Formed – 1945
of Members – 75
ities – Waters on the River Little Ouse.
h Bank – Downstream from Wilton
ge, Lakenheath, to a point opposite old
of the Green Dragon (known as the Wash)
ox. 3 miles. Blackdyke. At the end of the
rete fen drove. Pumping Station — the
to the west of the pumping station to the
bridge. Available for hire to local clubs

adland Specimen Group

etary – V. Bellars
e Trees, New Road, Fritten, Great
outh

eham AC

etary – H.E. Mortram
am Road, Matteshall
surer – Mr. B. Fanthorpe
Neatherd Road, Dereham
0362 2094

bership – Unrestricted
of Members – 800

s & District A.C.

etary – Mr. M.R. Howard
sefield Road, Diss, Norfolk
0379 51494

bership – Unrestricted
of Members – 500
ities – Club waters on Waveney and also
ss Mere. Most species of coarse fish may
aught.

enham AC

etary – Mr. G. Twite
ack Street, Hempton, Fakenham, Nr.
nham
0328 63109

bership – Unrestricted
of Members – 200 +
ities – Fishing for Brown Trout (up to 2½
nd Dace (up to 12 oz) and also Roach
1½ lbs) on the River Wensum.

leston Wortwell & District AC

etary – Mrs. C. Smith
grims Way, Harleston
0379 853400

Membership – Unrestricted. Junior
membership available
Year Formed – 1940
No. of Members – 500-600
Facilities – 4 gravel pits at Weybread (North
Suffolk) near Harleston, Norfolk 5-6 miles of
the upper River Waveney near Harleston.
(Needham, Shotford, Mendham, Homersfield,
Denton). 2 miles of the tidal River Waveney at
Dunburgh, Gillingham Beccles. Weybread
No. 1 Pit, Weybread, Suffolk (near Harleston)
58 pegs available to hire for matches. River
Waveney at Beccles 60 pegs Dunburgh, 40
pegs available for matches.

Kings Lynn AA

Secretary – G.T. Bear
1 Cock Drove, Downham Market
Tel: 036 63 87114

Membership – Unrestricted. Junior
membership available
Year Formed – 1881
No. of Members – 500
Facilities – River Ouse. River Wissey,
Tottenhill Pits, middle level part of Stradset
Lake — Fosters End Pits. Babingley river.
Waters available to hire for matches.

Swaffham AA

Secretary – W.A. Boughen
3 Adastral Place, Swaffham, Norfolk
Tel: 0760 23312

Membership – Unrestricted
No. of Members – 272
Facilities – Two lakes at Broadmoor Common,
Pentney which are well stocked with coarse
fish.

Wroxham & District AC

Secretary – R. Westgate
32 St. Olaves Road, Norwich NR3 4QB
Tel: 0603 401062

Membership – Restricted
No. of Members – 150

NORTHAMPTONSHIRE

Britannia AC

Secretary – C.W. Gray
3 Coverack Close, Delapre, Northampton
NN4 9PQ
Tel: 0604 64489

Membership – Unrestricted
Year Formed – 1933
Facilities – Grand Union Canal, Castlethorpe
Bridge 64, to within 100 yards of bridge 62.

Desborough & Rothwell AC

Secretary – C. Parker
33 Eden Street, Kettering
Tel: 912 518316

Membership – Unrestricted
Year Formed – 1960
No. of Members – 200
Facilities – Small pond at Sudborough,
Northants.

Earls Barton AC

Secretary – B.F. Hager
113 Station Road, Earls Barton, Northampton
Tel: 0604 810 888

Membership – Unrestricted. Junior
membership available
Year Formed – Before 1890
No. of Members – 100
Facilities – 2 miles of the River Nene, from
White Mills Lock to Harwater Mill Lock,
(South Bank). The Dam, a 300 yd. stretch of
still water. Also a section of the River Nene
upstream of White Mills Lock at Earls Barton
— inc. back streams.

Irthlingborough AC

Secretary – P.W. Pratt
7 The Shortlands, Irthlingborough,
Northampton
Tel: 97 651137

Membership – Unrestricted
Year Formed – 1934
No. of Members – 400
Facilities – Approx. 2 miles of River Nene and
6 acre lake. The lake is not fully established
but still holds good rudd, roach and pike.
The river is improving, and is expected to
reach it's former glory of the sixties.

Northampton Nene AC

Secretary – S.H. Battison
36 Church Way, Weston Favell, Northampton
Tel: 0604 409 361

Membership – Unrestricted
No. of Members – 2000
Year Formed – Pre-1881
Facilities – Extensive stretches of the River
Nene in and around Northampton plus a
number of lakes

Rushden, Higham Ferrers & Irchester AA

Secretary – A. Webster
10 Barrats Close, Higham Ferrers

Membership – Unrestricted
No. of Members – 700
Facilities – Coarse fishing on some local rivers
and lakes. Strong match team.

Towcester & District AA

Secretary – I. Findull
62 Jenkinson Road, Towcester

Membership – Restricted
Year Formed – 1936
No. of Members – 500
Facilities – Approx. 7 miles River Tove and 5
small ponds.

Wellingborough & District Nene AC

Secretary – G.W. Barker
139 Knox Road, Wellingborough
Tel: 0933 22 3823

Membership – Unrestricted
Year Formed – 1869
No. of Members – 1500
Facilities – Day Ticket on Wellingborough
enbankment, (Nene). Nene — Two miles
upstream and 3 miles downstream of
Wellingborough. Nene — 300 yards Denford
Nr. Thrapston. Back Brook 1 mile plus.
Section of Nene 800 yards near Oundle. 700
yards Nene Barnwell Estate Water. R. Ouse at
Harrold 800 yards. Ditchford Lakes shared
with Rushden AC Sywell Res.

NORTHUMBERLAND

Bedlington & Blagdon AA

Secretary – S. Symons
8 Moorland Drive, Bedlington
Tel: 0670 822011

Membership – Restricted
Year Formed – 1956
No. of Members – 125
Facilities – River Blyth. Mid Northumberland. From Stannington village to Bedlington. Both banks with the exception of two small stretches on one bank which are privately owned. River consists of streams, flats, and deep pools gravel & rock bottom. Sea trout brown trout, grayling, perch, roach.

Big Waters Angling Club

Secretary – D. Emson
134 Salters Road, Gosforth, Newcastle upon Tyne NE3 3UP

Membership – Unrestricted. Junior membership available
No. of Members – 400
Facilities – River Tyne at Newburn, Marden Quarry Pond, Kimmer Lough, The Tweed Coldstream, The Till, Tiptoe, Ancrfot Ponds.

Chatton AA

Secretary – A. Jarvis
New Road, Chatton, Alnwick
Tel: 066 85 257

Membership – Restricted
Year Formed – 1911
No. of Members – 125
Facilities – Agricultural area. Clear water. All of Duke of Northumberland's preserves of River Till.

Glendale Grayling Club

Wooler

Facilities – Fishing on River Till, Breamish.

Ladykirk & Norham Improvement A

Secretary – R.G. Wharton
8 St. Cuthbert's Square, Norham, Berwick-on-Tweed
Tel: 0289 82467

Membership – Restricted to area. Junior membership available.
No. of Members – 30
Facilities – River Tweed only for Brown trout, grayling and roach.

NOTTINGHAMSHIRE

Barnstone Welfare A. Section

Chairman – Dr. P.B. Layne
Blue Circle Industrial, Experimental Plant & Products Dept, Barnstone Works, Barnstone
Tel: 0945 60501

Membership – Restricted
Year Formed – 1970
No. of Members – 49

Facilities – The water is a flooded worked-out quarry on the works site, established for about 15 years. It contains tench, carp, pike, bream, roach, perch, and rudd including specimen size fish (carp 22lb +, tench 7lb +, pike 32lb, bream 8lb +, roach 2lb +). Area of water can hold up to 150 anglers simultaneously. Children 15 or under are only permitted with an adult ticket.

Bottesford & District AA

Secretary – B.C. Cross
12 The Square, Bottesford

Membership – Unrestricted
Year Formed – 1890
No. of Members – 250
Facilities – Approx. 5 miles of the Nottingham Grantham Canal and a short stretch of The River Devon at Elston Grange.

Bridon Wire AC

Secretary – P. Ware
67 Albert Road, Retford
Tel: 0777 705748

Membership – Restricted to works members and associates
No. of Members – 40
Facilities – River Idle Fishery. River Trent. Two stretches of the River Idle are available for matches anytime. Thrumpton 25 pegs and Hardmoors 20 pegs.

Clipstone Colliery AC

Secretary – F.W. Welch
45 Seventh Avenue, Clipstone, Mansfield
Tel: 0623 34924

Membership – Unrestricted
No. of Members – 50
Facilities – Vicar water, approx. 7 acres.

Collingham AA

Secretary – J. Wilson
93 Breamer Road, Collingham, Newark
Tel: 0636 892700

Membership – Restricted
Year Formed – 1900
No. of Members – 200
Facilities – River Trent — right bank from Cromwell Weir to Besthorpe Parish Boundary, (except 2 short fields at Jolly Bargeman), approx. 4 miles.

Earl Manvers AC

Secretary – G.R. Dennis
29 Deabill Street, Netherfield
Tel: 0602 240201

Membership – Restricted
Year Formed – 1952
No. of Members – 70
Facilities – The water is known as Long Higgin. It is well known for it's open matches. It contains most fish — Roach, carp, chub, barbel, bream, bleak, gudgeon, perch. It is deep, 15 ft. in places. Waters hired out for matches. Maximum of 50 pegs.

Grafton AA

Secretary – Mr. K. Hill
102 Cavendish Road, Worksop
Tel: 0909 476944

Membership – Restricted to 25
Year Formed – Approx. 1946
No. of Members – 22
Facilities – 3 sections of the Chesterfield Canal (3-4 miles) including 2 locks 3-5 ft. deep, running through Worksop Town. Ty of fish — roach, chub, rudd, eels, bream.

Grafton AC

Secretary – Mr. R.A. Mee
157 Anston Avenue, Worksop

Facilities – Part of Chesterfield Canal.

Horse & Groom AC

Secretary – A.A. Bishop
13 Hazel Drive, Larkfield Estate, Nuthall
Tel: 0602 389728

Membership – Unrestricted
No. of Members – 60
Facilities – Erewash Canal Ilkeston. Plenty room for parking cars. Good fishing, carp roach, chub and bream.

Long Eaton Victoria AS

Secretary – D.L. Kent
18 Collingwood Road, Long Eaton
Tel: 06076 64813

Membership – Unrestricted within 20 mile radius
Year Formed – 1880
No. of Members – 650
Facilities – R. Trent — 1 Meadow (Long Eaton), good for chub, roach, but also carp bream regularly caught. R. Soar — 2 stretches — Kegworth & Radcliffe on Soar roach, gudgeon, dace, chub. R. Erewash — Above Long Eaton — developing roach, dace, chub. Erewash and Cranfleet Canals Good mixed fishery — excellent when Trent is in flood. Pond (Long Eaton) — excellent carp fishery and good roach, perch and pi (Strictly members only).

Mansfield & District AA

Secretary – A. Quick
158 Huthwaite Road, Sutton-in-Ashfield NG 2GX
Tel: 0623 511479

Membership – Unrestricted. Junior membership available
Year Formed – 1930
No. of Members – Approx. 800
Facilities – Ell Lake, Rainworth. Members only. Bleasby Gravel Pits, Members only. Both stocked with roach, bream, tench, car pike, perch. Scarcliffe Pond Day tickets. Roach, tench. R. Trent Besthorpe. Redland Gravel washer downstream 70 pegs. R. Tre High Marnham from Brownlow Arms, Clapper Gate upstream one field. Member may also fish Witham and District Federati waters. Wellbeck Lake; members in a 10 m radius of Mansfield only.
R. Trent, High Marnham and Besthorpe available to hire for matches 55 pegs and 7 pegs respectively.

Midland AS

Secretary – J. Bradbury
19 Ethel Avenue, Linby, Hucknall
Tel: 0602 634487

mbership – Restricted
ar Formed – 1908
of Members – 50
ilities – 1½ miles of River Trent.
veringham & Caythorpe. Approx. 12 miles
vn stream from Nottingham called The
ythorpe Stretch, Hoveringham Pastures
d Davisons Slope. Members only other than
tches. Predominantly roach, chub,
dgeon, other species now showing more
quently include perch, carp, bream and
e. Waters available for hire on application
he Secretary to a maximum of 140 pegs.

ttingham AA

retary – E.J. Collin
Radford Bld, Nottingham
0602 877558 or 782601

mbership – Restricted
ar Formed – 1890
of Members – 4000
ilities – River Trent. 6-7 miles bank.
twood Ponds — 4. Ponds in Trent Valley
5. River Derwent & River Soar.

ttingham Co-op Sports A. ction

retary – W.E. Parker
anelagh Grove, Wollaton   Tel: 288423

mbership – Restricted
ar Formed – 1950
of Members – 58
ilities – Small section of River Trent —
ow Trent Bridge at rear of works vehicle
npound. (6 to 8 pegs), 1 mile of River Soar
Ratcliff on Soar near Kegworth from Ford
ards Trent Lock.

ttingham & District F. of AS

retary – W. Belshaw
Springreen, Clifton, Nottingham
0602 216645

mbership – Unrestricted
ar Formed – 1908
of Members – 2000
ilities – All our fishing in the Nottingham
a of the River Trent at Clifton, Holme
rpoint, Radcliffe, Burton Joyce,
anthorpe and Hazelford Ponds at Home
rpoint, Radcliffe and Gunthorpe.

ttingham Stalkers Specimen roup

retary – S. Tytherley
Pearmain Drive, The Wells Road,
tingham

tford & District AA

retary – H. Oxby
Moorgate, Retford DN22 6RS
0777 701090

mbership – Restricted
ar Formed – 1902
of Members – 2,650
ilities – Approx. 5¼ miles Chesterfield
al.

yal Ordnance Factory AS

retary – K. Ingers
Brisbane Drive, Heron Ridge
0602 279241

Membership – Restricted
Year Formed – 1938
No. of Members – Employees of Factory only.
Facilities – Clifton South bank. 900 yards
above bridge, 1000 yards below bridge.
Entrance to waters 30 yards upstream of
bridge. (No parking for vehicles).

Sandiacre Alexandra AC

Secretary – E. Jones
12 Sudbury Avenue, Sandiacre NG10 5DB
Tel: 0602 399287

Membership – Unrestricted
Year Formed – 1941
No. of Members – 40
Facilities – On the Erewash Canal 2 miles
from the Basin Sandiacre to the tip Stanton
Gate.

Shaftesbury AC

Secretary – F.M. Lawrence
2 Rufford Road, Long Eaton
Tel: 0602 66857

Membership – Restricted
Year Formed – 1926
No. of Members – 38
Facilities – Approx. 600 metres of the River
Soar downstream from Ratcliffe Locks near
Kegworth Leics. The water is used basically
for members but the club does allow outside
clubs permission to match fish on vacant
dates. No day tickets issued for individual
fishermen.

Worksop United AA

Secretary – R. Whitehead
72 Dryden Dale, Worksop
Tel: 0623 81962

Membership – Restricted
Year Formed – 1850
No. of Members – 100
Facilities – Chesterfield Canal from Kilton Top
Lock at Bracebridge Worksop to
Humpbacked bridge at Ranby.

OXFORDSHIRE

Abingdon & District ARA

Secretary – R. Pitson
11 Finmore Close, Abingdon OX14 1HF
Tel: 0325 25140

Membership – Unrestricted. Junior
membership available
Year Formed – 1899
No. of Members – 500
Facilities – From Sandford Lock, downstream
including Radley & Nuneham waters approx.
2 miles of River Thames. Situated between
Oxford and Abingdon. Waters available to
hire for matches.

Abingdon & Oxford Anglers Alliance

Secretary – M.J. Ponting
4 Holyoake Road, Headington, Oxford
Tel: 0865 67008

Membership – Unrestricted
Year Formed – 1963
No. of Members – 2800
Facilities – 55 miles of fishing on the Rivers
Thames, Cherwell, Evenlode and Roy. 70
Acres of lakes at Cassington, Dorchester and
Abingdon. All within the area of Oxford,
Abingdon and Clifton Hampden Oxon.

Banbury & District AA

Secretary – P.M. Handley
2 Mannings Close, Sibford Ferris, Banbury
Tel: 029578 491

Membership – Unrestricted
Year Formed – 1892
No. of Members – 1000
Facilities – Extensive stretches of the Oxford
Canal and River Cherwell plus Chattercote
Reservoir and Sourland Pool.

Bicester & District Angling Alliance

Secretary – W. Barker
41 Ruskin Walk, Bicester
Tel: 086 92 43675

Membership – Unrestricted
Year Formed – 1963
No. of Members – 400
Facilities – River Cherwell, River Ray,
Greatmoor Lake, Trow Pool.

Burford AS

Secretary – L. Lavigne
16 Abingdon Close, Court Drive, Hillingdon
Tel: 0895 52208

Chinnor AA

Secretary – B. Helsdown
2 Ravensmead, Chinnor
Tel: 0844 52174

Clanfield AC

Secretary – F. Baston
Mill Lane, Clanfield

Culham AA

Secretary – R. Wiblin
33 Essex Street, Oxford
Tel: 0865 45727

Membership – Restricted
No. of Members – 175

North Oxford AS

Secretary – J. Humm
11 Summerfield, New Hinksey, Oxford
Tel: 0865 45051

Membership – Unrestricted
No. of Members – 900
Facilities – River Thames Godstow Lock to
Carrats Lawn about 4 miles. All nights on
towpath side some on other bank. Very good
chub, bream and roach fishing. Oxford
Canal, Oxford to Kidlington towpath side
good fishing in winter. River Cherwell at
Marston, one lake and a small stream.

Oxford A & PS

Secretary – A.F. Goodchild
44 New Cross Road, Headington, Oxford
Tel: 0865 69763

Membership – Unrestricted. Junior membership available
Year Formed – 1882
No. of Members – 850
Facilities – Dates and venues are available for hire. Contact secretary for details.

Radcot A & PC

Secretary – C.R. Neville
"Clanville", Bampton Road, Clanfield
Tel: 991 81 362 Secretary
991 81 220 Swan Hotel Radcot H.Q.

Membership – Unrestricted. Junior membership available
Year Formed – 1946
No. of Members – 200
Facilities – Radcot on Thames — Trout 1st April — 10th September. Coarse 16th June — 14th March. Available to hire for matches up to 150 pegs.

Remenham AS

Secretary – A.E. Fenn
59 Luker Avenue, Henley-on-Thames
Tel: 049 12 6490

Membership – Unrestricted (nomination and acceptance by committee)
Year Formed – 1938
No. of Members – 150
Facilities – River Thames at Henley.

Witney AS

Secretary – G.C. Kirk
49 Eastfield Road, Witney
Tel: 0993 5920

Membership – Unrestricted
No. of Members – 600

SHROPSHIRE

Big Waters AC

Secretary – M. Taylor
45 Weidner Road, Newcastle 4

Facilities – Marden Quarry, Whitley Bay

Bridgnorth AS

Secretary – T.R. Egan
80 Well Meadow, Bridgnorth,
Tel: 07462 4612

Facilities – 4 mile stretch of the River Severn on the West Bank, 1 mile above Bridgnorth.

Castlefields AC

Secretary – K.J. Ford
31 Albert Street, Castlefields, Shrewsbury
Tel: 0743 63738

Facilities – 2 pools. One mixed one carp only. Discretionary day tickets.

Dawley AS

Secretary – K. Brown
48 Fellows Close, Little Dawley, Telford
Tel: 0942 592611

Membership – Restricted to local people
Year Formed – 1926
No. of Members – 100 full, 350 Hon.
Facilities – 1 mile River Severn at Ironbridge. All common coarsefish, large barbell. 1 Pool (Withy) cat fish, carp, bream, pike. 1 pool (Horsehay). 2 pools Stirchley Pool. Waters available to hire for matches. River Severn maximum 80 pegs. Horsehay and Stirchley Pool maximum 40 pegs.

Ditherington AC

Secretary – G.E. Williams
6 Meadowbrook Cottages, Annscroft, Shrewsbury
Tel: 0743860 835

Membership – Unrestricted
Year Formed – 1930
No. of Members – 200 +
Facilities – Three stretches of River Severn around Shrewsbury. One stretch is owned by Society other two on long lease. All is contest water and is available for away clubs to book. Water holds very good head of barbel, chub, bream, roach, dace. Society has Game fishing on 2 stretches, also available. Also we rent a large pool near Shrewsbury — Sunderton.

Ellesmere AC

Secretary – W. Benkoff
Rose Cottage, Colemere
Tel: 093 922 317

Membership – Unrestricted
Year Formed – 1931
No. of Members – 300-350
Facilities – Rights on local meres and River Vyrnwy at Llanymynech. Private trout pool.

Iron-Bridge AS

Secretary – F. Wilcox
23 & 24 The Wharfage, Iron-Bridge, Telford
Tel: 095 245 3279

Membership – Restricted
Year Formed – 1887
No. of Members – 150
Facilities – Approx. 1 mile, left bank, in Iron-Bridge, and opposite Iron-Bridge Power Station.

Leighton Salmon & Coarse FS

Secretary – F. Wilcox
23 & 24 The Wharfage, Iron-Bridge, Telford
Tel: 095245 3279

Membership – Restricted
Year Formed – 1936
No. of Members – 200

Ludlow AC

Secretary – R.J. Deakin
9 Downton View, Ludlow 378 1JE

Membership – Restricted
Year Formed – 1908
No. of Members – 60
Facilities – River Teme north of Ludlow for some 1½ miles on both banks. Small river containing a good head of chub, dace, roach, grayling, trout and a few pike.

Old L.M.S. AC

Secretary – J.R. Thorpe
13 Hordley Avenue, Heathfarm, Shrewsbur
Tel: 0743 6303

Membership – Unrestricted
Year Formed – Before 1932
No. of Members – 130

Oswestry & District AS

Secretary – W. Jones
55 Laburnum Road, Oswestry

Membership – Restricted
Year Formed – 1928
No. of Members – 250
Facilities – River Vyrnwy. Llanymynech, Maesbrook and Melverley. River Severn Melverley and Nesscliffe. Shropshire Union Canal, Queen Head, Oswestry. Pool, Middleton, Oswestry. Permits are given to holiday makers.

G.K.N. Sankey AC

Secretary – P. Fox
6 Whitemere Road, Wellington, Telford
Tel: 0592 54403

Membership – Unrestricted
Year Formed – 1934
No. of Members – 120
Facilities – Shelton, Nr. Shrewsbury, River Severn. Also Rossal Nr. Shrewsbury, River Severn. Gressage Nr. Wellington, River Severn, Hawk Lake, Hawkstone Park, Hodr Shropshire.

Shifnal AC

Secretary – E. Mountford
"Woodside", Spout Lane, Benthall, Brosele
Tel: 0952 88303

Membership – Restricted
Year Formed – 1950
No. of Members – 100 Senior, 50 Juniors
Facilities – River fishing at Shrewsbury. Fitz Berwick and Buildwas. Canal fishing at Newport and pool fishing at Shifnal.

Shrewsbury & District Piscatoria S

Secretary – K.J. Ford
31 Albert Street, Castlefields, Shrewsbury
Tel: 0743 63738

Membership – Unrestricted
Facilities – Mainly River Severn in Shrewsbury area. Some pools in individual clubs.

Shropshire Anglers Federation

Secretary – P.C. Moody
65 Broadway Avenue, Trench, Telford
Tel: 0952 603779

Membership – Unrestricted – Individuals
Restricted – Clubs
Year Formed – 1923
No. of Members – 2000
Facilities – Coarse and Game, Berwick Est Shrewsbury — River Severn. Coarse only, Rossall Estate, Shrewsbury, River Severn. Coarse and game, Melverley, near Knocki Shropshire. Coarse only, Pentre Nr. Knock Shropshire.

mmerfields AC

retary – S. Harris
urnside, Brookside, Telford
0952 590605

mbership – Unrestricted
of Members – 160 Seniors – 100 Juniors
lities – Trench pool Reservoir, tench,
, roach, bream, perch, pike, dace and
. River Roden approx. ¾ mile at Roden,
, dace, roach, perch and a few pike. Day
ets on Trench pool only. Contests
nged also. Disabled anglers welcome on
ch Pool.

lford AA

retary – J. Sullivan
eckbury, Shifnal
095 287 334

m AC

retary – R.A. Salisbury
e Paddock, Whitchurch Road, Wem
0939 33720

mbership – Unrestricted at the committee's
cretion
r Formed – 1947
of Members – 230
lities – Hawk Lake is a long narrow lake of
ut one mile long. This is a day permit
er where they can be obtained from the
k off the Bailiff. We also lease two small
tches on the River Severn and one small
tch on the River Roden.

hitchurch AA

retary – B.W. Young
Smallbrook Road, Whitchurch
0948 2656

of Members – 100 +
ilities – Fenns pools: Sheaf pool 80 pegs,
pool 40 pegs, coarse fisheries. Roach,
am, tench, perch, rudd, eel, pike.

OMERSET

thampton AA

retary – A. Adams
Beech Avenue, Shepton Mallet
: 0749 3021

mbership – Unrestricted
r Formed – 1920
of Members – 3,500
ilities – Coarse fishing on the Bristol Avon
ten ponds and lakes in Bath and the
rounding area. Trout fishing on the
utaries of the Bristol Avon.

idgwater AA

retary – P.D. Summerhayes
aleigh Close, Bridgwater
0278 424118
licity Officer – R. Perrett
Weston Zoyland Road, Bridgwater
0278 56340

mbership – Unrestricted
r Formed – 1905
of Members – In excess of 1840

Facilities – Virtually all waters within a ten
mile radius of Bridgwater, including Huntspill
and Cripps Rivers, South Drain, Kings
Sedgemoor Drain, Bridgwater and Taunton
Canal between the River Parrett and bridge
on A361. Local Rhynes and ponds. Season,
period (7 days) and day tickets are all entitled
to use all waters and are listed on licence.

Chard & District Angling Club

Secretary – D. Lemon
38 Glanvill Avenue, Chard TA20 1EU
Tel: 0460 61281

Membership – Unrestricted. Junior
membership available
No. of Members – 150
Facilities – Coarse fishing at Perry Street
Pond, Perry Street, nr. Chard and Ash Pond,
Ash nr. Martock. Coarse and trout fishing at
River Isle at Donyatt and Ilminster, and River
Axe, Broom Bridge, nr. Chard.

Cheddar AC

Secretary – N.C. Cordery
'Applegarth' Mill Lane, Wedmore
Tel: 0934 712021

Membership – Unrestricted
No. of Members – 200
Facilities – Fishing on the River Axe, Hixham
Rhyne, North Drain and Cheddar Clay Pits.

Frome & District AA

Secretary – R.J. Lee
103 The Butts, Frome BA11 4AQ
Tel: 0373 61433

Membership – Unrestricted
Year Formed – 1931
No. of Members – 350
Facilities – Approx. 7 miles of the River
Frome above town and below — a mixed
coarse fishery. A small trout stream and 1
lake containing tench, bream, roach etc.

Ilchester & District AA

Secretary – R.M. Hughes
32 St Cleers Orchard, Somerton
Tel: 0458 72128

Membership – Unrestricted. Junior
membership available
Year Formed – 1957
No. of Members – 280
Facilities – River Yeo Ilchester, members also
permitted to fish Wessex Federation of
Anglers water, river Parret, Isle Langport and
shared water Westmoor/Southmoor, Thorney
Moor and Long Load drains Langport area.

Ilminster & District AA

Secretary – A. Green
10 Hill View Terrace, Ilminster
Tel: 04605 3363

Membership – Unrestricted
Year Formed – 1953
No. of Members – 100 Seniors, 100 Juniors
Facilities – I.D.A.A. control about 6 miles of
water from downstream of Ilminster. The
water holds roach, chub, dace, gudgeon,
rudd and some perch. A relatively fast
flowing river. A better winter river than a
summer one.

Langport & District AA

Secretary – Mrs. I. Barlow
'Florissant' Northfield, Somerton TA11 6SJ
Tel: 0458 72119

Membership – Unrestricted
Year Formed – 1957
No. of Members – 336 Adults & Juniors
Facilities – River Parrett, Yeo Corner to Oath
Lock on opposite bank to that held by Wessex
Federation. Slow to medium flow.

North Somerset Association of AC

Secretary – R. Newton
64 Clevedon Road, Tickenham, Clevedon
Tel: 02755 6107

Membership – Unrestricted
No. of Members – 2000
Facilities – Association of Weston-Super-Mare
& District AA, Highbridge AA and Clevedon
& District FAC.

Stoke-Sub-Hamdon & District AA

Secretary – M. Prescott
'Homemead' Rimpton Road, Marston Magna,
Yeovil
Tel: 0935 850426

Membership – Unrestricted
Year Formed – 1955
No. of Members – 250
Facilities – River fishing, coarse and trout, on
upper reaches of River Parrett.

Taunton Fly FC

Secretary – J.S. Hill
21 Manor Road, Taunton
Tel: 0823 71530

Membership – Unrestricted. Junior
membership available
Year Formed – Pre 1900
No. of Members – approx. 95
Facilities – 10 Miles of River Tone upstream of
French Weir, Taunton. Three separate
stretches totalling 2 miles on River Axe,
Devon.

Westland Freshwater AC

Secretary – B.E. Swain
108 Beechwood, Yeovil
Tel: 0935 28133

Membership – Restricted
Year Formed – 1965
No. of Members – 250
Facilities – Stretch of River Yeo at Mudford.
2 miles. Also a pool at Charlton Mackral.
Good dace and roach. Most other coarse fish
in small quantities.

Yeovil and Sherbourne AA

Secretary – N. Garrett
18 Springfield Road, Yeovil
Tel: 0935 71889

Membership – Unrestricted

STAFFORDSHIRE

Beresfords AC

Secretary – J.W. Robinson
1 Brookside Way, Wilnecote, Tamworth
B77 5LH
Tel: 021 783 3081/0827 54398

Membership – Restricted
Year Formed – 1938
No. of Members – 36

Blackfords Progressive AS

Secretary – T.W. Ponder
4 Long Croft, Huntington, Cannock
Tel: 054 35 6373

Membership – Unrestricted
Year Formed – 1935
No. of Members – 350
Facilities – Calf Heath Reservoir, 20 acres
sited by junction 12 of M6. Mixed coarse
fishery. Membership cards obtainable from
house at lake side and Cannock fishing tackle
shops.

Burslem Isaac Walton AS

Secretary – R.W.H. Burdon
77 Albany Road, Hardfields, Stoke-on-Trent
Tel: 0782 618807

Membership – Restricted
Year Formed – 1900
No. of Members – 100
Facilities – A length of the Caldon Canal to
the North East of Stoke-on-Trent, from Milton
to Hazelhurst Junction.

Burton Mutual AA

Secretary – D.J. Clark
7 Denton Rise, Burton-on-Trent
Tel: 0283 44734

Membership – Restricted
Year Formed – 1884
No. of Members – 1700
Facilities – Trent & Mersey Canal (Wychnor to
Claymills). River Dove apart from a few
hundred yards, Tutbury Weir to River Trent
— both banks including Ox-Bows. Branston
gravel pit. Various small stretches of River
Trent.

Burton-on-Trent Specimen Group

Secretary – R. Johnson
60 Eastern Avenue, Burton-on-Trent

Coton AC

Secretary – J.C. Cross
18 New Road, Coton in the Elms (B.O.T.)
Tel: 0283 761837

Membership – Unrestricted
Year Formed – 1950
No. of Members – 120
Facilities – River Trent, River Mease, Lake
Arrow Pool.

Durber's Tackle Fishing Club

Secretary – J. Durber
8 William Clowes Street, Burslem, Stoke-on-
Trent Tel: 0782 814941

Membership – Unrestricted
No. of Members – 35
Facilities – On affiliated waters i.e. Stoke City
& District Association waters, and anywhere
matches can be arranged on a peg fee basis.

Izaak Walton (Stafford) AA

Secretary – R. Wilton
Brook House, Brook Lane, Brocton
Tel: 0785 661429

Membership – Unrestricted
No. of Members – 1,713
Facilities – Staffs & Worcester Canal
(Stafford), 5 miles. Shropshire Union Canal
(Gnosall) 1 mile. Trent and Mersey Canal
(Nr. Stafford) 1½ miles River Sow (Stafford) 7
miles River Penk (Stafford) 2 miles. 2 Lakes
"Hopton Pools", (6 acres) nr. Stafford).

Kidsgrove & District AA

Secretary – Mrs. B. Rigley
95 Ian Road, Newchapel, Stoke-on-Trent
Tel: 07816 72240

Membership – Unrestricted. Junior
membership available.
No. of Members – Approx. 500 including
juniors
Facilities – Bathpool—Leg-o-mutton
pool—Clough Hall Lake, all at Kidsgrove.
Stoke-on-Trent Macclesfield Canal (Congleton
Station Cheshire Bridge 75 to 72). River Dove
from road bridge A50 at Doveridge
downstream right bank for 1 mile. Congleton
canal available to hire for matches. Apply to
Secretary.

Lamb AC

Secretary – P.H. Atkins
32 Chetwynd Avenue, Polesworth, Tamworth
Tel: 0827 894253

Membership – Restricted
Year Formed – 1928
No. of Members – 300
Facilities – 12 acre pool, mixed fishery. River
Anker, 50 pegs. River Mease 3 stretches,
good chub and roach fishing. River Tame,
new fishery on once heavily polluted river.

Leek & Moorlands FC

Secretary – D. White
20 Campbell Avenue, Leek
Tel: 0538 371526

Membership – Unrestricted
Year Formed – 1885
No. of Members – 600 Senior 500 Juniors
Facilities – Grayling and trout on Manifold at
Hulme End and Dove at Earl Sterndale. Trout
and coarse on Churnet around Leek. Coarse
— Crakemarsh Pool, Nr. Rocester and
Caldon Canal at Leek, Cheddleton and
Froghall.

Lichfield SC

Secretary – D.L. Sheldon
67 Purcell Avenue, Lichfield
Tel: 054 32 22372

Membership – Unrestricted
Year Formed – 1968
No. of Members – 30
Facilities – River Severn, Avon, Trent, Teme.
Under the control of Birmingham Anglers
Association.

Middleport W.M.C. AS

Secretary – K. Reed
63 Boulton Street, Wolstanton, Newcastle-
under-Lyme

Membership – Unrestricted
Year Formed – 1940
No. of Members – 250
Facilities – Canal. Approx. 5 miles in
Middleport to Etruia area. Roach fishing
mainly.

North Staffs Association of Anglers

Official – F. Basset
117 Hartshill Road, Stoke-on-Trent ST4 7NE
Tel: 0782 46633

Stoke City & District AA

Secretary – P. Johansen
31 East Crescent, Sneydgren, Hanley, Stoke
on-Trent
Tel: 0782 24840

Membership – Unrestricted. Junior
membership available
Year Formed – 1880
No. of Members – 700
Facilities – 11 miles Canals. T & M Canal,
Aston-Weston. S.U.C. Gnossall, Shebdon.
Acre lake near Eccershall. Rivers Severn,
Tern, Roden, Rheiw, Sow, Trout Lakes, Fly
only. Available for matches on S.U. Canal
area of Norbury Junction and Woodseaves.
250 pegs maximum.

SUFFOLK

Beccles AC

Secretary – W.D. Holmes
21 Glenwood Drive, Worlingham, Nr. Beccl
NR34 7DR
Tel: 0502 716180

Membership – Unrestricted. Junior
membership available
Year Formed – 1900
No. of Members – 120
Facilities – River Waveney, (certain parts).
Being a tidal water, this provides mainly
roach, bream, perch and pike fishing, from
boat or bank. We also control non tidal
stream at Barsham and hope to acquire righ
to gravel pits in future. Part of River Waven
at Beccles and club water at Barsham
available to hire for matches.

Bungay Cherry Tree AC

Secretary – I.R. Gosling
37 St. Marys Terrace, Fuxton Road, Bungay
NR35 1DW
Tel: 0986 2982

Membership – Unrestricted. Junior
membership available
Year Formed – 1935
No. of Members – 150
Facilities – The club controls three stretches
the River Waveney which are all non-tidal
waters. They also have a large gravel pit
which is well stocked with all species.
Shipmeadow stretch and Two mile stretch ar
available for matches on application to
Secretary.

mlingham & District AC

etary – B. Finbow
e Butts, Debenham, Stowmarket
0728 860123

bership – Unrestricted
of Members – 75
ities – Fishing on the River Deben and
t Lodge Ponds. Good quality tench,
bream, rudd and perch may be caught
e ponds. Quality roach up to 2 lbs and
pike can be caught in the River Deben.

ping Angling Preservation
iety

etary – G. Alderson
lover Close, Ipswich IP2 0PW
0473 211402

bership – Unrestricted, 30 mile radius
Formed – 1868
of Members – 1,200
ities – 10 miles of River Gipping 5 gravel
(owners of one). 1 lake (7 acres), boat
g only. (Club punts available). 1 mile of
r Stour (Essex). Various arrangements on
waters for members.

eat Cornard AC

etary – P. Franklin
Queensway, Gt. Cornard, Sudbury
0787 73766

nbership – Unrestricted. Junior
nbership available
of Members – 120
lities – River Stour, or trips to various
rs or lakes in Suffolk, Essex or Norfolk
. Waters hired out by advanced booking
, some 20-25 swims.

rleston Wortwell & District AC

retary – Mrs. C. Smith
Pilgrims Way, Harleston
0379 853400

nbership – Unrestricted. Junior
nbership available
r Formed – 1940
of Members – 500-600
ilities – 4 gravel pits at Weybread (North
olk) near Harleston, Norfolk 5-6 miles of
upper River Waveney near Harleston
edham, Shotford, Mendham, Hemersfield,
ton) 2 miles of the tidal River Waveney at
nburgh, Gillingham Beccles. Weybread
1 Pit, Weybread, Suffolk, (near
rleston) 58 pegs available to hire for
ches. River Waveney at Beccles 60 pegs
Dunburgh 40 pegs available.

rk Angling & PS

cretary – G.J. Amiss
Cricks Road, West Row, Nr. Bury St.
munds
: 0638 715976

mbership – Unrestricted

ng Melford & District AA

cretary – N. Mealham
Springfield Terrace, East Street, Sudbury
0787 77139

Membership – Unrestricted
Year Formed – 1949
Facilities – Approx. 7 miles of the Suffolk
Stour and tributaries. Top class coarse fishery
heavily stocked with all coarse species (except
barbel). Also some trout on certain stretches.
10 acre gravel pits (Starfield pits) containing
all species and size ranges bream, tench, and
roach to specimen proportions.

Saxmundham Sports AC

Secretary – J.T. Firman
15 Saxon Road, Saxmundham IP17 1ED
Tel: 0728 2638

Membership – Unrestricted
Year Formed – 1969
No. of Members – 200
Facilities – Sibton Lake. Approx. 3 acres
coarse fishing. Carp, tench, rudd. Clay pond
approx. ¾ acre carp, roach, tench

Sudbury & District AA

Secretary – W.J. Gabbey
13 Lambert Drive, Acton, Sudbury
Tel: 0787 71597

Membership – Unrestricted
Year Formed – 1912
Facilities – 2 Pits plus 7 miles of Suffolk Stour
in Clare-Long Melford, Sudbury, Gt.
Cornard and Henny. All fisheries easily
accessible. Good close parking some fisheries
are members only. Most all day ticket. Roach,
bream, tench, dace, chub, pike-zander and
rudd, carp. Some club bookings taken.
Matches most weeks on 1 water only.

Sudbury & District Specimen
Group

Secretary – B. Waldron
10 Lark Rise, Sudbury

Suffolk County Amalgamated AA

Secretary – G. Howard
4 Merrifield Road, Lowestoft
Tel: 0502 4024
Facilities – An association of the leading
Suffolk angling clubs.

Woodbridge & District AC

c/o Rod & Gun Shop
62 The Thoroughfare, Woodbridge
Tel: 039 432377
Secretary – J. Markham Tel: 03943 5315

SURREY

Basingstoke Canal (Surrey) AA

Secretary – M. Hatcher
80 Hillview Court, Guildford Road, Woking
Tel: 048 62 69736

Membership through affiliated clubs.

Byfleet AA

Secretary – L. Chapman
43 Edengrove Road, Byfleet
Tel: 09323 45414

Membership – Restricted
No. of Members – 650
Facilities – Stretches of River Wey

Carshalton & District AS

Secretary – J.F. Humm
39 St. Albans Road, Cheam
Tel: 01 644 2830

Membership – Unrestricted
Year Formed – 1919
No. of Members – 200
Facilities – Stretch of River Mole at
Betchworth

Cobham Court AS

Secretary – P. Aspin
Homelea, Oakfield Road, Cobham
Tel: 093 26 2450

Epsom AS

Secretary – J.C.J. Wood
"Ashlea" 26 Temple Road, Epsom KP19 8HA
Tel: 037 27 24839

Membership – Unrestricted. Junior
membership available
Year Formed – 1890
No. of Members – 332
Facilities – Two stretches of the Rivers Mole
and Wey, at Esher and Weybridge.
Containing a good head of all coarse fish.
Occasional brown trout. Newdigate
Brickworks Fishery.

Fishers Farm AC (F.W.S.)

Secretary – P. Martin
8 Stowell Avenue, New Addington, Croydon
Tel: 0689 41833

Membership – Unrestricted
Year Formed – 1975
No. of Members – 80
Facilities – Have our own stretch of water at
Chiddingstone.

Godalming AS

Secretary – M.R. Richardson
87 Summers Road, Farncombe, Godalming
GO7 3BE
Tel: 048 68 22791

Membership – Restricted
No. of Members – 1000 Senior, 700 Junior
Facilities – River Wey 8 miles. Two coarse
lakes 10 and 6 acres. Carp, tench, crucians,
roach in both. Two trout lakes at Winkworth
Arboretum of 4½ and 5½ acres.

Guildford AS

Secretary – G. Pank
72 St. Philips Ave, Worcester Park
Tel: 01 337 5692

Membership – Unrestricted. Junior
membership available
Year Formed – 1883
No. of Members – 600
Facilities – River Wey — most of the fishing
rights between Broadford Bridge, Shulford to
Triggs Lock, Sutton Green approx. 7 miles of
bank. Also Britten's pond, off Salt Box Lane,
Worplesdon carp lake. Waters available for
exclusive use by visiting clubs are from
Broadford Bridge to Stoke Wier (approx. 2
miles of bank comprising canal and river).

Horley Piscatorial Society

Secretary – D.J. Penny
63 Upfield, Horley
Tel: 029 34 71836

Facilities – 2 stretches of the River Mole and stillwaters.

Leatherhead & District AS

Secretary – R. Boychuk
22 Poplar Avenue, Leatherhead
Tel: 037 23 76771

Membership – Unrestricted
Year Formed – 1946
No. of Members – 653
Facilities – River Mole, approx. 3 mile of bank, 2½ on both banks. 3 Local ponds total 3 acres. Member of Group Angling Alliance, this offers 3 large pits, River Thames and 2 streams.

Leisure Sport AS

Manager – J. Newby
Thorpe Water Park, Staines Lane, Chertsey

Facilities – Extensive waters throughout the Thames Area.

Reigate & District AA

Secretary – Mr. D.J. Watts
20 Priory Road, South Park, Reigate
Tel: 073 72 41977

Membership – Unrestricted
No. of Members – 70
Facilities – Stretches of the River Mole at Bury's Court, Flanchford, Santon, Wonham. Also have stretches of water at Stamford Brook at Worplesdon.

Staines AS

Secretary – G.H. Brown
134 Page Road, Bedfont
Tel: 01 890 0261

Membership – Unrestricted
Year Formed – 1970
No. of Members – 65
Facilities – 3 Gravel Pits and River Colne.

Thames Fisheries Consultative Council

Secretary – A. Leaver
11 Chalgrove Avenue, Morden
Tel: 01 648 5424

Walton-on-Thames AS

Secretary – M.L. Campbell
4 Hennel Close, Dacres Road, London SE23

Membership – Restricted
Year Formed – 1896
No. of Members – 120
Facilities – Private lake and stretch of small stream fishing at Woking. Private lake and stretch of the River Mole at Cobham.

Wey Navigation A. Amalgamation

Secretary – I. Fraser
4 Elmgrove Road, Weybridge KT13 8NZ
Tel: 0932 49230

Membership – Unrestricted
Year Formed – 1968
No. of Members – 500
Facilities – 9 Miles of slow running Wey Navigation Canal from Thames Lock Weybridge, to Newark Bridge Ripley. Holding chub, roach, bleak, gudgeon, carp. Available to hire for matches.

Weybridge AC

Secretary – P. Dayman
61 Byron Road, Addlestone
Tel: 0932 53542

Membership – Restricted
Year Formed – 1900
No. of Members – 450
Facilities – River Wey, 1000 yards upstream of Wey Bridge (Wey Meadows) Roach, Chub, Carp. Wey navigation Canal. Eleven miles beginning at Weybridge (most coarse fish) Broadwater Lake, Outlands Park. (Members only).

Woking & District AA

Secretary – B.E. Candler
58 Nursery Road, Knaphill, Woking
Tel: 04867 81485

Membership – Restricted
No. of Members – 1020

SUSSEX EAST

Clive Vale AC

Secretary – D. Swain
81 Amherst Road, Hastings
Tel: 0424 713240

Membership – Restricted to people living in a 20 mile radius.
Year Formed – 1912
No. of Members – 700
Facilities – Clive Vale and Ecclesbourne reservoirs. River Rother. Day tickets available.

Compleat Angler

Secretary – V.W. Honeyball
The Cottage, Parkland School, Eastbourne
Tel: 0323 54598

Membership – Unrestricted
Year Formed – 1926
No. of Members – 800
Facilities – 20 miles of marsh drains on Pevensey Marshes i.e. Pevensey Haven, Wallers Haven. Approximately 6 miles River Cuckmere. Various other marsh drains and ponds.

Copthorne & DAS

Secretary – F.E. Munro
9 Medway Estate, Turner's Hill
Tel: 0342 715933

Membership – Restricted
Year Formed – 1928
No. of Members – 450
Facilities – Rowfant Millpond, Horse Pasture Lake, Worth, Little Rowfant Lakes, Claypit Godstone, River Eden, Haxted Mead, Cernes Farm, Prinkham Mead, River Arun, Bucks Green, River Mole.

Crowborough & District AA

Secretary – K.J.B. Wilson
'Elysium' 35, Southridge Road, Crowborou
Tel: 08926 4722

Membership – Restricted. Junior membersh
available
No. of Members – 150
Facilities – Local lakes, streams, rivers with
a 15 mile radius of Crowborough Cross.

Hastings Bexhill & District Freshwater AA

Secretary – G. Gutsell
14 Jameson Crescent, St Leonards on Sea
Tel: 0424 421422

Membership – Restricted to a 25 mile radiu
Year Formed – 1895
No. of Members – Approx. 600
Facilities – Local park reservoirs, Alexande
Park, Marsh and Drain waters on Romney
Marsh, affiliated to Rother Fisheries, River
Rother, lake waters at Catsfield Battle,
Wishingtree Reservoir leased from S.W.A.

Rye & District AS

Secretary – A.V. Curd
34 The Maltings, Peasmarsh, nr. Rye
Tel: 079 721 427

Membership – Unrestricted. Junior
membership available
Year Formed – 1920
No. of Members – 150
Facilities – Fishing on the Rivers Tillingham
Brede, and Rother. The latter being a well
known permanently pegged match water.
Most drains and dykes on the Romney Mars
All our waters are in or around Rye. Waters
available for closed events, club and league
matches only.

Seaford AC

Secretary – Mr. B. White
62 Eley Drive, Rottingdean, Brighton
Tel: 0273 38513

Membership – Unrestricted
No. of Members – Approx. 200
Facilities – Waters at Wallers Haven, at
Normans Bay, Old River at South Heighton,
Piddinghoe Pond at Piddinghoe.

South East Specimen Group

Secretary – P. Jones
50 Parsons Close, St Leonards-on-Sea

Wadhurst AC

Secretary – R. Stone
47 Medway, Crowborough
Tel: 08926 4779

Membership – Restricted
Year Formed – 1972
No. of Members – 150

SUSSEX WEST

Ash Angling Match Club

Secretary – P. Carter
83 Longfield Road, Horsham

mbership – Unrestricted
r Formed – 1979
of Members – 20

itish Airport Authority AC

retary – R.J. Patchett
Hardham Close, Ifield, Crawley RH11 0DP
0293 24351

mbership – Restricted
r Formed – 1972
of Members – 63
ilities – All lakes — Members only.

ssocks & District AS

retary – J. Piper
Ockenden Way, Hassocks
07918 4285

mbership – Unrestricted

ywards Heath & District AS

retary – S.F. Whetstone
st View, Lewes Road, Lindfield
6 2LT
044 77 3059

mbership – Unrestricted
r Formed – 1915
of Members – 500
ilities – Approx. 12 Miles of the River
e from Avins Bridge Road to Gold
ge, Newick. Balcombe. 5 Acres Burgess
3 acres.

nfield & District AS

retary – D.W. Newnham
Bungalow, Coombe House Lane, Bolney
7 5SG
044 482 434

bership – Unrestricted
of Members – 400
ilities – Tidal and non tidal River Adur
t 6 miles. One small lake 30 swims.
hester Canal (member Club of the
ciation). Two miles of Brooks at Upper
ing. Members of the Sussex Country AA.

rsham & District AA

retary – N. Farley
urst Avenue, Horsham
0403 60104

bership – Restricted to district of
ham
Formed – Approx. 1910
of Members – 850

worth AC

etary – D.A. Pugh
erry Tree Walk, Petworth
0798 42866

bership – Unrestricted
Formed – 1957
of Members – 200 +

oorough & Steyning AS

etary – M. Booth
th Lane, Houghton, Arundel
079 881 525

Membership – Unrestricted
Year Formed – 1919
No. of Members – 400
Facilities – 3 miles River Arun (Tidal) 1 Mile
River Rother. Bream, roach, chub, dace and
pike main species. 3 Miles River Adur. Same
species. Several small lakes.

Rother AC

Secretary – C. Boxall
4 Half Moon Cottages, Petersfield Road,
Midhurst
Tel: 073081 3897

Membership – Unrestricted
Year Formed – 1953
No. of Members – 300
Facilities – 1½ Miles of Western Rother
upstream of North Mill on South Bank. ¾
Mile of Rother upstream of Woolbeding
Bridge, North Bank. 1½ acre pond at Bepton,
1 Mile S.W. of Midhurst. 1½ acre pond on
north bank of Rother.

Stedham AC

Secretary – P.J. West
25 Park Crescent, Midhurst GU29 9ED

Membership – Unrestricted
Year Formed – 1934
No. of Members – 150
Facilities – Approx. 1 mile of West Sussex
Rother. 1 Small picturesque pond.

Sussex County AA

Secretary – Mrs. J. Cranford
5 Myrtle Terrace, Weavers Lane, Henfield
Tel: 0273 492714

Membership – Restricted

Sussex Specimen Group

Secretary – G. Jenner
60 Cuckmore Crescent, Gossops Green,
Crawley

Victoria AC

Secretary – J. Young
3 Sextant Court, North Beaument Park,
Littlehampton, West Sussex

Membership – Unrestricted
No. of Members – 130
Fishing on the River Arun and Fittleworth to
Shoplane dridge in Sussex.

Worthing & District Piscatorial Society

Secretary – R. Tunicliffe
79 North Lane, Portslade

Membership – Unrestricted
Year Formed – 1953
No. of Members – 650

TYNE & WEAR

Chester-le-Street & District AC

Secretary – T. Wright
156 Sedgletch Road, Houghton-le-Spring
DH4 5JY
Tel: 0783 848211

Membership – Unrestricted. Junior
membership available
No. of Members – 231
Facilities – Various stretches of lower River
Wear plus 5 miles of River Pont,
Northumberland.

North East Specimen Carp Group

Secretary – A. Rowell
59 Brookfields Cres., Chapel House

WARWICKSHIRE

Atherstone AA

Secretary – K. Horton
Glenavon, Dudley Street, Atherstone
Tel: 082 77 2554

Membership – Unrestricted
Year Formed – 1960
No. of Members – 200
Facilities – Approx. 6 miles of River Anker,
(mixed). Stretch of River Trent (Willington)
coarse. Etwall Brook, trout and coarse.

Lawford Lodge Farm FC

Secretary – W.J. Boileau
89 Wyken Avenue, Coventry Tel: 0203 444426

Membership – Restricted
Year Formed – 1953
No. of Members – 22
Facilities – Pit, Lawford Lodge Farm, Church
Lawford, near Rugby — 1 acre.

Royal Leamington Spa AA

Secretary – E.G. Archer
9 Southway, Leamington Spa
Tel: 0926 34185

Membership – Unrestricted. Junior
membership available
Year Formed – 1890
No. of Members – 850
Facilities – 12 Miles Grand Union Canal,
Warwick — Napton. River Leam at
Offchurch; Welsh's Meadow, Victoria Park in
centre of Leamington; River Avon, Guyscliffe,
Wasperton, River Stour at Alderminster. 12
miles of Canal available to hire for matches.

Hazeldine AA

Secretary – J.W. Hazeldine
8 Dudley Road, Sedgley, Dudley DY3 1SX
Tel: 0384 4629

Membership – Unrestricted. Junior
membership available
Year Formed – 1950
No. of Members – 3,500
Facilities – River Severn-Llanymynech.
Welshpool, Worcester, Chaceley. River
Avon, Stratford-on-Avon, Defford, Offenham.
River Mease, Clifton Campville. River Meese,
Tiberton. Shropshire Union Canal. Wheaton
Aston-Gnosall. Staffs and Worcs Canal,
Compton. Membership cards must be
obtained before fishing waters.

Hollingsworth AC

Secretary – J. Hubble
163 Elm Terrace, Tividale, Warley

Membership – Restricted
Year Formed – 1969
No. of Members – 20-25

Stratford-on-Avon AA

Secretary – D. Evason
School House, Ullenhall, Solihull, W.
Midlands B95 5PA
Tel: 05642 3260

Membership – Unrestricted
No. of Members – 495
Facilities – Club fishes on the 4 stretches of
the River Avon and also fishes on the River
Stow.

Warwick & District AA

Secretary – L.C. Sargeant
218 Warwick Road, Kenilworth
Tel: 0926 52769

Membership – Unrestricted
Year Formed – 1921
No. of Members – 700
Facilities – 7 Lengths River Aval. Approx. 8
miles Warwick to Hampton Lucy. Chub,
roach, dace, bream. 1½ Miles River Leam.
Specimen fish water — Cubbington. Length
of Grand Union Canal, Warwick.

WEST MIDLANDS

Beaufort Arms AC

Secretary – E. Bayliss
Richmond Croft, Hamstead, Birmingham

Membership – Restricted
Year Formed – 1945
No. of Members – 30
Facilities – Warwickshire River Avon at
Weston-on-Avon, 440 yards, but strictly club
members only.

Bedworth Ex-Servicemans AC

Secretary – R. Weatherill
6 Alfriston Road, Finham, Coventry CV3 6FN
Tel: 0203 411201

Membership – Unrestricted
Year Formed – 1969
No. of Members – 50
Facilities – No Waters at present. Besac is
affiliated to Birmingham Anglers Association,
and uses B.A.A. waters, and waters
belonging to other assocations for matches.

Birmingham Anglers Association Limited

Secretary – F.H. Bayley
100 Icknield Port Road, Rotten Park,
Birmingham B16 0AP
Tel: 021 454 9111

Membership – Unrestricted. Junior
membership available
Year Formed – 1883
No. of Members – 40,000
Facilities – 400 miles of fishing rights on the
rivers Anker, Arrow, Avon, Banwy, Cherwell,
Clun, Kemp, Ouse, Ithon, Ledwyche, Lugg,
Mease, Monnow, Onny, Perry, Roden,
Salwarpe, Severn, Stour, Swarbourn, Teme,
Tern, Thame, Thames, Trent, Trothy, Wyrnwy
and Wye also pools, gravel pits, canals and
trout fisheries. Waters only available for
matches to affiliated clubs.

Blue Ball AS

Secretary – B. Marsh
34 Hamilton Drive, Wordsley, Stourbridge
DY8 5EX
Tel: 0384 279598

Membership – Restricted
Year Formed – 1952
No. of Members – 40

Brewood AC

Secretary – F. Hodgkiss
290 Wolverhampton Road, Sedgley, Dudley
D43 1RD
Tel: 0902 850395 Headquarters

Membership – Restricted
Year Formed – 1965
No. of Members – Approx. 180 Seniors, 30
Juniors
Facilities – Approx. 50 acres, Chillington. Big
Pool, Chillington Estate, Codsall Wood, 2
Small pools on Chillington Estate, (8 pegs
each.) Clovery Hall Pool (10 acres)
Calverhall, Shropshire. Belvide Reservoir (80
acres), Stretton, Staffs. Approx. ½ mile Staffs
and Worcester Canal, Aldersley Codsall.
Approx. 1 mile Shropshire Union Canal,
Stretton, Staffs. (Guest tickets available to
members).

Caldmore Liberal AC

Secretary – J. Taylor
18 Villiers Street, Palfrey, Walsall WS1 4AW
Tel: 0922 39789

Membership – Unrestricted
Year Formed – 1970
No. of Members – 35

Coventry & District AA

Secretary – P. O'Connor
48 Loxley Close, Wood End, Coventry
Tel: 0203 612880

Membership – Unrestricted
Year Formed – 1914
No. of Members – 9,000

Crossways

Secretary – J. Deathridge
Crossways, College Road, Birmingham B44
Tel: 021 373 0771

Membership – Restricted
Year Formed – 1928
No. of Members – 64
Facilities – Venues on coarse fishing are in the
main on local rivers such as the Severn,
Trent, and the Avon. On sea fishing we have
purchased a 47 seater coach, therefore we
travel to all parts of Great Britain.

Crowhurst/Northfield AC

Secretary – F.W. Pearson
48 Green Acres Road, Kings Norton,
Birmingham
Tel: 021 458 3924

Membership – Unrestricted
Year Formed – 1953
No. of Members – 24
Facilities – Members of B.A.A.

Golden Throstle AC

Secretary – D.D. Phillips
28 Clayerdon Drive, Great Barr,
Birmingham, Warwick
Tel: 021 358 2067

Membership – Restricted
Year Formed – 1968
No. of Members – 40

Goldthorn Social AC

Secretary – E.J. Boleyn
36 Goldthorn Hill, Wolverhampton WV2 3H
Tel: 0902 339564

Membership – Unrestricted. Junior
membership available
Year Formed – 1930
No. of Members – 70

Hazeldine AA

Secretary – J.W. Hazeldine
8 Dudley Road, Sedgley, Dudley DY3 1SX
Tel: 0384 4629

Membership – Unrestricted. Junior
membership available
Year Formed – 1950
No. of Members – 3,500
Facilities – River Severn-Llanymynech.
Welshpool, Worcester, Chaceley. River
Avon, Stratford-on-Avon, Defford, Offenha
River Mease, Clifton Campville. River Mee
Tiberton. Shropshire Union Canal. Wheatc
Aston-Gnosall. Staffs and Worcs Canal,
Compton. Membership cards must be
obtained before fishing waters.

Hollingsworth AC

Secretary – J. Hubble
163 Elm Terrace, Tividale, Warley

Membership – Restricted
Year Formed – 1969
No. of Members – 20-25

Hughes-Johnson AS

Secretary – J.R. Coates
44 Warley Road, Oldbury, Warley
Tel: 021 552 1361 (day-time only)

Membership – Restricted (50)
Year Formed – 1930
No. of Members – 50

James Bridge Copper AS

Secretary – J.H. Bird
35 Simmonds Road, Little Bloxwich, Walsa
WS3 3PV
Tel: 0922 77043/21292

Membership – Unrestricted
Year Formed – 1974
No. of Members – 54

Kinver Freeliners

Secretary – R. Oliver
68 High Street, Kinver, Nr. Stourbridge
DY7 6ER
Tel: 038 483 3255

bership – Unrestricted
Formed – 1971
f Members – 60 Full, 45 Hon.
ities – Coarse, trout and salmon. River
n — Erdington — Bridgnorth — Quatt
veley. Coarse, Staffs — Worcs Canal —
ington — Stewpony — Gothersley.
se and trout, River Solwarpe, Droitwich.
se, River Avon, Wick. Trout, River
lode, Gloucestershire.

er Shenley AC

etary – B.G. Shaw
ove Lane, Gt, Wyrley, Walsall
0922 413893. Office — 0922 28241

bership – Unrestricted
Formed – 1965
of Members – 30 (Limit)
ities – Affiliated Members of Birmingham
Monthly meetings and 8 Contests per

iden Hall AC

etary – W.E. Brooks
enoak, Berkswell Road, Meriden CV7 7LB
0676 22371

bership – Restricted
Formed – 1971
of Members – 65
ities – 1 Acre pool in Meriden Hall
unds, stocked with 6 types of coarse fish,
pike or gudgeon. Visitors are only
ved if accompanied by member and prior
ce is given to Hon. Sec.

enix AC

etary – J.A. Mobley
Greenhill Road, Halesowen
021 422 1161

hbership – Restricted
r Formed – 1967
of Members – 40
ities – 2½ Miles of River Lugg near
eford, (Marden-Moreton). Good mixed
se fishing with some big chub. ¾ miles of
r Vyrnwy near Llanymynech (Salop).
ed coarse fishing with some good trout
occasional salmon. Waters available to
for matches. Up to 60 pegs on River
g, Herefordshire and 25 pegs on River
nwy, Salop. Apply to Secretary.

chmond AC

etary – L. Ball
ea Ford Road, Stechford, Birmingham
9TP

nbership – Restricted
r Formed – 1959
of Members – 35

all Heath Amateur Gardeners

etary – G.W. Beesley
Berkley Road, South Yardley,
ningham B25 8NL
021 772 0892

nbership – Restricted
r Formed – 1935
of Members – 1,200 (club) 42 angling
tion
ilities – River Anchor on the outskirts of
nworth. Good selection of coarse fishing
t Barbel).

Sutton Coldfield Specimen Group

Secretary – T. Barwell
Flat 19 Ayphodel, Hill Hook Road, Sutton
Coldfield

Union Locks AC

Secretary – D.R. Clarke
c/o Josiah Parkes & Sons Ltd.
Union Works, Willenhall
Tel: 0902 66931

Membership – Restricted to employees and
friends only.
Year Formed – 1960
No. of Members – 60 +
Facilities – Small Pool containing roach,
tench, carp and perch.

Whitmore Reans Constitutional AA

Secretary – R.H. Hughes
Star Chambers, Prince's Square,
Wolverhampton
Tel: 0902 25241

Membership – Unrestricted
Year Formed – 1907
No. of Members – Approx. 3000
Facilities – River and Canal fishing in
Staffordshire, Worcestershire, and
Shropshire.

WILTSHIRE

Ashton Keynes AC

Secretary – J. Parker
81 Donnington Road, Wootton Bassett
Tel: 079370 2028

Bradford on Avon & District AA

Secretary – J.B. Webster
Garland Farm, The Midlands, Holt, nr.
Trowbridge
Tel: 022 14 782170

Membership – Unrestricted. Junior
membership available
Year Formed – 1920
No. of Members – 750
Facilities – Middle reaches of Bristol Avon.
Bradford and Trowbridge area, including
tributaries 4½ miles. Kennet and Avon Canal
Avoncliffe to Semington, 4 miles. Provision
for visiting clubs at Barton Farm, Bradford on
Avon.

Calne AA

Secretary – R.J. Reeves
16 Wessex Close, Calne SN11 8NY
Tel: 0249 814516

Membership – Unrestricted. Junior
membership available
Year Formed – 1951
No. of Members – 150
Facilities – Control of most of the River
Marden, tributary of the Bristol Avon between
Calne and Chippenham. Noted for quality
roach and dace also perch, chub, some
bream with occasional tench and carp.
Facilities for disabled anglers.

Chippenham AC

Secretary – Mrs. M. Steel
21 Braemar Road, Calne
Tel: 0249 815903

Membership – Unrestricted
No. of Members – Approx. 400
Facilities – Waters on the River Avon. Fishing
for Roach, Dace, Chub and Tench.

Devizes AA

Secretary – B.K. Nisbeck
20 Blackberry Lane, Potterne, Devizes
SN10 5NZ
Tel: 0380 5718

Membership – Unrestricted. Junior
membership available
Year Formed – Early 1900
No. of Members – 568
Facilities – 15 Miles of Kennet and Avon
Canal from Ladies Bridge Wilcot to
Semington Road Bridge.

Horcott AC

Secretary – D. Reeve
82 Okus Drive, Swindon
Tel: 0793 34378

Downton AA

Secretary – Major D.S.M. Mackenzie
Rose Cottage, Charlton All Saints, Salisbury
Tel: 994 21764

Membership – Unrestricted
No. of Members – Approx. 100
Facilities – Fishing on the River Avon, plus
fishing at Charford Lions Fishery.

Isis AC

Secretary – J. McDonald
35 Hawkswood, Covingham, Swindon
Tel: 0793 694613

Membership – Unrestricted
No. of Members – 1,000
Facilities – Stretches of the Bristol Avon and
Thames, plus a number of lakes.

Lavington AC

Secretary – M.D. Gilbert
Gable Cottage, 24 High Street, Erlestoke
Tel: 0380 830425

Membership – Restricted
Year Formed – 1961
No. of Members – 125 Seniors, 75 Juniors
Facilities – Baldham River at Bulkington.
Coarse fishing, no tickets. Worton Brook at
Worton, coarse fishing no tickets. Erlestoke
Lake, coarse fishing day tickets available from
the Secretary or Water Bailif at Badgerland
Cottage Erlestoke or Rod and Reel Tackle
Shop, Devizes.

Swindon Golden Carp AA

Secretary – W. Gunter
65 Redbourne Road, Swindon
Tel: 0793 25753

Membership – Unrestricted
No. of Members – 80

Warminster & District AC

Secretary – D.M.M. Vickers
113 Westleigh, Warminster
Tel: 0985 215858

Membership – Restricted to local residents
Year Formed – 1961
No. of Members – 400
Facilities – 2 Small lakes, Dilton Marsh
containing coarse fish. 2 Large lakes.
Shearwater, Warminster, coarse fish. 1 Mile
River Wyley, trout fly only, Warminster. 1
mile River Brue, Lovington, coarse fish.

Wiltshire Fishery A

Secretary – M.J. O'Lone
c/o Humberts, 8 Rollestone Street, Salisbury
Tel: 0722 27274

Membership – Unrestricted
Year Formed – 1950
No. of Members – 290
Facilities – The Committee of the Association
includes members who have knowledge of
and fish on each of the 6 rivers in area viz:
The Upper Avon, Wylye, Nadder, Ebble,
Bourne and Upper Kennet and the still waters
fished by the various angling clubs. A
watchdog organisation protecting the interests
of riparian owners and fishermen in Wilts.

Wooton Bassett AC

Secretary – T. Strange
15 Shakespeare Road, Wooton Bassett
Tel: 0793 851178

Membership – Restricted
Year Formed – 1961
No. of Members – 200
Facilities – 1½ Acre Gravel Pit (Calne
Wiltshire). 1½ Acre lake (Wooton Bassett)
Brinkworth Brook (Tributary of Bristol Avon).

YORKSHIRE NORTH

Ben Johnson AC

Secretary – T.N. Cunliffe
Ben Johnson & Co. Ltd. Boroughbridge
Road, York YO2 5SS
Tel: 0904 798241

Membership – Restricted Employees and
Employees relatives.
Year Formed – 1947
No. of Members – 30
Facilities – We are an affiliated club to the
York Amalgamation of anglers who control
the fishing and hold the rights for various
local stretches on the Rivers Ouse, Nidd,
Derwent, Rye, Swale, along with 3/4 ponds.
Our own club has no control over any water.

Bishopthorpe & Acaster AC

Secretary – R. Baker
2 Harcourt Close, Bishopthorpe, York
Tel: 0904 706895

Membership – Unrestricted
No. of Members – 30
Facilities – Bridge Fields, River Ouse,
Bishopthorpe, York, 300 yards coarse fishery.

Boroughbridge & District AC

Secretary – G. Whitaker
9 Manor Drive, Kirby Hill, Boroughbridge

Membership – Restricted
No. of Members – 100
Facilities – River Ure. Tickets sold at 1
Topham Post Office Boroughbridge.

Ebor Specimen Group

Secretary – P. Thorpe
3 Pembroke Street, Burton Stone Lane, York
Tel: 0904 20094

Membership – Restricted
No. of Members – 5

Harrogate & Pateley Bridge AC

Secretary – C. Johnson
2 Briggate, Knaresborough
Tel: 0423 863065

Membership – Restricted
No. of Members – 150
Facilities – 1000 m. River Swale — coarse.
1000 m. River Ure — coarse/game.

Harrogate AA

Secretary – R. Pick
3 Norfolk Gardens, Tockwith
Tel: 090 15 445

Membership – Restricted
Year Formed – 1920
No. of Members – 100
Facilities – The club has fishing rights both
banks, river Nidd through Ribston Park Down
to the A1 at Walshford, then left bank through
Hunsingore down to Cattal Bridge.

Helperby AC

Secretary – Mr. J. Wiles Tel: 09016 660

Facilities – River Swale day permits.

Huttons Ambo AC

Secretary – S. King
1 Danby Cottages, Thornton-le-Clay, York
Tel: 065 381 596

Membership – Restricted
Year Formed – 1930
No. of Members – 100
Facilities – Day tickets obtainable from the
post office, open seven days a week. We have
about two miles of fishing in a beautiful
setting. Anglers only. No picnickers.
Occasional ramblers. Famed for back end
roach and dace fishing.

Milton & Norton AC

Secretary – M. Foggin
123 Welham Road, Norton Malton
Tel: 0653 4923

Membership – Restricted
Year Formed – 1920
No. of Members – 250
Facilities – Malton and surrounding area —
Basic coarse fishing (roach, chub, dace,
perch, pike). Although all waters do contain
some trout and grayling. River Derwent.
Local facilities include access to other fishing
— River Rye and Castle Howard Lake.

New Earswick AC

Secretary – M.L. Smith
42 Whitethorn Close, Huntington
Tel: 0480 28230

Membership – Restricted
Year Formed – 1948
No. of Members – 50
Facilities – The New Earswick Angling Cl
have the sole rights to fish a small pond w
is situated in the New Earswick Nature
Reserve. The pond contains pike, roach,
chub, crucian carp, bream, and tench. T
nature reserve is in the village of New
Earswick, on the outskirts of York.

Northallerton & District AC

Secretary – J.G. Easby
24 Quaker Lane, Northallerton DL6 1EE
Tel: 0609 2464

Membership – Restricted
Year Formed – 1920
No. of Members – 500
Facilities – All the clubs' waters for which
permits are available are situated on the R
Swale, central access point is at Morton
Bridge, near Northallerton. Day permits a
available from the village Morton-on-Swal
from 1 May — 28 February annually. The
waters hold mainly chub, pike, barbel, da
grayling, roach and trout. Re-stocking tak
place each year by the club ably assisted
the Yorkshire Water Authority.

Preston Park AC

Secretary – N.G. Wickman
7 Skelwith Road, Berwick Hills,
Middlesbrough TS3 7PT
Tel: 0642 211139

Membership – Unrestricted. Junior
membership available
Year Formed – 1949
No. of Members – 150
Facilities – 2 miles of trout, sea trout and
salmon fishing on River Esk at Danby,
between 5 arch bridge and Danby road
bridge. ¾ mile of coarse fishing plus odd
trout. Good grayling fishing on River Swa
at Gatenby. Between RAF Leeming River
Bridge and Mrs Stubbs water. Coarse fishi
pond in Coatham Stob Lane, near village o
Elton just outside Stockton-on-Tees, room f
about 14 anglers.

Richmond & District AS

Secretary – J. Legge
9 St. Johns Road, Wipswell, Catterick,
Garrison DLG 4BQ
Tel: 0748 833478

Membership – Unrestricted locally
Year Formed – 1912
No. of Members – 300
Facilities – River Swale from Low Oxque to
Great Langton. (Some private water in
between). Trout, grayling, dace, chub and
barbel fishing. Pond fishing also available a
Great Langton and Green Lane Scorton.
Carp, tench, roach, perch, rudd.

Rippon AC

Secretary – A.R. Trees
55 Borrage Lane, Ripon
Tel: 0765 3143

mbership – Restricted
ar Formed – 1831
. of Members – 40
cilities – Lumley Moor Reservoir. Trout —
tickets. River Laver. Trout and grayling
y tickets. River Ure. Trout and coarse. Day
ets River Skell.

edale Specimen Group

cretary – S. Lush
dge Farm, Butterwick, Brawley, Malton

carborough Mere AC

cretary – W. Scott
metery Lodge, 30 Dean Road,
arborough YO12 7JN
: 0723 76253

mbership – Restricted. Junior membership
ilable
ar Formed – 1935
of Members – 90
ilities – Scarborough Mere 16 acres. River
rwent 1 mile at Yedingham. River Derwent
iles at Whykham. Scarborough Mere
ilable to hire for matches. Book via
retary.

ipton AA

cretary – J.W. Preston
Beech Hill Road, Carleton, Skipton
23 3EN
0756 5435

mbership – Restricted. Junior membership
lable
r Formed – 1907
of Members – 250
lities – River Aire: 3 miles both banks at
leton & Skipton consisting of good trout
ng together with coarse fish in the deeper
ths. River varies from shallow, swift
ing water to deep, slow moving water in
ower reaches. Embsay Reservoir: 23
s trout only. Whinnygill Reservoir: 6
s trout and roach. Jennygill Reservoir: ½
trout only.

dcaster Angling &
eservation Association

cretary – D. Wilkinson
andfield Terrace, Tadcaster LS24 8AN
0937 834610

mbership – Restricted
r Formed – 1887
of Members – 160
lities – Good coarse fishing. We cater for
permit anglers and match anglers.
rox. 2½ miles of the Wharfe below
caster on both banks.

ensleydale AA

cretary – H.G. Leyland
Garth, Bainbridge, Leyburn
50210

mbership – Restricted
Formed – 1890
of Members – 94
lities – Approx. 4 miles of the River Yore.
miles of River Bain which is only a small
am. The River Yore is a much bigger river
plenty of pools. We have a small section
nks on Lake Semerwater (coarse fishing).

York & District Amalgamation of Anglers

Secretary – E. Woodward
Tel: 0904 58298

Facilities – Day permits available from:
G.E. Hill, 40 Clarence Street, York. Bulmers
Selling Service, Lord Mayor's Walk, York.
Anglers Corner, Walmgate Bar, York. Hookes
of York, 28 Coppergate, York. Mitre Pets, 214
Shipton Road, York. R.J. & B. Morley, 7
Bishopsthorpe Road, York. The Post Office,
Nether Poppleton, York. C.T. Hoe, Bakers
Shop, Fulford Road, York. The Post Office,
Stamford Bridge. Skip Bridge Filling Station.
Selby Angling Centre, 69 Brook Street,
Selby. P.H. & J.R. Smith, 28 High Street,
Knaresborough. Burton Sports Centre, Front
Street, Pontefract. Fred Alexander, The
Springs, Wakefield. Coates Bros. Sagar
Street, Castleford. E. Everett, 3 Flemingate,
Beverley. D. Holt, Weeland Road,
Knottingley. Roberts, 107 Long Street,
Easingwold. M. Spence, Market Place,
Pontefract. Ken Jackson's, Queen Street,
Morley.

York Youth Fishing League

Secretary – F. Jackson
6 The Glade, York, YO3 0LA
Tel: 0904 31180

Membership – Restricted
Year Formed – 1967
No. of Members – 30-40 per yr. Age 14-18
Facilities – The league is affiliated to York
Amalgamation of Anglers. All our matches
are fished on York water within 15 miles of
York.

YORKSHIRE SOUTH

Bristol Steel Corporation Stocksbridge Works Social Services AC

Secretary – H. Wade
52 Spink Hall Lane, Stocksbridge, Sheffield
S30 5FL

Membership – Restricted
Year Formed – 1953
No. of Members – 350
Facilities – The "Dam" is in a wood alongside
the River Don. We control the Dam (approx.
1 acre in size) and one mile of the River Don
from the bottom of the weir at Cherry Tree
Row to Deepcar Railway Bridge. Stocked with
coarse fish and all our waters are by permit
only. Restricted to outside members within a 6
mile radius of Stocksbridge.

Chapeltown & District AA

Secretary – J.W. Rowlinson
8 Brook Road, High Green, Sheffield S30
4GG
Tel: 0742 848242

Membership – Unrestricted. Junior
membership available
No. of Members – 300
Facilities – Westwood and Newbiggin
Reservoirs. Available for hire to member
clubs, Sunday mornings only.

Coal Industry Social Welfare Organisation

Secretary – J. Wood
25 Huddersfield Road, Barnsley
Tel: 0226 5241

Membership – Unrestricted
No. of Members – Open to general public
Facilities – Wintersett and Cold Hiendley
Reservoirs.

D.C. & M.W.S. Angling Section

Secretary – R. Battersby
83 Willow Road, Thurnscoe, Nr. Rotherham
Tel: 0709 893131

Membership – Unrestricted
Year Formed – 1950
No. of Members – 2000
Facilities – 3 Ponds consisting of about 6 acres
of water, this has been landscaped. Trout are
put in yearly. Also there are mirror, common,
leather and crucian carp, roach, chub,
bream, rudd, tench, perch, silver bream and
eels. Yearly permits are only £1.50.

Eastwood View W.M.C. AA

Secretary – A.W. Stubbs
27 Campbell Drive, Rotherham
Tel: 0709 71456

Membership – Unrestricted
Year Formed – 1970 AA Parent Club 1920
No. of Members – 290 AA Members + over
1000 in Parent Club
Facilities – We are associated with clubs that
control waters on the Rivers Trent, Witham,
Steeping, Yorkshire Ouse, and Lakes. Club
facilities include lounge, games and snooker
rooms and large concert hall which is
available for prize presentations, dancing etc.

Flanshaw AS

Secretary – L.D. White
Tel: 0924 66432

Facilities – River Dearne

Harlequin AC

Secretary – T.H. Haywood
25 Willow Grove, Thorne, Nr. Doncaster

Membership – Unrestricted
Year Formed – 1976
No. of Members – 35
Facilities – Trent, Winthorpe Lake, South
Forty Foot, Ancolme.

L.N.E.R. AC

Secretary – H.F. Smallman
35 Sycamore Road, Mexborough S64 9EW

Membership – Unrestricted
Year Formed – 1950
No. of Members – 43 + Permit holders
Facilities – The Watercourse of the Old River
Dearne, Pastures Road, Mexborough. A
stretch of 1 mile after the river had been
diverted, leaving a Spring Fed, slow moving
watercourse. Would be considered for
matches.

Ranmoor Piscatorial Soc.

Secretary – P.R. Cobbold
26 Renshaw Road, Ecclesall, Sheffield
S11 7PD
Tel: 0742 661258

Membership – Restricted
Year Formed – 1960
No. of Members – 130
Facilities – River Idle at Misson and Ordsall,
Nottinghamshire. River Upper Witham at
Long Bennington, Nottinghamshire. Wardlow
Mires, Tideswell, Derbyshire. Ordsall Fishery,
Retford, Nottinghamshire, Caythorpe Fishery,
Lincolnshire.

Sheffield Amalgamated AS

Secretary – A. Baynes
39 Sparken Hill, Worksop S80 1AL
Tel: 0909 474365

Membership – Unrestricted. Junior
membership available
No. of Members – Approx. 2,000
Facilities – River Trent at Girton, River Trent
at North and South Clifton, Waters available
to hire for matches.

Sheffield & District AA Ltd.

Secretary – J.W. Taylor
Reg. Office, 26 Wicker, Sheffield S3 8JB
Tel: 0742 24910. Home 872365

Membership – Unrestricted
Year Formed – 1869
No. of Members – 14,000

South Sheffield Specimen Group

Secretary – J. France
150 Badger Road, Woodhouse, Sheffield

Thorne & Moorends AA

Secretary – J. Armstrong
11 Houps Road, Thorne
Tel: 0405 814151
Facilities – Day permits for the 'Delves' Lake.

West Riding Specimen Group

Secretary – P. Creigton
3 Ashwood Grove, Great Houghton, Barnsley

YORKSHIRE WEST

Aireborough & District AA

Secretary – R. Holgate
64 Leeds Road, Otley LS21 1BT
Tel: 0943 461757
Membership – Restricted
Year Formed – 1900
No. of Members – 200 Seniors, 250 Juniors
Facilities – Yeadon Tarn — Coarse fishing.
Day tickets available, Nunroyd pond —
Coarse fishing, members only. Thorpe
Underwood — River Ouse, coarse fishery,
Members only.

Bingley AC

Secretary – P. Exley
5 Highfield Road, Frizinghall BD9 4HY
Tel: 0274 493409
Membership – Unrestricted
Year Formed – 1946
No. of Members – 600
Facilities – River Aire, Bingley area, 4
stretches (trout/coarse). River Wharfe, Ben
Rhydding and Kerby (trout/coarse). 1 Small
reservoir and 2 dams (trout only). 1 Small
lake (coarse only). As members of Leeds &

Liverpool local canal Association approx. 36
miles of canal available to members. River
Aire, Myrtle Park, Bingley, available for club
matches 30 pegs maximum.

Boston Spa AC

Secretary – A. Waddington
The Cottage, 12 The Village, Thorp Arch,
Wetherby Tel: 0937 842664
Membership – Restricted
Year Formed – 1840
Facilities – 2 Miles of fishing on North Bank,
River Wharfe and 2 miles on South Bank. The
South Bank (Boston Spa) is available on day
tickets from the Spa Baths, Boston Spa. The
river contains trout, grayling, dace, roach,
perch, barbel, chub, pike.

Bradford No. 1 AA

Secretary – C.W. Smith
44 Fleet Lane, Queensbury, Bradford
BD13 2JQ Tel: 0274 815630
Membership – Restricted. Junior membership
available
Year Formed – 1878
No. of Members – 3,216
Facilities – River Wharfe, Aire, Swale, Nidd,
Derwent, Ure, Calder. Also various lakes and
ponds within 45 mile radius of Bradford, plus
approx. 40 miles of Leeds—Liverpool Canal
from Leeds to Bank Newton, Nr. Gargrave.
River Swale Maunby; River Calder available
for 1 match per month. Details from R.W.
Naylor, 2 Fieldhead Drive, Guiseley, nr.
Leeds LS20 8DZ.

Bradford City AA

Secretary – A. Scaife
80 Whetley Hill, Bradford BD8 8NQ
Tel: 0274 47799
Membership – Unrestricted
No. of Members – 4,000
Facilities – River Ure, BoroughBridge,
Roecliffe, Langthorpe, coarse. River Swale,
Topcliffe, mainly coarse. River Ure, Worton,
fly only, trout, Aysgarth trout. River Wharfe,
Buckden, Appletrewick, Addingham, Burley,
mainly trout. River Aire, Bradley, Connonley,
Kilowick, mainly trout. Steeton, mainly
coarse. Reservoirs, Leeming at Oxenhope,
trout. Doe Park coarse, Denholme. Shipton
Lake, mixed.

Bradford Police AC

Secretary – J. Maddon
100 Harbour Road, Wibsey, Bradford
Tel: 0274 6789 39
Membership – Restricted
Year Formed – 1933
No. of Members – 70
Facilities – 2 mill dams in the city of Bradford.
Two acres and a half acre, both contain
coarse fish only (Perch, bream, carp, roach,
tench).

Brighouse AA

Secretary – P.M. Hoyle
155 Foxcroft Drive, Brighouse HD6 3UP
Tel: 0484 714691
Membership – Restricted
Year Formed – 1928
No. of Members – 1,100
Facilities – Brookfoot Lake, Brighouse. 3½
Acre gravel pit. Day ticket and match
bookings. (Carp, bream, roach, perch).
Calder and Hebble canal from Brighouse to
Salter Hebble, approx 5 miles. (Roach,
bream, tench, perch) River Calder, 4
sections. Total length, approx. 2 miles.
(Roach, bream, carp, tench). River Nidd.
Brookfoot Lake: Brighouse available to hire
for matches. Maximum of 40 pegs. Minimum
of 20 pegs.

Dean Clough AS

Secretary – G.R. Crabtree
5 Peabody Street, Lee Mount, Halifax
HX3 5EG
Tel: 0422 51469
Membership – Restricted
Year Formed – 1950
No. of Members – 160
Facilities – 2¼ Miles of Calder and Hebble
Navigation canal, mixed coarse fishery.

Ferrybridge Power Stations

Secretary – C. Greenwood
28 Byram Park Road, Byram, Knottingley
Tel: 0977 82541
Membership – Restricted
Year Formed – 1953
No. of Members – 80
Facilities – Brotherton Ings Pond. Originally
water-logged field which has been excavated
and stocked with roach, perch, tench, bream
and carp.

Hanging Heaton AC

Secretary – Stephen Kemp
35 Princess Road, Chickenly, Dewsbury
WF12 8QT
Membership – Restricted to 65 maximum
Year Formed – 1961
No. of Members – 60
Facilities – Man-made pond at Netherfield
Road, Ravensthorpe, Dewsbury 2 ponds at
Heckmondwike Town Centre.

Huddersfield AA

Secretary – C.A. Clough
38 Holly Bank Avenue, Upper Cumberworth
Tel: 048 488 764
Membership – Restricted
No. of Members – 75
Facilities – Boshaw and Holmstyes, game —
brown and rainbow trout. Longwood, coarse
— pike, roach, perch.

I.C.I. (Organics) Huddersfield A

Secretary – M. Senior
Orchard Farmhouse, Back Lane, Briestfield
Dewsbury WF12 0P8
Tel: 0484 37456 Ext. 214
Membership – Restricted
Year Formed – 1971
No. of Members – 70
Facilities – I.C.I. owned dam known as
Woodhouse Mill Dam, Leeds Road,
Huddersfield. Approx. half an acre. Stocked
with most species of coarse fish.

Ilkley & District AA

Secretary – J.A. Cockerill
31 Grange Estate, Ilkley LS29 8NW
Tel: 0943 608310
Membership – Restricted
Year Formed – 1937
No. of Members – 130 Seniors, 50 Juniors
Facilities – River Wharfe, from the Pack Ho
Bridge down to the Stepping Stones at Ben
Rhydding. Approx. 9 furlongs (both banks)
disused gravel pits, (2) at Ben Rhydding.
River, good trout and grayling fishing.
Coarse, also chub, dace. Gravel pits, carp,
tench, rudd, perch etc.

Keighley AC

Secretary – L.W. Brocklesby
11 Eelholme View Street, Beechcliffe,
Keighley
Tel: 0535 67699
Membership – Unrestricted
Year Formed – 1868
No. of Members – 800
Facilities – Leeds and Liverpool Canal.
Approx. 16 miles on the River Aire (day
tickets). 4 Miles River Worth. Whitefields
Reservoir, Steeton, Roberts pond, Beechcliff

rd River Wharfe (Addingham). Match
g for River Aire only, send S.A.E. Full
rs only.

s & District Amalgamates
ty of Anglers
ary – G. Copley
nt Pleasant, Middleton, Leeds 10
532 705059
ership – Unrestricted
Formed – 1889
Members – 9500
ties – Most Yorkshire rivers. High
es, game fishing, lowland reaches,
e fishing. Lake fishing, coarse and trout.

s and Liverpool Canal AA
ary – W.M. Troman
Royd, Shipley
274 583088
ership – Unrestricted
Formed – 1968
Members – 40,000
ties – Leeds and Liverpool Canal (towing
Leeds Office Lock to Top Lock,
ewton. 36 miles containing most
ies of coarse fish and brown trout.

ds Piscatorials
ary – B.C. Freer
enby Road, Leeds LS11 5RN
532 711413
ership – Restricted
Formed – 1968
Members – 55
ties – 4 Lakes, coarse only (Sherburn
1 Lake trout only, (Bramham Park). 2
stretches, mixed, (Nidd). 1 River
h, game only, (Trib. Ure).

ds Postal Sports Association
etary – H.A. Teanby
emont Gardens, Leeds LS10 2EP
532 771567
ership – Restricted
Formed – 1945
f Members – 45

erhills Old Boys AA
etary – S.C. Harrison
e Street, Bradford BD7 3HQ
ership – Unrestricted
Formed – 1884
f Members – 500
ties – Pilleys Lake, Eccleshill Bradford.
ods, trout and a few coarse fish. River
Apperley Bridge, short length, mixed
e fish.

ckintosh AC
etary – M. Russell
tree Mackintosh, Halifax
422 65761
ership – Restricted
Formed – 1962
f Members – 108
ties – We rent from the Y.W.A. a 500
stretch of canal from Sutterhebble to the
rhebble Lock.

ckton AC
etary – R. Newman
ill Lane, Ryhill, Nr. Wakefield
22 720 3895
ership – Unrestricted
Formed – 1957
f Members – 350
ties – Disused Barnsley and Wakefield
al. Roughly ¾ mile long. Contains perch,
h, pike, bream, tench, carp. Stocked
y with trout.

rley & District AS
etary – Mr. Elridge

---

7 Harthill, Gildersome, Morley
Tel: 0532 531306
Membership – Unrestricted at present
Year Formed – 1899
No. of Members – 27
Facilities – We are amalgamated to, and fish
the waters of Leeds & District, Amalgamated
Society of Anglers. These waters cover a wide
area in West & North Yorkshire.

New Ramblers AC
Secretary – D. Fulthorpe
19 Roundhay Gardens, Leeds LS8 4EG
Tel: 0532 620195
Membership – Unrestricted. Junior
membership available
No. of Members – 35
Facilities – Match fishing club. Affiliated to
the Leeds & District ASA.

Old Bank AC (W.H.C.)
Secretary – J.R. Brownhill
11 Water Royd Lane, Mirfield
Tel: 0924 499151 (Chairman)
Membership – Restricted
Year Formed – 1966
No. of Members – 66
Facilities – Hopton Dam in Mirfield (coarse
and trout).

Paris Piscatorial Society
Secretary – R. Sykes
1 William Street, West Vale, Greetland,
Halifax
Tel: 0422 79947
Membership – Restricted to 150 Members
Year Formed – 1978
No. of Members – 142
Facilities – The fisheries are situated at
Scholes Nr. Holmfirth, being approx. ¼ mile
apart. The fisheries consist of 3 dams. 1. Lee
Mills Dam, Scholes, approx. ½ acre
containing carp, tench, perch, bream, roach,
gudgeon. 2. Doob Royd Mill Dams each
approx. ½ acre. Top dam, trout only. Bottom
dam, tench, bream, gudgeon, trout.

Ryburn AS
Secretary – L. Kitching
44 Sellerdale Avenue, Wyke, Bradford
Tel: 0274 671994
Membership – Unrestricted
Year Formed – 1942
No. of Members – 350
Facilities – River Calder — Most fishable
lengths between Luddenden Foot and Copley,
through Sowerby Bridge Swamp and Milner
Royd Reservoirs (both small).

Saltaire AA
Secretary – W.M. Troman
7 Hall Royd, Shipley
Tel: 0274 583088
Membership – Unrestricted
Year Formed – 1867
No. of Members – 900
Facilities – Trout and grayling waters.
Grassington, from below weir to 2 fields
below Linton Bridge. Leeds and Liverpool
Canal. River Aire, parts of right and left
Bank. River Swale, Catterick Bridge. Tong
Park Dam.

Slaithwaite & District AC
Secretary – A. Bamforth
43 Binn Road, Marsden, Huddersfield
HD7 6HF
Tel: 0484 844119
Membership – Unrestricted. Junior
membership available
No. of Members – 906
Facilities – River Trent (Dunham and Sutton).
River Rye (Butterwick) Rye and Derwent, Old
Malton. 7 miles Hudds narrow canal. 20 Local

---

ponds/reservoirs. Waters available for
matches are Dunham Bridge, River Trent, nr.
Newark and River Derwent, Old Malton,
Yorkshire.

Spenborough & District AA
Secretary – J.P. Farrar
19 Harefield Drive, Birstall, Batley
Tel: 0924 475068
Membership – Unrestricted
Year Formed – 1955
No. of Members – 450
Facilities – 2 Open dams., i.e. Longbottoms
(at Birstall) and Mann Cleckheaton. Both well
stocked. Longbottoms has a very good head
of tench and roach, carp, perch, Mann Dam
contains roach, perch, carp and pike.

Town & Country Anglers
Specimen Group
Secretary – D. Fulthorpe
30 Roundhay Gardens, Leeds LS8 4EG
Tel: 0532 620195
Membership – Unrestricted. Junior
membership available
Year Formed – 1980
No. of Members – 17
Facilities – Fish throughout British Isles for
specimen fish. Affiliated to the Leeds &
District A.S.A.

Unity AC
Secretary – E.K. Mann
19 Busfield Street, Bradford 4 7QX
Tel: 0734 591834
Membership – Unrestricted
Year Formed – 1960
No. of Members – 200
Facilities – River Calder, Brighouse. River
Ure and Canal, Boroughbridge Lake,
Bradford. New water 1981.

Wakefield AC
Secretary – B.D. Harper
29 Victoria Crescent, Horsforth, Leeds LS18
4PT   Tel: 0532 584424
Membership – Unrestricted. Junior
membership available
No. of Members – 1500, 1000 juniors
Facilities – Newmillerdam Lake; Millfield
Lagoons, Horbury; Half Moon Lake,
Kirkthorpe; Walton Canal; Flanshaw Dam;
Mixenden Reservoir, Halifax.

West Riding Anglers
Secretary – H. Wigglesworth
84 Westfield Lane, Wrose, Shipley
Tel: 0274 598053
Membership – Restricted
Year Formed – 1901
No. of Members – 125
Facilities – River Wharfe (game and coarse),
River Swale (coarse).

Wetherby & District AC
Secretary – P.F. Burnett
10 Calder Close, Wetherby
Tel: 0937 62171
Membership – Restricted
Year Formed – 1910
No. of Members – 240 Seniors, 110 Juniors
Facilities – Approx. 5 miles of bankside
fishing on the River Wharfe around Wetherby
and 1 mile of the River Nidd at Skip
Bridge/Kirk Hammerton. Plus a small pond
near Pocklington.

Yeadon & District
Secretary – R. Holgate
64 Leeds Road, Otley
Tel: 0943 461757
Facilities – Day permits issued for Yeadon
Tarn.

WALES

CLWYD

Bodelwyddan AC

Secretary – R.G. Richardson
3 Ffordd Siarl, St. Asaph
Tel: 0745 582693

Membership – Unrestricted
Year Formed – 1975
No. of Members – 125
Facilities – Parts of River Elwy for game. Lodge Pools, Glascoed (Nr Bodelwyddan) for coarse.

Bryn-y-Pys AA

Secretary – H.V. Guest
Bryn-Hovah, Bangor-on-Dee, Wrexham

Membership – Restricted to local residents
No. of Members – 400
Facilities – River Dee between Overton Bridge and Bangor Bridge.

Colwyn Bay Victoria SAC

Secretary – Dr C.W. Haskins
20 West Road, Old Colwyn, Colwyn Bay
Tel: 0492 55011

Membership – Unrestricted
Year Formed – 1930
No. of Members – Varying 300-400
Facilities – Control fishing on 1 small freshwater pond.

Connah's Quay AC

Secretary – P. Roberts
42 Pinewood Avenue, Connah's Quay
Tel: 0244 815643

Membership – Unrestricted
Year Formed – 1970
No. of Members – 950
Facilities – Alyn River, 1½ miles at Rossett. Wepre Brook mixed fishing. Mostyn Pool: tench and carp. Paper Mill Reservoir, at Oaken Holt, trout fishing, fly only. All the above is member only fishing. Wepre Pool, coarse fishing especially carp. Special access and amenities which makes it ideal for the disabled, permits available.

Maelor AA

Secretary – K. Bathers
'Sunnyside', Hill Street, Cefn Mawr, Nr. Wrexham
Tel: 0978 820 608

Membership – Unrestricted, Junior membership available
Year Formed – 1910
No. of Members – 250
Facilities – 1 mile River Dee salmon, trout, grayling. Sunbank near Llangollen, both banks. 2 miles River Dee, trout, grayling, coarse fish Trevor, both banks.

Pilkingtons Recreational Club Angling Section

Secretary – G. Kenway
Kenrose, Allt Goch, Henllan Road

Membership – Restricted
Year Formed – 250
Facilities – Coarse fishing (on site). Local sea waters, river waters, lakes and reservoirs.

DYFED

Pembroke & District AC

Secretary – T.J. Cavaney
Kilnback House, Angle Village
Tel: 064 684 208

Membership – Partly Restricted
Year Formed – 1958
No. of Members – 250
Facilities – Bosherston Lily Ponds. About 20 acres for coarse fishing, but the club is mainly a Sea Angling Club.

GLAMORGAN MID

Abadare & District AA

Secretary – R. Hancock
11 Cobdon Street, Aberaman, Abadare
Tel: 0685 875209

Membership – Unrestricted
Year Formed – Before War
No. of Members – 930
Facilities – Senni River, Cynon River. Also Rivers Dare and Amman. Lakes in Country Park. Water Authority Reservoir, Nant Moel Cynon. Nanthir Reservoir.

Glyncornel AA

Secretary – J.M. Evans
126 Ystrad Road, Ystrad, Rhondda
Tel: 0443 439961

Membership – Unrestricted, Junior membership available. Also disabled
Year Formed – 1952
No. of Members – 100
Facilities – River Rhondda, trout fishing. Restocked with 1000 10inch fish annually. Any means of fishing. Darran Park Lake Ferndale, coarse fishing. No fly or spinning. Rhymmy Bridge Reservoir, fly fishing only. Good stock of fish 12 inch+also stocked every year. Darran Park Lake available to hire for matches.

Merthyr Tydfil AA

Secretary – C. Hughes
2 Wesley Close, Dowlais, Merthyr Tydfil

Membership – Unrestricted
No. of Members – 600
Facilities – Fishing on Taff, Taf Fechan, Taff (trout). Two local park lakes and manmade Mixed fisheries + 1090yds salmon trout and coarse fishing on River Usk above Usk town

New Duffryn AC

Secretary – D.F. Roberts
The New Duffryn Hotel, Aberbargoed
Tel: 0443 831635

Membership – Unrestricted
Year Formed – 1979
No. of Members – 30
Facilities – Negotiating for water at present.

Porthcawl SAA

Secretary – E. Fielding
75 Westminster Way, Bridgend CF31 4QX

Membership – Unrestricted
Year Formed – 1952
No. of Members – Sea 150, Coarse 200
Facilities – Sea shore angling for bass, flounder, whiting, codling. Sea boat angling for above, skate, ray, tope and mackerel.
Game – Wilderness Lake – rainbow trout.
Coarse – Pwl-y-Waun Lake, carp, roach, perch, bream.

Porthcawl SAC

Chairman – A. Birch
171 New Road, Porthcawl, GF36 5DD
Tel: 065 671 3975 HQ Sportsmans Club

Membership – Unrestricted
Year Formed – 1952
No. of Members – 450
Facilities – Wilderness Lake – game: rainbow trout. Mercies Lake – coarse: bream, roach, perch, carp. Day and weekly permits from Bridges Sports Shop, New Road, Porthcawl.

South Wales Switchgear AC

Secretary – G. Dingley
73 Meadow Close, Pengam, Blackwood
Tel: 0443 833642

Membership – Unrestricted, Junior membership available
Year Formed – 1962
No. of Members – 100
Facilities – River Sirhowy at Pontlanfraith – trout fishing. Feeder pond at Fochriw (near Merthyr Tydfil) coarse fishing. Holds a good head of coarse fish. Carp upto 12lb, chub to 6lb, roach perch, tench, rudd. This is also available for matches, 40 pegs maximum.

Taff AA

Secretary – H.T. Gwynne
87 Shirley Drive, Heolgerrig, Merthyr Tydfil
Tel: 0685 4506

Membership – Unrestricted
Year Formed – 1970
No. of Members – 128
Facilities – Reservoirs of the Welsh Water Authority.

LAMORGAN SOUTH

ute Angling Society

Secretary – L.V. Powell
'6 Clare Road, Grangetown, Cardiff

embership – Restricted
ar Formed – 1899
o. of Members – 30
cilities – River Taff, Cardiff, badly polluted at
esent. River Ely, Cardiff and River Rhymney,
Mellows. Some fish beginning to appear as a
ult of stocking. This is a new aquisition.
oadway Reen, Marshfield. Well stocked with
ach, bream, tench, chub and carp. Results
ry variable, probably owing to abundance of
ural foods.

LAMORGAN WEST

etal Box Coarse Fishing Club

cretary – J. Hall
Kingdom Owen Road, Cimla, Neath
: 0639 50375

embership – Unrestricted
ar Formed – 1970
of Members – 50
cilities – Square Pond, Briton Ferry

eath & Dulais Angling Club

cretary – A. Beasley
Neath Road, Tonna, Neath
0639 50878

mbership – Unrestricted
ar Formed – 1911
of Members – Adult 368, Junior 348
A.P. 38
cilities – Situated in an area of natural beauty.
cess from A465 and B4434. All fishable
ers listed on club ticket. Coarse fishing in
tom half of Neath Canal, from Neath Road
dge to Briton Ferry.

WENT

vmbran AA

retary – P.M. Gulliford
The Circle, Cwmbran
06333 5036

mbership – Unrestricted
r Formed – 1963
of Members – 250
lities – Trout – Afon Llwyd, 3 miles fly or
n fishing only, 9in. limit, 2 fish per day.
ws through new town, pleasant parklands.
rse – Mon. and Brecs. canal approx 5½
s, tench, carp, dace, chub, roach, rudd,
h, skimmer bream, eels. No bait restrictions.
ish, except eels, to be returned to water.
nbers only. No day tickets, on Blaen Bran
ervoir and Bigsweir Fishery
ober – December only) River Wye between
mouth and Tintern Abbey. Sea: Bristol
nnel, charter boat available.

ntypool AA

etary – A. Wakeham
Hilda's Road, Griffithstown, Pontypool
049 55 4743

Membership – Unrestricted
Year Formed – 1906
No. of Members – 600
Facilities – 15 Miles trout fishing River Afon.
Llwyd at Pontypool in an industrial area. 7 Mile
Solway Brook Usk in the heart of the country.
3½ Acres Pen-yr-Heol Reservoir. Mon. Canal
Coarse fishing plus Dace fishing on River Usk
during close season.

South Wales Switchgear

Secretary – G. Dingley
73 Meadow Close, Pengam, Blackwood
Tel: 0443 833642

Membership – Unrestricted, Junior membership
available
Year Formed – 1962
No. of Members – 100
Facilities – River Sirhowy at Pontllanfraith – trout
fishing. Feeder Pond at Fochriw (near Merthyr
Tydfil) coarse fishing. Holds a good head of large
coarse fish. Carp up to 12lb, chub to 6lb. Roach,
perch, tench, rudd. This is also available for
matches. 40 pegs maximum.

GWYNEDD

Bala & District AA

Secretary – D.M. Rees
21 Tremyffridd, Bala Tel: 0678 520812

Membership – Unrestricted, Junior membership
available
Year Formed – 1949
No. of Members – 300
Facilities – 3 Trout fishing streams stocked
regularly. River Dee 2 miles fly only, trout and
grayling. River Tryweryn approx 4 miles trout
and salmon. Bala Lake (700 acres) coarse and
game fishing. Small mountain lake stocked
regularly with brown trout.

Trawsfynydd Lake Management Committee

Secretary – H.K. Lewis
Manchester House, Trawsfynydd
Tel: 076 687 234

Membership – Unrestricted
Year Formed – 1953
No. of Members – 460
Facilities – Trawsfynydd Lake – 1200 acres of
reservoir. Water used to cool turbines of Nuclear
Power Station, thus ensuring warm water to
enhance fish production and rearing throughout
the year.

POWYS

Argae Hall AC

Secretary – J. Wilkes
Ponderosa, Argae Hall Caravan Park, Garthmyl

Membership – Unrestricted
Year Formed – 1977
No. of Members – 31
Facilities – Montgomery Canal from Berriw Lock
to Fron Post Office Garthmyl 4½ miles.

Lakeside AA

Secretary – Wendy P. Davies
Lakeside, Llangorse LD 7TR
Tel: 087 484 226

Membership – Unrestricted ?????
Facilities – Llangorse Lake ????

Llandrindod Wells AA

Secretary – A.H. Selwyn
4 Park Crescent, Llandrindod Wells
Tel: 0597 2397

Membership – Unrestricted
Year Formed – 1924
No. of Members – 100
Facilities – The fishing under the control of the
Association is on the River Ithon and is within
easy walking distance of the town. The length of
the fishing available is approx 4 miles.

Llanidloes & District AA

Secretary – J. Dallas Davies
Dresden House, Great Oak Street, Llanidloes
Tel: 05512 2644

Membership – Unrestricted
Year Formed – Pre War
No. of Members – 180
Facilities – River fishing on Severn, Clywedog,
Trannon and Dulas for trout, grayling, salmon,
dace, chub, and pike 2 lakes available with pike
perch and chub. Also Clywedog Reservoir – fly
only for both brown and rainbow trout. Stocked
at regular intervals throughout season (18th
March – 16 Nov).

Montgomeryshire AA

Secretary – R. Thomas
128 Oldford Rise, Welshpool, SY21 7TD
Tel: 0938 3488

Membership – Unrestricted, Junior membership
available
Year Formed – 1964
No. of Members – 300
Facilities – Extensive stretches of the River
Severn, including some tributaries and several
other waters offering excellent coarse and game
fishing for most species. Shropshire Union Canal,
River Banwy, Montgomery Canal, only the latter
is available for matches, approx 4 continuous
miles.

Newtown & District Fishing Club

Secretary – J.A. Walker
129 Lon Gwern, Trehafren, Newtown
Tel: 0686 27987

Membership – Unrestricted
Year Formed – 1938
No. of Members – 150
Facilities – Several miles of The River Severn,
with salmon, trout, grayling, pike, chub, dace
etc. Also several miles of canal containing coarse
fish. Also Fachwen Pool, 10 acres, stocked with
brown and rainbow trout up to 4lbs. 12 Acre
Llyn Tarw unique in that American brown trout
have bred naturally for years.

Welshpool & District Anglers Club

Secretary – Revd. R.H. Fairbrother
The Vicarage, Betws, Cedewain, Newtown
Tel: 068 687 345

Membership – Unrestricted
Facilities – The waters used by the club are those
managed by The Montgomeryshire Angling
Association. All members must be members of
M.A.A.

Coarse Clubs: Scotland

SCOTLAND

BORDERS

Coldstream & District AA

Secretary – E.M. Patterson
Market Square, Coldstream
Tel: 0890 2719

Facilities – River Tweed and River Leet.

Jedforest AA

Secretary – A. Whitecross
42 Howden Road, Jedburgh, Roxburghshire
Tel: 083 56 3615

Kelso AA

Secretary – Mr Hutchinson
53 Abbot Seat, Kelso
Tel: 057 32 3440

Facilities – Fishing on Rivers Tweed, Teviot and Eden for brown trout, grayling and roach.

Ladykirk & Norham AA

Secretary – R.G. Wharton
8 St. Cuthbert's Square, Northam
Facilities – River Tweed. Brown trout, grayling, roach.

Peebles Angling Improvement Association

Secretary – Blackwood and Smith W.S.
39 High Street, Peebles
Tel: 0721 20131

Facilities – Rivers Tweed and Lyne. Brown trout and grayling.

Whiteadder AA

Secretary – R. Welsh
Abbey Street, Bathans, Duns
Tel: 03614 210

Membership – Unrestricted
Year Formed – 1932
No. of Members – 500
Facilities – We control Whiteadder Water from thernside to the source, also its tributaries.

CENTRAL

Killin Breadalbane AC

Secretary – D. Allan
Main Street, Killin
Tel: 056 72 362
Membership – Restricted
Year Formed – 1881

No. of Members – 50
Facilities – Loch Tay, River Dochart, River Lochay, Lochan-Na-Larige for brown trout, perch, pike.

DUMFRIES & GALLOWAY

Commissioners of Royal Four Towns Fishings

Secretary – W. Graham
Glenelg, Hightae, Lockerbie
Tel: 038 781 220

Membership – Restricted
Year Formed – 1910
Facilities – 4½ Miles both banks River Annan from Shillahill Bridge to Smallholmburn.

Esk & Liddle FA

Secretary – R.J.B. Hill
Bank of Scotland Buildings, Langholm
Tel: 0541 80428

Membership – Unrestricted
Year Formed – 1855
Facilities – 30 Miles of bank fishing comprising different stretches of the Border Esk and the Liddle Water and of their tributary streams namely the Ewes Water, Tarras Water, Wauchope Water and the White Esk. Caters only for clubs and during the off-season viz. 1st November to 31st January.

Gretna AA

Secretary – J.G. Graham
126 Currock Park Avenue, Carlisle
Cumbria CA2 4DH

Membership – Unrestricted
Year Formed – 1932
No. of Members – 270
Facilities – River Sark – Scottish side from Gretna-Carlisle Road to Solway approx ¾ to 1 mile. River Kirtle both banks from Carlisle – Dumfries Railway line to Solway Shore, approx 3 miles.

FIFE

Primrose AC

Secretary – A. Cox
103 Whinnyburn Place, Rosyth KY11 2TR
Tel: 0383 415703

Membership – Unrestricted
Year Formed – 1978
No. of Members – 14

Elgin AA

Secretary – H.B. Fleetwood
St. Mary's, Dunbar Street, Lossiemouth IV31 6RD
Tel: 034 381 3142

Membership-Unrestricted
Year Formed – 1942
No. of Members – 1000
Facilities – River Lossie. 15 Miles (approx). Both banks from Calcots Railway Bridge on the North to the junction of The Leanoch Burn (Glenlatterach) on the South 2. The right or East bank from the point known as Coral Peel on the North to The Calcots Railway Bridge.

Lossiemouth AA

Secretary – T.B. Clark
Dunconusg, Stotfield, Lossiemouth
Tel: 034 381 2380

Membership – Unrestricted
Year Formed – 1958
No. of Members – 220 including Juniors

HIGHLAND & ISLANDS

Dingwall & District AC

Secretary – A. Shanks (official)
The Sporting Stores, Tulloch Street, Dingwall
Tel: 0349 62346

Membership – Unrestricted, Junior membership available
No. of Members – 200
Facilities – River Conon (lower beat). Fly fishing only for sea trout and brown trout. Loch Luicha (Upper Loch). Flyfishing and spinning. Brown trout, perch, char, pike.

STRATHCLYDE

B.S.C. Ravenscraig Works Freshwater & Sea

Secretary – J. McLaughlan
22 Cheviot Crescent, Wishawhill, Wishaw
Lanarkshire ML2 7PN
Tel: 069 83 61987

Membership – Unrestricted
Year Formed – 1978
No. of Members – 38 Full, 2 Retired, 14 Junior, 6 Associate

Shotts Bon-Accord AC

Secretary – J. Frew
26 St. Catherines Crescent, Shotts, Lanarkshire

Membership – Unrestricted
Year Formed – 1980
No. of Members – 18

TAYSIDE

Aberfeldy AC

Secretary – D. Campbell
Sports Shop, The Square, Aberfeldy
Tel: 088 74 354

Membership – Restricted
Year Formed – 1887
No. of Members – 170
Facilities – 3 Miles salmon, trout and grayling o River Tay. 1 Small trout loch.

Canmore AC

Secretary – E.S. Mann
44 Sheriff Park Gardens, Forfar

Membership – Unrestricted
Year Formed – 1977
No. of Members – 244 Adults, 104 Juniors
Facilities – Trout fishing. Rivers Dean, Kerbet, Noran, Lemno, Airneyfoul, Glenogil Reservoir Forfar Loch, and Rescobie Loch.

Rannoch & District AC

Secretary – J. Brown
The Square, Kinloch Rannoch, By Pitlochry
Tel: 08822 331

Membership – Restricted to local residents
Junior membership available
Year Formed – 1951
No. of Members – Approx 80
Facilities – Loch Eigheached near Rannoch Station. For brown trout and for perch.

Strathmore Angling Improvement Association

Secretary – New appointment pending

Membership – Unrestricted
Year Formed – 1940
No. of Members – 4000 approx, plus permit holders
Facilities – Rivers Isla, Dean, and stretches of Ericht and Dean. The association also runs their own fish farm and produces all their own stoc Salmon fishing available to season ticket holde and members.

SOUTHERN IRELAND

CO. CAVAN

Baillieborough Angling &
Tourist Association

Secretary – Mrs Mary McCabe
Lower Drumbanon, Baillieborough

Belturbet Angling Club

Secretary – Mr Barry Galligan
Kilconny, Belturbet

Cavan Tourism Association

Secretary – Mrs B. O'Hanlon
St Martins, Creeghan

Cavan Tourism Association

A. McGinnity
Cavan Town

Coarse Angling & Tourist
Association

Secretary – Mr Tony Lynch
Stradamesduff

Cootehill Chamber of Commerce

Secretary – Mr Liam Hayes
Bicycle Shop, Cootehill

Development Association

Secretary – Mr J. Cloane
Arvah Gowna

Killeshandra Holidays

Secretary – Mrs Bothwell
Lisnella, Killeshandra

CO. CLARE

Scarriff, Mountshannon &
Whitegate Angling Club

Secretary – Mr P. Cahill
Mountshannon

Ennis & District Coarse Angling Club

Secretary – Mr Brian Culloo

CO. CORK

Fermoy Coarse Angling
Tourism Association

Secretary – Mr Jack O'Sullivan
Fermoy

Bandon & Coarse Angling Club

Secretary – Mr David Wills
Wills
Bandon

Macroom Tourism Development
Association

Secretary – Mr Noel Hackett
Macroom

DUBLIN

Dublin Coarse Angling Club

Secretary – Mr Robert Smithers
2 St Helen's Terrace, Dublin 8

GALWAY

Angling Committee
Ballinasloe Chamber of Commerce

Secretary – Mr P. Lawless
4 Hillcrest, Ballinasloe

Palmerstown Stores

Mr Gerry Kenny
Portumna

Tackle Dealer

Mr Patsy Scanlon
Ballygar

CO. KILDARE

Angling Club

Secretary – Mrs E. O'Farrell
Prosperous

Athy & District Anglers

Secretary – Mr Jerry Sheahan
21 Clonmullin, Athy

KILKENNY

Barrow Valley Holidays

Secretary – Mrs Alice McCabe
Brandon View, Ballyogan, Graiguenamagh

CO. LAOIS

Ballinakill & District
Angling Association

Secretary – Mr Dennis Bergin
The Square
Ballinakill

Vicarstown Canal Development
Association

Secretary – Mrs M. Corbett
Vicarstown

CO. LEITRIM

Angling Tourism Association

Secretary – Mrs T. Kennedy
Glenview Farmhouse, Ballinamore

Carrick on Shannon Angling Club

Secretary – Mr Sean O'Rourke
Carrick on Shannon

Tourism Association

Secretary – Mr J.M. Mooney
Drumshanbo

Tourist Development Association

Secretary – Mr G. Taylor
Hyde Terrace, Mohill

LIMERICK

Mr John Morrison
42 Rossa Avenue, Limerick
or
Shannonside RTO
92 O'Connell Street, Limerick

LONGFORD

Clondra Development Association

Secretary – Mrs T. Casserly
Clondra

Lanesborough/Ballyleague
Development Association

Secretary – Mr Des Watts
Rathcline Road
Lanesborough

CO. MEATH

Angling Development Association

Secretary – Mr Jim Meade
Drumconrath

Enfield Angling Club

Secretary – Mr Brian O'Donahue
Baconstown, Enfield

CO. MONAGHAN

The Bawn & District Gun Club

Secretary – Mr John Clerkin
Cortubber PO, Castleblaney

Carrickmacross & District Anglers

Secretary – Mr David Shorthouse
Tullynaskeagh West, Carrickmacross

Mr G. Maguire
Ballybay

CO. OFFALY

Mr John Campion
Banagher

Shannonbridge Anglers Association

Secretary – Mr D. Kileen
Shannonbridge

CO. ROSCOMMON

Ballyforan Angling Club

Secretary – Mr J. Thompson
Ballyforan

Development Association

Secretary – Mr M. Mitchell
Abbey House, Boyle

Roosky & District Anglers

Secretary – Mrs Bridie Duffy
Roosky

Strokestown Angling Club

Secretary – Mr George Gearty
Strokestown

SLIGO

Ballymote Development Association

Secretary – Mr M. Wilcox
Keenaghan, Ballymote

TIPPERARY

Kilgarvan Anglers Club

Secretary – Mrs B. Fox
Brocka, Ballinderry, Nenagh

CO. WATERFORD

Cappoquin Angling Club

Secretary – Mr Jim Aherne
Upper Main Street, Cappoquin

CO. WESTMEATH

Athlone International Festival

Secretary – Mr Sean Egan
59 Connaught Street, Athlone

Mr Tony Mullen
Lowther House, Clonmore, Mullingar

ENGLAND

AVON

Bathampton AA

Secretary – D. Crookes
25 Otago Terrace, Larkhall, Bath
Tel: 0225 27164

Membership – Unrestricted. Junior
membership available
Year Formed – 1930
No. of Members – 2,300
Facilities – 10 Miles of fishing on Bristol Avon,
5 miles of trout fishing on tributaries of the
Bristol Avon 10 ponds and lakes offering
carp, tench etc. Hire out Newbridge —
Saltford — Kelston waters a total of 250 pegs.

BEDFORDSHIRE

Verulam AC

Secretary – J.K. Trew
128 Benson Close, Bramingham Wood, Luton
LU3 3QR
Tel: 0582 593798

Membership – Unrestricted. Junior
membership available
Year Formed – 1934
No. of Members – 600
Facilities – River Lea. 1½ miles, 2 stretches.
Small fast river, 5 miles from St. Albans
Gravel Pit at Smallford, 2 miles from St.
Albans. Deep lake, (big carp). Gravel Pit at
Frogmore, 5 miles from St. Albans, 3 Lakes,
8' deep. Converted watercress bed in St.
Albans, 5' deep. Coarse and game fish. April
1 — June 15. River Ouse, 8 miles north of
Bedford. 3½ miles in 3 stretches. Fast and
slow water.

BUCKINGHAMSHIRE

Iver Fly Fishers

Secretary – J. Frost
1 Coopers Row, Iver Heath
Tel: 0753 651790

CAMBRIDGESHIRE

Cambridge Trout Club

Secretary – S.R. Tubbs
The Old House, Hauxton, Cambridge
Tel: 0223 870240

Membership – Restricted
Year Formed – 1938
No. of Members – 21
Facilities – River Cam or Granta from Ickleton
to Duxford (about 2 miles).

Deeping St. James AC

Secretary – J. Cran
53 Castle Drive, Northborough, Peterborough
Tel: 0778 343691

Membership – Restricted
Year Formed – 1890
No. of Members – 1,112
Facilities – River Welland (Market Deeping
and Deeping St. James). Gravel pits and
millstream at Maxey and Market Deeping.
Trout pits at West Deeping.

Stowe Fly FC

Secretary – T.L. Hodson
11 Stanford Walk, Netherton, Peterborough
Tel: 0733 263965 (Home)
     0733 64734/5 (Office)

Membership – Restricted
Year Formed – 1974
No. of Members – 24
Facilities – Approximately 6 acres of still
water — old gravel pit.

Waterbeach AC

Secretary – A. Ballaam
14 Rothleigh Road, Cambridge
Tel: 0223 358911 Ext. 2649

Membership – Unrestricted
Year Formed – 1936
No. of Members – 450
Facilities – Approximately 5 miles on the
River Cam, 1½ miles on Swoffham Lode plus
a 15 acre trout lake (Membership restricted to
50).

Willow-Brook Fly-Fishers

Secretary – B. Barron-Clark
Orchard Cottage, Tansor, Peterborough
Tel: 08326 267

Membership – Restricted
Year Formed – 1958
No. of Members – 30
Facilities – The Willow-Brook from
Fotheringhay upstream to Apethorpe dam.

Cheshire AA

Secretary – F.R. James
34 Sweet Briar Crescent, Crewe CW2 8PE
Tel: 0270 69855

Membership – Unrestricted
Year Formed – 1918
No. of Members – 7,000
Facilities – Montgomeryshire 6½ miles. R
Severn and 1½ miles R. Camlad N. Staffs
Knypersley Reservoir 33 acres, Serpentine
lake 14 acres Cheshire and Shropshire,
Shropshire Union Canal 50 miles, Llango
Branch 40 miles, Cheshire Trent and Mer
Canal 7 miles. R. Dee 12 miles (in
conjunction with Dee AA) R. Dane 5 mile
(Somerford Booths Ches.).

Cheshire Specimen Group

Secretary – K. McNeil
21 Vale Road, Timperley, Altringham
WA15 7TQ
Tel: 061 980 3464

Membership – Restricted (selection by
invitation only)
No. of Members – 5

Congleton AS

Secretary – N.J. Bours
8 Norfolk Road, Congleton CW12 1NY
Tel: 02602 77284

Membership – Unrestricted. Junior
membership available
Year Formed – 1954
No. of Members – 350
Facilities – Several stretches of River Dane
Congleton area. 2 sections of Macclesfield
Canal. Several local pools. Day permits o
if accompanied by a member. Hiring out
on clubs stretch of Macclesfield Canal at
Congleton.

Davenham AC

Secretary – A. Cook
41 Fairfield Road, Leftwich Estate, Northw
CW9 8DG   Tel: 0606 41838

Membership – Unrestricted
Year Formed – 1954
No. of Members – 900
Facilities – 7 miles trout and coarse fishing
River Dane. 4 pits — carp, roach, perch,
tench, chub. River Dane — roach, dace,
perch and gudgeon.

Halton District AA

Secretary – K. Philcock
68 Belvoir Road, Widnes WA8 6HR
Tel: 051423 1627

Membership – Unrestricted
Year Formed – 1898
No. of Members – 200
Facilities – 3 local ponds coarse fishing on
½ mile River Banwy Llanfair Caerinion, ½
mile River Vyrnwy Meifod.

Irby AC

Secretary – Frank Evans
4 McAlpine Close, Upton, Wirral L49 6JR
Tel: 051 678 7619

Membership – Unrestricted
Year Formed – 1967
No. of Members – 600
Facilities – 25 small lakes and ponds (Wirr
area) S.U.C. at Aberbechan. River Severn
Aberbechan (small stretches). Montgomery
Canal, Aberbechan Bridge nos 150-153
available to hire for matches.

...mm AC

...cretary – J.S. Graham
... Boswell Avenue, Warrington WA4 6DQ
...: 0925 54942

...mbership – Restricted (Members only
...cepted after induction meeting). Junior
...mbership available
...ar Formed – 1946
... of Members – 1,700
...ilities – R. Bollin, Lymm — Several miles
...game and coarse fishery. Whitley
...ol, Warrington — 3 acre coarse fishery.
...age Pool, Whitley, Warrington — ¾ acre
...rse fishery. Wincham Brook, Lostock
...alam, Northwich — 1 mile river — game
...coarse species. Hatchmere, Norley, via
...rrington — 12 acre coarse fishery.
...mvale, Whitegate, Northwich — Unique
...ed fishery — American Brook, Brown and
...nbow trout, tench, chub, grayling, orfe.
...er Vrynwy, Llandrinio, Llanymynech,
...ys — ¾ mile river — mixed fishery. R.
...ern Llandrinio, Llanymynech, Powys — ¾
... river — mixed fishery. River Rhiw,
...afon, Berriew, Powys — ½ mile river,
...ed fishery, River Severn, Abermule,
...town, Powys — ¾ mile river, mixed
...cies. Hirings available as Lymm Dam
...casionally let out) 50 pegs maximum,
...chmere — 15 pegs maximum, Statham
... — 25 pegs maximum, R. Dane — 45
...s maximum, R. Vrynwy — 30 pegs
...imum. R. Severn — Llandrinio — 25 pegs
...imum, R. Severn — Abermule — 30 pegs
...imum.

...ntwich AS

...retary – R.P. Dainty
...ningside, 85 Broad Lane, Stapeley,
...twich
...0270 626536

...bership – Unrestricted
...of Members – 300
...ities – Derbyshire — Mid-Cheshire and
...Wales. Mainly river fishing providing
...llent trout, grayling, salmon and coarse
...ng.

...nce Albert AS

...etary – C. Sparkes
...a Lodge, Upton, Macclesfield
...0625 26311

...bership – Unrestricted
... Formed – 1954
...of Members – 5,000
...ities – Rivers Severn, Ribble, Lune,
...ey, Dee, Banwy, Dove, Mawddach, Trent,
...e, Dean Vyrnwy. In addition to numerous
...s, reservoirs and pools plus Macclesfield
...al and Welsh arm of Shropshire Union
...al.

...sett & Gresford AA

...etary – J.F.L. Coates
...aleside, Upton-By-Chester, Chester
... 1EP
...0244 26588

...bership – Restricted
... Formed – 1906
...of Members – 175
...ities – 2¼ miles, mainly both banks of the
...yn, between the villages of Rossett and
...ord, Clwyd, N. Wales.

Warrington AA

Secretary – J.S. Jackson
23 Nora Street, Warrington WA1 2JG
Tel: 0925 37525

Membership – Unrestricted
Year Formed – 1891
No. of Members – 13,000
Facilities – 134 miles canal fishing,
Bridgewater, Trent and Mersey, Shropshire
Union, Grey Mist Mere, Ackers Pit, River
Gowy, R. Alyn, R. Ribble, R. Dee, R. Severn,
R. Banwy, R. Vyrnwy, R. Roden, Rea Brook,
R. Cain, R. Dane, Cicely Mill Pool.

Winsford and District AA

Secretary – J.S. Bailey
22 Plover Avenue, Winsford
Tel: 060 65 3902

Membership – Unrestricted
Year Formed – 1900
No. of Members – 1,500
Facilities – River Weaver, River Dane, (coarse
and game river fishing). Pools — Top Flash
Marton Hole, The Ocean, New Pool,
Newbridge Pool, Sixes Hole (coarse fishing
with exception of Marton Hole which is a
game fishery).

Wyche AC

Secretary – F. McGarry
65 Queens Drive, Nantwich

Membership – Unrestricted
Year Formed – 1955
No. of Members – 1,350
Facilities – River Weaver, various, Nantwich,
trout, dace, roach, bream, chub, River Dee,
Holt, Nr. Wrexham, dace, roach, River
Banwy, Meifor, North Wales, trout, dace,
chub, roach, Osmere, Blakemere, Nr.
Whitchurch, bream, roach, rudd, perch,
pike, tench, Crewe, Aughtons Flash,
Thomassons Flash, bream, rudd, carp. Also
affiliated to Cheshire Anglers and ballot
permits, various other waters.

CLEVELAND

Esk FA

Secretary – H.B. Thomas
Angrove House, Great Ryton, Middlesbrough

Membership – Restricted
Year Formed – 1864
No. of Members – 60
Facilities – Yorkshire Esu. Waters between
Glaisdale, Egton, Grosmont.

Thornaby AA

Secretary – D. Speight
10 Stainsby Gate, Stainsby Hill, Thornaby
Tel: 0642 62099

Membership – Unrestricted
No. of Members – 1,000 +
Facilities – 50-60 miles on R. Tees, Swiral,
Ure, Eden.

CORNWALL

Bodmin AA

Secretary – Lt. Col. H.M. Ervine-Andrews
V.C.
The Old Barn, St. Neot, Liskeard
Tel: 0579 20799

Membership – Unrestricted
Year Formed – 1956
No. of Members – 400/500
Facilities – About 12 miles on the rivers
Camel and Fowey, with trout fishing on some
tributaries. There are salmon in the rivers at
all times but the best runs are the grilse in
summer and the winter fish in November and
December. Sea trout are best in July and
August. Riverside accom. is available.
Enquiries to Hon Sec. with S.A.E. please.

Bude AA

Secretary – Lt. Cdr. S.F.W. Blackall
5 Ward Close, Stratton, Bude EX23 9BB
Tel: 0288 4354

Membership – Unrestricted. Junior
membership available
Year Formed – 1933
No. of Members – 23
Facilities – About 8 kilometers of bank on the
River Tamar, plus about 2 km. of bank on the
River Claw, all in the Upper Tamar Valley
between the parishes of North Tamarton and
Kilhampton. There is some parking space.
The fish consist of wild brown trout, a few
wild rainbow trout plus some dace and
grayling. The fishing at North Tamarton is fly
fishing only.

Essa AC

Secretary – J. Webber
2 Rashleigh Avenue, Saltash
Tel: 075 55 5594

Membership – Unrestricted
Year Formed – 1977
No. of Members – 50

Liskeard & District AC

Secretary – B.G. Wilson
The Bruff, Rilla Mill, Callington

Membership – Unrestricted. Junior
membership available
Year Formed – 1950
No. of Members – 250
Facilities – 30 Miles of game fishing on the
River Fowey, Camel, Lynher, Inny, East
Looe, West Looe, and Seaton. Salmon, sea
trout and brown. All are spate rivers running
through well wooded villages mainly in East
Cornwall.

Lostwithiel FA

Secretary – S.E. Brewer
Hillhouse, Lostwithiel
Tel: 0208 872542

Membership – Unrestricted
Year Formed – 1936
Facilities – Fishing for salmon, sea trout and
brown trout — Bass in Estuary and sea fishing
on coast at Fowey.

Game Clubs: Cumbria

St. Mawgan AC

Secretary – T.J. Trevenna
Lanvean House, St. Mawgan, Newquay
Tel: 063 73 316

Membership – Restricted
Year Formed – 1960
No. of Members – 45
Facilities – Small brown trout on River Melanhyl. Only certain parts of the stream are club waters.

Wadebridge & District AC

Secretary – E.J. Renals
Coppins, Whiterock Close, Wadebridge
Tel: 020881 3239

Membership – Restricted
No. of Members – 140
Facilities – Fishing for Salmon and Trout on the River Camel. Average weight of Salmon: 10 lbs, Trout 12 lbs.

CUMBRIA

Alston & District AA

Secretary – L.S. Pattison
Belvedere, Park Lane, Alston
Tel: 049 81 222

Membership – Restricted to residents within reasonable distance of Alston. Junior membership available
No. of Members – 50
Facilities – Seven miles trout fishing on River South Tyne in Alston and Slaggy Ford.

Aspatria AC

Secretary – R. Baxter
25 Outgoing Road, Aspatria

Membership – Restricted
Year Formed – 1958
Facilities – Approximately 6 miles of fishing on River Eden.

Barrow AA

Secretary – D.M. Adams
The Old Post Office, Woodland, Broughton in Furness
Tel: 06576 581

Membership – Restricted
Year Formed – 1880
No. of Members – 230

Brampton AA

Secretary – T. Donockley
1 Denton Crescent, Low Row Brampton
Tel: 069 76 518

Membership – Restricted
Year Formed – 1870
No. of Members – 300

Burneside AA

Secretary – C.G. Walker
47 Dunmail Drive, Heron Hill,
Kendal CA9 7SG

Membership – Restricted
Year Formed – 1900
No. of Members – 60
Facilities – Middle reaches of the River Kent and Sprint and some small tarns.

Carlisle AA

Secretary – E. Cave
9 Brunton Crescent, Carlisle CA1 2AX
Tel: 0228 20833

Membership – Restricted
Year Formed – 1852
Facilities – 7 miles R. Eden.

Cockermouth AA

Secretary – Dr. J. Abernethy
5 Sunscales Avenue, Cockermouth
Tel: 0900 823570

Membership – Restricted to residents of Cockermouth Postal District for river fishing. Unrestricted for lake fishing. Junior members admitted.
No. of Members – 150
Facilities – River Derwent and River Cocker, salmon and trout fishing. Rainbow/Brown trout fishing on Cogra Moss hill lake. Day, Week and season tickets available.

Coniston & Torver Dist. A.A.

Secretary – D.E. Lancaster
'Wetherlam', Mount Pleasant, Greenodd, Ulverston LA12 7RF
Tel: 022 986 307

Membership – Restricted
Year Formed – 1953
No. of Members – 65
Facilities – Yewtree Tarn — Brown and rainbow trout (fly and spinning only) — Lake shore access — east of Coniston Lake on Brantwood estate. Fishing lease on land bordering Yewdale and Torver becks belonging to Hext Estates Ltd. (Tickets to Yewtree Tarn available 'The Tackle Shop', Tilberthwaite Road, Coniston, Cumbria, during normal business hours.

Grizedale Angling Club

Secretary – Alan Wilton
'Barrowfoot', Hawkshead, Nr. Ambleside
Tel: 09666 582

Membership – Restricted
Year Formed – 1966
No. of Members – 40
Facilities – 2½ miles of Grizedale Beck from Grizedale to Face Forge — offers brown trout, sea trout after July and occasional salmon. Fly and worm fishing.

Kent (Westmorland) AA

Secretary – J.C. Parkin
11a Blea Tarn Road, Kendal
Tel: 0539 22386

Membership – Restricted
Year Formed – 1845
No. of Members – 85. Seasonal Visitors
Facilities – Mainly open country. Wooded in places. 8 mile river both banks — 2 mile single bank. Trout, sea trout, salmon. Dry/wet fly — spinning — worm.

Keswick AA

Secretary – W. Ashcroft
Springhaven, How Lane, Portinscale, Keswick
Tel: 0596 72703

Membership – Restricted to residents only. Junior membership available
Year Formed – Over 100 years
No. of Members – 100
Facilities – Part of River Greta (trout and salmon). Part of River Derwent (trout and salmon). Derwent water (coarse fish and trout).

Kirkby Lonsdale & District AA

Secretary – G. Clough
Keepers Cottage, Burrow, Via Carn Forth, Lancs.

Membership – Part Restricted
Year Formed – 1929
No. of Members – 50
Facilities – 2½ miles, mainly both banks, upstream of Kirkby Lonsdale. Brown trout, sea trout and salmon. Fly only, except whe water is above a certain height when spinn is permitted.

Penrith AA

Secretary – R.F. Allinson
7 Scaws Drive, Penrith, CA11 88H
Tel: 0768 62256

Membership – Restricted. Junior membersh available
Year Formed – 1850
No. of Members – 400
Facilities – Rivers: Eden, Eamont, Lowther and Petteril. Mainly brown trout but small of salmon early and late season. Fishing generally fly only. Hayeswater Reservoir.

River Leven Lower Fishery

Secretary – J. Lightfoot
Hill Rise, Haverthwaite, Nr. Ulverston
Tel: 0448 31226

Membership – Restricted
Year Formed – 1956
No. of Members – 140
Facilities – From 1 mile downstream of Haverthwaite to Greenodd viaduct, both banks.

Sedbergh AA

Secretary – J.P. Lowis
Yarlside, Sedbergh
Tel: 0587 20868

Membership – Restricted
Facilities – Fishing on the Lune, the Rawth and the Dee; partly owned and partly rent The fishing is mostly brown trout, but if conditions are suitable there is a number o sea-trout in July, August and September, w a sprinkling of salmon.

Staveley & District AA

Secretary – D.A. Taylor
18 Rawes Garth, Staveley, Kendal
Tel: 0539 821002

Membership – Restricted
Year Formed – 1940
No. of Members – 100
Facilities – Kentmere Tarn 24 acres. Fly, Spinning and worm fishing allowed — fly only from boat. Season permits only (appl secretary). Upper River Kent 7 miles — weekly permits only (apply at local newsagent, Staveley).

ay & Dist. AC

tary – H. Riley
e Cross House, Tebay, Penrith
058 74 376

ership – Restricted
Formed – 1946
f Members – 114
ties – 17 miles of River Lune. Brown
sea trout and salmon. Best for salmon
st, September and October. Fly fishing
in April.

erston AA

tary – H.B. Whittam
ndhurst Road, Ulverston
0229 52322

ership – Restricted on Game
Unrestricted on Coarse
Formed – 1890
f Members – 400 +
ties – Canal — excellent — used by
for matches. ¾ mile River Crake —
ers only — salmon, sea-trout.
allow Tarn — trout (brown) members
Sandhall Ponds — trout (rainbow)
ers only.

dermere Ambleside &
. AA

tary – J.B. Cooper
one, Limethwaite Road, Windermere
096 62 3768

bership – Restricted to local residents 10
radius of Ambleside. Junior membership
able
Formed – 1949
f Members – 219
ties – Headwaters of Lake Windermere
Brathay, Rothay and Troutbeck rivers,
her with 3 tarns School Knott —
dermere, High Arnside — Skelwith
ge area and Moss Eccles — Far Sawrey
ed annually with brownies on put and
basis. Rydal Lake, coarse fishing only.
able for hire.

RBYSHIRE

bourne FFC

tary – F.W. Mellor
othby Avenue, Ashbourne DE6 1EL

bership – Restricted
Formed – 1920
ties – Fleumore and Beatley streams and
akes — Shirley Dam and Yeedersley Lake.

Birdsgrove Fly FC

tary – A.L. Jones
indmill Lane, Ashbourne
0335 42319

bership – Restricted
Formed – 1880
f Members – 39
ities – River Dove near Ashbourne.

esterfield AA

tary – B.E. Thorley
t. Augustins Avenue, Birdholme
0246 39541

Membership – Unrestricted
Year Formed – 1928
No. of Members – 1900
Facilities – Stretches of Rivers Trent, Idle,
Derwent plus stillwaters.

Derbyshire County Council

Secretary – O.W. Handley
'Osprey' House, Ogston, Higham,
Derby DE5 6EL
Tel: 077 383 3595

Membership – Restricted
Year Formed – 1959
No. of Members – Full Members – 450
(Access to all waters)
Season Ticket Holders – 950
(Coarse fishing only on lower Derwent).

Darley Dale Fly FC

Secretary – A.L. Carter
Overdale House, Biggin-by-Hartington
Tel: 029 884 561

Membership – Restricted
Year Formed – 1862
No. of Members – 55
Facilities – 4½ miles of fly fishing on River
Derwent.

Earl of Harrington AC

Secretary – J. Callaghan
12 Spencer Street, Alvaston, Derby
Tel: 0332 751126

Membership – Unrestricted
Year Formed – 1900
No. of Members – 1000
Facilities – River Derwent between Derby and
the Road Bridge at Borrowash.

Ecclesbourne Fly FC

Secretary – W. Smit
'Wayside', Longfield Lane, Ilkeston DE7 4DD
Tel: 0602 320698

Membership – Restricted maximum
membership 12
Year Formed – 1955
No. of Members – 12
Facilities – River Ecclesbourne between
Windley and Colour-works, Duffield.

Leek & District Fly FA

Secretary – A.K. Bridgett
34 Windsor Drive, Leek
Tel: 0538 373163

Membership – Restricted
Year Formed – 1970
No. of Members – 130
Facilities – 3 miles of River Dove from Thorpe
Road Bridge to the Stone Stile end of first
field below Viator Bridge, Milldale. 4 miles of
River Churnet between villages of Oakamoor,
Alton and Froghall.

Matlocks AC

Secretary – R.N.E. Walsh M.R.I.P.H.H.
5 Derby Road, Homesford, Matlock
Tel: 062 982 2535

Membership – Unrestricted. Junior
membership available
Year Formed – 1943
No. of Members – 250
Facilities – The club has a thriving game and
coarse fishery on the Derbyshire Derwent.
Matlock length, Matlock Bath length, 2 ponds
at Lumsdale, The Gas Works length at
Matlock, Darley Bridge length, Pic, Tor &
High Tor lengths, Oaker length, Darley Dale
Cricket Ground length, all members only.
Part of River Amber. Hire out Matlock Bath,
River Derwent matches at discretion, apply to
Secretary.

Moss Brook AC

Secretary – Derek Morton
17 Station Road, Eckington, Sheffield
S31 9FW
Tel: 0246 435163

Membership – Restricted to 70 members
Year Formed – 1959
No. of Members – 70
Facilities – The Mois Valley from White
Bridge downstream to Atco Works. 2 miles
River Mois — stocked at least once a year.

Okeover Fly FC

Estate Office, Okeover, Ashbourne

DEVON

Barnstaple & District AA

Secretary – M.J. Andrew
3 Wrafton Road, Braunton, North Devon
Tel: 0271 814474

Membership – Unrestricted C & G, Restricted
G
Year Formed – 1931
No. of Members – 300
Facilities – Coarse — ponds up to 2 acres in
size with small stretch of the river Jaw.

Kennick Flyfishers A

Secretary – P. Mugridge
29 Champernowne, Modbury, Ivybridge
Tel: 054 88 30522

Membership – Unrestricted
Year Formed – 1975
No. of Members – 140

Plymouth & District
Freshwater AA

Secretary – J. Evans
Spring Cottage, Hemerdon, Plympton

Membership – Restricted
Year Formed – 1947
No. of Members – 100
Facilities – 2 Day tickets issued for a small
section of the River Plym. Brown trout, sea
trout and a few salmon. Tickets issued by
D.K. Sports, Exeter Street, Plymouth.

S.W.E.B. (Torbay District) AC

Secretary – T. Holtom
Electric House, Union Street, Torquay
TQ1 4BN
Tel: 0803 26200

Membership – Restricted
Year Formed – 1973
No. of Members – 70
Facilities – None, but have knowledge and information about complete area.

Tiverton Fly FC

Secretary – J.M. Ford
c/o Country Sports, 9 William Street, Tiverton
Tel: 08842 254770

Membership – Restricted to people living in area. Junior membership available
No. of Members – 100
Facilities – Approx. 3½ miles of River Exe at Tiverton.

Upper Teign FA

Secretary – A.J. Price
Gibbons Meadow, Chagford
Tel: 064 73 3253

Membership – Restricted
Year Formed – 1870
No. of Members – 25
Facilities – Approx. 14 miles of River Teign from Chagford downstream to Dunsford. Brown trout fishing available to non-members by the season, week or day. 2 Day tickets per day available to non-members for salmon and sea trout.

DORSET

Christchurch AC

Secretary – D. Chislett
Nimro 8 Sports, 9 Castle Parade, Ilford, Bournemouth
Tel: 0202 478224

Membership – Unrestricted
Year Formed – 1938
No. of Members – 1800
Facilities – 40 Miles of Hampshire, Avon & Dorset Stour plus 5 lakes.

Dorchester Angling & Boating Society

Secretary – A. Beattie
5 James Road, Dorchester
Tel: 0305 66536

Membership – Restricted
Year Formed – 1977
No. of Members – 50
Facilities – Waters fished by club — sea from Poole, Chesil Beach to Brixham. Coarse and game fishing, most rivers and lakes open to public in Dorset, Hampshire, Somerset and Devon.

Dorchester FC

Secretary – J.J. Fisher
Rew Hollow, Godmanstone, Dorchester
Tel: 030 03 306

Membership – Restricted
Year Formed – 1877
No. of Members – 36
Facilities – Dry fly only. River Frome and side streams. Approx. 6 miles of chalk streams.

Ringwood & District AA

Secretary – J. Steel
30 Mansal Avenue, Ferndown
Tel: 0202 893748

Membership – Unrestricted. Junior membership available
Year Formed – 1949
No. of Members – 1000
Facilities – Hampshire Avon, 5 miles Ringwood area including Severals and Ibsley fisheries. Dorset Stour, 10 miles. Other rivers, 3 miles. 6 lakes including Broadlands and Moreys. Most waters available to hire for matches.

Wimborne & District

Secretary – J. Bass
16 Tennyson Road, Walford, Wimborne
Tel: 0202 883840

Membership – Unrestricted
Year Formed – 1950
No. of Members – 800
Facilities – Dorset Stour — about 10 miles. 2 trout lakes and 4 coarse lakes.

DURHAM

Barnard Castle FFC

Secretary – G. Richardson
25 Cecil Road, Barnard Castle
Tel: 0833 38202

Membership – Restricted
Year Formed – 1936
No. of Members – 30

Bishop Auckland AC

Secretary – L. Mallam
32 Low Willington Crook
Tel: 038889 6575

Facilities – Have fishing on River Wear at Newfield, Pagebank, Croxaatt, West Mills dam, Willington and Byers Green, 2 stretches of Browney. River Tees at Whorlton.

Chester-le-St. and District AC

Secretary – T. Wright
156 Sedgeletch Road, Houghton-le-Spring, Tyne & Wear
Tel: 0783 848211

Membership – Unrestricted
Year Formed – 1935
No. of Members – 500
Facilities – River Wear 4 miles game and coarse fish. River Pont 5 miles brown trout only.

Darlington Brown Trout AA

Secretary – G.E. Coulson
5 Grange Avenue, Hopworth Place, Nr. Darlington
Tel: 0325 720246

Membership – Restricted
Year Formed – Early 1900's
No. of Members – 550 +
Facilities – Middle to Upper reaches of Tees and Swale.

Darlington Fly FC

Secretary – F.C. Birkbeck
Flat 4 Nora Fenby House, 48 The Green, Cockerton, Darlington
Tel: 0325 63896

Membership – Restricted
Facilities – Egglestone and Abbey Bridge Tees, Coniscliffe and Croft. Six miles.

Durham Co. Fed. of Anglers

Secretary – W. Craigs
33 Cleveland Place, Peterlee, Durham

Ferry Hill & District AC

Secretary – N. Davies
16 Conyers Terrace, Ferry Hill DL17 8AT
Tel: 0740 51522

Membership – Unrestricted. Junior membership available
No. of Members – 700
Facilities – Control rights on Burnhope Reservoir and Blackton Reservoir. Rivers North Tyne, Tyne, Hear Tees, Swale and 2 ponds with coarse fish.

Hartlepool and District AC

Secretary – K. Hewitson
16 Heathfield Drive, Hartlepool, Cleveland
Tel: 69025/69882

Membership – Restricted to residents in Hartlepool postal area. 'Outside' member (non-voting) is at present unrestricted.
No. of Members – 200
Facilities – Tilery Lake coarse fishery. Lake Kenny, Hutton Henry; R. Wear, Durham; Balderhead Reservoir, Teesdale; 2 corporation Park Lakes in Hartlepool, Cleveland.

North West Durham AA

Secretary – J.W. Geddes
Snook Acres Farm, Witton Gilbert, Durham
Tel: 0385 710237

Membership – Restricted
Year Formed – 1925
No. of Members – 80
Facilities – Two reservoirs leased from the Northumbrian water authority. Smiddy Sh (40 acres) and Waskerley reservoirs (68 acres).

Willington & District AC

Secretary – R. Lumb
18 Shipley Terrace, Crook

Membership – Restricted
Year Formed – 1950
No. of Members – 130
Facilities – Willington and District Angling Club control some four miles of water on River Wear and some 2 miles of water on Upper Reaches. The waters are stocked annually with brown trout and provide so of the best trout and migratory Fishing on river.

ESSEX

Chelmsford AA

Secretary – D.C. Willson
66 Marconi Road, Chelmsford CM1 1QD
Tel: 0245 87014

bership – Unrestricted
 Formed – 1922
of Members – 2,000
ities – 3½ miles River Chelmer, Gt.
ham — tench, pike, roach, rudd, carp.
 14 miles of Chelmer and Blackwater
gation Canal. Several weir pools and
waters including Kingmill, Paper Mills
Hoe Mill. Broads Green Lake (near
t Waltham), Danbury Trout Lake
bow and Brown) and Boreham Mere
eries — bream, roach, tench, carp,
, pike.

ex Fly Fishers' Club

etary – A.J. Bloomfield
 Warricks, Little Leighs, Chelmsford

bership – Restricted
 Formed – 1966
of Members – 110
ities – Trout fishing — fly only — two
ation lakes mid Essex — new members
be sponsored by existing member.

OUCESTERSHIRE

th Cerney AC

etary – H.J. Franklin
rs Farm, South Cerney, Cirencester
0285 860 362

bership – Unrestricted
 Formed – 1936
of Members – 980

EATER LONDON

mere Trout Fishery

etary – J. Howman
nere, Felix Lane, Shepperton TWM 8NN
093 22 25445

bership – Unrestricted
 Formed – 1952
of Members – 90
ities – 2 Gravel pits — one 55 years old,
years old. Both landscaped with now
re trees. Stocked with rainbow trout.

il Service AS

etary – N.J. Day
Honor Oak Road, London SE23 3RR

bership – Restricted
 Formed – 1934
ities – Waters on Thames, Kennet and
way. Still waters in Middlesex and North
on.

don AA

etary – V.R. Cooke
Hoe Street, Walthamstow,
on E17 3AP   Tel: 01 520 7477 (Day)

bership – Unrestricted
 Formed – 1884
of Members – Approx. 18,000
ities – Extensive fishing rights in London
surrounding areas. Includes stretches of
rs Avon, Beult, Cam, Great Ouse, Stour,
mes, Cole, Lee, Little Ouse, Stort, Ver,
sum, Wissey plus lakes, canals and
voirs.

Rod & Line (Sundridge) Trout Lakes

26 Marishal Road, Lewisham, London SE13

The Thames Angling Preservation Society

Hon. Secretary – A.E. Hodges
The Pines, 32 Tile Kiln Lane, Bexley, Kent
DA5 2BB
Tel: Crayford 525575 (London) 2 525575
S.T.D. 0322 525575

Founded in 1838
To protect the fisheries of the River Thames.

GREATER MANCHESTER

Border Anglers & Naturalists (Mossley & Dist.)

Secretary – H. Garside
60 Queensway, Greenfield, Oldham
OL3 7AH
Tel: 045 77 5993

Membership – Restricted – Junior Members
Year Formed – 1971/2
No. of Members – Approx. 250
Facilities – Hollingrove Dam, Coarse fishing
— Greenfield Trout etc. River Tame,
Alexandra Mill length only, Uppermill
Claytons Pond Mossley area (Coarse fish),
River Tame Greenfield Mossley area short
lengths being developed for coarse fishing.
(Milton Mill area Roaches area). We are a
branch club for the Oldham and District AAA
and help control their waters.

Bury District AS

Secretary – F. Booth
142 Bury Road, Tottington, Nr. Bury,
Lancs BL8 3DX
Tel: 020488 2517

Membership – Unrestricted
Year Formed – 1903
No. of Members – Approx. 1300

Oldham & District Amalgamated AA

Secretary – H. Garside
60 Queensway, Greenfield, Oldham
OL3 7AH
Tel: 045 77 5993

Membership – Unrestricted – full membership
via clubs.
Year Formed – 1950
No. of Members – Approximately 350 to 400
counting all categories.
Facilities – Area Saddleworth, Oldham,
Stalybridge. Huddersfield Narrow Canal
(Coarse and Trout) Lock 24 Saddleworth — to
Bridge 85 Greenfield. Swineshaw Mill Dam
Stalybridge area (trout and coarse). A water
at Stakehill Nr. Oldham (Dam). Small pond at
Grotton Nr. Oldham (Coarse fish).

HAMPSHIRE

Bishops Waltham AC

Secretary – M. Creese
8 St. Andrews Green, Meonstoke
Tel: 048 97 664

Membership – Unrestricted
Year Formed – 1969
No. of Members – 83

Bishops Waltham Parrish FC

Secretary – B.R. Jerome
Rareridge, Rareridge Lane, Bishops Waltham
Tel: 04893 4137

Brockenhurst Manor Fly FC

Secretary – Mrs. J. Chessell
The Laurels, Beaulieu Road, Dibden Purlieu,
Southampton
Tel: 0703 842788

Christchurch AC

Secretary – B. Chislett
16 Old Milton Road, New Milton.
Tel: 0425 610304

Membership – Unrestricted. Junior
membership available
No. of Members – 1800
Facilities – 40 miles of Stour and Avon 9
stillwater coarse fishing lakes. 1 put & take
trout lake.

Houghton Club Ltd.

Fisheries Manager – V. Lunn
Willow Mead, Stockbridge
Tel: 026481 797

Petersfield & District AC

Secretary – G.A. McKee
25 North Lane, Buritom, Petersfield
GU31 5RS

Membership – Restricted
Year Formed – Approx. 1932
No. of Members – 170
Facilities – Sussex Rother — Petworth,
Fittleworth, Trotton, Durford Bridge. Arun —
Pulborough, Watersfield River Meon —
Titchfield, Chichester Canal. Westhammet
gravel pit, Hayling Island gravel pit. Hilsea
moat Portsmouth, Heath Lake Petersfield.

Ringwood & District AA

Secretary – J. Steel
30 Mansal Avenue, Ferndown
Tel: 0202 893748

Membership – Unrestricted. Junior
membership available
Year Formed – 1949
No. of Members – 1,000
Facilities – Hampshire Avon, 5 miles
Ringwood area including Severals and Ibsley
fisheries. Dorset Stour 10 miles. Other rivers 3
miles, 6 lakes including Broadlands and
Moreys. Most waters available hire for
matches.

Salisbury & District AC

Secretary – A.C. Amos
28 Dudley Avenue, Fordingbridge
Tel: 0425 52660

Membership – Unrestricted
Year Formed – 1941
No. of Members – 1900

Facilities – Coarse fishing at Steeple Langford, Petersfinger, Edington and Milford Lakes. Also on Dorset Stour, Eye Mead. Coarse/game on River Avon at Burgate, Charford and Salisbury River Nadder at Salisbury. Game only on River Avon at Durnford, West Amesbury and Upper Avon, River Wylye at Stapleford, Bapton and Wylye Village.

Southern Anglers

Secretary – T.A. Irons
7 Nelson Crescent, Horndean, Portsmouth
Tel: 0705 597017

Facilities – 1½ miles on River Rother.

Sutton Scotney & District AC

Secretary – R.V. Larcombe
5 Meadow Bank, Stockbridge Road, Sutton Scotney
Tel: 096 276 412

Membership – Restricted to 40

Wilton Fly FC

Secretary – C.B. White
1 Sudan Cottage, Bryces Lane, Sherfield English, Romsey
Tel: 0703 30511 Ext. 35

HEREFORD & WORCS

Hereford and District AA

Secretary – I. Astley
The Lindens, Bishopstone, HR4 7JG
Tel: 098122 283

Membership – Unrestricted
Year Formed – 1921
No. of Members – Approx. 700 adults and 600 children.
Facilities – Approximately 8 miles of the River Wye and 7 miles of the River Lugg near Hereford. (Distances expressed as single bank). Salmon, trout, and coarse fish (particularly chub, dace, roach, perch and pike).

Kidderminster & District AA

Secretary – M.R. Millinchip
246 Marlpool Lane, Kidderminster
Tel: 0562 63471

Membership – Restricted
Year Formed – 1892
No. of Members – 1800
Facilities – Bewdley. Above Bridge for about one mile. Bewdley. Below bridge for about three quarters of a mile. Winnalls. Below Stourport for about one mile. Stewpony Canal. For about one and a half miles.

Portobello AC

Secretary – J.R. Harries
17 Kingsbury Road, St Johns, Worcester
Tel: 0905 54598

Membership – Restricted
Year Formed – 1955
No. of Members – 85
Facilities – R. Tewe (¾ mile), Bow Brook (¾ mile) Mill pool — Reconstructed in 1971.

HERTFORDSHIRE

Amwell Magna Fishery

Secretary – G.A. Pusey
32 Benford Road, Hoddesdon
Tel: 099 24 67979

Membership – Restricted
Year Formed – 1831
No. of Members – 35
Facilities – Old River Lea at Easneye, between Ware and Stanstead Abbotts, Herts, Millstream to Stanstead Abbotts and River Ash to road bridge. Includes two weirs mostly both banks totalling 4½ miles.

Palmers Green AS

Secretary – P.G. King
32 Ashdown Crescent, Cheshunt, EN273
Tel: 0992 27238

Membership – Unrestricted
Year Formed – 1948
No. of Members – 41
Facilities – We are the managing club of the Waltham Abbey Angling Consortium of nine clubs. The W.A.A.C. has a private fishery of about 1½ miles of water on the Old River Lea and the Cornmill stream at Waltham Abbey, Essex. Palmers Green A.S. has a 1½ mile stretch on the New River between Ware and Hertford, in Herts. Palmers Green has ¾ mile trout fishery on River Mirmram at Tewin, Herts.

Upper Gade Flyfishers Association

Secretary – D.E. Crocker
Llwyn Celyn, Hollybush Close, Potter End, Berkhamsted
Tel: 044 27 2135

HUMBERSIDE NORTH

Driffield AC

Secretary – R.W.A. Todd
Messrs. Todd & Thorpe, Land of Green Ginger, Hull

Membership – Restricted
Year Formed – 1833
Facilities – Chalk streams arising from the Wolds and eventually draining into the River Humber. Brown trout. Dry Fly — Upstream Nymph after July.

Foston Fly Fishers

Secretary – R.B. Booth
Church Farm, Foston-on-The-Wolds

Hunsley Fly Fishers

Secretary – R.B. Booth
Seven Corners Lane, Beverley

Market Weighton AC

Secretary – T. Brown
19 Glenfield Avenue, Market Weighton
Tel: 06962 2779

Membership – Unrestricted
Year Formed – 1966
No. of Members – 45
Facilities – Waters within a radius of 15 m of Market Weighton. 2 ponds within 4 mil Market Weighton — well stocked all spec: River Foulness approximately ½ mile — mainly bream, roach and dace. Low Catto — R. Derwent ¾ mile — mixed fishery including trout and grayling.

Millhouse Fly Fishers

Secretary – M.A. Russell
c/o Wm Jackson & Son Limited,
40 Derringham Street, Hull
Tel: 0482 224131

Membership – Restricted
No. of Members – 21
Facilities – Fishing takes places for 1 mile Foston on the Wolds.

KENT

Canterbury & District AA

Secretary – N.S.N. Stringer
Riversdale, Mill Road, Sturry, Nr. Canterb
CT2 0AF
Tel: 0227 710830

Membership – Unrestricted. Junior membership available
Year Formed – 1928
No. of Members – 2,060
Facilities – Members — 200 acres Lakes, Fordwich & Westbere 8 miles River Stour Fordwich to Plucks Gutter. Day tickets — Grove Ferry — Plucks Gutter also availab to hire for matches.

Darent Valley Trout Fishers

Secretary – D.J. Rees
21 Ramus Wood Avenue, Farnborough
BR6 7HF
Tel: 0689 51888

Membership – Restricted by lease. Waiting sequence.
Year Formed – 1949
No. of Members – 36
Facilities – 3½ miles minor chalkstream — Shoreham to Horton Kirby — full range of natural insects including Mayfly — Brown rainbow trout and grayling — wet and dry and nymph — members may fish any day season 1st April to 30th September. We h all water on long leases. Excellent water quality produces up to 1000 fish per seaso waiting list — boats have car parking, toil — all fishing on private farmland.

Edenbridge AS

Secretary – D.T. Gallard
1 Shoebridge Cottages, Furnace Farm, Cowden
Tel: 034286 711

ership – Restricted
Formed – 1950
f Members – 700
ties – Both banks of River Eden from
d to Penshurst. River Medway at Ashurst
Vithyham. Lakes at Hever Castle and
1 Green.

t Anglers Consultative Soc.

tary – J. Peters
ens House, Sherbourne Close, Dorset
, Tunbridge Wells

gfisher Angling & ervation Soc.

tary – A. Burrows
ntley Close, New Barn, Longfield,
nouth

ties – Coarse fishing waters in Kent and
ut Lake near Shoreham.

dway Fly Fishers

tary – R. Stokes
nys Drive, Wigmore, Gillingham

shurst AS

tary – M.A. Minns
ntgomery Road, Tunbridge Wells
892 38625

ership – Restricted
ties – Private waters

e Anglers & Owners Assoc.

tary – M.E. Sutton
le Place Cottages, Brenchely

ership – Restricted
Formed – Pre War
f Members – 140
ties – Approximately 6 miles of double
some sections fly fishing only, other
ns spin or bait. No float fishing,
ots, keep nets etc.

NCASHIRE

rington & District FC

tary – A. Balderstone
wneley Avenue, Huncoat
254 33517

ership – Unrestricted
Formed – 1956
ties – Coarse and trout fishing on
voirs and rivers, salmon rivers.

tham AA

tary – A.R. Green
Post Office, Main Street, Bentham
7HL
0468 61650

ership – Restricted to 40. Junior
ership available
f Members – Locals + 40 Non Resident
ties – River Wenning Brown and Sea
. Booking essential. Goodenber Lake,
nly Brown and Rainbow Trout limited to
s only.

B.I.C.C. AC

Secretary – J. Worthington
46 Landside, Leigh
Tel: 0942 605273

Membership – Restricted
Year Formed – 1934
No. of Members – 45

Blackburn & District AA

Secretary – B. Hogarth
1 Moorfield Road, Leyland PR5 3AR
Tel: 07724 24018

Membership – Unrestricted
No. of Members – 200
Facilities – River Hodder, River Ribble, R.
Wenning, R. Aire, R. Lune and Parsonage
Reservoir Blackburn.

Bury District Angling Society

Secretary – F. Booth
142 Bury Road, Tottington, nr. Bury
Tel: 020 488 2517

Membership – Unrestricted. Junior
membership available
No. of Members – 1034
Facilities – Parker's, Elton Vale, Kirklees,
Tottington, Scholes Water, Tottington, Bury
and Bolton Canal, Crompton's, Smethurst
Waters, Woolford, Horse Shoe Lodge,
Ramsbottom, Bolholt Waters, Leaks Water,
Taylor and Nicholson's, Wikes Water,
Longcroft Waters trout only.

Darwen AA

Secretary – J. Priestley
24 Knowlesley Road, Darwen BB3 2NE
Tel: 0254 75348

Membership – Restricted
Year Formed – 1890
No. of Members – 64
Facilities – Fishing on Earnsdale and
Sunnyhurst Hey reservoirs stocked with brown
and rainbow trout. Permits also available from
'County Sports', Duckworth Street, Darwen.

Galgate AA

Secretary – W.R. Palmer
'Deepdale' 29 Ashford Road, Scotforth,
Lancaster
Tel: 0524 68472

Membership – Restricted to waiting list
No. of Members – 105 + (30 juniors)
Facilities – 5-6 miles of River Conder.

Lancashire Fly FA

Secretary – R. Hill
220 Pleckgate Road, Blackburn
Tel: 0254 48982

Membership – Restricted
Year Formed – 1909
No. of Members – 110
Facilities – Fishing rights on Rivers Hodder
and Lune also reservoir fishing.

Marsden Star AS

Secretary – M.J. Jackson
27 Albion Street, Earby, Colne
Tel: 028284 3333

Membership – Unrestricted

Year Formed – Circa 1900
No. of Members – 800
Facilities – 9 miles of Leeds and Liverpool
Canal between Long Ing Bridge and Bank
Newton also stretches of River Aire and
Calder and several small waters in Lancashire
and Yorkshire.

Northern AA

Secretary – G. Wilson
11 Guildford Avenue, Chorley
Tel: 02572 65905

Membership – Unrestricted
Year Formed – 1889
No. of Members – 12,000 Senior 2,000 Junior,
1,000 Pensioners
Facilities – Fishing on Lancaster Canal,
Glasson Dock and Arm. Parts of Leeds and
Liverpool Canal, Shropshire Union Canal,
Bridgewater Canal. Wide Hole, Macclesfield
Canal, Lower Peak Forest Canal. Also fishing
on stretches of the following rivers: Ribble,
Worthenbury Brook, Dee, Alyn, Calder,
Vyrnwy, Gilpin, Banwy, Severn, Weaver and
Old.

Padiham & District AS

Secretary – J.W. Whitham
232 Burnley Road, Padiham, Burnley
Tel: 0282 73156

Membership – Restricted waiting list. Junior
membership available
No. of Members – 80
Facilities – River Hodder stretches.

Preston Centre Federated Anglers

Secretary – G. Jones
1 Carnarvon Road, Preston
Tel: 0772 56862

Membership – Unrestricted
Year Formed – 1900
No. of Members – 4,000
Facilities – Fishing on Rivers Ribble, Wyre
and Rufford Canal near Preston. Maps
available from Secretary.

Staincliffe Angling Club

Secretary – B. Robson
8 Rylstone Drive, Barnoldswick, Colne BB8
5RG
Tel: 02828 12544

Membership – Restricted
No. of Members – 135
Facilities – Upper reaches of River Ribble

Todmorden AS

Secretary – D. Howorth
42 Hallroyd Crescent, Todmorden
Tel: 070 681 4443

Membership – Unrestricted
Year Formed – 1935
No. of Members – 280 + 250 juniors
Facilities – Fishing on two trout lakes one
coarse lake and 7 miles of Rochdale Canal.

LEICESTERSHIRE

Hinckley AC

Secretary – L.J. Aston
75 Forest Road, Hinckley
Tel: 0455 611586

Membership – Unrestricted
Year Formed – 1922
No. of Members – 800
Facilities – 5 miles of Ashby-de-la-Zouch
Canal, ¾ mile River Sence and three small
local pools.

Rutland Water Fly FC

Secretary – S.N. Parton
93 Parkside, Wollaton, Notts
Tel: 0602 787761/286693

Membership – Unrestricted
Year Formed – 1978
No. of Members – 120
Facilities – Organization to represent Rutland
fishermen and arrange competitions, social
events and winter meetings for its members.

LINCOLNSHIRE

Deeping St. James AC

Secretary – J. Cran Esq.
53 Castle Drive, Northborough, Peterborough
PE6 9DL
Tel: 0778 343691

Membership – Restricted within 20 miles
No. of Members – 60
Facilities – River Welland (Market Deeping
Several Fishery) available for matches.

Lincoln & District AA

Secretary – A.D. Gilbert
Tel: 0522 685709

Membership – Unrestricted
Year Formed – 1868
No. of Members – 6,321
Facilities – Fishing on Rivers Trent and
Witham, three lakes with area of 35 acres also
Old River Witham, Wainfleet Relief channel,
Steeping River, Rivers Till, Skerth, Barlings
and Fossdyke and Swanholme Lakes Complex.

Witham & District Joint AF

Secretary – R.H. Hobley
30 Gunby Avenue, Hartsholme Estate, Lincoln
Tel: 0522 683688

Membership – Unrestricted
Year Formed – 1914
No. of Members – 40,000 +
Facilities – Fishing on 120 bank miles
including River Witham, River Steeping,
Wainfleet Relief Channel, Fossdyke Canal,
Billinghay Skirth and Timberland Delph — all
good mixed coarse fishing. Swanholme lakes
at Lincoln — fly fishing for trout.

MERSEYSIDE

Brunswick AC

Secretary – Peter Hatton
42 Thornholme Crescent, Liverpool 11
Tel: 051 256 8975

Membership – Restricted
Year Formed – 1950
No. of Members – 12
Facilities – Montgomery canal Lannymynech
between bridges 92-94.

Crosby & District AC

Secretary – M. Cain
40 Buttermere Gardens, Crosby, Liverpool,
L23 0SF
Tel: 051-928 9364

Membership – Unrestricted. Junior
membership available
Year Formed – 1971
No. of Members – 60
Facilities – No Club Waters, but members of
Liverpool and Dist. AA, and N.F.A. Outings
held on alternate Sundays, by coach to
venues within approx. 100 mile radius.
Meetings fortnightly which are well attended
because of features such as talks, films, etc.

Hutton & District AA

Secretary – H.O. Palmer
143 Blue Bell Lane, Hutton
Tel: 051 489 4819

Membership – Restricted
Year Formed – 1886
No. of Members – 60
Facilities – River Dee, Bowling Bank, Nr
Wrexham, North Wales.

Irby AC

Secretary – Frank Evans
4 McAlpine Close, Upton, Wirral L49 6JR
Tel: 051 678 7619

Membership – Unrestricted
Year Formed – 1967
No. of Members – 600
Facilities – 25 Small lakes and ponds (Wirral
area) S.U.C. at Aberbechan. River Severn
Aberbechan (small stretches). Montgomery
Canal, Aberbechan, Bridge nos 150-153
available to hire for matches.

Liverpool & District AA

Secretary – John Johnson
97 Liverpool Road, Maghull.
Tel: 051 526 4083

Membership – Unrestricted
No. of Members – Approx. 1,500
Facilities – Salmon waters at Berwyn, on the
River Dee, Godabridge on the River Vyrnwy,
Leighton on the River Severn and Haughton
on the River Vyrnwy. Waters can be hired out
— apply to Club Secretary.

Maghull & Lydiate AC

Secretary – J. Johnson
97 Liverpool Road, (North) Maghull
Tel: 051 526 4083

Membership – Unrestricted
Year Formed – 1911
No. of Members – 182
Facilities – Swan Pool, Liverpool Road
Aughton. Burscough Brickworks, Abbey Lane
Burscough. Barton Brook, Altcar Merser's
Pool, Bells Lane, Lydiate Ainsdale Lake,
Ainsdale, Lancs, Moss Lodges, Skelmersdale,
(Joint ownership with Skem. Comrades).

NORFOLK

Norfolk & Suffolk Fly Fishers Society

Chairman – S. Walker
16 Duff Road, Norwich
Tel: 0603 49038

NORTHAMPTONSHIRE

Kettering FF

Secretary – F. Jaran
8 Cumberland Close, Northampton

Kettering & District Fly FC

Secretary – F. Arran
110a Abington Street, Northampton
Tel: 0604 27501

Mid. Northants Fly Fishers

Secretary – H. Cave
c/o Lowery Estate Agents, 24 Bridge Stre
Northampton
Tel: 0604 21561

Membership – Unrestricted
Year Formed – 1950
No. of Members – 150
Facilities – Does not control any water, bu
club fishes on Pitsford & Ravensthorpe,
Driycohe, Grafham Rutland, Eyebrook.

Mid Northants TFA

Secretary – H.F. Cave
Church End, Hall Park, Brixworth NN6 9
Tel: 0604 880503

Membership – Unrestricted. Junior
membership available
Year Formed – 1955
No. of Members – 180
Facilities – No water controlled by us. Ho
waters for fishing are Pitsford & Ravensth
Reservoirs.

NORTHUMBERLAND

Allendale AA

Secretary – J.W. Smith
Dalegarth, Allendale, Nr. Hexham
Tel: 043 483 375

Membership – Restricted to Parishoners o
Facilities – Allendale to Allenhead. Ticket
secretary or The Post Office, Allendale. 8
miles of river fishing. Brown trout, fly fish
only.

Aln AA

Secretary – F.J.R. Moir
Thistledowne, 49 Swansfield Park Road,
Alnwick
Tel: 0665 2771

Membership – Unrestricted
No. of Members – 150
Facilities – River Aln. 7 miles trout and se
trout fishing. Permits from Alnwick sports
centre, Narrowgate Alnwick. R.L. Jobson
Sons, Bondgate, Alnwick.

llington & Blagdon AA

etary – S. Symons
orland Drive, Bedlington
0670 822011

bership – Restricted
Formed – 1956
of Members – 125
ties – River Blyth. Mid Northumberland.
Stannington village to Bedlington. Both
s with the exception of two small
hes on one bank which are privately
d. River consists of streams, flats, and
pools gravel & rock bottom. Sea trout
n trout, grayling, perch, roach.

ingham AC

etary – T.H. Armstrong
4 Westlands, Bellingham, Hexham
0660 20455

bership – Restricted
of Members – 60
ties – Approx. 4½ miles River Tyne on
yside Estates on the upper North Tyne.
ng for brown trout, sea trout and salmon.
rly stocked with brown trout. Weekly
s are available for visitors on holiday in
arish of Bellingham only. Monday to
day inclusive, up till September 31 in
eason.

wick & District AA

etary – A.R. Manderison
estfield Avenue, Berwick-on-Tweed

bership – Unrestricted
Formed – 1927
of Members – 133
ties – Approx. 7 miles of River
eadder from Allanton to Canty's Bridge.
y fast flowing stream. Mixture of rock and
l bed. Fast weed growth.

tton AA

etary – A. Jarvis
Road, Chatton, Alnwick
066 85 257

bership – Restricted
Formed – 1911
of Members – 125
ties – Agricultural area. Clear water. All
ke of Northumberland's preserves of
Till.

ndale Grayling Club

er

ties – Fishing on River Till, Breamish.

twhistle & District AC

etary – J. Mason
Voodhead Park, Haltwhistle

bership – Restricted to Haltwhistle &
ct only. Junior membership available
f Members – 122
ties – Six miles of Tyne, Haltwhistle.
side of River S. Tyne, Haltwhistle Burn.

ham AA

etary – C. Sowerby
indsor Terrace, Hexham Tel: 0434 605355

ties – On River Tyne.

Ladykirk & Norham AA

Secretary – R.G. Wharton
8 St. Cuthbert's Square, Norham, Berwick-on-Tweed
Tel: 0289 82467

Membership – Restricted to area. Junior membership available
No. of Members – 30
Facilities – River Tweed only for Brown trout, grayling and roach.

Northumbrian AF

Secretary – P.A. Hall
25 Ridley Place, Newcastle upon Tyne

Membership – Unrestricted – Trout.
Restricted – Salmon
Year Formed – 1890
No. of Members – 2000
Facilities – Stretches of River Tyne & Coquet.
15½ miles of Duke of Northumberland preserves on Coquet.

South Tyne AA

Secretary – J.O. Moore
24 Strother Close, Haydon Bridge, Hexham

Membership – Restricted
Year Formed – 1879
No. of Members – 200
Facilities – South Tyne, Haydon Bridge

Upper Coquet Dalt AC

Membership – Restricted
Facilities – Extensive preserves on upper Coquet.

Wansbeck AA

Secretary – D.J. Bell
9 Bilton's Court, Morpeth
Tel: 0670 513478

Membership – Restricted
Year Formed – 1900
No. of Members – 500
Facilities – Trout fishing only. Certain stretches restricted to fly fishing only.
Spinning Worm on rest of water after 1st June in any year.

NOTTINGHAMSHIRE

Nottingham AA

Secretary – E.J. Collin
224 Radford Bld., Nottingham
Tel: 0602 877558 or 782601

Membership – Restricted
Year Formed – 1890
No. of Members – 4000
Facilities – River Trent. 6-7 miles bank.
Bestwood Ponds – 4. Ponds in Trent Valley
– 5. River Derwent & River Soar.

Nottingham Flyfishers Club

Secretary – H.J. Messer
23 Cavendish Road, The Park, East Nottingham
Tel: 0602 42899

Membership – Restricted
Year Formed – 1880
No. of Members – 97, of whom 45 fish
Facilities – River Meden — about 1 mile each bank through Thoreby Estate. A fifteen acre lake at Gibmere.

OXFORDSHIRE

Abingdon & District ARA

Secretary – R. Pitson
11 Finmore Close, Abingdon OX14 1HF
Tel: 0325 25140

Membership – Unrestricted. Junior membership available
Year Formed – 1899
No. of Members – 500
Facilities – From Sandford Lock, downstream, including Radley & Nuneham waters approx 2 miles of River Thames. Situated between Oxford & Abingdon. Waters available to hire for matches.

Radcot A & PC

Secretary – C.R. Neville
"Clanville", Bampton Road, Clanfield
Tel: 991 81 362 Secretary
991 81 220 Swan Hotel, Radcot H.Q.

Membership – Unrestricted. Junior membership available
Year Formed – 1946
No. of Members – 200
Facilties – Radcot on Thames — Trout 1st April — 10th September, Coarse 16th June — 14th March. Available to hire for matches up to 150 pegs.

SHROPSHIRE

Ditherington AC

Secretary – G.E. Williams
6 Meadowbrook Cottages, Annscroft, Shrewsbury
Tel: 0743860 835

Membership – Unrestricted
Year Formed – 1930
No. of Members – 200 +
Facilities – Three stretches of River Severn around Shrewsbury. One stretch is owned by Society other two on long lease. All is contest water and is available for away clubs to book. Water holds very good head of barbel, chub, bream, roach, dace. Society has Game fishing on 2 stretches, also available. Also we rent a large pool near Shrewsbury — Sunderton.

Ellesmere AC

Secretary – W. Benkoff
Rose Cottage, Colemere
Tel: 093 922 317

Membership – Unrestricted
Year Formed – 1931
No. of Members – 300-350
Facilities – Rights on local meres and River Vyrnwy at Llanymynech. Private trout pool.

Leighton Salmon & Coarse FS

Secretary – F. Wilcox
23 & 24 The Wharfage, Iron-Bridge, Telford
Tel: 095245 3279

Membership – Restricted
Year Formed – 1936
No. of Members – 200

Old L.M.S. AC

Secretary – J.R. Thorpe
13 Hordley Avenue, Heathfarm, Shrewsbury
Tel: 0743 6303

Membership – Unrestricted
Year Formed – Before 1932
No. of Members – 130

G.K.N. Sankey AC

Secretary – P. Fox
6 Whitemere Road, Wellington, Telford
Tel: 0592 54403

Membership – Unrestricted
Year Formed – 1934
No. of Members – 120
Facilities – Shelton, Nr. Shrewsbury, River
Severn. Also Rossal Nr. Shrewsbury, River
Severn. Gressage Nr. Wellington, River
Severn, Hawk Lake, Hawkstone Park, Hodnet
Shropshire.

Shrewsbury & District Piscatorial S

Secretary – K.J. Ford
31 Albert Street, Castlefields, Shrewsbury
Tel: 0743 63738

Membership – Unrestricted
Facilities – Mainly River Severn in
Shrewsbury area. Some pools in individual
clubs.

Shropshire Anglers Federation

Secretary – P.C. Moody
65 Broadway Avenue, Trench, Telford
Tel: 0952 603779

Membership – Unrestricted – Individuals
Restricted – Clubs
Year Formed – 1923
No. of Members – 2000
Facilities – Coarse and Game, Berwick Estate,
Shrewsbury — River Severn. Coarse only,
Rossall Estate, Shrewsbury, River Severn.
Coarse and game, Melverley, near Knockin
Shropshire. Coarse only, Pentre Nr. Knockin,
Shropshire.

SOMERSET

Bathampton AA

Secretary – A. Adams
38 Beech Avenue, Shepton Mallet
Tel: 0749 3021

Membership – Unrestricted
Year Formed – 1920
No. of Members – 3,500
Facilities – Coarse fishing on the Bristol Avon
and ten ponds and lakes in Bath and the
surrounding area. Trout fishing on the
tributaries of the Bristol Avon.

Chard & District Angling Club

Secretary – D. Lemon
38 Glanvill Avenue, Chard TA20 1EU
Tel: 0460 61281

Membership – Unrestricted. Junior
membership available
No. of Members – 150
Facilities – Coarse fishing at Perry Street
Pond, Perry Street, nr. Chard and Ash Pond,
Ash, nr. Martock. Coarse and Trout fishing at
River Isle at Donyatt and Ilminster, and River
Axe, Broom Bridge, nr. Chard.

North Somerset Association of AC

Secretary – R. Newton
64 Clevedon Road, Tickenham, Clevedon
Tel: 02755 6107

Facilities – Association of Weston-Super-Mare
& District AA, Highbridge AA and Clevedon
& District FAC.

Stoke-Sub-Hamdon & District AA

Secretary – Mr. M. Prescott
'Homemead' Rimpton Road, Marston Magna,
Yeovil
Tel: 0935 850426

Membership – Unrestricted
Year Formed – 1955
No. of Members – 500
Facilities – River fishing, coarse and trout, on
upper reaches of River Parrett.

Taunton Fly FC

Secretary – J.S. Hill
21 Manor Road, Taunton
Tel: 0823 71530

Membership – Unrestricted. Junior
membership available
Year Formed – Pre 1900
No. of Members – approx. 95
Facilities – 10 Miles of River Tone upstream of
French Weir, Taunton. Three separate
stretches totalling 2 miles on River Axe,
Devon.

Yeovil and Sherbourne AA

Secretary – N. Garrett
18 Springfield Road, Yeovil
Tel: 0935 71889

Membership – Unrestricted

STAFFORDSHIRE

Burslem Isaac Walton AS

Secretary – R.W.H. Burdon
77 Albany Road, Hardfields, Stoke-on-Trent
Tel: 0782 618807

Membership – Restricted
Year Formed – 1900
No. of Members – 100
Facilities – A length of the Caldon Canal to
the North East of Stoke-on-Trent, from Milton
to Hazelhurst Junction.

Burton Mutual AA

Secretary – D.J. Clark
7 Denton Rise, Burton-on-Trent
Tel: 0283 44734

Membership – Restricted
Year Formed – 1884
No. of Members – 1700
Facilities – Trent & Mersey Canal (Wychr
Claymills). River Dove apart from a few
hundred yards, Tutbury Weir to River Tr
— both banks including Ox-Bows. Brans
gravel pit. Various small stretches of Rive
Trent.

Kidsgrove & District AA

Secretary – Mrs. B. Rigley
95 Ian Road, Newchapel, Stoke-on-Trent
Tel: 07816 72240

Membership – Unrestricted. Junior
membership available
No. of Members – approx. 500 including
juniors
Facilities – Bathpool — Leg-o-Mutton Poo
Clough Hall Lake, all at Kidsgrove. Stoke
Trent Macclesfield Canal (Congleton Stat
Cheshire bridge 75 to 72). River Dove fro
roadbridge A50 at Doveridge downstrean
right bank for 1 mile. Congleton canal
available to hire for matches. Apply to
Secretary.

Leek & District Fly FA

Secretary – A.K. Bridgett
34 Windsor Drive, Leek
Tel: 0538 373163

Membership – Restricted
Year Formed – 1970
No. of Members – 130
Facilities – 3 Miles of River Dove from The
Road Bridge to the Stone Stile end of firs
field below Viator Bridge, Milldale. 4 Mi
River Churnet between villages of Oakam
Alton and Froghall.

Leek & District Fly FC

Secretary – E. Dennis
Rough Close, Stoke-on-Trent

Leek & Moorlands FC

Secretary – D. White
20 Campbell Avenue, Leek
Tel: 0538 371526

Membership – Unrestricted
Year Formed – 1885
No. of Members – 600 Senior 500 Juniors
Facilities – Grayling and trout on Manifol
Hulme End and Dove at Earl Sterndale. T
and coarse on Churnet around Leek. Coa
— Crakemarsh Pool, Nr. Rocester and Ca
Canal at Leek, Cheddleton and Froghall.

Stoke City & District AA

Secretary – P. Johansen
31 East Crescent, Sneydgren, Hanley, Sto
on-Trent
Tel: 0782 24840

Membership – Unrestricted. Junior
membership available
Year Formed – 1880
No. of Members – 700
Facilities – 11 Miles Canals. T & M Canal
Aston-Weston. S.U.C. Gnossall, Shebdor
Acre lake near Eccershall. Rivers Severn,
Tern Roden, Rheiw, Sow, Trout Lakes, Fl
Available for matches on S.U. Canal area
Norbury Junction and Woodseaves. 250 r
maximum.

Uttoxeter Fly FC
Secretary – I.E. Davies
The Coppice, Sunnyside Road, Uttoxeter
Membership – Restricted
Year Formed – 1880
No. of Members – 30
Facilities – River Dove, Rocester

SUFFOLK

Long Melford & District AA
Secretary – N. Mealham
Springfield Terrace, East Street, Sudbury
Tel: 0787 77139

SURREY

Godalming AS
Secretary – M.R. Richardson
Summers Road, Farncombe, Godalming
GU7 3BE
Tel: 048 68 22791

Peper Harow Park Fly FC
Secretary – Ms. M.E. Hide
Inglewood, Moushill Lane, Milford,
Godalming
Tel: 048 68 7954
Membership – Restricted
Year Formed – 1946
No. of Members – 30
Facilities – The water from Somerset Bridge
on the Elstead-Shackleford Road downstream
to the road bridge on the A3 at Eashing. Both
banks may be fished except a small stretch on
the North Bank, bordering Peper Harow
Community and there are three ponds at
Oxenford Farm, the smallest pond being
reserved for dry fly fishing only.

Clive Vale AC
Secretary – D. Swain
Amherst Road, Hastings
Tel: 0424 713240
Membership – Restricted to people living in a
5 mile radius.
Year Formed – 1912
No. of Members – 700
Facilities – Clive Vale and Ecclesbourne
Reservoirs. River Rother. Day tickets
available.

Crowborough & District AA
Secretary – K.J.B. Wilson
'Elysium' 35, Southridge Road, Crowborough
Tel: 08926 4722
Membership – Restricted. Junior membership
available
No. of Members – 150
Facilities – Local lakes, streams, rivers within
a 5 mile radius of Crowborough Cross.

SUSSEX WEST

Haywards Heath & District AS
Secretary – S.F. Whetstone
West View, Lewes Road, Lindfield
RH16 2LT
Tel: 044 77 3059

Leconfield Flyfishing Club
Secretary – Sir C. Wolseley Bt.
Estate Office, Petworth GU28 0DU
Tel: 0798 42502
Membership – Restricted
Year Formed – 1980
No. of Members – 70 full rods, 30 half
Facilities – There are 7 fully stocked trout
ponds totalling approximately 13 acres all of
which are situated on the Leconfield Estate at
Petworth.

Ouse Angling Preservation
Secretary – Dr. J.L. Cotton
Down End, Kingston Road, Lewes
Tel: 07916 4883
Membership – Unrestricted

Petworth AC
Secretary – D.A. Pugh
3 Cherry Tree Walk, Petworth
Tel: 0798 42866
Membership – Unrestricted
Year Formed – 1957
No. of Members – 200 +

Pitshill Flyfishing Waters
Secretary – R. Etherington
c/o Messrs. King & Chasemore
Lombard Street, Petworth Tel: 0798 42011
Membership – Restricted
No. of Members – 40
Facilities – Approx. 1½ miles of rain feed
river with a natural stock of brown trout and
sea trout. Also stocked with brown and
rainbow trout.

Rotherbridge Flyfishing A
Secretary – R. Etherington
c/o Messrs. King & Chasemore, Lombard
Street, Petworth
Tel: 0798 42011
Membership – Restricted
Year Formed – 1972
No. of Members – 50
Facilities – Approx. 4½ miles of rain feed
river with a natural stock of brown trout and
sea trout. Also stocked with brown and
rainbow trout.

TYNE & WEAR

Chester-le-Street & District AC
Secretary – T. Wright
156 Sedgletch Road, Houghton-le-Spring,
DH4 5JY
Tel: 0783 848211
Membership – Unrestricted. Junior
membership available
No. of Members – 231
Facilities – Various stretches of lower River
Wear plus 5 miles of River Pont,
Northumberland.

WEST MIDLANDS

Atherstone AA
Secretary – K. Horton
Glenavon, Dudley Street, Atherstone
Tel: 082 77 2554

Birmingham Anglers Association Limited
Secretary – F.H. Bayley
100 Icknield Port Road, Rotten Park,
Birmingham B16 0AP
Tel: 021 454 9111
Membership – Unrestricted. Junior
membership available
Year Formed – 1883
No. of Members – 40,000
Facilities – 400 miles of fishing rights on the
rivers Anker, Arrow, Avon, Banwy, Cherwell,
Clun, Kemp, Ouse, Ithon, Ledwyche, Lugg,
Mease, Monnow, Onny, Perry, Roden,
Salwarpe, Severn, Stour, Swarbourn, Teme,
Tern, Thame, Thames, Trent, Trothy, Wyrnwy
and Wye also pools, gravel pits, canals and
trout fisheries. Waters only available for
matches to affiliated clubs.

Fifty Nine Fly Fishers
Secretary – A.D. Stobo
"Everest", Arden Leys, Tamworth-in-Arden,

Solihull B94 5HU
Tel: 056 44 2723
Membership – Restricted
No. of Members – 100
Facilities – River Blythe, Warwickshire 4,500
yards. Double bank at Hampton in Arden.
River Blythe, 2,500 yards. Mainly double
bank at Temple Balsall. River Teme,
Worcestershire, 1 mile single bank,
Knightwick. (All waters stocked with trout
annually).

Golden Throstle AC
Secretary – D.D. Phillips
28 Clayerdon Drive, Great Barr,
Birmingham, Warwick
Tel: 021 358 2067
Membership – Restricted
Year Formed – 1968
No. of Members – 40

Goldthorn Social AC
Secretary – E.J. Boleyn
36 Goldthorn Hill, Wolverhampton WV2 3HU
Tel: 0902 339564
Membership – Unrestricted. Junior
membership available
Year Formed – 1930
No. of Members – 70

Hazeldine AA
Secretary – J.W. Hazeldine
8 Dudley Road, Sedgley, Dudley DY3 1SX
Tel: 0384 4629
Membership – Unrestricted. Junior
membership available
Year Formed – 1950
No. of Members – 3,500
Facilities – River Severn-Llanymynech.
Welshpool, Worcester, Chaceley. River
Avon, Stratford-on-Avon, Defford, Offenham.
River Mease, Clifton Campville. River Meese,
Tiberton. Shropshire Union Canal. Wheaton
Aston-Gnosall. Staffs and Worcs Canal,
Compton. Membership cards must be
obtained before fishing waters.

Kinver Freeliners
Secretary – R. Oliver
68 High Street, Kinver, Nr. Stourbridge
DY7 6ER
Tel: 038 483 3255
Membership – Unrestricted
Year Formed – 1971
No. of Members – 60 Full, 45 Hon.
Facilities – Coarse, trout and salmon. River
Severn – Erdington – Bridgnorth – Quatt
– Alveley. Coarse, Staffs – Worcs Canal –
Whittington – Stewpony – Gothersley.
Coarse and trout, River Solwarpe, Droitwich.
Coarse, River Avon, Wick. Trout, River
Evenlode, Gloucestershire.

Midland Fly Fishers
Secretary – D.M.P. Lea
11 Newhall Street, Birmingham
Tel: 021 2361751
Membership – Restricted
Year Formed – 1930
No. of Members – 60
Facilities – 3 Miles River Dee above
Llangollen, Glyndfyrdwy and Rhewl Beats.
Day permits and season tickets for Trout and
grayling only available.

WILTSHIRE

Bradford on Avon & District AA
Secretary – J.B. Webster
Garland Farm, The Midlands Holt, nr.
Trowbridge
Tel: 022 14 782170

Wiltshire Fishery A

Secretary – M.J. O'Lane
c/o Humberts, 8 Rolleston Street, Salisbury
Tel: 0722 27274

Membership – Unrestricted
Year Formed – 1950
No. of Members – 290
Facilities – The Committee of the Association includes members who have knowledge of and fish on each of the 6 rivers in area viz: The Upper Avon, Wylye, Nadder, Ebble, Bourne and Upper Kennet and the still waters fished by the various angling clubs. A watchdog organisation protecting the interests of riparion owners and fishermen in Wilts.

Wilton Fly FC

Secretary – C.B. White
c/o Keepers Cottage, Manor Farm Lane,
Great Wishford, Nr. Salisbury
Tel: 072 279 231

Membership – Restricted
Year Formed – 1877
No. of Members – 40
Facilities – 6 Miles wild brown trout and grayling, dry fly and upstream nymph. Chalk stream. River Wylye above Wilton. Full time river keeper.

YORKSHIRE NORTH

Secretary – M.J.R. Davies
26 Otley Street, Skipton BS23 1EW
Tel: 0756 2601

Boroughbridge & District AC

Secretary – G. Whitaker
9 Manor Drive, Kirby Hill, Boroughbridge

Danby AC

Secretary – Mr. Farrow
The Butchers Shop, Danby, Nr. Whitby
Tel: 02876 385

Facilities – Trout and grayling permits for River Esk.

Grosmont AC

Secretary – K. Porritt
Priory Park, Grosmont

Membership – Restricted
Year Formed – 1962
No. of Members – 30
Facilities – 200 Yards fishing on the River Esk, plus ¼ mile on the Murk Esk. Approx. 7 miles from the estuary and comprising of pools and running water.

Harrogate & Pateley Bridge AC

Secretary – C. Johnson
2 Briggate, Knaresborough
Tel: 0423 863065

Membership – Restricted
No. of Members – 150
Facilities – 1000 m. River Swale — coarse. 1000 m. River Ure — coarse/game.

Harrogate AA

Secretary – R. Pick
3 Norfolk Gardens, Tockwith
Tel: 090 15 445

Membership – Restricted
Year Formed – 1920
No. of Members – 100
Facilities – The club has fishing rights both banks, river Nidd through Ribston Park Down to the A1 at Walshford, then left bank through Hunsingore down to Cattal Bridge.

Harrogate Fly FC

Secretary – J.D. Tredger
18 St. Catherines Road, Harrogate
Tel: 0423 884249

Membership – Restricted
Year Formed – 1887
No. of Members – 40
Facilities – About 3 miles on River Lidd, downstream from Dacre Nr. Harrogate. Private club only. No day tickets except to member's guests.

Harrogate Hospitals AC

Secretary – J.H. Bouckley
209 Woodfield Road, Harrogate HG1 4JE
Tel: 0423 66948

Membership – Restricted to Hospital Employees
Year Formed – 1973
No. of Members – 22
Facilities – Small lake about 1 acre with inlet and outlet streams. Fly spinning only for Brown Trout.

Hawes & High Abbotside AA

Secretary – A.H. Barnes
Marridene, Gayle, Hawes
Tel: 096 97 384

Membership – Unrestricted. Junior membership available
Year Formed – 1860
No. of Members – 100
Facilities – River Ure, upper Wensleydale, from the approach side of Bainbridge to source of River Ure. Foss, Widdale, Cotterdale Duerley, both banks. No Sunday fishing. Trout and grayling. Limit 6 fish per day. No spinning.

Hutton Rudby FC

Secretary – C.R. Warwick
The White House, Hutton, Rudby
Tel: 0642 700623

Membership – Restricted
Year Formed – 1920
No. of Members – 35
Facilities – Fly fishing for trout. River Leven — between Skutterkewe and Crathorne. A small club leasing waters from various private estates.

Kilnsey AC B. Trout A.

Fly fishing only

Secretary – J.A. Croft
Throstles Nest Farm, Conistone, Skipton
Tel: 075 676 267

Membership – Restricted
Year Formed – 1840
No. of Members – 50
Facilities – Waters stretch from 1 mile to Netherside, 2 miles below Kilnsey on the River Wharfe and from 1 mile below Arncliffe to where the skirfare runs into the wharfe at watersmeet. Situated in the North Yorkshire Dales. Beautiful countryside. None on Sundays or Bank Holidays.

Linton Threshfield & Grassington AC

Secretary – H.T. Astley
Shiel, Raines Meadows, Grassington
BD23 5NB
Tel: 0756 752 720

Membership – Unrestricted. Junior membership available
No. of Members – 80
Facilities – 2½ miles River Wharfe. Brown trout, April/September, Grayling, October/February.

Long Preston AC

Secretary – J. Bowker
Pendle View, Long Preston, Skipton
Tel: 07294 276

Membership – Restricted
Year Formed – 1952
No. of Members – 35
Facilities – All fishing on River Ribble at Long Preston.

Nidderdale AA

Secretary – J. Dalton
Bracken House, Princess Road, Ripon
Tel: 0765 4004

Membership – Restricted
Year Formed – 1896
No. of Members – 530
Facilities – Water begins at Gouthwaite Reservoir and down to Dacre Banks. Approx. 6 miles of fishing. Our waters are restocked twice yearly with trout (brown and rainbow). The scenery and beauty of these waters make fishing a pleasant and relaxing sport in idyllic surroundings.

Northallerton & District AC

Secretary – J.G. Easby
24 Quaker Lane, Northallerton DL6 1EE
Tel: 0609 2464

Membership – Restricted
Year Formed – 1920
No. of Members – 500
Facilities – All the clubs' waters for which permits are available are situated on the River Swale, central access point is at Morton Bridge, near Northallerton. Day permits are available from the village Morton-on-Swale, from 1 May — 28 February annually. The waters hold mainly chub, pike, barbel, dace, grayling, roach and trout. Re-stocking takes place each year by the club ably assisted by the Yorkshire Water Authority.

Pickering Fishery A

Secretary – C. Hardy
3 Westbourne Grove, Pickering
Tel: 0751 72212

Membership – Restricted
Year Formed – 1892
No. of Members – 90
Facilities – Oxfold Beck and River Costa. Chalk streams, Pickering Beck. (Rain fed Ellerburn Lake 2½ acres spring fed).

Preston Park AC

Secretary – N.G. Wickman
7 Skelwith Road, Berwick Hills,
Middlesborough TS3 7PT
Tel: 0642 211139

Membership – Unrestricted. Junior membership available
Year Formed – 1949
No. of Members – 150
Facilities – 2 miles of trout, sea trout and salmon fishing on River Esk at Danby, between 5 arch bridge and Danby road bridge. ¾ mile of coarse fishing plus odd trout. Good grayling fishing on River Swale at Gatenby. Between RAF Leeming River Bridge and Mrs Stubbs water. Coarse fishing pond in Coatham Stob Lane, near village of Elton just outside Stockton-on-Tees, room for about 14 anglers.

Richmond & District AS

Secretary – J. Legge
9 St. Johns Road, Wipswell, Catterick,

ison DLG 4BQ
0748 833478

bership – Unrestricted locally
Formed – 1912
of Members – 800
ities – River Swale from Low Oxque to
t Langton. (Some private water in
een). Trout, grayling, dace, chub and
el fishing. Pond fishing also available at
t Langton and Green Lane Scorton.
o, tench, roach, perch, rudd.

pon AC

etary – A.R. Trees
orrage Lane, Ripon
0765 3143

bership – Restricted
Formed – 1831
of Members – 40
ities – Lumley Moor Reservoir. Trout —
ckets. River Laver. Trout and grayling
tickets. River Ure. Trout and coarse. Day
ts. River Skell.

tton AC

etary – M.B. Vallance
ham Hall, Farnham, Knaresborough
090 14 282
bership – Restricted
Formed – 1957
of Members – 40
ities – Approximately 500 yards of North
of the River Nidd at Scotton Banks,
t 2 miles west of Knaresborough.

en AC

etary – P. Stansfield
Seven, Sinnington YO6 6RZ
0751 31325
bership – Restricted
Formed – 1952
of Members – 30
ities – 2 Miles both banks of River Seven
w village of Sinnington. Trout and some
ling, fly only.

nington AC

etary – J.D. Hattersley
llow Rise, Kirkbymoorside
0751 31805
bership – Restricted
Formed – 1949
of Members – 30
ities – 1 Mile brook fishing.

pton AA

etary – J.W. Preston
eech Hill Road, Carleton, Skipton BD23

0756 5435
bership – Restricted. Junior membership
able
Formed – 1907
of Members – 250
ities – River Aire: 3 miles both banks at
eton & Skipton consisting of good trout
ng together with coarse fish in the deeper
ths. River varies from shallow, swift
ng water to deep, slow moving water in
ower reaches. Embsay Reservoir: 23
s trout only. Whinnygill Reservoir: 6
s trout and roach. Jennygill Reservoir: ½
trout only.

nsleydale AA

etary – H.G. Leyland
Garth, Bainbridge, Leyburn
50210

Membership – Restricted
Year Formed – 1890
No. of Members – 94
Facilities – Approx. 4 miles of the River Yore.
2-3 miles of River Bain which is only a small
stream. The River Yore is a much bigger river
with plenty of pools. We have a small section
of banks on Lake Semerwater (coarse fishing).

YORKSHIRE SOUTH

Cressbrook & Litton Fly FC

Secretary – J. Shirtcliffe
16 Storth Park, Fulwood, Sheffield SID 3QH
Tel: 0742 305703

Membership – Restricted
Year Formed – 1964
No. of Members – 61
Facilities – River Wye approx. 5 miles. Millers
Dale Nr. Buxton, Derbyshire.

Eastwood View W.M.C. AA

Secretary – A.W. Stubbs
27 Campbell Drive, Rotherham
Tel: 0709 71456

Membership – Unrestricted
Year Formed – 1970 AA Parent Club 1920
No. of Members – 290 AA Members + over
1000 in Parent Club
Facilities – We are associated with clubs that
control waters on the Rivers Trent, Witham,
Steeping, Yorkshire Ouse, and Lakes. Club
facilities include lounge, games and snooker
rooms and large concert hall which is
available for prize presentations, dancing etc.

Sheffield & District AA Ltd.

Secretary – J.W. Taylor
Reg. Office, 26 Wicker, Sheffield S3 8JB
Tel: 0742 24910. Home 872365

Membership – Unrestricted
Year Formed – 1869
No. of Members – 14,000

Sheffield Trout AA

Secretary – G.M. King
66 Harthill Road, Woodthorpe, Sheffield
S13 8AN
Enquiries to K. Pigot Tel: 74977

Membership – Restricted. Junior membership
available
Year Formed – 1893
No. of Members – 50
Facilities – The River Dove — Between
Hartington and Crowdicote, Derbyshire. The
River Amber at Wingfield, Derbyshire.

Sothal Fox Inn SAC

Secretary – L. Reynolds
63 Victoria Road, Beighton, Sheffield 19
Membership – Restricted
Year Formed – 1947
No. of Members – 56, Limited to 48 Fishermen

YORKSHIRE WEST

Bingley AC

Secretary – P. Exley
5 Highfield Road, Frizinghall BD9 4HY
Tel: 0274 493409
Membership – Unrestricted
Year Formed – 1946

No. of Members – 600
Facilities – River Aire, Bingley area, 4
stretches (trout/coarse). River Wharfe, Ben
Rhydding and Kerby (trout/coarse). 1 Small
reservoir and 2 dams (trout only). 1 Small
lake (coarse only). As members of Leeds &
Liverpool local canal Association approx. 36
miles of canal available to members. River
Aire, Myrtle Park, Bingley, available for club
matches 30 pegs maximum.

Bradford No. 1 AA

Secretary – C.W. Smith
44 Fleet Lane, Queensbury, Bradford
BD13 2JQ Tel: 0274 815630
Membership – Restricted. Junior membership
available
Year Formed – 1878
No. of Members – 3,216
Facilities – River Wharfe, Aire, Swale, Nidd,
Derwent, Ure, Calder. Also various lakes and
ponds within 45 mile radius of Bradford, plus
approx. 40 miles of Leeds—Liverpool Canal
from Leeds to Bank Newton, Nr. Gargrave.
River Swale Mounby: River Calder available
for 1 match per month. Details from R.W.
Naylor, 2 Fieldhead Drive, Guiseley, nr.
Leeds LS20 8DZ.

Bradford City AA

Secretary – A. Scaife
80 Whetley Hill, Bradford BD8 8NQ
Tel: 0274 47799
Membership – Unrestricted
No. of Members – 3,500
Facilities – River Ure, Boroughbridge,
Roecliffe, Langthorpe, coarse. River Swale,
Topcliffe, mainly coarse. River Ure, Worton,
fly only, trout. River Wharfe, Aysgarth trout.
Buckden, Appletrewick, Addingham, Burley,
mainly trout. River Aire, Bradley, Connonley,
Kilowick, mainly trout. Steeton, mainly
coarse. Reservoirs, Leeming at Oxenhope,
trout. Doe Park coarse, Denholme. Shipton
Lake, mixed.

Bradford Waltonians AC

Secretary – E.N. Williams
East Rombalds, Rombalds Lane, Ben
Rhydding, Ilkley LS29 8RT
Tel: 0943 607014
Membership – Restricted
Year Formed – 1883
No. of Members – 80
Facilities – Two stretches of River Wharfe.
Beamsley/Addingham, W. Yorks. Denton/Ben
Rhydding, W. Yorks. Three reservoirs —
Silsden, Chelker nr. Skipton and Winterburn,
Nr. Skipton.

Halifax & District AC

Secretary – F. Fox
52 Monkwood Road, Outwood, Wakefield
Tel: 0924 824597
Membership – Unrestricted. Junior
membership available
No. of Members – 180
Facilities – The upper River Calder and River
Hebden.

Halifax Fly FC

Secretary – Dr. I. Calvert-Wilson
Flat 2, Addington House, Halifax HX1 3EA
Tel: 0422 52692/52159
Membership – Restricted
Year Formed – 1949
No. of Members – 40

Hanging Heaton AC

Secretary – Stephen Kemp
35 Princess Road, Chickenly, Dewsbury
WF12 8QT
Membership – Restricted to 65 maximum.
No. of Members – 60

Facilities — Man-made pond at Netherfield Road, Ravensthorpe, Dewsbury. 2 Ponds at Heckmondwike Town Centre.

Hawksworth Fly FC
Secretary — J.M. Padgett
36 Tranfield Avenue, Guiseley, N. Leeds
Tel: 0943 75628/74315
Membership — Restricted
Year Formed — 1925
No. of Members — 16
Facilities — 1 small lake approx. 3 acres (bream and trout only) Hawksworth Mere.

Huddersfield AA
Secretary — C.A. Clough
38 Holly Bank Avenue, Upper Cumberworth
Tel: 048 488 764
Membership — Restricted
No. of Members — 75
Facilities — Boshaw and Holmstyes, game — brown and rainbow trout. Longwood, coarse — pike, roach, perch.

Ilkley & District AA
Secretary — J.A. Cockerill
31 Grange Estate, Ilkley LS29 8NW
Tel: 0943 608310
Membership — Restricted
Year Formed — 1937
No. of Members — 130 Seniors, 50 Juniors
Facilities — River Wharfe, from the Pack Horse Bridge down to the Stepping Stones at Ben Rhydding. Approx. 9 furlongs (both banks) disused gravel pits, (2) at Ben Rhydding. River, good trout and grayling fishing. Coarse, also chub, dace. Gravel pits, carp, tench, rudd, perch etc.

Keighley AC
Secretary — L.W. Brocklesby
11 Eelholme View Street, Beechcliffe, Keighley Tel: 0535 67699
Membership — Unrestricted
Year Formed — 1868
No. of Members — 800
Facilities — Leeds and Liverpool Canal. Approx. 16 miles on the River Aire (day tickets). 4 Miles River Worth. Whitefields Reservoir, Steeton, Roberts pond, Beechcliffe. 100 yard River Wharfe (Addingham). Match booking for River Aire only, send S.A.E. Full Members only.

Leeds & District Amalgamates
Society of Anglers
Secretary — G. Copley
6 Mount Pleasant, Middleton, Leeds 10
Tel: 0532 705059
Membership — Unrestricted
Year Formed — 1889
No. of Members — 9500
Facilities — Most Yorkshire rivers. High reaches, game fishing, lowland reaches, coarse fishing. Lake fishing, coarse and trout.

Leeds and Liverpool Canal AA
Secretary — W.M. Troman
7 Hall Royd, Shipley
Tel: 0274 583088
Membership — Unrestricted
Year Formed — 1968
No. of Members — 40,000
Facilities — Leeds and Liverpool Canal (towing path). Leeds Office Lock to Top Lock, Banknewton. 36 miles containing most varieties of coarse fish and brown trout.

Leeds Piscatorials
Secretary — B.C. Freer
18 Allenby Road, Leeds LS11 5RN
Tel: 0532 711413
Membership — Restricted

Year Formed — 1968
No. of Members — 55
Facilities — 4 Lakes, coarse only (Sherburn area). 1 Lake trout only, (Bramham Park). 2 River stretches, mixed, (Nidd). 1 River stretch, game only, (Trib. Ure).

Listerhills Old Boys AA
Secretary — S.C. Harrison
8 Lime Street, Bradford BD7 3HQ
Membership — Unrestricted
Year Formed — 1884
No. of Members — 500
Facilities — Pilsley Lake, Eccleshill Bradford. 40 Rods, trout and a few coarse fish. River Aire, Apperley Bridge, short length, mixed coarse fish.

Mackintosh AC
Secretary — M. Russell
Rowntree Mackintosh, Halifax
Tel: 0422 65761
Membership — Restricted
Year Formed — 1962
No. of Members — 108
Facilities — We rent from the Y.W.A. a 500 yard stretch of canal from Sutterhebble to the Sutterhebble Lock.

Monckton AC
Secretary — R. Newman
23 Mill Lane, Ryhill, Nr. Wakefield
Tel: 022 720 3895
Membership — Unrestricted
Year Formed — 1957
No. of Members — 350
Facilities — Disused Barnsley and Wakefield Canal. Roughly ¾ mile long. Contains perch, roach, pike, bream, tench, carp. Stocked yearly with trout.

Old Bank AC (W.H.C.)
Secretary — J.R. Brownhill
11 Water Royd Lane, Mirfield
Tel: 0924 499151 (Chairman)
Membership — Restricted
Year Formed — 1966
No. of Members — 66
Facilities — Hopton Dam in Mirfield (coarse and trout).

Paris Piscatorial Society
Secretary — R. Sykes
1 William Street, West Vale, Greetland, Halifax
Tel: 0422 79947
Membership — Restricted to 150 Members
Year Formed — 1978
No. of Members — 142
Facilities — The fisheries are situated at Scholes Nr. Holmfirth, being approx. ¼ mile apart. The fisheries consist of 3 dams. 1. Lee Mills Dam, Scholes, approx. ½ acre containing carp, tench, perch, bream, roach, gudgeon. 2. Doob Royd Mill Dams each approx. ½ acre. Top dam, trout only. Bottom dam, tench, bream, gudgeon, trout.

Ripponden Flyfishers
Secretary — H. Hamer
The Hollies, Greetland, Halifax HX4 8AX
Tel: 0422 72596/72427
Membership — Restricted
Year Formed — 1954
No. of Members — 35 Seniors, 6 Juniors
Facilities — 20 acre reservoir: Ryburn Reservoir, Ripponden. Wet and dry fly-fishing for brown trout. Fish average around 14 ozs. Spawning facilities good. Stocking done at around 3 year intervals, as deemed necessary. Boat available for members.

Ryburn AS
Secretary — L. Kitching

44 Sellerdale Avenue, Wyke, Bradford
Tel: 0274 671994
Membership — Unrestricted
Year Formed — 1942
No. of Members — 350
Facilities — River Calder — Most fishable lengths between Luddenden Foot and Cop through Sowerby Bridge Swamp and Miln Royd Reservoirs (both small).

Saltaire AA
Secretary — W.M. Troman
7 Hall Royd, Shipley
Tel: 0274 583088
Membership — Unrestricted
Year Formed — 1867
No. of Members — 900
Facilities — Trout and grayling water. Grassington, from below weir to 2 fields below Linton Bridge. Leeds and Liverpool Canal. River Aire, parts of right and left Bank. River Swale, Catterick Bridge. Tong Park Dam.

Slaithwaite & District AC
Secretary — A. Bamforth
43 Binn Road, Marsden, Huddersfield HD7 6HF
Tel: 0484 844119
Membership — Unrestricted. Junior membership available
No. of Members — 906
Facilities — River Trent (Dunham and Sutto, River Rye (Butterwick) Rye and Derwent, C Malton. 7 miles Hudds narrow canal. 20 Lc ponds/reservoirs. Waters available for matches are Dunham Bridge, River Trent, Newark and River Derwent Old Malton, Yorkshire.

Unity AC
Secretary — E.K. Mann
19 Busfield Street, Bradford 4 7QX
Tel: 0734 591834
Membership — Unrestricted
Year Formed — 1960
No. of Members — 200
Facilities — River Calder, Brighouse. River Ure and Canal, Boroughbridge Lake, Bradford. New water 1981.

West Riding Anglers
Secretary — H. Wigglesworth
84 Westfield Lane, Wrose, Shipley
Tel: 0274 598053
Membership — Restricted
Year Formed — 1901
No. of Members — 125
Facilities — River Wharfe (game and coarse River Swale (coarse).

Wetherby & District AC
Secretary — P.F. Burnett
10 Calder Close, Wetherby
Tel: 0937 62171
Membership — Restricted
Year Formed — 1910
No. of Members — 240 Seniors, 110 Juniors
Facilities — Approx. 5 Miles of bankside fishing on the River Wharfe around Wethe and 1 mile of the River Nidd at Skip Bridge/Kirk Hammerton. Plus a small pon near Pocklington.

Yorkshire Gamefishers
Association
Secretary — M.J. Townsend
31 Marriot Grove, Sandal, Near Wakefield
Tel: 0924 252405
Membership — Unrestricted
No. of Members — 70
Facilities — Regular meetings at the Walton Hall Sports Club, Walton Nr. Wakefield.

ALES

.WYD

delwyddan AC

retary – R.G. Richardson
ordd Siarl, St. Asaph
0745 582693

nbership – Unrestricted
r Formed – 1975
of Members – 125
lities – Parts of River Elwy for game. Lodge
s, Glascoed (Nr Bodelwyddan) for coarse.

cain Fly Fishing A

retary – E. Williams
Maes Cilan, Cilcain, Mold
035 282 554

nbership – Restricted
r Formed – 1969
of Members – 40
lities – Day tickets – £3, week ticket i.e. Mon-
incl. £12 for fishing on 5 reservoirs which
12 acres.

nnah's Quay AC

retary – P. Roberts
Pinewood Avenue, Connah's Quay
0244 815643

nbership – Unrestricted
r Formed – 1970
of Members – 950
lities – Alyn River, 1½ miles at Rossett.
pre Brook mixed fishing. Mostyn Pool: tench
carp. Paper Mill Reservoir, at Oaken Holt,
it fishing, fly only. All the above is member
fishing. Wepre Pool, coarse fishing
ecially carp. Special access and amenities
ch makes it ideal for the disabled, permits
ilable.

andysul AC

retary – A. Jones
p-y-Jones, Llandysul
055 932 2317

ngollen AA

retary – W.N. Elbourn
Chapel Street, Llangollen
enquiries by letter please.

nbership – Unrestricted
r Formed – 1946

Maelor AA

Secretary – K. Bathers
"Sunnyside", Hill Street, Cefn Mawr, Nr. Wrexham
Tel: 0978 820 608

Membership – Unrestricted, Junior membership
available
Year Formed – 1910
No. of Members – 250
Facilities – 1 Mile River Dee salmon, trout,
grayling. Sunbank near Llangollen, both banks. 2
Miles River Dee, trout, grayling, coarse fish
Trevor, both banks.

Rhyl & District AA

Secretary – H.I. Jones
Belmont, 51 Pendyffryn Road, Rhyl
Tel: 0745 50342

Membership – Restricted
Year Formed – 1944
No. of Members – 120 (limit)
Facilities – River Elwy: The Association owns 3
stretches and rents 1 other stretch. River Clwyd:
The Association rents 4 stretches. In addition the
Association rents a well stocked reservoir. Both
rivers hold trout, sea trout and salmon. Personal
guests of members only. Each member is allowed
2 guests per season on some waters.

Wrexham & District AA

Secretary – G.I. Franks
132 Oak Drive, Acton Park, Wrexham
Tel: 0978 51343

Membership – Restricted
Year Formed – 1899
No. of Members – 65
Facilities – 4 Miles of River Alyn (tributary of
Welsh Dee) from Llong near Mold, downstream
to Hope.

DYFED

Aberystwyth AA

Secretary – Dr J.D. Fish
P.O. Box 15, Aberystwyth
Tel: 0970 828433

Membership – Unrestricted, Junior membership
available
No. of Members – approx 200
Facilities – Exclusive rights on approx 14 miles of
The River Rheidol and some rights on The River
Ystwyth. Both rivers well known for their runs of
sea trout and salmon. Brown trout and rainbow
trout fishing in 10 lakes up to 40 acres. Some
lakes stocked others have good populations of
wild fish. Caravan holidays arranged by
Association. Boat fishing available on lakes.

Ammanford AA

Secretary – A.S. Usherwod
49 High Street, Ammanford
Tel: 0269 2173

Membership – Restricted
Year Formed – 1919
No. of Members – 250
Facilities – 5 Miles on the River Loughor also
fishing on The Rivers Marlais, Amman and
Cennen.

Carmarthen & District AC

Secretary – H. Evans
25 Maple Crescent, Carmarthen
Tel: 0267 31945 evenings

Llandilo AA

Secretary – D. Richards
Llysnewydd, Ffairfach, Llandilo
Tel: 055 82 2672

Membership – Restricted
Year Formed – 1964
No. of Members – 230

Llanilar AA

Secretary – M.M. Hamblin
Delmar, Llanilar, Nr. Aberystwyth
Tel: 097 47 305

Membership – Unrestricted
Year Formed – 1956
No. of Members – 400
Facilities – 9 Miles mainly with bank: River
Ystwyth. Sea trout and salmon.

Pembrokeshire Anglers A

Secretary – M. Gibby
22 Greenfield Close, Haverfordwest,
Pembrokeshire

Membership – Unrestricted
Year Formed – 1957
No. of Members – 250
Facilities – Approx 15 miles on River Western
Cleddau. Part leased from local farmers, part
owned. In beautiful wooded valley.

Talybont AA

Secretary – J.S. Hughes
Lerry Tweed Mills, Talybont
Tel: 0970 86 235
Membership – Unrestricted
No. of Members – 71
Facilities – 4 Lakes in the Anglers Retreat area,
above Talybont. Fishing also on 1 mile of the
River Lerry and ¾ mile of River Einion at
Furnace.

Teifi Trout Association

Secretary – C. Jones
Emlyn House, Newcastle, Elymn
Tel: 0239 710405

Membership – Unrestricted
No. of Members – 500
Facilities – 10 Miles of salmon, sea trout and trout
fishing around Newcastle Emlyn including
Cenarth.

Tregaron AA

Secretary – G.R. Phillips
c/o Barclays Bank Ltd, Tregaron SY25 6JL
Tel: 09744 207

Membership – Unrestricted, Junior membership
available
Year Formed – Pre 1914
No. of Members – 97

GLAMORGAN MID

Abadare & District AA

Secretary – R. Hancock
11 Cobdon Street, Aberaman, Abadare
Tel: 0685 875209

Membership – Unrestricted
Year Formed – Before War
No. of Members – 930

Glyncornel AA

Secretary – J.M. Evans
126 Ystrad Road, Ystrad, Rhondda
Tel: 0443 439961

Membership – Unrestricted, Junior membership
available also disabled
Year Formed – 1952
No. of Members – 100
Facilities – River Rhondda, trout fishing.
Restocked with 1000 10inch fish annually. Any
means of fishing. Darran Park Lake Ferndale,
coarse fishing. No fly or spinning. Rhymmy
Bridge Reservoir, fly fishing only. Good stock of
fish 12 inch+also stocked every year. Darran
Park Lake available to hire for matches.

Merthyr Tydfil AA

Secretary – C. Hughes
2 Wesley Close, Dowlais, Merthyr Tydfil

Membership – Unrestricted
No. of Members – 600
Facilities – Fishing on Taff, Taf Fechan Taff Fawr
(trout). Two local park lakes and manmade pond.
Mixed fisheries+1090yds salmon trout and
coarse fishing on River Usk above Usk town.

New Duffryn AC

Secretary – D.F. Roberts
The New Duffryn Hotel, Aberbargoed
Tel: 0443 831635

Membership – Unrestricted
Year Formed – 1979
No. of Members – 30
Facilities – Negotiating for water at present.

Ogwr AA

Secretary – F.J. Hughes
20 Hoel Glannant, Bettws, Bridgend
Tel: 0656 722077

Membership – Unrestricted
Year Formed – 1969
No. of Members – 300
Facilities – Ogwr River, Garw River

Osprey Fly Fishers

Secretary – G. Wride
13 Pencerrig Street, Pontypridd
Tel: 0443 404589

Porthcawl SAC

Chairman – A. Birch
171 New Road, Porthcawl, GF36 5DD
Tel: 065 671 3975 HQ Sportsmans Club

Membership – Unrestricted
Year Formed – 1952
No. of Members – 450
Facilities – Wilderness Lake – game rainbow trout.

Taff AA

Secretary – H.T. Gwynne
87 Shirley Drive, Heolgerrig, Merthyr Tydfil
Tel: 0685 4506

Membership – Unrestricted
Year Formed – 1970
No. of Members – 70
Facilities – Reservoirs of the Welsh Water
Authority.

GLAMORGAN SOUTH

Cowbridge & District AA

Secretary – H.W. Roberts
Greystones, Llanelthian, Cowbridge
Tel: 044 633241

Membership – Restricted
Year Formed – 1975
No. of Members – 100
Facilities – River Thaw

GLAMORGAN WEST

British Steel Corp. Sports & Social Club, (Angling Section)

Secretary – C.D. Jones
B.S.C. Sports & Social Club, Groes, Port Talbot
Tel: 0639 883161 Ext. 3368

Membership – Unrestricted, Junior membership
available
Year Formed – 1970
No. of Members – 662
Facilities – Eglwys Nunydd. Regularly stocked,
plenty of fish. Available for matches if sufficient
notice is given.

Llangyfelach & District AA

Secretary – M.L. Griffiths
3 Aldwyn Road, Cockett, Swansea
Tel: 0792 581711

Membership – Unrestricted
Year Formed – 1940
No. of Members – 250
Facilities – Llan River, 6 miles. Restocked every
year.

Neath & Dulais Angling Club

Secretary – A. Beasley
10 Neath Road, Tonna, Neath
Tel: 0639 50878

Pyrddin AA

Secretary – D.M. Jones
4 Moorlands, Duffryn Cellwen
Nr. Neath SA10 9HU

Membership – Restricted
Year Formed – 1952
No. of Members – 50
Facilities – The river we control runs into the main
Neath River. A number of small tributaries run
into our river from the Brecon Beacons. The
nature of our waters is that it drops from 900ft.
above sea level to approximately 100ft. above
sea level in a matter of 3 miles, and it contains a
number of waterfalls which prevent salmon
entering the waters controlled by our society.
The nearest main road is approx ½ mile away.

Tawe & Tributaries AA

Secretary – K. Jones
21 St. David's Road, Ystalyfera, Swansea
Tel: 0639 843916

Membership – Restricted to those residing in area
Year Formed – 1925
No. of Members – 280
Facilities – Tawe River, Twrch River

GWENT

Cwmbran AA

Secretary – P.M. Gulliford
16 The Circle, Cwmbran
Tel: 06333 5036
Membership – Unrestricted
Year Formed – 1963
No. of Members – 250
Facilities – Trout – Afon Llwyd, 3 miles fly or
worm fishing only, 9in. limit, 2 fish per day.
Flows through new town, pleasant parklands.

Pontypool AA

Secretary – A. Wakeham
7 St. Hilda's Road, Griffithstown, Pontypool
Tel: 049 55 4743

Membership – Unrestricted
Year Formed – 1906
No. of Members – 600
Facilities – 15 Miles trout fishing River Afon.
Llwyd at Pontypool in an industrial area. 7 Mile
Solway Brook Usk in the heart of the country.
3½ Acres Pen-yr-Heol Reservoir.

Usk Town Water Fishery Association

Secretary – C.E. Brain
56 St. Julians Road, Newport Tel: 0633 5558

Membership – Restricted
Year Formed – 1921
No. of Members – 9

GWYNEDD
Bala & District AA

Secretary – D.M. Rees
21 Tremyffridd, Bala Tel: 0678 520812

Membership – Unrestricted, Junior membership
available
Year Formed – 1949
No. of Members – 300
Facilities – 3 Trout fishing streams stocked
regularly. River Dee 2 miles fly only, trout and
grayling. River Tryweryn approx 4 miles trout
and salmon. Bala Lake (700 acres) coarse and
game fishing. Small mountain lake stocked
regularly with brown trout.

Bangor AA

Secretary – W. Barton Tel: 0978 780384

Membership – Unrestricted
Year Formed – 1945
No. of Members – 50
Facilities – Information and Permits available from
The Stores, Bangor on Dee, Tel: 0978 780430
4-5 miles of Dee.

Cambrian AA

Secretary – E. Evans
Garth, Tyddyn Gwyn, Manod
Blaenau Ffestiniog LLH1 HAL

Membership – Restricted to residents of Blaenau
Ffestiniog postal area
Year Formed – 1885
No. of Members – 243
Facilities – Mountainous area around Ffestiniog
Gamallt Lakes, Dubach-y-Bont, Morwynion,
Manod Lake, Dubach Lake, Barlwyd Lakes,
Cwmorthin Lake, Cwm Foel and Cwm Corsio
Brown trout.

...fni AA

...etary – W.J. Williams
...nant, Gaerwen, Anglesey Tel: 024 877 765

...mbership – Restricted
...r Formed – 1952
...of Members – 200 Adults, 50 Juniors
...lities – Reservoir 173 acres. Public water
...ply. 12 boats available and unrestricted bank
...ng available.

...ccieth Llanystumdwy & ...trict AA

...retary – G. Hamilton
...awel, Llanystumdwy, Criccieth LL52 0SF
...076 671 2251

...nbership – Restricted
...r Formed – 1927
...of Members – 235 Senior, Junior and O.A.P.
...lities – 10 Miles of single and double bank
...ng on rivers Dwyfor and Dwyfach.

...lgarrog AA

...retary – F.A. Corrie
...aylor Ave, Dolgarrog, Conwy
...049 269 651

...nbership – Unrestricted (Restricted Salmon)
...r Formed – 1950
...of Members – Salmon 100, Trout 300
...lities – Conway River, Hill Lakes

...lgellau AA

...retary – W.E. Roberts
...Muriau, Cader Road, Dolgellau LL40 1SG
...0341 422360

...mbership – Unrestricted
...r Formed – 1947
...of Members – 162
...ilities – Llyn Cynwch-23 acres – contains
...wn trout and is restocked annually with
...bow trout. Considerable stretches of River
...ion – full details given on fishing permit.
...ntains brown trout and there is a good run of
...gratory fish. 1 Mile on Mawddach River.
...uary fishing for migratory fish.

...lwyddelan FA

...cretary – T.V. Jones
...awel, Dolwyddelan LL25 0ST Tel: 06906 223

...mbership – Restricted
...ar Formed – 1940
...of Members – 90
...cilities – Approx 2 miles double bank late
...son, salmon and sea trout on the Lledr from
...wyddelon to Pont y Pant. Permits: weekly
...ets to resident visitors, i.e. staying in house or
...el village. (Not tents or caravans). A limited
...nber of visitors season tickets are also issued.

...laslyn AA

...rmit Secretary – R.J. Gauler
...dge House, Aberglaslyn, Beddgelert
...l: 076 686 229

...embership – Unrestricted
...o. of Members – 200
...cilities – Beddgelert – Porthmadog. Fast rock
...waters. (Permits and licences from above).

...anrwst AC

...cretary – D.C. Thomas
...wlas, 30 Llwynbrith, Llanrwst LL26 0HH
...l: 0492 640596

Membership – Restricted
Year Formed – 1933
No. of Members – 200
Facilities – River Conwy – Both banks for approx
1¼ miles upstream from Llanrwst Bridge, Non
tidal waters. Weekly temporary membership
allowed until 19th Sept. of any season. Waters
mainly hold salmon and sea trout. There are also
brown trout.

Prysor AA

Secretary – D.G. Williams
Bryn Gwyn, Trawsfynydd Tel: 076 687 310

Membership – Unrestricted
No. of Members – 370
Facilities – Prysor River – brown trout fishing.
Eden River – salmon and sea trout. Small
Mountain Lakes – brown trout.

Pwllheli AA

Secretary – G.W. Pritchard
30 Lon Ceredigion, Pwllheli Tel: 0758 3531

Membership – Restricted to locals
Year Formed – 1954
No. of Members – 170
Facilities – Rhydhir River and Erch River

Trawsfynydd Lake Management Committee

Secretary – H.K. Lewis
Manchester House, Trawsfynydd
Tel: 076 687 234

Membership – Unrestricted
Year Formed – 1953
No. of Members – 460
Facilities – Trawsfyndd Lake – 1200 acres of
reservoir. Water used to cool turbines of Nuclear
Power Station, thus ensuring warm water to
enhance fish production and rearing throughout
the year.

Wygyr FA

Secretary – F.J. Gough
Glanrafon, Mountain Road, Llanfechell LL68 0SA

Membership – Restricted
Year Formed – 1952
No. of Members – 30
Facilities – 2 Miles of rivers, fishing both banks.
Open fields and wooded areas. Wild brown trout
and sea trout when running. Fly only, no
worming or spinning.

POWYS

Corris & District AA

Secretary's – A.D. Woodvine and B. Rowlands
"Ty Isaf" Ceinws Tel: 065 473 273

Membership – Unrestricted
Year Formed – 1972
No. of Members –
Facilities – 5 Acre Lake, "Glanmerrin" Nr.
Machynlleth. Stocked annually with brown trout.
Most of River Dulas North (Dovey Tributary).
Very good runs of sea trout and some salmon.
Brown trout which is quite small usually. River
runs from Machynnleth through Corris.

Llandrindod Wells AA

Secretary – A.H. Selwyn
4 Park Crescent, Llandrindod Wells
Tel: 0597 2397

Membership – Unrestricted
Year Formed – 1924
No. of Members – 100
Facilities – The fishing under the control of the
Association is on the River Ithon and is within
easy walking distance of the town. The length of
the fishing available is approx 4 miles.

Llanidloes & District AA

Secretary – J. Dallas Davies
Dresden House, Great Oak Street, Llanidloes
Tel: 05512 2644

Membership – Unrestricted
Year Formed – Pre War
No. of Members – 180
Facilities – River fishing on Severn, Clywedog,
Trannon and Dulas for trout, grayling, salmon,
dace, chub, and pike 2 lakes available with pike,
perch and chub. Also Clywedog Reservoir – fly
only for both brown and rainbow trout. Stocked
at regular intervals throughout season (18th
March – 16 Nov).

Montgomeryshire AA

Secretary – R. Thomas
128 Oldford Rise Tel: 0938 3488

Membership – Unrestricted, Junior membership
available
Year Formed – 1964
No. of Members – 300
Facilities – Extensive stretches of the River
Severn, including some tributaries and several
other waters offering excellent coarse and game
fishing for most species. Shropshire Union Canal,
River Banwy, Montgomery Canal, only the latter
is available for matches, approx 4 continuous miles

New Dovey Fishing Association

Secretary – D. Morgan-Jones
Plas Machynlleth Tel: 0654 2721

Membership – Restricted
Year Formed – 1929
No. of Members – 63
Facilities – 15 Miles both banks sea trout and
salmon. Known as one of the best sea trout rivers
in the country Season opens 1 April and closes
17 October. Main runs of fish from June to
October.

Newtown & District Fishing Club

Secretary – J.A. Walker
129 Lon Gwern, Trehafren, Newtown
Tel: 0686 27987

Membership – Unrestricted
Year Formed – 1938
No. of Members – 150
Facilities – Several miles of The River Severn,
with salmon, trout, grayling, pike, chub, dace
etc. Also several miles of canal containing coarse
fish. Also Fachwen Pool, 10 acres, stocked with
brown and rainbow trout up to 4lbs. 12 Acre
Llyn Tarw unique in that American brown trout
have bred naturally for years.

Welshpool & District Anglers Club ·

Secretary – Revd. R.H. Fairbrother
The Vicarage, Betws, Cedewain, Newtown
Tel: 068 687 345

Membership – Unrestricted
Facilities – The waters used by the club are those
managed by The Montgomeryshire Angling
Association. All members must be members of
M.A.A.

Game Clubs: Borders – Central

SCOTLAND

BORDERS

Coldstream & District AA

Secretary – E.M. Patterson
Market Square, Coldstream
Tel: 0890 2719

Facilities – River Tweed and River Leet.

Earlston AA

Secretary – W.W. Lothian
10 Westfield Street, Earlston
Tel: 089 684 559

Membership – Unrestricted, Junior membership available
Year Formed – 1900
No. of Members – 100
Facilities – 3 Stretches of water on River Leader, approx 3½ miles. 1 Stretch of River Tweed at Gledswood approx 1 mile. 1 Stretch of River Tweed at Leaderfoot approx 200 yards day tickets only for Gledswood and Monday, Tuesday, and Wednesday day and night stretch at Leaderfoot. Daily and season tickets on 3 stretches of Leader.

Eckford AA

Secretary – Mr Lothian
10 Westfield Street, Earlston
Tel: 089 684 559

Facilities – Leader for brown trout.

Eye Water AC

Secretary – W.S. Gillie
Market Place, Eyemouth
Tel: 0390 50038

Facilities – Brown trout fishing on eye water.

Galashiels AA

Secretary – R. Watson
41 Balmoral Avenue, Galashiels

Facilities – Fishing on Tweed at Gala, starting Craigs Compensation Pond.

Gordon FC

Secretary – W.A. Virtue
Kirkaig, Manse Street, Galashiels

Facilities – River Earn, tributary of Tweed for brown trout.

Greenlaw AC

Secretary – A. Lamb
Waterford, Wester Roon, Greenlaw
Tel: 036 16 246

Membership – Unrestricted
Year Formed – 1880
No. of Members – 100
Facilities – River Blackadder – approx 10 miles. Arable countryside.

Hawick AC

Secretary – R. Johnston
Kelvin, 6 Raeson Park, Hawick
Tel: 0450 2266

Membership – Restricted
No. of Members – 250 Local, 75 Visitor and Day and Week Tickets
Facilities – 6 Lochs, 3 purely brown trout and the other 3 containing pike and perch as well as brown trout. River Teviot and tributaries (adding up to over 100 miles), mainly brown trout but some grayling and autumn salmon.

Jedforest AA

Secretary – A. Whitecross
42 Howden Road, Jedburgh, Roxburghshire
Tel: 083 56 3615

Membership – Restricted for salmon
No. of Members – 200
Facilities – 2½ Miles of the River Teviot, Jed and Oxnam. Trout, sea trout and salmon on Teviot. Day tickets for sea trout and salmon restricted to 3 tickets per day. No Sunday fishing on any of our waters.

Kelso AA

Secretary – Mr Hutchinson
53 Abbot Seat, Kelso
Tel: 057 32 3440

Facilities – Fishing on Rivers Tweed, Teviot and Eden for brown trout, grayling and roach.

Lauderdale AA

Secretary – D.M. Milligan
2 Sidegate Mews, Haddington
Tel: 062 082 5161

Membership – Unrestricted
No. of Members – 30
Facilities – River Leader and tributaries.

Ladykirk & Norham AA

Secretary – R.G. Wharton
8 St. Cuthbert's Square, Northam

Facilities – River Tweed. Brown trout, grayling, roach.

Melrose & District AA

Secretary – J. Broomfield
"Ravensbourne", Douglas Road, Melrose
Tel: 089 682 2219

Membership – Unrestricted
Year Formed – 1938
No. of Members – 76 Local, 87 Visitors
Facilities – Day permits are available on Ravenswood stretch, approx 1 mile and Cow Pool, approx 440 yards, both on River Tweed near Melrose. Fly Fishing permitted only. No price permits issued, and applicants must be members of parent body. 6 Rods only allowed any one time, i.e., 1 hour before sunrise to 1 hour after sunset.

Peebles Shire Salmon FA

Secretary – Blackwood and Smith W.S.
39 High Street, Peebles
Tel: 0721 20131

Facilities – River Tweed for salmon fishing only

Peeblesshire Trout FA

Secretary – D.G. Fyfe
39 High Street, Peebles
Tel: 0721 20131

Membership – Restricted to residents of Peeblesshire
No. of Members – Approx 500
Facilities – 25 miles of the River Tweed and 5 miles of the River Lyne in Peeblesshire.

Selkirk & District AA

Secretary – A. Murray
40 Ragburn Meadows, Selkirk
Tel: 0750 21534

Facilities – Ettrick and Yarrow Waters, a distance of approx 80 miles. Lindean Reservoirs. Brown and rainbow trout.

St. Boswells & Newtown AA

Secretary – R. Black
Kilgraden, St. Boswells, Melrose TD6 0EP
Tel: 083 52 3271

Year Formed – 1930
No. of Members – 90
Facilities – Approx 5 miles on River Tweed. Detailed on permits

St. Boswells AA

Secretary – R. Black
Kilgraden, Spring Terrace, St. Boswells
Tel: 0835 23271

Facilities – Brown trout on Tweed

Yetholm AA

Secretary – A.J. Turnbull
c/o Messrs. J. & D.W. Tait
The Square, Kelso
Tel: 04674 2311

Facilities – Fishing for brown trout on River Bowmont.

CENTRAL

Allan Water Angling Improvement Association

Secretary – P.J. Nicholls
5 Lister Court, Bridge of Allan

404

mbership - Restricted
r Formed - 1899
of Members - 550
ilities - Fishing for brown trout, sea trout and
e. Virtually uninterrupted fishing from the
n Bank Hotel, Green-loaning to where the
r joins the River Forth.

ckridge AC

retary - A. Neil
Murdostown Crescent, Harthill

mbership - Unrestricted
r Formed - 1945
of Members - 180
ilities - Hillend Loch lies between Bathgate
Airdrie. Easy access from main road. Lily
ch lies at back of Brald Farm. Only entrance
Loch about 1 mile. Both Lochs contain good
ck of brown trout (6000 every year). All bank
ing. No restriction of tackle.

lin Breadalbane AC

retary - D. Allan
n Street, Killin
: 056 72 362

mbership - Restricted
r Formed - 1881
of Members - 50
cilities - Loch Tay, River Dochart, River
chay, Lochan-Na-Larige for brown trout,
ch, pike.

arbert & Stenhousemuir AA

retary - M. Arthur
Old Bellsdyke Road, Larbert
: 032 45 2581

mbership - Restricted
r Formed - 1947
. of Members - 70
cilities - Loch Caulter, Reservoir

llibody & Cambus SAC

retary - J. Meer
8 Carseview, Tullibody, Clackmannanshire
: 212714

mbership - Unrestricted
r Formed - 1977
. of Members - 34

UMFRIES & GALLOWAY

nnan & District AC

cretary - W. Jackson
Closehead Avenue, Annan, Dumfriesshire
l: 04612 2616/2060

mbership - Restricted
. of Members - 1300
cilities - 1 Stretch of River Annan 3 Lochs
nted. Rainbow trout and brown trout stocked
arly.

nnandale & Egremont FC

cretary - P.A.W. Hope Johnstone
nnandale Estates Office, St. Anns,
ckerbie, Dumfriesshire
l: 057 64 317

Membership - Restricted only if membership
is full
Year Formed - 1974
No. of Members - 60 If membership falls below
this figure, weekly or day tickets available
Facilities - 9 Fishing points on River Annan

Commissioners of Royal Four Towns Fishings

Secretary - W. Graham
Glenelg, Hightae, Lockerbie
Tel: 038 781 220

Membership - Restricted
Year Formed - 1910
Facilities - 4½ Miles both banks River Annan
from Shillahill Bridge to Smallholmburn.

Dalbeattie AA

Secretary - G.D. Bomphray
7 Urr Road, Dalbeattie DG5 4DH
Tel: 0556 610421

Membership - Restricted
Year Formed - 1919
No. of Members - 160 Adults
Facilities - Dalbeattie Reservoir. Brown and
rainbow trout. 1½ Miles of River Urr. Salmon,
sea trout, brown trout.

Gatehouse & Kirkcudbright AA

Secretary - D.A. Lamont
37 St. Mary Street, Kircudbright DG6 4AE
Tel: 0577 30492

Membership - Restricted
Year Formed - Pre 1970
No. of Members - 100
Facilities - Lochenbreck Loch, Laurieston 34 acre
loch stocked on a put and take basis. Brown,
rainbow and brook trout averaging 12-16oz.

Gretna AA

Secretary - J.G. Graham
126 Currock Park Avenue, Carlisle
Cumbria CA2 4DH

Membership - Unrestricted
Year Formed - 1932
No. of Members - 270
Facilities - River Sark - Scottish side from Gretna-
Carlisle Road to Solway approx ¾ to 1 mile.
River Kirtle both banks from Carlisle - Dumfries
Railway line to Solway Shore, approx 3 miles.

Mid-Nithsdale AA

Secretary - R.W. Coltart
49 Drumlanrig Street, Thornhill
Tel: 0848 30464

Membership - Restricted
Year Formed - 1897
No. of Members - 200
Facilities - 4½ Miles of River Nith. Salmon, sea
trout and brown trout. Gravel bed and grass
bank with easy access to the river.

Newton Stewart AA

Secretary - J. Stuart Coy
Park Cottage, Creetown, Newton Stewart
Tel: 067182 332

Membership - Restricted
No. of Members - 250
Facilities - 3 Lochs and 3 Rivers. Lochs are
stocked regularly with brown trout, brook trout
and rainbow trout. Rivers hold salmon and sea-
trout.

Upper Annandale AA

Secretary - J.B. Black
1 Rosehill Grange Road, Moffat DG1D 9HT
Tel: 0683 20104

Membership - Restricted
Year Formed - 1926
No. of Members - 300
Facilities - River Annan. 4 Miles both banks from
Meeting of Waters, Beattock to Railway Viaduct,
Wamphray. ½ Mile right bank at Johnstone
Bridge Parish Church 6 Miles both banks from
Lochbrow Farm Johnstone Bridge to mouth of
River Kinnel excluding Jardine Hall & Applegarth
Manse Waters. River Kinnel - 1 mile upstream
from junction with River Annan; left bank and
part only of right bank.

FIFE

Ballingry AC

Secretary - W. Duncan
162 Stenhouse Street, Cowdenbeath KY4 9DL

Membership - Restricted
Year Formed - 1919
No. of Members - 31
Facilities - Hold competitions on Loch Leven
(Kinross), The Meadows (Crosshill) and Loch Fitty
(Kingseat Fife).

The Canmore AC

Secretary - L.W. Mitchell
33 Halbeath Road, Dunfermline
Tel: 0383 31561

Membership - Restricted
No. of Members - 27
Facilities - Fly fishing on Loch Leven and Loch
Fyth (Fife).

Dunfermline Artisan AC

Secretary - J. Jamieson
154 Wedderburn Street, Dunfermline
Tel: 0383 20442

Membership - Restricted
Year Formed - 1910
No. of Members - 81
Facilities - Controls local reservoir approx 50
acres. Fly fishing only.

Eden AA

Secretary - J. Fyffe
67 Braehead, Cupar
Tel: 0334 53588

Membership - Unrestricted
Year Formed - 1904
No. of Members - 700
Facilities - Approx 9 miles of River Eden (best
May, June and July). Good dry fly fishing for
trout. Good salmon and sea trout (Aug, Sept,
Oct, part Nov). All legal methods. No Sunday
fishing.

Kelty Artisans AC

Secretary – A. Japp
73 Croftangry Road, Kelty
Tel: 0383 830635

Membership – Restricted
Year Formed – 1922
No. of Members – 24
Facilities – Club fishes solely on Loch Leven.

Nairn Thistle AC

Secretary – H. F. Greig
24 James Grove, Kirkcaldy KY1 1TH
Tel: 0592 62584

Membership – Restricted
Year Formed – 1971
No. of Members – 35

Primrose AC

Secretary – A. Cox
103 Whinnyburn Place, Rosyth KY11 2TR
Tel: 0383 415703

Membership – Unrestricted
Year Formed – 1978
No. of Members – 14

St. Andrews AC

Secretary – P.F. Malcolm
54 St. Nicholas Street, St. Andrews
Tel: 0334 76347

Membership – Restricted
No. of Members – 120
Facilities – Cameron Reservoir. Brown trout fishing. Approx 100 acres. Bank and boat fishing. 4 Miles from St. Andrews. Particulars available from secretary.

Townhill AC

Secretary – J.A. Macdonald
5 Witchbrae, Dunfermline
Tel: 0383 20634

Membership – Restricted
Year Formed – 1902
No. of Members – 50
Facilities – Small reservoir approx 4 miles north of Dunfermline. Fly fishing only. Bank fishing only. Stocked annually with 500×9in. brown trout.

GRAMPIAN

Aberdeen & District AA

Secretary – Messrs. Clark & Wallace
14 Albyn Place, Aberdeen
Tel: 0224 53481

Membership – Restricted
Year Formed – 1947
No. of Members – 600
Facilities – Brown trout and salmon on River Don. Sea trout and salmon on River Ythan.

Elgin AA

Secretary – I. Mackay
49 Bailies Drive, Elgin, Morayshire
Tel: 034 45168

Membership – Restricted, Junior membership available
Year Formed – 1942
No. of Members – 450
Facilities – River Lossie. 15 Miles (approx). Both banks from Calcots Railway Bridge on the North to the junction of The Leanoch Burn (Glenlatterach) on the South 2. The right or East bank from the point known as Coral Peel on the North to The Calcots Railway Bridge.

Forres AA

Secretary – P. Garrow
2 Robertson Place, Forres IV36 0BU

Membership – Restricted
No. of Members – 180
Facilities – Parts of River Findhorn from Red Craig Pool to Estuary.

Fyvie AA

Secretary – G.A. Joss
Bank House, Fyvie, Turriff AB5 8PB
Tel: 065 16 233

Membership – Unrestricted
Year Formed – 1910
No. of Members – 50
Facilities – Water situated on River Ythan, North Bank from Peath Bridge situated ½ mile South of Fyvie Village stretching 3 miles southwards to Fetterletter Farm, Woodhead, Fyvie. Permits may be obtained during business hours at Clydesdale Bank Limited, Fyvie and also Vale Hotel, Fyvie, Spar Supermarket and Ythan Bar, Fyvie and also Sheiling Tor Cafe, Fyvie.

Inverurie AA

Secretary – T.H. Dunderdale
9 Rutherford Folds, Inverurie
Tel: 0467 20842

Membership – Unrestricted
Year Formed – 1928
No. of Members – 85
Facilities – Water owned by Gordon District Council, administrated by Inverurie AA. 6 Miles on River Don and Urie (salmon, sea trout, brown trout). Permits available from J. Duncan 4 West High Street, Inverurie Tel: 0467 20310.

Laurencekirk & District AA

Secretary – R. Stewart
68 Provost Robson Drive, Laurencekirk
Tel: 056 17 680

Membership – Restricted
Year Formed – 1956
No. of Members – 100
Facilities – We control 6 miles of The Luther Water and 7 miles of The Bervie Water. Both rivers are excellent for salmon and sea trout and brown trout fishing. Both rivers are within the Parish of Laurence Kirk.

Lossiemouth AA

Secretary – T.B. Clark
Dunconusg, Stotfield, Lossiemouth
Tel: 034 381 2380

Membership – Unrestricted
Year Formed – 1958
No. of Members – 220 including Juniors
Facilities – Approx 4 miles of shore fishing, mainly for sea trout and salmon approx 1½ mi of river fishing from both banks of The River Lossie. (Trout and salmon). The sea and shore fishing is mainly for sea trout, although some members bait fish for other sea fish. Flounders mackerel etc.

River Ugie AA

Captain Curzon, Daluaine, Rhynie, Huntly, Aberdeenshire AB5 4HL
Tel: 04646 638
Facilities – Privately owned fishing waters. Perm available on application to Captain Curzon.

Westhill and Elrick AC

Secretary – R. Findlay
49 Henderson Drive, Elrick, Skene
Tel: 0224 741704

Membership – Restricted (to 30 members)
Year Formed – 1978
No. of Members – 27
Facilities – This is under negotiation. Rights to mile brown trout on Urie.

HIGHLANDS & ISLANDS

Abernethy Angling Improvement A

Secretary – A.D. McLaren
Rothiemoon, Nethybridge
Tel: 047 982 204

Membership – Restricted
Year Formed – 1966
No. of Members – 100
Facilities – Salmon, sea trout and brown trout fishing over a 4 mile stretch of The River Spey between boat at Garton and Nethybridge (both banks). Permits restricted to local residents or visitors with established residing in the Parish of Duthil.

Assynt AC

Secretary – S. McClelland
Baddidarroch, Lochinver, Lairg
Tel: 057 14 253

Membership – Restricted (3 Months residence in year)
Year Formed – 1956
No. of Members – 100
Facilities – 34 Hill Lochs and 4 Lochs available locals only, experimental sea trout project (Loch Roe), rivers available to local members 2 days per season.

Dingwall & District AC

Secretary – A. Shanks (official)
The Sporting Stores, Tulloch Street, Dingwall
Tel: 0349 62346

Membership – Unrestricted, Junior membership available
No. of Members – 200
Facilities – River Conon (lower beat) Fly fishing only for sea trout and brown trout. Loch Luichar (Upper loch), Fly fishing and spinning. Brown trout, perch, char, pike.

...noch & District AA

...tary – W.A. Macdonald
...e Street, Dornoch
...082 281 301

...bership – Restricted to Dornoch and District
...ents
...f Members – 130
...ale, Loch Laoigh, Loch Buidhe, Loch
...ale, Loch Lannsaidh boat and bank fishing.
... fishing at Littleferry. Arrangements can be
... for Loch Cracail, Loch Lard, Loch
...ain, Loch Ghobhair and Loch Evelix.

...t William AA

...etary – A.E. Reece
...edere, Alma Road, Fort William
...0397 2068

...bership – Restricted
... Formed – 1900
...f Members – 50
...ties – River Nevis – 6 miles of fishing for
...on and sea trout. Fly and worm only.
...ning not allowed. Short river giving good
... May to September in spate conditions. Day
...s available from tackle shops in Fort
...am.

...spie AC

...etary – Mr D.W. Melville
...a Vista, Main Street, Golspie
...040 83 3272
...bership – Unrestricted
...f Members – 50
...ities – Game fishing at Loch Brora for
...on, sea trout and brown trout. Also fishing at
...Lundie, Loch Horn and Loch Farlay for
...n trout only.

...irloch AC

...etary – T.A. Bell
...massie Wood, Gairloch, Ross-shire
...044 583 247

...bership – Restricted
... Formed – 1967
...f Members – 50
...ities – Leased from Gairloch Estate Gairloch.
...im Lochs for brown trout River Kerry for
...on and sea trout. Loch Maree, 1 beat salmon
...sea trout (boat only) Fionn Loch. 1 Boat for
...n trout. Boats 12 in all on brown trout lochs.

...ghland Omnibuses ...ployees AC

...etary – D.J. Mackay
...Dell Road, Inverness
...0463 30136

...bership – Restricted
...r Formed – 1975
...f Members – 30
...ities – Game fishing in Rivers and Lochs in
...county and other counties North and West of
...rness. We do not control any waters. Sea
...ng – round the North and N. West Coasts of
...tland.

...erness AC

...etary – J. Fraser
...Hawthorn Drive, Inverness
...0463 36193

Membership – Restricted
Year Formed – 1920
No. of Members – 350 Senior, 430 Junior
Facilities – Both banks of the River Ness within the
town of Inverness, approx 3 miles.

Isle of Bute AA

Secretary – S.W. Squires
2 Timber Cottages, Mount Stuart, Isle of Bute

Membership – Unrestricted
Year Formed – 1967
No. of Members – 72
Facilities – Open shore line – variable sandy
beaches and rocks. Cod, flatties, mackerel,
pollock, haddock. South of Island high rocky
shore line – good wrasse Loch Fad and Loch
Quein – trout. Both lochs wooded and easily
accessible fly fishing only. Loch Ascog – Course
fishing – pike and perch. Same nature as above.

Lairg AC

Secretary – J.M. Ross
Post Office House, Lairg, IV27 4DD
Tel: 0549 2010 – 0549 2025 (Day)

Membership – Restricted to residents in immediate
area. Junior membership available.
Year Formed – 1960
No. of Members – 35
Facilities – Loch Shin, Sutherland. Large
expanse – some 18 miles long. 7 Boats available
for hire, equipped with outboard motor.

Loch Achonachie AC

Secretary – M. Burr
The Tackle Shop, Cromartie Buildings,
Strathpeffer
Tel: 099 72 561

Membership – Restricted
Year Formed – 1955
No. of Members – 130
Facilities – River Conon (Upper Beats). Brown
trout and salmon, 1 April to 30 Sept Loch Meig
brown trout only. Fly fishing only. 1 May to
30 Sept Loch Achonachie and River Blackwater
brown trout and salmon. Spinning allowed.
1 April to 30 Sept.

Loch Brora AC

Secretary – J. Mackay
Ataireachd Ard, Lower Brora, Sutherland,
KW9 6PZ
Tel: 883 512

Membership – Restricted
No. of Members – 100
Facilities – 2 Boats on Loch Brora. Sea trout,
salmon, char, brown trout River Brora, tenancy
for salmon. Minimum 3 weeks AA (72 rod/days).

Nairn AA

Secretary – Mrs W.R. Mackay
36 Mill Road, Queenspark, Nairn, Nairnshire
Tel: 0667 53768

Membership – Unrestricted
Year Formed – 1921
No. of Members – 201 Adults, 60 Scholars,
52 O.A.P.
Facilities – River Nairn. Approx 7¾ miles from
mouth of river to Whitebridge, Cawdor.

North Uist AC

Secretary – D.L. Cockburn
19 Dunrossil Place, Lochmaddy, North Uist
Tel: 089 63 205

Membership – Restricted
Year Formed – 1952
Facilities – All Lochs on North Uist Estates
controlled by Factor, North Uist Estates,
Lochmaddy, North Uist Permits for all fishing can
be obtained at Estate Office, Lochmaddy.

Orkney Trout FA

Robert Windwick
17 Hermaness, Kirkwall
Tel: 0856 4104

Shetland AA

Secretary – A. Miller
3 Gladstone Terrace, Lerwick, Shetland Isles
Tel: 0595 3729

Membership – Unrestricted
Year Formed – 1920
No. of Members – 441
Facilities – Over 1000 Lochs, both sea and fresh
water scattered throughout the "mainland" island
of Shetland. No river fishing as such, but all
freshwater lochs have brown trout of varying
sizes. Sea trout and grilse of varying sizes in the
sea lochs and voes throughout the year, but best
in Spring and Autumn

South Uist AC

Secretary – Dr. I. Logan Jack
Griminish, Benbecula
Tel: 2215 2068

Membership – Restricted to residents only
Year Formed – 1950
No. of Members – 75
Facilities – Over 300 lochs in Benbecula and
South Uist. Fly fishing for salmon sea trout and
brown trout. Some fishing restricted to members
only by agreement with owners but daily/weekly
permits are available for visitors on nearly all
club waters at approx £1.00 per day or £3.00
per week. Boats available to visitors at approx
£1.00 per day. Seasons: brown trout, 15 Mar to
30 Sept, salmon/sea trout 1 Feb to 30 Oct.

Soval AA

Secretary – E. Young
The Rectory, Stornoway, Lewis
Tel: 0851 2204

Membership – Restricted
Year Formed – 1959
No. of Members – 60
Facilities – Lochs on Soval Estate

Strathspey Angling Improvement Association

Secretary – G. Mortimer
61 High Street, Grantown-on-Spey
Tel: 0479 2684

Membership – Restricted
Year Formed – 1913
Facilities – 7 Miles double bank fishing on the
River Spey. 12 Miles double bank fishing on the
River Dulnain. Both rivers salmon, sea trout and
brown trout. 5 Stocked lochs (rainbow, brown
trout).

Thurso AA

Secretary − J. Robertson
23 Sinclair Street, Thurso
Tel: 0847 2819

Membership − Restricted
Year Formed − 1959
No. of Members − 290
Facilities − Beat No. 1 on the River Thurso. Salmon and sea trout, also brown trout. Strictly fly only. Area is open country. Water is of a peaty colour, i.e. clear with brown tint. The Association was granted this stretch of water by Lord Thurso.

LOTHIAN

Edinburgh Walton AC

Secretary − M.W. Thomson
21 Heriot Row, Edinburgh EH3 6EN
Tel: 031 225 6511

Membership − Restricted
Year Formed − 1874
No. of Members − 60
Facilities − Competitions and outings to numerous waters within 50 miles of Edinburgh.

Leukaemia Research Fund AC

Secretary − Mrs J.C. Oag
Rowan Cottage, 75 Main Street, Ratho EH28 8RT
Tel: 031 333 1080

Membership − Restricted
Year Formed − 1977
No. of Members − 40
Facilities − No Club Waters

North Berwick AC

Secretary − G.B. Woodburn
29 Craigleith Avenue, North Berwick, E. Lothian
Tel: 0620 3120

Membership − Restricted
Year Formed − 1907
No. of Members − 50

South Queensferry AC

Secretary − B.D. Plasting
53 Sommerville Gardens
Tel: 031 331 1605

Membership − Unrestricted
Year Formed − 1974
No. of Members − 50
Facilities − No waters controlled. Variety of social events, the club is affiliated to the Scottish Federation of Sea Anglers. The club is also a founder member of the Eastern Region of that body.

St. Mary's AC

Secretary − J. Miller
6 Greenbank Loan, Edinburgh, EH10 5SH
Tel: 031 447 2192

Membership − Restricted, Junior membership available
No. of Members − Approx. 60
Facilities − St. Mary's Loch, Selkirkshire, Loch o' the Lowes, Selkirkshire. Game fishing clubs may be given permission to hold matches on Lochs, but this must be pre-booked in writing to the secretary stating number of anglers. No coarse fishing matches allowed.

STRATHCLYDE

Avon AC

Secretary − T.M. Hamilton
69 Lockhart Street, Stone House, Lanarkshire
Tel: 0698 793517

Membership − Unrestricted
Year Formed − 1903
Facilities − Fishing available on 11 miles of trout river.

Ayre AC

Secretary − P. Mack
8 Pine Brae, Ayr
Tel: 0292 60275

Membership − Restricted
Year Formed − 1970
No. of Members − 400+
Facilities − River Ayr, Town stretch 1½ miles upstream (10 miles). ½ Mile and 2 lochs.

B.S.C. Ravenscraig Works Freshwater & Sea

Secretary − J. McLaughlan
22 Cheviot Crescent, Wishawhill, Wishaw
Lanarkshire ML2 7PN
Tel: 069 83 61987

Membership − Unrestricted
Year Formed − 1978
No. of Members − 38 Full, 2 Retired, 14 Juniors 6 Associate

Castle AC

Secretary − E.W. Griffiths
35 William Street, Johnstone

Membership − Restricted
Year Formed − 1909
No. of Members − 160
Facilities − Strathclyde area. River Black Cart, 2½ miles. Brown trout and some coarse fish.

Dalrymple AC

Secretary − J. Black
Portland Road, Dalrymple

Membership − Restricted
Year Formed − 1945
No. of Members − 40
Facilities − ½ Mile water on River Doon

Dreghorn AC

Secretary − D. Muir
6 Pladda Avenue, Broomlands, Irvine
Tel: 0294 213137

Membership − Unrestricted
Year Formed − 1912
No. of Members − 500
Facilities − The club controls approx 6 miles of salmon, sea trout and brown trout fishing on The River Irvine ending at the confluence of the Annick and Irvine rivers which is just outside the town of Irvine. Both the River Irvine and River Annick (main tributary) can be fished on both banks upstream from the confluence for about 6 miles. The River Annick contains some salmon as well as sea trout and brown trout.

Drongan Youth Group AC

Secretary − M. Harvey
19 Lane Crescent, Drongan
Tel: 029 258 840

Membership − Unrestricted
No. of Members − Over 250
Facilities − It is a country area and flows into t River Ayr.

Drumgrange & Keirs AC

Secretary − S.J. Taylor
9 Carsphairn Road, Dalmellington

Membership − Unrestricted
Year Formed − 1902
No. of Members − 200
Facilities − 5 Miles of river fishing (both banks) the River Doon between Dalmellington and Pa Species: Salmon, sea trout, brown trout. Regu restocking of all species. Best from June onwa

Finlas F.C.

Secretary − W.A. McMillan
27 Miller Road, Ayr
Tel: 0292 64002

Membership − Restricted
Year Formed − 1900
No. of Members − 30
Facilities − Loch Finlas. Hill loch served by Residential Lodge.

Hamilton AC

Secretary − J. McBride
198 Trossachs Road, Cathkin, Rutherglen, Glasgow

Helensburgh AC

Secretary − J.F. McCreath
37 Bain Crescent, Helensburgh
Tel: 0436 4850

Membership − Restricted
Year Formed − 1945
No. of Members − 70
Facilities − Helensburgh Reservoirs Nos. 1, 2 a 3. Finlas Water.

Hurlford AC

Secretary − J. Miller
25 Knowehead Road, Hurlford, Kilmarnock
Tel: 0563 35122

Membership − Restricted
Year Formed − 1904
No. of Members − 180
Facilities − River Irvine 4½ miles both banks. Woodland and meadows, pools and streams. Stocked annually with brown trout and sea tro River Cessnock (tributary of Irvine) 3 miles bo banks − few salmon. Stocked annually with bro trout only.

Kilmarnock AC

Secretary − H. Grubb
33 Lochnagar Road, Bellfield
Tel: 0563 27574

Membership – Unrestricted, Junior membership
available
No. of Members – 400
Facilities – Craigendunton Reservoir, Burnfoot
Reservoir, River Irvine, Drumtree and Borland
Waters, River Lugar: Millerston Stretch about
5 miles.

Kilmaurs AC

Secretary – J. Watson
Four Acres Drive, Kilmaurs KA3 2ND
Tel: 056 381 267

Membership – Unrestricted
Year Formed – 1924
No. of Members – 300 approx, including Juveniles
Facilities – R. Annick – Cunningham Head Dam to
Chapeltown Bridge. R. Glaisert – Water Meetings
to Bloakholm Bridge. Both above waters contain
trout (stocked annually). Some sea trout and
salmon June – October North Craig
Reservoir – brown trout.

Kilwinning Eglinton AC

Secretary – M.S. Tudhope
5 Viaduct Circle, Kilwinning
Tel: 0294 53652

Membership – Restricted
Year Formed – 1905
No. of Members – 500
Facilities – River Garnock from Dalgarven to
estuary approx 4 miles. River Lugton from
Montgreenan to its entry into River Garnock,
approx 4 miles.

Kintyre Fish Protection & AC

Secretary – Rev. J.A.M. McFie
Lochend Manse, Campbeltown PA28 6EN
Tel: 0586 2605

Membership – Restricted
Year Formed – 1949
No. of Members – 70 Senior, 30 Junior (under 17)
Facilities – L. Lussa: Hydro Board Reservoir 7
miles approx North of Campbeltown, loch fed by
burns passing through mainly peaty land. Loch
surrounded by young forests of spruce, fir, larch
etc. Loch Auchalochy: Set in the hills about
1 mile north of Campbeltown, this loch is part of
the public water supply. This loch is fed by
streams which pass through land with a good
concentration of lime. Loch Ruan: A small loch
approx ½ mile East of Loch Auchalochy. Loch
Crosshill: A local authority reservoir about a mile
south of the town centre (fed by peaty streams).
Coniglen Water: flows through village of
Southend (approx 5 miles club controlled) mainly
spate water.

Kyles of Bute AC

Secretary – A. Morrison
Kenteith Kames, Tighnabruaich Tel: 070 081 458

Membership – Restricted
Year Formed – 1960
No. of Members – 50
Facilities – Loch Ascog, stock: Rainbow trout and
native brown trout. Fly only Upper and Lower
Powder Dams, stock: rainbow and native brown.
Fly and bait. Tighnabruaich Reservoir: brown
trout. Fly and bait, no spinning on club waters.
Permits available at 5 local shops and post office.
£1 per day. Fishing lochs, set in quiet scenic
surrounding, readily accessible. Private hotel
and chalet accommodation available in
surrounding area, (not associated with club).

Lamington & District Angling Improvement Association

Secretary – J. Hyslop
Donnachie Cottage, Biggar, Lanarkshire
ML12 6EP
Tel: 0899 20616

Membership – Restricted to residents in immediate
area
Year Formed – 1922
No. of Members – 100/120
Facilities – River Clyde, 9 miles both banks from
Roberton/Thankerton. Species: brown trout and
grayling. Regularly stocked. Visitors permits
day/weekly/season available, from Secretary and
Bailiffs.

Lanark & District AC

Secretary – A. McLean
137 St. Leonalds Street, Lanark
Tel: 0555 4879

Membership – Unrestricted
Year Formed – 1930
No. of Members – 200
Facilities – From Kirkfieldbank Bridge to
Eastersills Farm.

Lochgilphead District AC

Secretary – D. MacDougall
23 High Bank Park, Lochgilphead
Tel: 0546 2104

Membership – Restricted
Year Formed – 1930
No. of Members – 90
Facilities – Hine Hill Lochs, located approx 4
miles from Lochgilphead.

Penwhapple FC

Secretary – J.H. Murray
3 & 120A Dalrymple Street, Girvan
Tel: 0465 2039

Membership – Restricted to area ratepayers
Year Formed – 1926
No. of Members – 50
Facilities – A beautiful hill loch (Penwhapple
Loch), of 14½ acres. Stocked annually with
brown trout. Situated 4 miles from Girvan with 5
boats available. Fly fishing only. Available for
matches mid-week only maximum number 20.

Port Glasgow AC

Secretary – I. Tucker
39 Marloch Avenue, Port Glasgow, Renfrewshire
Tel: 0475 705012

Membership – Restricted
No. of Members – 225
Facilities – 72 acres Lower Loch Gryffe, 10 acres
Knocknairshill, 24 acres Harelaw, 6 acres Mill
Dam. All Reservoirs set in hills. Good scenery
acid waters. Near factories and housing schemes.

Rowbank AC

Secretary – A.C. Wilson
C. Davidson & Son, 15 Forbes Place
Paisley PA1 1UT
Tel: 041 889 3459

Membership – Restricted
Year Formed – 1870
No. of Members – 110

Facilities – Rowbank Reservoir, 97 acres
Barcraigs Reservoir, 175 acres. These reservoirs
completed in 1870 and 1916 respectively. Have
now acquired a natural appearance. They are
situated above the village of Houston and are
surrounded by wooded and agricultural land. Fly
fishing only for trout.

Shotts Bon-Accord AC

Secretary – J. Frew
26 St. Catherines Crescent, Shotts, Lanarkshire

Membership – Unrestricted
Year Formed – 1980
No. of Members – 18

Stewarton AC

Secretary – J.L. Sharp
13 Morton Road, Stewarton, Ayrshire
Tel: 0560 84138

Membership – Restricted
Year Formed – 1930
No. of Members – 400
Facilities – The type of water we have consists
mainly of small rivers in a region that is used
mainly for dairy farming. We also have a loch
which is stocked annually.

Strathgryfe AA

Secretary – F. Sinclair
"Dunedin", Port Glasgow Road
Kilmacolm PA13 4QG
Tel: 050 549 2435

Membership – Unrestricted, Junior membership
available. Limit of 100 non-local members
Year Formed – 1900
No. of Members – 200
Facilities – River Gryfe and tributaries in vicinity
of Kilmacolm.

Tobermory AA

Secretary – A. Brown
Stronsaule, Tobermory, Isle of Mull
Tel: 0688 2381

Membership – Unrestricted, Junior membership
available
No. of Members – 75
Facilities – Mishnish Lochs, 1½ miles N.W. of
Tobermory, 100 acres – wild brown
trout – 3 boats for hire. Aros Loch – 20 acres –
Rainbow and brown trout in Forestry Comm.
Ass. Park 1 mile south of Tobermory.

United Clyde Angling Protective Association Ltd

Secretary – J. Quigley
15 Auchter Road, Cambus Court, Wishaw,
Strathclyde

Membership – Unrestricted, but by application
Year Formed – 1887
No. of Members – 170
Facilities – The Association is the largest trout
angling association in Scotland. Approx 60 miles
of trout and grayling fishing, from Motherwell to
Kirkfieldbank, Carstairs to Thankerton and
Roberton to Crawford, all on the River Clyde.

TAYSIDE

Aberfeldy AC

Secretary – D. Campbell
Sports Shop, The Square, Aberfeldy
Tel: 088 74 354

Membership – Restricted
Year Formed – 1887
No. of Members – 170
Facilities – 3 Miles salmon, trout and grayling on River Tay. 1 Small trout loch.

Brechin AC

Secretary – D.E. Smith
3 Friendly Park

Membership – Restricted
Year Formed – 1875
No. of Members – 120
Facilities – Loch Saugh, 13 acres brown trout, rainbow trout. Border Holes, 3 acres brown trout, rainbow trout. Westwater 4½ miles, brown trout, sea trout, salmon.

Canmore AC

Secretary – E.S. Mann
44 Sheriff Park Gardens, Forfar

Membership – Unrestricted
Year Formed – 1977
No. of Members – 244 Adults, 104 Juniors
Facilities – Trout fishing. Rivers Dean, Kerbet, Noran, Lemno, Airneyfoul, Glenogil Reservoir, Forfar Loch, and Rescobie Loch.

Killin Breadalbane AC

Secretary – D. Allan
12 Ballechroisk, Killin, Perthshire
Tel: 056 72 362

Membership – Restricted to residents of Killin
No. of Members – 70
Facilities – River Dochart, River Lochay, Loch Tay and Lochan Larige. All available to hire for matches.

SOUTHERN IRELAND

CLARE

Kilamley & District Angling Club
Secretary – F. Healy
Farrow, Kilmaley, Ennis

Kirriemuir AC

Secretary – H.F. Burness
13 Clova Road, Kirriemuir
Tel: 057 52 3456

Membership – Restricted
Year Formed – 1919
No. of Members – 176
Facilities – River South Esk, 7 miles (both banks). Salmon, sea trout River Prosen, 1 mile approx. Salmon, sea trout. River Isla, small beat. Salmon, sea trout

Loch Rannoch Conservation Association

Secretary – S. Fordham
Cluain na Coille, Dall, Rannoch Station
Tel: 088 22 379

Facilities – A conservation association which regulates the fishing on Loch Rannoch on behalf of its owners.

Montrose & District AC

Secretary – G.S. Taylor
Brago, 14 Russell Street, Montrose BD10 8HS
Tel: 0674 3904

Membership – Restricted
Year Formed – 1947
No. of Members – Lessees of River South Esk Water at Bridge of Dun. Lessees of River North Esk at Graigo. Salmon, grilse, sea trout, finnock, both waters South Esk, approx 1½ miles both banks North Esk, south bank only 2 miles.

Pitlochry AC

Secretary – R. Harriman
"Sunnyknowe", 7 Nursing Home Brae, Pitlochry
Tel: 0796 2484

Scarriff, Mt Shannon & Whitegate AA

Secretary – Padraic Cahill
Mt Shannon, Scarriff

Sixmilebridge AC

Secretary – G. Murphy
41 Fergus Park
Ennis

CORK

Blarney & DAC
Secretary – S. Kelleher
Lisduff, Whitechurch, Blarney

Castle AA
Secretary – D. Papazian
St Judes, Earlwood, The Lough, Cork

Membership – Unrestricted to locals, Junior membership available
Year Formed – 1884
No. of Members – 120
Facilities – Loch fishing (with boats). Superb fishing in beautiful surroundings in Perthshire. River fishing for salmon and trout on The River Tummel above and below Pitlochry Dam and Loch Fastcally. Loch Bhac, fly only, rainbow, brown and brook trout; Loch Garry, Loch Kinardochy, trout. Port-na-Craig – salmon.

Rannoch & District AC

Secretary – J. Brown
The Square, Kinloch Rannoch, By Pitlochry PH16 5PN
Tel: 08822 331

Membership – Restricted to local residents, Junior membership available
Year Formed – 1951
No. of Members – 80
Facilities – Loch Eigheached near Rannoch Station. For brown trout and for perch.

St. Fillans & Lockearn AA

Secretary – J. Waspharrow
Rainoch, 4 Carnview, St. Fillan
Tel: 076 485 219

Membership – Restricted
Year Formed – 1928
No. of Members – 150
Facilities – Loch Earn, both shores. River Earn ¾ of mile North side the complete stretch. South bank, approx ½ mile. All fishing closed on the 6th October.

Strathmore Angling Improvement Association

Secretary – New appointment pending

Membership – Unrestricted
Year Formed – 1940
No. of Members – 4000 approx, plus permit holders
Facilities – Rivers Isla, Dean, and stretches of Ericht and Dean. The association also runs their own fish farm and produces all their own stock. Salmon fishing available to season ticket holders and members.

Castlelyons TAC
Secretary – R. O'Mahoney
Castlelyons

Coachford AA
Secretary – E. Hayes
Madrid, Coachford

Cork TAA
Secretary – J. Riordan
Jalna, Bishopstown Avenue, Model Farm Road, Cork

Frmoy TAA
Secretary – P.J. O'Reilly
6 Church Place, Fermoy

Irishtown FC
Secretary – M.J. O'Regan
Fishermans Rest, Bandon

ildorrery AC
ecretary – S. Dennehy
ermoy Road, Kildorrery

ilworth & DTAC
ecretary – J. Nash
ally, Kilworth

Mallow TA
ecretary – Kevin Healy
3 O'Sullivans Place, Mallow

wenabue TAA
cretary – J. Kelleher
0 St Philomena's Terrace, Carrigaline

iverstown & DAA
ecretary – J. McGrath
 The Rise, Bishopstown

undays Well FC
cretary – M.F. Lane
elmore, Cherry Grove, Model Farm Road,
ork

ONEGAL

inlough & DAA
ecretary – V. Battisti
asa-Mia, Sligo Road, Maheracar, Bundoran

UBLIN

albriggin & Skerries FC
cretary – P. McDermott
ul

lane & Kilcock AA
cretary – T. O'Callaghan
 Sarsfield Park, Lucan

londalkin AA
cretary – N.E. Nolan
heen House, Nangor Road, Clondalkin

odder AA
cretary – R. O'Hanlon
 Braemar Road, Churchtown, Dublin 14

uiness AC
cretary – T. Kennedy
 Violet Hill Drive, Glasnevin, Dublin 11

bridge AC
cretary – D. Johnson
 Avondale Park, Raheny, Dublin 5

can SA
cretary – B. Murray
 Chalet Gardens, Lucan

ALWAY

llinasloe TAA
cretary – B. Larkin
sfield Road, Ballinasloe

ornomona & DAA
cretary – Dr E.J. Sullivan
namona

Corrib Brotherhood AA
Secretary – Peader O'Dowd
88 Prospect Hill, Galway

Galway & Corrib AA
Secretary – E.J. Lloyd
7 Kylemore Park, St Mary's Avenue
Nr Salthill

Headford & Corrib AA
Secretary – Kevin Duffy
Main Street, Headford

Loughrea AA
Secretary – J.J. Mitchell
Waterview, Loughrea

Moycullen AC
Secretary – E. O'Sullivan
Carrigdhoun, Moycullen

Oughterard AA
Secretary – J.P. Lydon
The Square, Oughterard

Tuam & DAC
Secretary – S. Smyth
Ulster Bank House, Tuam

KERRY
Flesk & DAA
Secretary – P. O'Donovan
25 Kigh Street, Killarney

Lough Lein AA
Secretary – J. Tarrant
98 Countess Grove, Killarney

Pretty Polly AC
Secretary – D. J. O'riordan
58 Park Road Estate, Killarney

Waterville AA
Secretary – R. Rudd
Westgate, Waterville

LOUTH
Drogheda & DAA
Secretary – D. Clinton
35 Hillview, Drogheda

Dundalk SAA
Secretary – L.W. Doran
Harristown, Ardee

MAYO
Ballinrobe & DAA
Secretary – D.F. Kellegher
Beale Road, Ballinrobe

Ballina & DTAA
Secretary – E. Brogan
Sligo Road, Ballina

Cong & DAA
Secretary – J. Hopkins
Cong

Cross (Co Mayo) AC
Secretary – L. O'Dea
Cross, Claremorris

Lough Conn AA
Secretary – Dr Brendan Mulloy
Crossmolina

Lough Mask AA
Secretary – P. Heneghan
Treew, Tourmakeady, Claremorris

MEATH
Duleek AA
Secretary – J. Curley
Larrix Street, Duleek

Gormanston & DAC
Secretary – J. Collier
Station House, Gormanston

Navan & DAA
Secretary – P. Smith
Dunmoe, Navan

SLIGO
Collooney AA
Secretary – J. O'Hora
St Mary's Green, Collooney

Lough Arrow FPA
Secretary – Mrs Norah Hart
Annaghloy House, Castlebaldwin

Sligo AA
Secretary – J. Clarke
4 Wolfe Tone Street, Sligo

TIPPERARY
Cahir & DAA
Secretary – P. O'Donnell
Uper Cahir Abbey, Cahir

WESTMEATH
Brosna AA
Secretary – M. Murphy
9 Old Ballinderry, Mullingar

Inny TAA
Secretary – J. Nally
Green View, Multyfarnham

Lough Derravarragh AA
Secretary – A.W. Mills
Ballynacargy

Lough Ennell AA
Secretary – N. Black
Hornbeam House, Portloman, Slanemore,
Mullingar

Lough Glore AA
Secretary – T.B. Meehan
Coolure, Coole

Lough Owel TPA
Secretary – W. Harvey-Kelly
Clonhugh, Multyfarnham

WEXFORD
Enniscorthy & DTAA
Secretary – P.R. Griffin
Bellefield Cottage, Enniscorthy

Lough Garman S&RAA
Secretary – A. Lennon
Alanna, Coolcots

WICKLOW
County Wicklow AA
Secretary – W.A. Hannon
106 Ardmore Park, Herbert Road, Bray,
County Wicklow

Dublin TAA
Secretary – F.J. McCann
Beechwood House, The Dowry, Manorkilbride

ENGLAND

AVON

Albatross SAC

Secretary – C.J.C. Wood
33 Stanbury Avenue, Fishponds, Bristol
Tel: 0272 570421

Membership – Unrestricted at present
Year Formed – 1975
No. of Members – 40
Facilities – We have a full year of booked trips for deep sea angling to venues on the South and West coasts, also Wales. We also have a shore and competitions section taking part in Club and Federation organised trips and matches.

Bristol SA

Secretary – M.J. Bacon
41 Grass Meers Drive, Whitchurch, Bristol
Tel: 0272 830621

Membership – Restricted
Year Formed – 1950
No. of Members – 45
Facilities – The club concentrates on boat fishing at South West Coastal venues. 2 Trips per month on a regular basis catering for up to 10 members a time.

Bristol Shark Club

Secretary – W.J. Dunstone
Home Farm, Courtlands Lane, Bower Ashton, Nr. Bristol
Tel: 0934 862063

Membership – Restricted
Year Formed – 1963
No. of Members – 30
Facilities – Deep sea fishing in Bristol Channel and South Coast.

Brunel SAC

Secretary – K. Reed
27 St. Michaels Avenue, Clevedon BS21 6LL
Tel: 0272 872101

Membership – Restricted
Year Formed – 1971
No. of Members – 35

Merchant Arms SAC

Secretary – H.E. Rushton
23 Cornish Walk, Stockwood. Bristol
Tel: 0272 837511

Membership – Unrestricted
Year Formed – 1973
No. of Members – 70
Facilities – Wide range of Sea Angling Wreck, Reef and Shark. Also very keen to enlarge beach casting section. Have own club van. Fish mostly in Devon and Cornwall.

Pioneer SAC

Secretary – C. Jones
11 Longway Avenue, Whitchurch, Bristol
Tel: 0272 837191

Membership – Unrestricted
Year Formed – 1975
No. of Members – 120
Facilities – Anywhere on the English or Bristol Channels, Welsh Coast and Irish Sea. Both boat and shore fishing.

Weston-Super-Mare AA

Secretary – G.A. Crossman
3 Little Orchard, Uphill, Weston-Super-Mare
Tel: 0934 31129

Membership – Unrestricted
Year Formed – 1952
No. of Members – 200
Facilities – Club House and organised boat and shore matches in Devon, Somerset and Avon.

BEDFORDSHIRE

Bedford SAC

Secretary – K. Harding
168 Honey Hill Road, Bedford MK4 04PD
Tel: 0234 211001

Membership – Unrestricted
Year Formed – 1965
No. of Members – 40
Facilities – Most of fishing is done on the East Coast. Lowestoft, Felixstowe area. We have our own club boats at Felixstowe.

The Hawks SAC

Secretary – E. Clarke
20 Southwood Road, Dunstable
Tel: 0582 660455

Membership – Restricted
Year Formed – 1980
No. of Members – 12. Accept another 15
Facilities – None. Sea and beach fishing. We fish all around the coast.

BERKSHIRE

Bisley & District SAC

Secretary – M.L. Smythe
79 Moordale Avenue, Bracknell
Tel: 0344 27042

Membership – Restricted
Year Formed – 1976
No. of Members – 120

Mortimer SAC

Secretary – T. Godward
Norkett, Basingstoke Road, Riseley, Reading
Tel: 0734 882840

Membership – Unrestricted
Year Formed – 1970
No. of Members – 45
Facilities – Sea fishing only. Mainly boat fishing using charter boats, south and west coast. Have own mini-bus for travel.

Pioneer SAC

Secretary – D.J. Belson
15 Risborough Road, Maidenhead
Tel: 0628 73120

Membership – Restricted
Year Formed – 1978
No. of Members – 20

S.K.F. UK Limited SAC

Secretary – S. Burgoyne
4 Atherstone Road, Bedfordshire
Tel: 0582 597384

Membership – Restricted
Year Formed – 1974
No. of Members – 30
Facilities – We run monthly trips to the coast where we book charter boats from Bradwell and Lowestoft (winter) and Folkestone and Newhaven (summer).

Sperry Bracknell SAC

Secretary – M.S. Raine
2 Longmoors, Bracknell
Tel: 0344 53767

Membership – Restricted
Year Formed – 1975
No. of Members – 50

BUCKINGHAMSHIRE

Bed's & Buck's SAC

Secretary – T. Rainer
11 Forest Road, Windsor
Tel: 07535 57701

CHESHIRE

Maccfishers Deep Sea AC

Secretary – C.P. Creighton
32 Greystone Road, Great Boughton, Chester
Tel: 0244 35413

Membership – Restricted
No. of Members – 30
Facilities – Fortnightly chartered sea fishing trips to North Wales and Anglesey.

National Supply SAC

Secretary – E. Cookney
2 Tamworth Close, Hazel Grove, Stockport
Tel: 483 6990

Membership – Unrestricted
Year Formed – 1976
No. of Members – 30

rth Cheshire Sea Anglers

retary – Dave Rothwell
Vest Vale Road, Timperley
061 928 8378

nbership – Unrestricted
r Formed – 1969
of Members – 53
lities – Monthly boat excursions (Yorks,
cs, and N. Wales coasts). Monthly beach
petitions. 2 weekend trips per year.

nce Albert SAC

retary – Malcolm Forster
tage Street Nursery, Macclesfield
0625 25693

nbership – Restricted
r Formed – 1973
of Members – 12

ddish SAC

retary – H. Thomas
Churchill Crescent, N. Reddish, Stockport
061 432 6608

mbership – Unrestricted
r Formed – 1970
of Members – 25

oodley SAC

retary – Glenn Jones
Poleacre Lane, Woodley, Stockport
061 494 1240

mbership – Unrestricted
r Formed – 1978
of Members – 18
cilities – All coastal waters in U.K.

ORNWALL

de & District SAA

retary – A.J. Inch
rview, Poughill, Bude
0288 3018

mbership – Unrestricted
r Formed – 1963
of Members – 80

allington SAC

retary – R. May
ke Road, Kelly Bray, Callington
057 93 2414

mbership – Unrestricted
r Formed – 1969
of Members – 60
cilities – As a S.A.C. we control no waters.
r main areas are the Cornish Coastline,
s Devon with all the tidal rivers, both boat
d shore.

ambourne AA

retary – Mrs. J. Williams
Enys Road, Camborne

amelford & District SAC

retary – P. Davey
evarthian, 4 Victoria Road, Camelford
32 9TH
084 02 3751

Membership – Unrestricted
Year Formed – 1978
No. of Members – 70
Facilities – We control no waters being a sea
angling club. We fish from shore (rocks),
beach and from the club boat.

Carnhell Green SAC

Secretary – Mrs. V. Cook
14 Penhale Road, Carnhell Green, Camborne

Essa AC

Secretary – J. Webber
2 Rashleigh Avenue, Saltash
Tel: 075 55 5594

Membership – Unrestricted
Year Formed – 1977
No. of Members – 40

Fowey AC

Secretary – D.C. Shelley
Castledore, Tywardreath, Par
Tel: 072 683 2613

Membership – Unrestricted
Year Formed – 1958
No. of Members – Less than 100
Facilities – Estuary and Sea.

Hayle SAC

Secretary – A.G. Dowrick
10A Tresdale Parc, Connor Downs, Hayle
TR27 5DX
Tel: 0736 4343

Membership – Unrestricted
Year Formed – 1979
No. of Members – 95
Facilities – As we are a sea angling club we
do not actually control any waters. Our
members are able to fish anywhere in
Cornwall, but are subject to N.F.S.A. rules.
Many species of fish are available.

Heathcoats SAC

Secretary – Mrs. C. Roberts
28 Condurrow Road, Beacon, Camborne

Helston & District SAC

Secretary – R. Coombs
1a Penventon View
Tel: 032 65 4672

Membership – Unrestricted
Year Formed – 1968
No. of Members – 100
Facilities – Our fishing area (locally) centres
around the Lizard Peninsula for all sorts of
fishing, from the Wrasse mackerel and garfish
etc. from the rocks to the bass beaches and
Helford River. Boat fishing depends on
availability of boats but if possible such spots
as the Manacles and around the Lizard are
very good.

Helston Royal British Legion Club

Secretary – M. Jennings
16 Hermes Road, Helston

Year Formed – 1974
No. of Members – 28
Facilities – Boat, rock and beach fishing.

Herbert AC

Secretary – H. Saunders
Avalon, Hallan Moor, Lanner

Launceston Sea Anglers

Secretary – L.H. Harrison
47 St. Leonards Road, Lanstephan,
Launceston

Membership – Unrestricted
Year Formed – 1978
No. of Members – 20

Liskeard & District SAC

Secretary – R. Wallbank
c/o 6 Donierts Close, Liskeard PL14 4HS
Tel: 0579 45263

Membership – Unrestricted
Year Formed – 1972
No. of Members – 85
Facilities – This club has permits to fish
E.C.C. Ports, docks at Fowey and Par and is
hoping to arrange permits to fish War Dept.
Jetties at Jupiter Point Antony, and Thancks
Oil Fuel Dept, Torpoint,

Looe SAC

Secretary – D. Snell
Sunnybank, Trewidland, Liskeard

Lostwithiel FA

Secretary – S.E. Brewer
Hillhouse, Lostwithiel
Tel: 0208 872542

Membership – Unrestricted
Year Formed – 1936
Facilities – Fishing for salmon, sea trout and
brown trout — Bass in Estuary and sea fishing
on coast at Fowey.

Mawnan AC

Secretary – D. Woodgate
Bareppa, Mawnan Smith, Falmouth

Mevagissey SAC

Secretary – G.E.M. Stuart
1 Lower Well Park, Polkirt Hill, Mevagissey

Membership – Unrestricted
Year Formed – 1964
No. of Members – 150
Facilities – Sea fishing only

Mounts Bay AS

Secretary – D.J.E. Cains
37 Treassone Road, Penzance TR18 2AU
Tel: 0736 67709

Membership – Unrestricted
Year Formed – 1946
No. of Members – 102. 55 Seniors, 47 Juniors
Facilities – The local fishing is excellent from
either pier, rock, beach, or boat. Many
competitions are held each year for both
members and non members. The club is
affiliated to both the National Federation of
Sea Anglers and the European Federation of
Sea Anglers.

Newquay Royal British Legion AC

Secretary – R.G. Addison
6 Stanways Road, Newquay TR7 3HF

Membership – Restricted
Year Formed – 1970
No. of Members – 40

Perranporth SAC

Secretary – A.D. Naylor
16 Tregundy Road, Perranporth
Tel: 087 287 3764

Membership – Unrestricted
Year Formed – 1971
No. of Members – 50

Porthleven SAC

Secretary – D. Ward
43 St Peters Way, Porthleven

Raleigh SAC

Secretary – D.G. Livick
9 Coombe Park, Cawsand
Tel: 0752 822117

Membership – Restricted
Year Formed – 1974
No. of Members – 94
Facilities – Shore fishing in general and plenty of reef fishing. Secretary is charter boat owner. Affiliated to N.F.S.A. and R.N. + R.M.S.A.A. and Plymouth command membership.

Rame Peninsula SAC

Secretary – P. Carne
100 West Street, Millbrook, Nr. Torpoint
Tel: 0752 822 16

Membership – Restricted
Year Formed – 1977
No. of Members – 45
Facilities – Sea Angling only. No restrictions.

Redruth SAA

Secretary – Mrs. L. Cockerill
Flat 1, Paynters Lane, End, Illogan, Redruth

Roche AC

Secretary – D.E. Minards
63 Porth Bean Road, Newquay
Tel: 063 73 5669

Membership – Restricted
Year Formed – 1960
No. of Members – 400
Facilities – Disused clay pits and stone quarries in Mid. Cornwall. 8 Pools in all ranging from 1½ acres to 7 acres. All our pools are fully stocked with a full range of fish. The pools are totally covered in trees and natural cover.

St. Ives AS

Secretary – D. Hugo
Flat 4, Suncrest Flats, Fernlea Terrace, St.Ives

St. Newlyn East

Secretary – D. Ford
1 Mertha Road, Newquay

South Crofty SAC

Secretary – L.A. Hocking
5 St. Martins Crescent, Camborne

Tintagel SAC

Secretary – G. Tagg
Clonmore, Atlantic Way, Tintagel

Truro City AC

Secretary – Mrs. L. Cofer
22 Treverbyn Road, Truro

Volunteer AC

Secretary – G. Eley
56 Dennis Road, Liskeard
Tel: 0579 45633

Membership – Unrestricted
Year Formed – 1968
No. of Members – 32

DERBYSHIRE

Chesterfield Deep Sea AC

Secretary – Tony Hutchinson
5 Hunloke Avenue, Boythorpe, Chesterfield
Tel: 0246 77744

Membership – Unrestricted
Year Formed – 1968
No. of Members – 40

Great Longstone SAC

Secretary – P. Askew
Standhill Cottage, Gt. Longstone, Bakewell
Tel: 062987 319

Membership – Restricted
Year Formed – 1972
No. of Members – 55

DEVON

Axminster SAC

Secretary – L. Pursey
63 Lea Combe Axminster
Tel: 0297 32444

Membership – Unrestricted
Year Formed – 1964
No. of Members – 50

Babbacombe SAA

Secretary – A. Hern
29 Westhill Road, Torquay, Devon
Tel: 0803 312455

Membership – Unrestricted
Year Formed – 1966
No. of Members – 200
Facilities – N.F.S.A. South Devon. Section. C. Lyme Regis to Plymouth. (Main fishing in Babbacombe).

Bideford & District AC

Secretary – V.B. Eveleigh
21 Capern Road, Bideford, Devon EX39 3
Tel: 023 72 2470 Club: 023 72 77996

Membership – Unrestricted
Year Formed – 1964
No. of Members – 300 Male, 45 Female
60 Juniors, 100 Associates
Facilities – The only area the club controls fishing on is a club lake situated at Langtr Nr. Torrington, Devon. We have of course wonderful coastline for sea fishing. Game fishing is available. The club has a headquarters open to members of Angling Clubs producing proof of AC membership

Blackhorse SAC

Secretary – D. Dolby
7 Pugsley Road, Tiverton, Devon
Tel: 08842 57489

Membership – Unrestricted
Year Formed – 1974
No. of Members – 50 +
Facilities – Situated Equi-Distant South and North Coast, about 25 miles. Because of availability of each coast, the fishing is ver variable. Bait is easily obtainable.

Brixham SAC

Secretary – M. Coopman
Brixham SAC Clubhouse, Castor Road, Brixham
Tel: 080 45 3930

Membership – Unrestricted
Year Formed – 1913
No. of Members – 800
Facilities – Weigh-in facilities only. Open s angling. Available to all free of charge.

Budleigh Salterton SAC

Secretary – D. Baker
11 Moorfield Close, Exmouth

Challaborough SAC

Secretary – J. Cooper
119 Langley Crescent, Southway, Plymouth
Tel: 0752 779421

Membership – Unrestricted
Year Formed – 1978
No. of Members – 67
Facilities – The club is run on an April — September basis with a strong shore section We fish the Bigbury Bay area fishing generally very good, with a wide variety of fish, a Club House with weighing facilities and bars for social events.

Dawlish SAC

Secretary – L. Loram
82 Churchill Avenue, Dawlish

...eter Surfcasters Specimen ...oup

...retary – K.J. Hughes
...reen Lane, Redhills, Exeter
...0392 76810

...nbership – Restricted
...r Formed – 1979
...of Members – Maximum 20

...mouth SAA

...retary – P. Moffat
...awn Road, Exmouth, Devon
...03952 71095

...nbership – Unrestricted
...r Formed – 1919
...of Members – 120
...ilities – Sea and estuary fishing. (Waters
...under our control). Various fishing from
...nder, silver eels, plaice in estuary to
...sse, bass, conger, all to be caught from
...re especially Straight Point. Garfish
...ack, wrasse, bass, mackerel from pier
...mit needed to fish from pier available from
...ward on pier.

...racombe & District AA

...retary – J. Jobson
...Labbett's, 61, 62 High Street, Ilfracombe
...0271 62974

...mbership – Unrestricted
...of Members – 175

...e Ivybridge SAC

...retary – J. Cragg
...Voodhey Road, North Prospect, Plymouth
...: 0752 779504

...mbership – Unrestricted
...r Formed – 1968
...of Members – 70 +
...ilities – Knowledge of shore areas. S.
...von and Cornwall. Contacts with
...fessional Boat Angling Skippers/private
...ts, river/inshore/reef (Eddy Stone etc.),
...cking. Many record holders amongst
...mbership including 6 national and 2 world.
...en meetings 8 p.m. 1st. Tuesday in month.
...tors welcome. London Hotel, Ivybridge.

...ngsbridge & District SAC

...retary – D. Screech
...a Fore Street, Kingsbridge

...ndon & Manchester Assurance ...C

...retary – J.J. Mackenzie
...don & Manchester Assurance Co. Ltd.
...nslade Park, Exeter EX5 1DS
...: 0392 52155 Ext. 3601

...mbership – Restricted to employees of Co.
...relatives
...r Formed – 1977
...of Members – 21

...aritime AC

...retary – B. Harvey
...inewood Road, Milbur, Newton Abbot

Okehampton SAC

Secretary – W. McPhee
37 Hillfield, South Zeal, Okehampton
Tel: 083 784 660

Membership – Unrestricted
Year Formed – 1978
No. of Members – 20

Paignton SAA

Secretary – C. Holman
61a Higher Polsham Road, Paignton
Tel: Sec. 0803 552471, H.Q. 553118

Year Formed – 1955
No. of Members – 450

Plymouth City Transport SAC

Secretary – J. Cooke
31 St. Georges Terrace, Stoke, Plymouth
Tel: 0752 54539

Membership – Restricted
Year Formed – 1966
No. of Members – 20
Facilities – Deep Sea Fishing out of Plymouth.

Plymouth Co-op SAC

Secretary – I. Blagdon
41 Beatrice Avenue, Keyham, Plymouth
Tel: 0752 59670

Membership – Restricted
Year Formed – 1969
No. of Members – 57
Facilities – Devon and Cornish Coast.

Plymouth Federation of SA

Secretary – T. Matchett
5 St. Michaels Avenue, Keyham Barton, Plymouth
Tel: 0752 52434

Plymouth SAC

Secretary – J. Hrydziuszke
64 Dale Gardens, Mutley, Plymouth
Tel: 0752 261253

S.W.E.B. (Torbay District) AC

Secretary – T. Holtom
Electric House, Union Street, Torquay
TQ1 4BN
Tel: 0803 26200

Membership – Restricted
Year Formed – 1973
No. of Members – 70
Facilities – None, but have knowledge and information about complete area.

Salcombe & District SAA

Secretary – M. Durrans
Quay House, Union Street, Salcombe
Tel: 054 884 2513

Membership – Unrestricted
Year Formed – 1947
No. of Members – 70
Facilities – Club limits Plymouth to Brixham fishing mainly in Salcombe estuary and inshore marks. Many competitions and trophies for visitors. Week long festival in October open to all.

South Devon SAC

Secretary – F. Folland
42 Pathfields, Totnes
Tel: 0803 864702

Membership – Restricted
Year Formed – 1973
No. of Members – 65
Facilities – Fish the South Devon Coast from both boat and shore.

Starcross Fishing & Cruising Club

Secretary – I.D.: Birdseye
Regent House, Starcross, Exeter

Membership – Unrestricted
Year Formed – 1959
No. of Members – 325

Tavistock SAC

Secretary – D. Thyer
36 West Street, Tavistock, Devon
Tel: 0822 3924

Membership – Unrestricted
Year Formed – 1968
No. of Members – 50
Facilities – Sea areas of Plymouth, Rock (Cornwall), Newquay, Dartmouth. No control of fishing.

Teignmouth SAS

Secretary – R. Treacher
26 Deer Park Avenue, Teignmouth TQ14 9HD
Tel: 062 67 5650

Membership – Unrestricted
Year Formed – 1922
No. of Members – 150
Facilities – Sea angling facilities, boat and shore, including River Teign.

Torbay ASA

Secretary – P. Rowe
59 Kenwyn Road, Torquay
Tel: 0803 211375

Membership – Unrestricted
Year Formed – 1950
No. of Members – 200
Facilities – We fish the coastal area of South Devon, rich in many species throughout the year.

Torbay Hospitals' SAC

Secretary – J.H. Freeman
13 Quinta Road, Babbacombe, Torquay
Tel: 0803 35832

Membership – Restricted
Year Formed – 1977
No. of Members – 25
Facilities – Sea fishing non-controlled. Club waters i.e. within Section C of N.F.S.A. waters (South Devon) i.e. Coastal area between Rame Head, Plymouth and Beer Head, Sidmouth (Seaton). Boat fishing-sailing to any distance within the stated coastline. Rivers — Exe (to the Lock), Teign (to Bypass Flyover), Dart (to Totnes Bridge) and Tamar (to Suspension Bridge).

Torquay SAA

Secretary – C.F. Finch
14 Clifton Road, Paignton
Tel: 0803 312455

DORSET

Badger SAC

Secretary – D.J. Morgan
8 Coombe Road, Shillingstone, Blandford
Tel: 0258 860 332

Membership – Unrestricted
Year Formed – 1976
No. of Members – 30
Facilities – We have 2 sections to the club, one for shore anglers, one for boat anglers. We fish an area from West Bay to Mudeford. We hold at least 6 open competitions for beach anglers a year, and about 12 boat trips

Boscombe & Southbourne SFC

Secretary – E. White
14 Clifton Road, Southbourne, Bournemouth

Bournemouth & District SAA

Secretary – B.J. Whitfield
26 Egdon Drive, Merley, Wimborne
Tel: 0202 886461

Membership – Unrestricted
Year Formed – 1910
No. of Members – 150
Facilities – Sea fishing throughout the year from shore, pier and boat. Club waters extend from Southampton to West Bay.

Christchurch Royal British Legion AC

Secretary – H.G. Aldous
8 Whitehayes Road, Burton, Christchurch
Tel: 0202 482797

Membership – Restricted
Year Formed – 1968
No. of Members – 50
Facilities – Local tidal waters; Needles to Swanage inc. Poole and Christchurch Harbours; boat and shore with trips further afield.

Cock & Bottle S.A.G.

Secretary – H.G. Dyer
153 Whitefield, West Morden, Wareham
Tel: 092 945 440

Membership – Unrestricted
Year Formed – 1977
No. of Members – 28
Facilities – Beach competitions. Mudeford to Chesil Bank including all Poole harbour. Boat comps: Poole, Swanage, and Weymouth. Visitors welcome.

Dorchester Angling & Boating Society

Secretary – A. Beattie
5 James Road, Dorchester
Tel: 0305 66536

Membership – Restricted
Year Formed – 1977
No. of Members – 50
Facilities – Waters fished by club — sea from Poole, Chesil Beach to Brixham. Coarse and game fishing, most rivers and lakes open to public in Dorset, Hampshire, Somerset and Devon.

Greyhound Inn SAC

Secretary – R.A. Rawles
22 Orchard Street, Blandford Forum

Membership – Restricted
Year Formed – 1979
No. of Members – 12
Facilities – Our membership consists of regular customers of the Greyhound Inn only. We formed the club amongst the members who wish to go fishing and at present we have full membership.

Poole Dolphins

Secretary – J. Gilbert
56 Dale Valley Road, Oakdale, Poole

Sandford Legion SA

Secretary – G. Cox
6a Gordon Close, Upton, Poole
Tel: 0202 625067

Membership – Restricted
Year Formed – 1976
No. of Members – 30
Facilities – Poole Harbour beach fishing. Dorset Coast, Kimmeridge private boat fishing.

West Bay SAC

Secretary – P. Page
8 Pine View, Bridport
Tel: 0308 25281

Membership – Unrestricted
Year Formed – 1951
No. of Members – 400
Facilities – Monthly club beach contests range from Portland to Seaton. Boat contests are held monthly and are fished in a radius of 9 miles east and west to 3½ miles out. Some 40 trophies are fished for annually.

ESSEX

Admiral Vernon SAC

Secretary – T.E. Nicklin
63 Downing Road, Dagenham, Essex RM9 6NA
Tel: 01 595 4298

Membership – Restricted
Year Formed – 1977
No. of Members – 12

Aristocrat AAA

Secretary – W.R. MacDonell
19 Kitkatts Road, Canvey Island
Tel: 037 43 62618

Membership – Unrestricted
Year Formed – 1977
No. of Members – 30

Atlanta Boat AC

Secretary – E. Malby
4 Eton Road, Clacton-on-Sea
Tel: 0225 24770

Membership – Unrestricted
Year Formed – 1972
No. of Members – 180
Facilities – Fishing off Clacton, between Holland-on-Sea and Jaywick Sands, inside Gunfleet Sands. The club has its own winc on west pier beach.

Becmain AS

Secretary – R. Smith
46 Short Crofts Road, Dagenham
Tel: 01 592 0348

Membership – Unrestricted

Birchanger SAC

Secretary – K.C. Sturgeon
258 Birchanger Lane, Birchanger, Nr Bisho Stortford, Herts
Tel: 0279 815638

Membership – Unrestricted
Year Formed – 1972
No. of Members – 18

Brentwood SAC

Secretary – E.W. Negus
79 Cranston Park Avenue, Upminster RM14 3XD
Tel: 040 22 23389

Membership – Unrestricted
Year Formed – Approx. 1970
No. of Members – 80
Facilities – Own club boat moored at South

Canvey Island SAC

Secretary – L.J. Stoker
'The Anglers', 11a Crescent Road, Canvey Island SS8 7JY

Membership – Restricted
Year Formed – 1926
No. of Members – 100
Facilities – Thames Estuary out to line of Margate to Clacton. The club has its own 3 diesel fishing boat (CISAC 1) which is ope to guests as well as members. Fishing is ve good. Summer — flounders, bass, large ee soles, skate. Winter — large channel whitir and good size cod.

Chelmsford AA

Secretary – D.C. Willson
66 Marconi Road, Chelmsford CM1 1QD
Tel: 0245 87014

bership – Unrestricted
Formed – 1922
of Members – 2,000
ities – 3½ miles River Chelmer, Gt.
ham — tench, pike, roach, rudd, carp.
14 miles of Chelmer and Blackwater
gation Canal. Several weir pools and
waters including Kingmill, Paper Mills
Hoe Mill. Broads Green Lake (near
t Waltham), Danbury Trout Lake
bow and Brown) and Boreham Mere
eries — bream, roach, tench, carp,
h, pike.

cton SAC

etary – W. Marples
Old Road, Clacton-on-Sea
0255 28652

bership – Unrestricted
Formed – 1902
of Members – Approx. 250
ities – Fishing on 9 miles of local
hes. Also 2 compounds housing 100
s.

ringham SAC

etary – G.W. Roberts
tt Golf Club, Orsett
0375 891302

bership – Restricted
Formed – 1960
of Members – 35

ggers Deep Sea AC

etary – N.C. Sparrow
oley Road, Stanford-Le-Hope
037 56 43586

bership – Two classes of membership —
and associate. Full membership is
icted to 32 members but associate
bership is always available.
Formed – 1975
ities – Headquarters are based at
enham Football Club. The club runs four
fishing trips each month to Bradwell,
, Herne Bay and Southend. Weekend sea
ing trips run annually to different parts of
country.

adnought DSAS

etary – W.H. Flack
aternoster Hill, Waltham Abbey
0992 711758

bership – Unrestricted
Formed – 1911
of Members – 80
ities – Sea club. No waters.

n Park Hornchurch & trict AS

etary – P.W. Darling
osslyn Avenue, Harold Wood, Romford
04023 43246

bership – Restricted
Formed – 1936
of Members – 300
ities – 4 lakes in locality, 3 stretches on
olk Stour, 1 stretch River Roding.

Green Line Social Club (Angling Section)

Secretary – R.P. Rate
3 First Avenue, Grays RM16 1JR
Tel: 04026 7307

Membership – Unrestricted
Year Formed – 1976
No. of Members – 34
Facilities – Sea fishing only.

Harlow Owls SAC

Secretary – B. Hickey
145 Westfield, Harlow
Tel: 0279 31366

Membership – Unrestricted
Year Formed – 1978
No. of Members – 24

Harrow SAC

Secretary – R.J. Biscoe
32 Sheepcotes Road, Chadwell Heath
Tel: 01 599 4431

Membership – Restricted
Year Formed – 1970
No. of Members – 26
Facilities – Essex and Kent coasts.

Havering Sea Anglers

Secretary – P. Berry
417 St Marys Lane, Upminster
Tel: 040 22 20525

Membership – Unrestricted
Year Formed – 1976
No. of Members – 30
Facilities – Mainly boat fishing in the year
1981. 12 Sunday boat trips and 4 Saturday
wrecking trips.

Jolly Fisherman SAC

Secretary – J. Ray
c/o Jolly Fisherman PH, Southend Pier,
Eastern Esplanade

Kelvedon & District AA

Secretary – T. Ladkin
68 Western Road, Silver End, Witham
Tel: 0376 83504

Membership – Unrestricted
Year Formed – 1948
No. of Members – 1200
Facilities – Roach, dace, chub, perch in 7½
miles of River Blackwater between Stisted and
Wickham Bishops. Plus stretch of River Stour
and 11 stillwaters in Silver End Birch, Tiptree
areas. Sea fishing trips organised.

Lafarge SAC

Secretary – Mr. L. Emms
9 Limerick Gardens, Upminster
Tel: 040 22 50930

Membership – Unrestricted
Year Formed – 1977   No. of Members – 19

Leigh & Westcliff AAS

Secretary – E. Illsley
3 Homestead Road, Hadleigh, Benfleet
Tel: 0702 555219

Membership – Unrestricted
Year Formed – 1916
No. of Members – 82
Facilities – Open sea, pier and beach.

Milton Hamlet AAS

Secretary – Mrs S. Carter
141 Tankerville Drive, Leigh-on-Sea
Tel: 0702 712414

Membership – Unrestricted
Year Formed – 1921
No. of Members – 60

Rayleigh Anglo'd SAC

Secretary – D. Withers
59 London Road, Rayleigh
Tel: 0268 770528

Membership – Restricted
Year Formed – 1977
No. of Members – 60 + Juniors
Facilities – Our club mainly fish the Essex and
Kent coastlines. Our main interest is offshore
boat angling but we do hold regular beach
and pier competitions.

Rayleigh SAC

Secretary – Mrs L. Godwin
6 Cheddar Avenue, Westcliff-on-Sea SS0 0HJ
Tel: 0702 529297

Membership – Restricted
Year Formed – 1975
No. of Members – 80 +
Facilities – We do not control fishing, as we
are a sea angling club. We generally fish the
Thames Estuary and outer river marks in
summer.

Shark '25' Deep Sea F.C.

Secretary – M. Walker
10 Lodge Hall, Harlow CM18 7SU
Tel: 0279 33721

Membership – Restricted
Year Formed – 1965
No. of Members – 25
Facilities – No fishing areas. We use charter
deep sea boats on east and south coast.

Shell Club AS

Secretary – J.W. Deaves
28 Rainbow Lane, Stanford Le Hope
SS17 0AS
Tel: 037 56 2107

Membership – Restricted
Year Formed – 1930
No. of Members – 300
Facilities – We have a 30 acre lake called 'The
Warren', Wharf Road, Stanford-Le-Hope and
the club is a works club. We have a varied
coarse fishery (carp, tench, bream, roach,
perch). Only a small amount of bank is
measured for members, the remainder is open
to public on day ticket basis.

Shoeburyness & Pierhead AAS

Secretary – E.S. Gonning
124 Shoebury Road, Thorpe Bay
Tel: 0702 588356

Membership – Restricted
Year Formed – 1946
No. of Members – 100
Facilities – Sea fishing from chartered boats and from pier and foreshore in the borough, also fishing within an area controlled by the M.O.D. Because of this the membership is vetted and restricted.

Shore House Angling Group

Secretary – G. Govier
173 Church Road, Shoeburyness
Tel: 03708 3496

Membership – Restricted to local Residents
Year Formed – 1978
No. of Members – 23

Southchurch SAC

Secretary – R. Hart
33 Thurston Avenue, Thorpe Bay

Southend AAS

Secretary – R. Threadgold
67 North Crescent, Southend-on-Sea
Tel: 0702 351545

Membership – Unrestricted
Year Formed – 1900
No. of Members – 100
Facilities – Boat fishing Thames Estuary (club and open competitions), pier fishing Southend Pier (club and open competitions), beach fishing mainly Southend areas, club meetings first Friday each month Naval and Military club, Royal Terrace, Southend.

Southend Pier Junior AA

Secretary – B. Macgregor
133 St James Avenue, Thorpe Bay SS1 3LW

Membership – Unrestricted – Age limit 17
Year Formed – 1972
No. of Members – 60
Facilities – Southend Pier and local beaches.

Thorpe Bay AA

Secretary – R.C. Porter
120b Eastern Esplanade Tel: 0702 66116

Membership – Unrestricted
Year Formed – 1970
No. of Members – 50

Walton-on-Naze SAC

Secretary – T. Chalk
10 Greengates, Webley Road, Little Clacton
Tel: 0255 860751

Membership – Unrestricted
Year Formed – 1902
No. of Members – 300
Facilities – Walton Pier, Walton Beaches and coastal waters within area.

West Essex SAC

Secretary – M.T.J. Tebbutt
22 Regent Road, Epping CM16 5DL

Membership – Restricted – Reviewed annually
Year Formed – 1978
No. of Members – 36
Facilities – Fishing south and east coasts — boat fishing mainly N.F.S.A. affiliated.

GLOUCESTERSHIRE

Cotswold & District AC

Secretary – Gary Sutton
368 Swindon Road, Cheltenham
Tel: 0252 29097

Membership – Unrestricted
No. of Members – 25

Eastington Deep Sea AC

Secretary – D. Cordrey
Priding Villa, Priding, Saul, Gloucester
Tel: 0452 740711

Membership – Unrestricted
No. of Members – Approximately 30
Facilities – Meetings for booking trips on first Monday of each month at H.Q. The Victoria Inn, Eastington, Nr. Stonehouse, Gloucester.

GREATER LONDON

Barking Sea AA

Secretary – E.J. Mallows
14 Merritt Point, Maplin Road, Canning Town, London E16 3QG
Tel: 01 474 5087

Membership – Restricted
Year Formed – 1977
No. of Members – 16

Bracklesham Caravan & Boat Club

Secretary – Ernest Munns
35 Emanuel Avenue, Acton, London W3
Tel: 01 992 9391

Year Formed – 1976 Affiliated to N.F.S.A.
No. of Members – 30-40
Facilities – Fish direct off Bracklesham Bay (Sussex) and Littlehampton. All sea fishing in 14 ft. to 16 ft. dingys. All our members are strictly caravan owners of above private club.

The Crepitus SAC

Secretary – G.J. Cant
6 Devonshire Gardens, Chiswick, London W4
Tel: 01 994 4077

Membership – Unrestricted
Year Formed – 1955
No. of Members – 31
Facilities – Boat fishing trips each month (Sundays) to agreed venues including Deal, Brighton, Newhaven and Littlehampton.

Crystal Palace AA

Secretary – W.E.S. Beattie
175 Hermitage Road, Upper Norwood, London SE19 3QJ
Tel: 01 653 0232

Membership – Restricted
Year Formed – 1924
No. of Members – 200 Seniors 25 Juniors
Facilities – Intermediate Lake — Crystal Palace Park. (Still water fishery. All major coarse fish).

Gilfin Deep Sea AC

Secretary – T, Lipscombe
83 Beech Road, Feltham, Middlesex TW14 8AJ
Tel: 01 890 8972

Membership – Restricted
Year Formed – 1970
No. of Members – 20
Facilities – All our fishing is deep sea, consisting of rough ground and wreck fish on Decca boats up to forty miles out to sea Weather permitting. Sea ports fished — Newhaven, Brighton, Littlehampton and Plymouth. We also take guests.

Hounslow Sea AC

Secretary – D. Reynolds
26 Victoria Gardens, Heston, Hounslow, Middlesex
Tel: 01 570 8138

Membership – Unrestricted
Year Formed – 1978
No. of Members – 30
Facilities – We fish all venues. E.g. Folkestone, Deal, Brighton, Newhaven, Plymouth, Rye and Havant. We are a mid-week club.

L.T. Elephant & Castle AS

Secretary – P. Scott
Flat 3, 9 Penford Street, Brixton, London SE5 9JA
Tel: 01 274 0358

Membership – Unrestricted
Year Formed – 1977

New Studio Club AS

Secretary – D.M. Edwards
51 Poplar House, Wickham Road, Brockley London SE4 1NE
Tel: 01 691 4011

Membership – Restricted
Year Formed – 1939
No. of Members – 260

Otis SAC

Secretary – K.J. Stenson
46 Stockwell Park Crescent, London SW9
Tel: 01 274 6041

Membership – Restricted
Year Formed – 1975
No. of Members – 50

Office — London
communications Region
ateur Sports Association —
p Sea Angling

tary – H. Nuelle
rntwood Lane, Tooting,
on SW17 0AJ
1 946 2758

ership – Restricted
Formed – 1970
f Members – 600
ties – All deep sea, east and south coast.

ensbourne & District SAC

tary – D.A. Lowe
dpoll Way, Erith DA18 4BX
1 310 8976

ties – Most of clubs fishing done on the
-East coast, Kent and Sussex.

EATER MANCHESTER

Cross Sports & Social SAC

tary – J. Hollingworth
nold Avenue, Gee Cross, Hyde, Tameside

ership – Restricted
f Members – 12

wood AS

tary – B.J. Hargreaves
ctor Street, Heywood, Lancs.
706 622445

ership – Unrestricted
f Members – 200

chester Saltwater Specimen
up

tary – Roy Brierley
nters Avenue, Atherton, Manchester
9EF
0942 874583

ership – Restricted
Formed – 1977
f Members – 12 + Reserves
ties – Two national anglers council grade
angling instructors are full time
ers.

nrakers SAC

tary – M.J. Lawler
irway, Castleton, Rochdale, Lancs

ership – Unrestricted
Formed – 1976
f Members – 46
ties – Deep sea wreck fishing.

enix Sea Angling

tary – J.C. Beaumont
vern Drive, Swinton, Lancs.
37 3295

ership – Restricted
Formed – 1976
f Members – 24

Urmston SAA

Secretary – R. Brierley
1 Chanters Avenue, Atherton, Manchester
M29 9EF
Tel: 0942 874583

Membership – Unrestricted
Year Formed – 1976
No. of Members – 100 +
Facilities – 5 fully qualified N A C instructors
— free lead moulding equipment —
comprehensive trophies for competitions —
discount on fishing tackle from local dealers.

Ye Olde Nelson SAC

Secretary – P.A. Owens
51 George Henry Street, Salford,
Lancs M5 2QT.
Tel: 061 737 1110

Membership – Unrestricted
Year Formed – 1976
No. of Members – 30

HAMPSHIRE & ISLE OF WIGHT

Armfield & Ringwood SAC

Secretary – D. Smith
85 Ash Grove, Ringwood BH24 1XT
Tel: 042 54 78694

Membership – Unrestricted
Year Formed – 1967
No. of Members – 60
Facilities – One of three founder member
clubs of Wessex Angling Consortium. Area
fished from Milford Shingle bank to Poole
Harbour. Strong beach and boat sections with
recently formed dinghy section.

Bembridge AC

Secretary – R. Green
22 Downsview Road, St Helens, Ryde
Tel: 098 387 2214

Membership – Unrestricted
Year Formed – 1960
No. of Members – 110
Facilities – Sea Angling by boat.

Bishops Waltham AC

Secretary – M. Creese
8 St. Andrews Green, Meonstoke
Tel: 048 97 664

Membership – Unrestricted
Year Formed – 1969
No. of Members – 83

Civil Service Sea AC (Southern)

Secretary – T.J. Skittrell
2a Cracknore Road, Freemantle,
Southampton
Tel: 0703 28677/781721

Membership – Restricted to members of
C.S.S.C.
Year Formed – 1980
No. of Members – 20
Facilities – Boat angling Needles area and
Sussex coast, fishing out of Littlehampton.
Beach fishing Hampshire coast.

East Cowes AC

Secretary – R. Gustar
36 Ash Road, Newport, Isle of Wight
Tel: 0983 524757

Membership – Unrestricted

Eastleigh Rodbenders SAC

Secretary – A.M. McCall
63a Portswood Road, Portswood,
Southampton SO2 1FT
Tel: 0703 550681

Membership – Unrestricted
Year Formed – 1975
No. of Members – 73
Facilities – Beach fishing throughout the coast
of Hampshire, Sussex and East Dorset
including Solent waters. Deep sea fishing
from Littlehampton, Lymington, Poole and
Southampton. Dinghy fishing on Hamble,
Itchen and Solent waters. Special trips to
Plymouth, Shorehay, Dungeness, and
Southampton Docks.

Elmore AC

Secretary – D.R. Dixon
1 Andrews Close, Bishops Waltham,
Southampton
Tel: 048 93 4994

Membership – Unrestricted
Year Formed – 1957
No. of Members – 310
Facilities – Boat fishing in eastern Solent,
mainly members boats but club owns 3 for
hire to members. Beach fishing from
Langstone Harbour to Hurst point including
Portsmouth Harbour. Club built own
headquarters on sea front in 1979 and has
boat compound for 150 boats.

Emsworth SAC

Secretary – M.E. Hampton
39 Keats Close, Cowplain
Tel: 070 14 4027

Membership – Unrestricted
Year Formed – Approx. 1958
No. of Members – Approx. 100

Esso Fawley SAC

Secretary – E. Entwistle
Beaulah, Nash Road, Dibden Purlieu,
Southampton
Tel: 0703 845272

Membership – Restricted
Year Formed – 1955
No. of Members – 132

Factory Sports & Social Club

Secretary – C.L. Anders
95 Stansted Road, Southsea
Tel: 0705 815978

Membership – Restricted
No. of Members – 30

Folland Sports & Social Club Angling Section

Secretary – W.A. Rawles
63 Firgrove Road, Freemantle, Southampton
Tel: 0703 783010

Membership – Restricted
Year Formed – 1945
No. of Members – 100

'Ford Force & Anglers'

Secretary – J. Coulson
30 Northolt Gardens, Southampton

Membership – Unrestricted
Year Formed – 1979
No. of Members – 30

Fountain Lake AC

Secretary – T.D. Gregg
146 Whale Island Way, Portsmouth PO2 8EW
Tel: 0705 691565

Membership – Restricted
Year Formed – 1966
No. of Members – 120
Facilities – Beach fishing available Hayling
Beach, Haslar Wall, pier and South Parade
pier. F.L.A.C. mainly boat fishermen fishing
in Solent area, south of Isle of Wight.

Gipsy Queen Sea AC

Secretary – E. Maggs
161 Whitworth Road, Gosport

Membership – Restricted
Year Formed – 1977
No. of Members – 36
Facilities – Solent and Needles area of the
channel.

Golden Hind SAC

Secretary – J. Pearse
43 Underwood Road, Bishopstoke
Tel: 0703 610181

Membership – Unrestricted
Year Formed – 1979
No. of Members – 14

Gravatom AC

Secretary – R.P. Eccleston
108 Carisbrooke Road, Rowner, Gosport
PO13 0NZ
Tel: 0329 288260

Membership – Unrestricted
Year Formed – 1976
No. of Members – 16

Greyfriar SAC

Secretary – M. Metherell
4 Windsor Close, Alton
Tel: 0420 84818

Membership – Unrestricted
Year Formed – 1969
No. of Members – 30
Facilities – Boat fishing from south coast ports,
Beach fishing from Eastbourne to Chesil.

Hamble Social SAC

Secretary – A. Spridgeon
26 Beech Gardens, Hamble, Soton
Tel: 042 122 2328

Membership – Restricted
Year Formed – 1978
No. of Members – 30
Facilities – We concentrate entirely on deep
sea fishing mainly around the Needles area.

Havant Avengers SAC

Secretary – I. Bayliss
12 Knox Road, Stamshaw, Portsmouth
Tel: 0705 65650

Membership – Unrestricted
Year Formed – 1975 (Affiliated to N.F.S.A.
1976)
No. of Members – 42
Facilities – We do not control any waters as a
sea club but we run a very competitive match
programme both shore (beach/pier) and deep
sea boat via charter craft, along a wide length
of coast line, throughout the year. Monthly
club meetings are held for update of latest
news etc. Visitors from other areas and new
members always welcome.

H.C.B. AC

Secretary – D.A. Andrews
11 Vincent Avenue, Shirley, Soton

Membership – Restricted
Year Formed – 1966
No. of Members – 40

H.M.S. Dolphin SAC

Secretary – A.G. Wood
16 Shenley Close, Catisfield, Fareham
Tel: 032 94 43070

Membership – Restricted
Year Formed – 1966
No. of Members – 100
Facilities – Two boats which can accommodate
10 rods — fishing in Solent and out to Nab
tower. Fishing from the beach within H.M.S.
Dolphin which is at the entrance to
Portsmouth Harbour.

Island Plastics AC

Secretary – B.E. Ward
Hunters Lodge, Fernhill, Wootton
Tel: 0983 883305

Membership – Restricted
Year Formed – 1960
No. of Members – Approx. 40

Isle of Wight AS

Secretary – Mrs. S.J. Jackson
70 Hunnyhill, Newport PO30 5HN
Tel: 0983 524419

Membership – Unrestricted
Year Formed – 1930
No. of Members – 68
Facilities – The Society does not control
fishing but is concerned with sea fishing (a
separately formed branch is called the I. W.
Freshwater Angling Society) around the
Island, which incorporates all kinds of shore,
estuary, river and deep sea angling.

I. O. W. Youth
& Community FC

Secretary – C.G. Williams
Cowes Youth Centre
Tel: 0983 292829

Membership – Restricted
Year Formed – 1976
No. of Members – 40
Facilities – Isle of Wight sea and shore.

Kingsbury SAC

Secretary – E. Barnes
2 Monroe Close, Gosport
Tel: 070 17 84706

Membership – Restricted
Year Formed – 1978
No. of Members – 25

Lymington & District SFC

Secretary – B. Greenwood
2 Boldre Lane, Lymington
Tel: 0590 74390

Membership – Unrestricted
Year Formed – 1936
No. of Members – 200-250
Facilities – Our club waters are from Hill
Head, Gosport, Hants to Ringstead Bay,
Dorset. All docks and harbours between the
two points inclusive. Boat angling up to
approximately 15 miles from all shores.

Maypole SAC

Secretary – J.W. Lawson
106 Lower Northam Road, 'Argonaut' Hed
End
Tel: 048 92 2229

Membership – Restricted
Year Formed – 1979
No. of Members – 38
Facilities – Poole, Plymouth, Solent at
Littlehampton. The Maypole club comes
under Wessex area regarding specimen fi

Moneyfield Angling Section

Secretary – P.R. Merritt
183 Copnor Road, Portsmouth
Tel: 0705 64667

Membership – Unrestricted
Year Formed – 1969
No. of Members – 70

Plessey Radar Angling Society

Secretary – F.D. Deakin
19 Horseshoe Close, Northwood,
Cowes PO31 8PZ
Tel: 294141 Ext. 135 (Day) 296357 (Eve)

Membership – Unrestricted, Except applic
must become associate member of Sports
Social Club if outside company.
Year Formed – 1964
No. of Members – 60
Facilities – Charter boat trips. Own club b
(16ft.) for Solent and river fishing. Shore
fishing all round island including tidal riv
and estuarys. No club on island has contro
waters.

Plessey (Havant) S & S C
Angling Section

Secretary – K.L. Lodge
'Kencodia' 5 Brenchley Close, Portchester
Tel: 0329 237080

Membership – Restricted
Year Formed – 1965
No. of Members – 68
Facilities – We control no waters but we b
fish and boat fish, at least once a month. C
also has a junior section.

...rtchester Sporting AC

...retary – R.J. Toomer
...Cooper Grove, Portchester
...0705 381690

...mbership – Restricted
...r Formed – 1960
...of Members – 70
...lities – Mainly area surrounding
...smouth but competitions are held at
...estone (Kent) and other areas further
...d each year.

...rtsmouth Elim Church Anglers

...retary – J.W. Lummis
...Maylands Road, Bedhampton, Havant
...0705 486549

...mbership – Restricted
...r Formed – 1979
...of Members – 20
...lities – South coast sea fishing from shore
... boat.

...ders AC

...etary – P. Macaire
...Victoria Road, W. Cowes
...0983 296697

...bership – Restricted
... Formed – 1971
...of Members – 120
...lities – All fishing is on beach, river or
... or from boats. No control held over
...rs. All public coastline around island.

...yal Aircraft Establishment ...d-week ASC

...etary – Albert Bore
...eir Avenue, Cove, Farnborough
...4 0BH
...0252 513863

...bership – Unrestricted
... Formed – 1970
...of Members – 62
...lities – Venues cover Ramsgate to the Isle
...ight.

...ndown & Lake Angling Society

...etary – F. Clarke
...Culver Way, Yaverland, Sandown
...0983 404142

...bership – Unrestricted
... Formed – 1937
...of Members – 240
...lities – Pier beach and boat. Open
...petitions controlled from club hut on pier.
...S.A. Rules.

...a Angling For all Disabled

...etary – D. Baldwin
...eats Road, Bitterne, Southampton
...0703 444354

...bership – Unrestricted
... bodied accepted as helpers can also fish
... club.
... Formed – 1977
...of Members – 35
...lities – Solent River (sea), Portsmouth area
...ding Isle of Wight (Nab Tower), Needles
... (all sea fishing) boat and shore.

The Shanklin AS

Secretary – P.A. Monk
74 Park Road, Ryde
Tel: 0983 64485

Membership – Unrestricted
Year Formed – 1932
No. of Members – Approx. 45
Facilities – Open sea along all the Shankline
sea front and fishing from the pier when open
in summer season. We also hold competitions
at any point on the Isle of Wight beaches and
piers.

Solent Rod Benders SAC

Secretary – J.J. Kavanagh
12 Mansel Road East, Millbrook. Southampton
SO1 9DN
Tel: 0703 785108

Membership – Unrestricted
Year Formed – 1980
No. of Members – 14
Facilities – We fish as far as Brighton and
Weymouth all beaches between these two
places.

Southampton SAC

Secretary – R. Trent
49 Lytham Road, Bitterne Park, Southampton
Tel: 0703 551492

Membership – Unrestricted
Year Formed – 1934
No. of Members – 200 +
Facilities – The club has competitions every
other Sunday either on the shore, pier, boats
or docks. The club has 4 boats of its own for
any members use. A strong junior
membership of over 25%. Fee £2.50 per
annum — Junior £1.25.

Southern Gas (Soton) SAC

Secretary – P.J. Noyce
34 Laundry Road, Southampton
Tel: 0703 779989

Membership – Unrestricted
Year Formed – 1979
No. of Members – 12

Southern Vectis SAC

Secretary – R.J. Russell
8 Park View, Wootton
Tel: 0983 882133

Membership – Restricted
Year Formed – 1976
No. of Members – 32

Southsea SAC

Tel: 0702 25508

Stamshaw Lake AC

Secretary –
Ranelagh Road, Stamshaw, Portsmouth
Tel: 070 14 58440

Membership – Restricted
No. of Members – 187
Facilities – We do not control any waters. We
fish Portsmouth harbour and surrounding area
from our own boats.

Swan Sea AC (Basingstoke)

Secretary – H.T. Brooks
47 West End, Sherbourne St John,
Basingstoke
Tel: 0256 850558

Membership – Restricted
Year Formed – 1972
No. of Members – 30
Facilities – Deep sea angling mostly south
coast (Isle of Wight) some beach fishing
outings. (Club is affiliated to N.F.S.A.).

Temperature AC

Secretary – R.G. Scovell
20 Cross Street, Sandown
Tel: 0983 405340

Membership – Restricted
Year Formed – 1976
No. of Members – 50
Facilities – Fish all round the island both
shore and boat. In winter, fish the River
Medina and Newtown & Bembridge harbour
for flounders.

Vectis Boating and FC

Secretary – M.T. Sawyer
27 Salters Road, Ryde

Membership – Unrestricted
Year Formed – late 1800's
No. of Members – 50 full members – 100
associates/juniors etc.
Facilities – Solent: Portsmouth Harbour,
Norris Castle, Southsea — Bembridge. The
area enclosed by these land marks is not
controlled by the club but is used for
competitions and specimen fish trophy
awards.

Vectis Stone AC

Secretary – R.W. Cooke
90 St Thomas Square, Newport
Tel: 0983 528958

Membership – Unrestricted
Year Formed – 1971
No. of Members – 180
Facilities – No control of any areas. We fish
all shores of the Island and sometimes
Hampshire. Boat fishing in Needles, Nab
Tower and St. Catherine's areas.

Waterside AC

Secretary – B. Harman
40 Cowper Road, Southampton
Tel: 0703 463206

Membership – Restricted
No. of Members – 40
Facilities – Shores around Solent. Hired boat
from Lymington out to the Needles.

Western Wight AC

Secretary – R.A. Pearson
The Quorn, Moortown Lane, Brighstone
Tel: 0983 740078

Membership – Unrestricted
Year Formed – 1967/8
No. of Members – 411

Sea Clubs: Hereford – Kent

HEREFORD & WORCESTERSHIRE

Evesham Sea AC

Secretary – L. Bourne
99 Woodlands, Evesham
Tel: 0386 47928

Membership – Unrestricted
Year Formed – 1978
No. of Members – 18

HERTFORDSHIRE

Inland Sea Anglers

Secretary – J. Hardwick
69 Dunlin Road, Hemel Hempstead
Tel: 0442 47117

Membership – Restricted to over 14 years old
Year Formed – 1967
No. of Members – 40
Facilities – We fish the English Channel from Newhaven, Littlehampton, the East Coast from Bradwell and Brightlingsea in Essex. Beach fishing for members all round Kent and Suffolk, Essex coast.

HUMBERSIDE NORTH

Bridlington Shore Anglers

Secretary – S.C. Morland
57 Lambert Road, Bridlington
Tel: 0262 74603

Membership – Unrestricted. Junior membership available
No. of Members – 120
Facilities – Shore Angling Club only, organise three club matches per week between October and March inclusive and a one day open festival.

Hull Rock AC

Secretary – K. Massey
10 Lowther Street, Hull

Membership – Unrestricted
Year Formed – 1945
No. of Members – 30-40

Willows Deep Sea Angling

Secretary – W. Fullard
94 Digby Garth, Noddle Hill Way, Bransholme, Hull HU7 4NW

Membership – Restricted
Year Formed – 1955
No. of Members – 21
Facilities – Filey to Hornsea boat and beach fishing, our boat is kept in Bridlington Harbour.

HUMBERSIDE SOUTH

Cromwell SAC

Secretary – D. Fukes
39 Daubney Street, Cleethorpes

East Halton SAC

Secretary – W. Kay
'Beckside', Thornton Abbey Road, Ulceby, Nr. Brigg

Grimsby & Cleethorpes Humber SAC

Secretary – D.T. Maultby
196 Chichester Road, Cleethorpes

Membership – Restricted
Year Formed – 1955
No. of Members – 125

KENT

Blue Circle (Sittingbourne) AC

Secretary – P.L. Savison
6 Grove Park Avenue, Borden, Sittingbourne
Tel: 0795 21294

Membership – Unrestricted
Year Formed – 1965
No. of Members – 25
Facilities – Kent coast, Sheerness to Dungeness.

Broadstairs and St. Peters Sea AA

Secretary – L. Withey
5 King Edward Avenue, Broadstairs
Tel: 0843 62670

Membership – Unrestricted
Year Formed – 1922
No. of Members – 258
Facilities – Club waters are North Foreland area, good fishing all the year round. All species except shark. Local council charge launching fee, and fishermen with trailer boats advised to launch from Palm Bay which at the moment is free. Club affiliated to N.F.S.A. 3 day festival Sat, Sun, Mon, 10th, 11th, 12th October, 1981.

Broadstairs Viking Shore AS

Secretary – R. Jones
25 Dumpton Park Drive, Ramsgate

Membership – Unrestricted
Year Formed – 1964
No. of Members – 53
Facilities – This is a rock ranging club using waters in the North Foreland area, viz, Botany Bay, Joss Bay, Stone Gap, Broadstairs Jetty, Dumpton Gap and the Colburn. Members fish from rocks or bays at low water. Fish: Cod, Bass, Eels. Club year starts December 1st each year. All welcome. N.F.S.A. affiliated. Has two N.A.C. Sea Angling instructors (qualified) in club.

Dartford Ramblers Sea Anglers Assoc.

Secretary – J.F. McKenzie
10 Taunton Close, Barnehurst DA7 6NN
Tel: 01 829 3056

Membership – Restricted – male only
Year Formed – 1947
No. of Members – 80

Deal Angling Club 1919

Secretary – C.R. Smith
35 The Strand, Walmer, Deal
Tel: 03045 63441

Membership – Unrestricted
Year Formed – 1919
No. of Members – 450 (350 senior 100 junior
Facilities — We have a large club H.Q. with weighing in area and licenced bar etc. at 13 The Marina, Deal, Kent.

Deal & Walmer AA

Secretary – Deal & Walmer AA
Headquarters Deal Pier (South Side), Deal

Membership – Unrestricted
Year Formed – 1904
No. of Members – 300
Facilities – Four miles of beach fishing, also pier and boats. Competitions monthly. Membership fee £4.00 for anglers. A club cabin at the end of the pier where anglers may make hot drinks etc., also lockers. For further details write to, The Secretary at H.Q

Dover Sea AA

Secretary – J.P. Shearn
14 Priory Road, Dover
Tel: 0304 204722/203520/821856

Membership – Unrestricted but must be approved by a member of the committee.
Year Formed – 1903
No. of Members – 530
Facilities – Southern Breakwater (when wind are less than force 6), entrance via. Prince Wales Pier — Toll 20p + boat fee of 60p return. Admiralty Pier free to all anglers. Beaches and rocks to East and West of Dov

Duke of Wellington SAC

Secretary – M.F. Carter
4 Maine Close, Dover
Tel: 0304 211197

Membership – Unrestricted
Year Formed – 1965
No. of Members – 35
Facilities – Fishing from Dover breakwater.

Dymchurch & District AC

Secretary – R.B. Knowles
14 York Road, Kennington, Ashford
Tel: 0233 25223

Membership – Unrestricted
Year Formed – 1959
No. of Members – 80 +
Facilities – Sea fishing both boat and beach between Folkestone and Rye Bay.

Fairness Sea AC

Secretary – J.S. Jarvis
19 Stirling Way, Ramsgate
Tel: 0843 586808

Membership – Unrestricted
Year Formed – 1976
No. of Members – 19

Folkestone Yacht & Motor Boat Club

Secretary – N. Clover
39 Queen Street, Folkestone

embership – Unrestricted
ar Formed – 1973
. of Members – 376
cilities – Fishing in Dover Straits

ravesend & District SAC

cretary – B. East
St Dunstan's Drive, Gravesend
: 0474 52114

mbership – Restricted
ar Formed – 1963
. of Members – 60
cilities – Charter boat angling —
lkestone, Herne Bay, Newhaven, Plymouth
ach competitions each month.

erne Bay AA

cretary – H.G. Chalk
Central Parade, Herne Bay
: 02273 62127

embership – Unrestricted
ar Formed – 1903
. of Members – 320
cilities – Boat fishing for tope, bass, cod,
ts, eels, whiting etc. Beach fishing for cod,
ls, flats etc.

orton Kirby Sea Anglers

cretary – D.R. Luxford
Harold Road, Hawley, Nr. Dartford
l: 0322 29684

embership – Restricted
ar Formed – 1977
. of Members – 52

othfield & District AC

cretary – J. Martin
yndon Way, Lyminge, Folkestone
l: 0303 862764

embership – Unrestricted
ar Formed – 1973
. of Members – 100 approx.
cilities – Fresh water, ¾ mile dyke on
mney Marsh at Old Romney and limited
cess to various private lakes. Sea fishing,
ore club competitions at Dungeness and
ver breakwater. Boat competitions on
artered boat off Dungeness.

le of Sheppey AA

cretary – S. Harrison
0 St Georges Avenue, Sheerness
l: 07956 66299

embership – Unrestricted
ar Formed – 1950
. of Members – 90
cilities – Beach fishing at Thames, Medway
d Swale. Sea fishing from boat on Thames
tuary, Medway and Swale. Boat compound
· club members with boats under 14ft. 16ft.
·kney Longliner for club members.

ingsdown AC

cretary – T.D. Cousins
Balmoral Road, Kingsdown, Nr Deal
l: 03045 3832

Membership – Restricted
Year Formed – 1948
No. of Members – 175
Facilities – Sea angling boat club.
Competitions for members only, two day
festival mid October. 17 boat competitions.
Club hut on beach.

Lenham W.M.C. SAC

Secretary – A.B.G. Boorman
1 Douglas Road, Lenham, Nr Maidstone
Tel: 0622 858627

Membership – Restricted
Year Formed – 1980
No. of Members – 30

Maidstone & District Motor Services Sports & Social Club

Secretary – L. Day
16 Sheppey Road, Maidstone
Tel: 0622 45847

Membership – Restricted
Year Formed – 1978
No. of Members – 90
Facilities – Sea angling on Kent coast and
waters.

Manufacturers Hanover Sea AC

Secretary – R. McInnes
28 Stuart Close, Hextable, Swanley
Tel: 0322 62940

Membership – Restricted
Year Formed – 1979
No. of Members – 20

New Beach Sea AC

Secretary – B.J. Sisley
54 Halsted Walk, Allington Farm, Maidstone
Tel: 0622 61086

Membership – Restricted
Year Formed – 1966
No. of Members – 200 + juniors
Facilities – Rye bay area. Club boats and 40
private boats. Also rescue boat maintained 24
hours with advice from Coast Guard. Club
house with bar, full time steward and coast
guard officer.

Orpington & District Sea AC

Secretary – R. Sewell
23 Sandybury, Orpington
Tel: 0689 50404

Membership – Unrestricted
Year Formed – 1974
No. of Members – 44
Facilities – Coach each month to south coast
for boat fishing.

Page Heath SAC

Secretary – R.R. Skinner
171 Homesdale Road, Bromley
Tel: 01 464 1479

Membership – Unrestricted
Year Formed – 1975
No. of Members – 36

Parkwood SAC

Secretary – P. Flynn
32 Cambridge Road, Wigmore, Gillingham
Tel: 0634 31731

Membership – Restricted
Year Formed – 1978
No. of Members – 50

Penguin AC

Secretary – D. Palmer
3 White Wood Road, Eastry, Sandwich
Tel: 0304 611829

Membership – Unrestricted
No. of Members – 40

Ravensbourne & District SAC

Secretary – D.A. Lowe
67 Redpoll Way, Erith DA18 4BX
Tel: 01 310 8976

Membership – Unrestricted
Year Formed – 1976
No. of Members – 60
Facilities – Approximately two boat trips and
two beach competitions per month. Yearly
fishing trip to Ireland.

Ramsgate Beachcasters SAS

Secretary – R. Dutfield
27 St Davids Road, Ramsgate
Tel: 0843 57673

Membership – Unrestricted
Year Formed – 1976
No. of Members – 50
Facilities – Beach fishing

Royal Ramsgate Invicta AA

President – D. Campbell
6 Goodwin Road, Ramsgate

Sandgate AS

Secretary – P. Chidwick
96 Dallas Brett Crescent, Folkestone

Membership – Unrestricted
Year Formed – 1904
No. of Members – 150
Facilities – Sandgate and Hythe beaches all
types of flat fish, bass cod, whiting and pout
Boat trips for all types of fish.

Seabook SAS

Secretary – B.J. Uden
57 Shepherds Walk, Hythe
Tel: 0303 65221

Southern Circuit SAS

Secretary – A.R. Sinden
53 Taylor Street, Southborough, Tunbridge
Wells

Membership – Unrestricted
Year Formed – 1944
No. of Members – 40
Facilities – Sea anglers organising fishing
competitions around Kent coast between
Gravesend and Eastbourne.

Southern Counties SAA

Secretary – G.E. Hills
4 St. Aidans Way, Gravesend
Tel: 0474 22994

Membership – Unrestricted
Year Formed – 1979
No. of Members – 100
Facilities – Mark and wreck fishing from
Ramsgate, Folkestone, Rye and Falmouth
Beach fishing around Kent coast. New
members always welcome.

Tenterden & District Angling & Preservation Assoc.

Secretary – D.M. Burt
26 Aragon Close, Ashford TN23 2DH
Tel: 0233 36657

Membership – Restricted
Year Formed – 1920
Facilities – Fishing on River Rother, adjoining
dykes and streams, and local ponds.

Whitstable & District AS

Secretary – D. Woolnough
82 Regent Street, Whitstable
Tel: 0227 264488

Membership – Unrestricted
Year Formed – 1928
No. of Members – 100
Facilities – Sea fishing only

White Cliffs Sea AC

Secretary – G.L.A. Smith
73 Markland Road, Dover
Tel: 0304 205249

Membership – Unrestricted
Year Formed – 1967
Facilities – Monthly club competitions on
Southern breakwater, beach and all night
competitions throughout the year.

Woodcroft SAC

Secretary – D.D.S. Reeve
43 First Avenue, Bexleyheath
Tel: 01 303 0423

Membership – Restricted
Year Formed – 1976
No. of Members – 30

LANCASHIRE

British Aerospace AS Preston

Secretary – W. Stammers
3 Cottam Lane, Ashton Preston

Membership – Restricted
No. of Members – 100 +

Loveclough AC

Secretary – L.J. Thomas
5 Victoria Street, Haslingden, Rossendale
Tel: 07062 28424

Membership – Unrestricted
Year Formed – 1973
No. of Members – 100
Facilities – Fishing on two waters in the
Rossendale Valley both fed by the River Limey.

Sefton Deep Sea AC

Secretary – A.K. Harrison
31 Derby Street, Colne
Tel: 0282 862160

Membership – Unrestricted
Year Formed – 1968
No. of Members – 40
Facilities – Mainly boat fishing with occasional
beach fishing.

LEICESTERSHIRE

Bowling Green Sea AC

Secretary – C. Brown
3 Westfield Avenue, Ashby-de-la Zouch
Tel: 0530 414518

Membership – Unrestricted
Year Formed – 1970
No. of Members – 30
Facilities – Fishing at Whitby, Staithes and
Holyhead. Winter fishing under negotiation.

Rugby Sea AC

Secretary – Mrs. V. Lax
8 Attfield Drive, Whetstone
Tel: 0533 848327

Membership – Unrestricted
Year Formed – 1968
No. of Members – 75
Facilities – Boat and beach fishing all over the
country. Coach trips on Saturdays and two 2
day trips each year.

LINCOLNSHIRE

Lincoln Imps Sea AC

Secretary – R.W. Hodges
2 Falcon Close, Eagle, Lincoln

Membership – Unrestricted
Year Formed – 1979
No. of Members – 53
Facilities – Various fishing venues i.e., —
Anglesea, Gt Yarmouth, Bridlington, Whitby
— general fishing and wrecking.

Royal Air Force Scampton

Secretary – M.L. Carey
36 Sandwell Drive, Lakeside Park, Lincoln
Tel: 0522 686669

Membership – Unrestricted
Year Formed – 1979
No. of Members – 40

Skegness Sea AC

Secretary – S. Kinning
'Westward Ho' Everingtons Lane, Skegness

Membership – Unrestricted
Year Formed – 1958
No. of Members – 100 +
Facilities – Beach and small boat fishing off
Lincolnshire coast.

MERSEYSIDE

Irby AC

Secretary – Frank Evans
4 McAlpine Close, Upton, Wirral L49 6JR
Tel: 051 678 7619

Membership – Restricted
Year Formed – 1967
No. of Members – 800
Facilities – 25 Small lakes and ponds (Wirral
area) S.U.C. at Aberbechan. River Severn
Aberbechan (small stretches).

Liverpool Cormorants SAC

Secretary – John Allcock
97 Barford Road, Longview, Liverpool 13

Membership – Unrestricted
Year Formed – 1964
No. of Members – 35
Facilities – Coast of North Wales and
Lancashire. Also east coast. Frequent boat
trips.

Maghull & Lydiate AC

Secretary – J. Johnson
97 Liverpool Road, (North) Maghull
Tel: 051 526 4083

Membership – Unrestricted
Year Formed – 1911
No. of Members – 182
Facilities – Swan Pool, Liverpool Road
Aughton. Burscough Brickworks, Abbey La
Burscough. Barton Brook, Altcar Merser's
Pool, Bells Lane, Lydiate Ainsdale Lake,
Ainsdale, Lancs, Moss Lodges, Skelmersdal
(Joint ownership with Skem. Comrades).

NORFOLK

Association of East Anglian SA

Secretary – Mrs. Audrey London
3 Green Yard, Cromer Hall, Cromer

Cromer & District SAC

Secretary – D. Burdett
11 Carrington Road, Cromer
Tel: 0263 511156

Membership – Unrestricted
Year Formed – Probably 1945-1950
No. of Members – approx. 80
Facilities – We fish on all beaches along the
local coastline between Cley-next-Sea and
Happisburgh. Mainly sandy terrain with som
areas of rock.

Dereham AC

Secretary – H.E. Mortram
Yaxham Road, Matteshall
Treasurer – Mr. B. Fanthorpe
11a Neatherd Road, Dereham
Tel: 0362 2094

Membership – Unrestricted
No. of Members – 800

Harleston Wortwell & District A

Secretary – J.C. Adamson
"Yew Villa", Roydon, Diss, IP22 3EG
Tel: 0379 3952

Membership – Unrestricted
Year Formed – 1940
No. of Members – 700 +
Facilities – 4 gravel pits at Weybread (North Suffolk) near Harleston, Norfolk 5-6 miles of the upper River Waveney near Harleston. Needham, Shotford, Mendham, Homersfield, Denton). 2 miles of the tidal River Waveney at Dunburgh, Gillingham Beccles.

Kings Lynn SAC

Secretary – E. Jermyn
'The Ferns', Church Lane, Roydon, Kings Lynn

Membership – Unrestricted
Year Formed – 1961
No. of Members – 85
Facilities – Sea Fishing on East Coast from Weybourne to Dunwich.

Stalham & District SAC

Secretary – M.R. Moorhouse
Kingarth Union Road, Smallburgh, Norwich
Tel: 0603 331

Membership – Restricted
Year Formed – 1974
No. of Members – 60
Facilities – Open beach fishing.

NORTHAMPTONSHIRE

Corby Silver Band SAA

Secretary – M. Campbell
4 Byron Road, Corby

Membership – Restricted
Year Formed – 1977
No. of Members – 25
Facilities – We are only a section and do not control any waters. However we fish all round Britain from Hartlepool down the East Coast to the South Coast and Wales.

Daventry "Sea Kings" AC

Secretary – C.M. Enstone
9 The Fairway, Daventry NN11 4NW
Tel: 032 72 71595

Membership – Unrestricted
Year Formed – 1978
No. of Members – 70
Facilities – Club trips are run on an average of one every four weeks. Venues include Brighton, Newhaven, Folkestone, Conway, Great Yarmouth, etc.

Kettering & District D.S.A.C.

Secretary – M.J. Coe
9 Ennerdale Close, Kettering NN16 8UQ
Tel: 0536 515496

Membership – Restricted
Year Formed – 1974
No. of Members – Fluctuates between 30 & 90
Facilities – The club runs at least one trip to the coast each month, sometimes more. Winter fishing is mainly on the East Anglian coast with the N. East, South and Welsh coasts also being visited in the summer. The

Club only caters on an organised basis for boat anglers although a number of members organise fishing trips in winter. There are club Trophies for Points, Aggregate Weight, Unusual Catch and a number of the more popular species. The Club is affiliated to N.F.S.A.

Rod & Reel (Kettering)

Secretary – K. Pilcher
5 Gough Close, Kettering
Tel: 912 511279

Membership – Restricted
Year Formed – 1976
No. of Members – 25
Facilities – All Coastal Waters.

NOTTINGHAMSHIRE

Awsworth Sea AC

Secretary – C.J. Nicol
22 Barlow Drive, Worth, Awsworth
WG16 2RR
Tel: 0602 328128

Membership – Unrestricted
Year Formed – 1975
No. of Members – 15
Facilities – None at present. We have a boat fishing club and charter boats all over the U.K. We are launching a coarse fishing section during 1981 as we are obtaining some local waters.

Mansfield & District Sea AA

Secretary – J. Godley
7 Misters Road, Newstead Village
Tel: 0623 753765

New Houghton Deep SAC

Chairman – R. Gregory
The Bungalow, Rotherham Road, New Houghton, Nr. Mansfield
Tel: 0623 810512

No. of Members – 40

Newstead Deep SAC

Secretary – J. Godley
7 Musters Road, Newstead Village
Tel: 0623 753765

Membership – Restricted
Year Formed – 1978
No. of Members – 40
Facilities – All our fishing is Deep Sea and Wreck fishing. Winter fishing at Lowestoft. Summer fishing at Whitby. Arrangements are being made for weekend fishing, Kinsale Ireland.

Nottingham Sea Specimen Group

Secretary – A. Booth
137 Main Road, Watnall NG16 1HF
Tel: 0602 384396

Membership – Restricted
Year Formed – 1973
No. of Members – 15
Facilities – Boat bookings on daily and weekly charters with the emphasis on better than average sea fishing.

Plough Inn D.S.A.C.

Secretary – J.B. Hyde
8 The Oval, Ordsall, Retford DN22 7SE

Membership – Restricted
Year Formed – 1972
No. of Members – 24

Warsop Deep Sea Angling

Secretary – C.H. Millership
22 Glebe Avenue, Warsop, Mansfield
Tel: 0623 842006

Membership – Restricted
Year Formed – 1978
No. of Members – 24
Facilities – Fish to N.F.S.A. Rules on location at Whitby or any other wrecking locations at sea.

Westfield Deep Sea AC

Chairman – R. Teece
188 Alfreton Road, Sutton-in-Ashfield
Tel: 0623 56688

Membership – Restricted
Year Formed – 1963
No. of Members – 35

Dog & Partridge SAC

Secretary – P. Thompson
44 Park End, Bodicote, Banbury

Membership – Unrestricted
Year Formed – 1970
No. of Members – 25

Osney SAC

Secretary – P.S. Robinson
34 Duke Street, Oxford Tel: 0865 43493

Membership – Restricted
No. of Members – 18
Facilities – Club Headquarters, The Malbrough Arms, St. Thomases Oxford.

Oxford & District AA

Secretary – P. Weston
18 Linden Road, Bicester Tel: 08692 44533

Membership – An Association of 40 member clubs
Year Formed – 1930
Facilities – River Thames at Shifford, Medley Folley, Donnington, Iffley, Sandford and Clifton Hamden. Bookings for club matches welcomed.

Thames Valley SA Alliance

Secretary – P. Stone
16 Rose Hill, Oxford Tel: 0865 777841

SHROPSHIRE

Bulls Head SAC

Secretary – L. Latham
33 Penistone Close, Donnington, Telford
Tel: 0952 603968

Membership – Restricted
Year Formed – 1974
No. of Members – 8
Facilities – No controlled waters — fish mainly Welsh coast.

Dawley SAC

Secretary – P.J. Green
2 Talbot Close, Wrockwardine Wood
TF2 7AP
Tel: 612023

Membership – Restricted
Year Formed – 1971
No. of Members – 8
Facilities – N/A Sea angling only. We fish all waters from Lands End to John O'Groats and further.

Oakengates SAC

c/o Rose & Crown, AS Ketly Bank, Telford

Red Lion SAC

Secretary – P.J. Stanton
92 New Road, Wrackwardine Wood, Telford

Shropshire SAC

Secretary – C.H. Day
100 Thompsons Drive, Whitchurch
Tel: 0948 4441

Membership – Unrestricted
Year Formed – 1962
No. of Members – 74
Facilities – Irish Sea fishing — Almwch, Conway, Rhyl etc and distant trips to Brixham, Plymouth, Deal and Portugal.

SOMERSET

3 BS SAA

Secretary – R. Lambert
14 Julians Acres, Berrow
Tel: 787444

Membership – Unrestricted
Year Formed – 1976
No. of Members – 120
Facilities – Coastal waters of the Bristol Channel along the Burnham and Berrow shore line. Charter boat facilities available from Burnham-on-Sea. Fishing the reefs of Hincley Point and Brean Down.

Blackdown SAC

Secretary – P.F. Milton
13 Churchfields, Wellington TA21 8SD
Tel: 082 347 6453

Membership – Restricted
Year Formed – 1975
No. of Members – 75
Facilities – Sea Angling only. We do not control any waters.

Bridgwater SAC

Secretary – O. Syms
101 Holford Road, Bridgwater
Tel: 0278 423043

Membership – Unrestricted
Year Formed – 1965
No. of Members – 87
Facilities – 16 Charter boat trips annually from Plymouth, Minehead and Ilfracombe. Boat Festival at Ilfracombe. Beach and boat matches under auspices of Bristol Channel Federation of Sea Anglers. Monthly club beach matches in local area.

Chard & District Angling Club

Secretary – D. Lemon
38 Glanvill Avenue, Chard TA20 1EU
Tel: 0460 61281

Membership – Unrestricted. Junior membership available
No. of Members – 150
Facilities – Coarse fishing at Perry Street Pond, Perry Street, nr. Chard, and Ash Pond, Ash, nr. Martock. Coarse and trout fishing at River Isle at Donyatt and Ilminster, and River Axe, Broom Bridge, nr. Chard.

Hinkley Point SAC

Secretary – J.A. Fidoe
9 Willow Walit, Bridgwater
Tel: 0278 55896

Membership – Restricted
Year Formed – 1970
No. of Members – 60
Facilities – Fishing throughout the country. Particularly the south side of the Bristol Channel (Hinkley Reefs) near power station. Own boat for club members moored at Porlock/Minehead for deep fishing in the Channel.

Kings Billy SAC

Secretary – M. Patrick
7 Woodland Road, Frome
Tel: 0373 71534

Membership – Unrestricted
Year Formed – 1976
No. of Members – 35
Facilities – Deep sea venues from Dartmouth to S.W. Wales to 60 miles out when Wrecking. Beach from Poole to Weston-Super-Mare.

N.F.S.A. Misterton AC

Secretary – J. Bloomfield
16 Southmead Crescent, Crewkerne

Membership – Unrestricted
Year Formed – 1971
No. of Members – 24
Facilities – Westbay Bridport, Lyme Regis, Weymouth, Brixham, Dartmouth, Beir Regis.

Rainbow SAC

Secretary – P.N. Southword
16 Howard Road, Yeovil
Tel: 0935 21438

Membership – Unrestricted
Year Formed – 1974
No. of Members – 60
Facilities – We fish from Poole Harbour to Brixham and use some of the best charter skippers on the South Coast. We have an excellent past record of species and anyone is welcome to fish with us.

Taunton Vale SA

Secretary – K. Dawe
90 Belmont Road, Taunton
Tel: 0823 74433

Membership – Unrestricted
Year Formed – 1975
No. of Members – 75
Facilities – Beach and boat fishing from Dorset, Somerset, Devon and Cornwall.

Tor SAC

Secretary – R.W.G. Musgrave
18 Mildred Road, Walton, Nr. Street
Tel: 0458 42957

Membership – Unrestricted
Year Formed – 1958
No. of Members – 60

Westlands Sports SAC

Secretary – J. Robinson
15 Crofton Park, Yeovil
Tel: 0935 71818

Membership – Unrestricted
Year Formed – 1965
No. of Members – 50
Facilities – Club matches are fished on the Chesil Beach, Poole, Bristol Channel and Weymouth Bay areas mainly.

STAFFORDSHIRE

Buccaneers Deep SAC

Secretary – J.B. Gwynne
208 Anchor Road, Longton, Stoke-on-Trent
Tel: 0782 324014

Membership – Restricted
Year Formed – Reformed as Buccaneers D.S.A.C. — 1975
No. of Members – 14

Burton-on-Trent DSAC

Secretary – R.M. Holmes
15 Collinson Road, Barton Under Needwood, Burton-on-Trent DE13 8JJ
Tel: 0283 713317

Membership – Restricted
Year Formed – 1971

Swordfish Marine SAC

Secretary – D.T. Cliff
31 Bell Lane, Barlaston Park, Stoke-on-Trent
Tel: 0782 3279

Membership – Unrestricted
Year Formed – 1976
No. of Members – 70
Facilities – Anywhere in Great Britain.

SUFFOLK

Bungay Cherry Tree AC

Secretary – I.R. Gosling
87 St. Marys Terrace, Fuxton Road, Bungay
NR35 1DW Tel: 0986 2982

Long Melford & District AA

Secretary – N. Mealham
Springfield Terrace, East Street, Sudbury
Tel: 0787 77139

Saxmundham Sports AC

Secretary – J.T. Firman
15 Saxon Road, Saxmundham IP17 1ED
Tel: 0728 2638

SURREY

Ebbisham SAC

Secretary – D. Jenkins
Stane Way, Ewell, Epsom KT17 1PN
Tel: 01 393 7584

Membership – Unrestricted
Year Formed – 1977
No. of Members – 13
Facilities – Charter boat fishing only from various Marinas along the South coast wtih occasional trips further afield i.e. Plymouth.

Fishers Farm Angling Club, SS

Secretary – D.M. Shulver
Montacute Road, New Addington,
Croydon CR0 0JF
Tel: 0689 41833

Membership – Restricted
Year Formed – 1975
No. of Members – 80

The Huntsman SAC

Secretary – R. Milner
Vale Road, Sutton
Tel: 01 661 9883

Membership – Unrestricted
Year Formed – 1978
No. of Members – 38
Facilities – From Plymouth to Dover throughout the year.

SUSSEX EAST

Birling Gaps AC

Secretary – D. Roper
Southfield, Polegate BN26 5LY
032 12 5994

Membership – Unrestricted
Year Formed – 1950
No. of Members – 7
Facilities – The English Channel

Brighton Trades Labour Club

Secretary – R. Scrase
165 Bear Road, Brighton

Membership – Unrestricted
Year Formed – 1963
No. of Members – 25
Facilities – A 27 foot boat, with 22 H.P. diesel engine, based at Brighton Marina. Range of about 20 miles covered — all types of fish caught all year round.

Crowborough & District AA

Secretary – K.J.B. Wilson
'Elysium' 35, Southridge Road, Crowborough
Tel: 08926 4722

Membership – Restricted. Junior membership available
No. of Members – 150
Facilities – Local lakes, streams, rivers within a 15 mile radius of Crowborough Cross.

Daltons D. S. A. C.

Secretary – R. Price
168 Wiston Road, Brighton BN2 5PS
Tel: 0273 689976

Membership – Unrestricted
Year Formed – 1976
No. of Members – 18
Facilities – All the members are boat owners and we fish the Brighton area.

East Hastings SAA

Secretary – D.W. Brockington
c/o East Hastings SAA
The Stade, Hastings
Tel: Office — 0424 426644
    Club Room — 0424 430230

Membership – Unrestricted
Year Formed – 1908
No. of Members – 1200 angling, 1400 social
Facilities – Large modern clubhouse with bar, tea bar, changing rooms, toilets and showers, boat repair workshops, five winches, 34 club boats for members' use, lockers, outboard storage space, etc. Joining fee £5.00. Membership £7.50 per annum or £10.00 per annum for boat owners. Reduced fees for juveniles and O.A.P's.

Eastbourne AA

Secretary – C. Parsons
Eastbourne AA
Tel: 0323 23442

Membership – Unrestricted
Year Formed – 1905
No. of Members – 700
Facilities – Open sea fishing. Good sport to be had all the year round.

Eastbourne Fishermans Protection Society and Club

Secretary – G.J. Pearson
21 Beltring Road, Eastbourne BN22 8JH
Tel: 0323 36852

Membership – Unrestricted
Year Formed – 1960
No. of Members – 55
Facilities – Channel area ranging from Beachy Head to Pevensey Bay.

Eastbourne Nomads AC

Secretary – Mrs L. Woods
65 Greenleaf Gardens, Polegate BN26 6PF
Tel: 032 124817

Membership – Unrestricted
Year Formed – 1929
No. of Members – 150
Facilities – Beach and pier.

Harbour AC

Secretary – K. Luxford
50 Oakdene Crescent, Portslade

Membership – Unrestricted
No. of Members – 230

Hastings & St Leonards AA

Secretary – G. Wall
Marine Parade, Hastings
Tel: 0424 431923

Membership – Unrestricted
Year Formed – 1895
No. of Members – 1,762
Facilities – Pier and beach.

Hove Deep Sea Anglers

Secretary – R.E.L. Robinson
Clubhouse, Western Esplanade,
Hove BN4 1WB
Tel: 0273 413000

Membership – Unrestricted
Year Formed – 1908
No. of Members – 335 men + 160 ladies

Pevensey Bay Aqua Club

Secretary – Mrs J. Miller
'Coasters' Marine Terrace, Pevensey Bay

Membership – Unrestricted
Year Formed – 1966
No. of Members – 200
Facilities – Beach, Berths for boats, 2 motor winches, bar, own car park.

Queens Head AA

Secretary – G. Fenner
25 Courtlands Ashton Rise, Brighton
Tel: 0273 606045

Membership – Restricted
Year Formed – 1959
No. of Members – 70
Facilities – Apart from away venues we fish Brighton — Hove beaches giving seven miles of sandy bottoms which yield big bags of fish during both summer and winter.

Rye SAC

Secretary – R. Coates
10 Battle Crescent, St Leonards-on-Sea

Membership – Unrestricted
Year Formed – 1977
No. of Members – 100 +
Facilities – We hold monthly boat and beach competitions, with an open beach competition once a year. Rye Bay and channel waters are fished from the boats. Dengemarsh Beach for the shore competitions.

Sir Robert Peel AC

Secretary – Charles Barden
15 Clarke Court, Wasingham Road, Hove
Tel: 0273 725 802

Membership – Restricted
Year Formed – 1908
No. of Members – 25
Facilities – Launch boats from a shingle beach. All types of sea fish to be caught.

St Leonards SAA

Secretary – R.J. Towner
'Yolinar' Churchwood Road,
St Leonards-on-Sea
Tel: 0424 51652

Membership – Unrestricted
Year Formed – 1901
No. of Members – Fluctuates between 150-200
Facilities – We have a number of club and private boats beached at Warrior Square, St Leonards. Fish the English Channel and hold frequent morning, all day and evening competitions. Entry fee to membership £1.00 then £3.50 per annum thereafter.

SUSSEX WEST

Bexhill SAC

Secretary – R.S. Bage
4 Glyne Barn Close, Bexhill-on-Sea
Tel: 0424 212887

Membership – Unrestricted
No. of Members – 160-180
Facilities – From the foreshore at Galley Hill, Bexhill-on-Sea. Club boat available for hire.

Bognor Regis Amateur AS

Festival Secretary – B. Spriggs
8 The Midway, Feltham, Bognor
Tel: 0243 864842

Membership – Unrestricted
No. of Members – 90

Bognor Regis Surfcasters AC

Secretary – B. Howlett
125 Oving Road, Chichester
Tel: 0243 782984

Membership – Unrestricted
Year Formed – 1960
No. of Members – 50
Facilities – Beach Angling from Selsey Bill to Shoreham. Open and closed club competitions.

British Airport Authority AC

Secretary – R.J. Patchett
21 Hardham Close, Ifield, Crawley RH11 0DP
Tel: 0293 24351

Membership – Restricted
Year Formed – 1972
No. of Members – 63
Facilities – All lakes — Members only.

Elmer Sands Boating & AC

Secretary – H.T. Emerson
35 Shrubbs Drive, Middleton-on-Sea, Bognor Regis
Tel: 024 33 4614

Membership – Restricted
Year Formed – 1948
No. of Members – 60
Facilities – Within sight of and launched from Elmer Sands and from beaches between Climping and Southdean.

Licensed Victuallers Deep SAC

Secretary – E.E. Doree
1 Norfolk Court, Sea Lane, Rustington
BN16 2SQ
Tel: 090 62 5653

Membership – Restricted to Licensed Victuallers and Allied Trades
Year Formed – 1959
No. of Members – 50
Facilities – We have vacancies for Licensed Victuallers or members of Allied Trades. Our existing members, all of whom are very experienced anglers, are always ready to help if necessary to give instruction to newcomers. Alternate venues – Littlehampton, Brighton and Deal fortnightly always on Wednesdays.

Pagham Offshore AC

Secretary – P.S. Isom
4 Mallard Crescent, Pagham, Bognor Regis
Tel: 024 32 2106

Membership – Restricted
Year Formed – 1973
No. of Members – Approx. 60
Facilities – A Boat Only club. Have a launching slipway, electric winch, boat and car park. Fish caught ususally — tope, conger eels, bass, black bream, skates and rays, dogfish, cod etc.

Pulborough & Horsham DSA

Secretary – C. Denyer
40 Warren Hamlet, Sullington RH20 3NL
Tel: 09066 4739

Membership – Unrestricted
Year Formed – 1964
No. of Members – 25
Facilities – Main ports — Littlehampton and Shoreham — mark and wreck fishing. Other ports according to demand.

Selsey Bill FC

Secretary – P.W. Cooper
2 Ruskin Close, Selsey
Tel: 024361 4048

Membership – Restricted
Year Formed – 1965
No. of Members – 52

Selsey Tope Fishers Specimen Club

Secretary – R.G. Horrod
28 Beach Road, Selsey
Tel: 024 361 4544

Membership – Restricted membership by invitation only
Year Formed – 1965
No. of Members – 30

Shoreham AC

Secretary – K. Weaver
5 Thornhill Way, Mile Oak, Portslade
BN4 2YY
Tel: 0273 415132

Membership – Unrestricted
Year Formed – 1949
No. of Members – 137

Sussex Offshore Sea Anglers

Secretary – A. McTaggart
80 Parkside Avenue, Littlehampton
Tel: 090 64 24385

Membership – Restricted
Year Formed – 1976
No. of Members – 10
Facilities – Dungeness (Cod fishing) 16 trips per annum. Dartmouth (Wreck/banks) 5 2-da trips per annum. Keyhaven and Portsmouth (Summer fishing) 10 trips per annum.

Worthing Deep SAC

Secretary – B.J. Devitt-Spooner
128 Aldsworth Avenue, Goring-by-Sea, Worthing   Tel: 0905 44456

Membership – Restricted
Year Formed – 1975
No. of Members – 22
Facilities – Boat fishing booked each month. Facilities for weighing specimen fish. Affiliated to N.F.S.A. Eligible for specimen fish medals.

WARWICKSHIRE

Cotswold SAC

Secretary – B.T. Hart
9 Butlers Road, Long Compton
Tel: 060 884 617

Membership – Unrestricted
Year Formed – 1973
No. of Members – 30
Facilities – Coastal Waters. South Coast. Mainly day trips, charter.

Vikings SAC (Leamington Spa)

Secretary – V.P. Alcock
44 Newburgh Crescent, Warwick
Tel: 0926 42417

mbership – Restricted (70)
ar Formed – 1971
. of Members – 70
cilities – We have no waters but we go to
coast every 3 weeks. Trips to Folkestone,
lwch, Plymouth, Swansea. Minehead,
erystwyth, Keyhaven and many more.

IDLANDS WEST

ossways

retary – J. Deathridge
ssways, College Road, Birmingham B44
: 021 373 0771

mbership – Restricted
ar Formed – 1928
of Members – 64
ilities – Venues on coarse fishing are in the
n on local rivers such as the Severn,
nt, and the Avon. On sea fishing we have
chased a 47 seater coach, therefore we
el to all parts of Great Britain.

nes Bridge Copper AS

retary – J.H. Bird
immonds Road, Little Bloxwich, Walsall
3 3PV
0922 77043/21292

mbership – Unrestricted
r Formed – 1974
of Members – 54

ngswinford Deep SAC

retary – H. Sanders
udley Road, Kingswinford, Nr. Brierley
, DY6 8BS

mbership – Restricted
r Formed – 1980
of Members – 18

lers Arms SAC

retary – A.K. Cheadle
each Avenue, Woodcross, Bilston
090 73 76518

mbership – Restricted
r Formed – 1975
of Members – 18

ILTSHIRE

on SAC

retary – D. Mayo
t. Aldhelms Road, Bradford-on-Avon

tish Rail SAC Westbury

retary – B.A. Morris
eur De Lys Drive, Southwick, Trowbridge

mbership – Unrestricted
r Formed – 1974
of Members – 30

ce Eight SAC

retary – D.K. Galliers
eech Grove, Trowbridge
022 14 62348

Membership – Unrestricted
Year Formed – 1977
No. of Members – 45
Facilities – Boats booked along various ports
on the South Coast, i.e. ground and wreck
fishing.

Salisbury Anchor SAC

Secretary – L.H. Woolford
449 Devizes Road, Salisbury
Tel: 0722 27797

Membership – Restricted 200
Year Formed – 1965
No. of Members – 80
Facilities – From Hengistbury Head,
Christchurch, Dorset to West Bay, Bridport
(shore). Poole Bay and Weymouth for boats.

Wreck SAC

Secretary – A.R. Vallis
26 Coronation Road, Durrington
Tel: 52486

Membership – Restricted
Year Formed – 1975
No. of Members – 30

YORKSHIRE NORTH

Filey Brigg AS

Secretary – K.C. Carpenter
18 Ash Grove, Filey YO14 9LZ

Membership – Unrestricted
Year Formed – 1925
No. of Members – 100
Facilities – Filey Brigg, Deep water, long
ridge of Rocks Best Mark June to September.
Very good float for pollack, mackerel
coalfish, good flatfish from shore and boats in
Summer. Mackerel from mid July to end
September, cod from September to March.
All baits obtained locally. Festival held every
year first week September.

Scarborough Rock Anglers Society

Secretary – H. Dobson
1 Uplands Avenue, East Ayton, Scarborough
YO13 9EU
Tel: 0723 72495

Membership – Unrestricted
Year Formed – 1901
No. of Members – 162
Facilities – Sea Fishing

South Cliff AC

Secretary – E. Appleby
Duntrune, 19 Bedale Avenue, Scarborough
Tel: 0723 61275

Membership – Unrestricted
Year Formed – 1911
No. of Members – 83
Facilities – Rock Angling Club boundaries,
Whitby West Pier to South Landing,
Flamborough (40 miles).

YORKSHIRE SOUTH

Barnsley SAC

Secretary – D. Northcliffe
20 Broadway, Barnsley Tel: 0226 5119

Membership – Unrestricted, max. 36
Year Formed – 1959
No. of Members – 36
Facilities – The club has two sections — the
largest is the Sunday section with 36
members. The Thursday section, with a
membership of 12 caters for businessmen etc,
able to take advantage of early closing day.
Most fishing done East Yorkshire Coast but a
3 to 4 day annual trip is run with venues as
diverse as Kinsale, Ullapool, Plymouth, Arran.

The Brecks SAC

Secretary – R.J. Stanley
15 Saville Road, Whiston, Rotherham
Tel: 0709 60967

Membership – Restricted
Year Formed – 1978
No. of Members – 30
Facilities – The Breck Sea Anglers specialise
in wreck fishing on the Yorkshire Coast,
mainly, from Whitby and Scarborough. These
being 10 or 12 hour trips every 2 weeks, from
June to October, and are members of the
N.F.S.A.

California SAC

Secretary – G. Swithenbank
54 Princess Street, Staincross, Barnsley
Tel: 0226 385324

Membership – Restricted
Year Formed – 1967
No. of Members – 24
Facilities – Day trips to East Coast (Whitby,
Bridlington). Boat. Annual trip for one week.
Usually a South Coast Resort.

Eastwood View W.M.C. AA

Secretary – A.W. Stubbs
27 Campbell Drive, Rotherham
Tel: 0709 71456

Membership – Unrestricted
Year Formed – 1970 AA Parent Club 1920
No. of Members – 290 AA Members + over
1000 in Parent Club
Facilities – We are associated with clubs that
control waters on the Rivers Trent, Witham,
Steeping, Yorkshire Ouse, and Lakes. Club
facilities include lounge, games and snooker
rooms and large concert hall which is
available for prize presentations, dancing etc.

Hemingfield Deep Sea FC

Secretary – G. Bradley
1 Coronation Terrace, Hemingfield, Barnsley
Tel: 0226 759329

Membership – Restricted
Year Formed – 1965
No. of Members – 24
Facilities – Being a sea fishing club, we do no
control any waters. We have 8-10 trips a year,
mainly on the East Coast. Whitby is the most
popular, along with Bridlington,
Scarborough, Hartlepool. In September we
have a weeks eld Tel: 0484 36430

Taverners SAC

Secretary – A.M. Long
318 Killinghall Road, Bradford 2

Membership – Unrestricted
Year Formed – 1980
No. of Members – 15
Facilities – We are affiliated to the National Federation of Sea Anglers and we fish all around Gt. Britain.

Yorkshire Bank Ltd. SAS

Secretary – D.A. Bentley
c/o Yorkshire Bank Ltd. O & M Dept
20 Merrion Way, Leeds LS2 8NZ
Tel: 0532 441244

Membership – Restricted
Year Formed – 1976
No. of Members – 30

Yorkshire Wreckers SAC

Secretary – K.L. Alderson
6 Kenmoor Crescent, Cleckheaton
Tel: 0274 872172

Membership – Unrestricted
Year Formed – 1970
No. of Members – 50
Facilities – Wreck fishing, mainly on Yorkshire Coast. Also weekend trips to Mevagissey, Plymouth and Scotland. Affiliated to N.F.S.A. Yorkshire and British Conger Club.

YORKSHIRE WEST

Brighouse Sea AA

Secretary – T. Spink
1 Alfred Street, Brighouse
Tel: 0484 712979

Membership – Unrestricted
Year Formed – 1967
No. of Members – 26
Facilities – Sea or shore. Approx. 2 hours travel to East or West Coast.

Hemsworth M.W. SAC

Secretary – H. Hargreaves
52 Second Avenue, Fitzwilliam, Pontefract
WF9 5BA
Tel: 0977 612867

Membership – Restricted to 32
Year Formed – 1975
No. of Members – 24
Facilities – We sea fish at Whitby at least 12 matches a year.

I.C.I. (Organics) Huddersfield AS

Secretary – M. Senior
Orchard Farmhouse, Back Lane, Briestfield, Dewsbury WF12 0P8
Tel: 0484 37456 Ext. 214

Membership – Restricted
Year Formed – 1971
No. of Members – 70
Facilities – I.C.I. owned dam known as Woodhouse Mill Dam, Leeds Road, Huddersfield. Approx. half an acre. Stocked with most species of coarse fish.

Keighley AC

Secretary – L.W. Brocklesby
11 Eelholme View Street, Beechcliffe, Keighley
Tel: 0535 67699

Membership – Unrestricted
Year Formed – 1868
No. of Members – 800
Facilities – Leeds and Liverpool Canal. Approx. 16 miles on the River Aire (day tickets). 4 Miles River Worth. Whitefields Reservoir, Steeton, Roberts pond, Beechcliffe. 100 yard River Wharfe (Addingham). Match booking for River Aire only, send S.A.E. Full Members only.

Leeds City Seadogs

Secretary – H.W.E. Charnock
2 Swardale Green, Swarcliffe, Leeds LS14 5HL
Tel: 0532 600971

Membership – Restricted
Year Formed – 1979
No. of Members – 12 members, 3 reserves
Facilities – We do not control any waters. We use mainly the East Coast, but occasionally cross to the West coast.

Mackintosh AC

Secretary – M. Russell
Rowntree Mackintosh, Halifax
Tel: 0422 65761

Membership – Restricted
Year Formed – 1962
No. of Members – 108
Facilities – We rent from the Y.W.A. a 500 yard stretch of canal from Sutterhebble to the Sutterhebble Lock.

Norristhorpe SAC

Secretary – T. Sheard
6 West Park Terrace, Healey Batley
Tel: 0924 478619

Membership – Restricted
Year Formed – 1975
No. of Members – 30
Facilities – Have a club boat moored at Whitby, for inshore fishing.

Primrose Hill SAC

Secretary – H. Raby
22 Lawton Street, Primrose Hill, Huddersfield
Tel: 0484 36430

Taverners SAC

Secretary – A.M. Long
318 Killinghall Road, Bradford 2

Membership – Unrestricted
Year Formed – 1980
No. of Members – 15
Facilities – We are affiliated to the National Federation of Sea Anglers and we fish all around Gt. Britain.

Yorkshire Bank Ltd. SAS

Secretary – D.A. Bentley
c/o Yorkshire Bank Ltd. O & M Dept
20 Merrion Way, Leeds LS2 8NZ
Tel: 0532 441244

Membership – Restricted
Year Formed – 1976
No. of Members – 30

Yorkshire Wreckers SAC

Secretary – K.L. Alderson
6 Kenmoor Crescent, Cleckheaton
Tel: 0274 872172

Membership – Unrestricted
Year Formed – 1970
No. of Members – 50
Facilities – Wreck fishing, mainly on Yorkshire Coast. Also weekend trips to Mevagissey, Plymouth and Scotland. Affiliated to N.F.S.A. Yorkshire and British Conger Club.

WALES

CLWYD

odelwyddan AC

cretary – R.G. Richardson
fordd Siarl, St. Asaph
: 0745 582693

mbership – Unrestricted
ar Formed – 1975
. of Members – 125
ilities – Parts of River Elwy for game. Lodge
ls, Glascoed (Nr Bodelwyddan) for coarse.

olwyn Bay Victoria SAC

cretary – Dr C.W. Haskins
West Road, Old Colwyn, Colwyn Bay
0492 55011

mbership – Unrestricted
ar Formed – 1930
of Members – Varying 300-400

nfair P.G. Club
anfairpwll SAC)

retary – S.R. Walburn
Tan-y-Bryn, Rhos-on-Sea
ilities – All year round bass, plaice, conger,
ss may be caught from Brittania Bridge to
Newydd.

kingtons Recreational Club
gling Section

retary – G. Kenway
rose, Allt Goch, Henllan Road

mbership – Restricted
of Members – 250
lities – Coarse fishing (on site). Local sea
rs, river waters, lakes and reservoirs.

d Cow Deep SAC

retary – J. Kendall, (acting)
Cow Inn, Penybryn, Wrexham
0978 263986

mbership – Restricted
Formed – 1978
of Members – 25

DYFED

Aberystwyth SA & Yacht Club Angling Section

Club House, The Harbour, Aberystwyth

Endeavour Deep Sea Group

Secretary – Mrs B. Haigh
2 St. Davids Wharf, Pen-yr-Angor, Aberystwyth
Tel: 0970 612818

Membership – Unrestricted
Year Formed – 1965
No. of Members – 100 paid up clubs
300 paid up personal members
Facilities – Three 36ft. boats operating on a cost
sharing 20 mile radius of Aberystwyth. Private
wharfe recently completed. Extensive clubhouse,
restaurant, dinghy and car park in construction
on harbourside.

Fishguard & Goodwick SAC

Secretary – J. Harries
6 Heol Emrys, Fishguard
Tel: 0348 872600 after 1800 hrs

Membership – Unrestricted
Year Formed – 1955
No. of Members – 50
Facilities – Very good area for sea fishing with 2
breakwaters within the bay, free to club
members, but a charge made to visitors.
Excellent facilities for launching of boats.
2 Storm beaches within 6 miles and excellent
wrasse fishing at Strumble Head and surrounding
cliffs. Hire boats available at Lower Fishguard.

Pembroke & District AC

Secretary – T.J. Cavaney
Kilnback House, Angle Village
Tel: 064 684 208

Membership – Partly Restricted
Year Formed – 1958
No. of Members – 250
Facilities – Bosherston Lily Ponds. About 20 acres
for coarse fishing, but the club is mainly a Sea
Angling Club.

Tenby & District AC

Secretary – B. Ryan
Leechway, Tenby

Membership – Unrestricted
Year Formed – 1975
No. of Members – 180
Facilities – Local beaches and boat fishing.

GLAMORGAN MID

Aberaman Ex-Servicemans SAC

Secretary – E. Salway
37 Aman Street, Cwmaman, Aberdare CF44 6PD

Membership – Unrestricted
No. of Members – 42

Cynon Valley SAC

Secretary – K. Davies
109 Cardiff Road, Aberaman
Aberdare CF44 6UT

Membership – Unrestricted
Year Formed – 1975
No. of Members – 27

New Duffryn AC

Secretary – D.F. Roberts
The New Duffryn Hotel, Aberbargoed
Tel: 0443 831635

Membership – Unrestricted
Year Formed – 1979
No. of Members – 30
Facilities – Negotiating for water at present.

Porthcawl SAA

Secretary – E. Fielding
75 Westminster Way, Bridgend CF31 4QX

Membership – Unrestricted
Year Formed – 1952
No. of Members – Sea 150, Coarse 200
Facilities – Sea shore angling for bass, flounder,
whiting, codling. Sea boat angling for above and
skate, ray, tope and mackerel.
Game – Wilderness Lake – rainbow trout.
Coarse – Pwl-y-Waun Lake, carp, roach, perch,
bream.

Porthcawl SAC

Chairman – A. Birch
171 New Road, Porthcawl, GF36 5DD
Tel: 065 671 3975 HQ Sportsmans Club

Membership – Unrestricted
Year Formed – 1952
No. of Members – 450
Facilities – Wilderness Lake – game: rainbow
trout. Mercies Lake – coarse: bream, roach,
perch, carp. Day and weekly permits from
Bridges Sports Shop, New Road, Porthcawl.

Victoria SAC

Secretary – R. Jones
14 Parkfield Road, Ynyscynon Park
Aberdare CF44 0JL

Membership – Restricted
Year Formed – 1979
No. of Members – 14
Facilities – South Wales Coast

Wanderers AC

Secretary – G. Thomas
44 Rhydypenau Road
Cardiff

Membership – Restricted

GLAMORGAN SOUTH

Cardiff SAC

Secretary – G.E. Jones
34 Coveny Street, Splott, Cardiff
Tel: 0222 373 730

GLAMORGAN WEST

Welsh Shark, Tope Skate & Conger Club

Secretary – E. Woods
1 Parc Glas, Skewen, Neath

GWENT

Blackwood SAC

Secretary – C.G. Thomas
7 Ty-Deganerys, Bloomfield Road, Blackwood
Tel: 0495 226062

Membership – Restricted
Year Formed – 1979
No. of Members – 14
Facilities – The Gower Coast from Swansea to
Tenby. Teignmouth, South Devon. Aberystwyth,
West Wales. Plymouth (wrecking and reefing).

Cwmbran AA

Secretary – P.M. Gulliford
16 The Circle, Cwmbran
Tel: 06333 5036

Membership – Unrestricted
Year Formed – 1963
No. of Members – 250
Facilities – Trout – Afon Llwyd, 3 miles fly or
worm fishing only, 9in. limit, 2 fish per day.
Flows through new town, pleasant parklands.
Coarse – Mon. and Brecs. canal approx 5½
miles, tench, carp, dace, chub, roach, rudd,
perch, skimmer bream, eels. No bait restrictions.
All fish, except eels, to be returned to water.
Members only. No day tickets, on Blaen Bran
Reservoir and Bigsweir Fishery
(October – December only) River Wye between
Monmouth and Tintern Abbey. Sea: Bristol
Channel, charter boat available.

Gwent & District SAC

Secretary – C. Kenmore
61 Pant Glas, Pentwyn, Cardiff
Tel: 0222 734545

Spencer Works Deep Sea AC

Secretary – M. Osborne
7 Brecon Walk, Southville, Cwmbran

Membership – Unrestricted
Year Formed – 1978
No. of Members – 30
Facilities – This club fishes mainly from Plymouth,
Swansea and Pembroke.

GWYNEDD

Amlwch & District SAC

Secretary – E.W. Roberts
47 Maes Mona, Amlwch, Anglesey

Membership – Unrestricted
Year Formed – 1976
No. of Members – 65-70
Facilities – all round the coast of Anglesey. Mostly
shore, rock fishing, some beaches. Also boat fishing.

Associated Octel SAC

Secretary – J. Davies
Amlwch, Anglesey
Tel: 0407 831265

Membership – Restricted to Employees of
Associated Octel only
Year Formed – 1976

Bangor City AC

Secretary – M.L. Partridge
1 Lon Isaf, Menai Bridge, Anglesey
Tel: 0248 713867

Membership – Unrestricted
Year Formed – 1965
No. of Members – 60

Holyhead & District AC

Secretary – G. Hefin Jones
8 Moreton Road, Holyhead, Anglesey LL65 2BG
Tel: 0407 3821

Membership – Unrestricted
Year Formed – 1951
No. of Members – 100
Facilities – As we are a Sea Angling Club we do
not have control of any area. Our members
however, have right of access to certain areas,
i.e. Penrhos Estate, Raven's Point, Porth-y-
Gorwel, Silver Bay, Bryn-y-Bar.

Marine SAC

Secretary – P. Gannon
President – S. Stewart
Swolaimon, Richmond Hill, Holyhead
Tel: Sec. 0407 2385, Pres. 0407 2304 ext 15

Membership – Restricted

Port Dinowic SAC

Secretary – R. Rossen
27 Rhuven, Rhinlas, Bangor
Tel: 0248 51963

University College of North Wales SAC

Secretary – P.J. Coates
c/o Student Union, Deiniol Road, Bangor

Membership – Restricted
Year Formed – 1973
No. of Members – 42
Facilities – Meetings in Students Union. Trips
using Union facilities. Boat trips on local charter
boats.

SCOTLAND

BORDERS

Eyemouth SAC

Secretary – G.B. Crookston
Deanhead Drive, Eyemouth, Berwickshire

Membership – Unrestricted
No. of Members – 20

Gala SAC

Secretary – L. Thin
Aster Court, Galashiels, Selkirkshire TD1 2LN
Tel: 0896 55088

Membership – Unrestricted
Year Formed – 1976
No. of Members – 40
Facilities – Fishing is normally off the South East coast of Scotland, and the North East Coast of England, but have occasional trips to Luce Bay and Clyde Coast.

Whiteadder AA

Secretary – R. Welsh
Abbey Street, Bathans, Duns Tel: 03614 210

Membership – Unrestricted
Year Formed – 1932
No. of Members – 500
Facilities – We control Whiteadder Water from Cranside to the source, also its tributaries.

CENTRAL

Alloa & District SAC

Secretary – R. Mitchell
Meadowgreen, Sauchie by Alloa
Clackmannanshire Tel: 0259 21 3415

Membership – Unrestricted
Year Formed – 1967
No. of Members – 50
Facilities – We fish inland sea lochs and the open sea. We are in the process of getting a boat of our own.

Falkirk Sea Angling Club

Secretary – B. Treeby
6 Parkfoot Court, Falkirk, Stirlingshire FK11YY
Tel: 0324 27805

Membership – Unrestricted
Year Formed – 1970
No. of Members – 50
Facilities – Club hold boat outings every 3 weeks when outings fish marks on both East and West Coast with Stonehaven and Fairlie being the most popular venues. We generally have 3 boats booked over the year and have a membership which includes a good number of juniors.

Tullibody & Cambus SAC

Secretary – J. Meer
228 Carseview, Tullibody, Clackmannanshire
Tel: 212714

Membership – Unrestricted
Year Formed – 1977
No. of Members – 34

DUMFRIES & GALLOWAY

Dalbeattie & District SAC

Secretary – J. Moran
12 Church Crescent, Dalbeattie

Membership – Unrestricted
Year Formed – 1972
No. of Members – 150
Facilities – Miles of coastline. Rock fishing for dogfish, conger, skate, cod, pollock etc. Beach fishing, flatfish and bass.

Kirkcudbright & District SAC

Secretary – D. Ross
Muithill Cottage, Kirkcudbright, Kirkcudbrightshire
Tel: 0557 417

Membership – Unrestricted
Year Formed – 1956
No. of Members – 60
Facilities – The club fishes the Solway Firth from Stranraer on the West to Annan on the East.

Loch Ryan SAA

Secretary – R. Smith
Millbank Road, Stranraer

FIFE

Buckhaven & District SAC

Secretary – J. Forsyth
142 West High Street, Buckhaven
Tel: 0592 713688

Membership – Unrestricted
Year Formed – 1976
No. of Members – 55
Facilities – The club has its own fenced off compound on the foreshore at Buckhaven. Most members have their own boats which lie on the beach inside the compound from May – November. Although there is no harbour now, launching from the beach is quite easy. Visitors are welcome and will be taken out in members boats if possible. Fish to be caught cod, wrasse, whiting and flats.

Oysart Sailing Club

Secretary – H.F. Greig
24 James Grove, Kirkcaldy Tel: 0592 62 584

Membership – Unrestricted
Year Formed – 1968
No. of Members – 150

Firth of Forth
(H.M.S. Cochrane) SAC

Secretary – R.R. Coombes
H.M.S. Cochrane, Rosyth
Tel: 0383 41212, ext. 2973/2873

Membership – Restricted
Year Formed – 1975
No. of Members – 37

Kingfisher AC

Secretary – W.M. Laurie
29 Atholl Terrace, Kirkcaldy KY2 6LY
Tel: 0592 68373

Membership – Unrestricted
Year Formed – 1970
No. of Members – 30

Nairn Thistle AC

Secretary – H. F. Greig
24 James Grove, Kirkcaldy KY1 1TH
Tel: 0592 62584

Membership – Restricted
Year Formed – 1971
No. of Members – 35

Primrose AC

Secretary – A. Cox
103 Whinnyburn Place, Rosyth KY11 2TR
Tel: 0383 415703

Membership – Unrestricted
Year Formed – 1978
No. of Members – 14

GRAMPIAN

Aberdeen Thistle SAC

Secretary – Mrs M. Baker
c/o 40 Thistle Street, Aberdeen
Aberdeenshire AB1 1XD
Tel: 0224 50910

Membership – Unrestricted
Year Formed – 1968
No. of Members – 65
Facilities – Boats sail mainly from Stonehaven, (15 miles south Aberdeen). South of Aberdeen all fishing is off rocks. Good cod fishing. (Care should be taken when fishing above, check locally). North of Aberdeen the ground is all beaches fairly shallow. 33 Miles North is Peterhead North & South breakwaters. Good mixed fishing.

Elgin SAC

Secretary – D. Clarke
24 Bezack Street, New Elgin, Elgin, Morayshire
Tel: 0343 46889

Membership – Unrestricted
Year Formed – 1979
No. of Members – 45
Facilities – Sea fishing, Stonehaven McDuff – Whitehills, Buckie, Wick, Scrabster Loch Layford, Lochinver, Ullapool, Aultbea Gairloch, Sky. Will travel anywhere in own Mini Bus.

Lossiemouth AA

Secretary – T.B. Clark
Dunconusg, Stotfield, Lossiemouth
Tel: 034 381 2380

Membership – Unrestricted
Year Formed – 1958
No. of Members – 220 including Juniors
Facilities – Approx 4 miles of shore fishing, mainly for sea trout and salmon approx 1½ miles of river fishing from both banks of The River Lossie. (Trout and salmon). The sea and shore fishing is mainly for sea trout, although some members bait fish for other sea fish. Flounders, mackerel etc.

Westhill and Elrick AC

Secretary – R. Findlay
49 Henderson Drive, Elrick, Skene
Tel: 0224 741704

Membership – Restricted (to 30 members)
Year Formed – 1978
No. of Members – 27
Facilities – This is under negotiation. Rights to mile brown trout on Urie.

HIGHLANDS AND ISLANDS

Harris SAC

Secretary – W.D. Cameron
Harris Hotel, Harris, Western Isles
Tel: 0859 2154

Membership – Unrestricted
Year Formed – 1963
No. of Members – 20

Highland Omnibuses Employees AC

Secretary – D.J. Mackay
35 Dell Road, Inverness
Tel: 0463 30136

Membership – Restricted
Year Formed – 1975
No. of Members – 30
Facilities – Game fishing in Rivers and Lochs in the county and other counties North and West of Inverness. We do not control any waters. Sea fishing – round the North and N. West Coasts of Scotland.

Isle of Bute AA

Secretary – S.W. Squires
2 Timber Cottages, Mount Stuart, Isle of Bute

Membership – Unrestricted
Year Formed – 1967
No. of Members – 72
Facilities – Open shore line – variable sandy beaches and rocks. Cod, flatties, mackerel, pollock, haddock. South of Island high rocky shore line – good wrasse Loch Fad and Loch Quein – trout. Both lochs wooded and easily accessible fly fishing only Loch Ascog – Coarse fishing – pike and perch. Same nature as above.

Kingsmills Sea Angling & Sports Club

Secretary – D.I. Kewley
31 Inshes Crescent, Inverness
Tel: 0463 34171 (office) 0463 38459 (Home)

Membership – Restricted
Year Formed – 1972
No. of Members – 115

North Uist AC

Secretary – D.L. Cockburn
19 Dunrossil Place, Lochmaddy, North Uist
Tel: 089 63 205

Membership – Restricted
Year Formed – 1952
Facilities – All Lochs on North Uist Estates controlled by Factor, North Uist Estates, Lochmaddy. North Uist Permits for all fishing can be obtained at Estate Office, Lochmaddy.

North West Skye SAC

Secretary – L. Shurmer
13 Skinidin, By Dunvegan, Isle of Skye IV55 8ZS
Tel: 047 022 380

Membership – Urestricted
Year Formed – 1971
No. of Members – 37

Orkney Islands SAA

Chairman – J. Adam
44 Quaybanks Crescent, Kirkwall, Orkney

Shetland AA

Secretary – A. Miller
3 Gladstone Terrace, Lerwick, Shetland Isles
Tel: 0595 3729

Membership – Unrestricted
Year Formed – 1920
No. of Members – 441
Facilities – Over 1000 Lochs, both sea and fresh water scattered throughout the "mainland" island of Shetland. No river fishing as such, but all freshwater lochs have brown trout of varying sizes. Sea trout and grilse of varying sizes in the sea lochs and voes throughout the year, but best in Spring and Autumn

Shetland Association of Sea Anglers

Secretary – A. Leslie
65a Burgh Road, Lerwick, Shetland
Chairman – M.S. Mullay
c/o Information Centre, Alexandra Wharf, Lerwick, Shetland
Tel: 0595 3502

Membership – Unrestricted
Year Formed – 1970
No. of Members – 150
Facilities – Fishing around almost 100 islands with a coastline of 3000 miles. Fairly strong tides and depths to 60 fathoms. Excellent fishing from good baskets of haddock, whiting, mackerel, ling, coalfish and cod etc to record-breaking skate (226lb) and porbeagle shark (450lb).

Stornoway SAC

South Beach Quay, Stornoway

LOTHIAN

Edinburgh Thistle SAC

Secretary – G.A. Walker
5 Broomhouse Crescent, Edinburgh

Grouse Beaters SAC

Secretary – W. Todd
5 Oxgangs House, Edinburgh
Tel: 441 4599

Membership – Unrestricted
Year Formed – 1968
No. of Members – 40
Facilities – Waters fished are West Coast Scotland, namely Largs, Fairlie, Gareloch East Coast Scotland, Eyemouth, Berwick Stonehaven. South West Scotland, Luce Bay Drunmore.

Leukaemia Research Fund AC

Secretary – Mrs J.C. Oag
Rowan Cottage, 75 Main Street, Ratho EH28 8
Tel: 031 333 1080

Membership – Restricted
Year Formed – 1977
No. of Members – 40
Facilities – No Club Waters

Musselburgh & Fisherrow SAC

Secretary – B. Ball
20/21 Meadow Field Drive, Edinburgh
Tel: 031 661 5546

Membership – Unrestricted
Year Formed – 1961
No. of Members – 108
Facilities – We boat fish and shore fish all year round and travel all over Great Britain.

Newliston Arms Hotel SAC

Secretary – R. Maxwell
3 The Glebe, Kirkliston
Tel: 333 2135

Membership – Unrestricted
Year Formed – 1980
No. of Members – 33

South Queensferry AC

Secretary – B.D. Plasting
53 Sommerville Gardens
Tel: 031 331 1605

Membership – Unrestricted
Year Formed – 1974
No. of Members – 50
Facilities – No waters controlled. Annual subscription: £4.80+£2.00 joining fee (Seniors £2.00 (Junior subscription). Variety of social events, the club is affiliated to the Scottish Federation of Sea Anglers. The club is also a founder member of the Eastern Region of that body.

STRATHCLYDE

Albion SAC

Secretary – E. Lally
120 Mirren Avenue, Hardgate, Dumbartonshi
Tel: 041 377 5949

Membership – Restricted
Year Formed – 1970
No. of Members – 89

Ardrossan & District SAC

Secretary – I.B. McClymont
41 Corrie Crescent, Saltcoats KA21 6JL
Tel: 0294 61830

Membership – Unrestricted
Year Formed – 1968
No. of Members – 105
Facilities – The facilities available are numerous, species of fish are many. Hired boats are available all the year round and the surroundings are beautiful. Most parts of the Clyde are fishable irrespective of weather conditions from both boat and shore. Species: cod, haddock, whiting, eels, wrasse, dogfish, flounder, plaice, dab, shark, rays and skate. Any shoreline open to the public is fishable free.

Arran SAA

Chairman – N.C. McLean
Corlin Villa, Kilmory, Brodick, Isle of Arran

Arran Seafishing Association

Secretary – A.N. McLean
Kiddery
Tel: 077 087 240

Ayr SAC

Secretary – R.C. Steel
4 Inchmurrin Drive, Kilmarnock, Ayrshire
Tel: 0563 20779

Membership – Unrestricted
Year Formed – 1970
No. of Members – 50

Beith & District SAC

Secretary – A.H. Wilkie
7 Ash Drive, Beith, Ayrshire

Membership – Unrestricted
Year Formed – 1978
No. of Members – Unknown – Club is reforming
Facilities – Easy access to all Clyde boat and shore marks. Boat available at Ayr, Irvine, Fairlie, Largs, Courock and Greenock.

The Bellshill SAC

Secretary – A. McLuckie
Kirklee Road, Mossend, Bellshill
Lanarkshire ML4 2QN
Tel: 0698 748769
Membership – Restricted
Year Formed – 1978
No. of Members – 24

B.S.C. Ravenscraig Works Freshwater & Sea

Secretary – J. McLaughlan
2 Cheviot Crescent, Wishawhill, Wishaw
Lanarkshire ML2 7PN
Tel: 069 83 61987
Membership – Unrestricted
Year Formed – 1978
No. of Members – 38 Full, 2 Retired, 14 Juniors Associate

Clyde Specimen Hunters SAC

Secretary – I. Mitchell
42 Hillside Road, Mansewood, Glasgow
Tel: 041 632 9317
Membership – Restricted
Year Formed – 1980
No. of Members – 20

Drumfork SAC

Secretary – Mrs J. Lambert
Lever Road, Helensburgh, Dunbartonshire
Tel: 0436 2083
Membership – Restricted
Year Formed – 1968
No. of Members – 55

Facilities – Gareloch and Loch Long Sea water. Excellent fishing all year round from both boat and shore. Bait can be dug locally. No bait on sale.

Firth of Clyde SAA

Secretary – J. Galt
22 Helmsdale Avenue, Blantyre
Lanarkshire G72 9NY
Tel: 0698 822415
Membership – Unrestricted
Year Formed – 1968
No. of Members – 50

Giffnock North AAC (Angling Sect.)

Secretary – J. Trainer
51 Orchard Park Ave, Giffnock, Glasgow
Tel: 041 638 1520
Membership – Restricted
Year Formed – 1979
No. of Members – 27
Facilities – Mainly Clyde coast from Gourock to Girvan and beyond.

Glasgow and District SAC

Secretary – E. Ledger
61 Coldstream Drive, Burnside, Rutherglen
Glasgow, G73 3LJ
Tel: 041 647 2996
Membership – Unrestricted
Year Formed – 1973
No. of Members – 60
Facilities – Boat booking service for all members. Boats booked on an alternate basis (i.e. Saturday 1 week, Sunday the next week). Junior section with own trophies to fish for.

Govan AC

Secretary – T.L. Blunn
19 Southcroft Street, Glasgow G51 2DQ
Tel: 041 440 0085
Membership – Restricted
Year Formed – 1979
No. of Members – 18

Irvine SAC

Secretary – J.G. Macnab
27 Wilson Avenue, Irvine, Ayrshire KA12 0TW
Tel: 0294 76886
Membership – Unrestricted
Year Formed – 1969
No. of Members – 60
Facilities – We are 1 section of a large group of clubs under 1 roof, (Irvine Winter Sports Club), which has canoeing yachting, sub aqua, sand yachting. We do not control any fishing waters but fish all the year round. Boat and shore fishing in Scotland and England.

Johnstone Castle SAC

Secretary – J. Reilly
34 Poplar Avenue, Johnstone, Renfrewshire
Tel: 0505 25420

Kyle SAC

Secretary – R. Sutherland
c/o Ayr Yacht & Cruising Club
South Harbour Street, Ayr, Ayrshire
Membership – Unrestricted
Year Formed – 1976
No. of Members – 25 Seniors, 18 Juniors
Facilities – We fish The Firth of Clyde area from both boat and shore. This area is one of the safest for boat angling and one of the most productive areas on the West Coast for catchers, both from boat and shore. Type of fish mostly cod in winter, also flat fish and conger, spur, dogs and various others.

Lennox SAC

Secretary – R.N. Elder
191 Crosslet Road, Dumbarton

Mull of Galloway Big Game Club

Secretary – J.T. Scott

7 Carmel Avenue, Kilmarnock
Ayrshire KA1 2NY
Tel: 0563 35482
Membership – Unrestricted
Year Formed – 1970
No. of Members – 10 - 15
Facilities – We are a Sea Angling Club and fish mainly from our members own boats in an area from Port Patrick down the South West Coast of Scotland including Port Logan and round the Mull of Galloway into Luce Bay. Most of the fish we catch are returned to the sea. Species caught include common scate, tope, thornbuck ray and conger eel.

Newton Mearns SAC

Secretary – J.E.C. Macbeath
Pollock Castle Estate, Newton Mearns
Glasgow, Renfrewshire
Tel: 041 639 5836
Membership – Unrestricted
Year Formed – 1977
No. of Members – 20
Facilities – We do not control waters. We fish the West Coast. Portpatrick, Ayr, Troon, Gomock, Helensburgh. All boat fishing. Club has trophies for biggest total catch, best fish of year league cup, junior cups, club championship fished on single outing, plus runner-up shields.

Prestwick SAC

Secretary – M. Templeton
"Trebor", 15 Teviot Street, Ayr

Saltcoats SAC

Secretary – E. Donnell
4 Fleck Avenue, Saltcoats, Ayrshire
Match Secretary – W. Coulston
Tel: 0294 67800

Shotts Bon-Accord AC

Secretary – J. Frew
26 St. Catherines Crescent, Shotts, Lanarkshire
Membership – Unrestricted
Year Formed – 1980
No. of Members – 18

Stevenston AA

Secretary – A. McAllister
1 Lochlea Road, Saltcoats, Ayrshire KA21 6EB
Tel: 0294 602461
Membership – Unrestricted
Year Formed – 1975
No. of Members – 30
Facilities – The West Coast of Scotland including some of the sea lochs and the islands of the Great Cumbrae and Arran.

TAYSIDE

Halliburton SAC (Affiliated to Scottish Federation SA)

Secretary – John Jackson
104 Millfield Road, Arbroath, DDH 4H2
Tel: 0241 73640
Membership – Unrestricted
Year Formed – 1977
No. of Members – 28
Facilities – Arbroath, fast becoming a popular town in Eastern Scotland. Giving both shore and boat anglers ideal fishing. Boats sailing to Bellrock Lighthouse, skippers contacted from harbour. Ragworm Lugworm cockle and mussel obtained on local beaches (no bait provided). Local tackle dealer. Has limited stock of tackle. Species: cod, haddock, ling, conger, plaice.

Plough SAC & NER

Secretary – R.W. Fraser
19 Lorimer Street, Dundee, Angus
Membership – Restricted
Year Formed – 1975
No. of Members – 26
Facilities – 3 Miles of Stonhaven rough terrain. Very good fishing.

SOUTHERN IRELAND

CLARE

Lisdoonvarna-Fanore SAC
Secretary – Mr James Linnane
24 Tullyglass Crescent, Shannon
Tel: 061-74595

CORK

Aghada SAC
Secretary – Liam Hyde
Ballykenneally, Ballymacoda

Ballycotton SAC
Secretary – Jack Desmond
Hill Road, Whitegate

Celtic SAC
Secretary – John O'Sullivan
36 Evergreen Blds

Clonakilty SAC
Secretary – Mrs Peg Jayes
Ahidelake Bungalow, Clonakilty
Tel: Clonakilty

Cobh SAC
Secretary – Mrs Mary Geary
18 Plunkett Terrace, Cobh

Cork Sea Anglers SAC
Secretary – Michael Magee
'Journey's End', off Pouladuff Road, Cork

Courtmacsherry SAC
Secretary – Dirmuid O'Mahony
Courtmacsherry

Crosshaven SAC
Secretary – John Martin
7 Roman Street, Cork

Evergreen SAC
Secretary – Billy Rice
7 Whitebeam Road, Togher, Cork

Irish Shark SAC
Secretary – Eddie Cullen
1 Glenview, South Douglas Road, Cork

DONEGAL

County Donegal River, Lake & SAC
Secretary – Mr D. Borland
Tamney House, Tamney, Letterkenny
Tel: Tamney 55

Downings Bay SAC
Secretary – Ms Caroline McKeon
c/o Beach Hotel, Downings
Tel: Downings 5

Fahan SAC
Secretary – Mr S. Fullerton
'The Orchard', Ardaravan, Buncrana
Tel: Buncrana 79

Gweedore SAC
Secretary – Mr H.T. Boyle
c/o Seaview Hotel, Bunbeg
Tel: Bunbeg 18

Killybegs SAC
Secretary – Mr E. O'Callaghan
St. Catherine's Road, Killybegs
Tel: Killybegs 288

Leabgarrow SAC
Secretary – Mr D. Boyle
Leabgarrow, Arranmore, Co. Donegal
Tel: Arranmore 12

Lough Swilly SAA
Secretary – Mrs F O'Connor
Rathmullen, Co. Donegal
Tel: Rathmullen 64

DUBLIN

Achill SAC
Secretary – Mr John O'Shea
6 Raphoe Road, Crumlin, Dublin 12
Tel: 01 501975

Aer Lingus SAC
Secretary – Capt. J.V. Smith
'Wycuffe', Millview Road, Malahide, Co. Dublin

Belgard & District SAC
Secretary – Mrs N Carroll
118 New Ireland Road, Rialto, Dublin 8
Tel: 757585

Borough SAC
Secretary – T. Butler
'Seaview' 17 Newtown Park, Blackrock,
Co. Dublin
Tel: 887791

Castletown SAC
Secretary – T. Farrell
101 Shelmartin Avenue, Fairview, Dublin 3

CIE SAC
Secretary – R. Kerins
3 Albert College Lawn, Glasnevin, Dublin 9

Clondalkin PM SAC
Secretary – N. O'Connor
3 Kippure Avenue, Greenpark, Walkinstown,
Dublin 12

Dalkey SAC
Secretary – A. Harty
10 Beaumont Crescent, Dublin 9

Dolphin Richview SAC
Secretary – P. McCartin
5 Bawnville Erne, Tallaght, Co. Dublin

Donabate SAC
Secretary – J. Carton
Burrow Road, Portane, Co. Dublin

Dublin City SAC
c/o British Legion Club
4 Sir John Rogerson's Quay, Dublin 2

Dublin Metropolitan Garda AC
Secretary – M. Maher
23 Dangan Park, Kimmage, Dublin 6

Dundrum & District SAC
Secretary – R. Dalton
86 Hillview Court, Ballinteer, Dublin 16

Dun Laoghaire SAC
Secretary – Mrs S. Bolster
136 Beaumont Road, Dublin 9
Tel: 373872

East Coast Ladies SAC
Secretary – Mrs M. Hayden
22 Moatefield Avenue, Dublin 5

Edenmore AC
Secretary – M. Forrestal
91 Edenmore Avenue, Raheny, Dublin 5

Erins Isle SAC
Secretary – B. Kinsella
29 Abbotstown Road, Finglas, West Dublin 11

Erne SAC
Secretary – A. Ryan
3P Pearse House, Pearse Street, Dublin 2

Fiat SAC
Secretary – J. Gavin
82 Ardmore Drive, Artane, Dublin 5

Fitzwilliam SAC
Secretary – E. Garland
64 Riverside Park, Bonnybrook, Dublin 5

Garda SAC
Secretary – B. Prendergast
78 Glasnevin Park, Dublin 11

Guinness SAC
Secretary – T. Kennedy
48 Violet Hill Drive, Glasnevin, Dublin 11

ammond Lane SAC
cretary – B. Lawless
Pidgeon House Road, Ringsend, Dublin 4
681358

arp SAC
cretary – S. Jenkins
Verbena Park, Sutton, Dublin 13

owth SAC
cretary – P. Gaffey
7 Howth Road, Dublin 3
: 332138

chicore SAC
cretary – P. Wilson
Dunsink Drive, Finglas, South Dublin 11
usiness)
: 787118

dependent SAC
cretary – T. Duffy
Kildonan Drive, Finglas, West Dublin 11
: 342532

sh Fishing Club SAC
cretary – T. Sullivan
Thomond Road, Ballyfermot, Dublin 10

nights of Silver Hook SAC
cretary – L. O'Driscoll
Brookwood Avenue, Dublin 5

ansdowne SAC
cretary – M. Cunningham
Orwell Gardens, Rathgar, Dublin 14

ever Bros SAC
cretary – M. Ennis
Castletimon Road, Coolock, Dublin 5

ucan SAC
cretary – T. Connolly
Turret Road, Palmerstown, Dublin 20
l: 267801

alahide SAC
cretary – K. Friel
Texas Lane, Malahide, Co. Dublin

errystown SAC
cretary – K. Mulligan
Willington Avenue, Templeogue, Dublin 12

oolbeg SAC
cretary – B. Maher
Brian Avenue, Marino, Dublin 3

hoenix SAC
cretary – J. P. Kelly
Inbhir Ide, Malahide, Co. Dublin

aheny & District SAC
cretary – C. Denvir
Ardilea Road, Artane, Dublin 5

andymount SAC
cretary – J. O'Brien
tonehurst, Enniskerry, Co. Dublin

emperit SAC
cretary – M. Kearney
Ashwood Road, Ashwood, Clondalkin,
o. Dublin

ix O SAC
cretary – R. Reynolds
O'Rourke Park, Sallynoggin, Co. Dublin

outh Shore SAC
cretary – F. Baxter
OA Spencer Street, North Strand, Dublin 3
el: 747236

tillorgan SAC
o W. O'Brien
Woodley Park, Dundrum, Dublin 14

St. Helena's SAC
Secretary – H. Halpin
12 Valley Park Road, Finglas, South Dublin 11
Tel: 346674

Vikings SAC
Secretary – J. Farrell
173 Rathgar Road, Dublin 6
Tel: 972427

Waterfront SAC
Secretary – R. Kelly
166 Thomond Road, Dublin 10

Wolfe Tone SAC
Secretary – J. Cully
285 St. Michael's Estate, Inchicore, Dublin 8

Woodbine SAC
Secretary – Mrs J. Shanahan
209 Brandon Road, Dublin 12
Tel: 501612

KILKENNY
P.J. Sweeney (SAC)
2 Nuncio Road, Kilkenny

CO. LOUTH
Achill Shark Club SAC
Secretary – Mr Hugh Mullin
Sportshall, Dundalk
Tel: (042) 35322

Harp Lager SAC
Secretary – K. O'Connor
14 The Laurels, Dundalk

WEXFORD
Blackwater AC
Secretary – M. Tobin
'Kilmacoe', Curracloe, Enniscorthy

Kilmore Quay SAC
Secretary – J. Monaghan
Ballyteigue, Kilmore Quay
Tel: 053 29734

Kilmuckridge SAC
Secretary – J. Hayden
St. David's, Kilmuckridge, Gorey

New Ross & District SAC
Secretary – M. Browne
9 Chapel Street, New Ross, Wexford

Saltee SAC
Secretary – C. Manning
1 Avondale Drive, Wexford

Wexford SAC
Secretary – L.D. Meyler
'Garryowen', Rosslare, Strand
Tel: 053 32181

Wexford & District SAC
Secretary – M. Guerin
Whitewell House, Mulgannon

WICKLOW
AGL AC
Secretary – E. Ryan
26 Oaklands, Arklow

Arklow SAC
Secretary – T. O'Farrell
31 Abbeyville Estate, Arklow

Bray SAC
c/o K. Sinnott
129 Newcourth Road, Bray

Greystones Ridge AC
Secretary – M Doyle
27 Sugarloaf Crescent, Bray
Tel: 868706

John Paul II SAC
Secretary – M. Fortune
5 Brennan's Parade, Bray

Kish Bank SAC
Secretary – J. Byrne
119 Charnwood, Bray

Wicklow Bay SAC

Secretary – D. Gillespie
4 New Street, Wicklow

GALWAY
Carna Angling Association SAC
Secretary – Mr Duncan Brown
Mweenish, Carna
Tel: Carna 44

Clifden Boat and SAC
Secretary – Mr Paddy Pryce
Main Street, Clifden
Tel: Clifden 106

Galway Bay SAC
Secretary – Mr Tony Flannery
18 Rockmount Road, Highfield Park, Galway
Tel: 091 22851

MAYO
Allergan SAC
Secretary – Mr Peter O'Donnell
c/o Allergan Limited
Westport
Tel: Westport 562 563

Ballina SAC
Secretary – Mr Thomas Melvin
Bunree, Ballina
Tel: 096 22494

Belmullet SAC
Secretary – Mr Paddy Leech
Belmullet
Tel: Belmullet 500 (B)
Tel: Belmullet 157 (H)

Clew Bay Ladies SAC
Secretary – Mrs Mary Tarmey
Tubber Hill, Westport
Tel: Westport 68

Currane SAC
Secretary – Mrs Teresa Walsh
Currane, Achill
Tel: Currane 208

Grainne Uaile Ladies SAC
Secretary – Mrs Alice McNamara
Dugort PO, Achill
Tel: Dugort 1

Killala Bay SAA
Comp. Secretary – Mr John Walkin
Tone Street, Ballina
Tel: 096 22442

Louisburgh SAC
Secretary – Mr J.J. Philbin
Bridge Street, Louisburgh
Tel: Louisburgh 65

Newport SAC
Secretary – Mrs Margaret Moran
Ross, Kilmeena, Westport
Tel: 098 41105

Westport Boat SAC
Secretary – Mr Martin O'Donnell
Shop Street, Westport
Tel: Westport 277

Westport Centurions SAC
Secretary – Mrs M. Conlon
'Rossmalley', Rosbeg, Westport
Tel: Westport 371

Westport SAC
Secretary – Mr Liam Golden
Bridge Street, Westport

CO. SLIGO
Inniscrone and District SAA
Secretary – Mr Jim Bryne
Alpine Hotel, Inniscrone
Tel: 096 36144

Inniscrone Shore AC
Secretary – Mr Peter Byrne
Inniscrone Angling Centre
Tel: 096 36144

NATIONAL ANGLERS' COUNCIL

in association with – The National Federation of Anglers · The National Federation of Sea Anglers · The Salmon and Trout Association

SUPPORTED BY SWAN VESTAS

PROFICIENCY AWARDS

The Scheme's aim The National Angling Coaching Scheme is angling's official training scheme backed by more than four hundred qualified instructors in coarse, sea and game fishing. It is run by the NAC for the national angling bodies – The National Federation of Anglers, The National Federation of Sea Anglers and The Salmon and Trout Association.

Proficiency Awards are a development of the National Angling Coaching Scheme. They set targets of achievement for all anglers from basic to advanced level in each branch of the sport.

The aim is to help anglers become more proficient at their sport and educate them as conservationists who understand the water environment and the need for its protection.

Emphasis on Ecology Proficiency Awards are primarily aimed at improving angling performance and techniques but special emphasis will be placed on the waterside code.

This draws special attention to the protection of the water environment, the bankside habitat, the need to avoid litter, regulations affecting fishing, respect for riparian owners' property and the need for every angler to act as a guardian of the waterside heritage.

The Awards There are three levels of awards – Basic (Bronze), Intermediate (Silver) and Advanced (Gold).

Anglers must take these awards through an NAC approved instructor and must complete a practical test at the waterside and a written examination. There will be a minimum period of time which must elapse between the taking of any two awards. There will also be minimum ages for direct entry.

Anglers who qualify will receive–

● *An NAC Certificate confirming their level of achievement.*
● *Badge (a sew-on badge) issued only to anglers who have qualified through the Scheme.*
● *A presentation tackle box from the supporters of the Scheme, Swan Vestas.*

Every angler who qualifies will be entered in the National Angling Awards Register.

He will be entitled to receive an Awards Newsletter and will be made a member of any National Angling Awards Club which may be established as the number of holders grows.

Award winning anglers will also be able to take part in special events organised for them.

The National Anglers' Council reserves the right to make any changes in the Proficiency Awards Scheme which it deems necessary.

How to enter The Awards Scheme is educationally designed to improve the proficiency of anglers in three stages. The first stage, or Bronze Award, is open to all anglers over the age of 11 years. It is especially suitable for schools and will fit easily into a school time-table. There are also Silver and Gold Awards.

Young people at school and teachers who are interested in the Awards Scheme should contact the National Anglers' Council at the address given.

Anglers over sixteen years of age who wish to take the Bronze Award must be affiliated to the NAC either through personal or club membership of the appropriate national angling body: National Federation of Anglers, National Federation of Sea Anglers, Salmon and Trout Association. Proof of membership through production of a current card will be required by the NAC Instructor involved and there will also be a registration fee payable on the date of application.

NATIONAL ANGLERS' COUNCIL,
11 Cowgate, Peterborough PE1 1LZ
Telephone 0733-54084

Index – Companies and Organisations

Index – Coarse Day Permit Waters

Index

ex to the waters appearing in the Day Permit
hing Section.

Index

Index to the waters appearing in the Day Permit Fishing Section

your very own water authority
for just £4.95!

**The updated 1982 Fishing Handbooks —
fondly known as 'The Angler's Bible' fact packed in
soft or hardback.**

Here's three unique publications covering Coarse, Game
and Sea Fishing for just £4.95 each. They'll tell you about all the
places to get the most out of your particular sport — maps, where
to fish, the organisations, clubs, water authorities, tuition and rod
records. Plus a wealth of articles by experts and where to buy all
the accessories you need; even the most obscure items.
Or there's the complete Compendium in Hardback for just £8.50

COARSE FISHING

A 224 page bible of information packed with facts, articles
and advice by coarse fishing experts. It tells you where to go, what
you can expect to catch and where to buy everything you could
possibly need, for your sport, plus all the names, addresses and
phone numbers. At just £4.95 it's the answer to a fisherman's prayer.

GAME FISHING

Where to go, who to contact and hotels to stay in, all listed
alphabetically by county with all the addresses and phone
numbers, plus of course the type of game fishing available.
224 pages, price £4.95.

SEA FISHING

A fact finder with articles by experts. In 224 pages it
brings you details of shore spots, boat charters and the
quality of fishing available plus where to get everything you
need. Price £4.95.

HARDBACK EDITION

The complete works — all three softbacks combined together
in one big 448 page edition. It's the most comprehensive Fishing
Fact Finder available and at just £8.50
it's a great catch.

*Available from bookshops.
Or contact: Beacon Publishing,
Jubilee House, Billing Brook Road,
Weston Favell, Northampton NN3 4NW
Telephone (0604) 407288.*

THE LEADING
LIGHT

BEACON PUBLISHING
You won't find it anywhere else.